CONTRIBUTORS

ROBERT SOMERLOTT, the editorial consultant for this guidebook, has lived in Mexico for more than 20 years. The author of 14 books, he has had articles appear in *American Heritage* and *The Atlantic*, among other publications. He is also a regular contributor to the travel section of *The News*, Mexico City's English-language daily.

ROBERT CUMMINGS, a resident of Mexico for the past eight years, has written numerous travel articles as well as a novella, and is currently working on a novel.

CANDACE LYLE HOGAN, a freelance writer and editor currently living in New York City, is the contributor of the "Weekend in Baja" section. She has explored Baja California over the last 40 years from her home base in La Misión.

ROBIN LLOYD has lived in Mexico for 16 years and is a correspondent for *The News*, Mexico City's English-language daily, and for *Vallarta Today*. He is also the editor of *VNN* (*Vallarta and Nayarit News*) and the author of five books. His articles and photographs have appeared in *Life, Time,* and *Newsweek*.

MITCHELL NAUFFTS, a freelance writer and editor based in New York City, writes frequently about Mexico. He is also a founding editor of *Turnstile*, a biannual literary review.

JACKIE PETERSON has worked as a reporter for the travel section of the *San Francisco Examiner* and as an editor for both *The News*, Mexico City's English-language daily newspaper, and the *Sacramento Union*. Currently a resident in Mazatlán, she reports on Mexico's resort areas on a freelance basis.

LARRY RUSSELL, a resident of Mexico City since 1973, is a frequent contributor to the travel sections of Mexico's *Vogue* and *Progreso* magazines. He has also, in collaboration with his wife, produced, written, and performed the musical scores for a number of documentary films about Mexico.

SUSAN WAGNER, the travel editor of *Modern Bride* magazine for 10 years, has worked on the staff of *Travel & Leisure* magazine and written a series of guidebooks to Mexican resorts and innumerable articles on the country. She attended graduate school in Mexico and returns there frequently.

CELIA WAKEFIELD has lived in Mexico for many years, the past 16 in San Miguel de Allende, and travels extensively throughout the country. She has written articles for *The Atlantic, Saturday Review, Newsday,* and *Punch.* She is also the author and photographer of *High Cities of the Andes.*

THE BERLITZ TRAVELLERS GUIDES

AUSTRALIA

CANADA

THE CARIBBEAN

ENGLAND & WALES

FRANCE

GERMANY

GREECE

HAWAII

IRELAND

LONDON

MEXICO

NEW YORK CITY

NORTHERN ITALY AND ROME

PORTUGAL

SAN FRANCISCO &
NORTHERN CALIFORNIA

SOUTHERN ITALY AND ROME

SPAIN

TURKEY

THE BERLITZ TRAVELLERS GUIDE TO MEXICO 1993

ALAN TUCKER
General Editor

BERLITZ PUBLISHING COMPANY, INC.
New York, New York

BERLITZ PUBLISHING COMPANY LTD.
Oxford, England

THE BERLITZ TRAVELLERS GUIDE TO MEXICO 1993

Berlitz Trademark Reg U.S. Patent and Trademark Office
and other countries—Marca Registrada

Copyright © Root Publishing Company,
1990, 1991, 1992, 1993

All rights reserved.
No part of this book may be reproduced or transmitted in any form or by any means, electronic or mechanical, including photocopying, recording or by any information storage and retrieval system without written permission from the publisher.

Published by Berlitz Publishing Company, Inc.
257 Park Avenue South, New York, New York 10010, U.S.A.

Distributed in the United States by
the Macmillan Publishing Group

Distributed elsewhere by Berlitz Publishing Company Ltd.
London Road, Wheatley, Oxford OX9 1YR, England

ISBN 2-8315-1772-9
ISSN 1057-4786

Designed by Beth Tondreau Design
Cover design by Dan Miller Design
Cover photograph © Dennis Hallinan/FPG International
Maps by Mark Stein Studios
Illustrations by Bill Russell
Fact-checked in Mexico by Patricia Alisau
Copyedited by Cynthia Sophiea
Edited by Mitchell Nauffts and Lisa Leventer

Printed in the United States of America
1 3 5 7 9 10 8 6 4 2

THIS GUIDEBOOK

The Berlitz Travellers Guides are designed for experienced travellers in search of exceptional information that will enhance the enjoyment of the trips they take.

Where, for example, are the interesting, out-of-the-way, fun, charming, or romantic places to stay? The hotels described by our expert writers are some of the special places, in all price ranges except for the very lowest—not just the run-of-the-mill, heavily marketed places in advertised airline and travel-wholesaler packages.

We indicate the approximate price level of each accommodation in our description of it (no indication means it is moderate in local, relative terms), and at the end of every chapter we supply more detailed hotel rates as well as contact information so that you can get precise, up-to-the-minute rates and make reservations.

The Berlitz Travellers Guide to Mexico 1993 highlights the more rewarding parts of the country so that you can quickly and efficiently home in on a good itinerary.

Of course, this guidebook does far more than help you choose a hotel and plan your trip. *The Berlitz Travellers Guide to Mexico 1993* is designed for use *in* Mexico. Our writers, each of whom is an experienced travel journalist who either lives in or regularly tours the city or region of Mexico he or she covers, tell you what you really need to know, what you can't find out so easily on your own. They identify and describe the truly out-of-the-ordinary resorts, restaurants, shops, activities, and sights, and tell you the best way to "do" your destination.

Our writers are highly selective. They bring out the significance of the places they *do* cover, capturing the personality and the underlying cultural and historical resonances of a city or region—making clear its special appeal.

The Berlitz Travellers Guide to Mexico is full of reliable and timely information, revised and updated each year. We would like to know if you think we've left out some very special place. Although we make every effort to provide the most current information available about every destination described in this book, it is possible too that changes have occurred before you arrive. If you do have an experience that is contrary to what you were led to expect by our description, we would like to hear from you about it.

A guidebook is no substitute for common sense when you are travelling. Always pack the clothing, footwear, and other items appropriate for the destination, and make the necessary accommodation for such variables as altitude, weather, and local rules and customs. Of course, once on the scene you should avoid situations that are in your own judgment potentially hazardous, even if they have to do with something mentioned in a guidebook. Half the fun of travelling is exploring, but explore with care.

ALAN TUCKER
General Editor
Berlitz Travellers Guides

Root Publishing Company
330 West 58th Street
Suite 504
New York, New York 10019

CONTENTS

This Guidebook	vii
Overview	1
Useful Facts	16
Bibliography	26
Mexico City	**35**
Teotihuacán	104
Getting Around	110
Accommodations	115
Dining	123
Nightlife and Entertainment	140
Shops and Shopping	144
Side Trips from Mexico City	**157**
Cuernavaca	161
Taxco	167
Puebla and Cholula	170
Tula	181
Valle de Bravo	186
The Colonial Heartland	**195**
Querétaro	200
San Miguel de Allende	210
Guanajuato	223
Morelia	234
The Western Highlands	**254**
Guadalajara	258
Pátzcuaro	271
The Copper Canyon	**285**
The Baja California Resorts	**297**
Los Cabos	312
The Pacific Resorts	**332**
Mazatlán	335
Puerto Vallarta	357
Tenacatita	377
Barra de Navidad	379

CONTENTS

Manzanillo	381
Ixtapa/Zihuatanejo	392
Acapulco	406
Puerto Escondido, Puerto Angel, Huatulco	433
The Gulf Coast	458
Oaxaca	489
Mayan Mexico	514
The Yucatán	521
Chiapas	547
Guatemala	564
The Yucatán Caribbean Resorts	601
Cancún and the Tulum Corridor	603
Isla Mujeres	640
Cozumel	647
Historical Chronology	667
Index	675

MAPS

Mexico	xii
Mexico City	42
Downtown Mexico City	52
Mexico City Environs	158
Puebla	171
The Colonial Heartland	196
Querétaro	201
San Miguel de Allende	211
Guanajuato	224
Morelia	235
The Western Highlands	256
Guadalajara	259
The Copper Canyon Area	286
Baja California Norte	301
Baja California Sur	308
Mazatlán	336
Puerto Vallarta	358
Ixtapa/Zihuatanejo	393

Acapulco Area	408
The Acapulco Strip	417
Veracruz	461
Northern Gulf Coast	469
Southern Gulf Coast	476
Oaxaca City	491
Oaxaca State (detail)	506
Yucatán Peninsula	516
Northern Chiapas State	549
Guatemala	566
Cancún	606
Isla Mujeres	641
Cozumel	648

OVERVIEW

By Robert Somerlott

Robert Somerlott has lived in Mexico for more than 20 years. The author of ten books, he has had articles appear in American Heritage *and* The Atlantic, *among other publications. He is also a regular contributor to the travel section of* The News, *Mexico City's English-language daily.*

For many visitors the most surprising discovery about Mexico is its foreignness. Travellers from the United States who thought they were just going next door are particularly astonished. Even if they have read books on Mexico, seen films set there, and studied photos of the country, they are seldom prepared for the reality that greets them. Europe, even for first-time visitors, seems familiar by comparison.

The surprise often springs from the vivid colors and odd contrasts that abound in Mexico. You climb into an ordinary taxi in Mexico City, for example, and suddenly notice that the driver has transformed his dashboard into a shrine. The Virgin of Guadalupe, the country's patroness saint, lit by twinkling bulbs, presides over a bed of plastic flowers. When the taxi stops for an ordinary traffic light, an extraordinary quartet of fire-eaters leaps into the street to entertain. Or you get on a modern, unusually handsome subway only to discover as you change lines that the station is built around an Aztec temple complete with sacrificial altar. More remarkable still, it is not a set or reconstruction; the temple was once, centuries ago, just that, and the tens of thousands who pass it daily take this incongruity for granted. Or, driving on a new highway in the middle of nowhere, you suddenly overtake a procession of people walking on the shoulder of the road. Their dark, earthy faces are framed by straw hats and handwoven shawls, and they carry banners and religious icons. Oddly, this procession does not seem to end.

You drive on, mile after mile, passing a multitude of men and women, many carrying babies. They are joyous, exalted; they sing, chant, and laugh as they trudge through the dust and heat and rain. You have come upon a religious pilgrimage to one of Mexico's several great shrines, where the pilgrims are counted in the hundreds of thousands and walk for days, sleeping at night in the open. You suddenly realize that the deep and powerful impulse that draws millions of Mexicans across fields, through marshes, and over mountains is far older than the religion whose banners they bear. While today the destination may be a church instead of a sacred well, the force that sets this human river in motion is unchanged and, as ever, awe-inspiring.

The sounds in Mexico are often as unfamiliar as the sights. In the middle of the night in an isolated hill town all the bells of all the churches suddenly begin to clang and peal at once. No, it is not a harbinger of revolution, or even an alarm. More than likely, a festival has just started, or a local *fútbol* team has won an important match, or a dignitary has arrived on an official visit. But what does it matter, really? Bells are made for ringing, and Mexico is a land of thousands of bells speaking to one another. In the same town, the shouts of vendors selling strawberries or crab or fresh asparagus mix with the melody of the scissors grinder and the off-key brass of a ragtag band as it marches down a street for no discernible reason.

Mexico, it quickly becomes clear, is not a European country. It is not even really what is today called a "Western" country. Instead, it is a unique blending of cultures based on a civilization that built great and beautiful cities when northern Europe was a wilderness peopled by barbarians.

Mexicans, a traveller soon discovers, express themselves publicly, in rites, rituals, rallies, and fairs. Every town and every parish has its own saint to honor, its own anniversaries to commemorate, its own special reasons for flying banners. Octavio Paz once asked the mayor of a poor village how the town's income was spent. "Mostly on fiestas, señor," was the reply. "We are a small village but we have two patron saints."

The richness of life in Mexico is evident in its streets and plazas, in a gathering together, in a sense of community that has nothing to do with conforming. Families are close, and clan ties are binding, even when disrupted by hardship and migration. But beyond the family, outside the home, lies another life, a necessary world of public ritual, where people stand close as fireworks shriek and explode in the night. "Viva México!" they shout—but the cheers are not for the government; Mexicans distrust all government. No, the cheers are for the land, for the people, for their families and way of life.

Mexicans are quite different from their neighbors to the north and south for reasons that are both historical (as you will see throughout this book) and racial. The first human inhabitants of the Americas were nomadic hunters from Asia who followed the herds they depended on over a broad isthmus that has long since been submerged under the shallow Bering Sea. We know little about these first "Americans," migrating as they did tens of thousands of years ago, but the evidence indicates that included in these various migratory waves of prehistoric peoples were many racial types. Later and larger migrations were comprised primarily of Mongoloid racial types, and they played the largest part in determining the physical traits of succeeding populations.

From the time of the last great migration (which ended around 9000 B.C.) until the arrival of the Spanish in the 16th century, there was no meaningful contact between the Old World and the New. The Americas, supporting a very small population relative to the rest of the world, developed independently and in isolation.

Civilization here rose in conjunction with the development of corn (maize), which became the food staple of much of the Americas (as it remains today). The Maya called its kernels the "sunbeams of God." Other Mesoamerican people displayed equal reverence toward this life-sustaining plant. (The picture of a lone man hoeing his mountainside patch of corn is a profound symbol of Mexico.)

Some 3,000 years ago a mighty culture suddenly rose and flourished on an unlikely piece of real estate, the swamps of coastal Tabasco, just west of the Yucatán Peninsula. These people today are known as the **Olmecs**, and in many respects theirs can be considered the "mother culture" of Mesoamerica. While much of their history and accomplishments remain unknown, we do know that the Olmecs invented the first form of writing used in the Americas, a numerical system later adopted and vastly expanded by the Maya; that they were the first Mesoamerican people to devote themselves to astronomical studies; that they originated many of the religious concepts and customs that came to characterize Mesoamerican civilization; and that they also became accomplished at jade carving and developed methods of transporting huge boulders great distances.

About 2,000 years ago there was a stirring of collective activity throughout Mesoamerica. It was then that **Teotihuacán**, America's first true city, rose and flourished in the Valley of Mexico some 30 miles northeast of the modern capital. Its builders, who erected such imposing monuments as the Pyramids of the Sun and Moon, were in all likelihood descendants of primitive villagers native to the area. Their name for themselves remains a mystery, but today they are called "Teotihuacanos." Within a century these vigorous people had come to dominate a huge region, sending trading parties out in all directions, some as far as present-day Guatemala. (In addition, trade goods, if not the traders themselves, found their way north up the great rivers of what is now the southwestern United States.)

Over the next several centuries various cultures rose and flowered throughout Mesoamerica: Teotihuacán and Xochicalco in the central highlands, the Zapotec centers in Oaxaca, and, most resplendent of all, the Classic-era cities of the Maya in the southeast. The Maya, whose earliest ceremonial centers were concentrated on the shelf of land bordered by the Pacific and the uplands of southern Chiapas and Guatemala, and whose ascendancy was roughly contemporaneous with that of Teotihuacán, were the first people in the world to develop the mathematical concept of zero, and their use of numbers and a calendar based on astronomical observation was far superior to the cumbersome systems that prevailed in Europe at the time.

The **Classic era**, as this period of widespread culture and knowledge in Mesoamerica is called, began to draw to a close about A.D. 600, and three centuries later had ended completely. The great cities and ceremonial centers were abandoned; no one knows exactly why—although there are theories. A great plague or plagues has been suggested as one possible cause; a series of crop failures—leading to a rejection of traditional religion—is another. Other experts believe that the maintenance of so many priests and temples simply became too much, that these great civilizations were destroyed by nothing more than excessive taxation. At the same time barbarian peoples from the north were roaming the land, yet their presence, according to the experts, seems not to have been the primary cause for the abandonment, which started in the north and progressed to the south and east, of one city after another. In any case, by the end of the Classic era several qualities that would remain constants in the Mexican character were already evident: a devotion to ritual, a belief in the importance of pilgrimage, a fondness for bold color, and a love of exuberant music and dance.

In the tenth century the country suffered the invasion of a warrior people called the **Toltecs**, who bequeathed it an infusion of much-needed vitality as well as a variety of new styles of art. The ancient ruins at **Tula**, northwest of Mexico

City, and **Chichén Itzá**, in the Yucatán, are their greatest surviving monuments.

The Toltec conquest, however, proved only to be the prelude to the rise of the **Aztecs**, a fierce imperialistic society with a particularly bloodthirsty religion. After only a century of Aztec rule, the stage was set for the arrival of Hernán Cortés in 1519.

The saga of the Conquest has been told and retold. Still, one important fact is often neglected: The conquistadors were defeated and put to flight by the Aztecs. Their eventual victory became possible only after they allied themselves with an army of natives, the Tlaxcalans. **Tenochtitlán**, the magnificent Aztec capital (over which Mexico City was built), was surrendered to Cortés on August 21, 1521.

Following the victory of the conquistadors, it was left to the missionaries of the Church to subdue and secure the rest of the country over the next two decades. Employing tactics and rhetoric perfected during the long, grim decades of the Inquisition, the missionaries set about their task—one they were oddly suited for, believing as they did that Satan was a living presence, an insidious enemy who lurked invisibly at the shoulder of every would-be convert whispering foulness into his ear. Native books, art, buildings, and customs were seen as being steeped not just in sin but in even more dangerous magic. In the end, there was not only fanaticism but fear behind the missionaries' destruction of some of the most glorious art ever created.

(Among the Mayan and Aztec materials destroyed were documents, so-called codices, painted or written on strips of pounded bark or parchment. Only three Mayan codices are known to have survived; all are in European museums. Other codices that remain in Mexico are post-Conquest copies of the originals.)

For almost three centuries Spain held sway over her New World colony, imposing on it her religion, art, and institutions—and still Mexico is only superficially Spanish. It is a curious fact, and one that is implicitly acknowledged on October 12, Columbus Day: In Mexico, it is not so much Columbus who is honored as it is the people of Mexico themselves, the unique Mexican race, or *raza,* and so the day is known here as the Día de la Raza. It is an entirely appropriate holiday, for today's Mexicans are mostly *mestizos,* a mixture of Indian and Spanish. Of course, the proportion of the mix is impossible to determine and varies from region to region. Then, too, there are the purely Mayan or Zapotec people, or those of other native groups, as well as the purely Spanish, or *criollo.* (Other, smaller European admixtures are present as well—French, Irish, and German, most notably. The African influence is relatively small. Slaves from the Indies sometimes reached the Gulf Coast, and a few were imported, but the Spaniards were afraid of black slavery in New Spain, being nervous about rebellions. Chinese were brought into the north as railroad builders; Lebanese entered the southeast first as peddlers and later as storekeepers.)

During the centuries of colonial rule New Spain, as Mexico was called, was an intellectually somnolent land. Education was reserved for the privileged few, and what little was offered to the poor suffered a terrible blow when the Jesuits, the best and most selfless teachers, were expelled by the Spanish Crown in the 18th century. At the same time Spain was careful not to permit the growth of an indigenous governing class. Mexico paid heavily for this after she gained her sovereignty in 1821: Her leaders had no experience in government, and little understanding of compromise and practicality.

The 19th century was a time of violence, hardship, and loss. The United States invaded Mexico in 1846 and walked away with half its territory two years later. The French marched in 16 years later and, with the help of Mexican conservatives, put the puppet emperor Maximilian on a spurious (and wobbly) throne. Throughout the period Church and State battled without mercy.

The modern Mexican state emerged from a bloody, brutal revolution that raged from 1910 into the 1920s, a struggle comparable in its ferocity to the U.S. Civil War. It was a revolt of the poor, the landless, and the disenfranchised, and when Mexicans speak of "the Revolution," they are referring to this total upheaval of society, not the earlier struggle for independence from Spain. The 1920s witnessed a strike by the clergy; the priests and nuns locked up the churches and departed. Parishioners shot the locks off church doors and conducted their own services, which brought the clergy rushing back, only to be expelled again—this time against their will. The subject remains a touchy one.

Today Mexico has laws on its books and articles in its constitution sharply limiting the powers of the Church and clergy. Clerics recently were granted the right to vote, but they may not hold political office. The Church's ownership of real estate is highly restricted, and it may not buy radio or television stations, although "special" religious rites, such as a Mass celebrated by the Pope, may be broadcast. New churches may be built only by special permission (almost never granted), and the Church may not offer primary education. Convents are illegal but a few small ones are tolerated.

OVERVIEW

In recent years authorities have winked at the Church's small violations of the law and constant testing of limits. But the anti-clerical laws remain official and are usually enforced. Oddly enough, the majority of people in this overwhelmingly Catholic country support the restrictions. They recall the clerical abuses of power, and every school child knows that a Pope once declared the Mexican constitution null and void.

The Mexico of today is the product of long and tragic tumult. The sculpted bronze figures you see in public squares across the land are almost always of men who fought for a losing cause: Cuauhtémoc, the last Aztec ruler, tortured and slain; Hidalgo, Aldama, Allende, and Jiménez, martyrs in the struggle for independence at the start of the 19th century, executed or beheaded; José María Morelos, who continued the fight for independence, executed in 1815; Vicente Guerrero, staunch defender of the rights of the people, first against Spain, then against the rich and powerful of his own country, treacherously executed in 1831; Francisco Madero, the first president of modern Mexico and a great liberal reformer, murdered with his vice president in a Mexico City alley in 1913; Emiliano Zapata, land reformer and hero of the peasants, shot in cold blood in 1919; President Alvaro Obregón, early defender of constitutional government, assassinated three weeks after his re-election in 1928. Their ideas and causes ultimately may have triumphed, but they themselves came to tragic ends, most of them believing their cause was lost. They are Mexico's true heroes, and there is a certain melancholy appropriateness to this in a nation too often beset by turmoil and trouble.

There is a saying here that goes, "Once the dust of Mexico has settled on your heart, you will find peace in no other land." Certainly, the traveller who discovers Mexico for the first time is likely to return again and again. One trip is not enough to comprehend it—perhaps a lifetime is not sufficient, for its character is like a Mayan temple, built up layer upon layer, the newest façade hiding but not destroying the earlier ones. Nor do the centuries quietly vanish when their time is up; in Mexico they linger on, the past mixing with the present, complicating judgments and making predictions all but impossible.

Most visitors come initially for the glorious beaches or the magnificent pre-Columbian ruins. We hope that after experiencing the pleasures of those you will prolong your stay or return to see the less publicized attractions we have chosen, such as the romantic streets and alleys of Guanajuato or the Indian color and serenity of Pátzcuaro.

Mexico is a bargain. Prices change and exchange rates fluctuate, so it is more of a bargain some years and in some seasons than others. Still, all things considered, a Mexican vacation is one of the best travel buys in the world. When this book labels something as "expensive," it usually means an amount that would be considered moderate in New York or Paris, and cheap in Tokyo.

Another reason to go to Mexico is the Mexican people themselves. Mexicans, in general, are fond of foreigners, especially their northern neighbors on the continent. Full of a lively curiosity, tolerant and accepting of different kinds of behavior and tastes, they are generally a kind and courteous people.

Often, it's true, Mexican politicians and intellectuals sound as xenophobic as any in the world. The media here ring with screams about imperialism, arrogance, and exploitation. From a Mexican viewpoint, however, there is often good reason for this screaming. Mexico, after all, has suffered grievously at the hands of foreigners. The United States stormed onto its soil not once but several times, and claimed a large part of it as its own. The French also invaded, and the British, although less involved, are not innocent. Alas, Spain's conduct was simply unspeakable. And yet, despite this discouraging record, ordinary Mexicans like their foreign neighbors. No wonder the feeling is usually mutual.

If a visitor makes the least attempt at uttering a few Spanish words, however badly, Mexicans will go to extraordinary lengths to understand and be of help. A few gestures may inspire an entire pantomime. You'll find no snobbery here, no sense that those who do not speak the native tongue are considered little more than savages.

Almost everyone strives to be helpful. If a car is mired on a country road, suddenly half a dozen men appear from nowhere to push it out. When their efforts fail, someone fetches a team of oxen. Strangers will guide you, be infinitely patient in repeating directions, and sometimes even walk you to your destination. (This can lead to a sort of courtesy disaster when an informant doesn't really know the way but won't be so rude as to disappoint you. Truth must not interfere with politeness.)

Mexicans are often surprisingly familiar with the United States and Canada, at least on a second- or third-hand basis. After all, a chief export of the country is its own sons and daughters for labor abroad. Is there anyone, even in the remotest village, who doesn't have at least one cousin who has crossed two or more borders to find work? Or an uncle living in Los Angeles?

Because these temporary laborers and new immigrants are often exploited, the guilty American conscience expects hostility in return from Mexicans. Mexican fatalism usually prevents this: What happened was the fault of the system, the government, or just bad luck. Nothing personal, and all in all it wasn't so bad. *Así es la vida*—such is life! Why nourish bad feelings? This kind of fatalism moves like a tide through Mexican life, softening its hard edges and making bad times and economic failures bearable. Resignation may be an enemy of progress, but it is also a balm for the wear and tear of daily living.

There is one facet of the national character you probably won't understand, and it may ultimately annoy you, so be prepared. The Mexican concept of schedules and punctuality is a pre-Columbian mystery. At times it seems incredible that the ancestors of these people calculated the world's most accurate calendar. What is two o'clock? Well, it's two until it's three o'clock, clearly. Also, it's two when it's no longer one o'clock. Novelist Carlos Fuentes writes of an old man who wove palm hats as he walked from village to village. Thus, a certain village became two hats away, another one three. Each to his own clock, and you cannot expect a person to keep "English time," which is what the exact time is called.

All the jokes and stories about *mañana* are understatements. In part, the answer that your train/letter/money order will be there *mañana* is simple courtesy, a desire not to disappoint. In part, it is optimism. But it also stems from a belief that you will not take such a word as "tomorrow" literally. *Mañana* is a dream, a hope, a kindness—as well as a way of getting rid of an aggressive, impatient person.

In the end, you must simply relax and adopt this Mexican virtue of fatalism.

Touring Mexico

This book, intended as an introduction to a large and varied country, is *selective* rather than complete. Only the best and most interesting places have been chosen. There is no point in muddying its contents with destinations few people would willingly choose. It also omits places—including a few of Mexico's larger cities—that are simply pass-through points en route to somewhere else. **Monterrey**, for example, Mexico's northeastern metropolis, has some attractive neighborhoods and an admirably renovated downtown section, but it remains a place for business, not for leisure or discovery. Many other large and prosperous cities are omitted for the same reason, among them Torreón, Durango, Ciudad Victoria, and León.

A different type of omission is neatly summed up by the famous remark of Dr. Johnson: "Worth seeing? Yes, but not worth going to see." Some places, even though attractive, are too remote or difficult to reach to be considered here. The once-flourishing mining towns of **Real de Catorce**, south of Monterrey, and **Alamos**, southeast of Ciudad Obregón, are examples. They are interesting if you happen to be in the neighborhood but for most people not worth a special and awkward trip, so they are only covered briefly as side trips from border routes. Many archaeological zones also fall into this category. Dedicated ruins buffs will easily find them in more specialized reference publications.

Two colonial silver cities, **San Luis Potosí** and **Zacatecas**, have attractions that are also not described in detail below because they, too, do not quite justify the trip. If you find yourself in their vicinity, however, do not neglect those handsome towns.

On the other hand, the **Copper Canyon** (and its train), also remote from usual destinations, is special. Its breathtaking natural beauty and the opportunity for adventure it affords justify a trip to Mexico's dusty northwest corner, so we discuss this experience in detail.

Our exploration of Mexico begins with the capital, **Mexico City**, the country's hub and crossroads. The world's largest city is full of both annoyances and charm. Its traffic is manic, its pace distinctly un-Mexican. Traditional Mexican courtesy is put to the extreme test here. Individuals in the D. F. (Distrito Federal, as Mexico City is officially known) are usually as kind and courteous as people in the provinces, even though as city dwellers they must be wary. But courtesy is not a usual trait of crowds, of mobs at the subway, of people rushing desperately to board the bus to get home.

For all its problems, there is much to admire and enjoy in the capital. The great Zócalo (main plaza) is a masterly achievement in urban design, with its cathedral, its fine government palace, and, hidden just around a corner, the once-great Templo Mayor of the Aztecs. The National Museum of Anthropology is the country's finest "archaeological zone," and ranks among the great museums of the world. The pyramids at nearby **Teotihuacán** are marvels of ancient achievement. Finally, the city itself is a museum of people and life, filled with quaint neighborhoods, odd little shops, and unexpected vistas.

Mexico City is also the jumping-off point for a number of short trips, five of which are outlined here: flower-filled **Cuernavaca** and the lovely ruins of **Xochicalco** nearby; picturesque **Taxco**, town of noted silversmiths; staid **Puebla** and the huge pyramid in neighboring **Cholula**; a northward loop including the National Museum of Viceregal Art in **Tepotzotlán**, the ruins of ancient **Tula**, and the 16th-century monastery at **Ixmiquilpán**, with its strange Indian murals; and an excursion to **Valle de Bravo**, a wooded and verdant resort on a man-made lake in the mountains west of the capital, with the Aztec shrine of **Malinalco** an added bonus.

That is as much as most travellers will be able to explore from the Federal District. Those with more time may also want to visit **Tlaxcala**, with its fanciful architecture, and the mysterious pre-Columbian ruins of **Cacaxtla**.

Travellers often talk about discovering "the real Mexico," and while every part of the country is equally real, the sort of place they usually have in mind turns out to be in the historic **Bajío**, the colonial heartland located more or less north of the capital. Although the Bajío lacks Mexico's two greatest attractions for foreign visitors—beaches and ancient archaeological ruins—it is indeed "the real Mexico," as well as the best place to discover what the country as a whole is doing and thinking. The Bajío comprises only an eighth of Mexico's land but produces most of its food. And it is here, in the mining towns of **Guanajuato, Querétaro, San Miguel de Allende**, and **Morelia**, that you'll see the finest colonial architecture and get the strongest sense of Mexico's colonial heritage.

The valley encircling **Guadalajara** blends into the Bajío without any sharp geographical separation, but Mexico's second city lies far enough west of the capital to have developed its own ways and style. Although it is difficult to rate historical suffering, this area, the **Western Highlands**, probably bore the worst of it during the Conquest, with the barbarity of the conquistadors reaching special depths of sadism. Fortunately, the city of Guadalajara and the surrounding Jalisco region were spared from later foreign incursions. The invasion route taken by the armies of the United States lay far to the east, and the struggles with the French were north and south of Mexico City. Guadalajara also largely avoided the depredations of bandits in military uniforms during the years of revolutionary turmoil.

This comparatively benign history shows in its architecture, its style, and its people. Here is a friendly and vital city, one where sightseers will want to linger but not remain too long—its charms are many, but not infinite. Still, the Guadalajara area has the largest English-speaking expatriate colony in the world: one in the city itself and a second in residence in the small towns along the shore of **Lago de Chapala**. An ideal climate is a powerful attraction, it seems.

Mexico's other celebrated lake, **Pátzcuaro**, is east and slightly south of Chapala, situated among rugged mountains rather than in a fertile valley. With the change in terrain there also comes a change in the people—from the cowboys (real or rhinestone) of Guadalajara to the sober Tarascans of Michoacán. Writer and intellectual Andrés Henestrosa has said, "Mexican songs are Indian inside, European outside—Spanish melody and Indian melancholy." Nowhere does that seem truer than in Pátzcuaro. But if the people are sober, their great market is a riot of color. Ultimately, Pátzcuaro seems outside of time, an Indian Brigadoon only superficially affected by passing fancy.

The mountainous route between Pátzcuaro and Mexico City, via Morelia, is scenic country well worth exploring if you have a car, but not otherwise. You'll want to be able to stop, get out, look around, and breathe deeply—a luxury that buses simply don't offer. The towns themselves are not especially attractive, but the trip is lovely.

Far to the southeast lies **Oaxaca**, just as Indian as Pátzcuaro but utterly different in temperament. Whereas the Tarascan people seem reserved and as cool as their mountain lake, the Zapotec folk of Oaxaca are outgoing, lively, warm, and curious. In forested Pátzcuaro you are aware of shadows; the Valley of Oaxaca, on the other hand, is flooded with sunshine. Centuries ago two ancient cultures, the Zapotecs and later the Mixtecs, flourished in the valleys that converge at the city of Oaxaca. Today the ruins of their many ceremonial centers, including the great **Monte Albán** and **Mitla**, stand as a reminder of that former glory. Two thousand years ago at Monte Albán the Zapotecs began to reshape a mountaintop, creating in the process ancient Mexico's only necropolis, a true city of the dead. Later, the Mixtecs added to Monte Albán's vast honeycomb of tombs and created for their dead some of the most exquisite jewelry ever fashioned, treasures now displayed in Oaxaca's museums. But the charm of Oaxaca is by no means confined to archaeology. Today's city offers fascinating architecture, colorful craft markets, and the pageant of daily life around its welcoming plaza.

The **Gulf Coast** region is the least visited of those discussed here, but also the most varied. **Veracruz** is a burst of marimba music, a city full of gaiety and celebration. Some of the more sober descendants of old, respectable families

(Spanish, of course) lock their doors at *Carnaval* time and insert earplugs, but that staid face is not the one that Veracruz—either the city or the state—usually shows the public.

To the north of Veracruz, two archaeological sites deserve special attention: **Zempoala** and magnificent **El Tajín**, the latter considered by many to rival some of the Mayan sites for beauty and mystery.

Our exploration of the Gulf Coast north of Veracruz ends at sleepy **Tuxpan**, a town with no particular beauty—and certainly little in the way of excitement. What it does have is character and a graceful, unhurried river. Farther north lies the modern port of Tampico, which we do not cover. Its attractions are exclusively for sportsmen, especially sportsfishermen, although it does have good hotels and restaurants because of its status as a prosperous center for the petroleum industry.

To the south of Veracruz are the slightly dubious attractions of **Lago de Catemaco**, not one of the more charming destinations in this book. Fortunately, the big lake, nestled among volcanoes, makes up for the somewhat grubby town. At any rate, Catemaco is the start of a beautiful drive or bus ride east to **Villahermosa**, the gateway to the Mayan world and a handsome city with a remarkable outdoor archaeological museum full of Olmec artifacts.

Ancient Mesoamerican culture reached its zenith in the jungles of the **Yucatán** at such magnificent ceremonial centers as **Chichén Itzá, Uxmal**, and others. Oddly enough, the Maya seem to have done best where the soil was poorest and the climate most inhospitable. **Palenque**, in the northern part of the state of Chiapas, while perhaps the most elegant Mayan ruin, is on the edge of a jungle so dense that no one knows what other ruined cities might be concealed there.

Today the Maya, fighting to keep their ancient traditions alive, survive not only near the great centers their ancestors erected but also in the highland fastness of **San Cristóbal de las Casas**, capital of the state of Chiapas, where the surrounding hamlets remain virtually untouched by the modern world.

They are also found to the southeast, in **Guatemala**, a country with very different traditions. Ancient legend has it that a Mayan miracle took place here at **Tikal**, the largest and in some ways most impressive of the Mayan cities. And while today the Maya struggle to come to terms with modern divisions that are artificial and political—and over which they had no control—Tikal remains a magnificent reminder of the continuity of Mayan culture as well as a natural complement to explorations of Uxmal, Palenque, and Chichén Itzá. Apart from the Mayan interest, Guatamala's crafts markets, exploding with color, dazzle like fireworks. The landscape, too, can be awe-inspiring, as attested to by the sight of Lake Atitlan shadowed by its volcanoes at sunset.

Mexico's beach and saltwater resorts are by far the country's most popular attractions with visitors, their names synonymous with pleasure and sometimes glamour. **Cancún, Cozumel, Acapulco, Ixtapa/Zihuatanejo,** and **Puerto Vallarta** are just the major ones, but we cover a number—**Mazatlán, Manzanillo, Puerto Escondido**—that are more modest in size and some, such as **Isla Mujeres** and **Barra de Navidad**, that are small and/or little known.

Of course, sand and sea are international, and so are the vacationers who flock to find both in Mexico, including Mexicans themselves. Yet each resort has its own special identity and flavor. Cancún, for example, has a close Mayan neighbor in **Tulum**, one of the last outposts of Mayan greatness and a surprising, if overrun, bonus for vacationers. In fact, none of the big resorts we cover is merely a "hotel culture" (though Cancún comes close). Cozumel has a strong island character all its own, and Acapulco is one of Mexico's largest and most vibrant cities. In all of them you'll find more than clear water, warm sand, and palm trees: They also share the warmth of Mexico.

Baja California, a very special place and the subject of many books in its own right (see the Bibliography for two of them), is not covered as is, say, the Colonial Heartland; instead, we describe it briefly as a possible weekend getaway from Southern California and as a route to the **Los Cabos** resorts—which are discussed in detail.

Mexican Cooking

In recent years Mexican cooking has been given its rightful place among the great cuisines of the world. Corn and beans remain the staples of the land, but they are handled with infinite variety, supplemented and spiced ingeniously. Only a few dishes are as fiery as legend claims; much of the pepper (chile) is reserved for green or red sauces served on the side, and can be tasted with caution by the newcomer. The national herb, cilantro (coriander), lends its distinctive flavor to everything from soup to roast turkey, producing the characteristic tang of Mexico. But it is impossible to generalize about the national cookery, for Mexico has at least a half dozen different cuisines: Yucatecan, Tarascan, Poblano, Veracruzana, food of the Texas border and of the Western Highlands.

Travellers who feel that Mexican food is simply not to their taste need not worry. "International cooking" (sometimes with a Mexican accent) is offered in most places where foreign visitors dine.

Mexican Crafts

In the discussions of various regions in this book there is much mention of crafts and shopping. Because we cover the subject piecemeal throughout the book, perhaps a broader look here will be of value.

In many countries travellers find shopping to be incidental. They may well pick up some souvenirs or buy a destination's famed specialties—jades in the Orient or perfumes in Paris, for example.

Mexico, as in so many things, is different. Shopping in the craft markets, or at least browsing, is one of the decided pleasures of visiting the country. (The same is true in Guatemala, where crafts are not far behind Tikal as an attraction. Almost all of highland Guatemala dazzles with handmade or decorated textiles; vendors in open-air markets expect to sell their wares at about one-third the asking price.) But the Mexican scene is often so rich that visitors find it confusing. What to look for?

First, a few words on those things you *cannot* buy. It is illegal to purchase and take pre-Columbian art and artifacts out of the country. Not surprisingly, Mexican authorities hold a very serious view of the matter; such an offense can lead to heavy fines and imprisonment.

Then why, you might ask, are all these vendors jumping out of the bushes at archaeological sites and offering me carvings? Why aren't they arrested? The answer, of course, is simply that they are offering nothing but fakes. If you find an object attractive and reasonably priced, buy it as contemporary art—but don't think of it as old. Reproductions of ancient works, especially ceramics and clay sculptures, are created in studios under government license. Shops everywhere offer them, especially in the resort centers. Often they are lovely, striking, and unusual. Enjoy them for what they are—not what someone *says* they are—and you won't be disappointed.

Mexico expresses its character in its handicrafts, which are often beautiful and quite fragile. Nowadays the best are quickly shipped all over the country and soon appear on shelves in Mexico City and Acapulco. On the other hand, if you want to search for the best at the source, here are some tips:

- *Silver.* Mexico City, Taxco, Guadalajara, and Oaxaca
- *Tinware.* San Miguel de Allende
- *Blankets and rugs.* Tlaxcala, Oaxaca, San Miguel de Allende, Pátzcuaro, and Guatemala
- *Clothing.* Morelia, Pátzcuaro, Mérida, Guadalajara, San Miguel de Allende, Mexico City, and Guatemala
- *Ceramics.* Oaxaca, Pátzcuaro, Tonalá, Puebla, and Mexico City
- *Hand-blown glass.* Guadalajara
- *Lacquerware.* Pátzcuaro, Morelia, and Uruapan
- *Copperware.* Mexico City, Guadalajara, San Miguel de Allende, and Santa María del Cobre (near Pátzcuaro)
- *Brass.* Mexico City and San Miguel de Allende
- *Woodcarving.* Paracho (Michoacán) and Pátzcuaro
- *Gold filigree.* Mérida

Every region of Mexico has its special character and unique attractions, as you will see in this book. Each traveller will find places that become personal favorites—be they ruins, dazzling beaches, tile-encrusted palaces, or fragrant plazas.

Yet there is something more in Mexico, an elusive quality, that makes the whole more than the sum of its parts. Writer Charles Flandrau, after sojourning through the country early this century, understood this, and no one since has expressed it quite so well: "The most notable sight in Mexico is simply Mexico."

USEFUL FACTS

When to Go

Mexico is a fine year-round destination, but the various seasons have different attractions. Winter—December through March—is ideal because of the generally cool, dry weather. It's an especially good time to visit the Gulf Coast and Yucatán, which can get unbearably hot and humid at other times of the year. On the other hand, it's also the peak tourist season, when demand for all services is greatest. Discounts vanish, many prices rise sharply despite controls, and major beach resorts get crowded. Archaeological zones are also heavily visited at this time of year.

April and May usually are not crowded, but spring is also the hottest, driest time of year in many places. The highland regions grow dusty and the land turns brown.

Summer, the second most popular season for visitors, brings rains that are usually brief but often torrential. Mornings and early afternoons tend to be clear and lovely. Summer, even on the coasts, is not as warm as spring.

Fall has temperate weather, with the rains continuing until the end of September. October and November are appealing, uncrowded months. This is also hurricane season on the Caribbean coast, so weather there, usually pleasant in fall, is a matter of luck.

Mexico City closes down during Holy Week (the week before Easter), as millions of its inhabitants rush for the beaches. Avoid the resorts at this time. The capital, on the other hand, is an attractive alternative then, even though some businesses will be closed. Throughout the country all forms of transportation are packed at Easter.

Entry Documents

In theory, U.S. and Canadian citizens need only proof of citizenship and a tourist card to enter Mexico. Ironically, as free trade among the three countries moves closer to becoming a reality, immigration requirements, even for short-term visitors, seem to have been tightened. Instances of U.S. and Canadian citizens being threatened with stiff fines for trying to enter Mexico without a passport have become increasingly common of late. As naturalized citizens and Europeans *must* present a valid passport, and all travellers will find that a passport is invaluable for transactions in banks and money-exchanging offices, we strongly suggest that every visitor to Mexico, regardless of nationality, brings theirs along. Tourist cards are issued at Mexican consulates, border crossings, major airports, and by some travel agencies. There is no charge for the card, which is stamped on entry and which must be turned in, along with a departure tax (currently $12 per person), when you leave the country. The length of permissible stay listed on the card is determined by the official issuing it. The time can be extended, not to exceed 180 days, at tourism offices throughout the country.

See "Around Mexico by Car," below, for information on documents needed to bring a car into Mexico.

Arrival at Major Gateways by Air

The major carriers providing direct service to Mexico are Mexicana, Aeroméxico, Continental, American, Delta, and United. With few exceptions international travellers will have to make connections in the United States. (Canadian Airlines International, which offers direct Toronto–Mexico City flights three times a week, is an exception.)

Mexicana offers direct service to Mexico City and Guadalajara (with connections from the capital to every major city in the country) from a number of U.S. cities, including New York, Miami, Chicago, Dallas–Fort Worth, Denver, San Francisco, and Los Angeles. It also offers direct service to Cancún from New York and Los Angeles. Aeroméxico offers direct service to Mexico City and Cancún from New York, Miami, Houston, and New Orleans, and to Mexico City only from Los Angeles. Continental flies direct from its Houston hub to Mexico City and Guadalajara as well as most of the major resorts, including Acapulco, Cancún, Cozumel, Ixtapa/Zihuatanejo, Los Cabos, and Puerto Vallarta. American, which routes the bulk of its Mexico service through Dallas–Fort Worth and Miami, offers flights to Mexico City, Guadalajara, Acapulco, Cancún, Cozumel, and Puerto Vallarta. Delta offers daily flights to Mexico City and Acapulco from its Dallas–Fort Worth hub. United flies daily to Mexico City from Chicago and San Francisco, as well as infrequently to Cancún from Chicago and Washington, D.C. The relatively new international airport in León (in the Colonial Heartland) is serviced daily from Houston by Continental, from Los Angeles by Mexicana, and from Chicago three days a week by Mexicana. Aeroméxico offers a daily León–Los Angeles flight with a stop in Hermosillo, and flies the same route three times a week with a stop in Puerto Vallarta. For further information contact your travel agent or any of the airlines mentioned above.

Taxis with regulated rates are available at the capital's airport. There is metro (subway) service from the airport, but it can be confusing for passengers with little command of the language arriving in Mexico for the first time.

Some hotels in outlying cities will arrange to have a driver meet passengers at the customs exit gate at the Mexico City airport and transport them directly, thus bypassing a stopover in the capital.

Flights leave daily from Mexico City for Guatemala City. See the Getting Around section at the end of the Guatemala chapter for information on travel to that country.

Around Mexico by Air

Mexico City is the air hub of the country, and air service anywhere is often routed through the capital. There is, in addition, good service from the D.F. to all the larger resorts. For the other regions described in this book the airport gateways are: Morelia, León, and San Luis Potosí for the Bajío (Colonial Heartland) region; Guadalajara for the Western Highlands and Pacific coast resorts; Veracruz and Villahermosa for the Gulf Coast region; Villahermosa, Mérida,

Cancún, and Tuxtla Gutiérrez for the Mayan region; and Chihuahua and Los Mochis for the Copper Canyon.

Around Mexico by Train

Service is relatively limited and tends to be slow. As in most affairs, everything is linked to the capital. There is good but not rapid service from the D.F. to Veracruz, Guadalajara, Querétaro, San Miguel de Allende, Pátzcuaro, Monterrey, Nuevo Laredo, and Oaxaca. While the trains are constantly being upgraded, they are not really a practical option for touring the country. If you are not travelling overnight, get a ticket that is first-class special (*primera especial*), which will guarantee you a comfortable seat.

Around Mexico by Bus

The bus is the donkey of motor vehicles in Mexico, able to get to the most remote backwater. Good service will be provided on a bus that runs first class (*primera clase*); ask for direct service (*directo*) to avoid too many stops and detours. Nevertheless, be prepared for the toilet to be out of order and dress for the air-conditioning to be likewise—or else working overtime. Bottled drinks are generally available, but on a long trip you should carry some sort of snack; some bus-station restaurants are less than appetizing.

Second-class buses (*segunda clase*) are often identical to first-class vehicles except for the number of stops they make (although some are older and a bit more rickety). A second-class bus may stop anywhere along the road to load or unload things, including passengers, bundles of newspapers, chickens, goats, or a hundred pieces of handmade pottery on the way to market. They may also be jammed to the roof: Try to grab a window seat if you can. Finally, don't get too discouraged; travelling like this can be fun and colorful or simply fast and uneventful.

A new and far superior class of service began operating in 1991. *Premier de lujo,* or *super de lujo,* offers vehicles equipped with rest rooms, reclining seats, and attendants who serve refreshments. Although expanding rapidly, this service now operates only between the largest Mexican cities and the U.S. border. Two good lines are **ETN** (Tel: 5/567-3773 or 5/273-0251) and **Primera Plus** (Tel: 5/587-5200 or 5/271-2724); inquire before purchasing another type of ticket—this is much the best choice and worth the price difference.

Rest rooms in bus stations are usually called *sanatarios*

yet tend to be anything but sanitary; be prepared for at least a twinge of culture shock.

Around Mexico by Car

Travellers driving into Mexico will need car permits, which are issued free of charge by Mexican customs at the border. The document is valid for 90 days and can be extended by any customs office in the country; official tourism offices in major Mexican cities will refer motorists to the proper authorities for extensions. Only the principal driver needs a permit; passengers need only a tourist card.

The driver must also sign a credit card voucher and a pledge saying the car will not be left in Mexico. The $10 charge is payable only with an internationally recognized credit card issued in a country other than Mexico. Cash is not accepted. Proof of ownership and a valid driving license are necessary.

Drivers without a credit card must present other documents: their license plus one copy, the original car title, the current operating registration, a U.S. insurance policy valid for at least two months after the date of the border crossing, and legal proof of citizenship with a copy. (Have any necessary copies prepared *before* you reach the border.) Additionally, if the car is not fully paid for, the bank or other lien holder must authorize the use of the car in Mexico for a specific period of time. Because these rules have resulted in such slow crossings (one to 3 hours), changing them is under consideration; inquire at a Mexican consulate.

Mexican auto insurance is required by law; short-term policies are sold on the U.S. side near all border crossings. AAA and Sanborn's are reliable, but so are others. All insurance transactions are closely regulated by the government and rates are uniform. *On no account should you drive in Mexico without proper Mexican insurance.* Uninsured drivers go to jail if involved in an accident. You may *not* leave Mexico without the vehicle. If for any reason you cannot take the car back across the border, contact the U.S. embassy or nearest consular agency for instructions.

Once you are equipped with a car permit and Mexican insurance, only two more items are essential: a large measure of optimism and another of patience. Optimism is important, as the first few hours driving through northern Mexico may prove disappointing; it is the least attractive region of the country. Patience will be helpful as you encounter poorly marked highways, unexpected *topes* (speed bumps) that force you to slow to a crawl, and free-ranging livestock oblivious to car horns and shouted imprecations.

Similarly, the condition of rest rooms in Pemex stations (Pemex is the governmental gasoline monopoly) may range from offputting to appalling. At such moments, remind yourself about cultural differences and then tell yourself that matters will improve—as indeed they will.

There are countless tricks and techniques to driving in Mexico, but essentially everything comes down to common sense, courtesy, and a little more caution than you would exercise on more familiar ground.

If your car develops trouble at any point, the Green Angels may come to your rescue. The "Angels" are government-subsidized crews in green-and-white pickup trucks who roam Mexico's main highways looking for travellers in need of assistance. The service is free, but motorists will have to pay for any gasoline, oil, or replacement parts.

If you find yourself in need of a Green Angel, pull off the highway and raise the hood of your car; this will alert any passing repair crew. If there's a telephone nearby, call the national hotline of the **Secretary of Tourism**, Tel: (5) 250-0132; they will radio-dispatch a patrol to you as quickly as they can. Passing truck drivers are also good about stopping and placing calls for you or rendering other assistance. In fact, foreign drivers are frequently surprised by the number of good Samaritans on Mexico's highways.

Low-quality gasoline is one good reason to opt for renting a car rather than using your own. If you're taking your own vehicle you'll face the frustration of trying to find the unleaded gas that most foreign cars use. Pemex has introduced a new unleaded gas called Magna Sin, which can be found along all the usual tourist routes but not on side roads. (Signs posted beside major highways announce the availability of Magna Sin ahead.) Regular Mexican leaded Nova will do in a pinch, without poisoning your engine, until you can find the higher octane. (Some drivers have their U.S. antipollution package disconnected before crossing the border.) Expect coughs and sputters from the lower-octane mix, however.

The prudent driver will get out of the car at gasoline stations and check the pump to make sure it is set at zero before delivery begins. If possible, order the same amount of gas every time you stop (e.g., half a tank, three-quarters of a tank), and count your change.

Getting to the more interesting parts of Mexico can be a long and expensive proposition. Combining means of transportation is probably your best bet: flying in, renting a car and driving to a particular destination, turning it in and taking a train, plane, or bus to the next spot, et cetera. Rental cars from companies with recognizable names are widely available, though they will be more expensive than in North America. If you want a car with an automatic transmission, you must ask ahead; they aren't standard issue.

Readers thinking of driving into Mexico from the U.S.–Mexico border will want to consult the Getting Around sections at the end of the Colonial Heartland, Western Highlands, and Gulf Coast chapters, as well as the Mazatlán section of the Pacific Resorts chapter. Under the "Driving Down from the Border" heading in each of these chapters you will find much useful information concerning preferred routes, accommodations (usually motor inns), and places to eat.

Except within a large city do *not* drive at night. The reasons are legion.

Local Time

Mexico is never on daylight saving time. Most of the country is on central standard time (Winnipeg, Chicago, Dallas), with the exception of the far west—Sonora, Sinaloa, Nayarit (the mainland coast north of Puerto Vallarta)—and southern Baja California, which are all on mountain standard time (Calgary, Denver). Northern Baja California is on Pacific time and is the sole exception to the daylight saving rule: It always keeps the same time as Los Angeles.

Currency

The monetary unit is the peso, indicated by a dollar sign and sometimes the abbreviation M.N. (*moneda nacional*). The exchange rate fluctuates in relation to the U.S. and Canadian dollars. Denominations of bills are 1,000; 2,000; 5,000; 10,000; 20,000; 50,000; and 100,000. The coins that matter are 100; 200; 500; 1,000; and 5,000. Smaller coins of no real value are much in circulation, weighing down purses and wearing out pockets. (On January 1, 1993, bill denominations are scheduled to lose three zeroes and new bills are to be introduced. Additionally, coins are going to be phased out. Both old and new bills will be honored for an indefinite period of time.) As this book went to press the exchange rate was about 3,000 pesos to the dollar.

Traveller's checks and foreign currency should be exchanged at banks or private exchange offices (*casas de cambio*) for the best rate. Most banks exchange only during early business hours. Airport exchange offices also give good rates.

Major credit cards are accepted in most larger establishments, except gasoline stations. You will see the familiar logos posted on doors or windows. If you don't, ask before trying to charge.

Room Rates

Hotel room rates listed in this book are for double rooms, double occupancy, for the 1992–1993 winter "high season," that is, from December 1992 through Easter 1993. These rates, which are provided in U.S. dollars, include taxes but not meals, unless otherwise noted. (A 10 percent VAT tax applies to all goods and services, including hotel rates, in Mexico.) Service charges may not be legally added to quoted room rates. At press time some hotels were expecting to raise prices by 10 to 15 percent in 1993, so rates quoted should be used as general guidelines only. Inquire about actual costs before booking. (Note too that travellers may get a discount of 10 to 15 percent merely by asking "Hay descuenta?")

Time-shares

Selling time-shares in condominiums has become a thriving business at almost all Mexican resorts. These units offer endless variations concerning length of time involved, price, and quality. One danger to be aware of comes from high-pressure salespeople, usually native speakers of English, who stampede customers into hasty or careless decisions. The brevity of a resort vacation may impel people toward imprudent purchases. It is essential to ask thoughtful questions, to consider printed (as opposed to oral) information, and to comparison shop before signing anything.

Electric Current

Electricity in Mexico is supplied at 110 volts, alternating current, as in the United States and Canada. The same type and sizes of sockets and plugs are also standard in all three countries.

Telephoning

The international code number for dialing directly to Mexico is 52. While long-distance calls within Mexico are cheap, international calls are expensive because of taxes. It is easiest to telephone through hotel switchboards, but all towns have *larga distancia* telephone offices where prepaid calls can be put through.

Business Hours

There is no simple answer to this mystery. The day seems to start soon after 9:00 A.M., but it may be an hour later. Most of the country pauses for a two-hour break at 1:00 or 2:00 P.M., which means that business generally resumes between 3:00 and 4:00 P.M. Some offices will close at 5:00 P.M., which is a modern—and foreign—custom. Many establishments in Mexico City ignore the siesta, others keep it faithfully, and so far most attempts to change the old custom in the interest of efficiency have failed. Closing hour for most stores is commonly 7:00 or 8:00 P.M.

Museums and other public institutions that stay open on Sundays usually close on Mondays. Major archaeological zones are open seven days a week; inquire locally about smaller sites.

Holidays

Official holidays, when most businesses and all offices are closed, are: January 1, New Year's Day; February 5, Constitution Day; March 21, the birthday of Benito Juárez; May 1, Labor Day; September 16, Independence Day (but the celebration starts the night before); November 20, Anniversary of the Revolution; and December 25, Christmas.

Not official but close to it are: Holy Week, the week before Easter (with work slowly grinding to a halt as the week progresses and stopping completely on Thursday); May 5 (Cinco de Mayo), Anniversary of the Battle of Puebla; December 1, the presidential state-of-the-union report (*el informe*)—banks close; November 2, Day of the Dead; and December 12, Feast of Guadalupe, patroness saint of Mexico.

Also important are: May 10, Mother's Day; and October 12, Columbus Day, called Día de la Raza in Mexico.

Every town has its patron saint and takes a day to a week to celebrate his or her feast. Other religious holidays include: January 6, Three Kings Day, the traditional day of Christmas gift giving (but losing ground to Santa Claus); January 17, St. Anthony's Day, the traditional day for the blessing of animals; February 2, Candelaria, a rite of spring and the day candles and seeds are blessed; Carnaval (Mardi Gras), which is movable, with the best parties in Veracruz, Mazatlán, Mérida, and Guadalajara; late May or early June, Corpus Christi Day, with fairs and rites throughout the country; and December 16–23, the long Christmas prelude, celebrated with processions, parties, much singing, and nativity plays.

Safety

Beware of pickpockets, especially at public celebrations and on public transportation. The metro in Mexico City is a favorite hunting ground for dips and cutpurses; museum entrances are another haunt. Public streets in general are comparatively free of violence, but normal precautions should be taken.

Smaller cities are usually so safe that the only danger is in becoming careless. Theft of valuables from automobiles is common, however, so be careful where you park and leave nothing tempting in plain sight. Cameras and the like should be locked in the trunk.

Taxes

The onerous one is the I.V.A., called "Eva," a 10 percent sales tax on almost everything. By law it is supposed to be included in marked prices and quoted rates, but often it isn't. Ask if something is without tax, *sin* I.V.A. (*sin "Eevah"*), or if the tax is included, *con* I.V.A. (*con "Eevah"*).

Health

High altitudes can play strange tricks on your system. Avoid too much exertion, overeating, and heavy drinking while your body is adapting to the change in its oxygen supply. Alcohol seems to work more swiftly and potently in the highland areas, and can sneak up on you if your usual habitat is located at sea level or thereabouts.

In most places tap water is not purified. The old admonition "Don't drink the water" always seems hardest to remember when you have a toothbrush or an iced drink in your hand. Potable water is provided, in jugs or bottles, by all decent hotels and restaurants. In better establishments ice is made from purified water, but when in doubt, skip the ice.

The bulk of medical opinion is against taking any medicine in advance as a preventive for diarrhea. Rest and moderation are the best cure in almost every case. (The Spanish word for pharmacy is *farmacia*.) Most major hotels have a house doctor on call if you do get sick. However, they are usually prepared to treat only minor illnesses, and will recommend a specialist or hospital if necessary. The U.S. embassy in Mexico City also keeps a list of doctors on hand for emergencies; Tel: (5) 211-0042.

If you come to Mexico for a diving vacation make sure your medical insurance includes diving accidents; some dive operations in beach resorts do not carry their own insurance. In any event it's always better to be covered before setting out from home.

Dressing for Comfort

Tennis shoes, running shoes, or the like are strongly recommended. In all highland areas and even on the Gulf Coast a sweater or jacket will be needed on many nights, as will a windbreaker in Mexico City and at similar altitudes in winter. Informality in dress is the norm, but some restaurants in the capital and elsewhere have dress codes: coat and tie for men, cocktail dress or the like for women. Mexico City is the only truly dressy place in the country, and even there casual wear usually prevails, except in business.

It is no longer necessary for women to cover their heads before entering churches. One dress taboo remains, however: Shorts are not acceptable except in a beach or sports situation.

Rainwear will be needed in the late spring, all summer, and most of the fall.

For Further Information

The following is a list of Mexican government tourism offices in several major U.S., Canadian, and U.K. cities: 405 Park Avenue, Suite 1401, New York, NY 10022 (Tel: 212/755-7261, Fax: 212/753-2874); 2707 North Loop West, Suite 450, Houston, TX 77008 (Tel: 713/880-5153, Fax: 713/880-1833); 70 East Lake Street, Suite 1413, Chicago, IL 60601 (Tel: 312/565-2778, Fax: 312/606-9012); 10100 Santa Monica Boulevard, Suite 224, Los Angeles, CA 90067 (Tel: 310/203-8191, Fax: 310/203-8316); 2 Bloor Street West, Suite 1801, Toronto M4W 3E2 Ontario (Tel: 416/925-0704 or 1876, Fax: 416/925-6061); 1, Place Ville Marie, Suite 2409, Montréal H3B 3M9 Québec (Tel: 514/871-1052, Fax: 514/871-3825); 60–61 Trafalgar Square, London WC2N 5DS (Tel: 071/734-1058, Fax: 071/930-9202).

For further information on Guatemala contact the **Guatemala Tourist Commission**, 299 Alhambra Circle, Suite 510, Coral Gables, FL 33134; Tel: (800) 742-4529.

BIBLIOGRAPHY

MARIANO AZUELA, *The Underdogs* (1916). A sweaty, gritty novel of the revolutionary upheavals between 1911 and 1920, and a book that changed the course of Mexican literature.

JOSEPH ARMSTRONG BAIRD, JR., *The Churches of Mexico* (1962). A knowing survey of the major architectural achievements of New Spain.

BARBARA BALCHIN DE KOOSE, *Guatemala for You.* A detailed handbook to the country, published in 1989.

BIBLIOGRAPHY 27

SYBILLE BEDFORD, *Sudden View.* A sharp-eyed woman's travel memoir of Mexico, originally published in 1954.

IGNACIO BERNAL, *Mexico Before Cortés: Art, History, and Legend* (1963). A capsule history by the former director of Mexico's famed National Museum of Anthropology.

———, *The Olmec World* (1969). An elegantly written introduction to Mesoamerica's first great culture.

EMMET REID BLAKE, *Birds of Mexico* (1972). The abundant avian life of Mexico presented by a distinguished ornithologist. Illustrated.

ANITA BRENNER AND G. R. LEIGHTON, *The Wind That Shook Mexico* (1943). A long-repressed nation violently enters the modern world. Memorable photographs illuminate the text.

FRANCES CALDERÓN DE LA BARCA, *Life in Mexico* (1843). A series of shrewd, gossipy, and witty letters penned by the Scottish-Bostonian wife of Spain's first ambassador to the newborn Mexican Republic. Delightful, and in some ways oddly contemporary.

JORGE CASTANEDA AND ROBERT A. PASTOR, *Limits to Friendship: The United States and Mexico* (1989). Two informed viewpoints—often in disagreement, always thought-provoking.

MICHAEL D. COE, *The Maya* (fourth edition, 1987). A reliable introduction to the ancient Maya by a reputable scholar.

———, *Mexico* (third edition, 1986). A companion volume to Coe's book on the Maya, and a similarly reliable introduction to the highland cultures of ancient Mexico.

MAURICE COLLIS, *Cortés and Móctezuma.* Thoughtful speculation about the history of the Conquest as well as insights into its two major figures.

MIGUEL COVARRUBIAS, *Indian Art of Mexico and Central America* (1952). The appreciative views of an artist-scholar. Some theories are now outdated, but the main points remain valid, and the author's illustrations are unsurpassed in the field.

———, *Mexico South: The Isthmus of Tehuantepec* (1946). A colorful visit to a corner of Mexico as it was yesterday and almost is today. Illustrations by an outstanding artist.

NIGEL DAVIES, *The Ancient Kingdoms of Mexico* (1982). An excellent introductory survey of all the major pre-Columbian cultures except the Maya.

———, *The Aztecs* (1973). A political history of the last pre-Hispanic conquerors of Mexico.

———, *The Toltecs* (1979). An account of pre-Aztec conquest and culture.

BERNAL DÍAZ DEL CASTILLO, *The Discovery and Conquest of Mexico*. Also published as the *Bernal Díaz Chronicle*. An exciting eyewitness account by one of Cortés's soldiers. Essential; basic to everything ever written about the era.

HARRIET DOERR, *Stones for Ibarra* (1978). A penetrating novel of life and death in an isolated mining village.

ERNEST EDWARDS, *A Field Guide to Mexican Birds* (1972). For on-the-spot identification, where and how to watch, and what to look for.

ANDRE EMMERICH, *Art Before Columbus* (1963). The best and most concise introduction, one that untangles a complex field.

———, *Sweat of the Sun and Tears of the Moon* (1968). The use and veneration of precious metals in pre-Columbian art.

CARLOS ESPEJEL, *Mexican Folk Crafts* (1978). A wide-ranging survey that is short on text but lavish in photographic illustrations by F. Catala Roca.

CHARLES M. FLANDRAU, *Viva Mexico* (1908). These traveller's tales sometimes cross the line into fiction, but always to the reader's enlightenment.

CARLOS FUENTES, *The Death of Artemio Cruz* (1962). A powerful and complex novel of the betrayal of revolutionary ideals by politicians and businessmen. A novelist, essayist, and diplomat, Fuentes is the strongest voice currently speaking for Mexico.

———, *The Good Conscience* (1959). An intelligent and observant boy grows up in the provincial city of Guanajuato.

———, *The Old Gringo* (1984). A fictional speculation about the last days of celebrated American author and social critic Ambrose Bierce, who vanished into the Mexican revolution. Replete with pointed observations about Mexico, gringos, and life in general.

THOMAS GAGE, *A New Survey of the West Indies*. An account published in 1648 by the first English observer to report on

New Spain. He found little to his liking, establishing a British tradition.

CHARLES GALLENKAMP, *The Maya* (1976). Ancient Mayan life and art, with a postscript about the Maya in modern times.

GRAHAM GREENE, *The Power and the Glory* (1940). After half a century, this novel of the suppression of the Church in Mexico still crackles with suspense. It has been denounced by many Mexicans, who charge that it, as well as Greene's lesser work, *Another Mexico* (in some editions titled *The Lawless Roads*), were subsidized by foreign oil companies wishing to destabilize Mexico.

BERTITA HARDING, *Phantom Crown* (1934). A biographical work about Maximilian and Carlota.

MARIAN HARVEY, *Mexico's Crafts and Craftspeople* (1973). Where and how Mexican popular arts are fashioned and who makes them. Many photographic illustrations by Ken Harvey.

———, *Crafts of Mexico* (1987). A survey, appreciation, and explanation.

MCKINLEY HELM, *Man of Fire*. Mexican muralist José Clemente Orozco is presented in full color in this critical biography.

C. BRUCE HUNTER, *A Guide to Ancient Maya Ruins* (1974). Practical, portable, and now available in a revised up-to-date edition.

———, *A Guide to Ancient Mexican Ruins* (1977). A companion volume to Professor Hunter's book on ancient Mayan ruins. With site maps and halftones.

JONATHAN KANDELL, *La Capital*. A vivid "biography" of Mexico City that breathes with life, color, and the curiosities of history.

JOYCE KELLY, *The Complete Visitor's Guide to Mesoamerican Ruins*. A sensible and extensive work designed for the serious archaeology buff.

DIANA KENNEDY, *The Cuisines of Mexico*. Of the many books on Mexican cookery, this is the most popular with foreigners and the most representative of the country's varied regions.

JOSEPH WOOD KRUTCH, *The Forgotten Peninsula*. A keen and wise observer examines Baja California.

Diego de Landa, *Yucatán: Before and After the Conquest*. Friar Diego's eyewitness work, written in the mid-1500s, is basic to all Maya studies.

D. H. Lawrence, *The Plumed Serpent* (1926). Lawrence redesigned Mexican mythology to fit his own views, but the atmosphere of Lake Chapala and the Mexican characters he evokes make the story rewarding.

———, *Mornings in Mexico* (1927). Lawrence wrote most of these observations and ruminations in Oaxaca; the city's serene atmosphere lends the book a touch of peace uncharacteristic of the author's work.

A. Starker Leopold, *Wildlife of Mexico* (1959). Much of this work, written for hunters, has been rendered passé by game laws and extinction. Yet the information that abounds in its illustrated pages remains informative.

Oscar Lewis, *The Children of Sánchez* (1961). A profound and moving portrayal of slum life in Mexico City. This true account by an anthropologist caused a sensation in Mexico when first published. Now a classic.

———, *Five Families* (1959). A cross-section of Mexican life in readable form.

———, *Pedro Martínez* (1964). The harsh life of Mexico's farms and villages.

Malcolm Lowry, *Under the Volcano* (1947). A cult classic for a generation, this disturbing novel of foreigners in Cuernavaca has moved into the mainstream of literature.

Salvador Madariaga, *Heart of Jade* (1944). Tinged with mysticism and crammed with adventure, this novel gallops across the Mexican landscape during the Conquest.

———, *Hernán Cortés* (1948). A biography of the conqueror.

J. Patrick McHenry, *A Short History of Mexico* (1962). A concise, handy review, from pre-Conquest to 1960, unusually sympathetic to the Church.

The Metropolitan Museum of Art, *Mexico: Splendors of Thirty Centuries* (1990). With an introduction by Nobel Prize-winner Octavio Paz, this book is a photographic splendor in itself. From Preclassic fertility figurines to Frida Kahlo.

Tom Miller and Carol Hoffman, *The Baja Book III: Map Guide to Today's Baja California*. The best overall practical guidebook for someone planning to drive the length of Baja California.

Minutiae Mexicana. This series of pocket-size booklets in English (usually available at tourist centers in Mexico and sometimes in the United States) deals in summary form with everything Mexican, from bird lore to witchcraft. Many titles, all carefully prepared.

SYLVANUS G. MORLEY, *The Ancient Maya* (revised by George W. Brainard and Robert J. Sharer, fourth edition, 1983). A distinguished Mayanist explores the field for beginners.

WRIGHT MORRIS, *Love Among the Cannibals* (1957). A witty novel about the lives of some jaded Los Angeles show-business types after they move down to the Acapulco of the 1950s to find themselves.

PATRICK OSTER, *Mexicans* (1989). A portrait of a people through the profiles of 20 individuals.

HENRY B. PARKES, *A History of Mexico* (1960). A balanced, straightforward work that has become almost standard for English-language readers in this field.

OCTAVIO PAZ, *The Labyrinth of Solitude* (1962). Sharp, sometimes startling insights into Mexican life and character by a great contemporary writer and philosopher. A Mexican monument.

The *Popul Vuh,* or sacred writings of the Quiché Maya. Pre-Hispanic history, legend, and theology interwoven into a fascinating literary tapestry. Also known as the *Book of the Tiger Priests* or the *Book of the Counsel.*

WILLIAM H. PRESCOTT, *History of the Conquest of Mexico.* This masterpiece, first published in 1843, has some faulty and doubtful judgments, yet remains the unsurpassed epic of the Spanish Conquest.

JOHN REED, *Insurgent Mexico* (1914). What a "red" gringo firebrand saw, or wanted to see, in the Mexican Revolution.

ALAN RIDING, *Distant Neighbors* (1988). A U.S. journalist turns a penetrating eye on the Mexico of yesterday and today.

JUAN RULFO, *Pedro Páramo* (1955). The living and the dead mingle elusively in this fictional masterwork of Mexican literature.

LINDA SCHELE AND DAVID FREIDEL, *A Forest of Kings: The Untold Story of the Ancient Maya* (1990). A fascinating, revisionist look at ancient Mayan society by a sometimes controversial authority on Mayan hieroglyphs and her collaborator.

EDWARD SIMMEN, ED., *Gringos in Mexico*. Fifteen U.S. authors, including such unlikely companions as William Cullen Bryant, Edna Ferber, and Jack Kerouac, rub elbows in this short-story collection.

JEAN-MARIE SIMON, *Guatemala: Eternal Spring, Eternal Tyranny*. (1987). A disturbing report on repression in Guatemala told in strong words and powerful, moving photographs.

LESLEY BYRD SIMPSON, *Many Mexicos*. Lively and sometimes trenchant essays on Mexican history, from Cortés through the 1960s. Indispensable.

BRADLEY SMITH, *Mexico: A History in Art*. The story of the country from earliest times as revealed by artists both known and unknown. Fine reproductions make this a lovely way to study history.

REX SMITH, ED., *Biography of the Bulls*. Everything a beginning aficionado needs to know about bullfighting. The concentration is on Spain, but the information also applies to Mexico.

ROBERT SOMERLOTT, *Death of the Fifth Sun* (1987). This fictional autobiography of Malinche, Cortés's mistress and guide, gives a different view of the Aztec world.

JACQUES SOUSTELLE, *Arts of Ancient Mexico*. A short but solid survey lavishly illustrated with black-and-white photographs.

———, *Daily Life of the Aztecs* (1961). A less-than-vivid treatment is saved by accurate, telling details.

JOHN STEINBECK, *The Pearl*. A timeless story about a Baja California fisherman and his covetous neighbors. The village life is sharply revealed.

JOHN STEINBECK AND EDWARD RICKETTS, *The Sea of Cortés*. A leisurely but interesting journey along the coast of Baja California.

MARIA STEN, *The Mexican Codices and Their Extraordinary History*. Fascinating stories and explanations of the "painted books" of the pre-Hispanic epoch. An introduction to ancient American writing.

JOHN L. STEPHENS, *Incidents of Travel in Yucatán*. Stephens and draftsman Frederick Catherwood were explorers in the Maya region. Their work, published in 1843, was dismissed as Marco Millions exaggerations. Time has made fools of the critics.

FRANK TANNENBAUM, *Mexico: The Struggle for Peace and Bread* (1950). The outstanding foreign work about Mexico's continuing revolution.

FRANCES TOOR, *A Treasury of Mexican Folkways* (1947). As packed as a piñata with sayings, customs, songs, superstitions, and other lore, this is the foremost work in its field.

MANUEL TOUSSAINT, *Colonial Art in Mexico* (1949). This pioneering work is the cornerstone of Mexican art history. Architecture, painting, sculpture, and a glance at popular arts.

B. TRAVEN, *The Bridge in the Jungle* (1938). An ironic parable of cultural collisions in the form of a novel.

———, *The Rebellion of the Hanged* (1952). The author wrote six novels of revolt set in Mexico's jungles. This, the fifth, is the most powerful.

JOHN KENNETH TURNER, *Barbarous Mexico* (1909; reprinted 1969). Early in this century, the author, a muckraking journalist, penetrated slave camps in southern Mexico and exposed the horrors of the Porfirio Díaz dictatorship, causing a furor in the United States.

GEORGE C. VAILLANT, *The Aztecs of Mexico* (1941). An early work in the field, and still the most complete and interesting for the general reader.

VICTOR W. VON HAGEN, *The Aztec, Man and Tribe* (1961). A popular historical survey with informative illustrations.

BERNARD DE VOTO, *The Year of Decision* (1961). The parts of the book dealing with the U.S.–Mexican War provide a brief but incisive treatment of this tragedy.

JACK WILLIAMS, *The Magnificent Peninsula: The Only Absolutely Essential Guide to Mexico's Baja California*. Well, maybe not the *only* guide (see the Miller-Hoffman book), but a practical one; with photographs.

ERIC WOLF, *Sons of the Shaking Earth* (1959). The land, people, history, and culture of Mexico and Guatemala.

BERTRAM D. WOLFE, *The Fabulous Life of Diego Rivera* (1963). This biography of the tempestuous genius fully lives up to its title. Crammed with wine, women, and outrage.

RONALD WRIGHT, *Time Among the Maya* (1989). A thoughtful and articulate traveller in Belize, Guatemala, and Mexico.

AGUSTIN YANEZ, *The Edge of the Storm* (1947). A living, breathing, but fictional creation of a Mexican village. Mexico's first major psychological novel.

MICHAEL ZAMBA, *A Guide to Living in Mexico* (1989). Practical, sensible information for prospective retirees and others.
—*Robert Somerlott*

MEXICO CITY

By Larry Russell

A resident of Mexico City since 1973, Larry Russell is a frequent contributor to the travel sections of Mexico's Vogue *and* Progreso *magazines. In collaboration with his wife, he has also produced, written, and performed the musical scores for a number of documentary films about Mexico.*

Like wagon-wheel spokes to a hub—an immense hub—all major highways in the Republic of Mexico lead to its capital, Mexico City. Officially known as the Distrito Federal (D.F.), the most populous city on the planet is situated in the Valley of Mexico (called the Valley of Anáhuac in pre-Conquest days) on a site that was chosen in the 14th century by the Aztecs for what would soon become Tenochtitlán, their storied capital. Today the D.F. sprawls over a flat, sun-baked plateau that rises 7,347 feet above sea level and covers 573 square miles. It is surrounded by three forested mountain chains, which dramatically set the stage for 17,883-foot Popocatépetl (Smoking Mountain) and 17,338-foot Iztaccíhuatl (pronounced EE-sta-see-watl, and meaning "Sleeping Woman"), the two perpetually snow-capped volcanoes that dominate the valley's southeastern horizon. On a clear day the panoramic views from the city are breathtaking.

With the climatic effects of its semitropical latitude offset by its altitude, Mexico City has a temperate and invigorating climate that can be divided into two seasons: a dry season, which stretches from November through early May, and a wet season, which lasts from mid-May through October. (The tail end of the dry season, when there are few cleansing rains, may be the least comfortable time of year here.)

Temperatures average 60°F over the course of the year, and seldom rise above an average of 75°F in the hottest months (June and July) or fall below an average of 45°F during the coolest months (December and January). Nights are always cool, and there's a marked temperature contrast between sunny and shady places, as well as between the heat of midday and the chill of early morning and evening.

According to the latest census figures, fully a quarter of Mexico's 88 million people lives in the D.F. Whereas the 1930 census counted only a million inhabitants in the entire metropolitan area, and there were fewer than five million in 1960, the net growth rate of the capital's population today is 1,000 residents *daily*. Projections for a decade from now run as high as 30 million inhabitants.

As a result, the D.F. pulsates with a vibrant energy that makes it a compelling place to visit. In countless ways it epitomizes the best of Mexico—except in the quality of its air. Though Mexico City is notorious for its pollution, the seriousness of the situation has inspired determined—if somewhat belated—action on the part of the people in power (and the D.F. is where most of the nation's powerful live). As of 1989, every vehicle registered in the Republic of Mexico was banned from circulating in the capital one day a week, Monday through Friday. Called "Hoy No Circula," what began as a program to reduce car emissions during the winter months (the city's peak pollution season because of thermal inversions and the lack of rainfall) has been extended "indefinitely"—for obvious reasons. According to recent estimates the ban keeps nearly half a million vehicles idle each day it is in effect, eliminating almost 3,000 tons of particulate matter from the valley's sometimes poisonous stew of pollution.

(After drivers hoping to get around the restrictions began registering their cars in other states, Mexico City's pollution prevention and control department announced that cars from outside the city, and even the country, would be subject to the ban as well. The day on which such out-of-state cars are banned is determined by the last number on the license plate: Cars with plates ending in the number one or two are banned on Thursdays, those ending in three or four on Wednesdays, five and six on Mondays, seven and eight on Tuesdays, and nine and zero on Fridays. In March 1992 the "Hoy No Circula" campaign was extended to two days of restriction per five-day period, eliminating 40 percent of the normal traffic flow. The restrictions may fluctuate depending on contamination levels.)

In fact, many of the country's persistent problems are being addressed with renewed vigor by a breed of younger politicians led by 44-year-old Harvard-educated Carlos Salinas de Gortari. A hands-on president midway through his six-year term, Salinas has utilized the virtually unlimited powers of his office to order Pemex, the government-run petroleum monopoly, to immediately supply unleaded gasoline to every gas station in the nation, and to make it mandatory for all auto-assembly plants and public-transportation vehicles to install emission converters. Recently Salinas disbanded SEDUE, Mexico's Urban Development and Environmental Secretariat, which had long been considered a paper tiger, and instigated the creation of a new governmental group answering directly to him. The goal of the group is to "deal a death blow to corruption in governmental bureaucracy and to dedicate all that is necessary to acquire a healthy ecological equilibrium."

When it comes to crime in the streets, on the other hand, Mexico City is safer than New York, Hong Kong, São Paulo, or Rome. (According to government statistics, Mexico City has fewer per capita crimes of violence than any other city in the world with a population exceeding a million people.) Moreover, visitors enjoy a privileged status here, and not only because Mexicans have a long tradition of hospitality to strangers. As most Mexicans realize, tourism represents one of the few reliable sources of foreign currency and nonpolluting employment.

A visit to Mexico City today is like stepping into an enormous melting pot of history and cultures. Sadly, the blending of these cultures was usually forced and involved much bloodshed. Perhaps the plaque at the Plaza de las Tres Culturas in Tlatelolco says it best: "On the 13th of August, 1521, defended by the heroic Cuauhtemoc, Tlatelolco fell under the power of Hernan Cortez. It was neither a triumph nor a defeat, but the painful birth of the mixed race that is the Mexico of today."

One of the legacies of this painful past is the inherent sense of fatalism that seems to lurk within the souls of most Mexicans. In the D.F. this fatalism is nowhere more evident than in the wild and often reckless style of driving that prevails among its residents. (Public-transportation drivers, oddly enough, are usually the worst offenders.) The local saying here is that if you can drive—and survive—in Mexico City, you can drive anywhere.

To those who have spent time here, it is not just macho boasting. In fact, as a visitor quickly learns, if you scratch a typical Mexico City native you'll find a soulful anarchist. Little wonder, then, that the city itself seems to mirror this side of the Mexican character, from its colorful, bustling street markets (*tianguis*), where the distinctive sound of the penny whistle signals the arrival of the itinerant knife-sharpener, to busy street corners where groups of traditionally attired Indians perform their native dances. Elsewhere, shabbily dressed street musicians congregate in residential neighborhoods to perform on their dented saxophones, beat-up clarinets, and toy-size drums while a skinny kid collects the coins that residents rain down on them from their windows; balloon vendors with their fabulous bunches of brightly colored helium-filled *globos* seem to defy the laws of nature by staying earthbound; barrel organists in funky khaki uniforms grind away in front of cantinas; bell-clangers lead the garbage trucks on their daily routes as if they were drum majors leading a parade; and Indian women, squatting on the sidewalk, sell handmade tortillas at twice the price of the government-controlled *tortillerías* ("The sweat from the palm of the hands is the secret ingredient," say the connoisseurs).

The almost palpable energy in the air is enhanced by telling contrasts on every street and around every corner: sleek limousines parked cheek by jowl with unimpressed burros; chic boutiques selling international designer originals as barefoot Indian women hawk handicrafts made the night before on the sidewalk out front; a gourmet dining in an elegant French or Japanese restaurant while, down the street, a gourmand munches on tacos served from a portable grill set up on the sidewalk.

And yet, despite these contrasts, Mexico City is no longer just a great Third World capital. Today it is a cosmopolitan *world* capital, one that need not take a back seat to any of the great metropolises in the quality of its architecture; the quality and diversity of its museums, art galleries, public parks, and zoos; the variety and exuberance of its cultural presentations; the range of its hotels, restaurants, and shopping; and the efficiency of its public transportation. And, among the great cities of the world, it stands far above the others in one respect: the warmth of its hospitality.

MAJOR INTEREST

Museums
Museo Nacional de Antropología

Museo del Templo Mayor
Museo Rufino Tamayo
Museo de Arte Moderno

Sights
The historic Zócalo area
Palacio de Bellas Artes
Plaza de las Tres Culturas
Central Paseo de la Reforma
The canal rides of Xochimilco
The pyramids of Teotihuacán

Neighborhoods
The Zona Rosa for shopping and café life
Polanco for dining and shopping
Coyoacán and San Angel, quaint colonial villages with beautiful vintage residences
El Pedregal's spectacular homes

Parks
Alameda
Chapultepec

Ancient Mexico City

"Mexico City has almost always been the largest city in the world," writes Fernando Benítez, octogenarian Mexican historian and author. "At the height of the Roman empire's glory, Teotihuacán, as Mexico City was then known, was acknowledged to have been more populated and much more splendid than Rome. It was the capital of an empire that stretched from what is today the northern border of Texas beyond the southern boundaries of the country we know as Guatemala."

In the early 14th century, some 600 years after Teotihuacán had been mysteriously abandoned by its priest-rulers and inhabitants, a nomadic tribe calling themselves the Mexicas (pronounced meh-SHEE-kas) left their ancestral home of Aztlán in search of greener pastures. According to their mythology, they would recognize the site of their new home when they came upon an eagle perched on a nopal cactus with a serpent in its beak.

After years of wandering, the Mexicas stumbled upon this apparition sometime around 1325, at a spot that is now buried under the Plaza de Santo Domingo, in Mexico City. At the time, however, the future site of Tenochtitlán, as the Mexicas were to call their new home, was nothing more than an uninhabited, snake-infested island located some 30 miles from the fabled pyramids of Teotihuacán in the southern reaches of a vast, shallow lake. Over the next two centuries, the Mexicas—whom their neighbors dubbed Aztecs, or "people from Aztlán"—worked feverishly to expand the limits of their island city, draining portions of the lake, creating landfills, and constructing causeways to the shore. (Only in recent years, with the construction of the underground metro system, have some startling remains of Tenochtitlán been uncovered. See the Templo Mayor section below.)

By the time Columbus arrived in the New World, the Aztecs had created, in addition to their magnificent city, a far-reaching empire, and were even then engaged in trying to expand it by bringing coastal lands around present-day Acapulco under their control. When, in 1519, a 34-year-old Spanish sea captain named Hernán Cortés led a band of 550 soldiers and 22 mounted horses inland from their landfall just north of what is today the city of Veracruz, he found a city larger and more spectacular than any existing in Europe at the time. Reliable estimates put the population in excess of 200,000, many of whom lived on man-made plots of land connected to the main island by an intricate series of canals. Despite their admiration for the material accomplishments of the Aztecs, however, the self-styled *conquistadores* were appalled by the natives' religion, driven as it was by human sacrifice, and so promptly set out to subjugate and convert the city's inhabitants to Christianity. (Another theory is that the Spaniards greatly exaggerated the human sacrifice factor in order to justify their actions.)

Eventually the victorious Spanish—with the assistance of an estimated 10,000 Tlaxcalan Indian warriors (dedicated enemies of the Aztecs), gunpowder, and a decimating smallpox epidemic—destroyed virtually every visible aspect of Aztec civilization and over the ruins of their great temples and the emperor's palace built their own cathedral and a palace for Cortés. In fact, most of the foundations of the 16th-century structures here were erected using the sturdy building stones taken from toppled Aztec temples.

From the first, the city—which the Spanish named México (after the Aztecs' name for themselves)—functioned as the capital of New Spain. Nevertheless, the city grew slowly in its formative years, and only regained the population levels of Tenochtitlán early in our own century. Physically, however, Mexico City spread ever wider as the great lake, Texcoco, was drained, filled, and built over.

As it turned out, it was not a very practical site for heavy construction, and the old buildings almost immediately began to settle into the soft underbelly of the ancient lake bed—a process that has been continuing for centuries now. Frequent pumping of underground water and periodic flooding since the 16th century have also contributed to the city's "settling"—by some estimates more than 23 feet during the last century alone. Experts claim the situation has been stabilized by the use of modern engineering techniques and the installation of an ingenious drainage system that has permanently eliminated flooding. Still, while the avant-garde skyscrapers that are constantly going up seem to be in fine shape, you'll see many old colonial-era churches and buildings tilting at odd angles, especially throughout the historic downtown area.

The frequent earthquake activity in the region also has done its share of damage to the foundations of many slowly sinking structures. Although dozens of newer buildings were devastated by the 1985 quake, the city's skyscrapers weathered the shocks thanks to their high-tech "floating" foundations. Most of the colonial structures were unscathed as well; some even lean less than they did before the quake.

Mexico City Orientation

It may be difficult for the first-time visitor to form a mental image of the city, what with its rambling vastness seemingly devoid of a sensible street plan, with many of its major thoroughfares crisscrossing diagonally, and with cul-de-sacs punctuating every neighborhood. Once you get your bearings, however, it is surprisingly easy to find your way around the areas of interest.

The two main arteries in Mexico City are the 27-km (17-mile)-long **Avenida Insurgentes** (in-sur-HEN-tays), one of the longest urban thoroughfares in the world, which basically runs north to south; and the 15-km (9-mile)-long **Paseo de la Reforma**, the eight-lane tree-lined Champs-Elysées of the Americas, which starts out by running parallel to Insurgentes in the northeast, curves and intersects the latter just north of the Zona Rosa, cuts through Chapultepec Park—the city's magnificent public space and the site of the Museo Nacional de Antropología and other great cultural institutions—and finally turns southwest, where it eventually becomes Federal Highway 15 and continues on to Toluca, 30 miles away. The Zócalo, the Zona Rosa, and Chapultepec Park are all within a 15- to 30-minute walk of the intersection of Reforma and Insurgentes, and it's here as well that you'll find clustered most of the best hotels, restaurants, major foreign embassies, airline sales offices, and other visitor attractions. (The Reforma intersection is also where Insurgentes Norte becomes Insurgentes Sur.)

The Zócalo serves as the eastern boundary of the area of most interest to visitors, and Chapultepec Park does the

Mexico City

same to the west. The northernmost point of interest in the central urban area is the **Basílica de Nuestra Señora de Guadalupe** (Basilica of Our Lady of Guadalupe), which is reached by following Paseo de la Reforma to its beginning at the Tlatelolco traffic circle (about 6 km/3½ miles from the intersection of Reforma and Insurgentes) and continuing north on Calzada de Guadalupe for two blocks.

Avenida Insurgentes Sur leads to all the major attractions in the southern part of the city, including the **Siqueiros Cultural Polyforum**; the **Plaza México** (the bullfight ring); the residential colonial neighborhoods of **Coyoacán** and **San Angel**; the avant-garde architecture of the elegant residences in **El Pedregal**; the archaeological sites of **Copilco** and **Cuicuilco**; **University City**, with its famous murals; **Reino Aventura** (Mexico's Disneyland); and the canals of **Xochimilco**. The last, 25 km (16 miles) south of the intersection of Reforma and Insurgentes, is the southernmost boundary of the areas of most interest.

The **Zócalo** is the heart of the old city. Besides the many historical sites, including the cathedral and the excavations of the central Aztec temple complex, the surrounding area is home to the financial district. Colonial in feel and appearance, the narrow cobblestone streets are jammed with all types of shops. It is a bit seedy, perhaps, but picturesque nevertheless and always churning with vitality. The Zócalo itself is off limits to vehicular traffic, and pedestrian malls are scattered throughout the area, making it ideal for strolling and window-shopping. One of the ancient streets leading west from the Zócalo is Calle Madero. Only a few blocks long, it changes its name as it crosses Eje Central Lázaro Cárdenas and becomes Avenida Juárez. At this point the preponderance of 17th- and 18th-century colonial architecture merges with a dash of the Art Nouveau and other more contemporary styles. The elegant Palacio de Bellas Artes (Palace of Fine Arts) is on the right, and to the left, towering above the hustle and bustle, is the Torre Latinoamericana (Latin American Tower), a modern 44-story skyscraper with an observation deck on the 42nd floor and a restaurant, the Muralto, with panoramic views from most every table occupying the entire 41st floor.

Continuing west on Avenida Juárez you'll pass the always pulsating **Parque Alameda Central**, abounding with voluptuous statues, bubbling fountains, and young couples courting, before arriving at Paseo de la Reforma. Avenida Juárez continues for another block and ends at the massive Monumento a la Revolución in the Plaza de la República, but if you follow Reforma south and west you'll soon come to its intersection with Avenida Insurgentes. After passing Insurgentes, Reforma becomes the northern boundary of the **Zona Rosa** (Pink Zone), which is to Mexico City what SoHo is to New York or Chelsea is to London. The U.S. embassy is on the right at the next traffic circle, and straight ahead is the entrance to **Chapultepec Park**, to the north of which is the fashionable **Polanco** district. On the other side of the park, Reforma leads into the exclusive residential district known as Las Lomas de Chapultepec (*lomas* means "hills" in Spanish), where you'll find a few excellent restaurants and the last of the city's sand-castle–like, Art Nouveau mansions surrounded by an ever-increasing number of high rises.

We start our discussion with the area north of the Zócalo and then move toward the historic downtown area. After discussing the Zócalo and Alameda Park areas, we follow Paseo de la Reforma southwest to the Zona Rosa and then Chapultepec Park (and, to its north, the Polanco district).

After that we discuss the attractions along Insurgentes Sur—the Siqueiros Cultural Polyforum, then the Plaza México bullfight ring and the Coyoacán and San Angel districts—each a neighborhood in its own right, and interesting for their archaeological and historical sites, their many small museums, and the variety of crafts for sale. Finally, a bit farther south still, we discuss University City, with its famous O'Gorman mural, the archaeological sites of Copilco and Cuicuilco, and the canal district of Xochimilco.

The great pre-Aztec site of **Teotihuacán**, located northeast of the city center, is discussed in a separate section after the coverage for Mexico City proper.

NORTH OF THE ZOCALO
Plaza de las Tres Culturas

Site of the ancient city of Tlatelolco, 2½ km (1½ miles) north of the Zócalo, the plaza is, physically and chronologically, a good starting point for a day's tour that might include La Basilica de Nuestra Señora de Guadalupe, another 2½ km farther north of the plaza, and end back in and around the Zócalo itself.

The Plaza de las Tres Culturas (Plaza of the Three Cultures), inaugurated as such in 1964, is located at the northern end of Paseo de la Reforma (called Reforma Norte at this point). Examples of pre-Hispanic, colonial, and modern architecture are represented here by, respectively, Aztec ruins, the Templo de Santiago Tlatelolco, and the sleek marble skyscraper housing the Foreign Ministry.

Tlatelolco, as the area has been known since pre-Hispanic times, was once an island in an immense swampy lake, and was already inhabited when the Aztecs arrived in 1325. In fact, it was the most important commercial and market center in the Valley of Anáhuac, and the Aztecs, being the Tlatelolcans' nearest neighbors, were its best customers, albeit begrudging ones. (It wasn't until 1473 that the island's inhabitants were forcefully annexed into the Aztec empire.) By the time the Spanish arrived in 1519, much of the lake between Tlatelolco and Tenochtitlán had been filled and built over, and it was here that Cortés and his troops came to marvel at the size and order of the native market. (It was also here that the last Aztec emperor, Cuauhtémoc, made his final stand against the Spanish.)

The Aztec ruins, which are not particularly impressive, are embedded at ground level in the northern outdoor patio of the high-rise Exteriores (Foreign Ministry) complex. You can see part of what was once a pre-Hispanic **ceremonial center** as well as the remains of a **palace,** the walls of which were built of basalt and *tezontle,* the reddish-colored blocks of solidified lava characteristic of the native architecture of the period. There are, in addition, two smaller Aztec structures, one of them a square *tzompantli* (wall of skulls) near which thousands of human skulls were discovered, each with holes bored through the temples, presumably the result of having been displayed side by side on poles mounted around the sides of the building.

The **Templo de Santiago Tlatelolco,** with a plain façade typical of the fortresslike churches of the 16th and early 17th centuries, was built in 1609 out of materials taken from an old Aztec pyramid. On the pendentives of the cross vault inside there's an interesting Indian carving of the four evangelists. The church, along with the Colegio de la Santa Cruz, which was founded in 1535 by Franciscan missionaries to teach the sons of the Aztec nobility Spanish, Latin, and Christianity, became a center for the study of native culture; it was here that Fray Bernardino de Sahagún wrote *A History of Ancient Mexico,* his famous work on the history, beliefs, and religions of pre-Hispanic Mexico.

You can get to the Plaza de las Tres Culturas on the metro (the number 3 line, Tlatelolco station stop), or you can take the Indios Verdes bus north anywhere along Avenida Insurgentes and get off at the Monumento a la Raza stop, then walk two blocks east. By car, take Reforma Norte to the third traffic circle north of Alameda Park (which is where Reforma Norte ends).

La Basílica de Nuestra Señora de Guadalupe

The Basilica of Our Lady of Guadalupe, located north of the Plaza de las Tres Culturas on Calzada de Guadalupe, the continuation of Reforma, is considered to be the holiest Christian shrine in all of Latin America. According to legend, Juan Diego, an Aztec who had converted to the Christian faith, was on his way to Mass one cold December morning in 1531, crossing the hill known as Tepeyac, when a vision of the Virgin Mary appeared before him and requested that a church in her honor be built on the spot. When the shaken Diego related this miraculous encounter to the bishop, Juan de Zumárraga, the skeptical bishop asked Diego to show him proof. Three days later the Virgin appeared again and instructed Diego to gather roses, which she then caused to bloom in the frozen ground before him. Shocked at finding roses blooming in winter, Diego bundled them under his cloak and hurried before Zumárraga, where he let the roses tumble to his feet. To the astonishment of both men, stamped upon the peasant's cloak was an image of the Virgin. Needing no further proof, the bishop ordered the church built.

The miracle surrounding the construction of the church was especially significant, in retrospect, for it marked the turning point in the Spanish missionaries' attempts to convert their new subjects to Catholicism. And, as it happened, the apparition occurred on the exact spot where the Aztecs' temple to Tonantzin, their earth goddess, had stood before it was destroyed by the conquistadors.

(It was also here, in the original church, that the Treaty of Guadalupe Hidalgo was signed in 1848, ending the Mexican War; under the terms of the pact, Mexico ceded all or parts of New Mexico, Colorado, Utah, Arizona, Nevada, and California to the United States—reducing her territory by more than 50 percent while, at the same time, enlarging that of her northern neighbor by more than 25 percent.)

The original church was completed in 1533 and subsequently enlarged several times to accommodate the thousands of pilgrims who came in a never-ending stream to worship at the site of the miracle. By 1970, however, the shrine had shrunk so far into the area's spongy subsoil, and had tilted so perilously as a result, that it was declared a safety hazard and closed to the public. In 1976 an ultramodern basilica designed by the great Mexican architect Pedro

Ramírez Vázquez (whose achievements include the National Museum of Anthropology in Chapultepec Park) was consecrated on the west side of the same plaza, while the original structure was eventually shored up and opened to the public as a museum of religious artifacts.

The exterior of the new basilica resembles a huge, futuristic circus tent, while the interior is starkly ornate, embellished with glitter but strangely devoid of icons. When its massive doors are opened as many as 40,000 worshipers can participate in the Mass, including those jammed into the immense **Plaza de la Américas** outside, surpassed in size only by the Zócalo. The shrine boasts no paintings, no statues, no cupolas, and just one relic: the miraculous cloak. (No satisfactory explanation has ever been given as to why the cloak itself has not long since deteriorated.) An underpass near the altar allows visitors to view the revered image without disrupting services; moving walkways prevent anyone from lingering too long. The basilica is open to the public from 6:00 A.M. to 8:00 P.M. daily.

Outside, the plaza is a constantly changing stage for a steady stream of humanity—worshipers, priests, vendors selling religious paraphernalia, and tourists. Many pilgrims cover the last mile or so of their journey on their knees—which often end up bruised and bloodied—as an act of penance. In addition, the annual anniversary of the second apparition, December 12, is a national holiday, and draws tens of thousands of worshipers to the shrine.

At the end of the plaza and to the right, a winding walkway leads up the hill to a few tiny chapels. One of the more charming is the exuberant, Baroque-style **Capilla del Pocito**, inside of which is a well said to have first bubbled up during one of Juan Diego's apparitions. Built in the 18th century, the chapel is actually two chapels, the larger one distinguished by its blue-and-white tiled domes and its impressive paintings of the Virgin by Miguel Cabrera.

At the top of the hill is the **Capilla de las Rosas**, built to commemorate the place where Diego gathered his miraculous roses. Inside the chapel is a mural by Fernando Leal depicting the legend of the miracle.

From the basilica you can take a taxi south to the historic Plaza de Santo Domingo, which is a five-minute walk north of the Zócalo, or, for music, to the Plaza de Garibaldi (at its best in the evening), a little to the north and west of the Plaza de Santo Domingo.

Plaza de Garibaldi

This large public square, located on Eje Central Lázaro Cárdenas between Calles República de Honduras and República de Peru, four blocks north of Bellas Artes, is the musical heart of the capital and a must to visit—at least briefly. Surrounded by cantinas, restaurants, nightclubs, and food stalls, you'll know you're getting close when you see dozens of mariachis gathered on the street, all of them ready to offer their musical services for a fee. For better or for worse, it's hard to tell the different mariachi bands apart: Each player wears black silver-studded skin-tight pants and a short brocaded jacket along with his embroidered wide-brimmed sombrero. On cool evenings a serape is added to the costume, each with its own unique woven design and color scheme. Up close, however, there is a touch of seediness to the mariachis—as there is to the neighborhood in general. The plaza at one time was a pickpocket's haven, but this is no longer the case. Just take normal precautions.

In the plaza itself, the cacophonous sounds of trumpets, violins, guitars, and vocalists fill the air. Dozens of bands playing different tunes in different keys simultaneously compete with one another for the attention of would-be customers, and it is quite natural for local businessmen, relaxing after office hours with friends and a few tequilas, to hire a band to accompany them while they sing along. (It could be said that singing is Mexico's national pastime.)

Mariachis are always eager to provide some soulful music announcing one's desire, be it there on the spot or, better yet, under the balcony of the object of one's affection, wherever she may reside. Once a fee is agreed upon (and it is generally rather expensive) the entire group will pile into a taxi, with the *guitarrón* (a large, pregnant-looking guitar that fills the role of the bass) usually propped on the roof and held by an arm extended from an open window. Then, resembling nothing so much as the Keystone Kops, the mariachis will follow your car to the agreed-upon destination. (No matter the hour, neighbors never complain. While the sound of three trumpets, three guitars, two violins, and a choir of voices under your window is bound to get your attention, in Mexico it's exceedingly bad form to protest having your slumber interrupted. In fact, a ban on serenades after midnight was imposed by a mayor of the D.F. some 30 years ago. His successor lifted the ban as his first official act in office, to overwhelming public acclaim.)

Of course, an hour later they'll be back on the plaza ready for more good-natured competition with the other mariachis assembled there. Even at the height of the tourist season there are usually a dozen musicians for every visitor, so it is a buyer's market. Don't hesitate to bargain during negotiations; it's expected.

Of the four nightclubs around the plaza, **Tenampa** is the most authentic and least exploitative. The energy level inside this huge and sleazy two-room establishment is always high, with three circulating quartets offering serenades. Fortunately, the service is swift and bouncers are placed strategically inside and out to discourage undesirables, so don't worry about giving it a try.

That same intensity of energy prevails throughout the rows of taco, torta, and tamale stands jammed together on each side of a narrow paved corridor north of the plaza. Delicate digestive tracts will best be served, however, by limiting the experience to looking and savoring the smells.

Diagonally across Eje Central Lázaro Cárdenas from the plaza is the famous old **Teatro Blanquita**, where top Mexican entertainment is presented nightly. Singers and musical groups, who normally would command fees ten times what they earn at the Blanquita, keep in touch with the grass-roots segment of their public by appearing here between engagements at the more expensive nightclubs in the D.F. and provinces. The government-controlled admission charge makes a night at the Blanquita one of the capital's great bargains. (Many people choose to attend the 7:30 P.M. performance at the Teatro and then visit the plaza afterward.)

The Plaza de Santo Domingo to the Zócalo

Legend has it that the Plaza de Santo Domingo was the spot where, in 1325, the Aztecs saw an eagle perched on a nopal cactus with a serpent in its beak. According to Aztec legend, just such a sight—the central image on the modern Mexican flag—was supposed to mark the place where these nomadic warrior people were to settle down and build a great city.

Located two blocks south and three blocks east of Plaza de Garibaldi, between Calles Belisario Domínguez and República de Cuba, this beautiful old colonial square is steeped in history. Most of the materials used in the construction of its old buildings were taken from the remains of the emperor Moctezuma's two palaces, which stood in the middle of what is now the plaza until the Spanish under Cortés demolished them in 1521. It was also the site of the first Dominican monastery in the Americas, built in 1539. Today, in the fountain in the center of the square, there is an attractive statue of Doña Josefa Ortíz de Domínguez, better known as La Corregidora, the most famous heroine in Mexican history. (See the Querétaro section of the Colonial Heartland chapter for a more complete description of her role in the Mexican struggle for independence.)

The square itself is bounded on the north by the church of Santo Domingo, on the east by the Casa Chata (the former courthouse of the Inquisition) and the Customs House, on the south by a number of rather run-down colonial-era homes, and on the west by the famous arcade known as the **Portal de los Evangelistas** (Arcade of the Scribes), where public scribes set up their tiny portable desks and chairs and, for a fee, pound out anything from legal forms and students' theses to love letters on their ancient typewriters, thereby carrying on a centuries-old tradition. (Seventeenth-century evangelist missionaries were the first scribes here, and hoped by offering their services to win the confidence—if not the conversion—of the local populace.) Flanking them on the sidewalk are a dozen antique printing presses churning out posters, business cards, wedding invitations, and what not, all offering same-day service and decent quality at very reasonable prices.

The Baroque-style **Iglesia de Santo Domingo** was originally a Dominican convent, built between 1716 and 1736. The Neoclassical main altar within was designed by Manuel Tolsá, and is considered one of the prolific Spanish master's best works.

The **Casa Chata** was locally infamous as the headquarters of the Inquisition from its arrival on Mexican shores in 1571 to its abandonment in 1820. During these bleak years the building was known as the Palacio de la Inquisición. A major renovation of the structure was completed in 1736, elevating it to one of the city's most elegantly sober Baroque buildings. In 1822 it became a military academy, then, from 1855 to 1954, it served as the Escuela Nacional de Medicina. When the school moved to larger quarters, the **Museo de Historia de Medicina** was established here, and today is one of the historic zone's interesting, albeit lesser known, sites. The history of medicine in Mexico is illustrated here from 13th-century native herb lore to modern science. Note the still-prominent crest at the top of the façade commemorating the original occupants—Tribunal de la Inquisición—as well as the engraving above the main gate, which translates as "Rise, Lord, and judge your house." Open 10:00 A.M. to 6:00 P.M. weekdays; closed weekends.

The **Antiguo Edificio de la Aduana** (Customs House) now

Map 1 (Top)

- Plaza de las Tres Culturas
- Templo de Santiago Tlateloco
- Museo de San Carlos
- Monumento a la Revolución
- Museo de la Almeda
- Monumento a Cristóbal Colón
- Plaza de Garibaldi
- Parque Alameda Central
- Zócalo

Streets: INSURGENTES NORTE, MOSQUETA, GLORIETA SAN MARTIN, CALLE RAYON, PASEO DE LA REFORMA NORTE, REPUBLICA DE ECUADOR, REPUBLICA DE HONDURAS, PUENTE DE ALVARADO, RAMOS ARIZPE, COLON, HIDALGO, CALLE DE BRASIL, REPUBLICA DE ARGENTINA, TACUBA, JUAREZ, CALLE CARDENAS, REP. DEL URUGUAY, CALLE PINO SUAREZ, CORREGIDORA, MILAN, BALDERAS, ARCOS DE BELEN, EJE LAZARO CARDENAS, JOSE MARIA IZAGAZA, SAN PABLO, ROMA, BARCELONA, RIO DE LA LOZA, FRAY SERVANDO TERESA DE MIER

Map 2 (Bottom)

- Plaza de Garibaldi
- Iglesia y Plaza de Santo Domingo
- Secretaría de Educación Pública
- Edificio Central de Correos
- Museo Nacional de Arte
- Escuela Nacional Preparatoria
- Palacio de Minerva
- Nacional Monte de Piedad
- Museo del Templo Mayor
- Palacio de Bellas Artes
- Casa de los Azulejos
- Catedral Metropolitana
- Templo de San Francisco
- Palacio de Iturbide
- Museo Nacional de las Culturas
- Palacio Nacional
- Zócalo
- Departamento del Distrito Federal
- Suprema Corte de Justicia
- Museo de la Ciudad de México
- Hospital de Jesús de Nazareth
- Iglesia de Jesús de Nazareth

Streets: REPUBLICA DE HONDURAS, CARMEN, REPUBLICA DE PERU, ARGENTINA, BELISARIO DOMINGUEZ, REP. DE BRASIL, REPUBLICA DE CUBA, VENEZUELA, GONZALEZ OBREGON, HIDALGO, CALLE PALMA, JUSTO SIERRA, SAN ILDEFONSO, TACUBA, CINCO DE MAYO, GUATEMALA, MADERO, MONEDA, GANTE, 16 DE SEPTIEMBRE, CALLE SEMINARIO, CORREGIDORA, V. CARRANZA, REPUBLICA DE URUGUAY, MANZANARES, REPUBLICA DEL SALVADOR, CALLE ALLENDE, ISABEL LA CATOLICA, PINO SUAREZ, EJE LAZARO CARDENAS CENTRO, JOSE MARIA IZAGAZA, CALLE DE 20 DE NOVIEMBRE, SAN PABLO, FRAY SERVANDO TERESA DE MIER serves as office space for the Secretariat of Public Education, and inside has a fine David Alfaro Siqueiros mural entitled *Patricians and Patricides*. The three-story building is constructed of *tezontle,* the Aztecs' favorite construction material and the closest thing to an earthquake-proof building material.

Walk one block east on Calle Luis González Obregón (a continuation of Calle República de Cuba) until you come to Avenida República de Argentina, then turn north. At number 28, on the left side of the street, is the entrance to the impressive **Secretaría de Educación Pública** (Ministry of Public Education) building. Once an elegant cloister for nuns of the rather liberal Conceptionist order, it has two interesting patios within surrounded by mural-covered galleries.

Following the Mexican Revolution, poet-philosopher José Vasconcelos, the newly appointed Minister of Public Education, was directly responsible for commissioning a number of native-born artists and encouraging them to make their creative statements on the walls of government buildings in order to promote the development of Mexican cultural values. In the process a powerful Mexican artistic tradition was born.

To his later credit, Vasconcelos turned over most of the wall space at the Ministry of Public Education to a young artist by the name of Diego Rivera, who was just back from years of study in Paris, and who proceeded to paint some of his most important early works here. The results are striking. All the murals in the ministry (with the exception of one or two each by Montenegro, Charlot, O'Gorman, Mérida, de la Cueva, and Amero) are by Rivera, and, taken as a whole, create an epic visual poem of Mexican life, from pre-Hispanic times to the future—or, at least, Rivera's vision of the future. The emphasis of the 235 separate panels is (as would become the artist's trademark) on social struggle, and together they reveal an extraordinarily talented young artist who had not yet succumbed to the bitterness and cynicism that would influence his later work.

As you leave the Ministry of Public Education turn right and head back to Calle González Obregón and then left (east) at the corner, where the street's name changes to San Ildefonso. Closed to traffic, the street is part of the old university area and is dominated by the block-long 16th-century former Jesuit seminary that once housed the **Escuela Nacional Preparatoria** (National Preparatory School). Now part of the National University, it is still known by its earlier name.

To enter one notably beautiful building in this enormous

complex go south on Calle Cármen for one block, then take a right on Calle Justo Sierra and look for number 16 in the middle of the block. Restored in 1982, the ancient *tezontle* façade frames an elegant entrance that leads to the cradle of the modern Mexican mural (*muralismo*) movement (follow the signs marked "Anfiteatro Boliver"): Minister Vasconcelos's initial commission was given to Ramón Alva de la Canal, who, in 1921, painted the first true Mexican fresco on one of its walls. José Clemente Orozco painted some of his best early murals here between 1923 and 1926. But the building's most notable work was created by Rivera over the stage in the auditorium. Begun in 1921 and completed two years later, *La Creación,* Rivera's first mural, is hardly recognizable as his by those acquainted only with his later murals, in which he developed his distinctive style of caricaturing well-known historical figures as either villains, victims, or heroes.

When you're ready to leave, head west on Calle Justo Sierra for half a block and take a left on Calle República de Argentina, which becomes Calle Seminario just beyond the fenced-in Aztec ruins on your left. The Zócalo is straight ahead.

THE ZOCALO

Although no longer the geographical center of Mexico City (the growth of the D.F. has been to the west and south), the Zócalo site was and still is the capital's heart—and for good reason. Perhaps nowhere else in the Western Hemisphere has so much history been enacted as on the stage of this huge square.

On the spot where the great Catedral Metropolitana now dominates the Zócalo, majestic Aztec temples once stood, upon the high altars of which human sacrifices were performed wholesale. After the surrender of Tenochtitlán, Cortés ordered the pyramids razed and the Aztec idols broken into chunks. On a portion of the ruins he then had the foundation for a cathedral laid. The huge plaza in front of the cathedral—today the second largest public square in the world after Moscow's Red Square—was modeled after Madrid's central plaza and has remained basically the same for nearly five centuries.

As it has been throughout its existence, the Zócalo is Mexico City's political and religious center. It is surrounded by, in addition to the cathedral, El Sagrario Metropolitano, an appendage to the cathedral, on the north; the Palacio Nacional and the Suprema Corte de Justicia on the east; the

Departamento del Distrito Federal (city government offices, including the office of the mayor of the D.F.) to the south; the entrance to the Portal de los Mercaderes (Merchants' Arcade), between Calle Madero and Calle 16 de Septiembre to the west and the Nacional Monte de Piedad at the northwest corner, where Calle Cinco de Mayo meets Calle República del Brasil. The fascinating Templo Mayor and its adjoining museum, the site of recently uncovered Aztec ruins, are located a block north and east of the Zócalo behind the cathedral.

While Plaza de la Constitución is the square's official name, everyone simply calls it the "Zócalo." (*Zócalo* is the Spanish word for "pedestal." In 1843 the government commissioned a monument to Mexico's independence here, and a *zócalo* was subsequently constructed in the middle of the great square. For various reasons, the project never materialized, and the pedestal was finally removed in the waning years of the 19th century—but by then the nickname had stuck. Today every main square in every provincial Mexican town is also called the "zócalo," in imitation of the capital's grand public space.) Unemployed tradesmen congregate daily along three sides of the cathedral looking for work. Each displays a hand-lettered sign stating his specialty. There are usually also a few groups of strolling native performers or costumed families dancing in circles, playing wooden flutes, and shaking their ankle castanets while the youngest member of the troupe passes the hat—except that it's more likely to be a feathered receptacle.

Every evening at 6:00 you can watch the presidential guards march out of the National Palace and ceremoniously lower the national flag from its gigantic flagpole in the center of the square. An especially fine vantage point for viewing this patriotic scene is the seventh-story rooftop restaurant of the **Hotel Majestic**, the entrance to which is located at the corner of Madero and República del Brasil, across the square.

Catedral Metroplitana

Tilting this way and that after centuries of settling into the soft subsoil of the Zócalo, the Baroque-style Catedral Metroplitana—the oldest and largest ecclesiastical structure in Latin America—symbolizes as much as any single building in Mexico the brutal suppression of native culture by Cortés and his conquistadors. The original structure, begun in 1525, was built by Aztec survivors of the Conquest under Spanish supervision, with many of the original *tezontle* foundation stones salvaged from their ruined temples. (It wasn't mere coincidence that the site chosen for the cathedral lay directly on top of the leveled foundations of demolished temple bases.)

Political strife and fire halted construction of the cathedral often over the years, and it wasn't until 1813 that it was finally completed. As a result, generations of architects and artisans contributed to the final product. And yet despite the combination of seemingly incompatible architectural elements—ranging from ancient Greek to Spanish Baroque to French Neoclassical—the exterior of the cathedral is a remarkably harmonious synthesis of these different styles and impulses. The contributions of Manuel Tolsá certainly helped bring all the styles together. Tolsá, a brilliant Spanish sculptor/architect, created the elegant main façade of white marble and gray sandstone as well as the domed stained glass ceiling within, both completed in 1813.

As was so often the case with many early colonial-era structures, the indigenous artisans, attempting to follow the instructions of their Spanish supervisors, unconsciously created a new style—a sort of "Indian Baroque"—that was, and remains, unique to Mexico. Today it is most brilliantly evident in **El Sagrario Metropolitano** (The Metropolitan Sacrarium), the annex attached to the cathedral that was designed as a depository for consecrated relics. A creation of Spanish architect Lorenzo Rodríguez, the annex was begun in 1749 and completed 30 years later, possibly explaining why the interior decor is pure Neoclassical while the exterior is one of the best examples of the extremely ornate Churrigueresque style. Shaped like a Greek cross under a central dome, the interior has some noteworthy attractions, such as the baptismal font, to the left of the main altar, with its embedded golden rays.

The interior of the cathedral, on the other hand, is so dark and gloomy that it actually comes as a relief to visit the basement crypts, which are interesting for the 16th-century Gothic ribbing around their vaults (they weren't completed until 1623). This is where you'll find the remains of most of the archbishops of Mexico City, including those of Juan de Zumárraga, the first prelate of New Spain (and the man responsible for ordering the destruction of all Aztec codices that crossed his path, as well as the construction of the original shrine built in Guadalupe's honor).

The cathedral and its adjoining chapel are illuminated at night on national holidays, creating truly startling shadow-and-light effects. On these occasions the Mexican flag flies from its façade and, despite the ostensible separation of

Church and State, the ardently nationalistic churchgoers of the D.F. join in the noisy celebration. The cathedral itself, like all religious buildings in Mexico, is owned by the government.

Templo Mayor and Museo del Templo Mayor

The Templo Mayor, or Great Temple, once the ceremonial heart of the Aztec capital of Tenochtitlán, is located northeast of the cathedral at the corner of República de Argentina and República de Guatemala. It was here, over a period of 80 years, that the Aztecs erected a 150-foot-high pyramid in honor of Huitzilopochtli, their supposedly bloodthirsty god of war, and Tlaloc, the age-old Mesoamerican god of rain, at the summit of which countless human sacrifices were offered. Prisoners of war were the usual victims, but if a military campaign failed to produce a sufficient number, slaves would be purchased from Aztec slave-owners to fill the priests' quotas. Convinced that the sun would not rise and the world would end if the gods were not satisfied, their scribes recorded sacrificial statistics that, even by today's jaded standards, were mind-boggling. Bernal Díaz recorded a conversation between Móctezuma II and Cortés on the latter's first visit to Tenochtitlán (at which point the Spaniards were still being treated as honored guests) in which the Aztec emperor boasted that, on the occasion of the dedication of the most recent incarnation of the Templo Mayor, his priests had sacrificed 20,000 individuals.

Little wonder then that the Spanish, despite their own deviousness and greed, had no trouble recruiting other Indian tribes as their allies. With the help of an estimated 10,000 Tlaxcalan warriors, sworn enemies of the Aztecs, and a smallpox epidemic, Tenochtitlán, the chief stronghold of the Aztec empire, was forced to surrender in 1521, after which the victorious Spanish quickly went to work razing the magnificent architectural accomplishments of their Aztec enemies, including the Templo Mayor. (Ironically, the very first colonial structure on the site of the razed temple was the public gallows, completed in 1522. Given their loathing of human sacrifice, the victorious Spaniards had a curiously liberal attitude toward capital punishment, with even common thiefs seen fit to hang.)

Over the ensuing centuries the rubble from the ruined Aztec city sank deeper and deeper into the subsoil under and around the Zócalo. Then, on August 13, 1790, 269 years to the

THE ZOCALO AREA

day after the final defeat of the Aztec empire, a construction crew working on a restoration project at the cathedral unearthed the famous **Aztec calendar stone**. Weighing 24 tons and measuring nearly 12 feet in diameter, this basalt marvel of pre-Hispanic artistry depicts the Aztec concept of the cosmos, and is now proudly displayed at the National Museum of Anthropology in Chapultepec Park.

In 1900 and again in 1913 additional Aztec artifacts were unearthed in other excavations. But this door to the Aztec past wasn't completely opened until February 1978, when workmen from the city's light and power company, digging just six feet below ground level, uncovered the massive stone disk—ten feet in diameter and weighing eight tons—of Coyolxauhqui, the Aztec moon goddess.

With this discovery experts were forced to agree that, contrary to the long-held belief that the Templo Mayor was buried forever under the nearby cathedral, the actual site of the central temple complex had indeed been found. The light and power company's project was immediately halted and excited archaeologists took over. After five years of careful excavation work, all four sides of the Templo Mayor were exposed; several other temples were also uncovered, along with thousands of statues and relics, some in a remarkable state of preservation—though many of the artifacts (some of them 600 years old) had to be given immediate treatment to prevent them from crumbling into dust upon contact with the air.

The quantity and quality of the finds unearthed at the Templo Mayor site far surpass anything previously found from this period of Mesoamerican history, and new discoveries continue to be made almost daily. The whole site probably will never be explored completely, however; the massive cathedral itself is adjacent to what archaeologists speculate could be some of the most impressive discoveries, but the cathedral site is, and will remain, off limits.

The uncovered ruins of the Templo Mayor are located at Calle Seminario 8, an outdoor museum complex that is far more extensive than archaeologists had originally dared dream. Look, in particular, in the stage 2 area for the *piedra de sacrificios* (sacrificial stone); the nearby chac-mool, to date the oldest piece discovered at the site, reclines calmly with its receptacle for human hearts held snugly against its belly. Also included within the uncovered ruins area is a recently constructed scale model of the original ceremonial center, complete with a network of canals.

Adjacent to the eastern boundary of the excavated area is the **Museo del Templo Mayor**, a masterpiece of the versatile architect Pedro Ramírez Vázquez, whose achievements include the National Museum of Anthropology and the Basilica of Our Lady of Guadeloupe. Objects of all sizes and every description are displayed in the cool, muted interior here, including several life-size ceramic figures known as the Eagle Warriors; giant stone serpent heads; obsidian knives (which were used by Aztec priests to remove the hearts from their sacrificial victims); sacrificial altars; and, the pièce de résistance, the stone disk of the moon goddess Coyolxauhqui, the discovery of which was responsible for this extraordinary exhibition. (Also on display is a wooden club about the length of a standard-size baseball bat with a doughnut of black obsidian blades ringing its thicker end. According to one Spanish scribe, a strong man swinging this weapon could decapitate a horse.) Additional exhibits feature ancient cultures that existed in the Valley of Mexico long before the arrival of the Aztecs, and one section of the museum is devoted to the country's geology, flora, and fauna.

The museum is open from 9:00 A.M. to 6:00 P.M. daily, except Mondays, but the ticket office closes at 5:00 P.M. On Sundays and holidays closing time is one hour earlier. English-language tours can be arranged in advance; Tel: (5) 542-1717 between 9:00 A.M. and 4:00 P.M. to make reservations.

Also on the Zócalo

One block south and another block east of the Templo Mayor site, at Calle Moneda 13, is the **Museo Nacional de las Culturas**, a.k.a. Antigua Casa de Moneda (Ancient Mint), once the site of one of Móctezuma's palaces. Rebuilt in the early 18th century to house the Royal Mint, the structure became the National Museum of Natural History in 1865 and the National Museum of Anthropology in 1940. When the latter moved to its present location in Chapultepec Park in 1964, the National Museum of the Cultures was established in its place. Its building painstakingly restored to its former colonial glory, the museum contains a variety of ethnographic displays from all over the world, including traditional ceramics, artwork, crafts, costumes, and tools. A Rufino Tamayo fresco graces the entrance to the museum. Open Tuesday through Saturday from 9:30 A.M. to 6:00 P.M., Sundays from 9:30 A.M. to 4:00 P.M.; closed Mondays. Tel: (5) 512-7452 or 0165. Admission free.

The dominant structure on the Zócalo is the **Palacio Nacional**, the elegant façade of which, handsomely set off by the wrought-iron railings of its many balconies, is made of gray sandstone and rose-colored *tezontle* and stretches nearly the length of the eastern side of the plaza. More than a magnificent architectural creation, the palace is the official residence of the executive power of the government, with the president of the Republic making his most important pronouncements from its center balcony.

The first known structure to occupy the site was the palace of Móctezuma II, who reputedly had an elaborate aviary installed as the centerpiece of a huge garden that took up the entire inner courtyard. After the Conquest, Cortés had Móctezuma's palace destroyed and, as reward for a job well done, was given the deed to the land by the king of Spain. He then had a new palace built from the rubble of the old, which, upon its completion, became the seat as well as the symbol of the Spanish Crown's power in New Spain.

Cortés himself lived in, as well as governed from, the palace. In 1529, upon his return from a journey to what is now Honduras, his friends staged a bullfight in the patio (which more or less coincided with the dimensions and location of Móctezuma's splendid patio)—allegedly the first bullfight to be held in the Americas. In 1562, years after Cortés had sold the deed back to the Crown, the palace became the official residence of the viceroys who ruled New Spain. A public riot touched off by an increase in grain prices badly damaged the structure in 1692, and what you see today is mostly the result of extensive renovations done in the early 18th century. After Mexico gained its independence from Spain in 1821 the palace became the official residence of the president of the Republic, a function it served according to the whims of the titular head of state until 1884. (Both Agustín de Iturbide, the fledgling republic's self-appointed emperor, and Maximilian of Austria, who was appointed emperor by Napoleon III after France invaded Mexico in 1860, chose to live elsewhere.)

In 1884 luxury-loving President-for-Life Porfirio Díaz moved the official presidential residence back to Chapultepec Castle (which had been renovated by Maximilian after his temperamental wife, Carlota, was attacked by bedbugs on her first night in the palace), and the historic old building was converted into government offices. (A restored colonial hacienda in Chapultepec Park, Los Pinos, has served as the official presidential residence for the past half century.) Although renovations have altered its interior considerably over the years, and a third story was added in 1927, the National Palace continues to serve as the working headquarters of the executive branch.

Access to the main patio is through the palace's massive entrance, high above which hangs the famous church bell struck by Father Miguel Hidalgo in his home town of Dolores to proclaim Mexico's independence in 1810. Ornate arches surround the patio; to the left an elegant staircase leads up and past a memorable **Diego Rivera mural** depicting his interpretation of modern Mexican history. Rivera often linked contemporary events with incidents and episodes from different eras. Easily recognizable in this particular work are such leading figures of 20th-century capitalism as J. P. Morgan, John D. Rockefeller, and Cornelius Vanderbilt—all menacingly portrayed. Not surprisingly, given Rivera's political inclinations, the heroically drawn figure of Karl Marx stands out among the "villainous" capitalists. The mural on the northern wall of the patio, also by Rivera, depicts Mexico's history from pre-Hispanic days through the Revolution. The Rivera murals can be viewed from 9:00 A.M. to 6:00 P.M. daily. Admission is free.

The **Museo Recinto Homenaje a Benito Juárez**, located on the first floor of the palace, displays a small collection of memorabilia belonging to Mexico's great reform leader. Juárez, who died on the premises in 1872 while serving his second term as president, carried on an extensive correspondence with his U.S. counterpart, Abraham Lincoln (with whom he is often compared), and their letters to each other are on view as well. The entrance to the museum (which temporarily closed for repairs) is through the door on the northern, or Calle Moneda, side of the palace. It's open Monday through Friday from 10:00 A.M. to 6:00 P.M.

At the southern perimeter of the Zócalo, opposite the cathedral, are the offices of the city government, the **Departamento del Distrito Federal**, including the office of the mayor of the D.F. Built in 1532, the structure was originally a town hall and served over the years as a grain exchange, a city jail, and the national mint. Part of the building was destroyed in the civil uprising of 1692 and then rebuilt between 1720 and 1724. The third and top floors were added much later. The indigenously flavored Churrigueresque façade features a number of ornately carved coats of arms, including those of Christopher Columbus and Hernán Cortés.

The **Portal de los Mercaderes** (Merchants' Arcade), located on the west side of the Zócalo, still retains its old pillars but no longer has the stalls where merchants once sold their wares. Built in 1524, the arcade was constructed after local merchants petitioned the newly established colonial government to erect a portico over the broad sidewalk as protection against the morning sun and bad weather.

During the arcade's first two centuries of existence, public scribes would set up their portable shops here (before they moved to the arcade of the Plaza de Santo Domingo).

Today the cramped, narrow stalls of the past have been replaced by cramped, narrow shops selling jewelry—perhaps the most visible vestige of a guild system (in which a neighborhood consisting of several blocks confines itself to selling one particular product) that prevailed among the Aztecs. The system allegedly is the only indigenous custom adopted by the founders of New Spain. Ambulatory vendors, displaying their wares on the sidewalk, change daily. All conceivable items, ranging from cut-rate "genuine" Rayban sunglasses to cures for intestinal worms, are vigorously hawked here.

Most of the commercial establishments in and around the Zócalo offer a ten-percent discount off the listed price if you pay in cash rather than with a credit card. You should also be aware that, in general, prices are much lower here than elsewhere in the city.

Located on the northwest corner of the Zócalo, between Calles Cinco de Mayo and Tacuba, is the imposing **Nacional Monte de Piedad** (National Pawnshop, translated literally as "National Mountain of Mercy"), occupying the site of a former Aztec palace where the conquistadors were first housed as guests by Móctezuma II. (It was on the roof of the palace—nothing remains of it—that Móctezuma was said to have been stoned to death by his furious subjects as he attempted to calm their anger over his acquiescence to the Spaniards. Because the only documentation ever uncovered pertaining to Móctezuma's demise came from Spanish scribes, some historians feel the story might have been made up to hide the emperor's murder by Cortés.) Today the National Pawnshop (all pawnshops in Mexico are government owned) offers myriad unredeemed goods for sale. Chandeliers, antique books, office machinery, dentist chairs, artwork, antique jewelry—just about every item imaginable is available in this huge colonial building, which during business hours always seems to be teeming with humanity. Every so often public auctions—at which great bargains supposedly are available—are held to clear out the merchandise. (Although they're advertised as "once-a-month" events, it is not uncommon for "once-a-month" to become "once every few months.")

The **Suprema Corte de Justicia**, the seat of judicial power in Mexico, is located at the corner of Avenida Pino Suárez and Calle de la Corregidora, on the southeastern corner of the Zócalo. During the viceregal period (1535 to 1821) the site was occupied by the Mercado del Volador, an open-air market to which fresh fruits and vegetables were brought along the Acequia Real (Royal Canal) from Xochimilco's floating gardens, 16 miles to the south. The present structure, with its somber Baroque façade, was built in 1929 and completely remodeled in 1940.

Inside are three murals by José Clemente Orozco and one by his U.S. contemporary, George Biddle. Orozco was commissioned in the early 1940s to paint a series of murals in the building, but his third, *Injustice,* a powerful presentation of judges snoozing in court, executed in vivid colors on the landing of the second floor, was considered highly inappropriate by his sponsors and the rest of the proposed series was unceremoniously canceled. You'll find the Biddle mural at the entrance to the library.

On the stretch of Corregidora between the National Palace and the Supreme Court you can see a reconstruction of a segment of the walls that used to surround the old Acequia Real.

SOUTH OF THE ZOCALO

Three blocks south of the Zócalo, at the corner of Avenida Pino Suárez and Calle República del Salvador, is one of the area's more interesting landmarks, the **Museo de la Ciudad de México** (Museum of the City of Mexico). Built in 1526 as a residence for Cortés's cousin, the mansion was remodeled in the 18th century for the count and countess of Santiago de Calimaya and carried their name until it became a museum early in 1964.

The building alone, built of dark red volcanic stone, is worth a visit. The centerpiece of the façade is the count's family crest, decorated with ornately sculpted cannons and gargoyle-like figures. The cornerstone, salvaged from an Aztec ruin, is a sculpted plumed serpent's head that peers menacingly at the passing scene. (Legend has it that Cortés placed the stone here with his own hands.)

The museum's displays cover the history of the city from earliest pre-Hispanic times to the present, although the emphasis begins with the founding of Tenochtitlán. Especially interesting are the models of the ancient Aztec capital, with people going about their work, shopping in the markets, or simply watching as Aztec nobles are carried by in ornate chairs. Depicted in another model is the colonial capital of New Spain, with miniature versions of many still-extant buildings, including the one housing the museum.

Upstairs are four additional rooms devoted to the history of the city, including an outstanding collection of 19th-century lithographs and photographs. Open 9:30 A.M. to 7:30 P.M. daily, except Mondays. Guided tours are available from 9:30 A.M. to 5:00 P.M. Monday through Friday.

Diagonally across the street from the museum is the fortresslike **Iglesia de Jésus**, with its entrance on Calle República del Salvador. The church's early Baroque-style façade is topped by a tile-faced cupola, while the plaque on the outside wall of the apse commemorates the first meeting between Hernán Cortés and Móctezuma II—an encounter that, according to Bernal Díaz del Castillo, took place here on November 8, 1519, when it was still the site of an Aztec temple.

Inside is a superb (but unfinished) mural by Orozco depicting the Conquest, and another by him, entitled *Apocalipsis,* that covers the walls and ceiling behind the dome. (Work on the former was interrupted by Orozco's death in 1949.) The remains of Cortés are also, allegedly, interred here, in an urn identified only by a small bronze plaque on a wall of the tallest altar.

Adjacent to the church is the **Hospital de Jésus**, which was founded by Cortés in 1524 and completed in 1535. Believed to be the first hospital established in the Americas, it is worth visiting if only to see its inner courtyard. Permission to enter this serene 16th-century patio will be granted graciously at the admittance desk; walk straight into the hospital and take your first left.

One block south on Avenida Pino Suárez is the Pino Suárez metro station, where an **Aztec temple** was uncovered during construction on the metro in 1968. The temple, which dates from the 14th century, has been preserved as an integral part of the concourse. There is also an entrance here to a subterranean pedestrian walkway that leads back to the Zócalo. Expect lots of activity in this tunnel at all times—everything from wall-to-wall art exhibitions and sidewalk entrepreneurs to droves of people simply going about their business.

WEST OF THE ZOCALO

The **Palacio de Iturbide**, located at Francisco Madero 17, four blocks west of the Zócalo, is the most elegant structure in the neighborhood, its architecture a curious fusion of indigenous Baroque and Italian touches. The façade is constructed out of *tezontle* and gray sandstone, and the massive, beautifully carved doors open onto an equally striking courtyard. Designed by Francisco Guerrero y Torres and completed in 1780, it was for many years the residence of a Spanish marquis and, later, a count. Then, in 1822, it became the "palace" of its most famous occupant, Agustín de Iturbide, a successful army colonel who won control of the government after Spain granted Mexico its independence the previous year. No stranger to megalomania, the victorious Iturbide had himself crowned emperor and from his palace ruled the country for ten months, during which time he managed to alienate most of his "subjects." A "sabbatical" in Spain followed, but an attempt by the Spanish government to renege on its agreements with newly independent Mexico prompted the Spanish-born Iturbide to again offer his services to his adopted countrymen, who had already had quite enough of him. Needless to say, Iturbide was surprised upon his return to find that the provisional government had condemned him in absentia to death by firing squad, and so it was that he met his maker in February 1824.

The palace became, in the decades that followed, a hotel, an office building, and a shopping plaza. In 1965 the interior was restored and turned into the administrative offices of a branch of the Banco Nacional de México. A permanent exhibition of colonial religious art on the ground floor is open to the public during regular business hours.

As you leave the Palacio de Iturbide continue west on Calle Madero; between Calle Gante and Eje Central Lázaro Cárdenas you'll see what remains of an immense Franciscan monastery, built over the site of what had been Emperor Moctezuma's botanical garden and menagerie. Cortés personally supervised construction of the project, which covered several city blocks when it was completed in 1524. As the headquarters of the Franciscan order, it was the largest ecclesiastical complex in the Americas during the 16th century. In 1856, during a period of intense anticlerical sentiment in Mexico, the government of Benito Juárez demolished most of the complex, leaving only the church—the **Templo de San Francisco**—standing. The façade is a magnificent example of the merging of the Churrigueresque and Indian styles. Sadly, the church has sunk so deeply into the marshy soil over the centuries that the building's original ground floor is now the basement.

The **Casa de los Azulejos** (House of Tiles), across the street from the church of San Francisco at Calle Madero 4, was built in 1596 as a palace for the count of Orizaba. Legend has it that one of the later counts had a son who did not measure up to his father's standards. One day the father reproached his son for his lack of ambition and ended by telling him, "Son, you will never have a house of tile." Stung by his father's criticism, the boy went on to marry a wealthy woman and then tiled the palace from top to bottom with glazed blue-and-white Puebla *azulejos*—to match the sky, as he later told the curious.

In 1904 two brothers from the United States, Walter and Frank Sanborn, opened the first soda fountain in Mexico a few doors away. The enterprising brothers then installed a piano and hired a pianist who specialized in Viennese waltzes, and Mexico City's elite responded to the novelty. Ladies who rarely entered commercial establishments were soon stepping out of elegant horse-drawn carriages to refresh themselves at **Sanborn's** with those amazing concoctions called ice-cream sodas. Walter, a licensed pharmacist, set up a pharmacy in the rear of their large store, arranged so that customers had to pass the tempting beverages and piles of sandwiches (then unfamiliar to Mexicans) in order to reach it.

By the end of the First World War the Sanborns had taken over the Casa de los Azulejos and spread an enormous amber-colored glass roof over its patio and installed a grand piano. What had been a popular drugstore soon became the most elegant public establishment in the city. In time the Sanborns added a perfume department, silver shop, and fur department to cater to their ritzy clientele.

Nowadays a property of Walgreen Pharmacies, the Casa de los Azulejos is a comfortable place to relax after a morning of exploring the Zócalo area. The coffee is good, and there's even a 1925 Orozco mural winding up the wall of the stairwell.

Diagonally across the street from Sanborn's, on the corner of Madero and Lázaro Cárdenas, is the 44-story **Torre Latinoamericana**, at 594 feet Mexico's third-tallest skyscraper (the PEMEX building and Hotel de México, both in the capital, now rank one and two, respectively). The enclosed observation deck on the 42nd floor affords panoramic views of the entire Valley of Mexico (on a clear day), and the **Muralto**, on the floor below, is an adequate restaurant. The building's innovative "floating" foundation, designed by Frank Lloyd Wright, has withstood numerous earthquakes while preventing it from sinking into the soft subsoil underlying much of the city. The observation deck is open from 10:00 A.M. to 11:00 P.M. daily.

Before you cross the avenue and begin to explore the Alameda Park area, there's another interesting cluster of buildings two blocks north on Lázaro Cárdenas. The elegant mansion at the corner of Lázaro Cárdenas and Calle Tacuba is home to the D.F.'s **Edificio Central de Correos** (Central Post Office). Designed by the Italian architect Adamo Boari, whose masterpiece, the Palacio de Bellas Artes, is directly across the street, it was built between 1902 and 1907 and opened a year later. As post offices go, you'd be hard-pressed to find a more elaborate one. Particularly noteworthy are the sumptuous details of the building's exterior and the carved woodwork and bronze handrails of the main stairwell inside.

The beautiful Neoclassical building next door at Calle Tacuba 5 is the former **Palacio de Minería** (Palace of Mining), a creation of the multitalented Spanish émigré Manuel Tolsá. Begun in 1797, it took 16 years to complete, and served as a school for mining engineers until 1945. (It continues to house the Faculty of Engineering.) In addition to its stately façade, the palace boasts a splendid patio and an exquisitely carved staircase. There's also a good 19th-century mural inside by the Spanish artist Rafael Ximeno y Planes.

On the Plaza Manuel Tolsá here, the public square separating the two wings of the former palace, you'll find the ornate three-story **Museo Nacional de Arte**. Designed by another Italian architect, Silvio Contri, the building was inaugurated in 1910 as the Palace of Communications and Public Works, later became the repository for the National Archives, and finally, in 1984, assumed its present function. The exhibition rooms, which are reached by climbing a magnificent marble staircase, contain more than 700 works of art, most dating from the 14th century to the mid-20th century, including a number of the finest paintings by the Mexican landscape artist José María Velasco. The museum is open from 10:00 A.M. to 6:00 P.M. daily, except Mondays.

In the plaza itself you'll find what is undoubtedly its namesake's most famous sculpture, the 29-ton, 15½-foot-tall "**El Caballito**," as it is popularly called. The massive statue depicting the despised Bourbon king Charles IV (1788–1808) astride his horse—what many consider to be the finest equestrian statue in the world—was cast in 1803 and placed in the Zócalo opposite the cathedral while Tolsá was creating the cathedral's magnificent Neoclassical dome. The odyssey of the "Little Horse" didn't begin in earnest, however, until after independence was achieved in 1821. Then, in order to protect it from the anti-Spanish sentiments of the people, Tolsá had it encased in a wooden globe and moved to the relative safety of a courtyard on the old university campus a few blocks away. There it sat until 1852 (the wooden globe was removed in 1824), when it was painstakingly moved—15 days to travel a little more than a mile—to the intersection of Paseo de la

Reforma and Calle Bucareli. It arrived at its present—and, let's hope, final—destination in 1978, and today is one of the capital's more popular attractions.

THE ALAMEDA PARK AREA
The Palacio de Bellas Artes

Located at the corner of Juárez and Lázaro Cárdenas, this huge, opulent building designed by Adamo Boari is a Mexico City landmark as well as the nation's foremost cultural center. Eclectic in design—the building itself is a fusion of Neoclassical and Art Nouveau elements—the Bellas Artes (bay-yas AR-tays) is noted for its excellent acoustics and is home to both the world-famous Ballet Folklórico and the National Symphony Orchestra.

Construction of the building, which was begun in 1904, was halted by the Revolution, and its plans were subsequently modified a number of times before its completion in 1934—hence the mixture of styles. Today the ground floor contains a number of spacious galleries that are used for temporary exhibitions, while the second floor has a permanent gallery featuring the works of 19th- and 20th-century Mexican masters. (The Bellas Artes has served as the headquarters of the National Institute of Fine Arts since 1946.)

But it is the murals in the **Museo Nacional del Palacio de Bellas Artes** on the second, third, and fourth floors that make this such a fascinating and worthwhile stop. Here you'll find the most extensive display of Mexican *muralismo* anywhere in the world, with works by Rufino Tamayo, Juan O'Gorman, José Clemente Orozco, David Alfaro Siqueiros, Jorge Camarena, and Diego Rivera lined up one after the other. Rivera's reworked version of *Man at the Crossroads* (1934), the original of which was commissioned for New York City's Rockefeller Center but was painted over after the artist's sponsors got a look at its graphic political message (they objected, among other things, to John D. Rockefeller being depicted as a devilish capitalist), is just one of the treasures here. Open from 10:00 A.M. to 6:00 P.M. daily, except Mondays. Guided tours in English are available during the same hours, but not on Sundays. Tel: (5) 520-9060, ext. 3324, for reservations. Admission is free.

Unfortunately, it is estimated that the Palacio de Bellas Artes has sunk more than 15 feet into Mexico City's soft subsoil since it was opened in 1934, and it continues to sink at the rate of about three and a half inches a year, despite a number of innovative engineering schemes that have been implemented to halt its downward progress. The principal building material, extremely heavy Italian marble (the type used by Michelangelo), has so far defied modern technology. The prognosis is that by the turn of the century the original second floor will become the first floor.

Lovers of dance—which includes most Mexicans—will tell you that the richness and diversity of Mexican culture is nowhere more apparent than in their favorite art form. While most regional folk dances have remained unchanged since the 14th century, the Spanish influence, as exemplified by flamenco and the Dance of the Moors and Christians, has also figured prominently in this rich tradition. Perhaps the best way to experience the full spectrum of dance in Mexico is to see a performance by the **Ballet Folklórico de México**, which takes the stage three times a week at the Bellas Artes. Authentic costumes, superb dancers, outstanding choreography, and masterfully performed traditional music all combine to make this an unforgettable experience. The Bellas Artes's 22-ton Tiffany crystal curtain, its stained glass portraying the snow-capped volcanoes of Popocatépetl and Iztaccíhuatl at dawn and dusk—effects achieved with special lighting—is displayed prior to each performance.

Performances are held Wednesdays at 9:00 P.M. and Sundays at 9:30 A.M. and again at 9:00 P.M. Reservations should be made in advance through your hotel, a travel agency, or at the box office on Calle Violeta, which is open from 10:00 A.M. to 5:00 P.M. daily; Tel: (5) 520-1701. You'll get the best views from seats on the first (lowest) balcony.

Parque Alameda Central

Bordered by Avenida Hidalgo to the north, Avenida Juárez to the south, and Bellas Artes to the east, the park is a pleasant four-block stretch of greenery in the midst of the perennially clogged streets of the capital. Filled with ornate fountains, Neoclassical marble sculpture, wrought-iron benches, courting young lovers, ice-cream and balloon vendors, and towering poplar trees (the park's name is derived from *álamos,* the Spanish word for poplars), it's a good place to relax after a morning of sightseeing.

Dating back to 1596, it is also the capital's oldest public park. The western section, known as the Plaza del Quemadero (Square of the Burning Stake), was where heretics were burned during the Inquisition. Later, in the 19th century, the park became *the* fashionable place for Sunday promenades (see Diego Rivera's *Dream of a Sunday After-*

noon in the Alameda in the nearby Museo Mural Diego Rivera). Since the Revolution, however, Alameda has been a people's park. Families and couples, mostly working class, congregate for picnics under the poplars, enjoying the free weekly concerts of classical, jazz, rock, folk, and martial music.

During the Christmas season, and especially in the days before the Day of the Three Kings (January 6), the normally lively park becomes even livelier, as dozens of Santa Clauses line up next to their plush crimson chairs set on gaily decorated portable stages and wait to pose with passersby for a small fee. Each Santa brings his own photographer with a shoe-box camera, and traditionally one Santa is always on stilts.

Much of the park's voluptuous statuary was brought from Italy by Porfirio Díaz during his long tenure as president (1872 to 1911). The large semicircular marble monument to Benito Juárez that faces Avenida Juárez was also commissioned by Díaz.

The **Museo Nacional de Artes y Industrias Populares** (National Museum of Folk Arts and Crafts), housed in the former church of Corpus Christi (inaugurated in 1587 and renovated a century later) at Avenida Juárez 44, directly across from the park's Juárez Monument, is a government-run shop and museum that displays and sells traditional arts and crafts from different regions of the country. The museum section is on the second floor, with its entrance at the rear of the building, and is open from 10:00 A.M. to 6:00 P.M. daily, except Mondays. Displayed pieces are for sale on the first floor and mezzanine at prices comparable to what you would pay in the villages of their origin. Among the items for sale are sweaters and ponchos, hand-carved masks, onyx chess sets, hand-blown glassware, bark paintings, and a variety of ceramics. The silver jewelry here is less expensive than it is in Taxco, where it is made, and the wooden toys from the state of Michoacán are especially charming. Also of interest is the ceramic Tree of Life, a traditional wedding gift fashioned in the shape of a candelabra and characterized by intricate decorative motifs featuring angels with trumpets, assorted biblical characters, and flowers. The most ornate come from Metepec, in the state of México. Beautifully carved wooden chests from Olinala, Guerrero, and the hard-to-find Huichole Indian yarn paintings from Nayarit are available here at reasonable prices and can be counted among the best buys in folk art anywhere in Mexico. Tel: (5) 521-6679.

If you follow Avenida Juárez three and a half blocks to

the west you'll come to **FONART**, a branch of the immense government-run operation that sells native arts and crafts at just about wholesale. Here you'll find handicrafts in precious, semiprecious, and garden-variety materials such as silver, onyx, glass, shell, leather, clay, wood, wax, papier-mâché, and even sugar. The government coordinates the manufacture, distribution, and sale of these goods, and also regulates their prices. The rural artisans are, in effect, subsidized—which is an absolute necessity if these craft traditions are to survive.

The **Museo Mural Diego Rivera**, located just north of FONART on the corner of Calles Balderas and Colón, is the new home of the recently restored Diego Rivera masterpiece *A Dream of a Sunday Afternoon in the Alameda*. Most certainly the capital's smallest museum, it was built for the sole purpose of housing the mural after its previous home, the landmark Hotel del Prado, was all but leveled in the 1985 earthquakes. (The hotel has since been torn down.) When the mural was first unveiled in 1948 it created an uproar because of a placard carried by one of its figures that stated *"Dios No Existe"* ("God Does Not Exist"), a quotation from a lecture given by the Mexican philosopher Ignacio Ramírez. As a result of the outcry, the mural was covered and remained so until 1956, when Rivera, a devout Communist, finally consented to paint over the objectionable words, substituting in their place the phrase *"Conferencia de la Academia de Letran de 1836"*—a reference to the lecture in which the controversial words had been pronounced. (The chubby young boy with the bulging eyes standing in the front row is a self-portrait.) Open 10:00 A.M. to 6:00 P.M. daily, except Mondays; Tel: (5) 521-1016.

The **Museo Franz Mayer**, housed in the 16th-century Hospital de San Juan de Dios, one block north and two blocks east of the Museo Mural Diego Rivera at Avenida Hidalgo 45, boasts an extraordinary collection of mostly applied antique art, including ceramics, crystal, furniture, clocks, and Talavera ware. Mayer, a German-born financier who lived most of his life in Mexico as a Mexican citizen, bequeathed this collection of 16th- and 17th-century antiques from England, China, Spain, and Holland to his adopted country upon his death in 1976. Mayer's legacy to Mexico is considered to be one of the finest collections of its kind in the world.

The museum's noteworthy library houses mostly collectors' items, including 770 different editions of *Don Quixote*, as well as many books whose binding, typography, and illustrations are more valuable than their text. There are also numerous reference works on the particular applied arts that Mayer collected as well as books on painting, engraving, and sculpture. Photographing without flash is permitted. Open 10:00 A.M. to 5:00 P.M. daily, except Mondays.

Next door to the museum is the seriously tilting **Templo de la Santa Veracruz,** Mexico's answer to the Leaning Tower of Pisa. Although this 16th-century Baroque relic has been restored and continues to function as a church, taking a dramamine pill before you enter might not be a bad idea. Built in 1527 under the direction of Cortés, this is one of the oldest churches in Mexico. The exceptionally impressive image of Christ on the crucifix over the altar was a gift from Pope Paul III to King Charles V of Spain, who, in turn, gave it to Cortés to inaugurate this venerable place of worship. The interior has a number of beautifully tiled walls, especially behind the "Lady Chapel," to your left as you enter. The remains of the master architect Manuel Tolsá are also interred here.

Before you head down Reforma, make a short detour to the **Museo de San Carlos**, located at Avenida Puente de Alvarado 50 (Puente de Alvarado is the continuation of Avenida Hidalgo), two major intersections west of Templo de la Santa Veracruz. Housed in a beautiful Neoclassical structure that was designed by Manuel Tolsá in 1806 as an aristocrat's residence, the building itself is noteworthy for its unusual two-story oval patio and elegant stairway, while the museum's permanent collection on the second floor includes works by El Greco, Rubens, Bosch, Goya, and Van Dyke. Open 10:00 A.M. to 2:00 P.M. and 4:00 P.M. to 6:00 P.M. daily, except Mondays. Tel: (5) 535-1246. (As of this writing the museum was under renovation but was due to reopen in early 1993.)

If you walk two blocks south on Calle Ramos Arizpe you'll come to the square known as the Plaza de la República and, in the middle of it, the nation's largest monument, the **Monumento a la Revolución**. Originally, this massive arch was designed to be the ceremonial entrance to a lavish legislative palace in which President-for-Life Porfirio Díaz was to hold court. By the time the arch was completed, however, the Revolution had begun and Díaz had fled into exile. Today the monument is the final resting place for five of Mexico's most revered revolutionaries: Buried in crypts under the monument's immense pillars are Francisco "Pancho" Villa; President Francisco Madero, who succeeded Díaz only to be assassinated two years later; President Venustiano Carranza, himself a victim of modern Mexico's bloody birth; President Plutarco Calles, founder of the ruling PRI party; and President Lázaro Cárdenas, the man responsible for nationalizing the oil industry and implementing agrarian reform on a large scale.

The **Museo Nacional de la Revolución**, located in the basement of the monument, presents a well-organized permanent exhibition entitled "50 Años en la Historia de México (1867–1917)." Open 9:00 A.M. to 5:00 P.M. daily, except Mondays. Weekday evening hours are from 5:00 to 8:00 P.M. Tuesday through Sunday. Tel: (5) 546-2119.

The huge peach-colored building forming the northern border of the Monumento a la Revolución is the **Frontón México**, a 4,000-seat arena featuring professional jai alai every night except Mondays at 7:00. There is a dress code.

CENTRAL PASEO DE LA REFORMA

One long block south of the Monumento a la Revolución via Calle Ignacio Ramírez is Mexico City's great thoroughfare, the seven-and-a-half-mile Paseo de la Reforma. Originally called the Paseo del Emperador, after Maximilian, who during the course of his brief and ill-fated reign ordered this grand boulevard built along the lines of the Champs-Elysées, Reforma was completed in 1865 and renamed in 1877 in honor of the great reforms in government and civil rights initiated by Benito Juárez. Once exclusively residential, today it has become *the* chic address for everything from elegant hotels and foreign embassies to the sleek new office towers of national and multinational corporations.

It's also at this point that Reforma, as it proceeds on its stately way to Chapultepec Park and the southwestern environs of the D.F., becomes a veritable open-air museum of monumental statuary. The four principal monuments here are located at *glorietas* (traffic circles) spaced about a half mile apart and serve as the hubs of major intersections. The first of these, where Calle Ignacio Ramírez intersects Reforma features the **Monumento a Cristóbal Colón** (Christopher Columbus), created by the French sculptor Charles Cordier and donated to the city by Don Antonio Escandon in 1877. The second *glorieta,* at the intersection of Reforma and Avenida Insurgentes, holds the **Monumento a Cuauhtémoc**, the last Aztec emperor, who is portrayed complete with plumed robe, feathered headdress, and spear in hand. The monument itself was designed by Francisco Jiménez and completed in 1887 by Ramon Agra (the figure of Cuauhtémoc was sculpted by Miguel Noreña).

The third *glorieta* is dominated by Mexico's most celebrated monument, the **Monumento a la Independencia**, better known as "El Angel," a 150-foot column surrounded by sculpted figures and surmounted by a golden-winged angel. Begun in 1901 under the direction of Antonio Rivas Mercado and completed in time for the centennial of the Republic in 1910, this startlingly beautiful landmark has become the most recognized symbol of the city. (According to historian Fernando Benítez, the monument's nickname is a misnomer: "Angels are traditionally sexless, and the golden figure is definitely female and was originally referred to correctly as 'La Victoria.' ")

The final *glorieta* before Chapultepec Park is at the intersection of Reforma and Río Mississippi to the north and Sevilla to the south. For the last dozen or so years the circle has featured the Fuenta Plan Cutzamala, an avante-garde structure that served as a fountain. The *glorieta* was originally occupied by a bronze sculpture of the Roman goddess Diana; first displayed in 1943, Diana became a bonafide landmark in 1964 when the local version of the League of Democracy protested her "immoral nakedness" and demanded that a skirt be placed on the lower part of her body. The fastening of a loincloth caused a successful public protest the following year and the loincloth was removed, but she was shunted off to a less conspicuous spot where she remained until, mysteriously, she disappeared a few years ago.

But now Diana's back, unveiled with little fanfare on July 5, 1992. At an estimated 110 feet tall, the gleaming sculpture is a beautiful addition to the city's skyline. However, the capital's ongoing intrigues with its statues continue, as the Fuente Plan Cutzamala is now among the missing.

The Zona Rosa

"Zona Rosa" ("Pink Zone") is the unofficial name for a roughly triangular 29-block area southwest of the Alameda Park neighborhood. It is bordered by Paseo de la Reforma to the north, Avenida Insurgentes to the east, Avenida Chapultepec to the south, and Calle Florencia to the west. An exclusive residential district from the late 19th century through the 1950s, today the Zona Rosa is home to some of the nation's best art galleries, boutiques, antiques shops, bookstores, hotels, restaurants, discotheques, bars (including gay bars), and nightclubs. Not surprisingly, just about every type of item imaginable is for sale somewhere within its borders, including clothing and jewelry of the highest quality (with prices to match). It is also the location of the **Mercado Artesanías Insurgentes**, an old-fashioned market that houses more than 200 stalls selling a variety of native handicrafts, silverwork, leather goods, onyx, and earthenware. Situated at the corner of Calle Florencia, between Calles Londres and Liverpool, the market is accessible from both those streets as well. Every Saturday the **Plaza del Angel**, a shopping mall located between Calles Londres and Hamburgo, features a flea market specializing in antiques.

In the years after the Second World War a smattering of small cafés began to infiltrate this neighborhood of luxurious two-story residences. Writers and artists such as Octavio Paz, Carlos Fuentes, and Rufino Tamayo soon were spending leisurely afternoons and evenings in these cafés enjoying each other's conversation and company. (One of the regulars from the old days, writer Luis Guillermo Piazza, is given credit for coining the name Zona Rosa. In Mexico, areas designated for legalized prostitution are called "Zonas Rojas," or red zones. Because some of the first cabarets to open in the area in the early 1950s offered entertainment bordering on the risqué, Piazza came up with the name "Zona Rosa." The rest is history.) The Pink Zone's first hotel, El Presidente, opened on the corner of Calles Hamburgo and Amberes in 1956, after which it was just a matter of time before most of the residents sold their properties and fled to the peace and quiet of the suburbs. Many of their homes were converted into chic business venues. (El Presidente was seriously damaged in the 1985 earthquake, and is still undergoing renovation.)

The buildings throughout the Zona Rosa reflect the turn-of-the-century taste for Art Nouveau, a style known in Mexico as "Porfiriato" (after Porfirio Díaz, who was president during the period in which the neighborhood came into its own). These elegant survivors of modern urban planning are appreciated today as nostalgic reminders of the neighborhood's formerly genteel character. Most of the Zona's north–south side streets are now off limits to vehicular traffic, creating lovely pedestrian malls lined with welcoming cafés. In fact, umbrella-shaded tables prevail to such an extent that it is sometimes difficult to determine where one café ends and another begins. During lunchtime the eateries and bars are crowded with tourists and local businesspeople, who eventually give way to the evening crowd. But the Zona hardly ever sleeps. As the last revelers are wandering home in the early morning light, the local businesspeople are returning to the neighborhood for their breakfast *juntas* (meetings).

BOSQUE DE CHAPULTEPEC

Spread over 40 square miles just west of the Zona Rosa, Chapultepec Park—in Spanish, Bosque (Forest) de Chapultepec—is one of the largest public parks in the world. Once an island in a swampy lake of dozens of islands, the park has ancient *ahuehuete* trees that were already a hundred years old by the time the Aztecs made their way to the Valley of Mexico in the early 14th century. In the two centuries that followed, Aztec emperors used the virgin forest as a hunting and recreation ground, only to give way to the victorious Spanish viceroys, who constructed vacation homes throughout the forest during the three centuries of the colonial era.

Today Chapultepec Park is a people's park, a place where tens of thousands of Mexico City residents come daily to decompress from the hustle and bustle of the world's largest metropolis. The great branches of the *ahuehuetes* meet high above wandering pathways to form lush green arcades; elsewhere, grassy stretches of open space attract sunbathers and picnickers (although in many areas of the park the grass has taken a beating). Signs prohibiting this and that are nowhere to be seen; the residents of the capital have a magnificent public space to live up to, and, for the most part, they do so with respect and appreciation.

The park itself is divided into three sections. The first (*primer*), or easternmost, section is home to the Museo Nacional de Antropología and the Museo Rufino Tamayo, both of which are located on the north side of Paseo de la Reforma. On the other side of Reforma, due south of the Museum of Anthropology, are a number of attractions: Lago Menor, where ducks and swans vie for the right-of-way with rowboats rented by the hour; Lago Mayor, where the National Ballet performs *Swan Lake* every April; the Museo de Arte Moderno and the Monumento a los Niños Héroes (Monument to the Boy Heroes), both due east of the lakes; the Castillo de Chapultepec (Chapultepec Castle), perched on a steep hill and looking like something out of an illustrated book of fairy tales, and the Museo de la Lucha del Pueblo Mexicano por la Libertad (Museum of the Struggle of the Mexican People for Liberty), a.k.a. the Museo del Caracol because its odd exterior resembles a snail, both southeast of the lakes; the Parque Zoológico de Chapultepec (the zoo), where the first pandas outside of China to be conceived naturally and in captivity were born, and the Jardín Botánico (Botanical Gardens), both due west of the lakes; the Auditorio Nacional (National Auditorium), due west of Calzada Molina del Rey; and Los Pinos, the presidential residence since 1938, at the extreme southern portion of this section where Avenida Constituyentes meets Calzada Molina del Rey.

The newer, middle section of the park, the *segundo sección,* is bordered by the Periférico Sur to the east and south and Reforma to the north and west. In addition to an amusement complex dominated by a huge roller coaster, this section of the park is home to two other museums, the Museo de Historia Natural and the Museo Tecnológico de Comision Federal de Electridad, as well as the Lerma Terminal de Agua, an exhibition hall for a number of Diego Rivera murals.

The third (*tercer*) section of the park, less crowded than the other two, is bordered by the huge Panteón Dolores (Dolores Civilian Cemetery) to the east, Avenida Constituyentes to the south, and the lovely residential neighborhood known as Lomas Virreyes to the north and west. This section is largely undeveloped and alternates between hilly, forested terrain and green pastures carpeted with wildflowers. It is also crisscrossed by bridle and foot paths that meander through great clumps of ferns, and is a favorite with the capital's equestrian crowd. (Public stables here rent horses by the hour.) The pastoral clearings host frequent *fiestas de cumpleaños* (birthday parties), which are easily identified by the vividly colored balloons strung between trees to mark the boundaries of the party. This section of the park is home to the Atlantis Dolphinarium as well, where superbly trained dolphins and sea lions delight the relatively few spectators who find their way here.

Museo Rufino Tamayo

The best way to see Chapultepec Park is to start early in the day with a visit to this museum, which houses the personal collection of one of the greatest Mexican painters of the 20th century. Tamayo, an orphaned Zapotec Indian, is credited, along with Diego Rivera, José Clemente Orozco, and David Siqueiros, with bringing international attention to 20th-century Mexican art. An exile in the United States during much of the 1940s and 1950s, when he refused to join the politically oriented *muralismo* movement led by Rivera and Siqueiros, he returned to Mexico in 1959, where he continued to create paintings—and later prints and sculpture—true to the tenets of the modernist movements that dominated the international art world for most of this century. He inaugurated the museum bearing his name, the first in the country to be financed by private corporations, in 1981, and passed away, at the age of 91, in the summer of 1991.

To get to the museum, follow Paseo de la Reforma south and west. After you pass Mariano Escobedo, on the corner to your right will be a large signboard with the latest information on the museum's temporary exhibitions. Take a right on Calzada Mahatma Gandhi and walk the few hundred yards to the strikingly modern structure that houses the collection. The Sculptors' Patio at the front entrance is graced by a large Henry Moore. Inside, the first thing to catch your eye will be a major Picasso—part of the museum's permanent collection. While the Tamayo Room is limited to some of the master's lesser efforts, the other nine galleries are filled with splendid works by his contemporaries, both foreign and Mexican, including Marc Chagall and José Chávez Morado, and frequently host travelling exhibitions. Open 10:00 A.M. to 6:00 P.M. daily, except Mondays.

To continue your exploration of the park, walk back to Reforma, which runs in a straight line through the northeastern corner of the park, and follow the sidewalk to your right or take your pick from a steady flow of public transportation vehicles heading in the same direction. All buses and *peseros*—the light green collective taxis—will stop in front of the National Museum of Anthropology, the next stop after the first traffic light.

Museo Nacional de Antropología

The National Museum of Anthropolgy is one of the great museums of the world, and in itself is reason enough to visit Mexico City. At the very least it deserves the better part of a day of your time.

Designed by Pedro Ramírez Vázquez, this deceptively simple rectangular structure is generally considered to be the greatest achievement of modern Mexican architecture, and certainly is one of the most harmonious settings ever conceived for the exhibition of antiquities. The exterior of the second floor, for example, is dominated by a window lattice reminiscent of traditional Mayan ornamentation. And, of course, no truly "Mexican" building would be complete without a patio. In the case of Ramírez Vázquez's design, the patio is surrounded by almost two dozen exhibition halls and is dominated by a huge inverse "umbrella." Resting on a single reinforced-concrete column decorated with reliefs depicting the history of Mexico and stabilized by special steel stays, this massive concrete cover is designed to catch rainwater and then channel it into the reed-filled pond at the opposite end of the patio.

Standing permanent sentry duty on a marble plinth at the entrance to the museum is a huge, unfinished basalt monolith representing either Tlaloc, the god of rain, or his sister, the water goddess, Chalchiuhtlicue. By all accounts the largest single-piece sculpture (weighing in at 165 metric tons and standing 23 feet tall) created in Mexico before the arrival of Columbus, this massive monolith was uncovered in a riverbed near the town of Coatlichán, some 30 miles northwest of the capital, and dates back to the heyday of Teotihuacán. Transported to its present site with great logistical difficulty (it made the trip on a specially constructed tractor-trailer that was escorted by the Mexican army), the statue was greeted by thousands of passersby as it finally rumbled through the downtown area on the afternoon of April 16, 1964. Then, almost a month before the rainy season usually begins, the skies opened up and a tremendous downpour drenched the astonished onlookers—rain, as it turned out, that continued intermittently for three days.

The exhibition rooms inside are laid out in such a way that you can visit them in any order you choose, but to appreciate fully the treasures of this great museum you should probably start with the **Orientation Room**, straight ahead as you walk through the reception hall, where a 15-minute overview of Mesoamerica's ancient cultures is offered along with guided tours in English, Spanish, German, and French at half-hour intervals. Although the tours cover just a small portion of all there is to see, they provide a valuable introduction to the pre-Columbian history of the region as well as the museum itself.

(As is the case in most museums throughout the country, all signs in the Museum of Anthropology are in Spanish only. A well-stocked bookstore on the left as you enter the reception hall has a good selection of illustrated guidebooks in English, however.)

To the right of the Orientation Room is a **Rufino Tamayo mural** depicting the eternal struggle between good and evil. (Other Mexican painters whose works are exhibited in the museum include José Chávez Morado, Matías Goeritz, Carlos Mérida, and Pablo O'Higgins.) Near the Tamayo mural are the temporary exhibition halls, where recent discoveries from ongoing excavations are displayed. These new additions to the museum's collection arrive on a regular basis; the Templo Mayor site near the Zócalo, for example, recently has produced a series of important pre-Hispanic relics.

CHAPULTEPEC PARK

The rest of the ground floor is divided into collections classified by either region or culture. These include rooms devoted to **Teotihuacán**, **Tula**, the **Mexica** (Aztec), **Oaxaca**, the **Gulf Coast**, and the **Maya**. What is probably the most popular piece in the museum is on display in the Mexica Room: the famous **Aztec calendar stone** (which is reproduced in miniature and sold in almost every souvenir shop in Mexico). This 24-ton basalt disk was unearthed during a restoration project on the Metropolitan Cathedral back in 1790, and then for years was left propped against one of the cathedral's walls. More recently, experts have concluded that it is not so much a calendar as a vision of the Aztec cosmos, and was probably carved in the early years of the 16th century.

Other well-known pieces in the museum's collection include **El Luchador**, an Olmec wrestler, and a huge Olmec head from the Late Preclassic period (about 200 B.C.). The famous Aztec **obsidian monkey**, one of the 140 priceless artifacts stolen during the Christmas Eve robbery of 1985, was recovered in 1990 and is now back on display (along with a new state-of-the-art alarm system installed as a safeguard).

Outside the Maya Room a small temple in a lovely garden contains three striking murals depicting Mayan warriors engaged in battle. These are reproductions of the originals, which were discovered in 1947 in the jungles of southernmost Mexico at a site known as Bonampak, and are considered to be some of the best preserved specimens of their type unearthed so far. Painted sometime around A.D. 800, the murals depict Mayan warriors as aggressors in a violent confrontation and further discredit the long-held belief that the Maya were dedicated pacifists.

The second floor is devoted to ethnology exhibits illustrating the lifestyles of Indian groups in Mexico today, and is arranged so that its rooms relate as closely as possible to those below. Exhibits on this floor include maps, photographs, examples of arts and crafts, religious objects, farm and fishing implements, everyday wear, native costumes and ceremonial dress, and a number of life-size replicas of traditional shelters created by Indian craftsmen.

The Museum of Anthropology has a passable **restaurant** and **cafeteria**. Large weekend crowds make the best time to visit the museum a weekday (other than Mondays, when it's closed). Open from 9:30 A.M. to 6:00 P.M. Tuesday through Saturday, and on Sundays and holidays from 10:00 A.M. to 7:30 P.M. English-speaking tours are conducted from 10:00 A.M. to 2:00 P.M. Tel: (5) 553-6381.

Parque Zoológico and Jardín Botánico

Directly south of the museum and across Reforma is the entrance to the main body of the park. Immediately to the left is a children's zoo; you can rent rowboats at the large manmade lake to the right. At the southwestern corner of the lake is the **Casa del Lago**, a colonial-era mansion-cum-theater that presents concerts, plays, readings, films, and round-table discussions on a variety of topics; admission to all events is free. Daily workshops in painting, music, dance, drama, and arts and crafts, also free, are conducted on the large patio in front of the theater's entrance. The chess and checker boards set into stone tables and scattered about under the ancient lichen-covered *ahuehuete* trees are yet another popular draw.

Nearby is the entrance to the **Parque Zoológico de Chapultepec**, which first opened in 1923. The credit for creating the first public zoo in history goes to Móctezuma II, who caged six jaguars sent to him as tribute and installed them on this very site at the beginning of the 16th century. He later moved the large aviary from his palace in the center of Tenochtitlán here in order to keep the jaguars company and then began to add other species to his collection. Eventually he allowed his favored subjects to visit the compound, and thus was born the concept of a public zoo.

For quite a while the zoo's most celebrated inmates were the pandas. A gift from the Chinese government, the first pair arrived about a 15 years ago. Fame is fickle, however. The newest crowd favorite seems to be the six kangaroos that were donated by the Australian government. Open 9:00 A.M. to 5:00 P.M. Wednesday through Sunday.

Just outside the entrance to the zoo is a depot from which a miniature train departs for its leisurely trip around the entire first section of the park. Tickets are sold at the depot itself, and a complete round trip takes about 45 minutes.

On the western side of the zoo is the **Jardín Botánico**, the origins of which also date back to the reign of Móctezuma II, who is supposed to have puttered around an herb garden on the site. West of the gardens is a small, recently inaugurated park that has one requisite for admission: You must be at least 50 years old. Inside its fenced-off confines are comfortable benches, beautiful tropical flora, and an ever-present choir of songbirds.

South of this small park-within-a-park a pathway known as the **Calzada de los Poetas** (Poets' Walk) is lined with statues of some of Mexico's greatest writers and poets. At the end of the walk, to the east, is the Móctezuma Ahuehuete Tree—with a circumference of almost 50 feet, the largest tree in a park filled with large trees. Besides being a natural wonder, the tree is an inspiration to all the health-conscious joggers who jam the path that winds past it. The grassy knoll nearby serves as a workout area for fledgling matadors, who cape imaginary bulls under the tutelage of their trainers as the sun rises to warm the always chilly morning air.

Continuing in a southerly direction, you'll come to the **Monumento Nezahualcoyotl** (nez-a-wahl-COY-o-tal) on Avenida Heroico Colegio Militar, the favored route for the capital's hordes of joggers. Nezahualcoyotl, the 15th-century poet-king of Texcoco, is the man most often credited with supervising the planting of the area's *ahuehuete* trees. Nearby you can see the remains of an ancient **aqueduct**, another civic improvement reputedly instigated by Nezahualcoyotl. On the other side of the aqueduct you can either enter a tunnel and wait your turn for the elevator to Chapultepec Castle or follow the winding pathway to the top.

Castillo de Chapultepec and the Museo Nacional de Historia

The hill of Chapultepec has been the site of one kind of fortress or another since the days when the Toltecs occupied the valley, almost 1,000 years ago. In 1521 an anonymous Spanish chronicler wrote: "The Emperor Moctezuma gazes every sundown at his canalled capital surrounded by lakes... from his fortress high on the hill. Here he is borne in his jewel-encrusted litter after dinner to smoke tobacco treated with amber and to feast his eyes on the great temples of the pagan gods in the city plaza, washed with the colors of sunset." By the end of the 18th century a combination fort, granary, and summer residence for the Spanish viceroys had been built on the site. That structure was converted into a military college in 1840, almost 20 years after Mexico won her independence from Spain, and in 1847, with U.S. troops threatening to overrun the college, six cadets—soon to be known to posterity as the Niños Héroes (Boy Heroes)—provided the young Mexican republic with its newest martyrs by leaping from the precipice wrapped in Mexican flags rather than surrendering to the invading troops. (If you walk toward the south and east, you'll soon come to the six towering marble columns of the **Monumento a los Niños Héroes**. Inaugurated in 1952, the columns frame a large statue of a defiant Mother Mexico holding a dead son in her arms; another son at her feet is alive and ready to defend her. The remains of the young martyrs are buried within the monument.)

The Neoclassical design of the present-day castle dates back to France's short-lived (1864–1867) domination of Mexico. Austrian Archduke Maximilian and his wife, Carlota, sent to rule Mexico by Napoleon III, almost immediately took up permanent residence in the castle, rather than in the National Palace, after Carlota was attacked by bedbugs on her first night in the latter. Maximilian then ordered a complete remodeling of the castle, with results that today can be seen in the design of its gardens, winding stairways, and intimate patios.

After Maximilian was overthrown and executed, the new president, Benito Juárez, reestablished the presidential residence in the National Palace. His successor, President-for-Life Porfirio Díaz, moved the presidential residence back to the castle, where it remained until the populist Lázaro Cárdenas ascended to the presidency in 1934. Cárdenas viewed living in a castle as "undemocratic" and had the presidential residence moved to Los Pinos, an abandoned hacienda nearby, where it remains to this day. At the same time Cárdenas ordered the castle converted to its present function: home to the **Museo Nacional de Historia.** Today the museum houses a collection of historical memorabilia dating back to the days of the Conquest—blood-stained uniforms, swords, and the like—along with a number of outstanding examples of Mexican *muralismo,* including Orozco's *Benito Juárez and the Reform,* David Alfaro Siqueiros's *The Revolution,* Jorge Camarena's *The Constitution,* and Juan O'Gorman's *Themes of the Revolution.*

Upstairs are exhibits featuring period furniture and clothing, clocks, coins, and jewelry, but perhaps the most interesting pieces are the two horseless carriages—one an ostentatious coach designed especially for the ill-fated Maximilian and the other a stark black coach favored by Benito Juárez (the latter was literally the seat of the provisional government for a short period following Maximilian's demise).

Before leaving the museum be sure to take a stroll around the outside patio for a look at the opulent French-style furnishings left behind by Maximilian and Carlota. The panoramic views of the city and, on good days, Popocatépetl and Iztaccíhuatl, are well worth the climb. The museum is open from 9:00 A.M. to 6:00 P.M. daily, except Mondays.

Located just below the castle is the **Museo de la del Pueblo Mexicano por la Libertad** (Museum of the Struggle of the Mexican People for Liberty), also known as the Museo del Caracol, after its snail-like shape. You enter this glass-walled structure, which is tucked into the hillside, from the top and then walk down a winding ramp past a variety of three-dimensional models depicting historical events, as well as other materials from Mexico's revolutionary past. At the bottom of the hill you can rest on one of the chairs in the small circular garden known as the Audiorama while listening to recorded classical music. Open 10:00 A.M. to 4:00 P.M. daily, except Mondays; Tel: (5) 553-6391.

Turning north and heading in the direction of Paseo de la Reforma, you'll soon see the unmistakable silhouette of the glass-faced **Museo de Arte Moderno**. The building itself is actually two low, circular buildings connected by a short corridor and surrounded by a fenced-off sculpture garden. The well-lit interior is dominated by a white marble staircase and an elegant glass dome. One section of the museum is devoted to contemporary art trends of the past two decades and includes photographs, engravings, and sculpture. Another area displays Mexican fine art from the late 19th century through the 1960s. On permanent display are the works of Diego Rivera and his wife, Frida Kahlo; Rivera's mentor, José María Velasco; and such celebrated contemporaries as Tamayo, Orozco, and Siqueiros. Open 10:00 A.M. to 6:00 P.M. daily, except Mondays, and until 9:00 P.M. Wednesdays.

The Second and Third Sections

The newer sections of the park, although not far as the crow flies, are difficult to get to on foot. Your best bet is to walk to Paseo de la Reforma and then take any bus marked "Reforma" heading west. The last stop before the bus leaves the park will be Plaza Petroleos, where the imposing Fuente de Petroleos stands as a monument to President Cárdenas's nationalization of the oil industry in 1938. If you'd like to do more exploring in the park get off here and follow the long paved path south to the **Museo de Historia Natural de la Ciudad de México**. After the inspired architecture of the museums in the older section of the park, this series of ten drab-appearing domes will come as a bit of a letdown. Inside, however, a modern design and effective lighting enhance the displays of dinosaur skeletons, as well as exhibits on the creation of the universe, the evolution of aquatic and terrestrial life, and an illustrated breakdown of Mexico's mineral wealth, flora, and fauna. Open 10:00 A.M. to 5:00 P.M.

Tuesday through Saturday; 10:00 A.M. to 6:00 P.M. on Sundays. Tel: (5) 516-2848.

Just outside the front entrance to the museum is another miniature railroad depot. Although the tracks crisscross the middle section of the park, you'll soon discover that everything of interest in this section is easily accessible on foot. To the southeast, on the other side of a small artificial lake, is the entrance to the **Parque de Juegos Mecánicos** (amusement park), with its awe-inspiring roller coaster known as "La Montaña Rusa" ("The Russian Mountain"), and the **Museo Nacional de Tecnológico de la Comisión Federal de Electricidad** (Federal Electrical Commission Technological Museum). Modern achievement in communications, transportation, and industry, and an explanation of the electromagnetic theory, are some of the subjects presented in dioramas in this roomy, contemporary museum. The museum's fine **planetarium** offers presentations at 11:00 A.M., 1:00 P.M., and 6:00 P.M. Tuesday through Saturday. Regular hours on those days are from 9:00 A.M. to 5:00 P.M. and on Sundays from 9:00 A.M. to 1:30 P.M. Closed Mondays. Tel: (5) 516-0964.

Also in this section of the park is the **Lerma Terminal de Agua**, a large nondescript building that serves as an exhibition hall for a number of Diego Rivera murals depicting the importance of water. His best work here, though, is a mosaic at the bottom of the outdoor fountain in front of the terminal, with its dominating figure of Tlaloc, the rain god of the central highlands. On the same traffic circle as the fountain is the **Lago Chapultepec**, a restaurant with panoramic views of the lake from every table, good food and service, and live dinner music. (See Dining, below.)

The paved paths to the west and south of the fountain will lead you to sights of interest having to do with water, that most precious of commodities in this often parched land. The **Fuente de Nezahualcoyotl** and the **Fuente de los Dioses** are long stone walls carved with bas-relief murals of Aztec gods and symbols submerged by cascading water. To the south of these fountains, the Cárcamo, or municipal waterworks, boasts a rare Rivera sculpture dedicated to Tlaloc.

Still farther south, Avenida Constituyentes is filled with a constant stream of taxis, both private and collective. If you'd like to visit the third, and least developed, section of the park, take a taxi about half a mile west to the entrance to the Dolores Civilian Cemetery. From there, follow the road due north and you'll soon find yourself in the heart of this urban oasis. The path to the left leads to the **Dolphinarium** (open 10:00 A.M. to 6:00 P.M. daily, except Mondays), the one to the right to the **stables** and equestrian areas. If you've had enough park exploring for the day and want to head back into town, cross Constituyentes and hail a taxi heading eastward; it's a five-minute ride to the Zona Rosa.

Polanco

The *colonia* (neighborhood) of Polanco stretches along the northern perimeter of the first section of Chapultepec Park (the section that includes the National Museum of Anthropology and the Rufino Tamayo Museum), and extends as far as Avenida Ejército Nacional to the north, Avenida Mariano Escobedo to the east, and the Periférico Norte to the west.

Soon after the Conquest mulberry trees were imported from Spain and planted on what became the Hacienda de los Morales, the first silkworm farm in the Americas. Most of the area remained relatively undeveloped until about 40 years ago, when a new generation of wealthy Mexicans began to carve up the empty fields for their mansions and estates. Many of the homes were built in the classic Art Nouveau "sand-castle" style, with carved stone trimmings proliferating around windows and façades. As was the case throughout the D.F., preparations for the 1968 Summer Olympic Games led to urban expansion and changed considerably the character of the four main east–west avenues in the neighborhood: Campos Elíseos, Presidente Masaryk, Horacio, and Homero.

Although it is still an exclusive residential district, the graciously opulent homes and colonial-style mansions here (which tend to be clustered on the tree-lined streets running north to south across the avenues) have been joined by sleek, modern high-rise office buildings and condominiums; fashionable hotels and restaurants; one of the capital's largest department stores; a number of chic boutiques; a variety of nightclubs; and, of all things, an authentic Jewish shopping district where the choicest fruits, vegetables, and kosher products are available (though at slightly higher prices than you'll find elsewhere in the city). The **Deportivo Chapultepec** (Chapultepec Sports Club), well known for its elegant tennis facilities and open to the public, is located in Polanco's northwest corner. The **Conservatorio Nacional de Musica** is about 1 km (½ mile) away on Avenida Presidente Masaryk.

On Avenida Campos Elíseos, next to the rear entrance of the Stouffer Presidente Chapultepec, the **Centro Cultural de Arte Contemporaneo** houses rotating exhibitions of 20th-century painting on its two lower floors. The upper two floors contain the **Centro Cultural de Arte Prehispanica**—more than 400 art objects dating from 1000 B.C. to A.D.

1521—and the **Centro Cultural de Arte Fotografía**, whose permanent collection spans the entire history of photography, including works by Henri Cartier-Bresson, Man Ray, Edward Weston, and other greats. Open 10:00 A.M. to 6:00 P.M. daily, except Mondays, and until 8:00 P.M. Wednesdays. Tel: (5) 203-5820.

Hipódromo de las Américas

The Art Deco–style Hipódromo, Mexico City's only thoroughbred racetrack and one of the most charming racetracks anywhere, was built in 1943 after the Second World War shut down U.S. tracks, and was a hit right from the start. The track, located just north and west of Chapultepec Park, is unique in that it operates year-round (except for Easter Week and the last two weeks of the year), with the caliber of thoroughbreds on a par with all but the best tracks in the United States. Favorites win about 35 percent of the time. The track's oval is seven and a half furlongs, and the fountains and ponds of the beautifully landscaped infield are home for dozens of flamingos and swans. Pari-mutuel betting, state-of-the-art tote boards, and numerous TV monitors make the Hipódromo a very comfortable place to make your contribution to the betterment of the breed.

If you're going to spend an afternoon here, you might consider a table at one of the track's five first-class restaurants. At the elegant **Derby Club**, 15,000 pesos (per person) will get you a table with a glassed-in bird's-eye view of the finish line. Another possibility is the equally elegant **Jockey Club** (men must wear ties). The real bargain here, though, are the plush sky boxes, which go for 75,000 pesos and have room for up to 16 people; food and drink service is available, and each box has a color TV for monitoring the action. And, as in all the restaurant areas, betting windows are just a few feet away.

You can make reservations for any of these alternatives by phoning (5) 557-4100; an English-speaking agent will handle your request. There are 11 races a day on Tuesdays, Thursdays, and Sundays, and 12 each on Fridays and Saturdays; the track is closed Mondays and Wednesdays. Post time is 5:00 P.M. on Tuesdays, Thursdays, and Fridays, and 2:30 P.M. Saturdays and Sundays.

A steady stream of collective taxis leaves from the metro's Tacuba station or passes westward along Paseo de la Reforma marked either "Hipódromo," "Legaria," "San Isidro," or "Defensa Nacional." Any of these will drop you near the main entrance. If you're driving, take Periférico Norte and exit on

Calzada Legaria. Turn left at the stop light; straight ahead is the massive Hipódromo parking lot. Taxis are always available after the last race.

THE SOUTHERN DISTRICTS

There are a number of things to see and do along Insurgentes south of its intersection with Reforma. Down past the Polyforum Cultural Siqueiros and the Plaza México bullfight arena are two interesting neighborhoods to either side of the Monumento a Alvaro Obregón: Coyoacán to the east and San Angel to the west. Both neighborhoods, besides being good for walking, offer small museums, historical sites, cafés, and markets.

Farther south on Insurgentes is University City, with its interesting art and architecture, the archaeological sites of Copilco and Cuicuilco, and Mexico City's version of Disneyland, Reino Aventura. Finally, beyond Reino Aventura to the southeast—but still accessible by metro—is the canal district of Xochimilco.

Polyforum Cultural Siqueiros

In 1965 Mexico's famed patron of the arts, Manuel Suárez, commissioned David Alfaro Siqueiros, the equally famous muralist, to create the world's largest indoor mural on a 50-acre tract he happened to own near the Plaza México bullfight ring, 5 km (3 miles) south of the intersection of Insurgentes and Reforma.

Suárez was a self-made millionaire who had ridden with Pancho Villa during the Revolution, introduced the cement industry to Mexico, built the first highway from the capital to Acapulco (where he subsequently made a fortune from his real-estate holdings), and fathered 23 children. Siqueiros had been an officer in the Spanish Civil War and then had led a mob in an abortive attempt to assassinate Leon Trotsky in 1940. After spending a few years as a political prisoner in a Mexican jail for his outspoken criticism of the government, he received a presidential pardon in 1964 and agreed to take Suárez's commission with the understanding that he would have complete artistic freedom.

Siqueiros soon had drawn up plans for an elliptical 12-sided structure and went about painting it with the help of some two dozen apprentice-disciples. Suárez took exception to the participation of the assistants, however, as well as to the rather violent anti-capitalistic messages suggested by the design of the mural. The clash of their titanic egos eventually prompted Siqueiros to insist that the developer stay away from the work-in-progress. Suárez's response to this arrogant demand was to order the construction of a tower right next door—from which, upon its completion, he continued to spy on the artist at work below. Fortunately, Suárez allowed the work to continue, and in 1971, after six years of intensive labor, the Polyforum Cultural Siqueiros was inaugurated.

The 12 walls of the structure, each measuring some 820 square feet, are covered with huge, vividly painted human figures that seem to leap out with brutal vitality at passersby. (The sculptured iron fence surrounding the Polyforum also was designed by Siqueiros.) Inside, the mural entitled *The March of Humanity on Earth Toward the Cosmos* is said to be the largest in the world (Siqueiros painted this one entirely himself). The oval-shaped stage is, in actuality, a huge turntable on which more than 1,000 people can stand, inspecting Siqueiros's creation around and above them, as the platform slowly revolves 360 degrees (a full circle takes 15 minutes).

Downstairs is a multi-use theater, the outer corridor of which serves as a sort of museum for the display of native arts and crafts, while on the level below there is a branch of FONART (see Shops and Shopping, below) and a number of art galleries. Open 10:00 A.M. to 3:00 P.M. and 4:00 to 7:00 P.M. daily.

Nearby, the 51-story **Hotel de México**—known to locals as "El Elefante Blanco"—stands as a monument to one man's ego and vanity. After a few months of spying on Siqueiros from his lofty vantage point, Suárez, who was none too anxious to become the laughingstock of the capital, decided to enlarge his tower, surely believing that nothing would be more fitting than to build the world's tallest hotel next door to the world's largest indoor mural. The result of this logic is a monstrous structure with more than 1,300 rooms that, until recently, was destined never to be occupied. Under construction for 24 years, it was finally sold by the Suárez estate in 1988 (Suárez himself died at the age of 95 in 1987) to the group of businessmen responsible for organizing Mexico City's World Trade Center. From the looks of the exterior, it seems that virtually no progress has taken place in the last year, and the target date for opening, early 1992, has come and gone. It seems as though El Elefante Blanco is indeed cursed, and it continues to be known to some as the tallest eyesore south of Houston. Still, the top floor of the building, which has been functioning as a revolving restaurant for the past 20 years, affords terrific views of the city on a clear day (especially if your visit coincides with the monthly window washing). There is also a nondescript restaurant on the ground floor.

Plaza México

Traditionally, one of the few public events to start on time in Mexico is the weekly presentation of the bullfights at the 60,000-seat Plaza México, located 2 km (1¼ mile) south of the Polyforum on Insurgentes Sur. Promptly at 4:30 P.M. every Sunday a lone horseman in medieval costume prances his steed across the ring and follows the ancient custom of requesting permission of the authorities to conduct a "running of the bulls."

The Plaza México, reputedly the world's largest bullring, has been the principal bullring in the capital since 1946. During the dry season (November through May) the best matadors in the country appear here; the rainy season, on the other hand, is the time for *novilleros* (amateurs) to fight younger, smaller bulls, and for spectators to take their chances with the weather as well as the caliber of the artistry.

A good way to attend the bullfights, especially on Sunday, when it's always difficult to get a taxi in the D.F., is on a tour conducted by an English-speaking guide. The standard Sunday tour includes a morning performance at Bellas Artes by the Ballet Folklórico, followed by a gondola ride in Xochimilco, lunch, and then the bullfights in the afternoon. (If you're on your own, have lunch at Las Cazuelas, two short blocks east of Plaza México; see Dining, below.) All travel agencies and most hotels can make arrangements for you. The fee includes transportation and a reserved seat on the shady side of the ring, which should keep you out of harm's way of beer showers generated by disgruntled fans, most of whom seem to prefer the sunny side.

Coyoacán

The Monumento a Alvaro Obregón is about 4 km (2½ miles) south of the Plaza México on Insurgentes Sur. To the right as you head south is the San Angel area; to the left, or east, is the Coyoacán area. First, Coyoacán.

The quickest and least expensive way to get here from the Zócalo area is by metro; take line number 3 from the Zócalo's Pino Suárez station to the Miguel Angel de Quevedo station, one stop south of the Coyoacán terminal. As you exit you can turn west on Avenida M.A. Quevedo and walk 15 minutes to the **Monumento a Alvaro Obregón**, though the appeal of this monument has been diluted somewhat now that its main attraction—Obregón's severed hand and wrist, pickled in a glass container—has been removed. If you choose to bypass the monument, head north on Avenida Universidad upon leaving the metro and then take the first right onto Avenida Francisco Sosa for the most scenic entrance to Coyoacán.

The tiny 18th-century Baroque-style church on the north corner of Universidad and Francisco Sosa, the **Capilla de San Antonio Panzacola**, looks entirely out of place among the modern structures lining both sides of Universidad. But then the scenery begins to change: As narrow, cobblestoned Francisco Sosa heads toward Coyoacán center, the architectural creations of the 20th century give way to moss-stained stone walls hiding low-slung colonial mansions from prying eyes. Over the entrances to most of these mansions you'll find the centuries-old coats-of-arms of their former aristocratic residents. Coyoacán has always attracted the elite of Mexican society.

The settlement of Coyoacán can be traced back to the ninth century, when Toltecs moved into the area. They were followed, in turn, by Chichimecs in the 12th century and Aztecs in the 14th (the Aztecs built their vacation homes here). Later, Cortés established Coyoacán as the provisional capital of New Spain while the ruined Tenochtitlán was being rebuilt as the Mexico City of the Zócalo area. Today it is a mellow, unspoiled oasis filled with colonial buildings and peaceful gardens. At times it seems as if an ocean separates the serene ambience here from the intensity of the urban sprawl surrounding it.

Cramped Avenida Francisco Sosa suddenly opens up onto the large and attractive **Plaza Central**, which consists of the Jardín Centenario and Plaza Hidalgo. The largest building on the plaza, at its northeastern corner, is the so-called **Delegación Coyoacán**, which houses the offices of this quaint municipality. Constructed in 1522, the building originally served as Cortés's first residence, from which he governed the colony until his palace (an earlier version of today's Palacio Nacional) was completed. His coat-of-arms can still be seen embedded in the façade. The 16th-century **Templo de San Juan Bautista** overlooks the plaza, its plain, fortresslike exterior providing no indication of just how lavish and ornate the reconstructed interior is.

From Plaza Hidalgo walk north along either Aguaya or Centenario and then turn right on Calle Londres. The **Museo Frida Kahlo**, Londres 127, is located in the house where the eminent painter was born in 1907 and later lived with her husband, Diego Rivera. The house became a popular gathering place for artists, writers, poets, and intellectuals in the 1930s and 1940s: Among its more illustrious guests at one time or another were Leon Trotsky and D. H. Lawrence. Neither its lively history nor its bright blue exterior and cheery garden prepare the visitor for the ethereal and sometimes macabre self-portraits by Kahlo displayed within, however. Kahlo, who was afflicted by polio as a young girl and later was involved in a serious trolley-car accident, lived much of her life in pain—a fact that is clearly reflected in her art. A number of Rivera's drawings and mementoes of their life together are also on exhibit, as are a number of Mayan and Toltec sculptures and ceramics in a hut in the garden. Open 10:00 A.M. to 2:00 P.M. and 3:00 to 5:00 P.M. daily, except Mondays. Admission is free, as are the 11:00 A.M. guided tours on weekends.

Two blocks north and two and a half blocks east of the Kahlo museum, at Calle Vienna 45, the **Museo León Trotsky** is where the great revolutionary lived in exile and was eventually murdered by an assassin in the employ of his archrival, Joseph Stalin. Here, first impressions do tell the whole story, with the house resembling nothing so much as a fortress. The high bare walls are broken only by an equally tall and stark steel door; even the doorbell is hard to find. (It's to the left of the entrance, obscured by ivy.) Keep ringing. Once inside the compound you feel surrounded by a melancholy gloom that hangs heavily over the weed-choked garden and the small moss-covered monument to Trotsky designed by his friend Juan O'Gorman (Trotsky's ashes are interred within along with his wife's, who died in Paris in 1962).

Inside, the rooms have been left much as they were at the time of the assassination. Dozens of large bullet holes—courtesy of a prior attempt on his life allegedly led by the painter David Alfaro Siqueiros—pockmark the walls of Trotsky's bedroom. On August 20, 1940, Jaime Ramón Mercader del Río, an agent of Stalin's posing as the boyfriend of Trotsky's secretary, appeared at the door with a request that Trotsky read a paper of his. Granted admission to Trotsky's study, he then proceeded to smash the founder of the Red Army across the skull with the blunt end of an alpine ice pick he had concealed under his coat. Trotsky's shattered eyeglasses still lie on his desk where they fell. The museum has been enlarged to include the residence next door, and there is now a 10,000-peso admission fee. Open 10:00 A.M. to 5:00 P.M. daily, except Mondays.

To get to the **Museo Nacional de las Intervenciones**

(Museum of Foreign Interventions), head south on Calle Morelos for three blocks, turn left (east) on Xicoténcatl, and continue in the same direction across División del Norte until you come to the museum, which is housed in the former convent of Churubusco on the corner of Calle Vicente de Agosto. The Franciscans were responsible for building the original structure on this site in the years immediately following the Conquest, and it later became the base for their missionary activities in China, Japan, and the Philippines. It was renovated in 1768, and 79 years later became the scene of the so-called Battle of Churubusco, where badly outnumbered Mexican troops were overwhelmed by the U.S. army as it closed in on Mexico City.

Today the museum houses eight exhibition rooms filled with the memorabilia of Mexico's anti-colonialist wars, including captured weapons, blood-stained uniforms, documents, photographs, drawings, and a tattered 1847 version of the "Stars and Stripes" captured by Mexican troops. The emphasis throughout is on the bravery of the Mexican soldier rather than on the villany of the various aggressors. One of the rooms has a 19th-century carriage that belonged to General (later President) Santa Anna, who led the attack on the Alamo. There is also a lovely garden inside the walls of the former convent with a monument to the fallen defenders of the Battle of Churubusco. Open 9:00 A.M. to 6:00 P.M. daily, except Mondays.

Back on División del Norte there are usually plenty of cruising taxis. To complete your tour of the Coyoacán area, flag one heading south and have it drop you off in front of the Museo Anahuacalli, the towering pyramid-shaped structure on Calle Museo, about 2 km (1¼ miles) south of the Museum of Foreign Interventions. (This is a bit off the beaten path; either have your taxi wait for you—a half hour on the meter will cost about 10,000 pesos—or backtrack to División del Norte to catch a taxi for the 20-minute ride back to the hotel zone or Zócalo after your tour of the museum.)

Taking its name from the Aztec word for the Valley of Mexico, the **Museo Anahuacalli** was designed by Diego Rivera and built out of *tezontle*. Much of its ornamentation is derivative of Toltec and Mayan designs, and the overall effect is at once impressive and appropriate. The museum is filled with well-preserved artifacts—many dating back to the Preclassic period—from Rivera's own collection. For the most part these artifacts fall into three broad categories coinciding with the three most important cultures to arise from the Valley of Mexico: Teotihuacano, Toltec, and Aztec.

The largest room in the museum, on the second floor,

served as Rivera's studio toward the end of his life and is preserved just as it was at the time of his death. On one long wall there is even an unfinished mural with the likenesses of Stalin and Mao Tse-tung charcoaled in. The museum is not without its controversy, however. Serious rumors persist about an anonymous craftsman who churned out excellent replicas of ancient Mesoamerican artifacts for the actress Dolores del Rio, a close friend of Rivera's, and who was later introduced to the great muralist himself. (The extensive collection of vaguely pornographic artifacts is particularly suspect.) Nevertheless, the museum is well worth a visit, if only to appreciate Rivera's achievement as the architect of the building. The artist died before he could realize his vision of designing a cultural complex. The upstairs terrace of the museum affords a view of the staked-out plan for the structures that were never built. High weeds engulf the whole area, which resembles a barely excavated archaeological site after 35 years of neglect. Open 10:00 A.M. to 2:00 P.M. and 3:00 to 6:00 P.M. daily, except Mondays.

San Angel

This beautiful neighborhood just west of the Monumento a Alvaro Obregón was known in pre-colonial days by the Indian name Tenanitla, meaning "at the foot of the stone wall"—an allusion to the vast lava field to the south now known as El Pedregal (discussed below). Later, Spanish aristocrats built their gracious walled mansions here, and the area experienced its glory days in the 17th and 18th centuries. After Mexico gained its independence in 1821, San Angel continued to be popular, especially with writers and artists, who spent their leisure time in country residences here. Today, despite having been engulfed by the rapidly expanding D.F., San Angel retains much of its small-town charm and character.

Taxis aside, the easiest way to get from Coyoacán to San Angel is to take the number 56 or 116A bus, both of which can be boarded at the prominently marked *parada* (bus stop), just west of the Plaza Hidalgo on Avenida Hidalgo. The buses make the trip in less than 15 minutes, stopping right in front of the Exconvento del Carmen, which houses a small museum called the **Museo Colonial del Carmen**, and its adjacent church. Located on the east side of Avenida Revolución, just north and east of the Plaza de San Jacinto (the site of the Bazar Sábado; see below), the structure, which was built between 1615 and 1628, is a fine example of the ecclesiastical architecture of the period. On the other side of the main entrance is a beautiful garden graced by a lovely tile fountain and a number of ancient fig trees planted by the convent's founding friars and nuns.

Inside the museum are frescoes in various stages of disintegration. In a number of instances the topmost layer of paint has faded to reveal a totally different mural below it and yet a third below that, with probably a century elapsed between the first application of paint and the last. The basement crypt is the most popular attraction here, however. If you've seen Guanajuato's mummies and were favorably impressed, then you're in for a treat. If not, view at your own risk the horrified expressions on the mummified skulls of the 18th-century monks and nuns who were victims of a severe earthquake. The small room in which they had congregated was hermetically sealed by the violent upheaval, and more than a century later their well-preserved remains were discovered by a workman. The adjoining church also has some excellent 18th-century religious paintings by the Spaniard Cristóbal de Villalpando. Open 10:00 A.M. to 5:00 P.M. daily, except Mondays.

A few blocks north of the Museo Colonial del Carmen, on the same (east) side of Avenida Revolución at number 1608, is the sleek, modern **Museo de Arte Alvar y Carmen T. de Carrillo Gil**, named for the Yucatecan doctor, and his wife, who befriended Orozco, Siqueiros, and Rivera. The museum houses an outstanding collection of the artists' earlier murals and mounts exhibitions of the work of some of their foreign counterparts, including the likes of Picasso and Paul Klee. The Gil Museum has earned a reputation for consistently exhibiting only the finest art. Open 10:00 A.M. to 6:00 P.M. daily, except Mondays.

From the museum head south on Avenida Revolución back to the Museo Colonial del Carmen and then climb the short hill to the **Plaza de San Jacinto**. Mounted on a wall on the western side of the plaza is a plaque that reads: "In memory of the Irish soldiers of the heroic Battalion of Saint Patrick, martyrs who gave their lives for the cause of Mexico during the unjust North American invasion of 1847." The San Patricio Battalion was made up of deserters, most of them Irish-Catholic immigrants, from General Winfield Scott's army. Brutalized by the harsh treatment dispensed by their officers and lured by Mexican promises of citizenship and free land, they switched sides and fought against their former comrades-in-arms at the Battle of Churubusco. Eventually, superior discipline and firepower resulted in victory for Scott's troops, and the 71 members of the battalion were summarily tried and hanged in the plaza. Today, besides being a delightful public space, the plaza is the site of a very busy open-air art show every Saturday.

In the northwest corner of the plaza, an artisans' cooperative known as the **Bazar Sábado** takes up two floors of an 18th-century mansion. Here you'll find dozens of small shops arranged around an oval-shaped patio offering every kind of handcrafted item imaginable. Many of the artisans are immigrants from Europe and the United States who have been drawn to Mexico by the richness of its folkloric heritage. The bazaar is open from 10:00 A.M. to 8:00 P.M. every Saturday, and visitors can partake of an excellent afternoon buffet in the patio featuring traditional Mexican cuisine for non-Mexican palates (i.e., not too spicy). A marimba band in the native costumes of Chiapas adds just the right touch to this lively scene.

Outside the entrance to the bazaar you'll encounter Indian women squatting on the sidewalk selling their handicrafts at about half the cost of what you would pay inside. They expect—and look forward to—haggling over prices; the prices inside are fixed.

From the intersection of Avenida Revolución and Calle Altavista, just north of the plaza, it's a ten-minute walk (seven blocks) up the latter to the **Museo Estudio Diego Rivera** (entrance on Calle Palmas). Designed by architect-muralist and longtime Rivera friend Juan O'Gorman in 1933, the artist's studio was opened to the public as a museum in 1986, on the 100th anniversary of Rivera's birth. This rather bizarre studio-on-stilts, which actually consists of two studios—Rivera's blue one was connected to his wife Frida Kahlo's crimson-colored one by an overhead bridge—sticks out like the proverbial sore thumb in this neighborhood of discreet colonial mansions, and has been the cause of more than a few arguments. The continually changing exhibitions of the master's works, on the other hand, are almost always greeted with enthusiasm. Open 10:00 A.M. to 6:00 P.M. daily, except Mondays.

Diagonally across the street is the **San Angel Inn**, the landmark 17th-century hacienda that for years has been one of the capital's most elegant restaurants. It was perhaps inevitable, given its outstanding architectural elements and colorful history (the San Angel served as headquarters for General Antonio López de Santa Anna during Mexico's war with the United States and was used for the same purpose by Emiliano Zapata and Pancho Villa 64 years later), that the inn would become a stop for tour buses. As a result, the quality of the food and service has dropped considerably. Still, a stroll through its grounds will give you a little taste of what hacienda life must have been like for the privileged few who enjoyed it during the long centuries of Mexico's colonial domination. (The management of the inn frowns upon blue jeans and sneakers; if you plan on stopping here, wear something a little less casual.) Open 1:00 P.M. to 1:00 A.M. daily; Tel: (5) 548-6746.

There is a taxi stand right outside the entrance to the inn. Taxis also cruise Avenida Revolución.

Copilco

The Preclassic archaeological site of Copilco is located about 1 km (½ mile) south of the Insurgentes Sur turnoff for the Plaza de San Jacinto, just north of University City. A sea of petrified lava, its frozen flow black and lavender, is the graveyard of the ancient Cuiculco culture, buried by a catastrophic eruption of nearby Xitle (Little Smoking Mountain) sometime around the beginning of the Christian era. Ten feet below the lava, excavations here in 1917 uncovered several tombs, pottery, clay figurines, and stone implements dating back as far as 1500 B.C. Today three tunnels created by the original excavations have been converted into a museum, and several of the tombs are displayed in the same position and condition in which they were found, complete with the ceramic, stone, and bone objects found with them.

The site is open Tuesday through Sunday. The trip on the number 3 metro line from the Zócalo area (get off at the Copilco stop) is 20 minutes, quicker than most taxis. If you prefer to drive, take the "Copilco" exit off Avenida Insurgentes Sur (about 2 km/1¼ mile south of the Monumento a Alvaro Obregón) and turn left onto Avenida Copilco. Turn left again almost immediately and follow the signs. The entrance to the site is at Calle Victoria 54.

Ciudad Universitaria

Four decades ago, after 20 centuries of abandonment, the same lava-strewn moonscape that supports Copilco was transformed into a marvel of architecture, artistry, and urban planning. Today it is the setting for one of the largest and most modern universities in the world.

About 16 km (10 miles) south of the Zócalo, where six centuries ago the Aztecs built temples to their gods, rise contemporary temples, shining structures of glass and steel. The Universidad Nacional Autónoma de México (UNAM) is the oldest university in the New World, dating back to a September 21, 1551, edict of King Phillip II of Spain. Officially opened in 1553, it became a unified entity in name only as its facilities were soon scattered throughout the ever-expanding city. Miguel Aleman, one of Mexico's most productive presidents (1946–1952), instigated a concerted national project in which every building was planned to complement the whole, setting a local precedent for organization and teamwork. Ten thousand laborers worked under the direction of 150 architects and engineers and, in 1954, University City was inaugurated. Today more than 300,000 students are taught by 18,000 professors, who in turn are assisted by 2,000 researchers.

One of the most impressive cultural complexes anywhere in the world, its five square miles contain 80 university buildings; the **Sala Nezahuacoyotl Concert Hall**, an acoustically innovative, ultramodern theater; and the Estadio Olímpico, a 100,000-seat stadium inaugurated in time for the 1968 Olympic Games and site of the 1986 World Cup Soccer final. In traditional Mexican fashion, no decent-size wall has gone unpainted, and the works of every great 20th-century Mexican muralist painter can be found here.

With such an overwhelming amount of color and form commanding your attention, the ten-story **Central Library**, built in the shape of a rectangular prism, is the structure that catches the eye before all others. Juan O'Gorman utilized a combination of stone, colored cement, tile, and blown glass to create this startlingly dramatic architectural masterpiece.

Southwest of the library is the low-slung administration building called **La Torre de la Rectoria** (rectory). The wall facing Avenida Insurgentes is covered by a boldly executed three-dimensional mural by David Alfaro Siqueiros, combining painting and high-relief sculpture and creating a perspective-in-motion when viewed from a moving vehicle.

The **Estadio Olímpico**, built to resemble the crater of a volcano, serves as Diego Rivera's canvas: striking reliefs evoke the spirit of athletic competition from pre-Hispanic times to the present. Other significant murals to look for here are those by Francisco Eppens, José Chávez Morado, Matias Goeritz, and Federico Silva. A mass of volcanic rock next to the Sala Nezahualcoyotl features sculptural forms carved out of the frozen lava by Ignacio Asunsolo, Manuel Felguerez, and Helen Escobedo.

To get to University City take the number 3 metro line to the "Universidad" stop (the last stop). By bus, walk to Insurgentes Sur and take either the 17, 17A, or 17B bus; from Coyoacán take the number 19A bus west on Calle Centenario. A university-run bus swings by the city bus stop to pick up passengers interested in making a circuit of the campus, with stops at all the major buildings. Service daily, including weekends.

El Pedregal

To the west and south of the stadium, extending over an area bounded by Avenida Universidad, Boulevard de la Luz, the Periférico, and Calle Zacatépetl, you'll find the exclusive residential neighborhood of El Pedregal ("the field of stone"), where some of the finest examples of contemporary Mexican residential architecture hide behind an encircling wall. While the ancient lava field itself spreads to the east and south under University City and Coyoacán, it is here in El Pedregal where it is most noticeable. Formed almost 2,000 years ago when nearby Xitle erupted with tremendous force and devastating consequences, the area was a stark and almost surrealistic moonscape. About 40 years ago the architect Luis Barragán began to encourage wealthy clients to purchase land here and then built them innovative, elegant residences that were adapted to the irregular and dramatic terrain. Other architects began to follow Barragán's lead, and in time the neighborhood became one of the most desirable addresses in the city. Today the overall effect is stunning: El Pedregal can hold its own with the world's most exclusive neighborhoods.

The best way to see El Pedregal is by taxi. If you're going to drive, head south on Insurgentes Sur to Avenida Universidad, just before the stadium. Follow Universidad until you come to Paseo del Pedregal, then take a left. Courteous guards at the entrance to this walled-in community will screen visitors briefly—usually no more than a glance into the car—and then wave you in. A leisurely tour of the neighborhood takes about 15 minutes.

Cuicuilco

The earliest evidence of true civilization in the Valley of Mexico was uncovered at the archaeological site of Cuicuilco, just southeast of El Pedregal, during the construction of dormitories to house athletes participating in the 1968 Olympic Games. To everyone's surprise, under the almost ten feet of lava that had engulfed much of the surrounding area construction workers discovered a circular temple base that, when it was finally uncovered, proved to be almost 60 feet high and 41 feet in diameter. Further excavation and study revealed evidence of irrigation canals at the site and established the platform as having been built around 500 B.C., predating the first civic structures at Teotihuacán (see below) by some 300 years. The artifacts found here also indicated that the inhabitants of Cuicuilco had combined farming with subsistence activities such as hunting and fishing, and had abandoned the site in the first century B.C., just prior to the last volcanic eruptions. Everything else about these early inhabitants of the valley remains shrouded by the mists of time. The small **Museo de Sitio y Zona Arqueológica de Cuicuilco** exhibits samples of the pottery uncovered here, as well as a map detailing all the Preclassic sites that have been discovered in Mexico to date. Open from 9:00 A.M. to 4:00 P.M. daily, except Mondays.

Cuicuilco can be reached by following Insurgentes Sur south (follow the "Cuernavaca" signs) to the "Villa Olímpica" exit; make a U-turn back on to Insurgentes and head north. The site is enclosed by a green wrought-iron fence; the temple base is a short hike down a winding gravel path.

Reino Aventura

Reino Aventura, a recently renovated 100-acre amusement park on the southern edge of the city, is Mexico's answer to Disneyland. Reopened on July 4, 1992, it is now an ecological and cultural theme park that compares favorably with its U.S. and European counterparts.

State-of-the-art innovations include robots that serve refreshments and a most creative computerized maintenance plan. There are 23 rides in all; four water shows a day featuring trained dolphins and Keiko the killer whale; five ethnic villages (Mexican, Swiss, French, Polynesian, and African), and more.

The official address is Carretera Picacho-Ajusco km 1.5. About 24 km (15 miles) from the Zona Rosa, it is easily accessible via the Periférico Sur. The 30-minute taxi ride will cost about $12. Open Thursdays and Fridays from 10:00 A.M. to 6:00 P.M. and Saturdays and Sundays from 10:00 A.M. to 8:00 P.M. The $16 admission fee covers rides and performances.

XOCHIMILCO

The perfect way to experience both grass-roots Mexico and the feeling of Aztec Mexico, when Tenochtitlán was spread out over islands large and small connected by a network of canals, is to treat yourself to a Sunday afternoon gondola ride in Xochimilco (so-che-MEEL-ko).

The Toltecs took refuge here after the fall of Tula, about 900 years ago. According to historian Fernando Benítez, these Toltecs, renowned for their craftsmanship in stone, continued to speak their own dialect when the settlement came under Aztec rule, as interpreted from one of the few surviving Aztec codices. Signed by "Ixtixcochitl," a 16th-century Aztec historian, the same codice revealed that a tribe of Chichimec, known as the Chinampanecas, related to the Aztecs, settled here in the 13th century and spoke Náhuatl. The end of the codice states that Cortés and his band of invaders burned down the village on their march to Tenochtitlán.

The Chinampanecas created a system of cultivation here that tremendously increased the agricultural yield and established Xochimilco as the main source of produce for the Valley of Mexico, hence the Náhuatl name "Xochimilco," which means "the sowing place of plant life." They planted crops on small rafts covered with mud and water held together by a retaining screen of interwoven reeds, which were eventually anchored to the lake bottom by the growth of roots. The abundance of water and the fertilizing effect of the mud enabled these "floating gardens" to produce up to seven crops a year.

The Chinampanecas laid out the first *chinampas,* as the nursery beds became known, in the deepest part of the freshwater lagoon of Xochimilco, which merged with the saltwater lagoon of Texcoco. The Aztecs conquered the area, after many years of resistance from the inhabitants, in order to feed the growing population in their capital, Tenochtitlán, 20 miles to the north. The Aztecs greatly increased the number of *chinampas* and established a waterways route from Xochimilco to today's Zócalo in the D.F. This system continued for centuries after the Conquest, until landfill developments changed the mode of transportation to the overland routes that prevail today.

Today only five canals from the once-great Aztec city remain—all of them in Xochimilco—and the traffic on them is so heavy (especially on weekends) that at times they resemble nothing so much as bumper-car rides. But don't let that discourage you. Even though the waters are as murky as those in Venice, there are no unpleasant aromas emanating from them. Rather, the soft afternoon breezes—scrubbed free of the capital's notorious smog by prevailing winds—carry the aromas of freshly rolled tortillas, tacos, and a dozen other delicacies sold by Indian women out of their crude flat-bottomed canoes. Elsewhere, gondolas filled with mariachi or marimba bands glide by, auditioning for a chance to serenade you for a small fee as you glide along the waterways.

A standard-size gondola, with room for eight, costs the

same regardless of the number of people in your party. Each *remero* (licensed gondolier, of which there are more than 300 in Xochimilco) provides a cooler filled with beer and soft drinks (you have to supply your own wine or Champagne). At the conclusion of the ride you pay the *remero* for his time as well as the beverages consumed—and, of course, you should tip him. A few hours and a few beers cost the equivalent of about $25. You can also rub shoulders with the locals on one of the larger gondolas, which hold about 50 people. An hour's cruise on one of these costs approximately 2,000 pesos (the official government-set rate), and they're not tourist traps; in fact, on weekends, nine out of ten of the larger gondolas are filled with Mexican families out for a picnic or lovers sharing a bottle of wine.

For those who would rather cruise the canals in relative solitude, the gondolas at Xochimilco are for hire every day of the week, at all hours. Still, it is well worth investigating the Sunday tours, which are offered by all the major travel agencies and many of the city's hotels. These tours usually include a morning performance of the Ballet Folklórico at Bellas Artes; a few hours in Xochimilco, with lunch and a gondola ride included; and either an afternoon bullfight at the Plaza México or a tour of the murals at University City.

Xochimilco has more than its gondola rides to recommend it, however. The public **market** here is always bustling with activity, and the fruits, vegetables, and flowers for sale are probably the freshest and cheapest in all of Mexico. In fact, most of the produce and flowers for sale in the hundreds of markets throughout the capital are grown right here, as they have been since pre-Hispanic times, when they were transported by boat along the canals and later the Acequia Real (Royal Canal) to the Zócalo area. (You can still view a portion of the Acequia Real at the southeastern corner of the Zócalo, between the National Palace and the Supreme Court; see the Zócalo section, above.)

Xochimilco's zócalo is one of the most charming in the entire country, its delicate *huexote* trees providing a lovely contrast to the more conventional species planted throughout the square. The 16th-century **Parroquia** (parish church) **San Bernardino**, with its fortresslike appearance and an elaborate altar canopy inside, is well worth a visit, as is the **Escuela de Bellas Artes de Xochimilco**, located in the Barrio de la Concha at Avenida Constitución 600, with its murals by Manuel Tolsá (*Apotheosis*) and Acevedo Navarro (*Romantic Muses*).

A cab ride of a few minutes will take you to the village of Santa Cruz Acalpixan and the **Museo Arqueológico de**

Xochimilco, which is built into the side of an ancient pyramid at Avenida Tenochtitlán 17. (You'll recognize it by the white wall enclosing a large garden.) Inside, a fine collection of an estimated 800 pre-Conquest artifacts are on permanent display. Another permanent exhibit features prehistoric fossils. Open 10:00 A.M. to 5:00 P.M. daily, except Mondays.

Los Manantiales, an immense restaurant—it has seating for 1,000 diners—with an outrageously ugly exterior but surprisingly good international-style food, is a few minutes' walk from the gondola docks over a short bridge. It caters to tourists, which simply means that the hygienic standards here are superior to those maintained at the many food stands and smaller restaurants scattered around town. (In general, the food in Xochimilco is highly regarded by the locals.)

Although it's 25 km (16 miles) south of downtown Mexico City, Xochimilco is easily accessible via the metro. Take the number 2 line to the Tasqueña stop, locate Gate J, and board the number 140 bus, which will drop you in the heart of the Xochimilco market after a 20-minute ride. Or you can take one of the *peseros* marked "Embarcaderos" lined up outside the Tasqueña station and be at the gondola docks in ten minutes. A regular taxi from the downtown area takes approximately 40 minutes and costs the equivalent of $18.

TEOTIHUACAN

If you were limited to visiting only one archaeological site in all of Mexico, Teotihuacán (tay-oh-tee-whah-KAHN) would not be a bad choice. Situated about 50 km (31 miles) northeast of downtown Mexico City, Teotihuacán was once the religious and commercial center of a great highland civilization (also known to us as Teotihuacán) that predated the Toltecs by 1,000 years and the Aztec empire by almost 1,500 years. In fact, the Classic period of Mesoamerican civilization in Mexico's central highlands was dominated by Teotihuacán, whose influence was felt as far away as Oaxaca, the Yucatán (the Classic Mayan civilization there was roughly its contemporary), highland Guatemala, and, to the northwest, Zacatecas. And yet, even as late as the early years of our own century all this had yet to be discovered and Teotihuacán was considered merely a local culture roughly contemporaneous with the Aztecs.

Today the evidence indicates that Teotihuacán developed from villages that made their initial appearance in the Valley of Mexico sometime around the middle of the first millennium B.C. By 300 B.C. a small township had been established on the site, and for the next 800 years Teotihuacán flourished, reaching an estimated population of 150,000 by A.D. 600, making it perhaps the world's first true urban center. Then, for reasons still unknown, the city was abandoned during the eighth century. For years the most popular theory concerning the demise of Teotihuacán held that it had fallen to marauding northern tribes, but a more recent theory maintains that its demise was probably the result of what today would be called poor resource management, or, more simply, that it outgrew its available resources.

All the generally accepted names in the immediate area, including "Teotihuacán" (in the Nahuatl language, "the place where men became gods"), were coined by the Aztecs when they discovered the ruined city more than five centuries after it was abandoned. By then most of the ceremonial structures—thought to have been brightly painted—had been buried under a thick layer of dirt and debris. The Aztecs believed that the mounds of earth lining the main avenue at the site were actually the tombs of the deceased giants responsible for building the city in the first place, and named this central axis the Street of the Dead. (The Aztecs also helped themselves to the art treasures left behind by the Teotihuacanos—many of which are among the objects being uncovered in the ongoing excavation of the Templo Mayor site in the heart of downtown Mexico City.)

To date only an estimated one-tenth of this ancient city has been uncovered—a remarkably low percentage when you consider that several hundred murals, more than 2,000 residential complexes, 80 temples, and more than 700 workshops have already been discovered. (There are several "archaeological" Teotihuacáns, numbered I to IV, with the latest beginning around A.D. 650 and lasting less than a hundred years.)

As was the case elsewhere in Mesoamerica, the pyramids of Teotihuacán originally were built as platforms for ceremonial temples. However, no tombs have yet been linked to these structures—which distinguishes Teotihuacán from Palenque and Monte Albán. In fact, Teotihuacán is unique, as far as ancient Mesoamerican ceremonial sites go, in that the murals uncovered to date do not contain the slightest hint of thematic violence. Instead, the religious symbolism of the artwork found at Teotihuacán revolves around the stars, the rain god Tlaloc, and the benign, plumed serpent-god, Quetzalcóatl.

Visiting Teotihuacán

A good starting point for your visit to Teotihuacán is the **Unidad Cultural**, a small complex at the southernmost entrance to the site (opposite the Ciudadela and Temple of Quetzalcóatl) that contains shops, rest rooms, a second-floor restaurant, and a good museum offering concise overviews of what is to follow. You might consider having lunch before you begin, as restaurants in the area are few and scattered. **La Pirámide**, located on the second floor of the Unidad Cultural, offers adequate, moderately priced Mexican and international-style cuisine. If you're looking for better fare, with prices to match, the best can be found at the nearby **Villa Arqueológica** (follow the signs on the access road ringing the site), one of a chain of fine Club Med–operated hotels at Mexican archaeological sites. In addition to its fine food, the Villa Arqueológica has an excellent archaeological library with books in several languages, tennis courts, and a swimming pool. (The other advantage of the place, should you decide to stay here, is that you can start your exploration of Teotihuacán early in the morning, before the tour buses from the capital arrive. See the Accommodations section for Mexico City, below.)

Pirámide Charlie's, a branch of the popular Carlos 'n' Charlie's chain, is a five- to ten-minute walk north of the Villa Arqueológica. For a more romantic setting try **La Gruta**, a restaurant built inside a massive natural cave. To get there, walk to the Pyramid of the Sun, turn east and walk through Parking Lot D to the access road, and then turn left. Signs for the restaurant soon appear on the right-hand side of the road. Both the food (Mexican geared to tourist tastes) and music, which is enhanced by the cave's great acoustics, contribute to the charm of the place.

The most typically Mexican restaurant in the area, **El Gran Teocalli**, is located about 2 km (1¼ mile) from the Unidad Cultural in the village of San Juan Teotihuacán (follow the signs to the "México Libre" highway). Chicken enchiladas are the specialty here, and they live up to their reputation. The marimba music in the background is also good. For real grass-roots cuisine (tacos, tortas, and the like) there are numerous food stands—some of them quite charming—set up across from the southernmost entrance to the site.

With lunch out of the way, begin your tour at the **Unidad Cultural museum**. In the vestibule stands a full-size copy of the colossal statue of Chalchiuhtlicue, the goddess of rivers and lakes, the original of which, now on display in the National Museum of Anthropology, was unearthed near the Pyramid of the Moon. While you're here, look especially for the ornately decorated stone death-mask inlaid with jade, garnets, and other gemstones—one of the finest examples of Mesoamerican art ever uncovered.

Outside the entrance to the museum is the beginning of the mile-long **Calle de los Muertos** (Street of the Dead), a kind of Via Sacra that serves as the axis around which the site was planned. The reasons behind its almost exact north–south orientation (it's actually aligned 15°30' east of true north) are still debated, though it's generally agreed they had to do with astronomical alignments (including the rising of the Pleiades on the days of equinox).

Directly opposite the Unidad Cultural across the Street of the Dead is the **Ciudadela** (Citadel), one of the most interesting architectural groupings at Teotihuacán. This immense quadrangular complex is bounded by four platforms (three of which have two stories) surmounted by smaller temple platforms. Entrance to the complex is via a broad staircase, which leads down to a sunken patio. It was quite common in Mesoamerican cultures for already existing structures to be covered over and built upon rather than demolished. In the case of the Citadel, excavation revealed that its main pyramid had been built over an older (c. A.D. 200), much more impressive structure, the **Templo de Quetzalcóatl**, now partially revealed at the rear of the complex. To reach the temple, walk across the patio to the squat temple platform with a staircase. On the far side of the platform you'll come upon the façade of this masterpiece of the Classic period, with its sculpted stone heads of the feathered serpent-god, Quetzalcóatl, and the even more stylized figure of the rain god, Tlaloc.

From the Citadel proceed up the Street of the Dead to the massive **Pirámide del Sol** (Pyramid of the Sun), which, together with the Pyramid of the Moon, dominates the entire site. Believed to have been constructed during the first century B.C., the pyramid has a base only ten feet shorter on each side than the Pyramid of Cheops but is less than half as tall. Nevertheless, it is the largest pre-Columbian structure in the New World to survive relatively intact (the great pyramid in Cholula being larger but in ruins).

The pyramid itself consists of five superimposed platforms and is ascended by a double staircase that merges to form a single staircase two-thirds of the way up. Although the climb to the summit is a strenuous one, the view once you get there is breathtaking—if you have any breath left. Spread out below with a startling geometric exactness is all that remains of this more than 2,000-year-old city. Unfortunately, the mammoth gold statue that used to stand at the summit of the pyramid (it may have been placed there by the Aztecs) was ordered removed by Juan de Zumárraga, the first archbishop of Mexico City. In its stead is a stone "cap" placed there by the archaeological team that reconstructed the pyramid more than a half century ago.

The next major attraction to the north is, aesthetically speaking, the most striking at Teotihuacán: the **Plaza de la Luna** (Plaza of the Moon). An imposing patio surrounded by a variety of even more imposing platforms, the plaza is a worthy lead-up to the **Pirámide de la Luna** located at the end of the Street of the Dead. Consisting of four sloping levels, and situated on a rise (which makes it appear as if it's the same height as the larger Pyramid of the Sun), the Pyramid of the Moon is the most harmoniously designed structure in this ancient city. Archaeologists have managed to reconstruct the façade and massive staircase of the pyramid, which was built around the same time as the Pyramid of the Sun, so that at least an impression of its original splendor remains.

On the west side of the plaza is the **Palacio del Quetzalpapálotl** (Palace of the Quetzal Butterfly), to date the only roofed structure to have been uncovered at an archaeological site outside of the Maya region. First discovered in 1962 and subsequently restored, the building's rooms are arranged around a patio whose elaborately carved pillars feature stylized representations of birds and owls, as well as the butterflies that lend the palace its name.

Two other half-buried structures in the plaza area are also worth a look. The **Palacio de los Jaguares** (Palace of the Jaguars), due north of the Palace of the Quetzal Butterfly, has a portico with some well-preserved murals depicting jaguars in plumed headdresses blowing into plumed conch shells. As you exit this courtyard a modern tunnel to the right leads you to the second- or third-century **Palacio de los Caracoles Enplumados** (Palace of the Plumed Shells), distinguished by its bas-reliefs of feathered seashells with mouthpiece-like devices (presumed to be instruments) and red and green parrots ejecting streams of blue liquid, presumably water. (The overall effect is best viewed from the southeast exit to the Street of the Dead.)

To get to the last worthwhile stop at Teotihuacán, turn left (east) at the Pyramid of the Sun, walk through Parking Lot 2, and then follow the road to the ruins of the residential quarter of **Tepantitla**, about 1 km (½ mile) from the Street of the Dead. En route you'll pass a room adorned with a mural depicting elegantly dressed priests in headdresses, before coming to the walls of what was once an atriumlike structure. Here you'll find the remains of the most famous mural of the Teotihuacán III period (A.D. 350–650), *The Paradise of Tlaloc,* which depicts human figures sunbathing and chasing butterflies—the Teotihuacanos' vision of a state of grace.

GETTING TO TEOTIHUACAN

You'll need an early start to enjoy this day away from the hustle and bustle of the city. Teotihuacán is about a 100-km (62-mile) round trip, but unquestionably worth the effort. Buses leave the D.F. at frequent intervals from the terminal across the street from the Indios Verdes metro station, line 3. The buses are marked "Pirámides-Teotihuacán." The last bus back to the capital leaves at 6:00 P.M. from the main entrance to the site, next to the Unidad Cultural. There is also regular bus service to Teotihuacán from the Terminal de Autobuses del Norte, which can be reached via the number 17 or 17B bus, or on line 5 of the metro.

All major travel agencies and most hotels offer tours to Teotihuacán, with prices varying depending on the itinerary involved. You might also consider renting a taxi for the day. (If you do, expect to pay around $60—which, split three or four ways, is a very reasonable price for the added convenience.) You can even stay overnight at the site at the Villa Arqueológica (see the Accommodations section, below).

If you are driving, head north on Avenida Insurgentes and follow the signs to Highway 85D. At the 15-km (9-mile) mark take the toll road rather than the free road toward Pachuca. At the 25-km (16-mile) mark, bear right for Teotihuacán after paying your toll. Follow the signs to Highway 132.

You may want to turn off at the 34-km (21-mile) mark and follow the signs to **Tepexpán**, less than a mile away, where a small **museum** (open 10:00 A.M. daily; closed Mondays) houses the fossil remains of mammoths unearthed nearby. These remains have been dated to approximately 8,000 B.C. The most amazing remains on display, however, belong to what is reputed to be the oldest human being ever discovered on the continent, remains that were unearthed from under a layer of saltpeter and are thought to correspond to a period of drought that occurred some 10,000 years ago, during the waning stages of the last Ice Age.

From Tepexpán return to Highway 132 and continue another 4 km (2½ miles) for the next side trip. Exit to the right and follow the road to the towering fortresslike walls of the monastery and church of **San Agustín Acolman**, now a museum (open daily from 10:00 A.M.; closed Fridays).

Among the first New World communities founded by the Augustinians, the monastery and adjoining church were begun in 1539, completed in 1560, and restored in 1735. As a result, they are a stylized mixture of the Gothic and Baroque. At the end of the vast nave and around the cloister are unsigned murals depicting a group of monks, probably the dignitaries of the order. The murals themselves are believed to have been painted toward the end of the 16th century. The main altarpiece, Baroque in design, has paintings dating from the 17th and 18th centuries, while the side altarpieces are typical of the Churrigueresque style.

The second floor has two arcades enlivened by paintings from the 19th century, a library with a collection of theological works, and an exhibition room displaying pre-Hispanic artifacts uncovered during 20th-century excavations.

To the right of the church, level with the first floor of the monastery, is a small open-air chapel with a picturesque arch framing its entrance. Inside, a well-executed fragment of a mural portrays Saint Catherine. The monastery itself, with its cramped cells, gives you a feeling for the austere life led by the monks.

After San Agustín Acolman it's back to the highway for the final 13 km (8 miles) to Teotihuacán.

GETTING AROUND

The Metro

Mexico City has an outstanding public transportation system, with the sparkling metro one of the capital's pride and joys. Belgian-designed and -built, the trains run on rubber wheels from one brightly lit station to the next; the entire network covers a distance of 93 miles, and is still being expanded.

As of this writing the fare is 400 pesos. It's best to buy tickets in blocks of five, to avoid long lines. The maps posted in every metro car are quite comprehensive, and a symbol/color system is employed so that it is not necessary to understand Spanish. To change lines follow the signs that say "Correspondencia" and look for the name of the terminal station that is on the line you want as well as in the direction you are going. Avoid rush-hour trips (7:00 to 10:00 A.M. and 5:00 to 8:00 P.M.) if at all possible. During these hours cars are segregated by sex, although a female may accompany her male companion on a "male only" car. Cumbersome luggage is not permitted during rush hours, smoking is prohibited at all times, and classical music fills the air most of the time. Maps and general assistance are sometimes provided at information desks in all the major stations.

On Saturdays all lines operate between 6:00 A.M. and 1:30 A.M. On Sundays and holidays all lines operate between 7:00 A.M. and 12:30 A.M. On weekdays all lines operate between 6:00 A.M. and 12:30 A.M.

Peseros

Peseros, collective taxis (usually Volkswagen *combis*) that are painted pale green, run up and down the major avenues. They charge 550 pesos a person minimum, and extra if you travel beyond a certain point: 700 pesos for anything over 10 km (6 miles), and 1,000 pesos for any distance over 17 km (11 miles). When the driver has room aboard he cruises slowly and holds up his fingers outside his open window to indicate the number of available seats; you can get off at any point along the set route. Say *"Baja, por favor"* when you wish to get off. *Peseros* are safer than buses because there is no standing room allowed, cramping the style of potential pickpockets.

Buses

Take buses at your own risk. There is no maximum capacity, so they often resemble cattle cars. And although the fare is an extremely reasonable 400 pesos (have exact change ready before boarding, as drivers do not make change), buses are a pickpocket's paradise. Still, they're an efficient way to travel if you know precisely where you and the bus are going (the drivers tend to be reckless, however). Buses only pick up and discharge passengers at *parada* signs, and will stop only when the buzzer at the rear exit is pressed or someone bangs on the roof.

Taxis

Volkswagen Beetle taxis are the least expensive. Make sure the driver turns on the meter after you get in. If he doesn't, settle on the price in advance (many meters are allegedly "broken"). If there is no meter reading at the end of the trip, by law you owe nothing. Also, a photo I.D. of your driver must be pasted over the glove compartment; if you don't see one, leave the taxi at once.

While *sitio* taxis (radio cabs that are not allowed to "cruise") charge more, their drivers are also usually more knowledgeable about the city. (Private limousines, with commercial license plates and hooded meters, are found parked outside major hotels. They charge about three times the normal fare, but most of their drivers speak some English. They will also hire out by the hour.) In general, fares for private taxis are about a third of what you'd expect to pay north of the border, and drivers do not expect a tip. Nighttime prices are about 10 percent higher. A *libre* sign in the window means the taxi is available. Strangely enough, a lighted front beam at night indicates the taxi is occupied, while no beam means it's available—but good luck distinguishing a "no-beam" as a taxi in the dark.

Any taxi is authorized to take passengers *to* the airport, although only those belonging to the airport concession are permitted to bring passengers into the city *from* the airport. In other words, don't be lured into jumping from your place in line to flag down an empty city taxi as you're waiting to get out of the airport.

Car Rentals

Renting and driving a car in the capital is not recommended unless you are a veteran Mexico City driver and do not mind paying twice what the same car would cost to rent in the United States or Canada. Consider only the major international agencies. Vehicles from private agencies often are mechanically unreliable, and road service, in the event of a breakdown, is unpredictable.

Long-Distance Buses

Mexico's long-distance bus network is both excellent and inexpensive. All first-class buses—usually called *autobuses de lujo* to distinguish them from *primera clase,* which in Mexico means second class—have co-pilots; most have rest rooms and air-conditioning (many, in fact, are *over* air-conditioned, so be sure to bring a light sweater or jacket along); and some (most notably on the Mexico City–Acapulco run) even have stewardesses. If there's a drawback (other than the tendency of even the tiniest *señora* to recline her seat to its limit), it's that most of the personnel speak Spanish only.

Indeed, so popular is this mode of transportation with Mexicans themselves that it is almost always necessary to make reservations in advance. (This is especially true over long holiday weekends, during Holy Week, and from December 15 to January 6, when schoolchildren and bureaucrats have vacation.) In Mexico City travellers can make reservations and purchase tickets (*boletos*) in advance through one office: **Greyhound de México**, Paseo de la Reforma 27; Tel: (5) 535-4200. A number of the major travel agencies, including **Central de Autobuses** (Plaza del Angel, Calle Londres, Zona Rosa; Tel: 5/533-2047), will make the reservations for you and even deliver the tickets to your hotel. This is a great service, as the major bus lines and their ticket desks are all located on the outskirts of the city in one of four immense terminals, each servicing a cardinal direction. These are (clockwise from the north): the **Terminal Central de Autobuses del Norte**, Avenida de los Cien Metros 4907 (metro line 5 to the Autobuses del Norte stop); the **Terminal de Autobuses de Pasajeros de Oriente** (or TAPO), Calzada Ignacio Zaragoza 200 (metro line 1 to the San Lázaro stop); the **Terminal Central de Autobuses del Sur**, Tasqueña 1320 (metro line 2 to the Tasqueña stop); and the **Terminal Poniente de Autobuses**, Avenida del Sur 122 (metro line 1 to the Observatorio stop).

The major long-distance bus lines are:

- **Autobuses de Oriente (ADO)**, with service to Matamoras, Reynosa, Pachuca, Puebla, Tampico, Teotihuacán, and Tula from the Terminal Central del Norte (Tel: 5/587-8233); and Campeche, Cancún, Mérida, Oaxaca, Palenque, Veracruz, and Villahermosa from the Terminal de Oriente (Tel: 5/542-9654).
- **Estrella de Oro**, with deluxe nonstop service to Acapulco, as well as service to Cuernavaca, Taxco, and Zihuatanejo from the Terminal Central del Sur (Tel: 5/549-8520).
- **Omnibus Cristóbal Colón**, with service to Oaxaca, Salina Cruz, Tapachula, Tehuantepec, and Tuxtla Gutierrez, as well as connections to Guatemala and Central America, from the Terminal de Oriente (Tel: 5/542-7263).
- **Omnibus de México**, with service to Chihuahua, Ciudad Juárez, Durango, Guadalajara, Guanajuato, Morelia, Querétaro, San Luis Potosí, San Miguel de Allende, and Tampico from the Terminal Central del Norte (Tel: 5/567-6756).
- **Transportes Chihuahuenses**, with Pullman express cruisers to El Paso, Texas (connecting with Greyhound), as well as service to Chihuahua, Ciudad Juárez, Durango, Querétaro, and Zacatecas from the Terminal Central del Norte (Tel: 5/587-5377).
- **Transportes del Norte**, with direct express service to Laredo, Texas (and Greyhound), as well as service to Durango, Matamoras, Monterrey, Saltillo, and San Luis Potosí from the Terminal Central del Norte (Tel: 5/587-5511).
- **Tres Estrellas de Oro**, with direct express service to Guadalajara (continuing on to Mazatlán and Tijuana), as well as Irapuato, Puerto Vallarta, and Querétaro from the Terminal Central del Norte (Tel: 5/567-8157).
- **ETN**, with service to San Miguel de Allende, Guadalajara, Guanajuato, León, Querétaro, San Luis

Potosí, and Morelia, from the Terminal Central del Norte (Tel: 5/567-3773). In addition to some of the above cities, ETN also services Toluca, Colima, and Manzanillo from the Terminal Observatorio (Tel: 5/273-0251).
- **Primera Plus** services many of the same cities as ETN (Terminal Central del Norte, Tel: 5/587-5200; Terminal Observatorio, Tel: 5/271-2724).

The Mexican National Railway

Although it's not a well-known fact, Mexico's national railroad, the Ferrocarriles Nacionales de México, offers direct rail service to 16 major cities and three border towns from the capital, and vice versa. In other words, it's possible to traverse the country by rail from north to south and coast to coast in relative comfort and safety, although some trains have no club cars, so you must bring your own food.

The Estación Central de Buenavista, located on Avenida Insurgentes Norte, a few blocks north of its intersection with Paseo de la Reforma, is the *only* station with connections to all 19 destinations. For those with limited finances and the luxury of time (punctuality has not yet been elevated to a virtue by the National Railway), it's a great way to travel.

To ensure your comfort, buy a *primera especial* (first-class) ticket, which not only guarantees you a seat in an air-conditioned or heated car (not always the case with second class), but makes you eligible to purchase a berth on a *coche dormitorio* (sleeping car). If you're travelling alone and don't want to share a cabin with a stranger, ask for a *camarin,* a stateroom for one, or an *alcoba,* a stateroom for two (be advised that a "stateroom" in this instance means a Murphy bed that swings down over the toilet, completely filling the small cabin); a *compartimiento* is the same but slightly roomier. A *gabinete* is as good as it gets: three beds, a bath, shower, and room service.

You can purchase tickets for any destination at any of the windows in the Buenavista Station, or from most travel agencies in town. The ticket office at the station is open from 6:00 A.M. to 11:30 P.M. Monday through Saturday, and from 6:00 A.M. to 9:30 P.M. on Sundays. Try to avoid waiting until the last minute, as long lines are the rule.

The English-language *Official Railway Guide,* issued by the Ferrocarriles Nacionales de México, is revised on an annual basis (or whenever fares change). For a free copy, write to: *Official Railway Guide,* 1500 Broadway, Suite 810, New York, NY 10036.

ACCOMMODATIONS

Most of the best hotels in the D.F. are centrally located and within walking distance of each other; they range in style from elegant contemporary to intimate colonial. With two exceptions (the Fiesta Americana Aeropuerto and the Villa Arqueológica at Teotihuacán), the ones recommended here can be found within an area bounded by the Zócalo to the east and Chapultepec Park to the west. Generally speaking, the more moderately priced accommodations will be found north of Paseo de la Reforma in the neighborhoods around the U.S. embassy. The "Big Four"—the Sheraton María-Isabel Hotel & Towers, the Westin Camino Real, the Nikko México, and the Stouffer Presidente Chapultepec—each with more than 600 rooms, are all west of the U.S. embassy. The Stouffer Presidente, farthest west, and the Sheraton, right next door to the embassy, are less than two miles apart, and all are within walking distance of the first section of Chapultepec Park, the chic Polanco shopping area, and the Zona Rosa. Expensive by local standards but with rates about 20 to 30 percent lower than what you would expect to pay for comparable accommodations in New York or London, they offer everything a seasoned traveller expects from a luxury hotel. Just as luxurious are two smaller, more sedate hotels located geographically in the middle of this cluster: the Clarion Reforma, with fewer than 100 rooms, and the Marquis Reforma, the city's newest hotel. Both specialize in pampering their guests.

The better hotels in the D.F. all have air-conditioning, but it's usually not needed here except for a few days in early May just before the rainy season commences. The months of peak occupancy are December through March (especially Christmastime) for the luxury hotels, and July and August for the more moderately priced ones.

The rates given below are *projections* for December 1992 through the spring of 1993. Unless otherwise indicated, rates, which are given in U.S. dollars, are for double rooms, double occupancy; the 10 percent VAT has been added. As rates are subject to change, it's a good idea to double-check before booking.

The international telephone code for Mexico is 52; the area code for Mexico City is 5.

Chapultepec Park Area

The **Camino Real**—one of Mexican architect Ricardo Legoretta's masterpieces—is a stark two-story structure that covers a city block facing the eastern perimeter of Chapultepec

Park. Outside, the Camino Real is one of the best examples of "Mexican minimalism," a term coined by Legoretta himself when asked to describe his austere designs. Inside, the parquet floors in the huge lobby provide an ideal background for a mural by Rufino Tamayo and a Calder stabile in yellows, purples, and shocking pinks.

The Camino Real's 677 rooms and 36 suites are spacious and comfortable, and each is equipped with a marble bath. The hotel is also home to two of the D.F.'s finest restaurants: **Fouquet's of Paris** (arguably just as good as the chain's Paris flagship establishment) and **Azulejos**, featuring one of the best Sunday-brunch buffets in town. In addition, the hotel has four other restaurants, a 24-hour coffee shop, the very popular **Cero Cero** discotheque, a nightclub, four bars, four swimming pools, and rooftop tennis courts. The Camino Real is within walking distance of the outstanding museums in Chapultepec Park and is only a ten-minute cab ride from the shops and cafés of the Zona Rosa or the shopping district known as Plaza Polanco, making it an ideal site from which to explore and enjoy Mexico City. For visitors planning to explore a wider area, the hotel has a garage and in-house travel agent; valet service and car rentals are also available.

Avenida Mariano Escobedo 700, 11590 D.F. Tel: 203-2121; Fax: 250-6897; in the U.S. and Canada, Tel: (800) 228-3000. $228.

The 38-floor Japanese-built and -operated **Hotel Nikko México** opened its doors in 1987. Like the other major luxury hotels in the D.F., it is a huge affair, with 750 rooms, two bars and four restaurants (featuring excellent Japanese, Mexican, and French cuisine), a nightclub and discotheque, an in-house travel agent, laundry and dry-cleaning services, a jogging track and fully equipped gym (complete with sauna), three tennis courts and rooftop swimming pool, and a heliport. While the lobby resembles a modern, ostentatious shopping mall, and the hotel's overall atmosphere is somewhat impersonal, the rooms are large and tastefully decorated. The top floors of the hotel are reserved for those who desire the royal treatment, or a reasonable facsimile: Private registration, an exclusive clublike lounge, and private secretarial services are among the extras. There are also two authentically decorated, and very costly, "Japanese" suites in this part of the hotel. The 37th floor is reserved for women only and has 24-hour security and a special concierge.

Avenida Campos Elíseos 204, 11560 D.F. Tel: 203-4020 or (800) 9-0888; Fax: 255-5586 or 4272; in the U.S. and Canada, Tel: (800) 645-5687. $228.

As you enter the modern, 30-story **Stouffer Presidente**

Chapultepec, next door to the Nikko, you find yourself in a beautiful five-story pyramidal lobby with a skylight ceiling and a luxurious garden. The Presidente has 617 rooms and 40 suites decorated in a colonial style with modern touches. Some offer panoramic views of Chapultepec Park. Of the hotel's five restaurants, **Maxim's** is the best. The live music in the lobby bar attracts a young singles crowd most nights, and a number of exclusive boutiques line the mezzanine. The hotel also has a nightclub featuring top entertainment, a popular disco, banquet and convention facilities, a travel agency, and a parking garage.

Avenida Campos Elíseos 218, 11560 D.F. Tel: 327-7700 or (800) 3-2777; Fax: 250-9130; in the U.S. and Canada, Tel: (800) 472-2427. $184.

The pastel-hued Art Nouveau façade of the new **Hotel Marquis Reforma**, a 20-minute walk east of the Presidente, does not prepare you for its subdued, tasteful interior. The rooms, many of which overlook Paseo de la Reforma, are decorated with rich woodwork, polished brass, and chrome finishings. Designed to withstand earthquakes that measure up to 9.0 on the Richter scale, the hotel has 125 rooms and 85 luxurious suites. Among the features of the Marquis Reforma are a small, modern fitness center with an indoor jogging track, personal facsimile machines and computers in every suite, and closed-circuit surveillance. The service, too, is good; there are two English-speaking employees for every occupied room, and the staff is quite knowledgeable about Mexico's history as well as the best places to visit in the D.F.

Paseo de la Reforma 465, 06500 D.F. Tel: 211-3600; Fax: 211-5561; in the U.S., Tel: (800) 235-2387. $176.

Also on Reforma, a five-minute walk east of the Marquis Reforma between the Monument to Independence and Chapultepec Park, the **Clarion Reforma** offers 16 comfortable rooms and 80 beautiful suites, most with sauna and Jacuzzi, and all with great views of the park. A small member of the Choice Hotels International chain, this is easily the city's finest, most luxurious small hotel. The rather hip Holiday Inn decor is so understated that the superb amenities might take you by surprise. **Bellini's**, on the second floor, is one of the nicest Italian restaurants in the D.F.

Paseo de la Reforma 373, 06500 D.F. Tel: 207-9075 or (800) 9-0000; Fax: 208-2719; in the U.S. and Canada, Tel: (800) 228-5151. $190; with sauna and Jacuzzi, $228.

Zona Rosa

The **Hotel Aristos**, which has been upstaged in luxury and popularity by newer hotels, has 350 large, nicely decorated rooms; those on the upper floors afford great views of Paseo de la Reforma. Other amenities here include two restaurants, a bar, a nightclub, a disco, an in-house travel agent, laundry service, and a garage.

Paseo de la Reforma 276 (entrance on Calle Copenhague), 06600 D.F. Tel: 211-0112 or (800) 9-0102; Fax: 525-6783; in the U.S. and Canada, Tel: (800) 223-0888. $115.

The **Century Zona Rosa** offers marble baths and private balconies in all 142 of its rooms. A heated swimming pool, two restaurants, car-rental desk, garage, and an African safari–style bar that's a bit garish but fun round out this likable establishment.

Calle Liverpool 152, 06600 D.F. Tel: 584-7111; Fax: 208-4845. $118.

A member of the Westin Hotel chain, the 435-room **Westin Galería Plaza**, wrapped in a smoked-glass exterior, has an attractive lobby with a splashing fountain as its centerpiece. Facilities and services include a rooftop swimming pool, a sundeck, three restaurants (gourmet French, Mexican, and international), a lobby bar, a disco, a shopping arcade, and a travel desk.

Calle Hamburgo 195, 06600 D.F. Tel: 211-0014; Fax: 207-5867; in the U.S. and Canada, Tel: (800) 228-3000. $168.

The recently refurbished **Krystal Zona Rosa** has 302 large and comfortable rooms, a swimming pool, a restaurant, a bar, a nightclub, a shopping arcade, and a Japanese restaurant that's very popular with businesspeople at lunchtime.

Calle Liverpool 155, 06600 D.F. Tel: 211-0092; Fax: 511-3490. $142.

The **Royal Zona Rosa** is a pleasant family-style hotel with 162 comfortable rooms, two restaurants, a piano bar, a nightclub, a movie theater, shops, an in-house travel agent, laundry service, a swimming pool, and a garage.

Calle Amberes 78, 06600 D.F. Tel: 525-4850 or (800) 9-0209; Fax: 514-3330. $141.

The **Plaza Florencia**, a comfortable ultramodern hotel facing one of the busiest streets in the Zona Rosa, has 140 spacious (and soundproof, according to management) rooms, a restaurant, nightclub and bar, and a garage.

Calle Florencia 61, 06600 D.F. Tel: 211-3189; Fax: 511-1542. $111.

When it opened as an Art Deco showpiece in the late 1950s, the Geneva, as it was then known, was *the* hotel for foreign tourists and visiting dignitaries in Mexico City. After slipping a bit in subsequent decades, it was purchased by the Calinda chain, which spruced up the deteriorating old landmark and restored much of the charm of its heyday. The 346 rooms of the **Calinda Geneve Mexico** encompass a range of styles and decor (a pre-registration check of the room you have been given is advisable; rooms overlooking the street can be noisy), and the "jungle bar," located at the back of the lobby in an area that resembles a giant greenhouse, is a popular meeting place for locals. The facilities and services here include two restaurants and a jazz bar; tobacco, beauty, and barber shops; an in-house travel agent; a car-rental desk; and laundry service.

Calle Londres 130, 06600 D.F. Tel: 211-0071; Fax: 207-6422; in the U.S. and Canada, Tel: (800) 228-5151. $85.

For those who prefer to have cooking facilities in their rooms, the following Zona Rosa establishments are recommended.

The six-year-old **Marco Polo** offers a sophisticated European atmosphere in a sleek, modern structure with 64 beautifully designed rooms. The four penthouse rooms, which are larger and have better kitchen facilities, are well worth the extra cost. The Marco Polo also has a restaurant and piano bar, small meeting rooms, laundry service, and a garage.

Calle Amberes 27, 06600 D.F. Tel: 207-1893. $143; penthouse suites, $158.

The charming seven-story **Suites Amberes**, located in the heart of the Zona Rosa, offers 28 large suites, all with kitchenettes and balconies. There is also a good restaurant and piano bar on the premises.

Calle Amberes 64, 06600 D.F. Tel: 533-1306; Fax: 207-1509. $88.

Around the U.S. Embassy

Comfortable, modestly priced accommodations are the rule north of the Zona Rosa in the vicinity of the U.S. embassy. Though this area is a bit farther from the shops and great restaurants in the heart of the Zona Rosa, for most people the added savings will more than make up for the slight inconvenience.

The **Sheraton María-Isabel Hotel & Towers**, next door to the U.S. embassy, is conveniently located a few minutes' walk from the heart of the Zona Rosa. The gaudy, block-long lobby, with lots of polished wood and brass and ornate chandeliers, is a good example of how a space ought not be used. There are more than 700 spacious minimally decorated rooms and suites in the hotel as well as three restaurants, one of which, the **Veranda**, offers great views of "El Angel" and rather offbeat entertainment while you dine. The hotel's bustling **Bar**

Joronga, often with strolling mariachis, is popular with locals and singles. Other services and facilities include a rooftop pool, two tennis courts, an in-house travel agent, two bars, a nightclub, a garage, laundry and valet service, a fully equipped gym, banquet and convention facilities, and a variety of shops.

Paseo de la Reforma 325, 06500 D.F. Tel: 207-3933 or (800) 5-0205; Fax: 207-0684; in the U.S. and Canada, Tel: (800) 325-3535. $230–$255.

The moderately priced and always full **María Cristina** is an oasis of charm just a few blocks from the embassy. Chairs and tables are set out for relaxing on the lovely, grassy grounds, and there's a central patio with a fountain as well. The 150 or so rooms are on the small and plain side (ask for one overlooking the courtyard or the lawn), but the bathrooms are bright and modern and all rooms are equipped with cable TV. In addition, the hotel has a restaurant and piano bar, a tobacco shop, an in-house travel agent, laundry service, and a garage.

Río Lerma 31, 06500 D.F. Tel: 703-1787; Fax: 566-9194. $55.

El Romano Days-Inn Diana has 166 adequate rooms, a restaurant, a nightclub and bar, a disco, and a garage.

Río Lerma 237, 06500 D.F. Tel: 211-0109; Fax: 511-0693. $71.

The **Bristol**, though not much to look at from the outside, has 92 plain but pleasant rooms and 62 comfortable suites, and offers good value for the money. Facilities and amenities include a restaurant, a lobby bar, a garage, and laundry service.

Plaza Nécaxa 17 (at the corner of Río Panuco and Río Sena), 06500 D.F. Tel: 533-6060; Fax: 208-1717. $60.

The **Hotel del Angel** has 100 comfortable if modest rooms, and also offers good value for the money. Facilities and amenities include a rooftop restaurant with a view of the nearby Monument of Independence, a video bar, an in-house travel agent, a garage, and laundry service.

Río Lerma 154, 06500 D.F. Tel: 533-1032; Fax: 533-1027. $49.

The Zócalo Area

A beautiful Art Deco–style lobby with a stained glass Tiffany dome and old-fashioned cage elevators is the pride and joy of the **Howard Johnson Gran Hotel**, conveniently located on the Zócalo. The 99 rooms and 25 suites here, on the other hand, are not nearly as elegant as the lobby. (Try not to get a room with a view of a brick wall.) The hotel does offer adequate and friendly service, however, as well as great views of the Zócalo from the rooms on its upper floors, an in-house travel agent, a restaurant and bar, and a garage.

Avenida 16 de Septiembre 82, 06000 D.F. Tel: 510-4042; Fax: 512-2085; in the U.S. and Canada, Tel: (800) 654-2000. $71.

The **Best Western Majestic Hotel** offers pleasant colonial décor in a 16th-century building overlooking the Zócalo. Some of its 85 rooms are rather cramped, so a pre-registration check is advisable. There are sweeping views of the historic Zócalo area from the rooftop restaurant, and the hotel also has two other restaurants, a lively bar, an in-house travel agent, and laundry service. Many guests reserve rooms overlooking the Zócalo well in advance of the 15th and 16th of September, when Independence Day celebrations draw thousands to the square.

Avenida Madero 73, 06000 D.F. Tel: 521-8600; Fax: 518-3466; in the U.S. and Canada, Tel: (800) 528-1234. $81.

The **Monte Carlo**, a spotlessly clean hotel housed in a 17th-century building, is very popular with visiting foreign students. (D. H. Lawrence lived here for two years during the late 1920s.) For about $21 a night you can get one of the large, airy, no-frills rooms surrounding the hotel's courtyard. The Monte Carlo is only a few minutes' walk from the Zócalo.

Calle República de Uruguay 69, 06000 D.F. Tel: 521-2559. $21.

Other Choices Downtown

Located just north of Alameda Park and one block west of the Franz Mayer Museum, the **Hotel de Cortés** is housed in a 16th-century convent that in the 18th century was used as a hospice; today it is a national monument. Behind its fortresslike façade, the 20 rooms and seven suites, all clean but sparely furnished, are clustered around a truly lovely tree-shaded patio. The Cortés stages a great folkloric show in its courtyard every Saturday evening. (See Dining, below, for more on the Cortés.)

Avenida Hidalgo 85, 06300 D.F. Tel: 518-2181; Fax: 512-1893; in the U.S. and Canada, Tel: (800) 528-1234. $89.

The modern, 25-story **Holiday Inn Crowne Plaza** is always pulsating with activity—usually because it's hosting yet another convention or tour group. Located halfway between the Zona Rosa and Alameda Park on Paseo de la Reforma, the hotel has five nightclubs that often headline top-quality entertainment (see Nightlife and Entertainment, below), which makes it a focal point of nightlife in the D.F. Other installations include a swimming pool, three restaurants, two bars, a disco, an in-house travel agent, a solarium, and a garage.

Paseo de la Reforma 80, 06600 D.F. Tel: 705-1515; Fax: 705-1313; in the U.S. and Canada, Tel: (800) 465-4329. $176.

The ultramodern **Sevilla Palace**, also on Paseo de la Reforma, was built by local businessmen, and has a very Spanish flavor. It has 415 spacious rooms, a number of expensive boutiques, a rooftop pool, a health club, a gym, restaurants and bars, and a garage. The lobby is especially pretty, with lots of plants and a bubble elevator.

Paseo de la Reforma 105, 06030 D.F. Tel: 566-8877 or (800) 7-0070; Fax: 535-3842; in the U.S. and Canada, Tel: (800) 732-9488. $123.

The original decor of the **Emporio México**, on Paseo de la Reforma near the Zona Rosa, was early Space Age. Some of the rooms were left more or less intact during renovation a few years ago, and "garish" is the only word to describe them; a pre-registration check is advisable. All the rooms in the Emporio have Jacuzzi baths, however, and the hotel also has a restaurant, a bar in the lobby, and a garage.

Paseo de la Reforma 124, 06600 D.F. Tel: 566-7766; Fax: 703-1424. $75.

The **Vasco de Quiroga**, across the street from the Benjamin Franklin Library (an excellent English and Spanish library affiliated with the U.S. embassy), about a ten-minute walk from the Zona Rosa, offers 50 comfortable rooms and lovely colonial decor. It also has a restaurant, spacious bar, and laundry service.

Calle Londres 15, 06600 D.F. Tel: 546-2614; Fax: 546-4202. $59.

The 271-room **Hotel Casa Blanca**, right off Reforma a block south of the Monument to the Revolution, is a modern high rise with clean, well-furnished rooms, two restaurants, a rooftop pool and sundeck with large-screen TV, and four bars, three with live entertainment.

La Fragua 7, 06030 D.F. Tel: 566-3211; Fax: 705-4197; in the U.S. and Canada, Tel: (800) 826-6842. $96.

Located in a quiet residential neighborhood across the street from the back entrance to the first section of Chapultepec Park, about a ten-minute cab ride from the Zona Rosa, the two-story colonial-style **Park Villa** offers 45 clean, comfortable rooms, a nice garden area, a decent restaurant, handy parking, and reasonable rates.

Gomez Pedraza 68, 11560 D.F. Tel: 515-5248. $67.

Outlying Areas

Reached directly via overhead ramp from the international airport terminal, the five-year-old **Fiesta Americana Aeropuerto** advertises itself as "the only hotel with its own adjoining airport." Whether or not you consider that an advantage, there are 480 large rooms here, a cozy lobby usually filled with business travellers, a nightclub featuring live entertainment, a bar, a number of restaurants with average food, a gymnasium, an in-house travel agent, and a garage.

Boulevard Puerto Areo 502, 15520 D.F. Tel: 762-4088; Fax: 785-1034; in the U.S. and Canada, Tel: (800) 223-2332. $138.

Northeast of the city at the Teotihuacán archaeological site (a five-minute walk from the Pyramid of the Sun, the Club Med–operated **Villa Arqueológica** is a small but comfortable hotel with 40 simple, tastefully decorated rooms, a good restaurant and bar, a library well-stocked with archaeological titles, a swimming pool and tennis court, pleasant grounds, and a one-of-a-kind location.

Club Med, San Juan Teotihuacán, Tel: (595) 6-0750; in the U.S., Tel: (800) 258-2633; in Canada, Tel: (514) 937-7707. $60.

DINING

Mexico City offers more than 30,000 registered restaurants, among which you will find not only regional *restaurantes* featuring exquisite native delicacies (and, often, live regional folkloric music from various corners of the country) but superb international-style dining rooms as well. At the same time, on almost any street corner in the D.F. you will find women selling *carnitas* (chunks of roasted pork), tacos, and enchiladas. (Resist the enticing aromas: It's definitely risky to eat street food in Mexico if your digestive system is not primed.) Many people say that the best Mexican food is found at the tiny stalls, or *fondas,* in neighborhood markets, but going out to a special restaurant is a national pastime.

Many of the best restaurants in the D.F. were created by folks who had never run one before but who liked to eat, happened to own a prime location for a restaurant, and ventured to learn the business through trial and error. Other bistros are manned by European chefs who came to Mexico to direct the kitchens at the large international hotels and then fell in love with the country and decided to try their luck with their own establishments. The dining-out scene in the capital has been enriched by their daring. Most owners of the better restaurants have in common a passion for food, people, and a flair for showmanship. As Jane Pearson Fernández, the owner of the Piccadilly Pub and Sir Winston Churchill's, puts it: "Every day you have to put on a show that appeals not only to taste but to all the senses."

The sheer number of dining establishments in the D.F. guarantees a virtually unlimited range of culinary experiences. You can, for example, feast in former haciendas and 19th-century French-style mansions complete with lush gardens and exotic peacocks. Or you can embark on a gastronomic journey of the country by eating in the city's *fondas,* where you can sample such regional specialties as *cochinita pibil* (roast pork in barbeque sauce) from the Yucatán, *enmoladas de mole negro* (chicken with black *mole* sauce) from Oaxaca, or *albondigas de armadillo* in *salsa de huitlacoche* (armadillo meatballs in a sauce made with a rare and exceptionally flavorful black fungus). Often the menus will sound like the lyrics to a song in an ancient language: *garnachas* (fried tortillas covered with sour cream and chile sauce), *pambazos* (a fried roll filled with beans, hot sausages, and chiles), *pelonas* (a *pambazo* made in Puebla), *totopos* (the original nacho), or *chicharrones* (fried pork rinds). Even the foreign chefs here have been influenced to some extent by traditional Aztec and Mayan fare. As a result, certain ingredients will show up on the menus of trendy international eateries with some frequency, among which are the aforementioned *huitlacoche* (sometimes spelled *cuitlacoche*), which grows on corn; *cilantro* (coriander), sometimes referred to as Chinese parsley; and *flor de calabaza,* the flower of the yellow squash plant.

There is an old Mexican saying that goes, *"Todo se aregla en la cama o en la cantina"*—"Everything can be fixed in the bed or in the bar"—which in practice means that in the D.F. more important business deals are closed over lunch tables in the Zona Rosa than are concluded in the glass skyscrapers lining Paseo de la Reforma. Recently, these "business" lunches (which often used to wind up as wild soirées, with the tequila being shared liberally with members of the strolling mariachi band) have been replaced by working breakfasts—one reason you may find yourself standing in line for breakfast at your hotel at 8:00 A.M.

The better Mexico City restaurants also tend to be on the snobbish side. You can almost always count on excellent service at these establishments, but many will insist on relatively formal dress. (In the *fondas,* on the other hand, you can wear what you like.) When in doubt, phone the captain and ask about the dress code—it's better to get this information over the phone than at the door.

The prices of most dishes in exclusive restaurants will be

lower than they would be in comparable restaurants in big cities in the United States, Canada, or Europe. Imported wines, on the other hand, are pricey and can cost more than your entire meal; most restaurants will have a local wine list, however. Major credit cards are accepted in all D.F. restaurants unless otherwise noted. (Most will attempt to avoid American Express but will acquiesce if it's the only one you offer.)

A final word: Margarita aficionados should be aware that it's almost impossible to get a frozen margarita in Mexico City, where margaritas are usually served in champagne-style glasses with bits of ice floating around on top. Many Mexicans dining out like to down a couple of tequilas straight instead, with a *sangrita* (spicy tomato juice) as a chaser. They say it "opens the appetite." Remember, though, that the effect of alcohol on your system is accelerated in the D.F. because of the altitude; new arrivals in the city also should be careful not to eat much.

The restaurants listed below all cater to international guests. They claim to use purified water in all drinks as well as in their ice cubes, and also maintain that all vegetables and fruits on their menus are disinfected. This claim notwithstanding, it's best to avoid iced drinks—and fresh strawberries, even though they taste as good as they look (don't ask).

Most restaurants in the D.F. open from 1:00 P.M. to 1:00 A.M. The locals start to pour in from 2:00 P.M. on; to guarantee a table for lunch, get to the restaurant you've chosen by 1:00. Dinner crowds peak at about 9:30 P.M. Many restaurants are closed Sunday evenings, and are listed accordingly. A phone number accompanies the listing only if reservations are recommended; the area code in Mexico City is 5.

Zócalo Area

They say you don't really know the people of Mexico City until you have crowded into a traditional dining room such as the one at the **Hostería de Santo Domingo**, which claims to be the oldest restaurant in the country. (In the 18th century the building served as a Dominican seminary.) The service at this perennially popular establishment is almost always swift, but on Sunday afternoons you'll still have to wait in a line that stretches around the block. A perfect chow stop for those who have been busy touring the central historic district, the Hostería is located north and west of the Zócalo at Belisario Domínguez 72. Tel: 510-1434.

For sightseers looking for a bite to eat in the immediate vicinity of the Zócalo, the **Hotel Majestic**, Avenida Madero 73, offers some of the best views of the capital's main plaza from its rooftop restaurant. Its Sunday lunch, which begins at 1:00 P.M., includes a splendid buffet of Mexican dishes served casserole style.

Del Centro, located in the Howard Johnson Gran Hotel, the Art Nouveau landmark adjacent to the Zócalo, offers tasty Mexican and international dishes as well as a Sunday brunch that might be preceded by an English-language tour of the nearby Templo Mayor site and National Palace. Open weekdays from 7:00 A.M. to 11:00 P.M. and on weekends from 1:00 to 11:00 P.M. Tel: 521-5325.

Located three blocks west of the Zócalo at the corner of Motolinia and Cinco de Mayo, **Bar Alfonso** occupies the second floor of a stately old building facing a street that has recently been converted into a pedestrian mall. The high ceilings, brass chandeliers, wood paneling, and superb service are a perfect complement to the delicious Mexican-Continental fare served here, which includes such traditional favorites as *cabrito,* paella, and *camarones* (shrimp) à la vinaigrette. If you're planning on stopping for lunch, go early: The place is jammed with businesspeople most days of the week. Open daily from 1:00 P.M. to midnight. Tel: 512-7598.

Café de Tacuba, at Calle Tacuba 28 in a colonial-era building that originally was a Dominican convent, recently celebrated 80 consecutive years in business at the same location. The Tacuba is renowned for *enchiladas al horno* (stuffed rolled tortillas baked in a hot sauce) and its freshly baked *pan dulce* (assorted pastries), which locals munch on with a *café con leche* in the evenings. Part of the café's charm undoubtedly comes from its efficient, rather matronly waitresses, dressed a bit coyly in colorful regional dress, complete with outsize bows in their hair. Open from 8:00 A.M. to midnight daily, except Mondays. Tel: 518-4950. There is a branch in Polanco, at Calle Newton 88.

El Danubío, a few blocks south of the Zócalo at República de Uruguay 3, is a serious eatery with an emphasis on huge portions of seafood at reasonable prices. Popular with middle-class Mexicans, El Danubío also has an impressive cold counter featuring lobsters, crabs, clams, and baby eels. Open from 1:00 to 9:00 P.M. daily, except Sundays, when it closes at 6:00 P.M. Tel: 512-0976.

Southeast of the Zócalo at Regina 159, **Don Chon** is famous for such pre-Hispanic palate teasers as *iguana en salsa verde* (iguana in pumpkin-seed sauce), *león en salsa de ajonjali* (puma leg in sesame sauce), *albondigas de armadillo en salsa de nuez* (armadillo meatballs in walnut sauce), as well as such delicacies as *tepexcuintle* (prairie dog), stuffed chrysanthemums, ants' eggs, wild boar, snake, and venison. For the less adventurous, the *quesadillas de flor de calabaza* (squash-flower quesadillas) or the *tacos de salpicon de venado* (deer-salad tacos) are unforgettable. Open 10:00 A.M. to 6:00 P.M. daily. Tel: 522-2170.

Located one block south of the Torre Latinoamericana on Avenida 16 de Septiembre near the corner of Eje Central Lázaro Cárdenas, and first opened for business in 1892, **Prendes** is a huge, stately establishment with antique black lacquer chairs and a black-and-white tiled floor. The waiters look as though they were sent over by Central Casting, and the walls are adorned with murals of celebrated clients past and present: ex-President-for-Life Porfirio Díaz, Walt Disney, Frida Kahlo, Pancho Villa, and Gary Cooper. Leon Trotsky had his last supper here, and Señor Sánchez, the father in Oscar Lewis's classic *The Children of Sánchez,* worked here as a food buyer for the last 30 years of his life. The always-fresh seafood is the specialty. The place is usually packed at lunchtime but thins out considerably after 5:00 P.M. Open from 2:00 to 10:00 P.M.; closed Mondays. The refurbished, upscale Fronton México has a branch of Prendes that is open from 2:00 P.M. to 2:00 A.M.; closed Mondays.

Both entrances to **Restaurante Vasco**, a block north of Prendes, are equally camouflaged. In its 64th year of continual operation, Vasco is the perennially "in" place for scores of locals, but to look for it is to understand how it has managed to remain relatively unknown to tourists. Just east of the House of Tiles is a narrow north–south walkway called Pasaje America. Look for a wall plaque on the left that says "Madero no. 6" at the southern end, and you've found one entrance. The northern entrance is marked "Cinco de Mayo no. 7."

To get to the main dining room, climb the two flights of stairs or use the ancient elevator and walk through a large atrium, nearly the size of a ballroom. The dining area itself combines Art Nouveau and Art Deco touches, with a highly polished parquet floor, gilt-edged adornments on the stone pillars and woodwork, and crystal chandeliers. There are other, less ornate, dining rooms upstairs. The two lovely co-hostesses run a tight ship, and the waiters would be at home in a private English club. Service is impeccably swift and the five-course *comida corrida* is traditional Mexican-Spanish cuisine at its finest. Open from 1:00 to 6:00 P.M. daily. Tel: 512-3465.

Built soon after the Conquest, the building that houses the **Hotel de Cortés**, at Avenida Hidalgo 85 near Alameda Park, originally served as a convent and 200 years later as a hospice for the needy. Declared a national monument a few years ago, it's now a regular stop on the local version of the Grey Line Tour. Nonetheless, it's worth a visit. An oasis in the midst of urban blight, it provides a welcome respite from the rigors of museum-hopping, with a pretty tiled patio rimmed with flowers and a gushing fountain as its centerpiece. The patio also serves as a stage for a twice-nightly folkloric show featuring dancers and musicians in regional dress. The flickering candlelight creates such a romantic atmosphere that the restaurant's "typical Mexican menu," not much better than your average airline fare, often goes unnoticed. Tel: 512-2181.

If you're looking for something different, you'll find it at **Mesón del Cid**, a little bit of Old Spain located two blocks west and south of Alameda Park at Humboldt 61. Dishes such as charcoal-broiled Cornish hen with truffles, Costa Brava salad, and a superb gazpacho earn raves from contented customers. The fun happens on Saturday night, however, when a memorable medieval-style feast is offered along with live entertainment supplied by a robe-clad *estudiantina* (student's choir). Closed Sundays. Tel: 521-1940. Open from 1:00 P.M. to midnight daily, except Sundays.

If hot, spicy food doesn't agree with your stomach but your palate craves the exotic, **Círculo del Sureste**, offering the best in Yucatecan cuisine in a very informal setting, is just the ticket. *Cochinita pibil* and *pollo pibil,* two of the delectable specialties of the house, are marinated overnight in a sauce made from *naranja agria* (sour orange) and *achiote* (a spice made from the seeds of the annetto tree). To top it off, try a glass of Xtabentun (shtah-ben-TOON), a Yucatecan liqueur flavored with honey and anise. The restaurant is located slightly off the beaten path at Lucerna 12, five blocks south of the large traffic circle where Bucareli, Juárez, and Paseo de la Reforma intersect. Open from 11:00 A.M. to midnight daily, except Sundays, when it closes at 6:00 P.M. Tel: 546-2972.

That many artists, intellectuals, and restaurant operators flock to "La Casa Paco," as the locals call it, is all you need to know about the **Fonda de San Francisco**. The fresh flowers on the tables and in the wall recesses are changed every day, and the *sopa de flor de calabaza* (squash flower soup), the *crepas de jaiba* (crab crepes), and the delicious *sopa de queso* (cheese soup) are as good to look at as they are to eat. Located about ten blocks west of the Monument to the Revolution at José Velásquez de León 126, near the phone company building, La Casa Paco is closed Sundays. Tel: 546-4060.

The Zona Rosa

José Loredo, the creative chef-owner of **Loredo** (and the son of the restaurant's founder, the late José Ines Loredo) prepares traditional Mexican dishes with a special flair. To start your meal, try his *sopa mixteca,* a savory vegetable soup flavored with bone marrow, and then move on to the *carne asada a la tampiquena* (grilled strips of beef), one of Mexico's best-known dishes and one that Papa Loredo is said to have invented when he lived in Tampico. If you're really hungry, the *fuente de mariscos,* an immense cold platter of shellfish, will satisfy all but the murderously ravenous. Hamburgo 29, at the eastern edge of the Zona Rosa; closes Sundays at 6:00 P.M.

Focolare, at Hamburgo 87, is known as "the Restaurant of the Three Suns" because it features gastronomic specialties from three distinct regions of the country: Veracruz, Oaxaca, and the Yucatán. It also serves a breakfast buffet (as a marimba band plays in the background) and a different kind of *mole* sauce every day of the week. Things pick up on Friday and Saturday nights, when there's a Mexican folk-dancing show and a simulated cockfight. (The restaurant is full of tour groups on Saturdays, so you may want to come another day if you're hoping for an intimate meal.) On either side of the restaurant as you enter are two smaller rooms: **El Trumpo**, an English pub–type bar, and **La Pirinola**, a piano bar. Open from 7:30 to 1:00 A.M. weekdays and from 9:00 A.M. weekends. Tel: 511-2679.

Alfredo's, located in the arcade between Londres and Hamburgo, is the best of the many restaurants strung out along this always-bustling alley. Sicilian-born Alfredo, 28 years at the same location, personally supervises the kitchen and is justly famous for his alleged namesake specialty: fettuccini Alfredo. Open daily from 1:00 to 11:00 P.M.; closed Sundays. Tel: 511-3864.

Shirley's, in the Plaza Comermex on Calle Londres, between Calles Niza and Génova, is a sure bet for tourists with queasy stomachs. In business for half a century, Shirley's always draws a lunchtime line for their famous buffets, featuring traditional Mexican cuisine (not too spicy) as well as U.S.-style dishes (including the city's best homemade apple pie). The friendly, efficient service and impeccably clean premises should dispel any lingering homesickness. Shirley's other locations are at Paseo de la Reforma 108 (near the Holiday Inn Crowne Plaza) and the corner of Periférico Norte and Reforma in Polanco.

Bellinghausen was owned by the Austrian restaurateurs of the same name until 1962, when Chef Enrique Alvárez took over the management of this bustling steak-and-seafood establishment at Londres 95. Sizable servings of crayfish spiced with paprika and olive oil, shrimp in garlic sauce, and a notable red snapper in a light chile sauce are among the specialties that make this a favorite meeting place of Mexican businesspeople, who favor the outdoor patio dining area. Open from 1:00 to 11:00 P.M. daily, except Sundays. Tel: 207-6149.

Located at the corner of Londres and Niza in what was once the official residence of the U.S. ambassador, **La Calesa de Londres** is a fine restaurant with the stately atmosphere of days gone by. It's especially recommended for beef lovers: The restaurant's owner raises his own cattle on a ranch in Chihuahua, an area famed for its quality beef. A string trio performs nightly in the cozy wood-paneled bar. Open from 1:00 P.M. to 1:00 A.M. every day except Sunday, when it closes at 6:00 P.M. Tel: 533-6625.

The two-story **Chalet Suizo**, Niza 37, is the place for Swiss-Bavarian cuisine. The portions are generous and the waitresses in their pretty peasant dresses along with the ethnic decor combine to create an atmosphere reminiscent of an Alpine chalet. A Zona Rosa landmark, the Chalet Suizo is open daily from 12:30 P.M. to midnight. Tel: 511-7529.

Named for Luis Buñuel's first film, *An Andalusian Dog,* **El Mesón del Perro Andaluz**, at Copenhague 26, used to cater to the capital's filmmakers and other artists. Now it's one of a trio of affiliated outdoor eateries, each with its own front-row seats to a colorful parade of Mexican streetlife. Next door, **El Mesón la Marisqueria del Perro Andaluz** serves tempting seafood. Across the alley, Italian chef Mario Saggese prepares the pasta dishes at his **El Perro d'Enfrente**. All three are open from 1:00 P.M. to 1:00 A.M. daily. Tel: 533-5306.

A number of restaurant critics put **Estoril**, at Génova 75, among Mexico's finest restaurants. Oaxacan chef Pedro Ortega learned to cook from his Indian mother, who taught him the recipe for his divine *crepas de huitlacoche* (corn-fungus crepes) and chicken in black *mole* sauce, which he makes every Thursday and Friday. His *perejil al Estoril* (fried parsley) is rumored to have aphrodisiacal qualities and the *huitlacoche* mousse is memorable. Open from 1:30 to 11:00 P.M. daily, except Sundays. Tel: 208-9311. There's a branch of Estoril in Polanco in an elegant old mansion at Alejandro Dumas 24. Reservations, jackets, and ties are required. Open 1:30 to 10:30 P.M. daily, except Sundays and Mondays. Tel: 531-4556.

Champs-Elysées, across Paseo de la Reforma from the U.S. embassy at Amberes 1, serves a kind of Mexicanized French cuisine in an otherwise typically French atmosphere. Whether by design or accident, the combination works. Tables up front (*"una mesa en frente, por favor"*) offer great views of the passing scene on Reforma. Open weekdays from 1:00 to 11:00 P.M.; closed weekends. Tel: 514-0450.

Popular with business executives for the past 33 years, **Passy**, a garden restaurant with French decor at Amberes 10, is housed in a 19th-century mansion on the Zona Rosa's most elegant street. The crab pancakes, seafood in a shell, and coq au vin are so good that Passy will, in all likelihood, be serving them for another three decades. Wear a tie. Open 1:00 to 11:00 P.M. daily, except Sundays. Tel: 208-2087 or 207-3747.

Honfleur, at Amberes 14A, is one of the handful of truly worthy French restaurants in Mexico. Tasty delicacies in subtle sauces are prepared in genteelly elegant surroundings by Cordon Bleu chef-in-residence José Rodríguez, who creates poetry with his soufflés. The service here is as fine as the cuisine. Open from 1:00 to 11:00 P.M. daily; closed Sundays. Tel: 533-2115 or 1181.

Yug, on the western edge of the Zona Rosa at Varsovia 3, is a neighborhood-type vegetarian restaurant that offers a variety of meatless Mexican dishes. Yug's baker makes fresh brown bread daily, and papaya, carrot, orange, and alfalfa juice are available year-round. There's also a whole-grain bakery on the premises. Tel: 574-4475.

La Lanterna, a few blocks west of the Zona Rosa at Paseo de la Reforma 458 (between Calles Burdeos and Lieja), features traditional Italian food and great pizzas. The pasta is made fresh on the premises every day. Closed Sundays. Tel: 207-9969.

Near the U.S. Embassy

The embassy district is north of Paseo de la Reforma, opposite the Zona Rosa.

Housed in a beautiful 19th-century mansion at Río Sena 88, its patio framed by classical sculpture and lush greenery, **Les Moustaches** is one of Mexico City's most stunning restaurants. It offers more than elegant decor, however; you quickly get the feeling you have walked into another world as you are ushered to your table. At Les Moustaches everyone is treated like a visiting dignitary. Start your meal with the smoked-salmon soup or spicy shrimp bisque. End it with flaming baked Alaska or the amaretto soufflé. Jackets and ties are required, and reservations are recommended. Open weekdays from 1:15 P.M. to 1:00 A.M.; closed weekends. Tel: 533-3390.

Grass-roots cuisine at its best can be enjoyed at **El**

Caminero, one block north of the U.S. embassy at Río Lerma 138. Although it looks suspiciously like a greasy spoon, don't be put off by the cramped, no-frills interior. The lunchtime crowds in business suits come for one thing and one thing only: tacos in every conceivable variety. You'll probably have to stand as you're munching yours, though; there are only a few stools at the counter in this landmark eatery.

Las Fuentes, at Río Pánuco 127, two blocks north of the Monument to Independence, is a roomy, comfortable, and sparklingly clean vegetarian restaurant—the best of its kind in the capital. French-American owner Monsieur Philipe, who somehow manages to greet every customer, takes pride in personally purchasing his produce every day at dawn in the Merced market. The result is the absolutely freshest food in town—and the largest helpings. Breakfasts are great (served from 8:00 A.M.), and prices are very reasonable. Las Fuentes is crowded at lunchtime, but the service is so good you shouldn't have to wait more than a few minutes, even if the line winds out the door and onto the street. There's also a retail shop here that stocks a wide variety of top-grade health foods. Open 8:00 A.M. to 6:00 P.M. daily. Tel: 525-7095.

Polanco

You can enjoy the atmosphere of "a thousand and one Arabian nights" and dance until dawn with Mexico's Middle Eastern community at **Adonis**, Homero 424. The food here—falafel, raw and fried kibbe, tabouleh, fish with nuts, stuffed grape leaves dipped in tahini, date pie, and other Middle Eastern favorites—is the real thing. Open 1:00 P.M. to midnight Wednesday through Saturday, and from 1:00 to 6:00 P.M. Sundays. Tel: 531-6490.

Chef Jacques Bergerault came to Mexico in 1957 to open the kitchen of the famed Las Brisas in Acapulco. Today he and his sons, Jacques and Federico, run the **Café de Paris**, Campos Elíseos 164, one of Polanco's more courtly establishments, and one especially dedicated to pleasing its customers. In fact, Bergerault himself goes to the market twice a week to find the best available ingredients for his daily specials. Begin with *croustade d'oeufs de caille palois* (tart stuffed with quail's egg) and follow it with the *pato al cilantro* (duck cooked in fresh coriander). The original Café de Paris, now in its fourth decade of continual operation, is hard to find. Tucked away under the Río Mississippi overpass at Parque Melchor Ocampo 14, just a few blocks north of the U.S. embassy (and so always packed at lunchtime with embassy administrative personnel), the restaurant is housed in a rather run-down centuries-old building (whereas the Polanco location would appear very much at home in a chic Paris neighborhood). The quality of the cuisine and service is impeccable at both Cafés de Paris. Open from 1:30 P.M. to midnight Monday through Saturday and until 6:00 P.M. on Sundays. Tel: 531-6646 (Polanco) and 528-8997 (original).

El Parador de José Luis, long an institution in the Zona Rosa, has now brought its Mediterranean food and Spanish decor to Campos Elíseos 198. Try their *tapas*. El Parador is also a good place to rest after a strenuous day of shopping in Polanco's expensive boutiques, or to indulge in a serious paella (but give the chef an extra 45 minutes to prepare it). Tel: 533-1840.

El Fongoncito is the name and tacos are their game. With two locations on opposite sides of Calle Leibnitz at numbers 54 and 55, a block from the rear entrance to the Camino Real, El Fongoncito draws taco aficionados from near and far, who gorge themselves on the legendary *tacos al pastor*. The constant beehive of activity requires a permanent crew of four policeman to control the traffic until the wee hours of the morning. An electronic sign records the number of tacos prepared; 4,495,620 as of July 1992. If you beat the house record, the tacos are free.

Just as the Camino Real can claim to be the best hotel in the D.F., the hotel's **Fouquet's of Paris** can legitimately claim to be one of the best French restaurants in the city. Superb service at lunch as well as dinner, live music, and spectacular flaming dishes make this a favorite with socialites, diplomats, and members of the Mexican communications industry. An excellent choice for a special occasion. Open weekdays from 7:30 to 10:00 A.M., 2:00 to 4:30 P.M., and 8:00 to 11:00 P.M.; Saturdays from 8:00 to 11:00 P.M.; Sundays from 2:00 to 4:30 P.M. Tel: 203-2121.

Meals at the Camino Real's **Azulejos** restaurant are served on an enclosed terrace overlooking a swimming pool. The Sunday brunch here is one of the best in the city. Open daily from 7:30 A.M. to 11:00 P.M. Tel: 203-2121.

Piccolo Suizo, diagonally across from the Camino Real at Mariano Escobedo 539, resembles an Alpine log cabin. It's been a popular meeting place for the neighborhood's many business executives for 30 years. The house specialties are *fondue de queso* (cheese fondue) and *pato al orange* (duck in orange sauce). Open 12:30 P.M. to 1:00 A.M. daily. Tel: 531-1298.

Las Mercedes, located one block north of the Camino Real at the corner of Darwin and Leibniz, is the place for hearty, traditional Mexican breakfasts, tasty meat dishes, and delicious hand-made tortillas. The portions are huge and the service impeccable, which perhaps explains why it's popular with local businesspeople during the week and families on the weekends. Tel: 208-8922.

The **Hacienda de los Morales**, on the western edge of Polanco (technically in Colonia Chapultepec Morales) at Vásquez de Mella 525, is celebrating its 25th anniversary in 1993. Originally the site of Mexico's first silkworm farm, the restored 17th-century hacienda is worth a visit for its architecture alone, with colonial-era fountains, chapels, paintings, and furniture. Considering all the bustling activity created by the conscientious, fast-moving staff as they serve hundreds of diners, the food is exceptionally good. The cold walnut soup especially is to be savored. A string quartet sets a nice, semiclassical mood in the comfortable lounge. Reservations, jackets, and ties are required after 6:00 P.M. Open 1:00 P.M. to midnight daily. Tel: 254-5000 or 540-3225.

Located in a neo-colonial home at Molière 50, not far from the Polanco hotels, **Isadora** is usually packed for lunch and dinner. Chef Carmen Ortino named her restaurant after the flashy, rebellious dancer because she, like the great Duncan, is a passionate performer—of the culinary arts. Reservations are advised, especially if the lovely Carmen is orchestrating one of her seasonal food festivals. A great choice in any season, however, is her ravioli stuffed with *huitlacoche* and covered in a light chile and corn sauce (*raviolis relleno de huitlacoche en salsa de chile poblano*). Open from 1:30 to 5:00 P.M. and 8:30 to 11:00 P.M. Monday through Saturday; closed Sundays. Reservations advised; Tel: 520-7901.

The **King's Pub**, an authentic Irish pub where informality reigns, is within walking distance of the Nikko México and Stouffer Presidente Chapultepec at Arquímedes 31. Irish-Mexican owner Pepe Meehan makes all his guests feel at home with his personal brand of blarney. Count on enjoying the best prime rib south of Kansas City, or try one of his "McMeehan burgers," the safe salad bar, and the draft beer. There's also live dinner music upstairs in the evenings. Open daily from 1:00 P.M. to 1:00 A.M. Tel: 254-2655.

If you have to limit yourself to just one Mexican restaurant, make it the **Fonda del Recuerdo**, Bahía de las Palmas 39, where four strolling bands play *veracruzano* folk music—simultaneously. Not a place to propose marriage, perhaps, but a terrific spot where the fiesta never seems to end. Known for its giant portions (truckloads of fresh seafood arrive daily from Veracruz), the house offers specialties that include a drink called the "torito"—guanabanana and mamey juice mixed with *aguardiente*. The Fonda del Recuerdo has menus in English and features everything from tortilla soup to crabmeat turnovers. There's also a babysitter on hand in a tot-lot to entertain your children. Open from 9:00 A.M. to 11:00 P.M. Monday through Saturday and until 6:00 P.M. Sundays. Tel: 203-0095.

The Argentinian steak house **La Tablita**, at Presidente Masaryk and Torcuato Tasso, serves choice cuts of meat prepared with special herbs and red-wine sauce. Dining here is something like eating in a greenhouse; the smell of steak cooking on individual braziers fills an atrium alive with the chatter of shoppers and well-dressed businesspeople. Try the cheese turnovers (*empanadas*). The service is superb. Tel: 250-2522.

El Buen Comer, Edgar Allen Poe 50, a small French bistro in the garage of a private home where the customers all seem to know each other, specializes in quiches and fondues. French Cordon Bleu chef Roger Marcellini, the founder of this intimate hideaway, and his son and daughter attend to the cuisine. Their beef bourguignon is made with tender morsels of steak, and the house wine is from the vineyards of Tequisquiapán, Querétaro. Open 1:00 to 6:00 P.M. daily, except Sundays. Tel: 203-5337.

At Temístocles 12, a few minutes from the Nikko México and Stouffer Presidente hotels, **La Palma** is an excellent choice for a typical Mexican meal. Tastefully decorated in elegant but unpretentious colonial style, this restaurant offers a variety of exotic, hard-to-find dishes. Especially recommended are *tacos de jaiba* (crabmeat-filled tacos), *huauzontles en anchol* (mixed greens in red chile sauce), and *sopa criolla La Palma* (bean soup with vermicelli). The delicious handmade tortillas are reason enough to eat here. Open 1:00 P.M. to midnight Monday through Saturday and until 6:00 P.M. on Sundays. Tel: 250-9881.

Rincón Argentina accepts no reservations, but nobody seems to mind. The wooden benches installed on the sidewalk for patient patrons, many of them business executives, are always filled at lunchtime. The wide variety of meats here is outstanding, and the restaurant's interior, featuring mahogany paneling and framed photos of Argentinian soccer teams, is a bit cramped but cozy. Try the *pascualina,* a pastry tart filled with ham and spinach, and the *morcilla,* a black pudding. The Chilean Santa Marta Cabernet Sauvignon is the perfect accompaniment to a meal here. Open from 1:00 P.M. to midnight Monday through Saturday and until 7:00 P.M. on Sundays. Tel: 254-3750 or 3964.

Sir Winston Churchill's, in the western part of Polanco at Boulevard Avila Camacho 67, is not just for those needing a quick fix of bangers and mash. This oasis in an old Tudor mansion is one of the finest, as well as most attractive, eating places in the city. The walls are paneled with mahogany; the tables are set with fresh flowers and cranberry-glass goblets; and the fireplace may be roaring. In this regal setting you can indulge in a tender rib eye, a rare piece of roast beef, or a flaming skewer of shrimps in herb butter. Among the many sinful desserts is a cappuccino mousse with whipped cream. The Irish coffee is great and the wine cellar well stocked. If you don't have time for dinner, go for tea. Private dining rooms are available for up to ten people. Coats and ties required. Open from 1:00 P.M. to 1:00 A.M. Monday through Saturday; closed Sundays. Reserve; Tel: 520-0585 or 0065.

Lago Chapultepec is a large, glass-walled restaurant on the shore of Lago Mayor in the second section of Chapultepec Park. A landmark for years, when it was called Restaurante del Lago, it was closed for more than two years due to a labor dispute. Under new management, it's now better than ever. It would be worth coming here for the beautiful setting alone, but the food is delicious and the service superb; a jazz trio plays danceable music. Caviar and smoked salmon are staples on the international menu, and the wine list is extensive. Casual clothing is acceptable until sundown, when jackets and ties are required. Open 8:00 A.M. to 2:00 A.M. Monday through Saturday, and from 11:00 A.M. to 4:00 P.M. Sundays. Tel: 515-9585.

Lomas de Chapultepec

Lomas is a luxurious residential neighborhood in the western D.F. that begins where Paseo de la Reforma swings south and west beyond Chapultepec Park. Magnificent trees and beautiful old mansions line the boulevard here, and it's just 20 minutes by taxi from the Zona Rosa (your restaurant will be happy to call a cab for you after dinner).

The **Villa Reforma**, Paseo de la Reforma 2210, has become a favorite gathering spot of the Lomas gentry. Sumptuous breakfasts, Mexican-style nouvelle cuisine, and dining on a glass-covered terrace are just three of the reasons for its popularity. It closes early after a great Sunday brunch. Open 8:00 A.M. to 1:00 A.M. weekdays, 9:00 A.M. to 1:00 A.M. Saturdays, and from 9:00 A.M. to 6:00 P.M. Sundays. Tel: 596-0128.

Colombian-born Guillermo Gomez fell in love with his beautiful partner and wife, Elizabeth, in Victoria, Canada; then, in a daring moment, they decided to move to Mexico City and try their luck as restaurateurs. The result of their decision is the romantically chic **Isla Victoria**, located at Monte Kamérun 120 in a small mansion on a tree-lined residential street. The menu offers daily specials such as

Colombian chicken soup served with capers, cream, and avocado; or *marminto,* a cream of mushroom and shrimp soup served in a bowl covered with a puff-pastry dome. Dress is semiformal (chic semiformal, of course); if you manage to look as if you've stepped out of a fashion magazine you will be treated as an honored guest. Children are not allowed. Open 1:00 to 11:00 P.M. daily, except Sundays. Tel: 520-5597.

Insurgentes Sur, San Angel, and Points South

Located on Torres Adalid, two blocks east of Insurgentes Sur near the Siqueiros Cultural Polyforum, **Suntory** is the oldest, most elegant, and most expensive of the capital's many Japanese restaurants. Authenticity reigns in this lovely setting: Rock gardens and cascading fountains surround the private dining rooms, and kimono-clad waitresses and *teppanyaki* chefs contribute to the feeling you've somehow been transported to the Far East. Open Monday through Thursday from 1:00 to 5:00 P.M. and 7:00 to 11:00 P.M.; Fridays and Saturdays from 1:00 to 11:30 P.M.; and Sundays from 1:00 to 6:00 P.M. Tel: 211-0092. There's another Suntory at Monte Urales 535 in Lomas de Chapultepec, just west of Polanco. The hours are the same; Tel: 540-0785.

Mazurka, the one and only Polish restaurant in the city, is located at Calle Nueva York 150, four blocks west of Insurgentes Sur in the neighborhood of the Polyforum, but it's hard to find; taking a taxi will save you a lot of aggravation. The Polish owner, Tadeusz Podbereski, is a gracious host who speaks passable English and takes great pride in suggesting the ethnic specialties of his Polish-born chef, including *ges* (duck baked with wild-rice stuffing) and *kaczka* (goose baked with sour-apple stuffing and topped with blueberries). Señor Podbereski is also certain to tell you how much Pope John Paul II loved his *bigos* (sweet-and-sour cabbage stuffed with smoked meats and sausage) when he visited Mexico a few years ago. The restaurant's Old World atmosphere is enhanced by Art Deco touches, slightly frayed red velvet drapes, and a chamber group that performs mostly Chopin in the evenings. A branch has opened recently near University City at Copilco 3. Both are open from 1:00 P.M. to 1:00 A.M. Monday through Saturday and until 5:00 P.M. on Sundays. Tel: 523-8811 or 548-7471 (Copilco branch).

For a genuine slice of Mexican life try **Las Cazuelas**, two blocks east of the Plaza México bullring at Avenida San Antonio 143. Delicious home-style cooking at reasonable prices accounts for the line of customers waiting to be seated during peak hours. The trick is to get there before

1:30 P.M., when most Mexicans are still digesting their *almuerzo* (the "snack" eaten between breakfast and lunch). In business since 1916, Doña Emilia Perez de Sotelo, the original owner, began her career as a taco street vendor, selling her wares from a *cazuela* (casserole). She was so successful she soon added more casseroles and eventually progressed to this sit-down restaurant with colorful, hand-painted tiles and furniture and strolling mariachis singing their hearts out. Lined up on both sides of the entrance are about two dozen huge, steaming earthenware *cazuelas* filled with various stuffings for tacos. The *machitos de carnero* (lamb sweetbreads) and *pipian con pollo* (chicken drowned in a squash-seed sauce) are worth the wait, and fruit-flavored pulque—the fermented juice of the maguey plant (before it's distilled to make tequila)—is the beverage of choice. Moderation is advised, however, as this delicious concoction tends to sneak up on the unwary. Tel: 563-3956.

With a quaint brick fireplace as its centerpiece, **La Casserole**, Insurgentes Sur 1880, near the San Angel area, serves Mexico City's best French provincial cuisine in an intimate setting. Some of the delectable specialties of the chef include *huachinango papillote,* squab, partridge, and fresh-baked garlic bread covered with melted cheese. Their chocolate mousse is delectable. Open from 8:00 A.M. to midnight daily, except Sundays. Tel: 524-5949.

Lancer's, at Insurgentes Sur 2018 (and elsewhere), is an above-average steakhouse with a bright, perky atmosphere and waitresses dressed like Scottish lasses. You can get a good breakfast, bowl of soup or salad, or fish dish here, but the big draw is the meat, especially the prime rib. Open from 8:00 A.M. to 11:00 P.M. daily; until 10:00 P.M. on Sundays.

Located between Avenidas Insurgentes Sur and Revolución at Avenida de la Paz 45, a few blocks east of the Plaza de San Jacinto, **Los Irabien** is one of the very best restaurants in the capital, as well as a convenient stop for breakfast, lunch, or dinner on your way to or back from the lovely colonial villages of Coyoacán and San Angel. The Irabien family is dedicated to excellence and caters to more than just your taste buds. Beautiful works of art, including originals by some of Mexico's finest painters, are discreetly interspersed among the spectacular potted plants, antique Mexican furniture, and carved wooden statues. Walls colored in unusual, subdued hues serve as the perfect background for these visual treats. The dining area itself is very comfortable, with every seat offering a fine vantage point of the rest of the room; a pianist performs at lunch and dinner.

Los Irabien's kitchen is under the supervision of inventive

master chef Enrique Estrada. One of his many delicious creations is a liver pâté presented atop a sculpted gelatin, itself a work of art. His *sopa de mariscos* with Pernod is memorable, as are two dishes from the nouvelle cuisine section, both featuring *huachinango* (red snapper): *huachinango en nopalitos al mojo de ajo* (spineless cactus leaves filled with filet of red snapper and fried in garlic) and "El Rey del Caribe" (red snapper topped with *huitlacoche* and *flor de calabaza*). Open daily from 8:00 A.M. to 1:00 A.M. Tel: 660-2382 or 0876.

Two blocks west of Insurgentes Sur at Pedro Luís de Ogazon 102 in San Angel, **Dos Puertas** (Two Doors) comprises several comfortable dining areas surrounded by enclosed gardens. The kitchen here puts out an amazing variety of fine Mexican and international cuisine, starting with breakfast; rotating art exhibitions enhance the elegant atmosphere of the place. Open 8:00 A.M. to 1:00 A.M. Monday through Saturday, and until 5:00 P.M. Sundays. Tel: 548-9361.

King's Road, located a block east of the landmark San Angel Inn at Altavista 43, serves some of the best beef in the D.F. The prime rib and the U.S.-style steaks at this English pub–type restaurant are excellent, as are the breaded frog's legs. A pianist provides appropriate background music for all meals. Open 1:00 P.M. to 1:00 A.M. Monday through Saturday and until 5:00 P.M. Sundays. Tel: 660-1632.

An ideal place to have lunch en route to University City or Xochimilco is the award-winning **La Cava**, Insurgentes Sur 2465, just south of the university and the Avenida San Jerónimo exit. Diners can choose from its extensive menu of Mexican, Spanish, and international-style entrées in an enclosed dining room overlooking a patio with a cascading fountain, or on the patio itself. There are, in addition, a number of private dining areas able to accommodate up to eight people—the perfect place to have a small celebration. Open 1:00 P.M. to 1:00 A.M. Monday through Saturday, and until 6:00 P.M. Sundays. Tel: 550-0852.

Mauna Loa, San Jerónimo 240 (the main avenue leading to El Pedregal), is about a half-hour's taxi ride south of the Zona Rosa, but it's worth the trip. Equally delicious Szechuan, Cantonese, and Temujin specialties are brought to your table by attentive waiters, and the nightly entertainment features Hawaiian music, hula dancers, and potent tropical drinks. Open 7:30 A.M. to 1:00 A.M. Monday through Saturday, and until 6:00 P.M. Sundays. Tel: 548-6884.

Another good choice for lunch in the southern D.F. is the **Antigua Hacienda de Tlalpan**, at Calzada de Tlalpan 4619. A restored 17th-century hacienda surrounded by two acres of beautiful gardens, it was once a stagecoach stop on the Acapulco road and, later, a weekend retreat for President-for-Life Porfirio Díaz. Today it's more likely to be filled with shoppers who have spent the morning at PERISUR, the capital's largest shopping mall, just a five-minute cab ride to the east. The food, mostly international, is better than average, but the grounds alone are reason enough to stop while you're exploring the surrounding area. Open 1:00 P.M. to midnight Monday through Saturday, and until 6:00 Sundays.

NIGHTLIFE AND ENTERTAINMENT

Mexico City after dark can be exciting, but selectivity is the key factor. Keep in mind, moreover, that the mile-and-a-half altitude in the D.F. tends to make each cocktail about twice as intoxicating as it would be at sea level.

Most nightclubs, like most major restaurants, are closed Sunday evenings.

The *Tiempo Libre,* a very informative weekly publication, lists all the current events in the D.F.; the latest edition is available at newsstands every Friday.

The area code in Mexico City is 5.

Cocktail Lounges and Hotel Bars

Live music in most lounges commences at 8:00 P.M. and continues until the 2:00 A.M. closing time (a few remain open longer). Most of the best cocktail lounges are located in the major hotels.

If you visit only one bar in Mexico City, make it the **Bar L'Opera**, located near the Palacio de Bellas Artes at the corner of Cinco de Mayo and F. Mata. In business at the same site since 1905, this historic tavern is worth a visit even if you're a teetotaler. It's an old-style cantina, admitting only men until 1975, when Mexico passed a law allowing women to patronize cantinas. The velvet-covered booths, garish wallpaper, antique chandeliers, and hand-carved wood paneling were allegedly purchased lock, stock, and barrel from a New Orleans bordello just after the turn of the century. True or not, the generous drinks and free-wheeling camaraderie have prevailed ever since the days when Porfirio Díaz would drop in to down a few tequilas with his cronies. Other celebrated customers have included Pancho Villa, who, peeved at his merrymaking troops, rode through the swinging doors one day in 1911 and allegedly put a bullet in the ceiling; the muralist Diego Rivera; and, more recently, the Nobel Prize–winning Gabriel García Márquez, who, according to the waiter Santiago, nurses a beer for hours while gobbling the bar's famous *botanas* (assorted snacks). "But he's a good tipper." Open daily, except Sundays, from noon to midnight.

The **Jorongo Bar** is a perennially popular night spot in the Sheraton María-Isabel, featuring the best in ethnic music (mostly mariachi) and jammed nightly in and out of season. It is also the closest thing to a singles bar in the D.F. Next door to the U.S. embassy at Paseo de la Reforma 325, across the street from the Zona Rosa.

The **Majestic Bar**, on the seventh floor of the hotel of the same name at Madero 73 on the Zócalo, offers superb views of the cathedral and the National Palace, especially on weekends, when both are floodlit. With the sounds of mariachi music always swirling through the bar, the Majestic is not the place for intimate conversations, however.

Don't be dissuaded by the sleazy appearance of **Tenampa**—if it's a slice of Mexico City life you're looking for, this is the place. The three or four strolling trios get an early (1:00 P.M.) start at this huge establishment, often playing simultaneously as they circulate among the hundreds of tables, and usually wait until the last customer is gone, sometime around dawn, before wrapping it up. Believe it or not, the constant cacophony is tolerable, and as the tequila flows the camaraderie gets mellower. Bouncers prevent undesirables from entering, so it's a safe scene. Credit cards are not accepted, however. North of Alameda Park on the Plaza de Garibaldi.

Club 25, in the Holiday Inn Crowne Plaza, is a rooftop bar with panoramic views from every window, making it an especially popular place for sunset watching. Open 5:00 to 9:00 P.M. daily. Paseo de la Reforma 80.

The always crowded **Gatsby's**, in the Stouffer Presidente Chapultepec, is both chic and cozy, and features live ethnic music played through a well-modulated sound system. Campos Elíseos 218, Polanco.

The Nikko México's most popular meeting spot is **Shelty**, a wood-paneled bar on the mezzanine that resembles a traditional English pub. Open 2:00 P.M. to 1:00 A.M. daily. Campos Elíseos 204, Polanco.

Discotheques

If you are fairly sober and presentable, you'll have no problem getting into any of the capital's discotheques. The normal cover charge ranges from 50,000 to 75,000 pesos, and major credit cards (with the exception of American Express in some places) are accepted. Most discos open at 10:00 P.M., but the real action generally doesn't begin until midnight. Closing time in most cases is 4:00 A.M.

Located in the heart of the Zona Rosa and always crowded, **Mekano**'s congenial clientele usually is equally divided between tourists and locals. At the corner of Hamburgo and Génova.

Cero Cero, in the Camino Real hotel, has been one of the most popular discos in the capital for the last 18 years, and features live as well as recorded music. The psychedelic lighting alone is worth a visit. Mariano Escobedo 700.

The intimate **Disco Club 84**, in the Stouffer Presidente Chapultepec, has a good sound system and sleek, modern decor. Frequented by youthful locals and tourists alike, it's at Campos Elíseos 218, across Paseo de la Reforma from the main entrance to Chapultepec Park. Open from 9:00 P.M. Thursday to Saturday only.

With its ultramodern decor, creative lighting, and excellent sound system, **Zazzy**, in the Nikko México, has become the new "in" disco in the D.F. Although it's usually crowded with a pleasant, youngish mix of locals and tourists, there is plenty of elbow room off the dance floor. It's next door to the Stouffer Presidente Chapultepec, at Campos Elíseos 204.

Magic Circus, north of the central historic district, is a bit off the beaten path, so it's best to take a taxi. The design and lighting are state of the art, and crowds of young locals congregate here nightly, but those with sensitive eardrums might consider visiting one of the two other discos, under the same management, connected to it. The **Rock Garage** is slightly smaller and features parts of classic cars as tables. The enthusiastic waiters weave in and out of this chic junkyard-like area with surprising efficiency—considering the rather bizarre obstacle course they have to deal with. **Privilege** is a bit more upscale than the other two, and insists on a dress code: Men must wear jackets but need not wear ties; no slacks are permitted for women. Calle Rodolfo Gaona 3.

News, very similar in decor and ambience to the disco of the same name in Acapulco (it's operated by the same people), is the hippest and largest disco in the D.F. Open only on weekends, from 10:00 P.M. to 4:00 A.M., it's near the El Pedregal neighborhood at Avenida San Jerónimo 252, next door to Mauna Loa (see Dining, above), about a half-hour's taxi ride south of the Zona Rosa.

Nightclubs with Floor Shows
Located on the mezzanine level of the always bustling Holiday Inn Crowne Plaza, **Barbarella** offers two shows nightly, Thursday through Saturday, featuring nationally known headliners. Popular with both locals and visitors, this modern,

comfortable room has a relaxed, friendly atmosphere. You can dance to live music between shows, and snacks are served. Open 9:00 P.M. to 3:00 A.M.; closed Sundays. East of the Zona Rosa at Paseo de la Reforma 80. Tel: 705-1515.

El Corral de la Moreria, at Calle Londres 161 in the Zona Rosa, is an intimate dinner club featuring top-quality Spanish music and flamenco dancing. Skip the authentic Spanish cuisine, though. Shows are at 11:00 P.M. and 2:00 A.M. nightly; open from 9:30 P.M. to 3:30 A.M. Tel: 525-1762.

El Patio, a massive landmark nightclub on Calle Atenas 9 near the Zócalo, features national and international headliners every other month or so. Shows here (two a night) are done on a grand scale. The Patio's neighborhood is a bit seedy but not dangerous; it is hard to find, however, so it's best to take a taxi. The normal schedule, between headliner bookings, offers dinner and dancing from 9:00 P.M. to 2:00 A.M. Closed Sundays and Mondays. Tel: 535-3904 to check on upcoming events.

A few blocks south of the Zona Rosa and one block west of Avenida Insurgentes Sur at Calle Oaxaca 15, colorful **Gitanerias** has been a favorite of flamenco devotees for some time now. Two shows nightly, at 11:30 P.M. and 2:00 A.M.; closed Sundays. Tel: 511-5283.

Las Sillas means "The Chairs" in Spanish, and there are more than a hundred in this intimate, friendly room—no two alike—for your sitting pleasure. You can dance to live music before and after the midnight show. Open nightly 10:00 P.M. to 3:00 A.M.; closed Sundays. In the Holiday Inn Crowne Plaza, Paseo de la Reforma 80. Tel: 705-1515.

Huge, very popular, and always crowded, **Marrakesh** is actually four clubs in one: Valentino's for dancing, the Morocco bar for a tame singles scene, Casablanca for top-quality entertainment, and La Madelon for dinner and after-dinner dancing to live music. Frequented by wealthy locals and visitors alike, Marrakesh is open from 9:00 P.M. to 3:00 A.M. nightly. In the Zona Rosa at Calle Florencia 36.

The **Plaza Santa Cecilia** is a traditional Mexican nightclub with four folkloric shows nightly. The room is huge and the food good, but patience is needed, as the service is not especially swift (to put it mildly). Shows at 8:30 P.M. and 2:30 A.M. Located north of Alameda Park on the Plaza de Garibaldi. Tel: 526-2455.

The entrance to **Señorial**, across the street from the Westin Galería Plaza in the Zona Rosa, resembles an enormous upended milk container. Its Sugar Bar, which features live rock music, is very popular with local businessmen, who often arrive in groups. There is a dress code. Open from

10:00 P.M. to 3:00 A.M. daily, except Sundays. Calle Hamburgo 188.

Maquiavelo, in the Krystal Zona Rosa, offers two floor shows nightly, at 10:00 P.M. and midnight, followed by very danceable music provided by a live orchestra until 3:00 A.M. A friendly ambience and attentive service are staples of this popular nightspot. Calle Liverpool 199. Open 10:00 P.M. to 4:00 A.M. Wednesday through Saturday. Tel: 211-3460.

Stelaris, on the top floor of the Holiday Inn Crowne Plaza hotel, is considered by many to be the best supper club in Mexico City. The superb food, excellent entertainment (often internationally known headliners), and spectacular views of the city make this a popular choice. There is a dress code. Open nightly 10:00 P.M. to 3:00 A.M.; closed Sundays. Paseo de la Reforma 80, east of the Zona Rosa. Tel: 705-1515.

Dining and Dancing

Fun always seems to prevail at **Chez 'Ar**, a brightly colored nightclub in the Zona Rosa. You can dance to a combo here from 9:00 P.M. to 3:00 A.M. nightly, except Sundays. Located in the Hotel Aristos, Paseo de la Reforma 276. **Yesterday's**, a comfortable, friendly ballroom also in the Hotel Aristos, is frequented by lots of young to fortyish singles four nights a week. The live music starts at 8:00 P.M. and continues until 2:00 A.M., Thursday through Sunday.

The **Torre de Oro** (Golden Tower), on the 22nd floor of the centrally located Sevilla Palace hotel, offers terrific evening views of the capital's skyline, including the recently inaugurated Bolsa (stock exchange) building. Live music, great for dancing, is served up by a good orchestra with an extensive repertoire of American "oldies but goodies." Crowded on weekends with both locals and tourists. Paseo de la Reforma 105. Tel: 566-8877 for reservations.

The great views offered by the **Muralto**, which occupies the entire 41st floor of the Latin American Tower, sometimes include the surrounding mountains and the Valley of Mexico, and are reason enough to drop by. In the evening the city spread out below appears at its best. The live music begins at 8:00 P.M., and there's a strict dress code for men (tie and jacket). Open 1:00 P.M. to 1:00 A.M. Monday through Saturday and until 10:00 P.M. Sundays. Tel: 521-7751.

SHOPS AND SHOPPING

Mexico City, which generates an abundance of artwork, high fashion, and handicrafts, is also the major market in the country for all types of traditional arts and crafts from outlying regional centers. Glassware and ceramics, for example, are only two of the many types of great buys that are available throughout the D.F.

Large stores and open-air markets devoted exclusively to regional handicrafts are scattered throughout the downtown area, with the products of the various states and regions usually separated into sections in each. At many of the markets Indian women wearing traditional garb work their looms on the sidewalks while waiting for customers. This should come as no surprise. Since Aztec times, the *tianguis* has been the economic heart of the Mexican pueblo, at once a place to barter goods and services, eat local dishes, and visit with friends. Traditionally, markets are the cheapest places to buy arts and crafts, regional clothing, foodstuffs, herbs, leather bags, and silver.

Only a few of the *mercados* in the D.F. have English-speaking shopkeepers and accept credit cards, however. If you possess a sense of adventure but just don't have the time to travel into the interior of the country, you can pay a guide to take you around some of these; you'll be able to pay for his time and car on the money you save. More important, you'll take home the memory of a real Mexican shopping spree.

The shops below are discussed first by type and then by neighborhood.

Crafts and Antiques Markets

The easiest market to shop is the **Centro Artesanal Buenavista** at Aldama 187, just off Insurgentes Norte near the Buenavista metro station and a few blocks east of the Guerrero station. The Centro is more like an American supermarket than a Mexican crafts market, and the prices are higher than in other markets; the vendors here welcome major credit cards, and there's even a place for your guide to sip coffee while you browse through the mammoth warehouse containing more than 80,000 items. Regional specialties such as carved lacquered chests from Olinala (in Guerrero), black pottery from San Bartolo Coyotepec (in Oaxaca), and copperware from Santa Clara del Cobre (in Michoacán) are available in abundance and at fair prices, and the selection of blown glass, brass, ceramics, silver jewelry, tablecloths, regional clothing, and gold (by the gram) is as good as in the Zona Rosa shops. Prices are fixed, and the vendors at the market will pack your purchases efficiently and get them to their destination safely. English is spoken.

If you're looking for a little adventure and have time to bargain, you will do better at **El Mercado de la Ciudadela**, at the corner of Balderas and Ayuntamiento, just a few blocks south of Alameda Park. Built in a former fortress, the market has two *fondas* where you can take a break and drink a beer or order a *comida*. Oaxacan Indians dressed in red *huipiles* sit on the ground, their offspring crawling around their feet as they work diligently on backstrap looms weaving bedspreads, tablecloths, and serapes. In the dozens of workshops inside the peach-colored walls, everything from silver baubles and hand-blown glass to Huichol beaded jewelry and rugs is being crafted as you wander among the more than 250 stalls here brimming with native handicrafts. Some shop operators will accept Visa or MasterCard, none American Express; most will honor traveller's checks and U.S. dollars. English here is limited to the basics, but nowhere else can you find such a well-priced and varied selection of masks (stall 65), copper (stall 80A), handmade guitars (stall 81), lacquerware (stall 60), traditional native clothing (stall 77), leather products (stall 85), and silver (stalls 30 and 82).

In the Zona Rosa itself is the **Mercado de Insurgentes**, with more than 200 vendors who know what travellers like and are eager to accommodate them. (The entrances to the market are on Calle Liverpool and Calle Londres.) This is an especially reliable bazaar for purchasing silver jewelry and native clothing. Bargaining is expected, and many stalls accept credit cards.

The **Saturday Antiques Market**, on Calle Florencia near the Reforma, is a flea market that sets up once a week on a patio in front of some antiques shops. As a rule, antiques are overpriced in Mexico, but there is always the possibility of coming up with an unexpected treasure that makes the hunt worthwhile.

The **Mercado de Antigüedades de la Lagunilla** (Sunday Thieves' Market) is located two blocks east of Paseo de la Reforma Norte and the equestrian statue of José Martí, beginning on Calle Rayón and stretching east for dozens of blocks. Amid the tangle of booths selling imported video and audio cassettes, foreign cheeses, hair spray, U.S.-made candy, blue jeans, Ray-Bans, and offbeat items too numerous to mention, you'll find some genuine antiques—and some possibly stolen from churches, so be careful. The vendors know what they have and offer few bargains as a result, but don't hesitate to quibble over the price of an item.

Clinging to the walls on either side of this labyrinth of stalls are Indians who have brought their wares—masks, bark paintings, wooden fish with pastoral scenes sketched on their sides, and the like—from their villages to sell to the buyers of the various crafts shops. The prices for these goods are generally very reasonable.

The **Bazar Sábado**, in an old colonial mansion on the northwest corner of the Plaza de San Jacinto in San Angel (see the main narrative above), was founded in 1960 by two imaginative entrepreneurs who wanted to give highly specialized artisans an arena in which to display their unusual crafts. At first staged in a small house in the neighborhood, the venture quickly outgrew its original setting as it mushroomed into a collective embracing more than 200 individual operations. Eventually the founding partners purchased the building in which it now resides, renovated it, and opened a new and improved Bazar Sábado in 1965, initiating in the process a Saturday tradition that has delighted countless visitors to the D.F.

The bazaar sprawls around a jacaranda-shaded patio where delicious Mexican cuisine geared to tourists' tastes is served buffet style. There is, in addition, a very good brunch served from 10:00 A.M. to noon and a more elegant sit-down lunch starting at 1:00 P.M., the latter accompanied by an excellent marimba band.

Inside, the bazaar is a two-story maze of cramped stalls. For the first-time visitor it's all but impossible to get oriented, and the polite but determined crowds of browsers leave many people feeling as if they'd gotten stuck in a revolving door. Don't despair; the bazaar is not as big as it sometimes seems, and the patio is never far away.

Government Arts and Crafts Stores

To promote the production of regional arts and crafts as well as to help artisans finance their work, the federal government and some state governments run their own shops. **FONART** shops (FONART is an acronym for the Spanish for "National Fund to Promote Arts and Crafts") can be found throughout the country, as well as at five locations in Mexico City: Avenida Juárez 89, Centro; Londres 136, Zona Rosa; Insurgentes Sur 1630 (in the basement of the Siqueiros Cultural Polyforum); Avenida de la Paz 37, San Angel (within walking distance of the Bazar Sábado); and Patriotismo 691, Mixcoac. (Mixcoac is a middle-class neighborhood a few blocks from the Plaza México bullring. There's not much here other than the FONART shop, so you'll probably want to take a taxi if you go.) The items for sale vary, but normally there is a good selection of ceramics, jewelry, regional clothing, and glassware. FONART shops accept all credit cards.

Located directly across from Alameda Park at Avenida Juárez 44, in a 16th-century structure that was originally the church of Corpus Christi, the **National Museum of Folk Arts**

and Crafts has a section open from 10:00 A.M. to 2:00 P.M. and again from 3:00 to 6:00 P.M. where you can choose from among the best for-sale display of regional clothing in town. There are also wonderful toys, jewelry, and seasonal arts here; at Christmastime an assortment of *nativitas* is for sale in ceramic or tin versions, and in November the museum has the best *calaveras* (skeletons) in the D.F.

CASART, Avenida Juárez 18C, was specifically set up to promote the artisans of the state of Mexico. This is one of the better places in the D.F. to purchase a set of unleaded ceramic dishes from Valle de Bravo or to find original items from Metepec, where villagers produce charming ceramic pieces.

An excellent sampling of the offerings of Michoacán, also a notable producer of crafts, can be found at the **Casa de las Artesanías de Michoacán**, Campos Elíseos 199 and Temístocles in Polanco, in front of the Stouffer Presidente Chapultepec and Nikko México hotels. The region's blue-and-white ceramics (popular with Mexican decorators), copper pots with silver filigree, hand-crocheted table coverings, and carved wood columns and chests are among the many tasteful items for sale here.

Arts and Crafts Stores

Located at the corner of Calles Ayuntamiento and Dolores, four blocks south of Alameda Park, the **Mercado de Curiosidades Mexicanos San Juan** is a modern city-run arts and crafts market, and an especially good option for travellers who have grown weary of the communication barrier, as most of the vendors speak a passable English and are willing to bargain. Stall 142, on the second floor, sells silver by the gram and semiprecious stones by the carat; stall 160 offers a huge selection of easily packed bark paintings. Good buys in leather products, silver jewelry, and hammocks also abound.

The **Galería Reforma** is the largest handicraft bazaar in the capital, if not the entire country. Located two traffic circles north of the intersection of Paseo de la Reforma and Avenida Juárez, this block-long store sells every conceivable handicraft item, all of them beautifully displayed. Allow at least an hour to browse through the countless aisles before you begin serious shopping, and don't forget your wallet: The prices here are reasonable, but there are no great bargains.

Feder's, at Lago Murítz 67, about a 15-minute cab ride north of the Zona Rosa, is difficult to find on your own, but most taxi drivers will know the spot. A restored 19th-century mansion houses this factory outlet, which offers a good selection of beautifully colored hand-blown glass and intricately designed wrought-iron vases, lamps, goblets, candelabra, and tables. Felipe Derflingher, the congenial owner-designer, has received numerous international awards for his creations. Expert packers, Feder's ships worldwide. (Feder's also has a stall at the Bazar Sábado; see Craft and Antiques Markets above.)

Located at Carretones 5, a 20-minute taxi ride north of the Zona Rosa and a bit off the beaten path, the large **Avalos** factory (taxi drivers sometimes refer to it as "Carretones") is well worth making an extra effort to visit. This is where most of the hand-blown glassware you'll see in the better Mexico City shops and restaurants is made. The brothers Avalos, Francisco and Camilo, along with their sister, Estela, who manages the retail shop on the premises, are heirs to a tradition started by their grand-uncles over a century ago. Estela will gladly arrange a free tour of the factory for interested visitors; she will also see to it that your purchases are well packed and shipped safely to the destination of your choice.

The Popular Markets

If it weren't for these *tianguis* (where every shopper gets a wholesale price) it would be impossible for most Mexicans to weather their country's ongoing financial crisis. Although they appear to enjoy making crafts, most Mexicans don't buy them. Instead, they prefer to decorate their homes with imported foreign items.

The **Mercado de Sonora**, at Avenida Fray Servando and Calle San Nicolas, about 6 km (4 miles) due east of Chapultepec Park, sells all you need to cast or uncast a spell, which is why it's affectionately known as "the Witches' Market." Vendors at some 30 stalls here hawk amulets, dried bats, good- and bad-luck candles, soap to make you rich, wreaths of garlic to protect your home against the dreaded *envidia* (envy), dried hummingbirds to make a man irresistible to the opposite sex, live animals for sacrificial purposes, medicinal herbs, and decks of tarot cards. The market also abounds with cheap ceramics, toys by the dozen, chickens, ducks, geese, songbirds, iguanas, baskets, and party supplies.

The **Mercado Cuauhtémoc**, at Río Lerma and Río Danubio, behind the Sheraton María-Isabel, is a small neighborhood fruit and vegetable market where you can sample Mexican cheeses and choose from a great variety of seasonings, among other things.

Inside the enormous **Mercado de la Lagunilla Unidad de Ropas**, located at República de Ecuador and Allende, a few blocks northwest of the Zócalo, you'll find enough clothing for sale to dress a regiment, including a variety of regional headwear, serapes, flamenco dresses, and authentic peasant skirts and blouses (not to mention such necessities as a chicken suit, complete with papier-mâché mask). You can also purchase tutus and tulle butterfly wings for your ballet-student daughter, as well as Superman, Batman, or Spiderman outfits. If you wish, Señor José Alducin (booths 89 and 90) will outfit you as any bird, complete with real feathers. He also makes normal clothing to order. At Typicos Estelita, in the same market (booth 87), you can transform yourself into a mouse, skunk, elephant, or mariachi musician. Esperanza Garcia (booth 134) sells all kinds of dresses, including eye-catching tango and Charleston outfits. (She also makes clothing for dolls.) Be sure to bring your measurements and a translator, however.

Nearby at Calle Allende 84 between Repúblicas de Honduras and Ecuador is the famed Mexican mask store, **Galería Eugenio**, a treasure house of dragons, goblins, religious statues, antique carvings, and, of course, masks. Señor Eugenio claims to have 10,000 in stock, and even if he's exaggerating a bit, it would take you a few days just to sort through those on display from floor to ceiling in the various rooms here.

Department Stores

There are only two department stores in the D.F. worth mentioning. Puerto Liverpool is less trendy than the Palacio de Hierro, but both are hipper than the American entry, Sears. The block-long **Puerto Liverpool**, with entrances on Avenida Horacio and Mariano Escobedo, the eastern boundary of the Polanco district, is a 10-minute walk north of the Camino Real hotel. The downtown **Palacio de Hierro** (Iron Palace) is located on the corner of 16 de Septiembre and Isabel la Católica, a few blocks west of the Zócalo, in a huge 17th-century structure. There's also a branch closer to the Zona Rosa at Durango and Salamanca. Both stores cater to people of some means, and international credit cards are welcomed. English-speaking salespeople are available upon request at both.

Perisur is the largest, most modern shopping mall in the entire country. It's located just north of the Cuicuilco archaeological site, about a 30-minute taxi ride south of the Zócalo via the Periférico Sur, the main highway to Cuernavaca.

Gifts for People With Everything

Yarn paintings created by the Huichol Indians of northwest Mexico make great one-of-a-kind gifts. Following the outlines of traditional designs (with plenty of leeway for personal expression), lengths of brightly colored yarn are glued to a board. Shooting stars, shamans, blue cows—the subject matter is uniquely Huichol and as fascinating as their culture (which, among other things, embraces the use of natural hallucinogenics such as peyote and "magic" mushrooms).

The Huichols also turn out a variety of ceremonial masks distinguished by their intricate beadwork. Generally speaking, masks are a plentiful folk-art item in Mexico, and enterprising itinerant middlemen roam the countryside buying the "used" masks of various indigenous people. These, in turn, are sold to shops catering to tourists throughout the Republic.

The **Tapetes Mexicanos**, in the Zona Rosa at Hamburgo 235, is the place to buy the world-renowned Temoaya rugs. Created by Otomí Indian artisans using an ancient technique, these hand-knotted wool carpets are known as "Mexican Persian rugs," with more than 50 styles and patterns inspired by Mexican folklore. Temoaya rugs are heirloom souvenirs that will last for generations.

Art Galleries

The **Zona Rosa** is the hub of the D.F.'s many outstanding art galleries, all of which remain open until 8:00 P.M.

Galería Arvil, Hamburgo 9 (between Florencia and Amberes), sells works by Mexico's finest artists, including Tamayo, Zuniga, and Toledo. Contemporary originals and prints, and a good art bookstore as well.

Galería del Circulo, Hamburgo 112, has works by Tamayo, Siqueiros, and Clement, as well as prints by Dalí and Picasso, among others.

Salon de Arte Plastica Mexicana, Hamburgo 202 and Havre 7, is a government-operated gallery featuring works by young Mexican artists.

Galería Tere Haas, Génova 2, is staffed by knowledgeable personnel, and specializes in paintings, graphics, and bronze sculptures. Zuniga, Castañeda, Amaya, Montoya, Nierman, among many others.

Galería Hardy, Génova 2J, is filled with contemporary art by talented unknowns and has an excellent art bookstore.

Galería Misrachi, Génova 20, features the masters— Tamayo, Siqueiros, Zuniga, Toledo, Coronel—as well as works by contemporary sculptors.

Galería Londres Chumacero, Estocolmo 30, has a fine collection of contemporary paintings, sculpture, and ceramics.

Galería Solaris, Estrasburgo 19B, sells paintings, sculpture, etchings, and tapestry by the likes of Bustamante, Sebastián, Griza, and Alcántara.

The **Asian Art Gallery**, Amberes 11, is noted for its fine collection of Oriental artwork, sculpture, jewelry, and handmade crafts.

Galería Honfleur, Amberes 14, sells contemporary paintings, sculpture, ceramics, and silver.

Galería Juan Martín, Amberes 17, has a large selection of strictly modern paintings by a variety of international artists.

Galería Aura, Amberes 38, sells contemporary paintings and sculptures by well-known artists.

Galería Estela Shapiro, Varsovia 23, at the western edge of the Zona Rosa, features works by internationally celebrated artists. The gallery also sponsors occasional shows by up-and-coming contemporary artists.

Near the Zona Rosa: Galería de Arte Mexicano, Milan 18, three short blocks southeast of the intersection of Reforma and Insurgentes, is one of the most prestigious galleries in the city. The owners choose their artists carefully and have their favorites, including such young Mexican artists as Pedro Friedenberg and Luis López Loza.

Galería Pecanis, Durango 186, a half dozen blocks south of the Zona Rosa, is a fine gallery featuring the work of lesser-known (but quality) Mexican artists. Contemporary paintings, engravings, and drawings make up the collection.

Casasola, Praga 16, a few blocks west of Calle Florencia at the western edge of the Zona Rosa, features a great photography collection of old Mexico, especially the Revolutionary period. You can have your purchases mounted while you wait.

Galería Summa Artis, on the mezzanine level of the Stouffer Presidente Chapultepec, is a chic gallery featuring the works of old Mexican masters as well as aspiring young artists. Paintings, sculpture, graphics, and signed and numbered lithographs fill out its impressive collection.

Coyoacán: You can find celebrated Mexican bullfight sculptor **Humberto Peraza Ojeda**'s works for sale at his Coyoacán studio, Cerra Blanco 14, Pedregal de San Francisco, about a half-hour's cab ride south of the Zona Rosa. The maestro has ranked among the world's elite artists for more than half a century now, and his sculptures have been given as gifts to a number of heads of state, including Ronald Reagan, Emperor Hirohito, and King Juan Carlos. By appointment only; Tel: 554-5955.

The Zona Rosa

Calle Amberes, one of the city's loveliest streets, is the location of several quality French restaurants as well as practically being an outdoor mall for designer boutiques: Guess? by Georges Marciano, Express, Aca Joe, Ruben Torres, and Ralph Lauren are just some of the well-known names you'll find here. Also here is Noi, a sophisticated dress shop for petites, and the ubiquitous Benetton. (At most of these boutiques international designer fashions are available for less than half their cost in New York or London.)

Tane, Amberes 70, with branches in the Camino Real, Nikko México, and Stouffer Presidente hotels; the San Angel Inn; at Edgar Allen Poe 68 (in Polanco); and in the Perisur shopping mall, is Mexico's most elegant jewelry and art shop, and a veritable museum of silver treasures. Tane specializes in handmade reproductions of antique pieces from around the world, and also sells sculptures by outstanding Mexican and international artists.

Los Castillo, with stores at Amberes 41, Londres 132, the Calinda Geneve Mexico, and Palmas 50 (next to the San Angel Inn), is the retail outlet of the famous Taxco silver dynasty, and offers quality merchandise at reasonable prices. Original designs in silver, gold, copper, and tin, as well as ceramic ware and furniture, make it an ideal choice for unusual gifts.

Paul Flato is an ex–New York City jeweler who has established an excellent reputation in Mexico City during his 25 years in business at Amberes 21 (Gloria Swanson was one of his celebrated clients). Ask to see his unusual Maximilian pendant watch.

Joyería Peyrelóngue, an exclusive jewelry store located right off the Reforma at Amberes 5, offers beautiful gold, silver, and crystal gift items, including Rolex, Cartier, and Mercie watches.

The place for onyx is **Muller's**, at the corner of Florencia and Londres. Guy Muller, owner and raconteur *extraordinaire,* will serve up interesting anecdotes about the role of onyx in Mexican history as you browse through his well-displayed selection of chess sets, book ends, tables, and sundry other items—all guaranteed not to stain. Muller's creations can be shipped safely to any U.S. or Canadian destination, and his is one of the few Zona Rosa shops open Sundays.

Girasol, Génova 39A, has been setting trends in women's fashion for more than two decades. Designer-owner Gonzalo Bauer utilizes appliqués and hand embroidery in bright colors. Also featured are his unusual, eye-catching leather accessories. There are branches in Polanco (Presidente Masaryk 318) and the Perisur shopping mall.

An old converted mansion at Hamburgo 203 is home for the **Mexican Opal Company**, where you can observe the opals being transformed into a variety of beautiful merchandise at the workshop on the premises. The well-trained sales staff speak English, Spanish, and Japanese. Tel: (5) 528-9263 for an appointment, be punctual, and ring the bell to the right of the always-locked entrance.

Flamma, in a restored Art Nouveau town house at the corner of Hamburgo and Florencia, sells only one product: candles. There are thousands of them, in a colorful, creatively designed array featuring superb craftsmanship with prices to match.

Coloniart is for the discriminating antiques collector only. Located at Estocólmo and Hamburgo, Coloniart offers no hidden bargains, only exquisite furniture, paintings, and sculpture, and all worth the exquisite prices. By appointment only. Tel: (5) 525-8928.

Marigen, with stores at Hamburgo 97A, Calle Copenhague 2C, and Calle Julio Verne 89 (in Polanco), sells the fashion creations of the internationally celebrated Josefa (very Mexican and very chic) and the jewelry of Donna Brown.

Polanco

The chic shopping district here on Avenida Presidente Masaryk only recently has come into its own. Nevertheless, the temples to designer clothing now number in double figures and include such notable establishments as **Esprit**, **Ferrioni Collection** (a Mexican operation that uses little Scottish terriers on everything in its line, from shoes to umbrellas), and **Amarras** (meaning "to tie" in Spanish and referring to the shop's practice of using the knot as the basic element of design in everything from its bathing suits to shorts and shirts).

For sophisticated leather goods in Polanco check out **Regina Romero**, at the corner of Presidente Masaryk and Julio Verne.

Auda Silversmiths, on Campos Elíseos, a few minutes' walk west of the Camino Real, is one of the best of the capital's many quality jewelry stores specializing in silver. Their creative designs, expertly crafted, are guaranteed to be conversation pieces. By appointment; Tel: (5) 511-1941.

Rodrigo R. Rivero Lake, at Campos Elíseos 199, opposite the rear entrances to the Nikko México and Stouffer Presidente hotels, is the most unusual of the capital's antiques shops. Señor Rivero, who speaks English, is a man with a mission: He searches the world for the rarest of collectibles. A love seat from India and ancient porcelain from China are two of the many eye-catching treasures on display. By appointment only; Tel: (5) 250-8673.

One of Mexico's most celebrated contemporary artists is Sergio Bustamante, the creator of stylized animal and bird sculptures in bronze, copper, and papier-mâché. He maintains a retail shop, the **Galería de Sergio Bustamante**, on the mezzanine of the Nikko México hotel, Campos Elíseos 204, and another in the Sheraton María-Isabel, Reforma 325. Consider his costly creations investments.

San Angel

Three of the most elegant shops in the D.F. can be found in this southern neighborhood near the San Angel Inn, where Altavista meets Diego Rivera and Santa Catarina: **Carlos Demicheles**, perhaps the most exciting Mexican designer on the international fashion scene today; **Aries**, for leather bags, valises, wallets, and portfolio cases; and **Tane** (see also the Zona Rosa), for exquisite silverware. Though they all can be found at other locations throughout the city, it is only here that the shops themselves are treasures of contemporary Mexican architecture. Other shopping meccas on Altavista are **HB Galería** for contemporary art; **Galería Kim** for contemporary art and sculpture; **Farre** for decorator housewares; and **Frattina** for women's designer originals.

Calle Madero

The D.F. is the nation's jewelry-making center. Today the old Calle de los Plateros (Street of the Silversmiths) is known as Calle Madero, but it remains faithful to its 16th-century origins: Shops specializing in custom-made silver and gold jewelry line the street from the Zócalo to Alameda Park.

Bazar del Centro

An old colonial mansion at Calle Isabel la Católica 30, just south of Calle Madero and a few minutes' walk from the Zócalo, is now a very pleasant three-level shopping center called the Bazar del Centro. **Aplijsa**, a prestigious jewelry store from Guadalajara, has opened a branch here and offers an outstanding assortment of jewelry in all price ranges. Other shops ringing the central patio feature quality silver, leather goods, ceramics, and a great variety of expertly crafted products from all over the country.

Salvador Sandoval, owner of both the Bazar del Centro and Aplijsa, purchased the building in 1985 and redesigned and refurbished the old mansion, retaining as much as possible of the original late-17th-century decor, including the entire façade, the iron railings, the exposed beams, and the brick walls. As a result, there is a dramatic contrast between the rather seedy neighborhood and what awaits shoppers behind the Bazar del Centro's massive doors. Tiled benches under graceful laurel trees dot the central patio, and often, during the day, artists work at their easels in view of the curious. In a rear patio more shops offer an assortment of arts and crafts, and a very comfortable pub, the **Cueva de Emiliano**, beckons the foot-sore with an ethnic setting and a decent margarita.

SIDE TRIPS FROM MEXICO CITY

CUERNAVACA, TAXCO, PUEBLA, TULA, VALLE DE BRAVO

By Robert Somerlott

The area around the capital has so much to offer that the problem becomes one of choosing among its many archaeological sites, villages, museums, caves, and colonial towns. In deciding, be aware that growth has smudged the luster of some places that once were more attractive.

Toluca, to the west, is one such example. Its famed market is commercial and common now, the modernized city itself of little interest. Not so the nearby pottery village of Metepec, which retains interest for its traditional ceramics, especially its *pulque* jars, trees-of-life, and earthen casseroles. South of Toluca, Malinalco, an Aztec temple site carved out of volcanic rock, draws archaeology buffs. And the scenic Valle de Bravo, though without archaeological sites and the like, is exceptional for an outdoorsy getaway vacation.

Cuernavaca, once an automatic choice, still has attractions, but it has its drawbacks, too, as we shall see. Likewise the famous old silver town of Taxco. The old spa town of Tehuacán can be crossed off your itinerary altogether now

that its resort hotel is shabby and neglected. The same can be said of the city of Pachuca, which is simply uninteresting.

Perhaps the most rewarding side trip in the area east of Mexico City, on the way to Veracruz on the Gulf coast, is Puebla, an early colonial town with very attractive ecclesiastical architecture, and nearby Cholula, a pre-Hispanic religious center.

Tlaxcala, while not of the highest interest, is nonetheless an appealing jaunt from Puebla for visitors who have the time. The archaeological zone of Cacaxtla, a short drive southeast of Tlaxcala, is noteworthy for its pre-Columbian murals.

The Museum of the Viceregal Period at Tepotzotlán and the archaeological zone at Tula can be visited either as a side trip from the capital or while you are en route to Querétaro and other northern colonial cities. Both are of somewhat specialized interest. North of Tula, and perhaps not appealing to everyone, is Ixmiquilpán: Though the town is unattractive, its ancient monastery contains some of the most unusual and fantastic murals in Mexico. Like Tula and Tepotzotlán, it is of special, rather than general, interest.

MAJOR INTEREST

Cuernavaca
Scenic beauty on the trip from Mexico City
Hotels and resorts
Pyrámide de Teopanzolco
Xochicalco ruins

Grutas de Cacahuamilpa

Taxco
Picturesque town scenes
Parroquia de Santa Prisca y San Sebastián
Silverwork

Puebla
Scenic beauty
Colonial buildings
Talavera ware
Imposing archaeological site at Cholula
Folk art church at Tonantzintla

Archaeological site of Cacaxtla, near Tlaxcala

North of Mexico City
Museo Nacional del Virreinata at Tepotzotlán
Toltec archaeological zone at Tula
Ixmiquilpán monastery

West of Mexico City
Scenic beauty
Picturesque town of Valle de Bravo
Folk pottery at Metepec
Aztec temples at Malinalco

Cuernavaca and Taxco are easy to combine in one swing south of the capital. The route can be varied by returning to Mexico City via Highway 55, Ixtapán de la Sal, Metepec, and the Toluca bypass. The small but unusual Aztec temple at Malinalco, an interesting sidelight, is also on this route. The trip, often done in one day, actually crowds two.

CUERNAVACA

The journey by car or bus to Cuernavaca from Mexico City takes from an hour and a half to two hours each way—depending on traffic—using the toll road, a route that passes through spectacular mountain scenery; the roadside settlements, on the other hand, look interesting from a distance but are unappealing on closer inspection. You'll want to make frequent stops to take in the views as the road first rises to magnificent heights, then plunges into the semitropical valley enfolding Cuernavaca.

Cuernavaca, now an industrial city of more than a million people, was a winter refuge that beckoned Aztec nobles, Cortés, Maximilian and Carlota, and a legion of their peers and admirers. Malcolm Lowry brought Cuernavaca's expatriate community vividly to life in *Under the Volcano*.

Today Mr. Lowry's famous title is much less appropriate: The great, beautiful volcano of Popocatépetl is obscured by a haze of pollution—not terrible, but becoming ominously frequent and serious due to industrial fumes and exhaust. Every weekend hordes of Mexico City residents flee to this verdant valley to draw breaths of air still relatively fresh. The weekend trippers arrive by auto, jamming the broad highways and overloading all facilities. Cuernavaca should therefore be avoided on weekends.

Along with traffic and industrialization, other menaces to charm have burgeoned: Kentucky Fried Chicken restaurants, electronic hullabaloo, a babel of signs, a glare of chrome and glass-box architecture. The so-called City of Eternal Spring can grate on all the senses at once. Yet there are attractions here, too, though often muffled or camouflaged.

Cuernavaca presents a paradox to the traveller: Two days can be too much here, and yet two weeks might not be enough, depending on how you approach this annoying city—and how you retreat from it.

The "eternal spring" of tourist brochures is almost true. In this Edenesque climate, a colony of retired Americans enjoys its comfort barricaded behind walls of high-priced real estate. Their affluent Mexican neighbors, who outnumber them by far, sip Scotch, not tequila, in residences where petals float on swimming pools and the servants are well trained.

Visitors will see no more of this than a cascade of bougainvillaea tumbling over the outside of a garden wall. Yet a few of the town's inns give a credible imitation of *la dolce vita*—and this is the reason for lingering. Rental houses and apartments, most of them attractive though high-priced, are available on a monthly or seasonal basis. Away from the congestion, life in Cuernavaca can be balmy.

The Central Plaza Area

The main square, or zócalo, is a small park with venerable shade trees and a graceful bandstand inherited from a more serene era. This is an inviting spot on weekday mornings or evenings, but bedlam when weekend visitors claim it. Adjacent is a more ample park that's alive with vendors and, sometimes, musicians. (The crafts displayed nearby are not local, and the markup is steep.)

Buildings facing the two public spaces range from ugly to acceptable; one of them, the **Palacio de Cortés**, is the city's most famous structure. This grim pile has been patriotically renamed the **Museo de Cuauhnáhuac**, recalling the original Aztec name of the city. (Spanish conquistadors found the word as unpronounceable in 1525 as modern travellers do today. Cuernavaca, which means "cow horn," was a stab at it.) The palace has been reconstructed so many times that it's hard to guess what it once looked like, although some old photos are displayed inside.

Hernán Cortés ordered the building's construction in 1527, having just received Cuernavaca as part of his personal fief. In the late 1920s Dwight Morrow, the U.S. ambassador to Mexico, who had a Cuernavaca residence, hit on the happy idea of commissioning the great Diego Rivera to paint murals in the old palace. Rivera took advantage of the commission to portray Mexico's history from the earliest days of its habitation through the Revolution of 1910, with an emphasis on the events of the Conquest. The results, exuberant and bold, are a national treasure; the rest of the museum pales in comparison.

One long block west of the plaza stands the **Templo de San Francisco**, begun in the mid-16th century. Here again we have a story of antiquity, destruction, and rebuilding. As in the palace, the murals inside the cathedral outshine the building itself. Very early and naïve frescoes show Spanish missionaries bound for Japan in a skiff, as perplexed sea creatures regard them with curiosity. The friars are also shown at their later martyrdom in Nagasaki.

El Museo Robert Brady, at Netzahualcóyotl 4, was established by the late artist Robert Brady in his former residence, which was once part of the cathedral complex. The Brady collection includes paintings, antique sculpture and furniture, and textiles, all presented as elements of a beautifully decorated home. The museum is open Thursdays and Fridays from 10:00 A.M. until 2:00 P.M. and from 4:00 to 6:00 P.M., and on Saturdays from 10:00 A.M. until 2:00 P.M.

For a simple lunch while exploring downtown, **Marco Polo**, a checked-tablecloth pizzeria facing the cathedral at Hidalgo 26, is a good choice.

Close at hand, the **Jardines de Borda** survive as a relic of the demolished palace of 18th-century silver king José de la Borda. The design is formal and attractive. Fluffy ducks preside at a pool, along one side of which is a porch with paintings portraying the love affair between Maximilian and a local beauty known as La India Bonita. Empress Carlota also resided here at the time, but neither gossip nor history has revealed what she thought of her husband's indiscretions.

Near the railroad station is the **Pirámide de Teopanzolco**, a small but interesting pre-Columbian structure that may well be 1,200 years old. Built by the Tlahuica people, who were later conquered by their distant cousins, the Aztecs, the temple was covered with earth by the local inhabitants of the area at the time of the Conquest in order to prevent its destruction at the hands of the Christians. Almost four centuries passed, during which time the hill became part of the landscape. Then, in 1910, artillery supporting the rebel Zapata was placed on top of the hill. The repeated firing of the artillery caused a mini-earthquake, dirt and rocks slid away, and the ancient temple was found—except that it was actually two temples, for one had been built over the other in the traditional manner.

Staying in Cuernavaca

Cuernavaca is replete with just-adequate hotels offering basic rooms to weekend visitors at inflated rates. A few places, none of them inexpensive, are special, however.

The luxury inn **Las Mañanitas**, a few blocks from the zócalo, is famed for its food, its rooms, and a glorious garden adorned with flamboyant birds. The restaurant is so popular that on weekends it causes traffic jams in the surrounding streets. The suites, with unnecessary but attractive fireplaces, are admirable.

In the hills known as Rancho de Cortés, about a 15-minute drive north of the center of town via Avenida Morelos and partially hidden on Calle Francisco Villa, is the **Calinda Cuernavaca Racquet Club**, which appears at first to be a posh country club in the colonial style. The nine tennis courts, four of them lighted, attract an international crowd, but the occupants of the 33 suites (with living rooms) are by no means all tennis addicts. The dining room, open to nonguests, is quite good, the service at night late and leisurely.

The **Hostería las Quintas**, much closer to town but still too far to walk, is less costly than the Racquet Club, less sporty, and even more beautiful in its tropical garden setting. The fine public restaurant is a lovely bower of blossoming shrubs.

Dining in Cuernavaca

Three of Cuernavaca's finest restaurants are in the hotels mentioned above; Las Mañanitas is especially recommended.

One of the best restaurants outside of the hotels is **La India Bonita**, at Morrow 6. Mexican food is so well presented in simple but attractive surroundings here that the place has become a Cuernavaca tradition. The prices are as pleasing as the savory spices. Tel: (731) 12-1266.

Harry's Grill, at Gutenberg 3 on the main plaza, is part of the faintly slapstick Carlos Anderson chain that specializes in collegiate humor and hearty fare. Moderate prices, good service. Tel: (731) 12-7679. Closed Mondays.

A café, ice cream parlor, and gift shop, **Sanborn's**, at the corner of Júarez and Abasolo, is another bland but reliable link in a national not-so-fast food chain.

Sumiya, in the area called Juitepec, 5 km (3 miles) south and west of town off the Cuautla road, bills itself as a replica of the Japanese imperial palace. Actually it is the former mansion of Woolworth heiress Barbara Hutton and once (briefly) the home of the Shah of Iran. The restaurant serves modified Japanese and international cuisine in surroundings that outshine the food. There's also disco dancing on Friday and Saturday nights. Reservations required; Tel: (731) 15-3055.

Tepoztlán

About 24 km (15 miles) northeast of Cuernavaca by a good highway (115D) is the village of Tepoztlán, with its twisting cobblestone streets, ancient ruins, and Aztec temples clinging to a steep slope. Tepoztlán kept its pre-Columbian heritage and language far longer than most villages in Mexico. In fact, as recently as a few decades ago it was still a magnet for anthropologists hoping to study the elements of the earlier culture that survived here. Today, Tepoztlán's isolation has been shattered by the outside world, yet despite the intrusion of souvenir shops, the hamlet remains both antique and primitive.

The **Templo y Exconvento de la Natividad de la Virgin María** (1559), a severe Dominican monastery dominating the center of town, is worth inspecting, especially the stone carving around the church portal. A small **museum** behind the monastery on Calle González displays some fine pottery and figurines, gifts from the noted archaeologist Carlos Pellicer.

On a steep hill above Tepoztlán the ancient temple of **Tepozteco** commands the heights and a sweeping panorama of mountains and valley. To get there follow Avenida Tepozteco, northeast of the municipal market, as it climbs the hill before dwindling to a rocky trail. Allow an exhausting hour for the ascent. The temple, which seems to have been dedicated to the bibulous god of pulque, a brewed alcoholic drink, is late Postclassic, built by people who were relatives and, later, subjects of the Aztecs. The zone closes at 4:30 P.M. sharp.

The **Hacienda Cocoyoc**, a few minutes' drive southeast of Tepoztlán on the Cuautla highway, is a big, sprawling resort set amid landscaped gardens, an old aqueduct, and falling water. Once a thriving sugar plantation, Cocoyoc was burned by Zapata during the Revolution, and was restored in the 1960s by the family that now owns it; amenities include a nine-hole golf course. Prices in this tropical retreat are just moderate enough to attract weekend crowds from the capital, but it is lovely on weekdays. Make sure your room or suite has good ventilation; Cocoyoc is warm.

The Ruins of Xochicalco

The words "pretty" and "delightful" are not ordinarily applied to pre-Columbian ruins. At Xochicalco no others serve so well. The site is beautifully situated in slightly rolling country broken by hills that are vivid green in the rainy season, brown and severe in the dry season—but always impressive no matter what time of year.

Xochicalco looks upon the heights of Mount Ajusco some 39 km (24 miles) southwest of Cuernavaca in the direction of Taxco, more than half the distance over a toll road and all of it paved. Take Mexico 95D toward Taxco and exit at the turnoff marked "Alpuyeca." Then follow signs (which are not prominent) to Las Grutas and Alpuyeca. Twelve kilometers (7½ miles) from the exit is the Xochicalco sign, where you turn right and climb the hill to the ruins. In Nahuatl, the Aztec language, the name means "House of Flowers"—highly appropriate, although what the original builders called their city (or themselves) is unknown.

This was not just a ceremonial center, but a true city of at least 10,000 people, and possibly twice that. Although much studied, the ruins remain shrouded in mystery. How did Maya-like figures, carvings, and glyphs arrive in this remote region so far from the main centers of Mayan culture? What kind of people lived here and left their sculptural calling cards? One important point is certain: Xochicalco was in flower at a time, about A.D. 700, when northern ceremonial and religious centers had been abandoned, and the flame of culture and learning had all but sputtered out in Mesoamerica. The comparison to European monasteries during the Dark Ages is irresistible. Was this the place where tradition and culture were preserved while barbarians ranged the land? It seems likely. The inhabitants of Xochicalco adopted the styles of earlier civilizations, such as Teotihuacán, changed them somewhat, then passed on these modified traditions as part of the foundation of a new culture and new ways of life that were established at Tula, quite a bit north of here, in the tenth century. The people of Xochicalco were both keepers and transmitters of that civilization.

The **Pirámide de la Serpeinte Emplumada** (Pyramid of the Plumed Serpent), the site's finest monument, displays superb relief sculpture—flowing lines in stone that are indeed as lithe as a serpent as they curve, coil, and finally rear up in fierce, dragonlike heads. An aristocratic figure, instantly recognizable as Mayan, sits crowned with a panache that blends perfectly with the long rhythms of the whole sculpture.

The site also boasts one of the finest ancient **ball courts** in Mexico, laid out in the usual shape of the letter I and more than 200 feet long. From the top of a partly excavated mound known as La Malinche, the view down toward a line of circular platforms is striking. A residential section elsewhere on the grounds comes outfitted with a steam bath. Walls and fortifications protect the impressive area now called the Acropolis.

Grutas de Cacahuamilpa

Between Taxco and Cuernavaca, and easily reached from either, is Cacahuamilpa (kah-kah-wah-MEEL-pah) Caves National Park. The park's enormous corridors and chambers form the largest known cave system in Mexico, and are comparable in extent to the Carlsbad Caverns in the United States.

The entrance to the *grutas* is an awesome mountainside gap that eerily resembles a gigantic architectural structure. The halls and connecting corridors beyond it unfold like a lunar landscape amid fantastic formations of stalactites and stalagmites.

The empress Carlota visited these caves in 1866 and wrote on a wall, "Maria Carlota reached this point." Eight years later, a man instrumental in driving her from Mexico, President Lerdo de Tejada, added to the same wall, "Sebastian Lerdo de Tejada went farther." Today conducted tours, in Spanish and lasting about an hour and a half, leave frequently from the entrance. Admission is restricted to escorted groups, but those suddenly struck by claustrophobia can turn back at any time and find their own way out.

To drive to the caves from Cuernavaca, a distance of 74 km (46 miles), follow the route to Xochicalco (see above), then continue past the archaeological zone on Mexico 166 for 25 km (16 miles). The caves are just before the junction of Highways 166 and 55. The trip, once you are past Cuernavaca's urban sprawl, is pleasant and scenic. For bus service, take the Zacatepec–México line leaving Cuernavaca's Pullman bus terminal. Bus service from Taxco is provided by the Flecha Roja line.

TAXCO

Located about 80 km (50 miles) southwest of Cuernavaca, Taxco, a picturesque and photogenic colonial silver town, has been rendered much less appealing to visitors by its very attractiveness and proximity to the capital. Tour buses belching exhaust bear down on its tiny plaza like predatory monsters. Day trips from as far as Acapulco, where tourists are misled by promises of exploration of a "colonial gem," fill its streets with bewildered shoppers. What they get instead is hours of travel and about 45 minutes at their destination. The bus driver is bribed to halt at a certain silver shop, then the herding—soon followed by the roundup for departure—begins. The town somehow manages to accommodate these day-trippers, who are, after all, its bread and butter, but much is lost by the crowding.

Another evil effect of living on tourism is the sense one gets of a town too spiffed up, too conscious of its own image. Taxco, with its white paint and black signs, has an unnatural uniformity akin to the waxy quality of a film set; it does not seem to be a living town. Still, it is undeniably picturesque, even romantic. And while this is especially true of the downtown area—things loosen up away from the town center—downtown is what everyone goes to see. In fact, that really is all there *is* to see, except for strolls through old neighborhoods that are quaint but unimposing. Such a stroll quickly makes it clear that Taxco's silver wealth did not stay in Taxco, but instead went to erect mansions elsewhere.

Besides silver, Taxco has another treasure: the **Parroquia** (parish church) **de Santa Prisca y San Sebastián**, which lifts its magnificent spires to the glory of God and God's self-proclaimed partner, a French miner named José de la Borda.

Taxco is the oldest mining town in North America and dates back to the days when Mixtec craftsmen hammered its silver into ornaments for Aztec nobles. Of course, the conquistadors were overjoyed to seize its mines, and the serpentine, corkscrew byways of today's town are a reminder of the meandering mining village that tumbled haphazardly down the mountain slope in the 16th century.

The output of silver during those years was substantial but hardly fantastic. Then, in 1716, José de la Borda wandered into town and struck it rich. Grateful, Borda presented the Almighty with the most opulent temple he could concoct. "God gives to Borda, and Borda gives to God," he announced, marking the score even. The church was begun in 1751 and completed in 1758, with the best Mexican architects, painters, and carvers of the day kept busy on it.

Ever since, Santa Prisca has been hailed as the apogee of 18th-century Mexican architecture. In 1945 Manuel Toussaint, Mexico's pioneer art historian, wrote: "A homogeneous work of art, and of a beauty which cannot be described, the church of Taxco dominates the delightful town . . . the interior is an astonishing Churrigueresque work of art, madness is held within bounds . . . reason inexorably controls the effect, and fantasy develops just so far as the restraints of reason permit." In 1991 Santa Prisca was burglarized and religious art valued at $2 million stolen. The thieves left behind many of its finest treasures, however, and first-time visitors will be unaware of the tragic loss.

Over the decades the silver in the mountains was steadily mined out. Although Taxco still mines some silver, its modern connection with the metal dates from the 1930s, when William Spratling, a North American writer and artist, introduced silversmithing as a local art and industry.

Buying Silver in Taxco

Taxco's centrally located silver shops are reliable; buyers will not have to worry that some base metal has been palmed off on them. Still, as with anything expensive, you should be cautious; check that the product bears the ".925" stamp, the government's requirement for purity in silver.

Silver as metal is sold by weight, the price set on the world commodity markets. All costs above weight should involve design and *real* overhead. Some shops on Taxco's Avenida John F. Kennedy add a guide or bus driver's commission without mentioning it. Among the better shops in the zócalo area, though, there is little difference in price above weight, and the advantage of buying in downtown Taxco is not price but the range of options, with more than 100 silver outlets to choose from. **Emma**, Calle Celso Muñoz 4, gleams with a wide selection of smaller gifts and remembrance items. Larger works of quality will be found at **Los Ballesteros**, Calle Soto la Marina 5, and **Los Castillo**, Plazuela Bernal 10. Many other good establishments are sprinkled throughout the area.

Agua Escondida, William Spratling 4A, is convenient for lunch or snacks when you're shopping or visiting the sights downtown.

Staying in Taxco

The cottages at the **Hacienda del Solar** perch atop a mountain in rustic but definitely aristocratic surroundings. Two meals a day are served in its dining room—the city's best restaurant—which is open to the public. The view is magnificent, and the cuisine features accents of Italy. The Hacienda is located 3½ km (2 miles) south of town just off the Acapulco road, Highway 95, which makes a U; near the tourism office is a short street leading to the hotel. You'll need a car or taxi to get there from the center of town. Cab fare is about the equivalent of $1.

The **Hotel Santa Prisca** is conveniently located one long block west of the famous church in the center of town.

Simple, inexpensive, but attractively colonial, this pleasant inn also houses a commendable dining room.

The **Restaurant La Taberna** serves good international cuisine at reasonable prices. It's located next to the post office on the main street, a thoroughfare whose name changes often and arbitrarily.

PUEBLA

In Puebla you feel close to the sky, a sensation that stems from more than being in one of the highest cities in the world. Happily, despite the fumes of the ubiquitous traffic, the air here is still unusually clear. But it's really the four great volcanoes towering above the plain—especially Popocatépetl, the Aztecs' "Smoking Mountain," and Iztaccíhuatl, their "Sleeping Woman"—that do the most to create this perception of elevation. Their perpetually snow-covered summits do indeed inspire that familiar fantasy of being able to reach out and touch them.

The 95-km (59-mile) drive from Mexico City east to Puebla via toll road 150 winds gently through pine-clad slopes and rugged outcroppings of rock that afford spectacular vistas. Puebla stands at the head of a fertile valley along the main trade route to Veracruz and the Gulf of Mexico. The location is strategic; every invading army—whether Spanish, French, or American—has had to storm the town on its way to the capital.

The people of Puebla are called *poblanos,* and the adjective *poblano* is especially linked to their tile-encrusted buildings, a style of architectural decoration gone joyously mad with color. They are just as proud of their *poblano* dress and style, and will boast to anyone who will listen that *mole* sauce, made with chiles and rich but not sweet chocolate, was invented here. Pride is also taken in the city's grid design, in which *avenidas* run east and west, *calles* north and south. This checkerboard of streets was made possible by the fact that there was no native city here before the Spanish arrived—an anomaly in the history of the Conquest—as well as by the fact that the land was flat. Puebla also has more churches than any other place in Mexico, which is either the cause of or the direct result of *poblano* solemnity.

Yes, this is a serious town, where eyebrows are frequently raised. Despite the city's apparently staid demeanor, however, a current of passion runs through *poblano* life. The thousands of students at its large university are second to

Puebla

0 — yards — 500
0 — meters — 500

N

- Museo de La Intervención

CALLE 7 NORTE
CALLE 5 NORTE
CALLE 3 NORTE

BLVD. HEROES DEL CINCO DE MAYO

AV. 20 PONIENTE
AV. 18 PONIENTE
- Exconvento de Santa Mónica
AV. 16 ORIENTE
AV. 14 ORIENTE
AV. 12 ORIENTE
CALLE 2 NORTE
CALLE 4 NORTE
AV. 10 ORIENTE

To Veracruz →

AV. 8 ORIENTE
CALLE 6 NORTE
AV. 6 ORIENTE
- Templo de Santo Domingo
- Casa del Alfeñique
AV. 4 ORIENTE
- El Parián
AV. 2 ORIENTE
- Palacio Municipal
- Templo de La Compañía
AV. REFORMA
- Plaza de la Constitución
AV. M. AVILA CAMACHO
← To Cholula
AV. 3 ORIENTE
- Universidad de Puebla
- Zócalo
- Cathedral
AV. 5 ORIENTE
AV. 7 ORIENTE
AV. 9 ORIENTE
AV. 11 ORIENTE
AV. 13 ORIENTE
AV. CINCO DE MAYO
AV. 15 ORIENTE
CALLE 2 SUR
CALLE 4 SUR
AV. 17 ORIENTE
BLVD. HEROES DEL CINCO DE MAYO
AV. 19 ORIENTE
AV. 21 PONIENTE

CALLE 7 SUR
CALLE 5 SUR
CALLE 3 SUR

AV. 25 PONIENTE REVOLUCION

AV. 29 PONIENTE

none in the vehemence and violence of their protests. The workers at the auto factory, the largest Volkswagen plant in the world, belong to a voluble and fierce union. The *poblanos,* like the volcanoes around them, are dignified and quiescent—but not always, and certainly not below the surface.

Visitors to Puebla should be prepared to see an abundance of ecclesiastical architecture, impressive and opulent rather than beautiful. There is fine ceramic work here as well, especially the glazed Talavera ware, and some residences flaunt tile work—gleaming and gay, a flash of fantasy—as exterior decoration. The museums are worth visiting but not worth lingering in. Puebla and nearby Cholula reward the visitor who spends a day between them, but only merit more time if you have a car and can explore a larger area.

Downtown Puebla

The city's main attractions lie within walking distance of the zócalo, the **Plaza de la Constitución**, a central square that ranks among the most spacious plazas in Mexico. It was planned, as was the whole downtown, by a Franciscan, Fray Julián Garcés, the first bishop of Tlaxcala, who had been assigned the task of locating a new city. According to legend, His Grace was blessed by the nocturnal visit of two angels whom he watched pace off with pole and line a plain ringed with volcanoes. Thus the city was positioned, and so acquired its full name, Puebla de los Angeles, in honor of its angelic surveyors.

American visitors walking through the plaza usually have no idea they are crossing a spot that should be hallowed ground in U.S. history. It was here, in 1847, that General Winfield Scott seized the city after the battle of Cerro Gordo. While Scott's main force moved on to attack Mexico City, Colonel Thomas Childs was left behind in Puebla's zócalo with a small group of U.S. wounded. Colonel Childs, with foresight, rounded up some cattle and a flock of sheep, then spurred his injured men to barricade their camp. Their work was hardly finished when the Mexican general Santa Anna attacked with 2,500 men, employing artillery and posting snipers on roofs that still overlook the plaza today.

The local populace was jubilant at the imminent destruction of the invaders, cheering the besiegers and wildly ringing the bells of the city's 60 churches and convents. The staunch Americans held their terrible position for 30 days, however, until the approach of a relieving army put Santa Anna to flight.

The bluish-gray **cathedral** looms over one side of the zócalo, a grim shadow on an otherwise lighthearted space. Twin towers, too far apart, impart a stumpy look to the structure. The gloomy exterior hides a splendid nave replete with marble, lovely wrought iron, and admirable woodwork. The **Palacio Municipal**, the second most impressive structure on the zócalo, was built at the turn of the century in the Spanish Renaissance style—yet another example of the city's long-lived admiration of Spanish models.

It is a relief to leave the sternness of the palace and cathedral and discover the totally delightful **Casa del Alfeñique**, at Avenida 4 Oriente and Calle 6 Norte. The "House of Almond Cake" is indeed a confection, with red tiles accented by black iron work, the whole tied together with sugar-colored masonry to create a *poblano* fantasy. Inside is a regional museum with an emphasis on pre-Columbian history and the indigenous costumes of the area, including *china poblana* dress, the most famous garb of the city.

El Parián, a market across the street from the Casa del Alfeñique, is a cobblestone mall where crafts and almost-crafts are sold. Ceramics are a good buy here, but you should be cautious about the displays of onyx boxes, figurines, bookends, and chessboards—most of the work is imitation and mass produced. The greens and shades thereof, sometimes palmed off as jade, are colored by dye, not nature.

A Churrigueresque riot of decoration at Calle 4 Norte and Avenida M. Avila Camacho, the **Templo de la Compañía** is also the tomb of the original *china poblana,* a not especially fascinating character, but one who looms inordinately large in the city's collective consciousness. She was perhaps a princess, perhaps Chinese, and perhaps kidnapped by pirates who sold her in Acapulco in 1620. Bought by a Puebla merchant family that later adopted her because of her beauty, sweetness, and virtue, she taught sewing in the Chinese manner, invented the embroidered peasant dress named after her, and was denied her wish to become a nun. Eventually, she devoted an already virtuous life to care of the poor and sick.

The **Capilla del Rosaro** in the **Templo de Santo Domingo**, two blocks north of the zócalo at Cinco de Mayo and Avenida 4 Oriente, is the high point of *poblano* religious ornamentation: Lustrous gold leaf, brilliant tiles, and enamel dazzle the eye. The sculpted Virgin on the altar, spangled in jewels, seems dressed by Tiffany's.

The **Exconvento de Santa Mónica**, six blocks farther north along Cinco de Mayo, was built in the early years of the 17th century as a sort of retreat where noble matrons could be properly chaperoned when their husbands were out of town. The women of Puebla rejected the idea, however, and the building, ironically, became a reformatory for prostitutes. Later it was turned into a convent-college.

The convent went "underground" after passage of the Reform Laws abolishing Church property in 1857, with the nuns remaining secluded in their 39-room establishment. Entrance to the convent was through a secret door in an adjoining house. It was closed by the government in 1934, and is now a museum devoted to religious art and sculpture, as well as to the lives of the sisters. Despite the hocus-pocus of the hidden door, the "secret" was doubtless more widely known in Puebla than is generally admitted today. You can enter the convent at Avenida 18 Poniente 103, just off Cinco de Mayo.

The **Museo de la Intervención**, a military museum housed in the Fuerte de Loreto, a 30-minute walk northeast of downtown, is mainly of patriotic interest to Mexicans, but military and history buffs will find an interesting diorama of the famous battle fought here on May 5, 1862. On that day badly outnumbered Mexicans, some armed with guns that had seen service at Waterloo almost 50 years earlier, turned back a heavily armed spit-and-polish French army. The battle itself, which is an involved and fascinating story, is remembered throughout Mexico every year on the fifth of May (Cinco de Mayo), a legal holiday. To visit Loreto and its sister fort of **Guadalupe**, take a cab from the zócalo or a "Fuerte" bus at Calle 16 de Septiembre and Avenida 9 Oriente. It's a short trip, and the fare will be inexpensive.

Talavera Ware

Talavera ware, both as dishes and as tiles, is almost synonymous with the Puebla area of Mexico, although it is also made elsewhere.

The product, unlike most folk pottery, is durable—a quite un-Mexican quality. Fragility, after all, is part of the national fatalism: Dishes will be broken anyhow, so why worry too much or fight too hard to prevent it? Investing in Talavera, on the other hand, demands faith in the future and optimism about the human condition.

Talavera is made of a mix of three clays, which used to be

kneaded together for days by men dancing barefoot in clay pits. Today machines have replaced the Talavera jig in more populated areas. Either way, the mixed clay is ripened for six months, kept under a damp cloth, and rekneaded every few days. (This, too, goes against the national grain—witness the quick methods of wine- and cheese-making generally used in Mexico.)

Finally, the clay is wheel-thrown or molded, and the tile or vessel allowed to dry in the shade for days. Slow, low-temperature firing comes next. Prayers are chanted before and during the opening of the kiln, and the Blessed Sacrament is invoked, even in today's highly commercial operations. Every piece is tested to ring true, and those with a faulty tone are thrown away. The glaze applied includes honey; the final product is cream-white. Traditionally, only two colors are used to decorate the piece: always white, with blue or yellow in older works, and a bolder color in modern pieces.

Puebla's Talavera factories usually will not admit visitors, but a few have found on-premises sales to be profitable. Inquire about admission at the tourism office, Avenida 5 Oriente 5, beside the cathedral. Or simply try at **Casa Rugiero**, 18 Poniente 111, or **La Guadalupaña**, 4 Poniente 911.

An especially interesting place to see fine Talavera is in the **Exconvento de Santa Rosa**, Calle 3 Norte 1203. The **Museo de Arte Popular Poblano** housed in the former convent is devoted to arts, crafts, and the kitchen—surprisingly fascinating displays. Not all the pottery is Talavera, but some of the best is. Any Puebla church will also have its own fine examples.

A score of shops in Puebla sell the ware, though not all of it is of high quality. Remember: The whiter the base, the better the work. Any piece with smoke marks should be rejected.

Staying and Dining in Puebla

El Mesón del Angel is Puebla's most attractive hotel, with beautiful grounds, balconied rooms, and a very good dining room open to the public. Its bold beams and rock-and-glass walls give it a California feeling, while its location northwest of the city center at Hermanos Serdan 807, almost at the toll gate entrance to Highway 190D (the highway to Mexico City), makes it especially appealing to motorists passing through as well as to business executives visiting the industrial zone. For other visitors, however, it is a long way from the center of town.

The **Hotel Lastra**, also of the first rank but older and less expensive than El Mesón, is in a quiet neighborhood about 3 km (2 miles) northeast of the zócalo at Calzada de los Fuertes 2633. The roof garden is lovely, but the rooms vary in quality in this traditional, much-remodeled inn. Its good restaurant is open to the public.

On the zócalo itself, the **Hotel Royalty Centro** is a convenient, comfortable, and pleasant choice—depending on which rooms are available. Some are cramped and stuffy; the suites are worth the higher rate. At its best the Royalty is quite nice, and the indoor-outdoor restaurant offers a satisfactory breakfast.

The **Hotel del Portal** is another pleasant if unpretentious hotel with an excellent plaza location. The rooms at the rear, though smaller, are quieter, and the ambience is colonial. The Del Portal has a bar and restaurant.

Poblano food is the specialty of the simple, attractive, and popular **Fonda Santa Clara**, Avenida 3 Oriente 307. The *mole* here is outstanding.

The fare at the **Restaurante del Parián**, Avenida 2 Oriente 415, rises above the threats of the "quaint" decor and menus printed on pieces of wood: The coyness, thankfully, does not extend to the fine *poblano* cuisine, with the *adobo* and *pipian* sauces especially noteworthy. (*Adobo* is a tangy blend of cumin, sour orange, chile, and a variety of other spices, as inspiration dictates; *pipian* also varies but starts out with a base of chiles and sesame seeds.)

Regional cooking in Puebla is usually tasty and tangy, but "Continental" dishes seem beyond local abilities. Visitors hungry for international fare should go to the Lastra or El Mesón del Angel, whose rather elegant restaurants are not limited to regional selections, although these are well prepared, too.

Cholula

The town of Cholula adjoins Puebla, the two now virtually one as a result of growth. In its pre-Hispanic heyday, however, Cholula was a center of trade as well as an important religious center, both a holy city and a place of pilgrimage dedicated to Quetzalcóatl, the Plumed Serpent. Its settlement dates back to 500 B.C., and a city-state (probably a satellite of Teotihuacán, though a very important one that outlived Teotihuacán by centuries) flourished here between A.D. 200 and 300. Various native conquerors appeared in later centuries.

Cortés, often mistaken for the god Quetzalcóatl by the indigenous people of Mexico, passed through Cholula on his way to Tenochtitlán in 1519 and ordered a merciless slaughter. He may have misunderstood the intentions of the local people—undoubtedly he was under intense pressure. Whatever the reason, the Spaniards and their Tlaxcalan allies perpetrated a bloodbath.

(Cholula means "place the waters spring from." When Cortés was threatening the city, its inhabitants appeared to believe that native priests could open the sides of the massive pyramid here to release an avenging water monster, perhaps a flood.)

Because of Cholula's sacredness to the local Indians, the Spaniards saw to it that Christian shrines were erected at almost every other corner of the town. One writer has described Cholula as "blistered with churches"—an inspired description. Churches were angrily laid across Cholula like the welts from a lash.

Today these squat domes and boxy towers cluster around the largest pre-Hispanic structure in Mexico: At least three immense temple bases, one atop another, and four lateral additions were erected here over the centuries, each built at the end of a 52-year religious cycle, according to custom. The result is known as **Tepanapa**, and although not as tall as Egypt's Pyramid of Cheops, it's almost twice as large at the base.

From a distance this structure appears to be a steep, oddly shaped hill, certainly not man-made. A church, dwarfed by this mini-mountain on which it perches, is meant to look triumphant; it doesn't. Steps and a trail lead up the side of the "hill" to the church, but despite its pretty white-and-gold interior it is not worth the climb. What *is* worth it are the views in every direction—they are magnificent.

The **Plaza de las Estelas** (Patio of Altars), in the archaeological zone itself, is enclosed on three sides by curiously modern-looking construction typical of Cholula: Broad stairways flank plain balustrades that are balanced by handsome walls. Bold fretwork designs support large panels, and on two stelae carved in bas-relief there are designs clearly derived from the religious center of El Tajín in northern Veracruz state. Wandering through the three main patios of Cholula, a visitor gets a sense of cosmopolitanism, of ideas and elements brought by pre-Columbian pilgrims who came great distances—though no one knows exactly what attracted these pilgrims to Cholula.

Much of the construction is of adobe brick, with pebble facings overlaid by stucco. This inexpensive technique, still used all over Mexico today with slight variations, does not ensure lasting results without constant upkeep. Thus, the method of construction itself has caused some of the deterioration and shapelessness of Cholula's pyramid. The adobe bricks are believed to have been made at a place about 30 miles distant. According to legend, 20,000 prisoners passed them along to Cholula hand-to-hand, bucket brigade style.

Miles of tunnels were cut into the great temple base in the 1930s, revealing even older construction. Feeble lightbulbs will allow you to find your way, but it is best to carry a flashlight as well. Here and there you'll notice traces of murals on what were once the exterior walls of older temples. Visitors may enter on their own, but a guide, who can be engaged at the entrance to the site, will certainly help to clarify this puzzling place.

A small **museum** in a red building across the street from the entrance to the site contains artifacts and an illuminating cutaway model of the pyramid. Studying this before actually exploring the tunnels of Tepanapa is helpful.

In Cholula itself, the **Villa Arqueológica**, several blocks south of the pyramid, is a very good hotel, with a pleasant, informal atmosphere and a reliable restaurant. This is also the only really good choice for lunch while exploring the ruins, although **Los Portales**, a shady café on the zócalo, will do for simple food and bottled drinks.

Around Puebla

The little parish church in the village of **Tonantzintla**, 4 km (2½ miles) south of Cholula, is perhaps the most delightful building in all of Mexico. The modest exterior gives little hint of the richness of craft and imagination that awaits the visitor inside. Local artisans, working in the finest native traditions, decorated the interior with such a blaze of folk art that entering the church is like stepping into a kaleidoscope. Sly cherubs with Indian features peer from the polychrome murals and gilding, and the power of undiluted primary colors makes the nave radiant, its angels in miniskirts complemented by an abundance of grapes and flowers.

Just half a kilometer beyond Tonantzintla on the same road glistens the façade of **San Francisco Acatepec**, Rococo *poblano* style gone mad. Every inch of the exterior of this amazing church is covered with green, yellow, blue, and red tiles worked in intricate patterns. The building is as ornate inside as out, a white-and-gold fantasy sculpted in a rarely used Arabian mode—sand and calcimine combined to produce a surface with the hardness and texture of extremely fine cement. The church was gutted by fire decades ago, and what now dazzles the eyes is a modern replica, but perfect down to the last detail.

Travellers with their own vehicles can continue on the same road and arrive in Puebla without returning to Cholula.

Tlaxcala

Mexico's smallest state, Tlaxcala, is 30 km (19 miles) north of the city of Puebla via Highway 119. Its borders follow almost exactly the frontiers of the ancient Republic of Tlaxcala, chief ally of Cortés in the conquest of Mexico. The tiny state is walled in by high mountains; views of La Malinche in particular are spectacular here.

The capital city shares the name of the state, and has two buildings of unusual interest. A short walk south of the zócalo, the **Exconvento de la Asunción**, once a Franciscan monastery, may be the oldest church extant in the Americas. The cedar beams and inlaid wood below the organ loft are remarkable examples of carving and decoration, and very Moorish in design and execution.

At the eastern end of town, 3 km (2 miles) from the central plaza, stands the famed **Santuario de la Virgen de Ocotlán**, frosted with ornately shaped and molded white plaster. The church was built in 1745 to commemorate a purported appearance of the Virgin on the spot two centuries earlier. The interior boasts polychromed and gilded wood carving, the work of Francisco Miguel Tlayotehuanitzin, an Indian sculptor who devoted 25 years of his life to this glorious achievement.

The archaeological zone of **Cacaxtla** is found near the village of Nativitas, 18 km (11 miles) southwest of Tlaxcala. Watch for a turnoff to the west about a mile north of the town of Zacatelco. (A sign says "Ruinas.") The site, newly roofed, is remarkable for its murals painted with a realism unknown in ancient Mexico outside the Mayan region. The murals were discovered in 1975; excavation has been slow, and so scholarly disputes about their provenance still simmer. Regardless of their uncertain origin, the site is well worth a visit.

NORTH OF THE CAPITAL

For an interesting and very full day of sightseeing by car, head north from Mexico City and make a loop that includes the Museum of the Viceregal Period at Tepotzotlán, the Toltec archaeological zone at Tula, and the monastery at Ixmiquilpán, with its strange, almost bizarre murals. (Because Ixmiquilpán is of less interest than the other two, it can be dropped to shorten the trip.) Both the museum and archaeological zone are on the way to Querétaro, so visitors planning to explore colonial Mexico might choose to include both places on their itineraries as they travel northwest.

Tepotzotlán

Tepotzotlán (teh-pote-so-TLAN) is practically a suburb of Mexico City, lying as it does just north of the Federal District on the west side of Highway 57. (It should not be confused with Tepoztlán, a town with a similar name located near Cuernavaca.) In 1584 the Jesuits established the Seminary of San Martín here, which thrived as both a school and missionary center. In the middle of the 18th century the original church and some of the monastery were replaced with the present structure, one of the most impressive examples of Churrigueresque architecture in the Americas. Both the façade and interior are nothing short of magnificent.

Churrigueresque, sometimes called ultrabaroque, is an ornate style of architectural decoration named for the Spanish designer José de Churriguera, who worked in the early 18th century. Transported to Mexico, his style instantly took root and flourished, the elaborateness of the Mexican versions wildly exceeding the first Spanish examples. This purely ornamental form, which dominated Mexican façades throughout most of the 18th century, is marked by madcap impulses. The law of gravity is defied by columns narrower at the base than the top, and open space is abhorred, except at the sides of a structure; these are left blank. Another Churrigueresque delight is the transmutation of materials: Stone and tile imitate cloth or wood. While these sculpted riots in stone, cascading over the façades of churches and erupting in altars, were beloved by the Mexican people, clerical and academic authorities were embarrassed by their excesses. Aware that European visitors thought the Churrigueresque "unrefined," the powers that be put a damper on the style near the end of the 18th century. The common people continue to love the style to this day.

In 1767, shortly after the glorious new seminary was completed, the Jesuits were expelled from Mexico by royal decree. The immense complex they had built at Tepotzotlán was put to various uses before it finally became the **Museo Nacional del Virreinata** (National Museum of the Viceregal

Period). The main buildings were restored to their 18th-century brilliance, and today the great corridors and chambers are filled with the finest examples of colonial art, including paintings, sculpture, furnishings, ceramics, and ornaments. One room is a treasure house of ivories brought by galleon from the Far East. The gilded nave of the church, which gleams like Aladdin's cave, has been criticized for its "barbaric splendor," and for good reason. Equally splendid are two smaller gold-encrusted rooms of the adjacent Holy House of Loreto, to the right of the nave. The whole bewildering spectacle is at once pagan and Catholic, and a treat for the senses.

There's a restaurant in one of the ancient patios, but its service is too leisurely if you are hurrying on to other destinations; a number of small cafés across from the church atrium are better for quick refreshments.

The Ruins of Tula

Tula, once the proud capital of the Toltec empire, lies 80 km (50 miles) north of Mexico City off Highway 57, the same road that leads to Tepotzotlán. At Tepotzotlán Highway 57 becomes a toll road; from there, follow it to the Tula exit, which is clearly marked on the right. The exit road, Highway 126, will take you through the modern town of Tula. Follow the signs to "Las Ruinas"; the turnoff is marked by a towering stone warrior sculpted in Toltec style.

Centuries before the Spanish had even imagined there might be such a thing as a New World, Tula was a fabled city. Legend has it that during its golden age the walls were bejeweled; songbirds would land on your shoulder to serenade you; squashes grew so big that a single one would feed a family for days, and cotton grew in a variety of brilliant colors, so there was no need to dye the cloth later. Though you will find no trace of such wonders today, what remains is nevertheless impressive.

Some time around A.D. 900, a nomadic tribe of people entered what is now Mexico from the north. This was a period that has since become known as Mesoamerica's Dark Ages, and it is likely that these invaders hastened the decline of the existing civilization. Calling themselves Toltecs, these warrior people began to intermarry with the vanquished tribes of the region, and in A.D. 968 they established their capital at Tula. Over the next three centuries the Toltecs flourished; their influence on the cultures of Mesoamerica was dramatic. In fact, the Toltec culture is considered to be one of the greatest of Mesoamerica, the successor to Teotihuacán and the predecessor of the Aztec.

Today only hints of this bygone glory are evident at the Tula archaeological zone. After leaving the parking lot, passing the museum, and following a dusty path a few hundred yards, you come to the back of the **Templo de Tlahuizcalpantecuhtli** (Temple of the Morning Star), with its giant warrior figures exposed to the sky. (The temple is also named for Quetzalcóatl, the legendary Mesoamerican god-hero, who was most often worshiped in the guise of a plumed serpent. Many experts believe he achieved his apotheosis in Tula.) While they once served as huge columns supporting a roof, today these so-called *atlantes*—each more than 15 feet tall and carved in four sections—stand stiffly at attention in full military regalia, their butterfly-shaped shields held closely to their chests. The workmanship is rough and rigid, which only adds to their considerable power. (One of the columns is a replica; the original is on display in the Museum of Anthropology in Mexico City.) Pieces of columns at the base of the temple are all that is left of what was probably a meeting hall. The front of the temple base features a set of steep stairs, and from the top you'll get a bird's-eye view of the whole site.

The ruins spread out below were the inspiration for Chichén Itzá in the Yucatán, and the similarities between the two are everywhere—from the type of sculpture commissioned to the architectural design of various buildings to the motifs characterizing the relief carvings. At right angles to the temple bulks the **Templo del Sol**, Tula's most ambitious structure. Here, too, the climb to the top affords striking views of the site, especially the giant statues on the platform of the Temple of the Morning Star.

You will also find two spacious **ball courts**, a ruin known as the **Palacio Quemada** (Burnt Palace), and several other structures at Tula. The relief carvings depict stealthy jaguars with outsized claws, eagles, serpents, and skulls and bones. Every detail typifies Toltec civilization; this was, after all, a military society, fierce, ruthless, and enamored of human sacrifice.

The **Museo de Tula** has a collection of ceramics and carvings, but the major pieces here are located outside, not in.

Bottled soft drinks are sold at the site, along with a variety of trinkets, but you'll have to go elsewhere for food. The best choice (apart from a picnic lunch) is the **Restaurant Tollan Campestre**, 4 km (2½ miles) past the statue marking the turnoff to the ruins on the way back to the toll road. You'll recognize it by the covered wagon on its roof.

Ixmiquilpán

Ixmiquilpán (eesh-mee-keel-PAHN) is about 50 km (31 miles) northeast of Tula. To get there, follow Highway 126 along the Río Tula; a few minutes past the little town of Tlahuelilpan you take a turnoff to the north. (You don't want to go to Pachuca.) This road ultimately joins the old Pan-American Highway 85. Ixmiquilpán is just north of the junction, and the **Exconvento de San Miguel Arcángel** (Monastery of the Archangel Michael) is in the center of town.

In 1555 Augustinian friars founded a church and monastery here in what had once been one of the capitals of the Otomí people. Nothing out of the ordinary was known about these missionaries until two decades ago, when the white paint was removed from a church wall and something truly extraordinary came to light.

As the paint came off, it became apparent that the friars had allowed their church to be frescoed with pagan murals. On panel after panel, Indians were depicted much as they had been in the ancient codices, engaged in life-and-death struggles against monsters. At least one of these dread creatures was a sort of centaur, a horse with arms, hands, and a bow. Elsewhere, twisting vines and other vegetation seemed to be part of the battle.

These murals were painted at a time when convents in Mexico were usually decorated with solemn monochromes. The only subjects deemed fit for display were grim portraits of saints and martyrs accompanied by a few lifeless flowers copied from prayer books. But at isolated Ixmiquilpán the walls had been allowed to blossom into life.

To this day there is no explaining these murals. When the Inquisition came to New Spain in the middle of the 16th century, the daring missionaries who allowed them to be painted must have had second thoughts and quickly covered the walls with whitewash. Apparently, they could not bring themselves to destroy the heretical works completely—and so some of the very few examples of 16th-century native art managed to survive. Today the murals delight the few travellers who know about this out-of-the-way monastery.

Restaurant Savino, by far the most attractive place for lunch, is on Highway 85 (Calle Insurgentes), 2 km (1¼ miles) east of town where a bridge spans the Tula river. A broad terrace overlooks the tree-lined stream.

The most direct route back to Mexico City from Ixmiquilpán is Highway 85. The capital is 155 km (96 miles) south over a very good road.

Travellers with an extra day or so who want to explore a truly off-trail spot will be rewarded in the Nahuatl-Otomí town of Pahuatlán and the neighboring village of San Pablito. From Ixmiquilpán take Highway 105 south to Pachuca, turning off on the Pachuca bypass to Tulancingo via Highway 130 east. The Pahuatlán road turns north 37 km (23 miles) east of Tulancingo, passing through the little mountain town of Honey (named for the Englishman who founded it) on its way to mountain-locked **Pahuatlán**, which itself seems frozen in an earlier century. The modest but appealing **Hotel San Carlos** on the main street has a swimming pool, terraces, magnificent views, and a restaurant featuring good regional specialties amid amiable confusion. The best rooms are at the rear of the second floor, and the finest of these is suite 201.

Ten kilometers (6 miles) north of Pahuatlán over an unpaved but adequate road is the charming village of **San Pablito**, home of the simple and gracious Otomí people, who make *amati* paper. This tough, fairly stiff substance is produced by endlessly pounding the boiled inner bark of wild fig trees. In the village, vats bubble over open fires and the sound of hammers on pulp provides a constant background accompaniment to life in this untouristed Indian hamlet. The end products of all this labor are decorations, bookmarks, mats, and envelopes.

WEST OF THE CAPITAL

As millions of Mexicans and a few foreigners have discovered, **Valle de Bravo** and its lake offer the visitor serene charm, a restful atmosphere, and relief from a hurried sightseeing pace. Located in a mountain valley 145 km (90 miles) west of Mexico City, it's a fine place to contemplate the view, admire the lake, and simply relax. For those who can't sit still, there's boating, horseback riding over mountain trails, a good golf course, and tennis courts. Still, most visitors will assign the trip a lower priority than the other side trips discussed in this chapter, as the area lacks many of the features that travellers in central Mexico find most appealing: major archaeological sites (though Malinalco, if small, is nevertheless fascinating), lofty colonial monuments, and extensive handicraft or folk art centers. The landscape, with a few exceptions, is pretty and romantic rather than spectacular.

In addition to Valle de Bravo, there are two spots of interest south of Toluca. The Aztec shrine at **Malinalco**, 104 km (64 miles) from the D.F., is not a major ruin, but it is a delightfully unusual one. **Metepec**, just south of the Toluca highway and 92 km (57 miles) from the capital, is justly famous for its pottery, even though it's unlikely to hold most visitors' interest for long.

An indefatigable traveller could cram all this into a single whirlwind day. A better plan is to spend a night in Valle de Bravo, then visit Metepec and Malinalco on the return trip to Mexico City; alternatively, the region can be explored in two one-day trips, returning to Mexico City each night. Two other possibilities: Stop in Valle de Bravo while en route to Morelia (see the Morelia section in the Colonial Heartland chapter that follows); or visit Metepec and Malinalco on the back route to Taxco and Cuernavaca. Highway 55, which winds south almost all the way to Taxco, passes through scenic countryside and the pretty spa town of Ixtapán de la Sal.

In each case, a car is essential, whether your own or rented (hiring a car and driver for the day is another option, though an expensive one). Independent bus travel is slow and roundabout, and especially difficult to Malinalco. Travel agencies in the capital offer organized trips, though not with any frequency. Such group travel is a poor second choice, especially to Valle de Bravo, where a true appreciation of the town depends largely on being free to wander, linger, and dally as you explore.

The Valle de Bravo part of this excursion is also much less desirable on weekends, when Mexico City residents seeking the relatively pure mountain air and clean waters of the lake crowd the limited facilities and stall traffic on the two-lane highway. Weekdays remain tranquil and untouristed.

The Route West

To explore the region immediately west of Mexico City, head west on Paseo de la Reforma. The handsome avenue meanders through the elegant Lomas section, where embassies and opulent private residences line its way. Then, after a less attractive area of urban sprawl, it merges with the Toluca road, Highway 15.

From here the route winds upward through pine forests onto one of the highest populated plateaus (8,400 feet) in the world. (Ice forms rapidly on the road surface here in winter; use caution during cold weather.) Among the trees dotting the slopes at this elevation are pitch pines, Mexico's answer to the sandalwood tree, whose fragrant wood was so treasured by the Aztecs that great quantities of it appear on ancient tribute lists. Everywhere along the road, both before and after the junction with Highway 130, which heads southwest into

Valle de Bravo, stretch scenic vistas dominated by the snow-capped peak of Nevado de Toluca, an extinct volcano towering some 15,000 feet above the surrounding plain. The road threads itself among mountain meadows lined with stone walls and dotted by small farms. The appearance of the people along the roadside also changes remarkably: These are dark-complexioned descendants of Mazahua Indians, who became vassals of the Aztecs in 1432. Today their clothing still has a homemade look, the women's skirts long and heavy. The area is famed for its fine wool, and traditional woven designs can be seen in the shawls and serapes often worn by the local residents in cool weather.

The immediate approach to Valle de Bravo is marked by homes and a few businesses that, with their steeply pitched tile roofs, decorated eaves, and generous use of wood and dressed stone, seem to have been transplanted from the Swiss highlands. Then, after more piney copses and mountain meadows, the town and its mountain-locked lake appear suddenly.

Created in 1947 as part of a huge hydroelectric project, the freshwater lake today is known as **Presa Miguel Alemán**, in honor of a former national president (the word *presa* refers to both the dam and the lake behind it). With a surface area just over 7½ square miles, the lake is not large; set off by steep slopes and rocky ridges, it is lovely, however, and the comparison to Alpine lakes is irresistible—which explains much of the area's newer architecture.

Valle de Bravo

The town of Valle de Bravo itself antedates the lake by at least six centuries, although none of its earliest structures remains. The first European to make his way to this Mazahua Indian center was a Spanish friar who established a mission here in 1530; it wasn't until 1850 that the settlement was elevated to township status. Eleven years later the name Valle de Bravo was adopted in honor of the patriot Nicolas Bravo, who commanded a troop of men from the region in defense of Chapultepec Castle during the U.S. invasion of Mexico. Growth has been rapid over the last two decades, as Valle de Bravo and the nearby residential community of Avándero became popular weekend and vacation destinations for Mexico City dwellers, but strictly enforced zoning and architectural codes have preserved much of its charm.

Drivers who stay on the continuation of the highway into town will soon come to the zócalo, with its fanciful bandstand. This is the place to park, get out of the car, and stretch your legs as the leisurely life of Valle de Bravo passes by. It's a pleasant, welcoming spot, with arcaded buildings and a typical village church to the north.

The main street, which runs along the east side of the zócalo, is Calle Bocanegra, but as you follow it north and east its name will change to Calle Toluca without warning. Not to worry: The compactness of Valle de Bravo compensates for its confusing lack of street signs. The best way to explore the town is on foot, starting with the arcaded buildings (*portales*) on Calle Bocanegra. Here you'll find the **Restaurant El Portal**, a comfortable establishment with an abundance of tile, bricks, and greenery, and fine for a snack or light meal. A block north on the same street is the courtyard of **El Vegetariano**, a restaurant filled on weekends with a Mexico City set that of course eschews meat.

Up and down the length of Bocanegra (and all around the zócalo) are a number of small shops specializing in carved and painted furniture, rustic home accessories, and, occasionally, antiques of dubious age but attractive design.

The **Mercado Artesanias** (Crafts Market) is an easy stroll from the center of town over cobblestone streets. Just follow Bocanegra three blocks north of the plaza, turn left (west) onto Durango, and walk to the second corner; immediately to your right will be the market. Getting there through the town's picture-postcard streets is really more rewarding than examining the merchandise, most of which is ordinary. However, the traditional Mazahua embroidery, from small pillowcases to large bedspreads, merits inspection. Much of the work is done by machine; nevertheless, embroidery remains a home industry of good quality. You'll also find durable pottery here, though it tends to be more modern than traditional in design.

After you've eaten and had a chance to amble through the market, you'll probably want to fetch your car and drive down to the municipal pier. The lake is visible from many street corners in the center of town, and if you can't see it, you'll find it simply by heading downhill; the return trip is a fairly steep climb, however.

The *muelle municipal* juts into the water from the southern edge of town. From here you can catch a boat ride on a launch that accommodates 25 passengers; hire a motorboat; or rent "water cycles," untippable paddle contraptions especially popular with youngsters. Water skiers can also hire speedboats at the pier, although the skis themselves are not always available; you'll want to inquire of the boat man before putting money down. The lake is not especially popular with swimmers, partly because of the weeds that grow up from the bottom, and partly because the water is cold, particularly during the summer rainy season. The standard launch trip around the lake, on the other hand, is memorable, and offers delightful views of the mountains, forests, and picturesque towns along the shore. Sailboats and the occasional windsurfer add their own splashes of color to the scene.

The restaurants **Los Pericos** and **La Balsa** have been built on pontoon rafts and are moored near the pier; they are almost identical in quality. Both have bars, passable fare, and refreshing views of the lake. While fish would seem to be the appropriate choice, the menu offerings do not include anything caught nearby. (Although both restaurants advertise a local catch, the fish is of the saltwater variety.) Still, sitting at a table in either one, with its gently rocking motion, is a pleasant sensation.

Restaurant Taberna del León, firmly planted on the shore at the head of the pier, is a better choice in terms of food than either of the two raft restaurants, as are the dining rooms in the town's main hotels, as long as you don't mind passing on the views.

Avándaro

The beautiful residential community of Avándaro ambles along the lakeshore southeast of Valle de Bravo. Although the official distance from the Valle de Bravo zócalo is 7 km (4 miles), the only way you'll know you've left one and entered the other is by the prevailing architectural style, which changes from the merely picturesque to affluent-romantic.

To get to Avándaro from the public pier in Valle de Bravo, follow the shore road south to its end at Calle Ameyal, then turn left (east). A block farther on is the **Iglesia Santa María**, an imposing structure housing a famed Black Christ. This life-size statue is celebrated as a miracle worker by the tens of thousands of the faithful who make their way to the church every May 3 to honor the image. Except for the statue, the interior of the church is bare nowadays, its walls scraped of paint in preparation for major restoration work.

Continuing on Calle Ameyal, follow the signs for Avándaro until you come to **La Cascada**, a frothy waterfall gushing over boulders and ledges on its way to the lake. A rocky path leads to the top of the cataract and a fine view of the extinct volcano known as Cerro Gordo.

From here the road, which becomes the Ruta del Bosque (a name no one seems to recognize), winds and curves among groves of pine, affording superb views of the lake at several points along the way. A short distance before you reach the entrance to the Hotel Avándaro Golf and Spa Resort (discussed below) is an establishment that rents saddle horses by the hour. Called "mountain ponies" locally, a name that belies their tameness, these mounts provide an ideal way to spend a few hours exploring the loveliness of the area.

Staying in Valle de Bravo

With tennis courts, a well-kept golf course, a large swimming pool, and a restaurant that maintains the area's best kitchen, the **Hotel Avándaro Golf and Spa Resort** exudes a pleasing combination of luxury and rustic charm. Located off the area's main drive, the cabin-style accommodations (doubled to 130 units two years ago) at this decidedly first-class establishment have rates that are as high as you'd expect, although they do include massages, saunas, herbal wraps, and a variety of exercise programs. (The owners of the hotel installed a small but very compact high-tech spa facility around the time the hotel expansion began.) Greens fees at the 18-hole course, sometimes praised as the most beautiful in Mexico, are extra unless you subscribe to one of the week-long spa programs.

The **Hotel El Parador**, about 3 km (2 miles) north of the Hotel Avándaro on the same Ruta del Bosque, occupies a large, grassy clearing in the woods. While its large bungalow suites have fireplaces that sometimes smoke and rooms that tend to be a little dark despite their big windows, it's a comfortable inn with reasonable rates, a swimming pool and tennis courts, and a fair restaurant. Note, however, that on weekends the Parador is a vacation mecca for some of the world's noisiest families.

You'll find the moderately expensive **Loto Azul Hotel-Club** at the other end of the lake. To get there, follow Calle Toluca north and east through Valle de Bravo, continuing on as it becomes a dirt road, until you come to the hotel's large cabins spread over a forested hillside. Built as a retreat by an Asian religious sect, the Loto Azul still has a touch of the Far East about it, although it is hardly monastic in its comforts. The unusually ample bedroom suites in the main hotel have fireplaces and large windows that either look into the woods or, in a few cases, toward the lake. The lake-view units, which are located on the second floor, must be requested, however. The restaurant is good, there's a swimming pool on the grounds, and, for an extra charge, you can use the steam baths.

Located at Juárez 101, in the center of town near the zócalo, the two-story **Casa Vieja** is a very simple family-style posada whose rates appeal to travellers on a budget.

Metepec

The pottery center of Metepec lies some 6½ km (4 miles) south of Toluca off Highway 55. While the burgeoning urban sprawl of the latter has almost swallowed the former, Metepec is still the source of delightful earthenware that is shipped all over Mexico. There is no need to search for the pottery markets. In fact, shops competing for the dollars and deutsche marks of visitors line the road from the highway turnoff all the way to the center of town.

First inspired by the ceremonial needs of the church, the pottery designs of Metepec were transfigured by local craftsmen, becoming gayer and gaudier. That evolution has continued to the present day, and what you'll find as a result is a polychrome riot in clay: skeletal mariachis, gaudy "Last Suppers" attended by jolly devils, flamboyantly glazed and painted creatures of both flesh and fantasy. The most famous ceramic creations of Metepec are its Trees of Life (*Arboles de Vida*), which can show almost anything as long as it has a vague connection with Adam and Eve and resembles, at least somewhat, a tree. Most of these elaborate pieces end up serving as candelabra, but they really have lost all function except as delightful decoration.

Apart from its pottery and some woollen goods from nearby towns, Metepec will not hold a traveller's interest for long.

Malinalco

While Metepec is merely a shopper's pause on the highway, Malinalco offers the traveller both a sense of mystery and a fleeting glimpse into the Aztec mind, making it among the most memorable archaeological sites in all of Mexico.

Leaving (or bypassing) Metepec, continue south on Highway 55. At the outskirts of the village of Tenango turn left onto the road to La Marquesa. Road signs for Chalma will begin to appear after you have driven 19 km (12 miles); follow the signs until you come to the directional markers for Malinalco. The road is narrow and frequently blocked by slow-moving vehicles; allow about an hour and a half driving time from Toluca. The ruins themselves are situated high on a hillside above the archaeological zone's parking lot. It will take you an additional half hour to climb the 400 feet to the site.

The **Temple of the Eagle and Jaguar Knights** (Templo I, or Templo Principal) is, in essence, a single sculpture, including stairs, balustrades, altars, and figures, hewn from the solid rock of the hill. A broad stairway leads to the temple platform and its only entrance, the latter flanked by a large serpent's head and the carving of an eagle knight. (The Eagle and Jaguar Orders were the two principal warrior societies of the Aztecs.) A huge drum with a pseudo–jaguar skin top sits on the opposite side of the door along with the remains of a carved jaguar knight. The doorway itself is carved to resemble a serpent's head, its tongue stretched out on the entry platform. This odd carving has been compared by guides and not a few wags to a doormat, but it seems far more like a predatory limb ready to scoop up anyone with the temerity to step on it. In Aztec legend, it represented the jaws of Tepeyolotl, the earth monster, and was meant to overawe and even terrify the young warrior acolytes who worshiped here. It is easy to believe that it did.

The gloomy interior of the circular room is 19 feet in diameter, with half of that given over to a stone bench running along the wall. Eagle and jaguar sculptures dominate, and the same fierce motifs are etched into the floor of the chamber. A modern roof, made of thatch, is an accurate copy of the original covering. Of course, like all the pre-Hispanic ceremonial structures in Mexico, the temple once was covered with stucco and painted in brilliant colors. Young Aztec nobles were initiated here, in a painful ceremony, into the Order of the Sun: The septum of the initiate's nose was pierced, then a jaguar fang or an eagle claw was inserted as a badge of honor and kinship.

Templos II and III, nearby, have not fared as well as their neighbor, primarily because their removable stones were carried off and used in the construction of a Christian church below the site. Templo I, an unbreakable monolith, offered no such readily available building materials.

Templo IV, just north of Templo I, fared better because it, too, was partly hewn from the solid rock of the hill. In the temple itself you'll find two altars in a spacious chamber, with a bench on three sides. As in Templo I, part of the dramatic effect comes from the realization that all this was painstakingly chipped from the living rock with stone tools (the ancient Mesoamericans never discovered the secret of metal tools). In the presence of such a labor-intensive achievement, one can't help but think of the Indian *kivas* of the southwestern United States or, even, of certain Egyptian tombs.

With the exception of bottled drinks and some questionable tacos, neither the archaeological site nor the village below has any real services for the visitor. But the site, with its magnificent views of mountainous countryside, is an ideal spot for a picnic.

Travellers heading back to Mexico City can save themselves time and mileage by avoiding Toluca and returning, instead, via the La Marquesa route described above.

GETTING AROUND

Cuernavaca
Several bus lines serve Cuernavaca from Mexico City, all departing from the Terminal del Sur on Calle General Vicente Guerrero. Autobuses Pullman de Morelos is the most convenient choice because of its downtown Cuernavaca depot. The second-class line, Flecha Amarilla, also goes to the center of Cuernavaca. All other bus lines stop at the edge of town, from which passengers must then take a taxi. Both Pullman and Flecha Amarilla have several departures every hour. Travelling time is just over an hour on weekdays, but less predictable on weekends due to traffic. Seats on the right side of the bus afford better views on the ride from the capital.

A car is a nuisance in the center of Cuernavaca, but you will need one for exploring outlying areas. A wider selection of rental vehicles is available in the capital, but Cuernavaca itself has half a dozen agencies, including Hertz.

Taxco
Regular bus service to Taxco is offered by several commercial lines from both Mexico City and Cuernavaca. Driving is also easy, and a new road has speeded up the last quarter of the journey. From the capital the trip takes a little more than 2 hours each way. Taxco is about 50 minutes from Cuernavaca.

Tour buses also depart frequently from Mexico City; the booking is usually done at the travel desks of hotels. Be sure to ask how much time is allowed in Taxco before reserving or paying for a tour.

On any bus going to Taxco or Cuernavaca from Mexico City, the right-hand side as you face front offers a much better view of the scenic mountains south of the Federal District.

Car rentals for Taxco trips are available in Mexico City and Cuernavaca. A car offers a much wider range of possibilities, but is not needed in Taxco itself.

Puebla and Cholula

There is good first-class bus service from Mexico City to Puebla. Autobuses del Oriente, usually shortened to ADO, has several buses an hour leaving from the Terminal del Oriente (TAPO). If you're taking the metro to the station, get off at the San Lázaro stop. The trip to Puebla takes about 2 hours, and, again, you should try to get a seat on the right-hand side of the bus for the best views on the way. A car is not needed for enjoying downtown Puebla, but bus service to Cholula can be confusing to newcomers. From the bus terminal, a prepaid (by zone) taxi is your best bet.

Tonantzintla is a short taxi ride from the zócalo in Cholula. A car is best for seeing Tlaxcala.

West of Mexico City

Most travellers headed in this direction will be driving. The road for Toluca and Valle de Bravo descends swiftly into a fertile valley a little less than an hour from the capital. Before Toluca proper, there is a prominent sign for Highway 130 and Valle de Bravo to the southwest. Follow Highway 130 for 40 km (25 miles), and then turn right at the well-marked turnoff; Valle de Bravo is another 33 km (20 miles).

Highway 55 heads south from Toluca through Metepec, and then on to Malinalco and other small villages on its way to the Taxco region. The junctions, coming from both Mexico City and Valle de Bravo, are well marked.

Those who want to visit only Malinalco, omitting Valle de Bravo and Metepec, should follow the Toluca road, Highway 15, to the village of La Marquesa, 35 km (22 miles) from downtown Mexico City, and turn left (south) at the Chalma turnoff. Chalma is 60 km (37 miles) distant, and Malinalco (follow the signs) is another 11 km (7 miles) beyond it.

ACCOMMODATIONS REFERENCE

The rates given below are projections for December 1992 through Easter 1993. Unless otherwise indicated, rates are for double rooms, double occupancy; the 10 percent VAT has been added. As rates are subject to change, it's always a good idea to double-check before booking.

▶ **Calinda Cuernavaca Racquet Club.** P.O. Box 401, Francisco Villa 100, **Cuernavaca**, Morelos 62000. Tel: (731) 3-6122; Fax: (731) 7-5483; in the U.S. and Canada, Tel: (800) 228-5151. $147.

▶ **La Casa Vieja.** Juárez 101, **Valle de Bravo**, México 51200. Tel: (726) 2-0338. $23.

▶ **Hacienda Cocoyoc.** Carretera Federal, km 32.5, **Coco-**

yoc, Morelos 62740. Tel: (735) 6-2211; Fax: (735) 6-1212. $192 (includes two meals).

▶ **Hacienda del Solar.** P.O. Box 96, Colonia el Solar, **Taxco**, Morelos 40200. Tel: (762) 2-0323. $79.

▶ **Hostería las Quintas.** P.O. Box 427, Avenida las Quintas, **Cuernavaca**, Morelos 62440. Tel: (731) 8-3949; Fax: (731) 8-3895. $74–$104.

▶ **Hotel Avándaro Golf and Spa Resort.** Fraccionamiento Avándaro, **Valle de Bravo**, México 51200. Tel: (726) 2-0003 or 0626; Fax: (726) 2-0627. $132 (includes two meals).

▶ **Hotel Lastra.** P.O. Box 649, Calzada de los Fuertes 2633, **Puebla**, Puebla 72290. Tel: (22) 35-9755; Fax: (22) 35-1501. $64.

▶ **Hotel El Parador.** Ruta del Bosque, **Valle de Bravo**, México 51200. Tel: (726) 2-1173. $94 (includes two meals).

▶ **Hotel del Portal.** Camacho 205, **Puebla**, Puebla 72290. Tel: (22) 46-0211. $79.

▶ **Hotel Royalty Centro.** Avenida Portal Hidalgo, **Puebla**, Puebla 72290. Tel: (22) 42-0204. $52; suites, $85.

▶ **Hotel San Carlos.** Calle 2 de Abril 26, **Pahuatlán**, Puebla 73100. Tel: (775) 3-1910. $45; suites, $60.

▶ **Hotel Santa Prisca.** P.O. Box 42, Cena Obscuras 1, **Taxco**, Morelos 40200. Tel: (762) 2-0980; Fax: (762) 2-1106. $42.

▶ **Loto Azul Hotel-Club.** **Valle de Bravo**, México 51200. Tel: (726) 2-0796; Fax: (726) 2-1192. $127.

▶ **Las Mañanitas.** P.O. Box 1202, Ricardo Linares 107, **Cuernavaca**, Morelos 62400. Tel: (731) 4-1466; Fax: (731) 8-3672. $92.

▶ **El Mesón del Angel.** Hermanos Serdan 807, **Puebla**, Puebla 72100. Tel: (22) 48-2100; Fax: (22) 48-7935. $135.

▶ **Villa Arqueológica.** 2 Poniente 601, **Cholula**, Puebla 72760. Tel: (22) 47-1966; Fax: (22) 47-1508; in the U.S., Tel: (800) 258-2633; in Canada, Tel: (514) 937-7707. $76.

THE COLONIAL HEARTLAND

QUERETARO, SAN MIGUEL DE ALLENDE, GUANAJUATO, MORELIA

By Robert Somerlott

North and west of the capital lies a pleasant and usually gentle land ringed by mountains. This is the traditional Mexico, where tile-domed churches rise from almost empty fields; where iron-and-tin bandstands and fountains shaded by Indian laurels and pepper trees invite the weary to stop and rest a minute. This is picture-postcard Mexico, the Mexico of song and film. At the mention of such towns as San Miguel de Allende and Guanajuato, a Mexican listener is apt to toss his hands in delight and exclaim, "*Ay, que preciosa!* How beautiful!" At the same time, and perhaps not surprisingly, the cities of the colonial heartland tend to be conservative, wary keepers of a heritage.

Charles Flandrau wrote at the start of this century: "Superficially, Mexico is a prolonged romance. For even the brutal realities—of which there are many—are the realities of an intensely pictorial people among surroundings that, to the Northern eye, are never quite commonplace." Such are the colonial highlands.

This is also where the nation's patriotic soul is enshrined (in Mexico it is easy and customary to speak of the soul), as well as where the bitter struggle for independence was

launched. Half a century later, the final siege against Maximilian was waged here, and then, in 1915, one of the bloodiest battles ever fought on the North American continent took place at Celaya, ending in the destruction of Pancho Villa's army.

MAJOR INTEREST

Colonial architecture and history
Scenic beauty
Handicrafts

Querétaro
Historic sights and buildings

San Miguel de Allende
Largely preserved colonial town
Handicrafts, especially metals
Houses and gardens
Study of Spanish language and arts and crafts

San Miguel environs
Spas
Santuario de Atotonilco
Templo de Nuestra Señora del Carmen in Celaya
Augustinian monastery at Yuriria

Guanajuato
Visual drama
Teatro Juárez

Morelia
17th-century architecture
Handicraft marketing centers

The cities of the colonial heartland ring an area known as the Bajío, a vast fertile basin. Multinational companies such as Campbell Soup have built packing plants in recent years, but it's not unusual to see strawberry fields crowding the houses in some towns.

The Food of the Bajío

The abundance of fresh farm products in the Bajío has not, unfortunately, fostered an outstanding regional cuisine. Perhaps this is because its agricultural abundance came late, and only with irrigation. It also might be that Mexicans in the area are as traditional in their diet as they are in their religion. Except in Morelia, where there is a Tarascan touch to the menu, no ethnic group has been able to preserve its special ways of cooking. (The true center for Tarascan cooking is west of the colonial region covered in this chapter.)

As a result, the food of the region is very much a cross-section. The better restaurants—and even some inspired cooks in market stalls—hold their own with any in the country, but the traditional dishes lack the variety and dash of those in other parts of Mexico. Visiting Mexicans often complain, and the more affluent end up patronizing foreign-style restaurants.

You will discover a few specialties, however. Celaya, equidistant from San Miguel and Querétaro, produces a thick, syrupy caramel confection called *cajeta,* made of goat's and cow's milk, which is packed in wooden boxes and shipped throughout Mexico and abroad. Querétaro cooks work with the *camote,* a relative of the sweet potato, candying it with sugar and lemon juice.

To praise a dessert a Mexican might exclaim, "Good as if made by a nun's fingers!" In the old days the best sweets were made in convents, which preserved Spanish rather than Mexican traditions. Nuns in the larger convents produced almond-paste candy, shaped and colored like little fruits and similar to marzipan. Today the same recipes are cooked up in home kitchens and appear for sale at fiestas throughout the year. Desserts and chicken dishes enhanced with walnuts and almonds have also slipped out of the convents into private kitchens. *Pollo en nogado,* for example, is a holiday treat made with chicken, walnuts, chiles, and cinnamon. *Ate de Almendra* is a sherry-and-almond glorification of sponge cake.

Chile sauces tend to be less fierce here than in other parts of the country, but it is not macho to admit it; besides, the next restaurant may slip you liquid fire. Beef, except when ground, stewed, or thinly sliced (as for *carne asada*), is often disappointing.

Beverages in the Bajío are not distinct from those in the rest of Mexico, though nonalcoholic *licuados* and *aguas* here rely a little more on strawberries, which are abundant. The state of Querétaro produces wine, and so does the Dolores Hidalgo neighborhood, but neither area is famous for it.

The Historic Heritage of the Bajío

This fertile region supported a sparse population in pre-Hispanic times. Pottery-making villages flourished as early as 500 B.C., but despite the high art they achieved in clay, they failed to progress to higher levels of civilization.

When the Spanish arrived they found the land occupied by civilized Otomí Indians in the south, but encountered fierce semi-nomadic Chichimecs a little farther north. Far to the west the Tarascans, who in time might have rivaled the Aztecs, had established outposts beyond their traditional base at Lake Pátzcuaro.

Silver accounts for the lightning thrust of the Spanish northward. Their hunger for ore from Zacatecas and, later, Guanajuato propelled soldiers and prospectors still breathless from destroying the Aztecs into the Bajío. Simultaneously, missionary priests who had reaped a harvest of souls in the west moved quickly eastward. So the sword and the cross marched together, impelled by different motives.

Silver barons and hacienda owners, often one and the same, multiplied their wealth in the 17th century. Native workers were recruited from afar and, as they mixed with local folk, lost their identity as Aztecs, Tlaxcalans, or Mixtecs. Intermarriage between Indian and Indian, as well as Spanish and Indian, produced the population that today characterizes the heartland. When a Mexican from the Bajío says he is of a certain descent, he is probably no more accurate about his ancestry than the typical sixth-generation North American.

Prosperity in the 1700s allowed the cities of the Bajío to embark on ambitious building programs; most of today's great structures date from that century. The same prosperity fanned the flames of independence, however, and in 1810 a revolt plotted in Querétaro and San Miguel blazed forth from tiny Dolores, now Dolores Hidalgo. During the violence-filled decades that followed, construction nearly ceased, leaving a virtual architectural blank from 1810 until about 1880. With the ascendancy of Porfirio Díaz to the presidency, a period of relative calm ensued. Once again, municipal governments turned their attention to dilapidated infrastructures, and a period of zealous rebuilding followed that lasted until soon after the turn of the century—when a new and different kind of revolutionary violence halted everything but destruction and bloodletting.

THE CITY OF QUERETARO

Querétaro, prosperous capital of the small state of the same name, is an oft-bypassed beauty. Motorists heading north for the U.S. border or south to Mexico City usually skirt it, sighing as they pass the unattractive industrial suburbs. The impression from a train is little better.

Querétaro

Tourists' neglect of the city cannot be blamed entirely on unfavorable first impressions. Though worthy and historic, Querétaro lacks the impact of other colonial cities. It can offer a rewarding two days, but seldom engenders a passionate attachment. Yet Querétaro, in its somewhat staid fashion, has attractions to offer.

The first clue that something special awaits is given to travellers approaching from the usual direction, south, on the Mexico City Highway 57 bypass. At the city's edge traffic abruptly ducks under an 18th-century **aqueduct** that towers incongruously above the freeway. It comes up so quickly, in fact, that most people are oblivious to the extraordinary structure looming over them. The aqueduct, built between 1726 and 1738, has more than 70 arches, some soaring to heights of 76 feet. Once the town's chief source of water, and reputedly the seventh-largest such structure in the world at 4,200 feet in length, the aqueduct still supplies the Fountain of Neptune at the center of the city.

Querétaro once stood astride a vital trade route to the Bajío and the silver-rich mountains protecting it. The Otomí people settled here at least 1,000 years ago; Aztecs assumed loose control of the city in 1446, turning it into their northernmost allied outpost against the hostile Chichimecs.

The conquistadors swooped down on it in 1531, making a quick alliance with an Otomí chief named Conin, but then had to deal with the more formidable Chichimecs. Legend has it that the newcomers and natives agreed to settle ownership by man-to-man combat, a bare-knuckle fistfight. There are variations of what happened next. In one version, there was a melee. In another, even as the champions of either side stood ready, an astounding red-and-gold cross carried by Saint James mounted on horseback flared across the sky; the local population reportedly converted on the spot. Querétaro has been a bastion of Catholicism ever since.

In the early 1800s the traditionally cautious town became a den of conspiracy. At the center of the plot to overthrow Spanish rule was Josefa Ortíz de Domínguez, wife of the *corregidor* (mayor). In September of 1810, Doña Josefa, already under house arrest, managed to warn her fellow plotters that their sedition had been discovered and that the Spanish authorities were ready to pounce. Her message, which, according to legend, was passed through a keyhole, ignited the revolt. Doña Josefa, usually called La Corregidora, is today the greatest female figure in the history of a country with few acclaimed heroines.

In 1848 Querétaro became the provisional capital of the nation while the U.S. Army was occupying Mexico City. The

Treaty of Guadalupe Hidalgo, which ceded almost half of Mexico's territory to the United States (what are now the states of California, New Mexico, and Arizona, and parts of Nevada, Utah, and Colorado), was signed here later that year.

Nineteen years after that national disaster, the beleaguered Emperor Maximilian, along with the remnants of his army, was cornered at the edge of town. After a three-month siege, Maximilian was captured, tried, and executed (an event recalled in a painting by Manet). On a happier day in 1917, the constitution that is still in force in Mexico was written and adopted in Querétaro.

The latest incursion into the city has been quite different from the hostile ones of the past. After the earthquakes of 1985, thousands of Mexico City residents sought solid ground and new lives here, enlarging and changing the city even as they adapted to its peculiar rhythms. In return, these newcomers have brought with them a tonic of sophistication, a delight in the performing arts, and a generally faster-paced lifestyle.

Plazas Obregón and Independencia

In colonial days Querétaro, as a major link between the provinces and the capital, came to dominate the artistic tastes of a huge area, developing a gay, exuberant style that was flashier and more sentimental than the capital's. For two centuries it supplied even faraway towns with painters and artisans.

Today touches of this antique extravagance are everywhere to be seen in Querétaro, from its grillwork and balconies to its cornices and doors. The old section of town is especially delightful for strolling and discovering these details.

Traffic has been banished from the downtown area, which, while a blessing, also causes many a snarl in outlying areas. Parking lots are hidden from the uninitiated, so the best course is to walk or take a taxi to the main plaza.

The spacious and pleasant **Jardín Obregón**, in the center of town, is adorned with a bronze statue of the Greek goddess Hebe, swans, gargoyles, and curlicues—all the mandatory signs of civic chic at the turn of the century (other Bajío towns were not nearly so stylish). The character of the city becomes apparent in this square, which is suspiciously tidy and well-ordered. There is a strange paucity of vendors here, a lack of the usual confusion and sprawling disorder. It's as if it were saying, This is a tightly governed town, a slightly gentrified town, a town aware of its image.

On the east side of the square looms the **Templo y Exconvento de Francisco**. Built in 1545, it has endured so much expansion and cosmetic surgery that what remains is little more than a hodgepodge. Still, the dome and tower are splendid. Inside, the nave harbors some dreadful sculpture and one exceptional statue, a polychrome Saint James by the local master Arce, who worked at the start of the 19th century. A glance at the organ loft reveals a fine iron grille (*reja*) enclosing the choir.

The 17th-century Franciscan monastery next door has become a regional museum that includes the former **Museo Pío Mariano**, with exhibits of war relics, several fine paintings (including two by the famed Baroque master Juan Correa), and a variety of colonial furnishings, among them chairs identical in design and discomfort to those sat upon in conservative Querétaro today. Elsewhere in the museum, huge music books are emblazoned with hand-drawn notations big enough to be read over the choirmaster's shoulder from the loft above.

While the museum's contents may be scant, the building itself is an exhibit, especially the central patio, with its carved arches and domes in the Moorish (*mudéjar*) style. The smaller Patio of Novices and the Orange Garden evoke a sense of antiquity and the monastic life. The building as a whole is typically Franciscan, strong and practical, handsome but never extravagant.

Leaving the museum and walking east along a very pretty pedestrian mall, you pass attractive shops with quite ordinary merchandise. This shaded and flowering street leads to the tiny but charming **Plaza de la Independencia**. Here, in bronze, stands Marqués de la Villa del Villar del Aguila, the benefactor who financed the Querétaro aqueduct. The marqués was also a keen hunter, which accounts for the lean stone hounds that cling to his monument. These particular animals are replacements; the original bronze canines were dognapped.

On the east side of the plaza the riotous façade of the one-time mansion of Don Tomás López de Ecala displays Querétaro exuberance run amok, with a pair of vulturine eagles signifying the owner's high rank, stone draperies, and tangles of wrought iron. Don Tomás appropriated part of the park in order to erect this astonishing edifice.

At least a score of other attractive colonial buildings, both religious and residential, enrich downtown Querétaro. For the visitor who chooses to explore on foot there are countless touches of charm—including a statue of La Corregidora in a vaguely Greek costume but wearing long drop earrings for an added touch of elegance. (The statue is one block north of the Jardín Obregón on Avenida Corregidora.) And although sitting and strolling are the town's chief pleasures, Querétaro does have four additional sites of special interest.

Santa Clara and Santa Rosa Churches

Santa Clara stands gracefully behind its own atrium one block west of the Jardín Obregón, with the **Fuente** (Fountain) **de Neptuno**—the modern terminus of the Querétaro aqueduct—lending it an air of distinction. The fountain, for many travellers, is their introduction to Francisco Eduardo Tresguerras, the Renaissance man of Mexican art. Born in Celaya, about 30 miles west of Querétaro, in 1759, Tresguerras, with one year of formal art training, became an architect, painter, sculptor, etcher, woodcarver, poet, and musician, leaving a legacy of work that remains the pride of the region. His prestige is so great, in fact, that dozens of buildings in various cities are proudly, and falsely, attributed to him by local boosters. As the fountain demonstrates, he possessed a particular talent for warming the cold, often sterile Neoclassical style in which he was forced to build by government decree. (The ruling clique of his day had become embarrassed by the flamboyant decoration of the Mexican High Baroque, or Churrigueresque, style and sought to tame and refine Mexican buildings by making them look vaguely Roman. Artistic strangulation generally resulted; Tresguerras saved many new structures from what would have been an otherwise arid fate.)

At Santa Clara he designed the fountain, although he did not create the sculpture. In the last years of the 1790s he redid the dome and tower of the church, and probably created the main altar and interior vaulting as well. The rest of the church, dating from its original construction in 1633, features Baroque ornamentation that is majestic to the point of being sublime.

The church itself is the only surviving structure of a huge religious complex that once stretched all the way to the Jardín Obregón, the main square. At one time 8,000 nuns and their servants found shelter here, in what was one of the richest religious communities in the world. Evidence of that wealth is abundantly obvious in the church's ornamentation and sculpture, the most famous piece of which is the beautiful *La Piedad* by Mariano Arce. That there were hundreds of such communities throughout the country explains in part the genesis of Mexico's anti-clerical laws.

Southwest of the center of town on Avenida General

Arteaga, a rather long six-block walk from the main square, stands the imposing **Templo de Santa Rosa de Viterbo**, the most unusual of Querétaro's many ecclesiastical monuments. In 1670 three pious young sisters were granted permission to construct cells for their religious devotions. Other aristocratic girls immediately wanted the same fashionable seclusion, and thus began the convent. In time the nuns became teachers and the convent a college. (Of Mexico's tens of thousands of nuns, most were simply women in retirement and seclusion, "extra" women in a society that had no use for unmarried ladies of gentility. The teacher-nuns at Santa Rosa were among the exceptions.) The college was eventually housed in its present building, which was completed in 1752. The dome is so ponderous that special flying buttresses had to be added to support it, creating in the process a strikingly theatrical exterior.

Tresguerras was employed to rebuild and redecorate the structure at the end of the century, but it is hard to say how much of the building is his. Certainly he did the outer ornamentation, the dome and tower, and the carvings in the sacristy. In the same room you'll find one of the best murals painted during the colonial period, often attributed to Tresguerras but probably the work of José de Páez. The mural depicts nuns and their pupils in an enclosed garden while lambs carry white roses that turn red upon contact with the blood of the Savior.

Convento de la Santa Cruz

East of the Jardín Obregón at the corner of Carranza and Acuña, the Convento de la Santa Cruz (Convent of the Cross) commands the highest ground in the city, the alleged spot where Saint James stopped the fight between conquistadors and Chichimecs, thereby settling the future of Querétaro. Nowadays the views of the town's roofs and many church towers are almost as dramatic.

The church was for many years headquarters for the missionary priests who went forth on foot to Christianize the vast area of New Spain that is now the southwestern United States. Among them was Father Junípero Serra, whose missionary activities (he founded the California missions of San Diego, San Luis Obispo, San Juan Capistrano, Santa Clara, and San Francisco, among others) have virtually assured him of sainthood while earning the condemnation of Native American rights activists. In the late 1600s the church was also home to more than 7,000 mostly scientific volumes—what was probably the largest library in the New World at the time. A century and a half later Maximilian used the adjacent convent as a barracks, only to have it become his temporary prison. Today mementos of the emperor are on display there.

The Convent of the Cross itself is a labyrinth of seven patios and rooms that are literally countless due to the fact that many are sealed and buried. The present structure, with expansions and rebuilding, dates to around 1650. Historically and spiritually it is the most important edifice in Querétaro and attracts pilgrims from all over the country who come to worship at the site of a famed miracle.

According to legend, Fray Antonio Margil de Jesús Ros (1657–1726) was an amazingly devout missionary who, among other feats, walked barefoot from present-day Guatemala to Texas. In a garden at the church he reportedly plunged his staff into the ground, where, like Aaron's rod, it took root. A tree soon sprang up that bore cross-shaped thorns, and it still thrives in the same courtyard alongside some of its offspring. Supposedly, this type of tree will grow nowhere else—which means it not only has to be protected from the usual souvenir hunters but also from seekers of holy relics, who would shred it to its last root if given the chance.

Cerro de las Campanas

Whether or not the Hill of the Bells is worth visiting depends on your sense of history and romance. Outwardly it is not much, and the whole site has been called ugly by some. But those fascinated by the story of Maximilian and Carlota will want to stand on the spot where their tragedy came to an end and modern Mexico began—or at least was reassured about its survival.

The hill rises between the university and the industrial zone at the western edge of town. The first thing to arrest the eye is a stone colossus of Benito Juárez, harsh and rough, appropriately made of unyielding granite. His words are inscribed below: "Between individuals as between nations, respect for the rights of others is peace."

The memorial to the emperor is down the hill at the spot where he was executed. In death as in life the two leaders do not meet. The Austrian government has erected a chapel here as well, and near its altar are three stone plinths marking the spot where Maximilian, with his two Mexican generals, faced the firing squad. (Juárez once observed that Maximilian was honored to die beside two gallant Mexicans who loved both their church and their country.) The chapel is ill-maintained, however, and from the beginning was cheap, even mingy, somehow suggesting that the emperor, for all his glamour, was as great an embarrassment to Austria as he was a plague to Mexico.

Opals

East of the city is one of the world's major veins of opals, a source of every grade of this lovely stone. The mines have been worked for more than a century now, so the mines is not as abundant as it was a few decades ago, when opals were offered on almost every corner of the city. But the mines continue to be worked, and Querétaro remains a cutting and marketing center for them—as well as for amethysts, topazes, and aquamarines from elsewhere.

Evaluating opals is a tricky business. Buyers should always avoid street vendors who have just made "wonderful finds." Perhaps the first dealer you should consult is José Ramírez, owner of his own opal mine, who for many years has had an outstanding shop, **Lapidaria Querétaro**, at the corner of Pasteur Norte and 15 de Mayo, north of the monument to La Corregidora. Both loose stones and stones in settings are offered, and lovely imported amethysts and topazes may also be inspected here.

To compare prices and quality go to **El Rubí**, a few steps west of the Jardín Obregón at Avenida Madero 3. This is a family affair run by three gracious sisters who are both welcoming and knowledgeable. Again, both set and unset stones are displayed.

The **Sociedad Cooperativa Otomí**, in the center of town at Cinco de Mayo 29, has a much smaller collection, as does **Opalo** at Corregidora 13 Norte, near Sears.

Opals and other stones at these (as well as other) established stores are the only Querétaro specialty worth the attention of shoppers. A better selection of art and craft products will be found elsewhere in Mexico.

Staying in Querétaro

Most of the modern Querétaro hostelries are strung out along Highway 57 to attract motorists travelling to or from Mexico City, and therefore tend to suffer from typical motel monotony, limited service, and isolation. An exception is the attractive **Holiday Inn Querétaro**, a very well run establishment two miles west of the center of town (on an access road east of Highway 57) that more than justifies its slightly higher prices with comfortable rooms, pleasant decor, and facilities such as lighted tennis courts. The Holiday Inn also has a fine Mexican/international restaurant with an ample selection of wines, gentle lighting, and music in the evenings. The cheerful coffee shop, La Capilla, serves good breakfasts.

Less complete in its offerings but perfectly acceptable is the **Real de Minas**, part of a chain of motor inns popular with Mexican business and government travellers. It, too, is near the highway, about a mile from the center of town.

Visitors arriving by bus or train may want a more central location (although the Holiday Inn is especially helpful about arranging transportation). On the Plaza de la Independencia in the historic district is the **Mesón de Santa Rosa**, an elegant and unusual colonial building that has been restored and adapted with taste. The dining room is rather formal, with both food and service seeming more European than Mexican.

Five blocks west of the main plaza at Guerrero Norte 10A is **El Señorial**, a conveniently situated and modern hotel with protected parking.

The **Hacienda Jurica**, 13 km (8 miles) northwest of the city off Highway 57, is a fashionable resort hotel that is particularly popular with vacationers from Mexico City. It offers an 18-hole golf course, squash and tennis courts, even a roller-skating rink. Not all rooms in this 17th-century hacienda are excellent, but most are.

La Mansión Galindo, another elegant resort, is located some distance to the southeast on the way to Mexico City. Take Highway 57 east for 37 km (23 miles) to the Amealco exit, and then follow Route 120 another 6½ km (4 miles). After the turnoff, the directions will be clearly marked. The hacienda dates from the 16th century, but not even the viceroys of that era imagined the luxury that the Galindo offers today: lighted tennis court, posh nightclub, and more. The Galindo is popular with the capital's film, TV, and political folk.

Dining in Querétaro

Querétaro's most fashionable restaurant is also its best. Situated near the northeastern entrance to the city, on the service road of the Mexico City–San Luis Potosí bypass just west of the aqueduct, **Gitano's** is gently lit and has impeccable service. Lobster and crayfish are featured on a varied menu, and violin music adds to the refined atmosphere. Open for lunch and dinner until 1:00 A.M. Expensive. Tel: (42) 13-7033.

The **Parilla Argentina Fogon Pampero**, near the entrance to the country club on Boulevard Las Américas, opposite the bullring, packs in local businessmen for afternoon feasts of, usually, beef. This rather plain place serves large (but not cheap) portions of hearty food.

For a simpler meal or snack while downtown, the **Flor de Querétaro**, a family spot at Juárez 9, Jardín Obregón, offers an inexpensive menu for a set afternoon dinner (the *comida corrida*), as well as à la carte Mexican dishes.

A little fancier, the **Fonda del Refugio** is a restaurant and sidewalk café located in the historic zone at Corregidora 26. The café is popular with the more affluent students from the local university, and outdoor tables here are at a premium. Traditional dishes are satisfactory, the attempts at international cuisine a bit riskier.

The dozen or so hole-in-the-wall counter-in-the-front spots scattered throughout the Jardín Obregón neighborhood are all right for tacos, tortas, and the like. One is much the same as another, but out-of-towners should confine themselves to bottled beverages.

SAN MIGUEL DE ALLENDE

The usual approach to San Miguel de Allende is from the southeast, by car or bus from Mexico City via Querétaro. Above the town the cobbled road suddenly widens into a balustraded *mirador* (overlook), where most drivers pause to admire the view. After shooing away the vendors of flimsy rugs, you gaze across a valley toward a pale lake and distant mountains. The town lies directly below, its domes and towers clinging to the slope of the Hill of Moctezuma, a pastel collage.

The collage image is obvious, of course. Everyone knows that San Miguel is an art colony, and one rather self-conscious of the fact. But visitors standing at this spot have been known to fall in love with the town instantly and not always reasonably. And why not? This is the prettiest town in Mexico, although many others are more spectacular, imposing, or exotic. And despite recent growth and urban sprawl, it remains a small city, easy to see and manage.

San Miguel can be "done" in just a few hours by a zealous sightseer with a checklist. Indeed, a few marathon bus tours out of Mexico City offer just such a production-line schedule. However, the town will not reveal itself in a series of snapshots; much of its charm is subtle and indefinite, the whole being more than the sum of its parts. Still, energetic

San Miguel de Allende

(map not to scale)

folks who do not enjoy sauntering, lounging, or soaking up ambience may grow restless after a day or two here.

San Miguel is a winter haven for a few hundred refugees from the cold and snow of the United States and Canada. In summer it is a cool and convenient retreat for people from Texas and the Gulf Coast region. Many of these visitors from the north return year after year, renting houses or apartments or booking the same rooms in favorite hotels, staying a month or two, or even three. They become possessive of the town, as well as strong supporters of its cultural and charitable activities. Others, again mostly from the United States or Canada, retire to San Miguel to live on pensions and investments. A much smaller expatriate group actually works for a living, painting, writing, or running small businesses.

There are fears, usually expressed from a distance, that San Miguel has become Americanized. Indeed, on any given morning during mid-summer or mid-winter Americans seem to occupy the south side of the main plaza as surely as they do the Alamo. But travellers wishing to avoid other visitors have only to detour half a block to be solidly back in Mexico. Mexicans outnumber foreigners here by a hundred to one, and all the guest rooms in town would fit easily into a single resort hotel in Acapulco. San Miguel, despite superficial indications to the contrary, is as Mexican as cactus.

The Plaza Area

Visitors standing on the south side of the main plaza (usually called *el jardín*) facing San Miguel's imposing parish church, **La Parroquia**, will find themselves surrounded by as well preserved a colonial town as there is. Despite the traffic and overhead power lines, its 18th-century character remains surprisingly intact, much of this due to the fact that San Miguel was declared a national monument in 1926. Since then, architectural change has been banned, signs regulated, neon forbidden.

At the same time, the preservation of the town is only in part the result of decrees. The 17th and 18th centuries saw the town grow wealthy from commerce and ranching, as well as from the tanneries that lined some of its streets. Eventually it changed its name to San Miguel el Grande (because it was by then the biggest San Miguel, of which there were more than a few, in the region) and assumed aristocratic airs. But civil upheaval and the Industrial Revolution brought ruin to the burghers of the 19th century. Gradually, the silver in the surrounding region was mined out and the silver trains stopped coming; the tanneries found themselves unable to compete in mass markets because the town lacked sufficient water. So San Miguel was bypassed by the times. The old buildings were left standing because there was no need and no money to replace them; cobblestones were left in place by a town that could not afford repaving.

Today almost everything dates from the 1700s, with the exception of the French-influenced details from the turn of this century (the landscaping, benches, and bandstand of *el jardín* for example) and an occasional sign of more recent prosperity. And since the town has never been reconstructed as a sort of museum, it has been saved from being self-consciously picturesque. In the long run, San Miguel's past misfortune has become the visitor's good fortune.

At the edge of La Parroquia's atrium rises a bronze statue of Fray Juan de San Miguel, the barefoot Franciscan missionary who founded the town in 1542, naming it for his own patron saint, the warrior archangel. The full name of the town was San Miguel de los Chichimecas, prematurely honoring those Indians the friar intended to convert. As it turned out, the angel's protection was needed; this was wild country, and the Chichimecs proved so stubborn that Indians from Tlaxcala had to be imported to serve the needs of the Spaniards.

The settlement, located astride the silver trails, thrived. Prosperity, however, meant rebuilding; nothing remains of the 16th-century village. A stone church was erected, then replaced. The oldest walls of La Parroquia may date as far back as 1620, but most of it, except for the famous façade, was built 60 years later.

Today La Parroquia is the most photographed, most painted church in Mexico, an astonishment of Neo-Gothic architecture gone mad—or Mexican. Ceferino Gutiérrez, a self-taught Indian stonemason, was commissioned in 1880 to create a new façade for the then-conventional church. In love with the Gothic architecture of Europe, he studied drawings, engravings, and postcards, admiring especially the cathedrals of Milan, Chartres, and Cologne. Though he was probably illiterate and knew nothing of drafting, Gutiérrez daily sketched his plans in the sand for workmen to follow, just as the great cathedral builders of Europe once had. The result is, in the truest sense of the word, fantastic. La Parroquia stabs the sky with its turrets and spires; everything is aimed heavenward. But that was the only aspect of Gothic style Gutiérrez grasped. The rest of his façade is massive, brooding, solid as a fortress.

Still, La Parroquia completely dominates the San Miguel

landscape, just as its humble builder dreamed it would. Its heavy bells, the largest almost six feet high, give it added authority and act as a constant sound track for the town, sounding early Mass at dawn, ringing rosary, signaling events, arrivals, and departures. The slender clock tower next door, rebuilt by Gutiérrez to match his church façade, adds its own strong bell voice as it announces the quarter hours. (Visitors should be warned that there are about 150 public bells in town; all are rung on various occasions and sometimes all at once.)

The interior of La Parroquia is less interesting than its façade. There is, however, a remarkable life-size statue of Our Lord of the Conquest, made by Tarascan converts at Pátzcuaro in the 16th century out of cornstalks and an enduring orchid-bulb glue, in a chapel to the left of the main portal. This powerful figure is venerated by the *conchero* dancers, who perform their ceremonial dances in flamboyant costume, accompanied by shell instruments, at various religious festivals throughout the year. More than 100,000 *concheros* are scattered over a wide region that was once Chichimec country, but apart from the religious customs and ceremonial dances that glorify their ancestral heritage, most *concheros* lead ordinary lives. The wild dancing warrior with hair to his waist may be, under his wig, the short-haired bank clerk who changed your money earlier in the day.

Across the narrow street that flanks La Parroquia to the west stands the **birthplace of Ignacio Allende**, the town's most famous citizen. This fine and well-proportioned mansion is now a museum open to the public. Allende himself was an aristocrat, but the "taint" of being born a *criollo*—a Spaniard born in Mexico—condemned him to second-class status in his own country. The Crown's discrimination against Spaniards born abroad gradually nurtured resentment and, eventually, rebellion. Allende, a career army officer, was one of the few trained military leaders among the insurgents and became their general, second in command only to Father Hidalgo. After the rebel forces disintegrated in 1811, he was captured, shot, and then beheaded by royalist forces. His beloved hometown of San Miguel el Grande was renamed in his honor by an independent Mexico in 1862.

San Miguel's three leading art galleries are all within a block of Allende's birthplace. Around the corner at Umarán 1 is the **Josh Klingerman Gallery**; facing the side of the church at Cuna de Allende 15 is the **Galería Atenea**; and on the north side of *el jardín* at number 14 is the **Galería San Miguel**. The number of artists living in San Miguel has declined over the last dozen years, but the town remains the nation's second-largest art market, surpassed only by Mexico City.

At the north end of the block-long colonial arcade facing *el jardín* on the west side rises the imposing **Casa del Mayorazgo de Canal**, now occupied by Banamex, the Bank of Mexico. (To visit a colonial mansion in San Miguel, all you need do is step into a bank. There are five of them established in palatial quarters, all located on the street running uphill from the north side of the plaza.) The grand entrance to this 18th-century mansion is on Calle de la Canal, which heads downhill from the northwest corner of the plaza. The carriage doors seek to overwhelm the caller with the family Canal's importance: The eagle signifies its baronial status, the helmets indicate that ancestors fought against the Moors in Spain. (Two helmets here; both the husband and wife's families earned the distinction, and flaunted it.) The residence itself was built sometime around 1740 on top of an older structure, then remodeled some 50 years later. Supposedly, Eduardo Tresguerras did the restyling. Regardless, it is a fine example of the Mexican "severe" style: dark red walls, black wrought iron, white trim and woodwork. All such buildings—and there are many in Mexico—were either built or spruced up around 1800.

The owner of the house at the time of the War of Independence was Colonel Narciso de la Canal, commander of the local Spanish garrison. When the rebels, led by his neighbor Allende and Father Hidalgo, marched on the town, the colonel prudently kept his soldiers in their barracks. Later, when the possibility of his elevation to the rank of count was brought up, serious questions about his true allegiance were raised, and the title remained unconfirmed when the colonel died, under arrest, in Querétaro. His true role in the rebellion is still unknown, but posterity has granted him the title that was withheld in life: His family is always called "the Counts of Canal" in San Miguel de Allende.

The **Templo de San Francisco**, an elegant structure with a disturbing note, graces the street named after it, one block east of *el jardín*. The delicately carved façade, with its abhorrence of a blank spot, is pure Churrigueresque, its columns tapering illogically toward their bases. Whenever you see this inverted column in Mexico you can instantly date the structure as having been built between 1720 and 1785; the odds against being mistaken are overwhelming. However, this particular church was caught in a period of stylistic flux. Begun in 1779, its bell tower was still unbuilt when the shift to the Neoclassical swept the country. The always ingenious

Tresguerras was brought in from Celaya to design a tower that would express the new style yet blend with the church's existing façade. Though he didn't quite manage this impossible task, he came close. The interior design is also mostly his, and features a nave bathed in light. The Enlightenment, which was late in coming to Mexico, is seen in the most literal terms here. The church of San Francisco, like many others of the era, was purged of its atmosphere of oppressive mystery.

A block to the north, an open plaza fronts the **Iglesia de Nuestra Señora de la Salud** (Church of Our Lady of Health). A gigantic seashell commemorating a mass baptism by sea water spans the entrance. In the middle of the shell an all-seeing eye set in a triangle celebrates both the omniscience of God as well as the Holy Trinity. Many people believe, sensibly enough, that the church must specialize in curing diseases of the eye.

The interior boasts two unusual details. Panels of an old wooden altar in the right transept show Jesus the Good Shepherd ministering to his flock while some of the sheep are menaced by a unicorn. The oddity here is the portrayal of a New Testament parable in a Mexican church, where the miraculous usually reigns supreme. There are also four startling paintings of the classic virtues under the dome; while they're not exactly pagan, they're certainly not Roman Catholic, either.

The church itself was built early in the 18th century as a chapel for the college next door, an institution radical enough to have educated several martyrs of independence, among them Allende. This is the only explanation for the odd decor of La Salud.

A block west the **Oratorio de San Felipe Neri** boasts silverwork designs chiseled into the stone of its façade. The designs are somehow appropriate, for San Felipe Neri stands in a neighborhood where pack trains from distant silver mines once halted for a night's lodging.

This otherwise ordinary church, San Miguel's largest, has two unusual features, neither immediately apparent. Attached to the building is the **Santa Casa de Loreto**. According to Catholic tradition, the house of the Virgin Mary was transported by angels to Loreto, Italy, where it still can be visited today. Here we have a replica of sorts, although some locals would have you believe it's the original. To enter this special sanctorum, walk to the left side of the altar, where impressive gates often bar the way; an attendant will usually fetch a custodian with a key.

The outer room, the Virgin's drawing room, contains

statues of Manuel Tomás de la Canal and his wife, who paid for the chapel; they are buried underneath their statues. After going down a narrow hall lined with Oriental tiles (brought by the Manila galleons to Acapulco), you'll enter a dazzling chamber, the Virgin's bedroom, where even the stonework is gilded. The tile is Spanish Talavera, laid in 1735.

The other unusual feature of San Felipe Neri rarely seen by visitors is the **Indian entrance** on the east side of the church. To get there, go through the wooden gate, which is almost always open, at the front of the atrium. On the other side is the simple but beautifully carved entrance, with its Indian cherubs and plumes etched in stone. Originally, this was the portal of an older church that was taken from its humble congregation by legal trickery. In time, a grand new building was raised on the site by the rich *criollo* parishioners. Time has given the story a fittingly ironic ending: San Felipe Neri is once again the main church for the townspeople of San Miguel de Allende, whose ancestors once entered it through what is now the side door.

One block west of the main plaza, the convent and church of **La Concepción**, usually called "Las Monjas," dominates its neighborhood. Here the remarkable but unoriginal imagination of Ceferino Gutiérrez is again apparent. His façade for La Parroquia borrowed from several Gothic cathedrals, just as here he re-created the dome of Les Invalides in Paris—not exactly but quite obviously. The dome is a century old; the church goes back an additional hundred years.

Almost all of the massive former convent behind the church has been taken over by the government and turned into a school of the arts, part of the national system. Properly known as the Centro Cultural "El Nigromante," it is generally called **Bellas Artes** and is the focal point of the town's cultural life, especially for music. It boasts a magnificent patio, one of the most ambitious such designs in the country, and a small covey of nuns remains secluded in a corner of the building, squeezed between the church and the art center. Remarkably, their convent survived the battles and anti-clerical campaigns of the 1920s, and was perhaps the only one in Mexico not to be "opened" by revolutionary troops. The existence of this marooned little convent is still illegal, but nobody seems to care.

Staying in San Miguel

San Miguel has been receiving travellers since the early 17th century, when every week mule and burro trains arrived with silver ore bound for the capital. Today ancient inns line two streets, and the visitor has a wide selection of hotels whose managements have a good idea of what foreigners want and expect.

Almost all the inns in town are small and have only two stories. (The town's single elevator is looked upon with suspicion.) There is no air-conditioning, but then it isn't needed at an elevation of 6,400 feet. It is best to have quarters within easy walking distance of the main square, since San Miguel distances are vertical as well as horizontal; the steep hill must be taken into account. A few otherwise good hotels are too far out or too far up.

The **Casa de Sierra Nevada**, Hospicio 35, occupies four colonial houses, one a true mansion, that have been converted into rooms and suites. Some have patios, roof terraces, and fireplaces, and all are decorated with fine crafts and colonial-style pieces. The tone is refined and international (a former First Lady of the United States is a frequent guest), and the emphasis is on personal service and attention. Guests may have breakfast in the excellent dining room (discussed under Dining, below), on a verdant patio, in their own rooms, or on their terraces. No credit cards are accepted, but personal checks may be used by prior arrangement. The inn is near the center of town, slightly but not formidably uphill.

On the same quiet street, a step higher in topography but a decided step lower in price, is the well-named **Hacienda de las Flores**, a garden inn with restful lawns and a heated swimming pool. The hacienda has a modest entrance typical of San Miguel—noncommittal until you are fully inside—but then it opens onto a building and landscape designed to blend in with the colonial town. The rooms, actually junior suites, are attractive, spacious, and have good views. The hotel's intimate lounge centers around a fireplace. Two meals are included in the daily rate. Children are welcome; credit cards are not.

Attracting the same type of knowledgeable clientele is the **Villa Jacaranda**, located a little farther from the plaza but on a level street at Aldama 53. The rooms and suites, some with private patios, are excellent, as are the classic films shown in the evening in a friendly lounge. The small heated swimming pool also has a whirlpool. (Villa Jacaranda's fine restaurant is discussed under Dining, below.)

La Puertecita, situated near the crest of the hill on Calle Santo Domingo, is the town's newest, most luxurious inn and spa, pampering its guests with Jacuzzis, a game and billiard room, fireplaces, and private patios and terraces with magnificent views. Health and fitness are the watchwords here, with aqua-aerobics offered in an extra-large pool and in-house masseurs and masseuses; smokers should look elsewhere. Twenty-four-hour room service and excellent food are available on call, and hotel vans will take guests to the local restaurant of their choice—or anywhere else for that matter. La Puertecita is an outstanding inn, expensive but not overpriced.

El Patio, another small hotel, offers its guests spacious colonial-style suites in the center of town on Calle Correo, a convenient but traffic-choked area just a few steps west of the post office. Its suites harmonize perfectly with the colonial ambience of San Miguel and its restaurant features Mexican cuisine in the same baronial building.

The **Villa Santa Monica**, on the south side of town at Calle Baeza 22, facing the Parque Benito Juárez, looks like the stage set for a Mexican operetta: tile roofs, an arcaded patio, and a lovely garden. The rooms are cheerful and comfortable, but the restaurant, which serves only breakfast and lunch, is merely so-so. Also, the inn is just beyond convenient walking distance from the center of town, especially at night.

Generations of art students and vacationing teachers have chosen the provincial surroundings at the **Posada de las Monjas**, two blocks downhill from *el jardín*. The new section is nicer than the older part up front. The new **Hotel Monte Verde**, two blocks farther from the plaza, at Voluntarios 2, combines modern comfort with colonial decor, and has a flowering central garden and a good restaurant. The attractive rates make it worth the longer walk.

One of the best buys in town is the unpretentious but more than adequate **Casa Carmen**, located a few steps from the central post office on Calle Correo. Heated rooms encircle a pretty patio. Guests return often to this friendly pension for both its accommodations and its food.

Dining in San Miguel

Because of tourism and the presence of the foreign community, San Miguel's restaurants surpass those of neighboring cities in both quality and number. Still, regional fare of distinction is scarce here, and most of the better dining places emphasize "international" food, a cuisine that is sometimes a little hard to pin down.

The **Bugambilia**, Hidalgo 42, is an exception and has clung staunchly to a Mexican menu for three generations. The dishes are classical: *tinga, sopa Azteca,* steaming *caldo de res* with a chunk of chewy stewing beef, *chiles en nogada* sporting the national colors. There is also guitar music in the attractive patio of this former private home, which remains a bit rustic and nicely plain. Closed Wednesdays. No credit cards.

The expensive **Restaurant Casa de Sierra Nevada**, in the hotel of the same name at Hospicio 35, has flair and imagination. Reservations are advised because the elegant dining room seats only 32 (though other seating is available in the less formal patio); there is also an intimate little bar off the far side of the patio. Soft classical guitar music; dress code evenings. No credit cards. Tel: (465) 2-0415.

The **Villa Jacaranda**, Aldama 53, also a hotel dining room, displays on its walls the various awards for excellence it regularly captures from travel magazines. The menu is international, the presentation and service meticulous. In addition to a cheerful main room with views of the patio, a glassed-in gazebo overlooks the leafy treetops of a nearby park. The atmosphere, food, and service justify the high prices.

Two blocks north and west of the plaza at Calle de Mesones 101, **La Hacienda de Pepe** is popular with San Miguel's foreign colony, especially for Sunday brunch. Its two rustic patios and handsome rooms resemble a movie set for *Ramona* or *Zorro*. The menu includes traditional Mexican and international dishes.

La Vendimia, half a block north of the *jardín* at Hidalgo 12, serves a limited menu of international specialties in a fine old town house. Excellent food and service.

Restaurante El Correo, in a historic residence across from the post office at Correo 21, is a simple but quaint dining room and coffee shop. The varied menu, including numerous breakfast selections, is moderately priced.

La Dolce Vita is a European-style coffee-and-pastry café, a place to browse through newspapers and magazines. Located on the second patio of Canal 21.

San Miguel tends to call it a night after a late supper. **Mama Mía**, a pizza emporium at Umarán 8, offers flamenco guitar music in a popular patio and various combos in a smaller bar. **Pancho and Lefty's**, Mesones 99, has a Texas saloon feeling, complete with a neon beer sign above the bar, and features changing entertainment: jazz, country and western, and combos. The town's discos cater to teenagers, although oldsters in their twenties do not arouse suspicion.

Shopping in San Miguel

Metalwork, especially in tin and brass, is excellent in San Miguel, and a good buy. The town's weavers also offer fine quality, but the selection is more limited here than elsewhere. Furniture making in colonial or provincial style is a local tradition, and you'll also find a wide selection of embroidered clothing and a small but good choice of leatherware.

Two reputable places create wonderful items in silver: **Beckman**, Hernández Macías 115, and **David**, Zacateros 53.

There are galleries and boutiques all around the main plaza and in any street within a block of it. Others line Calle Zacateros two blocks west.

The **Casa Cohen**, Reloj 18, is the country's best maker of cast brass and also offers other items of more than usual interest. **El Pegaso**, a gathering place for coffee drinkers located across from the post office, displays carefully selected clothing and other unusual goods. The **Casa Canal**, at the corner of Canal and the main plaza, is a virtual museum of provincial furniture; it is also a boutique.

Special Events and Studies

The frequent concerts and musical events in San Miguel range from soloists to symphony orchestras. The **Chamber Music Festival**, which features internationally known string quartets and offers master classes, is staged every August. Bellas Artes will be happy to provide information by mail (San Miguel de Allende, Guanajuato, Mexico 37700). A smaller but equally pleasing string festival is staged at Christmastime by a different sponsor. In addition, several theatrical performances are given each year, some in Spanish, others in English. Of course, art exhibits open with some frequency in this art colony.

On most Sundays at noon the **Biblioteca Pública** (Public Library) conducts a tour of local houses and gardens—an excellent opportunity to "see behind the walls." Not surprisingly, it's a very popular event. The library is on Calle Insurgentes between Hidalgo and Reloj.

For four decades special San Miguel schools have attracted students who are mostly English-speaking. The **Instituto Allende** on Calle Ancha de San Antonio offers a curriculum of fine arts, crafts, and Spanish. The School of the Art Institute of Chicago uses the Instituto's colonial-style campus for its study-abroad plan; students and teachers from the Rhode Island School of Design also come to San Miguel every winter. The Centro Cultural "El Nigromante" (Bellas Artes) offers classes in the arts and crafts, as well as some musical instruction. Two schools specialize in Spanish and related subjects only: The **Academia Hispano Americana**, at

Mesones 4, is quite traditional in its by-rote approach; the newer **Casa de la Luna**, Cuadrante 2, is more innovative.

AROUND SAN MIGUEL

North of the town is an area dotted with hot mineral springs bubbling from the ground. Naturally, spas and resorts have sprung up here, the most impressive being the **Hacienda Taboada**, 8 km (5 miles) north on the highway to Dolores Hidalgo. This spa offers an Olympic-size pool with geothermally heated water, 60 rooms done in Mediterranean decor, and all hotel services, as well as horseback riding and free transportation to and from San Miguel. Non-guests are admitted to the rather posh facilities every day from 9:00 A.M. until 6:00 P.M. Less costly and much less luxurious spas in the neighborhood (on the same highway as the Hacienda Taboada) include **La Gruta** and **El Cortijo**, both popular with the locals.

Nearby, but quite different from the picniclike gaiety of a spa, the hulking **Santuario de Atotonilco** is a repository of Mexican folk painting, offering a glimpse into a corner of Catholicism seldom seen. Although the main building was begun in 1754, a medieval grimness and chill seemingly centuries older pervade this sprawling maze of rooms and corridors. (Only the center section is open to the public.) Each year thousands of religious penitents trek to the shrine to attend "exercises," to cleanse themselves and be shriven. Little whips called *disciplinas* are available for those who want them, and discarded crowns of thorn are often found outside.

Inside, in room after room, walls and ceilings are frescoed with naïve but skillful murals charmingly executed. Never have pain, suffering, and penance been portrayed more cheerfully. Sometimes the themes of these murals stray from the religious: The naval battle of Lepanto, for example, appears on a chapel ceiling, and elsewhere legends mix freely with miracles. But the overarching theme is wickedness, remorse, and pain. Here you will confront the dark side of faith and be reminded of the days when saints mortified their flesh and starved themselves atop pillars.

The village of **Atotonilco** itself is also historically important, for it was here that Father Hidalgo seized the banner of the Virgin of Guadalupe and proclaimed her patroness and generalissima of the Mexican forces, an honor she unofficially holds to this day.

Fifty-two kilometers (32 miles) south of San Miguel via

Highway 51 lies the industrial and commercial center of **Celaya**. In the center of this otherwise uninteresting city stands the masterwork of Eduardo Tresguerras, the **Templo de Nuestra Señora del Carmen**, which was erected in 1807. Tresguerras, as architect, sculptor, muralist, and decorator, created a light-bathed interior that proved it was possible to inject warmth into the usually severe Neoclassical style. In a mural depicting the Judgment Day, the artist himself is shown emerging from a tomb, quite uncertain of his future.

Still farther south, 114 km (71 miles) from San Miguel over paved and pretty country roads (Highway 51 south to Salvatierra, then west toward Moroleón)—an easy one-day excursion or, alternatively, a stop on the way to Morelia (for which, see below)—lies the town and lake of **Yuriria**. The town is noted for its massive Augustinian monastery, which was begun in 1550 and completed in 1568. In the 18th century it was expanded to include a lofty cloister, buttresses, and a new main entrance. Today the building's impact is overwhelming, impressing the visitor as a prime example of the "fortified" religious centers of the early days of the colonial era. Several missionaries who were later martyred in Japan studied here while en route from Spain to the Far East. Ask to be admitted to the bell tower, which commands a sweeping view of the lake and countryside. Unfortunately, there are no especially worthwhile hotels or restaurants in the Yuriria area.

Viajes San Miguel, a travel agency in a courtyard at Sollano 3, almost on the corner of Correo, arranges local tours and explorations; they also handle national and international travel arrangements.

THE CITY OF GUANAJUATO

For most visitors from north of the border, Guanajuato is little short of astonishing. With its narrow, tortuous streets that lose themselves in flower-bedecked plazas, unexpected balconies and bridges, and red-tiled roofs that lie level with the street above, few places in the world seem as exotic to northern eyes. Guanajuato both eludes and inspires description. Travellers speak of similarities to the hill towns of Italy, to southern Spain, even to the Aegean islands—all close to the mark but none quite hitting it. The fact is, Guanajuato retains a peculiar combination of Mexican and European qualities that is unrivaled.

It was once the second-largest city in Mexico and one of the wealthiest in the world—no place in Latin America

Guanajuato

(map not to scale)

could match it for the sheer display of its riches. The treasure that poured from its silver mines is legendary and beyond reckoning. The opulent structures left behind are mostly relics of two eras: the silver-mad 18th century, and just prior to the turn of our own century, when great new strikes again filled the local coffers. As a result of the Mexican fondness for different styles in both these periods, Guanajuato today is a mélange of the Spanish, Moorish, Italian, and French. The styles are not mixed. Instead, they stand side by side in happy defiance of each other, bewildering and wonderful all at once.

Guanajuato is sometimes offered as a one-day excursion from Mexico City. Certainly, you can cover the highlights of this compact city in a day, but even so it requires a sightseeing marathon. Instead, at least two full days should be allotted, and twice that amount of time would not be misspent. The city's monuments are impressive, but the greatest pleasure is derived from simply wandering among its picturesque plazas and fountains and getting lost in its colorful maze of streets and alleyways.

Visitors exploring the town will look in vain for an art gallery or good bookstore. Guanajuato, despite its claims to the contrary, has no intellectual climate to speak of—and this includes the university. In such matters, the citizens are quite unlike the elegant, imaginative buildings of their city. Never having been situated on a trade route, Guanajuato is a closed, provincial town clinging tenaciously to its old ways and, in some matters, to its self-satisfied isolation. The folk who live in this dramatic cityscape did not create it, and today outside support sustains it. The state and national governments are the sponsors of the community's performing arts groups, for example.

Guanajuato is also devoutly religious, its Catholicism of a conservative bent. You need look no farther than the **Cerro del Cubilete**, a looming mountain 13 km (8 miles) outside the city, for proof. Atop it, at what is reputed to be the geographical center of Mexico, towers a gigantic statue of *El Cristo Rey* (Christ the King) that dominates the great valley below it. This is not only a religious monument but a striking symbol of the will of the local people, who by a large majority resisted the national laws limiting the power of the clergy.

Around in Guanajuato

Guanajuato crouches in a gorge, hemmed in by rock walls. Although it's the capital of the state of the same name, a university town, and a busy city of some 75,000 people, it can be reached only by car or bus. If you come by car, after one initial detour, suggested below, your vehicle should be safely parked and then forgotten during your stay here. Guanajuato is truly an ordeal for drivers.

Almost all traffic enters from the west, skirting the ghost town of Marfil. Once Marfil was rich beyond measure, a place where bullfights were staged in the private patios of mine owners' mansions and opera companies were imported to perform, but those days are long gone. Almost adjoining Marfil to the southwest is the **Hacienda San Gabriel de Barrera**, its lovely gardens with French-inspired landscaping. The remaining estate buildings are of some interest, but the gardens outshine everything else in the neighborhood.

At the edge of town, the **Carretera Panorámica**, a skyline drive that offers a spectacular introduction to the city, veers sharply to the right and is easy to miss. The road climbs steeply toward a titanic statue of El Pípila, a local hero of independence (his story is told below). At the statue, near stands heaped with souvenirs and junk, is a perfect place to view the magnificent gorge, the city, and the high hills with their fortified mines and scarred and rocky slopes—all this is spread out below in a spectacular panorama.

Silver was the only excuse for building a city in this improbable place, but of silver there was plenty. In fact, the monarchs of Spain were deluged with silver for the better part of two and a half centuries, and fully half of it came from this inhospitable canyon. The first major lode was discovered in 1548—just 20 years after the town was founded—a bonanza that was only the beginning of its long and happy affair with the metal.

From the statue of El Pípila, the Panorámica winds eastward and down, debouching in a neighborhood known as **La Presa**, where the streets are lined with edifices financed by the city's last great windfall from silver, at the end of the 19th century. Many are sumptuously French Romantic and Italianate, so grand it is hard to imagine them as formerly private homes. (They now serve as offices, public buildings, and apartment houses.)

Just past this district is the entrance to the **Avenida Subterráneo Miguel Hidalgo**. Some years ago, to relieve traffic, the city utilized a number of mine tunnels and an old riverbed to create an underground thoroughfare that runs through the heart of the city. As a result of serendipity, the engineers also managed to create an unusual visual experience for visitors: The thoroughfare twists among the foundations of the town, its roof reinforced by a tangle of old mine cables embedded in concrete and stone. The effect is at once romantic and eerie, and will stay with the visitor long after the many meals eaten and shops visited are forgotten.

Avenida Miguel Hidalgo goes underground near the *mercado,* an area where a car or taxi becomes a definite encumbrance. The market, which bears an incongruous resemblance to an Italian railway station, offers a profusion of foods, goods, and gimcracks. The crafts mezzanine is worth the climb, if only for a view of the jumbled colors below. The merchandise offered here includes fake antique bells, machine-made cloth, and mass-produced figurines appropriate as prizes at a shooting gallery and little else. The sad truth is, there are no worthwhile crafts in Guanajuato and no surviving craft tradition to speak of.

The Alhóndiga de Granaditas

A block up the hill from the market is the broad esplanade behind the Alhóndiga de Granaditas, where every year the **Cervantino**, an international festival of performing arts honoring the master, Miguel de Cervantes, is staged. The festival, which is held in late autumn, once glittered with the stars of the music and dance worlds. In particular, during the six years when Carmen de López Portillo was First Lady of Mexico, it enjoyed bountiful patronage; she even arranged the restoration and scrubbing up of part of the city to improve its setting. These days, artists still come to the festival from a score of countries, but it nevertheless seems to have lost its glitter.

Short farces and skits from Spain, some by Cervantes, are performed by students during the Cervantino. These romps, called *entremeses,* are essentially mime shows and were written to be played as comic relief between the acts of Spanish dramas; the broad jokes are funny in any language, however.

The fortresslike Alhóndiga de Granaditas, one of the most prominent buildings in Mexican history, looms over the esplanade. Originally built as a granary, it served as a refuge for Royalist supporters when Hidalgo's rebels attacked the city in 1810. With the confrontation threatening to swing in favor of the Royalists, Juan Martínez, a miner from San Miguel who would be known to history as El Pípila, tied a broad flagstone to his back, and, so shielded, braved enemy fire to set the wooden doors of the granary aflame (an action that cost him his life). Rebels surged into the building, where a hand-to-hand struggle and, ultimately, a butchery of the Spaniards ensued. The few survivors retreated step by step to the roof, only to be slain there. Even this was not the end of the horror, however. Days later, after 247 unarmed Spanish soldiers had been imprisoned in the building, a screaming mob broke in and murdered them all.

The slaughter changed the public's perception of the uprising. Spaniards throughout the country rallied in support of the Crown. When they finally recaptured Guanajuato, they retaliated with a bloodbath, killing every man, woman, and child they could get their hands on. If it hadn't been for a local priest, who stepped between the executioners and their intended victims holding aloft a cross as his only weapon, the massacre might have spread to other towns in the Bajío. But, as it was, the bloodshed in the Alhóndiga helped polarize Mexico for generations to come.

After the revolt ultimately failed, the heads of its leaders—Hidalgo, Allende, Jiménez, and Aldama—were sent back to Guanajuato and hung for ten years from iron hooks at the corners of the Alhóndiga. The hooks remain today.

A crafts museum has been set up in the building, its gaiety a welcome but odd note. In addition, Guanajuato painter Chavez Morado has dramatized the town's violent history in a series of powerful murals. There are also historical exhibits here, none of them especially fascinating, but one, a collection of small-town studio photographs that is ordinary at first glance, definitely worth closer inspection. It is a sweet and touching album of the city: newlywed couples stiff in their finery, awkward soldiers, and miners with their hair slicked down for the occasion.

Upon emerging from the Alhóndiga turn right and walk toward Calle Pocitos and the university. The building at Pocitos 47 is the house where the muralist Diego Rivera was born, and is now the **Museo Casa Diego Rivera**. The collection, not surprisingly, is meager, consisting of some old furniture and early Rivera practice pieces. What *is* surprising is not that the museum is modest, but that it exists at all—for years Rivera was persona non grata in his hometown. The town fathers despised the great painter for being an atheist, a leftist, and a mocker of the Church and society. Pious Guanajuato, which resisted the revolution Diego glorified, never forgave the sinner, and never had second thoughts about forcing his family, wicked liberals all, to leave the city. The little museum, needless to say, is of recent vintage.

The **Museo del Pueblo de Guanajuato**, Pocitos 7, was once the home of a noble Spanish family. On display are a number of good provincial paintings of the colonial era, as well as works by Hermenegildo Bustos, a 19th-century talent.

The many broad stairways of the **Universidad de Guanajuato** sweep upward toward a towering structure that is a less-than-happy mixture of Spanish colonial architecture and something else. The pale university building dominates a portion of the cityscape, an odd reversal of roles in light of the fact that the university has always been subservient to the interests of the city and its politicians. The school, in contrast, is tame and traditional.

Just to the east is the lovely **Templo de la Compañía**, an 18th-century Jesuit contribution to the city's beauty and an admirable example of Baroque architecture as it began to flower into the more elaborate Churrigueresque style. A block southeast the way widens into the charming, Italianate **Plaza del Baratillo**, where sunlight plays on a fountain Maximilian gave to a city that entertained him lavishly. Students live on the upper floors of the old buildings in this neighborhood, and much of the university's rather sedate social life is centered here. In addition, the University of Guanajuato produces some of the best *estudiantinas,* student musical groups akin to glee clubs, in the country. Students in the romantic beribboned costumes of Old Spain sing through the streets at least once or twice a month.

South of the Plaza del Baratillo is the **Jardín de la Unión**, one of the loveliest and most inviting little plazas in Mexico. As public squares go, this is a mere postage stamp, but the leafy low-branched laurels form a canopy that shades its pretty benches of painted iron. On the southwest side of the plaza two adjacent buildings present façades exemplifying the richest architectural periods of the city's history: the exterior of the Teatro Juárez is a Neoclassical dream, while next to it rises, a little feebly, the weathered **Templo de San Diego**, an exquisite 18th-century Churrigueresque fantasy in stone. In different languages the two façades proclaim the same thing: the affluence of their builders.

The **Teatro Juárez** is such a delightful building that only a curmudgeon would call some of it a little silly. The green columns of its façade, quarried locally, ascend majestically behind bronze lions. On the roof rest eight allegorical female figures, also bronze. Interestingly, these Hellenic ladies were the work of one W. H. Mullen of Salem, Ohio, and were purchased in the 1890s, an era when Mexico renounced all things Mexican.

The lavish interior is a marvel as well, its ceiling resembling a carpet out of the *Arabian Nights.* The stage curtain was reportedly copied from a backdrop at La Scala a century ago. Throughout the building the details and furnishings are ostentatious, overdone, and yet somehow perfect. The sightlines from the boxes of honor are so bad that half the stage remains obscured; no matter, its occupants were royally displayed to the rest of the house.

Porfirio Díaz, "president" of the so-called republic from 1876 to 1880 and again from 1884 to 1911, attended the opening night here, arriving by special train with his whole cabinet and a good part of the capital's diplomatic corps. Across the street, in the Posada Santa Fé, there hangs today a painting of that special occasion. In it, the distinguished spectators are not looking at the Italian singers on stage, but, naturally, at each other.

Back outside, Calle Sopeña becomes Avenida Juárez and makes for an interesting stroll as it heads northwest and slightly downhill past the Hotel San Diego. Branching off it are the narrow alleyways and "pocket" plazas that give Guanajuato such character. No matter where you walk in the city, however, you'll probably notice plaques with the dates "1885" or "1905" on them; these indicate the highwater marks of disastrous floods that hit Guanajuato in those years. (The river has since been diverted.)

The **Basilica Menor de Nuestra Señora de Guanajuato**, opposite the Plaza de la Paz, was erected in 1671 and has suffered so many changes that little of distinction remains. Housed in one of its chapels, however, sits a statue of the Virgin Mary purportedly hidden in a cave in Spain after the Moors invaded in A.D. 714. The statue, rediscovered eight and a half centuries later undamaged by either time or dampness, was declared miraculous. It was bestowed on the city in 1557 by Philip II, who was grateful for the flood of silver pouring in. The plain wooden figure is enhanced by a gemmed gown and a golden diadem weighing almost five pounds.

On the far side of the Plaza de la Paz you'll find the handsomest **town house** in Mexico, once the palace of the conde de' Rul, a Midas among millionaires. Not surprisingly, the ubiquitous Tresguerras was the architect of this severe, august mansion with its clean lines and perfect balance. The stone, a soft rose color, was the best the area had to offer. (The handsome patio is usually open for inspection.)

The grace of Tresguerras's simple design is made all the more striking by the close juxtaposition of the green and grandiose **Palacio del Gobierno**, its ornate decoration proclaiming its own importance.

The renowned **Callejón del Beso** (Alley of the Kiss) is a passageway and set of steps flanked by flowering balconies one block south of Avenida Juárez (turn onto Calle de Patrocinio at the charming Plazuela de los Angeles). A local legend tells of kisses stolen over balcony railings, a cruel father, and a girl whisked away to a convent.

The biggest indoor drawing card for visitors to Guanajuato is the **Museo de las Momias** (Mummy Museum), located next to the cemetery about half a mile west of the Alhóndiga. In fact, its turnstiles have proved to be the most profitable installation in town since the days of the first silver mine. About 60 "examples," as the cadavers are called, stand poised for inspection behind glass display cases. The exhibits are not mummies in the Egyptian sense, but corpses that have undergone a sort of tanning process due to exposure to chemicals in the ground before being dug up and thrust into show business.

The **Presa de la Olla** is one of two dams that have created artificial lakes near town. Picnickers come for the shade and breezes at the lakes, and rowboats are available for rent. The park area is located at the southeast corner of town, at the end of Paseo de le Presa.

The Silver Mines and the Silver King's Church

The **Valenciana Mine**, still operating and profitable, plunges 1,738 feet into the mountainside above Guanajuato. Old service buildings made of stone and tile remain, and visitors may look down a shaft whose mouth is supposed to represent the Crown of Spain. Far below, a black maze of tunnels twists and turns like the roots of a gigantic tree. Once the world's richest vein of silver, it yielded fully one-fifth of all the silver circulating in the world for nearly a century, and brought its owners, first the conde de Valenciana and then his son-in-law, the conde de Rul, unimaginable wealth.

Because it is an operating mine, visitors are not allowed to descend into the shaft of the Valenciana. Conditions and schedules for visits to other mines in the area change frequently; for up-to-date information, inquire at the state tourism office, located on the corner of Avenida Juárez and Cinco de Mayo. (Local guides will also have current information.) The Valenciana is located 4 km (2½ miles) north of town on the Dolores Hidalgo highway. Buses leave frequently from a spot near the municipal market; a cab costs the equivalent of $2 one-way.

Across the street from the Valenciana mine stands the church of the same name, which was begun by the conde de

Valenciana and continued by the conde de Rul with a little compulsory help from their mine workers during the second half of the 18th century. In the course of construction, silver dust and Spanish wines were added to the mortar, inspiring the comment that the count was not only bribing the Lord but "getting Him drunk at the same time." Nevertheless, the finished product reveals both wealth and superb craftsmanship. Connoisseurs of stone sculpture praise the elegant relief work around the church's main portal; the façade and interior carving are airy, and the pulpit is a masterpiece.

Staying in Guanajuato

Guanajuato's somewhat narrow range of hotels does not include any of Mexico's finest, and the difference between moderately priced hotels and budget accommodations here is not a step but a plunge. Travellers trying to cut costs would be advised to do it in other cities rather than here.

The **Posada Santa Fé**, built in 1862, faces the lovely Jardín de la Unión, an ideal location from which to explore the city. Rooms vary, and the first one offered you should not automatically be accepted. The interior rooms, untouched by sun, seem positively polar on winter nights. The hotel, which is on the expensive side, is nonetheless gracious, and its stately public rooms are rich with the charm of Old Spain transported to Mexico.

The **Hotel San Diego**, across the square from the Santa Fé, is a little less expensive than its neighbor. Its better rooms have patios or balconies with views of the town, the rooftop terrace is inviting, and the cellar-style bar romantic (and lively at times). There's also a dining room with a fine view from the two tables at the corner window, but the vista is the only reason to eat there; the hotel is much better than the restaurant.

Although the **Hostería del Fraile** has 36 rooms, it feels more like an intimate pension. You'll need to prepare yourself for the precipitous stairs, and take note that the outside rooms tend to be noisy while the inside ones are cramped. Still, its excellent location at Sopeña 3, near the Jardín de la Unión, its reasonable rates, and its pleasing details make this converted 17th-century mint a more than satisfactory inn.

The more expensive and mostly newer hostelries are found along the Dolores Hidalgo highway that leads to La Valenciana. Guests without a car will have to depend on the bus or wait, sometimes a while, for a taxi to arrive after one has been called.

As its name suggests, the **Castillo de Santa Cecilia** is a castle, albeit more Disney than medieval. Spacious lawns, gardens, terraces, a heated pool, and a nightclub boost the rates for good rooms. The hotel is more cheerful than its battlements would suggest, however.

The **Parador San Javier**, the largest of the hillside establishments, is a modern hostelry with colonial touches and boasts all the necessary conveniences of a high-quality inn. Some rooms have fireplaces, and there's a large pool, a disco, and a cocktail lounge as well. The place is a favorite of Mexico City residents who like to explore the provinces in style.

The **Motel Guanajuato**, like the Parador San Javier, offers its guests panoramic views from a perch high above the town. Modern and comfortable, as well as a little plainer and less expensive than its neighbors, it has a pool and quite a good restaurant.

On the opposite side of the city, about 2½ km (1½ miles) southwest of town on the Marfil road, the **Hotel San Gabriel de Barrera**, situated across a country lane from the famous gardens, is not cheap but is still an excellent value for those with a car who do not mind a ten-minute drive to the center of town. Everything is spacious at this former hacienda; the rooms, both public and private, are airy and bright; and the terraces overlook gardens and flowerbeds. There are tennis and swimming facilities as well.

Dining in Guanajuato

Keeping in mind that a trip to Guanajuato is for attractions other than cuisine, visitors should expect sustenance, not delight, from the town's dining establishments. Guanajuato cares little about the capricious tastes of tourists, and the local cookery lacks flair and imagination as a result.

The sidewalk café at the **Posada Santa Fé** is happily situated so that customers can ignore the mediocre fare and concentrate on the scene in the Jardín de la Unión instead. Nearby on the same plaza, try the **Casa Valdez** for snacks, breakfast, and a hearty soup. The best buys here, however, are soda fountain items and postcards.

The **Tasca de los Santos**, Plaza de la Paz 28, presents a Spanish-style menu featuring *fabada* and paella. It's not outstanding, but the reasonable prices are some consolation.

El Claustro, on the Jardín de la Reforma, one long block south and another block east of the Alhóndiga, is decked out like a Spanish tavern (Guanajuato seems to draw out the

Spanish side of Mexicans), and is popular with students. Egg dishes are the safest bet here.

Other downtown eateries are pretty much alike. Order simply and be patient. At the hillside hotels your choices are better. The Motel Guanajuato runs the best, most reliable kitchen in the region. The coffee shop at the Parador San Javier seems better than the dining room, perhaps because its simple surroundings keep expectations from rising too high. **Venta Vieja de San Javier**, across from the Parador, appeals more to the eye than the palate. The quality is not as high as the prices, but it offers more verve than most places.

As in most things, Guanajuato is restrained when it comes to nightlife. The Castillo Santa Cecilia offers decorous dancing every night except Sunday, with a minimum charge designed to cover supper and the entertainment. **El Pozo**, the club in the Parador San Javier, presents fairly good late-evening entertainment in an unusual setting complete with built-in waterfall.

MORELIA

Morelia, the most stately and handsome of Mexico's cities, is like the Roman god Janus or certain masks on Mayan temples: It faces two directions at once. That's because Morelia is among the most Spanish of Latin American cities. It looks like Spain, and sometimes it even *feels* like Spain, which is unusual in Mexico. Yet almost in its backyard are the communities and culture of the Tarascan Indians. But despite its profuse craft markets, its patriotic nods to pre-Columbian culture, and even its geography, Morelia remains solidly colonial in appearance and Mexican in its style.

In recent years Morelia has burgeoned into a city of about half a million people, spilling over its old boundaries and creating a ring of suburbs, developments, and industrial zones that isn't of much interest to the traveller. Inside this ring, however, lies another world.

Founded in 1541 by Don Antonio de Mendoza, New Spain's first and greatest viceroy, and christened Valladolid in honor of his home town, the city was designed to be the center of government and religion for a vast area (the modern state of Michoacán, of which present-day Morelia is the capital, constitutes only a part of that region). The city grew slowly, however, and it wasn't until the middle of the 17th century that it truly started to flourish. Even then, the optimism and foresight of its architects and builders, who laid out their little provincial town with a practicality and

spaciousness that are remarkable to this day and must have been revolutionary more than three centuries ago, was amazing. The results are obvious to anyone who has spent time in Mexico's other colonial gems. Unlike most of its contemporaries, Morelia is not only well preserved, it actually works. Its plazas and public buildings accommodate modern-day crowds easily and efficiently, and its lovely streets even allow you to get around by car.

The Cathedral

The first glimpse you get of this old city is of the domes, towers, and pinnacles of the imposing yet graceful cathedral. Begun in 1640 but not completed until 1744, its design was intended to be Plateresque, a style of decoration based on silver plate. During a century of construction, while a variety of architectural styles swept New Spain, the builders of Morelia's cathedral stuck to their plan, almost the only builders in the country to do so. The result is a beautiful example of Baroque ecclesiastical architecture made out of trachyte, a brown volcanic rock warmed by rose overtones. Carved overlays and low reliefs, not to mention a number of broad, plain areas, accent the six statues around the main portal. In addition to its two graceful towers it has an exceptional dome. While it is true that Mexico is a land bubbling with domes, this one is special; from inside, it seems to float above the nave, giving an impression of height far greater than it can actually claim.

Although Morelia never became as rich from silver as its founders had hoped, the cathedral once boasted a communion rail made of the precious metal. In 1858 the bishop of Morelia refused to pay a war assessment, however, and as a result his precious railing was ripped out and melted down. But the church has other treasures: paintings by a number of outstanding colonial artists as well as what is perhaps the best pipe organ in Latin America—a treat for both the ear and eye. Every May a festival held in the cathedral takes advantage of this marvel, with organists from many countries coming to play. In fact, Morelia has a rich musical heritage: Among other distinctions, it claims the first conservatory founded in the New World. Today a celebrated boys' choir helps to continue the tradition.

The Plaza de Armas Area

The idyllic **Plaza de Armas** (also called the Plaza de los Mártires, in honor of Mexico's slain patriots), a lovely square with a bandstand that is, in its modest way, as perfect as the adjacent cathedral, is the heart and hub of Morelia. This is the place to stroll, lounge, meet friends, and listen to band concerts.

Also inviting are the sidewalk cafés under the arcade across the street, where newspapers are read and politics discussed as students from the University of Michoacán, unusually purposeful for their age, hurry by.

The **Palacio de Gobierno**, the state capitol, faces the cathedral. Although an 18th-century structure, it could be 100 years older. (Morelia seems always to have been wary of newfangled architecture.) Inside, murals by one of Mexico's outstanding painters, the locally born Alfred Zalce, dramatically illustrate scenes from Mexico's past.

Two blocks north of the cathedral and plaza, at the corner of Guillermo Prieto and Santiago Tapia, is the **Museo del Estado**, the state museum. The building itself and the murals inside are better than the displays, which include the complete stock of a Morelian pharmacy circa 1868, Tarascan jewelry, and other artifacts.

In the opposite direction, on the corner of Allende and Calle Abasolo, an even better building houses the **Museo de Michoacán**. This former residence boasts beautiful Michoacán woodwork, starting with the front door. The arches are also unusually effective, as is the stairway. Once again, the structure, not the collection of historical items it houses, is the attraction here.

Three blocks east and two blocks south, at Avenida Morelos Sur and Aldama, is the **Casa Museo de Morelos**, the home of the hero for whom the city was renamed. Of all the early figures in Mexico's struggle for independence, José María Morelos was the most brilliant. Born in what was then Valladolid in 1765, he became a laborer on a hacienda when a young man. By almost starving himself to death he managed to make it through the Colegio de San Nicolás in his home town and became a priest. The revolt of 1810 was a call to greatness for Morelos, who emerged from obscurity to become the military genius of the rebellion. In a relatively short period of time, he raised, trained, and armed 9,000 men using captured equipment, and then gained control of virtually all of western and northern Mexico. Morelos, who stood barely five feet tall, cast a long shadow over Mexican history, both in his words and by his deeds, and Valladolid was renamed in his honor in 1828. The small museum is representative of a humble house of the hero's day.

Several impressive buildings are located along Nigromante a block west of the Plaza de Armas. The **Colegio de**

San Nicolás de Hidalgo is the second-oldest college in the New World, and the oldest one extant. The patriot Father Hidalgo studied and taught here, as did Morelos and Agustín de Iturbide, who would later proclaim himself Emperor of Mexico. The University of Michoacán, which now occupies part of the old building, is a descendant of this venerable institution.

The 17th-century **Palacio Clavijero**, across the street from San Nicolás, now houses a massive state library and industrial school. Its patio is magnificent and a must-see for visitors. At the end of the second block heading north, you'll come to the lovely **Jardín de las Rosas**—which isn't named for its abundant flowers but for the Templo y Conservatorio de las Rosas (Church and Conservatory of the Roses), the mellowed building across from this square. Once a girls' boarding school, it is now home to the Morelia Boys' Choir, whose singing can often be heard coming from this, the oldest music school in the Americas.

Three blocks east of Las Rosas stands the **Exconvento del Carmen**, now the government-sponsored **Casa de la Cultura**. Construction on the convent was begun in the late 1500s and continued for almost two centuries, producing a building of enormous proportions. The stairway and domed ceilings are especially noteworthy. Virtually next door to the former convent, the little **Museo de Arte Colonial** features an interesting series of displays, including a collection of religious figures made from cornstalks and sugarcane.

The Plaza Villalongín Area

The Parque y Plaza Villalongín, the most attractive strolling area in Morelia—high praise in a city where street after street vies for the attention of the visitor—is located about half a mile east of the cathedral on Avenida Madero Oriente. The small plaza itself is attractive, though a visitor can only marvel at the dreadfully kitsch sculpture of Indians and fruit here. The kindest word for it is memorable.

Beyond the plaza stands an **aqueduct** begun in 1785, an immense project designed to carry water more than a mile from the surrounding hills. Here you'll also find a shady promenade leading to the fanciful **Santuario de Guadalupe**, a church that's a bit of Morocco somehow Christianized and made Mexican. The neighborhood is woodsy, and a favorite Sunday spot for local families.

Staying in Morelia

When it comes to accommodations, there isn't a great range of choices in Morelia, but comfort, charm, and—in one case—luxury are available.

The city is walled off to the south by the steep slopes of the Santa María hills. On their crest, reached from the city via Calle Galeana, is a quiet neighborhood with lovely views and two secluded hotels. Both establishments are located a little more than 3 km (2 miles) south of town, past the Parque Juárez and across the Periférico, the main highway. Calle Tangaxhuan winds up the hill.

With spectacular views of the city and the long valley in which it is situated, the **Villa Montaña** is one of the country's better inns. Its bungalow units have all the amenities you'd expect in a first-rate establishment, including fireplaces, and some guests spend a good part of the winter here even though it isn't an inexpensive haven. The inn's dining room is also outstanding; see below.

Across the road, the **Posada Vista Bella** is less luxurious and less expensive, but quite satisfactory. It also offers, in addition to its regular units, a number of apartments for weekly or monthly rental, and a restaurant.

Downtown, just off the main plaza at Zaragoza 90, is the charming **Posada de la Soledad**, a former monastery that has been modernized with skill and taste. The patio garden, around which the hotel is built, is noted for its serene beauty. Not all of its 60 rooms are desirable, though; a few should be avoided because of kitchen noise, others because of leftover monastic chill.

The **Hotel Virrey de Mendoza** is Morelia's traditional choice for a good hotel on the plaza. Its style is colonial, the building old but recently remodeled and upgraded. The dining room under its covered central court is filled most nights.

The modern **Calinda Morelia Quality Inn**, 6 km (3½ miles) southeast of town on the Periférico opposite a shopping center, is well planned for comfort and convenience. Because its guests are more likely to be prosperous business travellers than tourists, its rates are designed for expense accounts, but the trained staff makes every effort to offer value for your money.

The cocktail lounges of the major hotels provide what entertainment the city has to offer, mostly piano music, with an occasional combo making an appearance.

You might also choose to stay in scenic Pátzcuaro, just to

the west (see the Western Highlands chapter) and make day trips to Morelia from there.

Dining in Morelia

The **Villa Montaña** keeps a fine restaurant and bar with a good wine selection. Non-guests should make reservations (small children are not welcome); Tel: (451) 4-0179. The menu is international—regional cookery appears to be taboo here.

Those who wish to sample the traditional dishes of the region will do well in the flowering patio or equally charming dining room of the **Posada de la Soledad**, just off the Plaza de Armas. Their special *sopa Tarasca* has the right zing, and the Pátzcuaro whitefish is delicate and flaky.

Los Comenzales, a simple, low-priced patio restaurant at Zaragoza 148, is devoted entirely to Michoacán and Mexican cuisine. Its fare is hearty rather than delicate, but the lengthy menu offers a good sampling of regional dishes. Try, for instance, *uechepos,* a slightly sweet cornmeal bread, or the little triangular tamales called *corundas. Ate Moreleon,* the most famous dessert item of the region, may appear in the form of any fruit paste, including pineapple, guava, mango, or papaya.

The **Restaurant Fonda las Mercedes** has an excellent kitchen, a colonial-style patio full of artwork and plants, and loads of charm. It is pleasant by day and enchanting by night, and the food is good enough to compensate for the slow service if you're not in a hurry. The restaurant is located three blocks west of the Plaza de Armas and half a block north at León Guzmán 47; Tel: (451) 2-6113.

The cafés under the arcade near the cathedral are better for snacks and sodas than for meals, but within their limits all are pleasing. Don't even think of trying to order when they're busy, however. Coffee or anything in a bottle will get to you; ordering anything else will be pressing your luck.

Shopping in Morelia

Morelia specializes in crafts from the various nearby Tarascan communities. Good quality can be found in a variety of stores, but the best choice is the fabulous popular arts market at the **Casa de las Artesanías** in the former Convent of San Francisco on Calle Humboldt, two huge floors crammed with items from all over the state. While buying here is not as exciting as going to a craft village and making your own discoveries, you will probably not find better bargains anywhere. The prices reflect real market value, and the selection is excellent. The only thing missing is the thrill of the hunt.

Michoacán lacquerware is an especially good buy here; the work is genuine and as lasting as this rather fragile craft can be. (In recent years there has been a lot of "forged" lacquerware—glossy auto paint sprayed on cheap wood—making the rounds. It takes a sharp eye and a bright light to spot the real thing.) On the other hand, you'll probably want to avoid the guitars; for those you must go to Paracho and search. (**Paracho**, noted for its woodcarvings and musical instruments, is a small town about an hour-and-a-half drive west of Morelia via Uruapan, where you turn north on Highway 37 for 25 km/16 miles. While its specialty is guitars, other quality handcrafted string instruments are also available.)

The Monarch Butterflies

In an awe-inspiring migration, 100 million monarch butterflies make their way annually from Canada and the United States to winter (early November until late February) in Michoacán's mountaintop forests of pine and oyamel trees. A visit to the groves at this time of year will be an unforgettable experience.

The most popular point of departure for the sanctuary is the little mountain town of **Angangueo** in eastern Michoacán, about 97 km (60 miles) east of Morelia via Highway 15, then a marked but unnumbered road going east from 15 just north of Zitacuaro. The site, a rugged and scenic slope, is followed by an arduous climb up a steep path to the groves. The altitude will probably make it necessary for you to pause frequently along the way in order to catch your breath. Go slowly.

The scene that awaits you is worth the effort. On top, the trees are literally coated with monarchs; the muted sound you hear is the rustling of millions of wings.

If you make the trip from Morelia, plan to be on the road no later than 7:00 A.M. However, the experience is worth a leisurely trip. If you decide to take your time, you can stay overnight in clean but simple accommodations in Angangueo itself at the **Posada Don Bruno**. The famous old Hotel San José Purua, once a favorite for monarch watchers, now opens only erratically and cannot to be counted on. On the western edge of Zitacuaro, about 20 km (12 miles) south of Angangueo, the rustic but comfortable **Rancho San Cayetano** has a good restaurant and pleasant rooms. The inn is situated about a five-minute drive west of Highway 15 on the paved road that leads to Presa del Bosque; posted signs will help you find its quiet location.

GETTING AROUND

Driving Down from the Border

The two routes discussed here both converge on San Luis Potosí, at the northern edge of the Bajío. The McAllen–Reynosa border crossing is especially popular with drivers coming from the U.S. Gulf Coast states. The Laredo–Nuevo Laredo crossing is the gateway to the most heavily travelled route to central Mexico. We will cover the first route in its entirety before turning our attention to the latter, which includes a brief discussion of hotels and restaurants in San Luis Potosí, and winds up in Querétaro.

McAllen–Reynosa

Although Reynosa has a few acceptable hotels, all the better choices are located on the U.S. side of the border in McAllen.

For years the route from Reynosa followed Highway 40 to China, Highway 85 south to Montemorelos and Linares, and then Highway 58 west to San Roberto, where it joined Highway 57. Nowadays, however, many drivers prefer going via Ciudad Victoria and Huisache Junction, a route that offers the advantages of a smoother road and lighter local traffic. Although most of the surrounding countryside hardly can be called scenic, it is more varied than the trip via Linares, and so it's the one described here.

Highway 97, the road to Ciudad Victoria, begins at the customs station in Reynosa. It's an adequate road, fairly fast, and heads due south through poor ranchland. At a crossroads 107 km (66 miles) south of Reynosa, it is joined by Highway 101/180, which then branches off to the west some 32 km (20 miles) farther south. Stay on Highway 101 as it heads inland through Jiménez and a number of other small towns until it reaches the slightly more prosperous citrus country around Ciudad Victoria, the attractive capital of the state of Tamaulipas.

Three kilometers (2 miles) north of Ciudad Victoria you'll spot **Paradise** on the left side of the highway. While less heavenly than its name, Paradise is nevertheless a welcoming establishment, its cool, muted dining room the perfect antidote to the glare of midday. In addition to its attractive restaurant, the inn also offers modern, comfortable overnight accommodations.

Perched in the foothills of the Sierra Madre Oriental,

Ciudad Victoria is a well-kept provincial capital with a number of handsome turn-of-the-century buildings. It's also your best bet for a lunch and/or gasoline stop; the roadside facilities between here and Huisache Junction, a 3½-hour drive to the southwest, are limited (although you'll pass two widely spaced Pemex stations along the way). In the center of town, facing the Plaza Hidalgo, stands the gracious **Hotel Everest**, with its cheerful, pleasant rooms, good dining room, and convenient coffee shop. On the same plaza, the **Hotel Sierra Gorda** is also a good choice for a meal (its kitchen specializes in regional cookery) or an overnight stay.

You'll notice that the surrounding hillsides become steeper as soon as you leave town heading south and west on Highway 101. (Road signs along this stretch say "Tula," which is not to be confused with the famed archaeological zone outside of Mexico City.) And, in fact, the first 62 km (38 miles) of the route follow a winding road that snakes along a succession of ridgelines. The going is slow but not particularly hazardous, and you'll be rewarded by a measure of coolness as you gain altitude. Gradually the ascent will level off and you'll begin the almost imperceptible climb toward the great *altiplano,* or central Mexican plateau, passing the settlements of Tula, Colonel, and La Viga along the way.

At the junction of Highways 101 and 80, turn right and follow the latter 58 km (36 miles) to Highway 57, the principal north–south route into Mexico City. You'll begin to see high mountains in the distance along this stretch, with Cerro San Cristóbal, the tallest peak in the area, rising some 7,000 feet a short distance to the south.

Highway 80 veers sharply to the south as it joins Highway 57 just beyond the village of Huisache. From the junction of the two you can follow Highway 57 through San Luis Potosí and Querétaro into Mexico City. (For route and accommodations information in and around San Luis Potosí, see below.)

Laredo–Nuevo Laredo

The route from Laredo/Nuevo Laredo to San Luis Potosí and Querétaro is the most heavily travelled route to central Mexico, and thus is the best maintained, has the most frequent emergency service, and boasts the nicest tourist facilities. For the most part, Highway 85/57 offers fast, easy travel (although traffic can be slowed by tractor-trailer trucks on certain two-lane stretches) all the way to San Luis Potosí, some 756 km (469 miles) distant. The scenery, on the other hand, is nothing to write home about.

There are plenty of decent accommodations in Laredo, but many travellers prefer to clear border formalities and spend the night in **Nuevo Laredo**, both to take advantage of slightly lower prices and to ensure there are no delays in the morning: Traffic tie-ups on the international bridges and long lines at Mexican customs can get anyone's vacation off on the wrong foot.

Set on attractively landscaped grounds 5 km (3 miles) south of the International Bridge on Highway 85, **El Río Motel** offers large, airy rooms smartly decorated with provincial furnishings and a restaurant noted for its Mexican specialties. The **Hacienda Motor Hotel**, 4 km (2½ miles) farther south on Highway 85, is of comparable quality.

The hotels in downtown Nuevo Laredo tend to be noisy and afflicted with a seedy border-town atmosphere. Students and other budget travellers often choose the **Hotel Siesta**, a plain but adequate establishment near the center of town at Ocampo 559. A little fancier and more expensive, if not noticeably better, is the **Hotel Reforma**, also downtown at Avenida Guerrero 822.

Leaving Nuevo Laredo on Highway 85, you will probably be waved through a customs checkpoint 18 km (11 miles) south of town. (When drivers are stopped, it's almost always to check for a car permit.) The surrounding countryside is flat and semi-arid, but the poor soil manages to support a few ranches raising sorghum. The only trees you'll see are Joshua trees, a relative of the century plant.

Sabinas Hidalgo, 136 km (84 miles) south of Nuevo Laredo, is the only town of any size before you get to Monterrey. Next to a large Pemex station on the right is the Ancira Café and Curio Shop, adequate for bottled drinks, packaged snacks, and breaking up the drive. The Café Los Jacales, across the street, is in the same league.

As you get closer to Monterrey, mountains flanking the highway at some distance add a little variety to the scene. The most famous peak is Cerro de la Silla (Saddle Mountain), which comes into view about 186 km (115) miles south of the border.

At the 214-km (133-mile) mark approaching Monterrey you'll come to a bypass on your right marked with an unofficial sign reading "Saltillo." This two-lane road, which has almost no services and is choked with trucks, reportedly has a high accident rate, and because it's a winding route, making passing risky, it probably won't save you any time. It does, however, provide an alternative for drivers who dread going through an unfamiliar big city. (Those who decide to take this bypass should follow the signs for Saltillo; the exit is marked, but heed the signs carefully to make sure you're in the correct lane.)

Travellers choosing instead to spend time in **Monterrey** will encounter a huge, burgeoning industrial city, the third largest in Mexico and by far the most Americanized. (A former president of the Republic once angrily accused it of being more Texan in spirit than Mexican.) It's also an expensive city, and not a place for budget travellers to linger.

Two of the more pleasant accommodations in Monterrey face each other across Highway 85, just after it has become Avenida Universidad, on the northern outskirts of the city. Those electing to stay at either place have a choice in the morning of continuing on through the city or backtracking 7 km (4 miles) to the bypass. The **Holiday Inn Monterrey**, Avenida Universidad and Calle 18 de Deciembre, is smart and moderately expensive, and offers good-sized suites, a large swimming pool, tennis courts, and a chic nightclub. The restaurant and coffee shop are also convenient for those passing through the city. Across the street, the **Royal Courts Motor Inn** is slightly less expensive, has a smaller swimming pool, and offers rather small but comfortably air-conditioned rooms.

The hotels in downtown Monterrey center around the Plaza Hidalgo. To get there, follow Avenida Universidad to the freeway and take the "Hidalgo" exit.

The **Hotel Ambassador** is one of the finest hostelries in the country. Built by the Westin Camino Real chain as a showplace for international business travellers, it is elegant right down to the details. The hotel has a lovely and inviting garden swimming pool, a very good coffee shop, and the outstanding **Pavillon Restaurant**, a little corner of Paris in Monterrey. A dress code is observed, and the restaurant is as expensive as you would expect in this luxury hotel. The **Ancira Sierra Radisson Plaza Hotel Monterrey** once saw Pancho Villa stable his horse in its lobby. Nowadays, the modernized Ancira retains an echo of its former Old World charm—a quality all too rare in Monterrey. While a little less costly than the Ambassador, it pampers its guests every bit as much.

Monterrey is connected to Saltillo by Highway 40, a good road that runs south and west for 85 km (53 miles) to its junction with the Saltillo bypass. **Saltillo**, just west of the bypass, is an attractive city with a few remaining colonial touches, but it doesn't really merit closer inspection unless you decide to stop for food and lodging, in which case it is less expensive than Monterrey and easier to explore.

The **Camino Real**, located 10 km (6 miles) southeast of town on Highway 57, offers very comfortable rooms and a range of amenities, including a well-managed restaurant. It is fairly expensive for the area, however. The much more reasonably priced **Posada San José**, on the opposite side of town, is a pleasing inn with a rooftop restaurant, a rooftop pool, and safe parking.

Highway 40 meets Highway 57 at a *glorieta* (traffic circle) north of town. In general, the latter is a fast road, but that's not the case as drivers navigate the curves and bridges immediately south of Saltillo. The road is subject to fogs here, and great caution must be exercised in such conditions.

Leaving the streams that generate much of this ground fog behind, the road plows through mile after mile of flat country dotted with cactus and ringed by distant mesas. Much of the area was a shallow sea in times fairly recent by geologic standards, and you'll get a real sense of travelling over a seabed encircled by the telltale rings of vanished shorelines. There is a Pemex station at San Roberto, 122 km (76 miles) south of Saltillo.

The cutoff to the ghost town of **Real de Catorce** is another 120 km (74 miles) south of San Roberto. For those who have an extra 5 hours for the excursion, it's a curious trip to a mountainside collection of mostly ruined buildings that was once a silver boomtown. There are, in addition, some simple restaurants and lodging houses in Catorce, although most visitors return to **Matehuala**, a little more than an hour's drive, for the night. Highway 57 bypasses Matehuala with no loss to travellers. However, many drivers bound for Mexico City, about a 7½-hour drive to the south, prefer to break the trip here, even though the choice of accommodations is better in San Luis Potosí, 178 km (110 miles) farther on.

On the Matehuala bypass, near a welcoming arch resembling a McDonald's sign, **Las Palmas** is the largest, most popular establishment. Its modern motel-type units are not overpriced, but its fairly good restaurant is. Las Palmas also has a large swimming pool, curio shop, and miniature golf course. The **Motel Hacienda**, a neighbor of Las Palmas, is much smaller but just as nice, with less of a truck-stop atmosphere. Its restaurant specializes in roast kid (*cabrito*) and other typically Mexican dishes. The **Motel Oasis**, also near Las Palmas, is economical and has a restaurant.

From Matehuala Highway 57 continues south through a barren and featureless landscape, with the Sierra Madre Oriental far to the east. Many of the roadside vendors you see will be selling snakeskins, while others offer caged birds fated to survive only briefly.

The town of **San Luis Potosí** lies west of the highway

inside a ring of heavy industry. For those who have the time, its picturesque colonial center repays exploration.

Three very good motels are conveniently located on Highway 57. The moderately expensive **Cactus Motel**, 1 km (½ mile) southeast of the traffic circle, offers excellent accommodations, saunas, a good restaurant, and a lively nightclub. It recently became a Howard Johnson franchise and has been remodeled. The **Hostal del Quijote**, on the west side of the road, 5 km (3 miles) southeast of the traffic circle, is one of the better highway inns between the border and the capital. It also maintains a good dining room, coffee shop, bar, and discotheque. The **Motel Santa Fé**, 1 km (½ mile) southeast of the traffic circle, offers adequate accommodations at economical rates as well as an attractive garden, a pool, and a restaurant.

In the center of San Luis Potosí, two blocks west of the Plaza de Armas on Avenida Carranza, the **Hotel Panorama** offers first-class rooms and a full range of services. Also on Avenida Carranza, another two blocks west of the hotel, is **La Virreina**, one of the better provincial restaurants in Mexico. While its Old World elegance is reminiscent of the turn of the century, diners in travelling clothes are made to feel welcome. The menu at La Virreina is international, but a variety of regional dishes will be prepared upon request.

South of San Luis Potosí Highway 57 is mostly a two-lane road until it meets Highway 110, 118 km (73 miles) distant. Signs pointing to the east read "San Luis de la Paz," to the west "Dolores Hidalgo." A right turn here will take you to San Miguel de Allende via Dolores Hidalgo, but this is neither the shortest nor the fastest way. For the shortcut continue south 15 km (9 miles) to the Los Rodríguez cutoff. A sign will point the way to San Miguel de Allende.

Querétaro lies 32 km (20 miles) ahead over Highway 57. On the northern outskirts of the city the bypass to Mexico City is a clearly marked left turn.

Querétaro

The most direct auto route from the capital is Highway 57, much of it a toll road. Count on the trip taking about 3 hours one-way. Daily rail service from Mexico City (approximately $8 one-way) leaves early in the morning and returns in the afternoon. Trains to all points leave from Mexico City's central station on Avenida Insurgentes Norte. Breakfast is included in a first-class ticket, a box lunch on the return trip. For attentive service, morning travellers should be at the dining room the moment it opens.

First-class bus service, which is faster than the train, is the usual choice for those not driving. There is good and frequent service from the capital to Querétaro, a major hub for almost all routes north and west, with about eight different buses leaving the D.F. every hour (fare approximately $5). The finest service, and the fastest, is offered by **ETN** lines (Tel: 5/567-3773) and **Primera Plus** (Tel: 5/587-5200). Both provide service to Querétaro from the capital as well as from Guadalajara. The fare is about double the first-class price. Buses depart Mexico City from the Central Caminero del Norte, also called the Terminal del Norte; the station is on Avenida de los 100 Metros, quite a way out on Insurgentes Norte. The metro stop for the terminal is Estación Terminal de Autobuses del Norte, more simply indicated on most system maps as TAN. Clearly marked city buses making limited stops also make the run to the terminal on Insurgentes.

Taking taxis is inexpensive and easier than trying to drive in Querétaro. Walking is also easy on the flat paving stones of this almost flat city. (Be sure to bring comfortable, thick-soled shoes, however.)

San Miguel de Allende

The most direct auto route from the capital to San Miguel is Highway 57 via Querétaro. As you near Querétaro, follow the signs to San Luis Potosí. The San Miguel cutoff is 25 km (16 miles) north of Querétaro. The entire trip will take about 3½ hours one-way.

One first-class bus leaves Mexico City every morning for San Miguel (fare approximately $7), arriving about 4 hours later. The line is **Tres Estrellas de Oro**; Tel: (5) 567-8157. **Primera Plus** and **ETN** buses, the best but at about double the first-class price, depart each morning from the capital as well as from Guadalajara. Primera Plus, Tel: (5) 587-5200; ETN, Tel: (5) 567-3773. Second-class bus service likewise departs from the capital's Terminal del Norte. Purveyors include Flecha Amarilla and Herradura de Plata. Both first- and second-class buses leave the D.F. every few minutes for Querétaro; San Miguel passengers failing to make a direct connection can go to Querétaro and change there.

There is little reason to have a car in San Miguel itself, but driving is the most practical way to explore the countryside. Car rentals are best arranged in Mexico City, however—rentals in San Miguel are uncertain and often unsatisfactory.

In town, comfortable thick-soled shoes are essential. Taxis are cheap and can be found near the *jardín* (they will seldom respond to phone calls).

Guanajuato

The relatively new international airport in León, 50 km (31 miles) northwest of Guanajuato, is serviced daily from Houston by Continental, from Los Angeles by Mexicana, and from Chicago three days a week by Mexicana. Aeroméxico offers a daily León–Los Angeles flight with a stop in Hermosillo. Taxis and *colectivos* are available to run visitors from the airport into Guanajuato; count on spending $15 for the former, less for a *colectivo*. Ground transportation to San Miguel and Querétaro, though more expensive, is also available. Cab fare to San Miguel de Allende will run about $50, but can be divided among as many as four passengers, depending on baggage.

A car is a great convenience for getting to Guanajuato and a nuisance afterward (except for guests at the outlying hotels). Bus travel is the usual choice from Mexico City (see Querétaro and San Miguel de Allende above). **ETN** runs a deluxe bus to and from the capital daily. For reservations in Mexico City, Tel: (5) 567-3773; in Guanajuato, Tel: (473) 2-3134. Second-class **Flecha Amarilla** has more daily trips to Guanajuato than any other line; Tel: (5) 567-8033 or 8173. **Tres Estrellas de Oro** is better but offers less frequent service; Tel: (5) 567-8157. Buses to and from San Miguel de Allende arrive and depart frequently. From the capital or Guadalajara insist on a direct (*directo*) bus.

Stout walking shoes are a must. Taxi service is cheap, courteous, and as efficient as the cramped streets will permit. There are also bus tours of the city, although they're usually conducted in Spanish only. Hotels will arrange for guide service if desired.

Morelia

Aeroméxico serves the Morelia airport daily from the capital. Car rentals are available at the airport, as are taxis and minibuses.

To reach Morelia by car from Mexico City follow Paseo de la Reforma through Chapultepec Park (west), staying on it as it becomes Reforma Lomas then joins Highway 15. The latter leads all the way to Morelia and is one of the most scenic routes in the country. For the last 103 km (64 miles), however, there are no roadside services; the last stop for gasoline and food is Ciudad Hidalgo. Allow 5½ hours for the drive.

Regular bus service is from the Terminal del Norte. Destinations include Guadalajara, Guanajuato, Pátzcuaro, and, of course, points in between. Visitors travelling directly to or from the capital will want to go via Toluca, the fastest, most scenic route. The fare is approximately $15. The **ETN** deluxe bus runs between the capital and Morelia morning and late afternoon for about $30 one-way. In Morelia, Tel: (451) 3-7440 for reservations; in Mexico City, Tel: (5) 567-3773.

Train service to Mexico City (approximately $19) is available but not recommended. There is also daily rail service to **Pátzcuaro** (see the Western Highlands chapter), but buses are a more dependable alternative for this short trip (40 km/ 25 miles) to the west.

Morelia is mostly flat, and thus an easy city for walking. Taxis are cheap and plentiful, but fares should be settled in advance to avoid unpleasant surprises.

ACCOMMODATIONS REFERENCE

The rates given below are projections for December 1992 through Easter 1993. Unless otherwise indicated, rates are for double rooms, double occupancy; the 10 percent VAT has been added. As rates are subject to change; it's always a good idea to double-check before booking.

▶ **Ancira Sierra Radisson Plaza Hotel Monterrey.** P.O. Box 697, **Monterrey**, Nuevo León 64000. Tel: (83) 45-1060; Fax: (83) 44-5226; in the U.S., Tel: (800) 333-3333. $177.

▶ **Cactus Motel.** P.O. Box 393, **San Luis Potosí**, San Luis Potosí 78090. Tel: (48) 22-1995; Fax: (48) 22-0550. $58.

▶ **Calinda Morelia Quality Inn.** Avenida de las Camelias 3466, **Morelia**, Michoacán 58270. Tel: (451) 4-1427; Fax: (451) 4-5476; in the U.S. and Canada, Tel: (800) 228-5151. $83.

▶ **Camino Real.** P.O. Box 55, Carretera 57, **Saltillo**, Coahuila 25000. Tel: (841) 5-2525; Fax: (841) 5-3813; in the U.S. and Canada, Tel: (800) 228-3000. $116.

▶ **Casa Carmen.** Calle Correo 31, **San Miguel de Allende**, Guanajuato 37700. Tel: (465) 2-0844. $46.

▶ **Casa de Sierra Nevada.** Calle Hospicio 35, **San Miguel de Allende**, Guanajuato 37700. Tel: (465) 2-1895. $121–$228.

▶ **Castillo de Santa Cecilia.** P.O. Box 44, Camino a la Valenciana s/n, **Guanajuato**, Guanajuato 36000. Tel: (473) 2-0485; Fax: (473) 2-0153. $83.

▶ **Hacienda de las Flores.** Calle Hospicio 16, **San Miguel de Allende**, Guanajuato 37700. Tel: (465) 2-1808. $131 (includes two meals).

▶ **Hacienda Jurica.** P.O. Box 338, Carretera 57, northwest of **Querétaro**, Querétaro 76100. Tel: (42) 18-0022; Fax: (42) 18-0136. $139.

THE COLONIAL HEARTLAND

▶ **Hacienda Motor Hotel.** P.O. Box 682, **Nuevo Laredo**, Tamaulipas 88000. Tel: (871) 4-4666; Fax: (871) 4-4521. $60.

▶ **Hacienda Taboada.** Kilometer 8, Carretera a Dolores Hidalgo, **San Miguel de Allende**, Guanajuato 37700. Tel: (465) 2-0850; Fax: (465) 2-1798. $123.

▶ **Holiday Inn Monterrey.** Avenida Universidad and Calle 18 de Deciembre, **Monterrey**, Nuevo León 66450. Tel: (83) 76-2400; Fax: (83) 32-0565; in the U.S. and Canada, Tel: (800) 465-4329. $86.

▶ **Holiday Inn Querétaro.** Carretera Constitución Sur 13, **Querétaro**, Querétaro 76010. Tel: (42) 16-0202; Fax: (42) 16-8902; in the U.S. and Canada, Tel: (800) 465-4329. $104.

▶ **Hostal del Quijote.** P.O. Box F-1893, **San Luis Potosí**, San Luis Potosí 78090. Tel: (481) 8-1312; Fax: (481) 8-6105. $108.

▶ **Hostería del Fraile.** Calle Sopeña 3, **Guanajuato**, Guanajuato 36000. Tel: (473) 2-1179. $43.

▶ **Hotel Ambassador.** P.O. Box 1733, **Monterrey**, Nuevo León 64000. Tel: (83) 40-6390; Fax: (83) 45-1984; in the U.S. and Canada, Tel: (800) 228-3000. $190.

▶ **Hotel Everest.** Calle Colón 126, **Ciudad Victoria**, Tamaulipas 87000. Tel: (131) 2-4050. $51.

▶ **Hotel Monte Verde.** Calle Voluntarios 2, **San Miguel de Allende**, Guanajuato 37700. Tel: (465) 2-1814. $46.

▶ **Hotel Panorama.** Avenida Carranza 315, **San Luis Potosí**, San Luis Potosí 78000. Tel: (481) 2-1777; Fax: (481) 2-5491. $60.

▶ **Hotel Reforma.** Calle Guerrero 822, **Nuevo Laredo**, Tamaulipas 88000. Tel: (871) 2-6250. $37.

▶ **Hotel San Diego.** P.O. Box 8, Jardín de la Unión, **Guanajuato**, Guanajuato 36000. Tel: (473) 2-1300. $54.

▶ **Hotel San Gabriel de Barrera.** Carretera Marfil, **Guanajuato**, Guanajuato 36000. Tel: (473) 2-3980; Fax: (473) 2-7460. $80.

▶ **Hotel Sierra Gorda.** Carretera 85 and Plaza Hidalgo, **Ciudad Victoria**, Tamaulipas 87000. Tel: (131) 2-2280. $48.

▶ **Hotel Siesta.** Ocampo 559, **Nuevo Laredo**, Tamaulipas 88000. Tel: (871) 2-4737. $33.

▶ **Hotel Virrey de Mendoza.** Portal de Matamoros 16, **Morelia**, Michoacán 58000. Tel: (451) 2-0633. $72.

▶ **La Mansión Galindo.** P.O. Box 16, Carretera 5, Amealco exit, **San Juan del Río**, Querétaro 76800. Tel: (467) 2-0050; Fax: (467) 2-0100. $161.

▶ **Mesón de Santa Rosa.** Pasteur Sur 17, Plaza de la Independencia, **Querétaro**, Querétaro 76000. Tel: (42) 14-5781; Fax: (42) 12-5522. $78–$95.

▶ **Motel Guanajuato.** P.O. Box 113, Carretera Dolores, km

2.5, **Guanajuato**, Guanajuato 36000. Tel: (473) 2-0689. $35–$43.

▶ **Motel Hacienda**. Carretera 57, km 618, **Matehuala**, San Luis Potosí 78700. Tel: (488) 2-0065. $37–$44.

▶ **Motel Oasis**. Carretera 57, km 617, **Matehuala**, San Luis Potosí 78700. Tel: (488) 2-0742. $31.

▶ **Motel Santa Fé**. Glorieta Juárez, **San Luis Potosí**, San Luis Potosí 78090. Tel: (48) 14-4774; Fax: (48) 14-4784. $75.

▶ **Las Palmas**. P.O. Box 73, **Matehuala**, San Luis Potosí 78700. Tel: (488) 2-0001; Fax: (488) 2-1396. $59.

▶ **Paradise**. Carretera 180, **Ciudad Victoria**, Tamaulipas 87000. Tel: (131) 2-2280; Fax: (131) 2-9799. $51.

▶ **Parador San Javier**. Aldama 92, **Guanajuato**, Guanajuato 36000. Tel: (473) 2-0626; Fax: (473) 2-3114. $81.

▶ **El Patio**. Calle Correo 10, **San Miguel de Allende**, Guanajuato 37700. Tel: (465) 2-1647; Fax: (465) 2-3180. $79.

▶ **Posada Don Bruno**. Calle Principal, **Angangueo**, Michoacán 61411. Tel: (725) 8-0026. $39.

▶ **Posada de las Monjas**. Calle Canal 37, **San Miguel de Allende**, Guanajuato 37700. Tel: (465) 2-0171. $44.

▶ **Posada San José**. Calle Manuel Acuña 240, **Saltillo**, Coahuila 25000. Tel: (841) 5-2303. $32.

▶ **Posada Santa Fé**. P.O. Box 191, Jardín de la Unión, **Guanajuato**, Guanajuato 36000. Tel: (473) 2-0084; Fax: (473) 2-4653. $84.

▶ **Posada de la Soledad**. Zaragoza 90, **Morelia**, Michoacán 58000. Tel: (451) 2-1888; Fax: (451) 2-2111. $58.

▶ **Posada Vista Bella**. P.O. Box 135, Calle Galeana, Lomas de Santa María, **Morelia**, Michoacán 58090. Tel: (451) 4-0284; Fax: (451) 4-0284. $46.

▶ **La Puertecita**. Calle Santo Domingo 75, **San Miguel de Allende**, Guanajuato 37700. Tel: (465) 2-2250; Fax: (465) 2-0424. $115–$184.

▶ **Rancho San Cayetano**. P.O. Box 23, **Zitacuaro**, Michoacán 61500. Tel: (725) 3-1926. $40.

▶ **Real de Minas**. P.O. Box 77, Constituyentes Poniente 124, **Querétaro**, Querétaro 76010. Tel: (42) 16-0444; Fax: (41) 16-0662. $76.

▶ **El Río Motel**. Carretera 85, **Nuevo Laredo**, Tamaulipas 88000. Tel: (871) 4-3666; Fax: (871) 5-1232. $61.

▶ **Royal Courts Motor Inn**. Avenida Universidad, **Monterrey**, Neuvo León 66450. Tel: (837) 6-2017. $71.

▶ **El Señorial**. Guerrero Norte 10A, **Querétaro**, Querétaro 43700. Tel: (42) 14-3700; Fax: (42) 14-1945. $31.

▶ **Villa Jacaranda**. Aldama 53, **San Miguel de Allende**, Guanajuato 37700. Tel: (465) 2-1015 or 2-0811. $97.

▶ **Villa Montaña**. P.O. Box 233, Calle Galeana, Lomas de

Santa María, **Morelia**, Michoacán 58090. Tel: (451) 4-0179; Fax: (451) 5-1423. $155.

▶ **Villa Santa Monica**. Calle Baeza 22, **San Miguel de Allende**, Guanajuato 37700. Tel: (465) 2-0451 or 2-0427. $155.

THE WESTERN HIGHLANDS
GUADALAJARA AND PATZCUARO

By Robert Cummings

Robert Cummings, a resident of Mexico for the past seven years, has written numerous travel articles as well as a novella, and is currently working on a novel.

The sophisticated residents of Mexico City have always looked upon Guadalajara as the overgrown village where their country cousins live, friendly folk who strum guitars by day and perform hat dances by candlelight in a land of swaggering cowboys and blushing señoritas.

Everyone knows the stereotype is silly, but it persists because it bears a grain of truth. More than most large cities, Guadalajara *is* a collection of villages. There are strong neighborhood loyalties here, a sense of closeness to the parish churches, and, in the midst of modernity, a love of and yearning for the soil. Songs about *mi tierra,* "my land," and *mi ranchita,* "my little ranch," never lack for listeners, and often bring a tear to the eye of these transplanted city dwellers. After all, this is the state of Jalisco, and Jalisco means ranches, cattle, and crops. There's a secret rodeo buckaroo lurking inside many a banker and attorney here, one that usually bursts forth as soon as the music starts.

Guadalajara is the chief metropolis of the Western High-

THE WESTERN HIGHLANDS 255

lands and the gateway to the mountains that surround it on every side but the east. The grassy ranch country of Jalisco, from which Guadalajara drew its early wealth and cowboy traditions, crinkles into hills just south of the city, ridges that frame Lake Chapala, the largest and most northerly of the highland lakes.

Southeast of Chapala the forested mountains of Michoacán rise sharply, becoming the peaks that cradle Mexico's loveliest lake, Pátzcuaro. It was along these shores that the Tarascan civilization arose eight centuries ago; the mountain villages here remain Tarascan to this day.

(Far to the west, and a world apart from Lake Pátzcuaro, Jalisco's booming coastal resort of Puerto Vallarta caters to sun worshipers from around the globe. See the Pacific Resorts chapter below for a closer look at it and some of its nearby smaller sister resorts.)

This crescent-shaped region, with spirited Guadalajara at one tip and colorful Pátzcuaro at the other, offers visitors some of Mexico's richest discoveries in colonial history, native crafts and cultures, and urban diversions.

MAJOR INTEREST

Guadalajara
Las Cuatro Plazas
Palacio de Gobierno
Cathedral
Museo Regional de Guadalajara
Teatro Degollado
Orozco murals at Instituto Cultural Cabañas
Mercado Libertad
Barrio de San Francisco
Mariachi music
Nightlife and entertainment
Ceramic centers of Tlaquepaque and Tonalá

Around Guadalajara
Barranca de Oblatos
Tequila
Lago de Chapala area

The Tarascan Country
Scenic beauty
Picturesque town and lake of Pátzcuaro
Tzintzuntzán colonial town and archaeological site
Craft villages around Pátzcuaro
City of Uruapan
Paricutín volcano

The Western Highlands

0 — miles — 25
0 — kilometers — 40

JALISCO

León

GUANAJUATO

Irapuato

To Mexico City →

La Piedad

Zamora

MICHOACAN

Zacapu

To Capula

Lago de Pátzcuaro

Quiroga

Paracho

Janitzio

Tzintzúntzan

Angahuán

TZINTZÚNTZAN
ZONA
ARQUEOLÓGICA

▲ Paricutín

Pátzcuaro

Opepeo

Uruapan

Río Cupatitzio

Santa Clara
del Cobre

GUADALAJARA

Almost as populous as Chicago, Guadalajara is Mexico's second-largest city. But unless you're caught in rush-hour traffic, it's likely to feel much smaller. Maybe it's because there are no urban canyons, no skyscrapers, and even the moderately tall buildings are few and far apart.

It is true that there are more guitars per city block in Guadalajara than any other city would dream of listening to. And it's also true that despite the encroaching urban pressures and crush, these country cousins really are among the friendliest people in the Mexican Republic. Or perhaps it's just that they're the heartiest. In Jalisco it is sometimes hard to determine where heartiness ends and friendliness begins. The question becomes further confused by courtesy. The *tapatíos,* as the people of Guadalajara are nicknamed, are polite, smiling, and even courtly—insofar as the demands of surviving in the modern world permit.

Their style, however, can be confusing at times. You will be invited cordially, even enthusiastically, to "my house, which is *your* house," but you'll never learn the address. This is no more hypocritical than a friendly backslap at the club; it's merely a manner, a way of making life pleasant and gracious while staying safely uninvolved.

Perhaps *tapatío* cordiality, and the love of country values, is rooted in Guadalajara's unusually stable past. Founded soon after the Conquest on productive, gently rolling land, Guadalajara was bypassed by many of the storms of Mexican history. After some initial atrocities in the 16th century, ranch servitude here, though hardly an enviable condition, involved little of the suffering inflicted on native populations elsewhere in New Spain. The region also escaped the brutality of invasions, the social upheaval, and the violence that much of the country endured. Where other regions were forced to bow to sword and cross, Guadalajara had a chance to cultivate graciousness and romance—and it did so in abundance. Spain was remote, and life here casual.

Not surprisingly, its problems and dislocations have been more recent, a result of growth and industrialization. Guadalajara's major problem has been trying to reconcile its own explosive growth with its slow-paced, gracious traditions. Sometimes it manages to succeed; often it doesn't. In the spring of 1992 such a failure resulted in tragedy. Slipshod construction and maintenance by Pemex, the national petroleum company, caused a series of devastating blasts in a downtown residential area. The number of dead was large

but indeterminate, perhaps 400. Some officials were arrested and others expelled from office as the city struggled to rebuild and to cope better with the hazards of industrialization.

For all that, Guadalajara remains a pleasant, livable, charmingly robust city.

Las Cuatro Plazas

The Four Plazas, which surround the cathedral on all sides, are at the heart of downtown Guadalajara. Realizing it must yield to modernization, the city has nevertheless made major efforts to preserve the traditional grace and dignity of its historic center. The large, impressive area set aside as a result occupies about a dozen city blocks.

A good place to start exploring is the **Plaza de Armas**, on the south side of the cathedral at the corner of Morelos and Avenida 16 de Septiembre. This is a small, formal park where nothing distracts from the ornate bandstand, forged in Paris at the turn of the century and today a fanciful reminder of the Art Nouveau style that Mexican travellers brought back from France. Concerts are held here every Thursday and Sunday evening, and it is truly a pleasant place to linger on a wrought-iron bench enjoying the almost perpetual spring of Guadalajara while studying the domes, towers, and balustrades of the cathedral.

On the east side of the plaza stands the stolid **Palacio de Gobierno** (Government Palace), its 18th-century Baroque façade unusually severe. Inside is a dramatic mural by native son José Clemente Orozco that enfolds the viewer like a net. The subject is Father Hidalgo's abolition of slavery in Mexico, an act that was proclaimed from this very building.

The **Plaza de los Laureles**, which fronts the cathedral to the west, takes its name not name from its laurel trees, but rather for the wreaths reserved for Mexico's heroes. Its fountain, bubbling in the sunlight, adds a touch of life to this public space of stone. The **cathedral** seems to stare at the plaza with its two big round windows. An ungainly building, it is said to embrace no fewer than 14 distinct styles in the hash of its architecture. But *tapatíos,* having grown up with it, love it and proudly show it off to visitors. Actually, the ponderous structure is seen to best advantage from Avenida Juárez at night, when the yellow lights on its towers impart a magic glow. Inside are a number of good paintings, especially *The Assumption of the Virgin* by Murillo, which hangs near the entrance to the sacristy.

In front of the cathedral you can hire a horse and carriage

for $10 an hour or $20 for the standard tour of the neighborhood.

North of the cathedral a Doric rotunda graces the shady **Plaza de los Hombres Ilustres**. One block east, housed in a dignified 18th-century seminary building, is the **Museo Regional de Guadalajara**. The highlights of the collection—worth careful study—are the pre-Columbian figurines from the Western Highlands region. Fashioned by anonymous village sculptors, many are powerful representations of women at once fierce and compassionate; the animal figurines are also touched with genius. The second floor contains a collection of European paintings (mostly Spanish) assembled from the 19th-century collections of rich *tapatíos*. While most are not masterpieces, they are skillful and revealing of local tastes of the era.

When you're ready to leave the museum, turn left and walk east along the **Plaza de la Liberación** toward the imposing 19th-century **Teatro Degollado**, another source of local pride. Inside are murals inspired by Dante's *Divine Comedy,* gleaming chandeliers, and a profusion of gold leaf. The theater is the home of the **Guadalajara Symphony Orchestra** and the **Ballet Folklórico** of the university. The orchestra is well worth hearing, the ballet a blaze of color.

Continue strolling east through the long, narrow **Plaza Tapatía**, a model urban mall adorned with fountains and sculpture. The long thoroughfare is also a fitting buildup to perhaps the city's greatest treasure, the **Instituto Cultural Cabañas**, also called the Hospicio Cabañas.

Erected in 1801 as an orphanage, the building was the design of the talented Spanish architect-sculptor Manuel Tolsá, who was imported to head Mexico's first formal academy of the arts. While it's a fine and interesting building, no one pays much attention to it; the murals inside are what make it celebrated.

Working with a dark palette, chiefly grays and blacks befitting the atmosphere of its old chapel, José Clemente Orozco painted the frescoes inside in 1938 and 1939. Using details sparingly—a few thrusting lines portray a war horse, arrogant and apocalyptic, or what must be the sharpest barbed wire in the world, fangs of metal—Orozco managed to create a powerful protest against war and violence. The centerpiece of this breathtaking vision is his *Man of Fire,* painted on the interior of the dome high above. To be properly appreciated it should be viewed as the artist saw it. For this purpose, the institute provides benches so that visitors can lie down and gaze straight up. You needn't feel hesitant about this, but in case you do, the institute also provides mirrors; by all means use both methods. Either way, you'll feel as if you've come face-to-face with the gates to the inferno.

If you have time to see only one thing in Guadalajara, it should be this chapel.

Markets and Mariachis

Just south of the Instituto Cultural Cabañas, facing Calzada Independencia, sprawls the **Mercado Libertad** (Liberty Market)—actually a complex of many markets of many types. Although no one should miss it entirely, don't expect too much.

Visitors to the market should search out its color and life rather than merchandise. While there are displays of local weaving, glass, and leather goods, most are not first rate, examining the goods is frowned upon, and the bargaining that goes on could serve as an example to sharks. (One exception is **Artesanías Méxicanos**, Locales 313–316 in the main building, with leather work of good quality and a few other items.) Serious buyers will do better elsewhere; serious hagglers for whom the hunt is worth more than the prize will think they've found paradise.

At the southern end of the market is the old church of San Juan de Dios and, nearby, the **Plazuela de los Mariachis**, the famous "Mariachi Square." Here, at the many sidewalk cafés, customers may order drinks, food, and their favorite song. Day and night the musicians stroll among the tables or linger on the sidelines waiting to be hired. There is no charge for listening to what others have requested, but if you decide to become a patron yourself, ask the price in advance (this is not ordinarily a bargaining situation).

Mariachis are said to have originated in Guadalajara, and purists claim the city still has the best. Although they started out as string groups, featuring violins and a variety of guitars, these days their hallmark is brass. A traditional performance begins with a *sinfonía,* a gay little tune unconnected to the melody that will follow; this serves as an introduction, as well as the signature of that particular band. What follows is usually lusty and exuberant music, with hints of sadness and disappointment. While almost all mariachi musicians are accomplished instrumentalists, most usually are not talented vocalists. As a consequence, the mariachi tone is a little harsh, a little hoarse, and decidedly rough and masculine. The *gritos,* shouts often done in falsetto, are essential to a good performance.

Mariachi music is composed for streets, squares, and

spacious patios. Open air is as characteristic of the performance as the mariachis' flamboyant adaptation of cowboy clothing. Customers are often part of the act, joining in or even performing solo, using the hired band as accompaniment. It's not unusual for a host, or even more frequently a guest, to leave a private party, drive to the square, and bring back a carload of mariachis to play for an hour—or a night.

Mariachi music is heard all over Guadalajara. Aside from the plaza, the best bands can be heard in nearby Tlaquepaque in the zócalo (El Parián) and at major Guadalajara hotels. (The nightclub groups tend to sweeten their tone.)

Barrio de San Francisco

The Barrio de San Francisco, a corner of the downtown area five blocks south of the Plaza de Armas via Avenida 16 de Septiembre, is notable for two contrasting examples of ecclesiastical architecture, as well as for an old-fashioned garden that is both shady and welcoming.

The **Templo de San Francisco**, with a handsome Baroque façade that is at once ornate yet highly controlled, successfully combines Mexican Plateresque style with Flemish design elements. The twisting Salomonic columns are derived from the famous papal pillars at St. Peter's in Rome. The church, although remodeled in 1693, has stood here since 1554.

A modern street now separates the church from a smaller structure, the **Capilla de Nuestra Señora de Aranzazú** (Chapel of Our Lady of Aranzazú), to which it was once connected. The main altar and right secondary altar of the former chapel are sunbursts of Rococo gold leaf, fantastic and, in their very Mexican way, masterpieces of extravagance. The two churches, as well as half a dozen other structures now vanished, were part of a huge convent complex destroyed by the government's anti-clerical policies in the 1920s.

Sports and Spectacles

The Guadalajara bullring, or **Plaza Monumental**, is famed for its great international stars and dazzling pageantry in the winter season. In warm Guadalajara, where early afternoon skies are almost always clear, it is important to get a seat in the shade, however. The bullfights are held on Sundays in the ring just off Calzada Independencia; take any "Independencia" bus northbound and tell the driver you want to get off at the Plaza de Toros.

During the summer the Sunday thrills are at the **charreada**, Mexico's version of a rodeo, where the beauty of the costumes and horses is almost as important as the skill of the *charros*. The stadium is located south of the downtown area near one of Guadalajara's parks, **Agua Azul**. To get there, take the Avenida 16 de Septiembre bus.

Cockfighting is a national passion, often an occasion for reckless betting, and not always to the taste of visitors. Matches are held on Sundays at noon and again at 7:30 P.M., with special fights on holidays. The Plaza de Gallos, site of these furious combats, is on Calzada de la Revolución, 1½ km (1 mile) past the Technological Institute. Take any bus marked "Tlaquepaque."

Staying in Guadalajara

The **Fiesta Americana Guadalajara**, one of the most luxurious and modern hotels in Mexico, has helicopter service from the airport to the roof, glass elevators, panoramic views of Guadalajara from every room, as well as a nightclub and a lively bar with music. Mexican businessmen like to stay here as much for the amenities as for the animated cocktail lounge. The Fiesta Americana is located on Minerva Circle, about 20 minutes west of the city center, but *colectivos* run frequently to the downtown area. (The hotel's fine restaurants are discussed below.)

The **Holiday Inn Guadalajara**, a little farther out at the Plaza del Sol, west of Minerva Circle, is a modern and attractive hotel complex with gardens, lighted tennis courts, a sauna and whirlpool, and all the other amenities of a first-rate operation. The music in the hotel's nightclub is an added bonus.

Popular with families and Mexicans travelling on business, the **Hotel Malibu**, a bit north of Minerva Circle, is a jumble of annexes and courtyards, but rooms are ample and have all the essentials.

Unfortunately, attractive hotels in the downtown area are the exception. The colonial-style **Hotel Francés**, behind the Government Palace at Maestranza 35, is the most charming, its cocktail lounge a cheerful gathering place offering music and an international flavor. Some of the inside rooms overlook air shafts, but guests who are lucky enough to get a room facing the street wax enthusiastic about the Francés. The rates are reasonable, and parking in a public establishment two blocks away is provided. The restaurant **El Molino Rojo**, on the first floor, is good for breakfast or lunch, but usually deserted in the evening, although it's open for supper.

The **Hotel de Mendoza** is centrally located on tranquil Avenida Venustiano Carranza. The rooms here are airy and comfortable, the decor provincial with a colonial feel. While it is slightly more expensive than the Francés, the space and ventilation are better.

At the edge of the historic district on Avenida Juárez, halfway between the cathedral and the Liberty Market, the **Calinda Roma,** part of a chain of hotels, offers rooms typical of many large commercial establishments: carpeted and air-conditioned but with little character otherwise. The Roma has convenient basement parking, offers discounts to senior citizens, and is popular with tour groups.

With beveled glass windows, lovely old paintings, and countless small touches that make for a distinguished inn, the elegantly colonial **Quinta Real** is the city's finest luxury hotel. In fact, presidents have actually stayed in its presidential suite. All this attention to detail and personalized service does not come cheaply, however. The Quinta Real is located at the corner of Avenida México and Boulevard López Mateos, about ten minutes west of the center of town.

Situated on a hilltop overlooking Guadalajara, 6 km (3½ miles) south of the city on the road to Chapala, is **El Tapatío**. Winding up its second year of operation under new management, this high-tech health spa facility was built by the developers of the well-known La Jolla spa outside San Diego. The management claims that its staff outnumbers guests by two to one, which perhaps explains the astonishing dedication to massaging, exercising, and pampering that goes on amid the luxurious surroundings here. Packages are designed for week-long stays and bear price tags that reflect the personalized service guests receive.

Dining and Nightlife in Guadalajara

Typically, Jalisco fare is ranch fare—hearty, rather plain, with the emphasis on meat and fowl; local cooks seem to have a patronizing attitude toward vegetables. An à la carte order in the typical Jalisco restaurant is apt to be a slab of meat, some tortillas, chile sauce, and nothing else.

Cabrito (roast kid) is a regional specialty, as is *birria,* a hearty dish with chunks of goat, pork, or mutton, and sometimes all three in combination. It is best barbecued, although most Guadalajara restaurants steam it. On the other hand, *carnitas* (chunks of roast pork), a staple in Mexico, are reputed to be superior here. Another local favorite is *pozole,* half soup and half stew, made with hominy and pork and topped with onions, lettuce, and radish slices.

For Mexican cuisine at its absolute best try **La Hacienda**, a smart and sophisticated restaurant in the Fiesta Americana Guadalajara (Tel: 36/25-3434). Its serious rival in this field is **Río Viejo**, a handsome Guadalajara town house romantically furnished with antiques at Avenida de las Américas 302, a few blocks north of Avenida Vallarta in midtown (Tel: 36/16-5321). With less atmosphere and lower prices, **Los Otates**, Avenida de las Américas 28, at the corner of Morelos, serves traditional Mexican food with few surprises (Tel: 36/15-0481).

Most fine restaurants in Guadalajara pride themselves on their European or "international" dishes. The two most elegant restaurants in town are French: **Lafayette** in the Hotel Camino Real, Avenida Vallarta 5005, near the Malibu, and **Place de la Concorde**, in the Fiesta Americana. There is a dress code at both. For reservations at Place de la Concorde, Tel: (36) 25-3434.

Less expensive **La Fuente** has a refined atmosphere, tables set with crystal and linen, and an international menu. A bubbling fountain serves as the centerpiece for this town house located in a pleasant neighborhood at Avenida Plan de San Luis 1899. You can get there by heading north from Minerva Circle on López Mateos and turning right at the Columbus Fountain. Jacket and tie are suggested for men; Tel: (36) 24-7946.

La Copa de Leche, in the center of town at Juárez 414, was for years considered the city's finest restaurant. It has since been surpassed by others but remains a traditional standby. Good Mexican food and other dishes are served on the second floor. There's a different menu downstairs, mostly seafood and steaks, the former better than the latter. Tel: (36) 14-5347.

Visitors looking for American food and not-too-spicy Mexican dishes should try **Sanborn's** at Vallarta 1600. (Sanborn's is open every day of the year). **Luscherly**, at General San Martín 525 in a residential neighborhood off Niños Héroes, a main thoroughfare in the west-central part of town, has a Swiss chef who specializes in Continental cuisine, including snails and fondues. The decor is almost as impressive as the food: The intimate setting makes you feel as if you are dining in someone's tastefully decorated home. Reservations are a must; Tel: (36) 52-0509.

For nighttime entertainment and perhaps a taste of the

region's famed tequila, the two most popular places are **El Parián**, the courtyard in the main square in Tlaquepaque (see below), and the **Plazuela de los Mariachis** near the Liberty Market. Both are authentic rather than fancy.

All the major hotels have bars with entertainment. The best show with traditional music (and, of course, a hat dance) is at the **Holiday Inn**. Its two rivals are **El Pueblito Cantina**, in the Hotel Hyatt Regency across from the Plaza del Sol on the southwest edge of the city; and **La Pergola**, in the Hotel Sheraton, near Parque Agua Azul, a short distance south of the downtown area.

Atop the Hotel de Mendoza, in the center of town at Venustiano Carranza 16, you'll find the welcoming **El Compañario**, which offers twinkling panoramic views of Guadalajara and dancing after 9:00 P.M. Only couples and mixed parties are admitted, however.

Copenhagen is a cheerful spot to listen to a good jazz trio from 9:00 P.M. on. You can also dine here (paella is the house specialty), but a meal is not mandatory. You'll find Copenhagen in the center of town off Parque Revolución at Marcos Castellanos 140, near the university.

The **Hotel Francés** bar at Maestranza 35, one block from Avenida Juárez, is inviting for its conversation, background music, and convivial atmosphere. The "disco" next door is actually a modest nightclub with live music for dancing or just plain listening.

Shopping in Guadalajara

To find a wide range of crafts at fair prices, you should first visit the **Casa de las Artesanías de Jalisco**, a state museum and gallery devoted to the popular arts. Located in the Parque Agua Azul, it offers a range of work and provides a basis for comparison. There's another branch at the corner of Avila Camacho and 16 de Septiembre. In both places the quality is good, the prices reasonable.

In addition to the previously mentioned Artesanías Méxicanos in the Liberty Market, you might want to stop in at **El Charro**, Calzada Juárez 148, which has corralled a wild and woolly collection of cowboy and western clothes, from tooled boots to sombreros that could serve as parachutes. A few of the designs are outrageous, and the workmanship is excellent. Good silversmithing, including jewelry, plates, trays, and ornaments, can be found at **Plata Mex**, Independencia 910.

An interesting demonstration of the tequila distilling process can be seen in Guadalajara at the big **Tequila Sauza**

bottling plant, Avenida Vallarta 3273. Tours are conducted daily from 10:00 A.M. until 2:00 P.M., with courtesy samplings of the deliciously piquant drink offered to visitors. If you want to buy tequila to take home with you, remember that the smoothest varieties are those labeled "añejo" or "añejado" (aged).

To get to the Sauza plant, take the "Parque Vial" or "Plaza del Sol" bus on Juárez to the far (west) side of Minerva Circle. Then walk a few blocks farther west on Vallarta. Because taxis are not expensive, however, it's probably more convenient to hail one westbound on Juárez and tell the driver you want to go to Tequila Sauza. For the return trip, taxis are easy to find outside the bottling plant or near Minerva Circle. (The town of Tequila, 57 km/36 miles from Guadalajara, is discussed below.)

Tlaquepaque and Tonalá

San Pedro Tlaquepaque (tlah-keh-PAH-keh) is no longer a separate town but a continuation of the city to the southeast. Once famed as a pottery village, much of it has been turned into a psycho-ceramic nightmare heaped with crimes against taste committed in clay. Three-fourths of the stuff is dime-store junk, both gaudy and fragile, with glazes that threaten lead poisoning. In the middle of this mess you can find some good pieces, but it requires perseverance.

Dark, unglazed pottery, thought of as a Oaxacan specialty, is equally native to Tlaquepaque, and many pieces merit consideration. Good work is never glazed; the high sheen comes from a smothering process done in the firing: the darker and glossier the better. Shops and galleries in the pedestrian mall on Independencia have much the best offerings, and there's some imaginative work in metal and paper to be found here as well. The "antiques" on sale are also attractive, although usually manufactured last week. The **Ken Edwards** shop, Madero 75, presents the most appealing, whimsical earthenware in town.

At **Casa Canela**, Calzada Independencia 258, you'll find Talavera and Delft-inspired vases of remarkable quality—surrounded, of course, by garish ceramic souvenirs. Fortunately the glassware is better than much of the pottery, and local glassblowers achieve some beautiful and rare shades of red. Casa Canela has some fine examples, in addition to crystal balls in delicate hues for gazing.

Some of the most attractive glass can be found at **La Rosa de Cristal**, Calzada Independencia 232, where you can also observe the fascinating, eerie world of glassblowing.

The **Museo Regional de la Cerámica**, Independencia 237, will give you an idea of what you wish you could find along the streets outside. Across the street is the gallery **Sergio Bustamante**, with sculptures in various materials, much of it imaginative. Bustamante, a native son of Tlaquepaque, now has shops throughout Mexico and is expanding into the States as well.

Tlaquepaque buses, so marked, run along Calzada Independencia with some frequency. By car, head south on Calzada Independencia Sur and turn left on Calzada Revolución. At the traffic circle keep to the left of the gasoline station and stay on Revolución. You'll see signs for Tlaquepaque ahead. A right turn takes you to the central plaza, El Parián.

Tonalá, a ten-minute drive south of Tlaquepaque, has managed to keep its integrity. Maybe it's because the town actually makes things, rather than just selling them. Stoneware is especially good here, thanks to a recent tradition established by U.S. designers Ken Edwards and **Jorge Wilmot**. Wilmot's pieces, which are much more durable than the many imitations, are stamped with a "W." His studio is located at Morelos 80, not far from the church.

The **Bazaar El Caracol** boutique, Madero 19, specializes in cotton clothing and also offers metal work and archaeological reproductions.

Thursday and Sunday are market days in Tonalá, with displays of pottery overflowing the town square into the surrounding streets.

Buses to Tonalá run along Calzada Independencia and are clearly labeled. To get there by car, head east on Carretera los Altos and take the "Zapotlanejo Libre" exit.

AROUND GUADALAJARA
Barranca de Oblatos

The Barranca de Oblatos (*barranca* means "canyon") is an impressive 2,000-foot slash in the earth that has been cut by two rivers over the ages. In addition to its sheer beauty, it's interesting for the fact that the climate here changes as the gorge deepens, becoming positively tropical by the time you reach the bottom. Fruits such as papayas flourish in the canyon, and are harvested for the markets back in Guadalajara. For those interested in taking the journey, a cable car makes the descent to the bottom and back.

The "Barranca" bus runs north along Calzada Independencia Norte to the canyon rim and the cable-car departure point. If you're driving your own car, follow Independencia 11 km (7 miles) north until you reach the canyon (it's actually northeast but is marked "north"). Taxis, which are not expensive, are another option and can be hailed on Independencia; they'll be available at the canyon for the return trip.

Tequila

The town for which the famous liquor is named lies 57 km (35 miles) northwest of Guadalajara. It is a typical country town with dusty streets, a slow pace, and friendly people, which may appeal to travellers looking for authenticity. Most, however, will find it does not warrant a special trip unless they're already passing that way on Highway 15, the coastal route that heads north to the Arizona border. In that case, it is worth a stop to tour one of the distilleries, which are usually open to the public until 2:00 P.M.

Tours can be arranged ahead of time through travel agencies in major Guadalajara hotels. A tour takes about half a day and usually includes lunch; the overview of the tequila-making process is more complete than that given drop-in visitors.

Lago de Chapala

It is an easy trip from Guadalajara, about an hour south by car or bus (see the Getting Around section below), to Mexico's largest lake and its shoreline villages. The excursion merits a visit for those with the time, but be sure to explore Guadalajara first. The badly polluted lake, which is drying up at an alarming rate, is too dirty for swimming, almost useless for boating, and its fish died long ago. Only the magnificent views survive.

The town of **Chapala** has some attractive turn-of-the-century houses fronting the lake, worth a 30-minute walk or so. The villages farther west, Ajijic (ah-hee-HEEK) and Jocotepec, lost much of their innocence—and most of their charm—a generation ago, and now are advertised as places for "bargain retirement" and "bargain winter retreats." Actually, the bargains vanished at about the same time as the Chapala whitefish. Rentals here are expensive, hotel rates not low, and the restaurants and stores usually overpriced.

As almost everyone knows, a large colony of U.S. and Canadian retirees lives along the lake, enjoying the climate, the views, and one another's company. Over the years they've also established such things as an enterprising

English-language community theater, a weekly journal, and a chili cookoff.

In Chapala the traditional place for a drink or lunch overlooking the lake is the **Beer Garden**, at the foot of the main street; it's the roofed terrace on the right as you approach the head of the pier. The view and drinks are fine, the food only so-so.

For a meal or even an overnight stay in the area the best choice by far is **La Nueva Posada**, in the dusty village of Ajijic, about a ten-minute drive west along the lake from Chapala. The bar and dining room offer pleasant views of the lake, and the guest rooms have a rustic charm.

Buses are reputed to run along the lakeside highway. Their reliability may be gauged by the large number of hitchhikers, both Mexican and foreign, you'll see thumbing their way between the villages.

PATZCUARO AND THE TARASCAN COUNTRY

The lakeside town of Pátzcuaro (PAHTZ-kwah-ro), situated just west of Morelia (see the Colonial Heartland chapter) about halfway between Mexico City and Guadalajara, is the spiritual capital of the Western Highlands region, and is possibly Mexico's most purely Indian city. A city of almost 60,000 (at times it seems much smaller), it is, in the minds of many travellers, the heart of the most scenic corner of Mexico. For such people no other region equals Pátzcuaro and its environs for alpine beauty, and only the Mayan settlements in the southeastern part of the country rival it for being exotic and picturesque. The Tarascan people themselves, often under even greater pressure to change than the Maya, have been almost as successful in preserving their traditional ways, their language, and their artistic heritage.

The Tarascans (also known as the Purépecha) are an ancient people. According to legend they were one of the tribes that migrated into the region with the Aztecs. When they paused at Lago de Pátzcuaro, so the legend goes, the Tarascans went into the water to bathe. The Aztecs seized the opportunity to abscond with the Tarascans' clothes, and so began the undying enmity between the two peoples. In time, gods, speaking through hummingbirds, commanded the Tarascans to build a city on the shore of the lake. It was a thriving center by the time the Spanish arrived, and somehow managed to survive the atrocities committed by the conquistadors—horrors that are remembered by the Tarascans to this day.

There is one archaeological zone of medium interest in the region, Tzintzuntzán, as well as some smaller cities. Volcano buffs may want to visit the desolate world left behind by the eruption of Paricutín, Mexico's youngest volcano. In addition, the semitropical city of Uruapan is less than an hour's drive away.

Some travellers also use Pátzcuaro as a base for visiting Morelia, a short journey to the east, preferring the lakeside town's serenity and lower prices.

Pátzcuaro is in high country, located at an elevation of 7,000 feet; a warm sweater is a necessity, as will be a windbreaker on many occasions.

Pátzcuaro Town

Pátzcuaro rambles down the slopes of several hills toward the big lake of the same name. Its steep red-tiled roofs jut out over carved beams, lending it a slightly Oriental atmosphere, while its cobblestone streets lead to the two plazas around which the life of the town revolves.

The **Plaza Chica** (Little Plaza) is the first one you see on arrival; it is officially named the Plaza Gertrudis Bocanegra, after a local heroine of the War of Independence. The municipal market, which has some good handicrafts alongside the fruits and vegetables, starts at the square's southwest corner. Like Indian markets throughout Mexico, it is commercial, bustling with life, rundown, and colorful. Facing it on the north is a 16th-century Augustinian church that now houses the drafty **Biblioteca Pública**. Inside you'll find a dramatic fresco depicting the region's history painted by Juan O'Gorman, one of Mexico's leading muralists in the middle decades of this century.

A block to the south lies the **Plaza Grande**, known formally as the Plaza Vasco de Quiroga. This spacious square serves as the community's outdoor living room, a place where towering ash trees at least a century old provide dappled shade as well as a stately reminder of the forests at the town's edge. There's also a sense here that the town is on its best behavior; all is quietly Tarascan, and the sidewalk cafés are pleasant rather than lively.

Friday is market day. Early in the morning Indians from the surrounding countryside pour into town to sell and buy. They walk, come by canoe, or lead burros loaded down with pottery, lacquerware, cloth, carved wood, and hammered metal. Many of the women wear the traditional skirt made of yard upon yard of homespun wool, a garment that can weigh as much as 30 pounds. Pleated accordion style, the skirts are gathered in back and held by a belt so that they spread outward like a fan. Their shawls, or *rebozos,* are often distinctive to a particular village. Women from the town of Paracho, for instance, favor a scarf with a brilliant fringe designed to resemble the plumage of a hummingbird.

The serape, carried folded during the day, is a masculine item. Serapes tend to be dark in Pátzcuaro, coarse in texture, and relieved by simple designs in red. Male fiesta wear, which you probably won't see at the market, is usually an intricately embroidered shirt complemented by a hat decked out with gay ribbons.

Tarascan jewelry is also handmade, usually out of hammered silver fashioned into hollow globes and a variety of other shapes; various shades of crimson beads made of lacquered wood are popular as well.

A short walk uphill from the two squares and market is a spacious open area that was the town center centuries ago. In 1540 the Pope decreed that a cathedral be built in Pátzcuaro, and grandiose plans were drawn up. Only a portion of the nave was erected, however, before a terrible earthquake struck the town, damaging the new structure. The bishop of Michoacán, alarmed by this turn of events, decided to move his see to Valladolid (now Morelia). Today, the cathedral, known as the **Basílica de Nuestra Señora de la Salud** (Our Lady of Health), remains standing as a relic of that bygone age, and still serves the local community. It also houses a revered image of the Virgin made out of corn paste. A bit farther to the south is the **Templo de la Compañía**, another church built in the 1540s.

The **Museo de Artes Populares**, near La Compañía, was originally built in the 16th century as a Jesuit seminary. Today the museum inside is small but delightful, and boasts an antique kitchen, exquisite crafts, and a gracious patio.

La Casa de los Once Patios (House of Eleven Patios), half a block east of the plaza fronting the cathedral, was once a Dominican convent and is now a hive of crafts workshops, studios, and salesrooms. The sheer volume of work on display—including lacquerware, woven goods, pottery, woodcarving, embroidery, lace, and metalwork (especially copper)—makes it worth a visit.

A *mirador* (lookout) on the shoulder of **El Estribo**, the extinct volcano that walls off the town to the south, offers spectacular views of the lake and its seven islands. To get there, follow the cobblestone road that twists sharply upward from the Plaza Grande for a distance of about 4 km (2½ miles); it ends at a small park, a nice spot for a picnic.

Staying in Pátzcuaro

There are no deluxe hotels in Pátzcuaro, but there are several good places to choose from. The fanciest by far is the **Posada de Don Vasco**, a motor inn on the edge of town about 2 km (1¼ miles) north on Avenida de las Américas. It has a tennis court, cocktail lounge, what little nightlife the town offers, and a bowling alley (separate charge). As the most modern place in town, it is also the most expensive.

El Mesón del Gallo, in the center of town adjacent to the Plaza Grande, is a smaller operation with a little pool and garden area. One drawback: The rooms can be cold in the winter.

The rooms of the cheerful **Hotel Los Escudos**, also on the main plaza, are not large, but all have fireplaces.

Easily the most charming of the local inns, the **Posada de la Basílica**, at Arciega 6, facing the cathedral plaza, is at once rustic and homey, with fireplaces and a big patio that lets in the winter sunshine. The management is similarly helpful and friendly.

Dining in Pátzcuaro

Whitefish, delicate and flaky, is the specialty here; ask for the *pescado blanco*. Trout (*trucha*) is always fresh. The *sopa Tarasca,* rich and spicy but not peppery, makes an excellent first course.

Local restaurants, almost all of them located in hotels or inns, tend to be small, adequate, and pleasant but not special. Service can be casual.

Los Escudos, the dining room in the hotel of the same name, is satisfactory, as is its neighbor, **El Patio**, in the same category and also inexpensive.

The restaurant in the **Posada de la Basílica** offers a good breakfast and lunch as well as romantic views of the town—an almost Oriental panorama of steep tile roofs with quaintly upturned corners. A meal here will taste twice as good at a window table.

The restaurant in the **Don Vasco** is more elaborate than other places—not because it offers better food, just a more attractive room. Traditional entertainment is presented twice a week, including the famous Tarascan Dance of the Old Men.

Lago de Pátzcuaro

This beautiful mountain lake is about 12 miles long from north to south, its irregular shoreline dotted with Tarascan villages. The scenery is made even more interesting by the islands that break the lake's surface.

The largest and most famous of these is **Janitzio**, easily identifiable by the colossal statue of patriot José María Morelos (who deserved something better than this ungainly stone heap) crowning its summit. The island itself is the favorite destination for launches leaving regularly from the Pátzcuaro pier. The boat trip is lovely, the destination dubious. Nowadays, Janitzio is utterly commercialized, one tawdry shop after another, their ranks broken only by risky eateries. The island was once justly famed for its annual Day of the Dead celebration on November 2, but it is now entirely a tourist event and a crush; worse than spoiled, it has become offensive.

Likewise, the colorful fishermen with "butterfly nets" who were once emblematic of the region have all but vanished, except for arranged appearances in front of tour groups.

Tzintzuntzán

On the other hand, the drive north on Highway 41, along the eastern shore of the lake, is still a pretty trip. Tzintzuntzán (pronounced tsin-soon-SAHN, Tarascan for "place of the hummingbirds"), 21 km (13 miles) from Pátzcuaro, was once the capital of the ancient Purépecha people, ancestors of the Tarascans, who settled in Michoacán in the 12th century. When the Spanish arrived they estimated the population at 40,000—most of whom were soon liquidated or scattered.

Today the main points of interest are clustered around the southern entrance to the town.

The 16th-century **Templo de San Francisco**, mellow and splendid, was once the headquarters of Bishop Vasco de Quiroga, the most brilliant and sympathetic figure to emerge in New Spain in the decades immediately following the Conquest. After an outstanding career as a lawyer in the colony, a career that attracted the attention of Charles V, Don Vasco was chosen to mitigate the sufferings that recently had been inflicted upon the Tarascans. In order to employ the power of the Church in his task, Don Vasco took holy orders at a time when most men are ready to retire. He was 68 and a bishop by the time he arrived in Tzintzuntzán, and he quickly set about creating (or perhaps reorganizing) a communal and quite utopian society. As a result of his humane efforts, the bishop is still remembered as *Tata,* or "Father," by the people of the region.

Upon entering the huge atrium of the church you are immediately confronted by a reminder of the bishop—gnarled and venerable olive trees, planted by Don Vasco despite laws forbidding native production of olives. Also around the atrium are a number of small outdoor shrines, an echo of the long-ago times when the Tarascan people would purify themselves before entering their temples. The façade of the church is richly Plateresque, a beautiful example of the early handling of European themes by native artists.

Adjoining the churchyard is the studio of Luis Mandel Morales, an outstanding potter. His **Taller Alta Temperatura**, a ceramics workshop, is remarkable, if a bit hard to find. One of the small boys who frequent the church grounds will be happy to guide you to it for a tip.

On the other side of the highway rise the heights that are now protected as the **Tzintzuntzán Zona Arqueológica**. In 1500 the Purépecha people moved their capital from the vicinity of Pátzcuaro to Tzintzuntzán. Some construction at the site dates from this era, although much of it may be 200 years older. The zone is sometimes referred to as *las yácatas,* a Purépecha term for the five huge platforms that give the site its unique character. Unlike any other Mesoamerican temple bases, they are T-shaped, with short, rounded stems. The *yácatas,* which rise 40 feet above a cramped, paved plaza, functioned as a sort of acropolis in the decades before the Spanish conquest.

The formidable hill with its massive structures proved no barrier to the Spanish invaders, however, for the inhabitants, like the Aztecs a few years earlier, were demoralized by astrological predictions and offered little resistance. Their last king, Tangaxoan, was strangled before the eyes of his terrified subjects, and so many women were raped or forced into concubinage that the Purépecha began to call the Spaniards "sons-in-law," *tarascue,* either ironically or as a sop to their own battered pride. The Spaniards, in linguistic confusion, thought *tarascue* was the name of the people they had just conquered—hence the still slightly opprobrious term "Tarascan."

Unfortunately, the intervening years have not been kind to this "Place of the Hummingbirds." Still, the temple platforms remain an impressive sight, the views of the surrounding countryside even more so. The village of Tzintzuntzán itself is not attractive, but displays of the inexpensive local pottery and ingenious crafts made from local straw here are worth examining.

Quiroga, a few minutes' drive to the north, is of interest primarily for its main-street shops, which feature the town's fine lacquerware and woven furniture.

The Craft Villages

Villa Escalante, more commonly called **Santa Clara del Cobre**, is located 16 km (10 miles) south of Pátzcuaro. Bishop Quiroga introduced the art of coppersmithing to the region in the mid-16th century, and Santa Clara has thrived on it ever since. Here you'll find copper in every imaginable shape and form. There's also a little museum in town with prize-winning examples of the local specialty.

On the road to Santa Clara sits **Opepeo**, home to many skilled wood-carvers and furniture makers.

Capula, a 40-minute drive north and east of Pátzcuaro, is, like Tzintzuntzán, not an especially pretty village, but it does produce the most imaginative pottery in the region. To get there take Highway 15, which connects Quiroga and Morelia. The village is at the end of a side road heading north from the highway, about halfway between the two larger towns.

Uruapan

Uruapan (oo-roo-AH-pahn), a verdant semitropical city noted for its blossoms and luxuriant foliage, is located some 62 km (38 miles) west of Pátzcuaro, and the scenic drive from Pátzcuaro may be the best reason for visiting it. As the road descends from the 7,000-foot elevation of Pátzcuaro the scenery changes in only a few minutes from pine forests to lush hillsides checkered with coffee and banana plantations, as well as groves of lemon and orange trees.

At the northern entrance to town the **Parque Nacional Eduardo Ruíz** protects the headwaters of the Río Cupatitzio. Shady paths and rustic bridges make this a lovely place for a walk. At the end of the trail a cascade foams and seethes over rocks and ledges.

At the same end of town is a small museum that displays and sells local crafts, notably the lacquerware for which Uruapan is known. Another museum, located on the main plaza in a fine 16th-century building, features antique and modern Tarascan craft work.

Uruapan, despite its relatively fast pace, remains graciously provincial and still Tarascan enough to take pride in its local color; the annual fair, with locally produced crafts and toys, ranks among the best in Mexico, drawing a crowd during Palm Sunday week.

The **Mansión del Cupatitzio** is a hotel in a converted and expanded hacienda overlooking the national park, about a ten-minute walk from the zócalo. The rooms with park views are the best. The pool is well maintained, the restaurant satisfactory.

Downtown on the zócalo itself, the **Hotel Plaza Uruapan** occupies a parcel of land that is part of a shopping mall. Ask for a room on the top floor for views of the town and surrounding mountains from a private balcony. The bar, restaurant, and weekend disco are favorites with local businesspeople and commercial travellers.

La Pergola, a restaurant on the zócalo, is an unhurried spot with an extensive menu, but the broadly national dishes show the kitchen off to the best advantage.

Paricutín, the now-dormant volcano that raised havoc when it was born in a cornfield in 1943, is 39 km (24 miles) northwest of Uruapan. To get there, head north on Highway 37, the road to Paracho, for 18 km (11 miles), then turn left onto the road that leads to Angahuán. The village of Angahuán, where more Tarascan than Spanish is spoken, is at the end of the road about 19 km (12 miles) to the west. A guide—the most convenient way to see the volcano—will usually be waiting outside the village. If no guide is on duty, drive into the center of the village and someone will soon approach you. Just beyond town, but a little tricky to find, is the departure point for tours of the area, complete with a horse-rental stand and very basic overnight accommodations.

There is no access by car to the volcano itself, or to the villages it destroyed. Instead, it's a short ride by horseback (or a long hike) to the lava beds, a weird and lunar-like landscape. Of the first village, only part of the town church remains, the building buried in lava but the tower rising eerily above the blackness. Most visitors turn back after seeing this bizarre sight. To visit the crater itself requires an early morning start; the round trip, by horseback, takes most of a day. The ride to the village should not be daunting to inexperienced riders, however; the horses are gentle and know the routine.

Paracho, the first town north of Uruapan past the turnoff for Angahuán, is famous for its wood carvings, especially toys and miniature doll houses, and stringed musical instruments, especially guitars. Otherwise it has little to recommend it. None of its main-street cafés is particularly trustworthy or inviting, nor is any single guitar maker known as the best or most famous. Instead, musicians shopping here tend to spend hours visiting one shop after another, testing and comparing instruments as they go.

GETTING AROUND

Driving Down from the Border

The 1,520-km (942-mile) trip from El Paso–Juárez to Guadalajara requires careful planning, since acceptable overnight stops are not conveniently spaced. The average driving time, without stops, is 21½ hours, but that does not take into account possible dust storms, heavy rains, or snow in winter; this is a land of climatic extremes.

El Paso has a range of good accommodations, but drivers planning to go farther than Chihuahua the first day may want to have customs behind them before they start in the morning.

The fairly expensive **Hotel Plaza Juárez** is in the Pronaf Center in **Ciudad Juárez**, 3½ km (2 miles) south of the Bridge of the Americas at the corner of Avenidas Lincoln and Coyoacán. This is a gracious inn with a pool (heated in winter), a restaurant that serves spicy Mexican cuisine, a coffee shop with fast service, and a nightclub. The inexpensive **Motel Colonial Las Fuentes**, also on Avenida Lincoln, one long block closer to the bridge than the Plaza Juárez, offers good value for your money. The coffee shop next door is only adequate.

The **Paseo del Norte Restaurant**, located at 3650 Hermanos Escobar, not far from the Plaza Juárez, is an outstanding exponent of classic Mexican cuisine, with only a few concessions to the palates of Texans who cross the border to sample its fare.

From Ciudad Juárez, Highway 45 runs south across a slightly rolling semi-arid plain pocked with scrub vegetation. The few settlements along this stretch offer little in the way of tourist amenities. About 4 hours after leaving Ciudad Juárez you'll reach the more hospitable area around the city of Chihuahua. (For Chihuahua information and accommodations, see the Copper Canyon chapter below.)

Highway 45 continues south from Chihuahua through ranchland that's fertile only in comparison to what precedes and follows it. About an hour and a half southeast of Chihuahua the town of **Ciudad Camargo** huddles on the plain at the junction of two rivers that seem to run dry more often than not. The **Motel Los Nogales**, at Avenida Juárez 404, is acceptable, if overpriced for lack of competition. The **Cabañas Santa Rosalía**, at the corner of Abasolo and Juárez, is less costly and has a restaurant.

Seventy-one kilometers (44 miles) south of Ciudad Camargo, Highway 45 turns west, and should be followed only by travellers bound for Mazatlán. Others should continue south on Highway 49, the road to Torreón.

The next possible stop is **Ciudad Jiménez** (often simply called "Jiménez"). Though not much to look at, it begins to seem especially attractive when you take into account the fact that the next acceptable accommodations are nearly 292 km (181 miles) to the south in the so-called Triplet cities. The **Hotel Florido** is the best in Jiménez, though neither the hotel nor its restaurant is first class. The three other small inns in town will serve as ports in a storm.

Your goal the next day should be the attractive colonial city of Zacatecas, an 8- to 9-hour drive to the south.

From Jiménez, Highway 49 traverses another long stretch of infertile, windswept plain to the valley of the Triplet cities—Torreón, Ciudad Lerdo, and Gómez Palacio. Together the three are home to more than a million people. **Torreón**, little more than a century old and still unmellowed, was founded by British, French, and U.S. concerns active in dairy farming, mining, and smelting (today it is also a major transportation center). As a result, it is heavily North Americanized, and inevitably you will see the names of familiar fast-food restaurants lining the highway.

The **Hotel Gran Presidential Torreón**, with a restaurant, coffee shop, and pool, is the best the city has to offer in the way of roadside accommodations. To find it, follow Highway 40 5½ km (3¼ miles) east to the large equestrian statue of Pancho Villa at the traffic circle, then 1 km (½ mile) west on Revolución and 2 km (1¼ miles) south on Paseo de la Rosita. You'll find the **Hotel Palacio Real**, the traditional gathering place for Torreón business executives and civic leaders, in the center of town facing the main plaza. The hotel is also the location of the city's two fanciest restaurants, **La Fuente** and **Café de Paris**, the latter not noticeably French.

Highway 49 joins Highway 40 in Torreón. From here you follow the combined route south some 100 km (62 miles) to the junction just north of the village of Cuencamé, where they go their separate ways. Follow Highway 49 to Fresnillo and Zacatecas. (Highway 40 continues on to Durango, then becomes a rollercoaster through the mountains before it reaches the Pacific at Mazatlán.)

After passing through the picturesque old silver town of Fresnillo you come to Mexico's northernmost colonial city,

Zacatecas, which has retained and restored much of its 18th-century charm and is well worth a leisurely inspection—if not an overnight stay. This old silver-mining town has some of the prettiest colonial buildings in Mexico, wrought from pale pink stone. Especially notable are the cathedral, built between 1612 and 1752; the Patrocinio Chapel, which was erected on the summit of El Cerro de la Bufa, the mountain that dominates the town; and the graceful main zócalo. There's also the new **Museo Rafael Coronel**, next to the Exconvento de San Francisco, which houses a collection of more than 1,000 Mexican masks collected by the well-known painter from Zacatecas. The museum is closed Mondays.

Two of the newest hotels in Zacatecas are the **Paraiso Radisson Zacatecas** and La Quinta Real. The Radisson, across the street from the cathedral and the most convenient address for exploring the downtown area, incorporates the original façade of the restored colonial building it occupies. Some of its rooms have charming wrought-iron terraces and antique furniture. **La Quinta Real Zacatecas**, near the edge of town at Rayon 434, is an all-suites hotel built around a bullfight ring. It's a beautiful place and the service is excellent.

The **Hotel Aristos Zacatecas**, on a hilltop west of town off Highways 45 and 54, offers comfortable modern rooms and an adequate restaurant. Its finest feature, however, is the memorable vista of the city it affords. The **Hotel Gallery Best Western** is in town on Highway 45, at the corner of Boulevard López Mateos and Callejón del Barro. Pleasantly colonial in atmosphere, it has an indoor pool and a satisfactory restaurant.

From Zacatecas, Highway 54 continues south some 273 km (169 miles) through pleasant, temperate country to Guadalajara.

—*Robert Somerlott*

By Air

Several airlines fly directly between Guadalajara and the United States, including Alaskan Airlines, Aero California, American, Mexicana, and Aeroméxico. (Mexicana and Aeroméxico also offer frequent flights to Mexico City as well as other cities in the country.) From Guadalajara there are daily westbound flights to Puerto Vallarta. Transportation into the city from the airport is by cheap minibus or rate-controlled taxi (about $10 for the latter). Airport buses will also pick you up at your hotel and take you to the airport for departure. Car-rental agencies at the airport include Arrendadora de Automóbiles, S.A.; Albarran; National; Avis; Hertz; Budget; and Quick. All have offices in the city as well.

By Train

The only recommendable rail service to the capital is the night train, *El Tapatío,* which leaves Guadalajara at 7:55 P.M. and usually arrives in the capital the next morning at 8:10. Passengers should avoid buying the cheapest ticket, which is misleadingly called "first class." True first class is called *primera clase especial.* A choice of roomettes and bedrooms is also available; the service is fair, the dining car adequate. The fare is approximately $45, one-way; expect to pay an additional $20 for a sleeping compartment (*dormitorio*). *El Tapatío* arrives and departs in Mexico City from the central station on Calle Buenavista off Insurgentes Norte.

The *Del Pacifico* winds between Guadalajara and Mexicali on the U.S. border—a trip of about 33 hours. The fare is roughly $100, one-way; expect to pay an additional $20 a night for a sleeping compartment. The only rail depot in Guadalajara is on Avenida Washington, 15 blocks south of the Liberty Market near the Parque Agua Azul.

In and Around Guadalajara

Except in the central historic district, distances in Guadalajara are too great to be covered easily on foot. Taxis are plentiful, however, and not expensive. An excellent bus system runs from the center of town to the Minerva Circle hotel area and beyond. There's also good bus service to Tlaquepaque and Tonalá, with destinations marked on each bus.

Although there is regular bus service to Lake Chapala, the problem is getting around once you're there. The trip is probably best made by car or tour bus. The outstanding tour-bus company is Panoramex, which calls at hotels throughout Guadalajara.

ACCOMMODATIONS REFERENCE

The rates given below are projections for December 1992 through Easter 1993. Unless otherwise indicated, rates are for double rooms, double occupancy; the 10 percent VAT has been added. As rates are subject to change, it's always a good idea to double-check before booking.

▶ **Cabañas Santa Rosalía.** Juárez y Abasolo, **Ciudad Camargo**, Chihuahua 33700. Tel: (146) 2-0214. $26.

▶ **Calinda Roma.** Avenida Juárez 170, **Guadalajara**, Jalisco 44100. Tel: (36) 14-8650; Fax: (36) 18-1704; in the U.S. and Canada, Tel: (800) 228-5151. $83.

▶ **Fiesta Americana Guadalajara.** Avenida Vallarta and López Mateos, **Guadalajara**, Jalisco 44100. Tel: (36) 25-3434;

Fax: (36) 30-3725; in the U.S. and Canada, Tel: (800) FIESTA-1. $159.

▶ **Holiday Inn Guadalajara.** Boulevard López Mateos and Avenida Mariano Otero, **Guadalajara**, Jalisco 44100. Tel: (36) 34-1034; Fax: (36) 31-9393; in the U.S. and Canada, Tel: (800) 465-4329. $142.

▶ **Hotel Aristos Zacatecas.** Lomas de la Soledad, **Zacatecas**, Zacatecas 98040. Tel: (492) 2-1788; Fax: (492) 2-6908; in the U.S. and Canada, Tel: (800) 5-ARISTO. $72.

▶ **Hotel Los Escudos.** Portal Hidalgo 73, **Pátzcuaro**, Michoacán 61600. Tel: (454) 2-1290. $31.

▶ **Hotel Florido.** Avenida Juárez and 20 de Noviembre, **Ciudad Jiménez**, Chihuahua 33980. Tel: (154) 2-0186. $37.

▶ **Hotel Francés.** Maestranza 35, **Guadalajara**, Jalisco 44100. Tel: (36) 13-1190; Fax: (36) 58-2831. $63.

▶ **Hotel Gallery Best Western.** Boulevard López Mateos and Callejón del Barro, **Zacatecas**, Zacatecas 98000. Tel: (492) 2-3311; Fax: (492) 2-3415; in the U.S. and Canada, Tel: (800) 528-1234. $75.

▶ **Hotel Gran Presidential Torreón.** P.O. Box 1010, Paseo de la Rosita and Diagonal de las Fuentes, **Torreón**, Coahuila 27000. Tel: (171) 7-4040; Fax: (171) 2-4968. $84.

▶ **Hotel Malibu.** Vallarta 3993, **Guadalajara**, Jalisco 45040. Tel: (36) 21-7888; Fax: (36) 22-3192. $61.

▶ **Hotel de Mendoza.** Avenida Venustiano Carranza 16, **Guadalajara**, Jalisco 44100. Tel: (36) 13-4646; Fax: (36) 13-7310. $82.

▶ **Hotel Palacio Real.** Morelos 1280 Poniente, **Torreón**, Coahuila 27000. Tel: (17) 16-0000; Fax: (17) 16-8608. $61.

▶ **Hotel Plaza Juárez.** Avenidas Lincoln and Coyoacán, **Ciudad Juárez**, Chihuahua 32310. Tel: (16) 13-1310; Fax: (16) 13-0084. $82.

▶ **Hotel Plaza Uruapan.** Ocampo 64, **Uruapan**, Michoacán 60000. Tel: (452) 3-3700; Fax: (452) 3-3980. $44.

▶ **Mansión del Cupatitzio.** Uruapan, Michoacán 64430. Tel: (452) 3-2060; Fax: (452) 4-6772. $63.

▶ **El Mesón del Gallo.** Dr. José María Coss 20, **Pátzcuaro**, Michoacán 61600. Tel: (454) 2-1474; Fax: (454) 2-1511. $25.

▶ **Motel Colonial Las Fuentes.** Avenidas Lincoln and de las Américas, **Ciudad Juárez**, Chihuahua 32310. Tel: (16) 13-5050; Fax: (16) 13-4081. $63.

▶ **Motel Los Nogales.** Juárez 404, **Ciudad Camargo**, Chihuahua 33700. Tel: (146) 2-1247; Fax: (146) 2-4442. $30.

▶ **La Nueva Posada.** Donato Guerra 9, **Ajijic**, Jalisco 49920. Tel: (376) 5-3395. $54.

▶ **Posada de la Basílica.** Arciega 6, **Pátzcuaro**, Michoacán 61600. Tel: (454) 2-1108. $27.

- **Posada de Don Vasco.** Avenida de las Américas 450, Pátzcuaro, Michoacán 61600. Tel: (454) 2-0227; Fax: (454) 2-0262. $72.
- **La Quinta Real.** Avenida México 2727, **Guadalajara**, Jalisco 44100. Tel: (36) 52-0000; Fax: (36) 30-1797; in the U.S. and Canada, Tel: (800) 458-6888; in California, Tel: (800) 227-0212. $231.
- **La Quinta Real Zacatecas.** Rayon 434, **Zacatecas**, Zacatecas 98000. Tel: (492) 2-9104; in the U.S. and Canada, Tel: (800) 458-6888; in California, Tel: (800) 227-0212. $170.
- **Paraiso Radisson Zacatecas.** Hidalgo 703, **Zacatecas**, Zacatecas 98000. Tel: (492) 2-6289; Fax: (492) 2-6245; in the U.S. and Canada, Tel: (800) 333-3333. $130.
- **El Tapatío.** P.O. Box 2953, km 6.4 on Guadalajara–Chapala highway, Jalisco 45580. Tel: (36) 35-6050; Fax: (36) 35-6664; in the U.S., Tel: (800) 424-2440; in New York, Tel: (800) 431-2822. $146.

THE COPPER CANYON

RIDING THE CHIHUAHUA–PACIFIC RAILWAY

By Robert Cummings

It has been called the most scenic railroad trip in the world. No doubt there are rivals and other claimants, but it's hard to name one. The Chihuahua–Pacific weaves, snakes, and climbs through as wild and spectacular a countryside as you are ever likely to visit. High in the Sierra Madre of northwest Mexico, south of Ciudad Juárez and western New Mexico, the train skirts the brink of deep canyons, then rolls into the immense Copper Canyon (*Barranca del Cobre*) itself. Upon seeing it a rush of adjectives floods the mind: breathtaking, awe-inspiring, incomparable. In fact, four Grand Canyons could be dropped into this vastness, which is why it's sometimes called "the Grander Canyon."

There are two ways to do this trip. First—and the most popular way—is simply as an exciting rail journey. You get aboard at either end of the line and pass through a series of titanic canyons, getting out now and then to catch your breath and gape at the spectacular scenery that stretches as far as the eye can see. Then you detrain at the other end of the line, Chihuahua inland to the northeast, or Los Mochis, near the Sea of Cortés to the southwest. If the train is on schedule, the trip takes 13 hours, but 15 or more is not

unusual. It doesn't really matter, however, because the trip is worth taking whatever the length. Spending 13 to 15 hours, even in a comfortable coach, with stops too few and too brief, hardly does justice to the magnificence of the canyon, and totally omits the surrounding area, but if that's the only way your schedule permits, by all means do it.

On the other hand, an unhurried trip with overnight stops is far better. The Copper Canyon can and should be considered as a short vacation destination of unusual interest and beauty, something more than an excuse for a spectacular train ride. Ideally you should allow three or four nights for exploring the canyon itself, not counting time spent in Chihuahua or Los Mochis. Even one overnight along the way is better than a nonstop trip, which may leave you tired and dazed from taking in too much scenic beauty at a single stretch.

If it is to be one overnight, consider either Divisadero, the halfway point of the trip and a very appealing town, or Creel, five and a half hours from Chihuahua, and with more in the way of attractions. Visit both if possible.

A one-way ticket costs about $30 (first class is called "star service"), and there's a 15 percent surcharge covering unlimited stopovers in one direction. Seats on the train are comfortable, but dining car service has been interrupted in the past; it's a good idea to inquire prior to departure whether it is necessary to bring your own provisions. Frequently the heating system doesn't work or is inadequate, so in cold weather you might want to carry a lap robe. Recently a number of new deluxe coaches have been added, but few things about the Chihuahua–Pacific are certain or permanent. At the frequent five-minute stops along the route vendors hawk hot coffee, cocoa, and soft drinks. Although the train runs year-round, the best time to see the canyon is October, after the rainy season but before the weather turns cold. March and April, before the spring rains and heat, are also good, but be sure to avoid Holy Week, when all facilities and attractions are crowded.

The Railroad

Gouged out of ancient rock, thrown across plunging gorges, and bored through towering mountains, this seemingly impossible route was the dream of Albert K. Owen, a visionary who longed for a railroad connecting Kansas City to Topolobampo on the Sea of Cortés, partly in order to service a utopian community he was building at what would be the line's southern terminus. Launched more than a century ago, it was an impractical idea, even for the Gilded Age, but

Owen sank large amounts of money into the project. The beginning and end of the line presented no problems; the land there was flat. But in between rose the formidable Sierra Madre.

Fortunes were devoured trying to make the link. Finally the best engineering and financial minds in the United States pronounced the railroad an impossibility. The enterprise was shelved and almost forgotten. Only the first section, from Chihuahua to Creel, was put to use.

In the years after the Revolution Mexico gradually began to acquire ownership of her own railroads, and in 1939–1940 bought out the last of the foreign companies, among them the Chihuahua–Pacific. Mexican engineers studied and debated the ambitious project for 13 years before announcing their solutions to the daunting problems blocking the completion of the railroad.

The biggest one, of course, was the 160-mile stretch through the Copper Canyon, a land of rugged mountains and bottomless gorges inhabited only by the primitive Tarahumara Indians and a handful of missionaries. For eight years the construction work inched along. Thirty-nine bridges were built to span the chasms of the canyon and 86 tunnels were dug through its mountains. Finally, in 1961, the line was opened, making it possible to take what would soon be known as "the Train Ride in the Sky."

The Tarahumara

The railway did not replace a road; there were—and still are—very few through roads in the region. In fact, the surrounding countryside had been virtually isolated since the earliest days of its habitation. As a result, when the construction crews first encountered the local Tarahumara Indians, they found themselves among a Stone Age people.

The Tarahumara you will encounter are a sturdy people with sharply defined features and long coarse hair, which the men wear bound in a headband. They also wear rough white shirts and the *tapote,* a kind of loincloth. They are fabled runners who will hunt a deer by chasing it until the animal drops of exhaustion, and their strength is as great as their stamina. A favorite Tarahumaran game involves kicking a small ball while running a footrace; participants will run as much as 150 miles without a real rest, a feat of endurance that takes several days and nights.

Today many of the Tarahumara still live in caves and follow the seasonal migration patterns of their ancestors: In summer they live on the high cliffs, but when winter comes they retreat to the canyon depths, moving from colder to milder temperatures as they descend more than a mile to the bottom.

Taking the Train

First-class trains, known as *especiales,* make the trip daily, one southbound from Chihuahua, the other northbound from Los Mochis. They pass near Divisadero, but do not stop to exchange passengers. In other words, you'll have to wait about 24 hours at any stop along the line for the next train. And because the entire trip (without stopovers) takes longer than daylight lasts, you'll have to make a round trip to see everything in daylight. (Most travellers choose not to do this, although it can be a convenient plan depending on your next destination.) The best way to see the canyon is to take the *northbound* train, either from Los Mochis or El Fuerte, about 80 km (50 miles) to the northeast of Los Mochis (sit on the right side of the train for the best views). If you must leave from Chihuahua and do the trip straight through, you'll probably be disappointed when falling darkness obscures the views while you're still in scenic country. The longer days of summer lessen this problem somewhat.

Most travellers use **Los Mochis**, a modern agricultural center, as their boarding point. The town was founded in the last century by Albert K. Owen, the same man who pioneered the Chihuahua–Pacific Railroad, and was envisioned as a socialistic utopian settlement, grand in scale, noble in purpose. Owen's experiment failed, but 30 years later, in 1903, an American named Benjamin Johnson built Mexico's largest sugar mill here and literally put the town on the map. Today Los Mochis is a prosperous but unexceptional community.

Those who want to linger in Los Mochis a day or two may enjoy visiting **Topolobampo**, a small community on the coast 19 km (12 miles) south of town. The eastern terminus of the ferry to La Paz in Baja California Sur, Topolobampo offers a pleasant beach, swimming, and boat rentals for sportsfishing, which is famous here. Additionally, short cruises around the Bahía de Topolobampo can be arranged at the Hotel Santa Anita in Los Mochis. The scenic trip includes a visit to the **Roca de Farallón**, a low outcropping of sharp, wave-splashed stone where sea lions come to breed. There are no recommendable accommodations in Topolobampo itself, but drinks and snacks are available.

The **Hotel Santa Anita** in Los Mochis, part of the Balderrama hotel chain, offers comfortable lodgings at moderate rates. A five-story brick, glass, and steel structure, the hotel is nondescript modern with a few Mexican touches and smallish rooms. A travel agency in the hotel specializes in Copper Canyon excursions.

If you are planning on staying overnight in the canyon, it is *essential* to have confirmed hotel reservations before you step aboard the train. Once en route your alternatives are limited; hotels are few and there is no way to get to the next town if the first one is fully booked.

The train leaves the Los Mochis station at 6:00 A.M. If you have driven, hotels at either end of the line will arrange car storage. You can also have your car shipped from Los Mochis to Chihuahua. (The vehicles do not go on the passenger train but on a freight train that follows.) The cost is steep, however: about $250 to transport a compact model.

An alternate boarding point is the town of **El Fuerte**. Founded as a mission in the 16th century, then a vigorous mining town in succeeding centuries, today it is a quaint colonial town located in the middle of good fishing and hunting country on the Río Fuerte. El Fuerte has the **Posada Hidalgo**, a sister hotel of the Santa Anita in Los Mochis. The former mansion of a local politician, this rustic provincial inn is filled with antiques and gay Mexican decorations, and has a romantic, plantation atmosphere. Officially, the train is supposed to leave town at 8:26 A.M., but it never does. The good news is that you won't have missed much by avoiding the Los Mochis–El Fuerte leg.

East of El Fuerte the train begins its long ascent into the Sierra Madre Occidental. The fertile coastal plains of Sinaloa soon give way to a spectacular landscape of cliffs and buckled escarpments carved into a jumble of shapes by millions of years of wind and water. The whole complex is vast, a cluster of canyons of which the Copper is merely the greatest. As you look out the window of your coach or observation car, the average crest you see will be nearly 6,500 feet. Several rise to 9,000 feet or more, soaring above gorges that drop completely out of sight. The most spectacular contrast of this sort is the upthrust of **Monte Mohinara**, towering more than 12,000 feet above the rocky canyon bottom. The canyon floor itself enjoys a semitropical climate, while the heights above are often snow covered.

At about 12:30 P.M. you arrive in remote **Bahuichivo**, having crossed the state line into Chihuahua. There is a short stop here for sightseeing; it is also the first possible overnight break in the trip—and a good one. The **Hotel Misión** in Cerocahui, also part of the Balderrama operation, offers accommodations, food, guides, and a warm welcome to the back country. Situated in a quiet valley in the middle of inspiring scenery, it has a hacienda atmosphere, and sends a bus to meet the train, a trip of about 30 minutes.

The hotel's fertile valley, with its gentle climate, is carpeted with apple and peach orchards. In 1690 Juan María de Salvatierra, the first European to see the region, was so enchanted that he established a mission here. Today Cerocahui offers riding, two mines open to the public, a sparkling waterfall, and lofty mountain peaks. In addition, guests can take a motorized excursion down to the lovely Río Urique or visit the mission school, where you'll meet the shy Tarahumara. The charm of the hotel is further bolstered in the winter months by the pot-bellied stoves used to heat it.

From Bahuichivo the train climbs through even more spectacular country, plunging into tunnels and seemingly flying over bridges. The illusion of flight is especially convincing when the bridge is narrower than the train and nothing but space can be seen between you and a stream hundreds of feet below; the sensation is exhilarating rather than frightening.

Divisadero, the halfway point of the trip, offers views so overwhelming that a 15- to 30-minute stop is made. The great canyon winds around a big bend in the river here, making it even more dramatic, and from a promontory you can see the opposite rim a mile away. Beyond that are still more peaks and mesas. The air is bracing, the whole prospect magnificent.

The **Hotel Cabañas Divisadero-Barrancas**, a five-minute walk from the train stop, perches on the very edge of a sheer cliff commanding views across the canyon and of a pine forest below. The log-and-stone cabins and rugged dining room would have an almost ski chalet–type atmosphere were it not for the wonderful, restorative sense of quiet. (There are no radios, TVs, or phones here or in any of the other hotels in the immediate area.) The hotel is fairly expensive, though well worth it. Its management will be happy to arrange trips to Indian villages and into the canyon, as well as to a nearby waterfall.

Creel

This logging town with a frontier spirit five and a half hours from Chihuahua is the next major stop. Situated high in the Tarahumara Mountains, the most forbidding part of the Sierra Madre Occidental, Creel straddles the track. Nearby, huge stacks of lumber await shipment, scenting the crisp mountain air with an aroma of pine.

Creel is also known as the Indian capital of northern Mexico because of the concentration of Tarahumaras in the region. Roads, most of them quite rough, stretch out to all the major canyons from here, providing access to Tarahumaran villages, fantastic rock formations, a remarkable waterfall, mountain lakes, and old Jesuit missions.

The most difficult, yet rewarding, trip from Creel takes you 140 km (87 miles) northwest to the spectacular waterfall known as **Cascada Basaséachic**. The river here plunges in eerie silence 1,000 feet into Barranca (canyon) de Candameña—said to be the highest single-drop waterfall in North America. Your best bet is probably to take an organized tour (travel time is about four hours each way). Hotels in Creel arrange excursions to the falls, as well as to other natural attractions in the area. Though the trek on foot from the edge of the falls down to the canyon floor is a bit strenuous, the sight of the great silver ribbon of water springing far past the sheer cliff in a free fall is worth the effort.

Another local attraction, but more easily reached from Creel, are the "mushroom rocks" located outside the Indian village of **Basihuare**, 38 km (24 miles) south of town. Here you'll find a huge mountain dotted with outcroppings of rock, some reaching a height of 215 feet. All have been eroded by weather and beautifully colored by minerals in pinks and whites, making them seem as if they have "sprouted" from the side of the mountain.

Also nearby, about 20 km (12 miles) south of Creel, the Jesuit mission of **Cusárare** remains much as it was when it was founded in the 17th century. The interior, decorated with pigments made by the Tarahumara, is known for its life-size paintings. Abandoned in 1767, the mission was only recently restored to service.

Other points of interest around Creel include the **caves of Chomachi**, a series of mountain caverns that were once the home of Apaches; they remain mostly unexplored, although one is known to be six miles long. A tour of the caves, which begin about 10 km (6 miles) northeast of Creel and extend over a large area, could take anywhere from three to ten hours, depending upon how much exploring you want to do. About six hours should be devoted to a trip to **Sisoguichi**, a Tarahumaran village 29 km (18 miles) northeast of Creel centered around government medical facilities and a school; a Jesuit mission was founded here in the middle of the 17th century. **Lago Arareco**, about 7 km (4 miles) southeast of Creel, is a marvelous spot for swimming or rainbow-trout fishing. Allow about two hours for the trip to the mountain pond. Don't be put off by the words "tour" or "excursion" when used in connection with these places; there is nothing touristy, crowded, or spoiled about any of these wilderness spots.

Another highlight of the surrounding area is the village of **Norogachi**, about 77 km (48 miles) south and east of the Creel station. Sunday is fiesta day, when large numbers of Tarahumara dressed in traditional costume congregate here, giving the village a pre-Columbian air. About 40 km (25 miles) farther along the same road (118 km/73 miles south of the Creel station) lies **Barranca Batopilas**, the most beautiful canyon floor in the region. While the trip to the canyon is slow—almost seven hours by Jeep, truck, or bus—it is scenically as magnificent as the destination. Foliage changes as the trail descends, oaks and pines giving way to otate bamboo and Moctezuma cypress; you enter willow country as the cool temperate world becomes subtropical. The sheer cliff walls insulate this hidden land of ferns and wild roses, which flourish in the shadows of the precipices.

The isolated village of Batopilas is surrounded by colonial ruins from several different centuries: crumbling haciendas, mining installations, and a late-16th-century mission church, its fallen walls betraying majestic proportions. The people of this mountain oasis, both Tarahumara and their few Mexican neighbors, smile shyly and gravely in welcome.

The Parador de la Montaña or the Copper Canyon Lodge in Creel (both discussed below) will make arrangements for the trip as well as for simple overnight quarters (making this journey in one day is impractical). The modest, inexpensive **Hotel Batopilas** is your best bet, although there are a couple of other plain but adequate three- and four-room inns in Batopilas.

The stretch of road from Creel to Chihuahua is now paved and can be covered in a little more than two hours; in addition, small aircraft can be landed on a packed-earth landing strip outside of Creel. Many people from the United States drive to Creel, do some exploring, then take the train to the Pacific coast while their vehicle is shipped after them or stored in Creel to await their return.

In Creel the best hotel for your money is the **Parador de la Montaña**, a comfortable establishment close to the center of town. It has private baths (unlike some hotels in Creel), and a very good restaurant and bar. The **Copper Canyon Lodge**, about 30 minutes outside of town, is rustic but well equipped, with stone fireplaces in the guest rooms and a pleasant dining room. The lodge arranges excursions to many scenic attractions in the region—as do most Creel inns—and provides bus transportation to and from the station.

Chihuahua City

If you board the train the next afternoon you'll arrive later that evening in Chihuahua, a large and thriving city. The cathedral here is a fine building, begun in 1724 but so often delayed by Indian wars that it wasn't completed until a hundred years later. The **Museo Histórico de la Revolución en el Estado de Chihuahua**, housed in the former home of the outlaw-patriot Pancho Villa at Calle 10 Norte 3014, has Revolution-related documents, arms, and photos, as well as the automobile in which Villa was riding when he was assassinated in 1923. The museum's tiny gift shop also has a list of Villa's 25 wives and 25 children. Villa, born Doroteo Aranjo, owes this memorial to his widow Luz Corral, whom he married and divorced four times and who died in 1981.

Elsewhere in town, the collection of photos and farm implements of early Mormon and Mennonite settlers gathered in the **Museo Regional de Chihuahua** is completely at odds with the building that houses it, a 1910 mansion filled with Art Nouveau furnishings, a Louis XV dining room set, and an abundance of stained glass skylights and windows.

There is a good selection of hotels to choose from in Chihuahua, the most luxurious and centrally located of which is the **Palacio del Sol**, at Avenida Independencia 500. Less expensive and also in the center of town, at the corner of Avenida Independencia and Niños Heroes, two blocks north of the zócalo, is the good if unremarkable **Posada Tierra Blanca**.

In addition to the restaurants and coffee shops in its main hotels, Chihuahua has two fine and popular restaurants. Housed in a 19th-century brewery on Highway 45, two blocks north of the intersection of Juárez and Colón (at Juárez 3331), **La Olla de Chihuahua** serves up tastefully prepared steaks, seafood, and Mexican dishes (Tel: 14/14-7894). Nearby, at Juárez 3316, is the more elegant **Los Parados de Tony Vega**, a remodeled private residence with a good but fairly expensive selection of steaks and seafood (Tel: 14/15-1333).

GETTING AROUND

Aero California offers direct flights from Los Angeles to Los Mochis, Tijuana, La Paz, and Guadalajara. Aeroméxico flies from Tucson to Mexico City, Guadalajara, and Hermosillo; from Guadalajara to Chihuahua; and from Mexico City, Monterrey, Mazatlán, Los Mochis, Hermosillo, and Tijuana to Chihuahua. Mexicana flies from Dallas–Fort Worth to Chihuahua, and Continental flies from Houston to Chihuahua. Aero Leo López flies from El Paso to Chihuahua and from Chihuahua to Los Mochis.

A dozen major bus lines serve Chihuahua's Camionera Central, which is about 1½ km (1 mile) northwest of the city center.

You need both a ticket and seat reservation for the Copper Canyon train. Information, tickets, and reservations can be obtained from: Jefe, Ferrocarril Chihuahua al Pacífico, Apartado 46, Chihuahua City, Chihuahua 31000; or Jefe, Ferrocarril Chihuahua al Pacífico, Los Mochis, Sinaloa 81200. It is easier, however, to deal with an agent than directly with the railroad.

In Los Mochis, **Viajes Flamingo** in the Hotel Santa Anita is helpful; Tel: (681) 2-1613; Fax: (681) 2-0046. In Chihuahua, **Quezada Tours** in the Palacio del Sol is good; Tel: (14) 15-7141; Fax: (14) 15-7606.

ACCOMMODATIONS REFERENCE

The rates given below are projections *for December 1992 through Easter 1993. Unless otherwise indicated, rates are for double rooms, double occupancy; the 10 percent VAT has been added. As rates are subject to change; it's always a good idea to double-check before booking.*

▶ Copper Canyon Lodge. **Creel**, Chihuahua 33200. Reservations: Viajes Flamingo, Los Mochis, Sinaloa 81200. Tel: (681) 2-1613; Fax: (681) 2-0046. $144 (includes three meals).

▶ Hotel Cabañas Divisadero-Barrancas. **Divisadero**, Chihuahua. Reservations: P.O. Box 661, Chihuahua City, Chihuahua 31000. Tel: (14) 10-3330 or 15-1199; Fax: (14) 15-6575. $160 (includes three meals).

▶ Hotel Misión. Domicilio Conocido, **Cerocahui**, Chihuahua. Reservations: Hotel Santa Anita, Los Mochis, Sinaloa 81200. Tel: (681) 2-1613; Fax: (681) 2-0046. $151 (includes three meals).

▶ Hotel Santa Anita. P.O. Box 159, Leyva and Hidalgo, **Los Mochis**, Sinaloa 81200. Tel: (681) 5-7046; Fax: (681) 2-0046. $82.

▶ Palacio del Sol. Independencia 500, **Chihuahua City**, Chihuahua 31000. Tel: (14) 16-6000; Fax: (14) 15-9947. $104.

▶ Parador de la Montaña. Allende 114, **Creel**, Chihuahua

33200. Tel: (145) 6-0075; Fax (in Chihuahua City): (14) 15-3468. $63.

▶ **Posada Hidalgo**. Hidalgo 101, **El Fuerte**, Sinaloa 81820. Tel: (681) 3-0242; Fax: (681) 2-0046. $55.

▶ **Posada Tierra Blanca**. Avenidas Independencia and Niños Heroes, **Chihuahua City**, Chihuahua 31000. Tel: (14) 15-0000; Fax: (14) 15-8811. $64.

THE BAJA CALIFORNIA RESORTS
LOS CABOS

By Susan Wagner with Candace Lyle Hogan

Susan Wagner, the travel editor of Modern Bride *magazine for 10 years, has worked on the staff of* Travel & Leisure *magazine and written a series of guidebooks to Mexican resorts and innumerable articles on the country. She attended graduate school in Mexico and returns there frequently. Candace Lyle Hogan, a freelance writer and editor currently living in New York City, is the contributor of the "Weekend in Baja" section. She has explored Baja California over the last 40 years from a home base in La Misión.*

Baja California is so unusual—and the car trip from one end of it to the other so demanding—that it really calls for its own separate guidebook. We recommend a couple of good ones in the Bibliography. (You can also write or call the foremost "Baja" bookstore, John Cole's Book Shop, 780 Prospect Street, La Jolla, CA 92037; Tel: 619/454-4766.)

While we do provide limited background on the peninsula itself, as well as a suggested weekend itinerary from the States, it is for the resorts at Los Cabos (the Capes), at the southernmost tip of the peninsula, that we provide the most details. Comprising the towns of San José del Cabo and Cabo San Lucas, as well as the 18-mile highway corridor that follows the ruggedly beautiful stretch of coast between them, Los Cabos has an otherworldly atmosphere that distinguishes it from other Mexican resorts. The area is one of the most beautiful on earth, and everything, including the marine life, seems to be larger than life. In fact, this is the only Mexican Pacific resort that attracts large numbers of working scientists in addition to vacationers.

Generally speaking, Cabo San Lucas is the center of the resort scene and the departure point for sightseeing and deep-sea fishing fleets. San José del Cabo, quieter and more residential, is the location of most of the area's government offices, home of the area's *panga* fleets (for those who prefer to do their fishing closer to shore), and the locus of its planned golf course development.

Regardless of where you end up staying, the golden dawns will be followed by clear days and the breathtaking sunsets will give way to velvety night skies full of stars. Wonderful hotels, great weather, and plenty of fresh air and sparkling beaches—Los Cabos is the perfect rejuvenating tonic for those lucky enough to find their way here.

MAJOR INTEREST

Baja California
Rugged natural beauty
Desert flora and fauna
Deep-sea fishing
Whale watching

Los Cabos
Isolated resort hotels
Small-town resort atmosphere in Cabo San Lucas
Spectacular scenic beauty
Deep-sea fishing
Scuba diving
Whale watching
Championship golf

BAJA CALIFORNIA

If you travel the highway that stretches from Tijuana, just over the border from San Diego, south to Cabo San Lucas at the tip of the peninsula, you'll pass through 1,000 miles of rugged, sometimes forbidding terrain that is never less than spectacular and is often heart-stopping. This slender piece of land is only 30 miles wide at its narrowest point and no more than 140 miles at its widest. With the Pacific Ocean to the west and the long, narrow Sea of Cortés (known as the Gulf of California in the United States and Canada) to the east, a stunning beach or lovely seascape is never far away. The waters off Cabo San Lucas, where the two meet, are among the world's most fertile fishing grounds, their junction marked by a natural arch-shaped rock formation called El Arco.

People who haven't spent a lot of time on the peninsula tend to think of Baja as a huge cactus garden. Indeed, dozens of species of cacti and other plants—many of which cannot be found anywhere else in the world—flourish here, including 80-foot-high *cardóns,* the world's largest cactus, and the *damiana,* an herb alleged to possess curative and aphrodisiacal properties. Nevertheless, the Baja peninsula is the kind of place where smart visitors travel with a pair of binoculars at the ready. Around any corner you may come upon sea lions basking on the rocks offshore, gray whales frolicking in a bay, or fish jumping clear of the jade-green waters.

The indigenous people who lived here before the Conquest were unaware of the highly developed cultures that had flourished on the mainland before the arrival of the Spanish. Hernán Cortés himself came to the peninsula in 1535 and stayed searching for gold and pearls until 1537. By 1847 the United States had claimed Alta (Upper) California as its own, but Mexico's neighbor to the north decided not to acquire Baja, or Lower, California. In fact, except for the chain of missions built by the Jesuits, Franciscans, and Dominicans during the 1700s, the human imprint on Baja California is of relatively recent vintage.

It all started to change when Baja became a territory in 1931 and a state in 1952. (Baja California Sur became a separate state in 1974.) But until the Benito Juárez Transpeninsular Highway (Mexican Highway 1) opened a little more than two decades ago, much of this immense desert wilderness remained an isolated backwater. (Previously, most of the distance to Cabo was unpaved—or roads were nonexistent— and only four-wheel-drive vehicles could make the trip with any reasonable assurance of getting to their destination.) Today Highway 1, though only two lanes, is a smooth ride all the way down. The peninsula is still sparsely populated, however, and much of its primitive natural beauty remains unspoiled: Baja California is one of the few places in the world unmarred by vast road and rail networks, ports, or power lines. Though pockets of development are growing at the northern and southern ends of the highway, most of Baja is still heaven for naturalists and a world apart for the rest of us.

In stark contrast to the resorts of Los Cabos, most of Baja has been a "poor man's paradise" since the mid-1950s.

Longtime gringo aficionados of Baja complain that prices here (for land, restaurants, and hotels) are rising, and so they are, but it's still one of the cheapest tickets to easy pleasure in the world. Especially if you live near the border towns of California or Texas and are into rustic experience, an exotic vacation is much more affordable and close by than the Los Cabos area.

Combining an excursion into Baja with a Southern California trip, for example, you can get a taste of a different culture by driving just 30 miles south of the border, sampling the ocean views, the inexpensive cafés, and the abundant curio stalls along the highway. By taking side roads, getting out of the car, and hiking off the beaten path you can explore areas where bobcats roam and eagles nest. But off-road venturing is not for the faint of heart: Baja is wilder than, it seems, anywhere, and its terrain and weather change by the hour. All the way down the peninsula are coves, caves, cliffs, and valleys to discover, but it's imperative that you carry bottled water (canteens and a rattlesnake bite kit if you're hiking) and the means to repair your car should something go wrong. Travelling those 1,000 miles you'll go through every kind of climate imaginable (and several landscapes as well): rainy tropics and dry desert, rocky mountains and sandy beaches. Anyone of a mind to experience Baja for the adventure rather than for margaritas could start by taking a weekend trip across the border (to Rosarito or Ensenada, not hectic Tijuana) and talking with locals and bearded gringos who've been exploring for years. They'll give you the latest on which dirt roads are passable and which are flooded out; where the private property signs mean something and where they don't; where there are lively horses to rent and where you'll only get a nag.

Finally, because of Baja's remoteness visitors should bring plenty of cash or traveller's checks. Many fishing charters, meals, car rentals, and hotel accommodations still have to be paid for in cash, and patchy phone communications can make it difficult to get credit approval at those places that do accept cards.

A Weekend in Baja

Crossing the California border into Baja is accomplished with a smile, a nod, and a slow roll—the border guards will simply be looking through your car windows to make sure you're just a tourist (and not an importer of major appliances or furniture). After they wave you along, follow the signs that say "Ensenada Cuota" (not Ensenada Libre), and

don't worry that your route along the outskirts of Tijuana seems circuitous; the signs will lead you south to the new road, Highway 1D. (Although the new road is officially known as Highway 1D and the old road Highway 1, most people refer to them as simply the new and old road.) Soon you'll pass through a toll booth and begin to enjoy your first sea views, which become more spectacular the farther south you go.

Rosarito and Environs

After about 25 km (15 miles), take the first Rosarito exit and drive slowly through the town, which is lined with curio shops and stores. Rosarito has grown from a quiet fishing village known to a few *norteamericanos* for its great beaches and surf into the one major tourist city between Tijuana and Ensenada, with resort hotels, horseback riding, and organized bicycle rides and races. It's still possible to happen onto those unexpected "finds," however, including delicious lobster tacos at the little stands along the ocean side of Boulevard Benito Juárez or at the tortilla factory near the center of town on the east side of that main thoroughfare. One of the many good places to eat in town is **Los Pelicanos Restaurant and Bar**, right on the beach; try any variety of seafood here (about $13) or the quail in garlic sauce for $10. For lobster dinners you can't go wrong with **Vince's Lobster Trap** at 39 Boulevard Benito Juárez.

At the end of town on your right, drive into the parking lot of the **Rosarito Beach Resort Hotel**, an aging but fascinating survivor of more glamorous times. On the beach, with a pool, racquetball and tennis courts, and a gymnasium, the Rosarito was built in the late 1920s as the answer to Prohibition in the States, drawing Hollywood stars and famous athletes who came here to drink and gamble. The Mexican government soon put a stop to the illicit activity, but you can still see the vast room that housed the casino. The food is okay, the rooms so-so, but the ambience is pure old-fashioned fun. The best American breakfast deal in town ($5) is found here at the **Rosarito Restaurant and Bar**, which is also known for its 99-cent margaritas and its mariachi bands on the weekends. Some of the best shops for Mexican handblown glass, jewelry, and wood-carved sculptures line the street adjacent to the hotel.

If you continue south for 21 km (13 miles) down the old road you'll see on the right **Puerto Nuevo**, an enclave of more than 30 restaurants, almost any one of which can be recommended for the sweet, clawless Baja lobster, caught just off the coast. The most you'll pay for the delectable crustacean is $15, and a fish dinner will cost about $10. **Ortega's Restaurant** is the most popular, but the small and simple **Miramar** is probably the best choice for lobster.

The next town you'll come to is **Cantamar**, with a gas station, a grocery store, a hotel, and a bakery or two. But mainly it's residential, a hamlet for locals and long-term vacationers. ATV buffs love the leviathan sand dunes here.

Hop onto the new road at the next on-ramp heading south to enjoy the sea views, and keep an eye out for the rounded backs of frolicking dolphins and the spouts of gray whales. The whales migrate from their summer feeding grounds in the Bering Sea in October to their breeding grounds in Scammons Lagoon, halfway down the peninsula, arriving any time from late January into March. (The best time to see the whales close to shore is at dawn.)

Five kilometers (3 miles) south of Puerto Nuevo you'll see, off to the right, **Halfway House**. Named for its location halfway between Tijuana and Ensenada, this is the oldest bar and restaurant along this stretch (in operation for more than 60 years), still serving its standard Mexican fare as well as burgers and hot dogs. Surfers take respite here from the excellent waves at nearby Punta Mesquite, and photographers relish the ocean view from the house's garden.

La Misión

A little beyond the Halfway House, 30 km (19 miles) south of Rosarito and shortly beyond the kilometer 64 marker, take the La Misión exit. Turn left, and immediately on your left will be **La Fonda**, an oceanfront motel, bar, and restaurant known and loved by all. The food and drink here is good and moderately priced, the atmosphere easygoing. The staff is made up of locals, people who live in or near the charming valley of La Misión. The clientele consists of Americans and Mexicans who've known about the place a long time and keep coming back. As a result, accommodations must be booked at least two weeks in advance. Though the rooms are modest, the ones with sea breezes will put you in mind of Key West and Hemingway. No less romantic is La Fonda's verandah, where you can eat or drink overlooking the beach from an umbrella- or tree-shaded perch.

If one or two quiet overnights is your plan and relaxed beach walks your pleasure—the ocean here is good for wading but not swimming—stay at La Fonda. With this as your home base, you can spend the rest of the day and evening exploring Ensenada to the south, and still make the

56-km (35-mile) trip back that night with ease. You'll wake up in the morning to the sound of gulls and the sight of pelicans knowing you've slept at a place that is part of local history: More than 30 years ago La Fonda was built by a Mexican citizen for his American wife, Eve Stocker, whose prickly proprietorship earned her the nickname "Cebolla" (the Onion).

Just a two-mile walk south along the beach from the motel is **Punta Piedra**, a rock formation that juts out into the sea, forming an inviting little bay. If you're lucky you'll see dolphins teaching whales how to surf here. Plans for a hotel at Punta Piedra are in the offing, but for now the area remains relatively unspoiled. (You may have to pay to camp or park along the beach, but the price shouldn't be more than a couple of dollars. There's also a trailer park hookup nearby.) You can jog along the beach, explore the tidal pools, and sunbathe, but be careful when swimming: There's usually an insidious riptide. Ask at the motel about where to rent horses, which can be ridden inland a mile or two but not on the beach.

For organized recreation you can drive 12 km (7½ miles) south of La Fonda to **Baja Mar**, a Mediterranean-style resort offering golf, swimming, tennis, and bicycle rentals. (Twenty of its 100 privately owned villas are available for daily or weekly bookings; for information and reservations, call the **Tijuana Baja Information Center** at Tel: 800/225-2786, 800/522-1516, or 619/222-9099.)

If you feel particularly adventurous, take the old road from La Fonda south about 8 km (5 miles) and turn left onto a dirt road right before the short whitewashed bridge. (A little package store is on the left, a taco stand with good fast food on the right.) This is the entrance to the valley of **La Misión**, where the real people live (and some longtime American expatriates, too). The ruins of the Misión San Miguel de la Frontera, a Dominican mission built in 1787, are barely discernible on a hill to your left. Most of the bottom land is worked by a farming cooperative; on either side rise the sheer cliffs of flat-topped mountains called *mesas* (tables). Here hawks soar, their high-pitched "screee" echoing from one side to the other of this narrow valley. There's really no place to go, but never was driving a couple miles just to turn around more intriguing. The artist Robert D'Amore lives less than a half mile in, up a rather treacherous driveway leading to the top of a hill; his photographs offer insight into the specialness of the surroundings. One family, the Crosthwaites, settled the left side of this valley, which today means any child you see in La Misión is likely to be a descendant of an Irish sailor who jumped ship in the 1800s.

Ensenada

The large town of **Ensenada** is just 109 km (68 miles) south of Tijuana and 56 km (35 miles) south of La Fonda via Highway 1. (Keep your eyes peeled a couple of miles north of town for "The Smallest Bar in the World," a tiny monument to expatriate eccentricity.) In Ensenada you can charter a deep-sea-fishing boat or just look over the stalls at the fish market, alive with fresh sea creatures every morning. The charter-boat offices in the port area offer group fishing excursions for as little as $30 per person. Many stores along Avenida López Mateos (the main drag) book fishing trips, as well; it's best to shop around, as vessels and rates vary dramatically.

The Baja *Sun* and Baja *Times,* two English-language newspapers, are good sources of current information on Baja Norte and the west coast, as is the state tourism office located at Avenida López Mateos 1350-13B; Tel: (684) 6-2222.

Rowdy Mexican **rodeos** are staged almost every summer weekend on the charro grounds near the corner of Calle 2A and Avenida Blancarte, and **bullfights** are held at the Plaza de Toros on Avenida Sangines between Boulevard Lázaro Cárdenas and Avenida Cipres. One of Baja California's most esteemed wineries is **Bodegas de Santo Tomás**, Avenida Miramar 666, where you can tour the grounds for $1.50 and sample the Santo Tomás wines. Ensenada also hosts numerous sports and cultural events throughout the year, including bicycle races, yacht regattas, and the renowned Presidente-Sauza SCORE Baja 1000, the premier off-road-vehicle competition.

Nightlife has long been hot in Ensenada, and there are many good restaurants and hotels, with rates generally more affordable than those in the Los Cabos area. From top to bottom, however, Ensenada is fully booked on weekends. You can get information—and guarantee reservations at some hotels and motels—by calling the **Tijuana Baja Information Center** (Tel: 800/225-2786, 800/522-1516, or 619/222-9099). The **Hotel Bahía**, in town, continues to be popular for its clean, carpeted rooms and balconies overlooking the bay, but if you want to get out of town for the night try the **Estero Beach Resort**, 10 km (6 miles) south of Ensenada. The complex here includes tennis courts, horse rentals ($6 an hour), a campground, and a recreational-vehicle park as well, with spaces ($10 a night for two) available along the edge of a lagoon.

Up-to-date information on the more than 200 restaurants in Ensenada can be found in the two newspapers mentioned above. For elegant surroundings there is **El Rey Sol**, an Old World French-Mexican restaurant honored by the International Seafood Fair. Located at the corner of Avenida López Mateos and Avenida Blancarte, El Rey Sol is the place to breakfast on fresh stewed manta ray for about $6.

Thanks to inexpensive liquor prices, Ensenada's bars and cantinas are plentiful and popular. The most famous of them in the "drinking district" (avenidas Gastelum and Ruíz) is **Hussong's**, which was still frequented by scowling *vaqueros* (cowboys) and Zapata lookalikes in the 1950s but is now crowded with young Southern California fun-seekers, bikers, and surfers. If you're just passing through, any café along the main drag will do for a quick snack or good Mexican beer; for fresh tortillas made before your eyes, head for the **Restaurant Las Brasas**, on López Mateos near Avenida Gastelum, where barbecued chickens are spit-roasted over an open flame.

Before heading back to the States, take a side trip about 24 km (15 miles) southwest of Ensenada to **Punta Banda** and the area's most popular weekend attraction, **La Bufadora**, a tidal blowhole that makes a phenomenal groaning sound. From Ensenada turn west off Highway 1 right before Maneadero onto the road numbered 23. Along the way you'll pass wooden stands where jars of chile peppers and olives are sold, the Baja Beach and Tennis Club, and several campgrounds; La Bufadora is at the very end of the road.

El Calafia, a romantic cliffside restaurant with an outdoor seating area exposed to balmy breezes off the ocean, is a pleasant place for a meal on your way back to the border. Visible from both the old and new roads is a big sign with an arrow pointing to its location, about 8 km (5 miles) north of Rosarito and 16 km (10 miles) from the border itself.

Crossing back into the United States will take longer than coming in; be prepared for an hour-long wait. Border guards check for illegal aliens as well as contraband. It's a good idea to look them in the eye and state—before they ask you—your nationality, where you've been, and that you are returning only with those things you came with or bought—no fruits, vegetables, or pets.

—*Candace Lyle Hogan*

BAJA CALIFORNIA SUR

The rugged part of the Baja peninsula begins below Ensenada. In northern Baja California Sur (after Highway 1 swings to the east and cuts across the peninsula), Santa Rosalía, Mulegé, and Loreto are oases in the desert, with all three showing signs of becoming popular vacation spots. **Santa Rosalía**, about 700 km (496 miles) south of Ensenada, and the smallest of the trio, has a handful of tiny hotels housed in historic buildings as well as a number of rustic restaurants. The town was founded in the late 19th century by a French-owned copper-mining company, and so many of its buildings are French colonial in style. **El Boleo**, a colorful local establishment, is reputed to be one of the best bakeries in the state. Windsurfing on the beautiful Sea of Cortés shares the limelight with fishing here.

Sixty kilometers (38 miles) down the coast in **Mulegé**, a smattering of retirement homes is beginning to appear along the banks of the Río Mulegé, the most picturesque part of town and the departure point for its fishing fleets. Palm groves line the riverbanks here, and an 18th-century mission church, the **Misión de Santa Rosalia de Mulegé**, stands atop the hill overlooking town. While the unspoiled beauty of the subtropical surroundings is spectacular, the big draw is the outstanding dorado fishing.

Loreto, 85 km (55 miles) south of Mulegé, has been a sportsfishing mecca for years now, and recently has seen a number of major development projects started. Still, these pockets of development are few and far between, with most bordered by miles of arid desert and empty beaches.

Downtown Loreto has a sleepy look that hardly reflects the important role it played as one of the first Jesuit missions established in New Spain, and later as the first capital of the Californias. Small hotels such as the **Hotel El Oasis** and **Misión del Loreto** (both with pools and their own charter fishing fleets), conveniently located on the seaside promenade, are comfortable and friendly if rather expensive for what they deliver.

A handful of restaurants here cater to visiting fishermen as well as to locals. **Cesar's**, on the corner of Zapata and Benito Juárez, has been satisfying visitors for more than 20 years with hearty portions of seafood. Dark wood panelling and checkered tablecloths give it an Old West look. **El Nido**, on the outskirts of town near the highway at Salvatierra 154, is constructed of dried cactus. It has a pleasant, if dark, interior and is locally famous for serving superb cuts of meat. Sea-

food is the house specialty at **Playa Blanca**, a restaurant with a beautiful terrace at the corner of Hidalgo and Madero. **Alfredo's**, right on the seaside promenade, serves Mexican seafood dishes on an outdoor terrace overlooking the ocean. Its location almost directly across from the docks assures the freshness of its fish.

The **Museo de la Misiónes**, the only historical attraction in town, features displays illustrating what mission life was like. The mission is located at the far end of a paved promenade closed to traffic and lined by small souvenir shops.

In the Nopoló neighborhood, the opulent California mission–style **Stouffer Presidente Loreto**, one of the stars of the Stouffer chain and the only self-contained resort in the area, is a knockout. Spread out over a sprawling beachside property, where swimming conditions are ideal and just about every water sport imaginable is available, the Presidente has a pool and pretty gardens in which to relax, tennis courts, a couple of excellent seafood restaurants, a lively lobby bar, and a discotheque. The new 18-hole golf course nearby was designed by Joe Finger, and affords spectacular views of the rugged terrain hereabouts.

Arturo's Sports Fishing at the Presidente will arrange excursions even if you are not a guest at the hotel; Tel: (683) 3-0700, ext. 114. Another reputable outfit is **Alfredo's Sport Fishing**; Tel: (683) 3-0165 or 0832.

Tepui, one of the nicest trailer parks in Mexico, is 11 km (7 miles) south of town in Puerto Loreto (formerly known as Puerto Escondido). Tepui's restaurant is a popular stop for motorists. **The Moorings**, a small marina that charters large sailboats, is about a five-minute cab ride to the south. Boats are available by the day or the week; Tel: (683) 3-0818.

La Paz

Situated on the Sea of Cortés at the southern end of the Bahía de la Paz, this city of almost 200,000 is the capital and commercial hub of the state of Baja California Sur. La Paz was the first Baja city to be discovered by the "outside world," after fishermen and sportsmen began arriving more than 30 years ago. (The bar in the Hotel Los Arcos was John Wayne's favorite place to watch the fishing boats come and go.) Today La Paz ("The Peace") is still a sports-lover's paradise, but one with a few conspicuous touches of the good life. It's clear that the residents of this rugged, no-nonsense city, with the highest per capita income in the country, have given thought to the town's development. Today, not only fishermen and scuba divers are attracted to La Paz and its cordial atmosphere.

Most of the tourist attractions and small shops are located along its seaside drive *(malecón),* which here is called Paseo Alvaro Obregón, and the streets that branch off it. Heading the *malecón* at the corner of Marqués de León is **La Paz-Lapa**, a Carlos 'n' Charlie's establishment. As in all the Carlos Anderson restaurants, the decor is zany, the menu even zanier. Loud rock music usually keeps the bar jumping, but the back dining room, which sits on stilts over the water, is both quieter and cooler, thanks to ocean breezes.

The **Hotel Los Arcos**, a few blocks northeast of La Paz-Lapa along the *malecón,* offers plain but comfortable rooms overlooking the promenade and bay, as well as pretty public areas with plenty of Old World charm. **El Bermejo**, a popular restaurant specializing in seafood, is also in the hotel. The **Cabañas de los Arcos**, across the street, are detached one-story rooms and suites arranged around a shady garden and small swimming pool—the nearest thing to an oasis that La Paz has to offer.

A block behind the Cabañas de los Arcos at the corner of Bravo and Francisco Madero, **La Carreta** is one of the best shops in town for ceramics, hand-blown glass, and other handicrafts. Down the street, **Xtasis**, housed in a former perfume shop at Zaragoza and Agustín Arreola, is the disco of the moment. No shorts are permitted here, but just about everything else goes—until 5:00 A.M. on weekends.

The **Hacienda El Abajeno**, a picturesque colonial building overlooking the bay at the corner of Alvaro Obregón and Lerdo de Tejada, specializes in meat dishes, and is popular with residents as well as visitors (Tel: 682/5-9666). A few doors beyond, **El Quinto Patio** is similar in atmosphere to La Paz-Lapa: Diners dance when the inspiration hits, despite the fact that there is no formal dance floor.

The **Hotel La Perla**, a few blocks north along the *malecón,* is an old favorite. Its newly refurbished rooms and public areas feature an attractive desert decor, while the open-air restaurant downstairs, a favorite La Paz hangout, is one of the best places in town to people-watch.

Farther down the *malecón,* between 16 de Septiembre and Callejon La Paz, popular **El Campanario** offers light meals and snacks, while downstairs the **Okey Laser Club** features multiple dance floors, video screens, balloons, confetti, and the occasional live show or act. In an old building still farther along the *malecón,* across from the pier, **Ciao Italia** draws crowds for its delicious Italian dishes served in an attractive, modern setting (Tel: 682/5-6227).

The rather plain façades of the stores on 16 de

Septiembre (which runs inland from the *malecón*) and nearby streets often bely the quality of the merchandise inside. **Dorian's**, a two-story U.S.-style department store at the corner of 16 de Septiembre and 21 de Agosto, is almost as well stocked as its counterparts back home. There's also a small **Chinatown** tucked into the side streets and alleys between the *malecón* and Dorian's.

The true business district is located several blocks to the south of the *malecón,* and most tours of the city will include several sights in the area. The **Biblioteca de las Californias**, at the corner of Cinco de Mayo and Madero, features a fine collection of Spanish-language books and documents relating to the establishment of missions in and colonization of the Californias. A stop at the three-story **Museo Antropológico de Baja California Sur**, on the corner of Cinco de Mayo and Altamirano, is worthwhile only for the most enthusiastic history buffs. Most of the exhibits consist of illustrations or small pre-Columbian pieces, and explanations are in Spanish only.

Four blocks away at Altamirano and Degollado, the **Bismark II Restaurant** is favored by those who want to get top value for their money and don't care much about decor. Seafood is the specialty here. (Tel: 682/2-4854.) If you head west on Altamirano to Navarro, you'll come to a modern cultural complex where music and drama performances are staged frequently.

Two pretty hotels—La Concha and La Posada—are located at the opposite ends of town. **La Concha Beach Resort**, about a ten-minute cab ride northeast of town in the direction of Playa Pichilingue, is a little jewel of a place with a pretty beach that's ideal for swimming. The modern, tropical decor of the rooms and public areas lends the resort a contemporary look that most of the other hotels in La Paz lack, and the dining room overlooking the pool and beach is especially pleasant. At the other end of town just off the road to Los Cabos, the clean and cozy **Hotel La Posada de Engelbert** (founded by Engelbert Humperdinck) is situated on its own beautiful stretch of beach. This charming, rather exclusive, colonial-style hotel has 25 suites—some in separate buildings and all with fireplaces—a screened dining room that's popular with local businesspeople, and a marina next door.

Of course, fishing is still the main thing on everyone's mind in La Paz, but excursions to unpopulated, exquisitely beautiful islands in the Sea of Cortés such as **Espíritu Santo** also make for unforgettable days. Trips can be arranged through your hotel or through such travel agents as **Viajes**

Perla, 170 Cinco de Mayo, Tel: (682) 2-8666; or **Viajes Lybsa,** at the corner of Alvaro Obregón and Degollado, Tel: (682) 2-6001.

In addition, a car ferry links La Paz to Mazatlán, across the Sea of Cortés (about 18 hours; see the Mazatlán section in the Pacific Resorts section below for details). A ferry also connects La Paz with Topolobampo (about 8 hours), the town next to the small city of Los Mochis, where interested parties can catch the spectacular Copper Canyon train (see the Copper Canyon chapter above). The ferry office in La Paz is located on Calle Guillermo Prieto between Independencia and Reforma; Tel: (682) 5-3833 or 2-5258. Schedules and rates are subject to sudden changes, however, so it's best to call the office or check with a travel agent in advance.

LOS CABOS

Los Cabos, the premier Baja California resort area, lies at the tip of the peninsula where the Pacific meets the Sea of Cortés. Highway 1, one of the most scenic seaside highways in the world—and the location of most of the area's top-drawer resort facilities—winds some 37 km (23 miles) between the region's two principal towns, San José del Cabo and, to the southwest, Cabo San Lucas.

Vermilion mountains seem to rise out of the ocean itself and, just behind them, endless terra-cotta–colored desert landscapes stretch to the horizon. The visitor to Los Cabos can rent horses or ATVs and ride for miles in the desert, or take solitary strolls on beaches that extend as far as the eye can see. Rock formations jutting out of the water and a shoreline that is alternately craggy and gentle provide spectacular seascapes at every turn. **El Arco,** a towering arch-shaped rock formation off the coast at Cabo San Lucas, has become one of Mexico's scenic landmarks, and the pink dawns and soft sunsets that bathe it are breathtaking.

Exquisite beauty lies under the water as well. The waters off Los Cabos, one of the most fertile fishing grounds in the world, teem with marine life and provide a stunning payoff for scuba divers and snorkelers. (One of the deep underwater canyons has been protected as a marine refuge.) More than 850 species of fish are said to live in these waters, and sharp-eyed visitors catch glimpses of some of them without having to don scuba or snorkeling gear. Porpoises, whales (between January and March), manta rays, and sea lions are also frequently spotted in the coastal waters hereabouts.

Before Highway 1 opened, this part of the peninsula was accessible only by air or water. Most of the hotels were posh fishing "camps" for wealthy sportsmen and Hollywood celebrities who could afford to arrive by private plane or yacht. Even today Los Cabos is the kind of place where hotels list private airstrips and fishing fleets among their amenities, and fishing charts and boat-rental information feature prominently in the text of their brochures. The area has long been known to those who love to fish as Marlin Alley; several thousand blue, black, and striped marlin are caught here every year. Swordfish, sailfish, dolphin fish, yellowfin tuna, sierra (a large mackerel-like fish), black snook (a warm-water pike), wahoo, roosterfish, and other species are also among the sportsfishing prizes here.

Not surprisingly, life in Los Cabos seems to accommodate a fishing schedule (though this is changing). Everyone gathers in local bars or around hotel verandahs in the late afternoon to watch the boats come in with their catches and to listen to the day's fishing yarns over drinks. Early-morning fishing trips mean that dinner is generally served early and that box lunches for the next day may be ordered along with the meal.

Fishing is no longer the sole activity here, however. Seemingly overnight, Los Cabos has matured into one of the biggest stars on Mexico's resort map. Both towns have undergone successful face-lifts within the last few years, and the refurbished façades and new amenities are attracting great numbers of visitors. With a marina and several new shops, restaurants, and discos in Cabo San Lucas, and a few boutiques and restaurants either open or under construction in San José del Cabo, non-anglers now have a wide range of options from which to choose—certainly enough to fill a week-long vacation. At the same time, many people come to Los Cabos to escape all the glitter, and it remains one of the few resort areas in the world where the natural beauty of the place is still its principal attraction.

The Los Cabos climate is ideal. The average annual temperature is 75° F, with hot days and cool nights (be sure to bring a light sweater or shawl). Some hotels used to close in summer when limited diesel-generated electricity ruled out the use of air-conditioners, but today most hotel rooms are air-conditioned and only the Twin Dolphin closes (for the month of September).

Many of the major hotels and activities in Los Cabos can

be found just off Highway 1 between Cabo San Lucas and San José del Cabo. The majority of the hotels along the highway corridor are separated by vast parcels of land. Access to the various beaches is clearly marked by white signs with black letters and green symbols, and even those areas that have been fenced off for development are legally open to the public.

A final word about beaches. Though all are stunningly scenic, not all are good for swimming because of strong undertows. Ask at your hotel and follow their advice before you dive in.

San José del Cabo

San José del Cabo, the location of Los Cabos International airport, is the area's major banking and business center. Though the population of the town is listed as 30,000, you'll probably wonder when you see it for the first time if everyone has "gone fishin'"—which, in all likelihood, they have.

The tranquil face of the town belies its relatively eventful history. San José del Cabo had its own mission and presidio in colonial times, when Cabo San Lucas was still a village inhabited largely by Pericue Indians. But the local priest was slain by marauding Indians, who then proceeded to discourage early settlers of the area from staying. Pirates, who plundered Spanish galleons arriving from the Philippines, were another thorn in the side of settlers.

Today, under the watchful eye of Fonatur, San José del Cabo is being transformed from a sleepy village into a busy little town. Shops and restaurants are situated in old pastel-colored buildings, and the private homes sprinkled among them have housed generations of families. Family names are often displayed on plaques by the door, and residents sit on the sidewalks chatting and watching passersby.

Visitors usually begin a tour of San José along Boulevard Antonio Mijares, which links the "hotel zone" to the south with the small downtown area itself. The boulevard is divided by a landscaped mall, and ends just past city hall at a small plaza with a fountain. Start at the open-air souvenir stalls at the bottom, walk to the plaza, and turn left on Calle Zaragoza. **La Bamba**, a branch of a Cabo San Lucas store at Boulevard Mijares 33, starts off the liveliest part of the boulevard with original hand-painted sportswear for children and their mothers. The **Squid Roe** shop next door, a Carlos 'n' Charlie's outlet, sells unisex tee-shirts, hats, and shirts decorated with that chain's familiar motifs.

The **Iguana Bar and Grill** features barbecued ribs and a

good selection of Mexican dishes, and always seems to have a gaggle of people watching televised sports events from the States or dancing to records on the cement floor (Tel: 684/2-0266). At **Eclipse**, a new disco/bar a few doors down, a special suspension floor lets you dance until you drop—and then some. **Tropicana**, one of the town's most popular restaurant/sports bars, is located on the opposite side of the street at Boulevard Mijares 30. A spacious place with attractive dining rooms inside and out, it also features live music in the evenings (Tel: 684/2-0907). The Tropicana's two-story "inn," situated behind the restaurant, consists of 40 air-conditioned rooms with satellite TV, and also has a large pool with a swim-up bar. On the same side of the boulevard as Tropicana, **Cardon Design** offers a well-selected array of handicrafts, from lamps and ash trays to placemats and vases.

Galería El Dorado, at the corner of Mijares and Doblado, is a branch of a larger gallery in Cabo San Lucas that sells whimsical sculptures by Mario González, a prominent Mexican sculptor, as well as a variety of works by contemporary Mexican painters. **La Casa Vieja**, Boulevard Mijares 27, stocks women's resortwear by Josefa and Girasol, as well as a selection of tasteful decorative items.

For light lunches and dinners in an informal setting, try **Café Europa** on the main plaza. The aroma of freshly baked bread and pastries wafts through the windows of **La Baguette**, just a few doors down.

Hidden away behind the plaza at Boulevard Mijares 18 is **Damiana**, one of the most charming restaurants in the area. Dinner here is served in what was once the main room of this 19th-century colonial home, as well as on its flower-filled patio, and thick adobe walls keep it cool by day and romantic at night. Lobster, abalone, and shrimp are the house specialties. Oenophiles might want to sample the Baja wines on Damiana's wine list: the Santo Tomás winery, located just outside Ensenada in Baja California Norte, produces Chenin Blanc, Pinot Noir, and Cabernet Sauvignon (Tel: 684/2-0499.)

Calle Zaragoza, which climbs the hill to the left of the plaza, is another interesting dining and shopping area. **El Caracol**, at the corner of Allende and Zaragoza, features a selection of carefully chosen sportswear and accessories. **Antigua Los Cabos**, in an old home with a beautiful patio just up the street at Zaragoza 20, is one of the loveliest shops in town. Decorative items and souvenirs are displayed throughout, and occasionally works by local artists are also for sale.

Pietro, an intimate Italian restaurant with an especially charming decor, is a few doors up the hill near the colonial-style church (Tel: 684/2-0558). **La Fogata**, a longtime San José favorite at the corner of Zaragoza and Morelos, specializes in T-bone steaks.

Staying in San José

The European-style **Posada Terranova**, on Degollado between Zaragoza and Doblado, is a lovely small hotel with seven rooms, a tiny indoor restaurant and bar, and an open-air restaurant that's especially popular with locals and resident North Americans. Owned by a Mexican family of Italian descent, the Terranova is a charmer in an area where small hotels are the exception rather than the rule. However, it is definitely a "downtown" property, and thus about a ten-minute drive from the beach.

The **Stouffer Presidente Los Cabos**, at the southern end of Boulevard Mijares, is the first of about a dozen widely separated resort properties between San José del Cabo and Cabo San Lucas. But the Presidente is the place to stay if you want to be near the commercial district in San José (a five-minute cab ride), the golf course (also a five-minute cab ride), or if you want to dance. (The **Cactus Video Disco**, the town's only disco, is housed in a separate building just outside the entrance to the hotel.)

The property itself resembles a Mediterranean-style village, with tiled walkways lacing the grounds and a large pool area that is usually the center of activity. The beach is just a few steps away. Rooms are spacious and very comfortable, and some have small sitting rooms and patios.

San José to Cabo San Lucas

The **Hotel Palmilla** has been the darling of knowledgeable resort travellers since the 1950s. Designed and built by Abelardo Rodríguez, the son of a former president of Mexico, it was the first luxury hotel in Los Cabos and is the only hotel in the area to enjoy the Mexican government's highest rating, Clase Especial Gran Turismo. The rooms and suites are large and comfortable, and most have balconies with an ocean or garden view. (Many also have patios where you can breakfast overlooking the ocean; ocean-view rooms cost a bit more.) Fluffy robes and giant towels add to the appeal of the large tiled bathrooms, and neither telephones nor TV sets are on hand to interrupt the reverie.

The Palmilla's personalized service (there are three employees for every guest here), begins the minute you step in the door, and soon makes guests feel as if they're members of a private club. Not surprisingly, many return year after year (and request their favorite rooms), and a few have even married in the private chapel just up the hill. Tennis and paddle-tennis courts, horseback riding, and croquet are a few of the activities offered on the premises. The Palmilla also has its own fishing fleet, one of the best diving and water-sports centers in the area, and a beautiful uncrowded stretch of beach where good swimming and snorkeling conditions prevail.

As if all this were not enough, the Palmilla's owners are currently building a 900-acre resort on the property. When completed the resort will feature white stucco buildings with red-tile roofs, a tennis club, golf course, shopping/ entertainment village, and a health spa. The 27-hole championship golf course, designed by Jack Nicklaus and due to open by the time this book is in print, will offer unrivalled panoramas of mountains, desert, and ocean. Whether or not you golf, however, the Palmilla has a certain cachet and sophistication that other hotels and resorts in Los Cabos lack. For a perfect vacation in an idyllic setting, it's tough to beat.

Even though its driveway is marked by a tall freestanding gate in the middle of nowhere, **Da Giorgio's**, located a few miles west of the Palmilla, is hard to find. Standing atop a hill on the same side of the highway, this popular restaurant serves up homemade pasta, pizza baked in brick ovens, and a variety of other Italian dishes on an outdoor terrace or in a Mediterranean-style dining room.

Located almost midway between San José del Cabo and Cabo San Lucas, the 282-room **Meliá Cabo Real** resembles a small, futuristic city with all the creature comforts of home. Stone floors, a vaulted lobby, and tasteful decor that mixes pre-Columbian reproductions with Spanish touches lend the Meliá a certain stylishness often lacking in big hotels. A huge pool, two restaurants, three bars, and a water-sports center are just a few of its other amenities. When construction of the surrounding resort is completed it will have an 18-hole golf course designed by Joe Finger. The layout of the Meliá is designed to give its guests a feeling of wide-open spaces: The pool area, for example, is a five-minute walk from the lobby, and the hotel's beautiful beach (safe for swimming) is another few minutes' walk beyond that.

The **Hotel Cabo San Lucas**, about 8 km (5 miles) farther down the road in the direction of Cabo San Lucas, is sometimes referred to as "El Chileno" because it stands at the head of Punta Chileno. Situated on a 2,500-acre estate fronting a very pretty beach and Bahía de Chileno, this massive facility bears the mark of the visiting fishermen who made it famous: Everything is built on a grand scale and has a solid, masculine look about it. (It also has its own private airstrip.) The rooms and suites are especially spacious, and all have beautiful views, either of the ocean or of the lovely gardens on the premises; some also have fireplaces. Of course, everyone gathers in the bar in the late afternoon to sip margaritas and watch the fishing boats come in. The dining room, which overlooks the ocean, is one of the most attractive in the area, with a palm-shaded pool and native stone walls. The food, on the other hand, is rather plain.

The hotel's fishing fleet is anchored minutes away, or if you prefer you can take advantage of shooting on the premises. In addition, one of the most interesting boutiques in the Los Cabos area, with a well-chosen selection of exotic treasures and jewelry from the Far East, is located in the lobby.

As you travel along this stretch of road, be sure to stop at **Acapulquito** or **Costa Azul** beaches, before the Twin Dolphin Hotel, to watch the surfers.

The posh **Twin Dolphin**, located on a bluff another few miles to the west, looks like a private sporting club with an unusual modern architectural style. Its comfortable rooms and bungalows, surrounded by desert landscape and a cactus garden, overlook the ocean, and graceful sculptures dot the property and stand guard over the pool. The bar, with its comfortable leather furniture, paneled walls, and soaring ceilings, resembles an old-fashioned gentlemen's club, and the dining room's high ceiling lends it a touch of elegance and formality.

The top-of-the-line facilities at the Twin Dolphin include an 18-hole putting green, two tennis courts lit for night play, a fishing fleet of eight boats, and two miles of marked nature trails. Service is truly personalized (the newest employee on the staff has been with the hotel more than six years), and the sophisticated international resort crowd that can do without nonstop nightlife (and TVs and telephones) loves it here. The Twin Dolphin operates on a full American plan (three meals a day), and is closed for the month of September.

The natural beauty of **Playa Santa María**, next to the Twin Dolphin, is truly breathtaking. Vermilion-colored mountains tumble into the water at either end of the moon-shaped bay, and swimming and snorkeling conditions are almost always perfect. Watching the sun set from here is more than memorable. Bring your snorkeling gear, pack a picnic (but be sure to take your refuse with you when you leave), and make an unforgettable day of it.

Las Misiones, a condo/home development that's still under construction, includes one of the area's most beautiful restaurants, **Da Giorgio's II**, situated on a promontory that affords a rare unobstructed view of El Arco, an arch-shaped rock formation off the coast, and Lovers' Beach. Pools and multi-level walkways lead out to a point. The restaurant itself is open to the air, and the menu consists of Northern Italian specialties; service is still getting out the kinks at this writing.

Ground has been broken on Cabo del Sol, an 1,800-acre resort that begins just past the Twin Dolphin and surrounds Barco Varado (Shipwreck Beach). The resort will include an 18-hole championship golf course designed by Jack Nicklaus; eight of the greens will be on the water. The course will be open to the public.

Cabo San Lucas

Cabo San Lucas is a delight. In the old days the moneyed crowd that stayed at the posh hotels along the highway rarely ventured into the sleepy town, but today it's busy and on the move, with the greatest concentration of shops, restaurants, and discos in the area. Old buildings around the zócalo have been renovated and the plaza itself burnished to a grandeur it hadn't known previously. Victorian benches and lampposts, flowers, and an ornate bandstand now make it a pleasant place for watching the passing parade. Nearby, a marina with 200 slips for private yachts, a large hotel (the Plaza Las Glorias), condos, a shopping mall, and a pier for sightseeing boats have all opened recently, giving the entire downtown area a Mediterranean look and feel.

The population of Cabo San Lucas is approaching 25,000, but the town never looks crowded, even when cruise ships glide into its tiny harbor, and the sole traffic light, one of two in the entire area, still seems superfluous. At the same time, though everything seems to be scaled down in size, Cabo San Lucas is spread out, and some of the streets remain unpaved. There's a cluster of small businesses where the road enters town from the southeast; a second grouping of stores on Lázaro Cárdenas and surrounding the zócalo; and a third concentrated around the harbor.

The part of town of most interest to visitors begins at the Pemex station on the main highway and continues around the marina past **Playa Medano**, the closest thing to a town beach (where swimming conditions are ideal year-round), to the Hotel Solmar. Most shops and restaurants are located on the seaside highway, Boulevard Marina, Calle Cabo San Lucas, or on the side streets that link them. If you continue straight along the highway past El Squid Roe, Boulevard Marina swings to the left, hugging the water, while Lázaro Cárdenas goes up the hill to the zócalo. The street on the far side of the plaza, parallel to Boulevard Marina, is Calle Cabo San Lucas, the last paved street in this part of the downtown area.

Coconuts, the beachside restaurant at the Club Cascadas condominium complex, offers great water sports by day in addition to a varied menu of meat, seafood, and pasta. By night it's one of the most romantic spots in town, offering candlelight and soft classical music backed by the sound of waves. Tel: (687) 3-0337.

The pretty blue-and-white **Pueblo Bonito**, a new all-suites condominium/hotel, is right on Playa Medano. The meandering pool is the social center of the hotel.

The 190-room **Meliá San Lucas**, the next large resort property in the direction of town, is about a five-minute walk down the same beach. An attractive Mediterranean-style complex, the Meliá offers smallish rooms with ocean views, a big pool just a few steps from the ocean, and breezy public areas, including two restaurants and two bars.

Known for its lobster and abalone served in wine sauce, as well as for tasty hamburgers and light lunches, **Las Palmas**, next door to the Meliá, is undoubtedly the most popular daytime gathering spot in the Los Cabos area. The best tables are on the sundeck overlooking the beach, with panoramic views of the coast as well as the sometimes frenetic activity below (during spring break the restaurant sponsors a volleyball tournament that attracts more than 3,000 participants). Tel: (684) 3-0447.

The stretch of beach between Las Palmas and the Hacienda hotel is lined with rustic restaurants. **La Oficina**, a favorite breakfast spot, also serves romantic dinners at tin tables right on the sand.

The **Hotel Hacienda** was among the first on the Cabo scene. Today it's popular with travellers who aren't looking to spend top dollar and want to be near town (about a ten-minute walk around the marina). The rooms and suites are simply furnished but comfortable (though in need of refurbishing), and the beach, where you can enjoy just about any water sport imaginable, is practically at your doorstep.

To find what many think is the most refined dining spot in the area, head over to the Marina Sol condominiums, just up the hill from Las Palmas, and look for **Villa Alfonso**. Housed in an elegant colonial-style building about half a block from the beach, the restaurant bears the special touch of its owner, Alfonso Fisher, a native San Lucan and longtime restaurateur. The menu changes every night according to what is fresh or in season, and the presentation is impeccable. All dinners are prix fixe—about $30 per person before drinks and tip—and consist of seven courses. Those who want to make an evening of it can arrive early and spend time in the cozy bar or outside in the lush poolside garden. Closed Sundays; Tel: (684) 3-0739. Those who really fall in love with the place can spend the night. Villa Alfonso's is the only truly elegant bed and breakfast in town. Each of the 14 sumptuous rooms is decorated differently, and some have Jacuzzis.

El Pavo Real (The Peacock), down the hill in front of the Marina Sol condominiums, is another of the few refined dining spots in town. The chef is German, the meals are served under a breezy palapa, and the elegant surroundings will make you want to linger.

If good food in a less formal atmosphere is what you had in mind, head for **El Faro Viejo**, located in the trailer park of the same name just up the hill from Boulevard Marina at the corner of Rosario Morales and Matamoros. If it's your first time, don't set out to find this place after dark; instead, take a taxi. (While not far, El Faro is in the heart of a residential section with unpaved roads and few street signs.) Lunch and dinner menus change according to what's fresh at the market, but you can usually count on a selection of fish and meat entrées. Whatever your choice, the food will be delicious and the portions hearty. Plan on arriving early for a drink in the restaurant's lovely garden, complete with wrought-iron benches and Victorian-style lampposts. Reservations are necessary if you arrive after 7:30, but almost impossible to make; the restaurant doesn't have a phone, so you either have to stop by during the day to make them or have your hotel arrange them for you.

Back on Lázaro Cárdenas across from the marina you'll find **El Squid Roe**, a two-story Quonset hut decorated with neon on the outside and typical Carlos 'n' Charlie's memorabilia inside. Though the place caters to a young crowd, almost everyone will drop by for a drink sooner or later, and the beat goes on until 2:00 or 3:00 A.M. In fact, party lovers who start at the Giggling Marlin or one of the new clubs in town will more than likely end the evening with drinks and dancing here.

Circle the marina to the west and you'll come to the **Shrimp Bucket**, a breezy new restaurant named after the Mazatlán flagship of the popular Anderson chain. Seafood dishes head the menu at lunch and dinner, and the whimsical paintings will make you smile.

The sleek terra-cotta–colored **Plaza Bonita**, across the way from El Squid Roe, houses a number of stores and restaurants, including **Dupuis** for decorative items and **Casual Affair** and **Dos Lunas** for resortwear; **Lukas**, the area's most sophisticated disco (no cutoffs here); and **La Terraza**, on the second floor, which serves sushi, pizza, and a variety of Continental dishes. **Salsitas**, a lovely nouvelle Mexican restaurant run by the affable owner of Villa Alfonso, is just around the corner in the same complex. You can dine inside or out and feel like a millionaire as you watch yachts and fishing boats come and go in the marina; the food (breakfast, lunch, and dinner) is unusually good.

Casa Roberto, in the Plaza Aramburo on Lázaro Cárdenas, features a line of original sequined tee-shirts, as well as resortwear and accessories for women. **Zen-Mar**, farther up the street, features folk art from the state of Oaxaca, some of it designed and made to order for this store.

The **Hotel Mar de Cortez**, two blocks up Lázaro Cárdenas, is the place to stay if you're looking for economical accommodations in the middle of things. Locals call this clean, no-nonsense establishment the Mar De (pronounced MAR-day), and though the Mar de Cortez is strictly downtown, the new part of the hotel is especially pleasant. **Plaza Candido**, a mini-mall with several stores, is just a few doors farther up the street at the corner of Lázaro Cárdenas and Guerrero.

The **Mercado Mexicana**, recently opened nearby on Calle Hidalgo, is filled with typical souvenirs. Look for the archway painted with flowers just past **Papi's** restaurant—which, incidentally, serves the best cup of coffee in Cabo. **Capitán Lucas**, down Calle Hidalgo near its intersection with Boulevard Marina, uses the nautical motif to the hilt. Continental dishes dominate the menu. The restaurant is built to resemble the prow of a boat, and, as a result, the ambience in its dining room is cozy and intimate. Diners who really want to enjoy this place should wait until the live music (which often drowns out all conversation) is through for the evening.

The **Cabo Wabo Cantina**, on Calle Zaragoza (four blocks to the east and parallel to Calle Hidalgo), is owned by Sammy Hagar, a member of the rock group Van Halen. It's a tastefully decorated nightspot with a good dance floor, a clublike decor, and a concert stage for performances by touring rock acts.

Mama Eli, with a fine selection of decorative items, resortwear, jewelry, and accessories, is in a restored building on the zócalo itself.

Cabo's newest Mexican restaurant, **Mi Casa**, at the opposite end of the zócalo, is housed in an old building that evokes the charm and graciousness of an Old World hacienda. Innovative nouvelle dishes are the specialty here, and reservations are necessary, especially on weekends; Tel: (684) 3-1933.

There are several other good stores and restaurants along Boulevard Marina, which skirts the marina before heading out past the hotels at Land's End. **Nekri**, one of the most attractive stores in Cabo, offers an especially good selection of folk art and decorative items. The main branch of **Galería El Dorado**, a few doors down opposite the marina, sells sculptures in a variety of mediums.

The cavernous **Giggling Marlin**, overlooking the marina, is a Cabo San Lucas institution. Old-timers and those in the know love it here. The beer seems to flow from breakfast on, and once the sun sets there is usually a crowd dancing under the indoor palapa. It's the kind of place where anything goes: You can even have a souvenir photo of yourself taken while posing upside down like a hooked marlin.

Temptations, one of the best stores in town for women's resortwear and accessories, is just behind the Giggling Marlin. The owners claim to have the largest collection of hand-painted clothing in the state, much of it designed by California artist T. Jay, and their prices are significantly lower than what you'd pay for the same merchandise north of the border.

Just off Boulevard Marina, **The Shrimp Factory** has come up with a winning formula: Customers order their crustaceans by weight and size, along with their choice of three delicious sauces. Brave customers wash it all down with a "Bulldog," a tequila-based house concoction.

The **Río Grill**, a few blocks farther down Boulevard Marina, is a relatively new complex with a restaurant, bar, and tiny dance floor. The informal restaurant is under a palapa with shuttered windows, while the dance floor is under the stars.

Just up Boulevard Marina from the Río Grill, **Señor Sushi** is one of the most popular restaurants in Cabo San Lucas. Offering a mix of Japanese and Continental cuisine, it also has the town's best sushi bar. Locals congregate in the regular bar to watch televised sports events. Others simply come to linger over a delicious meal and watch the passing parade.

For delicious pizzas, homemade bread baked in a traditional brick oven, and some of the best Italian specialties in town, try **Romeo and Julieta**, just beyond Señor Sushi at the corner of Boulevard Marina and Subida del Cerro.

The rooms in the colonial-style **Plaza Las Glorias**, located on the marina across the street from Señor Sushi, are bright and pleasant, with cool tiled floors and rattan furniture. Most also have balconies overlooking the ocean. Guests who prefer to spend the day at the beach rather than at the pool (which is on the second floor of the hotel) are shuttled to Playa Medano by water taxi (a five-minute ride), and most of the area's fishing fleets and sightseeing boats, as well as a seaside souvenir market that caters to cruise-ship passengers, are right outside the door or within easy walking distance. (You'll want to shop the stalls in the market before buying anything. Prices for some items can vary as much as $20 from one stall to the next, and bargaining is a must.)

Like a regal sentinel standing watch at one of the best locations in Cabo, the **Hotel Finisterra** perches atop a hill overlooking the harbor on one side and the exquisite expanse of beach at Land's End on the other. One of the first hotels in Los Cabos, the Finisterra offers the best of all possible worlds: It's within walking distance of the fishing fleets, restaurants, and shopping, yet still provides its guests with the feeling of being away from—or above—it all. Everything about it is sensible, solid, and first class, and the personalized service and faithful attention to details are not lost on its guests, who keep returning year after year. A drink at the **Whale Watcher's Bar** here is an established tradition. The hotel recently opened a lavish beach club with a large swimming pool. A stone bridge connects the hotel to the beach below.

El Galeón, across from the ferry terminal not far from the Hotel Finisterra, serves Italian and Continental cuisine, the Spanish decor (and owners) notwithstanding. The food is complemented by sweeping ocean views and soft piano music in the evenings. Tel: (684) 3-0443.

Still catering to the fishermen who made it popular in the first place, the **Hotel Solmar** stands on a breathtaking beach farther out toward Land's End. The rooms here are breezy and comfortable, the restaurant and pool areas pretty, and the record catches on display in the dining room truly amazing. The Solmar is about a five-minute cab ride from town.

Though the beaches around **Land's End** are notorious for their dangerous surf and undertow, their breathtaking beauty more than makes up for the inconvenience of not being able to swim. Most visitors who spend the day soaking up the sun and exquisite scenery out this way will find it a day well spent.

Nightlife in the Los Cabos Area

With new restaurants and clubs opening all the time, the early-to-bed reputation of Los Cabos is dissipating.

Most hotels have live music in their lobby bars to get the evening off to a happy start. In San José del Cabo you can dance after dinner at the **Tropicana** and the **Iguana Grill**. **Eclipse** downtown and the **Cactus Video Disco** next to the Stouffer Presidente (open Thursday through Sunday) keep the beat going until well after midnight.

Of the two towns, Cabo San Lucas has the greater concentration of restaurants and nightspots. Those who like to have fun in a loud, informal atmosphere start off at the **Río Grill** or the **Giggling Marlin**, where you can drink, dine, and dance, then move on to **El Squid Roe**, where you can do the same after the others close.

Those who like their evenings a bit more formal gravitate to the sleek setting of **Lukas**, across from Squid Roe, or the clublike atmosphere of the **Cabo Wabo Cantina**, where you never know what famous or semi-famous rock group might drop in. Even when the music is recorded, Cabo Wabo has one of the best dance floors in town, with comfortable chairs and tiny tables facing the stage and a snack bar outside on a pleasant patio.

Sports in the Los Cabos Area

There are any number of sports options in Los Cabos, but fishing is the top attraction. If your hotel doesn't have its own fleet, there are a few outfits that can arrange anything from a 22-foot *panga* (skiff) to a fully equipped ocean cruiser.

- Los Dorados Fleet: (684) 3-1630
- Gaviota Fleet: (684) 3-0430
- Hotel Palmilla Fleet: (684) 2-0582
- Hotel Hacienda Fleet: (684) 3-0663
- Hotel Cabo San Lucas Fleet: (684) 3-0663
- Hotel Finisterra Tortuga Fleet: (684) 3-0366
- Hotel Solmar Fleet: (684) 3-0022
- Twin Dolphin Juanita Fleet: (684) 3-0522
- Pisces Fleet: (684) 3-0409 or 0249

Fishing fleets are moored either at their hotels or at the town end of the marina in Cabo San Lucas. Prices range from $260 to $700 per trip, depending on the size and type of boat. Most hotels will be happy to help you get a group together. When booking, check to see if live bait and lunch are included.

Old hands at this game charter boats in advance. Most companies ask you to fax them a copy of the check you've mailed ahead of time. Those who sign up to compete in such well-known events as the Bisbee Blue Marlin Tournament (which usually is held in October) book boats as much as a year in advance.

The following establishments offer all-inclusive fishing packages in the East Cape area, about an hour and a half north and east of Cabo San Lucas (all telephone numbers are in the United States): **Spa Buena Vista**, Tel: (310) 943-0869; **Punta Pescadero**, Tel: (800) 426-BAJA; and **Villa Spacienda**, Tel: (510) 254-4123.

Canoeing, parasailing, snorkeling, windsurfing, jet skiing, and waterskiing are also available. If your hotel doesn't have the equipment, call Cabo Acuadeportes at the Hotel Hacienda, Tel: (684) 3-0117; Pisces Water Sports, Tel: (684) 3-0409 or 0249; Victor's Aquatics in the Hotel Posada Real, Tel: (684) 2-0155; or just head over to Playa Medano, where all kinds of equipment can be rented.

Bahía de Chileno (the location of the Hotel Cabo San Lucas), Punta Palmilla, and Playa Santa María (next to the Twin Dolphin) are the best places to snorkel. Scuba-diving excursions to multicolored coral beds, underwater caves, and the largest coral reef off the west coast of the Americas can be arranged through Amigos del Mar, Tel: (684) 3-0022; Buzos del Cabo, Tel: (684) 3-0747; or the Hotel Palmilla dive shop, Tel: (684) 2-0582. The truly dedicated sometimes rent a boat and fish, scuba dive, and snorkel all in the same day. In addition, the giant waves at Costa Azul, halfway between San José del Cabo and Cabo San Lucas (just before you get to the Twin Dolphin), are perfect for surfing.

The big hotels all have tennis courts. Horses—an exhilarating way to enjoy the truly spectacular scenery in Los Cabos—can be rented at Marco's Horse Rentals in front of the Hotel Hacienda or at the Stouffer Presidente in San José del Cabo.

Hunting trips for white dove and quail can be arranged through the travel agent at your hotel. Duck and goose shooting is also superb here.

Excursions in the Los Cabos Area

One of the most popular excursions takes you by boat past hundreds of unconcerned sea lions to **El Arco**. Boats leave from the Cabo San Lucas harbor, and the round-trip fare is the equivalent of $6. You can also arrange for the boat to leave you at **Playa del Amor**, a sparkling stretch of white sand where you can dip your toes in the Pacific, walk a few yards up the beach, and then dip them in the Sea of Cortés (the boat will pick you up at a prearranged hour). If it's solitude you seek, however, don't do this on a Sunday or when a cruise ship is in town.

Viajes Los Cabos and other travel agencies in the area offer trips to Buena Vista and the East Cape area. The trip includes swimming and lunch at the Rancho Buena Vista Hotel, which also has bungalows and a large pool. Other trips or excursions include the village of **Santiago**, where there's a small zoo full of animals indigenous to the area; the old lighthouse at **Cabo Falso**; the picturesque mining town of **El Triunfo**, where silver, gold, and zinc are still mined; a number of mission churches; and sunset cruises of the bay leaving from the Cabo San Lucas harbor. Contact the travel agent at your hotel to arrange these and similar tours. Most will leave from your hotel lobby.

The trimaran *Trinidad* (Tel: 684/3-1477) offers whale-watching tours in season (January to March), as does the **Amigos del Mar** dive shop; Tel: 684/3-0022.

One of the most delightful trips you can do on your own involves renting a car and driving about an hour and a half north from Cabo San Lucas along the coast to the small town of **Todos Santos**. The desert countryside along the way is beautiful, and the combination of cactus forests backed by palm trees and the blue Pacific is especially breathtaking.

Once in Todos Santos you can visit the charming Hotel California (yes, the very one made famous in the Eagles' song) on Avenida Juárez, and enjoy a gourmet Italian lunch or dinner in the **Café Santa Fe**, a stylish and romantic restaurant owned by Enzo Colombo and his wife, Paula, an interior designer from New York. Salads are fresh from the garden and the lasagna is like none you've ever tasted before. The restaurant, which closes on Tuesdays, is on Marqués de León opposite the zócalo. Reservations are advised; Tel: (682) 4-0002.

GETTING AROUND

Driving Down from the Border

Auto insurance, which is a must, can be bought along the San Diego Freeway or right before you cross the border; U.S. insurance is not valid in Mexico. (See "Around Mexico by Car" in the Useful Facts section, above.) Posted speed limits are about 10 m.p.h. faster than in the States, and people often push 90 on the new road (Highway 1D). Don't speed in town though—they'll catch you.

Four-wheel-drive vehicles are best, but are not a cause for overconfidence. The Baja terrain is unpredictable, and if you get stuck off-road, you're stuck. On the other hand, Highway 1D is patrolled by the Green Angels, teams hired by the Mexican government to help motorists whose vehicles break down. And it's a fairly frequent occurrence when a friendly Mexican with a warm blanket appears out of nowhere to rescue a gringo. Of course, almost every Mexican male knows how to repair an American car—if only with tape and bailing wire.

Take extra gas. Although there are more gas stations along Highway 1D and near populated areas these days, they still run out of fuel sometimes and unleaded gas is not always available. Also take extra water for your car—it can get very hot along certain stretches of road.

The "old road," though *libre* (free) and beautiful, is full of twists and turns, often runs close to the edge of cliffs, is vulnerable to rock slides, and usually is occupied by slow trucks and limping, ancient cars. You'll need to take the old road to get off the beaten path, but the new road is just as beautiful, usually affords more breathtaking ocean views, and, regardless of the tolls, is the far better choice for getting from point A to point B.

In the past few years the Mexican governmnent has been working on the Northern Border program, an ambitious campaign to cut down the bureaucracy at border crossings and to upgrade the Mexican highway system. A new bypass road is under construction between San Diego and Ensenada; due to be completed some time in 1993, the road starts in San Diego, skirts Tijuana, and continues south. Two roadside service areas near Tijuana are scheduled for completion some time in 1993 as well. They will provide such amenities as a service shop for light repairs, a restaurant, and public restrooms.

—*Candace Lyle Hogan*

The easiest way to get to Los Cabos is by plane. (All flights arrive at the Los Cabos International Airport in San José del Cabo.) Aero California flies to Los Cabos from Los Angeles, San Diego, and Phoenix; Mexicana from San Francisco, Los Angeles, Denver, Mexico City, Guadalajara, and Puerto Vallarta; and Alaska Airlines from Seattle, San Francisco, Los Angeles, and San Diego.

As of this writing, passenger ferries are not running between Cabo San Lucas and the mainland.

Once you arrive in San José del Cabo you can either rent a car or take a taxi to your hotel. If renting a car, it's best to do so at the airport (Budget, Hertz, and others have desks there), as Cabo San Lucas is about 40 km (25 miles) distant. A *colectivo,* shared with others, will cost between $8 and $24, depending on the number of passengers.

Cabs, usually vans, can be called from most hotels. The average taxi fare for the 25-minute ride between San José del Cabo and Cabo San Lucas is about $18. There also are taxi stands at the plaza in Cabo San Lucas and in front of the church in San José del Cabo. The taxis in the latter are red and yellow; Cabo San Lucas taxis are blue or green and gray.

It's best to rely on cash or traveller's checks here, as credit cards are not accepted everywhere and stores that do accept them often charge extra to cover their costs. (MasterCard and Visa are the most widely accepted.) U.S. dollars can be used everywhere, but getting change for large-denomination peso or dollar bills is sometimes difficult. If you carry plenty of small bills, you should have no problem.

Remember: Baja California Norte is on Pacific standard time (the same as Los Angeles and Vancouver), but Baja California Sur is on mountain standard time (the same as Calgary and Denver)—1 hour earlier than Mexico City. Be sure to take this into consideration if you have to make a flight connection; airline representatives often forget to remind you.

ACCOMMODATIONS REFERENCE

The rates given below are projections *for December 1992 through Easter 1993. Unless otherwise indicated, rates are based on double rooms, double occupancy; the 10 percent VAT has been added. As rates are subject to change, it's always a good idea to double-check before booking. Because it takes about two weeks for a letter to reach Los Cabos, most hotel booking offices are located in the United States. Many hotels do not accept credit cards on the premises (you can use a card when booking in the U.S., however). Some have good swimming beaches, others offer them nearby; check with your travel agent if this is a concern. The telephone area code for Los Cabos is 684.*

San José del Cabo

▶ Hotel Palmilla. Carretera Cabo San Lucas, km 27.5, **San José del Cabo**, Baja California Sur 23410; or P.O. Box 1980, 4343 Von Karman Avenue, Newport Beach, CA 92660. Tel:

(684) 2-0582; in the U.S. and Canada, Tel: (800) 637-2226; Fax: (714) 851-2498. $200–$336, European Plan.

▶ **Posada Terranova**. Domicilio Conocido, **San José del Cabo**, Baja California Sur 22340. Tel: (684) 2-0504. $45–$52.

▶ **Stouffer Presidente Los Cabos**. Boulevard Mijares s/n, **San José del Cabo**, Baja California Sur 23400. Tel: (684) 2-0211 or -0327; Fax: (684) 2-0232; in the U.S. and Canada, Tel: (800) HOTELS-1. $121–$176.

▶ **Tropicana Inn**. Boulevard Mijares 30, **San José del Cabo**, Baja California Sur 23400. Tel: (684) 2-0907 or -1580; Fax: (684) 2-1590; in the U.S. and Canada, Tel: (800) 524-5104 or (510) 652-6051. $85.

On the Corridor

▶ **Hotel Cabo San Lucas**. P.O. Box 48088, Los Angeles, CA 90048. Tel: (684) 3-0644; in the U.S. and Canada, Tel: (800) 733-2226; Fax: (213) 655-3243. $150.

▶ **Meliá Cabo Real**. Carretera Cabo San Lucas, km 19.5, **San José del Cabo**, Baja California Sur 23410. Tel: (684) 3-0967; Fax: (684) 3-1003; in the U.S. and Canada, Tel: (800) 336-3542. $120–$215.

▶ **Twin Dolphin**. 1625 West Olympic Boulevard, Suite 1005, Los Angeles, CA 90015. Fax: (684) 3-0139; in the U.S., Tel: (800) 223-6510 or (213) 386-3940; in Canada, Tel: (800) 554-4500. $318 (includes all meals).

Cabo San Lucas

▶ **Hotel Finisterra**. P.O. Box 1, **Cabo San Lucas**, Baja California Sur 23401; or 4422 Cerritos Avenue, Los Alamitos, CA 90720. Tel: (684) 3-0100; Fax: (684) 3-0590; in the U.S. and Canada, Tel: (800) 347-2252 or (714) 827-3933. $108–$264.

▶ **Hotel Hacienda**. P.O. Box 48088, Los Angeles, CA 90048. Tel: (684) 3-0664; Fax: (684) 3-0666; in the U.S. and Canada, Tel: (800) 733-2226; Fax: (213) 655-3243. $101–$292.

▶ **Hotel Mar de Cortez**. P.O. Box 1827, Monterrey, CA 93942. Tel: (684) 3-0032; Fax: (684) 3-0232; in the U.S., Tel: (800) 347-8821; in Canada, Tel: (408) 375-4755. $38–$57.

▶ **Hotel Solmar**. Avenida Solmar s/n, **Cabo San Lucas**, Baja California Sur 23410. Tel: (684) 3-0022; Fax: (684) 3-0410; in the U.S., Tel: (800) 344-3349; in Canada, Tel: (310) 459-9861. $108–$198 (including dinner).

▶ **Meliá San Lucas**. Playa Medano, **Cabo San Lucas**, Baja California Sur 23410. Tel: (684) 3-1000; Fax: (684) 3-4020; in the U.S. and Canada, Tel: (800) 336-3542. $215–$402.

▶ **Plaza Las Glorias**. Boulevard Marina s/n, **Cabo San Lucas**, Baja California Sur 23410. Tel: (684) 3-1220; Fax: (684)

3-1018; in the U.S. and Canada, Tel: (800) 342-2644 or (713) 448-2829. $154–$182.

▶ **Pueblo Bonito.** P.O. Box 460, **Cabo San Lucas**, Baja California Sur 23410. Tel: (684) 3-1976; Tel: (684) 3-1995; in the U.S., Tel: (800) 262-4500; in Canada, Tel: (800) 654-5543. $135–$160.

▶ **Villa Alfonso's.** P.O. Box 3, **Cabo San Lucas**, Baja California Sur 23410. Tel and Fax: (684) 3-0739; in the U.S. and Canada, Tel: (800) 347-2252 or (714) 827-3933. $138–$165.

Elsewhere

▶ **La Concha Beach Resort.** Carretera Pichilingue, km 5, **La Paz**, Baja California Sur 23010. Tel: (682) 2-6544; Fax: (682) 2-6218; in the U.S. and Canada, Tel: (800) 999-BAJA or (310) 943-1369. $94–$138.

▶ **Estero Beach Resort.** P.O. Box 86, **Ensenada**, Baja California Norte. Tel: (66) 76-62325. $42; cottages, $100.

▶ **La Fonda.** P.O. Box 268, San Ysidro, CA 92073. Tel: (800) 225-2786 or, in CA, NV, and AZ, Tel: (800) 522-1516. Oceanfront double, $50; apartment for four, $60.

▶ **Hotel Bahía.** Boulevard Costero y Alvarado, P.O. Box 21, **Ensenada**, Baja California Norte. Tel: (66) 78-2101. $40–$55.

▶ **Hotel Los Arcos.** P.O. Box 112, Paseo Alvaro Obregón 498, **La Paz**, Baja California Sur 23000. Tel: (682) 2-2744; Fax: (682) 5-4313; in the U.S. and Canada, Tel: (800) 347-2252 or (714) 827-3933. $75.

▶ **Hotel El Oasis.** P.O. Box 17, Boulevard López Mateos, **Loreto**, Baja California Sur 23880. Tel: (683) 3-0112; in the U.S. and Canada, Tel: (714) 534-8630. $103.

▶ **Hotel La Perla.** P.O. Box 640, Paseo Alvaro Obregón 1570, **La Paz**, Baja California Sur 23000. Tel: (682) 2-0777 or 0821; Fax: (682) 5-5363; in the U.S., Tel: (800) 252-0100. $110.

▶ **Hotel La Posada de Engelbert.** P.O. Box 152, Playa Sur and Calle Nueva Reforma, **La Paz**, Baja California Sur 23000; Tel: (682) 2-4011; Fax: (682) 2-0663. $65–$75.

▶ **Misión del Loreto.** P.O. Box 49, Boulevard López Mateos 47, **Loreto**, Baja California Sur 23880. Tel: (683) 3-0048; Fax: (683) 3-0648. $60.

▶ **Rosarito Beach Resort Hotel.** Boulevard Benito Juárez, km 27.5, **Rosarito**, Baja California Norte. Tel: (66) 12-1106. In the U.S., P.O. Box 145, San Ysidro, CA 92073; Tel: (800) 343-8582, (800) 225-2786, or (800) 522-1516. $36–$55.

▶ **Stouffer Presidente Loreto.** Boulevard Misión de Loreto s/n, **Loreto**, Baja California Sur 23880; Tel: (683) 3-0700; Fax: (683) 3-0377; in the U.S. and Canada, Tel: (800) HOTELS-1. $99–$137.

THE PACIFIC RESORTS

*By Robin Lloyd, Mitchell Nauffts,
Jackie Peterson, and Susan Wagner*

Robin Lloyd has lived in Mexico for 16 years and is a correspondent for The News, *Mexico City's English-language daily, and for* Vallarta Today. *He is also the editor of* VNN *(Vallarta and Nayarit News) and the author of five books. His articles and photographs have appeared in* Life, Time, *and* Newsweek. *Jackie Peterson has worked as a reporter for the features section of the* San Francisco Examiner *and as an editor for* The News, *Mexico City's English-language newspaper, and the* Sacramento Union. *Currently a resident of Mazatlán, she reports on Mexico's resort areas on a freelance basis. Mitchell Nauffts also writes the Yucatán Caribbean Resorts section of this book, Susan Wagner the Baja California Resorts section.*

Some of the world's most sophisticated resorts, not to mention some of its most scenic, are to be found on Mexico's Pacific coast. A combination of summerlike temperatures year-round, plenty of sunshine, broad sandy beaches, and lively nightlife has made these resorts, collectively, the country's major drawing card for international travellers. While those who want to combine a bit of archaeology with their sun, sea, and sand tend to congregate in the Caribbean resorts of the Yucatán peninsula, and sportsmen/sybarites who relish the comforts of home head for Los Cabos at the tip of the Baja peninsula, the international traveller looking for a mix of sun and fun, bustling activity, and peaceful surroundings is drawn to the exciting string of resorts that dot the Pacific coast from Mazatlán down to Huatulco. And though the personality of each of these resorts differs from those of its sisters, they all share one thing in common: Almost everything a visitor will want to see or do is located on or just off the coast road that runs through town.

We cover the Pacific resorts in geographical order, from Mazatlán in the north to Huatulco in the south. For driving down to one or more of these spots from the western United States, Highway 15 heads south from Nogales on the U.S. border and passes through Mazatlán on its way to Tepic, in the state of Nayarit. There, Highway 200 becomes the principal coastal route, linking the rest of the Pacific resorts all the way down to the Guatemalan border. (See the Getting Around section at the end of our coverage of Mazatlán for more information on driving down from the border.)

Mazatlán is the resort for those who put an emphasis on sports and would rather not worry about dressing up or doing anything too fancy. Besides being a commercial city in its own right, it's a hodgepodge of things to see and do, and although they're all here, you have to look to find them. If you want to arrange for a charter fishing boat or a windsurfing lesson, the place is the El Cid Mega Resort's sports center on the beach; if you want to lie on a beach with plenty of company, head for the sand in front of the Playa Mazatlán or the Costa de Oro; if you like beaches that are quieter, put on your bathing suit and mosey over to the Camino Real; and if you don't want to see *anybody,* just travel north along Avenida Sábalo Cerritos and pick your spot. Mazatlán makes no demands.

Puerto Vallarta, perhaps the quintessential Pacific resort, combines the outgoing friendliness of a genuine small town with first-rate amenities. It's a favorite with discriminating travellers from the West Coast, who enjoy strolling around town before having dinner at one of its many charming restaurants. The shopping (including resortwear by nationally known local designers) is terrific as well, and a sprawling new marina complex has added an extra touch of glamour to the town that Taylor and Burton first put on the map. **Nuevo Vallarta**, just north of Puerto Vallarta, is a developing resort area with a long way to go.

The beautiful, remote Hotel Costa Careyes in **Careyes,** a small bay south of Puerto Vallarta, is all but out of business, at least for the time being. After it fell victim to the recession, its Italian owners decided to sell the 3,700-acre property. The land development company that built Puerto Vallarta's new marina complex mentioned above is looking into buying the Careyes property, but the plans for its future are unknown. There is still a Club Med property at Careyes, however.

334 THE PACIFIC RESORTS

Tenacatita, a huge complex hidden away at the end of a winding road off the coastal highway to the south of Careyes, is another resort hotel on a small bay. It's a modern, comfortable place, ideal for those who wish to spend a few lazy days on a flat, sandy beach in the middle of nowhere.

Barra de Navidad, a few miles farther down the coast in the direction of Manzanillo, is a grown-up fishing village that has retained some of its charm despite the fact that, for the moment at any rate, it is stuck somewhere between what it once was and what it might yet become.

The kind of vacation you have in **Manzanillo**, due west of Mexico City, depends on your choice of hotel. Elegant Las Hadas (where much of the movie *10* was filmed) sits high on a hill like the regal dowager she is. Affluent travellers from around the world who want to unwind in a self-contained resort far from the madding crowd return here year after year. Other, less formal resorts line the road leading into town. Be forewarned, however: Nightlife and shopping are not the chief attractions of Manzanillo.

Ixtapa/Zihuatanejo, on the long stretch of coast between Manzanillo and Acapulco (but closer to the latter), is a laid-back version of Acapulco. With its "Hotel Row"—a string of soaring high-rise structures lining Palmar Bay—Ixtapa is a modern mega-resort. The old fishing village of Zihuatanejo, one bay to the south, attracts those who prefer a more casual atmosphere. In this friendly, charming little town (about four miles from Ixtapa over a paved road) you never have to wear anything more than cutoffs, a tee-shirt, and sandals—and that's the way the affluent crowd that vacations here likes it.

Acapulco was the trailblazer of Mexican resorts. Today it's one of the world's most famous playgrounds and one of Mexico's larger cities and largest ports. The Las Brisas residential section in particular is a haven for sophisticated pleasure-seekers, movie stars, statesmen, and just plain folks who like to relax by day and party by night in the sprawling private villas overlooking the bay. Elsewhere in town, the wide variety of ethnic restaurants and shopping malls is hard to beat, as is the glittering array of discos.

Puerto Escondido and **Puerto Angel**, east of Acapulco and south of Oaxaca City, are slated for further development. For the moment they are mostly visited by young budget-conscious travellers, an international surfing crowd, and retirees who arrive in their RVs and don't need mugs for their beer. Still, the fishing and surfing *are* great, and neon lights and TVs scarce.

Last but not least is **Huatulco**, with its nine glorious bays.

Amenities here include a sprawling Club Med, the deluxe Sheraton and Club Maeva resort hotels, a new Holiday Inn, and a growing number of stores and restaurants. Those expecting nonstop activity and nightlife at their doorstep are likely to be disappointed; it will take a few years for Huatulco to mature into a full-service resort. Those looking to get away from it all, on the other hand, may find Huatulco's combination of five-star hotels and unspoiled surroundings just what the doctor ordered.

MAZATLAN

Mazatlán, on the Pacific coast due east of Baja California Sur's Los Cabos area, has attractions few Mexican resorts can match. For one thing, it's closer to the United States than any other major Mexican resort (and closer to Texas than to Acapulco), allowing *norteamericanos* from the West and Southwest to fly down conveniently for long weekends. It was a working city and busy seaport long before tourists discovered its miles of sandy beaches. And it is also the only Mexican beach resort with an established language school, enabling those who want to learn Spanish or improve their skills to combine their studies with a seaside vacation.

A city that today numbers 500,000 residents, Mazatlán does not depend entirely on tourism for its well-being. Still one of Mexico's leading ports (the largest between San Diego and the west coast of Panama), it receives frequent visits from cargo-liners, cruise ships, and ferries, to say nothing of the comings and goings of its own home-based shrimp fleet, the country's biggest—as a glance at any restaurant menu in town will reveal. Fortuitously situated at the mouth of the Sea of Cortés, it is also considered the deep-sea fishing capital of the mainland (more than 6,000 billfish are boated here every year) and is home to one of the country's largest breweries, Pacífico. Finally, it's one of the few Mexican resorts on the national rail network.

In spite of their city's commercial importance, however, *mazatlecos* tend not to take life too seriously. The typical native, often bearing the features and coloring of 19th-century forebears from France, Spain, and Germany, calls himself a *pata salada* (salty foot). The local attitude is friendly and informal. Mazatlán is the kind of place where

Mazatlán

you can live in cutoffs and go to bed early and not miss much. The musicians who play the bouncy, German-inspired music of the *banda tambora,* a brass band that moves to the perky beat of the *tambora* (bass drum), may launch into a tune in a parking lot (or anywhere else that moves them, for that matter) and set people to dancing on the sand. In February it's also the scene of one of the best *carnavales* in the world. Pageants, street dancing, fireworks, and parades are all part of the merriment as Mazatlán turns topsy-turvy for a week. (But be sure to reserve well in advance if you plan to join in the fun.)

A visitor's typical daily schedule here revolves around sports and the great outdoors. Mazatlán was one of the first Mexican resorts to attract visitors in substantial numbers— and has been successful at keeping them coming back— because there *is* so much of everything for everybody, including space. (There are almost 30 miles of beaches in the area.) Among the many activities offered here, duck, pheasant, and dove shooting are especially good (there are two hunts a day from October to April), and it is also one of the few Mexican resorts to allow surfing. The early-morning wave action at Los Pinos, in front of the 19th-century Fuerte (Fort) Carranza, has caused local surfers to nickname it "The Cannon."

MAJOR INTEREST
Zona Dorada resort-hotel area
Deep-sea fishing
Hunting
Surfing

The less-than-eventful history of Mazatlán—which in Nahuatl means "Place of the Deer"—is in keeping with its easygoing personality. The town was founded by the conquistador Nuño Beltrán de Guzmán in 1531. In the decades that followed, the Spanish garrison in the area was stationed 15 miles away at Villa Unión, and Mazatlán itself was merely a sentinel post. In the 19th century the troops of Napoleon III were based not here but at Malpica, a few miles due east, and gold and silver were mined at towns farther inland such as Rosarío, Copala, and Pánuco. In fact, the first municipal government here wasn't established until 1837.

But it was an event out of the Keystone Kops that finally put Mazatlán in the history books. In 1914, during the Mexican Revolution, General Venustiano Carranza's forces set out to destroy the fort on top of Icebox Hill (Cerro de la Nevería) with a homemade bomb fashioned from dynamite, stones, and nails packed in pigskin. Instead, the pilot overflew the target and the airsick bombardier dropped his charge on a downtown street—thereby earning Mazatlán the dubious distinction of being the second city in the world to suffer aerial bombardment (Tripoli was the first).

It wasn't until the 1950s, when it was discovered by deep-sea sportsfishermen, that Mazatlán truly came into its own, however. Happily, the emphasis on the outdoor sporting life has prevailed ever since.

Around in Mazatlán

The city and resort of Mazatlán together cover much of a 15-mile-long peninsula. Most visitors to Mazatlán congregate along the coastal strip that stretches from the old lighthouse on the southern tip of the peninsula to the new condominiums on the beaches to the north. The center of the action is the strip of high-rises between Valentino's Discotheque at Punta Camarón and the posh, private Balboa Club to the north—the Zona Dorada, or "Golden Zone."

The stretch of seaside hotels extending north from the Zona Dorada to the Camino Real are also popular. Large-scale development along here is imminent. Within this decade the El Cid Mega Resort will expand into the Marina El Sábalo, with new dockside homes and apartments. In a couple of years the Camino Real, once splendidly isolated atop the rocks at Punta Sábalo, will overlook the entrance to a yacht harbor in the neighboring estuary, site of the planned nautical complex, Marina Mazatlán. The marina will include hotels, restaurants, villas, sports clubs, and a golf course along a broad avenue on the inland side of the estuary. This thoroughfare will eventually link up with the new resort complexes and condominiums lining Avenida Sábalo Cerritos north to Punta Cerritos and the new four-lane toll road from Culiacán.

This entire area is relatively spread out in comparison with most Mexican resorts. As a result, the beaches in front of the Zona Dorada have an uncrowded feeling about them. (Many hotels also have roped-off areas on the beach to keep itinerant vendors from interrupting your siesta.) And, as is true of most resorts in Mexico, everything you'll need is on or just off the beach road, which changes names five times: At its southernmost point it is called Avenida Olas Altas, then sucessively becomes Paseo Claussen, Avenida Del Mar, Avenida Camarón

Sábalo north of Punta Camarón, and finally Avenida Sábalo Cerritos north of the Camino Real.

At the far southern end of town sits the old lighthouse (second-tallest in the world after Gibraltar's), perched on a hill called Cerro del Crestón. To the east are berthed the fishing fleets.

El Centro, Mazatlán's downtown area (and a busy one by Mexican resort standards), is inland from Olas Altas and south of the Monumento a los Pescadores (Fisherman's Monument), the city's most famous landmark, which faces the Bahía Puerto Viejo on Avenida del Mar.

The curving strip of coastline that follows Avenida del Mar north from the old Carranza fort to Punta Camarón—the beginning of the Zona Dorada—was the resort-strip successor to Olas Altas. Now itself eclipsed by the Zona Dorada and points north, it still boasts a variety of restaurants, nightclubs, hotels, and motels.

We begin with the older parts of town.

Olas Altas

This is where, in the 1940s, it all began. Back then celebrities such as Ernest Hemingway and Katharine Hepburn would watch the sun set into the Pacific from their rooms at the Hotel Belmar while their fans back in the States wondered where they had disappeared to. The fishing fleets were moored on the south side of Cerro del Vigía (Lookout Hill), and nothing but empty beaches, beaches, and more beaches spread out to the north. The somewhat seedy Belmar and the plain but clean **Hotel La Siesta**, on the waterfront nearby, are today funky and old-fashioned—La Siesta is the more appealing of the two—and remain popular with sportsfishermen who want to be near the fleets (you'll also find an older crowd of budget travellers here as well as students from the United States and Europe). These are not what anyone nowadays thinks of as resort hotels, however. La Siesta has a pleasant courtyard restaurant and a big paneled bar where fishermen gather to drink Pacífico from the local brewery. The beach, which is a little rocky here and sometimes pounded by fairly big waves, is just across the road.

While Olas Altas long since has lost its edge to the hotel strip to the north, visitors who want to stroll through the historic neighborhood behind the waterfront may well end up seeking a cold drink at a sidewalk table along the avenue. Or they may join those who have come specifically to eat at the one-and-only **El Shrimp Bucket**, the flagship restaurant of the ever-popular Carlos 'n' Charlie's chain, located in the

Hotel La Siesta. Local businessmen, fishermen, and tourists alike flock to this place, especially at lunchtime, and the portions of fish, meat, and poultry are large—as are the drinks. No one comes here for a *quick* bite to eat: The Shrimp Bucket is all about animated conversation and hearty, drawn-out meals. (Dinner may be accompanied by live music, which can keep some hotel guests awake later than they would like.) For nonfishermen who want to watch the sunset and see the day's catch on display, it's also a great place to stop in for a drink before heading over the hill to the pier. (And you can pick up a fisherman's box lunch here every morning at 6:00 A.M.)

While you're in the neighborhood, drive or climb the steep stairways to the heights of **Icebox Hill** for panoramic views of the entire city. Originally a military observation point, the hill got its name in the days before electric refrigeration, when local fishermen would store their catch in ice-filled caves in its side.

Downtown

A daytime or early evening stroll around the downtown area, inland from Olas Altas, makes for an interesting counterpoint to the neon glitz of the Zona Dorada. The old part of town is undergoing a massive restoration, which, when completed, will make it pleasantly photogenic. Already many building façades sport new coats of paint and the general atmosphere has brightened considerably.

The jewel of the restoration is the 19th-century **Teatro Angela Peralta**, on Calle Carnaval a few steps from the historic Plazuela Machado (where outdoor art shows and band music frequently brighten the scene on Sunday afternoons). Originally called the Teatro Rúbio, the opera house was renamed for a famous Mexican diva who died of tropical fever during an appearance here in the 1880s. By turn it became a vaudeville, burlesque, and movie house, and ultimately fell into disuse 40 years ago when a hurricane blew off its roof.

Restoration of the Neoclassical theater began in 1987 and is virtually complete. Though now air-conditioned, it retains features designed for the tropical theatergoer of yesteryear. The entry portico (which houses a second-floor gallery for occasional art exhibitions) leads to an open-air lobby. Inside the horseshoe-shaped house itself several tiers of balconies are edged by ornate wrought-iron railings designed for cross-ventilation. In addition to occasional appearances by touring groups, the theater hosts a range of events from symphony and opera to rock and reggae during Sinaloa's statewide cultural festival each November.

Charming restaurants and shops have sprung up all over the neighborhood, joining the historic **Doney** at Calle Mariano Escobedo 610, where diners sample Mexican specialties in the roofed courtyard of a Spanish marquis' former home. **La Mesa de Capitán**, which serves regional dishes as well as seafood, and the **Café Pacífico**, a snack bar with a billiards table, have opened on opposite corners facing the plazuela.

The block-long **municipal market** at the corner of Avenida Juárez and Calle Melchor Ocampo sells predictable Mexican souvenirs that can be bought elsewhere in less time than it takes to bargain for them here. With its blue and yellow spires, the giant Moorish-style **cathedral** on the zócalo is cool and imposing but of relatively recent vintage.

The **Museo Regional de Mazatlán** is housed in an old building at Sixto Osuna 76, a block east of Avenida Olas Altas. Assembled from the private collections of three prominent citizens, the museum exhibits are devoted to the ancient history of Mazatlán and the states of Sinaloa and Nayarit. The front gallery sometimes is given over to temporary art exhibitions. Open 10:00 A.M. to 1:00 P.M. and 4:00 to 7:00 P.M. Tuesday through Sunday.

The **Centro de Idiomas** at Calle Belisário Dominguez 1908 (Tel: 69/82-2053) offers both group and private instruction in Spanish. Prospective students can show up any Saturday morning at 10:00 A.M. to take a proficiency test and then begin study the following Monday. In addition to Americans of all ages, the center attracts Europeans, especially the Swiss. Those who want intensive Spanish can arrange for homestays with Spanish-speaking families.

From El Fuerte Carranza to Punta Camarón

Avenida del Mar, the coastal strip along the Bahía Puerto Viejo, was the site of the first true resort action in Mazatlán. The palm-lined drive parallels Playa Norte, a three-mile crescent of sand that hugs the the bay. (Be forewarned: The mostly local crowd hangs out at the southern quarter of the beach for a reason. A dangerous undertow—*resaca*—kicks in opposite the Aguamarina Hotel and extends north to Valentino's. The unpopulated stretch of sand is fine for strollers, but swimmers should avoid it.) Tucked amid private homes and apartments along the strand, a few popular restaurants draw lunchtime crowds (beginning around 1:30, with dinner starting around 8:00), but it's after dark when this area comes alive with bars, discos, and the nightclubs in two older hotels—**La Guitarra** in the Hacienda and **Bar el Navegante** in the De Cima—attracting both locals and visitors.

El Marinero, a plain, family-style seafood place at Cinco de Mayo 530, near the Mexicana Airlines office, caters to those who like quality in their food but don't want to pay extra for ambience or decor. Popular with local residents for years, it shares its number one ranking as Mazatlán's favorite seafood restaurant with the even plainer **Mamuca's**, Simón Bolívar West 404; the latter is is so popular that its tables often spill onto the sidewalk.

Some of Mazatlán's best-known restaurants are located along the stretch of Avenida del Mar that runs from the Fisherman's Monument to Valentino's. **El Patio**, Avenida del Mar 30, near the Fisherman's Monument itself, is informal and lively, with a woody South Seas atmosphere (and sometimes too-loud music blaring from its speakers). The seafood, steaks, and chicken dishes are all good, as are the few Mexican dishes on the menu. Tel: (69) 82-1709.

Anyone who comes to Mazatlán soon hears about **Señor Frog's**, Avenida del Mar 255. The tongue-in-cheek mood is set by the life-size papier-mâché frog that greets guests as they enter the dining room. Cruise-ship passengers, some direct from the ship, arrive revved up and ready to party, and many stay right through lunch and into dinner. Consequently, you can forget about having a quiet conversation or sparking a little romance on most nights in season—and don't come at all unless you're prepared for rowdy fun and pranks. If you want to try the great ribs, chicken, or meat dishes without the hubbub, go for lunch. The tables just inside the door and in the seaside dining room next to the bar are the best for watching the action, but there's usually a line of eager revellers waiting to get in from 8:00 P.M. on. Tel: (69) 82-1925.

A young crowd also frequents the **Toro Bravo Bar** up the avenue. Outside the line is always long, but once you get in you can join the group at the bar or take a spin on the mechanical bull.

The **Acuario Mazatlán**, one block east of Avenida del Mar at Avenida de los Deportes 111, offers those who don't scuba dive a look at the marine life inhabiting the waters around Mazatlán. Natural history films are shown in the adjacent auditorium, and separate bird and sea lion shows are staged outdoors throughout the day. The small botanical garden and zoo outside are also worth the time it takes to stroll through them. Open 10:00 A.M. to 6:00 P.M. Tuesday through Sunday; closed Mondays.

Punta Camarón

The opulent Moorish-style complex at Punta Camarón looks like a movie set and houses two restaurants, a bar, a disco, and several other attractions. **Bora Bora**, a discotheque-bar on the beach level, fills two palapas lit by flashing colored lights. Next door is the new indoor eatery, **Bali Hai**. Both draw a college-age crowd.

Upstairs, the multilevel **Sheik** has a reputation as one of Mazatlán's most elegant restaurants. The posh decor, spectacular views of the ocean, and soft piano music make it the kind of place you'll probably want to dress for. The menu is Continental, and reservations are recommended. Tel: (69) 84-4478.

If you find yourself in a dancing mood after dinner, head next door to **Valentino's Discotheque**. Newly redesigned, with shimmering mirrors and video screens, this longtime favorite is once again Mazatlán's "hot" disco. There are separate areas for dancing to rock 'n' roll and touch dancing, a laser light show, and a game room where you can play pool or backgammon.

The sleek **Mikonos** piano bar, at the southern end of the complex, offers light snacks at tables inside or under the stars. The views of the coastline all the way to town are unforgettable, especially at night, and the piano music is the best in town, hands down.

The Zona Dorada

The "Golden Zone," an oval-shaped parcel of land bordered by Avenida Camarón Sábalo to the east and Avenida Rodolfo T. Loaiza to the west, encompasses the largest concentration of shops and restaurants in Mazatlán, and some of its prime resorts, all within steps of the town's most popular beach, **Gaviotas**.

Los Sábalos, a gleaming white stucco hotel just north of Valentino's, sits in an oasis of green grass and rustling palms overlooking a meandering swimming pool and, beyond it, the sea. Its splashy setting and features such as clay tennis courts and a health club with saunas and Jacuzzis tend to compensate for the plain decor of its 185 units. Suites have wet bars and small refrigerators. Palapa-shaded tables for patrons of **Las Gaviotas Bar** and the adjacent **Las Olas** restaurant share striking views of the sunset. The young people who gather at **Joe's Oyster Bar**, well removed from the rest of the hotel's structure, enjoy their sunset views to the amplified sounds of rock 'n' roll.

The sprawling, 432-room **Hotel Playa Mazatlán**, one of the oldest beachfront hotels in Mazatlán, is located just up the road on the same beautiful stretch of beach. With three restaurants, a large pool area, and several shops, the Playa Mazatlán is considered one of the nicer hotels in town, and its beach is certainly one of the busiest. The rooms here are decorated simply but comfortably, with tiled headboards and night tables. Not all have ocean views, however. The hotel's Mexican fiesta night is the best in town, and every Sunday at 8:00 P.M. its terrace bar and restaurant sparkle under a shower of fireworks.

Visitors who like the convenience of a kitchenette might consider one of the motels in the area. While the **Hotel Suites Las Flores**, about a block north of the Playa Mazatlán, may lack the lavish public facilities of its two neighbors, it does have cheerful deluxe suites with stove and refrigerator in the same price range. And then, at half the cost, there's the **Casa Contenta**. This small, truly special hideaway tucked between two larger motels at the north end of Rodolfo T. Loaiza has seven one-bedroom units and a large beachfront house suitable for eight guests, all delightfully decorated in Mexican colonial style.

Shopping should not be the main reason you come to Mazatlán. Most places feature quantity rather than quality, or cater to a crowd that likes to take home tee-shirts. The handful of shops and boutiques that offer a better selection of items are located for the most part in or near the Zona Dorada on Rodolfo T. Loaiza or Camarón Sábalo. (The siesta is observed by many of these shops between 2:00 and 4:00 P.M.)

Designer's Bazaar, at Rodolfo T. Loaiza 7, specializes in resortwear, both casual and dressy, as well as decorative items with a flair. **Casa Roberto**, in the Playa Mazatlán mall, offers tasteful reproductions of antique furniture and a good selection of decorative items.

Hidden behind colonial-style arches, **El Viejo Mazatlán**, Rodolfo T. Loaiza 303, has a spacious showroom filled with ceramic pieces from Tlaquepaque and Tonalá, two of the country's foremost artisans' centers.

Indio's Gifts, Rodolfo T. Loaiza 311 (as well as at three other locations around town), is known for its attractive brass, leather, copper, and silver decorative items and jewelry, all beautifully displayed.

As you head north from Indio's, the first shopping arcade

on the right has two shops of special note for gift buyers: **La Troje**, with small decorative objects, and **Fela the Flower Lady**, well back of the street, where you often find Fela Muñoz fashioning bright paper flowers while her husband, Ciro, sits outside at his workbench creating fanciful metal wall sculptures (schools of fish, flying birds).

On a side street at Avenida de las Garzas 8, **La Pata del Gato** specializes in one-of-a-kind items, many made of fabric, while **Si Como No**, nearby at number 1, sells original artwork and antiques.

Maya del Pacifico, in the pyramid-like building at Rodolfo T. Loaiza 411, has leather goods and decorative items. Next door, a folkloric show featuring the flying *voladores* of Papantla is staged every night except Sundays in season (and on Tuesdays, Thursdays, and Saturdays the rest of the year). Dinner is included in the price of the show, about $30 per person.

The **Mazatlán Arts and Crafts Center**, nearby at Rodolfo T. Loaiza 417, is a brick two-story colonial-style mall with some 20 shops. When you get tired of shopping, you can head over to the **No Name Café** in the mall's patio for a light meal or quick snack, accompanied by pop music and sports highlights from several TV monitors. Evenings, the culinary specialties include barbecued chicken and ribs. For a quieter luncheon respite head across the road to **Pancho's**, at the beach end of Las Cabañas shopping arcade, where you can munch a hamburger while perusing the wares of vendors parading by on the sand below.

For a more substantial meal try **The Shrimp Factory**, on the corner of Rodolfo T. Loaiza and de las Garzas, where the assembly-line techniques perfected by Henry Ford are applied to the consumption of that delicious crustacean. Customers choose the size of shrimp and number of kilos they want, and then sit back and enjoy as their order arrives post haste with a choice of three sauces.

The ubiquitous **Aca Joe** is located at the corner of Avenida Camarón Sábalo and Gaviotas, across the street from the kiosk that sells English-language newspapers at inflated prices.

From the Balboa Club North to the Camino Real

The private Balboa Club, with lovely screened rooms overlooking the beach at the northern end of the Zona Dorada, luxuriates in quiet, walled seclusion from its more boisterous neighbors. Exchange privileges from a club at home or a letter from a member will get you a room or allow you entrance for a meal. Either arrangement must be reserved in advance.

Casa Loma, located six blocks east of the Balboa Club at Avenida Gaviotas 104, is a few minutes' ride from the Zona Dorada. With its elegant red-velvet-and-wood-paneled interior and its garden patio, this small restaurant is an anachronism, both in appearance and personality. The popularity of its Italian specialties has been proved over a dozen years, and people are still coming back. In fact, the place is so popular that the owners can afford to close it from June to October. Casa Loma is for those who like to dine early, however; closing time is 10:00 P.M. Tel: (69) 13-5398.

The **Costa de Oro**, a large, modern hotel with two swimming pools, two restaurants, a bar, and tennis courts, sits on the same pretty stretch of beach as the Balboa Club. Rooms are small but cozy, and some have balconies overlooking a garden. Only a few have ocean views, but the views from the public areas, especially the restaurant, go a long way toward making up for that lack. **La Carreta**, one of the best shops in town for decorative items, is part of the complex, as is **Tequila Sunrise**, across the beach road.

El Cid Mega Resort, about a quarter-mile north of the Balboa Club, is one of Mexico's largest and most complete resorts. Sprawling along both sides of Avenida Camarón Sábalo, it has everything from private homes and condos to a wide range of hotel accommodations (there are more than 850 rooms and 220 suites scattered among its main hotel building and two towers). Most rooms have balconies and ocean views, but those overlooking the main pool also afford glimpses of the sea in the distance. Looking for a bite to eat? El Cid has 14 restaurants and two bars, as well as a discotheque, convention center, an 18-hole championship golf course, and Mazatlán's finest water-sports and racquet facilities (17 tennis courts; the only squash and racquetball courts in the city).

The **Caracol Tango Palace** here is a sleek, state-of-the-art nightspot for those who like to dance and stay up late. Built in a circular shape that gives the place its name (*caracol* means "snail"), this multi-million-dollar extravaganza looks like a set for "Miami Vice." The clientele is mostly young and well-to-do, but anyone is welcome as long as they dress the part, which means no shorts or cutoffs.

Los Arcos, across the beach road from the northern end of El Cid, is popular with both visitors and locals. Mouthwatering marlin tacos, a great shrimp *ceviche,* and a decor featuring antiques from the colonial-era town of Concordia keep packing them in under the big palapa here.

The 71-suite **Luna Palace**, up the beach road a bit, is less than two years old and offers the usual amenities: refrigerators, microwave ovens, and built-in hair dryers. Each unit has a beach view.

The beautiful terra-cotta–colored **Pueblo Bonito**, a timeshare hotel next door to the Camino Real, is one of the prettiest places to stay in Mazatlán. Its spacious rooms are tastefully decorated, and all have ocean or garden views, large patios or balconies, color TV, and fully equipped kitchenettes.

The deluxe **Camino Real** stands apart from the other hotels in Mazatlán on its own promontory, Punta Sábalo, overlooking the ocean at the northern end of the main resort area. The few extra minutes it takes to get downtown are compensated for by its many special features: You can wake up to birdsong and fall asleep to the sound of waves; it has its own tiny beach where swimming conditions are almost always perfect; and the atmosphere is pleasantly relaxing, thanks to the absence of itinerant vendors and gaggles of people watching the parasailers. Though the rooms are just average, clean and standard size, the public areas in the Camino Real are outstanding, and the attractive lobby bar is an especially good spot for watching sunsets.

It is unusual for a relatively small hotel like the Camino Real to have not one but two restaurants that rate so highly with the locals. The more formal of the two, **Las Terrazas**, is a candlelit dining room offering Mexican and international specialties. **Chiquita Banana**, under a palapa just a few steps up from the beach, is a lively place to lunch and an informal yet romantic place to dine and dance to the sound of waves and live music at night.

Few restaurants in town are as romantic as **Señor Pepper**, across the beach road from the Camino Real. The candlelight and lace, polished wood and brass, and soft jazz music make it perfect for intimate conversation. The house specialties are juicy steaks grilled to perfection and lobster or jumbo shrimp. Reservations recommended. Tel: (69) 14-0101.

Sports in Mazatlán

Mazatlán is made for sports enthusiasts. Almost every hotel has a water-sports center, and most will be happy to make arrangements for you. If yours doesn't, or won't, go to El Cid; theirs is right on the beach.

Mazatlán is the deep-sea fishing capital of the mainland,

and the odds of catching something big here are stacked in the fisherman's favor. Striped marlin season runs from December through April; black marlin, May through June; sailfish, May through November. Tuna, dorado, bonita, yellowtail, and sea bass can be caught year-round. Boat rentals are available at most hotels or at the fleet headquarters just past Olas Altas. One of the best charter outfits here is **Flota Faro** (Tel: 69/82-4977). Prices range from $150 to $225, depending on the size of the boat.

Scuba-diving and snorkeling excursions also can be arranged at your hotel. **Deer** (Los Venados) **Island**, just off the beach between the Playa Mazatlán and El Cid complexes, is one of the best places in the area for both activities. The island is about a 20-minute ride by water taxi (the "Super Pato" leaves from the water-sports center at El Cid every other hour between the hours of 10:00 A.M. and 2:00 P.M.), and equipment can be rented there as well.

Parasail rides are available on the beach in front of the Hotel Playa Mazatlán.

Tennis players congregate at the Camino Real, Los Sábalos, and El Cid hotels (although the excellent facilities at El Cid are reserved for hotel guests and members only).

There are two golf courses in Mazatlán. The private **Casa Club** at El Cid features an 18-hole championship course that winds through the main hotel zone. The **Campestre Club**, a 20-minute drive via Highway 15 in the direction of the airport, is a nine-hole course open to the public. Greens fees are $18 for a double circuit (18 holes).

Hunting for duck, dove, and quail is another popular sport in the Mazatlán area. The bag limit is 20 birds per day, and there are two hunts (at $139 per hunt) a day from October to April. It costs an extra $40 for nonshooters. Contact the Aviles Brothers, Tel: (69) 81-3728.

Charreadas, Mexican rodeos, are staged at Lienzo Charro near the railroad station; watch for announcements around town. There is also a small bull ring in Mazatlán; the season runs from December 15 through April. Aficionados will want to ask when the better matadors are likely to appear, rather than taking a chance on less skilled apprentices.

Excursions from Mazatlán

Anyone who likes getting out of a resort and into the countryside for a change of pace can choose from a number of destinations around Mazatlán.

The six-hour "country tour" offered by most hotels includes two of the most picturesque villages in the area.

Concordia, only an hour to the east, is centuries away in feeling. The town, more than 400 years old, is today a crafts center where leather goods, wooden furniture, pottery, and tiles are made; most tours will allow you to watch many of the artisans at work.

Copala, in the mountains northeast of Concordia on Highway 40, is an old mining town with cobblestone streets and a history that dates back to 1571. The main reason to visit, besides the scenery, is a restaurant called **Daniel's.** More than two decades ago Dan Garrison accompanied his mother when she returned to her hometown to claim a family inheritance. They fell in love with the sleepy village and decided to stay. Mama Chavala, an excellent cook, put her skills to work and soon she and Dan had established a restaurant that eventually expanded to serve legions of diners. Although Mama Chavala is no longer alive, the Mexican-style food remains decent and reasonably priced; the pièce de résistance is the coconut-and-banana-cream pie, still made from mama's original recipe. To work off their meal diners usually stroll up the lane to the village square for a look out over the steep hillsides, many dotted with restored haciendas now housing artists and fugitives from Mazatlán's sultry summers. Daniel's also has a few rooms for customers unwilling to tackle the mountain road after dark.

Expect to pay roughly $45 per person for a packaged excursion to both Concordia and Copala which will include lunch. The same tour by taxi costs twice that, plus the price of lunch for yourself and the driver.

Rosarío, southeast of Mazatlán on Highway 15, is a large, modern town with a historic district that has been kept more or less intact. Founded in 1655, it's another of the mining towns where Mexico's wealth from silver and gold was and is visible. (The splendid altar in its cathedral is made of gold.) Stops along the way include the thermal springs at Aguacaliente and Villa Presidio, the latter the first settlement in the area. Expect to pay about $25 per person for this morning excursion.

Touring the **Laguna de Teacapán,** farther south of Mazatlán, is an unforgettable experience. This long, narrow body of water stretches along the coast for nearly 60 miles, and has been likened to the Amazon because of the vegetation that grows along its banks. The tour includes stops at the thermal springs of Aguacaliente and the old mining town of Rosarío, with a break for lunch on a primitive, palm-lined beach. Allow eight hours for the tour; the cost is approximately $45 per person.

Tours can be arranged in Mazatlán through **Marlin Tours**

(Tel: 69/14-2690), although **Alitur** (Tel: 69/83-7777) is the only outfit that goes to Daniel's in Copala. Most hotels in Mazatlán will also be able to arrange excursions for you. (Check with your travel agent if you have your heart set on one, however, as some tours are only offered in season.)

The 40-foot sailboat *Cosas Buenas* departs at 10:00 A.M. daily from the sportsfishing docks for a four-hour trip around the three islands (Venados, or Deer; Pájaros, Bird; and Chivos, Goat) off the coast before landing at Isla de los Venados for sunning, swimming, and lunch. This trip costs approximately $35 per person. A five-hour excursion by boat or catamaran to Isla de la Piedra (Stone Island), across from the Port of Mazatlán, is offered by several outfits through hotel tour desks. It runs about $30 per person and includes a broiled seafood lunch at a beach restaurant. For one-third the cost you can take a launch ($1 round trip) from the foot of Avenida Gutierrez Nájera, walk or ride (for about 70¢) from the landing dock to the ocean side of the island, stroll along the beach looking for shells and sand dollars, then pick a lunch spot from the string of beachfront restaurants (from $4 to $7, depending on what's cooking and what you order). Horseback riding is available at about $10 an hour.

Finally, you can take a cruise of the bay on the motor yacht *Fiesta*. Cruises leave daily at 11:00 A.M. from the pier near the lighthouse, and tickets can be purchased from any hotel travel agent as well as at the company's office at José María Canizales 5. The cost is approximately $10.

—*Jackie Peterson and Susan Wagner*

GETTING AROUND

Driving Down from the Border

The recommended entrance to western Mexico and the Pacific resorts is Nogales, Arizona–Nogales, Sonora. Travellers coming from Southern California will have a better trip if they stay on the U.S. side of the border until they reach Nogales. Mexican Highway 2, which begins in Tijuana and hugs the border for most of its distance, is a dubious choice because of its generally inferior condition and a shortage of services.

One popular itinerary calls for a short day from Nogales to Guaymas and a second, longer day to Mazatlán, allowing motorists to spend the night in attractive coastal locations. However, many travellers choose to bypass Guaymas the first day in order to avoid a long drive to Mazatlán on the second. This option saves more than an hour by avoiding the traffic and congestion of Guaymas. Either way, more than half the trip will be tedious driving through a seemingly endless landscape of brush and cactus, the scattered towns along the way raw in their newness and jerry-built to shelter a mushrooming population. Still, this route, Highway 15, has its charming moments, and toward the end of the journey it even has its charming hours. Travellers in a hurry to reach Mazatlán should carry picnic food, thus avoiding slow-service lunch stops.

The stretch from the border to **Hermosillo**, the modern capital of the state of Sonora and a pleasant place to take a break, takes a little less than four hours, much of it through semi-arid, sparsely populated countryside (but with adequate services for motorists). In Hermosillo itself, a good, if not very fast, lunch stop is the **Restaurant Villa Fiesta**, which specializes in regional dishes from northwestern Mexico. To find it, look for Calle Yañez near the *glorieta* (traffic circle) at the northern outskirts of town. Turn right onto Yañez and go half a block. For those in a hurry, Highway 15 is dotted with U.S.-style fast-food restaurants, most of them clean and quick if not especially appealing.

Travellers looking for lodging in Hermosillo will find the **Holiday Inn**, conveniently located on Highway 15 (Boulevard Kino 369) at the northern outskirts of town, to be the city's best hotel. Much less expensive is the plain but adequate **Motel El Encanto**, a few hundred yards south of the Holiday Inn at Kino 900.

After passing through more unchanging countryside south of Hermosillo, Highway 15 reaches the Pacific at the old fishing port of **Guaymas** (135 km/84 miles), now a low-key beach resort that's especially popular with sportsfishermen.

About 6 km (4 miles) north of Guaymas you'll come to a Y in the road, with the left (southeast) route marked "Ciudad Obregón." This is the Guaymas bypass. Except for a short stretch between Navojoa and Los Mochis, this route is a four-lane highway all the way to Culiacán. Whether or not you take the bypass, veterans of the trip recommend the toll (*cuota*) roads as the best choices, even though they are somewhat expensive.

For those not taking the bypass, the Guaymas highway continues inland through the old town; those who want a view of the sea or to spend the night must turn right on any of the side roads marked "Playas" or "Bahía San Carlos."

The **Hotel Playa de Cortés**, on lovely Bocochibampo Bay, is the traditional choice here, its reasonable rates reflecting the fact that, as a beach resort, Guaymas lacks the glamour of its cousins to the south.

Travellers looking for nothing more than a place to lay their heads at an economical price will find the **Motel Armida**, at the north entrance to the city, satisfactory. A notch down in both price and quality is the basic **Del Puerto**, at the corner of Yañez and Calle 19 in downtown Guaymas. It's simple and clean, with air-conditioning and a restaurant that specializes in seafood.

Those who arrive in Guaymas a few hours before the sun sets may wish to continue on to **Ciudad Obregón**, 125 km (78 miles) to the south. The land along this stretch is by nature desert, but irrigation has worked miracles in certain areas. Ciudad Obregón itself was founded in 1928 as the commercial and transportation center of this reclaimed agricultural region. Tortilla flat and rigidly geometrical in its layout, the city is a testament to bureaucratic lack of imagination. It does have a decent hotel, however. The plain and quiet **Nainari Valle**, on the highway at the corner of Alemán and Tetabiate, has, in addition to its modest rooms, a pleasant coffee shop and dining room.

Navojoa, older than Ciudad Obregón but of no more interest, is 68 km (42 miles) south over a stretch of road that is frequently choked with farm traffic. The best roadside inn in the area is the clean and air-conditioned **Nuevo Motel del Río**, located on the northern outskirts of town right off the highway.

From Navojoa, an interesting side trip, or even an overnight stop, is **Alamos**, the most picturesque town in this region. It's a 45-minute drive (55 km/34 miles) over a reasonably good road. Dating back to the earliest Spanish exploration of northwest Mexico, Alamos came into its heyday in the 18th century when gold and silver were discovered nearby. Its colonial buildings, many of them restored, are now protected by government decree. Alamos has also attracted a small foreign colony and become something of a vacation center. Its main export is the Mexican jumping beans harvested in the area.

Casa de los Tesoros, an unusually appealing inn, occupies a former convent one and a half blocks from the main plaza. This charming hotel has fireplaces in every room and a friendly, festive atmosphere. On the main square, the **Hotel Mansión de la Condesa Magdalena** is another inviting colonial inn.

Alamos's antique buildings and two romantic hotels supply the feeling of Mexico that most travellers hope for. The town is situated in Yaqui Indian country, and the natives, distinguished by their rugged profiles and jet-black hair, preserve much of their traditional way of life.

As you continue south on Highway 15 from Navojoa, it's about a two-hour trip to **Los Mochis**, 163 km (101 miles) distant. (For information about Los Mochis see the Copper Canyon chapter.) The best and fastest sections of the west coast highway connect Los Mochis with Culiacán, capital of the state of Sinaloa. After following Highway 15 south 85 km (53 miles) from Los Mochis to Guamúchil, you then have to make a choice.

Sinaloa 1, a toll road, is a superhighway running about 100 km (62 miles) to the outskirts of Culiacán, where signs at a junction direct you back to Highway 15. But as recently as 1988 the crime rate on the toll road was alarming; even daylight banditry was reported. This situation seems to have been remedied by strong police action. But if you are in doubt or have heard of recent incidents, follow the older, heavily travelled Highway 15 from Guamúchil to Culiacán.

There is little to entice visitors into stopping in **Culiacán**, except perhaps for lunch at the **Motel Los 3 Ríos**, a very pleasant establishment just off the highway north of the bridge as you approach the city. The motel is on the left (east) side of the highway. It will also do as a comfortable overnight stop.

Mazatlán lies 222 km (138 miles) farther south on Highway 15, about a three-hour drive through scrubland. A new highway, scheduled to open in 1993, may shorten the driving time by as much as an hour.

—*Robert Somerlott*

By Air

Service to Mazatlán is offered by Aeroméxico from Los Angeles and Tucson; by Alaska Airlines from Seattle, San Francisco, and Los Angeles; by Aero California from San Diego and Phoenix; by Delta through its Los Angeles hub; and by Mexicana from San Francisco, Los Angeles, and Denver. Schedules vary according to season, with the greatest number of flights departing from December through April. Air charters, especially from November through April, connect Mazatlán with Minneapolis, Houston, Oakland, and several cities on the U.S. east coast. For up-to-date information, consult a travel agent.

The Rafael Buelna Airport—where you'll find a number of car-rental agencies (Hertz, National, and Budget among them)—is about a half-hour's ride from the hotel zone. Aside from renting a car or going by taxi, *colectivos* are the only other option. If that's the way you decide to go, bite the bullet and be patient as yours drops off other passengers along the way.

By Train

Mazatlán is one of the few Mexican resorts you can reach by rail. Trains leave daily from Nogales and Mexicali on the U.S. border, with connections to Guadalajara and Mexico City. The *Tren Estrella* (Star Train) leaves Mexicali at 8:00 A.M. and arrives in Mazatlán at 8:00 the next morning. There's a brief layover north of Hermosillo as you wait for the train from Nogales (which leaves Nogales at 2:00 P.M.); then the two trains combined continue on their way to Mazatlán and, at the end of the line, Guadalajara. There is no dining car or sleeping accommodations; food is brought to passengers in their seats. The one-way fare to Mazatlán, including food, costs $40 from Nogales, $50 from Mexicali. For more information, contact Ferrocarriles del Pacifico, 10 Avenida Carrera Internacional, Nogales, Sonora, Mexico; Tel: (631) 2-0024.

By Bus

Tres Estrellas de Oro offers express air-conditioned bus service to Mazatlán from either Mexicali or Tijuana. The trip takes approximately 24 hours, and the one-way first-class fare is less than $50. From Nogales (on the Mexico side) the same service takes 16 hours and costs $35.

By Ferry

Ferry service linking Mazatlán with La Paz, capital of the state of Baja California Sur, 235 miles to the west, departs at 3:00 P.M. daily except Saturday from both cities. The service is operated by the SEMATUR group, whose offices in Mazatlán are located at the foot of Avenida Carnaval Sur; Tel: (69) 81-7020. (Tickets can also be purchased there.)

There are four categories of accommodations on most boats: *salon* (reclining seat); *turista* (bunk beds, four to a cabin); *cabina* (one bunk with bath); and *suite* (sleeping area, closet, and bath). The cost of the 18-hour trip ranges from about $20 to $60, depending on your choice of accommodations (a cabin for two runs about $105), and reservations are advisable. Tack on an additional $125 if you decide to take your car (more for larger vehicles).

In Town

Once you're in Mazatlán, getting around is a breeze. With the exception of the Zona Dorada, most hotels in a given part of town are within walking distance of each other. Taxi rates are slightly higher here than in other resorts in Mexico, however, and there are no meters (rates are set by zone), so check the rate before you get in. (Most hotels will post the going rates on a placard outside the lobby.) If your destination is not a well-known landmark, call before you go and get the name of the nearest one.

Another option is to hop aboard a *pulmonía*—or "pneumonias" as the locals call them—jaunty little golf cart–like contraptions. These charge about one-third to one-half less than taxis, but be sure to check the rate before boarding (again, there are no meters) and allow more time if you decide to go this route.

It's also easy to get around town by bus. Stops, a block or two apart, are often sheltered to protect waiting passengers from heavy summer rains. The sign on the front of the bus, whether white and yellow (first class) or blue (second class), indicates its destination. "Centro" or "Basílica" buses run through the Zona Dorada and end up downtown; those marked "Sábalo Cerritos" head back to the hotel zone. The fare is 800 pesos (26¢) one-way for the first-class bus, 600 pesos (20¢) for second-class. On both, just pull the cord for your stop.

Mazatlán is on mountain standard time (the same as Denver and Calgary), which is one hour earlier than Mexico City.

ACCOMMODATIONS REFERENCE

The rates given below are projections *for December 1992 through Easter 1993. Unless otherwise indicated, rates are for double rooms, double occupancy; the 10 percent VAT has been added. As rates are subject to change, it's a good idea to double-check before booking.*

▶ **Camino Real.** P.O. Box 538, Punta del Sábalo, **Mazatlán**, Sinaloa 82100. Tel: (69) 13-1111; Fax: (69) 14-0311; in the U.S. and Canada, Tel: (800) 228-3000. $120–$175.

▶ **Casa Contenta.** Avenida Rodolfo T. Loaiza s/n, **Mazatlán**, Sinaloa 82110. Tel: (69) 13-4976. $50–$150.

▶ **Casa de los Tesoros.** P.O. Box 12, **Alamos**, Sonora 85760. Tel: (642) 8-0010; Fax: (642) 8-0400. $61.

▶ **El Cid Mega Resort.** P.O. Box 813, Avenida Camarón Sábalo s/n, **Mazatlán**, Sinaloa 82100. Tel: (69) 13-3333; Fax: (69) 14-1311; in the U.S., Tel: (800) 525-1925; in Canada, Tel: (800) 344-0293. $95–$195.

▶ **Costa de Oro.** P.O. Box 130, Avenida Camarón Sábalo s/n, **Mazatlán**, Sinaloa 82110. Tel: (69) 13-5888; Fax: (69) 14-4209. From $60.

▶ **Holiday Inn Hermosillo.** Boulevard Kino 369, **Hermosillo**, Sonora 83010. Tel: (62) 15-1112; Fax: (62) 15-5721; in the U.S. and Canada, Tel: (800) HOLIDAY. $121.

► **Hotel Mansión de la Condesa Magdalena.** Obregón 2, **Alamos**, Sonora 85760. Tel: (642) 8-0221. $52.

► **Hotel Playa de Cortés.** P.O. Box 66, **Guaymas**, Sonora 85450. Tel and Fax: (622) 2-0135. $59.

► **Hotel Playa Mazatlán.** P.O. Box 207, Rodolfo T. Loaiza 202, **Mazatlán**, Sinaloa 82100. Tel: (69) 13-4455 or 4444; Fax: (69) 14-0366; in the U.S., Tel: (800) 222-4466; in Canada, Tel: (800) 247-5292. $75–$85.

► **Hotel La Siesta.** Olas Altas 11, **Mazatlán**, Sinaloa 82000. Tel: (69) 81-2640. $45.

► **Hotel Suites Las Flores.** Avenida Rodolfo T. Loaiza 212, P.O. Box 583, **Mazatlán**, Sinaloa 82110. Tel: (69) 13-5100; in the U.S., Tel: (800) 452-0627; in Canada, Tel: (604) 683-3238. $90.

► **Luna Palace.** P.O. Box 411, Avenida Camarón Sábalo, Privada del Camarón, **Mazatlán**, Sinaloa 82100. Tel: (69) 14-6006; Fax: (69) 14-9666; in the U.S. and Canada, Tel: (800) 352-7690. $90–$165.

► **Motel Armida.** Avenida Serdán s/n, **Guaymas**, Sonora 85450. Tel: (622) 2-3050. $42.

► **Motel El Encanto.** Boulevard Kino 900, **Hermosillo**, Sonora 83010. Tel: (62) 14-4730. $46.

► **Motel Los 3 Ríos.** P.O. Box 311, **Culiacán**, Sinaloa 80000. Tel: (67) 15-4040. $66.

► **Nainari Valle.** Miguel Alemán and Tetabiate, **Ciudad Obregón**, Sonora 85000. Tel: (641) 4-0940; Fax: (641) 3-4194. $46.

► **Nuevo Motel del Río.** Carretera 15 s/n, **Navojoa**, Sonora 85800. Tel and Fax: (642) 2-0331. $73.

► **Pueblo Bonito.** P.O. Box 6, Avenida Camarón Sábalo 2121, **Mazatlán**, Sinaloa 82100. Tel: (69) 14-3700; Fax: (69) 14-1723; in the U.S., Tel: (800) 262-4500; in Canada, Tel: (800) 654-5543. $120–$145.

► **Del Puerto.** Calles Yañez and 19, **Guaymas**, Sonora 85450. Tel and Fax: (622) 2-3408. $25.

► **Los Sábalos.** P.O. Box 944, Rodolfo T. Loaiza 100, **Mazatlán**, Sinaloa 82110. Tel: (69) 83-5333; Fax: (69) 83-8156. $95–$150.

NUEVO VALLARTA

Nuevo Vallarta, in the state of Nayarit 15 minutes north of Puerto Vallarta's international airport, started as an ambitious nautical-residential property about 15 years ago. The plan called for expensive hotels and condominiums built along artificial canals. A slow starter, Nuevo Vallarta accelerated a couple of years ago and is now the location of a newly developed tourist center emphasizing the preservation of the local ecology, overseen by the Jacques Cousteau Society. No buildings are permitted to be built any higher than the surrounding palm trees. The only major hotel in the area as of yet is the Jack Tar Village, an all-inclusive chain operation. A Radisson hotel will open by the end of 1992 and a Four Seasons Hotel and Resort is planned for the near future.

PUERTO VALLARTA

Puerto Vallarta, on the Pacific coast due west of Guadalajara, looks like a movie set: Sprawling white stucco houses crowned with red-tiled roofs and bougainvillaea spilling over their walls are stacked on a hillside overlooking the ocean. The tiny, compact town, complete with a bandstand and seaside promenade, nestles at the hill's base. There's almost always a perfect Pacific sunset over Mexico's largest bay, the Bahía de Banderas (Bay of Flags), with palm trees silhouetted against an orange-pink sky.

Puerto Vallarta, or "P.V.," has been the darling of the California crowd ever since Elizabeth Taylor and Richard Burton made headlines here in the early 1960s when he was filming *The Night of the Iguana*. Visitors love the easygoing way of life, which rarely requires getting dressed up, and though there are plenty of sophisticated facilities in and around town, Puerto Vallarta remains less citified than some of her sisters on Mexico's Pacific coast.

Like most Mexican resorts, P.V.'s coastal road threads its way into, through, and out of town past dramatically scenic cliffs, beaches, and rock formations. And because Guadalajara is

only 385 km (239 miles) to the east, *tapatíos* (as Guadalajarans call themselves) love Vallarta, with many of the wealthy among them maintaining homes here. As a result of this influx, much of the land south of town and north to the Nayarit border is becoming over-developed.

MAJOR INTEREST

Small old town with cobblestone streets
Bahía de Banderas sunsets
Boat trips to isolated beaches

Unlike many of the resorts on the Pacific coast, Puerto Vallarta did not start out as a fishing village in the 1500s. Founded in 1851, P.V. is, in fact, a relative youngster by Mexican standards. It remained unknown to the outside world until the 1950s, when Mexicana Airlines began to offer regularly scheduled flights into town. In the 1960s, after Highway 200 was opened, linking it to the rest of the country, Puerto Vallarta became even better known.

The influx of visitors from the States and Canada began in earnest after Taylor and Burton catapulted Puerto Vallarta into the international spotlight. By the end of the decade, one area overlooking the Río Cuale—which divides the town into northern and southern halves—was even nicknamed "Gringo Gulch," in recognition of the many vacation homes that had been built by foreigners there. Today clusters of condos and time-share units are going up on both sides of the river and, as a result, vacationers and sometime residents are more widely dispersed than they were in the old days.

This development has not been without its drawbacks, the most obvious being the swarms of OPCs (Outside Personal Contacts) that buzz around visitors whenever they go into town. True, you'll be offered a variety of free gifts, free meals, and heavily discounted tours. But there's a price to pay: You'll be asked to attend a "presentation" at the particular time-share property, where a salesperson will extol the virtues of the property—and take a couple of hours of your valuable vacation time to do it. If you have an interest in the time-share concept, it might be worthwhile; otherwise, a simple "No, thank you" will get you off the hook.

Getting around Puerto Vallarta couldn't be easier. Everything is built around the Bahía de Banderas, which extends from Punta de Mita in Nayarit to Cabo Corrientes in the south. The greatest concentration of hotels and two marinas are found north of the Río Cuale, in the direction of the airport.

The major shops and restaurants as well as a few small hotels are located downtown. (You can walk safely anywhere in town, but rubber-soled shoes are a must. Hard, leather soles slip on the cobblestone streets and smooth sidewalks.) Just beyond Playa de los Muertos, the town beach south of the river, the coastal road begins to climb. Two major hotels—the Camino Real and the Hyatt Coral Grand—as well as numerous condominiums line the road all the way to Playa Mismaloya and beyond. At Mismaloya you'll find the hotel La Jolla de Mismaloya on the beach. Unique jungle restaurants are situated off the road and up the hill to the east of Mismaloya, where *The Night of the Iguana* was filmed.

North of Downtown

The approach to town from the airport passes through the busiest area in Puerto Vallarta. Most of the major hotels and shopping malls and many of the area's huge developments are spread out along this stretch of Highway 200, which here is called the Carretera Aeropuerto. New places to stay, shop, and dine continue to spring up all along the highway.

The first sight in this new, modern Vallarta to draw your attention is Plaza Marina, a huge air-conditioned shopping mall featuring such ubiquitous names as Denny's, Woolworth's, Price Club, and McDonald's. South of Plaza Marina the 442-acre complex called **Marina Vallarta** is on its way to becoming a city within a city, with luxurious private homes, condos, and a scattering of time-share properties. Marina Vallarta boasts one of the finest marinas on the Pacific coast, with many of its 400 slips frequently occupied by visiting mega-yachts. An adjacent property, also being developed, will include moorings for another 600 vessels.

Four major hotels have taken advantage of the access to a par-72 championship golf course, beach clubs, tennis clubs, and spas. Of the four, only the three-story **Villas Quinta Real** is not situated on the beach, but its many repeat visitors don't seem to mind (the hotel flanks the golf course instead). The air-conditioned rooms at the Quinta Real, known to its admirers as the "Pink Hacienda," feature tile floors, hand-painted furniture, and original art, including masks by Sergio Bustamante, and its reasonably priced terrace restaurant offers one of the best menus in town.

The other three establishments, the **Hotel Conrad** (bearing the corporate name for all Hiltons in foreign countries), the **Meliá Vallarta**, and the **Marriott CasaMagna** have much in common. Each has a huge swimming pool, beautifully ed event of the evening—bullfighting, costs about $30. [You] needn't worry about the bulls: There is no blood and no [kil]ling.

Bogart's, a rather formal restaurant in the Krystal, is filled with fountains, shimmering mirrors, peacock chairs, and plants. The Continental cuisine is complemented by a number of Moroccan specialties, and soft piano music contributes to the romantic atmosphere. Make sure you bring a bundle of money, however; Bogart's is the most expensive restaurant in town. Reservations recommended; Tel: (322) 2-1459.

The Krystal has two other restaurants: **Tango** features Argentine steaks and decor, while **Kamakura** is strictly Japanese, complete with the dexterous *teppanyaki* chefs popularized by the Benihana chain. Both are open from 6:00 P.M. Tel: (322) 2-1459.

Christine, P.V.'s favorite disco, is also part of the Krystal complex. Though the discos in Vallarta are smaller and less flashy, with fewer videos and gimmicks, than those in other resorts, they're no less fun. Christine is still number one, in part because its competitors have gone out of business, but also because its laser lights, great sound system, and a variety of other features surpass those of her sisters in Ixtapa and Cancún. Christine's laser artists and audio-video experts show off at 11:30 each night when the disco opens. Before the hordes are turned loose on the dance floor, the kids in the control booth run every effect on the board, a spectacular show that lasts about ten minutes and is often accompanied by classical music. If you don't care for discos, at least go for the show: You can be in and out for the cost of just one expensive drink.

The owners of the Hotel Buenaventura (see below) bought and completely remodeled the defunct Hacienda del Lobo a few years ago. Renamed the **Hacienda Buenaventura**, and located right next to the Krystal Vallarta, it's a colonial-style charmer wrapped around a large swimming pool. All 155 rooms of the Hacienda are tastefully decorated and air-conditioned, and have either small balconies or patios. The public areas are also quite attractive, and its pretty brick-ceilinged restaurant, Los Portales, is open for breakfast and dinner. Because the Hacienda is a short walk from the beach through the grounds of the Krystal, it's also very reasonably priced and an excellent choice for travellers on a budget.

The **Fiesta Americana** is popular with group travellers. The soaring seven-story lobby with its palapa-style roof immediately puts guests in a party mood, and the free-form pool with an island in its middle is the perfect place to have

landscaped grounds, well-appointed rooms, a
very good restaurant. All have the usual conve
lobby as well, including car-rental and travel a
tiques, and small stores for sundries. And al
guests the same tennis and golf privileges mentio
Because of their similarities, the choice becon
atmosphere and loyalty. The Marriott is manag
parent chain, which is a joint investor with a Mexica
manufacturing company. Inside the hotel there i:
feeling of Mexico: You could be in California or N
an atmosphere that many guests find comforting. Th
owned and operated by a Spanish group, strives for ;
of Mexico and Europe, which results in a feeling of
the Conrad is, well, Hiltonish.

Apart from the hotels, Marina Vallarta is ideal for walk
broad promenade surrounds the boat slips, and is flanke
a number of restaurants, stores, and, unfortunately, 7-Elev
The best time to stroll is in the cool of the evening, when
lights of the buildings reflect on the water. You'll easily fi
the marina's landmark—the lighthouse at the Royal Paci
Yacht Club. The bar up top is ideal for viewing the entir
complex.

Continuing south you'll come to the city marina. There
will probably be a cruise ship alongside its single pier and
perhaps one or two others anchored out in the bay. This is
the marina where you board day cruises to beach hideaways
or charter deep-sea fishing boats.

Favored by a fairly upscale clientele, the **Krystal Vallarta**,
farther south, is one of Vallarta's top hotels. Built by the
Gershenson family and run by them as the Posada Vallarta
in P.V.'s early days, when it was *the* hotel in town, it was
taken over by the Krystal chain after the elder Gershenson's death. Expanded in all directions, today it resembles a
colonial village, with suites and villas (the latter perfect for
families), cobblestone streets, beautiful gardens, and a fleet
of electric carts to haul guests around in. Non-guests can
get a taste of this elegance by dining alfresco poolside. The
Krystal is also one of the few hotels in town that allows
horseback riding on its beaches.

Tuesday night is usually Mexican fiesta night at the Krystal.
The hotel has its own bull ring a short distance away, and
dinner is served buffet style at tables set up around the ring.
Go hungry, because there's an extensive selection of Mexican dishes from which to choose and you can go through
the line as many times as you like. The show itself, which
includes mariachis, folk dances, lasso artists, and—the fea-

one. Better yet, every one of its well-appointed rooms offers a view of the bay (and those gorgeous Puerto Vallarta sunsets), and just about any water sport you can think of can be arranged on the beach in front of the hotel.

The Fiesta Americana also has **Friday Lopez**, the only disco in town featuring live music, and **El Morocco**, one of the nicer restaurants in Vallarta. A chic and formal kind of place, with a Casbah setting and pretty Persian rugs, its specialties include lobster, red snapper, prime rib, steaks, and Moroccan dishes. Reservations are necessary; Tel: (322) 2-2010.

With a John Newcombe Tennis Center on the grounds, the sprawling **Continental Plaza**, down the beach from the Fiesta Americana, is the best tennis/hotel facility in town. Though hotel guests crowd the courts in pre-arranged groups, it's still easy for non-guests to reserve playing time. Three of the seven courts are under a roof, and some are lighted for night play.

The **Villa Vallarta Mall**, in the same complex as the Continental Plaza, makes for a pleasant shopping experience. Fiorucci and Mar y Mar, two of the best boutiques in town for women's resortwear, are here, as are Gucci and Cartier. In addition, just about any toilet article or sundry can be found at the air-conditioned supermarket on the street side of the mall. The **Place Vendôme**, P.V.'s most popular French restaurant, is located just outside the door. Locals are attracted by Place Vendôme's top-quality steaks, chateaubriand, and a variety of fish dishes. Open 6:30 to 11:30 P.M. Reserve; Tel: (322) 4-0123.

Farther south in the direction of town, the **Sheraton Buganvilias** is a nice enough hotel with six 13-story towers facing the ocean and beautifully landscaped grounds. Popular with travellers who feel comfortable with a name they know, the Sheraton has 500 air-conditioned rooms (many with balconies), a number of large meeting rooms, and a variety of stores off the reception area. It also has a family-run gourmet restaurant, **Las Gaviotas**, which serves up delicious Mexican and international cuisine with courteous service. Open for dinner only; Tel: (322) 2-3000.

The **Hotel Buenaventura** is a little jewel of a place within easy walking distance of town. Everything about it is compact, clean, and efficient, yet the Buenaventura has a big-time-resort look and feel about it. The hotel is very popular with Mexican businessmen and European visitors, who like it for its harmonious mix of atmosphere and proximity to town—a bit of everything for those who have to be near the action (there is no beach, however).

The unhurried feel of the neighborhood between the Buenaventura and town along Avenida México eases visitors into the hustle and bustle of the congested downtown area. **Alfarería Tlaquepaque**, at the corner of Avenida México and República de Chile, looks as if it's an old garage but is in fact one of the few genuine souvenir shops in Puerto Vallarta. If you like looking for old-fashioned ceramic or glass knickknacks, you'll love poking around this place. Christmas is a particularly good season to browse for decorations and unusual crèche figurines.

Downtown: The North Side

Roughly speaking, the north side of the downtown area (meaning north of the Río Cuale) encompasses everything from where Avenida México hits the cobblestones and becomes Avenida Díaz Ordaz (the seaside drive) to the river. Avenida Díaz Ordaz, the streets parallel to it—Morelos and Juárez—and the side streets between Calle 31 de Octubre and Calle Galeana constitute the main downtown shopping and dining district. The downtown area from Calle Galeana to the river also has some upscale shops and restaurants, but is largely commercial. This is where you'll find most of the airline offices and banks, as well as the open-air souvenir market. Much of the north side is tough on the ears and the feet. Its streets are too narrow for the number of vehicles using them, and the cobblestones don't make for comfortable walking. Still, no one seems to care.

Restaurant Row, which begins at Calle 31 de Octubre and extends along Avenida Díaz Ordaz to what was once the Océano Hotel, at the corner of Calle Galeana, is one of the most popular areas in town to shop, dine, and people-watch. Popular restaurants in this neighborhood include such old favorites as the **Red Onion**, **Il Mangiare**, **Mogambo**, and **Casablanca**. (McDonald's recently opened its second branch here, much to the dismay of the more established restaurateurs.) It's not hard to make a choice; in Vallarta all the restaurants display their menus at the door. It's a good way to find out if they're serving the kind of food you're looking for at the prices you're willing to pay. Intermixed with the restaurants are such popular boutiques as Aca Joe, Ruben Torres, and Express. (Because many of the better designers and artisans in the country have homes here, Puerto Vallarta merchandise generally has a unique look.)

With its tried-and-true formula solidly in place at the corner of Díaz Ordaz and Domínguez, the **Hard Rock Café** has been a hit ever since it opened. If you've already been to a Hard Rock, you know what to expect: The rear end of a pink Caddy hovers near the entrance, the inside features lots of polished brass and rock 'n' roll memorabilia, the hamburgers and fries taste just like Mom's, and the shots of tequila will set you back about $3.50.

Although the Hard Rock is just two blocks south of the city center's former hot spot, **Carlos O'Brian's Pawnshop and Restaurant**, it doesn't seem to have taken any business away from the latter. Lines form around the block at both establishments (arrive before 7:00 P.M. to avoid them), and patrons drift from one to the other throughout the evening. If anything, O'Brian's still has the edge in ambience, with all sorts of odd things hanging from the ceiling and a variety of unusual seating arrangements. O'Brian's has long been an institution in Vallarta, and that status remains soundly secure.

Las Palomas, on the corner of Díaz Ordaz and Calle Aldama, features simple Mexican meat and fish dishes. Decorated in colonial style, and open to the street and bay, it's a local favorite. (Try to wangle a table near the window in the bar; it's one of the better places in town to watch the sunset.) The small dining room on the other side of the bar is lit by candles at night. The quality of the food here often depends on the chef's mood, but the strategic location couldn't be better for those who like to people-watch. Tel: (322) 2-3675.

Sunsets in Puerto Vallarta are an event that shouldn't be missed. Purists like to watch them from places like El Set in the Hotel Conchas Chinas out on the highway south of town; Le Kliff, even farther out at Boca de Tomatlán; or Chez Elena in the Cuatro Vientos Hotel on the hill above Restaurant Row. Those who just want to enjoy the view without the benefit of food and drink can plop down on a bench along the seaside *malecón* (promenade).

El Panorama, a restaurant on the seventh floor of the Hotel La Siesta, high on a hill overlooking the *malecón* at Domínguez and Miramar, has it all, including a view of the bay and the hotel strip north of town that is nothing short of awesome. The food is consistently good and reasonably priced, and many of the dishes are prepared right at your table. Try the giant shrimp *flambé*—at almost a foot long (truly), they live up to their name. Open daily from 6:00 P.M. to midnight; the bar stays open until 3:00 A.M. Tel: (322) 2-1818.

The former Océano Hotel, at the corner of Díaz Ordaz and Calle Galeana, across the street from the statue of a boy riding a seahorse (Puerto Vallarta's best-known landmark), is where everyone used to meet before it was turned into condominiums. Though its lobby bar is long gone, the colonial-style restaurant is still intact. Simple Mexican dishes and Continental cuisine are served in an informal atmosphere, and live music accompanies dinner in the evenings. Reasonable prices and a vantage point overlooking the street make it one of the best places in town to have breakfast or lunch—as well as to get a feeling for what the old days in P.V. were like. The new name of the restaurant is **Tequila**, but it will be a long time before anyone calls it anything other than the Océano.

Around you is the city center, its plaza complete with a bandstand in front of city hall. Dominating the area is the cathedral (one of the most photographed in Mexico), **Nuestra Señora de Guadalupe**, completed in 1951 *sans* its unique crowned steeple. Added in the late 1960s, the steeple is said to be a copy of the crown worn by Mexico's Empress Carlota at her coronation in 1867.

Some of the most interesting shops in town are located close to the cathedral on Morelos and Juárez, the first two streets up from and running parallel to Díaz Ordaz. **Galería Uno**, Morelos 561, is one of the finest art galleries in the country. Owned by Jan Lavender, an American who has made Puerto Vallarta her home, the gallery sells paintings and sculpture by an impressive roster of Latin American artists. Visitors from around the world congregate here to see works by the likes of Manuel Lepe, Miguel Angel Ríos, and Colunga, and it is safe to say that every celebrity who comes to town visits at least once. (There's a branch of the gallery in the Marina Vallarta complex.) The Galería Uno print and poster gallery is in the Plaza Malecón, at the corner of Avenida Díaz Ordaz and Calle 31 de Octubre.

A block to the east, at Juárez 519, **Galería Pacífico** offers contemporary art and sculpture in a lovely patio setting. You'll find a permanent display of work by some of Latin America's finest artists here, as well as a gift shop with posters, art books, and the like.

St. Valentin, Morelos 574, is one of the best shops in town for handcrafted items, with bowls, platters, and other original tableware (along with whimsical folk art) from Oaxaca. Don't let the unimpressive façade deceive you; the collection of items inside is extensive.

Suneson's, Morelos 593, carries pieces by the famous Taxco silversmiths Los Castillo in addition to a wide selection of other top-quality silver jewelry, and is one of the best such shops in town.

La Azteca, featuring a wide selection of 14- and 18-karat gold, is an extremely reputable family-run store, in business for more than 30 years. It's well located at Juárez 244. **Villa María**, at Juárez 449B, offers an exceptionally good selection of decorative and gift items.

Vallarta Mía, one of the more interesting boutiques in town, is on the south side of Aldama between Díaz Ordaz and Morelos. (There's no name on the door, and the narrow entrance is a few steps up from the sidewalk, so it's hard to find.) Necklaces and bracelets made from what look like the painted rubber rings of jelly jars, silver conch belts in all sizes, and other avant-garde accessories are among the items sold here.

Sucesos Boutique, featuring original all-cotton clothing for women, is at the corner of Libertad and Hidalgo, with several branches around town. Many of the fabrics are painted by hand at a commune high in the mountains, and Arizonan Toody Competello does a terrific job selecting unusual accessories and hand-painted objets d'art to round out the collection. The personalized service includes a wealth of information about where to go in town, what to do, and what to avoid.

The Bridges

Downtown Puerto Vallarta is divided into north and south sides by the Río Cuale, which is crossed by two narrow bridges. Locals call the one nearest the bay, which is open to one-way traffic heading south, the "new bridge." The "old bridge," three blocks to the east, carries traffic going north toward the airport.

Agustín Rodríguez, running from one bridge to the other on the north side of the river, is the site of Vallarta's popular **flea market**, at the corner of Morelos and A. Rodríguez, near the new bridge. A covered mall with hundreds of small stores selling everything imaginable, this is the place to haggle. In fact, the local merchants love and expect it. They also win every time.

Farther down the street in the direction of the old bridge is **Chef Roger**, one of Vallarta's finest, if not fanciest, restaurants, and easily its most difficult to find. The address is Agustín Rodríguez 267, but you'll be better off looking for Centro Plumero (Central Plumbing)—the restaurant is right across the street. At one time a small hotel built around a charming patio, the restaurant has sacrificed none of the Mexican-European–style intimacy of its predecessor, while the gourmet dishes prepared by owner/chef Roger Drier more than justify its reputation among local aficionados of fine dining. Open for dinner from 6:00 P.M. daily, except Sundays. Tel: (322) 2-0604.

Paseo Río Cuale meanders through the parklike Isla Río Cuale under both bridges. If you have to go from one bridge to the other this is the place to do it. (Access to the little island is provided by a short staircase at either bridge.) The lush foliage down here also makes it the perfect spot to cool off on a hot day. The noises of the traffic above are subdued, and shoppers can browse to their hearts' content in the stalls and boutiques that line the promenade.

Le Bistro, one of Puerto Vallarta's most enjoyable restaurants, sits at the river's edge on Isla Río Cuale near the old bridge. Popular with affluent tourists and locals alike, Le Bistro's enameled walls and black-and-white floors give it a sleek California look. Soft candlelight at night, an imaginative menu, stylish service, and mellow jazz music in the background all add to the experience. Be prepared to wait in line, however; Le Bistro does not accept reservations.

Downtown: The South Side

The section of town south of the bridges is known as Emiliano Zapata. Jammed with good, inexpensive restaurants, interesting boutiques, small hotels, and trendy bars, the eight-block-square area is P.V.'s answer to Greenwich Village.

The main street, Olas Altas, starts at a central plaza and runs parallel to the beach. In the early days it served as Vallarta's "airport": Battered DC-3s with tourists on board would buzz the road in order to get the attention of the town's two taxis. The beach is **Playa de los Muertos** (Beach of the Dead), where, legend has it, sailing ships from Spain and Britain used to anchor to pick up their cargoes of gold and silver. On one tragic occasion, 285 natives were massacred here after they demanded their fair share of the valuable metal they were hauling. A few years ago city officials tried to change the name to Playa del Sol (Beach of the Sun), on the theory that "Playa de los Muertos" wasn't likely to attract tourists, but they had about as much luck as the city of New York did when it changed the name of Sixth Avenue to Avenue of the Americas.

Today Playa de los Muertos is a lively spot that's a little on the grubby side but still popular with the locals. It's also crawling with vendors, who sell everything from dresses and tee-shirts to silver jewelry and puppets. The rule here is simple: Don't buy anything. You'll do much better in the stores nearby, which sell higher-quality merchandise at lower prices. Fortunately, the overwhelming majority of beach vendors are well-mannered, and after a firm but polite "No" they'll continue on their way looking grievously wounded but nevertheless resigned to your decision. If, on the other hand, you enjoy the sport of it, by all means give it a shot. Just remember you haven't bought a "bargain" at all. And, regardless of your attitude toward ritual haggling, definitely avoid the attractively designed and even more attractively priced rugs: After the first washing, you'll own an attractively designed placemat.

The promenade along the beach is filled with restaurants, bars, and condominiums. You'll probably hear **Andale**, perhaps Vallarta's trendiest bar, before you see it—it's as popular as Carlos O'Brian's and the Hard Rock, and just as crowded with tourists, rowdy locals, and beach bums. The spirited dancing that characterizes the place fills the spaces between tables, as there's no dance floor, and is accompanied by lots of friendly pushing and shoving. But Andale's secret, safely removed from the crowds and noise, is its restaurant on the second floor. A relative newcomer to town, Sal, who runs the restaurant, spent most of his career as the food-and-beverage manager aboard cruise ships and now puts his talent to good use here. The portions are huge, the barbecue ribs fall apart at the touch of a fork, and the perfectly seasoned chicken is as good as any in town. Best of all, you can sit on the restaurant's small balcony overlooking Olas Altas and watch the revelers below from a safe distance.

Just a half block from Andale, at Francisca Rodríguez 130, across from the Hotel Marsol, is **Archie's Wok**. Archie was the late John Huston's personal chef for many years, and his tasty specialties include sweet-and-sour Singapore fish and *hoi soi* ribs. To guarantee the freshness of the fish, Archie sends his own boats out to do the fishing. It's a very unpretentious place and also has take-out service. Open 1:00 to 10:00 P.M.; closed Sundays. Tel: (322) 2-0411.

A couple of blocks south of Archie's is **El Dorado**, a four-story condominium with a reasonably priced restaurant and bar right on the beach. More than a restaurant, El Dorado is a Vallarta institution and heavily patronized by longtime locals. The food, mostly typical Mexican dishes, is okay, but their chicken soup is as good as a blood transfusion. El Dorado opens around 7:00 A.M. and closes when it feels like it—usually early in the evening. Tel: (322) 2-1511.

The Highway to Mismaloya and Beyond

From El Dorado the street leads inland to a long flight of stairs. If you're in good shape, you can climb them to another street, which will bring you to the coast road, Highway 200.

In the Hotel Conchas Chinas between town and the Camino Real, funky, rustic-looking **El Set** is one of the best places in the Puerto Vallarta area to have a light meal and watch the sunset. It's one of the oldest restaurants in Vallarta, and has an elevator to take you to its rocky beach, where you can explore the tidal pools.

The **Camino Real** is about ten minutes south of town by taxi but seems to be even farther, in part because there are no other hotels nearby. Visiting presidents and dignitaries stay here when they come to town (it has two presidential suites to accommodate them), and the Royal Beach Club, which opened in 1990, doubled the number of rooms to 337. The trademark modern architecture of the Westin chain—in this case a stylish arc-shaped building with thick adobe-style walls and arches—and the lush vegetation enfolding the hotel make the complex all the more appealing to an upscale clientele of all ages. The Camino Real also boasts **La Perla**, one of the loveliest restaurants in Puerto Vallarta. After 22 years of serving oustanding international cuisine, La Perla has made a dramatic switch to authentic Mexican food. The restaurant has been completely remodeled, and its walls decorated with the art of Sergio Bustamante, which may be purchased. What hasn't changed is the superior service, at prices you'd expect to pay in a top-notch restaurant. Reservations advised; Tel: (322) 3-0123.

Farther south along the coast road the only points of interest are condos and a few restaurants. Among them, **El Coral**, the dining room of the Hyatt Coral Grand, is considered one of the town's finest, with exquisite table settings and a lovely view of the ocean. Frequented by discriminating locals and visitors, the Coral Grand satisfies those looking for good food served in a quiet, refined, air-conditioned setting. Dinner is accompanied by soft piano music, and on weekends there is dancing at the bar outside. Tel: (322) 2-5191, ext. 1514.

The dark-orange-and-white complex split by the highway is the recently opened **Club Maeva Puerto Vallarta**. This latest addition to Club Maeva's all-inclusive resort properties includes 360 rooms and suites and a wide range of facilities for its guests. Half the property spreads out right on the beach; the remainder is just across the highway.

Mismaloya, the locale that put P.V. on the map with the filming of *The Night of the Iguana*, is just before Boca de Tomatlán (about a 15-minute cab ride from the center of town), and these days is the site of a hotel/condo complex. The condo section, off the main highway, offers an excellent restaurant, fantastic views, and a 1950s-style disco with a waiter who moonwalks better than Michael Jackson. The young crowd finds it dull, but the older folks love it.

The hotel itself occupies most of the beachfront, and is easily reached by following the turnoff a short distance south of the condo units. **La Jolla de Mismaloya** is very attractive, with wide corridors and beautifully appointed rooms, some with small kitchens. (The façade of the movie hotel is still standing, but you have to climb a hill to reach it.) The hotel has managed to retain the original charm of Playa Mismaloya without being obtrusive, and because it's so far out of town, every possible amenity and convenience has been provided, including three very good restaurants.

Additionally, there are two interesting restaurants deep in the jungle that are accessible by car (or taxi) from the village of Mismaloya: Chino's and Eden. (They're not hard to find as there's only one twisty road with signpost boulders painted with serpents and apples pointing the way.) You'll find **Chino's** at the end of a bamboo bridge spanning the river, with a beautiful waterfall nearby where local youths will be happy to dive for you in exchange for a couple of dollars. The food is outstanding if you haven't eaten that day and mildly interesting if you have. Beware the potent, overly garnished tropical drinks. Tel: (322) 4-2926, but the jungle telephone is very unreliable and you certainly won't need to make reservations.

Continue on past Chino's and you come to **Eden**, which used to be the most primitive of the jungle restaurants, until Arnold Schwarzenegger and company arrived to shoot up some 40 acres of jungle during the making of the movie *Predator*. They also blew up the original Eden in the process, and the owner was handsomely rewarded with funds to rebuild the restaurant. Indeed, one of the crashed helicopters is still there. The food compares favorably with Chino's. Eden is open only in the high season because the road is impassable the rest of the year.

Back on the main highway south of Mismaloya, on the bay side of the road, is **Le Kliff**, high atop a cliff overlooking Boca de Tomatlán, where the Río Tomatlán empties into the bay. Tablecloths and candlelight make this open-air restaurant a somewhat more formal spot for romance than some of its neighbors in the area, and the views of the sunset from here are truly out of this world.

Chee-Chee, 1 km (½ mile) south of Le Kliff, is a Polynesian-style restaurant. A steep, winding bamboo staircase with a breathtaking vista at every turn leads down the overgrown hillside to the restaurant before continuing on to a swimming pool and a dock extending into the bay. (Women guests here often feel as if they should be wearing a Dorothy Lamour–type sarong.) The staircase, while a boon for photographers, is not for the weak of heart: People of all ages find themselves huffing and puffing on the way back up. The food, which is reasonably priced, is just so-so, but people make the trip for the scenic splendor, not for the culinary experience. Chee-Chee is open for lunch and an early dinner. Tel: (322) 2-4697.

Chico's Paradise, just south of Chee-Chee, is perched above the Río Tomatlán, its giant boulders and flat rocks offering what seems to be an ideal spot for sunbathing. A word of caution, however: 11 tourists and two horses were swept to their deaths here within a two-year period. The Río Tomatlán, which swells with water high in the mountains, turns it loose without warning.) Chico's is also a prime example of what land developers can do to despoil the natural beauty of an area. The giant boulders now have rustic bridges built across them in a low-budget attempt to achieve a mini-Disneyland. And while the menu at Chico's is interesting, it's also a little on the pricey side. Your best bet is the black bean soup; try a bowl and you won't need to experiment with the drunken shrimp. Tel: (322) 2-0747.

Sports in Puerto Vallarta

Just about every water sport you can think of is available here, along with two other sports that you won't find at most other resorts: donkey polo and hunting.

Scuba-diving and snorkeling equipment can be rented in town or at most hotel beaches. Once you pick up your gear, head for Los Arcos at the southern end of the bay or Punta de Mita to the north. Any of these excursions can be arranged on the beach or at **Paradise Divers**, Olas Altas 443; **Divers de México** on Díaz Ordaz near Carlos O'Brian's; or at the **Dive Shop**, Díaz Ordaz 186.

Deep-sea fishing in the waters off Puerto Vallarta is also good. November to May are the months to catch sailfish, marlin, roosterfish, red snapper, snook, sea bass, tuna, and bonito. You can rent a boat through a travel agent, across from the Hotel Rosita downtown, or at the marina north of town on the airport road. Freshwater fishing excursions to the Canyon de Peña Reservoir, 112 km (69 miles) south of Puerto Vallarta, can also be arranged. If your hotel doesn't have a travel agent head downtown or to the Krystal Vallarta.

Hunting excursions for wild boar, wild turkey, duck, dove, quail, and pheasant can be booked through **Aventuras Agraz**; Tel: (322) 2-2969.

Before the new golf course at the Marina Vallarta opened, golfers had to make the 13-km (8-mile) trip to **Los Flamingos**, an 18-hole course that mewith around the inlets of a beautiful lagoon. Now both are popular, with condos and town houses beginning to sprout up around Los Flamingos.

Most hotels in P.V. have tennis courts. If yours doesn't, head over to the Plaza Vallarta, with its John Newcombe Tennis Center, north of town.

Sports buffs from the States who find themselves missing a daily diet of televised sports should check out El Torito, Ignacio Vallarta 290, south of the Río Cuale. You can pick up a schedule of games to be broadcast at the door—and with nine TV screens, you just might need it.

Excursions from Puerto Vallarta

There are a number of excursions available for those who want to get away from the getaway of Puerto Vallarta. The following sailboat cruises leave from the marina and ferry terminal north of town.

The *Serape* or 60-foot *Vagabundo* will take you on a beautiful day trip south along the coastline to **Yelapa**, a Polynesian-style village with a beautiful white-sand beach, a number of thatched-roof restaurants, and a jungle waterfall that cascades 150 feet into a crystal-clear pool (the last is for the well-conditioned hiker only). The boats leave between 9:00 and 9:30 A.M. and return by 4:00 P.M. The *Serape* excursion (no lunch) will set you back about $15; for $30 the *Vagabundo* serves lunch and has an open bar.

The trimaran *Bora Bora* cruises to **Las Animas**, another beautiful beach south of Boca de Tomatlán, and one accessible by water only. Fishing en route and snorkeling once you get there are part of the fun. Plan on spending $30 for this six-hour excursion.

For about $33 the trimaran *Cielito Lindo* takes visitors to **Huanacaxtle**, north of P.V. in the state of Nayarit, a primitive fishing village fronted by a deserted beach where you can sun, fish, and sail.

The catamaran *Shamballa* sails to **Playa Quimixto**, yet

another laid-back spot between Las Animas and Yelapa, for about $26.

There is also a day trip available to **Rincón de Guayabitos**, a primitive beach in the state of Nayarit. The tour includes lunch, stops at small villages, and an exhibition of Huichol Indian art that consists mostly of whimsical "paintings" woven out of concentric circles of fine yarn.

One of the more interesting excursions from Puerto Vallarta is to the old silver-mining town of **San Sebastián**, 145 km (90 miles) inland via a narrow, twisty road that takes four hours to negotiate (or you can fly there in 20 minutes from P.V.'s airport).

San Sebastián dates back to 1607, and shortly thereafter became the proud provincial capital of the state of Jalisco. At one point during the colonial era it supported some 40,000 inhabitants, most of whom were kept busy refining the ore into silver, which was melted down into ingots and transported by mule to the mouth of the Río Cuale, where it was loaded aboard ships bound for Spain.

Today the population is about 800, most of them agricultural workers, and there's very little in the way of organized activities for tourists. You can explore the abandoned silver mines or whoop it up with some of the locals at one of the town's many cantinas. Or you can play Trivia Quiz with Bud Acord.

A former Texan who has lived in Mexico for 21 of his more than 60 years, Acord literally rediscovered the **Hacienda Jalisco**, the former headquarters of the mining company that profited so handsomely during San Sebastián's heyday, and spent three years and half a million dollars converting it into a guest house, after which it became a favorite hideaway for the likes of John Huston, Elizabeth Taylor, Richard Burton, Peter O'Toole, and William F. Buckley, Jr. Huston, who had an eye for the finer things of life, once said, "Some day a movie company will find this place and the privacy will be gone." He was close enough: CBS has already shot stock footage here. For those who don't dally, there's still plenty of romance and privacy left.

The half-dozen rooms are arranged in pairs, with every other one sporting a fireplace. In the winter it can get very cold, leading to some spirited bidding on the fireplace rooms. The Hacienda has a dining room, but most guests prefer to eat in the kitchen, where the coffee bushes grow right outside the window. The food is always good, but don't expect a menu: The meal consists of whatever the chef has a mind to cook. Room rates depend on the size of your group, the time of year, and how many people are in residence. Have a travel agent check before you commit.

Another thing to keep in mind: Pickup by plane at the end of your stay at the Hacienda is done Mexican style—that is, you may request a pickup time but not see the pilot and his plane until a day or two later. It's wise to allow some leeway if you're on a schedule.

If you'd like more information about the Hacienda Jalisco, check at the in-house travel agency in your hotel or contact one of the many travel agencies in town. **Viajes Horizonte**, in the lobby of the Fiesta Americana, is especially good when it comes to local tours of this nature. Tel: (322) 2-3888.

GETTING AROUND

The following airlines service Puerto Vallarta's Gustavo Díaz Ordaz International Airport from the United States: Aéromexico offers daily nonstop service from Los Angeles as well as daily flights from New York City (J.F.K.), Houston, New Orleans, and Miami via Mexico City. Mexicana offers daily nonstop service from San Francisco, Los Angeles, and Chicago; flights from Denver and Dallas–Fort Worth via Guadalajara; and from J.F.K. via Mexico City. Continental offers daily nonstop flights from Houston, and American Airlines flies nonstop daily from Dallas–Fort Worth. Alaska Airlines offers direct service to Puerto Vallarta from its hubs on the West Coast.

When you arrive at the airport, you'll find the trip through Immigration and Customs surprisingly smooth. After you collect your baggage, it's a good idea to change some of your money into pesos at the airport *casa de cambio,* where you'll get a much better rate of exchange than at your hotel. Change as much as you want to—you can always change it back again at the same *casa de cambio* when you depart. Keep some dollars, however; many of the restaurants and stores in town will offer a higher rate of exchange to their customers.

Don't look for a taxi at the airport: There aren't any. Mexico's airports are federal property and the government controls transportation to and from them. Taxis are allowed to drop passengers off, but they're prohibited from picking anyone up. Instead, you'll have to settle for a *combi* (a VW minibus). There's a ticket booth out front; the cost of the trip is preset by zone (it's about $3 from the airport to town). Passengers are loaded and dropped off at their respective hotels in sequence. If this forced "togetherness" doesn't appeal to you, or if you're interested in going directly to your hotel, ask for an *"especial"*; for a few extra pesos you'll get your own private *combi*.

Unless you're planning on leaving town frequently, there's no need to rent a car in Puerto Vallarta; the best way to get around is by taxi. Public buses, tend to be dirty and crowded, but are also convenient and inexpensive. They stop every two blocks along the beach road and can be flagged down as well. Look for those saying "Pitillal," "Las Juntas," or "Ixtapa."

Guadalajara is a 5-hour drive over a good highway. The bus (first class) takes about 7 hours and costs about $10. The four bus stations in Puerto Vallarta are all on the corner of Insurgentes and Basilio Badillo, south of the Río Cuale.

—*Robin Lloyd*

ACCOMMODATIONS REFERENCE

The rates given below are projections *for December 1992 through Easter 1993. Unless otherwise indicated, rates are for double rooms, double occupancy; the 10 percent VAT has been added. As rates are subject to change, it's a good idea to double-check before booking. Puerto Vallarta is in the central standard time zone; the telephone area code is 322.*

▶ **Camino Real.** P.O. Box 95, Playa de las Ecstacas, **Puerto Vallarta**, Jalisco 48300. Tel: 3-0123; Fax: 3-0070; in the U.S. and Canada, Tel: (800) 228-3000. $160.

▶ **Club Maeva Puerto Vallarta.** Carretera A. Barra de Navidad, km 1, **Puerto Vallarta**, Jalisco 48330. Tel and Fax: 2-2105. $245 (all-inclusive).

▶ **Continental Plaza.** P.O. Box 36B, Playa de las Glorias, **Puerto Vallarta**, Jalisco 48300. Tel: 4-0123; Fax: 4-5236; in the U.S. and Canada, Tel: (800) FIESTA-1. $110.

▶ **Fiesta Americana.** P.O. Box 270, Carretera Aeropuerto, km 2.5, **Puerto Vallarta**, Jalisco 48300. Tel: 4-2010; Fax: 4-2108; in the U.S. and Canada, Tel: (800) (800) FIESTA-1. $185.

▶ **Hacienda Buenaventura.** P.O. Box 95B, Paseo de la Marina, **Puerto Vallarta**, Jalisco 48300. Tel: 4-6667; Fax: 4-6400; in the U.S. and Canada, Tel: (800) 223-6764. $66.

▶ **Hacienda Jalisco.** c/o Bud Acord, **San Sebastián**, Jalisco 48300. No phone. $35 (includes meals).

▶ **Hotel Buenaventura.** P.O. Box 8B, Avenida México 1301, **Puerto Vallarta**, Jalisco 48300. Tel: 2-3737; Fax: 4-6400; in the U.S. and Canada, Tel: (800) 223-6764. $66.

▶ **Hotel Conrad.** Paseo de la Marina Sur, **Puerto Vallarta**, Jalisco 48300. Tel: 1-0720; Fax: 1-0410 or 0411; in the U.S., Tel: (800) 445-8667; in Canada, Tel: (800) 268-9275. $115.

▶ **La Jolla de Mismaloya.** Carretera A. Barra de Navidad,

km 11.5, **Puerto Vallarta**, Jalisco 48300; or 301 East Colorado Boulevard, Suite 808, Pasadena, CA 91101. Tel: 3-0660; in the U.S. and Canada, Tel: (800) 322-2344. $160.

▶ **Krystal Vallarta**. Avenida de las Garzas, **Puerto Vallarta**, Jalisco 48300. Tel: 4-0202; Fax: 4-0222; in the U.S. and Canada, Tel: (800) 231-9860. $120.

▶ **Marriott CasaMagna**. Paseo de la Marina 5, Marina Vallarta, **Puerto Vallarta**, Jalisco 48300. Tel: 1-0004; Fax: 1-0956; in the U.S. and Canada, Tel: (800) 831-1000 or 3131. $231.

▶ **Meliá Vallarta**. Paseo de la Marina Sur, Marina Vallarta, **Puerto Vallarta**, Jalisco 48300. Tel: 1-0200; Fax: 1-0118; in the U.S., Tel: (800) 336-3542. $232.

▶ **Sheraton Buganvilias**. Carretera Aeropuerto 999, **Puerto Vallarta**, Jalisco 48300. Tel: 3-0404; Fax: 2-0500; in the U.S. and Canada, Tel: (800) 325-3535. $142.

▶ **Villas Quinta Real**. P.O. Box 81, Pelicanos 311, Marina Vallarta, **Puerto Vallarta**, Jalisco 48300. Tel: 1-0800; Fax: 1-0801; in the U.S. and Canada, Tel: (800) 362-9170. $140–$160.

TENACATITA

If you've ever wanted to know what it's like to vacation in the middle of nowhere, this is the perfect place to find out—though it's hard to imagine you would travel to Mexico just to come here. The Hotel Los Angeles Locos de Tenacatita is aptly named—only "crazy angels" know where it is. Nestled on a beautiful bay off Highway 200, about 190 km (118 miles) south of Puerto Vallarta and 87 km (54 miles) north of Manzanillo, Tenacatita's lone hotel is announced by a few small signs along the road that point the way to the big red billboard at the turnoff to its access road. If you blink, however, you can miss them all.

MAJOR INTEREST

Superb bay and beach
Utter isolation

Though the choice to put a hotel on the graceful curve of this lovely bay was a sane one, it's the snaking mile-and-a-half-long access road through thick jungle that makes the whole prospect of the place seem crazy. The property, now managed by the Fiesta Americana chain and called the **Fiesta Americana Los Angeles Locos**, was originally built by a Mexican labor union that wanted to provide restful vacations for its members. (Shortly after this workingman's paradise was completed, the union had to turn it over to Fiesta Americana.) The result was a low-rise deluxe hotel with 200 rooms arranged around a central pool area. Most rooms overlook the ocean, and all have balconies, color TV, and comfortable rattan furniture. The hotel attracts Mexican families, Canadians on group tours, and more than a few U.S. travellers, and to satisfy their palates, three open-air restaurants offer a choice of well-prepared Mexican and Continental cuisine. Every imaginable water sport is available as part of the package as well. There are also four tennis courts lighted for night play and horseback riding along the wide, sandy beach. The lap pool is built around an island bar where the bartenders are happy to hand you a drink as you paddle by—a practice that tends to limit the number of laps you may have had in mind. A tiny disco with live entertainment (sometimes) is the only other distraction from the beauty and solitude in Tenacatita. However, most guests choose to fall asleep to the sound of waves and wake up to birdsong.

The hotel used to require a seven-night-minimum package, but due to demand the policy was changed to a flat day rate or split days pro-rated from $112 for a full day. The price is fine if you plan to spend an entire day, arriving in time for breakfast; the half-day offer is on the expensive side (how many laps can you swim and how many horses can you ride in half a day, with time out for meals?).

With all this and lots of favorable publicity besides, it was only a matter of time before private homes and condos began to appear on the hillside overlooking the hotel. If you are truly "seeking serenity in a remote paradise" (which the brochures promise to deliver), do it while the serenity and remoteness still exist.

GETTING AROUND

The hotel is about 46 km (29 miles) northwest of the Manzanillo airport and 160 km (99 miles) southeast of Puerto Vallarta. The taxi fare from the airport is more than the one-way plane fare to Manzanillo from Guadalajara, but you can always rent a car. For an additional charge of $22 per person, one-way, the hotel will send a *combi* to the airport to pick you up—perhaps your best bet (arrange in advance through the hotel or a travel agent).

—*Robin Lloyd*

ACCOMMODATIONS REFERENCE

The rates given below are projections for December 1992 through Easter 1993. Unless otherwise indicated, rates are for double rooms, double occupancy; the 10 percent VAT has been added. As rates are subject to change, it's a good idea to double-check before booking. Tenacatita is in the central standard time zone; the telephone area code is 333.

▶ **Fiesta Americana Los Angeles Locos.** P.O. Box 7, Highway 200, km 20, **Tenacatita,** Jalisco 48980. Tel: 7-0220; Fax: 7-0229; in the U.S. and Canada, Tel: (800) FIESTA-1. Low season, $96; high season, $112.

BARRA DE NAVIDAD

Barra de Navidad (Christmas Bar) is well known to Mexicans, but the mainstream tourist has yet to discover it. The attraction here is sportsfishing; year-round catches include sailfish, dorado, tuna, and blue and black marlin. Visiting fishermen from north of the border favorably compare Barra to the Cabo San Lucas of 20 years ago.

MAJOR INTEREST

Fishing
Fishing-village atmosphere

The village of Barra de Navidad, 2 km (1¼ miles) off the main highway, is a quiet place built on a spit of land separating the ocean from a mangrove-lined lagoon. The cobblestone streets are narrow, dusty, crowded, and confusing, lined by row after row of open-air stores. The perfect, dark-sand crescent of a beach quarters a surprisingly large number of small hotels in the low- to moderate-price range as well as a number of excellent palapa-type restaurants, which attract customers from the posh Las Hadas Hotel 20 miles to the south in Manzanillo. One such restaurant, though nameless, sits on the east side of Calle Vera Cruz, a block back from the ocean. The restaurant is run by a charming woman named Esperanza, who opens her front door (most evenings), puts a few tables out on the sidewalk, and serves the best *pozole* imaginable. (*Pozole* is a marvelous mixture of hearty beef stock, hominy, mixed vegetables, shredded pork, cabbage, and sweet, fresh onions served with stacks of corn tortillas.)

The **Hotel Cabo Blanco**, on the edge of town, looks like a plush country club and is part of a pretty, developed (for this part of the coast) complex called Pueblo Nuevo that also includes condos, the area's only tennis courts, a yacht club, and a canal that leads to the ocean. (Six steps will take you from the edge of the hotel swimming pool to the canal.) The hotel's fine restaurant is guaranteed to leave a smile on your face. Try a large bowl of the tortilla soup, which, preceded by a small green salad, is a meal in itself.

At the hotel's beach club, a five-minute drive from the hotel, waterskiing, scuba diving and snorkeling, windsurfing, or sportsfishing boat rentals can all be arranged.

After a few days you'll feel as if you know everybody in town. With this kind of hospitable atmosphere, it's only a matter of time before Barra de Navidad becomes a resort destination attracting the discerning traveller.

GETTING AROUND
It's essential to have a car in Barra de Navidad in order to get around. Cars can be rented at the airports in Puerto Vallarta, Manzanillo (the closest air gateway, 13 km/8 miles to the south and east), or Guadalajara (see their respective Getting Around sections for further information).

—*Robin Lloyd*

ACCOMMODATIONS REFERENCE
The rates given below are projections *for December 1992 through Easter 1993. Unless otherwise indicated, rates are for double rooms, double occupancy; the 10 percent VAT has been added. As rates are subject to change, it's a good idea to double-check before booking. Barra de Navidad is in the central standard time zone; the telephone area code is 333.*

▶ **Hotel Cabo Blanco.** P.O. Box 31, Armada and Pueblo Nuevo, **Barra de Navidad,** Jalisco 48987. Tel: 7-0182; Fax: 7-0168. $40–$52.

MANZANILLO

Manzanillo is the only Mexican resort to have become a movie star before it was a well-known destination. The movie *10* catapulted it onto the map with even more effect than the gala opening of Las Hadas, attended by celebrities from around the world, a few years earlier.

Before Las Hadas, Manzanillo was little more than a sleepy tropical port surrounded by fertile farmland. The few visitors who came here were likely to be deep-sea fishermen, and the biggest decision anyone ever had to make was whether to eat the large tangy oysters from the bay or the small sweet oysters from the Laguna Cuyutlán.

Highway 200, the road linking Manzanillo to Puerto Vallarta, about 260 km (160 miles) up the coast, opened some 20 years ago, and things haven't been the same since. (In the interim, two more highways linking it to Guadalajara have been built, and a brand-new four-lane highway that will cut the driving time to three and a half hours is nearing completion.) With more than 20 miles of beautiful beaches, excellent weather (Manzanillo is on the same latitude as Hawaii), and a number of first-class hotels and resorts in addition to Las Hadas, Manzanillo is the perfect getaway for those who want to unwind in an exotic setting without the hustle and bustle of some of Mexico's larger vacation destinations.

MAJOR INTEREST

Las Hadas resort

Manzanillo's fresh-faced appearance belies its importance: Connected by rail to cities throughout the country, it is one of the busiest commercial seaports in Mexico. It is also one of Mexico's major deep-sea fishing ports, and lies at the heart of one of the most fertile agricultural areas in the country—lush papaya, banana, and coconut plantations stretch for miles inland from the coast.

Cortés named the small settlement he found here for the beautiful blossoming chamomile plants of the surrounding area. Soon after, he established Latin America's first shipyard in order to build boats for the further exploration of New Spain and the Philippines. (He found the area so much to his liking, in fact, that he eventually retired here.) By the end of the 16th century Manzanillo was one of the New World's leading ports, with much of that activity revolving around trade with the Far East. But as Spain's fortunes in the New World declined, Manzanillo was all but forgotten by the rest of the world.

That all began to change in 1974 when Anteñor Patiño, a Bolivian tin magnate, unveiled the opulent Las Hadas resort. Other hotels and condominium complexes have followed, but, overall, the growth of Manzanillo as a destination for international travellers has been slower than that of other Mexican resorts.

The ten beautiful miles of the beach-fringed Bahía de Manzanillo run in a graceful curve from northwest to southeast. Downtown Manzanillo, where the major banks and airline offices are located, is at the southeastern end of the bay. Las Hadas is located to the north. The smaller, scallop-shaped Bahía de Santiago lies to the west of Las Hadas, with the two bays separated by the Península de Santiago. To the north and west of Santiago Bay are Playa de Oro, the finest black-sand beach in Mexico; the airport; and the coastal highway leading to Barra de Navidad and points north, including Puerto Vallarta. For the most part, visitors confine themselves to the seven-mile stretch between Las Hadas and the downtown area. Pockets of development surround each resort complex in the area—among them Las Hadas, Club Maeva, Club Santiago, and the Hotel Sierra Radisson Plaza—but miles of relatively unspoiled beach lie between each busy pocket. Other attractions here are also spread out—so spread out, in fact, that it's best to rent a car if you plan on spending any time exploring; the roads in and around Manzanillo are good and getting around is easy.

From the Airport to Las Hadas

The ride from the airport to Las Hadas is a long (43 km/27 miles) but scenic one that passes through lush banana and coconut plantations. If excursions to nearby towns and villages are on your itinerary, this will be a good time to watch the road signs and get a feel for the lay of the land.

Although it's a bit off the beaten track at km 12.5 on Boulevard Costero, the coast road (about a ten-minute drive north of Las Hadas), **L'Recif** (The Reef) is worth checking out. Situated high on a promontory in the Vida del Mar condominium complex, this romantic restaurant offers spectacular views of the craggy coastline and terrific food prepared by a French-born chef. (The Sunday brunch here is legendary.) If you come for lunch, be sure to bring a camera and a bathing suit—there's a splendidly tranquil pool in a tiny garden on the premises where patrons can swim and sunbathe after their meal. Reservations recommended; Tel: (333) 3-0624.

What most visitors think of as Manzanillo starts at **Club Santiago**, on **Playa Miramar** (popular with bodysurfers, it's the first beach you'll see on the trip in from the airport). Club Santiago offers a variety of accommodations in a posh, country club–like setting, including one- to six-room beachfront villas, secluded cottages, and spacious condominiums. The huge pool has a shaded swim-up bar, and guests can dine on the beach at **Oasis**, a sleek, sophisticated restaurant under a soaring palapa that specializes in moderately priced French cuisine (Tel: 333/3-0937), or dance till they drop at the club's lively disco. There are also six tennis courts and a nine-hole golf course (open to guests only) on the premises. One of the greatest attractions at Club Santiago, however, is the marvelous seclusion it offers.

The small but fast-growing town of Santiago itself is the location of the **Centro Artesanal Las Primaveras**, one of the best handicraft shops in the area (it doubles as a flower shop). You'll find it at Juárez 40, between the church and Camacho Supermarket, facing the highway.

To the south and east of Playa Miramar, following the curve of the bay in the direction of Las Hadas and town, the **Olas Altas** and **Santiago** beaches are especially pretty and unspoiled.

Popular **Juanito's**, at km 14 on Boulevard Costero, offers pretty colonial decor, typical Tex-Mex fare, and what many say are the best hamburgers, hot dogs, and American-style malted milkshakes in town. (They also will place long-distance phone calls for you.)

Just down the road from Club Santiago in the direction of town, about a 20-minute drive from the airport, is **Club Maeva Manzanillo**, a picturesque and self-contained resort hotel spread over 90 acres. Its blue-and-white villas, some capable of accommodating up to six people, cluster around the resort's beautiful gardens. Available by the day or the week (when making your reservation, request a deluxe villa with a view), their no-nonsense interiors—bright blue tiles cover the floor and built-in couches and beds keep the living areas uncluttered—seem to have been designed with families in mind. You can even buy groceries at the supermarket on the premises and prepare meals in your villa's kitchenette.

Guests at Club Maeva tend to congregate around the pool, one of the largest in the country (the proprietors sometimes hold water-skiing exhibitions in it); a pedestrian walkway leads over the coast road to the beach on Santiago Bay. The 12 tennis courts are lighted for night play, and special activities for children are staged throughout the grounds. In fact, Club Maeva strikes the first-time visitor as a "user-friendly" playland where the whole family feels at home from the moment it arrives.

Playa La Audiencia

The **Hotel Sierra Radisson Plaza**, a new deluxe hotel property designed by the architect of Las Hadas, stands on Playa La Audiencia, a graceful moon-shaped beach and bay at the the head of the Santiago Peninsula. La Audiencia got its name from a reputed meeting between Cortés and the local Indians—its only claim to fame besides its great natural beauty. Nestled in a protective inlet within the larger Santiago Bay, the beach is washed by the gentlest waves in Manzanillo, making it an ideal place to snorkel and swim.

The hotel itself is a towering 350-room complex with four lighted tennis courts, five restaurants and bars, and 24-hour concierge service. Rooms are large and tastefully decorated, and the impressive public areas are spacious and airy. Perhaps best of all, the developers of this huge hotel have not been totally insensitive to aesthetic considerations: The white walls and tile roofs of the complex lend it a vaguely Moorish look, and its striking architectural design complements the natural beauty of the bay.

Las Hadas

It is entirely appropriate that *Las Hadas* translates as "The Fairies": The guests at this exquisite resort often feel as if they are vacationing in nothing less than an enchanted fairyland. The architecture of the Westin Las Hadas Resort is a unique blend of Moorish, Mexican, and Caribbean elements combined to create a gleaming white stucco village perched on a hill overlooking Manzanillo Bay. And while Señor Patiño built the place to meet the high standards of his wealthy and discriminating friends, he also priced it so that others could enjoy the luxury and beauty that prevail here.

Everything at Las Hadas is on a grand scale, with the luxury built in from the ground up. Most rooms and suites have an ocean view, and some have large private patios. Inside, marble floors and tiled baths keep the spacious rooms and suites cool and inviting. (Las Hadas also offers rooms in its Royal Beach Club, complete with gorgeous views, deluxe amenities, and complimentary afternoon cocktails around the pool.) The two swimming pools are attractively decorated with mosaics, while the larger is crossed by a suspended bridge and has two landscaped islands in the middle of it. Exquisitely carved fountains dot the gardened walkways lacing the complex, and the small bay nearby is ringed by a lovely beach where beach attendants rake the sand and prepare white cabaña tents for their pampered guests. If you get tired of walking to the beach or the pool, a chauffeured golf cart (Las Hadas uses a noiseless model so that other guests won't be disturbed) will respond to your summons. Las Hadas also has a private 18-hole championship golf course.

The open-air **El Terral**, where Dudley Moore and Bo Derek shared a romantic dinner, is one of the charming restaurants at Las Hadas; **La Cartouche**, the piano bar/disco that also appeared in the movie, is where you'll find the nightlife. Both are open to the public at night. The **Player's Club** at the Las Hadas marina, where live mariachi music livens up most nights, is also fun.

The 90-slip marina at the foot of the hill looks like a showroom for luxury yachts, and the condominium complex just across the seaside promenade, Marina Las Hadas, is managed by the hotel. The complex includes the **Marina Mall**, with its maze of chic shops, tiny restaurants, and outdoor cafés.

The Mediterranean-style **Plaza Las Glorias Manzanillo** is a picture-perfect luxury accommodation perched atop another steep hillside overlooking Las Hadas, the golf course, and Club Santiago. There are 85 "villas" with living room, bedrooms, and bath on the premises here, but you may opt for a traditional room if you wish. The rooms, most with large terraces, are bright and spacious, and the dining room offers a panoramic view and refreshing breezes by day and a romantic ambience with live music at night. The pool has its own swim-up bar and bridge (though it's not as big as the pools at Las Hadas or Club Maeva), and for guests who want to hit the beach, a shuttle bus runs between the hotel and Playa Santiago, a few minutes away. For those who would just as soon avoid paying top dollar and can survive without a beach right outside the door, the Plaza Las Glorias is one of the best lodging options in the area.

From Las Hadas to Town

Almost everything a visitor will want to see, do, or arrange can be found along **Playa Azul**, the seven-mile stretch of beach that rings Manzanillo Bay. With its gentle curves and gentler waves (more so the closer you get to town), Playa Azul has become a magnet for hotels and restaurants, which can be found on either side of the highway and become more concentrated as you near town. The dining establishments and discos along this stretch are as informal as they come—you're not likely to find the fast-track Mexico City crowd here. In fact, an older crowd of retired Americans seems to constitute the first shift at many of these places, though they fill up later in the evening with locals, especially on weekends. Generally speaking, Manzanillo doesn't attract night owls, serious shoppers, or those who like to be "seen."

El Vaquero Campestre, a garden-style restaurant in the Salahua neighborhood, across the main road and three blocks south of the Las Hadas turnoff, is a sister establishment of El Vaquero, a popular downtown restaurant famous for its steaks and grilled meats. You enter this village-like oasis through a gate and follow a cobblestone path to a collection of palapas. Steak and seafood are the specialties, and on occasion there's music for dancing. Retired gringos seem to be especially partial to this one. Tel: (333) 3-0475.

Papagayo's, at km 8.5 near the Cine Fiesta movie house, is an air-conditioned hangout popular with the locals. Seafood and pasta dishes are best here, and occasionally there is music for dancing between courses.

The moderately priced **Fiesta Mexicana Days Inn**, on the beach across from the Restaurant Barra de Navidad, is a tropical charmer that's large enough to be comfortable but small enough to be friendly and cozy. Its rooms, decorated with floral prints and bamboo furniture, have a homey look, and the pretty pool with swim-up bar and dining area shaded by towering palms are the focal points of its layout. Its convenient location near a cluster of popular restaurants makes it even more of a bargain.

Farther south, at km 7 on Boulevard Costero, you'll come to the ever-popular **Carlos 'n' Charlie's Colima Bay Café**, one of a chain of unserious and much-loved restaurants started by the late Carlos Anderson. The prevailing attitude here is "Come in and join the fun," although it's not as boisterous as some of its brethren in other Mexican resorts. If you like down-home cooking (barbecue ribs are the favorite) but hate loud fiestas, wait for a table out on the porch overlooking the water.

South of Carlos 'n' Charlie's on the coast road there's a cluster of good restaurants at the Crucero Las Brisas, or Las Brisas crossroads (you'll recognize it by its life-size concrete sailboat). **Ostería Bugatti** was one of the first restaurants on the scene here and is still one of the most popular. Everyone likes the comfortable bar, the leaded-glass windows, and the piano music that accompanies dinner, while the cozy interior is a perfect complement to the food. The live music for dancing after dinner starts at 8:00 P.M. Tel: (333) 3-2999.

Willy's, on the beach at Las Brisas, is one of the most popular places in town (along with Bugatti's and Oasis, in the Club Santiago complex). Tables spill out of the main building and its pretty porch onto a platform on the beach. Out front near the entrance, savory meats are cooked over a charcoal grill, and elsewhere on the grounds a mini–street market keeps the same hours as the restaurant. Amid all this happy confusion, Chef Michele whips up delicious French cuisine and tasty tropical treats. Even with a reservation you'll probably have to wait, but with all the activity around, waiting is part of the fun. Tel: (333) 3-1794.

El Vaquero (it's the one with a covered wagon on its roof) claims to serve the best meat in town. With its dark wood-paneled walls, red-checked tablecloths, and Wild West memorabilia, you'll think you've stumbled into a Colorado steakhouse. After you've chosen your steak by cut and weight, it is grilled to your specifications right at your table. It's a great idea, but the place does tend to get hot in the summer despite the air-conditioning. Tel: (333) 3-1654.

If you stay to the right at the Las Brisas intersection, you'll soon enter the Las Brisas zone on Avenida Lázaro Cárdenas. The **Condominios Roca del Mar** is a pretty condominium-style hotel with a strategic location on the southeastern corner of Manzanillo Bay. Small and modern, with a friendly family atmosphere, a pool, a wonderful beach, and spacious units complete with living rooms, dining rooms, and kitchens, this is a delightful, reasonably priced place to spend a few days. **Elena's** boutique, just off the reception area, has a limited but tasteful selection of resortwear and decorative items (open only in season).

The **Hotel La Posada**, right next door to the Roca del Mar and across the road from the yacht basin (the place to charter fishing boats), is the kind of establishment where you can let it all hang out, relax in the sun on the beach with your favorite book, and enjoy the gorgeous Pacific sunsets over a cold drink without ever having to put on your shoes. People who have the time to travel through Mexico by car or RV love this place, and guests and locals alike stop here to enjoy the hearty, cooked-to-order American-style breakfasts and catch up on the latest gossip. Bart Varlemann, the owner, is an

Ohioan who came to Manzanillo years ago, and he goes out of his way to make his guests feel right at home. (The bar works on the honor system.) La Posada is a cash-only operation.

Downtown

In the past there was little reason for visitors to head into downtown Manzanillo. Those who did usually visited the small **Mercado Municipal** (Municipal Market), where sundries and souvenirs are sold; shopped at the **Bázar El Dorado** in front of the main square; and ended up at the **Bar Social**, Calle 21 de Marzo and Juárez on the zócalo (known here as the Jardín Alvaro Obregón), or the patio bar of the **Hotel Colonial**, Avenida México 100, for a drink and a bite to eat. Both are throwbacks to the days when Manzanillo attracted sportsfishermen and little else. Though the hotel's former elegance has faded (the once-ornate building now houses an appliance shop), it's still the only decent lodging option if you must stay downtown.

On the other hand, for those who enjoy local color, exploring downtown Manzanillo can be a treat. Streets that not too many years ago could only be described as seedy have been cleaned up, and the newly landscaped zócalo area invites tourists to relax and watch the passersby and commercial action that animate this busy port town. **Club Nautico**, a restaurant perched on stilts over the water, is a pleasant place for lunch or dinner.

Nightlife in Manzanillo

Nightlife and shopping in Manzanillo can be summed up in a few words: There isn't much of either. What little nightlife there is centers around the hotels, a few restaurants, and **La Cartouche** at Las Hadas (for hotel guests only). **Boom Boom** at Club Maeva and **Solaris** in the Hotel Playa de Oro are the most popular hotel nightclub/discos. Outside the hotels, three lively state-of-the-art discos on Boulevard Costero draw young (and young-at-heart) crowds. **Enjoy**, at km 16, is the largest of the three and has the standard laser lights and video screens. **Oui**, at km 9, is more intimate and ranks as the favorite among locals, while **Disco Bar de Felix**, at km 8.5, has the atmosphere of a bar in the States. Ostería Bugatti, Papagayo's and L'Recif restaurants usually have music for dancing.

Shopping in Manzanillo

As we've noted, Manzanillo is not a shoppers' paradise. Most hotels have one or two boutiques. The best collection of shops is in the Marina Mall at Las Hadas: **Jaramar** for decorative items, **La Palma** and **María de Guadalajara** for resortwear, and **Tane** for exquisite silver jewelry are three of the best here. The air-conditioned **Plaza Manzanillo**, at km 11.5 on the Boulevard Costero, has a number of good boutiques offering trendy resortwear and accessories, the usual fast-food restaurants, a couple of places where you can get your film developed, and a well-stocked supermarket. **Rubén Torres**, located in a snazzy glass structure on the beach side of the coast road at km 13, sells resortwear for men and women in a variety of bright colors. The **Mercado Municipal** downtown on Avenida Cinco de Mayo is the place to bargain for typical souvenirs.

Sports in Manzanillo

Manzanillo is yet another Pacific Coast paradise for sportsmen—though water-sport centers offering water-ski boats, scuba diving, and snorkeling trips are not as visible here as they are in other resorts. Windsurfing boards can be rented at the Roca del Mar, and the conditions at that end of the bay are usually gentle enough for even the greenest beginner.

Of course, fishing was the reason behind Manzanillo's early popularity and remains one of its biggest draws. Sailfish and marlin (Manzanillo bills itself as the "Sailfish Capital of Mexico") are the prize catches, and November and December are the best months to catch them. Species such as sea bass, mackerel, giant tuna, and yellowtail are abundant year-round, with October through March being the busiest season. Your hotel will be happy to arrange a charter boat for you at the marina across the street from the Hotel La Posada; the price, ranging from $150 to $300, depending on the size of the boat, usually includes bait and tackle.

Most of the major hotels and resorts in Manzanillo have tennis courts. If yours doesn't, there are six at Club Santiago, four at the Hotel Sierra Radisson Plaza (all lighted), and 12 at Club Maeva (six of them lighted) open to the public. Call in advance for reservations (see the Accommodations Reference list below for telephone numbers).

The **Laguna Juluapán**, northwest of Club Santiago, is a nature preserve and favorite haunt of visiting bird-watchers. Club Maeva allows horseback riding on its beach (and will supply the horses), and travel agencies in town and at the hotels will be happy to arrange scuba and snorkeling excursions.

Excursions from Manzanillo

Colima, about 100 km (62 miles) northeast of Manzanillo, is the capital of the small state of the same name, and is known for its geared-down pace and friendliness. Be sure to check out one of the folkloric or theatrical performances, staged year-round in its **Casa de Cultura**. The **Museo de las Culturas Occidentales**, part of the Casa de Cultura complex, houses the country's largest collection of the famous "dancing dogs of Colima," clay sculptures considered sacred by the local Indians, as well as other zoomorphic figures unearthed at nearby archaeological sites. The **Museo Regional de Historia**, at Hidalgo and Reforma, displays archaeological finds as well as handicrafts from the state of Colima; occasionally it also stages exhibitions of paintings by contemporary artists from the area. Housed in an old building on Calle 27 de Septiembre at the corner of Regalado is the **Museo Universitario de Arte y Cultura Popular**, more informally known as the Museum of Dance, Masks, and Popular Art. It exhibits costumes worn for folkloric dances as well as other regional art, some of which is for sale. (None of these museums has display explanations in English.) Hours are usually from 8:00 A.M. to 2:00 P.M. and from 6:00 to 7:00 P.M. daily, except Mondays.

In the nearby colonial town of **Comala** (15 minutes by car), visitors can choose from a good selection of painted furniture, pottery, and wrought iron at the **Mercado de Artesanías**. Your hotel or one of the travel agencies in downtown Manzanillo will arrange a trip to both Colima and Comala if you decide not to drive yourself.

More adventurous travellers can head for the primitive seaside town of **Cuyutlán**, about 50 km (31 miles) south of Manzanillo, most of the trip via Highway 200. The lagoon and beautiful unspoiled beach here are reason enough to pack a picnic and make the trip, but the lucky visitor may reap a dividend: Every spring between March and May, especially as the moon waxes full, the beach here is subject to repeated visitations of the mysterious *Ola Verde,* or "Green Wave," a wall of water that sometimes reaches heights of 30 feet or more.

If your hotel does not have a travel agent, contact **Bahías Gemelas** at Las Hadas (you can also find them at km 10 on the Boulevard Costero); Tel: (333) 3-1000 or 0204.

GETTING AROUND

You can drive good highways from either Puerto Vallarta or Guadalajara to Manzanillo or ride the bus. ETN buses leave Guadalajara four times a day. Although flying is by far the most convenient way to get here, most international carriers do not offer direct service to Manzanillo, which means travellers will be routed through either Mexico City or Guadalajara, with some connections through the former requiring an overnight stay. Two carriers that do offer "direct" service to Manzanillo are Mexicana and Aeroméxico. Aeroméxico offers daily flights from Los Angeles via La Paz, and Mexicana flies daily via Guadalajara (these stops do not require a change of planes). Flying time from Los Angeles is 4 hours.

The airport is a long ride—about 43 km (27 miles)—from the major hotels, so relax and enjoy it; the plantations you'll pass along the way are lush and lovely. There are a number of car-rental agencies right at the airport (Avis, Budget, Hertz, and National among them), as well as a few in town. A taxi from the airport will cost about $18; a *combi* will make the same trip for about $10.

Once you've settled in, taxis or rental car are the best way to get around. Taxis are plentiful and easy to hail; if you don't find one waiting outside your hotel door, ask the hotel to call one. There's also a taxi stand downtown across from the zócalo on Avenida Morelos. As is the case any time you decide to take a taxi in Mexico, establish the price *before* you get into the cab.

—*Susan Wagner*

ACCOMMODATIONS REFERENCE

The rates given below are projections for December 1992 through Easter 1993. Unless otherwise indicated, rates are for double rooms, double occupancy; the 10 percent VAT has been added. As rates are subject to change, it's a good idea to double-check before booking. Manzanillo is in the central standard time zone; the telephone area code is 333.

▶ **Club Maeva Manzanillo.** P.O. Box 442, Carretera Manzanillo–Barra de Navidad, km 12, **Manzanillo**, Colima 28200. Tel: 3-0141; Fax: 3-0395; in the U.S. and Canada, Tel: (800) 431-2822; Fax: (914) 632-3496. $110 per person (all-inclusive).

▶ **Club Santiago.** P.O. Box 374, Carrizales s/n, Bahía de Santiago, **Manzanillo**, Colima 28200. Tel: 3-0413; Fax: 3-0768; in the U.S., Tel: (800) 525-1987. Condos, $93–$110; villas, $143–$165.

▶ **Condominios Roca del Mar.** P.O. Box 7, **Manzanillo**, Colima 28200. Tel: 2-0805; Fax: 3-2950. $92–$105.

▶ **Fiesta Mexicana Days Inn.** Carretera Manzanillo–Barra de Navidad, km 8.5, **Manzanillo**, Colima 28200. Tel: 3-1100; Fax: 3-2180. $66–$76.

▶ **Hotel Colonial.** Avenida México 100, **Manzanillo**, Colima 28200. Tel: 2-1080. $20–$30.

▶ **Hotel La Posada.** P.O. Box 135, Calzada Lázaro Cárdenas 201–204, **Manzanillo**, Colima 28800. Tel: 3-1899. $67 (includes breakfast); no credit cards.

▶ **Hotel Sierra Radisson Plaza.** Avenida de la Audiencia, **Manzanillo**, Colima 28200. Tel: 3-2000; Fax: 3-2272; in the U.S., Tel: (800) 333-3333. $165–$200.

▶ **Plaza Las Glorias Manzanillo.** Avenida del Tesoro, Fraccionamento Península de Santiago, **Manzanillo**, Colima 28200. Tel: 3-0440 or 0550; Fax: 3-1397; in the U.S. and Canada, Tel: (800) 635-8483. $80–$150.

▶ **Westin Las Hadas Resort.** P.O. Box 158, Rincón de las Hadas, **Manzanillo**, Colima 28200. Tel: 3-0000; Fax: 3-0430; in the U.S. and Canada, Tel: (800) 228-3000. $215–$300.

IXTAPA/ZIHUATANEJO

Ixtapa/Zihuatanejo, 208 km (129 miles) northwest of Acapulco, offers the best of two worlds. It is both old and new, and is really two destinations in one—visitors so inclined can get double their money's worth.

This resort duo is somewhat difficult to describe. Ixtapa is sprawling and modern—it didn't even exist before the early 1970s—and is where most visitors stay, shop, and play after dark. Zihuatanejo dates to the 16th century and is where most visitors dine and play during the day, as well as where the area's business is conducted. The umbilical cord linking the two is a smooth, gently sloping four-mile highway with little in the way of development.

This may also be one of the most relaxing resorts in the country. Experienced resort-goers will tell you that Ixtapa (particularly suited to parents with young children and disabled travellers because of the flat unbroken terrain of its beaches) has Acapulco's fine weather without that famous resort's crowds. (The average year-round temperature is 79° F, slightly cooler than Acapulco, and the best weather coincides

with the high season, December through April. The rainy season stretches from June through October, but the showers usually wait until evening.) Those who like life in the fast lane, on the other hand, won't find it here. Instead, the ambience is laid back, giving you the feeling of being delightfully marooned in the midst of a tropical paradise.

MAJOR INTEREST

Relaxed resort pace with good shopping and dining

Ixtapa
Superior beach along hotel strip
Dining
Shopping
Nightlife

Zihuatanejo
Tranquil small-town atmosphere
Secluded beaches

Ixtapa/Zihuatanejo spreads out along a 25-mile-long coastline characterized by scalloped bays and beautiful beaches, with Ixtapa to the west and north of Zihuatanejo. Ixtapa's two-mile-long hotel zone faces the Bahía del Palmar, which is edged by an expanse of flat beach known as Playa del Palmar. The coast is broken at the far (western) end of the hotel zone by the small mouth of the Laguna de Ixtapa and then continues in a westerly direction to Punta Ixtapa. This undeveloped western stretch of coastline is scooped out into coves and inlets and has a number of unspoiled beaches. **Playa Las Cuatas**, on the near side of the point, is a pretty beach with offshore rock formations that will remind you of Bermuda. The small moon-shaped **Playa Quieta**, in front of Club Med on the far side of Punta Ixtapa, is the departure point for the 15-minute boat trip to Isla Ixtapa (also called Isla Grande; see the Excursions section below). **Playa Linda**, the farthest beach from the Ixtapa hotel zone, is backed by trees that provide delicious (and welcome) shade. It's a perfect place for midweek picnics, but gets crowded on weekends.

At the other end of Ixtapa, **Playa Hermosa**, a crescent-shaped beach in front of the Westin Resort Ixtapa hotel, is perhaps the prettiest of all the beaches in the area. (You have to enter through the hotel to get there, however.)

Zihuatanejo, a centuries-old fishing village, is a five-minute drive to the southeast over a highway carved into the hills. The tiny town nestles on its own bay, and the downtown beach, though sometimes sprinkled with seaweed, is shaded in places and friendly everywhere. Few tourists sun here, but the passing parade on the *malecón* is always fun to watch.

Playa La Madera is a broad, flat stretch of dark sand that begins just south of town. (What may appear on a map to be a short walk from town is in reality quite a hike: A channel forces would-be sunbathers into a 15-minute detour. Most people take taxis.) A road behind the beach climbs a hill to such smaller hotels as the Catalina, Irma, and Sotavento; the Villas Miramar is at the bottom of the hill just across the street from the beach.

Along the curve of the Bahía de Zihuatanejo to the south, just a five-minute drive over a scenic, rolling road, is **Playa La Ropa**, a favorite of international travellers and the location of the Villa del Sol and Fiesta Mexicana hotels. Named for the clothes that washed up on it after a long-ago shipwreck, the broad beach here and calm waters makes this a favorite spot for a variety of water sports.

Playa Las Gatas, to the south, can be reached by a very rocky path from Playa La Ropa or by launch from the town pier. Swimming conditions are less than ideal due to the beach's rocky bottom, but it's a good beach for diving and snorkeling, and has a dive concession right on the sand. Tiny restaurants offer snacks and chairs for rent.

IXTAPA

Ixtapa is a baby on the Mexican resort scene—but what a baby. Selected for development a little more than 15 years ago by the government computers at Fonatur, Ixtapa was built with the comfort and convenience of large groups of travellers in mind. This is one place where you can drink the water and not worry about the ice cubes (the hotel zone has its own water purification plant).

Several high-rise hotels have been built on the curve of Palmar Bay, and it takes about 30 minutes to walk the length of Paseo de Ixtapa (also called Paseo del Palmar), the road that serves as the spine of the hotel zone. The beach is at your back door along this stretch, the waves are usually gentle, and the water warm, so you can dive right in without shocking your system. It is also one of the few stretches of beach in the country that is lit for nighttime strolls (although you should stick to the section in front of the hotels).

The Ixtapa shopping district, easily accessible from any of the hotels in the zone, is a maze of modern malls on the inland side of Paseo de Ixtapa. The **Palma Real golf course**, an 18-hole Robert Trent Jones–designed course, is at the eastern end of the hotel zone, an easy walk from any of the major hotels here. (From the Sheraton you can walk to the first tee of the Palma Real in minutes.)

Staying in Ixtapa

Situated on its own promontory at the southern end of the bay, the **Westin Resort Ixtapa** is the crème de la crème of Ixtapa hotels. Big, breezy, and beautiful, it stands apart from the other hotels here not only in terms of its location but in its architecture as well. Built into the hillside above **Playa Hermosa**, its pretty crescent-shaped beach, the Westin Ixtapa resembles a vast expanse of bronze-colored bleachers. There are four freshwater pools, complete with fountains and an aqueduct (the six suites in the hotel have their own private pools), seven restaurants and bars, a disco, four tennis courts, and an indoor shopping area. But perhaps the outstanding feature of the Westin Ixtapa is the fact that even its smallest room has its own terrace-like balcony where you can dine under the stars, relax in a hammock, or read in a chaise longue. (Together, the room and the balcony have many of the amenities of a small cottage.) And yet, in spite of the hotel's size, you will never feel as if you're just one more guest of a big operation.

About a 15-minute walk to the west, the towering **Ixtapa Sheraton** heads the row of hotels that make up Ixtapa's hotel zone along **Playa del Palmar**. The Sheraton itself is an attractive resort where efficiency and cleanliness are everywhere in evidence. Although the decor of its otherwise comfortable rooms is less than eye-catching, the soaring atrium lobby, glass elevators, mini-mall, and air-conditioned bar with live music all contribute to the home-away-from-home feeling that's a hallmark of this chain. And for golfers, the Sheraton is closer (within easy walking distance) to the Palma Real golf course than any other hotel in the zone.

The **Dorado Pacífico**, one of the costliest hotels ever built in Mexico, is also one of the few privately owned hotels in the country. The lobby and public areas are cool and spacious, with marble floors and comfortable chairs in bright colors, and the butterfly-shaped pool with swim-up bar is just a few steps from the ocean. Inside, the contemporary polished-wood decor lends the Dorado Pacífico a plush, tropical feel. Even walking to and from your room is a treat. Hallways are punctuated by floor-to-ceiling picture windows, and the glass elevators look out upon the attractive lobby. All rooms have terraces and ocean views.

Everything about the **Krystal Ixtapa** is upscale, including Bogart's, a branch of the well-known chain of restaurants, and Christine, its dazzling disco (both are discussed below). Each room here has its own private terrace, climate control, and color cable TV, and there are five bars and restaurants as well as lighted tennis and racquetball courts on the premises. In addition, the Krystal's weekly Mexican fiesta night, which combines lively folkloric shows with traditional music, Mexican food, and rope tricks, is one of the best in town. (If you're not staying here, check with your own hotel for the day and time, as well as how to make reservations.)

The sprawling colonial-style **Omni Ixtapa**, at the far end of the beach, is the newest hotel in Ixtapa. Although austerely decorated, rooms here are spacious and equipped with the usual amenities; all have balconies with sweeping views. An attractive multilevel lobby, beautiful pool area, and half-dozen bars and restaurants add to its appeal, and its choice location will be even more of an asset when the marina at the mouth of the nearby lagoon is completed. Right now the marina, which is surrounded by pastel-colored villas and condominiums, can accommodate 600 yachts. A shopping mall, an art gallery, and a disco are scheduled to be added to the complex by the end of 1992, and an 18-hole golf course skirting the marina is due to be ready for play by the end of 1993. The course will be laced with canals, and players will be transported from the club house to the marina by electric boats or rowboats.

Dining in Ixtapa

Almost all the major hotels in Ixtapa have one or more air-conditioned restaurants, but trying those outside your hotel is part of the fun of vacationing here.

Bogart's, in the Krystal Ixtapa, is easily the most outrageous restaurant in town. The experience begins on the sidewalk out front, where diners on their way to the front door pass between two flaming torches. The restaurant itself looks like a set from *Casablanca*: Everything—costumes, carved screens, peacock chairs, and more—could have been lifted from Rick's. A fountain dominates the center of the room, and soft music from a white piano provides the perfect accompaniment for a memorable dining experience. Pretend you're Bogie or Bergman and dress up for this one. Reservations advised; Tel: (753) 3-0333.

Le Montmartre, on the second floor of the Galería Ixtapa across from the Dorado Pacífico, is a wonderful surprise. This breezy, informal place looks like a plain but attractive room in somebody's home, and specializes in seafood with a French accent. If you're the kind of person who likes juicy steaks without fancy sauces, you'll find those here, too. Le Montmartre was one of the first restaurants in Ixtapa, and its popularity has grown along with that of the resort.

A few steps off Paseo de Ixtapa across from the Plaza Ixtapa, **Villa Sakura** is a little bit of Japan transplanted to Mexico's Pacific coast. (Be sure while you're here to stroll through the small Japanese garden outside.) Waitresses in kimonos serve delicious Japanese dishes, including tempura, sushi, *yakimeshi,* and a number prepared *teppanyaki*-style at your table. Tel: (753) 3-0272.

The hacienda-style **Lighthouse** boasts a nautical decor, a lovely flower garden, and the refined atmosphere of a stately home. Meat and fish dishes are its specialties, and after dinner you can climb to the top of the "lighthouse" for a panoramic view of Ixtapa and the bay. Tel: (753) 3-1190.

Getting to **Carlos 'n' Charlie's** is like following the clues in a treasure hunt. (It's hidden away at the far western end of the hotel zone next to the Posada Real.) Once you find it, however, the ambience is pure barefoot vacation, the interior rustic Polynesian. The fun begins as soon as the front door opens around noon and keeps rolling until the wee hours. The beach is a step away, so you can take a dip in the ocean or soak up the sun between courses at lunch, and after dinner you can dance in the tiny raised open-air disco overlooking the beach. Tel: (753) 3-0085.

Coco's Beach Club, tucked between Carlos 'n' Charlie's and the Posada Real, is one of Ixtapa's best-kept secrets. It's the kind of place where bamboo swings substitute for barstools and a secluded pool just over a tiny bridge in the garden outside allows diners to sunbathe as the spirit moves them. Don't be put off by the warehouse-like appearance of the place; once you've eaten here you'll want to come back again and again. Open for lunch and dinner. Tel: (753) 3-1685.

An odd combination of colonial style and neon touches, **Los Mandiles** stands by itself behind the Magic Circus disco. Informality reigns with the beer-drinking crowd at the bar, however, and the Mexican food is wonderful. You can dine either inside or out on the porch. Tel: (753) 3-0379.

Mac's Prime Rib, overlooking the boulevard on the second floor of Los Patios shopping mall, is one of the more popular places in Ixtapa. Owned by a former Mexicana Airlines pilot named McGregor, Mac's offers delicious meals in an attractive open-air setting and has one of the best salad bars in town. Mac's specialty? Prime rib from Montana and Nebraska, of course.

Also in Los Patios, **El Sombrero** is an Ixtapa tradition. The German owners serve up excellent Mexican seafood and meat dishes, and have been packing the place ever since the place opened. The Mexican colonial decor with copper accents provides a pleasant setting for delicious meals. Reservations are suggested in season; Tel: (753) 3-0439. Open for dinner only; closed Sundays.

Standing by itself on Paseo de la Roca, just past the Westin Ixtapa, the **Villa de la Selva** is one of Ixtapa's most elegant restaurants. Tables in this former home of one of Mexico's presidents are placed a discreet distance apart on one of two terraces surrounded by lush vegetation, and soft piano music fills the air. The candlelight, beautiful table settings, and tropical ambience put the Selva a cut above the rest—and the prices don't reflect it. Come here to watch the sunset, stay through dinner, and enjoy one of the most memorable evenings of your life. You'll need a reservation, however; Tel: (753) 3-0362 or 2096.

Although **El Faro** is the only place with a panoramic view of the entire bay, finding the restaurant on your own isn't easy. If you decide to drive yourself, head for the Westin Ixtapa and take the right turn just before the entrance to the hotel. Then climb the hill to the condo development at the top called Club Pacífica. Parking is an adventure because of the steep incline of the parking lot, but the trip is worth it. The dining area opens to the sea breezes, and the spectacular view is accompanied by soothing piano music at dinner. Unfortunately, the quality of the food has much to do with the mood of the chef. For the moment the best way to enjoy the view here is to have a drink at the bar below the dining room. Closed Sundays.

Shopping in Ixtapa

In a very short time Ixtapa has grown into one of the country's best spots for shopping. In fact, so many new malls have gone up in the hotel zone that it's hard to figure out where one ends and the next begins. When they're all completed Ixtapa will have more than 300 stores and boutiques, giving Cancún a run for its shopping money. Resortwear is the purchase of choice here, with handicrafts running a close second. (Surprisingly few stores in Ixtapa carry the usual Mexican souvenirs.)

La Puerta, Ixtapa's original mall, is directly across from the Stouffer Presidente; newer malls have been built around and behind it. To help you sort it all out, here are a few of the shops to look for:

In La Puerta itself, **Galería Florence** has a good selection of paintings and sculpture for serious collectors.

Aca Joe, Ralph Lauren, and Benetton (all stocked with goods made in Mexico), as well as **Luisa Conti**, an Italian designer of outrageous costume jewelry; **African**, selling cotton safari-style clothing; and **Wanda Ameiro**, featuring the stylish designs of a well-known Mexican designer, are all in **Las Fuentes** to the right of La Puerta.

Chiquita Banana, on the first floor of the Los Patios mall, next to Las Fuentes, offers an especially tasteful assortment of decorative and gift items. The terra-cotta–colored **Plaza Ixpamar**, behind Los Patios, houses **El Amanecer**, with its small selection of folk art, and Calvin Klein (for men), among others. Of course, with many more stores in addition to the ones mentioned here, you're sure to discover your own personal favorites.

Nightlife in Ixtapa

Ixtapa is the center of the area's nightlife. Though things wind down earlier here than they do in Acapulco, this former early-to-bed resort has nonetheless become popular with those who love late nights.

One of a chain of well-known discos, **Christine**, at the Krystal, is sensational. The crowd is generally well dressed and the place itself is attractive and exciting. Video screens, flashing lights, balloons, smoke, and other gimmicks are the rule, but they don't overpower conversations. Though the crowd for the most part is under 30, people of all ages feel comfortable here. In other words, Christine is worth the hassle at the door and the hefty cover charge—at least for an evening.

Near the Galería Ixtapa, **Magic Circus**, with its tiered, high-tech, Miami-disco look, also has a sophisticated atmosphere. Though its clientele is not quite as upscale as Christine's, it is every bit as fun. **Le Visage**, almost next door, is even less elaborate than Magic Circus but still a good time. Tables are spread over two levels around the dance floor, and laser lights add sparkle to the occasional theme parties here.

Last but not least, **Euforia** is Ixtapa's newest discotheque. Again, the usual disco works prevail, but the pièce de résistance is a jungle "volcano," its periodic eruptions adding a certain suspense to the evening.

The hotels in Ixtapa occasionally feature international

entertainers and hold Mexican fiesta nights on different days of the week (watch for signs at the various hotels or check at your own). In the off season, live music animates many a lobby bar.

ZIHUATANEJO

Zihuatanejo is long on charm. Today a resort as well as a fishing village, the town dates back to the 1500s, when it was an important center for New Spain's trade with the Far East. (In Nahuatl *Zihuatan* means the "place of the women"; it is believed the Cuitlalteca tribe that lived here was ruled by matriarchs.) Until Ixtapa came along, however, Zihuatanejo was little more than a remote haven for adventurous budget travellers who loved the barefoot lifestyle it had to offer. Although it now serves as Ixtapa's commercial center and has a resident population of more than 30,000, Zihuatanejo has managed to hold on to its charm and small-town ambience.

The town's hotels, restaurants, and shops line cobblestone streets and alleyways. It's both easy and rewarding to spend a couple of days exploring Zihuatanejo—and you'll never have to dress in more than cutoffs and a tee-shirt to do it.

Scenic scalloped bays and inlets—some backed by hills and cliffs—link Zihuatanejo's three beautiful but very different beaches, all ringing the bay to the east and south of town (there is also a beach with a delightful seaside promenade in front of town). **Playa La Madera**, closest to town, is small and flat. There isn't much to see or do here, but one of the town's coziest hotels, the Villas Miramar, is a few minutes' walk down the beach.

Up and over the hill, a ten-minute ride from La Madera, stretches **Playa La Ropa**, perhaps the area's most beautiful beach and a barefoot kind of place where celebrities come to get away from it all. La Ropa is lined with small hotels and bungalows, including the Villa del Sol and Fiesta Mexicana, about halfway down the beach. (In front of the Villa del Sol you can arrange your water-sport activities, especially water skiing.) **La Gaviota** beach club at the end of La Ropa is a great place to swim and grab a bite to eat.

Beyond La Ropa, **Playa Las Gatas** can be reached by a rocky path from La Ropa or by launch from the town pier. Legend has it that this was once the private bathing place of a Tarascan Indian princess. Today it's the most undeveloped beach of the three, though there are a handful of simple restaurants as well as a place to rent snorkel and diving equipment.

Staying in Zihuatanejo

Puerto Mío, overlooking the Zihuatanejo marina, is on the far side of the small bridge at the western end of the town's *malecón* (just past the Hotel Tres Marías), a ten-minute walk around the bay from downtown Zihuatanejo. Everything about this place is intimate and tasteful. Most of its rooms and suites have a view of the bay, the tiled bathrooms are cool and pretty, and the tiny dining room and large bar face a rocky mite-sized beach. A small nightclub up the hill from the main building and a mini-marina just outside the entrance complete the scene.

The **Villas Miramar** is a small, colonial-style accommodation with a few charming rooms surrounding a small pool and a couple of additional suites across the street on Playa La Madera. The guest-rooms have vaulted ceilings with fans, and the toilets and stand-up marble showers are in separate rooms. Clean, small, and friendly, the Villas Miramar is favored by seasoned resort-goers, so be sure to reserve well in advance.

La Casa Que Canta is an 18-suite hotel on a cliff at the town end of Play La Ropa, near the spot where La Ropa meets La Madera. The hotel's peaceful ambience (children under 14 are not permitted) and beautiful setting more than compensate for its location off the beach. The furnishings in the terra-cotta–colored suites (which are linked by winding paths) are handmade in the state of Michoacán; some are replicas of Frida Kahlo's furniture. Two pools sit on different levels down the hill, and a meandering path leads to the beach and **La Sirena Que Canta**, a small restaurant with a popular sister establishment on the town *malecón*.

The **Fiesta Mexicana**, a small property with 57 rooms and three suites, is located about halfway down Playa La Ropa—in fact, its dining area is literally one step from the sand. The all-white rooms have beds with mosquito netting, and the tiled bathrooms in the suites come with Jacuzzis. Although the entire property could use some refurbishing, the Fiesta Mexicana still offers good value for the money.

Also some distance from town on Playa La Ropa, the **Villa del Sol** rates as one of Mexico's most charming small hotels and just one of two in the country to be awarded membership in the Relais & Châteaux organization. Built and run by Helmut Leins, a German engineer who came to Zihuatanejo more than 20 years ago, the Villa del Sol is marked by a heady combination of tropical opulence and European panache. Royalty, statesmen, and celebrities from around the world are among the guests who enjoy the hotel's spacious, split-level rooms and famous dining room. The hotel's Bar Orlando, named after the bartender, is a popular watering hole for guests and non-guests alike.

Guests staying at the Villa de Sol may want to rent a car to get to and from town; otherwise, the front desk will be happy to call a cab for you. (Sometimes cabs line up at the taxi stand on the corner to your left as you leave the hotel.) Many guests book their favorite rooms for the following year as they leave. Those who want to settle down here can buy one of the few condominiums in front of the hotel. Children are not permitted between November 14 and April 30.

Near La Ropa, a collection of simple bungalows known as **Las Urracas** sits a few steps from the beach, shaded by lush foliage. The problem here is finding the owner. Once you do, you're "in" forever, but whether you will is anybody's guess. We leave you on your own. Tel: (753) 4-2052.

Dining in Zihuatanejo

Coconuts, in town at Pasaje Agustín Ramírez 1, is the essence of Zihua. Visitors like it and locals love it—the bar is a favorite hangout. If you want to find out who's in town and what they're doing, this is the place. Take time for a drink at the bar and then move over to a table under the stars (most of the restaurants in Zihuatanejo are open-air). You'll find as much company as you want here, or you can have a quiet, intimate dinner. Vegetarian and Continental dishes comprise the bulk of the menu, and reservations are advised, especially if you plan on dining late; Tel: (753) 4-2518.

The restaurant at the **Villa del Sol** is open to the public. Under a large palapa and almost on the sand, it is especially lovely at dinnertime, when soft music and the murmur of waves accompany your meal. You'll want to reserve ahead, however (ask for a table on one of the lower levels of the dining room), especially on Fridays, when their Mexican fiesta night draws people from miles around; Tel: (753) 4-2239.

There are, in addition, two pretty, informal restaurants on the hill between Playas La Madera and La Ropa, both with views of the bay. The **Bay Club** offers soft jazz in an outside patio/bar, as well as a Continental menu and soft candlelight in an upstairs dining room. The Polynesian-style **Kon-Tiki**, a little farther up the hill, has lots of bamboo and rattan, a menu featuring Mexican and international cuisine (as well as what many locals claim is the best pizza in town), and a spectacular view of the bay. It's also the place to go if you need a quick fix of televised sports from the States.

Other, less formal restaurants worth a try downtown include **El Sombrero**, **La Bocana** (a family-style place popular with local businessmen), and **La Casita**. **La Sirena Gorda** and **Casa Elvira**, on the *malecón*, are good places to watch passersby any time of day.

Downtown Zihuatanejo

Downtown Zihuatanejo has its share of funky stores, which slowly are being upgraded. You'll find an open-air souvenir market in front of the cathedral; **El Jumil**, on the *malecón*, with an excellent selection of exotic masks; and **La Zapoteca**, offering a wide array of textiles from Oaxaca. **Coco Cabaña**, at the corner of Guerrero and Alvarez, past Coconuts, has the best selection of folk art in town.

The **Museo Arqueológico de la Costa Grande**, at the end of the *malecón*, houses a small, private collection of pre-Columbian artifacts in a charming stone building by the sea. It is worth a visit, if only to see the building and watch the sunset from the patio.

Excursions from Ixtapa/Zihuatanejo

You can sail away aboard the 36-foot catamaran *Tequila* for a three-hour cruise of Zihuatanejo Bay (twice daily, November to May), with stops for swimming and snorkeling. The boat leaves from Playa Quieta, in front of Club Med in Ixtapa, at 11:00 A.M. and again at 5:00 P.M. To reserve, Tel: (753) 3-0007.

Excursions to **Isla Ixtapa** leave from Playa Quieta at 10:00 A.M. and return at 3:00 P.M., and include a seafood lunch, snorkeling, and swimming. Once there, you can follow the path to the other side of the island, where you can sun and swim in front of the island's only restaurant. The cost is approximately $16. Ferryboats also operate from Playa Quieta; the round-trip fare is approximately $4.

A coastal tour (offered by almost every travel agency in town) takes you to **Agua de Correa**, a typical fishing village untouched by time, and **Barra de Potosí**, a haven for birdwatchers, with a stop along the way for lunch and swimming. Coconut, mango, papaya, and lemon plantations line the road en route. Expect to pay about $26 per person.

All cruises and tours can be booked at your hotel, or with a local travel agent such as **Expoviajes de Ixtapa** (Tel: 753/3-0442) in advance.

GETTING AROUND

Mexicana offers daily flights from Los Angeles to Ixtapa via Guadalajara (no change of planes) and from San Francisco three times a week, also via Guadalajara. Aeroméxico flies from New York City's J.F.K. airport daily, with a change of planes in Mexico City, and three times a week from Houston with a stop in Mexico City but no change of planes. Delta offers nonstop flights from Los Angeles three times a week, and America West flies from Phoenix with connections in Mexico City. The flying time from Mexico City to the Zihuatanejo airport is approximately 50 minutes.

Budget, Dollar, Fast (Jeeps), and Hertz all have desks at the airport.

The cost of a *combi* from the airport to the hotels in Ixtapa and Zihuatanejo is about $7 per person. Don't buy a round-trip ticket, however. Taking a regular taxi back to the airport will gain you some sun time.

You can drive to Zihuatanejo from Acapulco in about 3½ hours, with two stops for security checks along the way. The bus trip takes 4 to 5 hours. Estrella de Oro (Tel: 753/4-2290 or 4-3802) and Estrella Blanca (Tel: 753/4-3477 or 4-3478) are the first-class lines.

It's about an 8-hour drive to Mexico City. (The best route follows Highway 200 along the coast to Acapulco, and then inland from there.) The bus to the capital takes 12 hours.

With a little effort you can walk just about everywhere in the Ixtapa hotel zone; buses make the run from the zone to downtown Zihuatanejo, with stops outside most hotels, but there is no set schedule.

Taxis are the easiest way to get around, and the major hotels have cabs waiting outside. The taxi stand in Zihuatanejo is in front of the Canaima restaurant on Calle Juan Alvarez, which runs parallel to the *malecón*.

If you decide to spend the day at Playas La Ropa or La Madera, ask your cab driver to come back for you at an appointed time; or walk to the taxi stand behind the Fiesta Mexicana. Don't count on finding a cab during the siesta (between 2:00 and 4:00 P.M.) or after 9:00 P.M.

If you rent a car for the day, be sure to visit the opposite ends of the resort—Las Cuatas and Playa Quieta to the west of the Ixtapa hotel zone and La Ropa to the east of Zihuatanejo. The road from the Bay Club to La Ropa is one of the area's most scenic drives.

—*Susan Wagner*

ACCOMMODATIONS REFERENCE

The rates given below are projections *for December 1992 through Easter 1993. Unless otherwise indicated, rates are for double rooms, double occupancy; the 10 percent VAT has been added. As rates are subject to change, it's a good idea to double-check before booking. Ixtapa/Zihuatanejo is in the central standard time zone; the telephone area code is 753.*

▶ **La Casa Que Canta.** Camino Escénico a la Playa La Ropa s/n, **Zihuatanejo**, Guerrero 40880. Tel: 4-2722; Fax: 4-2006. $170.

▶ **Dorado Pacífico.** P.O. Box 15, Paseo de Ixtapa, **Ixtapa**, Guerrero 40880. Tel: 3-2025; Fax: 3-0126; in the U.S. and Canada, Tel: (800) 44-UTELL; Fax: (402) 398-5484. $143–$165.

▶ **Fiesta Mexicana.** Playa La Ropa, **Zihuatanejo**, Guerrero 40880. Tel and Fax: 4-3776. $68.

▶ **Ixtapa Sheraton.** Paseo de Ixtapa, **Ixtapa**, Guerrero 40880. Tel: 3-1858; Fax: 3-2438; in the U.S. and Canada, Tel: (800) 325-3535. $121–$154.

▶ **Krystal Ixtapa.** Paseo de Ixtapa, **Ixtapa**, Guerrero 40880. Tel: 3-0333; Fax: 3-0216; in the U.S. and Canada, Tel: (800) 231-9860. $143–$220.

▶ **Omni Ixtapa.** Paseo de Ixtapa 5A, **Ixtapa**, Guerrero 40880. Tel: 3-0003; Fax: 3-1555; in the U.S. and Canada, Tel: (800) 44-UTELL. $214.

▶ **Puerto Mío.** Paseo del Morro 5, **Zihuatanejo**, Guerrero 40880. Tel: 4-3624; Fax: 4-2048. $185–$195.

▶ **Villa del Sol.** P.O. Box 84, Playa La Ropa, **Zihuatanejo**, Guerrero 40880. Tel: 4-2239; Fax: 4-2758; in the U.S., Tel: (800) 223-6510; in Canada, Tel: (800) 424-5500. $170–$242 (includes breakfast and dinner).

▶ **Villas Miramar.** P.O. Box 211, Playa La Ropa, **Zihuatanejo**, Guerrero 40880. Tel: 4-2106; Fax: 4-2149. $71–$81.

▶ **Westin Resort Ixtapa.** P.O. Box 97, Playa Vista Hermosa, **Ixtapa**, Guerrero 40880. Tel: 3-2121; Fax: 3-0751; in the U.S. and Canada, Tel: (800) 228-3000. $170.

ACAPULCO

Acapulco is still Mexico's most glamorous resort; its special brand of outrageous, unabashed fun is unlike anything you'll find elsewhere. Other resorts may have scenic beauty and deluxe facilities, but it is the people of Acapulco, who go out of their way to make sure every visitor has a good time, that sets it apart. While daytime here is glorious—there are 360 days of sunshine every year—it is the nightlife that is truly legendary. No one ever asks what you did during the day, but seemingly everyone will exhibit an interest in what you did—or are going to do—after dark.

Despite the fact that the good times have been rolling since the 1950s, when the highway down from Mexico City opened and international flights began to arrive, what is now a third generation of waiters, boat boys, car attendants, and so on does not seem to have tired of the merriment.

Likewise, rumors of its imminent demise owing to pollution and a plague of itinerant vendors have proved to be premature. Well aware of the tough competition and fickle loyalties of the travelling public, Acapulco's city fathers initiated a cleanup campaign that continues to work. City streets and public buses are swept daily; the waters of the bay are cleaner than they have been in years (growing pelican and whale populations are taken as signs of improving ecological health); and vendors have been legislated off the beaches and relocated in sidewalk markets.

At the same time, Acapulco has been accused of welcoming only the young. The accusation is unjust. Anyone can have the time of his or her life here, whether the goal is to party or simply to relax. The trick is in knowing what you want and where to find it. Ninety-nine percent of the time Acapulco is the one Mexican resort that will have it.

MAJOR INTEREST

Large-resort variety of activity
Legendary nightlife
Shopping, especially for resortwear and handicrafts
Cliff divers at La Quebrada
Sunsets and laid-back lifestyle at Pie de la Cuesta and Laguna de Coyuca

Acknowledged as one of the world's most beautiful bays, the Bahía de Acapulco has been compared with that of Rio de Janeiro, and it's easy to see why. The first glimpse of it, at Puerto Marqués as you come into town from the airport, never fails to take your breath away, regardless of how many times you've seen it.

The famous beaches ringing this beautiful bay come in all shapes and sizes, with rough or gentle waves, palapas or palm trees, utter seclusion or all the action you could want. Finding one that suits your own particular style is easy. The beaches between the El Presidente and Acapulco Plaza hotels, as well as Playa Caleta and Playa Caletilla in Old Acapulco, are the most congested and lively. The rest are

To Ixtapa/Zihuatanejo

Laguna de Coyuca

■ Hotel Ukae Kim
● **Pie de la Cuesta**

Playa Pie de la Cuesta

N

200 CALZADA PIE DE LA CUESTA

Mercado de Artisanias

EJIDO

Radisson Paraiso Acapulco

Fuerte de San Diego

DOWNTOWN ACAPULCO — zocalo

La Quebrada

Playa Hornos

Pier

COSTERA

Bullring
Plaza Caletilla

Playa Caletilla

Playa Caleta

Isla La Roqueta

PACIFIC OCEAN

more tranquil and perfect for relaxing. No matter which you choose, however, you can count on the sun being strong; sunbathers should proceed with caution and be sure to use double doses of sunscreen.

For all the fun available here, those who seek a vacation far from the madding crowds can have it. If this is what you have in mind, rent a private villa in the posh Las Brisas residential section or stay at Las Casas de Villa Vera, on the grounds of the Villa Vera Hotel & Racquet Club. If you want serious privacy at more reasonable prices, you can stay up in Old Acapulco or at the Hotel Ukae Kim, in Pie de la Cuesta, and sun at places like Beto's Beach Club at Barra Vieja, off the airport road before it starts to climb Las Brisas hill.

In addition to being Mexico's most glamorous resort, Acapulco is also one of its largest cities, with a year-round population approaching two million people, and boasts one of its deepest harbors. As a central cog in Spain's Mexico–Philippines trade route for almost 300 years, it has always been an important port. The Spanish galleons have given way to luxury cruise ships, but the area near the port facilities is still its commercial center (though it looks like a seedy tropical town). Fishermen mend nets on the beach and head out at dawn, and the same tacky souvenirs that were the resort's original take-home treasures are still sold at street stalls near the zócalo.

Great weather is Acapulco's ace in the hole. Sunshine is more dependable here than at the other resorts, and the average annual temperature is 80° F. In fact, only the humidity varies noticeably from one season to the next. Locals consider it cold when they have to wear long-sleeved cotton shirts, and no one would be caught dead in a jacket, tie, or socks unless he were heading for a formal private party or one of the top hotel restaurants.

"The Season" runs from the middle of December to Easter (when the humidity is usually at its yearly low). But even in the rainy season—May to October—showers are short and usually fall at night; the foliage is at its most glorious then as well. Prices for everything go down after Easter, but the same kinds of fun and activities prevail year-round. At the end of May an international music festival draws artists and spectators from around the world. The only time things might slow down is late September or early October, when improvements are made in anticipation of the coming season, but this pause is imperceptible to most visitors.

Daily schedules follow those of most tropical places. If you want to conduct serious business, plan on doing it between

10:00 A.M. and 1:00 P.M. Lunch is eaten between 2:00 and 5:00 P.M., and dinner usually begins around 9:00 P.M., unless you're going to a private home, in which case cocktails normally are served around 10:00 and dinner at midnight. Discos are liveliest between midnight and 2:00 A.M. With this kind of schedule, it's worth resetting your internal clock to take advantage of it all.

Gourmet dining à la Paris or New York—or even Mexico City—is *not* an Acapulco trademark. If you like delicate food with intricate sauces, you won't find it here—or in any Mexican resort, for that matter. The best entrées are generally simple seafood and meat dishes with fresh tropical fruit for dessert. So unless you're dying for French, German, Italian, Japanese, Chinese, or Thai food, all of which can be found in Acapulco, when you select a restaurant you'll really be choosing an atmosphere to suit your mood.

When it's time to get ready for dinner, remember that in matters of dress Acapulco is one of the most relaxed places in the civilized world. You can wear a ballgown to breakfast, stay in your bathing suit until way past midnight, or walk around in an outrageous costume and no one will bat an eyelash. Anything goes, as long as you make an attempt to cover the important places. Well-put-together resortwear will get you in anywhere; the flashier it is, the faster you'll be accepted.

Finally, it won't take long to discover that Acapulco is a place where you can shop until 4:00 A.M. (Many discos and some restaurants even have stores where you can shop until dawn.) Competition from resorts such as Ixtapa and Cancún has forced retailers to upgrade both the merchandise sold here as well as the stores in which it is displayed. Acapulco seems to have risen to the challenge, and malls with good shops—the sparkling, air-conditioned Plaza Bahía is one example—are springing up all over town. The best buys are resortwear, handicrafts, and decorative items.

Around in Acapulco

A result of no conscious plan, Acapulco has developed into one pleasurable area after another.

The Acapulco Princess and Pierre Marqués hotels are at the center of the action in the area lying between the airport and the bottom of the hill where Las Brisas presides. Travelling along this road, called the Carretera Escénica, is like reading a guidebook, with billboards announcing many of the most popular shops, hotels, and restaurants in Acapulco.

At the moment, the Las Brisas hill is the fastest developing area of Acapulco, with a handful of new restaurants and an opulent disco having opened in the last few years. As a result, those renting or residing in the neighborhood or staying at the Westin Las Brisas no longer have to go into town to dine or dance.

"The Strip" begins on the far side of the hill at the naval base and Hyatt Regency, and extends around the bay to Papagayo Park. This is where you'll find the lion's share of malls, shops, restaurants, bars, and discos, with the section between the naval base and the Diana traffic circle being the liveliest (the stretch west from the Diana traffic circle to Papagayo Park runs a close second). The greatest concentration of good stores is found on the Strip between El Presidente hotel and Plaza Bahía mall, and a string of great seaside restaurants begins just past Sanborn's, a drugstore/cafeteria near the Presidente, and extends west to the traffic circle itself.

Things settle down a bit between the underpass to the park and town. The relatively tranquil old part of town, which first attracted visitors here, extends from and includes Isla La Roqueta, Playa Caleta and Playa Caletilla, the yacht club, and the bull ring.

Pie de la Cuesta, a beautiful, unspoiled stretch of beach near what used to be the airport, and Laguna de Coyuca are a 15-minute drive north and west of the old town over a winding and spectacular cliffside road.

From the Airport to the Puerto Marqués Turnoff

There's not much of interest along the stretch of pancake-flat highway that leads from the airport to the coast road. (Most of the construction along the road consists of home sites, condos, and time-share units. Punta Diamante, a huge resort complex yet to be completed, lies between Puerto Marqués and the Princess.) Not much, that is, unless you're staying at the Acapulco Princess or Pierre Marqués hotels, or if you have a tee time at one of the two championship 18-hole golf courses that lie between them.

Many people who stay at the **Acapulco Princess** never venture off the premises. Built to resemble an Aztec pyramid, this bustling self-contained resort offers its guests an air-conditioned shopping mall, fresh- and salt-water pools, a broad beach (unsafe for anything but wading, unfortunately), horseback riding, several excellent restaurants (including gourmet **Le Gourmet**), and a disco. With more than 1,000 rooms, it's also one of the largest hotels in the country.

You may bump into conventioneers with name tags on their bathing suits, but it's still possible to find a quiet corner here.

The Princess is typical of what makes Acapulco hotels different from others around the country. Most of the rooms are more spacious, the public areas larger, the pool areas bigger and more lavishly landscaped, and the range of services and facilities available more extensive than what you'll find in resort hotels elsewhere.

The **Hotel Pierre Marqués Princess**, its sister establishment "next door," has a more laid-back atmosphere than its much larger neighbor. The rooms and suites at the Pierre Marqués are linked by sprawling green lawns and peaceful gardens, and you can sun at either of its two pools or on its beautiful beach (part of the longest beach in Acapulco). When you're ready for a little action, just hop the shuttle bus over to the Princess; guests at both hotels may charge meals and drinks in either to their rooms.

As the coast road begins to climb west toward Las Brisas you'll get a glimpse of tiny **Puerto Marqués**, where pirates once hid from Spanish warships. Today the relatively undeveloped beach here is usually crowded with Mexican budget vacationers swimming or floating around the quiet bay in an inner tube or on a Sunfish. Spending a day away from other gringos can be a refreshing change of pace, but you might want to avoid it on Sundays (too crowded) and you should be prepared for the swarms of kids who try to hustle business (they're on commission) for the beachside restaurants. Those who like to play the "I-was-there-when" game had better check out Puerto Marqués soon, because it, too, is slated for serious development in the near future.

The Hill Between Las Brisas and the Hyatt Regency

This is one of the hottest areas in Acapulco today, and every time you look it seems as if there is something new to see and do here. Restaurants, shops, discos, even a new tennis club—all have been built within the last few years. And no wonder: The views of the bay are spectacular, and Las Brisas residents, though they usually entertain among themselves and seldom leave their enclave, are a natural target for ambitious entrepreneurs. This new crop of pleasurable distractions promises to restore some of Acapulco's original glamour, and at the same time get the really upscale crowd to leave their villas and enjoy Acapulco by night again.

Although you'll need patience and sometimes will have to bite your tongue over brusque treatment at the door, you'll probably be glad you dined at **Madeiras**. Their policy is "reservations only," however, and they're busy enough to enforce it. (In fact, those who want to be sure of getting a reservation often call from home before getting on the plane.)

Once you're in, however, dining here can be an especially pleasant experience, particularly if you reserve a table by the railing overlooking the bay. (Seating is on several levels, all open-air.) The menu, primarily Mexican nouvelle cuisine, changes frequently according to what's fresh at the market, and the four-course meals are prix fixe. There are usually several seatings each evening; if you opt for the later one at 9:30, you'll arrive at your favorite disco just as things are starting to heat up. Tel: (74) 84-4378.

Miramar, a bigger place in nearby La Vista mall, offers the same views of the bay as those from Madeiras. A slightly older crowd congregates here, which probably explains why the atmosphere in its open-air dining room is more formal. Give yourself time to have a drink in the bar before you head downstairs for dinner. Although every table has a view, ask for one by the railing when you reserve; Tel: (74) 84-7874.

Mr. Frog's, also in La Vista, is a cool, moderately priced lunchtime getaway with a fine view, and an especially pleasant and informal place for dinner.

After dinner you might slip over to **Pepe's** cozy piano bar and sing along or grab the mike and belt out a number yourself. Pepe Valle, one of Acapulco's most popular restaurateurs, has put together a winning combination, with a bar downstairs overlooking the bay and a billiards room upstairs.

Extravaganzza is impossible to miss; in fact, the neon lights on its façade illuminate the entire hillside. Owned by Acapulco's disco king, Tony Rullan, this $4 million dazzler is as plush and sophisticated as they come, with a dance floor that overlooks the bay, a dramatic marble entrance, and a chic boutique. At $10, the cover charge is higher than at other discos, but the unforgettable experience you'll have here will be worth it.

Fantasy, another dazzling disco, is just down the road from La Vista mall. Floor-to-ceiling picture windows afford revellers a spectacular view of the bay, and confetti, laser light shows, and fireworks are just some of the tricks used to keep the place jumping.

There's a special treat for serious art collectors just up the hill from this cluster of shops, restaurants, and discos. Sculptor Pal Kepenyes has designed a home for himself in which he exhibits his abstract bronzes. The house, a work of art in its own right, with an outdoor sculpture garden and a view that extends to Pie de la Cuesta, has been featured in the pages of *Architectural Digest*. The versatile Kepenyes, who also designs jewelry and objets d'art, can be visited by appointment; Tel: (74) 84-3738 or 4738. It's more than worth the trip; call for directions.

A small all-white charmer with great views of the bay, **Kookaburra** is additional proof of the canny genius of Acapulco restaurateur Carlos Hill, who also owns Hard Times on the Costera. Here, the view serves as the decor, and the informal atmosphere encourages customers to linger. Steaks, seafood, and barbecue are served indoors or out. Tel: (74) 84-4418. The glass walls of air-conditioned **Italianissimo**, right next door, take full advantage of the spectacular view. The food, as you might expect, is Italian, and, as at Kookaburra, the view is what you come for. Tel: (74) 81-1380.

The new multilevel **Casanova**, owned by Mexican Arturo Cordova and his American wife, Pat, has added new style to the area across from the entrance to Las Brisas Resort. In fact, many residents and longtime visitors to Acapulco feel that this is the most elegant restaurant in town. Polished marble floors, exquisite flower arrangements, and tables inside or out on the balcony make dining on the Italian specialties here an unforgettable treat. Reservations two to three days in advance (in season) are advised; Tel: (74) 84-6815.

A longtime favorite and one of the first restaurants in this area, **Los Rancheros** is located down the hill in the direction of the Strip but has the same spectacular view as the more expensive places higher up the hill. It offers standard Mexican fare in an informal setting, but until it gets a new chef you'll be better off sticking to the bar and dining elsewhere.

Everything they say about the **Westin Las Brisas Resort** is true. Perched on the hill overlooking the bay, it has probably entertained more celebrities than any other resort property in the world. It's so exclusive, in fact, that guests have to wait at a reception building for the ubiquitous pink-and-white Jeeps to take them to their rooms. (Jeeps will also take guests to the resort's private beach club, **La Concha**, ten minutes away.) Many of the rooms (called *casitas*, or "little houses") have their own private pool, and the management makes sure each one gets fresh flowers every day. Morning rolls and coffee arrive through an unobtrusive window in one of the walls (so you can sleep as late as you like), and a fruit plate will be waiting in the mini-fridge when you come back after a day in the sun. Little things like this make Las Brisas one of the most relaxing and private resort hotels anywhere. (If you truly want to guarantee your privacy, check to make sure that your pool isn't visible from the *casita* above.)

In keeping with its exclusive character, Las Brisas does not allow non-guests to dine at most of its restaurants (there are five in all). Those who want to get a glimpse of this deluxe property, however, are welcome at their Mexican fiesta night, one of the most colorful events in town; at **El Mexicano**, overlooking the bay; and at La Concha's weekly "lobster night," in the hotel's posh beach club overlooking the ocean.

THE STRIP

The Strip is the heart of Acapulco. About 80 percent of the city's restaurants, discos, and boutiques are on or near it, and anyone who loves being in the middle of the action will want to stay in one of its hotels. Similarly, if you're looking to buy *anything* while you're in Acapulco, chances are you'll be able to find it here—even if it's tucked away among a host of other distractions.

Generally speaking, the Strip is the section of Avenida Costera Miguel Alemán (usually just called the Costera) that stretches along the bay from the naval base and the Hyatt Regency at the foot of Las Brisas hill west to the Radisson Paraíso Acapulco and the underpass at Papagayo Park. The beaches fronting the Strip hop from sunup to sundown, and then the restaurants and discos take over and keep things going until dawn.

Until a few years ago this whole stretch was divided into unmarked pockets of action separated by private homes or empty tracts of land. Now, with breathtaking speed, almost all these homes have been or are being replaced by hotels and malls, and the empty lots are giving way to condos in anticipation of the opening of the new highway to Mexico City.

From the Hyatt Regency to El Presidente

The Hyatt Regency; Chin-Chin and Flash Taco, two lively restaurants; and Baby O, Magic, and the News, three sensa-

tional discos, get the Strip off to a roaring start. All are clustered near the naval base, which is tucked away at the bottom of Las Brisas hill. The base is off limits to all but naval personnel, except when the *Cuauhtémoc,* Mexico's "tall ship," is in port.

The **Hyatt Regency** has a canny combination of qualities that enables it to be all things to all people. Financiers stay here when international bankers' meetings are held in Acapulco, and everybody else likes it because it's recessed from the highway and therefore quieter than some of the other hotels on the Strip. (The hotel grounds do abut the naval base, where maneuvers can get noisy—especially on a Sunday when you're trying to sleep late—so be sure to reserve a room on the beach side of the hotel.) A freshwater pool, a beach with good swimming conditions, and one of Acapulco's better shopping arcades make this a self-contained resort. It also has **La Cascada**, one of the best Mexican restaurants in town. Steaks, crepes, and flaming desserts are the specialties, and some form of live Mexican music as well as a friendly baby burro are usually on hand to keep things interesting. Tel: (74) 84-2888.

Chin-Chin, just a few minutes from the Hyatt, is an informal restaurant that serves light meals and snacks between rounds of backgammon or Loteria, a Mexican bingo game played with picture cards. Across the courtyard, **Flash Taco** is a sleek new taco place with an Art Deco look. Diners here have great views of the Baby O disco crowd across the street.

Acapulco disco-goers are accustomed to checking out two or three spots a night, and **Baby O** is always one of them. In fact, disco diehards invariably end up here to let their hair down after a warmup at, say, Extravaganzza. As a result, there's usually a line at the door. The choice tables are on the dance-floor level, and of those the choicest are the banquettes against the wall and the "caves" at each side of the dance floor. Squeezing as many people as possible into a banquette or "cave" is the modus operandi, so don't wear anything you can't afford to wrinkle. Videos, electronic message boards, and other effects are part of every evening. If you happen to be in Acapulco at the end of February or beginning of March when their Pajama Party is held, don't miss it (even if you have to buy a pair of pajamas at the door).

The **News**, just beyond the Hyatt Regency, has managed to do something different. While other discos look small, this one is large and prides itself on its innovative special parties and events. On a good night the News packs in some 2,000 souls, but even then there's plenty of room for everybody. Two giant bars, a restaurant, and a "Champagne Room" (you have to buy three bottles of domestic champagne-style wine or one imported bottle in order to sit here) are part of the fun.

The old Magic, across the Costera and a little bit closer to town, has been redecorated and renamed **Pasha**, after the popular Madrid disco. Waterfalls and a simulated snowstorm are the highlights in this multilevel place with two dance floors and numerous snack bars.

Cocula, down the Costera a bit in the direction of town at the sign of the sombrero, offers informal Mexican dining at its best. Have a drink in the unobtrusive air-conditioned bar under the steps (a secret the locals seldom reveal) while you wait for a table under the stars. The only view is of traffic on the Costera, but the do-it-yourself chicken and beef taco plates and the Bohemia beer more than compensate. Breakfast served at tables shaded by soaring palm trees is also lovely. Tel: (74) 84-5079.

The **Hotel La Palapa**, a soaring structure on the beach behind the CiCi amusement park, is favored by Canadians and groups, and has nothing but small—truly small—suites. (It does have one of the best beauty salons in town for manicures and pedicures, however.) The pool is a few steps from the ocean, and the hotel itself offers tranquillity just off the beaten path at reasonable rates. For those who don't mind getting their elegance elsewhere, La Palapa is a good bet.

The dance floor of **Bananas Ranas**, a disco/snack bar on the Costera in front of the Hotel La Palapa, is in a freight car that used to do service on the Acapulco–Iquala line. Also on the Costera, **CiCi**, a water-oriented park for children, is enclosed by a wall painted with blue-and-white waves. Inside you'll find a pool with a wave-making machine, water slides, and a dolphin show. The **Convention Center** across the way is equipped to accommodate everything from operas to rock concerts; unfortunately, its beautiful gardens and buildings are rarely used. Watch the marquee for special performances.

A roomy **Hard Rock Café** has opened in the colonial-style Antigua mall, next to the CiCi amusement park (just look for the giant guitar). Inside, dark wood paneling, checked tablecloths, and the familiar Hard Rock menu make you feel as if you're in your favorite hamburger joint back home. Loud, live rock music at night inhibits conversation, but it does keep the dance floor energized.

Esteban, a local designer, sells California-style evening clothes and avant-garde streetwear in a pretty shop with a garden about five blocks farther west in the direction of town. He also has an art gallery next door.

The **Acapulco Malibu Hotel**, another of the town's best-kept secrets, is across from the Centro Deportivo on a nice stretch of beach. The Malibu is a time-share hotel; that is, it rents rooms when their individual owners aren't in residence. One of the very few small hotels on the Strip, it was built by a Texas millionaire and his partners, who intended it to be a chic hideaway in the midst of Acapulco's high-rise hotels and condominiums. The rooms are large and octagonal, and most balconies have a view of the ocean. With a cozy, family-style atmosphere and a friendly staff that will make you feel at home the moment you walk in the door, the Malibu is a refreshing change of pace from the larger, more impersonal hotels in town.

Tabasco Beach, a beachfront restaurant outside the Acapulco Malibu, is a pleasant spot for a quick breakfast, lunch, or drink; the tiny bar is also one of the better places in town from which to watch the sunset, though it is in need of some refurbishing. **Anna's**, a boutique featuring trendy original designs, is a few doors down, and **Fiorucci**, with its selection of Mexican-made Italian styles, is across the street.

La Mansión, a two-story hacienda-style steakhouse about ten doors down from the Acapulco Malibu, has a sophisticated urban decor that reflects the fact it's part of a Mexico City chain. Prime cuts of beef are cooked at your table; it's expensive but worth it. Tel: (74) 81-0796.

Behind the Pizza Hut you'll find the **Gallery**, with the most opulent transvestite show in town, as well as **Alfredo's Tennis Club** and **Tiffany's Tennis Club**, where anyone may play.

The **Villa Vera Hotel & Racquet Club** is the snazziest hotel on or near the Strip, and the sole small deluxe hotel in town. Only minutes inland from the Costera, it resembles a bit of Beverly Hills transplanted to Acapulco. The clientele ranges from serious tennis players (the tennis facilities are easily the best in town) to the well-heeled set seeking plush accommodations and privacy in a beautiful setting far from the crowds—but not so far that they can't partake of the action on the Costera. Every one of the 90 rooms is different (some have their own pools and many have large tiled tubs); the dining room (Tel: 74/ 84-0333), with superb food and grand views of the bay, is one of Acapulco's most popular places for breakfast, lunch, or dinner; and the main pool is a favorite spot for the trendy singles crowd (it offered the first swim-up bar in the country). Water-sports lovers can use the facilities at the Maralisa, the Villa Vera's charming sister hotel down on the beach, with a breezy, pleasant seaside restaurant of its own.

The hotel—which now includes Las Casas de Villa Vera,

private homes on the premises available to rent—is owned by a young American woman who prides herself on running a first-class operation. Attention to detail is evident in everything, and guests are carefully looked after. The fact that everything—including the guests (who apparently come here *after* going through a weight-loss program back home)—is easy on the eyes and ultra-luxurious makes it that much more appealing. As a result, a good percentage of the guests return year after year.

At the top of the same hill, on the Carretera Panorámica, the Italian palazzo–style **El Campanario** offers Continental cuisine as well as 180-degree views of the bay and the city lights. It's a wonderful place for a drink, but when the restaurant gets crowded diners may have to call on their reserves of patience. By day, it's an oasis for people who like to relax around the pretty pool below the restaurant. The light lunch fare is tasty and the spectacular location seemingly puts you miles above the hustle and bustle of the Strip. Tel: (74) 84-8830.

From El Presidente to the Diana Traffic Circle

This is Acapulco's epicenter, with the action really picking up as the Costera climbs toward the Presidente and Condesa del Mar hotels. **Rubén Torres**, **Franco's**, and **Dancin'** are just a few of the "name" boutiques crammed in between some of Acapulco's best-known restaurants along this stretch. **Acapulco Joe**'s factory outlet is also in the area, with merchandise from branches around the country sold at discounts of 30 to 50 percent.

Sanborn's, the drugstore/cafeteria that no one seems to be able to do without, is situated at the top of the rise. Only a handful of locals know that the best malted milkshakes in town are served in the downstairs restaurant.

Carlos 'n' Charlie's, the king of Acapulco's racous restaurants, is just across the street from Sanborn's. Unless you're a well-known celebrity, however, you'll probably have to stand in a first-come, first-served line to get in. Of course, that fact doesn't seem to deter anyone, and crowds of all ages and nationalities begin to arrive by car, taxi, and horse-drawn carriage as soon as the door opens at 6:00 P.M. The "Cluck, Moo, and Oink" items on the menu give you some idea of what to expect once you get inside, and waiters' pranks and jokes are an integral part of the total experience. In fact, nothing is serious here except the no-nonsense food. Fair portions of chicken, ribs, and fish are the most popular items, but with all the activity and people-watching going on, few customers pay attention to what they're eating. Stop in at the air-conditioned bar before dinner; chances are you'll stay longer than you planned.

Acapulco Shalom, located a few doors farther down the Costera at the entrance to the Plaza Condesa mall, offers a tasteful selection of silver jewelry and decorative items (which they'll be happy to pack and ship for you), and is a great place for one-stop gift shopping.

The beachfront restaurants that have captured the hearts of Acapulco vacationers for years begin just west of Sanborn's. **Beto's Safari Bar** is popular with beer-drinking youngsters and budget travellers, but the open-air restaurant on the lower deck is another of the less well known delights in town. The prices at the restaurant are moderate and the food decent, and it's hard to resist the romance of a candlelight dinner under the stars with the Bahía de Acapulco just a stone's throw away. Ask for a table near the railing so you can watch the moonlight shimmer on the water.

Beto's, a separate establishment next door, is one of the oldest and best of these beachfront restaurants. Located at the bottom of a staircase leading down from the Costera, it somehow manages to look like the verandah of a private home. There are dining rooms on either side of the stairs and luncheon service under palapas on the sand (most restaurants along this stretch offer food service on the beach). Be sure to try one of the dishes here that are hard to find elsewhere: *quesadillas de cazón* (fried tortillas filled with baby shark meat), *pescado a la Talla* (marinated grilled fish), or red clams. Beto's also has live music for dancing if the spirit moves you. The left side of Beto's beach, **Playa Condesa**, is frequented by the local gay community.

Tables at **Barbas Negras**, an old steakhouse with a new open-air look, offer views of the Costera or the ocean. Their "Hall of Fame" room captures the glamour of Acapulco's highlife with photographs of celebrities who have visited over the years.

Mimi's Chili Saloon (no beach service here) is a powder-blue hoot that promises and delivers dynamite two-for-one strawberry and mango margaritas at happy hour. In fact, everything at Mimi's, from the hot dogs and hamburgers to the potato skins and country-fried chicken, is designed to make you drool. All of which makes it the place to go when you're dying for American-style fast food and don't feel like McDonald's.

There's no restaurant on this planet quite like **Paradise**, a few doors down from Mimi's. One of the pioneers of Acapulco's special tongue-in-cheek style of fun, Paradise is the kind of place where anything can happen at any moment. A woman may find herself attracting admiring wolf whistles one minute, then have a lei of fresh flowers thrown over her head as a chimpanzee puckers up to give her a sloppy kiss the next. The live salsa and rock 'n' roll music gets everyone feeling friendly in a hurry (and out on the dance floor sooner or later), and heaven help you if they find out it's your birthday or anniversary—you just may be picked up, chair and all, and carried off to the bandstand to the great amusement of the other customers. The drinks are big, the palapas keep you cool, and the party lasts well beyond sunset. Hefty portions of lobster, shrimp, beef, and red snapper (*huachinango*) are the specialties of Paradise, and lunch is the busiest time; if a conga line to the beach starts to form, forget your inhibitions and jump in.

Sergio Bustamante, an art gallery a few doors down from Paradise on the opposite side of the street, sells a variety of whimsical papier-mâché animals and other sculpture inspired by that Mexican artist's work. **Martí**, everyone's favorite sporting-goods store, is nearby—look for the larger-than-life statue of an athlete—as are Ralph Lauren Polo (made in Mexico) and the "real" Acapulco Joe.

The Diana (as it is known), where traffic circulates around a fountain topped by a statue of the huntress with her bow, is one of Acapulco's busiest intersections. Highway 95, the road from Mexico City, meets the Costera here, and it's the location of the only big gas station in town. (There are only three gas stations in the entire area: one at the bottom of the hill before the residential neighborhood of Las Brisas; the one here; and a third at the western end of town where the winding road to Pie de la Cuesta begins.)

From the Continental Plaza to the Acapulco Plaza

El Patio, across from the Continental Plaza hotel and west of the Diana, was one of Acapulco's first malls. **Gucci** and **Emil**, the latter a no-nonsense clothing store; **Shanghai**, a Chinese restaurant; and **Victor Salmones**, a sculpture gallery for serious collectors, are just a few of the better establishments along this stretch of the Strip. The **Galería Rudic**, around the corner on Vicente Yañez de Pinzón, is another good gallery, with a fairly extensive selection of paintings and sculpture by a number of Mexico's better-known contemporary artists.

Located just beyond the Continental Plaza hotel, the **Acapulco Plaza**, with more than 1,000 rooms and suites in three towers, a shopping mall with a variety of stores, four tennis courts, and two pools, is the biggest hotel on the Strip. Despite its size, however, the management somehow keeps the service personalized. **Maximilian's** in the hotel, one of two "gourmet" restaurants in Acapulco (the other, Le Gourmet, is in the Acapulco Princess), is the only air-conditioned one on the beach (reservations advised; Tel: 74/85-9050); and **Los Arcos** is one of the few places in town where you can eat Mexican food in an informal, air-conditioned setting. Dark paneled walls and wooden furniture give the place the look of a hacienda, and the make-your-own-taco platter is one of the best buys on the menu. The Oasis health club on the third-floor level of the hotel is just for adults, so you can tan, take a dip in the pool, get a massage, or simply relax in glorious peace and quiet.

While its rooms and suites could use refurbishing, this is still one of Acapulco's top addresses. The rooms in the main tower here are the most convenient: Although the suites in the smaller towers have their own registration desk, they are a considerable distance from the restaurants and the entrance to the hotel's beach (something you'll notice if you leave your sunscreen behind). If you do end up staying in one of the smaller towers, try to avoid the west side of the Catalina Tower—the music from the lobby bar can make taking that all-important siesta a virtual impossibility.

The **Acapulco Plaza Mall** has two floors of good boutiques: **Diva, Mar y Mar** (the big Mar y Mar store is across the street), and **Pasarela** (for glitzy Mexican-style evening clothes and accessories) are a few of the better shops. Pasarela also sells beautiful (but expensive) hand-beaded dresses.

Papacito's Last Call, tucked away in a corner of the mall at street level, is one of a handful of places in Acapulco that can be enjoyed by the late-night crowd that doesn't like discos. The place has a modern look, with sofas where you can lounge and order drinks and snacks, and the Mexican folk art hanging on the walls was clearly chosen by someone with a sense of humor. The frozen margaritas are marvelous and the fajitas superb; the live music lasts until 3:00 A.M.

The Acapulco Plaza also has a sports center where everything from scuba diving to deep-sea fishing excursions can be arranged, and the hotel's beach is one of the best places to try the parasail rides for which Acapulco is famous.

The two-story **Plaza Bahía**, on the Costera a few doors down from the Acapulco Plaza, is the first and only air-conditioned non-hotel mall in town. **Baby O** and **Apasia**, for trendy resortwear and accessories; **Galería 10/10**, an art gallery; and **Bazaar**, which offers a varied assortment of souvenirs and objets d'art, are among the best shops here.

ACAPULCO OFF THE STRIP
The Underpass to Town

After the Radisson Paraíso, which is located a bit to the west of the Acapulco Plaza, the Costera goes underground to accommodate **Papagayo**, a sprawling park with games for children and a cable car that connects it to the beach. The best thing about this piece of prime real estate, however, is the **aviary**, which is a wonderful place to keep cool on a hot day.

Super Super (with everything from shampoo to suntan lotion, food, wine, liquor, and film), Gigante, and Comercial Mexicana, the three best supermarkets in town, are just to the west of the Papagayo underpass and across the street from **Playa Hornos**, a palm-shaded beach beloved by Mexican vacationers, who rent beach chairs nearby and cool off in thatched-roof restaurants such as **Sirocco**.

You'll feel as if you're in France when you step into **Normandie**, on the corner of the Costera and Calle Malespina. This unassuming establishment has a time-tested reputation for excellent food; some even say it serves the best French cuisine in the country. Fresh-from-the-market ingredients become imaginative appetizers and entrées, and the eclectic decor somehow manages to be relaxing. You can choose to dine on the patio or inside in air-conditioned comfort—but only for dinner, and only from December to Easter (it's closed the rest of the year).

The **Mercado Municipal**, five long blocks inland from the Costera, is one of the most colorful open markets in the country. Local residents depend on it for everything from food to magic potions, and strolling through its crowded aisles will give you an idea of what life in this tropical port is like behind all the glitz. The best spot to enter the market and begin your explorations is through the flower section. Ask your taxi driver to leave you at the corner of Ruíz Cortines and Diego Hurtado de Mendoza. If you drive yourself, look for the sign just past the Sol de Acapulco that reads "San Jerónimo, Pie de la Cuesta, Mercado." Turn right and get ready to sit: The narrow street is always congested, especially weekends. Park wherever you can just before Ruíz Cortines, and give the attendant a few pesos to watch your car.

Although not readily apparent, the market *is* divided into sections. If you're looking for something in particular, learn its name in Spanish and ask directions. Handicrafts and souvenirs are in the covered area next to the flower section toward the back. The market, where bargaining is part of the fun, is at its best in November and December, when whimsical Christmas-tree ornaments can be bought for pennies. Saturdays between 10:00 and 11:00 A.M. is prime time throughout the year. If you just want to have a quick look, go on a weekday morning around 10:00 and ask your taxi driver to accompany you inside.

The **Museo Histórico de Acapulco**, in El Fuerte de San Diego, overlooks the Costera from its hill above the cruise-ship pier. Despite its name, which means "place where the reeds were destroyed," Acapulco has had a relatively uneventful history. It became a shipbuilding center and an important port for Spain's Far East trade after the Conquest, and though pirates plundered its shores on occasion, no major war or uprising has ever disturbed the city.

After the Spanish departed in the aftermath of the War of Independence, Acapulco was all but abandoned for the next hundred years. In fact, it was only after the first road from Mexico City was pushed over the Sierra Madre del Sur in 1927 that Acapulco began to awaken. Highway 95, the first superhighway, was inaugurated in 1955, but the real fun began in 1964, when direct international flights began to bring a host of celebrities and jet-setters into town.

A broad staircase across from the cruise-ship pier leads from the Costera to the museum, where the story of the fort and the town's history are displayed in a series of air-conditioned rooms once used to store ammunition. The clever design (created by experts from the Museum of Anthropology in Mexico City) is in many cases as interesting as the exhibits themselves. And though it only takes a few minutes to see everything, it's well worth a stop. The museum is open from 10:00 A.M. to 6:00 P.M. daily, except Mondays.

Downtown

There are few good reasons for visitors to explore downtown Acapulco. It looks like any tropical port, complete with a zócalo and mandatory bandstand where concerts are held on Sundays; a church (Nuestra Señora de la Soledad) with a charming exterior; and some major banks and stores, including Woolworth's and branches of Sanborn's and Emil. If you want to change a large amount of currency, you'll save some money by doing it at one of the downtown banks. **Terraza de las Flores**, overlooking the plaza, is the best—and only—German restaurant in town; its red cabbage, schnitzel, sauerkraut, and potatoes are delicious.

The **Mercado de Artesanías**, sometimes called the Flea Market, proffers the typical souvenirs you may already have found along the Costera. It covers several blocks of Calle Velásquez de León, behind the Woolworth's.

Fishermen mend their nets, much as they always have, across from the zócalo at the corner of Costera and Calle Iglesias. You can rent deep-sea fishing boats at Pesca Deportiva, opposite the zócalo next to the *muelle* (municipal pier).

Old Acapulco

Old Acapulco—the peninsular area that includes **Playa Caleta** and **Playa Caletilla**, as well as Isla La Roqueta (see the Excursions section below)—looks much the same today as it did in the days when Acapulco was rehearsing for international stardom. The pier between Caleta and Caletilla is undergoing a restoration; **Magico Mundo Marino**, the new aquarium here, is a wonderful way to spend a day. Besides the exceptionally well done marine-life exhibits, the aquarium has a pool with open and closed water slides for the kids, one of the breeziest restaurants in town, and a beach with good swimming conditions. There is also a concession on hand for jet skis and scuba-diving equipment. Avoid Sundays if you can, but don't miss it.

The aquarium is the departure point for the **Acapulco Zoo**, situated on **Isla La Roqueta**, making it one of the world's only island zoos (launches shuttle back and forth from 10:00 A.M. to 6:00 P.M. daily). Animals are kept in naturalistic state-of-the-art environments, and the many exhibits include a Serpentarium that climbs the slope of a gentle hill to the spot where Nene, a baby giraffe, munches serenely on nearby treetops. Visitors to the zoo can climb down and swim in tiny protected coves, or join the folks on the main beach. The more adventurous follow the mountainous path to Palao (see below under Excursions), a beachfront restaurant on the other side of the island with its own tiny beach.

You'll also find the bull ring, **Plaza Caletilla**, in this part of town. The bravest bulls and greatest bullfights are usually not seen in the tropics, but Plaza Caletilla offers the best of any Mexican resort—largely because it has the largest potential audience. The season runs from December through

Easter, but contests are staged sporadically. Seats by the railing (*barrera*), in the shade, are the best. Tickets can be arranged through your hotel or through any of the travel agencies in town.

In Old Acapulco you can see the world-famous Acapulco *clavadistas* (cliff-divers), men who make daring leaps from a 100-foot-high cliff at **La Quebrada** several times each day—once in the afternoon and two or three times at night. You can watch these spectacular athletes in comfort from the bar at the Hotel Mirador or, for a small fee, from La Perla, its nightclub. Or head for the steps in the cliffside park near the hotel. The "show" is free, but contributions are appreciated when the divers pass the hat. Ask at your hotel or call the Mirador for the times of the performances; Tel: (74) 82-1111.

PIE DE LA CUESTA

Pie de la Cuesta and Laguna de Coyuca are for those who like their scenery without the crowds. The fishing village of Pie de la Cuesta is a great spot to visit on Sundays, and one of the best places to watch the sunset any day of the week.

The area is a scenic 15-minute drive north and west of downtown along Calzada Pie de la Cuesta. There's a turnoff leading to what was once the old airport road—now lined with ramshackle restaurants—after the road comes down out of the hills. If you've come to see the sunset, choose one of the restaurants on the beach side, rent a chair or a hammock, order your coco loco, and get ready for one of the world's finest shows.

The entire area is a world apart from the resort just over the hills to the south. Many children here still get to school by dugout canoe, and in some places at certain times of the year the waterways are made impassable by lily pads. The long, flat stretch of beach is unspoiled and beautiful, but the surf is too strong for swimming.

Laguna de Coyuca, across the street from the beach, is a nature preserve much loved by bird-watchers, fishermen, and filmmakers (*Rambo II* was shot here). It's also a water-skier's idea of heaven and the perfect place to learn how to drop one ski. **Tres Marías** and, especially, **Tres Palmas** are the local cognoscenti's favorite hangouts. Order your lunch when you first arrive and it will be waiting for you after you ski or swim. Whether you waterski or not, be sure to ask one of the boatmen to take you on a tour of the waterways at the end of the lagoon. "Broncos"—small motorboats for one or two—and inner tubes can also be rented.

If you fall in love with the place (a distinct possibility), you can stay overnight at **Ukae Kim**, an attractive and romantic 18-room hotel on the beach side. (If you're only coming out for the day, be sure to arrange with the taxi driver who brings you out to pick you up at an appointed time.) Reserve a room overlooking the ocean; the beds are on raised platforms so you can catch the view. There is also a small restaurant and beach club at Ukae Kim—all far from the crowds; non-guests can use the beach club for a small fee, which also gets you a towel and lounge chair.

NIGHTLIFE IN ACAPULCO

From sassy to sophisticated, Acapulco's legendary nightlife truly offers something for everybody.

You can dine and dance at air-conditioned rooftop restaurants such as **Techo del Mar** in the Fiesta Americana Condesa hotel; **The Windjammer** (La Fragata) in the Radisson Paraíso Acapulco; and, in season, **La Joya** at the Continental Plaza. All of these still have the feeling of days gone by and attract an older crowd that likes dancing cheek to cheek.

Nightclubs such as **Banneret** in the Calinda Acapulco Quality Inn and **Numero Uno** in the Hyatt Regency feature floor shows with big-name entertainers. **El Fuerte**, in front of the Hotel Las Hamacas, on the Strip just before you get to town, is for those who like it spicy and Spanish, flamenco style.

The Convention Center offers the occasional spectacle; watch the marquee outside for upcoming events.

Acapulco's discos rank as one of its leading attractions, and you're definitely missing something if you don't go at least once. They're at their best between 12:30 and 2:00 A.M. on a weekend night. Otherwise, they're open every night of the year from 10:00 P.M. until the last customer goes home. Some discos have big crowds waiting, especially in season, but if you're well dressed and well behaved (and good at staring doormen down) you're likely to get in sooner than the rest. Once you're inside, tip the maître d' or waiter right away to ensure a good table and good service. If you can't get into the disco of your choice, try another one. Extravaganzza, Fantasy, Baby O, and the News are the current favorites, and are discussed above along with others.

SPORTS IN ACAPULCO

Most of the bigger hotels have centers where you can arrange just about every imaginable water sport. In addition, water-skiing boats are available at most every beach, as are parasail rides. Jet skis can be rented by the hour on the beach behind Mimi's Saloon or at the aquarium. The beach behind Mimi's is also the place to rent Broncos (one- or two-person motorboats).

Windsurfers and sailboats can be rented on the beach behind the Hotel Malibu and Diana traffic circle. Scuba-diving and snorkeling excursions can be arranged at **Arnold Brothers** (Tel: 74/82-1877) or **Divers de México** (Tel: 74/82-1398), both on the beach side of the Costera just before town. Surfing is not permitted on the beaches along the Strip, so diehards take their boards out to Playa Revolcadero, south and east of town just before the Acapulco Princess.

Fishing boats can be chartered through your hotel or at **Pesca Deportiva**, across from the zócalo near the municipal pier; Tel: (74) 82-1099. Sailfish, marlin, tuna, mackerel, and snapper are all prize catches in the waters around Acapulco. Divers de México will be happy to arrange a spot for you on a boat shared by others.

The area's two championship 18-hole golf courses are located between the Acapulco Princess and Pierre Marqués hotels; the **Club de Golf Acapulco**, a nine-hole public course, can be found across from the Hotel Elcano. Greens fees at the first two are the equivalent of $64, and tee times should be made at least a day in advance; Tel: (74) 84-3100. Greens fees at the public course are $14. Carts at the first two and caddies at the latter cost about $10.

EXCURSIONS FROM ACAPULCO

The catamaran *Aca Tiki* takes guests on day and sunset cruises of the bay. The boat, which its owners claim is the world's largest sailing catamaran, leaves from the pier near the Fort of San Diego. Reserve in advance to avoid being disappointed; Tel: (74) 84-6140 or 6786. Sunset cruises include drinks (Mexican brands), dinner, and a folkloric show.

Those who want to do it the way the locals do can sail around the bay on the *Fiesta Cabaret* (Tel: 74/83-1550), the *Bonanza* (Tel: 74/83-1803), or the *Hawaiiano* (Tel: 74/82-1217) at rock-bottom prices; each has its own pier past town on the way to Playa Caleta.

Ferryboats take passengers from the Caleta pier to **Isla La Roqueta**, where you can visit the zoo and lunch at **Palao**, on its own tiny bay. Palao serves tasty, simply prepared seafood and meat dishes, occasionally accompanied by marimba music. After lunch you can take a dip or walk through the jungle, with breathtaking views of the ocean along the way. More energetic visitors can climb to the lighthouse. The main beach at La Roqueta, a favorite Sunday excursion for visiting Mexicans, is a ten-minute walk from the restaurant when the boardwalk is in good repair. Otherwise, it's about five minutes by boat.

GETTING AROUND

A number of international carriers link Acapulco to cities in the United States. While many flights are direct, few are nonstop, and often passengers will have to deplane and go through customs in Mexico City. Those carriers that do fly nonstop to Acapulco include Continental, which offers daily flights from its hubs in Newark and Houston, and American and Delta, which offer daily flights to Acapulco from Dallas–Fort Worth and Los Angeles. Aeroméxico (from New York) and Mexicana (from Chicago) offer daily "direct" service to Acapulco, with a stopover in Mexico City for customs. Aeroméxico flies from Houston four times a week with a stopover in Mexico City.

Getting from the Acapulco airport into town is no cup of tea, either. Private taxis are not allowed to pick up passengers at the airport, so unless you want to pay $28 for an airport taxi you're stuck with taking a *combi* or a bus. Your best bet is to call your travel agent or hotel before leaving home and arrange to be picked up by private car. If, on the other hand, you do take a *combi* or bus, buy a one-way ticket: Taxis *are* allowed to take departing guests *to* the airport (the fare is about $13). Watch to make sure your luggage is loaded, but if you're travelling with a companion have him or her get on and claim a seat while you wait. Finally, be prepared to be patient; invariably, the *combi* or bus will make numerous stops before it drops you off. The good news in all this is that the trip in from the airport is scenic. Try to get a seat on the left side of the bus for the best views.

Acapulco is 416 km (258 miles) south of Mexico City. Driving down on the superhighway, Highway 95, a toll road (tolls are minimal), takes about 5 hours. Those who prefer a more scenic, leisurely trip travel the "old road," making stops in Taxco and Cuernavaca. Presently this route takes 7 to 10 hours (depending on traffic), without stops. A new highway that will cut the driving time to the capital to 3½ hours is scheduled to be completed by March 1993.

Buses—Estrella Blanca (the first-class line; Tel: 74/86-3735) and Flecha Roja (Tel: 74/82-0351 or 2184)—operate several runs daily between Acapulco and the D.F. at rock-bottom prices. The trip takes at least 8 hours. If you decide to do it, travel first-class—it's worth it.

Getting around Acapulco itself is a breeze. Taxis are the best choice now that there are parking meters on the Costera. If you choose to drive, you'll have to come back from the beach every hour and plug 1,000 pesos into the meter. If you don't, zealous traffic cops will take your license plate.

Taxis in large numbers cruise the Costera day and night. Fares are set by zone and are usually posted on placards outside hotel lobbies. An average point-to-point fare will cost in the neighborhood of $2 to $5. "Sitios"—those taxis that have paid for the privilege of standing in front of specific hotels—cost a bit more. Rates go up as the night progresses, but are generally far lower than rates back home.

City buses run from downtown to the naval base and beyond, but their schedules are erratic. The large yellow shelters with blue public phones are the stops.

—*Susan Wagner*

ACCOMMODATIONS REFERENCE

The rates given below are projections *for December 1992 through Easter 1993. Unless otherwise indicated, rates are for double rooms, double occupancy; the 10 percent VAT has been added. As rates are subject to change, it's a good idea to double-check before booking. Acapulco is in the central standard time zone; the telephone area code is 74.*

▶ **Acapulco Malibu Hotel.** P.O. Box 582, Avenida Costera Miguel Alemán 20, **Acapulco**, Guerrero 39868. Tel: 84-1070; Fax: 84-0994. $92.

▶ **Acapulco Plaza.** Avenida Costera Miguel Alemán 123, **Acapulco**, Guerrero 39868. Tel: 85-9050; Fax: 85-5493; in the U.S., Tel: (800) 626-0569. $145–$187.

▶ **Acapulco Princess.** P.O. Box 1351, Playa Revolcadero, **Acapulco**, Guerrero 39868. Tel: 84-3100; Fax: 84-8820; in the U.S., Tel: (800) 223-1818; in Ontario, Tel: (800) 268-7140; in the rest of Canada, Tel: (800) 268-7176. $285–$345 (includes breakfast and dinner).

▶ **Hotel La Palapa.** Fragata Yucatán 210, **Acapulco**, Guerrero 39850. Tel: 84-5363; Fax: 84-8399. $94–$120.

▶ **Hotel Pierre Marqués Princess.** P.O. Box 474, **Acapulco**,

Guerrero 39907. Tel: 84-2000; Fax: 84-8554; in the U.S., Tel: (800) 223-1818; in Ontario, Tel: (800) 268-7140; in the rest of Canada, Tel: (800) 268-7176. $205–$275.

▶ **Hyatt Regency**. Avenida Costera Miguel Alemán 1, **Acapulco**, Guerrero 39869. Tel: 84-2888; Fax: 84-3087; in the U.S. and Canada, Tel: (800) 233-1234. $185–$210.

▶ **Ukae Kim**. Pie de la Cuesta, **Acapulco**, Guerrero 39868. In the U.S., Tel: (619) 451-8838; Fax: (619) 673-8210. $75–$85.

▶ **Villa Vera Hotel & Racquet Club**. Lomas del Mar 35, **Acapulco**, Guerrero 39890. Tel: 84-0333; Fax: 84-7479; in the U.S., Tel: (800) 223-6510 or (213) 550-7373; in Canada, Tel: (800) 424-5500. $198–$291; villa with private pool, $435.

PUERTO ESCONDIDO, PUERTO ANGEL, HUATULCO

Isolated from the outside world by the Sierra de Miahuatlán, and overshadowed by such glittering stars of the "Mexican Riviera" as Acapulco, Puerto Vallarta, and Mazatlán, the Costa Oaxaqueña remained a place outside of time well into the 1970s. Like their ancestors before them, the region's Mixtec, Zapotec, and Chatino Indians worried a living from the narrow shelf of land between the mountains and sea, or pulled their harvests from the sea itself. As far as the international jet-set was concerned, Puerto Escondido and Puerto Angel were just names on a map; Huatulco didn't even exist.

For a steady trickle of gringo fishermen and surfers, on the other hand, the region's empty beaches, big waves, and nominal cost of living represented the pot of gold at the end of the rainbow. That accommodations generally ran to palapas and hammocks, and a fancy dinner was considered the day's catch and a couple of *cervezas,* only added to its laid-back appeal.

As international tourism picked up in the latter half of the 1970s, things began to change. Fresh from its success in Cancún, Fonatur, the government agency in charge of tourism, was given the go ahead to develop a state-of-the-art resort complex somewhere along the coast, and eventually settled on the tiny fishing village of Santa Cruz Huatulco. With the paving of Highway 200, the coast road, all the way to the Guatemala border in the early 1980s, the Costa Oaxaqueña was opened to growing numbers of Mexican vacationers, budget travellers, and the RV crowd. The lengthening of the Puerto Escondido airstrip and the completion of the Huatulco airport a few years later accelerated the region's transition from sleepy backwater to fledgling international resort destination.

Today the Oaxaca coast is poised between what it was and what the Mexican government is determined to see it become. Spring still brings a pall of smoke from burning fields, and sleepy hamlets dot the landscape; this is the state of Oaxaca, after all, where the roots of traditional Indian culture reach back thousands of years. And yet, the telltale signs of the 20th century—from the oil refineries of Salina Cruz to the satellite dishes and ATMs of Huatulco—clearly suggest what the future holds in store.

MAJOR INTEREST

Proximity of all three to Oaxaca City and surrounding pre-Hispanic ruins and handicraft centers

Puerto Escondido
Appealing mix of locals, expatriates, and sophisticated crowd of international travellers
Superior surfing at Playa Zicatela

Puerto Angel
Beautifully situated fishing village
Playa Zipolite

Huatulco
Spectacularly scenic coastline
Low-key resort atmosphere

Mindful of past criticism, Fonatur pledged to develop the **Bahías de Huatulco** with respect for the environment and sensitivity to the welfare of the local population. For the present, the three or four luxury hotels here, most of the good stores, and a championship golf course are concentrated around a beautiful bay backed by steep hills. No building may exceed six stories, and all must conform to a generic Mediterranean architectural style. Development in and around the other bays has been, and will continue to be, regulated. Throughout the 23-mile length and six-mile width of the resort zone large parcels of land have been set aside as nature preserves. If activities and social opportunities outside the hotels are still somewhat limited, the beauty of the setting is unforgettable. Fonatur is committed to keeping it that way.

Although Huatulco has been the chief beneficiary of Fonatur's efforts, Puerto Escondido and, to a lesser extent, Puerto Angel—linked to each other as well as to Huatulco by Highway 200—are also feeling the impact of Fonatur's economic clout. With an increase in the number of visiting tourists and a quadrupling of its population in little more than a decade, **Puerto Escondido**'s days as a quiet fishing village and surfers' hangout have gone the way of the Woodie. While fishermen and surfers still roll into town in beat-up Beetles and campers, they're outnumbered these days by vacationing sun-lovers and the occasional celebrity looking to escape the fast pace of the bigger resorts up the coast. A small but colorful population of European and gringo expatriates, a dozen good, relatively inexpensive restaurants, and a live-and-let-live attitude that seems to infect visitors and locals alike all help to explain Puerto Escondido's popularity with budget travellers and the knowingly untrendy.

Situated midway between Huatulco and Puerto Escondido at the southernmost point of the Costa Oaxaqueña, **Puerto Angel**, a rustic fishing village with accommodations to match, remains more or less what it always has been, despite a modest influx of well-heeled tourists. Inevitably, many of these tourists are discovering what for years was Puerto Angel's best-kept secret: Playa Zipolite, the most unfettered nude beach in Mexico.

For the moment, all three are ideal hot-weather destinations for those who can do without flash and glitter, and who don't mind packing it in early after a day at the beach. As often happens with good things, however, the word about these destinations—Puerto Escondido and Huatulco, in particular—is spreading. As a result, it's not unusual for the better hotels in either resort to be booked up to half a year in advance for the Christmas and Easter vacation periods, while the one singular accommodation in Puerto Angel is usually booked solid for the entirety of its ten-month season (July to the end of April).

PUERTO ESCONDIDO

Before it was "discovered" by surfers and budget travellers in the 1960s, Puerto Escondido was a quiet fishing village with a long, uneventful past. Today it's the kind of place that's big enough to have the amenities you expect to find in a resort—airport, car-rental agencies, a range of hotels and places to eat—but small enough so that people will remember your face, if not your name, the second time they see you.

The first hint that "Escondido" offers something in addition to the usual beach-resort pleasures comes at its small but modern airport. For an hour or two every morning the hangarlike building here fills with a colorful crowd of board-toting surfers. Of course, surfing is serious business, and Puerto Escondido boasts some of the most serious surfing in North America. The "Mexican Pipeline," as surfers call the stretch of **Playa Zicatela** where the best waves break, is famous for its warm water and reliable "swells" (a sustained period of good waves). The perfectly formed waves are shaped by the configuration of the continental shelf, which rises abruptly from a depth of 300 feet to 30 feet just offshore. The town hosts two major surfing competitions a year, one in August—July, August, and September are the big-wave months—and another in November. Nonsurfers take note, however: Zicatela's pounding surf and dangerous riptides are not to be treated lightly. Strong swimmers will want to exercise caution; everyone else should confine their swimming to the town beach or the beaches west of town (see below).

Around in Escondido

Town is a few miles east of the airport via Highway 200, the coast road. West of the airport Highway 200 sweeps north and west in the direction of Punta Colorado and, eventually, Acapulco, in the state of Guerrero. If the developers have their way, **Playa Bacocho**, which stretches all the way from the airport to the point, will be thick with condominium projects and luxury hotels by the end of the decade. For now, it's a ruggedly beautiful but desolate stretch of sand pounded by heavy surf and patrolled by small-time *bandidos*; visitors will be wise to avoid it.

With the Pacific to your right, you'll pass Escondido's only gas station, a number of inexpensive motor inns, and various commercial establishments on the way into town. **Bacocho**, the spiffy-looking subdivision perched on a steep bluff about halfway between the airport and town, is home to a number of expatriate Americans as well as a sizable community of affluent Mexicans who have built second homes here. (Its popularity has spawned a new residential area next door called Punta Esmeralda.) It is, in addition, the location of the

Best Western Posada Real and Fiesta Mexicana hotels (see below), the lodgings of choice for most tour groups and families despite their distance from the shops and restaurants that cater to tourists.

While the heavy surf makes Escondido's most spectacular beach too dangerous for swimming, there are a couple of smaller strands where the waves roll rather than detonate. Among these are **Playa Carrizalillo** and **Puerto Angelito**, located midway between the Bacocho neighborhood and town. (Small signs on the highway point the way. The former is reached by taking the right fork in the unpaved access road, followed by a short hike down a steep bluff. The left fork leads to a badly rutted road that spills rattled drivers and passengers onto the beach at Puerto Angelito. Or, for a few dollars per person, you can make arrangements with one of the local fishermen on the town beach to be dropped off and picked up at either location.)

There are two beaches at Playa Carrizalillo, and because they're somewhat difficult to reach, rocky, and lacking amenities (it's a long, sweaty hike back up the bluff if you get thirsty), they're often deserted. The water is warm, however, and the waves perfectly manageable; the smaller of the two is also good for snorkeling. The beach at Puerto Angelito, a curving stretch of flat sand backed by a stand of palms and washed by gentle waves, is a popular spot, especially on Sundays, when local families arrive in numbers. A small concession stand here sells snacks and soda.

The main intersection in town is another 1 km (½ mile) east of the turnoff for Carrizalillo and Puerto Angelito. Though tourists seldom explore it, the dusty grid of streets laid out over the hillside to the left of this intersection is where most of Escondido's full-time residents live and conduct their business. The fastest-growing part of town, it's also where you'll find the town's two bus stations (Flecha Roja and Estrella del Valle), as well as a number of very inexpensive restaurants. As none has yet to establish a reputation as anything other than adequate, however, your best bet is to ask around before striking out into the gastronomic unknown.

A right turn at the intersection (marked "Centro") will lead you down the hill to **Avenida Alfonso Pérez Gasga**, Escondido's main tourist zone, and Playa Principal, the town beach. Closed to vehicular traffic (parking is provided at either end of the street), the eight blocks of Pérez Gasga are lined with a dozen beachside restaurants, a number of shops offering well-designed resortwear and quality handicraft items—in addition to many more peddling the usual junk—and a couple of inexpensive hotels. Much of what passes for nightlife in Puerto Escondido is situated along this stretch as well, as are the Mexicana and regional airline offices, the Hertz office, and the only bank in town—which visitors will be wise to avoid. (Most places in town accept American dollars; the Hotel Santa Fe and Art & Harry's Bar & Grill, at opposite ends of the Zicatela beach road, will cash traveller's checks.)

Playa Principal, a swath of brownish sand backed by palms and the above-mentioned restaurants and hotels, is a good family beach with little or no surf and plenty of room to spread out. The waves pick up where the beach curves around the bay in the direction of Playa Zicatela, a stretch of sand known as **Playa Marinero**, but rarely are they big enough to discourage swimming. In fact, from the "tadpoles" at the far end of the beach—junior surfers who have yet to develop the skill or muscle to tackle the giant waves on the other side of the rocks—to the never-ending parade of people, Marinero is the liveliest spot in Puerto Escondido.

Motorists headed for Playa Zicatela or the Hotel Santa Fe will want to continue through the main intersection on Highway 200. After passing an open-air market and a number of low-budget accommodations and campgrounds the road heads uphill. The unmarked turnoff to the Santa Fe will be to your right after the second set of speed bumps (look for the building with a painted "Bungalow Marinero" sign). Calle de Morro, the rutted road leading down the hill and around the Santa Fe to the bungalows and guest houses strung out behind Zicatela, has lately attracted the attention of the state government. In fact, the powers-that-be in Oaxaca City have decided to turn it into a paved, two-lane circuit with access roads at either end of the beach. (They've also allotted funds for the installation of a new sewer system here.) The idea is to improve—and increase—the flow of tourist traffic at this end of town, an objective that, if realized, will likely force the establishments catering to surfers to go upscale.

For the time being, the scene along Zicatela remains more or less what it has been for the last decade or so. The Hotel Santa Fe, which is experiencing costly growing pains on the way to doubling in size, anchors the end closest to town, and is still the best accommodation in Escondido, if not the best the Costa Oaxaqueña has to offer (see Staying in Escondido, below). At the opposite end of the beach, the old Tres Ochos has been reborn as Art & Harry's Bar & Grill, a breezy hangout popular with expats and anyone with a similarly carefree approach to living (see Dining, Shopping, and Nightlife, below).

In between these two very different but equally hospitable establishments, visitors will find a dozen low-key accommodations dotting the hillside between the beach and the highway. Places like Las Olas, the Hotel Arco Iris, the Hotel Inés, and Rockaway Surfer Village have long been popular with fishermen, surfers, and budget travellers not especially choosy about where they sleep. Generally speaking, accommodations range from the very basic (bed and cold-water shower) to the not-half-bad (swimming pool, expansive views of the water), with rates in the $10-to-$20 range. As an added bonus, bibliophiles and Orange County Republicans can stop by the **Richard Milhouse Nixon Memorial Library**, next door to Las Olas, and browse its eclectic collection of paperbacks and memorabilia devoted to the 37th president.

More than just surfers enjoy the waters off Puerto Escondido. **Deep-sea-fishing** enthusiasts have known about the place for decades, with the fishing for tuna, sailfish, bonito, mahi-mahi, and roosterfish especially good in the spring. Boats—most of them open *pangas* (skiffs)—can be rented on the town beach or at the small marina at the western end of Pérez Gasga. The going rate is about $20 per person, per hour, and should include your tackle.

Horseback riding on Zicatela is another popular option. You can usually find well-behaved nags for rent for about $20 an hour at the farthest end of Playa Marinero, or you can contact the **García Rendon** travel agency on Pérez Gasga (Tel: 958/2-0114) or in the Posada Real (Tel: 958/2-0458).

Staying in Escondido

There is one obvious choice here; indeed, some would say it's the only choice. The **Hotel Santa Fe**, located at the eastern end of Playa Marinero between town and Playa Zicatela, is far and away the best accommodation—at any price—in Escondido. Owned and managed by Californians Paul and Robin Klever (along with more than two dozen silent partners), the Santa Fe is a delightful change of pace from the impersonal, characterless luxury hotels that have come to dominate the larger Mexican resorts. And although it's bound to lose a measure of intimacy after the number of rooms doubles sometime during the 1993 season, it's a safe bet the Klevers will figure out a way to preserve its special charm.

For now, the Santa Fe's 30 rooms are spread among a compact cluster of three-story Mediterranean-style buildings. Rooms are simply but tastefully decorated with regionally produced ceramics and textiles, and feature two double beds, large tiled bathrooms, ceiling fans, and air-conditioning. Most also have tiny balconies where guests can wile away the hours with a book or magazine. (There are no radios or TVs at the Santa Fe.) Palm trees and flowering plants surround the small pool area at the heart of the complex, which is where nonswimmers will want to cool off. (Nearby Zicatela is no place for dog-paddlers or little children.)

Even if you aren't able to book a room here—and they go fast, especially during the Christmas and Easter holiday periods—the restaurant at the Santa Fe is a wonderful place to eat a meal. The menu, though pricey by local standards, features an extensive selection of VegMex dishes, all expertly prepared and served with style. But the food is only part of the restaurant's appeal. The pretty palapa-covered dining room overlooks the pool area on one side and the endless expanse of the Pacific on the other. Off to the right, Escondido climbs a hill behind its palm-fringed bay, while down the beach to your left the surfers—as many as 30 or 40 at once if a good swell has moved in—do battle with waves that seem to have rolled in from Hawaii. When you tire of soaking up the view you can turn your attention to the always colorful parade that comes and goes on the beach below. And if that gets old, there usually will be two or three interesting characters sitting around waiting to strike up a conversation and buy you a beer.

Perched high on a bluff in the tidy Bacocho neighborhood, the **Best Western Posada Real** promises more than it delivers. For what a room here costs you expect something special, but except for its pretty grounds, the Posada Real is disappointingly average. The drab motel-style rooms are equipped with air-conditioning, battered TVs, and little else, while the public areas are pleasant enough if a bit down-at-the-heels. The hotel's restaurant is a little better, and can even be charming if you eat at a table under the *portales*. The hotel's location in semi-isolated Bacocho, on the other hand, will come as a disappointment to many, necessitating frequent trips in taxis. (The hotel does provide free transportation into town during the day.) It doesn't add up to much, and inevitably there seems to be a lot of grumbling among the tour groups that wind up staying here.

Located at the base of the bluff behind the hotel, **Coco's Beach Club**, a Polynesian-style restaurant fronted by a palm-shaded patch of lawn and an enormous free-form pool (open to the public), is probably the best thing about the Posada Real. Although pricey, Coco's is a nice spot for a light snack, afternoon cocktails, or an early dinner, and is especially romantic after the sun sets, when the jungle decor, flickering torchlight, and pounding surf enhance its splendid isolation.

The **Hotel Fiesta Mexicana** suffers many of the same shortcomings as the Posada Real. Situated at the opposite corner of the Bacocho neighborhood, it has a less-than-ideal location and changes too much for what it offers. Although it looks from the outside as if it's still under construction, it reveals a prettier face once you get past the lobby. Rooms are comfortable if relatively spare, with faux-marble floors, air-conditioning, and mosquito-netted double beds. (Ask for one of the newer rooms.) The lobby bar sometimes features live music, and the small but pretty pool area on top of the bluff is a relaxing spot for a bite to eat or a cool drink.

The Fiesta Mexicana also has a couple of recently resurfaced tennis courts (although only masochists play the game in Escondido's heat and humidity), and has built a new beach club on Playa Esmeralda, a relatively sheltered stretch of sand at the base of the bluff below the hotel. The club was meant to compete with Coco's, up the beach, but fails to do so. Unless you have a fondness for concrete and amusement parks, you'll probably want to head elsewhere for your afternoon margarita.

At the low end of the budget spectrum, there are a couple of lodging choices right in town on Pérez Gasga that are more than adequate. The **Hotel Las Palmas** overlooks Playa Principal and a pretty courtyard filled with palms and flowering shrubs. The two dozen glass-fronted rooms here are on the small side, but louvered doorways and ceiling fans add a touch of charm, and the hotel's patio restaurant facing the beach is a popular spot. The **Rincón del Pacífico**, right next door, is a virtual carbon copy of Las Palmas, with rooms a bit smaller, perhaps, even though it charges a few dollars more.

Dining, Shopping, and Nightlife

If first-rate accommodations are a little scarce in Puerto Escondido, unpretentious, reasonably priced restaurants are not. The same holds true for shopping: Serious shoppers will definitely want to spend a day or two in Oaxaca City, one of the country's leading handicraft and folk-art centers (see Getting Around at the end of this section). If, on the other hand, a few trinkets are all you're looking for, Escondido can take care of your needs. Unless otherwise stated, the establishments mentioned below are located on the pedestrians-only stretch of Pérez Gasga.

At the west end of the street (the end farthest from the Santa Fe), the **Posada d'Loren** serves charcoal-grilled seafood, beef, and poultry on a pretty, palm-shaded terrace overlooking the beach. The chicken and fish get the nod over the beef, which can be fatty, but at these prices it's hard to complain. The two-story **Nautilus**, nearby, has a few tables downstairs and a palapa-covered terrace upstairs with great views of the bay; seafood, chicken, and beef dishes monopolize the menu, and the service is pleasant if not especially speedy. Across the street and up a few doors, the **Bazar Ticun-Uman** and **Bazar Tamar** offer nice selections of Guatemalan textiles as well as ceremonial masks from the states of Oaxaca and Guerrero.

La Luna, down the street toward the Santa Fe, fills its tiny space with a colorful assortment of bathing suits and inexpensive jewelry, while slightly larger **Bamboleo**, next door, has Escondido's most interesting selection of resortwear. On the same side of the street overlooking the beach and still more palms, **Da Ugo** is the spot for a romantic, candlelit dinner. **Osteria Viandante**, a longtime local favorite nearby, dishes out garlicky Italian specialties.

Until recently the freshest grilled seafood in town was served in the Swiss Family Robinson–style surroundings of the **Perla Flamante**, near the east end of the street. With new management in place, however, there's no guarantee the same standards will be maintained. **Banana's**, at the far end of the closed-off section of the street, offers the usual burgers-and-nacho fare but does it well; it's also the place to watch televised sports events from the States.

After the ballgame, you might want to head over to **Tio Mac's**, across from Banana's, which most nights can be counted on to be the loudest—if not necessarily the most happening—place in town. Tiny **Sushi Max**, right next door, provides a welcome alternative to Escondido's usual grilled seafood fare in a contemporary Art Deco setting. The **Spaghetti House**, a casually rustic spot on the beach around the corner from Banana's, is popular with hungry surfers and travellers on a budget.

During the day sun-lovers on Playa Marinero gravitate toward **Liza's**, with its simple, inexpensive food served at tables right on the sand. And though locals love to complain about its prices, the **Santa Fe's** breezy palapa-covered restaurant, a bit farther down the beach, manages to attract its share of them regardless of the hour. Especially good here are the *huevos mexicana* (made with fresh eggs), the deep dish–style enchiladas, the three-cheese lasagna, and their deliciously refreshing *limonada*.

The low-key establishments along the Zicatela beach road, which almost every visitor to Escondido checks out sooner or later, are the special preserve of surfers and the local expatriate community. Because novelty is a much-appreciated commodity in a place like Escondido, where one sun-drenched day seems to blend into the next, the newest establishments also tend to be the most popular. For now, the newest and most popular is **Art & Harry's Bar & Grill** (formerly Tres Ochos), at the far end of the beach. Under the watchful supervision of Patty, Jeff, and Pablo, Canadian ambassadors *extraordinaire,* Art & Harry's offers huge portions from a saloon-style menu; a half-dozen clean, no-frills rooms; and a full slate of social activities, including hotly contested dart competitions and a weekly Frisbee golf game. **Cabo Blanco**, at the opposite end of the beach just up from the Santa Fe, is a mellower, tropical version of Art & Harry's, with a semi-secluded terrace surrounded by lush ferns and palms and a limited, reasonably priced menu. Pizza aficionados will want to check out **Cipriano's**, next door, where an amazing variety of toppings adorn pies baked in a wood-fired oven.

Of course, not everyone who comes to Puerto Escondido is content to spend the week in shorts, sandals, and a tee-shirt. For those who've packed an outfit or two, the flashiest disco in town is **Bacocho**, in the neighborhood of the same name, where a sometimes-stylish crowd of expatriate Americans and affluent Mexicans pays a $5 cover charge to dance the night away.

PUERTO ANGEL

Situated on a pretty little bay about an hour's drive south and east of Puerto Escondido (the trip involves one clearly marked turn), Puerto Angel is the kind of place where everybody knows their neighbors' business and visitors are welcomed cordially, if not enthusiastically. Long a favorite destination of globe-trotting budget travellers, in recent years this small fishing village has also begun to attract a growing number of well-heeled tourists. Even with the money that has poured into Huatulco and, to a lesser extent, Puerto Escondido, however, the region around Puerto Angel remains one of the poorest in Oaxaca. Adequate health care and public schooling are unavailable to most of its residents, while sewage systems and paved roads are virtually nonexistent.

As a result, the tourist "scene" here still rates two or three speeds slower than laid back, with accommodations ranging from simple and straightforward to rustic and communal. Daytime activities are pretty much limited to strolling around town, wiling away the hours at a palapa-covered restaurant, hiring a *panga* for a few hours of fishing, or heading out to Playa Zipolite, that rare thing in Catholic Mexico—a beach where nudity is tolerated. For those looking to spend a night or two, there is one exceptional *posada* in town, in addition to a couple of barely adequate hotels and any number of modest guest houses with basic rooms (bed, fan, cold-water shower) for rent. After that, you're on your own.

The town climbs a series of rumpled foothills at the point where curvy Highway 175, here called Avenida Principal, meets the Pacific. (Highway 200, the coast road, is approximately 11 km/7 miles north of town via Highway 175.) The town pier and a small navy base dominate **Playa Principal**, the uninviting beach at the end of the road. From here you'll want to follow bumpy Boulevard Virgilio Uribe (don't bother looking for street signs) around the west end of the bay in the direction of Zipolite. Most of the businesses and guest houses in town are found on the hillsides or side streets to your right. One of these, the 32-room **Hotel Soraya**, sits at the top of a short, steep hill directly across the street from the pier and Playa Principal. The Soraya's charmless rooms, furnished with saggy double beds and noisy ceiling fans, are reason enough to spend a few extra dollars on an air-conditioned room. In fact, the best that can be said about the place is that it will do in a pinch.

A few minutes' drive on Virgilio Uribe will bring you to a fork in the road. The right branch leads to Zipolite (see below). The left branch continues around the bay to the town cemetery and, just beyond it, **Playa Panteón**, the safest and most popular swimming beach in town. The two or three palapa-style restaurants on the beach here are more or less interchangeable, and can be relied on to produce tasty grilled seafood and poultry dishes. They're also your best bet for a meal in Puerto Angel as long as the prevailing breeze isn't carrying the aroma of untreated sewage.

Continuing up and over the hill in the same direction (follow the signs to the Hotel Angel del Mar), you'll come to what appears to be the end of the road. The cobblestoned drive branching off to the left climbs another steep hill to the Angel del Mar, a splendidly situated hotel fallen on hard times, while the sandy road to the right leads to Puerto Angel's best accommodation, the **Posada Cañon Devata**. Owned and operated by Mateo Lopez and his American wife, Suzanne, the *posada* has ten rooms spread out among several buildings dotting the slopes of a lushly forested arroyo. Each room is unique in terms of size and decoration, and all have paintings by the multi-talented Mateo. Suzanne and Mateo's commitment to sixties-style communitarian values is evident throughout: The secluded complex has an open-air dining room where breakfast and a very reasonably priced set-menu dinner are served family-style; a small ecumenical chapel for private meditation; and a modest gift shop featuring locally made handicrafts and Mateo's paintings. It all makes for a delightful getaway—and a popular one at that. The Posada Cañon Devata is closed for the months of May and June and is usually booked solid the rest of the year.

Backtracking toward Playa Panteón and the right branch of the fork, you'll see a sign pointing the way to **Zipolite**. If you don't have a car, spend a couple of dollars for a taxi; the little community of Zipolite is about 4 km (2½ miles) west of town, and seems double that when you walk it in Puerto Angel's steamy heat. If you do have a car, prepare yourself for a bumpy ride. Where the unpaved road comes to a T you can turn left and, for a few dollars, leave your car with one of the local families; there are also a couple of very informal palapa-style restaurants at this end of the beach. Or you can turn right, following the road around an empty field and past a long string of still more palapa-style restaurants to a magnificent stand of palms, a spot that appeals to backpackers and travellers in camper-vans. Just remember: Falling coconuts can leave nasty dents in automobiles—and heads.

The beach here is a long stretch of coarse-grained sand backed by rustic palapas where you can pick up a snack and rent a hammock for the night. It's also a place where bathing suits are shucked with aplomb and strolling vendors go about their business unperturbed. Over the years Zipolite's cheap, no-frills digs and anything-goes atmosphere have made it the toast of budget travellers the world over. In fact, if not for the music, which has changed with the times, you might think the Summer of Love had never ended. Except that these days the peace-and-love attitudes of many Zipolite devotees seem tinged with a hint of desperation. Chalk it up to the lean-and-mean nineties, if you want; just don't leave your valuables unattended. One final caution: Swimming conditions here range from tricky to treacherous; even standing in waist-deep water you'll feel the tug and pull of enormous sheets of water. It's okay for cooling off, but you'll probably want to keep your feet firmly on the bottom.

HUATULCO

By the time its nine bays and 23 miles of coastline are fully developed early in the next century, Huatulco is expected to have a population in excess of half a million people, with enough hotel rooms to accommodate more than two million visitors annually. At the same time, tougher zoning regulations will curtail the kind of haphazard development that has characterized other Fonatur projects. In fact, more than half the acreage here will be left in its natural state in order to preserve the area's distinctive flora and fauna. Still, when all the concrete has been poured and the last nail pounded, Huatulco, like Cancún and Ixtapa before it, will personify the term "hotel culture."

All that lies in the future. For the moment, Huatulco (officially known as the **Bahías de Huatulco**) is an undeniably scenic but still somewhat limited and spread-out resort destination. Everywhere you look condominiums, additional commercial space, and new roads are under construction, but unless you've rented a car or are prepared to drop a few dollars on excursions, you're likely to find yourself running out of things to do after three or four days. This will change, of course, but for now most of the commercial activity and recreational opportunities are concentrated in or around three distinct locations: beautiful scallop-shaped **Bahía de Tangolunda**, at the eastern end of the resort zone; **Santa Cruz Huatulco**, the fishing village a few miles to the west that initially attracted Fonatur's attention; and **La Crucecita**, where the government, at first, relocated local people whose land had been expropriated for the Bahías de Huatulco project, and now developing an appealing identity of its own.

Bahía de Tangolunda

The decision to site the first of Huatulco's luxury hotels on beautiful Tangolunda Bay was made early in the resort's planning stages. With its craggy outcroppings, golden-sand beaches, and jungle-covered backdrop, Tangolunda dramatically fuses the wild and the sublime, its raw beauty tamed yet somehow magnified by man's additions to the landscape.

Club Med opened its 500-plus-room **Club Med–Huatulco** in 1987, years before there was much of anything else here, and has watched as other big chains such as ITT/Sheraton and Holiday Inn followed its lead. This particular outpost of the chain offers casita-style lodgings in low-rise buildings perched above the pounding Pacific. Each room has two double beds, a private bathroom with shower, and a terrace with ocean views; ingenious sliding partitions that allow for greater privacy are optional. Four restaurants, a dozen tennis courts, four different beaches, and three swimming pools are among the facilities scattered around this sprawling complex; free jitney service gets you from one end to the other. Of course, the major attraction for Club Med guests is sports, in this case water sports. Swimming, windsurfing, snorkeling, sailing, and fishing are offered along with a variety of motorized and self-propelled contraptions; club-owned boats also take guests to secluded, almost surreally beautiful beaches for picnics and other fun. And golfers are only five minutes by taxi from Huatulco's championship course (see below).

Located a couple of hundred yards to the east, the **Sheraton Huatulco** is a handsome example of the "coastal" architectural style that Fonatur has mandated for Huatulco. Rooms here are large and breezily attractive, if somewhat short on charm, with all the comforts you expect of a five-star hotel plopped down in the wilds of Oaxaca, including private balconies or terraces, color cable TV, servi-bars, and 24-hour room service. There are, in addition, a number of bars and restaurants in the hotel, including the wood-trimmed, candlelit **Casa Real**, where the set menu featuring different international cuisines changes nightly, and an expensive cafeteria that specializes in regional buffets. The Sheraton has a lively pool area, four tennis courts, an excellent water-sports center, in-house travel and car-rental agencies, and a couple of good boutiques. If you're planning a visit during the peak holiday periods (Christmas and Easter), you'll want to book six months in advance; July and August, when Mexican families head for the beach, are less crowded but still busy.

The buff-colored, red-roofed **Royal Maeva**, next door to the Sheraton, resembles its neighbor but, like Club Med, has an all-inclusive policy. All rooms come with private terrace or balcony, servi-bar, and color cable TV, and a recent upgrading of the amenities has added 24-hour room service and imported liquors to the package. With three restaurants, four bars, a nightclub/discotheque, tennis courts, a fitness center, a complete water-sports center, and bilingual hosts to help keep things lively, the Maeva offers the spirited atmosphere of Club Med in plush, Sheraton-like surroundings.

Although there's no denying the natural beauty of Bahía de Tangolunda or the quality of the accommodations here, visitors are likely to be a little disappointed by the dining and shopping options available outside its hotels. For whatever reason, restaurateurs and boutique owners have been slow to move into Tangolunda's two colonial-style commercial complexes, while a couple of those that have, including Yalalag, the fine handicrafts boutique from Oaxaca City, have thrown in the towel after a year or so. Still, there are a number of decent options to explore—with more in La Crucecita (see below)—for those willing to make the effort.

Visitors who wander over to the **Plaza Huatulco**, directly opposite the Sheraton and Maeva, will find a couple of small convenience stores; Solarium and O'Healey's, two of the newest restaurants in Huatulco; and **Sebastian**, silver specialists from Taxco whose designs are beautiful and whose prices put the shops in Santa Cruz and La Crucecita to shame. (Sebastian also has shops in Cancún and Taxco.) **Solarium**, owned by the same Puebla man responsible for the Club Plaza Huatulco (see below), specializes in fresh seafood served outside under a handsome wood-timbered ceiling. As of this writing, it's also the only place in the Tangolunda area that serves a reasonably priced breakfast. **O'Healey's**, which took over the pretty space formerly occupied by Don Wilo (now in La Crucecita), is owned by Juan Ruíz Healey, a well-known news personality in Mexico City, and offers a limited menu of chicken, beef, and pork dishes, along with live entertainment on occasion.

A staircase between these two restaurants leads upstairs to **Savage**, the only disco open to the general public at this end of the resort area. The original $20 cover charge, which included your drinks, has dropped to $13 when there's a live show (there's no cover when the music is canned), but the place is still dead until the nightly entertainment at the Maeva ends (about 11:30 P.M.), at which point it usually fills with a young, well-dressed crowd and stays hopping until the early hours of the morning.

The modest reception area for the **Club Plaza Huatulco**, the only alternative to the big hotels on Bahía de Tangolunda, is tucked away on the ground floor of the same complex. The 12 large, tastefully decorated suites here have their own terraces (a few with Jacuzzis), kitchenettes, marble-tiled bathrooms, purified water taps, color satellite TV, and air-conditioning. And while its public areas are limited to the reception area and a small patio out back with a hot tub–sized swimming pool, no one seems to mind. In fact, if you overlook the shortage of decent views and a small problem with noise on the terraces—the choice terraces either look out on the neon palm trees of the discotheque next door or the perpetually noisy air-conditioning plant of the Sheraton across the way—the Club Plaza just might qualify as the best value in Huatulco.

The dining-out options improve somewhat in the **Punta Tangolunda** complex, located across the street a short stroll from the Sheraton. At the far end of the complex, **La Pampa Argentina** offers grilled South American beef served hot on a brazier under airy *portales*. It's a good gimmick, but the glowing brazier tends to raise the already-warm temperature at your table. The **Misión Fa-Sol** (closed during the off-season) and **Cavendish** are located back to back on either side of the complex a few steps up from La Pampa. The former specializes in seafood with a Spanish accent, while the latter is a quiet and fairly expensive establishment serving seafood and Continental cuisine. Neither is long on decor, though both offer comfortable seating outside and attentive service.

The gently rolling and well-maintained **Campo de Golf Tangolunda** sprawls over both sides of Boulevard Benito Juárez, the main road winding through the Tangolunda hotel zone. (The clubhouse is a very long walk or five-minute cab ride from the lobbies of the big hotels.) Now with 18 holes open for play, the course measures 6,400 yards from the white tees and 6,850 from the blue. Greens fees are $26, with a cart costing an additional $26. Caddies, when they're available, charge a very reasonable $12, and a set of rental clubs goes for $13. You'll have to pay with cash, however; the golf club does not accept credit cards.

Bahía de Santa Cruz

According to local legend the first Spaniards to explore the Costa Oaxaqueña in the 16th century erected a wooden cross on the beach here that no amount of effort by the natives could destroy. Eventually, after Spaniard and Indian alike had accepted it as a miracle, the cross was removed and broken up into six pieces, with one piece ending up in the possession of the Vatican and the other remaining in the local parish church in Santa María Huatulco, where it became an object of veneration. (The village of Santa María Huatulco, 34 km/21 miles west of the Bahías de Huatulco, is also where city hall and other municipal offices are located.) Today the fishing village of **Santa Cruz Huatulco**, located a few miles west of the high-priced Tangolunda area on the Bay of the Sacred Cross, has been transformed into a small but bustling commercial district with three banks, a busy marina, a couple of decent hotels, a string of beachside restaurants, and a lovely new zócalo. While visitors will find it merits an afternoon, its appeal as a destination in its own right is pretty much limited to budget travellers.

Although the colonial-style **Castillo Huatulco**, opposite the marina and a recently upgraded souvenir market, presents a charming exterior to the world, it's really just a motor inn in disguise. The public areas, especially the pretty pool with swim-up bar, are nicer than the rooms, which tend to be small and Spartan in decor, with tiny balconies, one-channel satellite TV, and bargain-basement linens. Then again, at a half to a third of what a Tangolunda room goes for, they can look pretty good. Throw in the usual four-star amenities, including tennis court, gym, and room service, and the Castillo Huatulco might pass muster for a night or two.

The two-story **Posada Binniguenda**, a few blocks down the street, is where everyone with business in Santa Cruz seems to stay. While the rather gloomy air-conditioned rooms won't win any interior-design awards, the Binniguenda does have a lovely patio with a fountain, a pretty swimming pool area, and a lively restaurant and bar. Guests at both the Binniguenda and the Castillo Huatulco have access to the no-frills beach at Bahía de Chahue (see below), with free shuttle transportation provided by the hotel.

Magic Circus, the other disco in Huatulco frequented by tourists, is located two blocks from the Posada Binniguenda; head for the water and look for the two-story building with the colorful mural painted on one of its exterior walls. No one is likely to mistake its small dance floor and sound-and-light effects for big-time flash, but the crowd here seems to like it that way, and the $8 cover charge is modest enough to allow the curious to decide for themselves.

The small Santa Cruz **marina**, opposite the Castillo Huatulco, is usually jammed with covered *lanchas* that take passengers on excursions to the different bays (see below). This is an option favored by the locals, and is often the most fun way to see the spectacular coastline in these parts. The Mexican people are courteous and quick to laugh, and will go out of their way to make a visitor feel at home. Prices are controlled by a local collective, and range from $10 to $30 per person, depending on the number of bays visited. During the rainy season, June through September, the seas can get choppy; visitors prone to seasickness will want to take precautions.

There are several seafood restaurants lining the tiny beach on the other side of the marina breakwater. One of them, the **Restaurant Francis**, a thatched-roof affair with a breezy view of the bay, is run by Ramon Gil, a restaurateur from Guerrero, who usually puts out a tub full of live clams for customers who like them au naturel. (The normal practice here is to sprinkle them with lime juice, salt, and chile sauce before sliding them down the hatch.) At lunchtime, the beach area in front of these restaurants comes alive with peddlers and food vendors. Often you'll see little girls dressed in their Sunday best selling such local delicacies as iguana-tail tamales and armadillo or snake tacos. (The girls' mothers will have made them fresh that morning.)

After lunch you might want to spend an hour or two poking around the nearby **Mercado de Artesanías**, recently installed in new but charmless concrete-and-metal stalls next to Santa Cruz Huatulco's lovely zócalo (also new). Oaxacan and Guatemalan handicrafts predominate here, but the selection is limited and prices have jumped noticeably since the "improvements." (You can buy anything you see here for less in Puerto Escondido.) Try stall number 9, which belongs to Maribel Díaz, for reasonably priced bags from Guatemala and hand-embroidered Oaxacan dresses made by her aunt.

La Crucecita

A chaotic and sometimes intimidating place for visitors just a few years ago, La Crucecita (The Little Cross) today is a beehive of commercial activity with a pretty new zócalo and, facing it, a handful of busy bars and restaurants offering choice seats on an always lively scene. (From the Tangolunda hotel zone, follow Boulevard Benito Juárez to the traffic circle at the head of Santa Cruz's main drag; La Crucecita is another 2 km/1¼ miles up and over the hill to your right. A more direct route between the two areas is likely to be completed by the time this appears.)

Visitors might want to start their exploration of La Crucecita with the obiligatory stop at the Anderson group's ½ **Carlos 'n' Charlie's**, tucked away in a modest storefront at the corner of Carrizal and Flamboyan, two blocks south of the zócalo. The usual menu (chicken, beef, and pork) and high jinks prevail here, although the atmosphere seems to be less fevered than at other outposts of the chain. The patio out back is an especially relaxing place to enjoy a late afternoon margarita. Tel: (958) 7-0005.

On the zócalo itself (also called Plaza Principal), the **Cactus Bar & Grill** has added sushi to what was already one of the more ambitious menus in the area. If you prefer your seafood cooked, try the *camaron à la Mechin* (giant shrimp grilled in a sauce of olive, onion, garlic, pimento, and jalapeño); the *filete a la Farrah* (red snapper sauted in a white wine-and-tomato sauce); or always tasty langosta. Tel: (958) 7-0648.

Don Wilo, on the opposite side of the plaza, is a home-grown three-story affair with a sometimes-raucous bar on the top floor, a restaurant serving seafood and a few regional dishes on the middle floor, and a pizzeria on the ground floor. The inviting **Palma Real**, at the corner of Calles Gardenia and Ocotillo, entices with its green-and-white decor and shady *portales,* and serves up unspectacular though reasonably priced Mexican specialties.

For the best bargain in town, walk one street over to Bugambilias and head toward the plaza, where the nameless barbeque chicken place on the corner does a brisk takeout business serving half a broiled chicken with a stack of fresh tortillas (less than $4).

Though it has been upgraded in the last year or so, shoppers are likely to be disappointed by the merchandise in La Crucecita, which still runs to tee-shirts and bikinis. Far more satisfying is the **Mercado 3 de Mayo**, on Calle Guamuchil half a block from the plaza, with bright red tomatoes, saucy yelllow mangoes, and pungent burgundy-colored chiles stacked in neat piles lining narrrow aisles. The state of Oaxaca is well known for its chocolate, earthen-baked corn tortillas (called *totopos*), and string cheese, which is sold as *queso Oaxaca* outside the state but is called *quesillo* here.

Oaxaca markets are also famous for their *herberas,* female herb sellers who seem to have a remedy for any ailment, even the evil eye. The Mercado 3 de Mayo usually has a few *herberas* on hand, but they don't appear regularly. If you'd like to get a closer look at these folk remedies and traditions, your best bet is to head for the market in Pochutla, just north of Puerto Angel on Highway 175, which has built a reputation on the potency of its herbs.

The Bays

No visitor to Huatulco should leave without first spending a day exploring some of its less developed bays and beaches. In addition to Tangolunda and Santa Cruz, three others are now accessible to visitors with cars: **Conejos**, due east of Tangolunda and lately the site of frenzied upmarket condominium development; **Chahue**, a wide, soon-to-be-developed crescent of sand situated between Tangolunda and Santa Cruz; and **San Agustín**, the westernmost and least accessible of the bays, only because the long unpaved road leading into it from Highway 200 becomes a quagmire in spots during the rainy season. (As a precaution to possible mechanical mishaps, it's probably a good idea to leave word with the front desk of your hotel before making a trip to San Agustín.) Conejos is for sightseeing only: Access to the small beach is restricted, and the surf much too rough for swimming. Chahue also catches its share of rough surf, though at times it's a wonderful swimming beach. San Agustín, the best of the three for swimming, has a modest collection of inexpensive palapa-style restaurants where you can grab a tasty lunch of grilled fish or shrimp.

For the moment the other bays and beaches in Huatulco can only be reached by water taxi, of which there are no shortage. Spots such as **La Entrega**, where a coral reef in shallow water is protected as a national park; **El Maguey**, where the warm, jade-colored water works like a tonic on frayed nerves and stressed-out psyches; and all-but-deserted **El Organo** are the essence of Huatulco. Boats depart from and return to the beach in front of the Sheraton daily, with the cost of such an excursion running about $15 per person. Or you can head over to the Santa Cruz marina, opposite the Castillo Huatulco, where a local cooperative runs *lanchas* to the same beaches, usually for a few dollars less per person. Regardless of the option you choose, it will be a day you long remember. Don't forget to bring extra pesos to pay for snorkel equipment and a fresh seafood lunch at a beachside restaurant, as well as a hat and sunscreen: You'll be out for the better part of the day, and if you don't already know it you'll soon realize the sun this far south can be hazardous to your health.

EXCURSIONS FROM THE OAXACA RESORTS

The most common excursion from any of these resorts is a trip to one of its sister resorts. Puerto Escondido is 370 km (229 miles) east of Acapulco via Highway 200. The turnoff for Puerto Angel (Highway 175) is another 74 km (46 miles) east of Puerto Escondido via the same highway, most of it straight and flat. Huatulco is 48 km (30 miles) east of Puerto Angel, again via Highway 200, most of it twisting and hilly.

Day trips to Manialtepec and the national park at Chacahua are especially popular with travellers staying in Puerto Escondido. Located 15 minutes west of town via Highway 200, **Manialtepec**, a glassy lagoon encircled by mangroves, is a favorite nesting and feeding ground for pelicans, herons, egrets, ibis, and the occasional spoonbill and parrot. A couple of local families run two- to three-hour tours of the lagoon, which usually include a stop at the narrow barrier beach protecting its fertile waters from the saltier environment of the Pacific.

At **Chacahua**, a much larger lagoon complex some 74 km (46 miles) west of Escondido, you're likely to see the same kind of birdlife as well as storks, flamingos, and the occasional alligator. Although *lanchas* are for hire at the little village here (where you can also grab a bite to eat at an open-air restaurant), most visitors choose to explore Chacahua's three lagoons with a tour. The best are run by Michael Malone and his wife, Joan Walker, from December through March under the name **Hidden Voyages Ecotours**. For further information about their tours—of which there are a variety, ranging in price from $32 to $40 per person—contact Turismo Rodimar, Pérez Gasga 905, Puerto Escondido, Oaxaca 71980; Tel: (958) 2-0734 or 0737. Other travel agencies in town offering trips to Manialtepec and Chacahua include **Excursiones García Rendon**, in the lobby of the Best Western Posada Real, Avenida Benito Juárez, Puerto Escondido, Oaxaca 71980 (Tel: 958/2-0114); and **Viajes Moar**, Pérez Gasga 100, Puerto Escondido, Oaxaca 71980 (Tel: 958/2-0315).

Done as day trips from Huatulco, Manialtepec and, especially, Chacahua, are long, tedious affairs involving too much time on the bus and not enough time viewing wildlife. Some outfits have offered them in the past, although their numbers are dwindling. Interested parties might try **Excursiones García Rendon**, Manzana 31, La Crucecita, Santa Cruz Huatulco, Oaxaca 70900 (Tel: 958/4-0025); or **TurHuatulco**, in the lobby of the Hotel Flamboyant, Calle Gardenia at the corner of Tamarindo, La Crucecita, Bahías de Huatulco, Oaxaca 70989 (Tel: 958/7-0105 or 0113; Fax: 958/7-0121). Either outfit also will be happy to arrange a tour of the bays, a horseback tour of the Huatulco countryside, or deep-sea-fishing excursions.

Day and overnight trips to **Oaxaca City**—one of Mexico's most colorful Indian centers and a serenely beautiful colonial city in its own right—as well as the splendid archaeological ruins at **Monte Albán** and **Mitla** can be arranged through a travel agent. From Puerto Escondido and Puerto Angel, the 250-km (155-mile) trip can be made by car or bus (the latter a long, often hair-raising ordeal) via Pochutla and Highway 175, a truly spectacular two-lane road that snakes through the cloud forests of the Sierra Madre del Sur. (Highway 131, the direct road from Puerto

Escondido, is unpaved for much of its length and prone to washouts and rock slides; avoid it if possible.) From Huatulco, Highway 200 to Highway 190, the old Pan-American Highway, is a longer (by about an hour) but also much less nerve-wracking route than either of the other two. Regardless of the route and your departure point, however, try to get an early start, especially during the rainy season. The coastal mountains attract moisture like a sponge; should you be on the road when the thunderheads let loose, you'll think you're driving through an automated car wash, with one critical difference: Car washes have guardrails.

For many people, flying from either Puerto Escondido or Huatulco will prove to be the more sensible option. With Aerovias Oaxaqueñas out of business, daily service to and from Puerto Escondido is now handled by **Aeromorelos** (Tel: 958/2-0789 or 0734). The 40-seat propjet leaves Escondido at 8:30 A.M. and arrives in Oaxaca City an hour later, with the one-way fare approximately $60. **Aerocaribe** also flies to Oaxaca City from Puerto Escondido, departing at 7:45 A.M. and arriving an hour and 15 minutes later; their one-way fare is also $60. **Aero Vega** (Tel: 958/2-0151) sends a seven-seater over the mountains every Saturday and Sunday at 7:30 A.M. and again at 9:30 A.M.; the one-way fare is $55.

GETTING AROUND

International air service into Puerto Escondido and Huatulco (Puerto Angel does not have an airport) is infrequent at best, with most flights routed through Mexico City (Mexicana and Aeroméxico are the main carriers) or Oaxaca City (see above); the flying time in either case is just under an hour. There are, in addition, charter flights from Dallas–Fort Worth, with feeder service from cities around the United States for those staying at the Club Med in Huatulco. For further information, Tel: (800) CLUB-MED.

Because the daily plane *from* Mexico City to Puerto Escondido turns around and, an hour later, becomes the daily plane *to* Mexico City, the scene at the Escondido airport usually borders on mass confusion. VW minibuses (*combis*) are an inexpensive and popular form of transportation to the various hotels around town but tend to fill up as fast as they unload. A taxi is a better option and will only cost a couple of dollars.

The fare from the Huatulco airport to the hotel zone, a 20-minute drive, is $7.50. Cab fare between Huatulco and Puerto Escondido is approximately $80, with drivers willing to carry up to four passengers; the fare from either to Puerto Angel is about half that. Taxis also can be hired by the hour for sightseeing excursions of the wild and beautiful coast in this region, but some ability to communicate in Spanish is recommended.

If you decide to rent a car—always an expensive proposition in Mexico, but the best way to get around—you can arrange to have it waiting at either airport, thereby avoiding the scramble for a cab or *combi* altogether. Budget and Hertz have desks at the Puerto Escondido and Huatulco airports, as well as downtown (though in the case of Huatulco, both outfits require confirmed plane reservations). The Sheraton and Maeva in Huatulco also have car-rental desks, and both run shuttles to and from the airport, as does the Santa Fe in Puerto Escondido, with advance notice.

—*Mitchell Nauffts*

ACCOMMODATIONS REFERENCE

The rate ranges given below are projections *for December 1992 through Easter 1993. Unless otherwise indicated, rates are for double rooms, double occupancy; the 10 percent VAT has been added. As rates are subject to change, it's a good idea to double-check before booking. The Oaxaca Resorts are in the central standard time zone; the telephone area code is 958.*

Puerto Escondido

▶ **Best Western Posada Real.** Boulevard Benito Juárez, Lote 11, Fracc. Bacocho, **Puerto Escondido**, Oaxaca 71980. Tel: 2-0185; Fax: 2-0192; in the U.S. and Canada, Tel: (800) 528-1234. $85–$95.

▶ **Hotel Fiesta Mexicana.** Boulevard Benito Juárez, Fracc. Bacocho, **Puerto Escondido**, Oaxaca 71980. Tel: 2-0150; Fax: 2-0115. $80.

▶ **Hotel Las Palmas.** Avenida Alfonso Pérez Gasga s/n, **Puerto Escondido**, Oaxaca 71980. Tel: 2-0230 or 0303. $23.

▶ **Hotel Santa Fé.** Calle del Morro, **Puerto Escondido**, Oaxaca 71980. Tel: 2-0170 or 0266. $50–$57.

▶ **Rincón del Pacífico.** Avenida Alfonso Pérez Gasga 100, **Puerto Escondido**, Oaxaca 71980. Tel: 2-0056 or 0193. $33.

Puerto Angel

▶ **Hotel Soraya.** Calle Virgilio Uribe, **Puerto Angel**, Oaxaca 70909. Tel: 6-0144. $19–$23.

▶ **Posada Cañon Devata.** C/o Mateo and Suzanne Lopez, P.O. Box 74, **Pochutla**, Oaxaca 70900. No phone. Single or double, $20; bungalow, $30.

Huatulco

▶ **Castillo Huatulco.** P.O. Box 354, Boulevard Santa Cruz s/n, **Bahía de Santa Cruz**, Oaxaca 70989. Tel: 7-0051; Fax: 7-0131. $40–$50.

▶ **Club Plaza Huatulco.** Lote 23, **Bahía de Tangolunda**, Oaxaca 70989. Tel: 1-0027 or 0035; Fax: 1-0007. $109.

▶ **Club Med–Huatulco.** P.O. Box 154, **Bahía de Tangolunda**, Oaxaca 70989. Tel: 1-0033; Fax: 1-0101; in the U.S. and Canada, Tel: (800) CLUB-MED. Rates upon request.

▶ **Posada Binniguenda.** P.O. Box 44, Boulevard Santa Cruz s/n, **Bahía de Santa Cruz**, Oaxaca 70989. Tel: 7-0077; Fax: 7-0284; in the U.S. and Canada, Tel: (800) 262-2656. $86.

▶ **Royal Maeva.** P.O. Box 227, Boulevard Benito Juárez s/n, **Bahías de Huatulco**, Oaxaca 70989. Tel: 1-0000; Fax: 1-0220; in the U.S. and Canada, Tel: (800) 262-2656. $145 (all-inclusive).

▶ **Sheraton Huatulco.** Boulevard Benito Juárez s/n, **Bahías de Huatulco**, Oaxaca 70989. Tel: 1-0055; Fax: 1-0113; in the U.S. and Canada, Tel: (800) 325-3535. $126–$165.

THE GULF COAST

THE STATES OF VERACRUZ AND TABASCO

By Robert Cummings

The coastal lowlands of Veracruz and Tabasco are wedged between the Bahía de Campeche (part of the Gulf of Mexico) and some of Mexico's steepest mountains. It is verdant, flower-filled country, with vanilla and coffee plantations perched on the low shoulders of mountains to the northwest, steamy rubber country to the southeast—the center of the first great Mesoamerican civilization, the so-called Olmec, which in the language of the Aztecs meant "the people of rubber"—and cattle ranches hacked out of the jungle in between.

The people of the region, with the exception of a pocket of Totonac Indians in northern Veracruz, share a number of qualities that set them apart from highland Mexicans as well as from the people of Chiapas and the Yucatán. The Caribbean influence is strong here, the impact of African cultures over the centuries more noticeable than in other parts of the country. Writers of popular songs delight in the area. *Veracruzanos* are reputed to be languorous but passionate, tolerant but fierce; these extremes often seem to resonate in the region's music, while its traditional dances can shift from courtliness to sudden abandon. It is also rumored elsewhere in Mexico that people from the Gulf Coast region are given to crimes of passion—an unsubstantiated rumor but one that makes them appear both dangerous and attractive. Katherine Anne Porter seemed to accept the notion of the archetypal *veracruzano* when she wrote, "They carry on their lives of alternate violence and lethargy with a pleasurable contempt for outside opinion." While she may have overstated the case, the people of the region do impress the visitor with their confidence and self-assurance.

Foreign travellers have never come to the Gulf Coast in great numbers, but Mexican vacationers, searching for bargains, beaches, and the exotic, swarm to the Gulf, where they quickly notice the regional differences. The coast dwellers are darker complexioned, they drink rum instead of tequila, and their speech is lisping and clipped. And where does that odd music come from?

MAJOR INTEREST

City of Veracruz
Fortress-prison of San Juan de Ulúa
Beaches
Lively zócalo scene
Fiestas

North of Veracruz
Mountain town of Jalapa
Ruins at Zempoala and El Tajín
Sportsfishing and scuba diving at Tuxpan

South of Veracruz
Lago de Catemaco scenery
Parque-Museo de La Venta in Villahermosa (Olmec sculpture)
Regional birds and lush vegetation

The historic port city of Veracruz, on the coast east of Mexico City, is the primary gateway for the Gulf Coast region. From Veracruz we consider the coast north as far as Tuxpan, and then south, including Lago de Catemaco, as far as the Villahermosa area in the state of Tabasco. Villahermosa is also the jumping-off point for the Palenque archaeological site and San Cristóbal de las Casas, the capital of the state of Chiapas (for both of which see the Mayan Mexico chapter).

You should be forewarned that the climate in this part of Mexico is intensely hot from May through September. In addition, in August the *nortes,* or "northers," common to the hemisphere arrive with little warning and drench the entire region, bending trees and sending the temperature plummeting in the process. Fine weather usually follows in the wake of a *norte.*

The best time to visit is from November through March. Even winter doesn't necessarily bring better weather, however—one reason the Gulf Coast's beach resorts have been eclipsed by their younger Pacific and Caribbean cousins.

THE CITY OF VERACRUZ

Veracruz, the most piquant of Mexico's cities as well as the most European of its ports, was nicknamed "Little Havana" in the days before Cuba turned forbidding. Actually, Veracruz was never so freewheeling, although it has always been a sailor's haven. To quote Katherine Anne Porter again, who had a bad time in Veracruz in her youth: "It is in fact to the passing eye a typical port town, cynical by nature, shameless by experience, hardened to showing its seamiest side to strangers."

In those days, maybe. Today, not really. Veracruz has been scrubbed up a lot in the last decade, which has enhanced its charm without lessening its zest. It is far more high-spirited than bawdy, and still a city flirtatious in every way.

Veracruz is also a town of balconies. Wandering down any street, you'll be distracted and delighted by them—long and narrow, short and obtrusive, many embellished by orange and yellow flowers that are startling in their vividness when seen against the pale-colored walls typical of the city's architecture. From these balconies the women of Veracruz call to street vendors, summon their children playing outside, or simply dry their long black hair in the sunshine.

The Plaza de Armas

The zócalo, also referred to as the Plaza de Armas or Plaza de la Constitución, is a vibrant public space (except in the heat of the day when it may turn languid) set off by a lacy iron bandstand, slender coconut palms, and tropical flowers so vivid they seem unreal. Most of the area is closed to vehicular traffic, the better to saunter, promenade, or, at fiestas, to dance. Arcades shelter the cafés around the edges of the plaza, and a table here is an observation point for a neverending show, of which the spectators themselves are a major part. The zócalo in Veracruz is a crossroads not only of the city but of the Caribbean and the world beyond. At any moment you might spot a group of Russian or Norwegian sailors, or maybe the polyglot crew of some ship registered in Liberia, wandering along shady arcades as French and Italian tourists, looking chic in their new tropical outfits, stop to check their maps.

Veracruz

| 0 | yards | 330 |
| 0 | meters | 300 |

To Fuerte de San Juan de Ulúa

AV. SAN JUAN DE ULUA

VIADUCTO

Estacion de Ferrocarril

N

CALLE MONTESINOS
CONSTITUCION
EMPARAN
JUAREZ
M. LERDO
ZAMORA
MOLINA

Bahía de Veracruz

PLAZA DE LA REPUBLICA

Plaza de Armas
Palacio Municipal
La Parroquia

PASEO DEL MALECON
SERDAN
ARISTA

CAMPANA
ZARAGOZA
MONTERO
LANDERO
AV. GOMEZ FARIAS
16 DE SEPTIEMBRE
PENA
XICOTENCATL
HERNANDEZ Y HERNANDEZ
FIGUEROA
BLVD. M. AVILA CAMACHO

Museo de la Ciudad

MORALES
CANAL
RAYON

Baluarte de Santiago

CINCO DE MAYO
INDEPENDENCIA

MARTIRES 25 DE JUNIO
DOBLADO

Parque Zamora

To Villa del Mar
To Mocambo

BLVD. CAMACHO

The row of cafés on Calle Miguel Lerdo, which is closed to traffic, begins with the venerable **Prendes**, the city's oldest restaurant and an ideal place to sip coffee or a bottled drink. While spending half an hour at an outside table here you can have your shoes shined, hear a marimba concert, purchase a hammock, test your strength, buy a lottery ticket, hear a recitation of patriotic poetry, admire the bunches of fantastic balloons sold by vendors in the plaza, or watch the world go by. On the other hand, if this sounds a bit overwhelming you can always retreat to the quiet of the dining room.

If Prendes, as proper as its garrulous elderly waiters, seems too stiff, you can move down the row of cafés, taking a half step down the social ladder at every doorway. The voices gradually grow louder, the spirits flow more freely; the last watering place on the block, while not raunchy, is certainly déclassé.

Cutting back across the zócalo, circling the bandstand, and passing the vendors of gardenias and bubble-blowing pipes, you will come to the greatest local sidewalk institution of all, the **Gran Café de la Parroquia**, which faces the unpretentious parish church, now a cathedral. Here, at any hour of the day from 7:00 A.M. until 1:00 A.M., you'll find a noisy potpourri of *veracruzanos*. As patrons struggle to be heard over the din, waiters circle the café in pairs, one with a steaming pot of coffee, the other with hot milk. Spoons bang or tinkle on glasses as customers signal for milk to be added to their cups of black brew. "Coffee must be sweet, hot, and strong as love," *veracruzanos* will remind you at every chance. It is an old saying that applies to this colorful city as well.

The coffee is excellent. Then again, it has to be—many of the men who drink it here also grow it, pack it, or ship it by the ton. Others concern themselves with oil or beef deals, both major contributors to the region's prosperity. But not everyone arrives with a briefcase. Store clerks come to read their newspapers hurriedly, while students from the university gather to argue, joke, and plot their intrigues.

The Gran Café serves breakfast and snacks as well, but the coffee ritual is its chief drawing card. Endless cups of coffee and endless talk help pass the long hours until the sun goes down and the city cools off.

The church across the street, **La Parroquia**, needs paint both inside and out, as do seemingly half the buildings in Veracruz. Of course, the salt spray from the sea only a block away has something to do with this, as do the city's torrential rains, *nortes,* and hurricanes. In a climate such as Veracruz's even the most vivid paint soon fades to a pastel color, and eventually to an indistinct gray. The church, which was dedicated in 1734, adds a softening touch of antiquity to the plaza but is not particularly interesting in itself—very few buildings in the city are. There is little in the way of art here outside of the art of living.

The Malecón

The *malecón,* which starts two blocks east of the zócalo, near a spot where crab sellers hawk their wares at the top of their lungs, is the city's long, winding shore drive. At the head of it, a long pier dotted with trashy curio shops and so-so seafood restaurants juts into the harbor. A monument nearby reminds the visitor that Veracruz was the first "European" city to be established in the Americas, as well as the site of the first democratic (European-style) assembly. For approximately $6 you can hop aboard a boat here for a tour of the harbor. (A trip to **Isla de Sacrificios** is worth making if you'd like to try the beach there. The island, a sandy, desolate little key, is 30 minutes away by launch, which will cost you between $5 and $8, depending on the boat. The destination itself isn't great, but the views of the city, the harbor, and the jungled coast are reasons for going. Do not make the trip on a windy day, however.)

The pier is interesting by day, but especially romantic and colorful at night, when lovers and families go strolling, pausing to watch sidewalk artists, gape at jugglers, or listen to the ever-present troubadours.

As the *malecón* curves south it becomes the Boulevard M. Avila Camacho, eventually leading to **Villa del Mar,** the most popular beach in the city and a good spot for sunning, wading, swimming, and playing games in the sand. The facilities are simple, but Villa del Mar is nevertheless inviting. There's also a public swimming pool here.

The Forts

There is little in the way of conventional sightseeing in Veracruz, certainly not enough to fill a day unless, in true *veracruzano* style, you spend an hour in a café before and after each attraction.

One of the few sights in town, the **Fuerte de San Juan de Ulúa** squats in the harbor like some grim, ugly curiosity. Although it looks close from the comfort of a café seat near the plaza, it's actually a long walk in the Veracruz heat. A taxi is a better idea, and it's easy enough to find one to take you back downtown once you get there.

The castle was begun in 1528 on the island where Juan de

Grijalva, the first Spaniard to land at what is now Veracruz, had come ashore a decade earlier. During the century that followed the fort did the town little good, as Veracruz became the victim of one raid after another by the likes of Drake, Hawkins, and Agromonte. The worst catastrophe occurred in 1683, when Lorencillo, a merciless buccaneer, captured the sleeping town. The inhabitants were herded into the church and held there for four days—during which many died—while his men methodically sacked their homes.

Finally, after other protective measures had failed, in 1746 the entire town was encircled by a wall with seven gates—one of them reserved exclusively for use by the viceroy of New Spain. The illusion of security was just that, however. Although Veracruz did manage to hold out for years during the War of Independence, thereby earning a measure of infamy as the last Spanish stronghold in Mexico, the seemingly impregnable gates and ramparts of San Juan de Ulúa itself fell easily to French bombardment in 1838 and were taken again by U.S. troops in 1846. They also offered little protection when U.S. forces landed once more in 1914, capturing Veracruz and killing nearly 200 Mexicans in the process—an incident known locally as the Massacre of Veracruz. (Although *veracruzanos* are too polite to mention it to visitors from the United States, they have not forgotten.)

When it wasn't being stormed by foreign invaders, this fierce-looking but impotent dinosaur did long service as a much-dreaded prison. High tides would sweep through the lower levels, forcing prisoners to stand with seawater up to their chins; such food as was provided would be lowered to prisoners by rope through manholes on the roof. Not surprisingly, incarceration here amounted to a virtual death sentence. Even today the atmosphere is dank and heavy, and while there are fine views of the city from the fort's roofs and battlements, an hour's visit is enough for most people.

A much smaller and less interesting redoubt is found in the center of town, on Calle Rayón and 16 de Septiembre, about six blocks southeast of the main plaza. This fortress, dedicated to Saint James and so known as the **Baluarte de Santiago**, is all that remains of the old city walls and gives the visitor an idea of Spanish defenses in New Spain. The cramped museum inside is of minimal interest.

The nearby **Museo de la Ciudad**, four blocks south of the zócalo at Zaragoza 397, is worth a short visit. The sidewalk outside the museum is inset with tiles recounting the exploits of Cortés in this region—images that were borrowed from Aztec codices. The museum itself is housed in a gracious 19th-century building, and its interior, one of the best in the city, gives a sense of what life among the wealthy of Veracruz was like a century ago. An Olmec head, not one of the greatest, is displayed downstairs along with other artifacts and relics, including a number of wonderful clay pieces from the area. Upstairs, 26 life-size wax figures sport costumes typical of Carnaval (Mardi Gras) in Veracruz. If nothing else, it's a gaudy and alluring advertisement for this raucous fiesta.

Mocambo and Boca del Río

About 9 km (5½ miles) south of the zócalo, beyond Villa del Mar and just outside the city limits, stretch the sands of Mocambo, a better beach than Villa del Mar and a well-developed resort zone: In addition to its fine hotels (see below), chair and umbrella concessions dot the beach. Food and drink, including the locally famous *coco locos*—coconuts addled with gin—are also available. The clean, freshwater pool is open to the public.

Boca del Río, a fishing village still farther south, is a community doomed to be swallowed by the encroaching city before long. In the meantime there is swimming near the mouth of the Río Jalapa, although fishing remains the chief attraction. You might also want to check out one of the rustic open-air restaurants near the river for a fresh fish dinner.

Staying in Veracruz

Veracruz is a magnet for weekend vacationers from Mexico City. The climate and beaches may not compare to those of Cancún or Acapulco, but Veracruz is much closer and cheaper. Therefore, hotel reservations are *essential* if your stay includes a weekend. While the city has enough hotel rooms for something always to be available (except during Carnaval or Holy Week), third-choice rooms in Veracruz can be depressing.

First choose between the beach and the plaza areas. The best hotels at either location are about equal in comfort. On the other hand, economy is much better practiced downtown. Whatever your choice, air-conditioning is a must year-round.

The **Hotel Emporio**, centrally located on the harbor, is the traditional first choice. It offers balconies with most rooms, splendid views, three swimming pools, a restaurant, and a nightclub. In addition, the management is experienced and willing to help with boat rentals, fishing information, and tours of the region. It is expensive only by the standards of downtown Veracruz.

The **Hotel Veracruz**, practically facing the zócalo at the corner of Independencia and Miguel Lerdo, is a comfortable, pleasingly decorated full-service hotel. In terms of both quality and price, it's a notch above the neighboring hostelries on the zócalo and, considering its location, surprisingly quiet. The hotel was built a generation ago to be the city's most modern luxury inn. Time has left it a touch old-fashioned but still very inviting.

The **Hotel Colonial**, right on the zócalo, is the city's best value. Newer rooms, mostly in the front, rate better than the others, but the older ones have been modernized and aren't bad. Rooms up front come with zócalo noise and music, while the rear section is quiet. Many rooms are equipped with refrigerators, and all are air-conditioned. The Colonial also has a sidewalk café and an indoor pool.

The **Prendes**, on the zócalo above and behind the famed restaurant of the same name, is pretty basic but has all the essentials. Some of the larger rooms, called "suites," are much the best, and zócalo noise doesn't seem to carry to any of the rooms except those directly overlooking the plaza.

The sprawling **Hotel Mocambo**, with terraces that seem to wander off to the sea, is the grande dame of the beachfront inns. The hotel offers a tennis court, three swimming pools, and lovely views of the Gulf from its rooms, mostly one- and two-bedroom suites on the beach. Best of all, like the Emporio, it is expensive only by local standards.

While the **Playa Paraíso**, on the beach near Boca del Río, is slightly more modern and luxurious than the Mocambo, it is also less gracious in style. However, suites with one and two bedrooms overlook the beach, and the views of the Gulf are memorable. A bar and restaurant that stay open until 1:00 A.M. (when there are customers) offer a touch of nightlife in this otherwise quiet neighborhood.

Dining in Veracruz

The word here is seafood, of course. The best-known regional sauce, *veracruzana,* is made from tomatoes, onions, olives, capers, garlic, and mild chile peppers. Cooking with fruits and the use of banana leaves as a wrapper are also common. Although the state is an important producer of cattle, local beef is usually not to the taste of foreign visitors.

Prendes, on the zócalo, is the traditional favorite, but a look at the unsanitary kitchen would discourage anyone from ordering a meal here. (It's a good place for coffee or bottled drinks, however.) Across the street from Prendes, in the Hotel Veracruz, **Restaurant 1942** offers fresh, steaming seafood with or without the spicy sauces of Veracruz.

La Bamba, formerly Lorencillo, at Boulevard Avila Camacho, near Rayón, overlooks the harbor. There's a South Seas touch to both the decor and the menu in this casual but nevertheless refined spot. Lunch will cost you about $15.

Garlic's, about 1 km (½ mile) south of La Bamba on Boulevard Avila Camacho, also seems about to sail into the bay, and draws an informally stylish crowd. A seafood platter will cost about $13. Tel: (29) 35-10344.

El Pescador, Zaragoza 335, has wood paneling that's presumably meant to resemble the interior of a stateroom on an old luxury liner, and a collection of flotsam—kegs, belaying pins, nets, lanterns, and so on—to further enhance the atmosphere. The seafood here is fresh and well prepared.

You'll find an exception to the usual Veracruz seafood menu at the **Submarino Amarillo** (Yellow Submarine), Boulevard Avila Camacho at the foot of Rayón. This upscale family restaurant is modeled after a typical U.S. steak house and features tender, thickly sliced steaks (about $9)—unusual in a region that range-feeds its cattle.

La Paella, located on the zócalo at Zamora 138, attracts travelling student types who appreciate the hearty set *comida,* usually four courses, at a thrifty price (about $6).

Veracruz Nightlife and Fiestas

Veracruz seems to wake up about an hour after the sun sets. That's when the zócalo begins to pulsate, couples drift toward the *malecón,* and the sidewalk cafés come alive. More formal—and costly—entertainment is provided at the Emporio, the Mocambo, and the **Torremar**, a resort hotel located on the beach near the Mocambo.

Veracruz also boasts the most famous **Carnaval** in Mexico. While not quite on the scale of the annual celebration in New Orleans, it remains happier, safer, and cheaper. The city turns delightfully mad, the floats are glorious, and the dancing never stops. Hotel reservations must be made, paid, and confirmed months in advance. Although the last three days are the climax of the celebration in Veracruz, most visitors try to arrive a week before Ash Wednesday.

After the fireworks of Carnaval, the city rests a little during Lent, then explodes again during Holy Week. The Easter crowds here are enormous, and accommodation arrangements likewise must be made far in advance.

NORTH FROM THE CITY OF VERACRUZ

Buses will do for point-to-point travel to major destinations along the coast north of Veracruz, but you'll need a car if you really want to explore the region, an area much visited by Mexicans but seldom seen by foreign visitors.

The coast here is dotted with small, rustic beach resorts, especially between Nautla and Tecolutla. While it ought to be interesting—and often gives that impression from the highway—it isn't. It is a fisherman's paradise, however, and various annual tournaments are a major attraction of the region. Accommodations and restaurants are uniformly simple and economical.

Jalapa

Jalapa (pronounced hah-LAH-pah, and also spelled Xalapa) is an easy day's excursion from Veracruz (take Highway 140), or can be visited en route to or from Mexico City. Poised high above the Gulf in the foothills of the Sierra Madre Oriental, some 100 km (62 miles) northwest of Veracruz, Jalapa was once the site of a thriving pre-Columbian town. But it came into its own as Veracruz became Mexico's most important port. (It's also near one of the important coffee-growing regions of the state.) With its relatively temperate location, Jalapa offered escape from the tropical fevers that plagued the lowlands around Veracruz, and eventually became the capital of the state for reasons of health. Even after the old tropical diseases were eradicated in the lowlands, Jalapa remained popular because of its comfortable climate and scenic beauty. To this day its mountain breezes promise rejuvenation to sun-struck inhabitants of, and visitors to, the coast.

Here, where the easterlies off the Gulf collide with the Sierra massif, light rainfall is frequent and persistent—a local weather phenomenon known in Spanish as *chipichipi,* for its pattering sound. The abundant moisture, good soil, and mild climate of the region are ideal for plants of all kinds, and the town, as a result, resembles nothing so much as an open-air floral conservatory where blossoms seem to explode into vivid color. Jalapa is justly famous as the "Flower Garden of Mexico."

It has also flowered in other ways. The University of Veracruz, in particular, has helped make Jalapa a lively cul-

tural center famous for its theater, dance, and the best regional symphony orchestra in Mexico. In addition, the **Museo de Antropología**, on the campus of the university, has a collection of pre-Hispanic art that is, according to many experts, second only to the national museum's vast collection in the D.F. Among its fascinating exhibits are a number of curious (and some think magical) wheeled "toys," smiling figurines of many different shapes and sizes, and a variety of ancient Olmec sculpture. There are also three giant carved Olmec heads on the campus itself, which is located on the southwest edge of town just off the highway to Mexico City. Coming from Veracruz, stay on Highway 140, ignoring the "Centro" signs, until you come to Avenida Xalapa at the far end of town. Turn left, not quite making a U-turn, and then go straight. Like most museums in Mexico, this one closes on Mondays.

Although Jalapa, like Rome, was built on seven hills, it feels more like the older neighborhoods in Naples, with its sloping streets twisting sharply into hidden alleys and courtyards lined by pastel-colored houses. One of the greatest pleasures it affords visitors is simply wandering around its main plaza area and discovering such attractive spots as the lively and informal **Café Escorial** on Pasaje Enríquez. The nearby **Agora**, a center for the performing arts and favorite gathering place of students, is always busy with music, conversation, and the sale of records, tapes, and books.

The **Café Parroquia**, Zaragoza 18, is a popular eating and drinking place near the Hotel María Victoria downtown. It specializes in regional Veracruz cuisine.

Those who would like to spend more time in this delightful city should consider checking in at the very good and reasonably priced **Hotel María Victoria**, located in the center of town behind the government palace, or the older, somewhat rundown (and even more reasonably priced) **Hotel Salmones**, also centrally located on Zaragoza. Both have, in addition, clean and more than adequate restaurants. The huge **Hotel Xalapa**, downtown at the corner of Victoria and Bustamante, has air-conditioned rooms, parking, a nightclub, and a coffee shop descriptively named "24 Horas."

Zempoala

The ruins of Zempoala are only 4 km (2½ miles) west of Highway 180, about 40 km (25 miles) north of Veracruz. It's an easy excursion from the city; if you have a car, a visit can be combined with a trip to Jalapa, or else as the first stop on a trip along the northern Gulf coast.

Zempoala was the first Indian city that Cortés and his men saw after their miserable bivouac on the beach of what is now Veracruz. The Spaniards were literally starving when they were befriended by Totonac warriors and led to this jungle city, and many of them initially mistook its gleaming stucco walls for silver. It was here that Cortés found his first friends among the native people, although the friendship between them would soon turn sour. But that still lay in the future when a delighted Bernal Díaz wrote in 1519: "We were struck with admiration. It looked like a garden with luxuriant vegetation." The local ruler, known to history as Chicomacatl and to the Spaniards as the "fat chief," welcomed the white men as allies against the Aztecs and presented Cortés with an obese bride—a lady whom Cortés "received with courtesy."

Today enough of the center of ancient Zempoala remains to give us an idea of pre-Hispanic life, although all but traces of its residential neighborhoods have long since vanished. It's clear, however, that it was the Totonac capital, a city of some 30,000 people who called it the "Place of Twenty Rivers" because of the many nearby tributaries of the Río Actopan, and that it rose to prominence about A.D. 1200 when Toltec warriors, advancing outward from the central highlands, pushed the Totonacs off their traditional lands and into this less fertile, less healthful region.

The base of its great temple, the **Templo Mayor**, is still in remarkably good shape. (When you multiply 13, the number of its tiers, by four, the number of its sides, you get 52, the mystical Mesoamerican number.) It was on these steps that Cortés had a violent encounter with Chicomacatl after the Totonac chief protested Cortés's decision to destroy the stone idols atop the temple base; Cortés held a blade to the chief's throat while his soldiers carried out the destruction.

The upper platform of the **Templo de las Chimenas** (Temple of the Chimneys), on the east side of the main plaza, offers the best view of the site, and from here you can locate another temple and a path leading to it through a field of sugarcane. Known as the **Templo de las Caritas** (Temple of the Small Faces), its ornamental features have been badly eroded over time; still, it's worth the short walk, if only for the up-close look at a field of cane.

The whole area, shaded here and there by low, graceful palms, is open for roaming and exploration, and the small museum on the site is worth a glance.

Papantla and El Tajín

Farther north Highway 180 turns sharply inland near Tecolutla, and after about 20 km (12 miles) comes to Papantla, 225 km (140 miles) northwest of Veracruz in the heart of vanilla country. Vanilla plants are temperamental and demand endless pampering and coaxing. Until this century the world depended on the patience of Papantla's farm workers, mostly Totonac Indians, for this remarkable flavoring. Sadly, the discovery of inexpensive artificial vanilla extract all but ruined the economy of this corner of Mexico. There is still a demand for the real thing, however, so the vanilla farmers hang on.

Papantla also benefits from tourism, with visitors coming to see the archaeological zone at El Tajín, as well as to view the famous *voladores* (flying dancers). The dance, at once a religious rite and a beautiful spectacle, is performed every Sunday at noon in the zócalo. Four colorfully costumed men symbolically dressed as eagles and macaws leap from a tall pole to which they are attached by ropes tied to their ankles; 13 swooping revolutions around the pole bring them safely to the ground (the four fliers multiplied by the 13 revolutions create the sacred number 52).

Papantla is a charming little city, still countrified and quite Totonac. The zócalo is a small jewel; just up the hill from it a striking concrete relief sculpture depicting the history of El Tajín and the Totonacs adds an unusual aspect to the scene. The **Hotel Tajín** is the best of the town's several inns. You'll want to pay a little extra for air-conditioning, which is easily affordable at the hotel's modest rates. Its simple and straightforward restaurant puts out adequate meals.

Travellers bound for the archaeological site of El Tajín who prefer better accommodations can continue northwest past El Tajín to **Poza Rica** and the **Hotel Salinas**, which offers larger and better-appointed quarters as well as a more extensive menu. Unfortunately, this medium-size city is a raceway of traffic and, in addition to carbon monoxide, is often plagued by the smell of oil from nearby refineries hanging heavy in the air. For travellers with cars it is perhaps a better idea to leave Veracruz early, take a quick look at Papantla, spend a few hours at El Tajín, and then continue on to the pleasant river town of Tuxpan (see below), which has a number of good hotels, for the night.

El Tajín, a bit west of Papantla, is the most spectacular pre-Hispanic center on the Gulf Coast and surely ranks among the finest archaeological sites in the country. Named for both lightning and the Totonac rain god, it was founded very early in the Classic era, about 200 B.C., and reached its zenith under the tutelage of Teotihuacán from A.D. 600 to 900. Toward the end of its history it came under the influence of the Toltecs, before being abandoned in the 13th century (which was considerably later than were most great Mesoamerican ceremonial centers).

The **Pirámide de los Nichos** (Pyramid of the Niches) here is a startling sight, at once unexpected and strange. Emerging from the lush jungle that surrounds the site, it is not particularly lofty, like so many Mesoamerican pyramids, but its design nevertheless catches the imagination. Comprising six platforms, the pyramid is tiered like a wedding cake, with each of its sides covered by row upon row of recessed rectangles, or niches, adding up to a total of 365—one for each day of the solar year (the exact number and their meaning are still debated). The pattern continues around the four sides of the pyramid, six layers of heavily outlined rectangles, dynamic and strong. The changing light of day constantly shifts the emphasis, creating different depths and shadows as the sun moves across the sky. Perhaps these openings are simply ornamental, a rhythmically repeated decoration—no one is really sure. What is clear, however, is that builders throughout El Tajín's history were fascinated by niches, even though their use varied over time. One of the most common motifs was to use the niche as a frame for an important design element—the abstract serpentine image of the rain god, for example. Nevertheless, over the centuries a significant change occurred in this approach. The early work is serene and confident; later relief sculpture, on the other hand, has a tense, even frantic quality, and sacrifice and self-mutilation begin to enter the picture.

This Toltec-inspired frenzy is most evident in the carvings from the **Juego de Pelota Sur** (South Ball Court), as well as in the details of a carved column now in the Tajín museum. The ball-court carvings, dating from about A.D. 1150, exhibit wild sculptural rhythms suggestive of an age of social turmoil, and feature the skeletal death god with ominous frequency. There is no established narrative in the six carved panels, nor even a prevailing theme. Some meanings are clear: Panel one illustrates human sacrifice in connection with the ball game; panel two has to do with blessed drunkenness and the native brew *pulque*; the third involves nature gods, including an eagle, and musicians playing shell instruments. Number four involves rain gods, while five and six depict initiation and consecration rites, including self-mutilation.

The complex known as **El Tajín Chico** stands about 300 yards north of the main pyramid on slightly higher ground.

The structures, unromantically designated "A" through "D," overlap and abut in many places, requiringg careful observation to distinguish among the individual buildings. Edificio "C" is the most eye-catching, adorned as it is with niches and step frets in the manner of the main pyramid; it is a variation on the niche theme, however, and not a replica. Nearby is a ball court, one of at least 11 at this compact site.

A little farther uphill and somewhat north and west is the **Edificio de las Columnas**, so-called because of an almost entirely vanished colonnade that once formed its façade. The columns' surviving drums are solidly banded with relief carving from the Early Postclassic era. The profusion of motifs and styles again suggests that El Tajín benefited from contact with many different cultures.

The Pyramid of the Niches is built over an older but similar structure that dates to about A.D. 300; archaeologists speculate that the more recent structure was built perhaps three centuries later, but the origins of El Tajín's early builders remain obscure. An unknown number of structures remain covered by earth and tropical vegetation. Fortunately, excavation continues at the site, and each year more of its mysterious but fascinating past is revealed.

Sometimes *voladores* perform their spectacular flying dance in the main plaza at El Tajín. For those lucky enough to catch such a performance, it is the perfect—not to mention original—setting.

Tuxpan

Tuxpan (TOOSH-pan), a pleasant fishing port rather recently made prosperous and prodded into the 20th century by the discovery of oil, lazes along a riverbank some 58 km (36 miles) northeast of Poza Rica. The feeling of an "oil town" is almost totally absent, with the exception of what amounts to a virtual second city built by the national petroleum company, Pemex, between Tuxpan and its beach near the mouth of the Río Tuxpan.

There are no attractions of particular interest to be seen here—although the colonial church and bridge are handsome. Nor is there much of anything to do other than saunter along the river admiring the palm trees and the view. For all its lack of specific attractions, Tuxpan is nevertheless quietly enjoyable, with much color and life on display in and around its two main plazas.

Launches serving as ferries ply the Río Tuxpan, affording a pleasant little boat ride with good views of the town. In the village on the opposite bank you'll find the Mexican-Cuban

Friendship Museum, located on the spot from which Fidel Castro returned to Cuba in a fishing boat; the rest, as they say, is history. The boat is being restored (or perhaps re-created) for visitors, but only great admirers of Castro are likely to enjoy the museum, which consists almost entirely of early photographs of Fidel and his fellow revolutionaries.

The Tuxpan beach, **Barra del Norte**, is easily reached by bus or car from town. The beach has good sand and warm, shallow water; the facilities are simple but adequate. The strand itself resembles the more famous ones on Padre Island in Texas, long stretches of coarse but unpebbled sand and (usually) gentle water lapping the shore. (Industrial installations by Pemex neither pollute the beach nor seal it off.)

Tuxpan is perhaps best known for its **sportsfishing**, including the annual tarpon tournament held in June. Information is available at the Club de Pesca (Tel: 783/4-0406). In addition, scuba divers enjoy the **Laguna de Tamiahua** and **Isla de Lobos** north of town. Tuxpan is a good headquarters for expeditions to both.

The **Hotel Sara**, the town's best, has tastefully decorated rooms with balconies and views of the town and river. The beds tend to be firm, even hard, so you might want to check this before registering. The Sara is about three blocks uphill from the center of town, and also has a cheerful restaurant.

On the main street a block above the river boulevard is the comfortable **Hotel Plaza**, older than the Sara and a bit worn but still a good buy. The Plaza's restaurant features seafood and serves good breakfasts.

Fischer Restaurant, at the western edge of downtown facing the river, is Tuxpan's best restaurant, high priced but attractively situated.

SOUTH FROM THE CITY OF VERACRUZ

Travelling south and east along the coast from Veracruz you'll pass through green, level ranchland speckled with Brahman cattle. These pastures have been wrested from the jungle, and defending them is a never-ending struggle. Now and then the horizon is broken by mountains tumbling down toward the sea.

By car or bus, the trip around the Bahía de Campeche—as this southwesternmost part of the Gulf of Mexico is called—is both lovely and pastoral. But there are only two destinations of interest in the region: the Lago de Catemaco area

and, farther east in the state of Tabasco, Villahermosa. For most travellers other towns along the route will be of little interest.

Catemaco

Both the town and lake are an easy one-day trip from Veracruz, lying just 145 km (90 miles) southeast of the city over a good road, Highway 180. There's also fast and frequent bus service to both.

The lake, created in prehistoric times by the eruption of a cluster of volcanoes, is an impressive body of fresh water some ten miles long. Two imposing volcanoes, **San Martín** and **Cerro Blanco**, both long extinct, rise to the north, forming a frontier of sorts: This is the northern limit of the tropical rain forest on the continent. Travellers will notice the change as they head southeast, with the greens becoming deeper and the timber taller with every hour of driving.

Lago de Catemaco, sometimes hailed as the most beautiful lake in Mexico, is certainly a contender for the title in a country where lakes are few. Although the town huddled on its western shore has some color and zest, it is not particularly attractive. Nevertheless, a walk along the lakeside promenade under the majestic trees can be pleasant, even romantic. In addition, enjoyable boat rides are offered from the town dock. The charge is by the boat, not by the passenger, so it's cheaper to go with a group; people at the docks usually will be happy to have you join them. The trip affords long, lovely views of green highlands and mountains rising on every side, sloping pastures dotted with humped Brahman cattle, and waterfowl, especially egrets, wheeling in the sky or skimming the water. Seen from the lake the town is romantically transformed. Your boat may not be allowed to approach the spider monkey colony established by the University of Veracruz on an island here, but even if the view is only through binoculars, you're likely to see some bizarre scenes of monkey life. Eleven other islands abound with vegetation, and lilies, hyacinths, and lotuses carpet the shallows of the lake.

The **Iglesia del Carmen** on the lake's eastern shore is interesting for its collection of *milagros,* drawings and photographs about miracles experienced by pilgrims to this shrine. The most evident pilgrims here, however, are the middle-class residents of Veracruz treating their families to a weekend at the lake. As a result, many of the hotels in town have kiddie water slides and such.

The hotel **Playa Azul**, located west of town on a gravel

road facing the lake, has extensive lawns and its own dock, as well as a dining room. The rather modest accommodations are priced above value, and a car is necessary to get around. The rooms farthest from the driveway are the best.

For those without a car, the **Berthangel**, on the south side of the zócalo in town, is tidy and has pleasant balconies—about as well as you can do here despite the rather cramped quarters. It also has a coffee shop.

Meal times tend not to be joyful occasions in Catemaco. The small restaurants on the lakeshore offer limited menus of freshwater fish along with guitar music and lake views. The Hotel Catemaco on the zócalo has good ice cream, however.

Not far from town are some beautiful waterfalls, one of which, **Salto de Eyipantla**, is truly spectacular. Before setting out, inquire about directions and road conditions; washouts are common, the mud often deep, and warnings rarely posted. The *tránsito* office, in city hall on the zócalo, will be happy to advise you.

Masks and skeletons are brought out every autumn on a date determined by the lunar cycles in order to celebrate a reunion of sorcerers on the slopes of Monte del Cerro Blanco. Outsiders are most unwelcome at this native religious conclave, but the tradition inspires the youngsters of Catemaco to dress up and caper about as witches (*brujas*) regardless of the season—a surprising show for visitors, whether encountered in the town's streets, plazas, or along its back roads.

VILLAHERMOSA

The name Villahermosa means "pretty town," but most writers have begun their descriptions of the city by declaring the name deceptive, the place unpretty, even ugly. That declaration is no longer accurate; Villahermosa is beginning to live up to its name.

Located nearly 485 km (301 miles) southeast of Veracruz (via Highway 180), this sleepy, depressed old Tabasco town boomed because of oil, a windfall prosperity that resulted in tacky overgrowth. In the 1960s the old rundown town was transformed into the modern rundown city. But since then Villahermosa has been consolidating its prosperity, building and remodeling. Unfortunately, inflation came with wealth, and Villahermosa remains one of the more expensive cities in Mexico.

Still, travellers to the region can get what they need here:

attractive, if sultry, surroundings for those visiting the city's remarkable archaeological park-museum, its more conventional regional museum, and its zoo. Villahermosa is also a convenient gateway to Maya country, with **Palenque** less than a two-hour drive from the city (see the Chiapas section of the Mayan Mexico chapter below).

In addition, the many lagoons, rivers, and inlets nearby support an abundance of birdlife, attracting bird-watchers from near and far. Not surprisingly, the plumage of the tropical species that flock to the region is often gorgeous, and flamingos, toucans, and parrots make for a resplendent natural show.

In Villahermosa itself, café life centers on the Plaza de Armas, with the **Café del Portal** the traditional gathering place. Many blocks of the downtown area are closed to traffic, and visitors can stroll down streets lined with buildings designed in a simple but distinctive Caribbean style.

Parque-Museo de La Venta

La Venta, the greatest of the Olmec centers, was established sometime after 1200 B.C.—at about the time of Moses—and reached its zenith around 600 B.C., becoming the fountainhead of art and culture in ancient Mesoamerica and predating the rise of the Maya by centuries. Everyone has seen pictures of the colossal Olmec stone heads sitting out in the jungle, but government officials felt that La Venta—about 80 miles west of Villahermosa in a swampy isolated area—and the two other principal Olmec centers, San Lorenzo and Tres Zapotes, were too remote for most visitors. As a result, the great sculptures produced by this mysterious and surprisingly advanced culture were assembled and brought to an open-air museum in Villahermosa, the Parque-Museo de La Venta; smaller works went to the city's regional museum. (There is nothing of interest left at the original sites.)

Instead of simply setting out a row of statuary, a Mexican poet-savant by the name of Carlos Pellicer Cámara designed a "natural" environment in which these works might be seen as their creators had intended. Starting with a parcel of land along the **Laguna de las Ilusiones**, Pellicer created, in effect, an Olmec jungle.

The environment is perfect, at once a frame for and an extension of the sculpture. Monkeys scramble about in the trees; browsing deer look up, hesitate, then vanish into the thickets; the snarl of a jaguar (safely caged) underlines the fact that the Olmec were "jaguar people," with the great felines playing a dominant role in their religion and art.

Small details have been considered as well. For instance, instead of directional signs, naked footprints that look as if they've dried in the clay paths point the way.

Perhaps the best way to visit the park is simply to stroll through it, coming upon the huge heads, altars, and other great monoliths by surprise, gradually growing used to the "Olmec line" and concept of monumentality without worrying about specific meanings and relationships. Then walk through it a second time more slowly, and, if possible, with the official guidebook and map in hand. These are sold at the entrance to the park, although the supply is not always reliable. With or without a guidebook, however, the monuments are compelling enough to repay careful scrutiny.

Of all the monuments in the park, Colossal Head #1 evokes the most comment. Carved almost 3,000 years ago, this single boulder was transported some 70 miles through the jungles to the original La Venta site—despite being over seven feet tall, more than six feet in diameter, and weighing 44 tons. Yet, according to experts, the great stone was somehow moved without the help of wheels or draft animals.

You will read and hear endless speculation about the heads, especially the three magnificent examples in the park. Are they kings? Beheaded ball players? The simple truth is that nobody knows. Even the most thoroughly researched printed material contains much conjecture presented as fact. The carved altars, for example, may be something else—thrones, perhaps. Of course, visitors to the park are free to form their own opinions while contemplating the beauty and haunting power of these ancient stone sculptures created many centuries before the rise of Periclean Athens.

Museums in Villahermosa

The **Museo Carlos Pellicer**, named for the Tabascan poet-savant who was director of an older museum here, has one of the best regional collections in the country. Also, as an adjunct of the Centro de Investigaciónes de las Culturas Olmeca y Maya, or CICOM, it is the perfect complement to the Parque-Museo de La Venta. The museum is filled with artifacts from a variety of locations, but the emphasis—and the best collection—deals with the surrounding region: Olmec and Mayan objects, including beautiful copies of Mayan codices. You should allow about two hours for viewing its extensive displays of artifacts, maps, exhibits, and photographs. The Museo Carlos Pellicer is located on the banks of the Río Grijalva, just west of the Prolongación de

Ocampe, an extension of Villahermosa's *malecón*. Tours begin on the second floor. Closed Mondays.

The **Museo de Cultura Popular**, at Zaragoza 810, displays a variety of Tabascan crafts, the most interesting of which are the masks and musical instruments used in native dances. A "modern" Chontal Mayan dwelling has been duplicated with branches, logs, and thatch, and a conversation between two women has been recorded in the native Chontal dialect to give more authenticity to the dwelling. Plagued by errant husbands, they complain about the "lazy drunkards." Closed Mondays.

The **Casa de los Azulejos y Museo de la Ciudad**, at the corner of Avenida Juárez and 27 de Febrero, is a zany jumble of objects and ideas a young Scots-Mexican brought back from a grand tour of Europe in 1885. Housed in the family home (transformed by an Italian architect into something not entirely French, Italian, Persian, Moorish, or Gothic), the collection is supposed to illustrate the history of Tabasco—but that seems to be beside the point. Closed Mondays.

The Villahermosa Zoo

Adjacent to the Parque-Museo de La Venta, and stretching along the esplanade bordering the Laguna de las Ilusiones, is a delightful public garden that is also home to the equally delightful Villahermosa Zoo. Here you'll find jungle animals and birds in a lush, tropical setting. The bands of monkeys, in particular, attract crowds of fascinated, wide-eyed children.

Behind the zoo runs the long esplanade with its lovely views of the palm-fringed lagoon—a perfect place to find the stray breezes that occasionally stir this tropical city.

The park-museum, zoo, and beautiful Laguna de las Ilusiones are grouped together on the west side of the city, occupying a broad area northeast of the prominent corner of Paseo Tabasco and Boulevard Adolfo Ruíz Cortines.

Day Trip to Comalcalco

The ruined Mayan city of Comalcalco, situated at the very limit of Maya country some 55 km (34 miles) northwest of Villahermosa, was in pre-Hispanic times a satellite of Palenque. The first centuries of its life span, which covered the years A.D. 550 to 1250, comprised its greatest era. Comalcalco is somewhat of an oddity in that it was constructed of brick—the only important Mayan center so built. Though the site has been badly ravaged by time, some elaborate structures survive, as do some fine examples of stucco art inspired by Palenque.

While the site itself is only of medium interest, the drive through the surrounding cocoa-growing countryside, still inhabited by the Maya, will add a great deal of value to the excursion. Of the two routes you can take, the more interesting begins by following Villahermosa's main drag, Boulevard Ruíz Cortines, then turning north onto Avenida Universidad. Follow the signs for "Comalcalco via Nacajuca" and, a little later, a sign that says only "Nacajuca." Almost at once you will find yourself surrounded by cocoa plantations. A little past the halfway point to Comalcalco, 42 km (26 miles) from Villahermosa, stands the village church of **Cupilco**, a cheerfully gaudy example of folk art and decoration featuring a profusion of flowers and angels.

As you approach the modern town of Comalcalco, a sign indicates the ruins via a bypass north of town. Take the bypass. You'll be heading toward Paraíso before turning at the ruins access road, which is clearly marked.

Daily tours to Comalcalco leave from all the major Villahermosa hotels. It is also possible to take a bus to the access road, but this is usually an unappealing option due to the heat and overcrowding on the un–air-conditioned vehicles.

Staying in Villahermosa

The outstanding hotel here is also the city's newest, the **Holiday Inn Tabasco Plaza**, east of the Parque-Museo in a new residential/shopping district on Paseo Tabasco. One of the best operations in Mexico, it reflects Villahermosa's recent prosperity and burgeoning internationalism, with servi-bars, balconies, spacious rooms furnished with subtle good taste, and a swimming pool. The dining room is excellent for well-prepared regional and Mexican dishes as well as international-style entrées, and the bar has live entertainment. It all adds up to an elegant but relaxed hostelry, and a sterling, if expensive, addition to the Holiday Inn chain.

The **Hotel Hyatt Villahermosa**, in the same fairly expensive price range, is also a decidedly first-rate hotel, with dining room, coffee shop, nightclub, and pool; located near the zoo on Juárez, just off Paseo Tabasco.

The **Hotel Cencalli**, a comfortable establishment situated in a gardenlike neighborhood near the Laguna de las Ilusiones, offers its guests (mostly tourists) good rooms, attractive tropical grounds and a swimming pool. The restaurant, with a bar and entertainment, is also recommended.

Located downtown at Calle Reforma 304 (part of the pedestrian mall closed to traffic), the **Hotel Miraflores** has air-conditioning, a bar, and a restaurant. This is a rare operation in Villahermosa—an inexpensive hotel that is still acceptable. It will do.

Because of a steady stream of business traffic, much of it international, Villahermosa's hotels are crowded and reservations absolutely essential.

Dining in Villahermosa

The first choice for good food and service in town is the Holiday Inn Tabasco Plaza's serene but gleaming dining room.

Overlooking the river in the same complex as the regional museum, **Los Guayacanes** is pleasant enough and serves good seafood. Tel: (931) 2-1530.

Capitán Buelo's riverboat restaurant serves lunch, in two sittings, on two separate trips; the first departs at 1:30 P.M., the second around 3:00. Go for the boat ride, not the food, although the meal is better and less expensive than you would expect from this kind of operation. Get the boat at the *malecón* and Zaragoza. Tel: (931) 3-5762.

Leo's, Paseo Tabasco 429, became so popular as a result of its service, informality, and substantial fare—beef and pork tacos, pastries, all-American hamburgers with fries, and the like—that a second branch has been opened in Mérida. Tel: (931) 2-4463.

As noisy as the Caribbean music it's named for, **Guaraguao** seems to boil with crowds and tobacco smoke. But the *sopa de mariscos,* Mexico's answer to bouillabaisse, may be worth it. Salt- and freshwater specialties at moderate prices. Avenida 27 de Noviembre 947; no reservations.

Los Pepes, centrally located at Madero 610, is the best of the open-air cafés and serves regional food at low prices. The ceiling fans help some, but nothing open to the outdoors is very appealing on a torrid Tabasco day.

GETTING AROUND

Driving Down from the Border

Most travellers heading down from the border want to cover the northeast corner of the country as quickly as possible; to avoid delay at the start of a long drive, you might consider clearing customs and spending the night in **Matamoros**, across the border from Brownsville, Texas, so you can set out early the next morning. (You should also be aware that from May to October travellers are at the mercy of summer downpours.) The modern **Hotel Gran Presidential** is located on Matamoros's major street, Avenida Alvaro Obregón, at the corner of Amapolas. In addition to an inviting tropical patio, it has a good restaurant, bar, and nightclub; its prices are high by local standards, however. **La Casona**, in the center of town at Independencia 513, is merely adequate, its rates reasonable. Restaurant, bar, swimming pool.

From Matamoros you proceed south on Highway 180/101, traversing pancake-flat country bristling with scrub jungle. Twenty-nine kilometers (18 miles) south of San Fernando, Highway 101 swings to the southwest and Ciudad Victoria (and from there on to the central highlands). Southbound drivers will want to continue on Highway 180, which eventually becomes a toll road about 21 km (13 miles) north of Tampico.

Tampico, situated between the Gulf and a vast estuary, is a modern but sometimes makeshift city that has mushroomed in size with the growth of Mexico's petroleum industry. Relics of its previous incarnation as a resort—old decaying hotels near its beaches, a few waterfront bars—remain as forlorn reminders of a raffish past. Sadly, pollution has killed the fish that once drew sportsmen to its waters, and the oil refineries have overpowered the town's sleepy charm and driven out much of its other industry.

The first attractive hotel you'll see is the **Posada de Tampico**, 8 km (5 miles) north of the city on Highway 180. A 300-unit operation with satisfactory if expensive rooms and a clean, efficient restaurant, it's probably best as a convenient stop for lunch. The next establishment down the road, the **Camino Real Motor Hotel**, near the northern edge of the city on Highway 180, which here is called Avenida Hidalgo, is far more luxurious. The restaurant is also good and the coffee shop satisfactory, although not very fast. Less costly and more than adequate is the **Hotel Impala**, near the zócalo downtown, with a restaurant that serves very fresh and savory seafood.

Highway 180 heads due south out of Tampico over a new bridge that replaced the unreliable ferry, which served the city badly for generations. The route passes through sparsely inhabited savannah and wetlands for 131 km (81 miles), until it reaches the village of Potrero del Llano, where Highway 180 joins Highway 127 and swings to the southeast for the final 42 km (26 miles) into Tuxpan.

—*Robert Somerlott*

Veracruz

All major airline service is via Mexico City. Mexicana is the chief carrier, with three flights to and from the capital daily, plus four flights a week to Los Angeles (with a Mexico City stopover). The Mexicana office in Veracruz is on the corner of Serdán and Cinco de Mayo. Aero Litoral, partly owned by Aeroméxico, has flights to Villahermosa, Tampico, and Ciudad del Carmen, in the state of Campeche. Ground transportation to and from the airport is by taxi, *colectivo,* or rental car. A taxi will cost about $7, the *colectivo* half that much. For the return trip from the city to the airport the *colectivo* is not always reliable.

Intercity buses arrive and depart from the Central Camionera, about 4 km (2½ miles) from downtown Veracruz and accessible by taxi or city buses running south on Avenida Cinco de Mayo. (They're marked "Camionera" in white paint on the windshield.)

First-class buses (the ADO line) depart almost every hour for Mexico City; the trip takes about 7 hours and costs about $13. Buses *from* the capital depart the Terminal de Autobuses de Oriente (TAPO) near the San Lázaro metro station. There is also good service from Veracruz to Lago de Catemaco, Villahermosa, Tuxpan, and Jalapa (which is on the northern route to Mexico City). There is, in addition, a special night bus to Mérida in the Yucatán, and another to Oaxaca. It takes about 14 hours to reach Mérida, a little less than 12 to Oaxaca. The fare to the former is approximately $29, while it's about half that much to Oaxaca. It is imperative, upon your arrival in this busy terminal, that you make a reservation for your next destination before heading into town.

Four trains a day run between Veracruz and the capital, two departing each city in the morning, one via Jalapa and the other via Córdoba. The trip takes about 12 hours. There's also a night express, with Pullman cars, via Córdoba that leaves both cities at 9:30 P.M. and arrives at the other end of the line at around 7:40 A.M. Travellers taking the night express have a choice of accommodations, and tickets should be purchased well in advance. The night sleeper, called the "Jarocha," offers the best service and costs about $37 from the capital.

The better highway to Veracruz from the capital is the southern (toll) route, Highway 150D, via Puebla and Córdoba. The alternate route, via Jalapa on Highways 140 and 129, is longer and slower. Both routes offer spectacular mountain scenery.

A choice of car-rental agencies is available in Veracruz, but none is of international reputation. Service at the airport and in the city is offered by Auto Laurencio, Autos Panamericana, Renta de Carros Veracruz, and Valgrande Rent a Car. Major credit cards are accepted. There is no real need to have a car in the city, however. Public transportation is fast and frequent, and taxis plentiful.

Villahermosa

Daily flights offered by Aeroméxico and Mexicana connect Villahermosa to Mexico City. Aerocaribe, a regional carrier, connects Villahermosa to Mérida, Cancún, and Oaxaca. Price-controlled taxis provide ground transportation from the airport to the city, about 10 km (6 miles) distant; the fare should be about $5.

ADO is the best bus line linking Villahermosa with Veracruz, as well as Mérida, Palenque, and San Cristóbal de las Casas in Chiapas. The trip to Mérida takes about 9 hours. The daily express bus to Oaxaca is about an 11-hour trip.

There is a Dollar Rent-a-Car office in the Holiday Inn complex; otherwise, none of the city's dozen car-rental agencies is known internationally. Two of the larger are Arrendadora de Autos Usumacinta, at the airport and the Hotel Cencalli in town, and Tabasco Auto Rent, which is also at the airport and in town, the latter at the Hotel Viva, Paseo Tabasco 1201. Both offer a variety of models and accept credit cards.

Tour buses leave regularly for the archaeological zones of Palenque and Comalcalco, with pickup service at all the major hotels.

Highway 180 is the best road to Veracruz and points north and west; it also runs into Campeche and points east via the coast. Motorists heading east on this route, however, are dependent on the ferry at Ciudad del Carmen, and are therefore at the mercy of the weather. The inland route, Highway 186, is the more dependable route to the Yucatán Peninsula.

ACCOMMODATIONS REFERENCE

The rates given below are projections for December 1992 through Easter 1993. Unless otherwise indicated, rates are for double rooms, double occupancy; the 10 percent VAT has been added. As rates are subject to change, it's always a good idea to double-check before booking.

▶ **Berthangel**. Zócalo, **Catemaco**, Veracruz 95870. Tel: (294) 3-0089. $35.

THE GULF COAST

- **Camino Real Motor Hotel.** Avenida Hidalgo 2000, **Tampico**, Tamaulipas 89300. Tel: (121) 3-8811; Fax: (121) 3-9226. $135.
- **La Casona.** Independencia 513, **Matamoros**, Tamaulipas 87300. Tel: (891) 6-3740; Fax: (891) 3-7375. $43.
- **Holiday Inn Tabasco Plaza.** Paseo Tabasco 1407, **Villahermosa**, Tabasco 86040. Tel: (931) 3-4400; Fax: (931) 3-5569; in the U.S. and Canada, Tel: (800) 465-4329. $125.
- **Hotel Cencalli.** Carretera 180, **Villahermosa**, Tabasco 86040. Tel: (931) 5-1999 or 1994; Fax: (931) 5-6600. $78.
- **Hotel Colonial.** Zócalo and Miguel Lerdo, **Veracruz**, Veracruz 91700. Tel: (293) 2-0193. $37.
- **Hotel Emporio.** Malecón and Xicoténcatl, **Veracruz**, Veracruz 91700. Tel: (293) 2-0020; Fax: (293) 1-2261. $99.
- **Hotel Gran Presidential.** Alvaro Obregón and Amapolas, **Matamoros**, Tamaulipas 87300. Tel: (891) 3-9440; Fax: (891) 3-2777. $84.
- **Hotel Hyatt Villahermosa.** Ruíz Cortinez and Paseo Tabasco 907, **Villahermosa**, Tabasco 86050. Tel: (931) 3-4444; Fax: (931) 5-5808; in the U.S. and Canada, Tel: (800) 228-9000. $125.
- **Hotel Impala.** Díaz Mirón 220, **Tampico**, Tamaulipas 89300. Tel: (121) 2-0990; Fax: (121) 2-0684. $53.
- **Hotel María Victoria.** Zaragoza 6, **Jalapa**, Veracruz 91000. Tel: (281) 8-0521. $43.
- **Hotel Miraflores.** Reforma 304, **Villahermosa**, Tabasco 86040. Tel: (931) 2-0022; Fax: (931) 2-0486. $43.
- **Hotel Mocambo.** P.O. Box 263, Carretera Mocambo, **Veracruz**, Veracruz 91700. Tel: (293) 7-1710; Fax: (293) 7-1660. $90.
- **Hotel Plaza.** Juárez 39, **Tuxpan**, Veracruz 61420. Tel: (783) 4-0838. $30.
- **Hotel Salinas.** Ruíz Cortinez 1000, **Poza Rica**, Veracruz 93240. Tel: (782) 2-2347; Fax: (782) 2-9680. $25.
- **Hotel Salmones.** Zaragoza 24, **Jalapa**, Veracruz 91000. Tel: (281) 7-5431. $25.
- **Hotel Sara.** Garizurieta 44, **Tuxpan**, Veracruz 61420. Tel: (783) 4-0010; Fax: (783) 4-0018. $35.
- **Hotel Tajín.** Domínguez 104, **Papantla**, Veracruz 93570. Tel and Fax: (784) 2-1062. $37.
- **Hotel Veracruz.** Independencia s/n and Miguel Lerdo, **Veracruz**, Veracruz 91700. Tel: (293) 1-2233; Fax: (293) 1-5134. $101.
- **Hotel Xalapa.** Victoria and Bustamante, **Jalapa**, Veracruz 91000. Tel: (281) 8-2222; Fax: (281) 8-9424. $85.
- **Motel Playa Azul.** Carretera Sontecompan, **Catemaco**, Veracruz 95870. Tel: (294) 3-0001 or 0042. $30.

▶ **Playa Paraíso**. Boulevard Veracruz Mocambo, Boca del Río, **Veracruz**, Veracruz 91700. Tel: (293) 5-5033. $90.

▶ **Posada de Tampico**. P.O. Box C-71, Carretera 80, km 7, **Tampico**, Tamaulipas 89300. Tel: (122) 8-0515; Fax: (122) 8-0855. $125.

▶ **Prendes**. Zócalo, **Veracruz**, Veracruz 91700. Tel: (293) 1-0241; Fax: (293) 1-0491. $35.

OAXACA

By Celia Wakefield

Celia Wakefield has lived in Mexico for many years, the past 15 in San Miguel de Allende, and travels extensively throughout the country. She has written articles for The Atlantic, Saturday Review, Newsday, *and* Punch. *She is also the author and photographer of* High Cities of the Andes.

The city of Oaxaca (wuh-HAH-kah) lies about 300 miles southeast of Mexico City geographically; in spirit it is a world away. There could be no more complete change from the frenetic traffic, bustle, and pollution of the capital than this lovely city in the Sierra Madre del Sur.

Some cities keep their essential character in spite of the passing of time. Although Oaxaca has mushroomed in size in recent years, it remains a semitropical oasis of quiet charm, a place where visitors return again and again to unwind in its gentle, springlike climate. Nobody seems to be in a hurry here, but there is always something to do—especially outside the city limits proper—whether it's visiting the native crafts villages for which the region is justly famous; exploring the magnificent archaeological sites at Monte Albán, Mitla, and elsewhere; or using the city as a gateway for vacations on the beaches of Puerto Angel, Puerto Escondido, or Huatulco (see the separate Pacific Resorts chapter for a more detailed look at these and other attractions).

MAJOR INTEREST

Oaxaca City
Main plaza and cathedral
Iglesia de Santo Domingo
Museo Regional del Estado, with finds from Monte Albán

Instituto de Artes Graficas de Oaxaca
Museo Rufino Tamayo
Museo de Arte Contemporaneo
Saturday market

Outside the City
Monte Albán
Mitla
Craft villages

OAXACA CITY

Oaxaca is easily reached by plane, train, bus, or car from Mexico City, though each of these may have its disadvantages: The seven-hour drive is through uninteresting country, the plane flight may be canceled for mysterious reasons, the train may be late, or the bus crowded. Any of these inconveniences will be forgotten, however, once this pleasant city is reached.

Oaxaca takes care of its guests in small but important ways. At the airport a *colectivo* van pulls up to carry passengers to their hotels for a minimal fee. (If it doesn't turn up instantly, wait for it; taxis charge five times as much.) A few years ago the city banned all vehicular traffic from the central downtown plazas. Now pedestrians amble freely under huge trees, rest in the shade on white wrought-iron benches, and listen to marimba music at the Rococo bandstand. Shopkeepers, passersby, and neighbors on park benches are liberal with information; old-fashioned courtesy has not gone out of style here.

How long will you want to spend in Oaxaca? There are several museums, churches, and markets to be explored, as well as two separate excursions to the important archaeological sites of Monte Albán and Mitla. Three days therefore should be the minimum. Travellers with special interests in crafts or archaeology will want to allow a day or two extra for visits to small weaving and pottery villages, or to the less well known archaeological sites at Cuilapán, Zaachila, Dainzú, Lambityeco, and Yagul.

Oaxaca is a city of about 300,000 people nestled in a valley at an altitude of a little over 5,000 feet. Actually, there are three Oaxacas: the state, the city, and the valley of the same name. In conversation, "Oaxaca" may refer to both the city and the surrounding valley, which includes the craft villages and archaeological sites most visitors come to see.

The valley was inhabited as long ago as 9000 B.C. In time, the Zapotec Indians developed an advanced civilization here, trading with the equally advanced Olmecs on the Gulf Coast, and built a number of impressive ceremonial centers. Foremost among these was the great center of Monte Albán, founded around 800 B.C. by a pre-Zapotec culture. The Zapotecs, in turn, dominated the valley from around the birth of Christ to A.D. 800. Their eventual decline was hastened by the arrival of the warlike Mixtecs from the north, who did not so much subdue the Zapotecs as assume the reins of an exhausted culture. Toward the end of the 15th century the fierce Aztecs made their presence felt, building a fort in the center of the valley and controlling its trade and tribute. Details of these migrations and shifts in power are obscure, but the Zapotecs, who were the first to leave an imprint on the Valley of Oaxaca, survived, and theirs is the language most often heard in its markets today.

The Spanish appeared on the scene in 1521, but it was some years before they were able to subjugate the indigenous population and establish a city on the spot where the Aztec fortress had been. As W. H. Prescott wrote in his classic *History of the Conquest of Mexico:* "Cortes obtained a grant of an extensive tract of land in the fruitful province of Oaxaca, where he proposed to lay out a plantation for the Crown.... He soon had the estate under such cultivation that he assured his master, the Emperor, Charles the Fifth, that it was worth 20,000 ounces of gold." In 1529 the emperor gave Cortés the title of Marqués del Valle de Oaxaca.

The Dominican friars were instrumental in building the colonial city, and by 1575 there were 160 churches in the valley. At the same time, the province flourished economically. Silkworms were imported from Spain, and silk spinning was profitable until the China trade undercut it. Cochineal dye from the region was in demand until the advent of artificial dyes in the 19th century. Cattle ranching and wheat farming were both suited to the mild, dry climate of the valley. Oaxaca prospered, in part because it supported very few people. As the population increased over the centuries, however, the forests were cut down and the once-rich soil was eroded. Today Oaxaca is one of the poorest states in Mexico.

Oaxaca is also famous as the birthplace of two of Mexico's most important political figures. Benito Juárez, a full-blooded Zapotec, was prominent in the reform movement of the 1850s and instrumental in the 1860s in ridding Mexico of the foreign rule of Emperor Maximilian. In 1861 he became the first and (so far) only Mexican president of pure Indian descent, and since his death in 1872 has been revered as his country's Abraham Lincoln. The house where he worked as a servant in Oaxaca City is maintained as a small museum. Local legend has it that Juárez did not die but rather disappeared into a lake in his native town of Guelatao, from which he will emerge some day to lead his Zapotec tribesmen once again.

Porfirio Díaz, another *oaxaqueño,* rose to prominence from the other end of the social spectrum, having always known wealth and influence. Although he governed his country as president for 30 years, from 1876 to 1880 and again from 1884 until the second year of the Revolution in 1911, his accomplishments have not been so honored in Oaxaca, where he is usually thought of as a ruthless dictator not deserving of memorials—though you will find a street named in his memory.

The Plaza de Armas

The Plaza de Armas, or zócalo, actually consists of two public squares, the large Plaza de la Constitución and the smaller Alameda de León, which is surrounded by the cathedral, a number of government buildings, and the post office. The **cathedral**, which was begun in 1553 and finally finished in the 19th century, is squat rather than soaring, solid rather than elaborate. It almost seems to huddle on its plot, its two flying buttresses ready to ward off the vicious earthquakes that have struck the city more than once. Nevertheless, the colonial clock on its façade still keeps good time.

The enormous main plaza is surrounded by arcades and café tables occupied from breakfast to late evening by people eating, listening to music, gossiping, reading newspapers, or simply nursing cups of coffee as they while away the hours. Jugglers entertain with brightly colored balls, guitarists tune their instruments. Two women, their *rebozos* worn turban-style, carry big flat baskets on their heads, balanced off-center in apparent defiance of gravity. Elsewhere, a small ragged boy recites a poem at the top of his lungs, stanza after stanza; payment is hoped for. For many, the best seats from which to take all this in are the tall chairs meant for shoe shines, spaced like thrones at the edges of flowerbeds and sidewalks. Business thrives. Except for running shoes, everything else seems to need a shine every hour or two.

The air in Oaxaca is soft, the climate mild, neither sultry nor cool (although a sweater or light jacket will come in handy in the early morning and evening). Against the sky over the zócalo float bunches of balloons arranged in the shapes of fanciful animals. The balloon vendors seem to float as well, wandering from spot to spot, seldom making a sale. Oaxaca's vendors in general are businesslike without being offensively pushy. They have apparently learned that "no" may actually mean "no," whether the prospective buyer is looking at a woven rug, an engraved machete, or a colorful necklace.

Iglesia de Santo Domingo and Museo Regional

The Iglesia de Santo Domingo, located five blocks north of the zócalo in an area free of traffic, was begun by the Dominicans in 1575 and finished about a century later; the Baroque façade was added another 100 years after that. The intricate ornamentation evident everywhere, however, makes it surprising it was ever finished at all. Dazzling golden scrollwork covers almost every inch of the interior, including the 11 chapels. Especially remarkable is the many-branched Tree of Jesse, a series of 35 detailed relief figures illustrating the lineal descent of Christ.

The **Museo Regional del Estado**, housed in the attached convent, has as its great prize the treasures from Monte Albán. Visitors who see nothing else in the city usually find their way to the **Tomb 7 collection**, discovered in 1932. The magnificent jewelry on display, dating from about A.D. 500, consists of gold, conch shell, turquoise, amber, obsidian, onyx, and glass worked into elaborate pieces by superb ancient craftsmen. (The filigree necklaces are often used as models for the jewelry sold in Oaxaca's downtown stores.) Like so much else in Oaxaca—the Rococo bandstand, the fine embroidery work, and the marimba music, with its extra trills and flourishes—the jewelry from Tomb 7 is above all elaborate and complex, suggesting that Indian craftsmen centuries ago may have originated the long artistic traditions of the region.

Instituto de Artes Graficas de Oaxaca

Oaxaca exerts a strong pull on its native sons; they often return, after they have become successful, to share their fame with their birthplace. A few years ago the painter Rufino Tamayo did just that by establishing a splendid museum of pre-Columbian art in Oaxaca. More recently, the artist Francisco Toledo opened a museum of graphic arts in the building that was his childhood home (he now lives in Mexico City) and filled it with hundreds of lithographs, aquatints, and silk-screened prints from his huge collection.

The museum, across the street from the church of Santo Domingo at Alcalá 507, opened in late 1989 under the auspices of the State of Oaxaca and the National Institute of Fine Arts. Its seven rooms surround a garden courtyard and are filled with an extremely varied collection, including works by the likes of Goya, Matisse, Picasso, and Rouault, as well as Mexican giants such as Rivera and Orozco. For every famous artist represented you'll also find something by one of today's emerging lithographers. Special exhibits from time to time only add to this first-rate museum's already considerable appeal. Admission is free; closed Tuesdays.

Museo Rufino Tamayo

A plaque in the Museo Rufino Tamayo tells the visitor, in less-than-perfect Spanish, French, and English: "This museum is dedicated to the millenary art which flourished in the area called now-a-days the Republic of Mexico, art entirely inspired (with the exception of Occidental Mexico) by Pre-Columbian religions and myths, which represents the deified forces of nature: the sun, the wind, the water, and a multitude of other natural phenomena. But if, in our time, the pieces exhibited in the niches of the museum impress its visitors, it is not for religious feelings, because the religions of ancient Mexicans, a long time ago have been forgotten. Rather they are moved by the aesthetic rank of the works, their beauty, power, and originality."

The plaque goes on to emphasize the point: "It is the first time that a Mexican museum exhibits the relics of Indian past in terms of aesthetic phenomena, in terms of works of art."

The pieces in this museum were assembled as a private collection by Rufino Tamayo, one of modern Mexico's most admired painters, and donated to the city of Oaxaca, his birthplace. Tamayo took care that the public would see the objects at their best: There are no catchall display cases of "black pottery from the valley" or "human figures, various" here. Instead, each piece has received careful consideration, is described individually, and is mounted against a background—light blue, perhaps, or rose or orange—that brings out its beauty. The museum, northwest of the zócalo at Morelos 503, is housed in an old mansion with a flower-bordered patio. The convenient benches around the patio are a good place to rest and admire the pre-Columbian figures of men playing musical instruments, the Colima dogs yapping in unison, a man in a coyote mask, or a fierce jaguar carved out of jagged volcanic rock. The Rufino

Tamayo Museum is what a museum should be but often is not: a place for quiet contemplation and unhurried reflection. Closed for the siesta, and on Tuesdays.

Museo de Arte Contemporaneo

This is the newest of Oaxaca's museums, inaugurated in March 1992. Housed in a magnificent 16th-century mansion at Alcalá 202, it is "a cultural project dedicated to developing a greater awarenes of plastic arts from the State of Oaxaca as well as Mexico and other countries." The colonial building with its fragments of original frescoes has been restored beautifully, and some original doors and windows remain. Its high-ceilinged rooms and spacious patio form an imposing background for the works of contemporary Oaxacan artists. Several galleries are devoted to paintings by Rufino Tamayo, others to Francisco Toledo, Rodolfo Nieto, and Francisco Gutierrez. One room holds rare 19th-century photographs, another contains an extensive art library. Admission is free; closed Tuesdays.

The Saturday Market

Outdoor markets are a way of life in Mexico, and the market in Oaxaca is one of the biggest and best known. Although it operates every day, it really comes alive on Saturday, when farmers, craftspeople, and merchants from the small villages of the great Valley of Oaxaca stream into town. D. H. Lawrence was so intrigued by the spectacle, in fact, that he devoted a chapter of *Mornings in Mexico* to it. In those days, some 60 years ago, Indians almost always travelled by foot or burro, arriving loaded with goods for sale or to barter. "A little load of firewood, a woven blanket, a few eggs and tomatoes," Lawrence wrote, "are excuse enough for men, women and children to cross the foot-weary miles of valley and mountain. To buy, to sell, to barter, to exchange. To exchange, above all things, human contact."

Today's participants are as likely to arrive by truck or ancient car as by burro or on foot. Also, the city has cleaned up and somewhat deromanticized the market. Food is no longer spread out haphazardly on the ground. Merchants are assigned stalls, and their wares are exhibited on wooden stands, shielded from the sun and rain by lengths of old canvas. What was once a wide-open area of color and activity has been turned into a maze of alleys (making it easy to get lost), with here and there an open patio. As is always the case in Mexican markets, the same types of goods are arranged near one another. Next to one sugarcane vendor is another sugarcane vendor and next to him yet another. There seems to be no special competitive atmosphere; instead, it's much like a department store where dresses or kitchen utensils are lumped together.

There is an endless variety of things to buy here, from shoelaces to coconuts. Still, for the visitor—especially one with a camera—the food area is by far the most interesting. All this food comes from the surrounding countryside, and is arranged artistically, best side visible, in small piles (*pilas*) of five, in mountains of gleaming color, or in bundles or baskets.

The food area may be splendid, but to get to it you have to walk through alley after alley of uninteresting pots and pans, tapes of rock music, men's pants, and automobile parts. Do not go to the Saturday market expecting a primitive Indian scene. Approach it, instead, as a remarkable chance to see how impressive a massing of objects can be: a hundred cold gray machetes, a thousand plastic shoes, a glittering mound of blood-red tomatoes, a barricade of papayas, a million dried shrimp in baskets shining golden in the sun.

One more word of advice: The market should not be visited in the early morning, despite the fact that this may be recommended to you. The vendors will still be streaming into town then, and many of the stalls will not yet be open. The best time to go is about 10:30 A.M.

Shopping in Oaxaca

Oaxaca City is noted for the variety of its local crafts—serapes woven in muted colors and intricate patterns; unusual green and black ceramics; machetes with elaborate designs incised into their handles; delicate filigree jewelry. The serious shopper will have a wide selection from which to choose, and the way to go about it will depend on your personality and frame of mind. Anyone who loves to bargain will head for the market, where the first price mentioned is always far higher than the final one. The aficionado of cottage industries, on the other hand, will head for the outlying crafts villages. The best of these are **Teotitlán del Valle** (on the way to Mitla; see below) for weaving, **Atzompa** for green pottery, or **San Bartolo Coyotepec** for black. The black pottery, which is unique to the area, is left unglazed and fired in subterranean ovens so that the smoke colors the clay. Tours to these villages can be arranged in town, and there are also frequent buses from the second-class bus station at the end of Calle Trujano. For those with their own cars, these places are all a short ride over good roads.

Anyone who dislikes discussing price will be best served in a shop, and Oaxaca has some good ones.

Yalalag de Oaxaca, at the corner of Avenida Morelos and Macedonio Alcalá, is excellent for black pottery and woven goods. Two other good shops are located at Calle 3 and Alcalá, on the pedestrian mall one block from the Presidente hotel. **Artesanias Copil** has the best collection of masks in town, while **Artesanias Itandehui** sells a variety of colorful things that make good gifts, including dolls and glassware.

Also on Alcalá, at number 203, **La Mano Mágica** is a friendly shop with a wide variety of carefully selected merchandise: ceramics, woven goods, clothes, paintings, and more. In fact, it's as good a place as any to get an overview of the local handicrafts before stocking up.

Casa Victor's, Porfirio Díaz 111, is housed in a 17th-century monastery that has been converted into a shop. The stark, battered building seems about to collapse, but the store boasts a large selection of woven goods, ceramics, and cut paper. **El Tecolote**, nearby, offers ceramic figurines and a variety of woven goods.

The unusual offerings at **El Cosijo**, on Calle García Vigil, include fanciful figurines and big papier-mâché skeletons decorated with feathers.

Some of Oaxaca's most interesting shops focus on specialty items. The **Cuchilleria Alcalá**, at Alcalá 206, contains nothing but knives and swords handcrafted in the unique Oaxacan style with engraved blades, some embellished with mottoes. The hundreds of cutting blades here are suitable for everything from slicing a lemon to decapitating an enemy.

Oro de Monte Albán, in the Palacio Santo Domingo, the shopping center on Alcalá, has specialized for more than 25 years in the art of manufacturing three types of traditional Oaxacan jewelry: colonial (based on colonial-period designs), filigree, and pre-Columbian (especially miniature reproductions of the jewels found in Tomb 7 at Monte Albán). Visitors are welcome to watch the craftsmen in the workshop across the street as they make the gold jewelry using the "lost" wax technique, a complicated, laborious process. Hot melted wax is poured into a rubber mold struck from a tin replica of the original design, and a plaster cast is made from the cooled wax impression. When heated in a kiln, the wax is "lost" into the surrounding plaster. The hollow cast then is placed in a centrifuge and connected to a crucible containing gold, which, when melted by a blowtorch, is forced into the mold by centrifugal force. The shattered plaster cast reveals the delicate gold miniature, which is then cleaned in acid and trimmed; finally, a chain loop is attached.

In the last few years the painted animals made by woodcarvers in the Oaxaca Valley have become known abroad, fetching astronomical prices in the United States. These whimsical, imaginative figures are carved from the local hardwood *copal* and painted in bright designs, mostly by carvers in three tiny villages close to Oaxaca City: Arrazola, San Martín Tilcajete, and La Union Tejalapan. Arrazola, home of Manuel Jimenez, most famous of the artisans, is at the base of Monte Albán. Your best bet is to take a taxi, since the driver usually will be able to locate the homes where carving is done (there are no visible signs). The animals are less expensive in the villages than in Oaxaca, but some carvers may refuse to sell at all, saving their work for financially profitable export. If your trip to the source proves frustrating, check the usual folk art shops in Oaxaca. One store, called **Jimenez**, at Alcalá 407, carries Manuel Jimenez's work exclusively. You can purchase a crazy rabbit, a mermaid, a giraffe with a long, long neck, or the Devil himself, for anywhere from $300 to $600, depending on size. Many of the wooden animals sold on the streets of Oaxaca by less well-known artists, on the other hand, are quite inexpensive—from about $10 to $30.

Clothing shops in Oaxaca usually carry either traditional ethnic designs in *huipiles* (sleeveless garments resembling tunics), *rebozos,* and skirts (which, though beautiful in a Mexican setting, may seem out of place at home), or abandon the ethnic for international styles. At **Creaciones Lixhi-Tuu**, Alcalá 402, Interior 5, modern designs are created using handwoven cotton procured from villages in the Oaxaca Valley that is then decorated with delicate embroidery and drawn work. The result is a fine blend of traditional folk art and current fashion.

Finally, when you have done all your shopping and wonder how to get it home, you can stop in at **The Open Door** office at Labastida 118-1, around the corner from the Presidente hotel. This answer to tourist prayers will pack and ship, translate and interpret, explain business practices and customs, help with banking, phone calls, documentation, and anything else you need. Open Monday through Saturday from 8:30 A.M. to 12:30 P.M.; Tel: (951) 6-0403.

Staying in Oaxaca City

The **Stouffer Presidente Oaxaca**, right around the corner from the church of Santo Domingo, is probably the most romantic, and certainly the most historic, hotel in Mexico. Originally the Convento de Santa Catalina (c. 1576), it was tastefully remodeled and converted into a hotel some years ago with no expense spared. Today it's a labyrinth of sunny, flower-filled patios and shadowy arcades surrounding a lovely, grassy pool area. The junior suites are decorated in rose or blue tile, with locally woven wall hangings. The single rooms tend to be a little monastic, perfectly adequate but not as nice as the doubles and junior suites. The building itself is a veritable museum, and offers its guests a tangible sense of Oaxaca's colonial past. Romantic music provided by accomplished musicians at mealtimes further adds to the atmosphere of the past.

The food at the Presidente is definitely international, with few traditional Mexican dishes on the menu. As one of the chain of Presidente hotels it has the advantage of expertise from the capital, however, and may bring in a guest chef to supervise from time to time. The food is beautifully presented in a manner worthy of the hotel's colonial style. The sauces, especially, are rich and elaborate, the garnishes attractive.

By Oaxaca standards the Presidente is expensive, but not by international or even national standards. It is especially popular with Europeans, so the atmosphere tends to be international, but the jeans-and-sandals set is also welcome.

The **Hotel Victoria** sits high on a hill north of town at kilometer 545 of the Pan-American Highway. As it is not within easy walking distance of the zócalo area, its guests frequently fly down from Mexico City, then rent a car for the sake of convenience and sightseeing. There are two sections to the complex; the newer—and much the better—one features bungalows with slick pine furniture, walk-in closets, and refrigerators. The hotel's Mixtec-decorated restaurant caters to foreign tastes, with traditional Mexican dishes modified to suit North American palates. Looking out on the panoramic view of the valley, the diner here can enjoy what D. H. Lawrence described as the "gleaming, pinkish-ochre of the valley flat, wild and exalted...." The Victoria also has a bar, disco, swimming pool, and is less expensive than the Presidente, though still high priced.

The **Fortín Plaza**, next door to the Victoria, features much white tile and marble, with Mixtec motifs. (The front rooms have the best views.) It also has a swimming pool and tennis courts, as well as a restaurant that specializes in seafood. Meals are served on a terrace overlooking the swimming pool, with soft tango music as an accompaniment from 4:00 to 8:00 P.M. every day except Sunday. Slightly less expensive than the Victoria, the Fortín Plaza nevertheless attracts affluent Mexicans from the D.F. as well as locally.

The moderately priced **Hotel San Felipe Misión Oaxaca**, in a new residential neighborhood five minutes north of the city by car, is an attractive, well-maintained member of the Misión chain of hotels. The rooms here are comfortable, if a bit bare, the lobby and public areas ample. It has all the usual amenities—swimming pool, bar, nightclub, convention hall—and the dining room and swimming pool overlook the city. The hotel also offers hourly courtesy transportation to and from downtown, a big advantage for guests who have not arrived by car. It's all a bit routine, not memorably different from hotels in other cities, but pleasantly far from the din of traffic. The Sunday brunch, lavish and well served, is worth going up the hill for even if you are not staying here.

The **Misión de los Angeles**, at Calzada Porfirio Díaz 102, a long walk north of the zócalo, is tropical, lazy, and spacious, with beautiful grounds ideal for strolling. The suites here have fireplaces and old-fashioned furnishings, and the hotel has a dining room, a nightclub, and, on weekends, a disco. The Misión appeals to an older crowd, many of them retirees from cold climates. It's in the same price range as the Victoria, but not quite as good.

The moderately priced **Calesa Real**, two-and-a-half blocks north of the zócalo, is a former colonial town house with 77 units and a central patio. The rooms are simple but charming, and there's a secure parking lot next door. The restaurant in the Calesa Real is the most Mexican of the hotel restaurants, in both atmosphere and menu, with few concessions to the tourist. The pork and chicken dishes are especially tasty, and the prices are moderate.

Located right on the zócalo the **Señorial** also has a secure parking facility for guests (at the rear of the hotel). Behind its colonial façade is a modern and busy, though somewhat impersonal, hotel. However, many visitors find it comfortable as well as convenient. The units vary greatly in size; the rates are moderate.

The **Hotel Las Golondrinas**, a small, two-story converted home, is a good choice for the budget-conscious traveller. The 24 rooms here, all of which open onto garden patios, are clean and well kept, the atmosphere informal. Although there is no restaurant, breakfast is served. In fact, the hotel's only shortcoming is its slightly inconvenient location—about five blocks from the main plaza.

The **Marqués del Valle**, next door to the cathedral, is a

dowager that has been deteriorating for a couple of decades. However, its rooms, which are pleasantly spacious, recently have been repainted, and the baths are big and old-fashioned. The public areas are another story—a hodgepodge of posters stuck on marble columns, cigarette dispensers, and soft-drink vending machines. Still, it is right on the zócalo, and its café tables are always occupied.

The **Hotel Parador Plaza**, on the other hand, is brand new, having opened in 1991. Located near the zócalo at Murguia 104, it is decorated in a breezy modern style, with large and airy rooms. Its restaurant specializes in regional dishes.

Dining in Oaxaca City

Oaxaca has its specialties, among them tamales wrapped in banana leaves and its own version of *mole,* the chocolate-chile sauce more often associated with Puebla. Also notable here is the *comida corrida,* the fixed-price meal of several courses served during the midday lunch hour (a good way to get a well-balanced dinner from soup to dessert for a reasonable price).

In contrast to the hotel restaurants discussed above, the dining room at the **Hotel Monte Albán**, opposite the cathedral, is only mediocre. But the evening show of regional dancing here, despite its amateurism—poor sound track, overlong intermissions—is an excellent opportunity to see traditional dances from various towns in Oaxaca state staged with grace and enthusiasm. You'll be asked to pay a small admission charge; dining is not required.

Oaxaca has a handful of very good restaurants that are not in hotels. The best one is also the newest, a dream of period atmosphere, delicious cuisine, and sensible, friendly service: the **Del Vitral**, listed in *Gastrotur,* a Mexican gourmet magazine, as "the best restaurant in Oaxaca and the southeast of Mexico." It's a short walk east of the zócalo on Avenida V. Guerrero, where it occupies the second floor of a magnificent turn-of-the-century mansion. An imposing staircase leads up to a balcony, a dining room facing the street, and the "stained glass" room to the left. The stained glass, which gives the restaurant its name, runs along one whole side of the room, an enormous window decorated with fountains, cupids, and trees. It was created by European craftsmen for the wealthy Zorrilla family, whose descendants own the restaurant and have refurbished it to splendid effect: A pale rose decor, opulent draperies, and huge chandeliers are just some of its elegant touches. The best thing about Del Vitral, however, is that it has not become "Continental" and snobbish. Many of the dishes are from old Oaxacan recipes, and prices are high but not outrageous. Tel: (951) 6-3124.

Las Chalotes, a couple of blocks from the zócalo at Fiallo 116, is a first-rate French restaurant. The atmosphere is decidedly Gallic, the food excellent, the prices moderate. The usual French favorites—quiche lorraine, *boeuf Bourguignon,* and the like—are offered along with somewhat more adventurous choices such as warm goat's cheese salad or couscous. Tel: (951) 6-4897.

One restaurant that has been doing well for a good many years now is **El Asador Vasco**, located on the second floor of a building on the west side of the zócalo. It caters to a European crowd and serves steak, chicken, and fish as well as a few regional dishes. Try for a table overlooking the plaza; it's an expensive place, but you're paying partly for the view—as well as for the musicians who wander among the tables. Reservations are important; El Asador Vasco can get very crowded and rushed Tel: (951) 6-9719.

The **Restaurante Bar Catedral**, one block from the zócalo at Garcia Vigil 105, is pretty, airy, and comfortable, with tables set out in a small patio. The lengthy, reasonably priced menu emphasizes meat: eight different steak entrées along with chops and chicken; it's also a good place for the *comida corrida*. At night there is piano music. Tel: (951) 6-3285.

The **Hostería de Alcalá**, Macedonio Alcalá 307, offers a varied menu that includes a number of Mexican specialties. Located in the patio of a renovated colonial mansion, it is a refreshingly cool place to eat and unwind after a morning spent shopping in the attractive stores that line this street. Tel: (951) 6-2093.

There are very few good Chinese restaurants in Mexico, so it's both a surprise and a pleasure to find **Quing Long**, on the second floor of the new shopping complex on M. Alcalá, across the street from the church of Santo Domingo. The extensive menu embraces three styles of Chinese cuisine: Szechuan, Cantonese, and Hunan, with the emphasis on spicy Szechuan. Prices for individual dishes are high, but there are two reasonably priced set dinners on the menu. Tel: (951) 6-0232.

El Mesón, just off the zócalo on Hidalgo, is a simple and clean open-fronted restaurant where *oaxaqueños* drop in for big buffet breakfasts, snacks, and fruit drinks. Every kind of fruit imaginable is displayed, along with regional dishes such as *tamales* in banana leaves, tacos, and steaming *mole* in big earthenware pots. A regular menu lists more familiar dishes—ham, eggs, fried potatoes, and the like. Portions are big, prices modest (no phone).

The small **El Decano** restaurant and bar at Cinco de Mayo 210 is clean and unpretentious, with appetizing food and a friendly atmosphere. Open every day from 8:00 A.M. to 1:00 A.M., this is a good place for breakfast or to try regional specialties. Tel: (951) 6-9284.

OUTSIDE THE CITY
Monte Albán

At the majestic ruins of Monte Albán, 10 km (6 miles) south and west of the city, everything is enormous and austere, the ambience of the site enhanced by the sheer mass of the stone structures and the perspective lent by the surrounding mountains. As anyone who has ever visited Monte Albán knows, it's not surprising that people should come from all over the world with the express purpose of seeing the ruins. The groups of tourists who walk to and fro here are dwarfed by the scene; but then, so would a crowd of thousands.

Monte Albán is the only pre-Columbian necropolis in Mexico. The hill on which it stands, 1,300 feet above the Valley of Oaxaca, was flattened and shaped by the original builders and then used as a base for the construction that ensued. Today buff-colored masses of stone—stairs, columns, platforms, colonnades, halls, and passages—surround the central plaza. Below ground are more than 200 tombs where the dead were buried along with their "companion sculptures" (meant to accompany them on their journey to the other world). The earliest writing (glyphs) yet discovered in Mexico was also found at Monte Albán.

The precise origins of this complex are uncertain. Construction of the site seems to have begun about 800 B.C., and it might have been an early outpost of the Olmec people; although no artifacts from that seminal culture have been found at the site, the presence of the flowing "Olmec line" in some of the sculpture suggests they had an early influence on local populations. The *danzantes,* in the so-called **Templo de los Danzantes** (Temple of the Dancers), low relief sculpture carved out of hard stone, are the best-known relics from this period, and exhibit physical characteristics suggestive of the jaguar motif in Olmec art. The naked *danzantes* writhe and crouch in unnaturally contorted positions, and may represent individuals with medical problems or physical malformations. Or, since some seem to be marked with a flowery design on the interior of their thighs or on the abdomen, they may illustrate the practices of a primitive sexual cult. Still other theories suggest that they represent prisoners who were ultimately sacrificed. In any case, they remain mysterious. After the earliest period, **Monte Albán I**, there was little further stone sculpting at the site, and pottery took over.

The period archaeologists call **Monte Albán II** began about 300 B.C., with a different group of Indians occupying the site and leveling the hilltop for the Great Plaza and the **astronomical observatory**, the arrow-shaped structure also known as Building J. The walls of Building J are inscribed with hieroglyphic inscriptions, probably recording the victories of Monte Albán's warriors in battle. The partly unroofed interior chamber may have been used for astronomical observations, although this is not certain.

About 400 years later the Zapotecs arrived and, over the next 800 years, created a brilliant ceremonial center, constructing, in the process, a huge patio surrounded by buildings. This period, known as **Monte Albán III**, was followed by years of decline, beginning about A.D. 1000. Although the reasons remain obscure, the decline was universal in Mesoamerica. Mixtecs from the north migrated into the Valley of Oaxaca at this time, a period known as **Monte Albán IV**, and began to build tombs at the site without displacing their Zapotec predecessors.

The last active period at the site, when it became a necropolis for Mixtec nobles, lasted from A.D. 1200 to the Spanish Conquest and is known as **Monte Albán V**. In 1932 **Tomb 7**, which dates from this period, was excavated, revealing the greatest haul of archaeological treasure ever found in Mexico. Today the gold necklaces, carved jaguar bones, turquoise mosaics, and heavy strings of pearls from the tomb are housed in the Museo Regional in Oaxaca City.

To the visitor Monte Albán looks like an enormous complex of flat patios, terraced walls, and stone steps leading upward to the sky. The **ball court**, in the form of the letter "I," is the first large structure apparent as you enter the area. The hoop through which the ball is supposed to have passed is missing, but the large stone in the center probably marks the game's starting point. Above the court is a small temple where dignitaries and judges presided, and tiers of grandstand seats on either side of the playing area are well preserved. It is not hard to imagine a contest here, differing from our modern sports events only in that the losers probably lost their lives as well.

Other structures include **El Palacio** (The Palace), a large residence with 13 rooms encircling a central courtyard, and those known rather prosaically as Buildings G, H, I, M, L, and P, which once served as temples, altars, and sanctuaries. Additionally, there are numerous mounds, tombs, and

Oaxaca State (detail)

- Ixtlán
- Natividad
- *SIERRA VILLA ALTA*
- Santa Ana del Valle
- Yagul
- Mitla
- Ruinas de Mitla
- PAN-AMERICAN HWY. 190

N

0 — miles — 10
0 — kilometers — 16

sunken patios. Though much of the site has been excavated and studied, a great deal remains to be explored. Perhaps most impressive of all, however, is the sense of history, mysterious and unrecorded, that hangs in the air. Best seen shortly before dusk, these massive relics of former civilizations lead most visitors to pause and reflect on the passing of time, and are sobering reminders of the ephemeral nature of our own world.

The Mitla Area

Mitla, like Monte Albán, is an archaeological site, but the two couldn't be more different in atmosphere. At Mitla there is no feeling of vastness or isolation, for the ruins, close to a thriving village, are approached through an avenue of stalls where vendors urge serapes, *rebozos,* ceramics, and little pots of mezcal on every passerby. At the head of this avenue—really a dirt road—the ruins appear high on a hill, with a church to one side. Even at the entrance to the site wares are offered insistently.

To get to Mitla requires more time and effort than the 15-minute drive to Monte Albán. The daily tours from the Presidente, Victoria, and Marqués del Valle hotels, minivans of eight passengers with a trained guide, are your best bet. It's also possible to get there by bus, which gives you a chance to mingle with passengers who often speak an Indian dialect rather than Spanish and carry their children tenderly on their laps. (Children receive particular attention in Mexico. They are uniformly well behaved—except for some of the spoiled city kids—and seldom ill treated. Fathers seem to take as much practical care of them as mothers, and older children mind the younger ones. Charles Flandrau, who visited Mexico early in this century and wrote a classic account of his experiences, suggested that all children should be Mexican until the age of 15.)

Along the 40-km (25-mile) road to Mitla (Highway 190, the Pan-American Highway) are turnoffs to Dainzú, Lambityeco, and Yagul (smaller archaeological sites), as well as the textile-craft villages of Teotitlán del Valle and Santa Ana del Valle. It would be easy to extend your visit to Oaxaca beyond three days in order to spend some time visiting any or all of them.

These three archaeological sites would be more crowded than they are were it not for the ruins at Monte Albán and Mitla. **Dainzú**, which was an occupied village site as early as 600 B.C., boasts three large patios and buildings, as well as 50 sandstone slabs bearing bas-reliefs of ball players in action that date from about 100 B.C. The small site of **Lambityeco**, which reached its zenith around A.D. 700, is noteworthy for its stucco busts of Cocijo, the Zapotec rain god, along with its portraitlike human heads. **Yagul**, a much larger site, has an acropolis comprising a cluster of tombs and palaces, most notably the Palace of Six Patios, as well as the ruins of a great fortress situated on the crest of a steep hill overlooking the site.

Two other sites, off a side road heading south from Oaxaca, are worth visiting separately. At **Cuilapán**, in addition to a pyramid and Zapotec tomb, there's a handsome 16th-century monastery and church, both outsized and incomplete, with rows of columns waiting for a roof, enormous empty courtyards, and half-built arches. According to legend, the Dominican monks who initiated the project kept enlarging their plans, always thinking of something to add, never able to call it done. One day they welcomed a stranger in a carriage who offered to complete the project before cock crow the next morning if the abbot would sign a paper afterwards. Realizing this was the Devil, and that with the paper he would sign away his soul, the abbot rose in the night before the work was completed and made a cock crow, thus winning the contest. He kept his soul, but the monastery and church were never finished; the work was destroyed every night and, eventually, the Dominicans gave up trying.

Zaachila, a small village and the last Zapotec capital in the valley, claims a huge unexplored pyramid that dominates the center of the town.

The two crafts villages on the road to Mitla—**Teotitlán del Valle** and **Santa Ana del Valle**—produce some of the most elaborate handwoven textiles in Mexico. The *huipiles,* sleeveless tunic-like garments for women, are woven in complicated patterns on pale or colored backgrounds, and often have embroidered overlays and bright fluttering ribbons. Aficionados can even identify the town of origin: in Teotitlán del Valle, for instance, doves, fish, and flowers are combined in a variety of artful designs. Likewise, chemical dyes, not the primitive cochineal and vegetable dyes, are used to produce unusual shades of red, purple, and green. (The traditional dyes, though not as varied, are more vibrant.) The serapes worn by Zapotec men are less elaborate, although they're sometimes designed with strident patterns for sale to tourists. The most attractive are woven out of undyed gray or black wool, and feature figures of animals, birds, or abstract patterns in pale colors. Rugs are a specialty of Teotitlán del Valle, and you may be surprised to see designs copied from paintings by Picasso and other modern masters in addition to more conventional Oaxacan motifs. Originally taken from illustrations in an art book left in the village, the copies have proved to be as popular as the more traditional patterns.

If your time is limited, instead of going to these individual crafts villages take the Mitla tour on a Sunday, when the town of **Tlacolula**, on the way, is crowded with buyers and sellers attending its weekly market. Wares from all the nearby villages are brought to town and then sold up and down the dirt road in front of the local church. Tlacolula is also a mezcal-producing center, and the neighborhood stores will offer tiny glasses (your choice of sweet or dry) as a softening-up gesture. There's a Gypsy-like air to the Tlacolula market, and everyone seems to wear his or her brightest skirts, shirts, and shawls.

Every tour bus or taxi that heads out this way also makes an obligatory stop to see the **Tule tree** at Santa María del Tule. What kind of a tree warrants such attention? Well, it's a superlative tree, the oldest living thing in Mexico—2,000 years old, according to some naturalists. It's also an *ahuehuete* tree (*Taxodium mucronatum*), which is variously translated as a water cypress or sequoia. While they're larger in girth than redwoods in the States, they're not as tall. A smaller tree of the same species, known as *el hijo* (the son), grows nearby; it's only 500 to 600 years old. The older tree is usually surrounded by crowds of onlookers—foreign, Mexican, Indian, children as well as adults—staring with concentrated interest. But what else can be done with such a landmark? It's even too big to photograph, unless you're carrying a wide-angle lens.

Mitla was a shrine long before the extant ruins were constructed, and was probably inhabited 1,000 years before the beginning of the Christian era. The latest explorations here show that it probably emerged in its present incarnation during the period known as Monte Albán I, but its greatest development occurred later, possibly at the time of Monte Albán's decline, when it was rebuilt by the Mixtecs and dedicated to Mictlán, the Lord of the Underworld. It remained in full flower until relatively late, and was still active at the time of the Spanish Conquest.

Today the ruins (those that were not destroyed after the Conquest to build a sugar mill and churches) appear to be almost perfectly preserved, and seem designed for a secular rather than religious use. Many of the structures date to about A.D. 1400. (Much older remains are still being explored in a larger area encompassing the town.)

The style of construction at Mitla also differs from that

found at Monte Albán. There is no relief carving here; instead, all the decoration takes the form of geometrically abstract mosaics precisely cut and fitted into walls. The effect is akin to stylized embroidery, beige on beige, monochrome and repetitive, set in a surrounding area of sand-colored rock. Here and there the effect may be broken by a scarlet or bright blue flower that has gained a foothold in a crevice of the lattice-like patterns. In the courtyards enclosed by these elaborately worked walls are a number of heavy columns; put your arms around a certain column, legend has it, and the space between your hands will reveal how long you have to live.

To the left as you enter the village of Mitla is the **Museo Frissell de Arte Zapoteca**. Formerly a private museum, it was started in the 1940s by Erwin Robert Frissell, a retired real-estate broker from Minneapolis to whom local farmers brought pottery unearthed in their fields. His collection of ceramic pieces arranged in chronological order is now the property of the University of the Americas and open to the public. In the patio of the same building, which was Frissell's home, **La Sorpresa** (The Surprise) serves an excellent fixed lunch, while across the street a small cafeteria offers à la carte dishes.

GETTING AROUND

Oaxaca is easily reached from Mexico City. (There are no direct international flights.) Both Mexicana and Aeroméxico make the 50-minute flight several times daily. There is also a night train with Pullman accommodations. Buses make the trip in 10 to 12 hours, and Highway 190, for those driving the 7 hours from the D.F. to Oaxaca, is a good one.

The beach resorts are a half-hour's flight from Oaxaca City. Puerto Escondido and Huatulco are served by Mexicana. Aerocaribe, a feeder airline of Mexicana, offers flights four times a week from Oaxaca City to Huatulco. Puerto Escondido can also be reached from Oaxaca City by car or bus over a spectacular, twisting mountain road, Highway 175, which plunges down the steep southern flank of the Sierra Madre del Sur and hits the Pacific coast at Puerto Angel. The direct Oaxaca–Puerto Escondido road, Highway 131, is still unimproved in places and better left to those in four-wheel-drive vehicles.

The city of Oaxaca is easily explored on foot. Taxis are always available near the cathedral, and rental cars can be obtained from Avis at the airport or from Hertz at Plaza Labastida (adjacent to the church of Santo Domingo).

Guided tours to the surrounding villages and archaeological sites leave from the Presidente, Victoria, and Marqués del Valle hotels. A *colectivo* from the Mesón del Angel (Mina 518) takes passengers to Monte Albán and picks them up later for the return trip to the city. Most cab drivers in town also will be happy to drop you off and pick you up again at an appointed time. (Note: Tomb 7 closes about an hour before the site itself does.) Taxis can be hired for about $10 an hour for trips to other sites and crafts villages.

The first-class bus station is at Niños Héroes de Chapultepec near Emiliano Carranza, but most of the buses to the surrounding villages leave from the second-class station across the railroad tracks at the end of Calle Trujano.

The train station is located on the west side of town on Calle Madero.

For the trip to the airport, seats in a van can be reserved at the office next to the Monte Albán Hotel or through one of the travel agencies in town.

When to go? The big tourist season is from January to March, but this is due as much to North Americans' desire to escape the snow as it is the belief that summer in Oaxaca is unpleasant. Summer *is* warmer, and there are brief tropical rains almost daily from June through September, but the altitude eliminates the sultry tropical heat you would expect at this latitude. If you decide to visit the city at Christmas time, be sure to make reservations well in advance.

There are a number of famous fiestas in Oaxaca, particularly the "Night of the Radishes," on December 23. This unusual celebration is marked by a competition among area villages to see which can fashion the most elaborate folk dance or creative depiction of a biblical story with figures made from the common garden radish. Another colorful fiesta that recently has attracted international attention features the Guelaguetza dances, honoring the ancient goddess of corn. The dates for the latter fall on two Mondays in July.

ACCOMMODATIONS REFERENCE

The rates given below are projections for December 1992 through Easter 1993. Unless otherwise indicated, rates are for double rooms, double occupancy; the 10 percent VAT has been added. As rates are subject to change, it's always a good idea to double-check before booking.

▶ **Calesa Real.** Calle García Vigil 306, **Oaxaca**, Oaxaca 68000. Tel: (951) 6-5544; Fax: (951) 5-9687. $41.

▶ **Fortín Plaza.** Pan-American Highway, km 545, **Oaxaca**, Oaxaca 68040. Tel: (951) 5-7777; Fax: (951) 5-1328. $79.

- ▶ **Hotel Las Golondrinas.** Tinoco y Palacios 411, **Oaxaca**, Oaxaca 68000. Tel: (951) 4-2126. $22
- ▶ **Hotel Parador Plaza.** Murguia 104, **Oaxaca**, Oaxaca 68000. Tel: (951) 6-4900; Fax: (951) 4-2037. $43.
- ▶ **Hotel San Felipe Misión Oaxaca.** Jalisco Sur 15, San Felipe del Agua, **Oaxaca**, Oaxaca 68020. Tel: (951) 5-0100; Fax: (951) 5-0900. $69.
- ▶ **Hotel Señorial.** Portal de Flores 6, **Oaxaca**, Oaxaca 68000. Tel: (951) 6-3933. $43.
- ▶ **Hotel Victoria.** P.O. Box 248, Pan-American Highway, km 545, **Oaxaca**, Oaxaca 68040. Tel: (951) 5-2633; Fax: (951) 5-2411. $84.
- ▶ **Marqués del Valle.** Portal de Claveria, **Oaxaca**, Oaxaca 68000. Tel: (951) 6-3295; Fax: (951) 6-6294. $44.
- ▶ **Misión de los Angeles.** P.O. Box 171, Calzada Porfirio Díaz 102, **Oaxaca**, Oaxaca 68050. Tel: (951) 5-1500; Fax: (951) 5-1680. $78.
- ▶ **Stouffer Presidente Oaxaca.** P.O. Box 248, Cinco de Mayo 300, **Oaxaca**, Oaxaca 68000. Tel: (951) 6-0611; Fax: (951) 6-0732; in the U.S. and Canada, Tel: (800) HOTELS-1. $115.

MAYAN MEXICO
THE YUCATAN PENINSULA AND CHIAPAS

By Robert Somerlott

"Whatever country this is, it is not Mexico."

The journalist John Kenneth Turner wrote this after visiting the Mayan region at the beginning of this century, and he was by no means the first to express the opinion. It is an observation that springs more from the senses than from any single political or even economic fact. And yet, wars have been fought and lives sacrificed to support or discredit such a view. In the Yucatán, these are fighting words.

From the foreign visitor's viewpoint, the contrast offered by the Mayan region is simply another example of the Mexican republic's diversity. And what diversity it is! Anyone who spends time in the southeastern region of the country will soon understand what Turner meant. The people here call themselves *yucatecos,* not *mexicanos,* and, after 3,000 years of history, are heirs to a cultural legacy that, if not wholly independent, is quite different from that of the rest of the country.

To which a Mexican might well reply that Hawaii is part of the United States, as little as it resembles Vermont or Montana.

Even so, the sense that this is another world persists. Whereas most of Mexico is a topographical tumult, with rugged mountains plummeting down to lush valleys and, even in the most barren regions, distant ridges and peaks looming against the horizon, the tortilla-flat Yucatán Peninsula is so unbroken that normally insignificant hills are considered major heights. Likewise, to foreigners as well as the majority of Mexicans, the plant, animal, and bird life here is nothing less than exotic. Spider and howler monkeys romp—and sometimes rampage—through the trees (a howler monkey chorus is unforgettable). Brocket deer, which resemble tiny antelope, appear in clearings, then vanish, while parrots and parakeets flash gold, red, and green through the foliage. Where the topsoil is thick enough, tropical trees such as kapok, ebony, and rosewood flourish. Zapote trees produce not only the chicle used in chewing gum but also wood so strong and enduring that zapote beams still support the stones in Mayan temples after 1,000, and in some cases 2,000, years.

On the rim of the classic Mayan region to the south, in the state of Chiapas, in highland Guatemala, and in western Honduras, craggy sierras rear up to elevations of 13,000 feet. In the high, temperate valleys of such ranges the highland Maya still tend their corn (maize) patches, much as they have for centuries. And while this corner of the Mayan world outwardly resembles other parts of Mexico, its atmosphere is altogether different.

Still, it was not in these friendly highlands that the magnificent Mayan centers flourished. Instead, with few exceptions, the flowering of Mayan civilization took place in the lowland areas of the Yucatán Peninsula to the north, a flat, featureless limestone shelf covered with a thin veneer of soil and tangled with stunted vegetation. No rivers flow through the northern Yucatán; for water in the long dry seasons both men and animals must depend on natural wells, places where the limestone has collapsed, revealing underground water below. These life-sustaining ponds and concealed streams, called cenotes, were the single most important factor in the foundation of pre-Hispanic Mayan settlements.

The Yucatán was—and is—raw, calcareous land, newly liberated (in geologic terms) from the sea—and a sense of the sea still lingers. Yet from this meager, infertile soil sprang one of the most advanced cultures to appear in the Americas, as well as some of humankind's greatest achievements. The ruins of ancient cities and ceremonial centers here rival any the Old World has to offer, and strike modern eyes with their beauty and originality.

MAJOR INTEREST

City of Mérida (gateway to Uxmal, Chichén Itzá, and other Mayan sites)

The Yucatán Peninsula

```
0        miles        40
0      kilometers      70
```

GOLFO DE MEXICO

Progreso
Dzibilchaltún
261
Mérida
Mayapán
18
Ticul
Uxmal
Kabah
Sayil
Xlapak
Labná
180
261
Campeche
Bahía de Campeche
Edzná
180
CAMPECHE
Ciudad del Carmen
186
186
To Villahermosa and Palenque

CHIAPAS   GUATEMALA

The greatest Mayan ruins
Uxmal
Chichén Itzá
Palenque (in Chiapas)

Smaller but important Mayan sites
Mayapán
Dzibilchaltún
Kabah
Sayil
Labná
Edzná (in Campeche)

San Cristóbal de las Casas and its environs in Chiapas

Besides these attractions (and in addition to the celebrated beach resorts of Cancún, Cozumel, and Isla Mujeres, which, along with the nearby Mayan sites of Cobá and Tulum, are covered in the Caribbean Resorts chapter), this region offers other delights: sparkling waterfalls, sweeping ocean views, mysterious caves, a score of lesser but fascinating archaeological zones, handsome native crafts, and colorful villages.

Although more than twice the size of the six New England states, the region that shares the Mayan heritage (including parts of Belize, Guatemala, Honduras, and El Salvador) is set apart from the surrounding area by mountains, jungles, and swamps. Even today, despite the advent of jet planes and high-speed highways, it is (or was until quite recently) a curiously isolated corner of the world. For the Maya themselves, of course, it simply was and still *is* the world. But outsiders living here have always felt this isolation.

"Yucatan is not an island," wrote Friar Diego de Landa in 1566, "but mainland.... It is not seen from ships until they come very close." The friar had to explain this even though he was addressing some of the best-educated men in Spain only a quarter of a century after one of the decisive battles of the Conquest had been fought on the site where the Mérida cathedral stands today. But because the region lacked silver and gold it had remained on the periphery of its Spanish rulers' collective consciousness.

Forty years earlier, Hernán Cortés, after conquering the Aztecs, had rashly decided to traverse this country overland. The consequences of his decision, which were faithfully recorded by Bernal Díaz, make for one of the most grueling travel accounts of all time, a succession of days in which all the Spaniards seemed to do was slash, chop, stumble, sweat, and pray.

The wilderness was so dense and inaccessible, in fact, that they had to institute stern ordinances to keep their Indian converts (and labor supply) corralled. In 1552 Governor Tomás López decreed that "the Indians must not live off in forests, but come into the towns together ... under pain of whipping or prison." So came about the hundreds of villages in the region that travellers can still see, each with its own outsize church crumbling away.

Prolonged assault on their language and customs notwithstanding, there remain about two and a half million native speakers of Maya today, the language fragmented into a dozen dialects that are not always mutually understandable. (University courses in Maya are offered by the state from time to time, but these seem to be token efforts.) Nevertheless, despite more than four centuries of persecution, the Maya have kept their ways surprisingly intact, contributing to a cultural gulf that still separates them from their Yucatec or "ladino" neighbors. (A *yucateco* is supposedly anyone native to the area, but the word often does not include the Maya—who are the most native of all. Instead, the Maya mysteriously call themselves *mestizos,* people of mixed blood, and describe all "Europeanized" folk around them as "ladinos." *Mexicanos,* a subgroup of the ladinos, are those who come from other parts of the country.) While the most obvious differences are in language and dress, religious differences, which are not instantly apparent, become clear on closer acquaintance.

Long treatises have been written on the distinctive Mayan way of life. Perhaps just one difference, concerning machismo, will illuminate the hundred other contrasts with mainstream Mexican ways. The Mayan male needs a woman to grind his corn and bear his children—he is incomplete without a wife. But he finds romantic love foolish and sexual conquest dishonorable. Success with several women would earn him no credit; in fact, Casanovas are considered contemptible. Similarly, a Mayan male is free to show affection to his wife in public without sacrificing his machismo; he has no need to display a masculine superiority or aloofness. At the same time, his dignity will not allow him the exuberant camaraderie most Mexican men enjoy with their male friends.

All of this is so different from the arrogant pride of mainstream machismo that the emotional understanding between the Maya and their neighbors is often tenuous. Some of the most basic words in life—"sex," "love," "honor," and "success"—become blurred in translation. As a result, the Maya and the more aggressive, acquisitive people around them have seldom communicated clearly except through violence. And although peace has long been maintained, the distance between them remains. For all that, the Maya are a friendly, gracious people with a lively curiosity about strangers.

Visiting Mayan Ruins

There are no real patterns to look for at ancient Mayan sites such as you might find in Gothic cathedrals or Turkish mosques, but a few features were frequently repeated. Whether or not traces of them remain will vary from site to site.

Often you will see sculpted creatures with long, trunklike noses, sometimes with right-angle kinks, representing the rain god or gods (*chac* or *chaques*). Sometimes, as at Kabah, the protuberant noses have fallen off, and the great round eyes now stand out as the main feature of these so-called *chac* masks.

Some temples were situated with much thought given to astronomical or solar orientation, such as the Castillo at Chichén Itzá, so that certain patterns of shadow or light appeared on a critical day, such as the summer or winter solstice. (Such effects can still be seen, although their frequency and impact are frequently exaggerated by on-site tour guides.)

Originally, Mayan buildings, statues, and pavements were painted in brilliant colors that have now faded. The color red, often meant to connote death, was applied to tombs and other surfaces, such as paving. All central plazas were paved, as at Uxmal, and sometimes the entire central area of a site had a cement floor, as at Tikal. The once-paved areas are now often planted with grass.

If you see a free-standing arch, as at Kabah, there's a good chance that a slightly raised road or causeway (*sacbeob*) once ran through it. Those temples that today appear squat usually had tall roofcombs to add height.

A stable water supply was vital. A few sites, such as Copán and Palenque, were established near streams. Those that were not were almost always situated near cenotes, as at Chichén Itzá and Dzibilchaltún, or close to a system of reservoirs, as at Tikal.

MERIDA

Mérida, tropical and Caribbean, is the gateway for visits to Uxmal, Kabah, and some lesser but fascinating ruins. It is also a possible headquarters for a day trip to Chichén Itzá (although it is much more satisfying to stay overnight at that magnificent site). Three days are enough to glimpse the highlights of the Mérida area. Five days are more reasonable, and a week is not too much.

Mérida has two nicknames, and both are clichés—"the Paris of the West" and "the White City." Neither is accurate, but both contain a germ of truth about this curious town.

From the beginning, the city, which was established in 1542, looked across flat country toward the sea. The markets for the raw materials taken from the jungle around it, including hemp and lumber, lay in Europe, not Mexico, and events in Spain loomed far larger here than the goings on in remote Mexico City. In the 19th century, when hemp exports brought great wealth to Mérida, the city sent its sons to Paris for cultivation; over time they brought back the French manners and styles that are still in evidence today. In fact, strolling or riding along Mérida's Paseo Montejo, its most elegant avenue, evokes not only France but far more the old French neighborhoods in Algeria. Here are the curlicues, fancies, and fripperies of both Paris and Tangier. Yet the "Frenchness" of Mérida is merely a patina; ultimately, the hemp barons adopted a style, not a civilization.

As to Mérida's reputation as "the White City," when the Spaniards first stumbled out of the jungle here they found a town called Tiho (the Mayan T'hó). This native settlement, which was constructed of gleaming limestone, impressed them as both splendid and lovely. So, with the perversity of their tribe, they promptly destroyed it. Francisco de Montejo the Younger, the chief destroyer, gazed upon the havoc his men had wrought and nostalgically recalled the white stone heaps of a Roman ruin near the Spanish town of Mérida. Hence the name of the new city that was built with the stone blocks of the old.

While the walls of Mérida are no longer uniformly white, the local people make up for it with their clothing. Mayan women billow like clouds in their *huipiles* (pronounced locally as "ee-pih-layz"), pale tunic-like dresses tipped by rainbows of embroidery. The men are usually clad in white trousers and loose white *guayabera* shirts. When the main plaza is thronged with scrubbed people in their scrubbed clothes, Mérida is still "the White City." (Like the Maya people, who always bathe more than once a day, Mérida takes pride in being "the cleanest tropical city in the world." Perhaps this is true, although the market area somewhat belies the claim.)

Plaza Mayor

The main square, variously called the Plaza Mayor, Plaza Principal, Plaza de la Independencia, and Plaza de Armas, is at the intersection of Calles 60 and 61, the geographic and commercial heart of the city. (Mérida, like most towns the Spanish built from scratch, was laid out as a grid: Odd-numbered streets run east and west, even-numbered ones north and south.) This spacious plaza, with its tall, dignified laurel trees, is the ideal place to linger and get accustomed to the tempo of the city. Like so many things in Mérida, even the laurels have a Caribbean connection. They were originally sent from India and were intended to embellish Havana. After they were salvaged from a shipwreck off the Yucatán coast, however, they were planted here. (*Yucatecos* have always been quick to snatch any gift from the sea.)

The **cathedral**, on the east side of the plaza, was begun in 1561 and is the oldest still in use in Mexico. Unfortunately, its age and size are its only real claims to distinction, as is the case with virtually all the extant colonial buildings in Mérida; they offer nothing special.

The Montejo family—father, son, and cousin—and their successors were the Spanish conquerors (some would say plunderers) of the Yucatán. Their palace, built in 1549, originally occupied the whole south side of the square. Today the **Casa de Montejo** is greatly reduced in size and serves as a bank. Its façade, however, is the single colonial landmark in Mérida that merits careful inspection.

In 1841 John Lloyd Stephens, the modern discoverer of the ancient Mayan cities, strolled into Mérida's plaza, where this building instantly arrested his attention. As he later described the relief carving he saw that day: "The subject represents two knights in armour with visors, breastplates and helmets, standing upon the shoulders of crushed naked figures, probably intended to represent the conquering Spaniard trampling upon the Indian."

Stephens was accurate but kind. In actuality, the relief is one of the most arrogant representations ever commissioned for a private residence; the skill of the Mayan slave artists who did the carving only makes the whole matter worse. To see this relief is to see the brutal attitudes of the conquerors starkly revealed. Looking at it another way, you might say that even Diego Rivera, master propagandist for Indian rights, never created a more scathing indictment of the conquistadors.

Caryatid-like Amazons, fierce and busty, lurk at windows nearby, where they uphold royal escutcheons. Again, the stonework is as admirable as the idea is repellent.

The Conquest was neither as easy nor as complete as the Montejo façade would have you believe. The Maya resisted the Spaniards with greater fierceness and success than the Aztecs, at first repelling the invaders entirely, then battling for three years before their defeat at Tiho. Even then their acquiescence was no sure thing, and skirmishing went on for more than a century. In fact, the final surrender of the last rebellious band didn't come about until 1697, and resistance continued for years afterward.

Even as Stephens was studying the Montejo palace, trouble was brewing among the people who had been crushed by the conquering stone foot. In 1846 the Maya arose with such ferocity that only the cities of Mérida and Campeche held out, in what became known as the "War of the Castes." The terrified whites implored Spain, England, and the United States to accept the Yucatán as a colony. Finally, a Mexican federal army rescued them in 1848, retaking the burned haciendas. Sporadic violence continued until 1901.

On the opposite side of the plaza, a world away from the savagery portrayed on the façade of the Montejo palace, is the leisurely society of Mérida's sidewalk cafés. It's true that the city is a center of industry and commerce; somehow, things must get done. Yet in its cafés unhurried patrons who are obviously men of affairs have seemingly endless time for endless coffees served as *grecos*—triple strength with hot water on the side. Here, haste is frowned upon, and voices and gestures modulated, although the nearby streets bustle with scurrying people.

The **Parque Cepeda Peraza**, at the intersection of Calles 59 and 60, two blocks north of the cathedral, is another shady spot for lingering over coffee or a cool drink. It's also an international crossroads for archaeology buffs—many of them young and travelling on tight budgets—the kind of place where you can witness unexpected reunions of people who last saw each other in Cuzco or Crete. Tourists sit scribbling postcards, music echoes from a cantina in a nearby patio, and Mérida's only aristocratic church, the Iglesia de Jesús, mellows in the tropical sunshine.

Around in Mérida

The appeal of Mérida does not lie in inspecting its local monuments. On heavily advertised city tours, guides struggle to fill up two or three hours, driving through gentrified neighborhoods, holding passengers captive at overpriced craft shows, and turning them loose on their own in the municipal market. It is far better, instead, to stroll the downtown area on your own or ride in one of the horse-drawn carriages that lend color to the city.

The **Paseo de Montejo**, which runs north from Calle 47, is lined with imposing homes and spacious gardens, a reminder of how patrician the rulers of this city have always been. Mérida is probably the only city in Mexico where old families trace their history not just to the Conquest, but to a specific conquistador. They have not intermarried with the Maya—although their men have certainly interbred. Nor have they formed marital alliances with the many immigrant Levantine merchants who dominate the city's dry-goods business.

At the intersection of Calle 43 and the Paseo stands one of the most opulent and Rococo of the old mansions, now the local **Museo Regional de Antropología**. The collection of Mayan artifacts, including a variety of stunning jewelry, is excellent, while the building itself is a different kind of treat. Closed Mondays.

The **Museo de Arte Popular**, Mérida's very obscure craft museum, can be hunted down on Calle 59 between Calles 50 and 48, west of the plaza. The medley of flamboyant folk art includes looms, baskets, hammocks, textiles, and papier-mâché Mayan figures disconcertingly reminiscent of outsize voodoo dolls. A government-run shop at the rear offers a good selection of reasonably priced items. Closed Mondays.

The 19th-century **Palacio de Gobierno**, on the north side of the main plaza, is noted for a series of dramatic murals by Fernando Castro Pacheco illustrating in grisly detail the history of the region. Three other works by the artist, decorating the main stairway, deal with more cheerful, Mayan subjects.

Shopping in Mérida

The city market, a short walk south from the main plaza, is a crowded, bustling, somewhat confusing maze of stalls and counters heaped high with the region's offerings. Articles made of henequen cord take a hundred different forms here, from the obvious, such as shopping bags, mats, and hammocks, to some quite surprising and imaginative neckties and belts. The rugs are both unusual and durable.

On the other hand, the best hammocks are made not from henequen but from linen, and built to last a lifetime. Besides the usual one-person size, you can choose from matrimonial hammocks, family hammocks, and hammocks seemingly designed for community siestas.

Much of the embroidery on display is machine-made, yet so intricate that the method of manufacture hardly seems to matter.

Mérida is one of the great centers for Panama hats, but the best, unfortunately, are not displayed in the market. The city's most famous hat shop is **La Casa de los Jipis**, located on Calle 56 between Calles 65 and 67. Some of the hats here are among the best in the world, so don't be surprised if the prices seem high.

Gold filigree, crafted much as it was in pre-Hispanic times, is offered in many shops. Caution is advisable, however, for traditional Yucatecan gold work is only 10-carat, not 14 as is often claimed. In some shops true 14-carat gold is sold, for which you will be able to get a written or printed guarantee.

Guayabera shirts are a Mérida specialty and can be found in a score of shops. **Jack**, at Calle 59 number 505, has an especially large selection. The loose-fitting cotton *guayabera* is worn for its coolness, and you'll be disappointed if yours is warm because of the overuse of synthetic fiber, so buy carefully.

Finally, there are good craft and popular arts stores to be found at the entrances to major archaeological sites near Mérida; while the prices will be a little inflated, they won't be larcenous.

Staying in Mérida

The **Holiday Inn** in Mérida lives up to its name, conjuring a spirit of cheerful leisure. The service is excellent, and its large and well-maintained swimming pool is especially welcome after hours of exploring ruins. Located in a quiet flower-filled neighborhood just off the Paseo, the hotel is convenient to fast transportation downtown. The clientele is international, as are the dining room, its two coffee shops, the cocktail lounge with entertainment, and the disco. It also has a lighted tennis court. Higher priced than other Mérida hotels, the Holiday Inn is still a top value.

El Conquistador, located in an expensive and busy commercial neighborhood halfway between the downtown area and the outskirts of the city, offers new and very good rooms and suites with private balconies on Paseo de Montejo. Although it's more than walking distance from the center of town, transportation along the Paseo is good. El Conquistador also has an indoor pool and a restaurant.

El Castellano is a modern high-rise on Calle 57 near the center of town, two blocks west of the main plaza. Rooms vary in size, but some of the best are on the upper floors, with panoramic views of the city spread out below. They are also quieter, almost hushed. The hotel has ample public areas, a pool, and a restaurant as well.

At the corner of Calles 57 and 60, three blocks north of the plaza, the charming **Casa del Balam** mixes colonial and Mayan motifs in its decor. The rooms here, arranged around a leafy patio, are clean, spacious, and air-conditioned; those on the top floor are quietest. The pool is tucked away in a shady, restful garden, and the hotel also has a very pleasant bar and restaurant.

The **Hotel Dolores Alba** is a friendly, family-run establishment in a converted town house three blocks east of the main plaza on Calle 63. The rooms are basic, but the atmosphere is pleasant. Not all rooms are air-conditioned, however, and some are small. Get the best or go elsewhere; only the *good* accommodations here are a bargain.

Located a block northeast of the plaza at Calle 62, the **Hotel Colón** has enough charm to compensate for its rather plain rooms. Stay in the newer, air-conditioned wing if you can.

The **Gran Hotel** on the lively Parque Cepeda Peraza is a favorite of students and thrifty travellers of all ages. The interior of the old building is adorned with the owner's eclectic collection of antique sewing machines, phonographs, radios, and curios. Like the collection, the hotel is left over from another age. Despite the noise and reliance on ceiling fans, however, its guests seem to enjoy its personality.

Dining in Mérida

Spicy and rich Yucatecan cuisine has little to do with the usual fare of Mexico, except for their common reliance on corn and chiles as basic ingredients. Marinades, seldom used in the rest of the country, add tantalizing, hard-to-recognize flavors to many dishes here. Foods prepared in a tangy orange marinade are a particular specialty. In addition, the word *pibil* appears frequently on menus and refers to the traditional barbecue pits of the Maya (although *pibil* cookery in restaurants is usually done by steam). Chicken and pork (*pollo* and *cochinita*) so prepared are tender and succulent. Lime soup (*sopa de lima*) is a rich chicken broth made glorious with lime juice and spices, then garnished in a hundred different ways. Sometimes it has pieces of chicken, tortilla chips, chopped tomatoes, and onions (creativity is the soul of a good *sopa de lima*). Foods served *escabeche* have been soaked in a marinade of onions, vinegar, and whatever spices inspiration dictates. Finally, the Lebanese and Syrians have been settled in the Yucatán for so long that many of their national dishes have also become standard fare here.

Los Almendros, a traditional Mérida favorite, is located two blocks north and four blocks east of the Plaza Mayor on the Plaza Mejorada. A rather plain establishment, it nevertheless presents a fine sampling of Yucatecan cuisine at reasonable prices. For an introduction to the regional fare, the combination plate is a good choice, offering samples of about four selections, including the region's famous sausages. Here and in other regional restaurants you should treat the side sauces with respect; while the cookery is not fiery, the sauces may be molten lava. Tel: (99) 21-2851.

Rather more elegant (and expensive) is **Las Palomas**, on Calle 56 between Calles 55 and 53, a 19th-century Spanish-Moorish town house that has been converted into a very good restaurant serving Yucatecan and European dishes. Tel: (99) 25-5690.

The **Chateau Valentín** is a distinguished restaurant with impeccable service and a tasty selection of international and Yucatecan offerings (although the regional fare has been somewhat adapted). Piano music adds to its elegant ambience. Calle 58 number 499. (This is in the Holiday Inn neighborhood, not downtown as its address might suggest.) It's expensive, and reservations are advised; Tel: (99) 25-6367.

For snacks, short orders, and good but rather standard desserts, **Leo's**, at Paseo de Montejo 460A and Calle 37, is modern, casual, and inexpensive.

The best Lebanese food in town is found in the hacienda atmosphere of **Alberto's Continental Patio**. Lunch and dinner from an international menu are served in this early-19th-century mansion, with the reasonable prices attracting local businessmen.

Excursions from Mérida

If your time is limited you *can* see Uxmal, Kabah, Sayil, and Labná in a one-day excursion, but it won't allow you to appreciate them fully. Uxmal by itself is enough to take in at one go, although it can be combined with Kabah. But that really should be the limit. (See the Getting Around section below.) Note, too, that all archaeological zones, regardless of size, are officially open seven days a week, though some may close "unofficially" on Mondays.

Mayapán and Ticul also can be combined in a one-day excursion. **Mayapán**, 51 km (32 miles) southeast of Mérida via Highway 18, flourished in the 13th and 14th centuries, and was an important Mayan city in the centuries leading up to the Conquest; unfortunately, not a great deal of it remains. Eleven kilometers (7 miles) south of Mayapán, the large village of **Ticul**, where native dress is still worn, is known for its handicrafts, especially its pottery and embroidery. Although both places are interesting, time should be allowed for them only after the major sites have been explored.

An excursion to the archaeological zone of Dzibilchaltún (see immediately below) certainly repays a half-day trip. But continuing north of Dzibilchaltún to the port town of Progreso is not worth the time or effort.

Most visitors skip the beautiful Mayan ruins at **Edzná**, a three-and-a-half-hour drive southwest of Mérida in the state of Campeche, because it does not fit conveniently into the usual itineraries. But devotees of Mayan ruins, provided they have extra time, will not want to miss the magnificent **Pirámide de los Cinco Pisos** (Pyramid of the Five Stories) and some newly excavated ruins there. While it's a convenient stop for drivers heading for the Yucatán from Villahermosa or Palenque, it will either require a day-long excursion or an overnight stay in Campeche, about 60 km (37 miles) northwest, for those coming from Mérida.

The most extensive, but least accessible, Mayan ruins are found at **Calakmul**, southeast of Edzná near the Guatemalan border. Barely explored, but known to contain a large number of stelae, Calakmul was inhabited from about 1500 B.C. until nearly A.D. 1600. Entwined in dense jungle forest, the site may not be open to tourists for many years to come, as excavation is proceeding at a slow pace.

To sum up, the sights nearest Mérida, in descending order of importance, are the archaeological zones of Uxmal, Kabah, Sayil, Labná, Edzná, Dzibilchaltún, Mayapán, and, for handicrafts, Ticul. Magnificent Chichén Itzá is a possible one-day trip from Mérida, but is better left as an overnight (at least) excursion. On the other hand, it's an easy overnighter from either Cancún or Cozumel.

The Postclassic Mayan site of **Tulum** (too-LOOM), on the

Caribbean coast, was a Mayan trading center from A.D. 1200 to 1450. Although it makes for a convenient excursion from Cozumel, and is easy enough from Cancún, it does not, in spite of its lovely setting, quite justify a five- to six-hour drive from Mérida itself. Those travelling between Mérida and the Caribbean resorts will find Tulum a delightful bonus, however (see the Caribbean Resorts chapter, below).

Dzibilchaltún

Dzibilchaltún (tsee-beel-chal-TOON), just north of Mérida, is often hailed as the site of the longest continuous human occupation in the Western Hemisphere. A settlement sprang up here not long after 1000 B.C., and a Mayan village was still standing on the spot in A.D. 1580 when the Spaniards erected a church to aid in the conversion of the local inhabitants.

The site is extraordinarily large, complex, and important. Between A.D. 700 and 1000 this may have been not only the largest of all Mayan centers but the richest, supported by a flourishing trade in salt from the nearby coast. (Postclassic Dzibilchaltún covered an area as large as modern Washington, D.C.) The city declined dramatically after A.D. 1000, yet still managed to live on; in fact, modest buildings were being erected right up until the time of the Spanish occupation. Its past glories should not lead a visitor to expect too much today, however. The site is interesting and well worth exploring, but the beauty and glory have long since vanished.

Dzibilchaltún (the name means "place where there are inscriptions on flat stones") is easily reached from Mérida by car, taxi, bus, or packaged tour. A guide is helpful but not necessary. Allow two hours for inspecting the ruins and on-site museum. Drivers should take Highway 261 (the Progreso road) from Mérida north for 15 km (9 miles), then turn east and continue 5 km (3 miles) to the village of Xcunya. The site, which is closed to visitors on Mondays, is just south of the village.

Inside the entrance to the site a path leads past a small, well-restored temple known, in the sometimes arcane terminology of the archaeologist, as **Edificio 38-sub.** In classic Mesoamerican fashion, the fallen masonry of a slightly newer temple, Edificio 38, which once covered the older building, is strewn around the surviving building.

A little farther on a sign points left (east) to the Temple of the Seven Dolls. The way is dotted with fallen and crumbling walls, and to the north rise a ruined platform and temple next to a good-sized building base, **Edificio 36**. A wide stairway faces south, commanding a view of the main plaza and the Spanish-built chapel with barrel vault huddling there, an incongruous and feeble architectural gesture dating from the 1590s.

Heading east, the rubble-strewn trail eventually passes a platform with a simple stela, then continues on to the famous **Templo de las Siete Muñecas** (Temple of the Seven Dolls—Edificio 1-sub), the most impressive structure at Dzibilchaltún. (The approach to the temple is over the remains of a *sacbeob,* one of the raised ceremonial roads the Maya built out of limestone and lime cement. Two such elevated roads are found at the site, both leading to the main plaza.) Other nearby structures, including a platform and stela, are all associated with the temple. Judging by the orientation of the stairways and these outlying structures, the temple itself seems to have been used for astronomical observations.

Built at the start of the Late Classic era (about A.D. 600), the temple was filled in not long after its completion and another building erected over it. The inner temple seems to have been forgotten for two centuries or more, but about A.D. 1300 the Mayan inhabitants of Dzibilchaltún tunneled down to the original temple floor and there cut an opening in the rubble. They then enshrined seven crude clay figurines in this pit, representations of human beings suffering various deformities. The tunnel was filled in, leaving a pipe or speaking tube (called a psychoduct) open to the outside world, apparently so the living could receive divine communication during healing rituals. (Similar tubes appear at a few Mayan sites, most notably at Palenque.)

From the Temple of the Seven Dolls return by the route you came; at the cutoff leading back to the entrance, however, turn left. A little farther on is the **Cenote Xlacah**, whose impressive surface area, more than 100 feet across, makes it one of the largest wells in the Yucatán and the most important in the ancient city.

The cenote, one of several in Dzibilchaltún, plunges 140 feet through the limestone amid a spacious but sadly ruined palace complex that was surely magnificent in its day. (One of its buildings contained 20 vaulted rooms.) Divers exploring the cenote have brought up skeletons, both bovine and human, one of them that of a Spaniard.

A collection of artifacts from the cenote are found in the small **museum** at the entrance to the site. In addition to these and the curious clay figurines from the Temple of the Seven Dolls, the collection includes hairpins, ornaments, and two beautiful fragments of Late Classic stelae.

UXMAL

The first U.S. traveller to visit this imposing ruined city south of Mérida was John Lloyd Stephens, who wrote in 1843, "We entered a noble courtyard with four great façades looking down upon it, each ornamented from one end to the other with the richest and most intricate carving... presenting a scene of strange magnificence."

Magnificence indeed! At Uxmal (oosh-MAHL) gigantic masks of snouted rain gods crowd upon one another in emphatic profusion, mosaics of amazing intricacy enfold whole buildings, and boldness of conception is combined with the most delicate masonry technique. Invariably, the visitor is struck by the deluge of carved symbolism applied to Uxmal's palaces, pyramids, and temples. At the same time, the decoration is daring and radical; potentially jarring combinations of geometric and floral patterns instead are magically combined to achieve a sublime harmony.

The prevailing architectural style at Uxmal is called "Puuc," a name taken from the Puuc hills, a series of low ridges that dominate this topographically monotonous region. Puuc architecture runs to thick walls decorated with thin stones set like mosaics. The most common motifs are the masks of the rain god Chac, often combined with diamond shapes; realistic representations of Mayan *na* huts; and geometric forms resembling Greek key decorations. The façades of buildings in this style are usually divided horizontally by a medial molding, with the top half given over to these ornate mosaics and the lower half left plain. Pure Puuc style is a Late Classic–era development, and is not confined exclusively to sites in the Uxmal area; in fact, lovely examples of it occur far to the south at Río Bec as well as to the northeast in the older buildings at Chichén Itzá.

The great center of Uxmal was rebuilt several times over the centuries, so it is impossible to date its structures with any exactness. Its zenith occurred between A.D. 600 and 900. The latest confirmed written date at the site is A.D. 909; its temples and courtyards were probably abandoned soon after that—for reasons that remain unknown.

Near the entrance to the site rises the imposing **Pirámide del Adivino** (Temple of the Magician). Constructed in five different stages, its exact function is unknown. (The name refers to a magical dwarflike figure in Mayan folklore.) A single mask on the temple suggests the influence of people from the central highlands. But the Toltecs, who greatly changed the architecture of the Yucatán, never occupied

Uxmal; it remains pure Maya. The three-room sanctuary atop the Magician offers a breathtaking view of the site and the surrounding jungle.

The **Cuadrángulo de las Monjas** (Nunnery Quadrangle), immediately behind (to the west of) the Temple of the Magician, is often hailed as one of the most beautiful structures, or complex of structures, in the New World. The four buildings that compose it are a triumph of decoration in stone. The work is mosaic, but on a scale not usually associated with mosaic art. Individual pieces may be more than three feet in length and so heavy that one man could never have lifted them into place.

The four buildings of the Nunnery may have served as a residence for priests; at least that is the traditional theory. The modern explanations of its name, however, are illuminating, if perhaps inaccurate: It was so named by the Spaniards because nuns make lace and the stonework is lacy; or because the atmosphere within its walls suggests the serenity of a convent.

The **ball court**, just south of the Nunnery, seems to have been constructed to accommodate a small—doubtless elite—group of spectators. Raised on a huge man-made platform a bit farther south, the small and, at first glance, plain **Casa de las Tortugas** (House of the Turtles) is likely to be overlooked amid the grandeur of the rest of the site. Still, in its own sober way, this is a masterpiece, at once pure in its proportions and discreet in its decoration (with the exception of the carved turtles that adorn the frieze on its upper ledge). The molding, especially, is beautifully managed, and the symbolism throughout is connected with rain and agriculture.

The **Palacio del Gobernador** (Palace of the Governor), which takes its name from the crowned figure in the center of the structure, is located next to the House of the Turtles and dominates the site. Set upon a stone platform and built in three sections, it is regarded, like the Nunnery, as one of the masterpieces of Mesoamerican architecture. The designs on its façade were inspired by weaving and the decorative arts and are combined with a variety of snakeskin patterns and representations of the rain god Chac (in total, some 20,000 mosaic elements were used in the frieze).

The three sections of the palace are joined by corbeled "arches." (Although not true arches in an architectural sense, they are as close as the Maya came to achieving that engineering feat and are often called "Mayan arches.") Corbeled arches such as these were created by gradually projecting stone blocks outward from each side until the arch came to a peak, but since these constructions did not support weight efficiently, the Maya would reinforce them with a beam near the top. Today many of the beams have fallen or rotted away, but the holes cut for them remain.

In addition, two sculpted works stand at the base of the broad stairway leading up to the palace—a two-headed jaguar on a small platform, perhaps a throne, and a phallic column that is an oddity in this otherwise classic Mayan site. (Phallic sculpture was rarely used to decorate lowland Mayan centers, although other examples are found at Uxmal, most notably serving as rainspouts. Instead, the theme seems to have been imported from the Veracruz area, where such work is not unusual. Plumed-serpent representations at Uxmal also suggest faraway influences that seem to have been introduced late and had little effect on the basic style.)

The **Gran Pirámide** (Grand Pyramid), a few steps west of the palace, is in poor condition, as is the small **Templo de las Guacamayas** (Temple of the Parrots) that sits atop it. The dedication here is to the sun. The pyramid is easy to climb, however, and affords both grand views and excellent photo opportunities.

A bit to the west is the ruined **El Palomar** (Dovecote). The nine triangular works of masonry that top it are fanciful Mayan roofcombs, which were often added to rather squat structures to create the illusion of height and grace. Like all of Uxmal, they were once painted in brilliant colors.

Three outlying groups of structures are in ruined condition, some of them little more than rubble. They include the Grupo del Norte (North Group), the Grupo del Cementerio (Cemetery Group), and the Casa de la Vieja (House of the Old Woman); beyond them lies the quite unerotic **Templo de los Falos** (Temple of the Phalli).

Uxmal is 77 km (48 miles) south of Mérida via Highway 180 to Umán, then Highway 261 south. If your itinerary only allows for a one-day excursion, you should leave Mérida early in the morning so that any climbing you do at the ruins is over before the hottest part of the afternoon. (See the Getting Around section below.) In addition, every night a dramatic, well-designed sound-and-light show is presented: one just after sunset in Spanish, a later one in English. (The English version is usually too late for visitors returning to Mérida.)

Staying at Uxmal

There are a number of good hotels with restaurants if you decide to stay overnight at Uxmal, and all of them are helpful in arranging further exploration of the area. None is inexpensive, however.

The **Villa Arqueológica Uxmal**, at the entrance to the ruins, follows the solid format of this chain, which is Club Med–connected but very unlike Club Med in personality. Tennis court, bar, restaurant, pool, air-conditioning, and pleasant grounds.

Across the highway from the ruins, the **Hacienda Uxmal** is gracious, tropical, and colonial. Long verandahs, ceiling fans, and wicker furniture lend it a real hacienda feeling, and many people think it's the prettiest hotel in the Yucatán. Though expensive by local standards, the price of a room here would be a bargain almost anywhere else.

The **Misión Park Inn Uxmal**, part of the Misión chain, is modern and comfortable, and all its rooms have air-conditioning. The better rooms also have balconies and striking views. Its popularity with tour-bus groups is an indication of its value, but it's less personal than the other hotels here. Located a mile from the archaeological zone.

Kabah

The fanciful city of Kabah (kah-BAH), located on either side of Highway 261, lies approximately 22 km (14 miles) southeast of Uxmal. Visitors approaching the zone from Mérida and the north will suddenly see a remarkable structure rising above the low, spiky vegetation on the left side of the road. This is the famed **Palacio de los Mascarones** (Palace of the Masks), also known as the Codz-pop (coiled mat) because of its vast array of masks with undulating noses, which vaguely resemble the curving lines of Mayan mats.

Even after the exuberant decoration at Uxmal, this structure comes as a surprise. The entire façade is covered with masks of the Mayan rain god Chac—row upon blank-eyed row, and mostly noseless now. Here is stone clamoring for rain, the most insistent statement made by any Mayan temple. The masks, like the decorative work at Uxmal, are in actuality large-scale mosaics: Each mask, of which there are some 250, comprises 30 separate carved and dressed stone elements. Obviously, the labor involved in running the "mask factory" must have been enormous. You will need a lot of imagination, however, to envision the palace in its former glory.

Kabah, which was contemporary with Uxmal, thrived from A.D. 600 to 900, when, for reasons unknown, it was abandoned. There are nine more or less excavated structures here, two of which are three-building complexes. One of the most intriguing is located across the highway from the Palace of the Masks: the **arch**, a white limestone structure standing stark and alone, is a beautiful work of corbeling that spans a distance of more than 15 feet. According to archaeologists, it once served as a monumental gateway to a *sacbeob,* or processional route, that ran all the way to Uxmal. These roads, of which there were more than a few in the region, were impressive achievements, cutting through dense jungle and crossing treacherous swamps. The Spanish, arriving more than six centuries after the arch was built, proved woefully inferior to the Maya when it came to building roads.

On the east side of the highway, about a quarter of a mile from the main cluster of ruins, is the **Tercera Casa**, often called the Temple of the Columns. A long ripple of carving, the temple is related artistically to the House of the Turtles in Uxmal, both making extensive use of engaged columns as decoration. A front terrace once served to catch rainwater for a nearby cistern.

The soil around Kabah is ungenerous, yielding stingy corn crops to slash-and-burn farming, which the Maya practice today much as they did during the heyday of this ceremonial center. All the more reason, therefore, to stand in awe of the religious and cultural forces that fueled the Maya's magnificent impulse to build here and elsewhere in the Yucatán. (Incidentally, at Kabah, Sayil, Xlapak, Labná, and other sites in the region, a high iron oxide content in the soil gives the crumbling structures a reddish tint that is especially noticeable in the early morning or late afternoon.)

Sayil, Xlapak, and Labná

Three other interesting Mayan sites built in the Puuc style can be included in a trip from Uxmal.

Sayil (sah-YEEL) is a neighbor of Kabah. To get to this site, head south on Highway 261 for 5 km (3 miles), then turn left. This road, marked "Oxkutzcab" (oosh-coots-cahb), takes you to Sayil, 4 km (2½ miles) farther on. Road signs with the names of the sites make finding them a simple proposition.

The Sayil archaeological zone is famed for its **Palacio**, a terraced, 70-room, three-story structure. Though it is huge and massive, the lightness of its design counteracts any bulkiness, lending it instead a feeling of elegance and airiness. A broad stairway rises gracefully to divide the structure; elsewhere, round columns, well-spaced doors, and lovely friezes impart a pleasing rhythm to its lower floors. Among the site's curiosities are sculptures of the "upside-down god," which are variously described as diving, falling, or descending. The Chac masks and accompanying scrollwork are particularly beautiful. Carved stelae date from about A.D. 850, Sayil's heyday. Another stela, probably much older and perhaps not even Mayan, is an exaggerated phallic figure. The site, which was abandoned in the tenth century, seems to have been inhabited as far back as A.D. 200, to judge from the ceramic evidence. There are several (out of several hundred) buildings accessible to the public; the rest are still locked in jungle.

Xlapak (shlah-PAHK) is 7 km (4 miles) farther along the road to Labná and makes for a quick visit, since there remains only one temple at the site; it is an almost perfect structure, however. Three great stone masks dominate the center of the symmetrical, beautifully proportioned building—not rare but somewhat unusual in Mayan architecture. The structure dates from about A.D. 800.

The small but quite wonderful ruins of **Labná** are just 3 km (2 miles) east of Xlapak; there will be a sign indicating a parking area and path to the right. Four major structures survive here. The chief one, the **Palacio**, is almost 535 feet long at its base and two stories high. Besides the stern masks of the snouted rain god, you can see examples of the Mayan "hut theme"—a sculpted representation of what seems to be a thatched dwelling. A date corresponding to A.D. 862 is inscribed on the extended nose of one of the palace's rain gods, possibly the last carving done at the site before it was abandoned.

The **Mirador**, rising south of the Palace, displays an elegant roofcomb; the severe complex nearby is called the **Edificio Este** (East Building).

Also near the Mirador, the famous Labná **arch**, often called "La Puerta" ("the Gateway"), is a fantasy in stone. A corbeled arch is stepped up to an almost Gothic point and flanked by sculpted lattice-work and a small room on either side. This altogether delightful monument once connected two courtyards.

Labná was a major religious center, and probably an important market center as well, with a resident population that approached 3,000—an estimate partly based on the capacity of the 60 cisterns that were dug to supply it with water in the dry season. The water works can still be seen, although the site has long been abandoned.

The Loltún Caves

These caves (*grutas*), comprising a series of dramatic chambers and corridors that honeycomb the limestone crust in this region, were known to ancient hunters as early as 2500 B.C. The prehistoric visitors left behind a variety of stone artifacts, as well as the remains of animals they had killed. Later on, the mysterious atmosphere, strange rock formations, and stalactites and stalagmites appear to have inspired a certain amount of religious awe among the Maya. Eventually, glyphs and steps were carved at the entrance, and a sculpted sentinel was placed nearby—a figure thought to date from 300 B.C.

Lights have since been installed in the caves, but only enough to illuminate the surroundings without compromising their mystery. You may enter only with a guided tour group, however. The tours, conducted in Spanish, leave from the entrance at 9:30 and 11:30 A.M. and 1:30 P.M., Tuesday through Sunday; allow two hours for the full tour.

The caves are 20 km (12 miles) east of Labná on the road to Oxkutzcab and can be visited as part of an excursion to Labná or when exploring Mayapán and Ticul.

Tours leaving from the Uxmal hotels cover all the above sites in a day, including Kabah, though sometimes omitting the caves. Such a trip allows for a cursory glance at everything, but is far too rushed for true archaeology buffs, photographers, and anyone else who simply might want the time to absorb the strange and unusual things they will encounter.

A better trip would be: a full day at the Uxmal ruins, ending with a late lunch and perhaps a swim. Return to the ruins for the sound-and-light show in the evening and stay overnight at an Uxmal hotel. The next day return to the ruins to reexamine their memorable nooks and crannies, then go on to Kabah. A third day could be devoted to the other sights of the region, including the caves in the morning, and ending either at an Uxmal hotel or back in Mérida that afternoon.

Edzná

Edzná (edz-NAH), a jungle-besieged ruin in the state of Campeche, is more remarkable than beautiful. Although not one of the greatest Mayan ceremonial centers, it claims an honored place in the second rank.

A car is necessary for visiting the site, which is 225 km (140 miles) south and slightly west of Mérida via Highway 180 and Highway 261, the Campeche road. There's a well-marked turnoff to your left at kilometer 14, and it's another 19 km (12 miles) down this secondary road to the ruins. Travellers headquartered at Uxmal—which is the smartest (as well as the most comfortable) way to do it in terms of accommodations—face a slightly shorter trip of 148 km (92 miles) over the same highway. For those visitors staying in the nearby city of Campeche (discussed below), it's only 68 km (42 miles) distant, again via Highway 261.

Unlike most of the other Mayan ceremonial centers discussed in this chapter, Edzná is so little visited that travellers are likely to find only iguanas and howler monkeys frequenting the ruins. However, a spate of new archaeological work and restoration may soon change this. Until it does, you will find hardly anything remaining of what was once the pride of Edzná—an elaborate system of canals used for flood control and irrigation. Nevertheless, Edzná's attractions make it worth the trip.

The ceramic evidence seems to indicate that a village was founded here several centuries before the beginning of the Christian era. The city didn't reach its zenith until the Late Classic era, however, when most of the structures extant today were erected, often over older buildings. The fact that it stood at a major crossroads of trade no doubt accounts for its eclectic artistic style, which combines elements of the Chenes, Río Bec, and even Puuc styles, in addition to an elegant simplicity all its own. (Chenes is an ornate architectural style named for a Late Classic site in the Yucatán; the Río Bec style, so-called after a center in Campeche, features rounded towers meant to convey the illusion of height; Puuc style is characteristic of the northern Yucatán, most notably Uxmal.) The impression is of a cosmopolitan place open to new ideas and fashions.

After paying a nominal fee to enter the archaeological zone, you pass several sculpted stelae that merit inspection. A little farther on, past a temple platform and door columns, the broad stairway to the **Gran Acropolis** becomes visible. It is best to save it for last, however; instead, continue on down the path for 50 yards or so until you come to a low temple platform on your left. In front of it you'll find a number of beautifully carved stelae, now lying broken and scattered on the ground but still graceful.

The **Templo de los Mascarones** (Temple of the Masks), south of the Acropolis, is one of the oldest structures at the site, and dates to about A.D. 300. Masks of Itzamná, the sun god, are immediately recognizable by his plump, slightly bulbous face; the lips are pursed to emit invisible sunbeams, and his single emerging tooth symbolizes spring and, in a larger sense, the rekindling of life. The god displays a rare human touch at Edzná: He is cross-eyed, in the finest tradition of Mayan beauty.

The area on the opposite side of the Gran Acropolis, to the north, may have been the civil or administrative section of this urban center; its chief structure, the **Palacio de las Cuchillas** (Palace of the Knives), was named for the extraordinary number of these implements recovered from within and around the building. Four rooms of the palace have plaforms that may have supported beds.

About 100 yards west is a lonely **arch**. Dating to about A.D. 800, and thus newer than most of Edzná's monuments, it was built in the Puuc style, possibly by conquerors who overran the area at the time. The arch was the latter-day entrance to a raised road leading to the main temple.

The Acropolis, a complex structure with cascading stairways and a variety of civic and residential buildings, dominates the low jungle landscape. It, in turn, is dominated by Edzná's most imposing monument, the Templo Mayor, or **Pirámide de los Cinco Pisos** (Pyramid of the Five Stories), which rises 124 feet from its base to the tip of its partially ruined but still elegant roofcomb. Archaeologists have deduced only recently that the temple was built in such a way as to allow the rays of the setting sun to penetrate the interior on certain days in order to illuminate the figure of the Mayan sun god, Itzamná, located in one of the temple's four rooms. The phenomenon occurs every May 1, 2, and 3, the beginning of the rainy season; and again on August 7, 8, and 9, the start of the harvest, according to the Mayan calendar.

The Pyramid of the Five Stories displays a restraint unusual in Mayan architecture, its arresting effect achieved by the spacing of its five stories and multiple doorways in combination with the powerful stone undulations of its central stairway. The top story offers a splendid view of a number of recently restored buildings around the Main Plaza as well as of unrestored mounds in the jungle that seem full of archaeological promise. Especially striking is the well-proportioned seven-tiered temple base on the south side of the Acropolis.

In fact, all the nearby buildings give willing and able visitors an opportunity for unusual views of one another, as well as of the main temple. If nothing else, Edzná offers the challenge of a lot of climbing. Therefore, appropriate shoes are a must, and insect repellent is a blessing (as is something cold to drink that you can carry with you; if you can find him, the caretaker also sells cold sodas).

Campeche

Campeche, capital city of the state of the same name, is the closest overnight stop for visitors to Edzná. (It can also provide a break in the long trip from Mérida to Palenque or Villahermosa.) The city, which is made to seem romantic and colorful in travel brochures, proves less appealing in reality. Here is a typical Caribbean backwater, complete with rusting metal roofs, scraggly palms, and tropical swelter only occasionally relieved by cooling sea breezes—despite the claims of its boosters.

Colonial Campeche, constantly endangered by pirates, once crouched behind walls eight feet thick and bristling with *baluartes* (forts). The city is still studded with the remnants of these stone redoubts and ramparts, though they hardly evoke the ghost of Blackbeard. In addition, two antique gateways to the city, La Puerta del Mar and La Puerta de la Tierra, also survive. The two chief examples of the city's modern architecture, on the other hand, have been aptly nicknamed "The Juke Box" and "The Flying Saucer" by the locals.

The **Museo de las Estelas** (Museum of the Stelae), in the Baluarte de la Soledad, displays a number of stelae carved by the Maya, while the limited **Museo Archeológico** is housed in the Baluarte de San Miguel, facing the sea on the outside of the city. To get to the latter, take a taxi or drive 4 km (2½ miles) along the seaside *malecón* in the direction of Lerma, then turn left (uphill) at the Camino Escénica sign. The museum has a few artifacts from Edzná and some memorable funerary figurines from the island of Jaina, a Mayan burial place.

For an eclectic collection—six rooms of curiosities ranging from fine Mayan jade jewelry to Spanish colonial art objects—search out the **Museo Regional de Campeche**, on Calle 59 in one of this modest city's better colonial houses. Closed Mondays.

The first choice for accommodations in town is the **Hotel Ramada Campeche** (formerly the Presidente), with balconies overlooking the Bahía de Campeche, a swimming pool and bar, and air-conditioning throughout. The adequate restaurant specializes in seafood, as it should in this fishing port.

Next door, and not quite as satisfactory, is the **Hotel Baluartes**, with many of its less expensive and slightly threadbare rooms overlooking not the sea but the parking lot. Restaurant, bar, and pool.

The **Hotel Lopez**, one block south and two blocks west of the zócalo on Calle 12, is a modest and inexpensive establishment popular with commercial travellers. Only the air-conditioned rooms are worth the price here.

CHICHEN ITZA

This sprawling ceremonial center thrusts itself up from the jungle about 120 km (74 miles) east of Mérida on Highway 180, not quite halfway to Puerto Juárez (Cancún and Isla Mujeres). Nothing in the Mayan world prepares the visitor for the architecture here: dynamic, full of force and energy. The lively structures at Uxmal authoritatively but serenely occupy the ground on which they rest. They are so self-contained it doesn't matter that they crowd each other; in a sense, they provide their own framing. But at Chichén Itzá the great monuments each seem to insist on—and get—their own space. As with skillfully executed stage sets, the illusion they create exceeds their physical dimensions. In fact, Chichén Itzá is so theatrical that dazzled visitors often call it perfect, the most beautiful of all the Mayan ruins. While no site is "perfect," what Chichén may lack in depth and subtlety it makes up for in drama.

Though it is quite easy to get lost at Chichén Itzá, literally as well as artistically, this does not mean that a guide is necessary. Most visitors will want to move at their own pace, taking time to form their own impressions; it is difficult to absorb a running commentary while trying to grasp the purely visual aspects of such alien and majestic surroundings. On the other hand, you might want to invest in a detailed guidebook to the ruins. The government handbook issued under the INAH (Instituto Nacional de Antropología y Historia) imprint, on sale at the entrance to the site, is invaluable.

Chichén Itzá (chee-CHEN eet-SAH) roughly translates as "place at the rim of the well of Itzá." Identifying the people known as the Itzá is not terribly important for fully appreciating the site. Knowing about the well, however, is crucial, for that is where the whole story begins.

The northern Yucatán, for all intents and purposes, is without rivers or lakes. The torrential rains of summer disappear as quickly as they fall, running to the sea or vanishing beneath the limestone underlying the soil. Instead, there is a huge and complex system of subterranean rivers in the Yucatán whose life-giving waters are, for the most part, inaccessible. Here and there the limestone has caved in, creating the natural wells or sinkholes called cenotes. To the ancient Maya a cenote was literally the wellspring of life and a sacred gift from the gods.

The great cenote at Chichén Itzá, the **Cenote Sagrado** (Sacred Cenote), is the most awesome of these sinkholes, a gaping mouth in the earth roughly 190 feet in diameter and slightly more oval than circular. Sheer or undercut sides drop 65 feet or more to the surface of the water, which fills the hole to a depth of some 35 feet. The cenote is so unexpected and surrounded by such solitude that it would seem menacing even without the stories every visitor hears. It's not unusual to see people stand at the little temple platform on the rim, glance down at its murky waters, blink, and take a step backward.

In pre-Hispanic times the cenote was a magnet for Mayan pilgrims who came to this spot to implore or appease the rain god. Dredging in modern times has brought up a trove of sacrificial objects, including gold, silver, copper, polished jade, and, more grimly, about 50 human skulls, some of them belonging to young children. All this must be kept in perspective. The cenote was a center of sacrifice for at least 1,000 years: A victim every 20 years does not suggest that maidens were hurled into the depths seasonally, as some writers have imagined and certain guides still insist today.

In time the mystique and sustaining power of the cenote impelled the Maya to erect a ceremonial center not far away, a center that flourished during the latter stages of the Classic period, from about A.D. 600 to 900. At that point the region was overrun by a people known as the Itzá, allies or perhaps cousins of the warlike Toltecs of the central highlands, whose great capital was Tula (they might even have *been* Toltecs; this is a subject for scholarly debate). At any rate, under their influence a new ceremonial center, strategically located between the Sacred Cenote and the older Mayan city, was built after A.D. 900.

Chichén Itzá, as it exists today, is a mostly Toltec-inspired creation built by Mayan skill and labor—"Toltec-Maya" is as good a term as any. Much of its drama derives from the Toltec imagery found at every turn: jaguars that are almost preternaturally ferocious, eagles devouring human hearts, snarling plumed serpents, low-relief portraits of great warriors. In fact, the Temple of the Warriors complex, with its intimidating colonnades, seems to have been lifted in its entirety from Tula. Toltec domination in the Yucatán was effective but brief, a case of "the flies conquering the flypaper." They were assimilated; they disappeared. Yet during their short tenure they revived the greatness of Mayan art, as Chichén Itzá attests.

Visitors to the site are often so eager to begin exploring that they forget to stop at the Service Unit located at the entrance. This is a mistake. You can get the latest orientation information there, as well as schedules giving the hours when certain temple interiors are open for inspection.

The Northern Zone

The effect of the northern complex, more Toltec-Maya than purely Mayan, is instantaneous and powerful, so theatrical that the word "operatic" immediately suggests itself. Where other Mesoamerican ceremonial centers seem to have been constructed more for the benefit of the gods than for the impression they created on humans, Chichén Itzá is nothing less than a gigantic and obviously intentional show.

The **Castillo**, or **Pirámide de Kukulcán**, holds center stage. Kukulcán is the Mayan name for the Plumed Serpent, the Mexican priest-god folk hero who was also the Quetzalcóatl of the Toltecs and then the Aztecs. Besides being a temple the structure is a literal calendar in stone. Its original steps coincided with the days of the solar year, a type of symbolism not unusual in Mesoamerica; time cycles and months were numbered in terraces and panels. To this day, in fact, you can witness a curious byplay of shadows on the temple steps at the time of the equinox. Some observers claim to see a representation of a serpent during a precise 34-minute period in the late afternoon; others, watching the same thing, remain skeptical. In any case, the structure reveals a knowledge not only of architecture but of astronomy as well.

The pyramid rises in perfectly proportioned stone terraces of diminishing size, which contribute to the illusion of height. (The structure was built according to the tradition of placing one temple atop an older one after a 52-year cycle. The first Toltec religious structure here was dedicated to the sun.) Eager and heat-resistant visitors who have no tendency to claustrophobia can enter the pyramid and climb an irregular stairway to the top; there they will discover, besides a magnificent view, a rather crude but powerful jaguar sculpture, apparently a throne, cut from a single piece of limestone and painted with vermilion cinnabar. The bared teeth are made from white flint, the eyes from green jade (as are the large discs representing spots on the body). Access to this inner temple is limited to certain hours, and the schedule is by no means fixed; be sure to inquire at the entrance to the zone for the hours it's open to the public.

Northwest of the Castillo lies the great **Juego de Pelota** (Ball Court), the largest in Mesoamerica. There appear to have been various versions of this ceremonial game. Courts were always built in an I shape, thereby creating "end zones," and scoring at first may have involved cornering a hard rubber ball at either end. Later, stone rings were added to the side walls, and a player could win the contest by knocking or kicking (not throwing) the ball through one of these small hoops. The improbability of managing this is clear: A player who actually "scored" won all the clothes and jewelry worn by the spectators. It is often assumed, as a result of certain carvings, that those who lost the game were "sacrificed." This interpretation is Eurocentric, however; it's just as likely that the *winners* could have merited what was seen then as an honor.

Attached to the ball court, on top of the south end of the east wall, stands the small but massive two-story **Templo de los Jaguares**. Twin-plumed serpent columns, feathered and fanged, glare across the ball court as they support the entrance and roof. Murals of a procession have long since faded, but some carving endures: Warriors of the 12th century display their nudity, demonstrating that the Maya, or at least the Toltec-Maya, were not always puritanical. A steep staircase at the south corner provides passage to the lower temple and the remains of a sculpted jaguar, perhaps a throne, for which the temple is named.

East of the main path leading to the Sacred Cenote, the **Templo de los Guerreros** (Temple of the Warriors) and the **Grupo de las Mil Columnas** (Group of the Thousand Columns) are second only to the Castillo in impressiveness and second to none in their fascination for visitors. In addition to comprising a huge complex of courtyards, platforms, terraces, and colonnades, the two signify a sharp change in the life of Chichén Itzá. Prior to their construction, small interior rooms were adequate to meet the needs of its inhabitants. At a certain point, however, there appears to have been a sudden demand for roofed areas and meeting halls protected from the rain—proof, according to some experts, that a large new military aristocracy had developed among the Toltecs. In fact, just such a warrior elite is depicted in full regalia in carvings throughout the site.

The so-called **mercado** (market), which rises about 200 yards southeast of the Castillo, was more likely a stone stage used for dance or theatrical performances. Just to the east of it efficient steam baths were built and no doubt used for both the ritual purification of priests as well as to accommodate the personal fastidiousness of the Maya.

Chichén Itzá seems to have been a gathering place rather than a continuously inhabited city, although it obviously could accommodate a large number of people. In addition to its many ceremonial buildings, there is a second cenote capable of supplying water year-round, as well as seven other ball courts (although not all were in use at the same time).

Over the years scholars have avoided public speculation about life at Chichén Itzá in its glory days. But one, Jacques Soustelle, has ventured to the edge of conjecture. Discussing the northern zone, Soustelle writes: "One is tempted to group the buildings... under two headings: the religious and ritual center, with the great ceremonial ballcourt, the Temple of the Jaguars, and the sacrificial monuments; and the meeting place of the Itzá warriors... whom one can imagine strolling through the colonnade and beside the pool on their way to the small ballcourt. The Temple of the Warriors, with the vast pillared hall before its façade, serves as a transition between the two centers, the one religious and the other secular, military and no doubt commercial."

Soustelle's speculations, whether wholly accurate or not, dovetail with the site's design and help a visitor to re-create the life that went on in the northern zone.

The Southern Zone

This area, called Chichén Viejo (Old Chichén), was the older ceremonial center that the northern Toltec-Maya zone replaced, and is built in the classic Mayan Puuc style, much in the manner of Uxmal (although Toltec embellishments were added to some of the buildings at a later date). While a fascinating and beautiful place, it does not have the instant impact of the northern group, in part because of its subtler architectural style, but mostly because the positioning of the structures does not result in the breathtaking vistas and contrasts that later Toltec planning afforded.

El Caracol (The Snail), with an interior stairway that spirals upward, is the most immediately striking structure in the neighborhood and was probably used by ancient stargazers. (Because a snail's shell is spiral-shaped, anything that winds upward—a road or stairway for instance—is likely to be called a *caracol* in Spanish.) In fact, the four apertures facing the cardinal directions at the top of the structure seem to confirm that it was constructed as an observatory. (Only three of the original apertures survive.) Although imposing and surprising, El Caracol is less than beautiful, inspiring Mayanist J. Eric Thompson to observe that the building "stands like a two-decker wedding cake on the square carton from which it came."

Indisputably lovely, on the other hand, is the ruined **Edificio de las Monjas** (Nunnery) and its adjacent annex.

(The modern name is simply a bit of Spanish fancy.) Unfortunately, in 1868 an eager archaeologist set off an explosive charge inside the Nunnery to speed his search and did irreparable damage to the structure.

The entrance to the annex is through the mouth of a stone monster. Such a door typifies the "Chenes" style, an ornate architectural style named for a site in the central Yucatán dating from the Late Classic era. Related to the Puuc style of Uxmal, Chenes is characterized by decorative doorways (variously defined as the gaping jaws of rain gods, earth monsters, and sky serpents), huge rain-god masks, ornamental scrollwork, and decoration below the medial molding.

Nearby, the exuberant decoration of the "church" reminds viewers that the ancient Maya abhorred a design vacuum. Half a dozen other, lesser structures, each with its own mysteries, are scattered elsewhere around the area.

Staying near Chichén Itzá

Mayaland, adjacent to the archaeological zone, is the traditional choice. However, its popularity with tour packagers has caused it to become increasingly noisy and crowded, and the too-heavy demands on the kitchen are often all too obvious on your plate. If you can somehow avoid the throngs, its bungalows are especially attractive, and most of the rooms are very comfortable (though a few seem cramped). Ask for a private balcony. Mayaland also has a pool, cocktail lounge, and a helpful staff skilled in making travel arrangements in the region.

The attractive **Hacienda Chichén** keeps its cottages open only in the winter and consequently relies on ceiling fans rather than air-conditioning. Rustic but gracious, it, too, is located in the archaeological zone. In fact, some of Chichén Viejo lies within the Hacienda's lovely gardens. Bar, dining room, swimming pool.

The fairly new and well-run **Villa Arqueológica Chichén Itzá** is on the East Access Road, just up the street from the Hacienda and Mayaland. As in all the branches of this Club Med–owned chain, the rooms are comfortable but far from spacious. The public areas, which include a pool, flower-filled patio, lighted tennis court, gift shop, and dining room that offers attractive, well-prepared food, more than make up for the somewhat cramped quarters.

The **Misión Park Inn Chichén Itzá**, in the nearby village of Pisté, is popular with families and tour groups. The atmosphere is vaguely colonial, the air-conditioning modern, and it has a swimming pool, adequate dining room, bar, and protected parking.

About 2½ km (1½ miles) east of the ruins, on the road to Valladolid, is the unpretentious **Dolores Alba**, with adequate accommodations at attractive prices. If air-conditioning is available (check first) it is worth the extra charge.

Some travellers, especially students, choose to stay in the small town of **Valladolid** itself, some 40 km (25 miles) east of Chichén Itzá. The town's attractions consist mostly of budget-priced hotel rooms and good bus service to the ruins. In addition, there are some colonial buildings here, as well as a cenote that is used as a public swimming pool.

El Mesón del Marqués, on the Valladolid plaza, is a former colonial residence with a number of new rooms. Most of its rooms, old or new, are air-conditioned, and there is a pool and pleasant patio restaurant. A popular arts shop here offers a good selection of regional handicrafts. The **Hotel San Clemente**, also facing the plaza, has less character but is at least as comfortable as the Mesón del Marqués.

The Balancanché Cave

This is an adventure for the dedicated who don't mind squeezing and crawling through narrow passages. Visitors who were less than delighted by the interior stairways at Chichén Itzá will definitely want to skip it. Others may find it rewarding.

The subterranean passages of this complex contain sacred urns dedicated to the Toltec rain god, and are believed to have served as a refuge during times of invasion. In addition, a pond at the end of a main passageway is home to blind fish. Cameras are banned, as are small children, the latter for good reason: The cave is eerie and tomblike.

Admission to the cave, which is about 5 km (3 miles) north and east of Chichén Itzá off Highway 180, is with a guide only; arrangements may be made at the cluster of buildings at the entrance to the cave.

PALENQUE

"The temples of Palenque... are exquisite rather than imposing; refined, rather than massive. They are quite content with the earth they stand on, and do not, like their predecessors, reach for the sky. Like precious jewels, they are beautiful and complete in themselves. The earlier gods, if they were gods, in

548   MAYAN MEXICO

the sculptures of Tikal, Copan and elsewhere seem to represent great natural forces, the forces that caused the maize to grow and the rain to fall; these gods here at Palenque are members of an elegant aristocracy that rules gracefully over the destinies of men."—Louis J. Halle, Jr.

The site at Palenque (pah-LEHN-keh), in the rain forests of northern Chiapas, is compact and remarkably harmonious. Although its structures do not all date from the same period, they are of a piece and share a common aesthetic tradition. Many people think this is the most beautiful cluster of pre-Columbian buildings in the Americas: To find its rivals you will have to travel to Greece, Turkey, or Southeast Asia.

For centuries Palenque was the proverbial "lost city in the jungle," known only through vague rumor and manuscripts that were as obscure as the city itself. In 1786, however, a Captain Antonio del Río was sent to investigate. After weeks in the jungle he and his men found what they were looking for and immediately set about driving spikes into the stucco sculpture in order to hang their hammocks and armor. They also dug a quite useless trench, doubtless seeking treasure, then gave up after del Río had "discovered all that was to be found." The captain, while perpetrating this archaeological mayhem, observed that the natives were "sullen and suspicious." He was one of the rare visitors who did not like Palenque.

The two men responsible for focusing the world's attention on the ruined city were John Lloyd Stephens and his friend Frederick Catherwood, the English artist and architect. After hacking their way through the jungle with the help of native guides, the two stumbled upon the ruins in 1840 and were so delighted by their find that they fired the last of their gunpowder into the air.

Although the original name of this Mayan ceremonial center is unknown, we do know that it was the capital of a large Late Classic–era kingdom. The modern name, which was borrowed from the nearest town, means "palisade," and otherwise seems to have no connection to the ancient city that dominated this corner of the world with its knowledge and culture. When, near the end of its reign, some fortifications were built, it seems that Palenque was already doomed. It fell, for reasons unknown, in A.D. 800, the first great Mayan city-state to fail and be abandoned to the jungle.

Today the ruins rest on a narrow shelf of forested land high enough to provide sweeping views of jungle, meadows, and, in the distance, flat savannah stretching toward the sea. It is, above all, a green world, with every shade from olive

through emerald present. The site is also compact; there's no need to hire a guide. Stop at the information center at the entrance to inquire about hours and regulations, however, as well as to buy the official INAH handbook to the ruins. Once inside the zone, be sure to take your time. Not only are you in the tropics, but the subtleties of Palenque do not reveal themselves at a glance. If at all possible, allow two days for the site; the pleasure lies not only in seeing, but in absorbing and relating. Palenque is alien and distinctive even to travellers familiar with other Mayan sites. A good plan, therefore, is to use the first day for exploring the Palace, the Temple of the Inscriptions, and Temple XIII. The rest can wait for the second day.

Most visitors are drawn immediately to the Palace, readily identifiable by its four-story tower, leaving the structures on their right for later. A wise choice; the Palace is the best introduction to Palenque.

The Palace

Much of this complex, which surmounts a huge rectangular platform, was the creation of Lord Pacal, the most famous ruler of Palenque. Ascending to power in A.D. 615 as a 12-year-old boy, he is said to have ruled until his death at the age of 80—a period that coincides with Palenque's most marvelous work. Augustus Caesar once boasted that he found Rome brick and left it marble. Lord Pacal's achievement was every bit as impressive: He found Palenque humble and left it magnificent.

Additions were made to the Palace by Pacal's son, Lord Kan Xul. Indeed, some of the finest reliefs here date from his reign, and the work merits close examination. Unfortunately, much of it has been eroded over the centuries and some destroyed. Visitors will need to do some restoration in their imaginations to appreciate fully the achievements of the Palenque stone carvers.

The landmark tower, which probably was used both for stargazing and keeping an eye on affairs on the plain below, is often called the **observatory**. The climb to the top, often rewarded with a refreshing breeze stirring through the windows, is not difficult, and the views of the flat green world spread out to the horizon are unforgettable. From here it's also immediately apparent that only the central area of Palenque remains—or at least that is all that has been uncovered.

A new surprise awaits around every corner of the Palace

complex—altars and thrones, hidden stairways, reliefs in stone and stucco. After a few hours you will even develop a sense for the unique Palenque line—smooth, serene, and quietly understated.

The **Templo de las Inscripciones** (Temple of the Inscriptions), adjacent to the Palace, perches dramatically above its green jungle backdrop on stone terraces stepped one atop another. Though beautiful in its own right, the structure is best known for the discovery made here in 1952 by the Mexican archaeologist Alberto Ruz Lhuillier. Noticing some holes in the temple floor and suspecting they were handholds, Ruz had a huge slab raised, which revealed a hidden stairway blocked with rubble. While the passage was being cleared, Ruz discovered the skeletal remains of five or six youths—apparently the sacrificial companions of a master who had been entombed beyond. But, of course, everyone knew that Mesoamerican pyramids and temples were never used as burial crypts. This wasn't Egypt, after all.

To everybody's surprise, a sepulchral vault was eventually uncovered, with the figures of the Nine Lords of the Night standing solemn watch in the chamber. When, after immense difficulty, the beautifully carved slab lid of the huge stone coffin was removed, Ruz found the skeleton of a large man as well as an extraordinary jade mosaic funerary mask. We now know, after decades of trying to decipher the ancient Mayan glyphs on the sarcophagus lid, that the bones are those of Lord Pacal. At the same time, Ruz made another interesting discovery: From the sarcophagus a sort of pipe, or hollow molding, wound up the stairs to the temple—apparently so that Lord Pacal could maintain postmortem communication with the world he had departed.

As was usual at that time, everything in the tomb was whisked off to Mexico City, where it is now on view at the National Museum of Anthropology. But the monolithic casket lid would not fit up the narrow, twisting stairs, and so it remains in Palenque, proof that the tomb was built before the temple.

Near the Temple of the Inscriptions is the much smaller **Temple XIII** (also known as the **Templo de la Calavera**, or Skull Temple), accessible by a hillside path from the top of the Temple of the Inscriptions, which means it isn't necessary to descend the steep steps of the Inscriptions, as most visitors do. This lesser temple is somehow connected with death; at least the main stucco decoration remaining portrays a death god. From here a short, steep path rejoins the main path from the entrance.

A group of four temples, each distinctive but all related in style, is a good start for the second day's viewing. This group is located just southeast of the Palace across a narrow stream, and includes the Temples of the Sun, the Cross, the Foliated Cross, and Temple XIV. Such names as "the Cross" derive from European conjecture about sculpted forms found at the temples. They have no connection to the original names of the buildings, which remain unknown.

The small **Templo del Sol** is a treasure. Besides being valued for its lovely proportions, it contains a masterpiece, a carved panel of Pacal deified. The **Templo de la Cruz**, the tallest of this group, with a crumbling but still glorious roofcomb, almost seems to serve as a pedestal for the architectural element above. The **Templo de la Cruz Foliada** and the badly damaged **Templo XIV** nevertheless offer examples of beautiful carving. Considered as a whole, the quartet embodies the genius of Palenque, with the Temple of the Sun, especially, speaking volumes about its creators.

The Northern Group

North of the Palace complex are five structures that share a single base. Although they're in sad condition, the view of the surrounding plain from here is lovely, and it's still possible to imagine how they once might have looked. Nearby, the **Templo del Conde** (Temple of the Count), named for a German nobleman who lived in the structure for a time and made extensive drawings of the ruins in the early decades of the 19th century, is in slightly better condition. While this group is too damaged to be compared with its better-preserved neighbors, time spent lingering here will not be wasted: There's an ineffable atmosphere here that is likely to haunt you for a long time to come.

The small Palenque **museum**, located east of the Northern Group, while not extensive—the best of the site's artifacts has gone elsewhere—boasts some beautiful carvings, ceramics, and bits of stucco decoration.

Staying and Dining at Palenque

Eight kilometers (5 miles) by paved road from the archaeological zone is the town of Palenque. Seeing this modern settlement after visiting the ruins is enough to make anyone pessimistic about human "progress." Fortunately, there are far better accommodations closer to the site.

Staying at the **Chan Kah Cabañas**, a group of cottages about 4 km (2½ miles) from the ruins on the entrance road to the site, will enhance your visit to Palenque. The Mayan-style bungalows are so well designed and ventilated that ceiling fans provide enough cooling; there's also a stream-fed pool. Ask for a cottage near the river. The alfresco restaurant is just adequate.

The **Hotel Nututun Viva** has a beautiful, woodsy location on the river, 5 km (3 miles) south of town on the way to the ruins. The air-conditioned hotel is good and very popular, though some rooms are dark and damp. The dining room has a delightful river view, and the food is good. While the hotel advertises swimming in the river, the rocks and shallow water make this an uninviting prospect.

Two of the hotels in town are geared to student and archaeological tour groups. **La Cañada**, with both cottages and rooms, has attractive grounds and a thatched-roof restaurant that's quite good. It's located on the street of the same name, just off Avenida Juárez, the main street, at the western end of town. The **Casa de Pacal**, facing the municipal park on Avenida Juárez, lacks charm but is modern, air-conditioned, and a good buy.

The **Misión Park Inn Palenque**, at the eastern end of town in a neighborhood known as Rancho San Martín de Porres, has lovely grounds and an attractive restaurant. Despite its rather small, sterile rooms, it is popular with tour groups and quite satisfactory.

Across town, on the way to the ruins, the restaurant **La Selva** is a jungle fantasy mansion come true, a marvel of thatch, knotted twine, and polished wood. The menu is extensive, the food carefully prepared, and there's entertainment and dancing in the evenings.

(For directions to Palenque, see the Getting Around section at the end of the chapter.)

Agua Azul

Visitors to the Palenque area who have extra time, or who are driving on to San Cristóbal de las Casas, should stop at the lovely series of *cascadas* known as Agua Azul. To get there, follow the Ocosingo road 58 km (36 miles) south from Palenque town, then turn right onto the dusty side road, which requires patience and a bit of skill to navigate but is only 4 km (2½ miles) long.

At the end of the road, the waters of the Río Tulija swirl and plunge through a web of cataracts and rapids. You can follow the riverbank upstream past several foaming cascades, where the perpetual mist from the falls gives the foliage a special lushness and little rainbows form when the sun shines. In all directions the mountains of the Sierra Madre de Chiapas present a spectacular backdrop.

There's not much in the way of facilities at the little park, and the mist and dampness make it a less-than-ideal spot for picnics. (There are drier, more comfortable places farther from the tumbling, swirling water.) Nevertheless, it's an excursion well worth the time and effort. And the road from Palenque past the falls turnoff all the way into San Cristóbal de las Casas is extraordinarily scenic.

SAN CRISTOBAL DE LAS CASAS

The mountain-ringed city of San Cristóbal de las Casas is situated at the southwestern edge of Mexico's Mayan region, in the center of the state of Chiapas. Here, in the fastness of the Sierra Madre de Chiapas, the native settlements sprinkled throughout the region seem almost like outposts. And, in a sense, that's exactly what they are. Ages ago the highland Maya pressed no farther; they decided that their world ended here.

Most travellers will appreciate San Cristóbal as a stopover. Those bound by car for Guatemala from central Mexico should take the highland route, Highway 190, which goes through San Cristóbal, rather than the sultry and uninteresting Highway 200 along the Pacific coast: The scenery will more than make up for the extra distance. Likewise, motorists covering Mexico in a great loop from the Yucatán back to Oaxaca will also want to stop here. As a sole destination on what is a long journey, however, San Cristóbal is a dubious choice for most travellers. Still, a few will be enchanted by this odd, tucked-away town and will end up staying and exploring the surrounding region for as long as possible. The only way to tell which group you fall into is to make the journey.

The first signs that you're approaching San Cristóbal de las Casas appear along the roadside—groups or families of Maya gathering or carrying firewood, waiting for rides, plodding patiently toward unknown destinations. Physically these highland Maya look much like their cousins in the Yucatán: short, sturdy, dark, with rather coarse jet-black hair and expressive almond-shaped eyes. But their garb is noticeably different. This is cool country, after all. No gauzy *huipiles* for these women; instead, their clothing is dark and plain. It is left to the male to be the peacock, a role he embraces.

In fact, the different groups of the region can be distinguished by the costumes the men wear. The Zinacantecos, for example, stand out in their beribboned straw hats, pink-striped serapes, and scarves soberly checked in gray but trimmed with magenta tassels. Even in winter they are likely to be barefoot, although at times you'll see them wearing *huaraches* made from discarded automobile tires. The Chamulas, on the other hand, sport white hats big enough for a Hollywood cowboy; under these hats they wear a bright kerchief wrapped around the head for warmth in winter and used as a sweatband in summer, an accessory for all seasons. Their serapes, among the most beautiful in Mexico, are worn over white tunics and white knee pants, and are usually woven of thick wool left a natural or bleached white (although they are sometimes dyed black).

The ancestors of both these Mayan groups were quite possibly the builders of Palenque and other lowland centers in the Classic period. If so, they were probably dispersed and became refugees in the mountains after their magnificent cities were abandoned in the ninth and tenth centuries. They encountered the Spanish for the first time when Diego de Mazariego established San Cristóbal in 1528. His successor unleashed a reign of terror in the region, but the Maya's suffering abated after the arrival of the bishop of Chiapas, Bartolomé de las Casas, and 35 fellow Dominicans in 1545. The bishop was a vigorous and effective defender of Mayan rights and even managed to get some of the worst laws against them repealed. As a result, the town was renamed for him during the era of anticlerical reform in Mexico in the 19th century, becoming simply "Las Casas"—a name that still is often used today.

The town held onto its isolation and old ways for centuries, its traditions more common to Guatemala than Mexico. Racial purity was maintained along with sharp class distinctions. Politically, San Cristóbal resisted independence, resisted union with Mexico, resisted *all* change. In 1890, as a punishment, the state capital was shifted to Tuxtla Gutiérrez, which subsequently outdistanced San Cristóbal in both size and wealth—though not in interest for travellers.

The racial and caste divisions are obvious even today in San Cristóbal. This is much more a city surrounded by Indians than an Indian city, and the easy cultural assimilation of Oaxaca or Morelia is virtually unknown here.

Around the Zócalo

The dark reds and oranges of tile roofs, steeply sloped to ward off the torrential summer rains, are what most visitors first notice about San Cristóbal. This is also a place of whites and pastels, pale lavenders warming to pinks. And everywhere, in any direction, you get a sense of distance and of being hemmed in by mountains.

Situated on the north side of the zócalo, the old **cathedral** has a Plateresque façade and some antique statuary. The building dates from the 16th century, with later additions—a big structure but not a major one.

A very helpful government tourism office can be found on the south side of the zócalo, opposite the cathedral. Nearby is the 16th-century home of Diego de Mazariego, which is older than the cathedral but in the same style. (Today it houses the Hotel Santa Clara.)

There are pleasant strolls in every direction from the plaza; the destinations matter less than the cobblestone streets themselves, which are lined with quaint façades offering glimpses of gracious courtyards. The homeowners of San Cristóbal appear to have taken special pride in the ironwork decorating their houses; it is unusually good.

The 17th-century **Templo de Santo Domingo**, located five blocks north of the zócalo at the corner of Calzada Lázaro Cárdenas and Calle Nicaragua, is the finest colonial building in the region. Its style was borrowed from a number of 16th-century churches in Guatemala, and its interior is embellished by a masterpiece of a pulpit and some extraordinary gilded screens. Housed in the cloister of Santo Domingo is the small **Museo Regional**, which displays lacquerwork, native costumes, and an illustrated history of San Cristóbal.

Outside is a Mayan **market**; on a bright, sunny day a stop here leaves you with the impression of having walked into a rainbow of sparkling colors blending and clashing. The vendors, mostly women, wear delicately embroidered blouses, bold sashes, and, in their hair, yarn that is almost Chinese red. Their offerings include brocade and embroidery work, leather goods, hammocks, bags, and jewelry. Children, bright-eyed miniatures of the vendors, scamper and play among the displays.

Adjacent to the church is the **Sna Jolobil** shop and museum, run cooperatively by Mayan women. Prices seem slightly higher inside than out, but the co-op offers better quality. The museum is open mornings only.

The municipal market, north and east of Santo Domingo, is less interesting for its merchandise than for its customers: In every aisle appear faces that might have been models for the carvings at Palenque or Uxmal.

Staying and Dining in San Cristóbal

Visitors in the winter will definitely want a room with a fireplace, an adequate supply of wood, and—equally important—sufficient kindling. All the hotels in town are colonial and provincial, and some are even rustic.

The **Posada Diego de Mazariegos**, an inviting provincial inn with ample rooms (some with fireplaces) arranged around large patios, occupies two converted colonial buildings a block north of the zócalo. The dining room is also the town's best restaurant. Added attractions include a bar, a coffee and pastry shop, and friendly service. Convenient parking, not easy to find in San Cristóbal, is provided.

The reasonably priced **Hotel Santa Clara**, right on the zócalo, is housed in the 16th-century Diego de Mazariego mansion and is charmingly decorated with tiles, iron work, and carved wood. The dining room is quite good, and there's a protected parking lot. The cold-water swimming pool is only for the hardy.

Not quite as good is the **Hotel Flanboyant**, centrally located two blocks north of the zócalo at the corner of Calle 16 de Septiembre and Primero de Mayo. All the rooms, which vary greatly otherwise, have fireplaces, and the hotel also offers a dining room and charming patio garden. (This is the former Hotel Español, enlarged and redecorated.)

Just southeast of town off Highway 190 is the inviting **El Molino de la Alborada**, a hacienda-style establishment with cottages. It's a small, intimate inn, with a fine kitchen to serve its guests. It also has a good stable—as well as an airplane landing strip. Although somewhat isolated, El Molino appeals especially to visitors with time to explore the countryside and the native villages, as well as simply to relax. The rates are quite reasonable considering all that is offered.

San Cristóbal has no outstanding restaurants. The best food can be found in the hotels: Mazariegos, Santa Clara, and Flanboyant, in that order. **Madre Tierra**, a few blocks south of the zócalo facing the Templo de San Francisco, offers a good breakfast with a health-food accent, and also serves lunch and dinner. **El Fogón de Jovel**, Avenida 16 de Septiembre 11, features regional cuisine and evening marimba music in a patio that is as colorful as it is chilly after sundown. The **Restaurant Plaza**, on a second floor overlooking the main square, is well-situated for observing life in the zócalo; its best offering is coffee and rolls with a view.

Exploring the San Cristóbal Region

Casa Na Bolom, northeast of the zócalo at Calle Vicente Guerrero 31, is a small, privately run museum that serves as a center for visiting anthropologists and archaeologists investigating the area. It is owned and supervised by Gertrude Duby, herself an anthropologist (and photographer) and the widow of Frans Blom. The couple is celebrated for their efforts to preserve the Lancandon Indian traditions and the rain forest in which they live, as well as for their explorations and studies of the Chiapas highlands. Museum tours are conducted, and a donation is expected. In addition, maps of the surrounding countryside can be bought at Na Bolom, and the staff is generous with their knowledge of the region and its people. (El Molino de la Alborada is also helpful and expert in making excursion arrangements for its guests.)

Native villages, lovely lakes, and forested mountains—all lie within reach of San Cristóbal de las Casas. **Zinacantán**, 11 km (7 miles) west of San Cristóbal, and **San Juan Chamula**, 10 km (6 miles) northwest, are two of the more interesting rural centers of the highland Maya. In both places the inhabitants go about their business seemingly oblivious to the presence of curious tourists. Both villages absolutely forbid the taking of photographs in their churches—Zinacantán bans cameras altogether, and offenders are dealt with harshly. San Juan Chamula's church, built over a pyramid on the main square, is worth a visit if only to observe the rituals enacted there, which fall somewhere between Christian and pagan practices. Reluctant to give up their traditional form of worship, the Chamulas compromised their religion in order to avoid annihilation by their Spanish conquerors.

There are no pews in the church; the faithful spread out across the floor to perform their healings. Scattered among the small groups are usually a chicken, lit candles, an egg, and a bottle of Coca Cola. According to one version of their beliefs, the "healer" passes the malady of the sick person to a chicken or egg, which then is taken outside and buried, thus trapping the disease. The Coke is sprinkled about like holy water.

The church, dedicated to Saint John the Baptist (father of Jesus Christ according to popular belief in Chamula), has no priest and holds no traditional Catholic Masses. Wooden statues of various saints have been banished to the back of the building in "punishment" for not saving another parish building that burned to the ground. Chamula policemen, dressed in traditional white tunics and pants, patrol the interior to make sure no photographs are taken. A modest admission fee is charged at the police station.

The lakes of the **Lacandon Forest** are also accessible from San Cristóbal, though a fairly long trip by car; allow a full day. To get to the Lacandon area, drive to the town of Comitán, 86 km (53 miles) southeast via the Pan-American Highway. (The highway actually bypasses Comitán, a pretty little town with adequate cafés around its plaza.) Fifteen kilometers (9 miles) south of Comitán you'll come to the village of La Trinitaria, where you turn left onto the paved road that leads to **Lagunas de Montebello National Park**; the park lies 36 km (22 miles) farther on. After entering the park the road forks. Go left to the **Lagunas de Colores** (Colored Lakes), which are lovely, tranquil, and a startling sight with their contrasting colors.

Of the 16 lakes in the park, those off the right fork are not as accessible from the road. If you do take the right fork, after almost 16 km (10 miles) you'll come to **Dos Lagunas**, two especially beautiful bodies of water surrounded by forest. It is advisable to return to San Cristóbal for the night. (Note: In 1992 the right fork to Lagunas de Montebello was being used as a logging road, heavy equipment making the dirt trail dangerous and impassable. Inquire locally before proceeding to the right [southbound]. If the road seems torn up, you should turn back at once and stick to the paved routes. Hiking, of course, remains possible.)

The San Cristóbal region is crisscrossed by bridle trails. Arrangements for **renting horses** may be made at El Recoveco, a shop on the San Cristóbal plaza. Reservations are taken at 7:00 P.M. for the next morning; information about trails and maps are also available. In addition, most local hotels will be happy to arrange horse rentals and provide relevant information.

Advice and help with all excursions in the region can be obtained at the tourism office on the zócalo in San Cristóbal.

GETTING AROUND

Mérida

Mexicana Airlines offers flights connecting Mérida with Mexico City; it also flies, via Cozumel, to Miami and Dallas–Fort Worth. Aeroméxico links Mérida with Mexico City, Villahermosa, and Miami. Aerotaxis Bonanza offers small-plane service from Mérida to Chichén Itzá, Cozumel, and Cancún. The Mérida airport is a ten-minute ride from the main plaza and is served by price-controlled taxis, which cost about $5. The inexpensive airport bus (marked "Aviación") departs from the corner of Calles 67 and 60, downtown.

All buses to other cities arrive and depart from the central terminal on Calle 69 between Calles 68 and 70. There is good first-class service to all major destinations, with ADO one of the larger and better lines.

The train from Mexico City, via Palenque, has sleeping cars, but even so it is recommended only for travellers with endless time, patience, and fortitude.

Most Mérida hotels have travel desks or offices that are happy to offer options for exploring the area. These hotel services also tend to be more reliable than the little storefront agencies that pepper the city.

Bus tours are another dubious option and tend to be mass movers, highly regimented, and overly fast-paced. Any guided tour with more than seven passengers is also questionable. In fact, nothing larger than a station wagon or minivan is recommended. Private cars with guides are available at Sindicato de Guía; Tel: (992) 3-2602.

A number of major car-rental agencies in Mérida serve visitors who prefer exploring at their own pace; expect prices considerably higher than in the United States and Canada. Public transportation by bus is available to all major sites; schedules can be obtained through hotels or at the tourism office, Teatro Peón Contreras, Calle 60 between Calles 57 and 59; Tel: (992) 4-9290 (the staff is most helpful).

Chichén Itzá

The first-class buses between Mérida and Cancún also serve Chichén, which is just off Highway 180. Most buses stop at the entrance to the ruins, while a few stop at the nearby village of Pisté, where taxis to the ruins are available. You can also use the sidewalk from Pisté to Chichén—about a 20-minute walk. Travellers arriving by bus or car from Isla Mujeres and Cozumel reach Chichén via the very good Cancún-Mérida highway. Chichén is about 200 km (124 miles) west of Cancún.

In addition, you can fly to Chichén Itzá with Aerotaxis Bonanza out of Mérida, or with Aerocaribe/Aero Cozumel from the Caribbean resorts.

Palenque

The nearest commercial airport is in Villahermosa, 151 km (94 miles) to the northwest. Car rentals are available in Villahermosa as well, and the ADO line offers good bus transportation to the site. (It's slightly more than a 2-hour drive from Villahermosa to Palenque.) Those with cars may wish to continue south on the beautiful mountain drive to

San Cristóbal de las Casas after exploring Palenque. (See the Getting Around section for San Cristóbal below.)

For the adventurous, there is Pullman rail service to Palenque from Mexico City as well as from Mérida. The posted length of the trip from the capital is 24 hours—which seems to be more a speed record than the reality. The train sways and shimmies, and while the part of the trip through jungle is interesting, more of it is dull.

At Palenque, *combi* buses ply the road from town to the ruins with reasonable frequency, and taxis will respond to phone calls from area hotels.

For exploring the ruins, tennis or running shoes will do nicely; boots are not necessary. A sun hat and insect repellent are advisable.

San Cristóbal de las Casas

There is no commercial airport in the San Cristóbal area, but Tuxtla Gutiérrez, 93 km (58 miles) to the west, is serviced by regular daily flights to and from Mexico City. In addition, cars may be rented at the Tuxtla airport. There is minibus service from the air terminal to the bus depot, where you can catch the ADO bus for San Cristóbal. The road to San Cristóbal climbs steeply, so it takes about 2 hours to make the journey by car, a little longer by bus.

There is regular bus service from San Cristóbal to Guatemala City, with connections from there to most Guatemalan towns. The border is 172 km (107 miles) southeast of San Cristóbal. Buses also run regularly between San Cristóbal and Palenque, a distance of 207 km (128 miles). Travellers making the trip from Oaxaca by car should prepare for a very long day's journey: about 630 km (391 miles).

ACCOMMODATIONS REFERENCE

The rates given below are projections *for December 1992 through Easter 1993. Unless otherwise indicated, rates are for double rooms, double occupancy; the 10 percent VAT has been added. As rates are subject to change; it's always a good idea to double-check before booking.*

▶ **La Cañada.** Cañada 18, **Palenque**, Chiapas 29960. Tel: (934) 5-0102 or 0411. $45.

▶ **Casa del Balam.** Calle 60 488, **Mérida**, Yucatán 97000. Tel: (99) 24-8844; Fax: (99) 24-5011. $110.

▶ **Casa de Pacal.** Avenida Juárez 8, **Palenque**, Chiapas 29960. $28.

▶ **El Castellano.** Calle 57 513. **Mérida**, Yucatán 97000. Tel: (99) 23-0100 or 0621; Fax: (99) 23-0110. $90.

- **Chan Kah Cabañas.** P.O. Box 26, Carretera Ocosingo, km 31, **Palenque**, Chiapas 29960. Tel: (934) 5-0318. $88.
- **El Conquistador.** Paseo de Montejo 458, **Mérida**, Yucatán 97000. Tel: (99) 26-2155; Fax: (99) 26-8829. $85.
- **Gran Hotel.** Parque Cepeda Peraza, **Mérida**, Yucatán 97000. Tel: (99) 21-7620 or 24-7622; Fax: (99) 24-7730. $44.
- **Hacienda Chichén.** Zona Arqueológica, **Chichén Itzá**, or P.O. Box 407, Mérida, Yucatán 97000. In Mérida, Tel: (99) 21-9212. $111.
- **Hacienda Uxmal.** Zona Arqueológica, **Uxmal**, or P.O. Box 407, Mérida, Yucatán 97000. In Mérida, Tel: (99) 24-7142. $86.
- **Holiday Inn Mérida.** P.O. Box 134, Avenida Colón and Calle 60, **Mérida**, Yucatán 97127. Tel: (99) 25-6877; Fax: (99) 25-7755; in the U.S. and Canada, Tel: (800) 465-4329. $127.
- **Hotel Baluartes.** Avenida Ruíz Cortines 53, **Campeche**, Campeche 24000. Tel: (981) 6-3911; Fax: (981) 6-2410. $50.
- **Hotel Colón.** Calle 62 483, **Mérida**, Yucatán 97000. Tel: (99) 23-4355; Fax: (99) 24-4919. $48.
- **Hotel Dolores Alba.** Calle 63 464, **Mérida**, Yucatán 97000. Tel: (99) 21-3745; Fax: (99) 28-3163. $28.
- **Hotel Dolores Alba.** 2½ km east of the ruins on Highway 180, **Chichén Itzá**, Yucatán. In Mérida, Tel: (99) 21-3745. $29.
- **Hotel Flanboyant.** Avenida 16 de Septiembre and Primero de Mayo, **San Cristóbal de las Casas**, Chiapas 29200. Tel: (967) 8-0045; Fax: (967) 8-0514. $38.
- **Hotel Lopez.** Calle 12 Norte 189, **Campeche**, Campeche 24000. Tel: (934) 6-3021. $21.
- **Hotel Nututun Viva.** Carretera Ocosingo, km 3, **Palenque**, Chiapas 29960. Tel: (934) 5-0161. $66.
- **Hotel Ramada Campeche.** Avenida Ruíz Cortines 51, **Campeche**, Campeche 24000. Tel: (981) 6-2233; Fax: (981) 1-1618. $98.
- **Hotel San Clemente.** Calle 41 206, **Valladolid**, Yucatán 97780. Tel: (985) 6-2208; Fax: (985) 6-3564. $27.
- **Hotel Santa Clara.** Plaza Principal, **San Cristóbal de las Casas**, Chiapas 29200. Tel: (967) 8-1140; Fax: (967) 6-0031. $44.
- **Mayaland.** Zona Arqueológica, **Chichén Itzá**, or P.O. Box 407, Mérida, Yucatán 97000. Tel and Fax: (985) 6-2777; in Mérida, Tel: (99) 21-9212; in U.S., Tel: (800) 451-8891 or (305) 341-9173. $90.
- **El Mesón del Marqués.** Calle 39 203 (zócalo), **Valladolid**, Yucatán 97780. Tel: (985) 6-2073; Fax: (985) 6-2280. $44.
- **Misión Park Inn Chichén Itzá.** **Pisté**, Yucatán 97752. Tel: (985) 6-2462 or 2513; in the U.S. and Canada, Tel: (800) 437-PARK. $90 (includes two meals).

MAYAN MEXICO

▶ **Misión Park Inn Palenque.** Rancho San Martín de Porres, Palenque, Chiapas 29960. Tel: (934) 5-0444; in the U.S. and Canada, Tel: (800) 437-PARK. $90.

▶ **Misión Park Inn Uxmal.** Zona Arqueológica, Uxmal, P.O. Box 407, Mérida, Yucatán 97000. In Mérida, Tel: (99) 4-7308; Fax: (99) 24-7308; in the U.S. and Canada, Tel: (800) 437-PARK. $90 (includes two meals).

▶ **El Molino de la Alborada.** P.O. Box 50, Periférico Sur s/n, San Cristóbal de las Casas, Chiapas 29200. Tel: (967) 8-0935. $27.

▶ **Posada Diego de Mazariegos.** María Adelina Flores 2, San Cristóbal de las Casas, Chiapas 29200. Tel: (967) 8-0513; Fax: (967) 8-0827. $81.

▶ **Villa Arqueológica Chichén Itzá.** Zona Arqueológica, Carretera Mérida–Valladolid, km 12, Chichén Itzá, Yucatán 97752. Tel: (985) 6-2830; Fax: (985) 6-2771; in the U.S., Tel: (800) 258-2633; in Canada, Tel: (514) 937-7707. $84.

▶ **Villa Arqueológica Uxmal.** Zona Arqueológica, Uxmal, or P.O. Box 449, Mérida, Yucatán 97000. In Mérida, Tel: (99) 24-7053; Fax: (99) 24-7023; in the U.S., Tel: (800) 258-2633; in Canada, Tel: (514) 937-7707. $71.

GUATEMALA

By Robert Somerlott

In the first installment of the *Star Wars* trilogy, Princess Leia flees to a hiding place in a remote galaxy somewhere on the nether edge of the universe. For the film's director the problem was where—on earth—could such an alien landscape be found? Eventually, he decided that the perfect background would be Tikal, the great ruined Mayan city hemmed in by the Guatemalan jungle. As a result, at least a few viewers were startled to recognize the towering Temple of the Giant Jaguar when it appeared on-screen. Of course, the choice was brilliant. Until intergalactic travel becomes possible, Tikal is about as far removed from our own world as you can get.

To a lesser degree, the same can be said for much of Guatemala. In a world growing smaller and more homogeneous, Guatemala has managed to keep its character, its color, and its oddity. In a sense, a visitor here has an opportunity to sample time travel, to see a vanishing way of life—not everywhere in the country, of course, and perhaps not always for long. Still, there remains an element of fantasy in this picturesque land where reality has often been brutal.

For travellers who have become intrigued by the Maya in Mexico, a trip into Guatemala is a rewarding excursion. While the modern political boundary between the countries may separate two very different and sometimes antagonistic governments, in the Mayan view of time the separation is merely a recent development. The Maya recognize the frontier only as they are forced to. In the remote jungles straddling the border, people, ideas, goods, and news flow steadily in both directions. Despite a profusion of dialects and other differences, the indigenous folk are one people, far more like each other than akin to their Mexican, or ladino, neighbors.

The Mayan presence in Guatemala is strong. You will see

them everywhere, a flashing display of color, their embroidered and appliquéd clothing as flamboyant as the plumage of the country's tropical birds. They and, of course, the ancient monuments of their ancestors, are the chief reasons for visiting Guatemala.

MAJOR INTEREST
Mayan people and their crafts
Scenic beauty, including Lago Atitlán
Museo de la Ciudad de Guatemala (Mayan carvings)
Mayan ruins of Tikal
Mayan ruins of Quirigá and Mixco Viejo
Colonial city of Antigua
Boat trips on the Río Dulce

For a small country, Guatemala is unusually diverse in its scenery and climate. The terrain includes jungles, high mountains, temperate highlands, savannah, and a desert. Although it's about the same size as Ohio and almost half the size of the United Kingdom, such comparisons are misleading for the traveller—fully a third of the country is accessible only on horseback or by safari. Most of its attractions, with the exception of Tikal and the Río Dulce, cluster in the pleasantly cool highlands in the south, so you can see a great deal of Guatemala in a short time. Tours planned and sold by agents or airlines tend to be either five- or eight-day trips. Five days hardly offer time enough to cover the highlights, but an eight-day tour, whether packaged or independent, is not unreasonably crowded for sightseeing. Another day or two might be added for the Río Dulce or other out-of-the-way excursions.

Such tight scheduling allows little leisure for appreciating and absorbing this quite foreign land, however, and rules out some pleasant experiences—such as watching a sunset on Lago Atitlán for the second or third time or seeking out picturesque villages. Still, the colorful surface of Guatemala can be skimmed in a little more than a week, which is about what most travellers will choose to devote on a first visit. Inevitably, some of them, charmed by the country, will return for much longer stays.

(Note: Some troubling events came to the public's attention in 1991 when the U.S. State Department alerted travellers to a marked rise in crime in Guatemala, including incidents of robbery and muggings. Two murders of foreign travellers were also reported. The incidents seemed centered in the most frequently visited areas: Guatemala City, Antigua, Panajachel, and Chichicastenango. There were, in addition, renewed confrontations between government troops and rebel

Guatemala

guerrillas in other regions. In the months following these reports, however, thousands of travellers visited the country and encountered no difficulties. As seasoned travellers are aware, U.S. State Department advisories tend to be ultra-cautious; Guatemala today is no more dangerous than most of the world's large cities. Nevertheless, the prudent traveller will want to keep abreast of news reports while considering a trip to Guatemala.)

A great cordillera of lofty peaks and ridges thrusting south from Mexico forms the rugged backbone of Guatemala. Along the Pacific these mountains merge with an ancient chain of volcanoes that almost edge the ocean, leaving only a narrow shelf of lush tropical land broken by swift rivers pouring down from the highlands. No roads run along this coastal shelf; instead, all highways here lead inland and upland.

Higher up on the slopes lies coffee country—some of the richest in the world—and, higher still, long valleys wind among mountain peaks. Here are huddled the cities visited by most travellers: Guatemala City, Antigua, Panajachel, and Chichicastenango. Surrounding these are orchards of peaches and apples as well as truck farms and pastures. But above all, this is corn (maize) country. No slope seems too steep or discouraging for a Mayan farmer to plant this venerated cereal. The rainy season in the highlands lasts from May through October, but even in those months the climate is pleasant rather than sultry.

On the northern side of this mountainous spine, which begins a gradual descent to the lowlands below, are more coffee plantations. Soon, however, the land starts to fall away more sharply, and eventually becomes the wild, inhospitable region known as the **Petén**. Jaguars, often feeding on wild pigs, still inhabit this jungle, and bands of monkeys chatter and howl in the dense foliage.

The Petén is the root of the Yucatán Peninsula, a little less flat than the Yucatán proper, but just as tangled, torrid, and wet. It was here, where opportunities would seem poorest, that the Classic Maya raised their magnificent city of Tikal.

The Maya

Little is known about the first human inhabitants of Guatemala; the area's subsequent history, however, is linked to that of southeastern Mexico, for geographically it is the same region.

Mayan civilization was definitely established here before

300 B.C., flourished, like much of Mesoamerica, between A.D. 300 and 900, and then suddenly declined. No one knows why, though there is a lot of scholarly speculation (see the Bibliography).

In the highlands of Guatemala groups of seminomadic Indians appeared at various times, fought, mingled, and interbred with the local populace. The "pure Maya" of these highlands are a myth. Throughout its human history various Indians peopled Guatemala—as they still do—but the Maya were so dominant that it is simpler for the purposes of this discussion to group them all together.

When the Spaniards arrived in 1523, along with their Indian allies from central Mexico, they found a large population warring among itself. The subsequent conquest of the region was led by Pedro de Alvarado, an especially bloodthirsty and gold-hungry lieutenant of Cortés. The Spaniards, abetted by local treachery and feuds, not only defeated the Maya but also drastically reshaped their whole society. The educated ruling class of the Maya was annihilated; the surviving peasants were forced out of their rural dwellings and herded into Spanish-style towns that bore a strong resemblance to labor camps; Spanish Catholicism was imposed on the indigenous population, often with the aid of fire and the lash.

Mayan resistance, often passive but occasionally violent, proved to be more than a match for the Spanish. When native gods were officially abolished, the people simply renamed them after Christian saints. Here, as elsewhere throughout Mesoamerica, paganism and Catholicism ran like parallel lines, never meeting but always closely related and often indistinguishable.

The Maya maintained their identity, as they do today, through the force of tradition, which is summed up by the Spanish word *costumbre*. Although it usually translates as "custom," the word implies immeasurably more. *Costumbres* are not exactly at the heart of their religion; indeed, they are far less flexible than the Maya's faith. Perhaps the word "kosher" comes closest to conveying some sense of the power of *costumbre*.

After the Conquest, Spanish colonial society in Guatemala was divided into castes. For almost four centuries there existed a form of apartheid here, although it was somewhat diluted because Spaniards were neither as puritanical nor as consistent as the Afrikaaners have been. Guatemalan independence from Spain, achieved early in the 19th century, made little difference in the lives of most Guatemalans.

Today in Guatemala, blood and custom continue to serve

as the basis for the division of society, even though the edges are a bit more blurred. The ladino segment of the population controls almost everything. Originally, the word "ladino" described someone who was crafty and cunning, a city slicker. Some Mayan people will tell you it still means that, although in everyday parlance it refers to all *guatemaltecos* who are "Europeanized." A ladino wears shoes, of course, and maybe a charcoal gray suit during business hours. Generally speaking, he is modern, regards mechanical and material progress as blessings, and admires novelties. Most ladinos are partly or entirely of European descent; skin color and features are important in Guatemala, although not as basic to classifying a person as proper shoes or a proper frame of mind.

In Guatemala, ladinos often tell you that an Indian is simply someone who chooses to call himself so. This pretense to equality, however, will not become a reality until the day all ladinos suddenly go blind. Guatemala is, above all else, a caste-conscious country. While there are no separate public facilities here, there are certainly separate bank accounts. Still, people on either side of this social and financial chasm are almost always courteous and gracious to visitors.

Guatemalan Food and Drink

Restaurant food throughout the country tends to be a blending of European and North American cuisine. In fact, you could travel extensively in Guatemala without ever suspecting the existence of a national cuisine. To sample local food you must therefore look for places advertising a *comida típica*. Such an establishment will usually call itself a *comedor* (eating place) rather than a *restaurante,* which sounds more pretentious to the ears of most Guatemalans.

Chuchitos are little tamales with a spiced meat stuffing; *pepian* is a fricassee with squash seeds in a rich, dark sauce; another unusual item is *guisquil,* a pearlike vegetable that grows on vines. *Pacaya,* also native to the country, is a vegetable with an unfamiliar, rather harsh tang. Bananas, fried, mashed, or prepared any number of other ways, play a major role in Mayan cuisine. Black beans, too, are prepared in various ways. Beef, except in expensive restaurants, is often tough, so it is usually cooked by simmering it in *guisados* (stews) or *caldos* (soup broths). Many foods usually considered Mexican are also standard in Guatemala, including enchiladas, guacamole, and *ceviche*. Corn tortillas are a national staple.

Local wines, usually concocted with grape concentrates,

orange pulp, and the like, should not be considered; imported vintages are expensive, so ask about price before you order to avoid sticker shock later. Good Guatemalan beer helps to offset the lack of wine. Gallo and Cabro, both medium light, are the most popular brands, and higher-priced Medalla de Oro is not really better. Moza, a rich, dark beer, is excellent but not always available. Local rum and *aguardiente,* both distilled from sugarcane, are commendable, and the local vodka is smooth enough. The prudent will stay away from the native whiskey.

GUATEMALA CITY

La Ciudad de Guatemala may be the hub of the country and the seat of its government, but it is certainly not its heart. As the major transportation center of the country, the capital becomes the inescapable destination of most travellers. The best visit is a brief one; a day will do nicely, and even that is not necessary unless there's a delay involving your flight to Tikal. Hotels in Antigua and Panajachel will arrange to have a driver and car meet you at the airport, or you can rent a car at the airport, convert some currency, and be on your way, skipping the city altogether.

While this might make the capital sound like a dreadful place, it really isn't—except perhaps in rush-hour traffic or by the glare of neon at night. In fact, Guatemala City has good hotels and restaurants and three worthwhile museums. But then, they're probably not what you came to see.

Nor is the city the best jumping-off point for visits to the surrounding countryside. Both the attractive town of Antigua and the delightfully located lakeside town of Panajachel are better choices.

Guatemala City teems with more than two-and-a-quarter million people packed into a space never meant to accommodate such an onslaught. You can see some impressive buildings downtown, but beyond them spreads an ocean of urban sprawl. Likewise, parks too often are inundated by waves of hurrying humanity. The city's saving grace is that much of this humanity is Mayan, which enables you to see wonderfully expressive faces and, sometimes, the flair and flash of native costumes.

Around in the Capital

Tours of the city sold by hotels are of dubious value, mainly because much time is wasted on uninteresting monuments.

Better to hire a cab by the hour at an agreed-upon price, or to take a series of cabs and be off on your own.

Before setting out you should know that Guatemala City is divided into 21 zones. A street address without a zone number is insufficient, as names and numbers may be repeated from zone to zone. Although addresses might sound complicated, they are logical and easy to find with a map.

Your exploration of the city should begin with the **Parque Aurora**, near the airport on the south side of the city, Zona 13, between 7 Avenida and 11 Avenida. Museums, a zoo, a racetrack, and an extensive handicraft market make this park a center of interest and activity.

The **Museo Nacional de Arqueológica y Etnología**, often referred to by its old name, the **Museo de la Ciudad de Guatemala**, is housed in a modern gleaming white building. The architecture is totally Spanish-Moorish, which is odd because the museum's contents are almost totally Mayan. This is more than just an incongruity; it's also a telling comment about the divided nature of the country.

For all that, the museum's extensive collection of Mayan carvings, the largest in the world, is magnificent. One of its highlights is a throne from the jungle city of Piedras Negras. In addition, masterworks in ceramics—masks, figurines, and a variety of containers and vessels—rival the achievements in stone. Many of the objects on display were the accessories, the fittings and utensils, found at Tikal. Studying them here makes it easier to reconstruct that magnificent city in the mind's eye. The ethnological section of the museum, which is devoted chiefly to native costumes, is also interesting and well presented.

Across the street, the **Museo de Historia y Bellas Artes** merits a short visit because of its fine interior, especially the main ceiling, and the paintings by Carlos Mérida; its historical section, however, is limited.

The **handicraft market**, located behind the Museum of History and Fine Arts, sells crafts from every part of the country. If nothing else, the prices here will give you a standard of comparison for shopping elsewhere; work of higher quality, especially fine weaving, can be found outside the capital. The colorful atmosphere and gay marimba music are the market's best offerings.

Except for its flamboyant native birds, the **zoo**, just north of the market, is nothing special.

Two other museums in the capital are also worth visiting. The **Museo Popol Vuh** occupies the sixth floor of a high-rise building known as the Edificio Galerías Reforma, Torre 2 (Zona 9 at Reforma 8). Its display of Mayan polychrome vessels, including a number of large burial urns, is dazzling. The items were once in a private collection, and great care went into choosing every piece. All the Maya-inhabited regions of the country are represented, and although works created between A.D. 150 and 900 predominate, there are also earlier and later examples of the Maya's pre-Columbian artistry.

Quite different, but just as delightful in its own right, is the **Museo Ixchel**, where the textile arts of Guatemala, especially weaving and embroidery, are honored. The clothing on display in this museum is gorgeous, and the whole show so imaginatively presented that it rises far above the usual crafts display. In addition, this valentine of a museum is located in one of the city's better neighborhoods, 4A Avenida 16-17, Zona 10, about a 15-minute walk west of the Museo Popol Vuh.

If you have extra time, the **Relief Map** (*Mapa en Relieve*) in the pleasant Parque Minerva, Zona 2, may prove interesting. This is a sprawling rendering of the country, 125 by 250 feet, in somewhat exaggerated relief (the volcanoes, as shown here, would tower over Mount Everest in the real world). It's a painless and unusual geography lesson, and useful if you're about to set out to tour the country.

A number of city landmarks, though touted by guides and local advertisers, have little interest or charm. These include the grim National Palace, the Metropolitan Cathedral, and the National Theater—all of them, at best, just time fillers. Guatemalans are extremely proud of the municipal buildings in their Civic Center; these structures are modern, functional, and handsome.

The archaeological site of **Kaminaljuyú**, meaning "Hill of the Dead," is in Zona 7, off Calzada San Juan on 23 Avenida. Until recently this was the outskirts of the city; now, however, it is a suburb. There is not a great deal left of the ancient center, which flourished from about 2,000 B.C. until 300 B.C. With the exception of two modest complexes, almost everything was leveled in the course of building the modern city. Of the five stratigraphic levels at the site, the deepest and earliest is probably Olmec, followed by a stratum of Preclassic Mayan artifacts. The pronounced influence of Teotihuacán shows up in more recent strata.

Kaminaljuyú can be visited weekdays from 8:00 A.M. until noon and from 2:00 until 5:00 P.M. Bring a flashlight. The caretaker, who expects a small tip, will unlock the entrance to a tomb that is the site's most interesting feature. Further excavation proceeds by fits and starts nearby, with a number of promising finds of statuary and ceramic ware.

Staying in Guatemala City

The capital has good accommodations in all price ranges except the very cheapest, which are miserable. A room tax of 17 percent will be added to your bill, and will not always be announced in advance. You should inquire beforehand.

In an attempt to avoid congestion, which sometimes overtakes them anyway, the newer and more luxurious hotels are located outside the center of the city. The better neighborhoods are Zonas 4, 9, and 10. A hotel in Zona 1 is likely to be economical but noisy, and there is little advantage to being in this, the old central area.

Throughout the country national taste favors the sleek, streamlined, and unmistakably modern; the more North American the better. International travellers, on the other hand, seem to prefer more charm and less plate glass. Both types of hostelries are mentioned here.

The **Camino Real Guatemala City** is excellent—as it should be for the prices it asks—and has restaurants, three bars with live entertainment, tennis courts, a gym, and swimming pools in assorted sizes. (Guatemalan luxury hotels, by the way, put a premium on sports and body-conditioning facilities.) The hotel is located in an upper-class neighborhood in Zona 10.

The multistoried **Hotel El Dorado Americana**, a block of masonry and glass featured in tourism publications as representative of "modern Guatemala," has everything the Camino Real–Biltmore has—bars, restaurants, and swimming pools—only fewer of them. In other words, this is a fine international hotel, with prices to match.

Expensive but less so than the Dorado or Camino Real, the **Conquistador Sheraton** delights guests with its flourishing orchids in the lobby. While it has most of the amenities, it does not feature all the gym and sauna facilities of its somewhat more lavish competitors. It does have a good location in Zona 4, however, as well as a very good restaurant (discussed below), and is popular with European groups.

The **Hotel Plaza**, also in Zona 4, is straightforward and a couple of notches above basic at a moderate price. Ask for a room overlooking the swimming pool; the rooms facing the parking lot can be noisy.

In Zona 1 near the cathedral, the **Hotel del Centro** is rich in wood paneling and wrought iron; everything is hushed and gentle—except the streets outside (although the night traffic does eventually die down). The parking garage is convenient, the restaurant and carpets good, and it's not hard to imagine you've been transported to Spain. The location explains its bargain rates.

In the same moderate bracket, and with the same problems of noise and congestion due to its location in Zona 1, is the **Pan American**. In the Art Deco era the Pan American was the capital's leading hotel. Today, if some of its elegance has faded, it makes up for it with an abundance of comfort and charm. The hotel's restaurant is discussed below.

The **Posada Belén**, a quiet, friendly, and welcoming little inn (just nine rooms), is the city's best pension. Although it, too, is located in the center of town, in Zona 1, its street is spared the worst of the racket. In addition, the management is happy to help with tours and excursions, and there's a library full of information about Guatemala.

Dining in Guatemala City

The restaurant in the **Pan American**, though not exactly elegant, offers a good introduction to Guatemalan cuisine and also serves a variety of foreign dishes, good coffee, and fine pastries at modest prices. The waiters are decked out in traditional village attire, and the woven wall hangings are added attractions. Tel: (2) 26-8079.

The posh neighborhood around the Camino Real–Biltmore in Zona 10, **La Zona Viva**, or "lively zone," is where you'll find dining, dancing, and the cabaret world of Guatemala. While far from the equal of Paris or Rome, it is surprisingly chic for Central America. There are not many rich people in Guatemala, but those who have money seem to have a lot of it, and they spend it freely. They also all seem to know one another, and where they meet is New York, Paris, or here in La Zona Viva.

Le Rendezvous, 13 Calle 2-55, Zona 10, is a transplanted bit of Montmartre, more bistro than haute cuisine, and offering indoor or patio service. It's very good, very French, and fairly expensive.

The **Puerto Barrios**, at 11 Calle and 7 Avenida, Zona 9, is decked out like a Spanish galleon, but the seafood is much better than the pirate rigging would indicate. The steaks are good, the shrimp and lobster better. Tel: (2) 34-1302.

Martin's offers fare that is uncommon in Guatemala, including such items as frog's legs and rack of lamb. Broiled salmon, also served here, is an exotic item in Central America. Reasonable prices have helped keep this august establishment, at 13 Calle 7-65, Zona 9, popular for almost two decades.

Located not in La Zona Viva but across the street from the

Conquistador Sheraton at Via 4, 4-36, Zona 4, is **Estro Armónico**. With a limited menu of seafood and meat dishes accompanied by light French sauces, it's as warmly provincial as its flickering hearth. And while less expensive than the better establishments of the more fashionable zone, it is not inexpensive. Tel: (2) 31-9240 or 36-3892.

The reasonably priced **Restaurant Altuna** is situated downtown in Zona 1, on Calle 5 between Calles 7 and 8. Paella and other Spanish classics are offered on the roofed patio of this charming colonial-style building, and the seafood is admirably fresh. Tel: (2) 51-7185.

All the leading hotels in Guatemala City have satisfactory restaurants. The best in the deluxe category, in the Sheraton, is the **Restaurante de las Espadas**, which specializes in broiled steaks, fish, and shrimp. It also has style and panache. Tel: (2) 31-2222. Among the moderately priced hotels, the dining room of the **Hotel del Centro** is a good choice. The food isn't quite as Spanish as the decor, but the atmosphere is genteel and comfortable. Tel: (2) 38-1281.

TIKAL

Tikal, the grandest of the ruined Mayan cities, is nothing less than awe-inspiring. Here, in the tangled and almost impenetrable jungle of northern Guatemala, you suddenly come upon the greatest human achievement of the Stone Age. For Tikal *is* a Stone Age creation, even though its magnificent structures were raised in the first centuries of the Christian era. Its builders used no metal tools, no draft animals, and no wheels (consequently, no pulleys). In order to accomplish these feats of engineering and construction, an army of laborers and artists had to be recruited, trained, and maintained not just for a few years, but for generations—an achievement as amazing as the buildings themselves.

To date, 3,000 buildings have been mapped near the Great Plaza of Tikal. Foundations of about 10,000 stone structures are known—impressive enough when read about, but mind-boggling when you are actually there in the jungle.

Tikal began to take shape around the **Gran Plaza** about 2,000 years ago on a site that probably was selected because it was higher than the surrounding swamps. The city reached its zenith of art and activity between A.D. 500 and 900, when it had at least 50,000 inhabitants. Then, suddenly and inexplicably, it was abandoned to the jungle.

Some dates at the site can be confirmed. Temple I, better known as the **Templo del Gran Jaguar**, bears a Mayan glyph corresponding to A.D. 741, which tests have confirmed as the probable date of construction. The steep, graceful temple, Tikal's most famous monument, rises a lofty 170 feet above the East Plaza and looms almost as high above the Great Plaza.

Nearby are plazas, terraces, and other buildings, including the tallest in the ancient Americas, **Templo IV**, which rises over 212 feet from its base to the tip of its roofcomb, and even looks down on those giants of the jungle, the ceiba trees (which were sacred to the Maya).

Tikal is simply too vast and complex for a detailed discussion here. Those planning to explore the city should arm themselves with archaeologist William R. Coe's clear and definitive guide *Tikal: A Handbook of the Ancient Maya Ruins,* published by the University of Pennsylvania Museum, Philadelphia, and in Guatemala by Editorial Piedra Santa. While it is usually available in English at the Tikal museum or in the town of Flores, it is safer to purchase it in advance. (For getting to Tikal, see the Getting Around section at the end of this chapter.)

Staying at Tikal

Visitors have a choice of staying at the Parque Nacional Tikal itself, on the lakeshore, or in **Flores**, the small capital of the Petén, an island town in Lago Petén Itzá that's connected to the shore by a causeway. Two other little towns, Santa Elena and San Benito, are located nearby on the mainland.

Accommodations at Tikal itself are Spartan and not always available. Despite the quality of these facilities, however, being a 20-minute walk from the ruins has its advantages. Besides the convenience, the jungle itself is an attraction. With its cacophony of bird and animal cries (especially at night), it seems to be a living, breathing entity. The experience has much to recommend it.

(Moonlight not only transforms the jungle but works magic on the ruins. Tikal is magnificent under a full moon, and although the zone is usually closed at night, exceptions are sometimes made. Spend a night or two if possible in Tikal or Flores. More extensive tours than the usual packages provide can be arranged here. In addition, a limited number of Jeeps are available for private exploring.)

A good, rustic choice right in the archaeological zone is the **Jungle Lodge**, built to house scientists and leaders of the Tikal excavation team but now privately owned. The inn is clean and refreshing, with shaded verandahs and ceiling fans. It also has an adequate dining room, bar, and a friendly, helpful management. The rooms have walls so thin, however, you can hear conversations next door, and the electricity is turned off between 10:00 P.M. and 6:00 A.M. Still, you are right on the edge of the ruins, and free to wander at will.

Other small inns in the zone are uncomfortable and, in some cases, unsanitary.

The Flores/Santa Elena/San Benito area is an hour's drive from the Tikal archaeological zone, with good transportation available by bus or van. With one exception the better hotels in the area are adequate but not luxurious. There is a certain oddity, even simple charm, about these hotels, however, and you do not entirely lose the sense of being in the jungle.

The **Maya Internacional** is a collection of thatched, rather romantic cottages right on the water. The cottages are simple, clean, and comfortable, and the management will arrange tours of Tikal.

Also on the shore of Lago Petén Itzá, the new **Camino Real Tikal** offers pleasant rooms, an attractive restaurant with satisfactory food, and the only real air-conditioning within 100 miles. The jungle setting, with views across the lake, adds charm; toucans may perch outside your window and spider monkeys at home in the tangled canopy are a fairly common sight. Some travellers may find its slick modernity at odds with the experience of exploring Tikal, however, and, of course, you sacrifice independent access to the ruins. The hotel does have car/Jeep rentals and offers guided tours to Tikal, about 30 minutes away by car.

If you have the time, boat rides on the lake are easy to arrange and an enjoyable way to spend an afternoon while you're in the area.

OTHER MAYAN RUINS IN GUATEMALA

Any archaeological zone in Guatemala will seem a bit anticlimactic after Tikal, and in fact the sites that dot official maps are mostly of minimal interest, or else are too remote to repay the trouble involved in getting there. However, three other sites can be recommended to enthusiasts, with the obvious reservation: None is another Tikal.

Quiriguá (kee-rhee-GWAH) is famed for its carved monuments, some of the finest in the Mayan world. Though not a large site, with its extant buildings of only secondary interest, it is the location of the largest carved Mayan monolith known—Stela E, nearly 36 feet tall and weighing some 65 tons. Almost a quarter of this massive stone remains buried, and the narrative carving on it is fascinating. Scattered elsewhere around the site, a dozen smaller works boast equally intricate detailing.

Quiriguá is a little more than three hours from Guatemala City by car, about 206 km (128 miles) of that being paved road. Highway CA 9 heads northeast from the city to the vicinity of Los Amates, at which point you take a dirt cutoff for 3½ km (2 miles). You'll want to pack a lunch before heading out, including anything you might want to drink. (You can also visit Quiriguá on the way to the Río Dulce; see below.)

Mixco Viejo (MEESH-ko VYEH-o), the capital of the Pokomam Maya, a warlike people who were eventually defeated by the conquistadors, was still a thriving urban center when the Spanish arrived in 1525, although it had been established many centuries earlier near the end of the Classic era. Today it's a beautiful site, and less well known than it should be. There are two Mayan ball courts here, one that's particularly impressive; a major temple structure; and a number of pyramids and platforms. Best of all, it's only 50 km (31 miles) north-northwest of Guatemala City, most of that over a paved road and the rest improved. You should allow an hour and a half by car for the drive—think of it as a good opportunity for a picnic and one of the prettiest short trips you can take in Guatemala. (If you decide to visit Mixco Viejo, make sure you have a reliable map with the two turnoffs marked by your hotel or the tourist office.) Bus travel to Mixco Viejo, on the other hand, is not a practical option.

A trip to **Zaculeu** (sah-koo-LEH-oo), situated in Guatemala's far western highlands just outside the modern city of **Huehuetenango**, makes for a very long one-day excursion from Guatemala City, or a slightly easier one from Panajachel (see below). Huehuetenango (way-way-te-NAN-go) itself is 264 km (164 miles) northwest of the capital. Allow three and a half hours each way.

Occupied for at least 1,000 years before the arrival of the Spanish, Zaculeu's divided stairs, dance platforms, and other ruins show signs of Mexican influence. Structure I is an impressive stepped pyramid with a temple atop it. There is also a handsome ball court here. Of the more than 40 structures officially listed, most are only grassy mounds today. Although the site is interesting and the surroundings attractive, this is a trip for dedicated enthusiasts only—or for those seeking a good excuse to visit another region of Guatemala.

The **Hotel Piño Montano**, just outside Huehuetenango,

resembles a motel, with a restaurant and pool in a garden setting. It's a simple but satisfactory establishment for those looking for a night's lodging near Zaculeu.

Travel agencies in the major hotels in Guatemala City offer regular tours to Quiriguá, Mixco Viejo, and a number of lesser sites. Clark Tours (see the Getting Around section below) also makes such arrangements and will be happy, in addition, to advise visitors about seeing Zaculeu, a site too remote to be included in most standard itineraries.

Copán

Located not in Guatemala but just across its eastern border in Honduras are the magnificent Mayan ruins of Copán, generally considered one of the half dozen greatest Classic Mayan centers. The trip is an ordeal, however, and casual travellers usually skip it. Archaeology buffs, on the other hand, will probably not want to miss it.

Copán ranks among the greatest and most beautiful pre-Columbian centers of Mesoamerica, and some authorities have hailed it as the highest intellectual and artistic achievement of the ancient Maya. For visitors the first stop in what is now a landscaped national park is the **museum** near the entrance, where information in English about the site may be obtained. You may also engage a guide here, an invaluable asset when visiting these complex and extensive ruins.

The Copán Valley, a fertile region at an altitude of 2,000 feet, is well watered by the Río Copán. The valley attracted the Maya long before the present age, and reached its greatness in the Classic era (dates on monuments indicate the site's heyday extended from about A.D. 450 to 800). During this period temples, altars, and one of the finest ball courts in America were constructed. The ruler Smoke Squirrel, the next-to-the-last known monarch of Copán, ascended to power in A.D. 747 and built a gigantic stairway of 2,500 stone blocks carved with glyphs—the longest single pre-Hispanic inscription found to date, and a treasury of Mayan sculpture. The carved stone stelae at the site (which the Maya call "stone trees") are graceful and elegant, one monument after another proclaiming the genius of Mayan artists.

The highlights can be covered in about three hours; but, of course, the more time the better in this rare and beautiful place.

Bus tours from Guatemala City leave early and often return after dark. Unfortunately, much of this long day is spent in transit, with hardly enough time for the ruins themselves. Reliable service is provided by **Clark Tours**, 7 Avenida 6-53,

Efidicio El Triángulo, 2nd floor, Zona 4, Guatemala City, C.A.; in Guatemala City, Tel: (2) 31-0213 to 0216. Clark is the most experienced provider, but the major hotels may have other good suggestions. The far better (and much more expensive) option is small-plane charter service, available through most large hotels and major travel agencies.

To visit Copán by car, take CA 9, the Atlantic Highway (see the Río Dulce section below). Turn south onto CA 10 near Río Hondo and follow it for 42 km (26 miles). You then turn left (northeast) onto Highway 21, a poor road, which will take you to the border of Honduras, 43 km (27 miles) farther on. There will be customs and immigration formalities at the border. Copán is another 13 km (8 miles) from the border via Honduras Highway 20.

The trip, which takes about four and a half hours from Guatemala City, can be combined with a visit to the ruins at Quiriguá to make a two-day archaeological excursion, with an overnight in Copán. The simple **Hotel Marina**, in the village of Copán on the main plaza, has adequate accommodations and a restaurant. The electricity is cut off at about 9:00 P.M., however.

ANTIGUA

Antigua, on first sight, reveals nothing of its former glory. It's a pretty town, 20 km (12 miles) west-southwest of Guatemala City, and is manicured and buffed for its many visitors, which it receives with a gracious nod. It's also decorous and proper, its residents quite aware that this is *the* (living) national showcase.

The wide cobblestone streets here are lined by colonial façades that you think must be old yet don't seem to have aged. These structures are, for the most part, single-story with red-tiled roofs, imparting a uniformity of height and style to some neighborhoods that makes them seem harmonious, if a bit monotonous. As a result, the profusion of flowering vines throughout the city adds a welcome touch of disorder. And everywhere you look the silhouette of a mountain looms in the background.

Because Antigua seems to have been created by a Latin American Norman Rockwell, with what some people see as a slightly artificial prettiness, many visitors find it difficult to fathom the cataclysmic past behind its genteel present. On the night of September 10, 1541, the original capital of Guatemala was obliterated by fire, followed by a terrible deluge of water released from the crater of a nearby volcano. The survivors dragged themselves to the apparently safe valley here and founded Santiago de los Caballeros de Guatemala, "Saint James of the Knights of Guatemala," as Antigua was then called.

The new capital, which was cradled in a valley dominated by three immense volcanoes, grew to become an important center of Spain's New World empire, second only to Mexico City and Lima in power. The city's business was to exploit—however ruthlessly—the whole Mayan region, and in so doing it became a metropolis of some 60,000 people.

Then the bad omens began. Several times in the early 18th century an irritable volcano by the name of Monte Fuego belched forth lava and ash, burying some inhabitants alive. Earthquakes set the town's massive arches trembling. According to contemporary accounts, Antigua descended into a vicious cycle of crime, violence, and oppression. There appears to have been a cruel Old Testament justice to what fate had in store for the town and its citizens.

In the summer of 1773 the earth came alive again and literally shook the city to death—not a quick death, but rather a prolonged agony that lasted more than a month, followed by week upon week of deadly aftershocks. Adobe walls melted under torrential rains, and plague soon haunted the ruins. The governor, believing the valley to be cursed, ordered an evacuation and removed himself and his capital to what is now Guatemala City, which was formally declared the new capital in 1776. (Exactly two centuries later the quake of 1976 would almost level *that* city.)

The archbishop fought the governor to save the old town but was himself forced to move. A few determined survivors nevertheless hung on among the ruins of Santiago. Gradually, a new town arose from the devastation; in the 19th century it began to prosper from the coffee trade and became known as Antigua Guatemala, "Old Guatemala."

Exploring Antigua

The town is laid out on a grid, with the north–south thoroughfares called *calles* (streets) and the east–west thoroughfares called *avenidas* (avenues). The point at which "north" (*norte*) becomes "south" (*sur*) and "east" (*oriente*) becomes "west" (*poniente*) is the cathedral on the south side of the plaza.

The tourist office, located on the south side of the plaza in what was once the Palace of the Captains-General, is manned by a most helpful and generous staff with access to up-to-the-minute information.

Sightseeing here is mostly a matter of inspecting ruins while you wander through tidy, quaint neighborhoods. Antigua has been preserved as a monument to earthquakes, and the city takes a perverse pride in these lingering echoes of destruction. The ruins, all dating from the 18th century, are impressive, though a little melancholy in the bright sunshine, and soon you begin to think of Shelley's Ozymandias. It's a fascinating, if not exactly jolly, way to spend time.

Start with the shell behind the present cathedral and continue around town—the remnants of ruin are everywhere. The **Monasterio de Santo Domingo** is worth a brief mention because it once was huge and fantastically rich. A silver statue of the Virgin here was reported to be the size of a tall woman, and a silver altar lamp was said to have been so weighty it took three men to raise it. (After one earthquake the Virgin was fruitlessly bribed with a crown of jewels.) At the corner of 2 Calle Oriente and 2 Avenida Norte, the **Iglesia y Convento de Capuchinas**, much of it still standing, affords memorable views from its roof.

The **Convento de San Francisco**, 7 Calle Oriente and 1 Avenida Sur, is an old rubble heap, but the adjacent **church** survived the frequent devastation and contains an extensive collection of votive paintings, signs, letters, and photos proclaiming the miracles performed by Brother Pedro de Betancourt, a 17th-century holy man entombed here. Those needing his intercession in their own affairs rap on the tomb to get his attention; the knocking is frequent, gentle, but persistent.

There are also two museums in Antigua. The venerable **University of San Carlos**, 3 Avenida Sur and 5 Calle Oriente, has an uninteresting collection of colonial objects, but the building housing it has a lovely patio. The nearby Museo de Santiago has little to recommend it other than its rough, almost medieval architecture.

Staying in Antigua

Antigua's inns tend to be high priced for what they offer; nevertheless, the town is often short of rooms, so reserve ahead.

One reason for the town's popularity is its admirable location, which is excellent for staging excursions into south-central Guatemala. Knowledgeable guides and drivers are available in town, and attractive villages can be found nearby with their help.

The **Hotel Aurora**, conveniently located four blocks east of the cathedral, offers the best value in accommodations in

Antigua, although it's not the most luxurious in town. This spacious old residence, built around a flower-filled patio, now houses a carefully run family operation and has all the necessities, but offers no public rooms or luxuries other than its own atmosphere and service. Breakfast is provided.

The **Hotel Antigua**, another colonial gem (at least in decor), is far more luxurious. Its beautiful lawns frame a swimming pool and a children's wading pool near nicely spaced bungalows, and the gardens' lovely but raucous parrots are rivaled in beauty only by the many rose bushes, trees, and hedges on the grounds. In addition, the dining room is cheerful and tastefully decorated. The hotel prides itself on its Sunday buffet, which is accompanied by music. Actually, Sunday, when it's crowded with day-trippers from the capital, is the least attractive day of the week at the hotel. Nevertheless, the inn is a rarity in Guatemala, and rare things tend to be expensive—but in this case not outrageously so. The inn is a five-minute walk south of the plaza on 8a Calle Oriente.

In the center of town on 5A Avenida Norte, a block north of the Parque Central, is the **Posada de Don Rodrigo**, a series of high-ceilinged rooms and a restaurant and bar clustered around several shady patios. This historic old residence is a little too heavy on shadowy atmosphere, but it is nonetheless a handsome inn. Only avid marimba-music aficionados should accept quarters facing the main patio, however—at least on weekends. There are also considerable differences in size, light, and ventilation among the room choices. No one section of the inn is best in its entirety, so look at the individual room offered before registering. The rustic dining room is colorful, but the food is unexceptional. The Posada is moderately expensive.

If you face the frequent scarcity of rooms in Antigua, you might choose the **Ramada Antigua**. To stay here is better than having to journey back to Guatemala City, and the hotel is not terribly overpriced. Still, this apricot-colored cube of cement at the edge of town gives the impression that several conventions are either just ending or threatening to begin. It is popular with the business and government crowd from Guatemala City, who enjoy the tennis courts and the illusion of being in North America. The Ramada is on the Ciudad Vieja highway at the southwest edge of town. (Its restaurants are discussed below.)

Scattered around Antigua are a number of modest pensions and rooming houses that accommodate travellers looking for economy over the long term and students studying

Spanish in Antigua. (Antigua beckons language students of all ages, many of whom live with local families.)

Dining in Antigua

El Sereno, the most stylish restaurant in Guatemala, welcomes you with candlelight, crystal, and a lovely fountain. The food, which has gourmet aspirations, is French and international, with some transfigured native dishes. The restaurant is expensive but memorable. El Sereno's elegant entrance is found at 6 Calle Poniente 30; closed Mondays and Tuesdays. Reservations advised; Tel: (9) 32-0073.

Doña Luisa Xicotencatl seems to have something of everything, including a devoted following of students and young people from the capital. The courtyard is an especially convivial place, and a number of the tables upstairs offer striking views of the nearby volcanoes. You check off your choices on a long paper menu, which includes such fare as chile con carne, sausages, Reuben sandwiches, pies, and cakes. The food is fair, the atmosphere casual, the prices moderate. 4 Calle Oriente 2.

Located on Calle 4A one block west of the Parque Central, **Welten** serves up international-style cuisine in a pleasantly floral and ferny patio environment. Prices range from moderate to expensive.

Alom La Creación, in the Ramada, presents international specialties with a German emphasis. It's open evenings only from 7:00 until 11:00 P.M. but claims it won't turn you out until you're ready to end the night. **Las Chimeneas**, in the same hotel, is a standard operation, with piano music and (usually) good service that becomes rushed on weekends. Both Ramada restaurants are at the expensive end of the scale. Tel: (9) 3-2011 to 2015.

Shopping in Antigua

Tourist prices tend to prevail in Antigua, but you can find some good buys and fine merchandise here, especially at the **weaving market** located next to the Jesuit church, Compañia de Jesús, 6 Avenida Norte and 4 Calle Poniente. Those searching for interesting textiles should also visit the nearby village of **San Antonio Aguas Calientes**, about 5 km (3 miles) to the east.

Jade is an Antigua specialty. The founder of the jade art and industry here is **Jades** (HA-dess), a large, beautiful shop at 4A Calle Oriente 34 (the building also houses a number of interesting working studios). Guatemalan jade is the real stone, by the way, and it's risky to buy it off the street unless you are highly knowledgeable; you can rely, on the other hand, on an establishment like Jades, which specializes in exquisite stones, finely set. The store has many other items of interest, including handwoven cloth and the best available coffee beans.

After checking out Jades, pause at the tempting candy shop on the opposite side of the street across from the gas station, where chocolate reigns in all its glory and many of its forms. This street, 4A Calle Oriente, also has several other worthwhile handicraft shops, all of them located between Jades and the main plaza.

Mayan women frequently come into Antigua to sell their work or their possessions on the streets. It's a mistake to turn away automatically; you just might miss the best buys in town.

LAGO ATITLAN AND PANAJACHEL

Half a century ago Aldous Huxley pronounced Lake Atitlán to be "the most beautiful of the world." Virtually every ad, brochure, and discussion of the lake begins with the great man's encomium. In fact, in the lakeside town of Panajachel you can find the Huxley quote printed in at least four different languages, at once challenging and offending countless travellers. (It seems that everyone has a personal candidate for "the most beautiful," and though the lakes are scattered from Finland to California, none ever seems to be Atitlán.)

Regardless of which is fairest of them all, Lago Atitlán, in all its changing moods, *is* unforgettably, hauntingly beautiful. This broad sweep of water, some 16 miles long and 11 miles wide, is framed by massive symmetrically shaped volcanoes whose eruptions created the basin in prehistoric times. The lake is relatively clean and remains good for water sports, but it is mainly enjoyed for its beauty, whether it's in the late morning, when a daily wind freshens and lightens its deep blue color, or in the early evening, when the rising mist tints it silver. At any time of day, however, lake watching is a local pastime.

A dozen towns and villages, predominantly Mayan and linked to each other by launches, hug the shoreline, although roads connect most places. (The Maya prefer to have their feet on the ground. They are neither fishermen, good swimmers, nor canny boat builders: *No es costumbre*. The lake is merely the limit of their cornfields. Accordingly, they do not create legends or sing songs about it, and its waters are not viewed as a resource.)

Panajachel

Of the lake settlements at Atitlán, the most interesting to travellers is Panajachel (pahn-ah-hah-CHEL), the only one with facilities for visitors. The town itself winds, sprawls, and ambles along the northeastern shore of the lake, as casual in its layout as it is in its approach to life. Being more Mayan than ladino, Panajachel has little of Antigua's tidiness, quaintness, and squared corners. There are no ruins, monuments, or museums here. Instead, the town draws visitors because of the beauty of its setting, the interesting variety of its people (both native and foreign), and the carefree atmosphere of easy living that prevails. As a headquarters for exploring the countryside, it is more centrally located than Antigua, and its accommodations are a better value.

Panajachel carries no heavy burden of history. There was a good-sized native population here when the Spanish marched into the region, but after one bloody battle the struggle was over, and only the resistance of custom and stubbornness remained to confound the conquerors. The town became a center for the Franciscans, who converted the local folk after a fashion. Otherwise, life, which chiefly meant raising corn, continued along its age-old path.

In our own century the lake has increasingly attracted tourists and vacationers. Day-trippers come from Guatemala City, travelling 115 km (71 miles) each way. Europeans, especially younger ones, also come in noticeable numbers, usually after visiting Tikal. (Many seem to be taking vague sabbaticals.) In addition, foreigners and wealthy people from the capital have bought or built homes here. These substantial holiday or retirement houses are planted comfortably between the commercial district and the shore.

There is also a small coterie of North American and European transients, mostly young, who maintain a 1960s lifestyle reminiscent of the vanished world of San Francisco's "Hashbury." You might call them "post-hippies," but the term somehow seems too emphatic. At any rate, they hang up their wind chimes, play their bamboo flutes, and contemplate the lake at sunset with great seriousness. The backpackers among them gaze uncomprehendingly at Mayan folk carrying loads in much the same way. (The Maya do it more efficiently; they have tumplines circling their foreheads to brace the burden.) A number of artists and writers are also drawn to the lake. While the mix of people is not homogeneous enough to be convivial, Panajachel is probably the liveliest little town in Central America.

The town's center, like the lifestyle it encourages, is somewhat haphazard. Street names are rarely posted and frequently change. The heart of town can be found at the corner of Calle Principal, the main street, and Calle Santander, which runs toward the lake. Along Calle Principal you will find a slow-service bank, a peaceful enough pool hall, and a stand that sells delicious Topsy ice cream. The **Maya Palace** craft shop, an excellent store, is still operating even though the old hotel of the same name has become an office building. You'll also find a book exchange, a chocolate shop, and some restaurants and snack shops along the main street.

The evangelical church on Calle Principal is far livelier than the pool hall, in part because Protestant missionaries have flocked to Guatemala in recent years and enjoyed great success. The authorities seem to like this particular foreign import: The missionaries take a less jaundiced view of the Guatemalan government than the Catholic liberation theology movement. Politics aside, you'll probably be startled to hear "Rock of Ages" pounded out on an electric keyboard and backed by guitars as a fervent congregation sings along in Spanish and Mayan.

Walking down Calle Santander toward the lake, you pass several blocks of cloth displays. Visitors are invited, even urged, to inspect the wares but are not badgered. The overall effect is flamboyant and dazzling, and the quality often high—here and there you'll come across machine-made junk—but in the face of such a profusion of merchandise it is hard to concentrate.

The town's beach on the lake is a pleasant, busy place, but more for strolling than sunbathing, since much of it is gravel and dirt. The swimming is best in the morning before the breezes stiffen and turn the water choppy (there is better swimming nearby at the Hotel Visión Azul beach; see below). Still, you can always peruse the wares offered by perambulating vendors here as you enjoy a cool drink in one of the beach's open-fronted restaurants, or even take a boat ride.

Instead of renting a boat, most visitors take the mail launch (really a passenger launch) across the lake to San Pedro de la Laguna and Santiago Atitlán. The roofed launch carries a couple of dozen people, mostly Maya, on each trip. Mayan women, who are often uneasy away from land, seem to draw comfort from hand-lettered signs posted by the captain: JEHOVAH OUR GOD IS UPON THE GREAT WATERS, one plaque announces in Spanish; another urges BE NOT AFRAID! Obviously, this is an evangelical boat.

San Pedro, sometimes the first destination, is also evangelical. Little wooden steeples poke at the sky, serving a town that was converted almost en masse before splintering into sects. Horses and mules replace men and women as beasts of burden here—definitely not *costumbre* and possibly the result of the new religion. Knotted wool rugs are a specialty of local artisans.

San Pedro's neighbor, **Santiago Atitlán**, is the largest and most colorful of the lakeside villages. Evangelical protestantism has made converts here, but many people combine Catholicism with adoration of a god called Maximón, represented by a stubby wooden figure smoking a cigar. Santiago is famed for weaving, embroidery on machine-made cloth, women's headgear called "halos" (to be worn wound around the head), and colorful shirts for men. The town market, though not a place to buy handicrafts, is nonetheless a colorful scene as the women, dressed in brilliant costumes, preside over their vegetable stalls. The parish church exhibits the starkness of Mayan temples, and is filled with strangely dressed statues of saints in village clothing. Inside, to the right of the main door, is a simple but touching memorial to villagers slain when the national army raided the town a decade ago.

About three hours should be allowed for lakeside exploring: a brief visit to San Pedro, about an hour in Santiago, and the rest of the time on the boat.

Staying in Panajachel

The hotels in town will be happy to offer advice and help with nearby excursions, hiring guides or drivers, and bus schedules.

The **Cacique** (kah-SEE-kay) **Inn**, located near the southern edge of town on the Sololá road, a continuation of the main street, is a fine value. The rooms, which have attractive stone fireplaces, are grouped around a swimming pool and a well-kept garden; the dining room is probably the best restaurant in the area and serves international food with some local touches; and the inn itself is relaxed and very well run. In addition, you can walk from the Cacique to the center of town.

About a mile south of town past the Cacique Inn, the lovely grounds and gardens of the **Hotel Atitlán** feature topiary sculpture. The views from the hotel are also impressive, making the bar an ideal place for a drink at sunset. The dining room, with alamo beams, seems more stately than cheerful, however, and the food is only satisfactory. Individual rooms do not have fireplaces, and town is a long walk away. Nevertheless, the views and the serene, secluded surroundings make this handsome inn a fine choice.

The **Hotel Visión Azul** appears to have been carved out of the same coffee plantation as its neighbor, the Hotel Atitlán. This comfortable place, with lawns and a number of rooms offering panoramic views of the lake and surrounding mountains, is also simpler than its elegant neighbor, and therefore less costly.

The **Rancho Grande Inn** is located in town, not far from the beach. The accommodations here are bungalows set in a garden, good but not special. A hearty cooked breakfast is included in the price. The only public room is the dining room at breakfast time, and the management is not especially helpful with information and arrangements. The attraction here is privacy and a fine location.

The **Hotel del Lago** overlooks the beach and was obviously designed with vacationers from Guatemala City in mind. Thick-pile carpets climb right up the sides of the bar, and the volcanic stone seems to come in a variety of designer colors. All the rooms have balconies and wonderful views of the lake, but the top-floor rooms are the best. The hotel also has a restaurant, nightclub, swimming pool, and two curio shops—and it is expensive.

The **Hotel Galindo**, on Calle Principal, proudly advertises its patio garden, which is a veritable jungle. Unfortunately, its rooms are small and far from bright, but it does have two things to recommend it: a location downtown and very low rates. The Galindo also rents out several lakeside cottages with kitchens.

Dining in Panajachel

All the dining spots here are informal, and most of them at least a little rustic.

Although its menu is limited, the **Cacique Inn** has the most consistent kitchen in town (Tel: 9/62-1205). Of the other hotels, the **Atitlán** is really selling its surroundings more than its food, which is only satisfactory. The views are lovely, however (Tel: 9/62-1429).

La Fontana, on Calle Principal, offers Italian-style cooking, with indoor and outdoor service. Both the service and the surroundings are pleasing.

El Bistro (called El Patio by many locals), about halfway between the main street and the beach on Calle Santander, features lake bass, salads, chicken, and steaks. Tables are set up in a small dining room and an adjacent garden.

The murky **Last Resort**—it will take a few minutes for your eyes to adjust to the gloom—is mainly a bar. Late in the evening it draws a young (and sometimes not-so-young) international crowd. The food runs to such offerings as ribs and pizza, and the sandwiches are generous—a welcome surprise, because Guatemala is the land of the stingy sandwich and the scant taco. It's hard to find this place in daylight, however, even though it's just off Santander not far from the public school. At night look for a bulb burning outside, or trail a likely-looking patron (the clientele will quickly become identifiable).

The **Circus Bar**, in a Hansel and Gretel–style house near the center of town, also serves food, mostly snacks that are good enough as well as inexpensive, and has live music many nights.

In addition, several eateries have been tacked up along the beach. Most of them are breezy places where you can enjoy something cool while watching the lake and beach. One of them, **Los Pumpos**, is worth trying for lunch. The building is cobbled together out of split bamboo, thatch, and, it sometimes seems, glue. Hanging inside are stuffed fish, nets, oars, glass pendants, and all manner of flotsam. If the Swiss Family Robinson had opened a café, this would be it.

CHICHICASTENANGO

Despite the effects of increased tourism, Chichicastenango, about 20 km (12 miles) north of Panajachel, remains the quintessential Mayan town, at once a confluence of paganism and Catholicism, of folklore and ancient traditions culled from the entire highlands region. No numbers or names identify the cobblestone streets here—and it hardly matters. This is a small place, and everybody knows how to get everywhere; as a result, you will not need a hired guide.

The market tradition of Chichi, as the town is often called, dates back to the pre-Columbian era. People from a wide area have always come here to buy, sell, or trade. Others come merely to watch the transactions—not only foreigners but Mayan villagers themselves, for whom this is, and always has been, life and excitement. One writer described Chichi as "anthropology in action." The town, transformed by the market, is hardly worth visiting on other days, however.

The main market is held on Sunday, but preparations

begin on Saturday afternoon (a smaller market is held on Thursday). Some visitors feel that the market is conducted for their benefit, that it's a craft show for tourists. And while it's true that ladino merchants are there to deal and give tourists what they want, another market, where cheap kitchenware, needles, dyes, and furnishings for primitive dwellings are sold, is operating for the townspeople at the same time. Your eyes should not be held entirely by those who want your attention; the sideshow is truly the main event. (It's not for nothing that the market tradition is centuries old. The merchants overprice their goods, usually asking about three times the amount they actually expect to get. Most sellers have a keen sense of humor, but after you've made your purchase you may feel they are laughing all the way to the bank over the price you paid.)

After checking out the market you should visit the local church, **Santo Tomás**. The rites here are not performances for the benefit of curious onlookers, and neither are they voodoo rituals. This is folk Catholicism, practiced with candles and overhung by incense. The chants, prayers, and costumes of the devout are strange, even alien, making Santo Tomás a grim place fraught with an almost palpable aura of belief in miracles and magic. (Taking photos inside the church is frowned upon by the natives, who can become very forceful in their objections.)

There's also a small **museum** of regional curios in town, nicely done, but it will occupy no more than half an hour of your time. The real museum is Chichi itself.

If you want to stay overnight you'll find the **Mayan Inn** to be outstanding. Although it faces the plaza, its terraces afford lovely views of the valleys around Chichi. The dining room is also very good, and the comfortable rooms are made charming and personal with a selection of antiques and native art. A marimba band plays in the patio on market days; its musicians are as good as everything else about this inn, which is well worth the fairly high tariff charged. (Rooms with a view of the mountains are more expensive.)

Slightly less costly but with less personality is the attractive and colonial **Hotel Santo Tomás**. It, too, has beautiful views and lovely grounds, and the comfortable dining room serves well-prepared food.

The **Posada Chugüilá** is, unfortunately, no better than the room you get, which may or may not have a private bath and can vary from cramped to spacious. Some have fireplaces; ask for one of those, even in a heat wave—they're the best the inn has to offer. The patio is comfortable; the restaurant serves hearty, rather heavy fare.

THE RIO DULCE

The relatively new Atlantic Highway (Carretera al Atlántico), designated CA 9, provides fast, easy access to a region of Guatemala that was, until recently, little known or explored by foreigners. Although the highway heads in a northeasterly direction toward the Caribbean coast, in the minds of most travellers it seems to go *down,* dropping in its course from temperate highlands to rain forest and the steamy tropics. The trip is usually made for one reason: to see the jungle and the somnolent Río Dulce as it meanders from Lago Izabal into the Gulf of Honduras and the Caribbean. (The river is also a possible stop on the way by car or bus to the ruins at Tikal.)

At minimum, this is an overnight trip from Guatemala City; driving time is a little more than four hours each way. Some travellers will wish to combine this excursion with a visit to the Mayan ruins at **Quiriguá** (see above), not far from the highway. (The Quiriguá turnoff is near the Texaco station at Los Amates, kilometer 205.)

For the Río Dulce, you continue on CA 9 past the Quiriguá turnoff until, just past the town of Morales, you reach the junction with the road to Fronteras, where you turn left (north). About 34 km (21 miles) farther on lies **El Relleno**, a small settlement at the water's edge—and not on most maps. There is a good general store here, Tienda Reed; Mrs. Reed, who speaks English, can help with car storage and advice. The local fire department (*los bomberos*) will also store and guard your car.

Once that is settled, all that's left is to hire a launch from among those you'll see moored nearby. In choosing a boat, be sure to select one with a strong motor. Some of the boats are underpowered, and although they manage the trip, what should be a leisurely excursion can become a slow boat to nowhere as the motor fights the current. You'll also want to agree upon a price in advance—it's usually not the first price suggested. The whole trip takes a little more than two hours, including a short stop at the **Castillo de San Felipe**, a 17th-century fortress built to fend off pirates. The boatman should understand that the castle stop is included in the price.

Downstream on the north bank of El Golfete, a broadening of the river that seems more like a tropical lake, is a reserve for those fantastic creatures, manatees (sea cows), which can weigh up to a ton. (Distant sightings of manatees by sailors may have been the origin of the mermaid legend.)

Soon the river narrows and then enters a gorge. Mangroves, their twisted, clawlike roots gripping the riverbank, line either side. Kekchi Indians have built a few primitive villages in the jungle here, their thatched huts with peaked roofs appearing every now and then in a clearing. But human intrusion into this region is, for the most part, barely noticeable, the silence broken only by the cries of a multitude of birds or a breeze rustling the tangled foliage.

With its cheerfully painted wooden houses and corrugated metal roofs, **Livingston,** the small town at the mouth of the Río Dulce, gives an appearance of gaiety. But it's not really interesting unless you can stay long enough to become acquainted with its people, a mélange of Caribs, ladinos, Kekchis, Lebanese, Chinese, and East Indians.

The surrounding area has not been notably successful in promoting itself or its beaches—other Caribbean resorts outdo this narrow strip of coast in both facilities and atmosphere, nor is Livingston cheap for what it offers—but there is good scuba diving, swimming, sailing, and fishing here.

Staying in the Río Dulce Area

Perched on a hill above the boat landing in Livingston, the luxurious and well-run **Tucán Dugu** is a striking building with white walls and tropical thatch. It also has a swimming pool and a beach. Jungle motifs and rich woodwork contribute to the exotic atmosphere of this expensive accommodation.

Upriver, at the El Relleno–Río Dulce crossing, the **Turicentro Marimonte** is a good hotel and resort situated on the banks of the river. The Marimonte has a swimming pool and marina, and is popular with boating enthusiasts from Guatemala City. It also has a satisfactory restaurant.

About a mile downstream from El Relleno is the quite special **Hotel Catamarán,** situated on a small island in the river. The Catamarán caters to visitors who want to explore the Río Dulce and surrounding jungle, as well as those simply in search of a South Seas atmosphere in a relaxed environment. Its swimming pool and marina are well maintained, the food is good, and the rates are more than reasonable for such an attractive and unusual jungle inn. The Catamarán will also be happy to arrange for your transportation from the capital.

GETTING AROUND

Getting There

Citizens of the United States may obtain a Guatemalan tourist card, required by law, for a small fee by presenting proof of citizenship (passport, birth certificate, or voting registration) at airline check-in counters in the States, Guatemalan consulates, or border crossing stations; naturalized citizens may need their certificate of naturalization. British Commonwealth and Canadian citizens should apply in advance, with a passport and round-trip ticket in hand, at a Guatemalan consulate.

Entering Guatemala with an automobile requires an additional permit as well as proof of ownership. There will be a small fee for the permit, and still another for fumigating the tires of your car and squirting a whiff of something inside.

There are three possible entry points into Guatemala from the north. Coming directly from Mexico by car, you can take either the lowland coastal route, Highway 200, through Tapachula, or the highland road, Highway 190, from San Cristóbal de las Casas, which crosses into Guatemala near Ciudad Cuauhtémoc. The highland route is cooler and much more scenic. If you choose the latter, you'll soon understand why Guatemala, with its pine-clad mountains and long auto tunnels, is sometimes called "North America's Switzerland."

A third possibility is to enter through Belize. This route should not be attempted in a conventional car, however; stick to four-wheel-drive vehicles with high wheel bases if you have your heart set on this option (even then, it will be a long, bumpy, exhausting trek).

Air service from abroad to Guatemala City, which has the country's only international airport, is frequent and dependable. Continental flies to the capital from Dallas, and American Airlines offers three flights a day from Miami and one a day from Dallas–Forth Worth. Mexicana, the Mexican national airline, offers a daily morning flight to Guatemala City from Mexico City. In addition, two airlines not widely known outside of Central America also deserve consideration. Aviateca, the Guatemalan national airline, flies to Guatemala City from Miami, Houston, New Orleans, Los Angeles, Mérida, and Mexico City, and offers good service, an admirable safety record, and a thorough knowledge of its home country. At times it also offers reduced fares and attractive travel arrangements, including special rates on hotels and car rentals. Lacsa, the fine Costa Rican operation, flies to Guatemala City from New York and Los Angeles (with a stop in Cancún), and often lures passengers away from the bigger carriers with its discount fares. (Lacsa is a favorite with Latin American travellers.) Aerocaribe has three flights a week to Tikal (Flores airport) from Cancún. Aeroquetzal, a local airline, flies the same route.

Currency

The national monetary unit is the *quetzal* (ket-SAHL), named for the shy jungle bird beloved by the Maya. A quetzal is divided into 100 *centavos*. The currency is relatively stable; you should be able to change back to dollars or other major currencies without incurring startling losses. The present exchange rate is five *quetzales* to one U.S. dollar.

The Guatemala City airport, La Aurora, is a convenient place to exchange currency—especially since banks in Guatemala can be quagmires of bureaucracy. Small denominations of U.S. dollars are generally accepted throughout the country. Hotels and the better shops almost always accept U.S. dollar traveller's checks.

Credit cards are accepted at establishments dependent on tourism, including the better hotels, restaurants, and car-rental agencies.

Local Time and Electric Current

Guatemala is on central standard time (the same as Winnipeg, Chicago, Dallas, and Mexico City) year-round, but does not change over to daylight saving time.

Electricity in Guatemala is supplied at 110 volts, alternating current, the same as in the United States, Canada, and Mexico. The same type and sizes of sockets and plugs are also standard in all four countries.

Travelling in Guatemala

A rental car is a pleasure but not a necessity in Guatemala. You will find Avis, Hertz, Budget, Dollar, and National both at the airport and in Guatemala City. If you decide to rent a car from one of these outfits, make sure you're not paying double for insurance. Many credit-card companies cover such insurance, or at least a part of it, automatically (check with your own card-issuing company). Once you rent the car, stay with the attendant as it's being checked for damages prior to taking it; be sure that every dent and missing hubcap is properly noted, or else you may end up paying for them.

Those who wish to know more about packaged tours to Guatemala should contact **Clark Tours**, 7 Avenida 6-53, Edificio El Triángulo, 2nd floor, Zona 4, Guatemala City, C.A.; Tel: (2) 31-0213 to 0216. Clark is the oldest and largest company in the field. The international travel company

Wagon-Lits may also have some attractive tours (Avenida Reforma 12-81, Zona 10; Tel: 2-31-3268; Fax: 2-34-6143), and **Aviateca**, the Guatemalan national airline, is usually helpful (Avenida Incapie 42-12, Zona 13; Tel: 2-34-7722 or 31-8222; in the U.S., Tel: 800-327-9832). Most hotels in the major cities will arrange for cars, drivers, and guides.

There is good, regular bus service from the capital to Antigua, Chichicastenango, and Panajachel. (Bus service to the Río Dulce region, on the other hand, is less than convenient, and the bus trip to Tikal is not only boring, it's an ordeal.)

First-class buses are your best bet. You can reach **Antigua** in an hour on the Preciosa line, 15A Calle 3-37, Zona 1. Buses depart hourly from 7:00 A.M. to 8:00 P.M., and a ticket costs about $3.

Panajachel service is provided by Rébuli, 20A Calle 3-42, Zona 1. Rébuli, a second-class line, offers regularly scheduled departures from 5:00 A.M. to 4:00 P.M., and charges $6 for a one-way ticket. Panajachel is a 4-hour journey one-way.

The **Chichicastenango** bus, also a 4-hour trip one-way, is for early risers. Buses leave at 4:30, 5:00, and 5:30 A.M., and the fare is about $6. Service is provided by Reinita de Utatlán, 20A Calle and 4A Avenida, Zona 1.

The 14-hour one-way endurance run that ends at Flores (**Tikal**) begins at 17A Calle 8-46, Zona 1. The line is Fuentes del Norte, the one-way fare is $14; the bus goes via the **Río Dulce**, so it's possible to break up the trip. The stretch from Guatemala City to the river is the easy part (see below for more on Tikal).

Second-class buses, often antique school buses that were retired from service in the United States long ago, stop anywhere you can flag them down. Baggage goes on the roof; birds and animals travel inside with the passengers. Still, they are satisfactory, even an adventure, for good-humored travellers going a short distance. After a while, however, the smells, pushing, crowding, fumes, and general slowness of the proceedings lose their charm.

In almost all Guatemalan towns buses arrive and depart from a central street near a main corner. Inquire locally.

Getting to Tikal

The easiest and most practical way for travellers to get to Tikal is by plane from Guatemala City. For a round-trip fare of $68, Aviateca offers regular morning and afternoon flights (the planes accommodate either 6 or 24 passengers) to the nearby town of Flores. From there you can get a bus, taxi, or *combi* to take you to a hotel or, if you so choose, the ruins themselves. A taxi will set you back about $42, a bus only $5. The largest hotel in the region, the Camino Real, provides courtesy transportation from the airport.

The ruins are also accessible by car, with the most common route starting in the capital and ending some 12 hours later. The least rugged vehicle available in Guatemala that is practical for the trip is a Suzuki model that looks something like a Jeep. Bus transportation over the same route is also available, but the inexpensive fare is no bargain when you figure in the day lost and the considerable discomfort (not to mention the boredom). An Aviateca flight is much the better choice.

Half-day tours of Tikal by Jeep or minibus, with air feeder service from the capital and lunch included, can be arranged in Guatemala City. You return to the capital in the afternoon. While this is better than nothing, it's hardly good enough. Not only will you be rushed at the ruins and miss much of what is best about them, you'll also miss the once-in-a-lifetime experience of nightfall and sunrise in the jungle. The tours also vary greatly in cost, ranging from $30 to $70, plus airfare. Clark Tours, Wagon-Lits, and Aviateca, discussed above, arrange tours.

Whichever way you choose to go, you should take a few items along with you: insect repellent, a sun visor or hat, a flashlight for viewing darkened chambers, and binoculars. The latter need not be especially powerful—the details you want to bring closer are not far away, just high overhead.

If you're arriving by plane and plan on going exploring as soon as you get to Tikal, be sure to eat a good breakfast before departing the capital; food is not served on the flight.

ACCOMMODATIONS REFERENCE

The rates given below are projections for December 1992 through Easter 1993. Unless otherwise indicated, rates are based on double rooms, double occupancy; the 17 percent VAT has been added. As rates are subject to change, it's always a good idea to double-check before booking. The international telephone country code for Guatemala is 502; the capital area code is 2. There are several other area codes within the country. In some jungle areas telegraph is the only way to contact hotels.

▶ **Cacique Inn.** Calle Embarcadero, **Panajachel.** Tel: (9) 62-1205. $52.

▶ **Camino Guatemala City.** Avenida Reforma 14-01, Zona 10, **Guatemala City.** Tel: (2) 33-4633; Fax: (2) 37-4313; in the U.S. and Canada, Tel: (800) 228-3000. $170.

GUATEMALA

▶ **Camino Real Tikal.** Calle Flores Remate, **Tikal**. Tel: (9) 50-0207 or 0208; Fax: (9) 50-0222; in the U.S., Tel: (800) 228-3000. $145.

▶ **Conquistador Sheraton.** Via 5, 4-68, Zona 4, **Guatemala City**. Tel: (2) 34-1212 or 36-4691; Fax: (2) 34-7245; in the U.S. and Canada, Tel: (800) 334-8484. $122.

▶ **Hotel Antigua.** 8A Calle Oriente, **Antigua**. Tel: (9) 32-0288. $110.

▶ **Hotel Atitlán.** Camino a Sololá, **Panajachel**. Tel: (9) 62-1441. $71.

▶ **Hotel Aurora.** 4A Calle Oriente 16, **Antigua**. Tel: (9) 32-0217. $35.

▶ **Hotel Catamarán.** Río Dulce. In Guatemala City, Tel: (2) 32-4829. $60.

▶ **Hotel del Centro.** 13 Calle 4-55, Zona 1, **Guatemala City**. Tel: (2) 30-0540; Fax: (2) 30-0208. $54.

▶ **Hotel El Dorado Americana.** 7 Avenida 15-45, Zona 9, **Guatemala City**. Tel: (2) 31-7777; Fax: (2) 32-1877. $154.

▶ **Hotel Galindo.** Calle Principal, **Panajachel**. Tel: (9) 62-1168. $18.

▶ **Hotel del Lago.** Calle Rancho Grande, **Panajachel**. Tel: (9) 62-1555. $110.

▶ **Hotel Marina.** González Bocanegra 100 ZP3, **Copán**, Honduras. Tel: 526-7676 (country code: 504). $34.

▶ **Hotel Piño Montano.** Pan-American Highway, km 259, **Huehuetenango**. In Guatemala City, Tel: (2) 64-1637. $48.

▶ **Hotel Plaza.** Via 7, 6-16, Zona 4, **Guatemala City**. Tel: (2) 31-6337 or 36-3626. $54.

▶ **Hotel Santo Tómas.** **Chichicastenango**. Tel: (9) 56-1061. $82.

▶ **Hotel Visión Azul.** Camino a Sololá, **Panajachel**. Tel: (9) 62-1426. $64.

▶ **Jungle Lodge.** Parque Nacional, **Tikal**. Tel: (9) 50-0204. $42.

▶ **Maya Internacional.** Santa Elena, El Petén. Tel: (5) 081-1276 or 1352; in Guatemala City, Tel: (2) 36-1920. $60.

▶ **Mayan Inn.** Chichicastenango. Tel: (9) 56-1176; in Guatemala City, Tel: (2) 6-0213. $87.

▶ **Pan American.** 9A Calle 5-63, Zona 1, **Guatemala City**. Tel: 2-6807. $69.

▶ **Posada Belén.** 13 Calle A 10-30, Zona 1, **Guatemala City**. Tel: (2) 51-3478. $34.

▶ **Posada Chugüilá.** Chichicastenango. Tel: (9) 56-1134. $28.

▶ **Posada de Don Rodrigo.** 5A Avenida Norte 17, **Antigua**. Tel: (9) 32-0291. $87.

▶ **Ramada Antigua.** 9 Calle Poniente and Carretera a

Ciudad Vieja, **Antigua**. Tel: (9) 32-0011; Fax: (9) 32-0237; in the U.S. and Canada, (800) 2-RAMADA. $170.

▶ **Rancho Grande Inn.** Calle Rancho Grande, **Panajachel**. Tel: (9) 62-1554. $41.

▶ **Tucán Dugu**. Lívingston. Tel: (9) 48-1572; Fax: (2) 34-5242. $74.

▶ **Turicentro Marimonte. El Relleno–Río Dulce.** In Guatemala City, Tel: (2) 31-4437. $70.

THE YUCATAN CARIBBEAN RESORTS

By Mitchell Nauffts

The Yucatán is among the most varied tourist destinations in Mexico, encompassing rural hamlets where time seems to stand still as well as bustling cities; impenetrable jungles as well as one of the longest coral reef systems in the world; the ruins of ancient city-states as well as state-of-the-art luxury hotels. Depending on your itinerary it can seem familiar one day and utterly exotic the next. But then, the Yucatán has always been a world unto itself: Though part of the Mexican mainland, for much of its history it has been isolated both geographically and psychologically from the rest of the country. Even today, linked to the outside world by modern highways and international flights, it manages to remain apart, retaining some of the mystery of its long and fascinating past.

Archaeological sites that conjure up this ancient glory—Chichén Itzá, Uxmal, Labná, Kabah, Tulum, and Cobá among them—dot the map of the peninsula and tantalize travellers who have the time to make detours. Those who don't can still hear the ancient Mayan language spoken in the streets of the peninsula's towns and villages, see natives wearing the traditional *huipil* (a white shift with embroidered neck and hemlines), and eat time-honored dishes such as *poc-chuc* (grilled pork) and *pollo pibil* (chicken seasoned with *anchiote* and baked in a wrapping of banana leaves).

Behind its tranquil façade, however, the Yucatán is undergoing profound changes. Many of these have been stimulated by a boom in tourism to the region, and to Cancún in particular. Two-lane highways that were all but deserted a decade ago today hum with a steady flow of buses and rental cars. At archaeological sites such as Chichén Itzá or Tulum, or natural aquariums such as Xel-há (south of Cancún) or Garrafón National Park (on Isla Mujeres), the crowds reach De-Mille-ian proportions by early afternoon. Even so, there are any number of beautiful spots and fascinating places that remain off the beaten track, as well as strategies that can be employed to avoid the worst of the crowds.

The Mexican portion of the peninsula comprises three states, each with its own distinct flavor: **Quintana Roo**, which covers the eastern third of the peninsula (including its long Caribbean coastline), and which these days is the area most obviously affected by the benefits and drawbacks of *turismo;* **Yucatán**, which takes in much of the northern third of the peninsula, including the charming colonial city of Mérida as well as two of the country's greatest archaeological sites, Chichén Itzá and Uxmal; and **Campeche**, the little-developed and infrequently visited state encompassing much of the western third of the peninsula. Travellers who plan to use Mérida as a gateway for the exploration of the many archaeological sites in the region will find it and the surrounding area covered in the Mayan Mexico chapter. The somewhat limited attractions of Campeche, both the city and the state, are covered in the same chapter.

The focus of this section, on the other hand, is the Caribbean coast of Quintana Roo, a sun-splashed region of powdery beaches and aquamarine water. A virtual terra incognita just 30 years ago, when it was still home to a scattered population of Mayan farmers and fishermen, *bandidos,* and poisonous snakes, the area today is so popular with international travellers that Mexican tourism officials are ready to rechristen it the Turquoise Coast. We begin our coverage with a look at **Cancún**, that monument to impersonal luxury and conspicuous consumption on the northeast corner of the peninsula, and then follow with a discussion of the **Cancún–Tulum corridor**, a onetime beachcomber's paradise that's getting its first taste of large-scale development. Next is **Isla Mujeres**, a small resort island off the coast northeast of Cancún that appeals to visitors looking for a low-key getaway. We end with a discussion of **Cozumel**, Mexico's largest island and the site of some of the finest diving and snorkeling in the Western Hemisphere.

CANCUN

Cancún, a long sandspit of an island situated off the northeast corner of the Yucatán peninsula, looks like Miami Beach, parties like Fort Lauderdale, and empties a visitor's wallet as quickly as New York City. A tiny fishing village when it was discovered in the late 1960s by Fonatur, the government agency in charge of tourism, it continues to grow after 20 years of pell-mell expansion and today attracts more than a million visitors annually. Like a bodybuilder on steroids, everything about it—the malls, the hotel pools, the hotels themselves—is big and getting bigger. Cancún is so big, in fact, that the government has announced its intention to cap the number of rooms at around 20,000 (there are some 18,000 at present). Given that Cancún already boasts one of the greatest concentrations of luxury hotels in the world, a cynic might see this as an admission of the obvious: Eventually every inch of the island that can be developed will be.

None of which has much to do with the "real" Mexico, whatever that might be. But then Cancún never had much to do with the real Mexico—other than the fact that it provides tens of thousands of jobs to real Mexicans. Instead, as the flagship of Fonatur's five mega-resorts, it was developed from scratch with an eye to the comfort and convenience of large numbers of tourists. Fonatur can pat itself on the back. Over the years Cancún has evolved into a kind of Disney World for hedonists, a place where drinking, dancing, and shopping take the place of rides; HBO and ESPN are beamed into every hotel room; and English is the lingua franca. Many people hate it, especially when beer-guzzling college kids descend en masse during spring break; others can't wait to return.

If it leaves cold many of those looking for the ever-elusive "real" Mexico, Cancún does have charms that even the most jaded traveller will appreciate, including beautiful white-sand beaches, abundant bird and marine life, and great weather. For snorkeling enthusiasts it's one of the top sites in the Caribbean, while Cozumel, with some of the best snorkeling and scuba-diving in the hemisphere, is only a 15-minute flight (or a two-hour car-and-ferry trip) to the south. And for archaeology buffs, photographers, and the merely curious, it's the resort gateway to a number of fascinating sites, including Chichén Itzá, Tulum, and Cobá.

(For a complete description of Chichén Itzá, see the Mayan Mexico chapter.)

MAJOR INTEREST

Cancún
Beautiful beaches
Luxury accommodations
Nightlife and shopping
Snorkeling around Punta Nizuc
Ruinas del Rey

Cancún–Tulum Corridor
Funky beach town of Playa del Carmen
Natural aquariums at Xcaret and Xel-há National Park
Diving and snorkeling at Akumal
Beaches at Chemuyil and Xcacel
Mayan ruins of Tulum and Cobá

Cancún's luxury hotels, many of its better restaurants, and most of its best boutiques are located in the *zona hotelera,* which stretches the length of a slender 14-mile-long island resembling the number seven. The island itself is connected to the mainland by two short bridges, one at each end of the "seven," and is washed by the Bahía de Mujeres to the north and the Caribbean to the east. To the west a huge saltwater lagoon system separates the island from the mainland. The unique geography of Cancún accounts for the two types of beaches in the hotel zone: those facing Isla Mujeres and the sheltered waters of the Bahía de Mujeres, and those exposed to the open Caribbean. The latter, with their soft white sand and brilliantly hued water, are especially beautiful but also subject to heavy, and sometimes dangerous, surf. Visitors are advised to pay close attention to the flag system employed by hotels on the Caribbean side of the island: A green or blue flag means it's safe to swim; a yellow flag means swim with caution; and a red or black flag signifies dangerous conditions, swim at your own risk.

The hotel zone's main drag, Boulevard Kukulcán (from the ancient Mayan name for the legendary Toltec hero-cum-serpent god Quetzalcóatl), heads due east from Cancún City across the northernmost bridge on its way to Punta Cancún, at the "elbow" of the "seven." From there the boulevard swings south for the eight-and-a-half-mile run to Punta Nizuc, where it makes a final turn toward the mainland and crosses the other bridge before meeting up with Avenida Tulum (Highway 307), the road to the airport and points south. Virtually everything of interest in the hotel zone is located on, or just off, Kukulcán, with distances along the boulevard indicated by kilometer markers positioned on the malls dividing its four lanes of traffic. (Downtown Cancún City is km 0 and the bridge at Punta Nizuc is km 23.)

The hotels and commercial complexes along the first few miles of Kukulcán, many dating back to the resort's early years, tend to be scaled-down in size and more modest in their pretensions than those built during the boom years of the eighties. Dense zoning and a mishmash of architectural styles combine to create a quasi–honky-tonk feel along the boulevard, while the informal restaurants in the area usually are more reasonably priced than those farther out on the island. This is also the home base for a variety of excursion craft and party boats, including the **Isla Mujeres shuttle**, which leaves from the **Playa Linda marine terminal** next to the bridge three times daily. (See the Getting Around section at the end of this chapter for shuttle details.)

The hotel zone begins to look almost residential as you near km 7.5 and the turnoff for the **Pok-Ta-Pok Golf Club**. The Robert Trent Jones–designed course is laid out on both sides of Kukulcán and takes up most of one of the arms of land separating Laguna Nichupté from the smaller Laguna Bojórquez. Time-shares and expensive private homes line many of the fairways, and a small Mayan ruin overlooks the water on the 12th hole. (The course is open to the public; for greens fees and tee times, see the Sports in Cancún section, below.)

Two of the prettiest beaches on the Bahía de Mujeres are located a few hundred years west of the golf course behind the Stouffer Presidente and Fiesta Americana Cancún hotels. Like all beaches in Mexico, these are government property and open to the public. Unfortunately, it doesn't always work that way in practice. If you have trouble getting onto either, you'll find the same powdery sand, jade-colored water, and gentle waves at **Playa Caracol**, situated just east of Punta Cancún between the Fiesta Americana and its sister hotel, the Fiesta Americana Coral Beach.

The **Punta Cancún** area is the closest thing to a hub that you'll find in Cancún's otherwise far-flung hotel zone. This was the site of the first shopping mall on the island—today completely overshadowed by the newer, upscale Plaza Caracol complex nearby—as well as a number of its original luxury hotels. Like fine wine, the Krystal, the Camino Real, and the Hyatt Regency have gotten better with age, in part because they've had to: The almost-new Fiesta Americana Coral Beach here has set standards of luxury that will be tough to surpass. The addition, across the boulevard, of a

state-of-the-art **convention center** on the site of the old center is further proof of the area's vitality, as is the nightly scene that unfolds along the shop-lined alleys of the Mayfair/Lagunas/Terramar/Caracol/Costa Blanca commercial complex.

Rounding the traffic circle at the point and heading south in the direction of Punta Nizuc you'll pass a solid wall of hotels and time-shares as well as a couple of busy marinas before reaching the **Plaza Flamingo** complex, at km 11, where Planet Hollywood is the newest addition to Cancún's nightlife. As recently as 1985 the long stretch of sand from here to Punta Nizuc was all but empty, with the Sheraton at km 12.5 the last of the big hotels before the dunes and scrub grass took over. Now the Sheraton is just one of a string of huge hotels lined up like battleships along the boulevard.

Generally speaking, the construction activity has been confined to the ocean side of Kukulcán, with most of the hotels set back from the road and surrounded by expanses of lawn (or, in the case of the Meliá Cancún and Oasis hotels, executive golf courses). But with a giant **handicrafts exposition** under construction opposite the Sheraton, this too is changing. Stores and restaurants out this way, on the other hand, are still scarce—or will be, at any rate, until the very large, very upscale **Plaza Kukulcán**, south of the Sheraton, is completed. In the meantime guests of these hotels must rely on taxis or public transportation whenever they want to do something off hotel grounds. (As a rule anything south of the Sheraton is more than walking distance from the stores and restaurants in the Punta Cancún area.) Fortunately, Cancún's public transportation system is inexpensive and efficient, and taxis are plentiful.

The **Ruinas del Rey**, one of the hotel zone's most interesting—and least visited—attractions, are situated between kilometer markers 17 and 18 at the widest part of the island. (Watch for a small sign on the lagoon side of the road.) The ruins, surrounded by lush jungle and overrun by harmless iguanas, are reminiscent of many small sites dotting the Quintana Roo coast and date to the Postclassic period (roughly A.D. 1100 to the early 16th century). The extant structures form two main complexes, the **El Rey group**, which lends its name to the site and was itself named for the large sculptured head discovered here by the English archaeologists Channing and Frost around the turn of the century; and, to the south, the smaller, less elaborate **Pinturas group**, named for an interior mural fragment that no longer exists. Most of the structures are low platforms with the remains of what were once rows of columns, and are organized along two broad avenues.

Structure 2, the site's only pyramidal mass, with rounded corners reminiscent of the two large pyramids at Cobá, squats on the northeast corner of the main plaza. (For a detailed description of Cobá, see the Cancún–Tulum Corridor section, below.) The most important structure here, **structure 3B**, is a few steps to the south on the same plaza, and appears to have been dedicated to the king or god for whom the site was named; if you look carefully you can still make out faint traces of mural painting on its façade and interior walls. There is a small entry fee to the site, and INAH-sanctioned guides usually are on hand to give tours for an additional fee.

Most days the only traffic out this way are the cars of sightseers who stop at the lookout point across the road; the beach below, **Playa del Rey**, is steeply sloped, usually deserted, and a perfect spot to picnic against a backdrop of pounding surf and electric-blue water. This, too, is destined to change: The Westin hotel group has plans to build a multimillion-dollar project north of the ruins on the lagoon side of the boulevard.

You'll find the last group of hotels and condos in the hotel zone clustered south of the ruins in the vicinity of **Punta Nizuc** (where, true to form, Club Med was the first hotel on the scene). Although conveniently located to the excellent snorkeling in the waters around the point, as well as the highway leading to Playa del Carmen, Tulum, and points south, these places are a *long* way from most of the stores, restaurants, and night spots in the hotel zone, and even farther from the affordable restaurants downtown. If you end up staying at one of them you'll want to think about renting a car for the duration of your stay; otherwise, be prepared to spend a lot of time on buses or money on taxis.

If you follow Boulevard Kukulcán west to Avenida Tulum and follow the latter north through town, you'll eventually come to **Puerto Juárez** (10 km/6 miles) and **Punta Sam** (15 km/9 miles). The former is the departure point for *passenger* ferries to Isla Mujeres, the latter the departure point for *automobile* ferries to the same destination.

In the opposite direction Avenida Tulum leads south from Cancún City to the airport and, in order, **Puerto Morelos** (the departure point for car ferries to Cozumel), **Playa del Carmen** (the departure point for passenger ferries to Cozumel), **Xcaret**, **Puerto Aventuras**, **Akumal**, **Chemuyil**, **Xcacel**, **Xel-há**, and **Tulum**—all points of interest in what has become known as the Cancún–Tulum corridor. A beautiful reef-sheltered stretch of coastline, the "corridor" has long been popular with budget travellers and a bohemian international crowd that revelled in its exquisite white-sand beaches and inexpensive palapa-style accommodations. Those days are nearly history, however. With planned upmarket resort properties like Puerto Aventuras and Playacar already in place and more to follow, it's only a matter of time before the corridor is transformed and its rustic charm disappears along with hotel rooms costing less than $100 a night. For those who like their sun and sand minus glitz and flashy trappings, the time to visit this special area—covered below, after Cancún—is now, before it's overwhelmed by development and industrial tourism.

Staying in the Zona Hotelera

From a vantage point on the southernmost tip of Isla Mujeres, Cancún's *zona hotelera* appears to float on the Caribbean like a realtor's vision of Emerald City: One high-priced ziggurat after another marches down the beach, with the density approaching Babylonian proportions around Punta Cancún. It's a sight that strikes terror in the hearts of budget travellers and intimidates just about everyone else. How do you choose from among so many lavish hotels? Do you go for the prettiest room? The biggest pool? The best beach? Or does it really matter?

If money is no object, then it really doesn't matter. At the top end of the market—and in Cancún's hotel zone there is no bottom end—almost every hotel, including those we discuss, delivers the goods. Rooms are comfortable, air-conditioned, and almost always tastefully decorated; the towels are soft and the TV is hooked up to a dish; and the activities begin before noon and continue well past the average guest's bedtime. For the most part even location is not an issue: Taxis and an excellent public transportation system pretty much put everything within reach.

Which leaves the matter of price. During the high season a room for less than $150 a night is as rare here as a gringo without a sunburn. We've included the Calinda Cancún, one of the few establishments to offer such an animal, and recommend that you book well in advance for the high season. The same holds true for most of the hotels mentioned below, although less-than-80-percent occupancy and a never-ending supply of rooms in the pipeline have made advance reservations a somewhat less urgent priority outside the peak Christmas and Easter holiday periods. In fact, recent off-seasons have seen a proliferation of very affordable package deals. If you don't mind sharing the pool or beach with young singles in their twenties and families on vacation, this can be a great time to visit. Just remember that hurricane season in the Caribbean usually begins in late August and can last well into October.

The **Club Las Velas Hotel Cancún**, on the lagoon just before the bridge, was one of the first deluxe hotels in Mexico to offer an all-inclusive program. (Prices include accommodations, meals and snacks, unlimited beverages, entertainment, use of all facilities, and tips and taxes.) A self-contained colonial-style village complete with tiled plazas, splashing fountains, and a profusion of bougainvillaea and hibiscus, Las Velas offers small but comfortable air-conditioned rooms in multi-story towers for one to three persons, or junior suites in two-story "villas" for up to four persons. The sprawling complex backs up to an arm of Laguna Nichupté, which here features jade-colored channels lined by mangroves—a watery maze ideal for exploring by kayak, canoe, or sailboat. Two pools and two small beaches, several restaurants (including one that stays open 24 hours), tennis courts, and a complete water-sports center round out the amenities. (Guests who want to swim in the ocean face a ten-minute walk to Playa Linda and the Bahía de Mujeres, on the other side of Kukulcán.) The daily schedule of activities includes water sports, aerobics, and Spanish classes, and the clientele is a diverse mix of all ages and temperaments, from young singles to retirees. With plenty of opportunities to meet and mingle, everyone seems to get along, and most guests return year after year.

The 470-room **Calinda Cancún Beach** (not to be confused with the Calinda Viva Cancún near Punta Cancún), the first hotel on the other side of the bridge, is perhaps the best bargain in the hotel zone. Rooms are pleasant if unspectacular, and come with color satellite TV, a choice of full- or king-size beds, and those harmless-looking but insidious contraptions known as servi-bars; the newer rooms in the tower next to the original building are much the better choice, however. When compared with the facilities at some of the theme parks masquerading as hotels elsewhere in the hotel zone, the Calinda's pool area and beach—the latter a flat stretch of sand lapped by the calm waters of the Bahía de Mujeres—may come as a bit of a disappointment, although they're more than adequate. The Calinda also has two restaurants, a couple of bars, a complete water-sports center, and in-house car-rental and travel agencies. Its location opposite the Playa Linda marina, a busy terminal for excursion boats and the **Isla Mujeres shuttle**, which chugs over to the "Isle of Women" three times daily, is a bonus, as is its proximity to downtown Cancún City and the eating and drinking spots near Punta Cancún, both just five minutes by taxi from the hotel's lobby.

Situated a few hundred yards west of the golf course within easy walking distance of the busy Punta Cancún area, the stylish, understated **Stouffer Presidente Cancún** was one of the first luxury hotels built in the hotel zone, and still attracts a loyal, well-fixed clientele. Surely one of the reasons is the hotel's jewel of a white-sand beach, shaded by palms and facing an expanse of shallow, brilliantly colored water. With its two swimming pools, five Jacuzzis, shimmering swim-through waterfall, and mandatory swim-up bar, the pool area is no slouch, either. Don't coming looking for loud music or a rowdy pool scene, however—guests of the Presidente like their sun served up with plenty of peace and quiet. The hotel's standard-size doubles, all recently remodeled, are priced according to view, with lower-floor rooms facing the lagoon and parking lot the least expensive and upper-floor rooms overlooking the Bahía de Mujeres the most expensive. All guests receive a complimentary newspaper and coffee with their wake-up call, although only guests who spring for one of the 15 club-floor suites will be able to read their paper on a balcony; most rooms here don't have them. Other club-floor amenities include a concierge, free Continental breakfasts, complimentary canapes in the evening, beefed-up security, and a variety of other services designed to make guests feel like visiting heads of state. The concept has been so popular, in fact, that the Presidente now offers the same kind of amenities in standard-size rooms (again, minus the balconies) on its fifth floor.

The 281-room **Fiesta Americana Cancún**, located opposite the Plaza Caracol complex on the Bahía de Mujeres, was the first of the chain's three hotels in Cancún, and the years—and an energetic management—have been kind to it. Every room here has its own terrace or balcony facing the bay, and all feature the chain's trademark rattan-and-pastel decor. The horseshoe-shaped Mediterranean-style complex cradles a pretty free-form pool dominated by a small island and palapa-covered restaurant. With loud (and often live) rock music piped through speakers in the afternoon, the pool area is especially popular with groups of young people. Things are a little quieter on the beach, a continuation of the one fronting the Stouffer Presidente, with the same powdery sand and multihued water. And when guests tire of soaking up the sun they're literally right across the street from the Mayfair/Terramar/Lagunas/Costa

Blanca/Caracol commercial complex, the greatest concentration of restaurants, bars, and stores in the hotel zone.

On the Bahía de Mujeres almost at the point itself, the 11-story all-suite **Fiesta Americana Coral Beach Cancún**, is the newest and, quite possibly, the most luxurious property in Cancún. From the seven-story atrium-style lobby to the seemingly endless corridors with their handsome artwork and muted lighting, the Coral Beach strives for the grand effect—and usually pulls it off. The standard room here is a junior suite with marble floors, separate living room and vanity areas, and a private bay-front balcony. (Although the views from the top-floor balconies are spectacular, guests with small children might want to request a room on one of the lower floors.) There are, in addition, 68 master suites equipped with in-room Jacuzzis and ten two-bedroom Caribbean suites. It's not until you start to poke around the premises, however, that the sheer size of the Coral Beach begins to sink in. Among the facilities and amenities at its guests' disposal are a 220-yard-long swimming pool, three swim-up pool bars, a handful of restaurants, an indoor tennis and racquetball complex, a health club and spa, a water-sports center, an upmarket shopping arcade, a barber shop and beauty salon, an indoor parking lot—well, you get the idea. In fact, with a new convention center under construction directly across the street, and the restaurants, bars, and stores of the Plaza Caracol complex a short stroll from the lobby, it's safe to say that the Coral Beach has something for everyone.

You'll find three of the hotel zone's best-known properties arranged around the point itself. Just east of the Coral Beach the low-slung **Camino Real** sits in splendid isolation, surrounded on two sides by the pounding surf of the Caribbean. A standard double in the main building comes with either a partial bay view or an ocean view (you'll pay a little more for the latter), a private balcony, and two doubles or a king-size bed; all rooms in the 16-story Royal Beach Club have balconies overlooking the ocean, as well as the usual complimentary club-floor services. Facilities spread out around the hotel's leafy grounds include a small saltwater lagoon, a pretty pool area, four lighted tennis courts, a shopping arcade, and a palm-fringed strech of beach facing the calm waters of the Bahía de Mujeres. (If you have the patience required to wade out to the end of the rock jetty, this is one of the best places in Cancún to snorkel.) What the Camino Real's many repeat guests really like, however, is the seclusion and privacy it affords—even as the point area buzzes with activity just minutes from its lobby.

Just around the point, the **Hyatt Regency Cancún** offers a somewhat different atmosphere. The hotel's spectacular 14-story atrium aside, the pool is the pièce de résistance here. Built-in lounges and drink tables allow guests to tan, cool off, and read the paper simultaneously, while the bar area upstairs overlooks the ocean and the nonstop activity at the Krystal Cancún pool next door. The Regency's standard double is offered at three prices—oceanfront, deluxe, and super-saver—and in-room amenities include color satellite TV, servi-bar, and hair dryer; most of the more expensive rooms also have private balconies. With its proximity to the stores and restaurants of the Punta Cancún area and room rates that are comparatively affordable, the Regency qualifies as one of the real bargains in the hotel zone. (Note that there are two Hyatts in the hotel zone. The Hyatt Caribe Cancún, the very first luxury hotel built on the island, is a few minutes' taxi ride to the south, in the direction of Punta Nizuc, and was completely renovated and reborn a few years ago as a posh "boutique" hotel property. This is also where you'll find the intimate **Blue Bayou** restaurant, one of Cancún's finest, specializing in Cajun cuisine.)

Everyone seems to stop in at the **Krystal Cancún**, next door to the Hyatt Regency, sooner or later. Maybe it's because it has a certain mystique—or maybe it's just to have their picture taken in front of the *faux*-Roman colonnade that overlooks the hotel's narrow strip of beach. Then again, when the live music starts to play in its lobby bars this is one of the liveliest spots in Cancún. Newly remodeled from top to bottom, the Krystal offers standard doubles with views of the lagoon—and a few, by request, with views of the ocean—along with the usual in-room amenities; none of the rooms has a balcony. Of course, an integral part of the Krystal experience is a romantic dinner at **Bogart's**, its *Casablanca*-inspired restaurant, followed by an evening of dancing at **Christine**, its flashy discotheque; see the Dining in the Zona Hotelera and Nightlife in Cancún sections, respectively, for additional details.

Located a couple of miles south of Punta Cancún at km 12.5, the **Sheraton Cancún Resort and Towers** is a sprawling, self-contained resort property with a little something for everyone, including three swimming pools, six tennis courts, half a dozen restaurants, and a shopping arcade. The more than 700 rooms here are spread among three seven-story "pyramids" and an eight-story "club" tower. Standard doubles are located in the pyramids and come with the usual amenities; none has a balcony, however, and fewer than half have ocean views. (To get a balcony you have to spring for one of the junior suites, which come with outdoor Jacuzzis and either an ocean or lagoon view.) The more expensive tower rooms all have balconies, as well as the usual club-floor amenities.

During the day the main pool is a noisy beehive of activity—and a rowdy hornet's nest during spring break—but there are two smaller pools on the grounds where a quieter, family atmosphere prevails. The Sheraton's Caribbean beach is also one of the widest and most gently sloping around, with less of an undertow than other beaches on this side of the island. And for archaeology buffs there's an 800-year-old Mayan ruin located on a high bluff at one end of the complex. Experts speculate that it functioned as a lighthouse for the sea-going Mayan traders who plied these often treacherous waters in the late Postclassic period. While the federal government has declared it off limits to all commercial schemes, guests and non-guests are welcome to explore it.

The **Cancún Palace**, half a mile south of the Sheraton, is a huge horseshoe-shaped hotel with more than 400 rooms and a multitiered pool area that always seems to be hosting a contest of some sort. In fact, unlike some hotels in Cancún, the Palace welcomes groups (they're notoriously aggressive promoters) and prides itself on its lively pool scene. The music doesn't start until 11:30 A.M., but when it does the activity is nonstop: volleyball, water polo, bikini contests, tequila contests—you name it, the Palace will try it. In pleasant contrast, the hotel's rooms and public areas are surprisingly attractive if not downright posh. There's a generous use of marble throughout, and every room has its own balcony, a pleasing peach-and-pastel decor, and large bathrooms with handsome wood trim. Seventy percent of the rooms face the ocean, with a variety of more expensively priced accommodations, from junior suites with Jacuzzis to lavish penthouses, also available. The hotel also is the home of **Los Golondrinas**, a casually intimate colonial-style dining room specializing in traditional (and pricey) Mexican dishes.

Last but not least, at km 16.5, the **Meliá Cancún** (not to be confused with its sister hotel, the Meliá Turquesa) is distinguished by its pyramidal Plexiglas roofline and a soaring atrium lobby filled with tall fluted columns, tropical vegetation, and clusters of attractive seat groupings. If the Spanish owners of this space-age château were hoping to create an oasis of civility in the middle of Cancún's vacation jungle, they've succeeded. Standard rooms, each with its own balcony, separate sitting area, and full range of amenities, display a similar attention to guests' comfort. In fact, if there's a single telling complaint about the Meliá it's that it is "beautiful but boring." Of course, with an 18-hole executive-style golf course in their front yard and another right next door at the Oasis, golfers may beg to differ. Greens fees at both run about $20 per person.

Dining in the Zona Hotelera

Maxime, next to the Hotel Casa Maya at km 5.5, puts you in mind of a French official's home deep in the tropics. (This was once the home of one of Cancún's mayors.) Pretty pastels and floral wallpaper, French country furniture, big picture windows, and better-than-average French cuisine make for a pleasant change of pace from the usual hotel dining experience—though you'll find the price of the soothing, refined ambience reflected in your bill. Reservations advised; Tel: (98) 83-0704 or 0438.

Everyone drops by **Carlos 'n Charlie's,** opposite the Casa Maya on Kukulcán, at least once while they're in Cancún, and no one seems to mind that the raised dining room gets hot or that the nachos-burgers-fajitas fare is a little pricey. But then, dinner is hardly the main event here. After a bite to eat most people head over to the open-air arena-like dance floor, either to watch or to become part of the boisterous crowd. The (sometimes) live music keeps the place jumping until the wee hours, and a no-reservation policy prevails, so be prepared to wait in line, especially on weekends.

Señor Frog's, right next door, is the second of the three Anderson group gold mines in Cancún, and the hottest (literally) singles' spot around. Live reggae music, an impossibly crowded dance floor, and no ventilation appear to be the keys to its success. Come for a casual lunch and enjoy the view; come to dance and be prepared to sweat.

Jalapeño's, located just before the turnoff to the golf course, is the kind of place where rowdy diners compete with the waiters to see who can make the most noise. The seafood is better than average, however, not to mention less expensive than at some of the fancier restaurants in the hotel zone; the restaurant also offers a reasonably priced breakfast and lunch menu. And, like Señor Frog's and half a dozen other places in Cancún, it has jumped on the reggae bandwagon, with a no-cover-charge policy and live music on weekends.

The greatest concentration of restaurants in the hotel zone is found in the Mayfair/Terramar/Lagunas/Costa Blanca/

Caracol complex just west of the point. Like its brethren in other cities, the **Hard Rock Café** here serves up rock-and-roll as religion along with burgers, sandwiches, and fajitas. Lines begin to form long before the live music starts at 11:00 P.M., and the Hard Rock doesn't take reservations; go early if you want to avoid the crush, or go for lunch and enjoy its dark, air-conditioned ambience in relative privacy.

For a completely different experience, head over to the pretty but partially vacant La Mansion–Costa Blanca mall, where two restaurants owned and operated by the same group have carved out niches for themselves. On the ground floor, the **Restaurante El Mexicano** offers mariachi and folkloric shows nightly, except Sundays, to go along with its pricey regional Mexican dishes (you're paying for the show). The mariachis play at 6:00 P.M., the folkloric ballet begins at 8:00; and there's live music and entertainment from 9:15 on. Tel: (98) 84-4261 or 3-2220 for reservations and ask for a table on the floor. Upstairs, **La Veranda**, an elegant room featuring wood trim and lots of glass brick, specializes in fresh seafood and quality prime rib at big-city prices. Open for dinner only; Tel: (98) 84-1272 or 1569 for reservations.

For the moment, the two-story glass-enclosed Plaza Caracol, right next door to the Costa Blanca mall, has more fine restaurants and upscale boutiques than any other commercial complex in Cancún. In no particular order, visitors can choose from among the following: **Karl's Keller**, which doesn't look like much when approached from inside the mall but has a breezy sidewalk café out back. Karl's specializes in authentic German cuisine (sauerbraten, wienerschnitzel, rouladen), and also has a little bit of everything else on the menu, including steaks, seafood, and standard Mexican dishes. The cozy, casually intimate **Casa Rolandi** features Swiss-Italian cuisine prepared in a wood-burning brick oven. Specialties include fish cooked in salt, charcoal-broiled lamb brochette, and goat with rosemary. It also has a good wine list. Reservations recommended; Tel: (98) 83-1817.

On the Bahía de Mujeres side of the mall you'll find the upscale and ever-popular **Savio's**, a pretty place with a green-and-white decor, lots of plants, and umbrella-shaded tables under an atrium-style arcade. Refined northern Italian cuisine shares the menu with such appetizers as sliced salmon in a dill vinaigrette, quail-liver pâté, cèpes, and oysters Rockefeller. Open for lunch and dinner; Tel: (98) 83-2085 for dinner reservations.

At the far end of the mall under the same arcade, trendy **Iguana Wana** gets your attention with black-and-white-checked tablecloths, lots of palm trees, and a bank of six TVs at the bar. In addition to steak, seafood, or nouvelle-style Mexican dishes, you can choose from a reasonably priced raw-bar/*tapas* menu featuring such items as mushrooms in garlic, crab-meat or conch fritters, and chicken wings. Iguana Wana is also one of the better spots in Cancún for a late-night snack; open for lunch and dinner; Tel: (98) 83-0829.

You'll find the original **Bogart's** on the far side of the Punta Cancún traffic circle in the Krystal (see the Staying in the Zona Hotelera section, above, for a description of the hotel itself). Though it is is no longer unique (others have opened in Ixtapa and Puerto Vallarta), the layout of this Bogart's somehow makes it more appealing than its successors. The decor is a Hollywood art director's idea of Moroccan, complete with peacock chairs, shimmering fountains, and live piano music. The prices may be high, the service a bit snooty, and the food not as good as it should be on some nights, but it's worth trying all the same. Tel: (98) 83-1133 for reservations.

For an altogether different experience head over to the **Hacienda El Mortero**, the Krystal's other "theme" restaurant, located a short walk from the hotel's lobby in the direction of Punta Nizuc. The ambience here suggests the gracious living of the colonial period, with the building itself a scaled-down replica of the 17th-century Hacienda El Mortero, in the northern state of Durango. Inside, crisp linens, pastel walls, and muted lighting enhance the stylish surroundings. The pricey menu features haute Mexican cuisine as well as a variety of international specialties, accompanied by the music of a polished mariachi band. It's not all that authentic but it is fun. Reservations recommended; Tel: (98) 83-1133.

Although it's the tamest of the three Anderson group restaurants in the hotel zone, you'll find the familiar menu and waiters' pranks at the **Guadalajara Grill**, on the boulevard at km 9.5. The dining room opens to the lagoon, there's a small dance floor under the stars, and the five fountains off the open-air terrace make this a popular spot for snapshots. Come for a sunset drink or a late-night twirl, but save your appetite for elsewhere.

Two of the most frequented restaurants in the hotel zone are tucked away on the southeastern corner of Laguna Bojórquez, half a mile to the south. Even though **Gypsy's Pampered Pirate** sits on stilts over the water, don't expect much of a view. Gypsy's customers are crowded together at closely spaced tables with only ceiling fans and open windows to keep them cool, and the simple menu is limited to fish, chicken, and lobster (the house specialty). The cramped quarters usually translate into mediocre service, with dinner slow to arrive and quick to be cleared. Which leaves Gypsy's reasonable prices and twice-nightly flamenco show as the likely reasons for its continued popularity. The shows (7:30 and 9:30 P.M.) last half an hour, feature three lovely young women, and are worth the $2 admission price. Gypsy's also serves one of the cheapest ($4.95) breakfast buffets in the hotel zone. Dinner reservations recommended; Tel: (98) 83-2015 or 2120.

Lorenzillo's, right next door, is a big, noisy barn of a place trimmed out with lots of dark mahogany, brass ship's fittings, and potted plants. Reserve a table outside overlooking the lagoon (and the large fish cruising for scraps), but go early and plan to have a drink at the bar. Despite the only average food and the sometimes-less-than-swift service, this was one of the first restaurants on the scene, and repeat visitors remain loyal to it; Tel: (98) 83-1254.

The most elegant restaurant in the handsome Plaza Flamingo is **Seryna**, a quiet and expensive *teppanyaki*-style Japanese place with a sushi bar; Tel: (98) 85-1155 or 83-2904. **Pat O'Brien's**, the newest drinking-and-dining spot in the same complex, is a New Orleans–based watering hole with a piano lounge and a pretty open-air patio overlooking the lagoon. Its basic saloon menu features a tasty steak sandwich, brochetes, fajitas, and salads, all for under ten dollars, and the lounge is the only place in the hotel zone where you can listen to live jazz (on occasion). **Los Rancheros** and **Mr. Papa's**, side by side with outdoor seating overlooking the boulevard, are good spots for reasonably priced burgers, burritos, and beer. There's also a fast-food courtyard here where you can munch on pizza, nachos, frozen yogurt, and Big Macs.

Non-hotel restaurants south of the Sheraton are few and far between, although that will change when the Plaza Kukulcán opens for business sometime during 1993. For now the sole exception to this state of affairs is the **Captain's Cove**, on the lagoon side of Kukulcán opposite the Fiesta Americana Condesa, Oasis, and Omni hotels. (There's another branch on the beach between the Hotel Casa Maya and Club International.) Nothing fancy here—just a pleasant dining room and porch open to the lagoon, expertly prepared ribs and steaks, and a good selection of fresh seafood. You'll want to come early for dinner: The Cove is an excellent spot for sunset watching, and they don't take reservations. They also offer a very good (and popular) breakfast buffet for only $5.

Shopping in the Zona Hotelera

Although it may come as a surprise to serious shoppers who haven't visited recently, Cancún's shops and boutiques in general, and those in the hotel zone in particular, have noticeably upgraded the quality of their merchandise over the last few years. Designer resortwear, leather goods and perfume, jewelry, and quality handicrafts are all widely available—at top-drawer prices.

Most people start their perambulations at the air-conditioned **Plaza Caracol**, where downstairs you'll find **Aca Joe**, with the best-folded selection of resortwear in Cancún; **Gucci**; **Fila**; **Boutique Soqui**, for jewelry and well-known Mexican designer labels (Sucesos, Girasol, Judith Roberts); **Toes**, for belts and sandals; **Alan's**, for Guatemalan bags and belts; **Las Mañanitas**, with a small but tastefully displayed selection of handicrafts; **The Leather Shop**, for handwoven blankets; and **Extra**, a five-and-dime with a little bit of everything, including archaeological guidebooks, makeup, suntan lotion, and a pharmacy. Upstairs, in addition to a pleasant little café under skylights, you'll find **Polo** by Ralph Lauren; **Guess**; **Cartier**; and **Xaman-Ek** (The Bird Sanctuary), with a large selection of papier-mâché handicrafts (mostly birds).

Next door the pretty but hard-to-find **La Mansion—Costa Blanca** mall offers some of the most interesting shopping in the hotel zone. **La Iguana**, right off the front entrance, has a terrific selection of lacquered platters and boxes from Olinala, in the state of Guerrero, among other handicraft items. The markup is steep, but the sales clerks make up for it with their knowledge and helpfulness. Opposite La Iguana, **Mayan** has an unusual (and unusually expensive) selection of Mayan-style artifacts made from a variety of materials, including jade, onyx, mother-of-pearl, and obsidian. Off the mall's interior patio **Via Veneto** offers a nice selection of jewelry and fine leather products. **Mordo** (with outlets in the Plaza Caracol and Plaza Flamingo) has a large selection of Mexican-made leather boots, shoes, jackets, and Western accessories. And, tucked away in the farthest reaches of the mall, **La Galería** is the place for etchings of Mayan carvings as well as limestone replicas of carvings by the artist Gilberto Silva.

Visitors staying farther out on the island who don't want to go as far as the Punta Cancún area can take care of most of their needs at the neo-Mayan–style **Plaza Flamingo**, km 11 on the boulevard opposite the Continental Villas Plazas. In addition to such well-known names as Guess, Gucci, Girbaud, Mordo (leather), Los Castillo (silversmiths from

Taxco), and **Gold's Gym** (free weights for serious body builders), shoppers will also find the following of interest: **Arte Mexicano**, with a good selection of lacquered wood trays from Olinala as well as the usual assortment of mass-produced onyx, glasswear, and the like; **Original 60**, for hip resortwear made from colorful Guatemalan textiles; **Bond** and **Michel Domet**, for shoes; **Martí**, a sporting goods store that carries everything from bathing suits to fishing tackle; **La Casa del Habano**, for Cuban cigars; and **Kodak Express**, for film and a good selection of American magazines.

CANCUN CITY

Downtown Cancún is no longer the rough-and-ready place it was in the early 1970s, when only 200 people—most of them construction workers—called it home. Today its resident population is closer to 400,000—spurred to a large extent by the lowest unemployment rate in the Mexican republic—and the city limits continue to expand to the north and west. What has been a boon for Mexican workers has also resulted in a bonus for tourists, as more and more of them venture farther into town and discover, among the many lively bars and colorful street performers, some very good restaurants.

One thing hasn't changed over the years, however. For reasons known only to a higher authority, the downtown area is a congested maze of cul-de-sacs and traffic circles. Fortunately, most of the restaurants and bars catering to tourists are within walking distance of the Plaza Jose Martí, at the intersection of Avenidas Cobá and Nader, or up the street and around the corner on or just off Avendia Tulum, the city's main north–south drag.

While a number of its neighbors have closed their doors in recent years, the **Fonda del Angel**, Cobá 32, has prospered by sticking to the basics: a plain but appealing decor, reasonably priced entrées, and great margaritas. The menu features traditional Mexican fare tailored to *norteamericano* tastes, and the ambience is as relaxed as the staff is solicitous. Come early and stay as long as you like; you'll never feel rushed here. Tel: (98) 84-3393.

La Dolce Vita, a few steps up at Cobá 87, is a busy tropical-style trattoria with an appealingly sophisticated atmosphere. White wicker furniture, pretty peach-colored linens, and waiters in black and white set the tone in the two rooms here—one a trellis-covered patio open to the street, the other an enclosed dining room with ceiling fans. The Italian specialties on the menu tend more toward nouvelle than home-style, though the chef sometimes uses garlic with reckless abandon. You'll want to dress up a little and make reservations a day or two in advance. Dinner only. Tel: (98) 84-1384.

The downtown hustle and bustle begins after you cross Avenida Nader heading toward Avenida Tulum. First up on the corner here is **Pizza Rolandi**, Cobá 12, serving breakfast and daily specials in addition to Cancún's best pizza. At the **Fish Market**, right next door, customers choose their fish or lobster from iced-down displays and then watch as it's baked or charbroiled to their liking on the spot; Tel: (98) 84-4180. **Risky Business**, around the corner, opens for happy hour at 6:00 P.M., stays open till the wee hours, and is a favorite late-night destination of young partyers, many of whom stumble up the street after it closes to have breakfast at **Mi Ranchito**. The latter is open for lunch and dinner as well, and offers the same kind of waiters' pranks, rowdy atmosphere, and tacos-fajitas-burger fare that you'll find at the Anderson group establishments in the hotel zone.

Souvenir hunters will want to rummage through the **Ki-Huic** market around the corner on Avenida Tulum. Ki-Huic's maze of stalls has every trinket you'd expect to find, at prices slightly higher than you'd pay for them in other resorts. (Everything has to travel a little farther to get to this corner of the Yucatán.) *Huipiles,* hammocks (usually machine made), and sisal bags are among the regionally produced items sold here.

Lined with inexpensive hotels and busy restaurants, the one-way side streets on the opposite side of Avenida Tulum lately have become crowded with budget-minded diners and visitors looking for a change of pace. In most cases reservations aren't needed (although we've included phone numbers for people who want to call ahead for directions). Among the more popular restaurants here is **La Posta**, Crisantemos 10, for Tex-Mex specialties and American-style cuts of beef in a setting that recalls Mexico's revolutionary past. Tel: (98) 84-2105.

Charming little **Cenacolo**, one street over at Claveles 26, bills itself as "the best-kept secret in Cancún," even though it's not that hard to find: Just take Claveles off Avendia Tulum and turn right at the corner. White stucco walls, candlelight, and soft music establish the mood for the lovingly prepared northern Italian specialties that follow, while the service is prompt without being obtrusive. The cappelletti fettucini with lobster sauce is a house specialty, and at $13 (before the wine) it's also a bargain. Tel: (98) 84-1591. On the next block over at Tuliapanes 20, **Don Emiliano** has been serving its moderately priced seafood, meat, and Mexican specialties for nine years. Don Emiliano is not as noisy as some of its neighbors on the street, and strolling guitarists enhance its mellow dinnertime atmosphere. Tel: (98) 84-4448.

Still farther off the beaten track but a longtime favorite nevertheless, **La Habichuela** (The Stringbean) offers a wonderfully relaxing atmosphere that's all too rare in this manically modern resort. Located down the block from the town square at Margaritas 25, two blocks west of Avenida Tulum, it has been around almost as long as Cancún has been a resort, and specializes in moderately expensive seafood, Yucatecan, and traditional Mexican dishes. This is a place you'll want to dress up for, and reservations are recommended. Ask for a table on the romantic garden patio, however, as the handsome wood-trimmed dining room is not air-conditioned. Tel: (98) 84-3158.

Back on Avenida Tulum, **Pop**, next to city hall, sells toiletries and sundries imported from the United States at exorbitant prices; it's also the closest thing to an American-style cafeteria in greater Cancún, with a reasonably priced menu that includes hamburgers and milkshakes as well as enchiladas and huevos rancheros.

Several shopping malls and a number of hotels popular with budget-conscious travellers—the Hotel América, on the southeast corner of Tulum and Cobá, is the nicest—have opened downtown in recent years. Generally speaking, their rates reflect the fact they're not on the beach, which can be anywhere from five to 20 minutes away by car or taxi, depending on the beach. But then, everything seems to be more economical downtown.

Nightlife in Cancún

With the exception of Acapulco, Cancún offers the willing visitor more nightlife than any resort in Mexico. The fun usually begins in the hotel zone, where most of the big hotels offer some kind of evening entertainment in their lobby areas. From there it's on to dinner and a floor show. The most lavish is staged at the Continental Villas Plaza, opposite the Plaza Flamingo, where Silvia Lozano's **Ballet Folklórico Nacional Aztlán** holds forth nightly at 7:00 P.M. The price is $48 per person and includes dinner, drinks, the show, and all tips. Other dinner shows in the hotel zone include the mariachi bands and folkloric ballet at the Restaurante El Mexicano in La Mansion–Costa Blanca mall, and the twice-nightly flamenco shows at Gypsy's Pampered Pirate, on the lagoon side of Boulevard Kukulcán between Punta Cancún and the Plaza Flamingo.

Visitors who'd rather star in their own floor show have a choice of three state-of-the-art discotheques in the hotel zone, all of which stay open until the sun comes up. **Christine**, at the Krystal Cancún, attracts a well-dressed crowd with money to spend. **Dady'O**, located just beyond Christine at km 9.5 on the boulevard, and **La Boom**, on the lagoon side of Kukulcán before the bridge, are popular with a slightly younger, less sophisticated crowd.

There are, in addition, any number of less formal spots popular with hard-partying singles. Casual attire is the rule at these places, and many charge a small cover. The current favorite seems to be **Tequila Sunrise**, overlooking the Hard Rock Café and the open area at the heart of the Mayfair/Terramar/Lagunas/Caracol/Costa Blanca complex. (This courtyard-like area functions as a sort of "quad away from campus" during spring break. Other favorites include the aforementioned **Señor Frog's**, with live reggae music nightly, and **Carlos 'n Charlie's**, with an open-air dance floor, taped rock 'n' roll, and the occasional live act. You'll find the last two conveniently located next door to each other on the lagoon side of Kukulcán, opposite the Hotel Casa Maya. **Jalapeño's**, also on the lagoon side of the boulevard, just before the turnoff to the golf course, is another popular spot featuring live reggae music.

Guests at the big hotels out past the Sheraton often start their evenings at **Sixties**, in the Marriot CasaMagna, where the deejay spins "classic" rock tunes from 6:00 to 10:00 P.M. nightly, and then move on to the **Guadalajara Grill**, on the lagoon between the Plaza Flamingo and Punta Cancún, where the scene is a little less feverish than those at Carlos 'n Charlie's or "Froggy's." As things begin to wind down in the hotel zone, the truly dedicated jump in cabs and head downtown, where they usually finish the evening dancing to (you guessed it) live reggae at **Cats**, Avenida Yaxchilán 12, or taped rock-'n'-roll favorites at **Risky Business**, Avenida Tulum 13A.

Sports in Cancún

In addition to its an extensive lagoon system, Cancún faces the northern fringes of the second-longest coral reef in the world (extending from Isla Contoy, 30 miles north of the resort, to the Gulf of Honduras, off the coast of Belize). It's no surprise then that the resort is a nearly perfect destination for watersports lovers. Waterskiing, windsurfing, scuba diving, snorkeling, deep-sea fishing, jet-skiing, even kayaking—all can be arranged at the marinas scattered around the hotel zone. If your hotel doesn't have a water-sports center the following will be able to help:

Marina Aqua Ray (Tel: 98/83-3007, 1763, or 1773), next to Lorenzillo's at km 10.5 on the boulevard, offers a full range of services, from guided tours of the bird-filled mangrove jungles rimming Laguna Nichupté ($35 per person) to waterskiing on the glassy waters of the lagoon itself ($60/hour). The **Royal Mayan Yacht Club** at Captain's Cove (closed Saturdays; Tel: 98/85-0391), midway between Punta Cancún and Punta Nizuc, is another full-service outfit renting everything from windsurfers ($60/day) to jet skis ($50/hour). **Marina Jet Ski**, on the lagoon opposite the convention center (closed Sundays; Tel: 98/83-0766), specializes in motorized equipment, from jet skis and waterski boats to flights on ultralights. **Krystal Divers**, at the Krystal Cancún (Tel: 98/83-1133, ext. 500), and **Scuba Cancún** (Tel: 98/83-1011), opposite Vacation Clubs International, near the bridge, will be happy to help with your scuba needs.

For snorkeling excursions to the reefs off **Punta Nizuc**—something every visitor to Cancún should do at least once—try the Marina Aqua Ray or Royal Mayan Yacht Club at Captain's Cove (see above); the **Marina Punta del Este** in front of the Hyatt Cancún Caribe (daily; Tel: 98/84-4551 or 7-4039); the yacht club at **Carlos 'n Charlie's** (daily; Tel: 98/87-4643, 4-5352, or 3-1304); the **Villas Cerdena Marina** (Tel: 98/84-4913) behind La Boom discotheque; or the **San Marino Marina** (Tel: 98/83-1379) behind the Plaza Nautilus. In addition to getting you out to the reefs, all will be able to supply you with snorkeling equipment (for an extra charge), though there's no guarantee it will fit properly.

Deep-sea-fishing boats can be chartered at most of the marinas listed above. Or try **Cancún Avioturismo** at the Casa Maya Hotel (Tel: 98/83-0315); **Sunset Tours** in the Sheraton (Tel: 98/85-0329, ext. 2020) or the Plaza Flamingo (Tel: 98/85-1113 or 1107); **Club de Pesca Pez Vela** (Tel: 98/83-0992); or the **Playa Linda marina** (Tel: 98/83-0062 or 0884).

Most of the big hotels and time-share resorts have their own tennis courts. This being the tropics, however, court time is at a premium during certain hours of the day (early morning and late afternoon). Although it's rarely a problem, tennis players who want to avoid getting shut out should check their hotel's court-reservation policy when booking a room.

The golf boom has yet to be lowered on Cancún, though it's swinging this way: As part of the multi-million-dollar property it plans to construct north of the ruins, the Westin hotel group will build a new championship course. In the meantime, the 6,700-yard **Pok-Ta-Pok Golf Club** at km 7.5 on the boulevard is a fine track, even if it tends to get burned out during the peak tourist season (which coincides with the driest time of the year). But then, as somebody once said, golf in the tropics is a game for mad dogs and Floridians. Greens fees are $50 per person; figure on another $30 for the cart. Generally speaking, you don't have to worry about reserving tee times, although it's not a bad idea. Tel: (98) 83-1230 or 1277; Fax: (98) 83-3358.

For those torn between the siren call of the links and Cancún's beautiful sand and water, the **Meliá Cancún** and **Oasis** hotels have their own 18-hole executive courses—a good way to get your fix without sacrificing the better part of the day in the process. Greens fees at both run about $20. For the Meliá, Tel: (98) 85-1114; for the Oasis, Tel: (98) 85-0867.

Finally, there are two outfits in the Cancún area offering guided horseback tours of the tropical forest. Located at km 11.5 of the Cancún–Chetumal highway (Highway 307), between downtown Cancún and the airport, the **Hacienda San José de las Vegas** (Tel: 98/84-0373 or a travel agent) runs four two-hour tours (8:30 and 10:30 A.M., and 12:30 and 2:30 P.M.) daily, except Sundays (when horses can be rented by the hour). The horses generally are well-behaved, and the price of the tour includes transportation to and from your hotel, the services of a bilingual guide, and beer and soda. At the **Rancho Loma Bonita** (Tel: 98/84-0861), located half an hour south of Cancún between Puerto Morelos and Playa del Carmen, visitors can choose between a five-hour jungle tour (one tour daily; departure time 8:00 A.M.) or horseback riding on one of the beautiful white-sand beaches in the area (daily from 10:30 A.M. to 3:30 P.M. or 1:30 to 6:30 P.M.). The cost includes transportation to and from your hotel, the services of a bilingual guide, lunch, and beverages. For both, it's recommended you bring a pair of long pants and tennis shoes; if you opt for horseback riding on the beach, be sure to bring a bathing suit and towel.

Excursions In and Around Cancún

Excursion boats of every size and shape ply the waters around Cancún, with the nearby island of Isla Mujeres their most popular destination. Many of these boats stop at El Garrafón, a sadly overcrowded marine park at the southern end of Isla Mujeres, for a couple of hours of snorkeling before heading on to a beach-lunch rendezvous and a slate of loosely organized activities elsewhere on the island. It can be a diverting way to spend a day (the changing shades of water in the Bahía de Mujeres are reason enough to go), but only if you're prepared to spend the day with rowdy Americans in their twenties. (For more on Isla Mujeres, see the separate section below.)

Fairly typical of these cruises is the one offered aboard the "SS *Stela*." The *Stela* departs daily at 9:00 A.M. from its own pier at Playa Tortugas (between the Hotel Casa Maya and Villas Tacul), swings across the bay and stops at Garrafón for an hour or two, drops its passengers for lunch at the Hacienda de Gomar (a pretty place with palapa-covered tables on the sand and a lawn area shaded by a stand of palms), then shuttles them into Isla's small downtown area for another hour or two of souvenir hunting before returning to Cancún in time for happy hour. An open bar and lunch is included in the price, approximately $42 per person. For reservations, Tel: (98) 84-2882 or 4-3095.

Other boats that do much the same thing include:

The air-conditioned *Tropical Cruiser* (Tel: 98/83-1488), which departs daily (except Sundays) at 8:30 A.M. from the Playa Langosta dock (next to Vacation Clubs International) and returns by 3:30 P.M. (they claim to be the first outfit to arrive at Garrafón, a factor worth considering). An open bar, use of snorkel equipment, and lunch at "Pirate's Village," a sort of beachside amusement park, are included in the cost, about $42 per person. The *Fiesta Maya* (Tel: 98/83-0389 or 3-1804) departs daily from its own pier on Laguna Bojórquez near the Stouffer Presidente; the $30 cost per person includes breakfast, lunch, a semi-open bar, and an hour and a half of snorkeling at Garrafón. The *Aqua II* (Tel: 98/84-1057 or 4-3194) departs daily (except Saturdays) from the Playa Linda marina (near the bridge) and includes a Continental breakfast, buffet lunch, and open bar for about $35 per person.

For something a little different you can take the same trip on a 60-passenger trimaran. The *Aqua-quin* (Tel: 98/83-1883 or 3-0100) departs daily from the Camino Real pier at 11:00 A.M. A buffet lunch, open bar, and snorkeling at Garrafón are included in the cost, about $40 per person.

The Isla Mujeres excursion can also be done after dark as a sort of theme party. The "Treasure Island" cruise departs every evening (except Sundays) at 5:30 from the Playa Langosta dock. A pretty sunset cruise across the bay is followed by dinner and dancing at Pirate's Village, with the boat returning to Cancún by 11:00 P.M. The cost per person is $42.

For reservations, Tel: (98) 83-1488. The same kind of evening with a Caribbean twist (different costumes, limbo contest, Afro-Caribbean dinner show) is offered on board the *Carnivale,* which departs from the Hotel Club Verano Beat dock, west of the bridge, daily at 6:00 P.M., returning by 11:00. Again, the cost per person is approximately $42. For reservations, Tel: (98) 84-3760.

A more sedate version of the standard sunset cruise is offered on board the *Columbus,* a 62-foot motorized replica of the *Niña* that tools around the lagoon while its passengers enjoy an open bar and three-course dinner (featuring charcoal-grilled steak or lobster). The *Columbus* sails daily (except Sundays) at 4:00 P.M. from the Royal Mayan Yacht Club opposite the Oasis and Omni hotels, returning around 7:30, with the cost per person approximately $50. Reservations recommended; Tel: (98) 83-1021.

In many ways, a trip to **Isla Contoy**, a remote national park and bird sanctuary north of Isla Mujeres, is a more worthwhile excursion than those mentioned above, affording those who take it the chance to see spectacular fauna above and below the water, as well as the scrubby *selva* of the northern Yucatán in a relatively undisturbed state. As an excursion from Cancún, however, it's a long haul there and back, with the time spent snorkeling and birding the first thing to be sacrificed (especially when rough water lengthens travel time to the island). You'll get more of both if you do Contoy as a full day trip from Isla Mujeres (necessitating an overnight on Isla itself). If your travel plans won't accommodate an overnight on Isla Mujeres but you're determined to see Contoy, the 50-foot motor yacht *Thundergoat* makes the trip daily (except Sundays), leaving from the Playa Linda dock at 9:00 A.M. and returning by 5:00 P.M. The cost of the excursion, about $80 per person, includes an open bar on the boat, snorkeling en route, and a full lunch on the beach. For reservations, Tel: (98) 87-1909 or 87-1862.

A day trip to **Cozumel**, Mexico's largest island and a world-renowned diving and snorkeling spot, is another popular option. The standard travel agency package will provide round-trip transportation to and from your hotel, a few hours' snorkeling at Chankanaab Lagoon National Park, a few hours' in the island's only town, a visit to a black-coral factory to see jewelry being made, lunch, and beverages for about $75 per person. Or you can get to know the island and its friendly inhabitants on your own: Aerocaribe (Tel: 98/84-2000), the "air bridge," flies to Cozumel from the Cancún airport—a 15-minute flight—nine times daily. (For more on Cozumel, see the separate section below.)

Sunset Tours (Tel: 98/85-1113 or 85-1107) or **Intermar Caribe** (Tel: 98/84-4266), both with a number of offices around town and in the hotel zone, will be happy to arrange any of these cruises and/or excursions. Or you can contact the travel agent at your hotel. Both also run day trips to the ruins at Tulum and the natural aquarium of Xel-há (see below); the impressive Maya-Toltec ruins at Chichén Itzá; and the beautiful Late Classic ruins at Uxmal, with a stop in historic Mérida for lunch and sightseeing (see the Mayan Mexico chapter for more on Chichén Itzá, Uxmal, and Mérida).

THE CANCUN–TULUM CORRIDOR

Although it would take several vacations to see and do everything Cancún has to offer, not everyone falls in love with its flashy façade and materialistic soul. For many, Cancún is simply too familiar to be much fun; after a few chance encounters with friends of friends from back home, some people begin to crave something different, something a little more... authentic. It wasn't too many years ago that excursions to the Yucatán's ancient Mayan sites offered just such an opportunity. And to a large extent they still do, especially if you rent a car and take the time to linger in some of the small towns and villages along the way. These days, however, the more spectacular sites—Uxmal, Chichén Itzá, and Tulum in particular—are thoroughly commercialized (Uxmal less so than the other two) and usually overrun by tour groups.

Similarly, the coast south of Cancún, with its beautiful white-sand beaches and sheltering offshore reef, was until recently the almost exclusive preserve of its Mayan inhabitants and a few beachcombers and affluent divers. But this, too, has changed. Fonatur is said to have targeted 28 sites along the coast for future development; new resorts, condominium complexes, and tourist attractions are multiplying like mushrooms; and the whole area is on the verge of being marketed under a label that travel agents will love: the Turquoise Coast.

But if the future of the Cancún–Tulum corridor is large-scale tourism, the present is still all about abundant sunshine, relatively uncrowded beaches, and a diverse if funky mix of accommodations. Development pressure aside, the area as a whole is worlds apart from the luxury (and expense) of Cancún, and is likely to appeal to visitors who are left cold by the latter's soullessness.

Heading south out of Cancún, Avenida Tulum becomes Highway 307, a smooth two-lane road that follows the coast to the archaeological site of Tulum, 131 km (81 miles) distant. Along the way you'll pass numerous dirt roads leading off to your left; generally speaking, the more potholed the road, the more deserted the beach at the end of it. There is regular bus service between Cancún and Tulum (and points in between), but schedules tend to be erratic and the broiling Yucatecan sun is a match for even the hardiest traveller. A rental car, on the other hand, will give you the freedom to explore the beaches and other attractions in the area at your leisure. Before leaving Cancún, be sure to fill the tank; gas stations in the corridor are relatively rare.

Puerto Morelos, situated some 36 km (22 miles) south of Cancún, is of little interest for travellers except as the departure point for *car* ferries to Cozumel—an option best exercised by those with plenty of time on their hands. The ferry makes the four-hour trip once a day and has been known not to run at all during extended stretches of bad weather.

Just south of the turnoff to Puerto Morelos, on the same side of the highway, you'll see a sign and wrought-iron gate marking the entrance to the **Jardín Botánico Dr. Alfredo Barrera Marin**. Natural-history buffs as well as those simply looking to beat the heat are welcome to explore the more than seven miles of trails and 150 acres of semi-tropical forest here. The gardens are open from 9:00 A.M. to 4:00 P.M. daily; admission is about $2. The turnoff for the **Rancho Loma Bonita**, which offers horseback tours of the surrounding *selva* and nearby beaches—another way to get acquainted with the rich flora and fauna of the area—is 12 km (8 miles) farther down the road. (See the Sports in Cancún section above for details on the ranch's guided tours.)

Playa del Carmen

Located 68 km (42 miles) south of Cancún, this oddly appealing town is the point of departure for *passenger* ferries to Cozumel and, at first glance, little more than that. (There are two ferry operations here; one makes the crossing to Cozumel in about 40 minutes, the other in half an hour. Boats leave frequently—more or less every other hour, on the half hour—and the fare is the equivalent of $7.) There's more to Playa (as everyone calls it) than meets the eye, however. While no one will mistake it for an oasis of glamour and luxury, it has become, thanks to its funky, kicked-back ambience and topless beaches, a very popular stop on the international backpacking set's endless-summer circuit.

Playa's two main streets are laid out at right angles to each other. Avenida Juárez, the paved street running perpendicular to Highway 307, is where the town's business and civic affairs are conducted. Avenida 5 Norte, the potholed street running parallel to the coast, is the town's self-proclaimed "hotel and convention zone." First-time visitors who bypass Avenida Norte and find themselves at the town plaza, just up from the ferry pier, will wonder what the fuss is about. With the exception of the inviting porch of the colonial-style **Hotel Molcas**—a perfect spot to cool your heels and quench your thirst—you won't see much to tempt you into spending a night. The fact that the Molcas is one of the more expensive hotels in town doesn't mean it's the best. While its public areas are elegant, if a bit worn, the rooms are disappointing—stuffy, a little dingy, and often in need of housekeeping. Don't despair; almost everything of interest in Playa is located north and west of the plaza on 5 Norte.

There's a secure parking lot where you can leave your car for a night or three at the north end of the plaza (the water and Cozumel are to the east). From there you'll want to head up the hill in the direction of the bus depot. Given the essentially footloose nature of Playa's foreign colony, the fortunes of commercial establishments seem to change as often as the tides. The open-fronted restaurants on the north side of the plaza are an example: In the last couple of years La Negrita has closed, as has Ziggy's. **Mascaras**, at the bottom of the hill, manages to hang on, serving tasty Italian specialties and pizza with inventive toppings at very affordable prices. Its breezy little bar is also nice.

At the top of the hill, 5 Norte heads off to your right (the bus depot is on the far northwest corner). Here, too, the names of restaurants change with some frequency, although the idea doesn't: fresh, inexpensive seafood served with cold beer and lots of hospitality. **Pez Vela**, on the northwest corner of 5 Norte and Calle 2, is louder than most and a popular local hangout. When the vines on the front-porch trellis of **La Tarraya**, at the beach end of the first cross street north of Avenida Juárez, shrivel up during the dry season, they take much of the restaurant's charm with them. But the food is decent regardless of the season, and the Caribbean rolls gently onto the sand just a few yards from its tables. For fast food on the run, try **Jimmy's Fajita Factory**, a hole-in-the-wall just down the street from Pez Vela where shish kebab, fajitas, and delicious chicken tacos come sizzling off the grill.

Heading north, away from the plaza and ferry pier, you'll pass a well-stocked market and, farther up the block, **Original 60**, a small boutique with a delightful selection of handicrafts and affordable resortwear made from Guatemalan textiles (they have a bigger store in Cancún). For an excellent meal (breakfast, lunch, or dinner) in a pretty rock-garden setting, try **Limones**, on the northwest corner of the next intersection. Though you'll pay a little more here, you won't regret it: The kitchen uses only the freshest ingredients, the service is first-rate, and the ambience is absolutely charming. And Limones pours the best cup of coffee between Cancún and Belize.

Playa has a variety of low-budget accommodations to choose from. One of the nicest is the **Copacabana**, one block north of Limones on 5 Norte. The plain one-story building sits amid attractively landscaped grounds and has seven rooms, each equipped with a double bed, hot-water shower, and ceiling fan. Best of all, the English-speaking owners Eduardo and Jorge Canto are extremely knowledgeable about the area, and also have some interesting things to say about the impact of tourism on Mexico's Caribbean coastline.

At the opposite end of the budget spectrum, the **Blue Parrot Inn**, on the beach two blocks north of the Copacabana, is a a funky full-service resort popular with southern Californians and assorted Europeans. Accommodations here range from rooms with private baths in a two-story hotel to rustic bungalows with kitchenettes. The Blue Parrot also has a breezy beachside restaurant and rooftop lounge, a full dive and windsurfing shop (windsurfing is taken seriously here), and a beautiful beach where topless sunbathing seems to be the rule.

If you were to continue north along the beach for another mile you'd find much the same ambience minus the bohemian quality at Las Palapas and the Shangri-La Caribe, two of the nicest accommodations in the Cancún–Tulum corridor. The entrance to both, however, is back through town and down a long rutted access road off Highway 307, about a mile north of Avenida Juárez. (The access road, which serves both establishments, is well-marked by a large sign for the Shangri-La and a more discreet sign for Las Palapas.)

The **Shangri-La Caribe** was one of the first upscale establishments on the Turquoise Coast. The original accommodations here were raised rustic-looking "huts" (one- and two-story) built around a small, shady "lagoon"; each had a comfortable double bed, hot-water shower, ceiling fan, and hammocks to relax in. Expansion later resulted in the creation of a mini-village on the beach, with charming, detached one-room huts surrounded by acres of sand. With a pretty, thatched-roof restaurant and a couple of bars, a swimming pool, a recreation palapa, a full-service dive shop (which also arranges excursions to nearby reefs), and a beautiful stretch of sand (topless sunbathing de rigueur), the Shangri-La has just about everything a refugee from colder climes could want. It also has a loyal clientele that returns year after year. For the regular high season you'll want to book two to three months in advance; for the Christmas and Easter periods, at least five months. (When reserving, ask for numbers 1 through 5, junior suites right on the beach; 7 through 11, which are one "street" back from the beach but feel as if they're on it; or 14 through 16, which are shaded by lovely palms.)

The overwhelming success of the Shangri-La eventually led to the opening of a similar compound called **Las Palapas** right next door. Where the Shangri-La has a somewhat "primitive" ambience owing to its palms and sand, Las Palapas has a more manicured look, with one- and two-story thatched-roof huts arranged in an orderly fashion around a grassy lawn and bocce court. (Las Palapas is German-owned, and caters to a European clientele.) Each hut is simply decorated with tile floors and a few pieces of rattan furniture, but the simplicity of the decor belies the touches that many travellers appreciate: plenty of hot water, firm mattresses and pillows, and powerful ceiling fans. The complex also has an elegant thatched-roof restaurant (no shorts or bathing suits allowed), a pool, a lively recreation palapa, and a great expanse of beach facing the fertile waters of the Cozumel "cut," the deep underwater canyon between Isla Cozumel and the mainland. Again, you'll want to book months in advance for the high season, with the huts closest to the beach (numbers 1 through 4 and 26 through 28) the most desirable—and expensive.

The newest accommodation in Playa is also its most conspicuously luxurious. The **Continental Plaza Playacar**, on the beach behind the ferry pier, is a Cancún-style complex with all the amenities old Playa hands traditionally have done without: private terraces, satellite cable TV, servi-bars, swim-up bars, a shopping arcade, and an Olympic-size pool. The idea, apparently, is to provide visitors with the best of both worlds: the comforts of Cancún in a more "authentic" setting. It is authenticity, however, that is likely to disappear as more and more luxury hotels like this one are built in the corridor.

South of Playa

Not everyone eager to escape Cancún's glitz and high prices will be enthusiastic about Playa del Carmen's scruffier charms. Those looking for something more opulent might want to take a look around **Puerto Aventuras**, located 30 km (19 miles) south of Playa and 98 km (61 miles) south of Cancún. Well aware of the explosion of property values that occurred as Cancún grew from empty sand spit to mega-resort, the developers of this 500-acre parcel on the Bahía de Fatima set out to create their own upscale oasis. When it's completed, Puerto Aventuras will boast two marinas, an 18-hole championship golf course, and hundreds of luxury villas and condominiums—all of it conforming to a grand master plan (including acreage set aside for an ecological reserve). For now, there are two pretty hotels here operated by the Oasis hotel group; a small commercial district with a couple of expensive boutiques as well as a **Carlos 'n Charlie's**; the **Museo CEDAM**, a small but interesting dive museum established by Mexico's Underwater Explorers' Club; and a nine hole golf course ($28 for 18 holes; $23 for a cart).

Before continuing south along the coast you might want to visit **Xcaret** (ish-car-ette), located 15 km (9 miles) north of Puerto Aventuras and 9 km (5 miles) south of Playa del Carmen. If any one thing symbolizes the changes in store for the Cancún–Tulum corridor, this once-magical place is it. A few years ago it was one of nature's jewels, a beautiful lagoon where the mixing of warm sea water with colder fresh water attracted multitudes of brightly colored fish to tidal pools tucked in among the rocks. Today all that is gone.

In its place you'll find a tropical amusement park in the making. The access road leading in from the highway—once an adventure in itself—has been smoothed and lined with palms and flowering shrubs. A new multipurpose building at the entrance has lockers, showers, and an expensive souvenir shop; visitors are charged 30,000 pesos ($10). Additional pre-Hispanic ruins have been excavated and restored, and explanatory plaques in Spanish and English erected. A curving man-made jetty now shelters a sandy beach, a water-sports center, and numerous beachside concessions. The charming wooden gangplanks over the tidal pools have been replaced by mortared limestone walkways, and the *cenote* and subterranean cave system have been blasted out and turned into an underground river ride. (Fins, mask, and snorkel rent for 15,000 pesos.) The fish—blue tangs, striped sergeant majors, triggerfish—still hang around, albeit in reduced numbers, but at this rate their days appear numbered. Elsewhere on the grounds, an "ecologically sound" dolphin show has been added for the amusement of day-trippers from Cancún, and heat-prostrated nags will transport you through the jungle at exorbitant prices. While it may be pointless to protest "progress," one can't help but mourn the passing of something that was truly wonderful.

The beach at **Akumal**, 7 km (4 miles) south of Puerto Aventuras, is one of the nicest in the area—a broad expanse of seldom-crowded sand with a collection of hotels and bungalows behind it. (There are three separate entrances from the highway here. The first, marked "Akumal," is the one most visitors will want. The Hotel Akumal Cancún is located at the end of the last one.) Once a prime nesting spot for green and loggerhead turtles (Akumal means "place of the turtles"), today it's a perfect beach for children or those with a fear of big waves—the reef at the mouth of the bay cuts down the surf while creating great snorkeling opportunities. In fact, Akumal's original claim to fame was as a scuba diver's paradise; for years it was the exclusive preserve of the Mexican Underwater Explorers' Club, founded by Pablo Bush Romero, developer of the Hotel Club Akumal Caribe (see below) and Puerto Aventuras. Though the hoi polloi is now welcome, the scuba diving is still outstanding: The water stays bathtub warm year-round, visibility approaches 200 feet, and the coral gardens in 80 to 100 feet of water are a kaleidoscope of brilliant colors and swirling fish.

While accommodations in Akumal are limited in comparison to Cancún, they're more than adequate. The **Hotel Club Akumal Caribe** (formerly the headquarters of CEDAM) offers its guests a choice between traditional rooms in a three-story "tower" or plain but well-equipped bungalows complete with air-conditioning, small refrigerators, and purified water bubblers. (They also rent a variety of condominiums.) The 130-room **Hotel Akumal Cancún**, just down the beach, is situated amid lush tropical vegetation and offers a wider range of facilities, including a pool, tennis courts, a gym, and a complete water-sports center, in addition to its pretty motel-style rooms. Both are popular with a Texas crowd that takes its scuba diving seriously, and both are just a two-mile stroll down the beach (only residents of the nearby condominiums are allowed to drive) from the **Laguna Yal Ku**, a beautiful U-shaped lagoon that has been described as Xel-há (see below) without the crowds.

From Akumal, Highway 307 continues south past one beautiful beach after another. The sign pointing the way to **Chemuyil** brags that it's "The most beautiful beach in the world." True or not, after a few hours lounging on the sand here, the last thing you'll want to do is argue the point. Chemuyil isn't particularly dramatic, nor does it front a string of posh hotels; the only accommodations are a few sandy campsites behind the beach and a block-style condominium complex. What it does have is beautiful white sand and water warm enough to soak in. Sadly, dozens of the coconut palms that helped makes this such a special place have fallen to the tree doctor's chainsaw; others are dying. (The Quintana Roo coast has been hit hard in recent years by a wind-borne fungus that has devastated its palms.) It's also more crowded than it used to be (especially on weekends). Then again, those wonderful wooden chaise longues are as comfortable as ever, and the friendly beach attendants still make it possible for you to spend a day here without having to lift a finger.

If Chemuyil *isn't* the most beautiful beach in the world, it's only because that honor belongs to **Xcacel** (ish-ca-cell), located 5 km (3 miles) south of Chemuyil on Highway 307. The crescent-shaped bay here wears a necklace of flour-fine sand, and the beach is usually deserted. (The water is calmer, and the bottom less rocky, inside the point to your left.) While the thatched-roof restaurant perched on a sandy bluff above the beach has gotten a little pricey (and is entertaining more tour groups on their way back from Tulum and Xel-há), it still can't be touched for gorgeous views or relaxing ambience. There are also 20 campsites here, along with clean rest rooms and cold-running showers. Most interesting of all, however, is the turtle project that has been developed behind the beach by a mother-and-son team from Galveston, Texas, in conjunction with a Mexican biologist. Pat (the mother) will be happy to fill you in on the marvelous work they're doing. It's human nature to want to improve on something that's already perfect; Xcacel seems unlikely to escape that fate. Those who like their sun and sand without frills will want to experience this spot before the inevitable changes descend on it.

Xel-há National Park, 4 km (2½ miles) south of Xcacel, is one of the best places in the country to see marine life. It's also one of the best places in the country to see other people, especially between 10:30 A.M. and 2:30 P.M. Still, this extensive lagoon system (which is fed by the largest creek on Mexico's Caribbean coastline) is undeniably beautiful, and if you get here early enough you might even find an empty patch of sand.

Naturalists will tell you it's the mixing of fresh water with the warm waters of the Caribbean that accounts for the profusion of fish. Most of the fish, however, steer well clear of the schools of human beings. The best place to see them is along the ropes that divide the lagoon into "swimming" and "no swimming" areas, with conditions best on bright, sunny days. Unfortunately, bright, sunny days also mean people wearing sunscreens and suntan lotion, which come off in the water and form a film on the surface, inhibiting the proper mixing of fresh and salt water. If you know you'll be snorkeling, do not apply suntan lotion until after you're through for the day.

Visitors who arrive snorkel-less can rent equipment once they've paid their admission (about $5); a mask and snorkel rent for about $8, with the fins costing an additional $8. There are also two overpriced restaurants on the grounds in addition to a number of overpriced boutiques.

Tulum

Tulum, perhaps the most visited and photographed archaeological site in the Yucatán, is the only extant example of a walled Mayan city—an architectural development that became necessary during the strife-torn Postclassic era. According to local legend, Mayan kings came to Tulum to vacation, and one look at the beautiful beach below this striking site makes it clear how such a legend was born. The truth, however, is somewhat less romantic. Tulum was an important trading outpost, well situated to handle the large cargo-laden canoes that plied the coasts of the Yucatán in the centuries before the Conquest, and probably housed a population of 500 to 600 people in its heyday.

The turnoff for Tulum is 16 km (10 miles) south of Xel-há; the archaeological zone itself is about half a mile off the highway. The parking lot, which is usually filled with tour buses, is right in front of the entrance to the site. Tickets to the site can be purchased in a booth to the left of the entrance, where you'll find rest rooms as well. (Use the latter only in cases of dire need.)

The parking lot is surrounded by an assortment of lean-to restaurants and souvenir stands; none is better than any other, and most are overpriced. Feel free to bargain for souvenirs, but don't forget that most of the stuff is mass-produced and can be bought elsewhere for less.

Although the surrounding countryside was populated as early as the Preclassic era, the Tulum that lies unveiled today dates back only as far as the Postclassic era (A.D. 1200–1500). It is an unusually compact site, containing more than 60 buildings, 20 of which are within the walls of the city. The site has not been completely excavated, and the partially buried rocks strewn around can make walking difficult, so be sure to wear sneakers or comfortable shoes that will not slip on hard surfaces.

The **Castillo**, the most impressive structure at Tulum, squats on a bluff overlooking some of the most beautifully tinted water in the Caribbean. Just a year or two ago, the short but steep climb to the top would have been rewarded by breathtaking views of the coastline to the north and the site itself, with the latter's fortified wall and corner guardhouses still standing silent sentry after more than seven centuries. The Postclassic structure atop this platform served as a combined temple and priests' residence, according to experts, although there is speculation that it might also have served as a lighthouse for coastal traders. Unfortunately, the wear and tear caused by hordes of day-trippers from Cancún has forced the government to limit access to the structure; these days, the Castillo can be photographed but not climbed.

Of somewhat greater archaeological interest is the **Templo del Dios Descendente**, immediately to the left (as you're facing the sea) of the Castillo. This structure is named for the partially eroded relief of an upside-down figure—commonly referred to as "descending" or "diving"—recessed in a niche above the temple's sole doorway. Descending gods were a fairly common decorative motif in the Late Classic and Postclassic eras, although their identities and significance varied from site to site and century to century. The god honored here is assumed to be Ah Macehcabob, the Mayan bee god, and as such is a cultural manifestation of the all-important role of commerce and trade in Postclassic Mayan society (honey being a valuable commodity then, as it is today).

The other structure of note at Tulum is the **Templo de los Frescoes**, due west of the Castillo in the direction of the entrance to the site. A two-story building with a columned façade and a boxy, carelessly constructed temple set atop its first story, the Temple of the Frescoes is distinguished by a well-preserved interior mural that portrays, among other things, a Mayan deity surrounded by bean pods and holding in its hands two images of the rain god, Chac—a telling indication of the importance of adequate rainfall to the Maya's prosperity. Here again, however, the huge number of tourists visiting the site has led to the structure being roped off from curious eyes and damaging camera flashes.

If you've rented a car for a day or two, plan your itinerary so that you hit Tulum either first thing in the morning (before

11:00 A.M.) or toward the end of the afternoon (after 3:30; the site closes at 5:00), thereby avoiding the worst of the crowds. (Generally speaking, this is good advice to follow for any of the archaeological zones in the Yucatán. During the high season in particular—from Christmas through Easter—they tend to get very crowded between the hours of 11:00 and 3:00—which can prove especially frustrating for amateur photographers in search of unobstructed shots. This is also the hottest part of the day, when climbing pyramids under the fierce Yucatán sun can seem more like torture than vacation.) Remember, however, that Cancún is about a two-hour drive north of Tulum. If you're planning on heading back to Cancún for the evening and save Tulum for the end of the day, you'll end up driving most of the way in darkness—an unpleasant prospect at best. If Cancún is your ultimate destination, better to do Tulum first thing in the morning and then make your way back up the coast, stopping to check out Xcacel or Chemuyil, Xcaret, and Playa del Carmen in the afternoon.

Cobá

Dedicated archaeology buffs will want to continue on to Cobá, 44 km (27 miles) north and west of Tulum over a smooth two-lane road. The drive, especially in the late afternoon, is beautiful, with lush jungle growth crowding the road surface on either side, an occasional toucan flying overhead, and tiny Mayan hamlets appearing out of nowhere just when you start to think that's exactly where you are.

You'll need to stay overnight to explore this site fully— Cobá is one of the largest, as well as one of the least explored, Mayan cities discovered to date. (Experts say it will take at least 50 years—and money the government doesn't have—to excavate it completely.) Such an itinerary will also allow you to explore the site in the late afternoon or first thing in the morning, thereby avoiding the oppressive heat of midday.

The **Villa Arqueológica Cobá**, a branch of the pleasant chain run by Club Med, is situated on the shores of Lake Cobá, a five-minute walk from the entrance to the archaeological zone. With cozy rooms, potable tap water, and a swimming pool to provide welcome relief from the heat and humidity of the surrounding jungle, the Villa Arqueológica is a veritable oasis. There's also a pretty restaurant in the hotel that serves regional Yucatecan specialties prepared with a French touch. More adventurous types can try one of the three restaurants in the tiny village of Cobá, which straggles up from the northern shore of Lake Cobá; simple and unpretentious, all three serve the same kind of regional specialties as the Villa Arqueológica for half the price.

The ancient city of Cobá (*Cobá* means "water stirred by the wind") once extended over a large area dominated by two shallow freshwater lakes, Cobá and Maconxoc, and for a time in the Middle Classic period (seventh and eighth centuries A.D.) was one of the most important Mayan centers in the northern Yucatán. Ample proof of this is provided by the now-ruined causeway, or *sacbé,* that stretched west some 60 miles through the jungle from Cobá to Yaxuná. Such causeways (*sacbeob* in the plural) were constructed of double retaining walls and a core filled with broken stone, the latter plastered over to provide a smooth surface, and were an integral part of the city's ceremonial life as well as communication links to other Mayan communities. The remains of 50 such causeways have been found in and around Cobá, with the one leading to Yaxuná the longest discovered in the Yucatán to date.

Although the jungle reclaims structures almost as fast as they are cleared, the archaeological zone of Cobá is pervaded by an almost palpable sense of history—a feeling that's enhanced by the lack of other people exploring the site. The two principal structures here, the Iglesia, which is located in the Cobá complex, and the Castillo, in the Nohoch Mul complex, are situated roughly a mile apart; a third structure of interest, the Conjunto Las Pinturas, is located approximately halfway between these two. Elsewhere, narrow pathways lead through thick vegetation to stelae in various states of decay; 32 stelae have been found at Cobá, 23 of which still bear some trace of carving.

The two pyramids are the main attraction, however, and, despite their imposing height, can be climbed with relative ease. The **Castillo,** or Nohoch Mul pyramid, with its 120-step ascent, is the tallest pyramid in the northern Yucatán (slightly taller than the Castillo at Chichén Itzá), and is topped by a simple Postclassic-era temple—an indication that the site was reoccupied by "Toltecized" Maya (in all likelihood the same people who built Tulum) centuries after the original Cobá culture collapsed. The 360-degree view from the top takes in a number of jungle-covered hillocks that poke their heads above the pancake-flat canopy; in many cases these are not hillocks at all but rather other structures that have not yet been excavated.

The **Iglesia,** a few hundred yards from the entrance to the archaeological zone, is similar in design and construction, though not as well preserved as the Nohoch Mul pyramid. Nor are the views from the top as sweeping. The ceremonial center surrounding it (much of it cloaked in jungle) is larger than the center at the base of Nohoch Mul, however, suggesting that it was, in fact, the more important structure.

Northeast of the Iglesia, in the direction of the Nohoch Mul complex, is the **Conjunto Las Pinturas** (Temple of the Painted Lintel). The lintel above the doorway is indeed painted, in a style reminiscent of the frescoes at Tulum, which would seem to date the building to the Late Postclassic era. In the immediate vicinity of the structure you'll also find a number of altars, damaged stelae, and a stone phallus carved from a single stone.

Cobá probably won't strike everyone's fancy; the small number of excavated structures, the distances between them, and the relative lack of tourist amenities will have some visitors wishing they were back in Cancún. Others will be charmed by the beauty and solitude afforded by the site as well as by the chance to escape—if only for the night—the bonds of civilization.

ISLA MUJERES

Isla Mujeres, a small island eight miles north of Cancún, is the kind of place where cutoffs and a tee-shirt pass for formal wear and a video bar is a restaurant dining room with a portable color TV. It's the perfect resort for those who love the beachcomber's life, and despite recent changes—mostly in the form of higher prices and an influx of tourists—has so far managed to resist the glitzy path blazed by its sister resort on the mainland. Most visitors are content to take the ferry over in the morning, grab a bite to eat, go for a swim, and head back to the mainland before nightfall; others discover they could spend a week or more here. It all depends on your frame of mind and your willingness to leave the comforts of home behind. The more willing you are, the more you'll like this scruffy little oasis.

MAJOR INTEREST

Unhurried island pace
Playa Norte

In Town

Although the Spanish explorer Francisco Hernández de Córdova landed here in 1517, until recently, Isla Mujeres—named for the statues of women that Córdova saw when he came ashore—was all but unknown to everyone except its Mayan inhabitants. In the centuries after the Spanish left, the island remained isolated and was only occasionally used as a refuge by the likes of Morgan and Jean Lafitte. The United States built a naval base here during the Second World War, increasing its exposure to the outside world a hundredfold, but its present-day popularity as a tourist destination came about as a result of the development of Cancún.

The island itself is only five and a half miles long and half a mile wide. Its only town is situated at the northern end of the island, and most of its hotels, shops, and restaurants are within easy walking distance of one another. Otherwise, don't expect to find any neon lights, traffic jams, or nightlife here. In Isla Mujeres a visitor can go barefoot right through dinner, and lingering over drinks and a meal is about all there is to do at night.

Avenida Gustavo Rueda Medina is the main road on the island. In town, Avenidas Juárez, Hidalgo, and Guerrero run parallel to it. The zócalo and city hall are tucked away at the southeastern end of town; the ferry dock, farther to the west, is the center of most of what action there is. Accommodations tend to be places where you change, shower, and catch some shut-eye. As a rule, they are clean, no-frill establishments, as well as a bargain compared to hotels in Cancún or Cozumel.

The **Hotel Perla del Caribe**, at the corner of Madero and Guerrero on the eastern edge of the downtown area, has three kinds of rooms: those with no views and no air-conditioning; those with air-conditioning but no views; and those with air-conditioning and ocean views. While the ocean on this side of the island is too rough for swimming, the Perla del Caribe does have a nice little pool overlooking the crashing waves as well as a stretch of sand, and its **Restaurante Barlovento** serves up decent seafood and chicken dishes at reasonable prices.

The **Posada del Mar**, at the candy-striped lighthouse just up from the ferry terminal, offers good-sized rooms with ceiling fans and air-conditioning. Those on the second and third floors also have balconies offering views of the Bahía de Mujeres. The best thing about the place, however, is its pretty public areas, which include a delightful pool area and a funky restaurant/bar where patrons sit on swings suspended from the ceiling. Still, what you're really paying for here is the location: You'll find an uncrowded stretch of beach just across the street, while Playa Norte (also known as Playa Los Cocos), one of the best beaches anywhere, is a five-minute walk to the north.

Most of the decent restaurants and interesting shops are located north of the zócalo on either Juárez, Hidalgo, or their cross streets. **La Sirena**, just north of the zócalo on Hidalgo, has the island's best selection of painted animals from Oaxaca, black pottery from San Bartolo Coyotepec, lacquered boxes and platters from Olinala, and Guatemalan textiles. And while the shop attracts a lot of day-trippers, it's much less expensive than anything you'll find in Cancún. The two-story peach-colored building across the street has been artfully converted into the **Casa del Arte Mexica**, a cool, elegant gallery filled with objets d'art inspired by ancient Mayan motifs. Batik wall hangings and clothing, limestone reproductions of the beautiful carvings from Palenque, and interesting jewelry make this one of the best boutiques on the island.

Cocos Frios, Hidalgo 4, is a great stop for inexpensive chicken tacos with cheese, and sometimes has live music. The **Méson de Bucanero**, farther up the street, has two dining rooms inside as well as a shady courtyard fronted by wrought-iron gates. Their very good, reasonably priced breakfast menu is offered daily from 7:00 to 11:00 A.M., followed by their regular menu from 11:00 A.M. to 11:00 P.M. **Pizza Rolandi**, directly across the street, offers an extensive menu of Italian dishes, steak, chicken, and seafood, in addition to pizza cooked in their trademark wood-fired oven. For a slightly more romantic atmosphere try **Gomar**, at the corner of Hidalgo and Madero, which has moved upstairs to make way for a tee-shirt and ice-cream shop. Lobster and charbroiled steaks are the specialties here, and the new location puts patrons above the noise and fumes of Isla's ubiquitous mopeds.

Playa Norte

Fringed by rustling palms at the northern end of the island, Playa Norte is an easy ten-minute walk from the ferry dock. Just head north on Rueda Medina, turn right on López Mateos at the entrance to the Nautibeach complex, and then left on the first street past the cemetery. Like a number of beautiful beaches along the Yucatán's Caribbean coastline, Playa Norte offers acres of satiny sand and warm, shallow water. It's the ultimate sandbox, and seems to have a strangely liberating effect on the sunbathers who find their way here: After an hour or two of sunning and soaking, inhibitions—along with a surprising number of bathing suits—seem to fall away.

That visitors will love Playa Norte is a given. The hotel situation at this end of the island, on the other hand, is somewhat less certain. Perched on a rocky islet at the far end of Playa Norte, the Del Prado, Isla Mujeres's biggest hotel, finally closed after years of serving up a special brand of rudeness. Since then, construction crews have been busy renovating and expanding the place (80 rooms in beachside "villas" have been added to the complex), ostensibly in time for the 1993 season, when it will reopen as the Spanish-owned **Costa Club**. Until it does, however, you're on your own.

The two-story **Hotel Na Balam**, right next door, couldn't be more different from its upscale neighbor on the point. In fact, this is one of those low-key hideaways people are reluctant to tell their friends about. Accommodations consist of 12 one-room suites decorated in no-frills fashion with aquamarine tile and sturdy wooden furniture; each has a small refrigerator and ceiling fan, and some have air-conditioning. Those on the ground floor have patios on the sand, and all face a modest fenced-in enclosure dotted with palm trees and wooden chaise longues. Although the last two years have seen the addition of an informal dining room and a small, very popular *palapa*-style bar on the sand—additions that have enhanced its already considerable appeal—Na Balam remains a charming oasis safely removed from the aggravations of the modern world.

For those willing to spend more, the other lodging option at this end of the island is the **Nautibeach Condominium-Hotel**, at the far end of Rueda Medina just past the lighthouse. In addition to its friendly pool area and good restaurant, Nautibeach has 34 two-bedroom units, 10 of which are rented to the public. All have kitchenettes and are pleasantly decorated, making them an especially attractive option for families on vacation. A minimum two-night deposit is required during the high season; ask for Humberto when making reservations.

Chez Magaly, the poolside restaurant in the Nautibeach complex, is the prettiest dining spot on North Beach, if not the island, as well as the most expensive. A rather limited menu of seafood dishes is offered along with spectacular sunsets, and the talking parrot at the bar will be happy to chip in if conversation at your table starts to flag. Closed Mondays; Tel: (98) 82-0259 for reservations.

Midway between Nautibeach and Na Balam is **Buho's**, a onetime beachfront disco that was resurrected as a restaurant (breakfast, lunch, and dinner) after Hurricane Gilbert blew through town. Though the food is only average, the breezy ambience and international clientele (when there is one) make this the kind of tropical watering hole Papa Hemingway would have loved.

South of Town

South of town the island becomes hillier, with the vegetation along its main road (a continuation of Rueda Medina) low and scrubby. The airport, which cannot accommodate commercial jetliners, is located about a third of the way down the island on its eastern side. Almost everything else of interest is located on its western, or leeward, side, facing the calm waters of the Bahía de Mujeres.

The beaches on the way to El Garrafón park, at the southern tip of the island, are relatively unspoiled, although recent years have seen an increase in the number of makeshift souvenir stands and little open-air restaurants. **Playa Lancheros**, 5 km (3 miles) south of the ferry dock, is a favorite with visitors to Isla Mujeres in spite of its tacky ambience: Though the three giant turtles and one "sleeping" shark kept in underwater pens just offshore are meant to amuse curious day-trippers, the whole setup is more sad than appealing.

Of marginally greater interest is **Mundaca's hacienda**—or what's left of it—the path to which is located across the road from the entrance to Playa Lancheros (taxi drivers know the spot). According to legend, a sometime pirate and full-time slaver named Mundaca built the hacienda and surrounded it with beautiful gardens at great expense in order to woo an island beauty known as La Trigueña (The Brunette). La Trigueña had other plans, however, and married a local lad. The spurned Mundaca slowly went mad as his beloved bore her husband one child after another, and after he died his hacienda was left to the jungle.

In the opinion of many locals, **Maria's**, an elegantly rustic restaurant about a mile (1½ km) south of Playa Lancheros, is the best dining spot on the island. Lunch and dinner are served under a cozy palapa overlooking the bay, and the French-inspired but reasonably priced food—seafood is the specialty of the house—earns raves. Maria's also has a few rooms to let, most of them cozy and quite attractive, if a bit musty. It's a good idea to phone ahead for reservations; Tel: (98) 82-0130.

El Garrafón, a national underwater park at the southern end of the island, was once a snorkelers' paradise. Unfortunately, today there are more people than fish—the park is usually packed with tourists who arrive in large groups (don't even think of going on Sunday)—and the beach has been turned into a miniature version of Coney Island, with dank dressing rooms, tacky snack stands, and overpriced snorkel concessions. The combination of people and protruding rocks makes it difficult to enter the water, and once you do you're likely to spend as much time dodging other snorkelers as looking at fish. If it's first-rate snorkeling you're looking for, try the wrecks at the mouth of the **Laguna Makax** south of town or, better yet, head over to Cancún or Cozumel; for a peaceful day at the beach, there are better choices elsewhere on Isla Mujeres.

From El Garrafón the road continues south for another quarter mile before it loops around and heads back to town along the windward side of the island. The narrow paths on your right cut through tangled undergrowth to the southernmost tip of the island and a partially reconstructed temple where native Mayan women worshiped the fertility goddesses Ixchel, Ixchebeliax, Ixhunie, and Ixhunieta long after the Spanish arrived in these parts. Today the views of the wave-tossed Caribbean to the east, Cancún (looking like a modern-day Emerald City) to the west, and the crashing surf below are well worth the short hike.

If it's not too late in the afternoon and you have a car or motorbike, you'll want to head back to town along the largely undeveloped windward side of the island. The road has been regraded and paved, and in spots the combination of rocky hillsides and craggy coastline—the pitted limestone formations that hug the beach are a geologic phenomenon known as ironshore—will put you in mind of the Scottish highlands. Take care, however: The small patches of sand on this side of the island are perfect for picnics or solitary sunbathing, but save any serious swimming for the protected beaches on the other side.

COZUMEL

Cozumel is the kind of place you fall in love with without knowing exactly why. Observant travellers sense its uniqueness immediately, but the *source* of that uniqueness takes some time to figure out. Eventually you realize that the Mayan culture is more alive here than elsewhere, and Mayan facial and physical characteristics are more prevalent. At the same time, the island, because it is an island, brings visitors into closer contact with the resident population, which seems to have a "live-and-let-live" attitude toward the divers, day-trippers, cruise-ship passengers, and others who make their way here. If you gear down to its own special pace, Cozumel will reveal itself gently and gradually; once it does, you'll want to come back again and again.

MAJOR INTEREST

Unsurpassed scuba diving
Snorkeling at Chankanaab Lagoon National Park
Strolling the *malecón* and back streets downtown
Unspoiled beauty of its windward coast

Although it's Mexico's largest island, measuring some 30 miles long and 10 miles wide, and has a population of 50,000, Cozumel was isolated from the rest of the country until relatively recently. As a result, you'll still hear Mayan spoken here with some frequency. Likewise, many of the local women still wear *huipiles*—not least because nothing beats the heat better. At the same time, Cozumel is the only place in Mexico where you're likely to see people wearing full wet suits in the zócalo. In fact, every other person here seems to have a diver's bag dangling over a shoulder, and advertisements for the rental of underwater video cameras fill every local newspaper and guidebook.

The strong cultural contrast between the Mayan presence and the mania for water sports stems from the island's history. The Maya first settled Cozumel around A.D. 300, and by the Postclassic era it was an important trading outpost as well as a pilgrimage site famous throughout the Yucatán for its shrines to Ixchel, the Mayan goddess of the moon and fertility. First Juan de Grijalva and then Cortés landed here in the years immediately preceding the Conquest, but it wasn't until 1543 that the Spanish gained firm control of the island.

In the late 1500s the island's population was decimated by smallpox and the few native survivors packed up and headed back to the mainland. After that tragedy, it was not until 1848 that Mayan refugees from the bloody War of the Castes began to slip back to their former island retreat. Cozumel remained isolated from the outside world, however, until the Second World War, when the United States built an air base on the island.

After Jacques Cousteau discovered **Palancar Reef** in the 1950s, scuba divers began to arrive in numbers, and they more or less had the island to themselves until about 20 years ago, when the first hotel opened in Cancún. Palancar Reef, off the southwestern coast of the island, is ranked among the top five dive sites in the world. But Palancar isn't the only underwater attraction here. Virtually the entire southwestern quarter of Cozumel is surrounded by the kind of underwater reefs that divers dream about, with visibility often exceeding 200 feet. Best of all, there seems to be a reef for every level of diving expertise. Beginners can head out to inspect a sunken plane in the "front yard" of the Hotel La Ceiba. At Palancar itself coral spires rise 60 to 80 feet from sloping reef walls, and elsewhere deep canyons wind through spectacular gardens of coral and sponge, home to groupers, giant turtles, and dozens of species of brilliantly colored fish. Little wonder then that more than 20 dive shops are listed in the Cozumel phone book—an enormous concentration for such a small place.

Inevitably, the face of Cozumel has changed as it has become a popular port of call for ships cruising the Caribbean. Most of the fishermen in the island's main town, San Miguel de Cozumel, who used to own homes along Avenida Rafael Melgar, the town's main street (and also its *malecón*) have sold out to make way for the shops that cater to cruise-ship passengers and day-trippers from the mainland. And though the merchandise offered here does not match the level of sophistication found in Cancún, it has been upgraded over the last few years.

In light of increasing competition from Cancún, about a dozen years ago the government decided to improve Cozumel's appeal to non-divers. Existing hotels were gradually refurbished and new investment encouraged, with dramatic results. Today the greatest concentration of hotels and condominiums is found at the northwest corner of the island, from the Meliá Mayan Cozumel south along the coast to the marina just north of town. The intersection of the cross-island road, Avenida Juárez, and the coast road is the undisputed center of activity on the island, with the major restaurants, stores, and discos all located within walking distance of the passenger-ferry pier. Several more luxury hotels, a handful of restaurants, some excellent beaches, and Chankanaab Lagoon National Park are located to the south of town, either right on or just off the coast road.

A good deal less than half the island is inhabited; the pancake-flat northern half of Cozumel, most of it jungle and scrub growth, is dotted with half a dozen small archaeological sites that are difficult to get to. Archaeology buffs will want to rent a Jeep or motorbike (or hire a taxi; drivers know the spot) to visit the Mayan ruins at **San Gervasio**, a recently restored Postclassic site situated in the middle of the northern half of the island. A self-guided tour to the ruins in the form of an easy-to-read map with brief descriptions of the various structures is available in town, as well as at the Cozumel Flea Market, Avenida 5a Norte between Calles 2 and 4 Norte. Guides are also available for approximately $10 at the site itself, though how informative they are depends a great deal on their mood. Find out beforehand if the guide you are about to contract speaks English; most do not. San Gervasio is closed Saturdays.

The beaches on the spectacular eastern side of Cozumel are, generally speaking, too rocky and rough for swimming, but picnics at spots such as Punta Chiqueros, Chen Rio, and Punta Morena offer an unspoiled and refreshing change of pace. (There's also an informal beachside restaurant at Punta Morena.) There are a number of small, protected coves where the swimming is fine, but you have to exercise caution. There are no lifeguards and very few people on this side of the island; if you get into trouble, help may be a long time arriving. Cozumel's windward coast is also popular with giant sea turtles, who lay their eggs in the sand here during the months of July and August.

NORTH OF TOWN

The **Meliá Mayan Cozumel** is one of the best hotel properties on the island. A large complex situated at the end of the coast road leading north out of town, it's a haven for well-heeled travellers who want to relax and don't care if they ever leave the premises. All rooms have balconies and ocean views, and the pool area and two restaurants are tastefully done. Its wide, palm-shaded and protected beach is perhaps its most appreciated feature, however, especially among parents with young children in tow. The Meliá Mayan is, in addition, a place where many of the island's pleasures "come to you." It stages great Mexican fiesta nights, for example, and a number of excursion boats leave from the pier right off the beach. There is also a small shopping arcade on the lobby level.

Other, less elaborate properties, favorites of the island's visitors in the early days of its popularity, line the road—the Costera Norte—from the Meliá Mayan south into town. Most feature the kind of friendly ambience that only family-owned properties offer. Guests are usually divers (or friends of divers tagging along with the group) who have been coming to Cozumel for years. The pink stucco **El Cozumeleño**, next door to the Meliá Mayan, is one such hotel. The rooms here are old-fashioned and quite spacious, as are the hotel's public areas, and those guests who aren't out diving or snorkeling usually spend the day lazing around the small but pretty seaside pool.

Even if you're not staying at this end of the island, lobster lovers will want to make the trip from town for dinner at **La Cabaña del Pescador**, a tiny thatched-roof place with seating for 15 and a reputation for serving the freshest lobster on the island. The tails are sold by weight, with prices averaging about $21 per person. And even though it's hidden away opposite the Cabañas del Caribe hotel, you'll want to arrive early: Seating is on a first-come, first-served basis. Open 6:00 to 10:00 P.M. nightly.

Puerto de Abrigo, the small marina south of the Hotel Mara and just north of town, is where fishermen weigh and show off their catches at the end of the day. It's also the place to arrange deep-sea fishing expeditions.

SAN MIGUEL DE COZUMEL
North in Town

San Miguel looks as if it belongs under a tropical Christmas tree: Everything is undersized, including its short, stocky residents, who look as if they've stepped out of a Mayan frieze.

The town itself is laid out in a grid. Avenida Juárez, the street that begins at the passenger-ferry pier and cuts east across the island, divides the town into northern and southern halves. Streets to the north of Juárez are even-numbered and ascend by twos. Those to the south are odd-numbered and also ascend by twos. Most of the best shops and restaurants are located along Avenida Rafael Melgar, the seaside drive.

While on the subject, know that San Miguel is the kind of

place that requires shoppers to *shop*. Resortwear and silver jewelry are the most popular purchases, but jewelry and small sculptures made from black coral are the real prizes. Cousteau was the first to discover this type of coral, and it's extremely valuable because divers have to go to great depths to bring it up (it also takes 50 years to grow just one centimeter). **Roberto's**, with two locations in town—121 Avenida 5a Norte (next door to the Sports Page) and 618 Avenida Rafael Melgar (at the Hotel Barracuda, south of the passenger-ferry pier)—is one of the best places to find it.

Los Cinco Soles, located "uptown" at the corner of Calle 8 Norte and Avenida Melgar in a beige colonial-style building, is the place to begin your shopping spree; from there you can work your way south. Behind the usual stacks of tee-shirts at Los Cinco Soles you will find an extensive selection of silver jewelry, clothing, and folk art by some of Mexico's most accomplished designers and artisans.

Attached to the shop is **Pancho's Backyard**, one of the few places on the island where informal dining manages to be refined. The contemporary *faux*-colonial decor is easy on the eyes, the cocktail lounge is a pleasant place to have a drink, and the menu features Mexican and Continental dishes prepared with health and fitness in mind.

One of the island's most pleasant surprises is the enchanting **Museo de la Isla de Cozumel**, located a block and a half south on Avenida Melgar, between Calles 6 and 4 Norte. Installed on two floors of a pink-and-white colonial-style building, the museum combines culture and cuisine in a setting overlooking the sea. Permanent exhibits include diving memorabilia and archaeological relics, while breakfast, lunch, and dinner are served on its upstairs balcony. The museum is open Saturday through Thursday, from 10:00 A.M. to 2:00 P.M. and again from 4:00 to 8:00 P.M. (Note: Most stores and restaurants in Cozumel observe the siesta.)

Aca Joe, everybody's unisex favorite, is on the corner of Melgar and 4 Norte; **Animal Fiesta**, right next door, has a charming selection of toys and children's clothing, all of it made in Mexico.

With a new location on the corner of Melgar and 2 Norte, **La Concha** has expanded its selection of quality Mexican handicrafts, all of it tastefully displayed, without sacrificing its reputation for quality. Now open until 9:30 P.M. most nights, it remains one of the better boutiques on the island.

Carlos 'n Charlie's & Jimmy's Kitchen, farther south on Avenida Melgar, is one of Cozumel's liveliest spots. The restaurant is situated on the second floor at the top of a staircase that leads up from a narrow doorway, but you'll probably hear the racket before you find the door. The later the hour, the rowdier the scene—the mostly young beer-drinking crowd comes revved up and ready to have a good time, so you'll want to get here early if a quick bite in relative peace is what you had in mind.

Two of San Miguel's most popular places to eat are located directly across the street from the municipal pier. **El Portal**, a small, informal café open on one side so that customers can watch the passing parade, is popular with local businessmen in *guayabera* shirts as well as tourists just off the boat. Next door and upstairs, the **Café del Puerto** is an eclectically decorated dinner spot with a South Seas atmosphere and a pricey menu featuring prime rib and lobster. Reservations recommended; Tel: (987) 2-0136.

Cozumel's most romantic restaurant, **Morgan's**, is one block east on Avenida Juárez in the old wood-frame customs house. The restaurant's interior has been polished to a polyurethane sheen that reflects the shimmering candlelight, making it the place to linger over dinner and concentrate on your dinner companion. Reservations advised; Tel: (987) 2-0584.

The **Sports Page**, one block north of Morgan's at the corner of Avenida 5a Norte and Calle 2, serves up nonstop sports programming and American-style hamburgers, both of which make it a popular home-away-from-home for armchair quarterbacks who hate to miss the Big Game.

South in Town

Back on Avenida Melgar, **Las Palmeras**, across the street from the passenger-ferry pier, is a popular stop for the hordes of day-trippers and cruise-ship passengers that descend on the island. Although the food is nothing special, the prime location, breezy decor, and reasonable prices are enough to keep packing 'em in.

Las Campanas, one of Cozumel's oldest shops, is tucked away behind Las Palmeras; head toward the plaza and turn right at the corner of the building. This is a good choice for typical Mexican souvenirs and embroidered Oaxaca wedding dresses.

Pepe's Centro, on Avenida 5a Sur, was one of the first restaurants in town, and for years was a local favorite. These days, however, the two-story **Pepe's Grill**, on the corner of Avenidas A. Rosado Salas and Melgar, has surpassed its predecessor in popularity. Pepe's manages to be informal and romantic at the same time, and has a certain elegance that most places in San Miguel lack. Although the wood-trimmed downstairs dining room tends to be more popular, you'll enjoy a bit more privacy upstairs. Reservations advised; Tel: (987) 2-0213.

The **Bazar del Angel**, on the far corner of the block, has a large selection of typical Mexican handicrafts behind its big plate-glass windows. While it may not be the best gift shop in town, you'd have to check out three or four others to find the variety of items it offers.

Donatello's, Avenida Melgar Sur 131, is one of Cozumel's newest restaurants as well as one of its most refined and sophisticated. The inviting tropical decor is peppered with European antiques, and soft piano music accompanies your meal. After a drink at the spiffy bar, you can enjoy one of the Italian specialties of the house either inside in air-conditioned comfort or outside in a small garden. And though you'll probably want to dress up a little, men need not wear jackets. Tel: (987) 2-2586.

Soberanis, four blocks south of the passenger-ferry pier in the hotel of the same name on Avenida Melgar, is a branch of a Mérida steak-and-lobster restaurant that has been popular with knowledgeable travellers for more than 25 years. Lunch and dinner are served in a casual atmosphere that's made even more enjoyable by the live music. You'll want to call ahead to make reservations; Tel: (987) 2-0246.

Located at the southern end of town on the corner of Avenida Melgar and Calle 11 Sur, **El Acuario** is the nearest thing to a "theme" restaurant in San Miguel. The restaurant was once an aquarium (thus its name), and its steak and seafood entrées are served in a mahogany-and-glass setting that incorporates some of the old tanks along with expansive views of the water. You can start your meal by taking a peek at the green turtles and dusky sharks kept in holding tanks out back. And if you'd like to do a little dancing after dinner, **Neptuno**, one of San Miguel's two discos, is right across the street.

There are, in addition, a number of small, unpretentious restaurants popular with local residents at this end of town. **La Choza**, two blocks east of the waterfront at Avenida 10 Sur and Rosado Salas, is said by many to serve the best Mexican food in town. **Santiago's Grill**, another block east at the corner of Rosado Salas and Avenida 15 Sur, is a popular hideaway locally famous for its steaks. Perhaps San Miguel's best-kept dining secret, however, is the garden patio at **Bon Appetit**, a new deli and restaurant at 621 Avenida 30, six cross streets back from the plaza via Avenida Benito Juárez (a cab is probably your best bet the first time you go hunting for it). The prix-fixe dinner menu here ($12.95) changes according to market availability, and includes homemade soup, salad, and a choice of four inventive and usually delicious entrées. Lunch is a less formal affair, with deli sandwiches on homemade bread and the day's soups the usual offerings. Open from 1:00 to 4:00 P.M. and from 8:00 to 11:00 P.M., Monday through Saturday; closed Sundays. Tel: (987) 2-1681 or 0453.

San Miguel itself is a good-size town for the Yucatán (about 35,000 residents), and getting bigger. Anyone spending more than a day on the island who *doesn't* stroll the streets that run parallel to Avenidas Melgar and 5a Norte/Sur—the first street east of Melgar—will be passing up the opportunity to see what the town was like before it was discovered by the outside world. The streets here are lined by pastel-colored wood-and-concrete structures, every third one of which seems to house a juice stand or tiny restaurant, while native men and women go about their daily chores seemingly oblivious to the swarms of visitors. As it has elsewhere in the Yucatán, however, "progress" is blowing through San Miguel like a tropical storm, with more and more of its residents selling out to make way for luxury hotels and businesses that cater to the tourist trade. While such changes were probably made inevitable by the explosive growth of Cancún, one cannot be faulted for feeling as if something irreplaceable is being lost.

SOUTH OF TOWN

Set back from the road on six and a half acres, the **Hotel Villablanca Beach Club and Sports Complex**, about two miles south of town, is popular with serious divers who have some money to spend (divers on a budget stay in smaller hotels in town). Spread around a couple of buildings on neatly landscaped grounds, the standard rooms come with a large double bed, air-conditioning, sunken tile bath, TV, and refrigerator. For those with a little more money to spend, a new wing of breezy, spotlessly clean master suites makes it an even more attractive option.

A half-mile farther south, next to the Budget Rent-a-Car office, **Ernesto's Fajita Factory** serves what just might be the best fajitas in the Yucatán. In the old days Ernesto's customers sat on stools under an open-air palapa, their mouths watering as mounds of freshly sliced onions, chicken, beef, and pork were grilled to order. The portions were huge and the beer ice cold—a combination that, over the years, proved to be very successful. In the last few years Ernesto's has tripled in size and added another branch on Melgar south of the ferry pier. They've also expanded their menu to include breakfast, lunch, and dinner specials. Quality has not been sacrificed to expansion, however.

It's easy to see why many longtime Cozumel hands think the eight-story **Fiesta Americana Sol Caribe**, just down the road, is the best hotel on the island. From its glassed-in elevators to the beautifully landscaped pool area, the Sol Caribe is a top-notch luxury hotel removed to the tropics. The cheery, light-filled rooms in the original building and a new ten-story tower overlook either the water and mainland to the east or a flat stretch of scrubby jungle to the west (those with a jungle view are considerably less expensive). Whichever side you choose, however, be sure to request a room on the higher floors—views from the first two floors are completely blocked by shrubbery.

La Ceiba, next to the cruise-ship pier, is a pleasant, no-nonsense kind of place designed for divers. It has two restaurants—the seaside dining room is particularly good—a tennis court and pool, and a small stretch of beach dotted by palm trees and palapas. The simple rooms here reflect the fact that guests at La Ceiba spend most of their time underwater: The whole area north of Paraiso Reef is superb for snorkeling, and there's even an upside-down plane wreck—put there during the shooting of a movie and later overturned by a storm—right off the hotel's beach.

The sprawling **Stouffer Presidente Cozumel**, south of the Sol Caribe and La Ceiba, about a ten-minute ride from the airport, is one of the old Cozumel favorites and usually the first of the large hotels on the island to fill up. Set well back from the main road on a lovely stretch of beach, the hotel has 259 rooms, each of which comes with a private terrace or balcony, air-conditioning, and color TV. In addition, its gourmet restaurant, **Arrecife**, is considered to be one of the best on the island. But it's the extra touches and amenities—including valet service, an in-house doctor, car rental and travel agencies on the premises, a complete water-sports center, and live entertainment most evenings—that set the Presidente apart from other hotels on Cozumel. As a result, it's a magnet for affluent Mexicans and North Americans.

The island's newest hotel, the **Cozumel Reef Holiday Inn**, is just beyond the Presidente off the coast road, which, for the time being, puts it closer to world-famous Palancar Reef than any hotel on the island. The large, breezy rooms here are decorated in pleasant pastels and have small balconies overlooking the water. Other amenities include a pretty pool area, tennis courts, an in-house car rental agency, a branch of the full-service Pro Dive outfit, a jogging trail carved out of the jungle, and a breezy restaurant right on the water. Though not quite as luxurious as the more expensive hotels on the island, the Holiday Inn delivers all the comforts of home in the midst of unspoiled nature.

From the Holiday Inn to the lighthouse at the southern end of the island only Chankanaab Lagoon and Playa San Francisco are of interest to visitors.

Chankanaab Lagoon National Park, about 15 minutes south of town, is a beautiful underwater marine park surrounded by shady botanical gardens. The swimming and snorkeling are truly wonderful (equipment can be rented on the beach), and amateur botanists love the extensive gardens, not least because the more than 400 species of plants here are clearly labeled. A replica of a Mayan hut in the middle of it all houses a small museum and is the perfect place to get out of the sun. (There's also a small boutique in the back.) With a palapa-covered restaurant that serves lunch and cold drinks from 10:30 A.M. to 4:00 P.M., Chankanaab is a great place to make a day of it.

Playa San Francisco, five minutes south of Chankanaab Lagoon, is the best beach on the island—no frills, just pretty blue-green water, white sand fringed by palm trees, and a couple of simple beachside restaurants serving snacks and cold drinks. You can rent inner tubes and snorkel equipment here as well, and there are a few gift shops and artisans' stalls for those who can't let an afternoon slip by without a little shopping.

From Playa San Francisco the coast road swings to the east as it cuts through miles of uninteresting scrub jungle. **El Cedral**, down a mile-long paved road on your left, is a tiny settlement of farm buildings and ruined huts that, except for a small Saturday market, is deserted much of the time. With the help of a guide and some patience, visitors can find a few Mayan ruins in the jungle at this end of the island, but whether they're worth the time and effort is another matter.

The road finally hits the stunning windward coast of Cozumel just north of **Punta Celarain**—the southernmost point of the island. On Sunday the lighthouse here is the scene of a fried-fish-and-beer bash, but those on mopeds or motorbikes will find the sandy track extremely difficult to negotiate. It's no problem in a regular rental car, however, and well worth the time it takes (about an hour round-trip, depending on whether or not you stop to sunbathe). The jungle scenery along the way is impressively varied, while the dune-backed beach is the best on the island. There are even a few spots where it's okay to swim, although caution should be exercised at all times.

Visitors who have rented mopeds or motorbikes should probably save Punta Celarain for another day. Instead, you can follow the paved road north along the coast, thrilling at the fabulous views of windswept sea and dense jungle. There is swimming at a number of protected *caletas* along this stretch as well as small roadside restaurants at **Playa Chiqueros** and **Punta Morena**. The cross-island road—which takes you past the turnoff to the ruins of San Gervasio and, eventually, into town—meets the coast road just north of Punta Morena. Would-be Indiana Joneses with four-wheel-drive vehicles who hoped to explore the windward coast north to Punta Molas at the tip of the island will have to find their thrills elsewhere. The sand track was bogging down too many rented Jeeps, necessitating long hikes out of the jungle and astronomical towing charges. You should allow three hours to circle the southern half of the island on a moped (less in a Jeep), not counting the excursion to Punta Celarain. And don't forget your sunglasses (eye protection against suicidal bugs) and sunscreen.

Nightlife on Cozumel

Divers like to dance, too. Life after dark, like everything else on Cozumel, exists—but on a smaller scale than in Cancún or Acapulco. There are two discos on the island, neither especially elaborate, but the energy needed to keep the beat going until dawn (on weekends) is there. **Scaramouche**, the smaller of the two, attracts a younger crowd and is usually more raucous. **Neptuno** is high tech and more sophisticated, with videos, lights, and the works. Both are on Avenida Melgar near the southern edge of town.

Mexican fiesta nights are held at the Meliá Mayan (Tel: 987/2-0411), the Sol Caribe (Tel: 987/2-0700), and the Presidente (Tel: 987/2-0322) hotels.

Sports on Cozumel

The world-renowned coral reefs off the southwestern quadrant of Cozumel teem with colorful marine life. What follows are brief descriptions of the largest of these reefs, starting with those near the cruise-ship pier and moving south in the direction of Punta Celarain.

Paraiso Reef is actually a series of reefs that begins just south of La Ceiba and extends almost as far as the Stouffer

Presidente. Situated about 200 yards offshore at an average depth of 40 to 50 feet, Paraiso is about a five-minute swim from the sunken plane in front of La Ceiba, and, at its southern end, is one of the best spots off Cozumel for night diving.

Chankanaab Reef, situated in 10 to 35 feet of water right offshore, is located just south of the lagoon of the same name. Like Paraiso, it is famous for its beautiful coral formations and colorful marine life, and it, too, is a good spot for night dives.

San Francisco Reef, a quarter mile long and situated in 20 to 60 feet of water, is located directly offshore from Playa San Francisco. The current that sweeps the wall here (depth unlimited) is less pronounced than at other underwater locations around Cozumel, which makes it a good spot for intermediate divers to practice their wall drift dive technique.

The **Santa Rosa Wall**, a drop-off that begins at 50 feet and plunges into bottomless depths, is located due south of San Francisco Reef. After Palancar Santa Rosa is Cozumel's second most popular dive spot, but a strong current is always a factor here; beginning divers will want to get their feet wet elsewhere before moving on to the Wall.

Palancar Reef, located about a mile offshore and stretching over three miles, is Cozumel's pride and joy; in fact, it's rated one of the top five dive sites in the world. The northern end of the reef is situated in about 40 feet of water, but gradually slopes into deeper water, with the wall dropping off to unlimited depths. Divers will encounter a fantasyland of bizarre coral formations, deep canyons, winding ravines, and countless tunnels and passageways. Visibility sometimes extends as far as 250 feet, and most people who are lucky enough to explore it say there's nothing like it.

Colombia Reef, a few miles south of Palancar, is almost as beautiful as its neighbor. Situated in 60 to 70 feet of water, with a dropoff to unlimited depths, this is the spot to see such impressive denizens of the deep as groupers, jacks, and giant turtles.

Maracaibo Reef, off the southern tip of the island, begins at 100 feet and has numerous crevices and caves. This is the most challenging of all the dive sites off Cozumel, and with travel time figured in will require a full day.

The entire underwater area from the cruise-ship pier to Punta Celarain has been designated a marine refuge; collecting, breaking, or otherwise damaging the delicate corals and sponges is strictly prohibited. Dives can be arranged through one of the more than 20 operators scattered around the island, and underwater still or video cameras can also be rented at a number of places in town. Listed below are a few of the better dive shops:

- **Aqua Safari**: Daily trips to Palancar Reef, scuba lessons, snorkel gear for sale. Avenida Melgar 39a; Tel: (987) 2-0101.
- **Blue Angel Divers**: Daily trips to Palancar, lessons, PADI certification, snorkel gear rentals. On the coast road near the Villablanca; Tel: (987) 2-1631 or 0931.
- **Caribbean Divers**: Daily trips to Palancar, lessons, equipment rental, night dives. Avenida Melgar 38b; Tel: (987) 2-1145.
- **Dive Paradise**: Day and half-day trips for novice, intermediate, and expert divers; twilight dives. Avenida Melgar 601 (across from the navy base); Tel: (987) 2-1007.

For a complete listing of Cozumel's dive operators, write: CADO, P.O. Box 414236, Miami Beach, FL 33141-0236.

Most dive shops run snorkeling excursions in addition to dive trips. Bringing your own equipment from home, however, is your best bet; shops sometimes run out of equipment, and the masks often don't fit as well as they should.

Waterskiing can be arranged through the Stouffer Presidente. Hobie Cats and jet skis are available at the Meliá Mayan. Windsurfers can be rented at the Presidente, Villablanca, Cabañas del Caribe, Meliá Mayan, and Divers' Inn hotels. The Meliá Mayan, La Ceiba, and Cabañas del Caribe hotels have dive schools.

Deep-sea fishing boats and sailboats can be rented at Puerto de Abrigo, the marina on the coast road about five minutes north of town. **Pez Maya**, a beautiful camp for bone fishermen and bird-watchers 80 km (50 miles) to the southwest at Boca Paila, the long fingerlike peninsula that stretches south from Tulum, can accommodate up to 16 guests at a time in rustic cabins. Guides will take you fishing or out to see the pelicans, spoonbills, and other species of waterfowl that flock to this natural aviary. For more information contact the Meliá Mayan Cozumel, Playa Santa Pilar, Cozumel, Quintana Roo, Mexico 77600; Fax: (987) 2-1599.

No golf course has been built on Cozumel as yet, but there is a miniature course next to the Hotel Barracuda. Some hotels have tennis courts, but the same stiff breeze that keeps Cozumel temperatures pleasant has discouraged the serious development of tennis facilities.

Excursions from Cozumel

Travel agents anywhere in town will be happy to arrange the following excursions.

The usual tour of the island includes stops at Chankanaab Lagoon for swimming and the ten-acre archaeological site of San Gervasio; make sure that any such tour you sign up for includes both.

The *Bonanza* offers snorkeling trips to Paraiso and Palancar reefs, with a stop for lunch at Playa Santa Rosa. Tel: (987) 2-0563 to make reservations.

The *Zorro* takes you to a deserted beach on Isla de Pasión, off the northern end of Cozumel, for swimming, snorkeling, and a picnic. Lunch is sometimes caught along the way and prepared on the beach; the cost is approximately $40. Contact Fiesta Cozumel Holidays (Tel: 987/2-0725) or Viajes y Deportes del Caribe (Tel: 987/2-0322) to make reservations.

You can also fly to Chichén Itzá—one of the greatest Mayan archaeological sites—for the day (about $100 per person) or take a day-long trip to the beautiful walled city of Tulum, with a stop at the natural aquarium of Xel-há (about $50 per person). Both trips depart at 8:30 A.M. (pickup at your hotel). The Tulum trip returns by 2:00 P.M., the Chichén Itzá trip by 6:00 P.M. Contact Fiesta Cozumel Holidays (Tel: 987/2-0725) or Turismo Aviomar (Tel: 987/2-0477) for further information.

GETTING AROUND

Cancún

American, Continental, United, Mexicana, Aeroméxico, and Iberia are the major international air carriers offering direct service to Cancún. American offers daily service out of its Dallas–Fort Worth and Raleigh hubs; Continental offers daily service from its Houston hub; United flies daily from Chicago and Washington, D.C.; Mexicana flies nonstop from Los Angeles, Dallas–Fort Worth, Miami, and New York, and direct (with a stopover in Mexico City) from San Francisco and Chicago; Aeroméxico offers nonstop service from New York (four times a week) and Houston (daily); and Iberia is now offering direct service from Miami, with New York and Los Angeles service scheduled for the near future. It's a 3½-hour flight from Chicago, Washington, and New York; 3 hours from Raleigh; 2½ hours from Dallas–Fort Worth; and 1½ from Miami. If Cancún is only one stop on your Mexican itinerary, arrange for it as part of your overall ticketing before you leave; individual domestic fares within Mexico can be costly.

Upon arrival in Cancún you must take a *colectivo* from the airport to the hotel zone (the length of the trip will depend on the number of stops it has to make). A ticket, which you buy at the airport, will cost about $8.

In Cancún buses run through the hotel zone along Boulevard Kukulcán until midnight. The downtown stop for the bus that returns to the hotel zone is across Avenida Tulum from wherever you got off. (A good bet is to stand across the street from the San Francisco de Assis grocery store and simply flag down the first bus that comes along.) If you see a bus coming, jump on. Otherwise, be prepared for a long wait; no apparent schedule is kept.

Taxis are always available outside hotels and the busier restaurants. If you don't see one in front of your hotel, walk down to Boulevard Kukulcán and flag one down. You may want to keep your eyes shut, however; many drivers here are new behind the wheel and view Boulevard Kukulcán as the course at Le Mans. Saying "*Más despacio, por favor*" will get them to slow down. If you're going anywhere other than downtown, check the price before getting into the cab.

The most difficult place to get a taxi is at the passenger-ferry terminal upon your return from Isla Mujeres. The law of the jungle applies here. Push to the front of the boat before docking and prepare to disembark like a sprinter coming out of the blocks. When the gate opens, run—don't walk—to the road and flag down the first taxi you can, then jump in to hold your place. This is a situation where you simply can't afford to be shy.

Isla Mujeres

Direct flights to Isla Mujeres from anywhere convenient are virtually nonexistent; instead, most travellers fly into Cancún International Airport and then take the airport van to the ferry at Puerto Juárez, which costs about $20. Bonanza Airlines runs an air-taxi service between the island and Mérida every Tuesday, Thursday, and Saturday; call the Hotel Perla del Caribe (Tel: 98/82-0444) for information and reservations.

Passenger ferries operate out of Puerto Juárez, about 15 minutes north of Cancún City by taxi. *Car* ferries leave from Punta Sam, another 10 minutes north of Puerto Juárez. The trip from either to Isla Mujeres takes about 45 minutes. Schedules are rather informal, but ferries leave every other hour or so. The fare for either is minimal. If you opt for the passenger ferry, try not to bring anything too heavy; there is no place to store luggage and this is a strictly carry-it-yourself operation. If you're bringing a car over, be sure to get there at least 45 minutes before departure; the ferry can handle only 25 cars, and it's operated on a first-come, first-served basis. If it's a rough day, the car ferry will give you the smoother ride.

The third ferry option to the island, the Isla Mujeres shuttle (no vehicles), leaves from the Playa Linda marine terminal opposite the Calinda Cancún Beach three times daily (at 9:00 A.M., 11:15 A.M. and 2:30 P.M.). The fare is $12 per person, round-trip, and includes beverages. For further information, Tel: (98) 84-6656 or 6846.

To explore Isla Mujeres take a taxi or rent a moped. Mopeds can be rented at Cárdenas Moto Rent, Avenida Guerrero 105-A (Tel: 98/82-0079); Ppe's Moto Rent, Avenida Hidalgo 19 (Tel: 98/82-0019); Joaquin Motos, Avenida Juárez 7 (Tel: 98/82-0068); or Rente Una Moto, Avenida Rueda Medina 3 (Tel: 98/82-0031).

It's easy to get around town on foot. To get out to El Garrafón or any of the beaches, however, spring for the moped. The hills on Isla Mujeres are not particularly steep, but there are several and the trip by bicycle is tiring.

Cozumel

American, Continental, and Mexicana are the major international carriers offering direct service to Cozumel. American offers daily service from its Dallas–Fort Worth hub; Continental offers daily service from its Houston hub; and Mexicana flies direct (with a stopover in Cancún) from Miami, Los Angeles, New York, San Francisco, Chicago (also daily), and Dallas–Fort Worth (four times a week).

Aerocaribe links Cancún and Cozumel with 15-minute flights that depart every other hour. It also makes the seven-minute flight to Playa del Carmen every other hour. The car ferry from Puerto Morelos leaves early in the morning (the time changes from week to week), and the trip takes approximately four hours; the fare is about $5 per car. A passenger ferry—either the Water Jet or the slower *Cozumeleño*—leaves Playa del Carmen approximately ten times daily, with departures at 5:30, 7:30, 10:15, 11:00 A.M., and noon, and 12:15, 2:30, 5:30, 6:30, 7:30, and 9:00 P.M. Schedules are subject to change, and the fare is the equivalent of $7.

Private taxis are the way to get from the airport to your hotel on Cozumel. If you're staying on the north end of the island, the trip takes about five minutes. Trips to the southern part of the island take longer but rarely exceed 15 minutes.

Taxis are also the best way to get around the island, but

you have to be armed with patience—there aren't enough cabs to go around, so it's a seller's market. Taxi schedules also seem to center around drivers' appetites, with cabs tending to get scarce at lunch/siesta time and at night after 9:00 P.M.

Cars, Jeeps, and mopeds can all be rented in San Miguel, but you'll want to inspect the vehicle to make sure it's in working order before you sign the contract. You might also want to take your moped for a test drive to see whether you can handle it; loose sand or gravel on roadsides can cause serious accidents. Renting a Jeep or Volkswagen Safari is sometimes the better part of valor.

Public buses stop at the hotels on the coast road. Signs on the front of the rickety vehicles read "Hoteles," and though they are inexpensive, their runs tend to be sporadic.

ACCOMMODATIONS REFERENCE

The rates given below are projections for December 1992 through Easter 1993. Unless otherwise indicated, rates are for double rooms, double occupancy; the 10 percent VAT has been added. As rates are subject to change, it's a good idea to double-check before booking. Cancún, Isla Mujeres, and Cozumel are in the central standard time zone; the telephone area code for Cancún and Isla Mujeres is 98, for Cozumel it's 987.

Cancún

▶ **Calinda Cancún Beach.** Boulevard Kukulcán, **Cancún**, Quintana Roo 77500. Tel: 83-1600; Fax: 83-1857; in the U.S. and Canada, Tel: (800) 228-5151. $138–160.

▶ **Camino Real.** P.O. Box 14, Boulevard Kukulcán, **Cancún**, Quintana Roo 77500. Tel: 83-0100; Fax: 83-1730; in the U.S. and Canada, Tel: (800) 228-3000. $230–$240.

▶ **Cancún Palace.** P.O. Box 1730, Boulevard Kukulcán, km 14.5, **Cancún**, Quintana Roo 77500. Tel: 85-0533; Fax: 85-1593; in the U.S., Tel: (800) 346-8225; in Canada, Tel: (800) 826-6017. $160–$175.

▶ **Club Las Velas Cancún.** P.O. Box 1614, Boulevard Kukulcán at Galeón, **Cancún**, Quintana Roo 77500. Tel: 83-2222; Fax: 83-2118; in the U.S. and Canada, Tel: (800) 223-9815 or, in New York, Tel: (212) 545-8469. $268–$328 (all-inclusive, run of the house) or $328–$388 (junior suite).

▶ **Fiesta Americana Coral Beach Cancún.** Boulevard Kukulcán, **Cancún**, Quintana Roo 77500. Tel: 83-2900; Fax: 83-3173; in the U.S. and Canada, Tel: (800) FIESTA-1. $287.

▶ **Fiesta American Cancún.** P.O. Box 696, Boulevard Kukulcán, **Cancún**, Quintana Roo 77500. Tel: 83-2700; Fax: 83-2502; in the U.S. and Canada, Tel: (800) FIESTA-1. $210.

▶ **Hyatt Regency Cancún.** Boulevard Kukulcán, **Cancún**, Quintana Roo 77500. Tel: 83-0966; Fax: 83-1438; in the U.S. and Canada, Tel: (800) 233-1234. $225–$253.

▶ **Krystal Cancún.** Boulevard Kukulcán, **Cancún**, Quintana Roo 77500. Tel: 83-1133; Fax: 83-1205; in the U.S. and Canada, Tel: (800) 231-9860. $195–$218.

▶ **Meliá Cancún.** Boulevard Kukulcán, **Cancún**, Quintana Roo 77500. Tel: 85-1160; Fax: 85-1085; in the U.S. and Canada, Tel: (800) 336-3542. $270–$306 (add $10 to guarantee an ocean view).

▶ **Sheraton Cancún Resort and Towers.** P.O. Box 834, Boulevard Kukulcán, **Cancún**, Quintana Roo 77500. Tel: 83-1988; Fax: 85-0083; in the U.S. and Canada, Tel: (800) 325-3535. $165–$207 (double); $220–$255 (tower); $287–$310 (junior suite with Jacuzzi).

▶ **Stouffer Presidente Cancún.** Boulevard Kukulcán, km 7.5, **Cancún**, Quintana Roo 77500. Tel: 83-0200; Fax: 83-2515; in the U.S. and Canada, Tel: (800) HOTELS-1. $195–$240.

South of Cancún

▶ **Blue Parrot Inn.** P.O. Box 64, **Playa del Carmen**, Quintana Roo 77710. For reservations, contact: 460 Blue Springs Avenue, Orange City, FL 32763. Tel: (800) 634-3547 or (904) 775-6660; Fax (in Playa; address to "Caja 20"): (908) 4-4564. $55–$60 (hotel rooms, palapas); $75–$80 (bungalow); $100 (bungalow with kitchenette); $145–$175 (beachfront villa).

▶ **Continental Plaza Playacar.** Fracc. Playacar, km 62.5, **Playa del Carmen**, Quintana Roo 77710. Tel: (987) 2-1583 or 1100; Fax: (988) 5-1403 or 1065; in the U.S., Tel: (800) 88-CONTI. $165.

▶ **Copacabana.** C/o Sr. Eduardo Canto, P.O. Box 103, **Playa del Carmen**, Quintana Roo 77710. $35.

▶ **Hotel Akumal Cancún.** P.O. Box 28, Cancún, Quintana Roo 77500. Tel: (98) 84-2272; Fax: (987) 2-2567. $88.

▶ **Hotel Club Akumal Caribe.** For reservations, contact: P.O. Box 13326, El Paso, TX 79913. All reservations must be made through the El Paso office (the country code when dialing the United States from Mexico is "95"). Tel: (800) 351-1622; in Canada, (800) 343-1440. $100 ("tower"); $77 (bungalow).

▶ **Las Palapas.** C/o Arrecife Caribeño, S.A. de C.V., P.O. Box 116, **Playa del Carmen**, Quintana Roo 77710. Tel: (987) 2-2977; Fax: (5) 379-8641 (in Mexico City). $157 (includes breakfast and dinner; full payment must be received 30 days before arrival).

THE CARIBBEAN RESORTS

▶ **Shangri-La Caribe.** C/o CVI/Turquoise Reef Resorts, P.O. Box 2664, Evergreen, CO 80439. Tel: (987) 2-2888; in the U.S., Tel: (800) 538-6802; in Canada, Tel: (303) 674-9615; Fax: (303) 674-8735. $100–$140 (includes breakfast and dinner).

▶ **Villa Arqueológica Cobá.** P.O. Box 710, Cancún, Quintana Roo 77500. No local phone; in the U.S., Tel: (800) CLUB-MED; in Canada, Tel: (514) 937-7707 or (416) 960-5224. $62–$75.

Isla Mujeres

▶ **Hotel Na Balam.** Calle Zazil-ha 1, **Isla Mujeres**, Quintana Roo 77400. Tel: 82-0279. $55–$65.

▶ **Hotel Perla del Caribe.** Avenida Madero 2, **Isla Mujeres**, Quintana Roo, 77400. Tel: 82-0444; in the U.S., Tel: (800) 358-6454. $52–$76.

▶ **Nautibeach Condominium-Hotel.** Avenida Rueda Medina, **Isla Mujeres**, Quintana Roo 77400. Tel: 82-0259; Fax: 82-0487. $110 (two-night minimum).

▶ **Posada del Mar.** Rueda Medina 15, **Isla Mujeres**, Quintana Roo 77400. Tel: 82-0044; Fax: 82-0266. $50.

Cozumel

▶ **La Ceiba.** P.O. Box 284, Carretera a Chankanaab, km 4.5 **Cozumel**, Quintana Roo 77600. Tel: 2-0844; Fax: 2-0065; in the U.S. and Canada, Tel: (800) 777-5873. $132.

▶ **El Cozumeleño.** P.O. Box 53, Playa Santa Pilar, **Cozumel**, Quintana Roo 77600. Tel: 2-0149; Fax: 2-0381; in the U.S. and Canada, Tel: (800) 437-3923. $128.

▶ **Cozumel Reef Holiday Inn.** P.O. Box 207, Carretera a Chankanaab, km 7.5, **Cozumel**, Quintana Roo 77600. Tel: 2-2622; Fax: 2-2666; in the U.S. and Canada, Tel: (800) HOLIDAY. $150–$225.

▶ **Fiesta Americana Sol Caribe.** P.O. Box 259, Playa Paraiso, km 3.5, **Cozumel**, Quintana Roo 77600. Tel: 2-0555; Fax: 2-1301; in the U.S. and Canada, Tel: (800) FIESTA-1. $135–$175.

▶ **Hotel Villablanca Beach Club and Sports Complex.** P.O. Box 230, **Cozumel**, Quintana Roo 77600. Tel and Fax: 2-0865; in the U.S., Tel: (800) 780-3949. $55–$77.

▶ **Meliá Mayan Cozumel.** Playa Santa Pilar, **Cozumel**, Quintana Roo 77600. Tel: 2-0411; Fax: 2-1599; in the U.S. and Canada, Tel: (800) 336-3542. $135–$175.

▶ **Stouffer Presidente Cozumel.** Carretera a Chankanaab, km 6.5, **Cozumel**, Quintana Roo 77600. Tel: 2-0322; Fax: 2-1360; in the U.S. and Canada, Tel: (800) HOTELS-1. $132–$275.

CHRONOLOGY OF THE HISTORY OF MEXICO AND GUATEMALA

The Beginnings

- **50,000 B.C.**: Wandering hunters and food gatherers cross into the Americas from present-day Siberia over a land bridge, long since submerged, that anthropologists have dubbed "Beringia." Little is known of these Stone Age peoples, but over the course of tens of thousands of years various racial types arrive and become diffused over both the northern and southern continents of the Americas.

  At Tepexpán, near Mexico City, the skeletal remains of a young woman have been discovered near those of a mammoth that was killed with flint-tipped weapons. This so-called Tepexpán Man has been dated to about 12,000 B.C.
- **9000 B.C.**: End of the Ice Age; large Pleistocene fauna such as mammoths and mastodons become extinct.
- **7000 B.C.**: Domestication of maize begins. After maize, squash, chile peppers, and beans become staples of the Mesoamerican diet—much as they are today.
- **2300–1800 B.C.**: Pottery is introduced; clay figurines begin to be fashioned.

The Preclassic Era

- **1800 B.C.**: Small villages are established in the Valley of Mexico (around present-day Mexico City), among them Ticomán, Copilco, Tlatilco, and Zacatenco. Many clay figurines are produced, especially fertility images of women.
- **1200 B.C.**: The **Olmecs**, an advanced people of mysterious origins, establish their first great ceremonial center, San Lorenzo, in the Gulf region. Subsequently, their influence spreads over much of Mesoamerica and becomes especially evident at Monte Albán, near present-day Oaxaca City. Jade carving, giant stone heads, and other major stone sculpture are produced.
- **800 B.C.**: The first structures that can be called architecture rise at Cuicuilco and Cerro de Tlapacoya, in the

Valley of Mexico. The Maya establish themselves throughout the Yucatán Peninsula and the highlands of Chiapas—an area they occupy to this day.

- **700 B.C.**: The Maya, influenced by the Olmecs, build an elaborate ceremonial center at Uaxactún, in present-day Guatemala.
- **600 B.C.**: Olmec civilization reaches its apex at La Venta (in today's Tabasco). Hieroglyphs, numerals, and a calendar are developed.
- **500 B.C.**: In western Mexico, artisans create remarkable clay figurines.
- **300 B.C.**: America's first true urban civilization, Teotihuacán, begins to develop in the Valley of Mexico. In Guatemala construction begins at Tikal, where building will continue for the next 1,000 years.

The Classic Era

- **200 B.C.–A.D. 900**: Cities and ceremonial centers are established throughout Mesoamerica, in conjunction with a complex theology.
- **200–350**: The urban center of Teotihuacán covers six square miles and boasts more than 150,000 inhabitants in what is perhaps the largest pre-industrial city anywhere in the world. Centers in the Mayan region, on the Gulf Coast, and in Oaxaca continue to expand. Monte Albán, Palenque, Uxmal, and other centers enter their greatest era.
- **650–750**: Teotihuacán experiences irreversible decline. Eventually, internal dissension and other factors facilitate the destruction of the great city by nomadic invaders. Farther south and east, however, other great Mesoamerican civilizations continue to flourish. Tikal, Copan, and Chichén Viejo are deserted. Xochicalco survives, spanning the Late Classic and Postclassic eras.
- **750–900**: The great Mesoamerican centers experience decline, collapse, and, most often, abandonment, for reasons still debated (see Overview).

The Postclassic Era

- **900–1200**: Semibarbaric **Toltecs** migrate southward (where they came from remains unknown), supplanting older cultures while becoming civilized themselves. Their influence extends south as far as the Yucatán, where temples are built and the ancient cult of the plumed serpent flourishes. Perhaps the best-known incarnation of the plumed serpent, Topiltzin-Quetzalcóatl, a priest-king, is supposed to have been born among the Toltecs in 947.

Another warrior people, the **Mixtecs**, move into the valleys near the ancient ceremonial centers of Cholula and Monte Albán. Their knowledge of metalworking—first gold, and then copper and silver—improves and spreads; as forms of writing are refined, they begin to record their history.

- **c. 999**: Topiltzin-Quetzalcóatl flees, promising to return. Warrior kings succeed him at Tula, the Toltec capital.
- **1325**: **Aztecs** (theories conflict as to their geographical origins) arrive in the central highlands of present-day Mexico and establish their capital, Tenochtitlán, on an island in Lake Texcoco. The settlement will evolve into what is today Mexico City.
- **c. 1400**: *Chinampas,* so-called floating gardens that improve agricultural efficiency, facilitate the Aztec domination of the central highlands.
- **1440–1500**: Aztec domination extends throughout what is now Mexico.
- **1502**: Móctezuma II is crowned god-emperor of the Aztecs. Disturbing omens punctuate his reign, seeming to foretell the return of the plumed serpent-god Quetzalcóatl.
- **1517**: The expedition of Hernández de Córdova sails along the Yucatán coast.
- **1518**: Juan de Grijalva, following up on Córdova's discoveries, explores much of the Atlantic coast of Mesoamerica and reports back to his king on its vast size. The population of the region at the time—a figure unknown to de Grijalva—is put at 25 million by modern scholars. Grijalva names the region New Spain.
- **1519**: Hernán Cortés, a Spanish adventurer, lands on a Veracruz beach with 555 soldiers and 16 horses—animals unknown and terrifying to the inhabitants. After a grueling march over the Sierra Madre Oriental punctuated by skirmishes with local tribes, Cortés and his men enter the island city of Tenochtitlán. Although initially welcomed as the returning serpent-god Quetzalcóatl, Cortés soon seizes Móctezuma and takes him hostage.
- **1520**: The ineffectual Móctezuma is slain by his own people, and the Spaniards are driven from the city.
- **1521**: Cortés, with an army of Indian allies, returns and besieges the Aztec capital. Eventually, Tenochtitlán falls to the invaders.
- **1523**: Pedro de Alvarado, Cortés's chief lieutenant, begins a prolonged conquest of what is now Guatemala.

- **1524**: Cortés kneels to welcome 12 Franciscan friars, who immediately set out to Christianize the country—a task they accomplish with astonishing speed.
- **1525**: Cuauhtémoc, Móctezuma's successor, is executed by the Spanish; he is the last Aztec emperor. Vast amounts of Aztec treasure are shipped off to Spain.

New Spain

The Spanish Crown moves quickly to exploit and evangelize its new colony. A caste system is established, with Spaniards born in Spain at the top; pure-blood Spaniards born outside the motherland, called *criollos,* next; people of mixed race, or *mestizos,* below that; and pure-blooded Indians, or *indios,* at the bottom.

Native art, which is viewed as diabolical, is ruthlessly destroyed. Weakened by plagues, Indian resistance collapses. The few surviving native painted books, called codices, are taken back to Europe; not a single pre-Columbian codex remains in its country of origin.

- **1530**: Construction of the National Cathedral in Mexico City begins.
- **1531**: Juan Diego, a humble Aztec convert, sees a vision of the Virgin on a hill north of Mexico City—a miracle that promotes the conversion of, and gives solace to, dark-skinned people throughout New Spain, because this Virgin is herself dark skinned.
- **1535**: Antonio de Mendoza is named the first viceroy of New Spain; he will establish the pattern for Spain's administration of its New World colony.
- **1542**: Enslavement of Indians is outlawed, only to be replaced by new ways of obtaining their forced labor.
- **1554**: A new mining process increases silver output. Silver pours into Spain's coffers for the next two and a half centuries, doubling the Western world's supply in the process.
- **1565**: A plot to establish an independent Mexican kingdom, to be ruled by Cortés's son, is nipped in the bud.
- **1571**: The Inquisition begins its work in Mexico City.
- **1651**: Sor Juana Inés de la Cruz, destined to become New Spain's greatest poet, is born.
- **1700–1800**: Baroque art and architecture are fostered by the Church. Ornate, fanciful architectural decoration— the Churrigueresque style—flowers, only to be supplanted by the Neoclassical style at the end of the century.

CHRONOLOGY 671

- **1767**: The Jesuits are expelled from the colony by royal order.
- **1776**: Earthquakes destroy the old capital of Guatemala (now Antigua). Guatemala City is founded three years later.
- **1808**: In Europe, France invades Spain, precipitating a crisis in Spain's New World colonies.

The Struggle for Independence

- **1810**: The Querétaro Conspiracy arises as patriots in the Bajío region discuss and partly plan an uprising designed to overthrow Spanish rule. At the same time, Miguel Hidalgo y Costilla, a priest from the obscure town of Dolores, raises the cry of independence and leads a ragtag army against the Crown. The struggle continues for 11 years.
- **1811**: Hidalgo and other rebels are defeated and executed. José María Morelos, Hidalgo's student and successor, continues the war but is himself captured and executed (1815).
- **1821**: Independence for Mexico is proclaimed by Agustín de Iturbide and Vicente Guerrero (though Spain withholds its recognition until 1836). Guatemalan independence is also proclaimed; its status in regard to Mexico is left unclear.
- **1822**: Iturbide establishes himself as "emperor," but is deposed the following year. After Iturbide's fall, Guatemala follows its own course.
- **1824**: Mexico drafts a democratic constitution, and Guadalupe Victoria is proclaimed president.
- **1833**: General Santa Anna is elected president. Over the next two decades this mountebank, who styles himself "His Serene Highness," will be in and out of power—to Mexico's great detriment.
- **1835**: Texas declares and wins its independence from Mexico.
- **1838**: France blockades and bombards Veracruz to collect outstanding debts owed by the fledgling Mexican government.
- **1846**: The United States invades Mexico.
- **1848**: The Treaty of Guadalupe Hidalgo results in Mexico ceding almost half its territory to the United States.
- **1854**: Santa Anna sells parts of what are now the states of Arizona and New Mexico to the United States in order to

raise money for the suppression of liberal democracy in Mexico.
- **1855**: The bitter War of Reform, pitting liberals against the old establishment, breaks out. The Church battles against liberal reform.

Democracy vs. Dictatorship

- **1857**: A new constitution separating Church and State is adopted. Civil war continues and Church landholdings are seized. Pope Pius IX nullifies the Mexican constitution.
- **1859**: Benito Juárez, a full-blooded Zapotec Indian and liberal politician from Oaxaca, helps to draft the Reform Laws, which call for the nationalization of Church property, the closing of convents, and the liberation of religious expression. He is elected president two years later.
- **1862**: England, Spain, and France seize Veracruz to collect debts. Spain and England soon withdraw, but France invades and is defeated at the battle of Puebla—a military victory commemorated every year on May 5.
- **1863**: A second French invasion results in the capture of Puebla and Mexico City. Juárez flees north, while the Church and Mexican conservatives welcome the French.
- **1864**: The French and Mexican conservatives proclaim Austrian Archduke Maximilian Emperor of Mexico. War continues.
- **1867**: Royalist troops are defeated at Querétaro, and Maximilian is executed. Juárez is reconfirmed as president and enters the capital in triumph. He heads a liberal government until his death in 1872.
- **1871**: Liberals win military victory in Guatemala. Railroad construction begins.
- **1876**: General Porfirio Díaz is elected president.
- **1884**: Díaz, out of office four years, returns to the presidency and governs as virtual dictator until 1911. Dubbed the "Porfiriate," it is an era of foreign investment in Mexico, economic progress for the ruling class, and political repression.

Revolution and the Emergence of Modern Mexico

- **1910**: Francisco I. Madero, the son of a wealthy northern

family, campaigns against Díaz for the presidency—aided militarily by Emiliano Zapata—but is soon arrested. Díaz begins his eighth term in office.
- **1911**: Díaz, under pressure, resigns.
- **1912**: Madero is elected president. Invasion is feared as U.S. troops mass at the border.
- **1913**: General Victoriano Huerta stages a coup, and Madero is assassinated. Civil war breaks out and Huerta flees. In the south, Zapata leads an armed struggle for land reform.
- **1914**: U.S. troops seize Veracruz, killing nearly 200 Mexican defenders. In the north, Venustiano Carranza, an elderly landowner, forms a constitutionalist army. A power struggle ensues among Carranza, Zapata, and Pancho Villa, a peon turned general and warlord.
- **1915**: At the Battle of Celaya, troops of Carranza and General Alvaro Obregón defeat the forces of Villa and Zapata.
- **1916**: The United States recognizes the Carranza government. In retaliation, Villa raids Columbus, New Mexico. U.S. troops cross the border into Mexico.
- **1917**: Carranza is elected president under a new reform constitution. In Guatemala an earthquake devastates the capital.
- **1921**: Gen. Alvaro Obregón, revolutionary hero, becomes president. He is later assassinated by a religious fanatic.
- **1920**: Guatemalan dictator Manuel Estrada Cabrera is overthrown after 22 years of calamitous rule.
- **1924–1928**: Labor unions become a strong institutional force during the presidency of Plutarco Calles. During the same period, the Church is more sharply restricted, and the old anticlerical laws are once again enforced. *Cristeros,* religious militants in armed rebellion against this trend, are gradually suppressed. The Partido Revolucionario Institucional, or PRI, destined to become the dominant political force in Mexican life, emerges.
- **1934**: Lázaro Cárdenas is elected president. During his six-year term he nationalizes the railroads and petroleum industry (among other sweeping social and political reforms)—to the consternation of the international business community.
- **1940**: Avila Camacho wins an orderly election. Reform in the postwar period continues at a slower pace.
- **1945**: José Arévado becomes president of Guatemala and initiates democratic reforms.

- **1954**: In Guatemala Colonel Carlos Armas seizes power with the help of the United States. Years of tumult follow.
- **1968**: The hosting of the Summer Olympic Games brings new prestige to Mexico; the favorable publicity is marred by the violent suppression of student demonstrations.
- **1973–1978**: Mexico rides a wave of prosperity, thanks to soaring oil prices in the wake of the OPEC oil embargo.
- **1976**: Great destruction is caused by an earthquake in Guatemala.
- **1982**: President López Portillo nationalizes the banking system; Mexico is thrown into economic crisis as oil prices worldwide plunge.
- **1985**: Mexico City is devastated by earthquakes.
- **1986**: Vinicio Cereza, elected president of Guatemala, institutes a struggle for peace and greater democracy.
- **1988**: Carlos Salinas de Gortari is elected president in the first hotly contested national election in modern Mexican history. Amidst charges of widespread fraud, opposition parties on both the right and left make inroads into PRI political dominance.
- **1989–1990**: President Salinas intensifies his political and economic reforms. The powerful oil workers union is brought under legal control.
- **1991–92**: Mexico, the United States, and Canada debate a free-trade pact that would create the world's largest economic union. Political reform and greater freedom of the Church is advanced under President Salinas.

—Robert Somerlott

INDEX

Academia Hispano Americana, 221
Aca Joe: Cozumel, 652; Mazatlán, 345
Acapulco, 14, 334, 406, 408 (map), 425
Acapulco Joe, 421
Acapulco Malibu Hotel, 420, 432
Acapulco Plaza, 424, 432
Acapulco Plaza Mall, 424
Acapulco Princess, 412, 432
Acapulco Shalom, 422
The Acapulco Strip, 417 (map)
Acapulco Zoo, 427
El Acuario, 654
Acuario Mazatlán, 342
Adonis, 132
African, 400
Agora, 470
Agua Azul: Chiapas, 553; Guadalajara, 264
Agua de Correa, 404
Agua Escondida, 169
Akumal, 608, 634
Alamos, 10, 352
Alan's, 619
Alberto's Continental Patio, 527
Alfarería Tlaquepaque, 364
Alfredo's: Loreto, 309; Mexico City, 129
Alfredo's Tennis Club, 420
The Alhóndiga de Granaditas, 227
Los Almendros, 527
Alom La Creación, 585
El Amanecer, 400
Amarras, 154
Ancira Sierra Radisson Plaza Hotel Monterrey, 245, 250
Andale, 369
Angangueo, 241
Animal Fiesta, 652
Las Animas, 373
Anna's, 420
Antigua, 581, 597
Antigua Los Cabos, 315
Antiguo Edificio de la Aduana, 51
Antigua Hacienda de Tlalpan, 139
Apasia, 424
Aplijsa, 155
Aqua Safari, 660
El Arco, 312, 326
Los Arcos: Acapulco, 424; Mazatlán, 346
Aries, 155
Arrecife, 656
Arte Mexicano, 620
Artesanias Copil, 498
Artesanias Itandehui, 498
Artesanías Méxicanos, 262
Art & Harry's Bar & Grill, 443
El Asador Vasco, 503
Asian Art Gallery, 152
Astronomical Observatory, 505
Atitlán, 590
Atotonilco, 222
Atzompa, 497
Auda Silversmiths, 154
Avalos, 149
Avándaro, 188
Avenida Subterráneo Miguel Hidalgo, 226
La Azteca, 366
Aztec Calendar Stone, 59, 81
Azulejos, 116, 133

Baby O, 418, 424
Bacocho, 436, 443
La Baguette, 315
Bahía de Santa Cruz, 449
Bahías Gemelas, 390
Bahías de Huatulco, 434
Bahía de Tangolunda, 446
Bahuichivo, 290
Baja California, 14, 298
Baja California Norte, 301 (map)
Baja California Sur, 307, 308 (map)
Baja Mar, 304
Bajío, 11, 198
Balancanché Cave, 547
Bali Hai, 343
Los Ballesteros, 169
Ballet Folklórico de México, 70
Ballet Folklórico Nacional Aztlán, 622
La Balsa, 188
Baluarte de Santiago, 464
La Bamba: San José del Cabo, 314; Veracruz, 467
Bamboleo, 442
Banana's, 442
Bananas Ranas, 419
Banneret, 429
Bar Alfonso, 126
Barbarella, 142
Barbas Negras, 422
Bar Joronga, 119
Bar el Navegante, 342
Bar L'Opera, 140
Barra de Navidad, 14, 334, 379
Barranca Batopilas, 293
Barranca de Oblatos, 269
Barra del Norte, 475
Barra de Potosí, 404

675

INDEX

Barrio de San Francisco, 263
Bar Social, 388
Basihuare, 292
Basilica Menor de Nuestra Señora de Guanajuato, 230
La Basílica de Nuestra Señora de Guadalupe, 47
Basílica de Nuestra Señora de la Salud, 273
Bay Club, 403
Bazaar, 425
Bazaar El Caracol, 269
Bazar del Angel, 654
Bázar El Dorado, 388
Bazar Sábado, 97, 147
Bazar Tamar, 442
Bazar Ticun-Uman, 442
Beckman, 221
Beer Garden, 271
Bellas Artes, 217
Bellinghausen, 129
Bellini's, 117
El Bermejo, 310
Berthangel, 478, 486
Best Western Majestic Hotel, 121
Best Western Posada Real, 440, 456
Beto's, 422
Beto's Safari Bar, 422
Biblioteca de las Californias, 311
Biblioteca Pública: Pátzcuaro, 272; San Miguel, 221
Bismark II Restaurant, 311
El Bistro (Panajachel), 590
Le Bistro (Puerto Vallarta), 368
Blue Angel Divers, 660
Blue Bayou, 613
Blue Parrot Inn, 631, 665
La Bocana, 404
Boca del Río, 465
Bodegas de Santo Tomás, 305
Bogart's: Cancún, 613, 617; Ixtapa, 397; Puerto Vallarta, 362
El Boleo, 307
Bon Appetit, 654
Bond, 620
La Boom, 623
Boom Boom, 388

Bora Bora, 343
Bosque de Chapultepec, 77
Boutique Soqui, 619
Bristol, 120
El Buen Comer, 135
La Bufadora, 306
Bugambilia, 219
Buho's, 645

La Cabaña del Pescador, 651
Cabañas de los Arcos, 310
Cabañas Santa Rosalía, 280, 282
Cabo Blanco, 443
Los Cabos, 14, 297, 312
Cabo San Lucas, 316, 319
Cabo Wabo Cantina, 322, 325
Cacaxtla, 11, 179
Cacique, 589
Cacique Inn, 590, 598
Cactus Bar & Grill, 451
Cactus Motel, 247, 250
Cactus Video Disco, 316, 325
Café Escorial, 470
Café Europa, 315
Café Pacífico, 341
Café de Paris: Mexico City, 132; Torreón, 280
Café Parroquia, 470
Café del Portal, 479
Café del Puerto, 653
Café Santa Fe, 327
Café de Tacuba, 126
El Calafia, 306
Calakmul, 528
La Calesa de Londres, 130
Calesa Real, 501, 512
Calinda Cancún Beach, 610, 664
Calinda Cuernavaca Racquet Club, 164, 193
Calinda Geneve Mexico, 119
Calinda Morelia Quality Inn, 239, 250
Calinda Roma, 265, 282
Callejón del Beso, 230
El Caminero, 131
Camino Guatemala City, 598
Camino Real: Cancún,

612, 664; Mazatlán, 347, 355; Mexico City, 115; Puerto Vallarta, 370, 376; Saltillo, 245, 250
Camino Real Guatemala City, 574
Camino Real Motor Hotel, 484, 487
Camino Real Tikal, 578, 599
El Campanario: Acapulco, 421; La Paz, 310
Las Campanas, 653
Campeche, 539
Campo de Golf Tangolunda, 449
La Cañada, 553, 561
Cancún, 14, 602, 603, 606 (map)
Cancún Avioturismo, 624
Cancún City, 620
Cancún Palace, 614, 664
Cantamar, 303
Capilla de Nuestra Señora de Aranzazú, 263
Capilla del Pocito, 48
Capilla del Rosaro, 173
Capilla de las Rosas, 48
Capilla de San Antonio Panzacola, 92
Capitán Buelo, 483
Capitán Lucas, 322
Captain's Cove, 618
Capula, 277
El Caracol: Chichén Itzá, 545; San José de Cabo, 315
Caracol Tango Palace, 346
Cardon Design, 315
Careyes, 333
Caribbean Divers, 660
Carlos 'n' Charlie's: Acapulco, 421; Cancún, 615, 623, 624; La Crucecita, 451; Ixtapa, 398; Puerto Aventuras, 633
Carlos 'n' Charlie's Colima Bay Café, 386
Carlos 'n Charlie's & Jimmy's Kitchen, 652
Carlos Demicheles, 155
Carlos O'Brian's Pawnshop and Restaurant, 365

INDEX 677

Carnaval, 467
La Carreta: Mazatlán, 346, La Paz, 310
Carretera Panorámica, Guanajuato, 226
Cartier, 619
La Cartouche, 385, 388
Casa del Alfeñique, 173
Casa del Arte Mexica, 643
Casa de las Artesanías, Morelia, 240
Casa de las Artesanías de Jalisco, 267
Casa de las Artesanías de Michoacán, 148
Casa de los Azulejos, 66
Casa de los Azulejos y Museo de la Ciudad, 481
Casa del Balam, 526, 561
Casablanca, 364
Casa Canal, 221
Casa Canela, 268
Casa Carmen, 219, 250
Casa Chata, 51
Casa Cohen, 221
Casa Contenta, 344, 355
Casa de Cultura, 390
Casa Elvira, 404
La Casa del Habano, 620
La Casa de los Jipis, 525
Casa del Lago, 82
Casa Loma, 346
Casa de la Luna, 222
Casa del Mayorazgo de Canal, 215
Casa de Montejo, 522
Casa Museo de Morelos, 237
Casa Na Bolom, 558
Casanova, 415
La Casa de los Once Patios, 273
Casa de Pacal, 553, 561
La Casa Que Canta, 402, 406
Casa Real, 447
Casa Roberto: Cabo San Lucas, 322; Mazatlán, 344
Casa Rolandi, 616
Casa Rugiero, 175
CASART, 148
Casa de Sierra Nevada, 218, 250
Casasola, 152

Casa de los Tesoros, 352, 355
Casa de las Tortugas, 532
Casa Valdez, 233
Casa Victor's, 498
Casa Vieja, 190, 193
La Casa Vieja Gallery, 315
La Cascada, 188
Cascada Basaséachic, 292
La Cascada Restaurant, 418
La Casita, 404
La Casona, 484, 487
La Casserole, 138
El Castellano, 526, 561
Castillo: Cobá, 639; Chichén Itzá, 543; Tulum, 637
Los Castillo: Mexico City, 153; Taxco, 169
Castillo de Chapultepec, 83
Castillo Huatulco, 450, 457
Castillo de Santa Cecilia, 233, 250
Casual Affair, 322
Catedral Metroplitana, 56
Catemaco, 477
Cats, 623
La Cava, 139
Cavendish, 449
Caves of Chomachi, 292
Las Cazuelas, 137
El Cedral, 657
La Ceiba, 656, 666
Celaya, 223
Cenacolo, 621
Cenote Sagrado, 541
Cenote Xlacah, 530
Central de Autobuses, 112
Central Library, 99
Central Paseo de la Reforma, 74
Del Centro, 126
Centro Artesanal Buenavista, 145
Centro Artesanal las Primaveras, 383
Centro Cultural de Arte Contemporaneo, 87
Centro Cultural de Arte Fotografía, 88

Centro Cultural de Arte Prehispanica, 87
Centro de Idiomas, 341
Century Zona Rosa, 118
Cero Cero, 116, 142
Cerro Blanco, 477
Cerro de las Campanas, 207
Cesar's, 307
Chacahua, 454
Chahue, 452
Chalet Suizo, 130
Las Chalotes, 503
Chamber Music Festival, 221
Champs-Elysées, 130
Chan Kah Cabañas, 552, 562
Chankanaab Lagoon National Park, 657
Chankanaab Reef, 659
Chapala, 270
El Charro, 267
Chateau Valentín, 527
Chee-Chee, 372
Chef Roger, 367
Chemuyil, 608, 634
Chez 'Ar, 144
Chez Magaly, 644
Chiapas, 514
Chichén Itzá, 5, 13, 541
Chichicastenango, 591, 597
Chico's Paradise, 372
Chihuahua, 294
Las Chimeneas, 585
Chin-Chin, 418
Chino's, 371
Chiquita Banana: Ixtapa, 400; Mazatlán, 347
Cholula, 11, 176
La Choza, 654
Christine: Cancún, 613, 623; Ixtapa, 400; Puerto Vallarta, 362
Ciao Italia, 310
CiCi, 419
El Cid Mega Resort, 346, 355
Los Cinco Soles, 652
Cipriano's, 443
Circulo del Sureste, 128
Circus Bar, 591
Ciudad Camargo, 279
Ciudad Jiménez, 280
Ciudad Juárez, 279
Ciudad Obregón, 352
Ciudad Universitaria, 98

INDEX

Ciudad Victoria, 243
Clarion Reforma, 117
Clark Tours, 596
El Claustro, 233
Club de Golf Acapulco, 430
Club Maeva Manzanillo, 383, 391
Club Maeva Puerto Vallarta, 370, 376
Club Med–Huatulco, 446, 457
Club Nautico, 388
Club de Pesca Pez Vela, 624
Club Plaza Huatulco, 448, 457
Club Santiago, 383, 391
Club 25, 141
Club Las Velas Hotel Cancún, 610, 664
Cobá, 638
Coco Cabaña, 404
Coconuts, 320, 403
Coco's Beach Club, 398, 440
Cocos Frios, 643
Cocula, 419
Colegio de San Nicolás de Hidalgo, 237
Colima, 390
Colombia Reef, 659
The Colonial Heartland, 195, 196 (map)
Coloniart, 154
Comala, 390
Comalcalco, 481
Los Comenzales, 240
El Compañario, 267
La Concepción, 217
La Concha: Acapulco, 415; Cozumel, 652
La Concha Beach Resort, 311, 331
Concordia, 349
Condominios Roca del Mar, 387, 392
Conejos, 452
Conjunto Las Pinturas, 640
El Conquistador, 525, 562
Conquistador Sheraton, 574, 599
Conservatorio Nacional de Musica, 87
Continental Plaza, 363, 376
Continental Plaza Playacar, 632, 665

Convento de San Francisco, 583
Convento de la Santa Cruz, 206
Copacabana, 631, 665
Copala, 349
Copán, 580
La Copa de Leche, 266
Copenhagen, 267
Copilco, 98
Copper Canyon, 10, 285, 286 (map)
Copper Canyon Lodge, 293, 295
El Coral, 370
El Corral de la Moreria, 143
El Cortijo, 222
El Cosijo, 498
Costa Azul, 318
Costa Club, 644
Costa de Oro, 346, 355
Coyoacán, 91
Cozumel, 14, 602, 627, 647, 648 (map)
El Cozumeleño, 651, 666
Cozumel Reef Holiday Inn, 656, 666
Creaciones Lixhi-Tuu, 499
Creel, 291
La Crucecita, 446, 451
Cuadrángulo de las Monjas, 532
Las Cuatro Plazas, 260
Cuchilleria Alcalá, 498
Cuernavaca, 11, 157, 161
Cueva de Emiliano, 156
Cuicuilco, 100
Cuilapán, 509
Culiacán, 353
Cupilco, 482
Cusárare, 292
Cuyutlán, 390

Dady'O, 623
Dainzú, 508
Damiana, 315
Dancin', 421
Daniel's, 349
El Danubío, 126
David, 221
El Decano, 504
Deer Island, 348
Delegación Coyoacán, 92
Departamento del Distrito Federal, 62

Deportivo Chapultepec, 87
Derby Club, 88
Designer's Bazaar, 344
Disco Bar de Felix, 388
Disco Club 84, 142
Diva, 424
Dive Paradise, 660
Divisadero, 291
La Dolce Vita: Cancún, 620; San Miguel, 220
Dolores Alba, 547
Dolphinarium, 86
Doña Luisa Xicotencatl, 585
Donatello's, 654
Don Chon, 126
Don Emiliano, 622
Doney, 341
Don Vasco, 274
Don Wilo, 452
El Dorado, 369
Dorado Pacífico, 396, 406
Dorian's, 311
Dos Lagunas, 559
Dos Lunas, 322
Dos Puertas, 139
Downtown Mexico City, 52 (map)
Dupuis, 322
Dzibilchaltún, 529

Eclipse, 315, 325
Eden, 371
Edificio Central de Correos, 68
Edificio de las Columnas, 474
Edificio Este, 536
Edificio de las Monjas, 545
Edzná, 528, 537
Elena's, 387
Emil, 423
Emma, 169
Emporio México, 122
Enjoy, 388
Ensenada, 305
La Entrega, 453
Ernesto's Fajita Factory, 655
Los Escudos, 274
Escuela de Bellas Artes de Xochimilco, 103
Escuela Nacional Preparatoria, 54
Esprit, 154
Estadio Olímpico, 99
Estebán, 419

INDEX 679

Estero Beach Resort, 305, 331
Estoril, 130
El Estribo, 273
Estro Armónico, 576
Euforia, 400
Exconvento de la Asunción, 179
Exconvento del Carmen, 238
Exconvento de San Miguel Arcángel, 183
Exconvento de Santa Mónica, 174
Exconvento de Santa Rosa, 175
Extra, 619
Extravaganzza, 414

Fantasy, 414
El Faro, 399
El Faro Viejo, 321
Farre, 155
Feder's, 148
Fela the Flower Lady, 345
Ferrioni Collection, 154
Fiesta Americana (Puerto Vallarta), 362, 376
Fiesta Americana Aeropuerto, 123
Fiesta Americana Cancún, 611, 664
Fiesta Americana Coral Beach Cancún, 612, 664
Fiesta Americana Guadalajara, 264, 282
Fiesta Americana Los Angeles Locos, 378, 379
Fiesta Mexicana, 402, 406
Fiesta Mexicana Days Inn, 386, 392
Fiesta Americana Sol Caribe, 656, 666
Fila, 619
Fiorucci, 420
Fischer Restaurant, 475
Fish Market, 621
Los Flamingos, 373
Flamma, 154
Flash Taco, 418
Flores, 577
Flor de Querétaro, 210
Focolare, 129
La Fogata, 316

El Fogón de Jovel, 557
FONART, 72, 147
La Fonda, 303, 331
Fonda del Angel, 620
Fonda del Recuerdo, 134
Fonda del Refugio, 210
Fonda de San Francisco, 128
Fonda Santa Clara, 176
El Fongoncito, 133
La Fontana, 590
Fortín Plaza, 500, 512
Fouquet's of Paris, 116, 133
Franco's, 421
Frattina, 155
Friday Lopez, 363
Frontón México, 74
La Fuente: Guadalajara, 266; Torreón, 280
Las Fuentes: Ixtapa, 400; Mexico City, 132
El Fuerte, 290
El Fuerte Carranza, 341
El Fuerte Nightclub, 429
Fuerte de San Juan de Ulúa, 463

El Galeón, 324
La Galería, 619
Galería de Arte Mexicano, 152
Galería Arvil, 151
Galería Atenea, 214
Galería Aura, 152
Galería del Circulo, 151
Galería El Dorado, 315, 323
Galería Estela Shapiro, 152
Galería Eugenio, 150
Galería Florence, 400
Galería Hardy, 151
Galería Honfleur, 152
Galería Juan Martín, 152
Galería Kim, 155
Galería Londres Chumacero, 151
Galería Misrachi, 151
Galería Pacífico, 366
Galería Pecanis, 152
Galería Reforma, 148
Galería Rudic, 423
Galería San Miguel, 214
Galería de Sergio Bustamante, 155

Galería Solaris, 151
Galería Summa Artis, 152
Galería 10/10, 425
Galería Tere Haas, 151
Galería Uno, 366
Gallery, 420
Garlic's, 467
El Garrafón, 646
Gatsby's, 141
La Gaviota, 401
Gaviotas, 343
Las Gaviotas Bar, 343
Las Gaviotas Restaurant, 363
Giggling Marlin, 323, 325
Da Giorgio's, 317
Da Giorgio's II, 319
Girasol, 153
Gitanerias, 143
Gitano's, 209
Gold's Gym, 620
Los Golondrinas, 614
Gomar, 643
Le Gourmet, 412
Gran Acropolis, 538
Gran Café de la Parroquia, 462
Gran Hotel, 526, 562
Gran Pirámide, 533
El Gran Teocalli, 106
Greyhound de México, 112
Grupo de las Mil Columnas, 544
La Gruta, 106, 222
Grutas de Cacahuamilpa, 167
Guadalajara, 11, 254, 258, 259 (map)
Guadalajara Grill, 617, 623
La Guadalupaña, 175
Guanajuato, 11, 195, 223, 224 (map)
Guaraguao, 483
Guatemala, 13, 564, 566 (map)
Guatemala City, 571
Los Guayacanes, 483
Guaymas, 351
Gucci, 423
La Guitarra, 342
Gulf Coast, 12, 458
Gypsy's Pampered Pirate, 617

La Habichuela, 622
La Hacienda, 266

INDEX

Hacienda El Abajeno, 310
Hacienda Buenaventura, 362, 376
Hacienda Chichén, 546, 562
Hacienda Cocoyoc, 165, 193
Hacienda de las Flores, 218, 250
Hacienda Jalisco, 374, 376
Hacienda Jurica, 209, 250
Hacienda de los Morales, 134
Hacienda Motor Hotel, 244, 251
Hacienda El Mortero, 617
La Hacienda de Pepe, 220
Hacienda San Gabriel de Barrera, 226
Hacienda San José de las Vegas, 625
Hacienda del Solar, 169, 194
Hacienda Taboada, 222, 251
Hacienda Uxmal, 534, 562
Halfway House, 303
Hard Rock Café: Acapulco, 419; Cancún, 616; Puerto Vallarta, 364
Harry's Grill, 164
HB Galería, 155
Hermosillo, 351
Hipódromo de las Américas, 88
Holiday Inn Crowne Plaza, 121
Holiday Inn Guadalajara, 264, 267, 283
Holiday Inn Hermosillo, 351, 355
Holiday Inn Mérida, 525, 562
Holiday Inn Monterrey, 245, 251
Holiday Inn Querétaro, 208, 251
Holiday Inn Tabasco Plaza, 482, 487
Honfleur, 131
Hospital de Jésus, 65
Hostal del Quijote, 247, 251
Hostería de Alcalá, 503
Hostería del Fraile, 232, 251
Hostería las Quintas, 164, 194
Hostería de Santo Domingo, 125
Hotel Akumal Cancún, 634, 665
Hotel Ambassador, 245, 251
Hotel del Angel, 120
Hotel Antigua, 584, 599
Hotel Los Arcos, 310, 331
Hotel Aristos, 117
Hotel Aristos Zacatecas, 281, 283
Hotel Atitlán, 589, 599
Hotel Aurora, 583, 599
Hotel Avándaro Golf and Spa Resort, 189, 194
Hotel Bahía, 305, 331
Hotel Baluartes, 540, 562
Hotel Batopilas, 293
Hotel Buenaventura, 363, 376
Hotel Cabañas Divisadero-Barrancas, 291, 295
Hotel Cabo Blanco, 380
Hotel Cabo San Lucas, 317, 330
Hotel Casa Blanca, 122
Hotel Catamarán, 594, 599
Hotel Cencalli, 482, 487
Hotel del Centro, 574, 576, 599
Hotel Club Akumal Caribe, 634, 665
Hotel Colón, 526, 562
Hotel Colonial: Manzanillo, 388, 392; Veracruz, 466, 487
Hotel Conrad, 360, 376
Hotel de Cortés, 121, 127
Hotel Dolores Alba, 526, 562
Hotel El Dorado Americana, 574, 599
Hotel Emporio, 465, 487
Hotel Los Escudos, 274, 283
Hotel Everest, 243, 251
Hotel Fiesta Mexicana, 441, 456
Hotel Finisterra, 324, 330
Hotel Flanboyant, 557, 562
Hotel Florido, 280, 283
Hotel Francés, 264, 267, 283
Hotel Galindo, 590, 599
Hotel Gallery Best Western, 281, 283
Hotel Las Golondrinas, 501, 513
Hotel Gran Presidential, 484, 487
Hotel Gran Presidential Torreón, 280, 283
Hotel Hacienda, 320, 330
Hotel Hyatt Villahermosa, 482, 487
Hotel Impala, 484, 487
Hotel Lastra, 176, 194
Hotel del Lago, 590, 599
Hotel Lopez, 540, 562
Hotel Majestic, 56, 125
Hotel Malibu, 264, 283
Hotel Mansión de la Condesa Magdalena, 352, 356
Hotel Mar de Cortez, 322, 330
Hotel María Victoria, 470, 487
Hotel Marina, 581, 599
Hotel Marquis Reforma, 117
Hotel de Mendoza, 265, 283
Hotel de México, 90
Hotel Miraflores, 483, 487
Hotel Misión, 290, 295
Hotel Mocambo, 466, 487
Hotel Molcas, 630
Hotel Monte Albán, 502
Hotel Monte Verde, 219, 251
Hotel Na Balam, 644, 666
Hotel Nikko México, 116
Hotel Nututun Viva, 553, 562
Hotel El Oasis, 307, 331

INDEX   681

Hotel Palacio Real, 280, 283
Hotel La Palapa, 419, 432
Hotel Palmilla, 316, 329
Hotel Las Palmas, 441, 456
Hotel Panorama, 247, 251
Hotel El Parador, 189, 194
Hotel Parador Plaza, 502, 513
Hotel La Perla, 310, 331
Hotel Perla del Caribe, 642, 666
Hotel Pierre Marqués Princess, 413, 432
Hotel Piño Montano, 579, 599
Hotel Playa de Cortés, 351, 356
Hotel Playa Mazatlán, 344, 356
Hotel Plaza: Guatemala City, 574, 599; Tuxpan, 475, 487
Hotel Plaza Juárez, 279, 283
Hotel Plaza Uruapan, 278, 283
Hotel del Portal, 176, 194
Hotel La Posada, 387, 392
Hotel La Posada de Engelbert, 311, 331
Hotel Ramada Campeche, 540, 562
Hotel Reforma, 244, 251
Hotel Royalty Centro, 176, 194
Hotel Salinas, 472, 487
Hotel Salmones, 470, 487
Hotel San Carlos, 184, 194
Hotel San Clemente, 547, 562
Hotel San Diego, 232, 251
Hotel San Felipe Misión Oaxaca, 501, 513
Hotel San Gabriel de Barrera, 233, 251
Hotel Santa Anita, 289, 295
Hotel Santa Clara, 557, 562
Hotel Santa Fe, 439, 456
Hotel Santa Prisca, 169, 194
Hotel Santo Tomás, 592, 599
Hotel Sara, 475, 487
Hotel Señorial, 501, 513
Hotel Sierra Gorda, 243, 251
Hotel Sierra Radisson Plaza, 384, 392
Hotel Siesta, 244, 251
Hotel La Siesta, 339, 356
Hotel Solmar, 324, 330
Hotel Soraya, 444, 456
Hotel Suites Las Flores, 344, 356
Hotel Tajín, 472, 487
Hotel Veracruz, 466, 487
Hotel Victoria, 500, 513
Hotel Villablanca Beach Club and Sports Complex, 655, 666
Hotel Virrey de Mendoza, 239, 251
Hotel Visión Azul, 590, 599
Hotel Xalapa, 470, 487
Howard Johnson Gran Hotel, 120
Huanacaxtle, 373
Huatulco, 334, 433, 446
Huehuetenango, 579
Humberto Peraza Ojeda, 152
Hussong's, 306
Hyatt Regency, 418, 433
Hyatt Regency Cancún, 613, 665

Iglesia (Cobá), 639
Iglesia y Convento de Capuchinas, 583
Iglesia de Jésus, 65
Iglesia de Nuestra Señora de la Salud, 216
Iglesia Santa María, 188
Iglesia de Santo Domingo: Mexico City, 51; Oaxaca, 494
Ignacio Allende Birthplace, 214
La Iguana, 619

Iguana Bar and Grill, 314
Iguana Grill, 325
Iguana Wana, 616
La India Bonita, 164
Indio's Gifts, 344
Instituto Allende, 221
Instituto de Artes Graficas de Oaxaca, 494
Instituto Cultural Cabañas, 261
Intermar Caribe, 628
Los Irabien, 138
Isadora, 134
Isla Contoy, 627
Isla Ixtapa, 404
Isla de Lobos, 475
Isla Mujeres, 14, 602, 640, 641 (map)
Isla La Roqueta, 427, 431
Isla de Sacrificios, 463
Isla Victoria, 136
Italianissimo, 415
Ixmiquilpán, 11, 183
Ixtapa, 14, 334, 392, 393 (map), 395
Ixtapa Sheraton, 396, 406

Jack, 525
Jades, 585
Jalapa, 468
Jalapeño's, 615, 623
Jaramar, 389
Jardín Botánico, 82
Jardín Botánico Dr. Alfredo Barrera Marin, 629
Jardín Obregón, 203
Jardín de las Rosas, 238
Jardines de Borda, 163
Jardín de la Unión, 229
Jimenez, 499
Jimmy's Fajita Factory, 630
Jockey Club, 88
Joe's Oyster Bar, 344
La Jolla de Mismaloya, 371, 376
Jorongo Bar, 141
Josh Klingerman Gallery, 214
La Joya, 429
Joyería Peyrelóngue, 153
Juanito's, 383
Juego de Pelota, 543

682 INDEX

Juego de Pelota Sur, 473
El Jumil, 404
Jungle Lodge, 577, 599

Kabah, 534
Kamakura, 362
Kaminaljuyú, 573
Karl's Keller, 616
Ken Edwards, 268
Ki-Huic, 621
King's Pub, 134
King's Road, 139
Le Kliff, 371
Kodak Express, 620
Kon-Tiki, 403
Kookaburra, 415
Krystal Cancún, 613, 665
Krystal Divers, 624
Krystal Ixtapa, 397, 406
Krystal Vallarta, 361, 377
Krystal Zona Rosa, 118

Labná, 535, 536
Lacandon Forest, 559
Lafayette, 266
Lago Arareco, 292
Lago Atitlan, 586
Lago de Catemaco, 13, 477
Lago de Chapala, 12, 270
Lago Chapultepec, 86, 136
Lago de Pátzcuaro, 275
Laguna de Coyuca, 428
Laguna de las Ilusiones, 479
Laguna Juluapán, 389
Lagunas de Colores, 559
Laguna de Tamiahua, 475
Laguna de Teacapán, 349
Laguna Yal Ku, 634
Lambityeco, 509
Lancer's, 138
Land's End, 324
La Lanterna, 131
Lapidaria Querétaro, 208
Last Resort, 591
The Leather Shop, 619
Leo's: Mérida, 527; Villahermosa, 483
Lerma Terminal de Agua, 86

Lighthouse, 398
Limones, 631
Lívingston, 594
Liza's, 442
Loltún Caves, 536
Loredo, 129
Lorenzillo's, 618
Loreto, 307
Loto Azul Hotel-Club, 189, 194
El Luchador, 81
Luisa Conti, 400
Lukas, 322, 325
La Luna, 442
Luna Palace, 347, 356
Luscherly, 266

Mac's Prime Rib, 398
Madeiras, 414
Madre Tierra, 557
Magic Circus: Huatulco, 450; Ixtapa, 400; Mexico City, 142
Magico Mundo Marino, 427
El Maguey, 453
Majestic Bar, 141
The Malecón, 463
Malinalco, 11, 190
Mama Eli, 322
Mama Mía, 220
Mamuca's, 342
Las Mañanitas, 619
Las Mañanitas Hotel, 164, 194
Los Manantiales, 104
Los Mandiles, 398
Il Mangiare, 364
Manialtepec, 453
La Mano Mágica, 498
La Mansión, 420
La Mansion–Costa Blanca, 619
Mansión del Cupatitzio, 278, 283
La Mansión Galindo, 209, 251
Manzanillo, 14, 334, 381
Maquiavelo, 144
Maracaibo Reef, 659
Marco Polo Hotel, 119
Marco Polo Restaurant, 163
María Cristina, 120
María de Guadalajara, 389
Maria's, 645
Marigen, 154
Marina Aqua Ray, 624

Marina Jet Ski, 624
Marina Mall, 385
Marina Punta del Este, 624
Marina Vallarta, 360
El Marinero, 342
Mar y Mar, 424
Marqués del Valle, 501, 513
Marrakesh, 143
Marriott CasaMagna, 360, 377
Martí: Acapulco, 423; Cancún, 620
Martin's, 575
Mascaras, 630
Matamoros, 483
Matehuala, 246
Mauna Loa, 139
Maxime, 615
Maximilian's, 424
Maxim's, 117
Maya Internacional, 578, 599
Mayaland, 546, 562
Mayan, 619
Mayan Inn, 592, 599
Maya del Pacifico, 345
Maya Palace, 588
Mayapán, 528
Mazatlán, 14, 333, 335, 336 (map)
Mazatlán Arts and Crafts Center, 345
Mazurka, 137
Mekano, 142
Meliá Cabo Real, 317, 330
Meliá Cancún, 614, 625, 665
Meliá Mayan Cozumel, 650, 666
Meliá San Lucas, 320, 330
Meliá Vallarta, 360, 377
Mercado de Antigüedades de la Lagunilla, 146
Mercado Artesanias, 187
Mercado de Artesanías: Acapulco, 427; Comala, 390; Huatulco, 451
Mercado Artesanías Insurgentes, 76
El Mercado de la Ciudadela, 145
Mercado Cuauhtémoc, 149

INDEX 683

Mercado de Curiosidades Mexicanos San Juan, 148
Mercado de Insurgentes, 146
Mercado de la Lagunilla Unidad de Ropas, 149
Mercado Libertad, 262
Mercado Mexicana, 322
Mercado Municipal, 425
Mercado de Sonora, 149
Mercado 3 de Mayo, 452
Las Mercedes, 133
Mérida, 521
La Mesa de Capitán, 341
El Mesón, 503
El Mesón del Angel, 175, 194
Méson de Bucanero, 643
Mesón del Cid, 128
El Mesón del Gallo, 274, 283
El Mesón del Marqués, 547, 562
El Mesón la Marisqueria del Perro Andaluz, 130
El Mesón del Perro Andaluz, 130
Mesón de Santa Rosa, 209, 251
Metepec, 190
Mexican Opal Company, 154
El Mexicano, 416
Mexico, xii (map)
Mexico City, 10, 35, 39, 42 (map)
Mexico City Environs, 158 (map)
Mi Casa, 322
Michel Domet, 620
Mikonos, 343
Mimi's Chili Saloon, 422
Mirador, 536
Miramar, 303, 414
Mi Ranchito, 621
La Misión, 303, 304
Misión de los Angeles, 501, 513
Misión Fa-Sol, 449
Misión del Loreto, 307, 331

Misión Park Inn Chichén Itzá, 546, 562
Misión Park Inn Palenque, 553, 563
Misión Park Inn Uxmal, 534, 563
Mismaloya, 371
Mr. Frog's, 414
Mr. Papa's, 618
Mitla, 12, 510
Mixco Viejo, 579
Mocambo, 465
Los Mochis, 289, 353
Mogambo, 364
El Molino de la Alborada, 557, 563
El Molino Rojo, 264
Monasterio de Santo Domingo, 583
Monte Albán, 12, 504
Monte Carlo, 121
Monte Mohinara, 290
Monterrey, 9, 245
Le Montmartre, 397
Monumento a la Revolución, 73
Mordo, 619
Morelia, 11, 195, 234, 235 (map)
Morgan's, 653
El Morocco, 363
Motel Armida, 352, 356
Motel Colonial Las Fuentes, 279, 283
Motel El Encanto, 351, 356
Motel Guanajuato, 233, 251
Motel Hacienda, 246, 252
Motel Los Nogales, 279, 283
Motel Oasis, 246, 252
Motel Playa Azul, 477, 487
Motel Santa Fé, 247, 252
Motel Los 3 Ríos, 353, 356
Les Moustaches, 131
Mulegé, 307
Muller's, 153
Mundaca's Hacienda, 645
Muralto, 67, 144
Museo Anahuacalli, 94
Museo de Antropología, 470
Museo Antropológico de Baja California Sur, 311

Museo Archeológico (Campeche), 540
Museo Arqueológico de la Costa Grande, 404
Museo Arqueológico de Xochimilco, 103
Museo de Arte Alvar y Carmen T. de Carrillo Gil, 96
Museo de Arte Colonial, 238
Museo de Arte Contemporaneo, 496
Museo de Arte Moderno, 85
Museo de Arte Popular, 524
Museo de Arte Popular Poblano, 175
Museo de Artes Populares, 273
Museo Carlos Pellicer, 480
Museo Casa Diego Rivera, 228
Museo CEDAM, 633
Museo de la Ciudad (Veracruz), 464
Museo de la Ciudad de Guatemala, 572
Museo de la Ciudad de México, 64
Museo Colonial del Carmen, 95
Museo de Cuauhnáhuac, 162
Museo de Cultura Popular, 481
Museo de las Culturas Occidentales, 390
Museo del Estado, 237
Museo de las Estelas, 540
Museo Estudio Diego Rivera, 97
Museo Franz Mayer, 72
Museo Frida Kahlo, 92
Museo Frissell de Arte Zapoteca, 511
Museo de Historia y Bellas Artes, 572
Museo de Historia de Medicina, 51
Museo de Historia Natural de la Ciudad de México, 85
Museo Histórico de Acapulco, 426

684　INDEX

Museo Histórico de la Revolución en el Estado de Chihuahua, 294
Museo de la Intervención, 174
Museo de la Isla de Cozumel, 652
Museo Ixchel, 573
Museo León Trotsky, 93
Museo de Michoacán, 237
Museo de la Misiónes, 309
Museo de las Momias, 231
Museo Mural Diego Rivera, 72
Museo Nacional de Antropología, 79
Museo Nacional de Arqueológica y Etnología, 572
Museo Nacional de Arte, 68
Museo Nacional de Artes y Industrias Populares, 71
Museo Nacional de las Culturas, 60
Museo Nacional de Historia, 83, 84
Museo Nacional de las Intervenciones, 93
Museo Nacional del Palacio de Bellas Artes, 69
Museo Nacional de la Revolución, 74
Museo Nacional de Tecnológico de la Comisión Federal de Electricidad, 86
Museo Nacional del Virreinata, 180
Museo Pío Mariano, 204
Museo Popol Vuh, 572
Museo del Pueblo de Guanajuato, 228
Museo de la del Pueblo Mexicano por la Libertad, 84
Museo Rafael Coronel, 281
Museo Recinto Homenaje a Benito Juárez, 62
Museo Regional (San Cristóbal), 556
Museo Regional de Antropología, 524
Museo Regional de Campeche, 540
Museo Regional de la Cerámica, 269
Museo Regional de Chihuahua, 294
Museo Regional del Estado, 494
Museo Regional de Guadalajara, 261
Museo Regional de Historia, 390
Museo Regional de Mazatlán, 341
El Museo Robert Brady, 163
Museo Rufino Tamayo: Mexico City, 78; Oaxaca, 495
Museo de San Carlos, 73
Museo de Sitio y Zona Arqueológica de Cuicuilco, 101
Museo del Templo Mayor, 59
Museo de Tula, 182
Museo Universitario de Arte y Cultura Popular, 390

Nacional Monte de Piedad, 63
Nainari Valle, 352, 356
National Museum of Folk Arts and Crafts, 147
Nautibeach Condominium-Hotel, 644, 666
Nautilus, 442
Navojoa, 352
Nekri, 323
Neptuno, 654, 658
News: Acapulco, 418; Mexico City, 142
El Nido, 307
No Name Café, 345
Normandie, 425
Norogachi, 293
Northern Chiapas State, 548 (map)
Northern Gulf Coast, 469 (map)
Nuestra Señora de Guadalupe, 366
La Nueva Posada, 271, 283

Nuevo Laredo, 244
Nuevo Motel del Río, 352, 356
Nuevo Vallarta, 333, 357
Numero Uno, 429

Oasis Hotel, 625
Oasis Restaurant, 383
Oaxaca, 12, 489, 506 (map)
Oaxaca City, 454, 490, 491 (map)
Observatory at Palenque, 550
La Oficina, 320
O'Healey's, 448
Okey Laser Club, 310
Las Olas, 343
Olas Altas: Manzanillo, 381; Mazatlán, 339
La Olla de Chihuahua, 294
Omni Ixtapa, 397, 406
Opalo, 208
The Open Door, 499
Opepeo, 277
Oratorio de San Felipe Neri, 216
El Organo, 453
Original 60, 620, 631
Oro de Monte Albán, 498
Ortega's Restaurant, 303
Ostería Bugatti, 387
Ostería Viandante, 442
Los Otates, 266
Oui, 388

La Paella, 467
Pahuatlán, 184
Palace at Palenque, 550
Palacio: Labná, 536; Sayil, 535
El Palacio (Monte Albán), 505
Palacio de Bellas Artes, 69
Palacio Clavijero, 238
Palacio de Cortés, 162
Palacio de las Cuchillas, 539
Palacio del Gobernador, 532
Palacio de Gobierno: Guadalajara, 260; Mérida, 524; Morelia, 237
Palacio de Hierro, 150

INDEX 685

Palacio de Iturbide, 65
Palacio de los Mascarones, 534
Palacio de Minería, 68
Palacio Municipal, 173
Palacio Nacional, 60
Palacio Quemada, 182
Palacio del Quetzalpapálotl, 108
Palacio del Sol, 294, 295
Palancar Reef, 649, 659
Palao, 431
Las Palapas, 632, 665
Palenque, 13, 479, 547
Palenque Museum, 552
La Palma: Manzanillo, 389; Mexico City, 135
Palma Real, 452
Palma Real Golf Course, 395
Las Palmas, 246, 252
Las Palmas Restaurant, 320
Las Palmeras, 653
El Palomar, 533
Las Palomas: Mérida, 527; Puerto Vallarta, 365
La Pampa Argentina, 449
Panajachel, 586, 587, 597
Pan American, 575, 599
Pancho and Lefty's, 220
Pancho's, 345
Pancho's Backyard, 652
El Panorama, 365
Papacito's Last Call, 424
Papagayo, 425
Papagayo's, 386
Papantla, 472
Papi's, 322
Paracho, 241, 278
Paradise, 242, 252
Paradise Restaurant, 422
El Parador de José Luis, 133
Parador de la Montaña, 293, 295
Parador San Javier, 233, 252
Los Parados de Tony Vega, 294
Paraiso Radisson Zacatecas, 281, 284
Paraiso Reef, 658
El Parián, 267
Parián Market, 173

Paricutín, 278
Parilla Argentina Fogon Pampero, 210
Park Villa, 122
Parque Alameda Central, 70
Parque Aurora, 572
Parque Cepeda Peraza, 523
Parque de Juegos Mecánicos, 86
Parque-Museo de La Venta, 479
Parque Nacional Eduardo Ruíz, 277
Parque Zoológico de Chapultepec, 82
Parque Zoológico and Jardín Botánico, 82
La Parroquia: San Miguel, 212; Veracruz, 462
Parroquia San Bernardino, 103
Parroquia de Santa Prisca y San Sebastián, 168
Pasarela, 424
Paseo de Montejo, 524
Paseo del Norte Restaurant, 279
Paseo Río Cuale, 368
Pasha, 419
Passy, 131
La Pata del Gato, 345
El Patio Hotel, 219, 252
El Patio Mall, 423
El Patio Nightclub, 143
El Patio Restaurant: Mazatlán, 342; Patzcuaro, 274
Pat O'Brien's, 618
Pátzcuaro, 12, 250, 254, 271
Pátzcuaro Town, 272
Paul Flato, 153
Pavillon Restaurant, 245
El Pavo Real, 321
La Paz, 309
La Paz-Lapa, 310
El Pedregal, 100
El Pegaso, 221
Los Pelicanos Restaurant and Bar, 302
Pepe's, 414
Los Pepes, 483
Pepe's Grill, 653
La Pergola: Guadalajara, 267; Uruapan, 278
Los Pericos, 188

Perisur, 150
La Perla, 370
Perla Flamante, 442
El Perro d'Enfrente, 130
El Pescador, 467
Petén, 568
Pez Maya, 660
Pez Vela, 630
Piccolo Suizo, 133
Pie de la Cuesta, 428
Pietro, 315
Pinturas Group, 607
La Pirámide, 106
Pirámide del Adivino, 531
Pirámide Charlie's, 106
Pirámide de los Cinco Pisos, 528, 539
Pirámide de Kukulcán, 543
Pirámide de los Nichos, 473
Pirámide de la Serpeinte Emplumada, 166
Pirámide del Sol, 107
Pirámide de Teopanzolco, 163
La Pirinola, 129
Pizza Rolandi: Cancún, 621; Isla Mujeres, 643
Place de la Concorde, 266
Place Vendôme, 363
Plata Mex, 267
Playa del Amor, 327
Playa La Audiencia, 384
Playa Azul, 385
Playa Bacocho, 436
Playa Blanca, 309
Playa Caleta, 427
Playa Caletilla, 427
Playa Caracol, 605
Playa del Carmen, 608, 629
Playa Carrizalillo, 437
Playa Chiqueros, 658
Playa Condesa, 422
Playa Las Cuatas, 394
Playa Las Gatas, 401
Playa Hermosa, 396
Playa Hornos, 425
Playa Lancheros, 645
Playa Linda, 394
Playa Linda Marina, 624
Playa La Maderà, 395, 401
Playa Marinero, 438
Playa Medano, 319

686 INDEX

Playa Miramar, 383
Playa de los Muertos, 368
Playa Norte, 643
Playa del Palmar, 396
Playa Panteón, 444
Playa Paraíso, 466, 488
Playa Principal, 438, 444
Playa Quieta, 394
Playa Quimixto, 373
Playa del Rey, 608
Playa La Ropa, 401
Playa San Francisco, 657
Playa Santa María, 318
Playa Zicatela, 436
Player's Club, 385
Plaza del Angel, 76
Plaza de Armas: Guadalajara, 260; Morelia, 236; Oaxaca, 493; Veracruz, 460
Plaza Bahía, 424
Plaza Bonita, 322
Plaza Caletilla, 427
Plaza Candido, 322
Plaza Caracol, 619
Plaza Central, 92
Plaza Chica, 272
Plaza de la Constitución, 172
Plaza de las Estelas, 177
Plaza Flamingo, 607, 619
Plaza Florencia, 118
Plaza de Garibaldi, 49
Plaza Las Glorias, 324, 330
Plaza Las Glorias Manzanillo, 385, 392
Plaza Grande, 272
Plaza de los Hombres Ilustres, 261
Plaza Huatulco, 448
Plaza de la Independencia, 204
Plaza Ixpamar, 400
Plaza Kukulcán, 607
Plaza de los Laureles, 260
Plaza de la Liberación, 261
Plaza Manzanillo, 389
Plaza Mayor, 522
Plaza México, 91
Plaza Monumental, 263
Plaza Obregón, 203
Plaza Santa Cecilia, 143
Plaza de Santo Domingo, 50
Plaza Tapatía, 261
Plaza de las Tres Culturas, 45
Plaza Villalongín, 238
Plazuela de los Mariachis, 262, 267
Pok-Ta-Pok Golf Club, 605, 625
Polanco, 87
Polyforum Cultural Siqueiros, 89
Pop, 622
El Portal, 653
Los Portales, 178
Portal de los Evangelistas, 51
Portal de los Mercaderes, 62
Posada de la Basílica, 274, 283
Posada Belén, 575, 599
Posada Binniguenda, 450, 457
Posada Cañon Devata, 444, 456
Posada Chugüilá, 592, 599
Posada Diego de Mazariegos, 557, 563
Posada Don Bruno, 241, 252
Posada de Don Rodrigo, 584, 599
Posada de Don Vasco, 274, 284
Posada Hidalgo, 290, 296
Posada d'Loren, 442
Posada del Mar, 642, 666
Posada de las Monjas, 219, 252
Posada San José, 246, 252
Posada Santa Fé, 232, 233, 252
Posada de la Soledad, 239, 240, 252
Posada de Tampico, 484, 488
Posada Terranova, 316, 330
Posada Tierra Blanca, 294, 296
Posada Vista Bella, 239, 252
La Posta, 621
Poza Rica, 472
El Pozo, 234
Prendes Hotel, 466, 488
Prendes Restaurant: Mexico City, 127; Veracruz, 462
La Presa, 226
Presa Miguel Alemán, 186
Presa de la Olla, 231
Privilege, 142
Puebla, 11, 157, 170, 171 (map)
El Pueblito Cantina, 267
Pueblo Bonito: Cabo San Lucas, 320, 331; Mazatlán, 347, 356
La Puerta, 399
La Puertecita, 218, 252
Del Puerto, 352, 356
Puerto de Abrigo, 651
Puerto Angel, 334, 433, 435, 443
Puerto Angelito, 437
Puerto Aventuras, 608, 633
Puerto Barrios, 575
Puerto Escondido, 14, 334, 433, 435
Puerto Juárez, 608
Puerto Liverpool, 150
Puerto Marqués, 413
Puerto Mío, 402, 406
Puerto Morelos, 608, 629
Puerto Nuevo, 302
Puerto Vallarta, 14, 333, 357, 358 (map)
Los Pumpos, 591
Punta Banda, 306
Punta Camarón, 341, 343
Punta Cancún, 605
Punta Morena, 658
Punta Nizuc, 624
Punta Pescadero, 326
Punta Piedra, 304
Punta Sam, 608
Punta Tangolunda, 449

La Quebrada, 428
Querétaro, 11, 195, 200, 201 (map)
Quing Long, 503
Quinta Real, 265, 284
La Quinta Real Zacatecas, 281, 284
El Quinto Patio, 310
Quiriguá, 578, 593
Quiroga, 277

INDEX 687

Ramada Antigua, 584, 599
Los Rancheros: Acapulco, 415; Cancún, 618
Rancho Grande Inn, 590, 600
Rancho Loma Bonita, 625, 629
Rancho San Cayetano, 241, 252
Real de Catorce, 10, 246
Real de Minas, 209, 252
L'Recif, 382
Red Onion, 364
Regina Romero, 154
Reino Aventura, 101
El Relleno, 593
Le Rendezvous, 575
Restaurant Altuna, 576
Restaurant Las Brasas, 306
Restaurant Casa de Sierra Nevada, 220
Restaurante Bar Catedral, 503
Restaurante Barlovento, 642
Restaurante El Correo, 220
Restaurante de las Espadas, 576
Restaurante El Mexicano, 616
Restaurante del Parián, 176
Restaurante Vasco, 127
Restaurant Fonda las Mercedes, 240
Restaurant Francis, 450
Restaurant 1942, 467
Restaurant Plaza, 557
Restaurant El Portal, 187
Restaurant Savino, 183
Restaurant La Taberna, 170
Restaurant Taberna del León, 188
Restaurant Tollan Campestre, 182
Restaurant Villa Fiesta, 351
El Rey Group, 607
El Rey Sol, 306
Richard Milhouse Nixon Memorial Library, 439
Rincón Argentina, 135

Rincón de Guayabitos, 374
Rincón del Pacífico, 441, 456
Río Dulce, 593, 597
Río Grill, 323, 325
El Río Motel, 244, 252
Río Viejo, 266
Risky Business, 621, 623
Roberto's, 652
Roca de Farallón, 289
Rock Garage, 142
Rodrigo R. Rivero Lake, 154
El Romano Days-Inn Diana, 120
Romeo and Julieta, 323
La Rosa de Cristal, 268
Rosarío, 349
Rosarito, 302
Rosarito Beach Resort Hotel, 302, 331
Rosarito Restaurant and Bar, 302
Royal Courts Motor Inn, 245, 252
Royal Maeva, 447, 457
Royal Mayan Yacht Club, 624
Royal Zona Rosa, 118
Rubén Torres: Acapulco, 421; Manzanillo, 389
El Rubí, 208
Ruinas del Rey, 607

Los Sábalos, 343, 356
El Sagrario Metropolitano, 57
St. Valentin, 366
Sala Nezahuacoyotl Concert Hall, 99
Salon de Arte Plastica Mexicana, 151
Salsitas, 322
Saltillo, 245
Salto de Eyipantla, 478
San Agustín, 452
San Agustín Acolman, 109
San Angel, 95
San Angel Inn, 97
San Antonio Aguas Calientes, 585
San Bartolo Coyotepec, 497
Sanborn's: Acapulco, 421; Cuernavaca, 164;
Guadalajara, 266; Mexico City, 67
San Cristóbal de las Casas, 13, 554
San Francisco Acatepec, 178
San Francisco Reef, 659
San Gervasio, 650
San José del Cabo, 314, 316
San Juan Chamula, 558
San Luis Potosí, 10, 246
San Marino Marina, 624
San Martín, 477
San Miguel de Allende, 11, 195, 210, 211 (map)
San Miguel de Cozumel, 651
San Pablito, 184
San Pedro, 589
San Sebastián, 374
Santa Ana del Valle, 509
Santa Casa de Loreto, 216
Santa Clara Church, 205
Santa Clara del Cobre, 277
Santa Cruz Huatulco, 446, 449
Santa Fe, 442
Santa Rosa Church, 205
Santa Rosalía, 307
Santa Rosa Wall, 659
Santiago, 383
Santiago Atitlán, 589
Santiago's Grill, 654
Santo Tomás, 592
Santuario de Atotonilco, 222
Santuario de la Virgen de Ocotlán, 179
Savage, 448
Savio's, 616
Sayil, 535
Scaramouche, 658
Scuba Cancún, 624
Sebastian, 448
Secretaría de Educación Pública, 54
La Selva, 553
Señor Frog's: Cancún, 615, 623; Mazatlán, 342
El Señorial Hotel, 209, 252
Señorial Nightclub, 143
Señor Pepper, 347

INDEX

Señor Sushi, 323
El Sereno, 585
Sergio Bustamante: Acapulco, 423; Guadalajara, 269
Seryna, 618
El Set, 370
Sevilla Palace, 122
Shanghai, 423
Shangri-La Caribe, 631, 666
Sheik, 343
Shelty, 141
Sheraton Buganvilias, 363, 377
Sheraton Cancún Resort and Towers, 613, 665
Sheraton Huatulco, 447, 457
Sheraton María-Isabel Hotel & Towers, 119
Shirley's, 129
Shrimp Bucket: Cabo San Lucas, 321; Mazatlán, 339
The Shrimp Factory: Cabo San Lucas, 323; Mazatlán, 345
Si Como No, 345
Las Sillas, 143
La Sirena, 643
La Sirena Gorda, 404
La Sirena Que Canta, 402
Sirocco, 425
Sir Winston Churchill's, 135
Sisoguichi, 292
Sixties, 623
Sna Jolobil, 556
Soberanis, 654
Sociedad Cooperativa Otomí, 208
Solaris, 388
Solarium, 448
El Sombrero, 399, 404
La Sorpresa, 511
Southern Gulf Coast, 476 (map)
Spa Buena Vista, 326
Spaghetti House, 442
Sports Page, 653
Squid Roe: Cabo San Lucas, 321, 325; San José del Cabo, 314
Stelaris, 144
Stouffer Presidente Cancún, 611, 665
Stouffer Presidente Chapultepec, 116
Stouffer Presidente Cozumel, 656, 666
Stouffer Presidente Loreto, 309, 331
Stouffer Presidente Los Cabos, 316, 330
Stouffer Presidente Oaxaca, 499, 513
Submarino Amarillo, 467
Sucesos Boutique, 367
Suites Amberes, 119
Sumiya, 164
Suneson's, 366
Sunset Tours, 624, 628
Suntory, 137
Suprema Corte de Justicia, 63
Sushi Max, 442

Tabasco, 458
Tabasco Beach, 420
La Tablita, 135
El Tajín, 13, 472
El Tajín Chico, 473
Talavera Ware, 174
Taller Alta Temperatura, 276
Tampico, 484
Tane: Manzanillo, 389; Mexico City, 153, 155
Tango, 362
El Tapatío, 265, 284
Tapetes Mexicanos, 151
La Tarraya, 630
Tasca de los Santos, 233
Taxco, 11, 157, 167
Teatro Angela Peralta, 340
Teatro Blanquita, 50
Teatro Degollado, 261
Teatro Juárez, 229
Techo del Mar, 429
El Tecolote, 498
Temple of the Eagle and Jaguar Knights, 191
Templo de la Calavera, 551
Templo de las Caritas, 471
Templo de las Chimenas, 471
Templo del Conde, 552
Templo de la Compañía: Guanajuato, 229; Puebla, 173
Templo de la Cruz, 552
Templo de la Cruz Foliada, 552
Templo de los Danzantes, 504
Templo del Dios Descendente, 637
Templo y Exconvento de Francisco, 204
Templo y Exconvento de la Natividad de la Virgin María, 165
Templo de los Falos, 533
Templo de los Frescoes, 637
Templo del Gran Jaguar, 576
Templo de las Guacamayas, 533
Templo de los Guerreros, 544
Templo de las Inscripciones, 551
Templo de los Jaguares, 544
Templo de los Mascarones, 538
Templo Mayor: Mexico City, 58; Zempoala, 471
Templo de Nuestra Señora del Carmen, 223
Templo de San Francisco: Cuernavaca, 163; Guadalajara, 263; Mexico City, 66; San Miguel de Allende, 215; Tzintzuntzán, 275
Templo de San Juan Bautista, 92
Templo de Santa Rosa de Viterbo, 206
Templo de la Santa Veracruz, 73
Templo de Santiago Tlatelolco, 46
Templo de Santo Domingo, 173, 556
Templo de las Siete Muñecas, 530
Templo del Sol, 182, 552
Templo de Tlahuizcalpantecuhtli, 182
Temptations, 323
Tenacatita, 334, 377
Tenampa, 50, 141
Tenochtitlán, 5

SPILLANE

belts out another socker featuring a brand-new hero, counterspy
TIGER MANN,
who smashes into a Communist conspiracy involving UN delegates; CIA agents; ex-Nazi spies; a bold-bosomed, no-good beauty who's so kissable and so killable ... and winds it all up with a real gasper, with a Spillane-type switcheroo that will make mystery history!

"Tiger Mann, U.S. counterspy, keeps cold war at bay with his torrid gun. . . . Cordite and corpses abound." —*Saturday Review Syndicate*

"Simple, brutal and sexy. Like Mike Hammer, Spillane's latest hero, Tiger Mann, is a law unto himself." —*Kansas City Star*

"You'll thrill to the exploits of Tiger Mann as he recklessly pursues beautiful women and wicked spies leaving a trail of havoc behind him. If you like Spillane, you'll love this one."
—*Hartford Courant*

MICKEY SPILLANE

DAY OF THE GUNS

A SIGNET BOOK PUBLISHED BY
THE NEW AMERICAN LIBRARY

Copyright © 1964 by Mickey Spillane

All rights reserved. No part of this book may be
reproduced in any form without permission in writing
from the publisher, except by a reviewer who wishes
to quote brief passages in connection with a review
written for inclusion in a magazine, newspaper or
broadcast. For information address E. P. Dutton and Co., Inc.,
201 Park Avenue South, New York, New York 10003.

*Published as a SIGNET BOOK
by arrangement with E. P. Dutton and Co., Inc.,
who have authorized this softcover edition.
A hardcover edition is available from E. P. Dutton and Co., Inc.*

First Printing, May, 1965

SIGNET TRADEMARK REG. U.S. PAT. OFF. AND FOREIGN COUNTRIES
REGISTERED TRADEMARK—MARCA REGISTRADA
HECHO EN CHICAGO, U.S.A.

*SIGNET BOOKS are published by
The New American Library of World Literature, Inc.
501 Madison Avenue, New York, New York 10022*

PRINTED IN THE UNITED STATES OF AMERICA

To: The tigers of the world. There are still a few left. Some are dead and some will die, but the living ones be careful of. Those who know the inside story will get the message.

M.

DAY
OF THE
GUNS

Chapter 1

I looked past Wally Gibbons at the woman who had just come into the Cavalier Restaurant and felt the same as every other man in the place. Just to see her had a startling effect, but that low laugh and throaty voice was like the caress of fingertips across a naked stomach.

She was tall and auburn-haired with the edges of it curling around an upturned collar onto her shoulders and the wide-belted trench coat made you tingle because you knew she was all real beneath it. She had the lapels thrown back wide so that the flesh of her throat merged into the swell of her breasts before plunging into the black fabric of her dress.

Pedro, the maître d', bowed lower than was his usual habit, smiled more charmingly than he ever did to anyone else and led her past the tables of craning necks to the back of the room and into the alcove where the two stout men were sitting and hid her out of sight in the corner. Once she was there the table talk around us resumed, but the subject was the same, from the wishful thinking of the junior execs to the dirty cracks of the boys who liked to make like they'd been around.

Wally speared a piece of fish and grinned at me. "How about that," he said.

I grunted and picked up my drink.

"Come on, Tiger, don't play it down. Some broad, huh?"

"Swell," I said.

"Comes in here every once in a while. Never saw it yet when she didn't stop the action. I ran a piece about the mystery . . . just a U.N. translator, a sort of foreign-type career girl too dedicated to her job to be seen around much. Not that she doesn't get the offers."

Somebody at the next table made a snide remark and the others laughed. "Not that they wouldn't like to hand them out," I said.

Wally shook his head. "Hell, Tiger, I've seen it tried. Those English broads can knock you off your pins with two words and a look." He grinned at me. "Being a big columnist and all, I even tried it myself."

"And . . . ?"

"I got knocked off with two words and a look."

"Tough."

"Go give it a try, Tiger. You're not like in the old days, but from the word I hear you're still pretty active. I'd like to see you get bounced. Just once."

"Why?"

"Oh, you know . . . losers enjoy seeing winners get their lumps once in a while."

"I got enough to last me, buddy."

"So be a sport and give it a try. Hell, everybody else did. They're all waiting for a champ to come along. They'll hate your guts if you make out, but, man, they'll be looking up to you the rest of your life if you swing it."

"Forget it."

"Come on, Tiger . . ." he grinned again and shoved his plate away. "Her name is Edith Caine. London background, old family and all that. I understand she has plenty of private loot, so you can't use that approach. I've seen some Hollywood types make their pitch, and public personalities don't seem to sway her any, so that's out. All you can do is turn on the charm and whisper whatever the hell it is you whisper in their ears."

"Quit being a clown. I've had it."

"I'll write that you're a fink."

"So who knows me?" I laughed.

Wally put his drink down and stared across the table. "That, Tiger, is something I've always wondered about. Once or twice a year we get together and each time there's something different about you. At the wrong seasons you come in with a tan, I catch you in the shower last time and you got a new bullet hole in you that wasn't from the Army days, you have money to sit in on a big game and some funny pull in queer quarters. Now I'm a newspaperman and have ways of finding out things, yet I can't run you down in anything. I can't get past that discharge in '46. You might not even be alive, for all I know."

"I'm a spook."

"Sure. So go spook the broad. You're Tiger Mann, she's Edith Caine, go introduce yourself."

I put my drink down, swirled the ice around in my glass a second and took my hand away. "I don't need any introduction," I told him. "Her name isn't Edith Caine . . . it's Rondine Lund. She isn't English, she's Austrian and during the war she was a goddamn Nazi spy. She shot me twice in '45 and left me for dead, and if there's anybody in this world left that I'd like to kill, it's her. No, buddy, we don't need any introduction."

Wally couldn't answer. He sat there looking at me as though I was crazy, then his eyes squinched up to ask a question, but before he could he waved the thought away and said, "You're nuts." He pointed at my drink, then motioned to the waiter for another round. "Damn, what an actor you are. You almost get me believing you. After twenty years on the Broadway circuit in the newspaper business you'd think I could spot a line right off. Buddy, you should be in Hollywood, you and that crazy name of yours."

"The checker-outer," I said as the drinks came.

"Damn right. I have a reputation too, Tiger boy. She's been a news item since she got here six months ago. Everybody was flipping over the glamorpuss at the U.N., and right after she was on the cover of the Sunday-supplement section, I was assigned to do a piece on her. So did a few other columnists. So back we went through the British Embassy, the respectable Caine family in old London, a fashionable girl's school and a previous position in some obscure agency of the British government. She's twenty-eight, unmarried and untouchable. You're just finding out."

I leaned back in my chair and lit a smoke. "She's thirty-nine, an Austrian national and in '45 she tried to kill me."

"Okay, Tiger, tell me a story. I'll give you two minutes and have to blow. Maybe I can sell it to Paramount."

"Drop dead," I said.

Wally called for the check, signed it, and picked up his envelope off the spare chair. "When do I see you again?"

"Who knows? I'll call you."

"Anytime. You're always good for a laugh. If you ever run across any of the old gang, give 'em my regards. You going to be at the Group reunion this year?"

"Maybe."

"Try to make it. Terry Atkins and Bob Shiffer won't be there. Terry got killed down in Honduras during the flare-up and Ben got his from a cheap hood when they were cleaning up that narcotics ring in L.A."

"I heard about it."

"Brother, they can stuff the cop angle. One tour during the war with the O.S.S. was all I could take. I get scared."

"Who doesn't?"

"Yeah," he grinned. "Take it easy. I'll see you around."

He left then, and I sat back with the butt until it was down to the filter, then I squashed it out and got up from the chair.

The two fat guys had the look of importance about them, their clothes tailor-made for shape and the cigars the best. They were dignity and money with the subtle power of governments showing in their demeanor. They were speaking of the Common Market and exchange of trade when I walked up to the table and their eyes showed the intelligence of breeding and knowledge of affairs and they stood up when they realized I was about to join them.

But there was a hint of laughter there because they had evidently seen it happen before, knew why I was there and waited to see sudden death from a frosty glance and a few words.

I said, "Hello, Rondine."

Chapter 2

She was very good. Much better than I had expected. Her smile was lovely and forthright, and when the two men passed a quizzical look between them, I said, "Pet name," and held out my hand.

There was strength in her fingers, her smile a magical thing, and when I looked at her sitting there I could see why all the others wanted that crazy body so badly. She was woman all the way, bloomed to perfection and proud of the valley between her breasts and the way the tight-fitting dress dipped into her hips and swelled out against her thighs.

"It's been a long time, honey," I told her. I let her hand go and looked at the two men. "Tiger Mann," I said, shaking with them both. "Ridiculous name, but my father gave it to me."

One was Burton Selwick, the other Vincent Harley Case. Both were connected with the British legation, active at the U.N., both models of propriety and they invited me to join them. Pedro found another chair, brought a fresh drink, and we raised a toast to the beautiful, gorgeous killer sitting in the corner.

Selwick put his drink down and offered me a cigar. I shook my head and dumped the last butt out of my pack. "Are you in politics, Mr. Mann?" His voice had the crisp, cultured tone of an Oxford graduate that didn't quite conceal the subtle note of authority, a quality heard only behind closed doors at Downing Street.

I took the light he held out. "No . . . not politics." I looked across the flame at Rondine. She was sitting there with her chin propped on the back of her fingers, smiling. "You might call it . . . international business. Of a sort, that is."

"I see." He didn't really, but he said it.

"And how have you been, honey?"

"Fine, Mr. Mann."

"It used to be Tiger."

Her laugh was as deep as it ever was. "Fine, Tiger. And you?"

"Not bad at all. I'm surprised to see you again."

She made a gesture with her hands. "The world changes. Things happen."

I could still feel those two bullets going into my belly. "But we can still remember, can't we?" I said.

Her eyes were a peculiar shade. I tried to remember what they were like when I saw them last in the little room in Hamburg. Outside, the Eighth Air Force was plastering the city with block-busters and in another two minutes Cal Haggerty would be coming up the stairs with a tommy gun that would blow that goddamn nest of agents right off the face of the earth . . . only she had killed Cal too because she was quicker and had all the wiles of a woman going for her. You don't spray a naked broad with .45's without looking at her first and he had looked too pointedly and too long and had missed the Luger in her hand.

Vincent Case looked at his watch and snubbed his cigar out. "Well, you two, supposing we leave you to your reminiscing. We have to be back, but since everyone has adjourned for the weekend, you might as well stay, my dear. Mr. Mann, it was a pleasure." Unlike his partner, there was a slight Scottish burr to his words.

Burton Selwick said, "As for me, I'm afraid my day is ended. A few years after fifty can bring tiredness too easily, ulcers too abruptly, and strange pains that make one yearn for the heath and heather and the hearth."

Rondine shot him a sudden glance of compassion, but one so easily assumed. "Are you all right?"

"Just the usual complaint. Overwork, my dear. Too many

late hours, too much work and the usual complaints. I'll be happy to be replaced when the time comes."

"The doctor . . ."

He spread his palms out and smiled. "Exactly what I've just told you. Age, my dear. A few pills, a little administration, and I shall be quite well again to work another day."

I shook hands with them both. "Nice to see you," I said and watched them leave. Then I picked up a cigarette from her gold case, put it between her lips like I used to and lit it for her.

"Tiger," she said softly.

"Yes, dear," I said just as softly. "And now you're on your way down because I'm going to kill you just as dead as you thought you did me. Surprised? You shouldn't be."

She blew a thin stream of smoke at me, her eyes as steady as ever, not afraid. They had never been afraid. Determined, dedicated, but never afraid. "I was wondering when someone would come," she said.

"It's now, honey."

"I see. Can I explain?"

"No."

"How are you going to kill me?"

"I'm not sure yet," I said. "I think I'll shoot you."

"Why?"

I grinned at her, enjoying something I had thought about for almost twenty years. "It's not so much the past, sugar, but the present. You're back, you're here. Nobody knows it except me, maybe, but you haven't changed. Your damn setup is as good as it was then. You're still what you were, one of those tying the world into knots and you're in the right place to do it. U.N. translator? Hell kid you can speak seven languages and were trained in the greatest espionage school that ever existed. Right now you have a minor job but a key position to take what you want and wherever your information is going you got it made. With all the background and experiences you have it must be like making mud pies for you. Only now there's a difference."

"Oh?"

"Me. Now you can die. You left me with my belly torn out and figured me for dead. You suckered me into a beautiful love trap when I should have known better than to fall for a stinking Nazi agent and even when I let you off the hook . . . when I gave you a chance to get out when I could have killed you, you didn't take it . . . hell no, you gave me a pair of quick ones and blew. Honey . . . it wouldn't have mattered

... the war was over ... you could have made it if the hate wasn't inside you so deep nobody could get it out."

I put out my butt and sat back smiling at her as if it were just another luncheon conversation. "So now you die, kid. Whatever you're up to, tough ... you die."

Her face pulled together and the tip of her tongue wet her lips. "When?"

"Soon. I could do it right now, but first I find out what game you're playing and why. Then, pretty killer ... right in that smooth gut of yours."

"Tiger ..."

"Come on, honey ... you've had it too. No way out. Maybe you've had the face lifted and the gray dyed out, but this is the old soldier who dropped into Germany and made the big one. I don't go the mistake route twice. Kid ... you're dead. From this minute on, you're dead. I'd do it now only I want to enjoy it. I want to poke around some and blow your game before I put the big one inside your stomach."

I pushed my chair back, stood up and grinned down at her. A sudden, strange expression clouded her eyes, then passed.

"You were a great lover," I said. "Remember the bomb shelter?"

Her eyes were like twin arrows reaching for me.

"Remember the rainy night I lied to keep the Frenchies from finding you?"

Both of her hands were tightened into knots.

"They would have killed me if they had found out, Rondine. But we were lovers, one Nazi spy, one American spy. You showed your appreciation well. Ten minutes after we went to bed together you shot me. Twice. Ten minutes after you were rolling on that bed crying and moaning because you never had anything like it before you gave me two in the gut. That's real appreciation. Thanks a bunch. Now sweat."

The wetness that came in her eyes didn't bother me any. The quick motion of a sob that forced the cleft of her breasts apart had no effect at all.

I said, "Later, Rondine. I'll see you later. Just sweat."

They watched when I left. They knew I had been back there alone with her when nobody else was able to make it. They had seen the other two go, the essence of dignity and respectability, and now they saw a different type none of them could put their finger on and wouldn't really want to because I had to shave every day and looked at too many mirrors not to know what the others had seen.

Only those wouldn't talk any more. They couldn't. They were dead.

They came for me that night like I knew they would. I set it up beautifully and it was like the New York Giants pulling the Statue of Liberty play on the Packers. It was so damn old, with the dummy in the bed and all the archaic bits and pieces that went with the play that it was almost pathetic. I wanted to find out how fast they could run me down when nobody knew I was here or where I was, and they did a great job. Just great.

Except they missed.

I was outside on the window sill, forty feet above the street, hanging on to a rig I had snapped into the window washer's clamps, with a .45 in my fist for safety's sake and they came in the door with a key, smiling and joking like it was their room and the two of them pumped a full clip of slugs into the mound on the bed, each one going off with an almost inaudible *plop*, and the idiots were so sure of themselves and so anxious to be out of there they didn't check to see what they had hit. You don't catch a slug, even in your sleep, without a twitch or rearing up or some blood spilling out and the jerks didn't check it. They simply laughed some more, opened the door and walked out.

I gave them a full minute, opened the window, swung in and looked at the holes in the bedclothes. Tomorrow the housekeeper was going to be one teed-off broad. Maybe I'd even make a complaint. Fourteen shots had torn up three pillows under the blankets and left the room stinking of cordite.

I threw the chain on the door, double-locked it, fanned the fumes out of the room and climbed into my nice shot-up sack. Tomorrow was going to be full of surprises. For Rondine, anyway.

Chapter 3

Unless you've made a trip to the U.N. and sat in on a meeting of the General Assembly or the Security Council you don't know what you're missing. Outside on the door there's a quotation from Scripture . . . about turning swords into plowshares. There's not even a credit line . . . you'd think they had dreamed the possibility up. But considering the fact that ever since its inception the world has been at war, you'd think that this magnificent conglomeration of brains assembled from the world over were there for one purpose . . . not to make peace, but to figure out how many ways there were to kill. Hell, it's an old story, look at the record. We get stuck with the bills and the trouble. They scream for the gravy. But there are still some of us left. They can't kill us all.

Something had come up about Ghana and week-end passes had been canceled. I made a phone call from the lobby and an innocuous-looking guy had come out to show me to a spectator's seat. He gave me that funny look I always got when my calls had been routed and didn't ask any damn questions, but there was a distaste in his face when he saw my eyes.

Maybe he knew. Maybe he didn't. But he felt. I made sure of that.

The Russians were shouting that day. They didn't like what was coming up. It had to do with U.N. dues and some million-dollar trivialities and all I could think of was the slobs who didn't let Patton go ahead into Berlin and we had to split the spoils with pigs who later built the wall. We break our asses fighting and the striped-pants gang loses the peace.

Nothing much came out of it, but I found Rondine.

I came up behind her and said, "How much longer, honey?"

She was better than when we met. She looked around slowly, never hesitating in her translation, but the sudden widening of her eyes was enough to spell it out. The only thing that was wrong was that the wetness came back again and all I could think of was how much a woman could hate that she'd cry because one man didn't die.

I looked at the clock. The session was almost over. "I'll wait outside," I said.

She only took fifteen minutes. She came through the door composed and smiling as if death and terror were a daily occurrence. And they were. "Hello, Tiger."

"Tell me something."

"All right."

"Who did the face job . . . the plastic surgery? You look great. The lines don't show at all."

"They weren't supposed to."

"Your boys missed last night. I want you to tell them something. Will you?"

"Yes." Her eyes dropped to the floor.

"I could have killed them, baby. It would have been fun. Tell them they don't get a second chance. Neither do you."

"Tiger . . ." She was clear again. Beautiful as hell, woman all the way. She was almost as big as I was, soft luxurious woman I could fall into and kiss and love . . . only I wouldn't. "Are you hurt that badly?" she asked.

"It was a long time ago. The hurt is a long time gone."

"Revenge?"

"Nope."

"What then?"

"Satisfaction. I need it. I died too many times since you. All I want is you dead."

"I'm here."

"Uh-uh. I want your reason first. I want to see you scared again, then you die."

She did it too fast for me to stop her. She raised on her toes with her hands behind her head and her mouth was a hot, wet fire that pierced into me with a wild spurt of passion that sucked her body behind it, pressing it flat against mine. Before I could push her away she did it herself, then stood back and smiled, her teeth showing their white edges.

"Don't die again, Tiger," she said.

And when I smiled her eyes went dark and tightened at the corners because she read me right. "Don't worry, I won't," I reminded her.

The building on Fifth Avenue was a brand-new modern monstrosity that towered over Manhattan and on the sixteenth floor it housed one single office that bore the label, *THOMAS WATFORD, IMPORT-EXPORT*. I walked in, told the receptionist I'd like to speak to Mr. Watford, and no I didn't have an appointment, but he'd see me. She made the call, told me to go in and when I went through the door the gimlet-eyed guy in blue with the tight crew cut looked up, leaned back in his chair and said, "Ah, yes, Tiger Mann. Have a seat, Tiger."

I sat down.

"We heard you were in town," he said.

"Your agency has big ears."

"Not really. The trouble you leave behind you is easy to follow. It isn't appreciated."

"Tough, Mac."

The chair creaked forward and I wondered how many guys he had scared to death with that face of his. "We were aware that you knew of us. I don't like it."

"Then don't try to hide. We're pros too."

"Are you really?"

"You got a file on me."

"The rest of the group you represent, too. Very professional. You call yourselves patriots, don't you?"

I shrugged. "Not me. I used to, but no more. Now I just like the trouble. We get clobbered by all the pinkos and the liberals, but I gave up the patriot angle a long time ago. Too damn many patriots are going down the wide-open trail to Communism to suit me. They swallow the garbage, the promises, they lead the country down the garden path singing songs of peace and happiness behind the shoe-pounder and the do-gooders, but not me. I'm just one guy who likes trouble."

"Your bunch is going to get slammed by a Congressional investigation, Tiger."

"So go ahead. We're ready."

"Listen . . ."

"Who stopped the bit in Nicaragua? Who killed off the uprising in the Honduras? Who went into Colombia and Panama and put the squash on that deal? You slobs tried working it with papers and a couple of money twists when there were guns out in the open. Okay, buddy . . . get this, we're a power. We can push. We go right where it hurts those Commie bastards and we're not stopping. Like Hitler had commercial money behind him, we have top financing too. It's no Hitler job, but don't count us out. You're a secret tunnel here and we know the secret, so play ball or I'll blow the lid off this outfit now. Pretty?"

Watford sat back again, picked up a pencil and tapped it against the desk. "We heard what you had in mind."

"You know the way out. You're too big to break up. You know we can smear you if we want to. I'll break up this whole goddamn operation unless you cooperate and you can't afford to lose your cover. Too much is involved."

"Mr. Mann . . . you are a traitor."

"Not yet, friend. Not ever. Maybe in your eyes, but not ever. It's just that we're sick of some things and do them our own way."

"Illegally."

"The terminology is extralegal. We did it in 1776 too."

"This is 1964."

"So we'll do it again."

THOMAS WATFORD, IMPORT-EXPORT, was fed from Washington, D. C. It was a tight, secret agency that worked out of I.A.T.S. and what they had nobody was supposed to know.

But we knew.

The grand machinery of The Government vs. People Who Cared, I thought.

I said, "There's a girl in the U.N., a translator. Her name is Edith Caine. I want a check on her tomorrow."

"Personal, Tiger?"

"You might say that."

"Or else, I suppose."

I shrugged. "I got friends who think public agencies should be public information."

"No doubt. And where do I deliver this information?"

"I'll call you," I told him and left.

I took the bullets I had squeezed out of the pillows to Ernie

Bentley and five minutes later had a report on them. They were perfectly bore-marked for a ballistics check and the next time they showed up I'd know where they came from. They were 7.65-caliber Luger ammo fired from another make of gun; they were marked and filed away. I told Ernie thanks, left his office, ducked out the back way and took a cab back to the hotel.

Chapter 4

Edith Caine had a British passport. From the outside it looked good, backed up by the usual birth certificate and a phone call to London put her in the clear. Somehow she had made her way pretty well, but it isn't too hard to pick up a b.g. when you start back far enough. Somebody had died or was missing in her past and she had taken on from there. All I needed now was definite proof of identity. Two days at the outside. She was here and it could look easy. There was nobody to doubt her. Until she arrived at the U.N., cleared all the way, nobody had known her personally. She came out of London, picked up her job and was well liked. The pattern had a familiar ring to it. I had seen it during the war.

Wally Gibbons took time out to meet me for coffee and brought along four head photos of Edith Caine that had been taken for the papers. When he handed them over he said, "She tugs at the heart, doesn't she?"

"Yeah, man."

His grin turned curious. "What are they for?"

23

I tucked them inside my coat. "Reproduction. I want to get copies off to every plastic surgeon here and in Europe."

"What for?"

"To see who did a face job on her. It would have been one of the big ones."

"Come off it, Tiger. She needs a lift job like you need a hole in the head."

"If she had one I'll find who did it unless it was done behind the Curtain."

"You're sick, friend. You got something on that mind of yours again. Now I'm getting that trouble feeling like before and it scares me a little bit. You want to tell me about it?"

"Not yet."

He picked up his coffee, sipped it and studied me a moment. "I called your hotel this morning."

"Oh?"

"You had already left, but I was asked some questions by a certain Detective Tibbet. When I identified myself, and since we knew each other he mentioned a maid's complaint about a hatful of bullet holes in the bedding but no spent slugs. Any comment?"

I shrugged. "Lousy hotel. Who knows what happened after I left? Anybody hear any shots?"

"That's the funny part. No."

"Then let them figure it out."

"Will they?"

"I doubt it." I called for a refill and turned back to Wally. "Do something for me. Find out who Edith Caine is familiar with."

"How closely?"

"Personal relationships, business associations . . . anybody whose company she's in with any degree of regularity. Can do?"

"Why sure. Later you'll give me a breakdown on this I imagine."

"My pleasure."

"Okay, sucker."

The Army retired Colonel Charlie Corbinet a brigadier in '54, found a place for him in government, couldn't put up with his intelligence or his refusal to go along with certain proposals and eased him out in '56. The Russell-Perkins company took him on and now he rolled in millions.

But he still hadn't changed from when he was head of the

group that was dropped behind the lines during the war. He was older now, crustier than ever, but behind eyes that once were blue but now had the gray circle of age around their irises, he was the quietly determined probing person he ever was.

He held out his hand, said, "Well, Tiger, it's nice to know you're still alive."

"I had good training, Colonel."

We both laughed and you'd never realize that it had been ten years since we had seen each other. He told his secretary to cancel everything out for an hour and leave us alone, found a bottle, ice and mixer in a sideboard and poured us a drink. He held his glass up, looking into it. "To the old days, Tiger?"

"To now, Colonel."

Without moving his head, his eyes jumped to my face, then he nodded and accepted the toast. "This isn't a friendly visit, is it?"

"Not exactly. I want some information."

Corbinet sat down and waved for me to do the same. "I see. You know, Tiger, you aren't the first one to come back. Some of the others have done the same."

"I heard," I said.

"And I've heard about you. Not directly, of course, but I'm still in a position to pick up pieces of the action. Some of it had your stamp all over it. That business in Panama was very neat."

"We try."

"Your . . . group . . . can come to be well hated."

"That's already happened." I took a pull of the drink. As usual he had made it too damn strong.

"What can I do for you?"

"Rondine Lund. What happened to her?"

Corbinet didn't say anything for a moment. He watched me, thinking, then played with his glass. "Aren't you going pretty far back?"

"Maybe."

"Rondine, eh? You loved her, didn't you?"

I grimaced into my glass but the effect was bad. "So what?" I asked.

"So you almost spoiled the play at one time. Luckily the war was over."

"I paid pretty well for my indiscretions."

"Hell, you almost died for them."

"What about Rondine Lund?"

Corbinet leaned back and folded his fingers behind his head. "She dropped out of sight after the invasion. I heard the *maquis* caught her."

"Sure?"

He shook his head. "Nope. Too much was going on to check it out. She had lost her importance along with her war and we were being disbanded. You were still in the hospital when I got that much."

"From what source?"

"Price Richards in British Intelligence. He picked it up someplace and mentioned it over a drink as we were shipping out."

"If I contacted him . . ."

"No good," he interrupted. "Price died about three years ago."

"You think there's a way I can get past him to his source?"

"There's always a way," Corbinet said, "but it will take time. You don't cover twenty years in an hour, you know that. The *maquis* didn't keep records either." He took his hands down and leaned on his desk. "So it's Rondine again," he stated. "What would you do if you found her?"

"Kill her," I said simply.

"Well, I think it's going to take you a long time to find her."

I stood up and put on my hat. "Colonel . . . I think I *found* her."

Little tight lines pulled at the corner of his eyes. He was going over the list mentally, the ones dead Rondine had made that way, the two towns she pinpointed for destruction, the lives lost on the beach because she found a way to get inside somebody's mind and pry loose that critical bit of news.

All he said was, "Ah, yes, Rondine."

"I have to be sure. Colonel. Do you still have the contacts?"

Now his mouth tightened too in an expression I had seen before when the chips were down. "In a certain way . . . and I don't want this repeated . . . I'm in much the same position as you. Yes, I have the contacts."

It was my turn to study him. I put things into place in my head, remembering things I had come across about a certain former intelligence officer, about some peculiar strokes of luck in my own operations that seemed a little too coincidental, and there were a few times I had seen the mark of a fine hand that seemed somehow familiar employed in the same engagement I was involved in.

I felt a grin touch my mouth. "So I.A.T.S. never really did let you go, did they?"

"You think too much, Tiger. It's a new quality and an improvement over the old, but don't make yourself dangerous."

"It's the only way I'm appreciated, Colonel," I said. "I'll call you in a few days."

"Do that."

When I went out the door I covered the tiny lens set in the frame that photoed every visitor and laughed thinking of what the old boy would say when he saw the blank negative. Same old tricks.

At four o'clock I called Wally and asked what he had come up with. He gave me three names: Burton Selwick, with whom she apparently had a business connection; Gregory Hofta, another translator from Hungary with whom she was seen on numerous social occasions; and John Fredericks Talbot, a dashing-type Britisher who held a minor position with his embassy. There was a girl, Gretchen Lark, a U.N. secretary she frequently ate with and I took down their addresses, told him thanks and hung up.

My next dime got me Thomas Watford.

I said, "Tiger Mann. Anything on the Caine woman?"

"Possibly, but I think we had not better discuss it over the phone."

"Can you meet me?"

He said he would, named a bar on Sixth Avenue and told me he'd be there in an hour. That gave me time enough to get a line started on my three names.

With the last dime I called Barney Dodge and told him what I needed. He came right across with Burton Selwick's history and placed him as a man of more importance than his position indicated. It was assumed that he was one of those few people who could settle policy differences if they arose and could make decisions his government would back up without prior red tape. If he was a talker he'd be one fine source, but nothing ever pointed to him being loose-tongued. He said he'd give it a fast try and perhaps have some information that night.

It was about all I had time for. Office workers were beginning to hit the streets and were flagging down cabs from the corners. Rather than battle the crowd I started walking north toward the bar where I was to meet Thomas Watford, got there right on time, and that was where I made a mistake.

I should have been early.

Two of the boys he had with him were from a blue-card agency and I knew what they had in mind.

Nobody saw how they did it, but with nice, friendly gestures

27

they lifted the .45 from the rig, let me have a beer while the pressure of two service revolvers were against my side, then they escorted me out of there.

The room they took me to was an unmarked office ten floors from the street in a building in the middle Forties. There was a deadly quiet about the place, every other office window blank. You could rent places like this in any name for any length of time and nobody cared at all.

Then they took turns interrogating me. For two hours I let them waste their time and told them nothing, then it was Watford himself who grabbed the lead.

I said, "How long does this keep up?"

"Until you talk or we say stop. Take your pick."

"Good enough, kid. Tell me about the Caine girl."

"That's what caused the trouble. Where do you fit in with her?"

"I knew her when. It's personal."

"Balls. We checked her out back to when she was born. She never had any contact with you."

I shrugged.

"She's a British subject, Tiger. She's in a touchy and responsible position. The British get peeved when a check is run on their cleared personnel."

"How peeved?"

"Enough to get heat in our direction."

"Why? She's only a translator." I looked at him steadily.

"Your implication stinks," he said. "We're not letting anything happen that will foul up our relations with the British. We're not letting you pull one single stunt, buddy. Now do we talk?"

I pointed to the phone. "That connected?"

"It is."

"I assume you know your code calls."

Watford said nothing.

"Call the *circle fry* number. Tell him I said 'chow.'"

There was more surprise in his face than anything else, then the mask came on. He hesitated a few seconds, nodded and picked up the receiver. I heard him dial the right digits, mumble into the phone, make a few demands, listen carefully, then hang up.

When he turned around his face was tight and flushed. He said, "How do you do it, Tiger?"

I grinned at him. "Easy. A gentle form of blackmail. Now why this sudden heat on me?" I asked him.

The three of them passed a swift look around before focusing back on me again. "Because there's one hell of a security leak in the U.N.," he said.

I stretched, got up and walked to the door. Tomorrow they'd use a different place if they had to. I turned around and said, "It figures."

Chapter 5

John Fredericks Talbot had an apartment in Gramercy Park, an exclusive little oasis in the jungle of the city. Enough money lives there to keep the prowl cars on a steady circuit and patrolmen on the beat, and the only way to forestall an identity check is to make like you belong there and take the direct route.

I had made sure Talbot wasn't home with a phone call, then rang the downstairs apartment, introduced myself to the woman who answered the lobby door as a friend of Talbot's and asked her if she would give him a letter for me. She was very happy to and held the door open long enough for me to touch the safety button that would keep it in the unlock position. When Talbot answered the message he would simply be calling his superiors to see if there were any additional instructions for him and in the red tape of the organization little tricks like that happen all the time.

I made one trip around the block, came back to the building, went inside, after putting the lock on right, and up to Talbot's apartment on the top floor. Getting inside was no trouble at all.

With a pencil flash I spotted all the furniture, made sure

an exit was clear, then started the search systematically. John Fredericks Talbot had money, that was one thing. His clothes and accessories were the finest. He was regimented in his habits and everything indicated him to be as careful as a man in his position was supposed to be.

The garbage can in the kitchen held two empty beer cans and a fine pile of black, powdery ash. Talbot had burned some papers and made sure no one would ever know what they contained. Around the water level of the toilet bowl was another dark ring where he had flushed more of the same earlier. In all probability he had a maid, so it would have been done that day after she left.

It could be a necessary precaution in this job.

It could have been something else too.

Then I found the gun, a Colt Cobra in a belt holster, fully loaded and tucked inside one of his Chukka boots. Now there was something new to the pattern. Minor embassy employees don't go around New York armed.

I put the gun back, made sure everything was exactly in place and went back outside. Nobody saw me come in, nobody saw me go out. I was pretty good that way.

On the corner I flagged a cab, went back midtown to an address of Stephen Midros, found his apartment number and touched the button. Midros was one of the Hungarian freedom fighters who had gotten out to fight again and right now he was leading the battle from his position in exile and doing a good job.

The man who answered the door looked ten years older than he was. The gray hair and the scar down the side of his face did that much, but the age was mainly in his eyes. They had seen too much.

I said, "Stephen Midros?"

"Yes?"

"My name is Tiger Mann. I am going to mention one name. I think that will be more of an introduction."

He was coldly casual. "Very well."

"*George the Third.*"

There was a sudden warmth in his eyes, a recognition that meant even though we had never met we were friends of the same side and had fought for the same things. *George the Third* was a final identity signal only top inside people could possibly know. He didn't question the validity of my knowing it as I didn't his.

He answered, "*In truth,*" and held out his hand. The identity change had been completed. But like all Europeans, there were pleasantries first and it was only over a glass of wine that he asked the question.

"What business may I help you in, Mr. Mann?"

"There is a Hungarian translator in the U.N. named Gregory Hofta."

"Yes, I know of him."

"Any opinion?"

His shoulders moved in a characteristic shrug. "There has never been any need for inquiry. Why?"

"He is often seen with a British subject, another translator . . ."

"Ah," he smiled. "Edith Caine. Is that it?"

"That's it." I drank half the glass and waited.

"So, is this intrigue political or personal?" He grinned knowingly.

I didn't smile back at all. "It started from a personal angle, but it may have political repercussions. My interest is the Caine woman. There is a security leak in the U.N. somewhere and it could be there."

"But Hofta is not a Hungarian Communist," he said. "He was born in Budapest, but long ago became an American citizen. He was graduated from one of your larger colleges and has been with the U.N. since it was founded."

"Good cover if it is that way. I don't think I have to remind you of how planning for the future worked for the Nazis . . . or the Reds either for that matter."

His head furrowed in a frown. "But this connection . . ."

"What do you know of the two of them?"

He finished his wine, refilled our glasses and sat down again. "Generally I have seen them together at certain restaurants . . . Hungarian restaurants. Twice they have been at one of our gatherings, at a rally and again at a party one of my associates gave."

"How intimate were they?"

Midros spread his hands, searching for a word. "They seemed to be . . . well, more than . . . friends, shall we say? Other intimacies I cannot vouch for."

"Your organization is pretty tight, isn't it?"

"We have ways of finding things out, if that's what you mean."

"That's what I mean. Can you run a check on Hofta?"

"Yes, how far?"

"See who he left behind in Europe. Let's find out just how much of an American he really is."

I didn't have to explain any further. He got the connection

immediately with all its implications. He had a mind like a computer, too, and was putting things in their places right then. He nodded, offered me another drink I refused and said, "It will be done, Mr. Mann. I expect that you will contact me?"

"Yes."

Outside the rain was coming down harder, the reflected lights making a kaleidoscopic pattern in the asphalt streets. I ducked my head into it and walked to Broadway, then out over to my hotel. Out of habit I checked my box and saw the pink message slip there. When I slipped it open it read, "Edith called to get your number. Didn't give it to her knowing how hoople you are on the subject, but she said she can be reached at EN 2-7254 between four and six." It was signed, "Wally."

I felt a grin twist at my mouth, found a phone booth and dialed Charlie Corbinet's number. When he answered I said, "Tiger, Colonel. A quick favor."

"Shoot it."

"Get me an address from a phone number. EN 2-7254. How long will it take?"

"Five minutes." He didn't quibble about it.

A little less than five he called back. "It's a pay station in a bar and grill on Second Avenue called Lyon's. Anything else?"

"That's fine."

"Need help?"

"Did I ever?"

"Once that I remember."

"Those days are done with. Thanks." I hung up.

She was there, all right. She sat at a table in the back with Burton Selwick, engrossed in whatever he was saying, nodding and laughing like any interested woman would. I watched them for a full twenty minutes then crossed the street to another bar, dialed the number she had given me, told her I was available.

There was nothing devious about her voice. It was quiet . . . almost friendly with a peculiar touch of inquisitiveness in it. She would like to speak to me. Fine. I would like to speak to her too. Where? My hotel in an hour. Hell, she made the call, let her come to me. I hung up and went back outside.

He didn't take long . . . just enough time to pay the check and leave. I didn't wait for her. An hour from now she'd be there. But when he managed a cab I got in the one I had standing by and followed Burton back across town, down into Greenwich Village and waited while he told his taxi to hold while he went inside, then watched when he came back out with a tall brunette who had a million-dollar body and a walk to match. They got in the cab, drove to a restaurant on Fourteenth Street and got out.

For a few seconds Selwick just stood there holding his stomach, then the woman said something earnestly, seemed angry for a moment, then took his arm gently and led him inside. There was no two ways about it . . . the guy was hurting. Well hell, you don't jump from a killer to another broad without getting stomach pains. Rondine could give any guy a pain in the gut. I suffered from mine for months, only then she did it with bullets.

I didn't bother checking it out any further. I gave the driver my hotel and settled back to think about my date.

Things were looking up.

I sat there with my feet on the window sill looking out at the mist-shrouded roof of the city, thinking back twenty years, bringing her face back, the strange twist she could give to one eyebrow and the things we had said to each other in the dark.

Thinking of what kind of a fool I had been to expose an operation because one woman could do things to my insides and make my mind go against all the things it had been trained to do.

It had started back there, but it had ended back there too. The very thing I did made me try to prove something to myself and when Martin Grady had selected me along with several others to work in the same capacity through a civilian agency I had grabbed at the chance. There were forty when we started. Nineteen of the original group were left, but there were forty still, somebody always coming in as a replacement. The longer we lived, the better we got and the better our chances of staying alive.

Sure, the Washington agencies knew about our existence. I.A.T.S. kept a file on all of us as best it could, but none of it was explicit or important. They knew what we did only after we did it and nothing could be said because it was professionally done for the good of the country by experts in the field. It probably galled them though. It had, too. We moved in fast and hard when it was necessary and people had fallen and governments were toppled. Had we not been there it would have happened anyway, only millions of dollars and man-lives later.

By now Martin Grady would know I had hold of something and I'd get the word whether to process it or clear out, and, knowing how he hated any personal attitudes mixed in an operation, the word would be to get clear. He'd never take a chance on lousing up a job or losing a man to a pet hate. Only in this case he couldn't move me.

I wanted Rondine dead too badly.

There was a knock on the door.

I flicked off the light, swung around and sat there with the .45 facing the door and said, "Come in."

The knob turned, the door opened and there she stood, lovely, lovely Rondine. Beautiful as hell. With the same potential. Beauty and death inside the same shell. She still had that same hesitancy when she stepped inside a door and closed it, letting you have the full effect of the magnificence of her face and body, still the same habit of flipping open the coat so the impact of seeing the pressure of her breasts against a dress and the nipped-in waist and swell of her hips into thighs and calves of startling proportions, so that you could lose one important second of life.

I knew she couldn't see me, but I let her hear where I was.

I thumbed back the hammer of the gun and it was the loudest sound in the room.

"Here I am, Rondine."

She knew what I was holding. "Do I get it here, Tiger?"

"Maybe. It depends on how much you've sweated."

Rondine walked toward me, her hand feeling for the furniture. She hadn't adjusted her eyes to the darkness yet and it took a minute before she found a chair. Even in the dark, she sat down, crossed her legs with a graceful sweep that would have shown the whiteness of her thigh had the light been on, and in the dark I grinned, remembering that Cal had fallen for that same skin and had died for it.

"I think an explanation is in order," she said.

"Forget it, kid. The past is the past."

"But . . ."

"No buts. So you laid a couple in my belly. You knocked off a friend of mine and I tally it up to my own damn mistakes for letting you live when you were an enemy. No soap, kid, no explanations. I can understand the past. I hate, I pick up the pieces and wait my time out. Now it's here. You are as close to dying as you've ever been and you might make it."

"Tiger . . ."

"Shut up, doll," I said gently. "It's no time to explain. You have something going for you and before I knock you off I want to expose the whole bit. Then you go. Don't even talk to me. The last time you did I wound up sleeping in a shot-up sack. Your boys really came at me."

35

"You asked for it. You endangered . . ."

"Your situation? Why, sure, honey, that's what I'm here for."

"Tiger."

"I said shut up. It's my night to talk. Before, you always tried the great kiss and the roll in the hay to quiet me down, but no more, Rondine. How many times have I had you . . . or was it me who was had? Twenty? We were great together. Lovers who could love in the middle of a war. Love conquers all, we said. Great, just great.

"Everything went on the line for you, honey," I said. "Integrity, life . . . the works. I saved your ass and you tried to kill mine. For twenty years I've had it in the back of my head. All this time I thought you were dead, now it's fine to see you alive. Now I can take you right. No bed, no kiss, no talk is going to take you out of this one. First I bust up your play, whatever it is, then I take you. I'm a pro, kid, all the way. I've been practicing for a long time and it's my game right down the alley."

"Please . . ."

"Knock it off."

She could see me now, the rod in my hand and the expression on my face. There was nothing she could do and knew it. Very slowly she uncrossed her legs and sat there with her hands folded in her lap.

I said, "Send the boys for me. I'd like that. The next time I won't wait to have them prove a point. I'll put them down one by one and you'll be the last, the big one. Now get out of here."

She knew there was no use talking. She stood up slowly, looked at me, walked to the door and turned as if she were going to say something and thought better of it, then opened it, went out and it closed behind her.

It was a hell of a date. I let the hammer down on the .45 and put it away.

Chapter 6

I had laid out the trot lines, baited the hooks and now   had
to wait. Somewhere people would be meeting and policy set.
Action plans would be formulated with me as the target and
the second-guessing would be going on. In that great cluster
of buildings there would be worried people because they had
to step on a snake or get bitten and couldn't afford to lose.

So I waited for two days, knowing nothing would happen
yet because whatever was done had to be done deliberately
and carefully and things like that took time.

At nine in the morning on the second day a call came from
the lobby that a Mr. Toomey was there to see me and I invited
him up after he gave the recognition word that meant Martin
Grady had heard about me.

You never knew what to expect in the way of his agents.
This one was a good ten years older than me, a small man
impeccably dressed like the Madison Avenue types, briefcase
under his arm, rimless glasses and seemingly tired yet somehow good-natured. But in his past this one had knocked off
his share and probably would again. He could handle a blade

37

or a rod and would be adept at the peculiarities of the trade and follow orders right down the line.

I wondered what his orders were.

He sat in the chair I offered him with a sigh and looked at me with a single glance and I knew he was sizing me up all the way. He would have gone over the package Grady kept on me and knew every facet about my character and abilities, always allowing room for the little thing nobody knew about any of us.

"I presume you know why I'm here, Mr. Mann."

"Certainly. I've been waiting for you to show up."

"I see. Well, I'm here. We've had no report from you."

"You won't get one either."

"Mr. Grady understands that."

"Then what are his orders?"

Toomey smiled thinly and took the coffee I held out. "I think I'm going to surprise you."

"Nothing surprises me any more, buddy."

"This may." I caught the direct, humorous look in his eyes. "You can proceed, Mr. Mann."

"What!"

"Orders. Apparently by accident or coincidence you have disturbed something that needs disturbing. Your presence here has caused enough consternation in certain quarters that make an investigation profitable."

"Did Martin Grady know about it before I arrived?"

"No. However since every effort is being made to sidetrack you it's worth-while looking into."

"Does he know it's personal with me?"

"He realizes your motivation."

"A fuse, huh?"

Toomey nodded and smiled. "Correct."

"Then I can call on all the facilities of the command?"

"By all means."

I sipped my coffee slowly, then put the cup down. "One thing, Toomey."

"Yes?"

"What effort is being made to sidetrack me?"

His chuckle was quiet and low. "I'd hate to be on as many elimination lists as you are."

"Finish it."

"You're on the new Commie 'A' form."

"I was there a year ago."

"This is understood, Mr. Mann. You are now a primary target. On top of that I.A.T.S. wouldn't mind if you had an accident . . . oh, not a deadly one, but enough to retire you for a while. Then there's the British. Now you know how they don't care for any interference in their projects. They even dislike tying in with our own government agencies and the British can be a tough outfit. Frankly, between the Reds and the British, I'd rather have the Commies on my neck. They are predictable and not nearly as determined. So, Mr. Mann, you are to have your head. Find out why you are so well disliked."

"I can tell you now."

Toomey made a negative motion with his head. "You may think so, but you don't. Not yet."

"So I will."

"Mr. Grady seems to have great faith in your capabilities."

I grunted and picked up the coffee.

"If you want me, I'll be at the Chester Hotel," Toomey said. "Wilson and Standish are ready at the office in Newark if they're needed."

"I don't need anybody."

He got up, opened his briefcase and flipped a sheaf of bills on the table. "Perhaps not. At least, you'll need the usual. Call if you want anything at all."

"Sure. Thanks."

Toomey shrugged. "Orders. Now you have them too."

I met Charlie Corbinet for lunch at the Blue Ribbon on Forty-fourth Street and went upstairs where we could be alone, and after the beer came and while we waited for our meal, gave him a rundown on what happened. As long as he was still with I.A.T.S. I didn't have to tell him much . . . all I wanted to know was why our own people wanted me taken off a project.

He let me finish, then leaned forward, crossing his arms on the table. "This security leak at the U.N. is a big one. Right now we're in an arms race with the Reds and we have to retain control of key bases on foreign soil. Any information the Russians get on policy we establish with the various governments gives them an edge. We don't stand alone any longer. While we make policy with a government within a nation that same government can fall to the opposition, so we have to play it so that whatever we do is acceptable to . . . well, let's say both parties in British government. On top, we have to correlate our relationships with them and similar situations in other countries. This means there are a lot of angles to the game. Somebody in the U.N. has a hot pipeline in our basic policy structure and we're finding it hard to move. The goddamn Commies are always a jump up on us and overseas they're moving fast and hard and we're almost on the defensive. Right now a lot of agencies are trying to break through and if something interferes with their operation they're going to knock it out."

"It's Rondine, Colonel."

"Maybe."

"I'll find out."

"Expose her then."

"That won't be easy. She looks like a young kid. She's had a face job and everything to boot. Her background is damn near perfect, but you know and I know that it can be done."

"Go to England then, backtrack her."

"Nuts, friend, then I lose the bit here. It can be over before I get through. It'll be easier to work out where I can reach her."

"Okay, but it won't be her alone. If she's the one, she's getting her material from direct sources."

"She's in the position to do it."

The waiter came and set our plates down in front of us. When he left Charlie said, "Supposing it isn't Rondine?"

I started cutting into my lunch. "There's a good way to find out," I said.

"Oh?"

"But you wouldn't know about that. You never had Rondine in bed," I grinned at him.

I dropped him off at his office an hour later and went back to The Street. The Great White Way . . . brother, how it had changed. Where there used to be men and broads, now queers and jerks; the Black Muslims giving out papers . . . the guys who wanted to be kings. Okay, so be kings, only first take the crown away. Small bands like with Young Assassin on the back of their jackets trying to buck men who had guns in their hands and took the beaches, pimps peddling sixteen-year-old whores and finding the clientele that wanted them, cops who had to dress like babes in order to suppress the traffic, idiots who let the knotheads make passes at their wives because they were afraid to buck the trend. Now the slobs were on the loose and not too many wanted to do anything about it. Ha.

A mile away an international fiasco was in the making that would cover that lice who roamed and one of a few that wanted to stop it had the heat going high.

So try to stop that one.

I was glad it was raining.

Stephen Midros had left a simple note for me to meet him for supper at the Kubla Restaurant, a small side-street place that catered to those of Hungarian background. I got there a few minutes before seven, saw Midros facing me in a far booth and walked over.

There was another man with him I didn't know until Midros said, "I'd like you to meet Gregory Hofta, Mr. Mann."

He had a look of confidence about him, a polished cosmopolitan thing with a foreign air and his handshake was crisp and strong. *Hello, sucker,* I thought.

Midros said, "We are quite alone and unobserved here and very much among friends so we can be quite candid. First, sir, let me assure you that in what short time I had I did a thorough investigation of M. Hofta here." He smiled, watching me over his glasses, "And you too, Mr. Mann. You have quite . . . a reputation."

My eyes ran over Hofta quickly. He caught the move and nodded. "I don't mind. These things are sometimes necessary."

I played it as cool as I could. "And what do we find out, Mr. Midros?"

"Perhaps you had better tell him."

Hofta agreed with a nod and folded his hands on the table. "There are times when we must take chances in revealing certain things."

"I know the game."

"Very well. I have been working with I.A.T.S. for nine months now."

"Identify," I said.

He did the trick with his thumb and forefinger, their first recognition code.

"Confirm," I told him.

The next motion proved his point. For fun I answered him and he frowned.

"You seem to know quite a lot about our ways."

"I have to. But that makes you know about me, too, doesn't it?"

"Yes. So we'll continue. How much do you know about the security loss in the U.N.?"

"This much," I said. "Although I don't know the details of what's been divulged at this point, I understand the import of what's happening. I can deduce future events if the trend continues."

"Ah."

"And I know where it comes from."

His eyes narrowed briefly a moment. He waited.

I shook my head. "But you're not doing me out of the pleasure of slapping the lid on it personally. How about that?"

Hofta spread his hands in an impatient gesture. "You leave yourself in a position of danger. You realize what could happen?"

"Sure, buddy, but let's you offer the information."

"The American and British agencies are cooperating in a joint effort to find the leak. It comes from somewhere inside the two structures."

"Could you pinpoint it?" I asked him.

"No. It could come from the Embassy, the policy-making sections or out of the capitals themselves. Somehow the Russians always seem to know in advance what our decisions are regarding world situations and beat us to the punch in laying groundwork for their operations. Right now you can say we are in the stage of losing the cold war."

"That's how far up they are on us?"

"Precisely. In a few days something very big will come before the Security Council and if the Russians know our decision we will surely lose face in the eyes of the world if they move to make us rearrange our policy. That is why, Mr. Mann, if you have anything to offer, then do it now."

"Not now."

"The fate of many should not have to hinge on one man."

"Tough."

He looked at me, accepted the statement and said, "You told Stephen you had an interest in Edith Caine."

"Don't you?" I suggested.

"Doesn't everyone?" He smiled.

"Maybe more than you think."

"It is she you suspect," he stated flatly.

"Buddy," I told him, "I don't *suspect* anyone. I know."

"Then you can be dangerous to everyone."

"Midros . . ." I started.

"Yes, Mr. Mann."

"Am I to be doubted . . . or is my reputation no good?" I stood up and put on my hat.

"Sometimes . . . things change, sir."

"But not now," I said.

He looked at my eyes and saw something there. "No . . . not now," Midros repeated.

Chapter 7

I knew I had a tail when I got out of the cab. Since he was waiting a block away it meant there was a team staked out to pick me up no matter where I got off and that kind of a bit meant business. It meant that they were going to be careful, too, so I went in the newsstand for a paper and made the crowd that shielded me from anybody outside and called Toomey at the Chester. It only took thirty seconds and I got the message across fast. I felt better after that.

One tail took me to the hotel, another one picked me up inside. He didn't go up, but let a third check me through on my floor and as I went in the room he was going past the door.

Any time now.

But damn, there's no sense playing with these types unless you can have fun at it. They had tried for one hit and missed, now it was my turn.

This time I didn't hang on any window-washer's hook. I had chosen my floor deliberately and outside my window, two feet down, was an eighteen-inch parapet that ran around the whole building. I climbed out, shut the window behind me and went around to the third room that I had taken out in another name and popped it open.

Forty feet below me, the streets of New York were filled with theater traffic, the cabs an unending yellow stream and the noise one gigantic celebration of horn-blowing. It would have been louder had not the rain been a blanket over the whole scene.

So I saw the guy at my other door and he never saw me. He was working the lock and when I said, "*You!*" . . . he spun and fell on a dime and I missed with the .45 for the third time in twenty years and then I was in a tumble and roll because the bullet that creased my ear almost nailed me and I wasn't about to catch one.

From somewhere a slug blew out the light and in three short seconds of time there was nothing but the thunder of bullets blasting the semidarkness of the corridor apart and when it was over there was nobody there but me on the floor and Toomey on the other end.

Except for one thing.

A Tokarev 7.65-millimeter automatic was lying on the floor outside my door with little splatters of blood all round it with the hammer back in full reload-and-fire position.

I said, "Damn, you took your time."

Toomey grinned and pulled me to my feet. "I like to see my associates work."

I picked up the gun, looked at it and handed it to Toomey. It was an old job, but in perfect condition, a Soviet-built rod made in 1944, not the Czech slave-labor model . . . the one the officers wore during the war.

"Neat?" I asked.

"Neat," Toomey replied, "but it's a common piece. Ernie Bentley told me about your last bust. All 7.65's. Matter of fact, I know a lot of people who wear this rig."

"So do I," I said. "It won't help much. Chances are the blood types are all 'O' type."

"Chances are you better not try to find out. Come on, let's blow."

He stopped me by the exit staircase. "They went down here. No telling what floor they took out."

"I cased the place before I got here. Two floors down you can cut over to the other side of the building and take those exits down, too. They both open into the lobby and outside. If one of them's bleeding they won't stick around waiting for us to show."

"Want to go after them?" Toomey asked me.

I shook my head. "No. They'll be back. They have to come back. When they do I want it going all my way."

"You like this crap," he said, "don't you?"

"I love it," I answered.

Tomorrow I'd be asked to leave. One room at least. Tomorrow the whole goddamn city police force would descend on me for the job tonight and it was debatable whether or not it was to get me or get the heat on me that the whole play was pulled.

In a little while we'd find out.

Now here's the funny part. They were all watching me. They wanted to see what I was going to do . . . and hell, if they were smart enough, all they had to do was ask. I could have told them. Kill Rondine. That was all. For the sake of my own cover I'd break hers, but the initial emotion was simply . . . kill Rondine.

Everyone was sweating the security leak at the U.N. They even tried left-fielding me in, even Grady. But screw him too. Screw I.A.T.S. and the British and security and all the crap that goes with protecting a billion people. Goddamn, I was the one who caught the slugs. I'm the target now.

How simple can it get? One broad . . . that's all I asked. One lousy doll who needed a slug up her whoosis and who was going to get it from me and the whole world falls apart.

Hell, Grady even gave me orders.

Not really, though. I don't take those kind. He was just conforming. He had no choice either. I was going to nail Rondine beautifully and someplace I hit the tack and now everybody wanted to nail me.

That's the way I liked it.

When we hit the street we turned north and walked two blocks unhurriedly to a counter spot, then went in and ordered coffee. I said to Toomey, "You came on like gangbusters. How'd you know what the action was?"

"It figured. Besides, I was in contact with Grady a few minutes earlier. You're hot, Tiger."

"That's nothing new."

"Grady's contacts overseas got a message through. There's an all-out effort going on you. The Reds have you top-priority."

"*Thank you, Rondine,*" I half whispered.

"What?"

"Nothing. What's the scoop?"

"You have been ordered eliminated by any possible means immediately. From now on you'd better stay in the shadows."

"Think that accounts for the Tokarev?"

Toomey shrugged. "It's their pet weapon."

"Not in this country."

"Correction. This is not part of the *American* Commie setup. These are imports. You know they can get all the unregistered guns they want through diplomatic attaché cases."

"Then they weren't on their toes."

"Not necessarily. You were just up higher on yours. Martin says for you to go under cover."

"Nuts."

He drank his coffee and left a half a buck on the counter. "It's your neck."

"Damn right. Now do something for me. Run a check on John Fredericks Talbot and a U.N. secretary named Gretchen Lark."

Toomey wrote the names down, slipped them away and said, "Shouldn't take long."

"Who will you work through?"

He grinned and shook his head. "I'll do it my way. You want to get out of your hotel?"

"Yeah."

"I'll get your stuff moved over to the Chester in the room next to mine. I think your Mr. Watford will get us clearance on this."

"The local police aren't going to enjoy the interference."

"Friend, do I have to remind you that we're working on an international level or have you only one thing on your mind?"

"Knock it off."

"No, I can't. You may want that girl, but the complications of this affair are a little too big to make her the primary target. You are still in the group, still on assignment and still what you are. The years of training and experience you've had left their mark on you whether you know it or not and regardless of any emotional involvement, this is still . . . a case. Understand?"

"You took long enough to say it."

"Grady's instructions. I think he knows you better than you know yourself."

"Okay, okay," I laughed. "I'll keep it down."

But I wasn't about to. I could play it that way for Grady and the rest, but it was Rondine whom I loved and Rondine who had pumped two bullets into my belly and Rondine who had killed my friend and Rondine who was going to die and to hell with international complications.

Wally Gibbons was finishing off his column at his apartment when I got there. When he ended it, checked it through and stuffed it in a manila envelope he swung around in his chair. "Hell of a time to come calling."

I tossed a packet of photos on his desk. "Your shots of Edith Caine. I wanted to get them back to you."

"Do any good?"

"It'll be a couple of days before the reports come in," I said.

"Well, I don't wish you any luck. Frankly, I don't think you're going to have any either."

I sprawled out in a chair across the room. "You told me you researched the family."

"Thoroughly, buddy."

"You got the material around?"

"On the shelf right beside your head. That brown folder."

I reached up and pulled the piece out of the pile. It was a ten-page single-spaced summary with a couple dozen letters attesting to Edith Caine's background, copies of her birth certificate, school diplomas, recommendations from important people in England and a few general observations.

I said, "Brief me."

"Can't you read?"

"Sure, I will, but you give it to me first."

"Here we go again," Wally grunted. "Okay . . . fine English family. One of four girls and two boys. The oldest girl, Diana, was killed in the second air raid on London. The youngest son was in the R.A.F., shot down and killed in 1944. Ruth and Patricia Caine are both married to Army officers, Vernon, the oldest son, is still a bachelor and is in government service with the Admiralty. The father died in 1951, the mother is a dowager type who maintains the family residence, a sizable estate in the country with another place in London and is well recognized in English society. Not one smear on the family escutcheon; the stationery bears a coat of arms granted by old King John himself."

"So?"

"So this . . . if ever a more respectable bunch ever lived in merrie olde, it was the Caines. Prim and proper with never a breath of scandal. Always, the family has been connected with government service, putting in time with the military, emerging with officer rank in old regiments and what-not. Marriages have always been of their own class and they guard their reputation like we do Fort Knox."

"Ha."

"Laugh, but try to bust through the circle. You can't do it. It just doesn't have a loophole. Don't think British Intelligence didn't check every one of them out. They're no slobs. You don't get into government positions without one big security check."

"I can name a few who did."

"So can I, but they were exceptions."

"That's what I mean. Can I keep this awhile?"

"Be my guest," Wally said. He paused, looked at me seriously and frowned. "But . . . just in case, let's say . . ."

I waved him off. "You'll get the picture. You can be the hero."

He nodded, still frowning. "Tiger . . ."

"What?"

"I finally got a lead on *you*."

"How about that."

"Seems like you're a peculiarly important type of person."

"Oh?"

"Want to give it to me?"

"No."

"I'll find out anyway."

"Go ahead." I looked at him, expressionless.

"You make me nervous, buddy. What I heard is kind of frightening. Now I know why I could never get a line on you in all these years. It explains a lot of things if it's true."

I felt a grin cut the corner of my mouth. "It might be better if you kept it to yourself."

He nodded, not saying anything. I told him thanks for the package on Edith Caine and pulled myself out of the chair. At the door I turned and winked at him. He was still sitting there frowning and I knew what he was thinking. Maybe I would give him the story at that. He needed a little excitement in his life.

The invitation to visit the I.A.T.S. office downtown came from Thomas Watford through Toomey when he cleared the air about the affair in the hotel corridor. It was simply delivered, but the kind you didn't ignore.

Watford didn't bother introducing me when I came in. They were all seated at a conference table with an open chair on the end and he pointed to it and I sat down. Nothing else.

They weren't the striped-pants types, these. Two were field men I had seen before and the other pair matched them equally. The fifth was a big man, heavy in the shoulders with a tight set to his eyes and a hard mouth that had come out of years of war and intrigue. He had been a general once, during the war, now he showed up behind the scenes advising presidents and ambassadors on the fine hairline of action that can divide war from peace.

Hours before, the meeting had begun and decisions made. Although there were no papers showing on the table, the ash trays were full of butts and the room heavy with smoke. On a sideboard against the wall there was an empty water pitcher and another half full and all the glasses right side up with small pieces of ice still melting in their bottoms.

I nodded to them all in general and sat down. It was their play.

Watford said, "We'd like a statement from you about last night."

I waited a moment. "Simple. I was attacked."

"You were expecting it."

"In this business you have to expect anything."

"Come on, Mr. Mann. You had another room rented and we saw how you got into it. That's going pretty far."

"Maybe." I wasn't offering anything.

"Who were they?"

"Ballistics check the slugs?"

"Seven-six-five millimeter, a forty-five and thirty-eights." He tapped the table top with his fingertips. "We know where the last two came from."

"I take it Toomey gave you the gun we picked up?"

Watford nodded. "Unregistered. Russian make. There are a lot of war souvenir weapons like that in this country."

"And others brought in deliberately," I added.

He was noncommittal. "Perhaps." He glanced around, then said, "What about the first attack?"

"Can I make a phone call?"

"Need a lawyer?"

"Nope."

He pointed to a phone on the sideboard.

I got up, dialed Toomey at the Chester and asked, "You get the ballistics report on the test shot from the gun?"

Toomey was brief about it. "One of the ones used the first time. You're right in line."

"Thanks." I hung up and went back to my seat. "It was the same bunch who tried for the first hit."

For the first time the heavy guy spoke. He leaned forward to stare down the table at me, his mouth trying to hide the natural nasty curl of his lip. "It isn't our habit to divulge information of any nature, Mann, but there is a top level over us again who can alter the code of procedure. How your group manages to exercise such influence I can only guess. I don't have to like it and one day I'm going to be instrumental in breaking it, but at the moment we have instructions."

"Fine."

He ignored the sarcasm. "We ran a ballistics check on that gun too. It had been used before, once to kill one of our couriers and again to kill two supposedly minor British Embassy employees."

"Minor?"

"They happened to be members of British Intelligence."

"At least you know which side I'm on then."

"We don't need you, Mr. Mann."

"But you got me, brother. Now get to the point."

"Ah, yes, I will. We are very interested in uncovering the one who pulled the trigger. Since you seem to be a first-class target and insist upon offering yourself up for sacrifice, we're going to take advantage of the fact that you might be able to draw this person out in the open. Whatever happens to you is of no importance to us. In this case you are quite expendable and if you go down several purposes will have been served. One, another lead to this killer; two, the opportunity to rid ourselves of unwanted interference. Am I being blunt?"

"Not a bit," I said. "Only don't forget one thing."

"For instance?"

"This target doesn't fall easily."

"A matter we will help along if we can."

"You still haven't made your point," I reminded him.

He got a little red in the face and had to suck in his breath. "One of those British Intelligence men lived long enough to give us a description of his killer. Not a big man, thin, high forehead with rather long dark hair combed in the European fashion. He had a peculiar trait . . . he pulled the trigger of the gun with the second finger of his hand, not the forefinger."

"A pretty acute observation from a guy getting shot."

"He was a well-trained operator. There was another one with him, slightly taller, medium build. All he remembered was his mouth. He said he had a round mouth. That's a peculiar description and our man died before he could explain, but it should be apparent if he's spotted again."

"You have more than just that," I said.

The guy hesitated, then nodded slowly, the information coming out of him reluctantly. "A name. We think . . . not know . . . think, that the first one is a Red agent named Vidor Churis. Until now he has been assigned to and involved in the various situations in Central and South America."

He stopped then, and looked at me squarely. "I'm surprised you don't know him, Mr. Mann."

My eyes held his a long second. "I've heard of him," I said.

Heard of him? Hell, I had shot him two years ago and that's why he couldn't use his forefinger on the trigger. My slug had knocked the rod out of his hands before the warehouse explosion had blown us right through the walls of the place and ruining that deal on him had set him so far down in the party sights he had to accept piss-ant jobs in Chile doing leg work before they'd trust him with another big one. No wonder Churis was so anxious for a kill now.

"Have you anything to offer?"

"Uh-uh."

"Or is it that you won't?"

"I haven't. If I had I wouldn't."

For a second it looked like he would pop. Then he said, "Will you?"

"When the right time comes, yes." I tilted back in the chair. "It seems funny that you should be coming to me. Cooperation of this sort isn't usual."

Thomas Watford dragged in a hissing breath. "In our society and system of government people like Martin Grady can wield a sizable amount of influence."

"No doubt."

"Charles Corbinet's voice is listened to carefully."

"Good old Charlie," I said.

"In the latter case he's in a position of official authority, carefully covered, which you seem to know. I still can't understand why he prefers to trust you . . . or others in authority who seem to be swayed by Martin Grady."

"Simple bribery," I said.

One of the guys at the table said, "You bastard."

I grinned at him and set the chair back right. "The Commies used the bribery of exposure as queers on certain ones in high places to extract what they wanted. Sometimes there's good bribery, like the promise of results that can be gotten no other way. Keep it in mind. Now, is that all?"

"That's all for now," Watford said.

I looked down the table, fastening all the faces in my mind. They sat there hating the orders they had but not being able to do anything about it. I got up, poured a drink of water for myself, waved and left.

Chapter 8

It was Friday. The rain had stopped at last and the low scud hid the tops of the buildings above the twentieth floors. On the street people still carried their umbrellas and raincoats, not wanting to take a chance on the weather.

Outside the U.N. buildings the black limousines were pulling away from the curbs with taxis filling in the places they left. I waited ten minutes before Rondine came out, watched while she paused in the doorway until a tall brunette in a tan suede coat came out and they walked toward me together.

The brunette I had seen before. She was the one Burton Selwick had visited down in the Village and taken out to supper. When they reached the street I walked up and said, "Hello, Rondine."

It should have startled her, but didn't, that's how good she was. She turned her head almost casually, but her smile was a shade too tight to be real.

"Oh . . . Tiger," she said.

"Like a bad penny." I looked at the brunette.

"Gretchen Lark . . . Tiger Mann."

The brunette said, "How do you do, Mr. Mann. Or is Tiger a pet name?"

"My real one."

"Very picturesque. It has certain connotations," she smiled. Gretchen gave Edith a small puzzled glance then. "Rondine?"

"Now *that's* a pet name," I exclaimed. "We're real old friends."

Her eyebrows went up and her mouth pursed with a humorous, pseudo-knowing look and she laughed, "Well, then, I'll just say so long and leave you two old friends alone."

Edith said, "Oh, but . . ."

I just winked and grinned at her as if she had said the right thing and took Edith's arm. I thought for a moment she'd pull away when I felt the muscles harden under my fingers, but when I squeezed just a little bit she shrugged resignedly and said, "I'll call you tomorrow, Gretch."

"Do that. Good-bye, Tiger."

"See you," I said.

Most of the crowd had found taxis by then and we didn't have to wait. I flagged down a cruiser, eased Edith in, told the driver to take us to the Blue Ribbon on Forty-fourth and leaned back into the cushions with my beautiful killer beside me.

It was almost pleasant, that ride. It was almost like those times twenty years ago when we could sit and feel each other there in the dark and quiet and I could know the sensation of love long before the knowledge of hate. Neither of us spoke. We didn't have to. We knew what was in the other's mind and it was enough. I closed my eyes and thought about it and suddenly had to stop myself from reaching for her hand.

When the cab stopped at the intersection I could hear her breathing, forcing herself to keep control and I grinned because that's the way I wanted her to be. She knew she was going to die but didn't know when. My lovely Rondine was sweating inside.

At the restaurant I got out, paid off the cab and she stood there waiting dutifully, with perfect composure, knowing yet not being quite sure, that it wouldn't happen there. Rondine had always been like that. Even when she killed it had been with class. A lady, I thought. A lovely guise. It could cover almost anything.

We took a booth in the back, ordered a drink first, then steaks, and over the highball I grinned at her and she spoke for the first time. "You are making a big mistake, Tiger." There was ice in her voice.

"I'll take my chances on how I live or die, kid. No more mistakes for me."

Then for some reason the ice went out of her. There was a sudden heat in her eyes and the tip of her tongue moistened her lips before she sipped her drink. That was an old trick of Rondine's too. She could switch from hot to cold before you were aware of it and the new attitude almost made you forget the former one. She hadn't forgotten a thing.

When she tilted her head back I looked for the surgical scars, but the shadow of her chin obscured the region there. Later I'd find out.

"I don't understand your new technique, Tiger," she said. "You were going to kill me earlier."

"I still will, kitten, so keep sweating."

"Then why . . ." she made a motion of her hand around the booth.

"People have been telling me about you. I have feelers out. How'd you do it, Rondine?"

Her eyes creased in a frown. "Do what?"

"Get inside the Caine family."

Both her hands held the glass delicately and her eyes were steady on mine. "I was born into it. If you asked, then you would have found out."

"That's what I was told, but I have other ideas."

She flicked open her cigarette case, put one between her lips and waited for me to light it for her. Over the flame she said, "And they are?"

"A staid, respectable British family loaded with pride and tradition can have a lot to lose if somebody can jangle a skeleton in their closet. I wonder what they'd do or what they'd agree to do if they were suddenly confronted with something that could put them up to public ridicule and scorn to the point that they couldn't hold their heads up. Sometimes honor can tumble in the face of pride. It's an old dodge, sugar."

I knew I hit it right when her face went almost white. Tiny lines fixed themselves beside the corners of her mouth and eyes and her fingers nearly snapped the cigarette in two. For a few seconds her breath was caught in her throat and if ever she wanted to kill me it was then.

The laugh I made was the nastiest thing I ever heard. "What did you hold over their heads, Rondine?"

Through her teeth she said gently, "*I'd like to kill you.*"

"I know," I told her.

Only Rondine could have done it, that quick reversal of emotion, one second full of hate, the next totally calm and poised, thinking fast, ready with an answer. "Why don't you ask them?"

"I will. There are people working on it now. Before long I'll have all the facts and you'll fall. This minute pictures of you are all over the continent going to the offices of plastic surgeons and sooner or later I'll have the right one who did the face job. Or did you get it in Russia?"

Her smile was ambiguous. "Find out for yourself, Tiger."

"My pleasure."

The steaks came and we waited until the waiter left and then began eating to resume the pleasantries. It was like twenty questions now, the probing and parrying. It was fun being with her again, like the old days when we were on opposite sides, lovers, yet enemies, digging for information without wanting to hurt the other.

"Parents?" I asked casually.

"Richard and Agnes Caine: 1892 to 1951; 1896, still living." She smiled and went on, "Ruth, Patricia, Diana, sisters, Vernon, John my brothers. Both Diana and John were killed during the war. The dates of . . ."

"Never mind."

"You have a family crest," I started.

"Honorably won. Unicorns bearing a shield of red and blue with the bar dexter, beneath, an unfurled scroll with the insignia . . ."

"You're doing great," I cut her off. "You always were a quick study.

"Remember Cal Haggerty, Rondine?" I said abruptly.

She stopped eating, giving me a curious look. *Damn, she was better than ever!*

"Who?"

"You killed him, baby. You let him have it with a tommy gun. Right after you shot me."

She almost dropped her fork and the expression in her eyes was unreadable.

"Hurt to bring those things back? Hell, kid, I don't feel bad when I think about the people I knocked off. They all needed it. To your way Cal and I needed it too so don't feel bad about it." I stopped and picked up my drink and finished it. "Or does the thought scare you?"

Then she was back to normal again. "No," she said, "it doesn't scare me."

"It should, doll."

We finished eating then, not saying much more. I paid the bill and walked out with her and if anyone had looked we could have been nothing more than man and wife, not executioner and victim. On the corner of Broadway and Forty-fourth I whistled a cab over, gave her address and sat back, smiling to myself. She was on edge now and that's the way I wanted her.

Unconsciously, she had set her handbag between the two of us and I gave it a squeeze. There was a gun in there, all right. It was easy to wait until she glanced out the window to flip it open, finger the clip out of the small automatic, close it and drop the clip in my pocket without being noticed. Colonel Corbinet had trained us well and we kept up the practice.

She made no objection when I got out and followed her into the apartment, but she did make a point of speaking to the doorman and the porter inside. Both had a good chance to look at me and very deliberately she asked the porter the time and she made a pretense of setting her watch. No matter what I did now there would be personal and time identification by two people and my neck would be in the trap.

What Rondine didn't know was why I was there.

It wasn't to kill her. Not just yet.

She pushed the number twelve button in the elevator and I said, "Very nice, Rondine. Good thinking."

Rondine knew what I meant. She looked at me, smiled and said, "Do you blame me?"

"Not at all. You've had the training for it, haven't you?"

Her smile and the set of her face were peculiar. "Yes, I have."

Sure, admit it, kid. You've had the best. I already know, so why deny it?

She held the bag with her thumb and forefinger on the snaps, the other hand ready to dip into it if she had to and unless you were aware of those things you'd never notice the stance. It just wasn't quite the way a woman holds her purse. It would have been funny to see what happened if she tried it.

At her door I took the key out of her fingers, unlocked it myself and handed the key back. She walked in, held the door open and said, "A nightcap, Tiger?"

"Sure."

One switch seemed to turn everything on in the room. Three lamps blossomed into a soft glow and the haunting strains of Dvorak's *New World Symphony* chanted from hidden speakers. She threw her coat on the back of a chair, went behind the bar and reached for glasses and bottles. When she made the drinks she handed me mine, said, "Luck," sipped from hers and put it on the bar. Then she walked out of the room. I didn't worry. Her bag was still on the chair with her coat.

But she was clever. The door to her bedroom was open enough so that if I walked to the chair she'd see me. As long as I stayed at the bar where I was she'd play the game my way, thinking I was playing it hers.

Come, darling, I have seen the act before. It's nothing new. Remember Hamburg? Remember that little town in occupied France where you did the bit in a ripped-open pillowcase? Man, but were you hot then. All white, soft skin and flowing, soft flesh and lovely hair and all mine. Mine. Remember the things we did that night? If they knew, the names they'd call us, eh? But fun. Great. Love. Real, true love.

She came out in a quilted, blue housecoat and I didn't have to be told that there was nothing beneath it. Her legs were the same lovely flash of pink, beautifully molded like a dancer's, that melted into fabric before they revealed their true beauty; her waist pinched in and rising into the proud outthrusting of her breasts that were so deliberately Rondine's.

Oh, kid, I thought, *what the hell do you think you're pulling? This old soldier's been through the routine. Backwards and forwards. Don't give me the negligee and thigh deal. Hell, I've seen more naked broads than you have hair on your head. I've put them to bed, waked them up, left them gasping and two dying and now you're doing this to me? Nuts.*

"Nice," I said. "You'd make a great whore."

She stopped in mid-stride and smiled. "Thank you. Have you finished your drink?"

"I'm ready for another."

"So am I." She never saw the first one I poured down the drain, but I took the second one she handed to me, tasted it, then walked across the room to the windows. The apartment looked out on Central Park, the view taking in almost all of the giant rectangle that was so tightly laced together with the lights of taxis.

"Nice place, Rondine. Rent must go about a grand a month. Your U.N. job isn't about to keep you in a joint like this one."

"I have a private income," she answered simply. "I consider the position important enough to warrant the loss. My family feels the same way."

"Hell. I can think up an easier explanation."

"What would that be?"

I turned around and stared at her. She was standing in the middle of the room, the superb beauty of her turning my guts around. "You have a private income all right, but the source isn't the family. It's another government, a Red one."

She didn't challenge me. The small shake of her head was almost pitying.

Then I had another thought. "But maybe you are right, kid. Maybe it is the Caine family after all. Rattle that skeleton enough and they'll come across with anything." I paused a moment and grinned. "Perfect. Trace back your income and it fits the picture. What a wonderful setup."

The whiteness was there again, the fine lines back at her eyes, but only momentarily. The hate dissolved into the thinnest of smiles and she raised her glass to take a taste of her drink.

"In two days I'll have a pipeline into your family, kitten," I said. "If you could do it, so can I. You should know I'm not working alone. Behind me are others trained to the hilt and they'll get everything I want."

"Tiger . . ."

"How about your brother and sister who are dead? Maybe we'll have to go that far back if that's where the skeleton is. Want to tell me about them?"

"Damn you!" She threw the glass and it went past my head to smash against the wall. I never moved. "They're dead. You let my family alone." There was a harsh edge to her voice.

I let out a little laugh. "Honey," I said, "how you forget. You don't remember your old Tiger very well at all. I never let anything alone until I bury it personally. I want all the answers, sugar. I want you to fall hard and fast and I want to watch it happen. I loved you too damn much so I hate your guts the same way. So remember, girl."

I wouldn't let her talk. I said, "Remember all the things we were going to do after the war? The house on the ocean and the business together. How many kids did you say you wanted? Remember . . . four . . . and they'd look like both of us and we could teach them the things they should know and not the things they shouldn't? They'd never know how or where we met . . . we were going to fake a story about that one, but they would know how much we loved each other.

"Honey, was I ever a sucker for that. I pulled you out of the fire and nearly wrecked an operation doing it and then you shot me. Love? Hell, you don't know the meaning of the word. You grifted me for information and called it love. You suckered me, beautiful, but never again."

Her eyes had widened somehow and there was a lost expression on her face, but she was a great actress.

Suddenly she said quietly, "Do you still love me, Tiger?"

And just as quickly I told her. "Sure I do, Rondine. I always have. It isn't something you can turn off. After I kill you I'll go right on loving you like I always have but it won't make a damn bit of difference to me. The game is over. It's all cold, hard fact now."

"You really mean to kill me, don't you?"

"For certain, baby. You can be sure of it."

The music was coming to a close. The timing was right for what I wanted to do. I put my drink down and sat on the arm of a big chair and looked at her. "Take off that robe, Rondine."

If she had a drink in her hand she would have dropped it. She gave me a startled look and one hand went to her throat inadvertently to close the neckline that had been so deliberately opened.

She just stood there a second, then when I got up, took a step back and there was no place else to go because the couch was behind her pressing into her hips.

I walked the ten feet that separated us and stood there in front of her. "What's the matter, kitten? I've seen you naked before, dozens of times, from bedrooms to swimming in a river together. There's not an inch of you I haven't explored and you loved every minute of it. Don't play prude, not with me."

"Please . . ." The quiver of her mouth even looked genuine. If I hadn't seen her do it before I would have fallen for the act.

"Off," I said, "or do I do it for you?"

Her hands grabbed at the back of the couch and bit into the fabric. Rondine was scared silly. She had a right to be.

"Please . . ." she said again, "why . . ."

I grinned at her. "You thinking I'll jump you kid? Hell, I wouldn't throw a rock at you any more. I wouldn't give you another inch of myself. No, baby, I just want to see how far you went with the plastic surgery. Faces can be lifted, but women don't usually go all the way down to their shoes. The faces they show in the day . . . the rest they can hide in the night so why bother. But I'm curious about you, Rondine."

Ten seconds ticked by slowly before she moved. Her teeth bit into her lip and she made her decision. Her fingers came away from the couch, fumbled at the belt of her robe, loosened it, then with one sweeping motion she flung the housecoat wide and stood there like some new Joan of Arc challenging the mob.

The clock turned back twenty years instantly and it was the day Rondine and I were hiding in the loft in France with the *maquis* somewhere outside searching for her. There was a driving summer rain we knew had wiped out our tracks and in the exuberance of knowing we would make it together had felt the heady flow of happiness that turned into the wild, emotional waterfall of love and ecstasy. She had danced there in the loft and stripped off her clothes piece by piece and, in one final gesture before she flung herself at me, had stood there motionless, arms outstretched, every muscle in her body taut and vibrant, a luminescent, white, beautiful thing that was all mine.

And now she stood there again, breasts hard and proud, her belly trembling, the quiver seeming to run into her thighs, legs at a defiant angle, the auburn tint of her hair highlighted with gold, eyes flashing, daring.

"So you went all the way. The medics did a good job." There was a cold flat tone to my voice. "Paraffin injections, invisible surgery, hard diet and steady exercise can knock a lot of years off a person's appearance." I grinned at her again. "But they can't operate on memories, can they, kid?"

I stepped back, laughed and turned toward the door. I heard her curse me softly with something like a sob in her voice and she said, "Tiger . . . turn around."

She had the gun in her hand this time, the pocketbook open on the chair. "I could kill you right now if I wanted to."

"No you couldn't, Rondine. You forget too much." I reached in my pocket and took out the clip, looked at it and threw it at her feet. "Better try using bullets. You should know how they work."

Her mouth opened in surprise and she looked at the useless piece in her hand. I saw the tears start and like a kid she sort of crumpled to her knees on the floor and sat there crying with her head down.

She hated to be outguessed and that was the only way she could take it out on herself. But, Rondine had always been like that.

I got the hell out of there.

Downstairs, I walked to the corner, waited a couple of minutes for a cruising taxi and when none came by empty, turned west toward Broadway and started up the empty channel of the street. On either side the apartments rose flatly into the night sky, angular and drab, windows like dull yellow eyes sick of looking out at nothing. Cars were parked bumper to bumper along either curb, stacked there until morning, abrogating every law and violating every rule of common sense until the herd instinct took over at the de-witching hour of eight A.M. I never failed to wonder how the hell they got out of there. One big Caddie had pushed in the nose of a Volkswagen and tomorrow there would be one big bash on the sidewalk when the owners had it out. Halfway down the block somebody had swiped both tires off a Chevvie and left it on chocks. New York at night. Great place.

Traffic went opposite me so I didn't bother looking for a cab. All I could think about was Rondine.

Naked, lovely Rondine.

How could a woman devote her life to destruction? How could anyone so beautiful as her throw away the only good thing she had ever had? Sure, war could demand things of anyone, but out of war can come peace and decency if you have the sense to let it. Goddamn it, we could have had the world for our own, everything we ever wanted, only she was too warped and twisted inside to take it.

And now? The big now?

Warped and twisted? Balls . . . she was the essence of total depravity, a person who had gone from one scheme to another to recapture and keep the one thing a woman always wants . . . control. She needed it. But she'd never get it. That's why she cried.

For a pro I had gotten too lost inside my own head. There was too much night and too many thoughts and too much Rondine to stop and think of what she would do and I damn near died because of it. I didn't notice the car slowing down at first until the first shot came and missed, but I knew there would be others and went into a crazy dive toward the curb with the slug from a tommy gun slamming into the parked cars and whistling over my head. I had the .45 in my hand when my back hit the doors of a Buick beside me and let one go through the back window of the Ford racing off down the street.

But it didn't go any further than that. I was ready for the rest, ready for the second car that pulled up and the guy who jumped out when he thought I was concentrating on watching the Ford and when I turned and killed him with one smashing blow from the butt end of the Army Colt his eyes were white with the murderous horror of the moment. I shot through the window of the car and saw the driver slam up against the window and watched the car swerve into the others across the street and stand churning a moment before it stalled and the yelling from the windows started.

You never run. You walk. Nobody pays any attention when you walk near the scene of a killing. They only get civic when you run and not always then, except that they give descriptions. I took my time about lifting the guy's wallet before easing off down the block and by the time I heard the first siren I was already in a cab headed back toward Times Square and when I reached the Big Intersection I tapped the driver on the shoulder, handed him a buck and told him to let me out.

Down in the subway station I went into the men's room, went through the wallet and found thirty-two bucks in small bills stuffed in the money folder and not a card, scrap of paper or anything else. I was almost ready to toss it when I saw it was one of those secret-pocket types with a hidden compartment. I got my finger under the flap of leather, slipped it out and there was a brand-new thousand-dollar bill. I fingered it out, stuck it with the rest in my pocket, went out and tossed the wallet down between the tracks when nobody was watching and went up to the next level where the Coke machine was and had one.

Chapter 9

At nine P.M. I put a credit-card call through to London and, after a ten-minute wait, got Peter Johnson in our office there. He operated out of a fashionable haberdashery shop near Piccadilly Circus with a crew of four and after a four-month lay-off since the Berlin affair he was glad to get back on an assignment.

So far, he hadn't come up with anything on the Caine family outside of what Wally had given me, but was going to dig into the deceased Vernon and Diana Caine to see if there was any possibility of blackmail tactics being used against the Caines because of them. To date his research had been pretty thorough with no tangible results, so he wasn't especially hopeful about going back into the war years to find something new.

He did have one interesting piece of news though. In the general backtracking of Rondine Lund he had contacted a former *maqui* officer who said he had heard that the beautiful Rondine made two successful escapes from her captors at the war's end, and although he wasn't certain, he heard later she had been recaptured and shot. At that time she had been caught in a round up of Nazi collaborators when justice had been swift, burial quick and no reference made of identity after the act.

It wouldn't have been hard for Rondine to switch identities with some sucker. There were ways of working it. I had done it myself once. An unsuspecting woman gives the name of Rondine Lund and before she knows what's happening to her it's over. Exit Rondine, Enter Edith Caine.

I told Johnson to stay with it until I called and hung up.

The next call was through a relay and took five minutes before Martin Grady answered. As usual, he simply picked up the phone and held it without speaking, waiting for the caller to make the first move.

"Tiger here," I said.

"Is this necessary?" He had the cool, polished voice of a diplomat, but behind it was all the raw power of the man he was.

"Yes," I said. "I need to draw on all the resources. I.A.T.S. and the rest are looking for Vidor Churis. I want him first. He's in this area."

"Time element?"

"Now. This is a Class One."

"I'll have Newark call. Where can you be reached?"

"Tomorrow at exactly six P.M. I'll be at this number." I read it off to him. "It's a pay station in the Eighth Avenue subway."

I heard the click as the phone went dead, cradled the receiver and stepped out of the booth. In a few minutes from now the power of money would be doing what the power of great government organizations could not. Word would go out on a name and a description and whoever came out with the lead would find more money in his hand than he had ever dreamed of. Countless front men were used and nobody would be able to trace the inquiry back to its source or even want to, but there were those who knew about getting the word and what it meant, and even if they had to break down the payment to allocate some to others to bring the information to them it would be done. There would be one with a big bite, others with smaller bites, but everyone happy and all hoping to be the one on the fat end the next time.

But tomorrow at six there would be a line to Vidor Churis.

There was one strange note, however. Martin Grady didn't take direct contact casually. There was usually an explicit instruction or request to explain the urgency of the matter, or more likely a tone of disapproval for not having gone through the regular channels.

Maybe Grady was softening up. No, that wasn't it. Maybe he was smartening up. Could be age had given him insight into more than the big picture and he was considering personal feelings for once. In a way, he'd better. There were times when the big picture didn't give a damn . . . like twenty years ago with Rondine and me. There was even the possibility that he was going to teach me a lesson. If I hadn't learned it twenty years ago I'd learn it now, *so let out the rope.*

Screw him if he figured that way, I thought. I was too old at the business now. I'd been behind a gun too long and seen too many men fall in front of it. I had them plow into me and felt the fire of metal inside my skin too many times. I'd mixed it with the wild ones and the shrewd ones too many years to worry about anything now.

So okay, Grady, thanks for the rope. I'll use every inch of it you'll give me.

There was one contact I hadn't made yet, so before I left the phone I checked the number on my pad, dialed Gretchen Lark's place and waited through a half-dozen rings before she answered. She was breathless and coughing and when she said, "Yes?" it was as if I had interrupted something.

I had. I said it was me and she tinkled a laugh back.

"Tiger . . . the man with the funny name. I was just coming out of the shower. I'm all wet."

"Dry yourself off."

"I can't. I have no towel."

"You mean you're standing there dripping and naked and talking to me?"

"Well, it isn't exactly television, but you make me feel like it is."

"I think I can describe every inch of you."

"Don't do it!"

I laughed back at her. "Skin talk gets you sexy?"

"You know too much. How did you get my number? It's unlisted."

Rather than tell her I said, "No trouble when a guy really wants to meet a girl."

"Mr. Mann, please. You had a date tonight."

"Just seeing an old friend. Edith and I have been buddies a long time. Only buddies make strange combos."

"Tiger . . . I feel a proposition coming on."

"You're right."

"What about Edith?"

"I'm calling you, kid, not her."

"Did you two have a fight?"

"Come on, I don't fight with broads."

"I know, you're a tiger."

"So I've been told," I said. "Feel like getting dressed and going out?"

"Where?"

"Who knows? Maybe some slop chute. I feel like talking to a broad."

"And you picked me . . . just like that?"

"Just like that."

"You excite me, Tiger. I think I'll go."

"Naked?"

"No, I'll get dressed, but if you like you can come up and watch me."

"I'm too far away. By the time I get there you'll be ready."

"I'm a slow dresser," she said and hung up.

The cab dropped me off on her corner and I waited until it had pulled away before I turned and started walking toward her building. The last time I had waited in a taxi while Burton Selwick made the call, but this time I punched the button under her name and when the door buzzed, shoved it open.

Gretchen Lark lived on the top floor, three long, creaking flights up. And like she said, she was a slow dresser. Women can take two hours to put their faces on, but two minutes to get into clothes. Gretchen Lark had her face on. The rest was being smothered in a crazy beatnik cotton blanket robe that was all efficiency and no charm . . . but at least she had waited.

"Tiger man," she said when she opened the door. It wasn't my name. It was a deliberate dropping of the last letter and the capital and I let her see all the teeth in a smile and walked inside.

"Hello, baby. Should I say thanks?"

"It isn't necessary." She knew damn well what I meant.

There were framed oils on the walls, unframed canvases standing on the floor and two in easels with drape cloths hanging over them beside the skylights that faced the north side. Most of them were good, but a few were the expressionless scratchings of an artist that had no subject to paint.

I said, "Neat, but not gaudy."

"They'll never sell."

"What do you care. You're having fun."

"I can afford it."

She was laughing at me now, a tall, superlative doll with a shining brunette page-boy hair set that spilled around a nutty cotton robe that was no class at all. But she was laughing.

"Tiger . . . what do you think?"

"Good color composition," I said. "Brush strokes too hard and for Pete's sake stay off the palette knife; you just don't have the flair for it. The colored girl is lousy. No anatomy. No nothing there."

"I realize that."

"You can paint men, though," I told her. The one in the corner was a beauty except that it would never sell either. Realism can come to an end at times. There wasn't even a fig leaf and the exaggeration was too much to be believed. "You got a fetish," I said.

"No . . . only wishful thinking," she smiled.

"Someday you'll find out that technique can beat a ruler, kid."

"You're dirty."

"Why sure."

"I love it."

"Don't you all," I said.

"Would you like to watch me get dressed?"

"No. The reverse process is far more interesting. Hurry up."

Her smile was a teasing thing. "I knew you'd chicken out." She pointed to an icebox half hidden behind a curtain. "Have a beer while you wait."

"Thanks." She walked off into a bedroom at the far end of the room without bothering to shut the door. I found a Pabst, jacked it open and poured it into a glass to get a head on it. At least she drank like a man with the beer barely above freezing.

While I waited for her I toured the room, deciphering her tastes. It wasn't easy. Her book shelves were lined with everything from the classics to earthy mysteries, one entire shelf being given to treatises on international politics. About twenty books were in German, French and Spanish, all histories of each nation and their current role in politics. There were six volumes of a medical series and a stack of pamphlets from a New York school dealing with the aspects of being a legal secretary.

A real well-rounded broad intellectually as well as physically.

I flipped up the drape that covered a canvas and though

it was only partially done it was recognizable and even in these early stages, beautifully executed. It was a study of Burton Selwick.

Behind me Gretchen said, "How do you like it?" She came out, turned so I could button up the back of her dress and looked at the picture over her shoulder.

"It should be your best." Her flesh was warm under my fingers, firm and young. I tried not to touch her but couldn't help it. "Why don't you wear a brassière?" I asked her.

She let me finish buttoning and spun around. "Because I don't need it, Tiger." She smiled impishly. "Do I?"

I had to admit that she didn't.

With a sudden impulse she picked up a charcoal stick and swept in a line down the shoulder of the figure of Selwick. Just one line, but it added strength. Satisfied, she dropped the charcoal and wiped her fingertips on the drape cloth.

"This is for his wife," she said. "They have an anniversary in two months."

"How come he picked you?"

She took the beer from my hand and had a sip of it. "Sometime back I was exhibiting at the Conway Galleries and during lunch the office staff all went down with me. Mr. Selwick saw the studies I did of the President and a U.N. delegate and right then decided he wanted one of himself for his wife."

"Make much money?"

"Surprisingly enough, I do. That is, if an extra five thousand a year is much." She turned the drape down over the picture. "A few more sittings and I'll have it. The only trouble with Mr. Selwick is time. He works too much. He's not too well, either. Now finish your beer and let's go somewhere. If I'm going to be late-dated I want it to be in style."

There was a little place I knew buried on a side street that nobody could find unless they had been there before. The clientele is restricted to a chosen group because some of the things they sold there weren't on the approved list of the Pure Food and Drug Act. You simply went in a door that adjoined a dirty, vacant store window, down a hall to where the cellar door should be and when you knocked on that one a slot opened in a panel and you got a glimpse of a pair of eyes.

Gretchen's hand tightened on mine with a touch of fright.

Then the eyes crinkled in a smile as they recognized me and the door opened. The guy there was short, but broad in the shoulders with a face marked from years of dirty fighting. "Ah, Mr. Mann, it is good to see you again."

"Hello, Dell. How's everything?"

"Progressing, Mr. Mann. You would like your usual spot?"

"Please. The show on yet?"

"You are just in time."

We followed him down the stairs into the basement, went through an alcove, through another door and there was a scene from the middle of the Casbah right down to tinkling bells on the toes of the dancing girls to the burnooses of the waiters.

It was a huge place, with a center dance floor surrounded by tables occupied by people dressed in everything from evening clothes to beatnik outfits. A half-level up was a balcony divided into compartments, each with a heavily beaded curtain drawn across its front. But this Casbah joint had the benefit of modern air conditioning at least. Smoke was drawn off through ceiling ventilators and the only odor was that of some rich perfume. Whether it was deliberately introduced or was the conglomerate of that of all the women I couldn't tell, but was pleasant enough.

I pointed out the powder room to Gretchen and told her to hurry up. When she went through the louvered door I motioned Dell to one side where we were alone. "I'm after a man."

"Naturally. Otherwise you would not be here, no?"

"Only identification is a stiff right forefinger on the right hand. He may have an accent, but don't count on it. There's a possibility he'll be with another whose only distinguishing characteristic is a round mouth. I don't know what that means, but it should mean something."

"They have never been here."

"I don't expect they will. Pass the word."

"The usual fee?"

"We can throw in a bonus on this one."

Dell smiled gently and rocked on his heels. "I'll be happy to see what can be learned. We offer many accommodations here."

He nodded past me. "Here comes your lady. Very exquisite. You always did have good taste. What became of that stunning redhead?"

"She was killed in Mexico."

"So? Too bad. And the person who did such a thing?"

"I drowned him in a toilet bowl. It was a good ending."

"Very good," he said.

Dell turned us over to a bearded waiter who led us up the three steps to the balcony, went to the corner booth and held the curtains open for us.

69

After we sat down I gave him our order in rapid Arabic and flipped the curtain open so we could see what was going on downstairs..

The effect was showing on Gretchen's face. "In the middle of New York!" she said, awed. "And I thought I'd seen it all."

"Baby, there's a lot you haven't seen."

"But this place . . ."

"It's called the *Hall of the Two Sisters*. The atmosphere is exciting, the food authentic and you can arrange anything from a killing to a main-line pop without batting an eye."

"Incredible."

"Understand one thing. Nobody . . . hear that? Nobody comes in here unless they're cleared. Being with me clears you, but finger this place to anybody, talk about it and you can find yourself with a face full of acid or your fingers off down to the knuckles or tied to a table naked while a pack of goons work you into an idiot."

Her eyes were perfect circles of horror as she watched my face. I knew what she was seeing there. Everything I told her was the truth and she knew it.

"How . . . can it exist? The police . . ."

"Baby, in police work they sometimes let things exist. There are sources of information that can come out of queer places and rather than destroy them they utilize them. Forget it. That's not your line of work. Just keep in mind what I told you."

"Then you're a policeman?"

"Hell no," I said. "I'm in a business that takes me around and I get to know some strange people."

The drinks came then, tall and cool in oddly shaped glasses. Gretchen tasted hers, nodded with approval and took another sip. When she put it down she reached for a cigarette and let me light it. Through a gray stream of smoke she said, "And what *is* your business, Tiger?"

I shrugged. "Exploitation, to put it simply. The people I represent go into undeveloped areas and open them up. Five years ago it was rubber, then tin and tungsten, now we've located an untapped source of mahogany."

"You enjoy your work?"

"As long as you don't mind heat or cold, bugs, snakes, dry spells, cities or desert it isn't bad. How about you?"

"Oh, I'm satisfied."

"Why don't you stay with your painting?"

She lifted her drink again. "It isn't enough. I rather enjoy being with the U.N. Things are happening there that are important to the world."

"Nuts."

Before she could answer there was a clash of cymbals and immediately the flutes and drums started. Down on the floor the dancers came out, six of them, their only costume a headdress and gauzy veil. They were all dark-skinned and beautiful with hair black as coal, their bodies going in a frenzied motion that made you almost ignore their nakedness under the gauze.

Minute by minute the beat and rhythm of the music got more intense until it was one demanding tempo of seduction and the girls spun on bare feet so that the veils were wafted out in huge circles at their shoulders. Those at the tables below couldn't take their eyes from them and you could see the fine glisten of sweat on the foreheads of the men at the ringside. The women were the same way too and when I looked at Gretchen I could see the heat of it getting to her. There was a tight set to her body as if she were ready to go out there with them, ready to strip the clothes off her body and join the six. The tip of her tongue kept wetting her lips and the knuckles on the backs of her hands were white.

The man joined the dancers with a whip, an Arab in the loose white cotton of the desert tribes. He raised the lash, snapped it between the girls, twisted and spun in the rituals of the dance, every so often snaking the whip around the waist of a dancer to draw her to him and at the very moment of being ready to take her, changing his mind to go for another. One by one he tried them all, discarded them, then stood there, angry.

The drum beat was a signal. The girls stopped, then raced off the floor and in their place came the most exotic woman I had ever seen. She was evidently a Eurasian, combining the loveliness of the races. Each wrist and ankle was covered with bracelets that made music of their own as she came out in the classic motion of the dance.

And that was all she had on.

Her jet-black hair hung down to her waist and she could swirl it to cover or expose herself as she wished to. A look of greed and longing crossed the face of the Arab as he watched, then decided and went into motion with the whip. The lash snapped, ripped out and furled about her, to all appearances cutting her to ribbons, but it was as if she weren't there at all. No mark appeared on her bare skin at all, no welt showed and the girl's face simply smiled at the faces in the audience as she tinkled past the men and women who were plainly caught up in the act as if they were part of it. One woman was even half standing, her hands gripping the edges of the table and behind her a waiter hovered, waiting to restrain her if she moved. They had evidently seen it happen before.

The Arab was great with the whip, turning it into a living thing, then in a sudden climax he caught the girl up in the folds, this time refusing to let her go and slowly brought her close to him. The music went higher and higher, the tempo getting more furious as he wrapped her inside his cloak and with a sudden smash of the cymbals again the pair folded to the floor as the lights went out completely.

When they came back on again the floor was empty.

Gretchen said breathlessly, *"Good gracious!"*

"Stuns you, doesn't it?"

She looked at me, frowning. "How can you just sit there."

"I've seen it all before, kid." Then I grinned. "You almost joined the act."

Her face flushed and she licked her lips again, nervously this time. "I know. I felt like it. There's something . . . hypnotic about the whole thing."

"It's supposed to be."

"Inside, I feel like . . . I feel . . ."

"I know," I said.

"You know too damn much."

The bearded waiter came in, took the order I gave him and disappeared. Gretchen said, "How many languages do you speak?"

"Chow and girls I can order in almost any language. Conversationally I stick to English." It was a lie, but she didn't have to know it. Abruptly I said, "You know Edith Caine long?"

"Only since she came to the U.N."

"Close friends?"

"Pretty much. You know how girls are. How come you didn't take her out tonight? Have a fight?"

"We've known each other too many years. I rub her wrong. She ever tell you about her family?"

"A few times she's discussed them. They're quite important in England. Society, government and all that. She feels that she has to contribute something too and being part of the U.N. is the post she selected."

"Like the company?"

"The delegates?"

"More or less," I offered.

"Well . . . if you live on an intellectual plane—"

"Do you?" I interrupted.

"Yes, very much so. When you do you can find the work and the company fascinating. Considering that the people involved are all carefully selected and represent the highest order of culture and learning each country can bring here, working with them and sometimes adding to what they have is a satisfying thing."

"We've had nothing but wars, kiddo."

"True, but could we have had *bigger and more* wars if they hadn't been there?"

"It's a thought," I said. "How's Burton Selwick to work with?"

Gretchen made a face. "I'm not assigned to him often. Only twice have I had occasion to be with his staff. He's funny."

"How?"

"Oh, he has that staid British humor and isn't afraid to mix a little fun in with his work. All the girls like him. He's extremely intelligent. I had a professor like him once."

"Where?"

"College here in New York."

"Edith seems to think a lot of him."

"They're countrymen, that's why. Whenever they go out to lunch all they talk about is England. He uses her a lot after hours like all the rest of the Embassy bunch. That woman will work night and day without pay just to be 'doing her bit' as they say."

Sure, and doing her bit can get her a lot of inside information that can be diverted into other channels, I thought. Scratch another up for Rondine.

"She was always like that. Real close-mouthed, though."

"You have to be. Everyone is cleared security-wise and you don't last long if you talk out of turn. Look what happened last month and before that with that attaché."

The waiter came then with a steaming tray of strange dishes that had the pungent aroma of the Orient. He set them down, waited for a smile of satisfaction and went back through the curtain.

Gretchen asked, "What is it?"

"Maybe I'd better not tell you," I said. "Just eat it."

She gave a mock shudder of excitement and dipped her fork into her plate. What she tasted pleased her and we ate with small talk about the place itself. I pointed out a couple of politicians, an actor and two big hoods on the level below and gave her some background on the *Hall of the Two Sisters*. Before we finished Dell came up, spoke in my ear and when I shook my head, smiled and left.

"What did he say?"

I laughed and pushed my plate away. "He wanted to know if the lady and I were interested in sharing a room for the night. It seems that he has just the thing available."

"And you said no?" she teased.

"Sure. The beds are hard, the mirrors two-way and for a seat behind them somebody who goes for the oddball kicks pays Dell five yards. Besides, your place is better."

She leaned her elbows on the table, her chin cupped in her hands. "Tiger," she said, "you are completely overbearing and the picture of supreme over-self-confidence."

"So do we go to your place?"

"Certainly," she said.

The fire was still inside her, the picture of the dancers there in her mind. She let me unbutton the dress then shrugged out of it and stood in the soft light from the dresser and shed the black lace that was left. Slowly, she undulated across the room toward me, not dancing, but with the innate classic movement of every female who had ever lived and wanted just one thing. She was tall and sleek and stalked with the subtle grace of an athlete; breasts high and thrusting, swelled with excitement. Her belly was a concave region tense with excitement, merging with hips and thighs that were taut with demand. The Eurasian girl was just that compared to her . . . a girl.

"Now you," she said and reached for the buttons on my shirt.

In the living room the phone rang, a sudden discordant note. I looked at her and she shook her head. It rang twice more and stopped. Then her fingers were inside my shirt brushing my skin and I pushed her away to do it quicker.

Outside the Village had gone quiet and beside me Gretchen slept curled on her side, one arm flung across my chest. I lifted her hand, felt the pulse in her wrist steady, her breathing regular, dropped her arm on the bed and rolled out. I got dressed, threw the cover over her and walked to the door.

I looked back, said, "Nice. Very nice," then left.

Chapter 10

The story of the kill the night before was all over the morning papers. The pictures were there showing the guy on the ground and the one in the car. The accompanying story identified them as Tommy (Chum) Williams and the driver as Max Sweiber, both known hoods with police records whose regular base of operations was Chicago.

I put in a call to Thomas Watford and, when he wasn't in, told his secretary I'd be up there in an hour. Watford would know what I meant. He'd have everybody assembled, no doubt about that. I finished typing my report, dropped it in the mail chute beside the elevators and knocked on Toomey's door. He didn't answer so evidently he had already left on business of his own. He had a key to my room so I stuck a copy of the report under the empty bottom drawer of the dresser on the plywood dust panel where I told him I would and went downstairs for breakfast.

At nine-thirty, I finished, grabbed a cab to Watford's place and went in to the receptionist. She was smiling and busy, told me to go right in and nodded toward the door.

Just the two of them were there, Thomas Watford and the

heavy gun from I.A.T.S., and the look on their faces meant trouble. Both were seated at the desk going over a stack of papers and looked up when I came in with dark, foreboding glances and sat back, forgetting what they had been doing until I slipped into a chair across from them.

"You saw the ballistics report, I guess," I said.

Watford nodded. "*Your* gun, Tiger. The bullet checked with the one we already had."

"Now what?"

The big guy leaned forward, his attitude challenging. "Both dead men were armed, so in a way you're off the hook. The papers and the police are attributing it to an attempted gang rub-out and luckily someone saw the action from a window, said it was a deliberate attack, but couldn't identify the intended victim except to say that it was a man."

"Buddy," I stated flatly, "you're the one who wanted me to be the sacrificial cow. If it happens, don't point any fingers toward me."

"At this point we won't," Watford told me, "not as long as you cooperate."

I shrugged. "Who's holding back?"

"All right. What were you doing at that particular place at that particular time?"

"Visiting Edith Caine," I said.

Both of them exchanged quick looks.

"Why don't you check with her?"

Watford flipped the key on the intercom and gave his receptionist instructions. While he waited he said, "Someone knew how to find you."

"Sure. She told them. I left her place and she had time to make a phone call. If she had somebody on hand for such an eventuality it could have been an easy hit. Hell, there were two carloads of them. The first missed and the second was insurance. You get anything on the guys?"

It was the big guy's turn and his tone was reluctant. "A contract setup. They flew here out of Chicago two days ago. Nothing more than that and I doubt if there will be anything more than that."

The call came in then. Watford spoke briefly into the hushaphone on his desk and though nobody could hear what he was saying I knew the answer. He put the phone down and looked at his friend solemnly. "He was there," Watford said. "A friendly visit and the time fits."

"The local police going to move?"

"In this case we have jurisdiction."

I grinned at him a long moment. "Or does Martin Grady?"

I thought the big guy would bust. His face was a tight, florid thing filled with loathing of the big pro for the little pro and his hand slammed down on the desk. Very quietly, in spite of his rage, he said, "Damn Grady and the rest of you. I'm making a point of breaking up that clique!"

"You said that before. I think it's been tried several times."

"Money can't always buy everything."

"Almost everything," I said. "It couldn't buy me."

Neither of them spoke.

I said, "I asked you for information on Edith Caine. What did you find out?"

After a few seconds Watford said, "Clear. Security marks her clean. You have nothing there. I'd like to know what you expect to find."

"A killer, Tommy boy," I said. I got up and put my hat on, watching the guarded expressions on their faces.

Finally the big one said, "Whose?"

"It's a long story, friend, but mine among others," I told him. "Do you want a formal statement from me or will you handle this the usual way?"

"Do we have a choice?"

"Not really," I said.

"It isn't over yet, Tiger. They'll make another try."

"Naturally. This time I'll keep somebody alive long enough to talk about it."

"You do that."

"Why sure. Now I want a favor from your department."

"This isn't a joint effort on *our* part, Mann. You are to do the cooperating."

"Stow it, friend. If it doesn't work both ways count me out. It means you're too stupid to work with at all."

Watford ignored the insult, looked at the other one, then back to me. "What is it you want?"

"A tail on Edith Caine. Twenty-four hours, rotating teams and all contacts tailed individually. Secondary contacts tailed too and stake-outs on everyone involved."

"How long is this to last?"

"A week should do it."

Watford said, "You know what this will entail in personnel and cost involved, I imagine."

"If the government can finance Tito and underwrite wheat shipments to Russia I think it can stand a few grand and some men to protect its policies. If you want me to I'll put our own group on this, but that would mean losing a day in the race and I don't think any of us can afford it."

Neither of them answered me directly. Finally Watford asked, "What do you expect to find?"

"When it happens you'll know it. We'll consolidate our reports and pick it apart from there." I stopped and looked at them both. "Do we have a deal?"

"For a week," the big guy said.

"That should do it," I told him. "From now on I won't make any direct contact with you unless it's absolutely necessary, but if you get anything I'm at the Chester Hotel."

"Wide open?"

"You don't hide a target, friend, and that's what you want me to be. A pro won't find me too hard to locate, but for anybody else it won't be easy."

Watford had a satisfied look on his face. "I'm glad you're asking for it," he said.

"Don't hold your breath waiting for me to be scratched," I said.

"It's bound to happen. We'll all be better off when it does."

"Drop dead," I told him. But I was grinning.

I went downstairs and started walking back to the hotel. I stayed with the crowd, taking my time all the way, doing my thinking as I walked. A lot of things were beginning to tie in now, but the big apple hadn't been plucked yet.

It was cute, the way they were working it, calling in outside men rather than involve their own. Rondine wanted no strings tying her into this bit at all. She was passing it down the line to other hands and letting them make the contacts.

Everything figured out nicely. The try for a hit right after I met her. It wouldn't have been hard to find me where I was. Until I saw Rondine I wasn't using a cover at all. I was between assignments from Grady and marking time. I had two weeks in New York with plenty of loot in my pocket and I was going to enjoy myself. Until I saw her again. She sure worked fast, but then again, she had to. I could jeopardize her entire operation whatever it was and she didn't want to give me the chance. She knew damn well what I'd do.

She had had my hotel staked out when they made the second try that I spotted. When I made the tail I was thinking of it then because it's what I would have done myself. If I had played it cool I would have switched hotels after the first attempt, but I wanted her right out in the open where she'd be left cold.

They missed then too because I *was* smart enough to get the other room on the floor with the ledge around it, and that was something I did no matter where I stayed or whether I was on an assignment or not. For three years I had been on the Commie "B" list which meant a hit at any given opportunity, but being promoted to the "A" sheet, like they told me I was, meant an organized effort to nail me. Orders had been cut to kill this old soldier and by request from Rondine Vidor Churis had been given the job.

It was going to be nice to see him again. He had killed a friend of mine too.

There was a simple message waiting for me at the hotel and I had to laugh when I read it. I hadn't told Charlie Corbinet where I had moved to but he found me easily enough one way or another. It was coded in the old *Tike R* form we hadn't used since the war but couldn't forget because it was used more to set up interoffice dates than for business purposes. Charlie wanted to see me at two o'clock in front of the library building and I had twenty minutes to make it in.

Instead of going upstairs I called Toomey, got him in his room and told him my report was in and for him to be available right after six that night. Newark had already alerted him through Martin Grady and he said he'd stand by.

There was a cab in the slot outside, so I grabbed it and told the driver to drift by the library, spotted Charlie getting there right on schedule, waved him over and had him hop in.

I said, "Hi, Colonel. What's the good news?"

"You'll find out. Let's go to the British Embassy."

I gave the driver the message and sat back. When anyone was within listening distance Charlie Corbinet wasn't a talker. When we reached the embassy I paid off the driver and followed Charlie inside. He wasn't new to the place at all. He got the VIP treatment immediately and we were ushered upstairs to a private office furnished in dark-brown leather and mahogany and before we could get seated three men came in carrying briefcases and folders under their arms, shook hands quickly and were introduced to me.

One needed no introduction. He was Vincent Harley Case whom I had met with Rondine the first day I saw her again.

He said through a Glasgow accent, "Ah, Tiger Mann. Yes, we've already met through a mutual friend."

Charlie gave me a sideways look that could mean almost anything.

"Though I hardly expected to see you again under these—ah—circumstances."

79

"It's a small world."

"Not any longer, it seems. Please, sit down."

The chairs were pulled up around a low table, the folders laid out and it was the Colonel's time for explanation. Evidently they had expected him to come alone and weren't prepared for me.

Charlie said, "In view of the facts you're going to have to leave some things to my judgment, gentlemen. Without going into extreme details I can only tell you that Mr. Mann is an associate of mine, has served under my command and is, at present, engaged in activities that make his presence vital. Security on him is clear. I will vouch for him completely. Has anyone any objections?"

For just a moment there was an exchange of looks, a silent acknowledgment to accept Corbinet's opinion and Vincent Case nodded. "There is no reason not to go along with you, sir. After all, you are in an official capacity and our governments must work together. We can use all the help we can get."

Charlie glanced my way and I followed his lead, letting him do the talking. It was for my benefit that he reviewed the details, knowing I would put the pieces together in a hurry. I had to do more than that. I had to figure out just how deep he was with I.A.T.S. and what power he held. Damn, the agencies were smarter than I thought, getting him back in the ranks again. I wondered if he was over the big guy who stayed so close to Watford.

"As you know, yesterday we submitted certain prepared papers to the British regarding our joint efforts in the *Climax Project.* They contained false information deliberately planted to see if it was picked up." He paused and searched the faces of the others. "An hour ago our sources inside the Russian Embassy got word out that they had received news of our supposed intent and had called an emergency meeting of their delegates to counteract the proposal that was to be delivered today when the General Assembly convened.

"Since we did not follow it up with the true facts it was decided that the true proposal be discussed and agreed upon in secret, all members present not being allowed to confer with anyone until the time of the session this afternoon." Corbinet looked at his watch. "You gentlemen will be at that meeting in exactly forty-five minutes at an assigned place you will be given before I leave.

"This new proposal is not a vital one at this stage. It is what will be coming up within the week that will be of major importance. What we must do is find the source of this security leak and block it. We can't always be making last-minute decisions . . . we need time for discussion and communication, so this arrangement is in the way of a trial balloon. Is that understood?"

Again, there were acknowledging nods. Then the tall, thin one called Beaver said, "And Mr. Mann's part . . . ?" He let it hang there.

"Have you something to say, Tiger?"

"No offense intended," I said, "but I'd like you to run a security check on all your clerical help."

"Mr. Mann . . ." Case started.

I held up my hand. "Our people will do the same. I know they've been cleared once, but go through it again. There might have been new developments."

"Am I to understand that you have someone in mind?"

"You might try Edith Caine."

His frown deepened into a scowl and his eyes bit into mine. "I happen to know the family well."

"How well do you know Edith?"

"Quite well, sir."

"For how long?"

He drew himself up and there was an edge to his voice. "Ever since she was a child."

I knew I had him then. I said, "You recommended her for government service, didn't you?"

"Among others, yes. She came to see me, renew an old friendship and I was instrumental in bringing her here."

"Uh-huh. How long had it been since you had seen her before." He frowned again. "Well . . . I don't quite understand. . . ."

"How long, Mr. Case?"

He saw what I was getting at and his mouth tightened. "Not since she was eight or nine. Of course, her family had sent her to schools both in England and abroad. Since she was the youngest I rarely had occasion to do more than inquire about her . . . but this is sheer foolishness!"

I stood up. "Is it?"

"Indeed it is. However, to satisfy you we will check her through again. I hope it will satisfy you."

"It will," I told him.

Charlie took over then. He gave them an address, told them not to write it down and repeated the time of the meeting. There was nothing more. On the way out I managed to get in step with Case and take some of the sting out of what he had to do by reminding him a double check could not hurt and only clear everyone not involved once and for all and helped the possibility of stemming the leak. He finally gave me a friendly grin and admitted I was right.

I said, "Where's your sidekick today?"

"Sidekick?"

"Burton Selwick."

"Oh." He gave a sympathetic squint and said, "He had another attack last night. Took him to the hospital. Chap works too hard. He's been warned and knows better, but it's a demanding job."

"What's wrong with him?"

"Ulcers. He's going under the knife shortly. Right now he's at home, but if I know him he'll be present today."

"Tell him hello for me."

"I'll do that, Mr. Mann . . . and good hunting. I do hope you are mistaken in your premise, but if you aren't, well . . ."

"Sure," I said.

We separated at the elevator and Charlie Corbinet and I rode it down to the first floor. After picking up the hats and raincoats we went out to the street and without hesitation, he started north at a fast walk. I let him alone for a full block, knowing what he was doing . . . looking for a group to fall in behind so that when he spoke there would be no chance of being picked up by any mobile parabolic microphone that might be tracking us.

Three women and a kid were up ahead so we fell in behind him and I said, "Thanks for the party, Charlie, but that wasn't the rea   you wanted to see me. I'm short on time."

He tu   d his head and made a wry face. "You've opened up a dangerous avenue of thought."

"No kidding."

"After you left the other day," he said, "I made several calls to some old friends in British Intelligence. They aren't working at it now, of course, but I finally found one who tracked down an assistant of Price Richards. Luckily, he was a man with a remarkable memory and was engaged in liaison work with the French *maquis*. He did remember Rondine Lund and was able to fill me in on some of the details."

"A woman named Rondine Lund was shot," I said.

His eyes twinkled. "You're right there, boy. You still have your own ways, don't you?" Without waiting for an answer he went on, "Well, a year after the war she was caught up when the net went out for Nazi war criminals. Once again, by posing as the mistress of the one she was with, she managed to slip away because they considered her of no importance. However, sometime later she was recognized from a photo by one of our staff but by that time, naturally, she had made a successful escape.

"Now as a spy, with the war over, she never would have mattered, but there was a time, if you remember, she was in the company of several high officials of the Nazi Party who were never rounded up. These persons had access to documents we wanted and there was a possibility she could give us a lead to them, so an attempt was made to pick up her trail.

"It wasn't an easy job, several months were spent on it, she was identified and followed and the trail ended when she disappeared inside Soviet territory. A team of two was dispatched inside, one came back with the report that Rondine Lund was alive enough to kill his partner and there it ended because she had disappeared in the Soviet organization and there was no way of getting to her.

"By that time the documents we were after had been discovered by our men so there was no advantage in looking any further for Rondine. Naturally, there was no accusation of the murder of the agent because we couldn't let it out he was inside the Soviet line. So Rondine was dismissed and forgotten. The report was among many destroyed when we were burning the outdated paperwork and so ended Rondine."

"Until now," I added.

"It's hard to picture," he said. "I made a point to see Edith Caine."

"So did I. All over?"

Corbinet gave me a quizzical look.

I said, "Remember Carmen Bellotica? She was forty-two when they did the plastic on her so she could go back into Norway posing as her own sister who was fifteen years younger and pinpointed those Nazi installations for us. I saw her before she died and she looked like a kid. Surgery makes great strides during a war or in time of necessity."

"I remember her. And you think Edith Caine is Rondine Lund."

"I *know* it, Colonel."

"You'll need more than conjecture to swing it, Tiger."

"Don't worry. When I pull it off it will be all the way. I won't get myself messed up this time." Before he could say what he was thinking I added, "And I realize the importance of the job. I won't let personalities interfere. Digging out the security leak comes first, so don't lecture me. I'm over my first

83

mad and back at work. I'm under orders myself, so from now on it's cut and dried . . . but I'm taking a lot of real, personal pleasure in being on this one."

"Very good." He stopped, waited for the light to change and waved me across the street. "Incidentally, I heard about events on the street last night."

"Your cross-intelligence section is pretty good."

"No . . . I made the inquiry myself. That rub-out attempt was too close to Edith Caine's residence to be coincidental." A smile flirted with his usually tight mouth. "You have Mr. Watford and Hal Randolph in a sweat."

"That the big guy . . . the one with Watford?"

"Correct."

"Isn't he second in command of the Washington section of I.A.T.S.?"

Again, Corbinet smiled. "Nobody . . . nobody at all, is supposed to know that."

"Balls," I said. "You contact him?"

Charlie nodded. "This morning. He didn't appreciate it."

"Anything new?"

"Possibly one thing you might be interested in."

"Like what?"

"The staffs of all the agencies concerted their efforts on this one. When they have to they can dig hard and fast and getting to the contract killers who were hired wasn't an easy thing. But as always, there's an intimation at least, if not definite proof, of who was behind the attempted kill. One person in Chicago managed to come across with a small bit of information that has a peculiar tone to it in view of what we've just discussed."

"So?"

"It is suspected that the arrangement for those hoods was made by a woman. No names . . . no proof, but unsupported suspicion."

"But not unfounded?"

"No, not unfounded."

"We're getting there, Colonel."

"Your death is worth money to someone."

I put my hand on his arm. "Wait a minute." I looked around, spotted a small delicatessen with tables along one side and motioned for him to follow me. We went inside, sat down and ordered coffee and Danish. When it came I took the money I had picked from the dead guy's wallet, thumbed out the brand-new thousand-dollar bill and handed it to Corbinet.

"What's this?"

"One of the hoods I killed had this on him with some small

change. He wasn't the thousand-dollar type at all. Bills of this size generally have their serial numbers recorded and maybe you can trace it back."

He folded the bill slowly and put it in his inside pocket. "Nobody would make a mistake like that. Not in this business."

I shrugged. "Then get my grand back to me. I'll keep it as payment for getting shot at."

"Of course, if it's evidence, that's the end of it."

"The fortunes of the game, Colonel. I once found a million and a half in U.S. currency I had to turn in. I thought about it fifteen minutes before I figured it would only buy trouble. Remember?"

He smiled gently. "Quite well. You were younger then."

"I'll call you later then."

From across the table he gave me a direct stare, trying to read my face. "Vidor Churis?"

"Him."

"Every man available is on that pursuit."

"We have methods the agencies haven't."

"Yes, I know. Good hunting. I hope you're in shape."

"My kill record is pretty impressive. I'm still around."

"So I see. Shall we go?"

I found Wally Gibbons with a bunch of the guys from *The News* over in P. J. Moriarty's eating corned beef and cabbage. Brian gave me a nod from behind the bar, sent a beer over to the table for me and we shook hands all around. For a change the others were on assignments and couldn't stick around, so after fifteen minutes of small talk they paid up the tab, went back to work and left Wally and me alone.

Generally he was a laughing-boy type, always ready with a gag, but now he had no smile ready. There was a funny cut to his eyes and he kept looking at me from behind a cup of Irish coffee, then he said, "The more I dig the more I think about you, Tiger."

"Now what."

"Last night?"

"Good action. You want the story?"

"Buddy, I have it, but I won't run it until you come across all the way. You have something big going."

"Your pipelines are pretty tight. That's a closed circuit."

"To some, maybe. Not to me. I'm the thinking type. You want to talk about it?"

"Not yet. I haven't got all the answers ready. It would be like a joke without a punch line."

"You're a bastard."

"So I've been told. Many times."

He finished his coffee and reached for a cigarette. "I can give you something, friend."

"Go, man."

"John Fredericks Talbot. You know who he is?"

I shrugged, saying nothing.

"You recall the ASO deal in Poland?"

"I was there."

Wally started to pull on the butt and stopped. "Am I telling you something new?"

"Maybe." I took the top off the beer. "When they blew the legation building I got Connors and White clear, but that was all I was assigned to. Why?"

"Because Talbot was the inside man who nailed the assassins. You ever know George Gifford?"

"INS man in Paris?"

"That's the one. He was there at the time chasing some broad he had a big one for and she was running with Chevesky at the time. She got herself in a mess and George smuggled her out. Later she told him Talbot was on top of the business for six months posing as a Polish National and she got the lowdown on him from another broad he was sleeping with. Damn, the history of the world is made in a bedroom."

"From Eve through Caesar to now," I said.

"So while a member of British Intelligence, he was well planted and right there when the guns came out. He didn't expect the play and tried to stop it but it was too late. He hit the two Reds who got to Seliga, but they wound up dead."

"So why tell me?"

"Because one of the killers died slowly under Talbot's hands. He talked. He partially identified somebody implicated in the plot and it was a broad. That's where it ended. But now he's here, the guy is one of their top men. You bring Edith Caine into the picture and from what I know, what little you tell me and what I find out, I'm beginning to get some cold shivers. I don't like the action at all, Tiger."

"You just don't want to see a beautiful doll take a fall," I said.

"No, it's not that. The whole damn world is in a mess. One wrong move and somebody pushes the red button and you know what happens. One screwball with his finger on a switch triggers it and everything goes out of existence. The trouble is, you can be the catalyst and it scares me. I got that crazy feeling you can be the one."

"Never me, Wally. I think too much of my hide."

"Like hell you do. You got just one thing in your mind."

"Maybe," I said slowly. "I died a long time ago."

"Well *I* didn't." He dragged on the cigarette and stuffed the butt out in the ash tray. "Incidentally, I got the b.g. on Gretchen Lark. It wasn't too hard to do. I don't know why the hell I do your leg work for you."

"Because you want a story after the shooting's over, that's why."

"Okay, you're right. I'm chicken. You know her well?"

"We've met."

Wally nodded and fiddled with his coffee cup. "She's the intellectual type. Did you know she's gaining recognition as a painter?"

"I heard."

"Very scholastic. After high school she went into nurse's training, spent three years at the Center, then went back for her master's, then picked up two years' legal training at Shute College. She'd written four recognized papers on U.N. affairs before she went into her job."

"Good for her."

"She has a Ph.D. too."

"They're better smart."

"Better sexy too. I know two guys who laid her and they said it was great."

"How about that," I said.

"Oh, you slob. You bedded her down too, didn't you?"

"We were on top of the sheets. It wasn't exactly bedding."

"Some guys have all the luck."

"What else about her?"

Wally made a noncommittal gesture with his hands and said, "Nothing. Just general background you asked for. You want sex references?"

"The hell with that."

"Otherwise she seems to be a popular type, all ends tied, good, respectable American family and all that jazz. I scrounged the original clearance on her if you want to see it."

"No sweat."

"Okay, now for another piece. Burton Selwick."

"Oh?"

"The guy is sick. The office in London says he's about to be replaced. He's been hurting for the last year and they're really concerned about his health. He's had another ulcer attack but won't leave the job and his wife is raising hell so they're getting Smithwick to replace him. It's fairly common knowledge so I'm not talking out of turn. The only trouble is . . . he's a thinker and they'll face a heck of a loss when he goes. Selwick has been responsible for the tight relations between Britain and us for the last few years and whoever replaces him had better be good."

"And you're supposed to be a Broadway columnist," I said.

"Come off it, Tiger. In my own way I'm a thinker too. I wasn't in the code-and-cipher set like you were, but I had a personal interest in that goddamn war, too. I slogged behind tanks and got the crabs with the best of them. Maybe the only medal I got was the Victory Medal, but that was all I wanted. The ones you killed had names. The ones I knocked off were just uniforms. But I like it peaceful now."

"You haven't got it yet, buddy."

"It'll come. Now where do we go from here?"

I pushed the glass away and got up. It was starting to get late. "I'll give you a buzz when it happens. Stay on the ball."

"You got something working?"

"I got something working," I repeated.

"My story, remember?"

"Natch."

Chapter 11

The upheaval in the United Nations was already well under way when I got there. One of the nations from the Soviet bloc had entered its proposal on the subject under discussion and the United States delegate had countered with our own and was backed up by the entire Western group with such unanimous approval that the Soviets were thrown into a partial panic. It was totally unexpected and both proposals of such divergent nature, and the Western one so evidently the proper approach that the Soviets were passing notes and making hurried consultations and from some of the black scowls showing I knew they were wondering what went wrong with their inside track.

Burton Selwick was on his feet acknowledging Britain's acceptance of the United States' proposition, his voice thundering, yet persuasive. Two Russian delegates were trying to pull their usual stunts of attempting to disrupt the proceedings but were being ordered to quiet down. Some sort of signal passed between them simultaneously and, as one man, a dozen of them got up and began to file out of the room.

There was an immediate rush of reporters to the phones to

get the latest news to the press and it was plain that with this latest move the discussions were going to end in the general snafu that always accompanied the Soviet action.

Burton Selwick was still talking, but there was a hesitancy in his voice now. From where I stood I could see him plainly and there was a whiteness to his face and he pressed his hand against his side and held it there. Abruptly, he excused himself, sat down and leaned back in his seat tiredly. Two of his associates spoke to him, helped him to his feet and led him from the hall.

In the corridor they sat him down again and by the time I got there both Edith Caine and Gretchen Lark were at his side along with a dozen others. John Fredericks Talbot took up a position a little behind the group with four others and from their stance and demeanor I knew they were more than spectators or part of the party.

Someone asked for a doctor, but it was Gretchen Lark who told them it wasn't necessary, she was a nurse and familiar with the situation. She sent someone into an office who returned with a glass of water and some tablets, had Selwick take them and when the color returned to his face, helped him up.

There was too much hubbub to hear what they were saying, but Selwick and Edith spoke a few words, he said something reassuring to her, patted her shoulder with a smile and let himself be led away to a room. At the door Talbot and one other took up a post there, telling the reporters that it was a minor gastric attack and that everything was all right and well under control.

Toomey came out of nowhere, nodded and said, "What do you think?"

"He's been pretty sick."

"Yes, I know, but he was to be a key speaker today."

"What are you driving at?"

"He could have been out of action despite the Russian move. I'm wondering if that brought it on or not."

"Poison?"

"Not necessarily. There are other things . . . stimulants, irritants . . . that can incapacitate a man."

"I think I know a way of finding out."

Toomey glanced around him and said softly, "They fell for the gambit."

"I wonder if it can happen again?" I speculated.

"They aren't going to enjoy this development. Whoever steered them wrong is on the spot now."

"Unless he comes up with the new answer."

There was a half-smile on Toomey's face. "If it's worth mentioning, I caught a glimpse of Stovetsky's face a few minutes ago. He saw you standing there and he tightened up like a wrung towel."

"I saw him."

"Before K gave him this post he was assistant head of their secret police."

He wasn't telling me anything new.

"Talbot was watching you pretty closely, too."

"Good for him."

"You're playing this pretty close to your vest," Toomey said.

"Am I? You read the report. I.A.T.S. wants me to be a target so I'm trying to accommodate them. You have to push these slobs. They think they have the whole world by the tail and it'll yell when they give it a twist. It scares hell out of them to know we're loose and whenever we dump one of them we get a bonus. They don't like knowing there are people more ruthless than they are and like poverty protects Communism, money can protect capitalism. They push our bunch around knowing we go by the book because we like the public image of being good guys. Well damn it, the bad guys seem to have the edge these days and if you're going to be a bad one, be good and bad. That's the part they can't understand . . . people like us stepping out of character to enforce a principle and not a law. Believe me, buddy, when you play guns, nobody wants to be on the receiving end, no matter how bad or tough they are."

"Nice speech."

"Screw you, too."

"I'm too old for that nonsense. What's your next move?"

I looked at my watch. It was nearly five o'clock. "We split," I told him. "Wait at the hotel until I call you."

Toomey said "Roger," and sauntered off, looking for all the world like he belonged there.

Downstairs there was a public phone and when the two girls waiting had made their calls I dialed Charlie Corbinet's office and gave my name to his secretary.

The Colonel's voice was tight and I knew he had something. He said, "I checked that grand note through you gave me."

"Go on."

"Somebody was in too much of a hurry. The mistake was made. It becomes evidence now."

"Yeah?"

"That bill was part of a hundred thousand dollars given to the Russian delegates in exchange for rubles when they first came over for the present session."

"The finger points," I said.

"Definitely."

"How will you use it?"

"As a lever, Tiger. It will get you a certain amount of latitude of action from our own agencies. Just don't go too far and if there are positive developments be sure to let them handle the final phase."

"Is this official?"

"Nothing is official because as far as anyone is concerned neither I.A.T.S. nor you nor Martin Grady even exist. I had to do a lot of talking to get this concession."

"Thanks, Colonel. Let me know if you ever need a favor."

"Keep me informed," he said and hung up.

I stepped outside the booth, turning it over to an elderly guy in a bowler who thanked me politely. There was another behind him with his back half turned, apparently thumbing through an address book. I caught the slight motion of his finger and followed him when he gave a look of annoyance and went to the directory rack to look up a number.

Gregory Hofta.

I played the same game, making sure we were unobserved. I stayed behind him, waiting my turn and he spoke face down into the book while I put on the impatient, but casual act.

"There is trouble, my friend."

"What's the pitch?"

"There will be no moves until *they* have control again. They're calling a special meeting of the deputies at their Embassy tonight."

"You on this?" I asked him.

"By special instructions from Mr. Randolph."

"Target?"

"Edith Caine. I don't enjoy the assignment at all." He paused and thumbed through a few pages, found a number and began to write it down. "She was with Selwick before the session. He picked her up and they arrived together."

"Then you're thinking the same thing . . . Selwick's attack on the floor could have been arranged?"

"Let's say we are overlooking no possibilities. His previous attacks have been real enough."

"Where's Edith now?"

"Still upstairs with Selwick and the others. They'll be taking him out shortly. What happened isn't serious, but it will incapacitate him long enough to slow down proceedings."

"Why this contact?"

"One of the Hungarian nationals recognized an embassy clerk who works for Stovetsky. He was one of his chief agents and assassins when Stovetsky headed the secret-police section. His name is Alexis Minner and he was behind the scenes when the Russians tracked down the Freedom Fighters in Hungary. It was mentioned to Stephen Midros and I was told to pass it on to you."

"Thanks for the warning."

Hofta closed the book, passed by me to go to the phone booth and I completed the act, giving him time to get clear. When I was sure I had it made I went back upstairs and over to the door where John Talbot still talked to a lone reporter.

When he was finished I walked over and said, "Tiger Mann, Mr. Talbot."

There was an amused glint in his eyes. "Yes, I know you, sir. Can I . . . help you with something?"

"I'd like to see Edith Caine."

"At the moment she's occupied."

"It might benefit us both if you broke her loose a second. Just tell her I'm here."

"I'm afraid . . ."

"We missed each other on the ASO fiasco. I got Connors and White out. The chase was labeled *ROCKPILE*. Do I spell it out further for you?"

The amusement in his eyes disappeared and there was a hardness there and recognition, his mind going through the mechanics of whether or not to play it out. Then he made his decision. "I'll see her. Wait here a moment."

"Sure," I said.

Edith Caine came out alone, her face drawn. The fingers of both hands fidgeted nervously and she had chewed away most of her lipstick. But she was still lovely, still desirable. Only now she was scared.

Why scared, Rondine? Of me because your time's running out . . . or scared because you fluffed and gave the boys a bum steer and you know what happens when you muff a critical play. Or maybe you're scared because you got wind of what was going to come off and had to pull a cutie to slow down Burton Selwick and left yourself wide open if they check it through far enough. Espionage laws still provide a death penalty, baby, and you damn well know it.

I said, "Hi, doll."

Her nostrils made a tiny, flaring movement and when she saw my smile her eyes half shut. *Was she tired . . . or was her age showing now?*

"Mr. Talbot said you wanted to see me." Her head moved and she seemed satisfied that there were others passing by and she was safe for the moment.

"I just wanted to compliment you, Rondine. It came off pretty well. Good timing."

"What are you talking about?"

"Let's not kid each other." I let my grin go bigger. "Tonight I'll get a line on your boys."

"Boys?"

"Come off it, doll. You've had it. If it's worth anything to you I have a suggestion to make."

She said nothing, just waited.

"Make sure nothing happens to Burton Selwick. If it has to be, a simple rub-out can solve a lot of things. I don't have to go through the slow torture of making you sweat it out, kid. Either way will please me, but either way, your death will solve a lot of things. Clear?"

Before she could answer, the door behind her opened and Gretchen Lark stood there. "Oh . . . oh, hello . . . Mr. Mann."

"Hello," I said.

She looked at Edith and told her, "Mr. Selwick wants you a moment, Edith. Do you mind?"

Without a word she passed Gretchen and went through the door. I said, "How is he?"

Gretchen gave a sigh of relief. "Fine enough to throw dictation around. It was an ulcer attack, that's all. The doctor's orders were explicit, he was to stay in bed, but try to get him to do it. Right now he's back on his feet, but they'll try to keep him quiet if it's at all possible. It won't be easy."

"That's good."

She looked at me quizzically, her eyebrows going up. "What are you doing here?"

"Interested spectator. Quite a show."

"You must have some pull to make the audience."

"I'm getting favors returned. Look . . . they have a doctor with Selwick?"

"There's one there now."

"Then I guess everything's under control." I paused, grinned at her meaningfully and said, "When do I see you again?"

"You mean . . . *that's* why you're *really* here?"

94

"A guy has to try anything."

She let out a tinkly laugh. "Call me when I get squared away. I think it can be arranged."

I winked at her and she went back inside. The door closed and locked with a soft *click* and I walked away. So I'd see her again, all right, but not just for a bed routine. I wanted to know what the doctor's verdict really was and since Gretchen Lark had been a nurse, she ought to know.

The evening had come early to the city. It had clouded over again and the rain smell was back. The air felt sticky and in the east a sudden yellow glow of heat lightning brightened the sky momentarily and there was the distant rumble of thunder.

I caught a cab in the middle of the street and had him take me across town to the Eighth Avenue station, got there five minutes before six and held down the booth faking a call. Just before the hour I elbowed the receiver down until the phone rang then let it up.

The deep bass on the other end of the line belonged to Evans of the Newark control and when I identified he said, "There was a single lead through the ticket seller of a movie house that puts on foreign films."

"How was it established?"

"She remembered the right hand with the straight forefinger when he laid down his money. There was a purple scar on the palm and the back of the hand. At first she thought he was pointing at her. The second time she saw him she realized that it was a deformity."

"Any description?"

"Only the hand. That's all she remembered, the money, the ticket, the hand. She doesn't look at faces."

"It's a starter."

"They start a three-day run of a new Russian film tonight. There won't be another for two and a half weeks since they intersperse their program with Polish, Greek and Hungarian pictures."

"Right," I said, "I'll cover it."

"One other thing."

"Let's have it."

"Peter Johnson called from London this afternoon. They completed the check on the Caine family and they're clean. Getting a past on the deceased members wasn't easy . . . there's a natural reluctance to talk about the dead, but he found squadron mates of Vernon who were there when he was killed. Vernon Caine had nine victories flying Spitfires, was a squadron leader in his outfit, had several decorations and went in near Dover. He was positively identified and buried in the family plot near the town where he was born.

"There wasn't too much on Diana Caine. She had the usual schooling, all in England and was something of a wild one when she was young, which fact nobody seemed eager to discuss, but understandable. At the beginning of the war she joined a volunteer group in London. According to a former friend of hers it was to be where the excitement was and escape the pomp and protocol that was so much a part of her family. She was killed along with about seventy others during a raid on the docks."

"He find out what volunteer group it was?"

"No. It was before the call went out for women in the services or the outfits really got organized. Her bunch were collecting money and using it to establish mobile canteens for the defense workers on the docks. Johnson managed to locate some of the men who were employed there at the time and he got one piece of news that sounds interesting. Those girls gave more than their time. Their patriotism extended to the bedroom and they had a reputation for being willing to go to any extent to keep the boys happy. Think it means anything?"

"Maybe not to us," I said, "but to a family that puts virginity on a par with sainthood it might mean a lot. At least enough to be glad she's dead and not part of their immediate history. Get a report into Central right away, will you?"

"Already done. Is there anything you need?"

"Not yet."

"Very well. There's been one alteration made yesterday. Ernie Bentley has moved into the loft where Caldwell's was. You know the place?"

"Yes."

"We've consolidated and all armament and analysis will be worked through him now. He'll handle special equipment there too. His phone number remains the same."

"Okay and thanks." I hung up.

One lead now. The power of money had bought something, a natural. A man away from home who retained the tie by going to native-tongue movies. He was violating every rule in the book, but nostalgia had gotten the better of him.

Dillinger had made the same mistake and died because of it.

I called Toomey at the Chester and told him I was going on a stake-out at the theater and to wait there until I needed him. He didn't like the idea of me playing it alone but that was the way I wanted it and it was my chase and I was calling the shots. I told him to stay in my room in case Watford or Randolph called and that I would check in at intervals until something broke.

The feature at the *Grenoble Theater* didn't start until seven-thirty and the ticket window didn't open until seven, so I had a forty-five-minute wait. I wasn't going to stake out on the sidewalk where I could be spotted, but through the doors I could see the benches in the lobby and figured it would be better to pay my way in and wait. If necessary I could take a seat in the last row, let my eyes get accustomed to the dark and sit it out. If Churis showed he certainly wouldn't take a chance of walking down the aisle but would do pretty much the same thing I did. It just depended on who saw whom first.

In case Churis had a spotter going ahead of him, I cut out of the area and grabbed a cab to the Village. At Gretchen's place I told him to wait and went up the three flights to her apartment and knocked on the door.

Nobody answered, but inside a radio was playing softly and I tried the knob, pushed open the door and gave her a call in case she was in the shower. I edged my luck a little bit and walked on in. There was one light on in the living room; it was the radio behind the bar that was playing and nobody was home.

She had probably gone to the store, but I didn't bother to wait. I flipped over the drape cloth that covered Selwick's pictrue, saw the progress she had made on it, even to catching some of the realism of the sickness he had and made a mental note to tell her to pretty it up for his wife. Then I went back to the cab.

This time the ticket booth was open at the *Grenoble Theater* and I passed in two dollars, took the ticket and the change, found a spot in the shadows where I could watch the door and sat down with the .45 loose in the holster.

In twenty minutes the place was filled but there was no sign of Vidor Churis. I found a seat in the last row, sat through a garbled propaganda picture and wished K could have seen the reaction. The only reason the public was there was to hear something in their own language, but they laughed at the wrong places and could have been against the wall for it in Moscow.

During the intermission I double-checked the faces in the lobby, waited for the second show crowd to file in, took ten minutes to be sure he wasn't going to show and cut out.

One lousy lead and it wasn't paying off. I could feel that

funny sensation crawling up my back and walked it off down to Forty-second Street because you can't afford impatience when you're playing the game of big guns.

From a drugstore I called Toomey and broke him loose from the TV set. He said there had been one incoming call that our subject had left the U.N. complex, walked to the automat with John Talbot, then taken a cab to her apartment. Talbot had returned to the Embassy building and was presumed there still. Before going in he had been joined by two members of the British staff and Vincent Case, all cleared personnel.

A stake-out was in progress outside Edith Caine's apartment with a team on the street and one deployed inside the building somewhere. The call had come a half-hour ago so it was a good bet she hadn't left the apartment.

I told him to stay there and he wasn't anxious to argue about it. The rain that had been threatening all night had finally found its way through the smog and was angling down against the window outside the phone booth. All I wanted was for him to put a signal call through to Martin Grady with my initial negative-contact report and request a new approach if possible and an expedite order.

Now it was time to stick the needle in deeper.

I spotted the two stake-outs early and felt like telling them to take a refresher course. Both should have known better, they were old enough to have gone through the mill from both ends. One was smoking in a car and all the windows were frosted over from the humidity and the other was standing out of the rain trying to be inconspicuous. They could have walked or doused the butts but the weather got the better of them and they played it down. One day they'd die for being stupid if they stayed around that long.

The other one was on the floor below Rondine's making a pretense of waiting for the elevator, but actually watching the cables to see if the car stopped at her floor or not. If it had, he would have checked. I had to ride up and walk down six times before I had him clocked, made like I rounded the bend in the corridor to some apartment, then took the fire exit up to her floor.

I put my finger on the buzzer and waited. I touched it again and her voice said, "Yes?" from somewhere inside.

"Tiger, honey."

There was no hesitancy. She didn't try the peephole or call out again. No talking through the door. She swung it wide and stood there gorgeous and radiant in a sweeping white gown that accentuated every luscious curve in her body, showing the

V glint of chestnut and dagger pink of womanhood, proud and obstreperous in their anger at being accosted so deliberately and I said, "Can I come in?"

"By all means," Rondine smiled, and the smile went back to years ago when she could hook me with wet lips and the sight of a body that belonged to a lewd calendar and a voice that was a snare and a challenge all at once.

This time she looked at me, a quick glance that ran up and down me, knowing how I had reacted before, watching to see a visual sign of a sexual attraction. Maybe somebody else would have made the grade, but I had had the full treatment and nearly died for it. It didn't happen now.

I said, "Thanks, kitten," and walked on in.

She closed the door and followed me into the living room. This time the music was from Wagner . . . the *Love-Death* theme. Fitting, I thought. Nice. It went right with my mood. It had an undulating quality that seeped into your mind and set the scene so nearly perfectly that Hollywood couldn't have staged it better.

Rondine looked tired now. There were shadows under her eyes and lines down the sides of her mouth that seemed to pull the years together and inside I had that goddamn terrible feeling I had back in the loft when I had loved her so much.

She was as good as dead and I was going to do it. She knew it and I knew it and nothing would change it. If I missed again somebody else from Central would do it and without feeling, but if I did it the feeling would be there. So how do you want it, kid, from a stranger or someone who loved you so much he'd die for you?

I tossed my hat and coat on a chair, sat down against the arm of the sofa and stretched my legs out. There was a nervous quality in the way she moved and she tried to hide it by walking to the bar. "Drink?"

"Why not?"

"Scotch?"

"You made enough drinks for me before, kid. You know what I take. I haven't changed any. Just cheap bar whiskey and ginger ale and don't burn it." I was beginning to wish she'd quit the act in front of me. There wasn't any reason for it or sense to it. We were alone. It had all come to an end long ago, except for the climax. What was going to be done was going to be done.

I said, "How was your Mr. Selwick?"

Rondine put the drink on the table at my feet. "Well taken care of. He'll be at work again Monday as usual."

"I understand you had lunch with him?"

Her eyes darted my way. "Is there something wrong with that?"

"Possibly." I picked the drink up and tasted it. Good. She had the balance down pat. I said, "That was nicely timed for him to have an attack."

She frowned, not getting the point. "He's had them before."

"And you've had lunch with him before."

Then she realized what I was intimating and the glass in her hand shook visibly. I could sense her searching for words, but they didn't come. They couldn't get through the dark rage that suffused her face.

Before she could think of anything I changed the subject. "We have some information on Diana Caine, honey. Interested or do you know it all already?"

She couldn't help it. The glass dropped right out of her fingers and spilled all over the floor. One piece of ice skidded across the room and I kicked it back casually with my toe. There was a stricken look on her face and tight, corded lines ran down her neck into her shoulders.

I grinned at her, a nasty thing that twisted my mouth out of shape. "So you got to the Caine family through her. That just leaves one thing left and that can blow you, doll. Where is the real Edith Caine?"

She didn't answer. She sat there, her face a cross between horror and rage, hating me with everything inside her.

I said, "I'll spell it out for you then. Somewhere the right Edith is supposed to be in hiding. My bet is that she's dead. You wouldn't leave any loose ends like that around. So far all your recommendations are from people who knew Edith Caine as a child, not an adult. Because the family has always been above reproach they never considered that one of the Caines would be a phony and a plant. I bet the family is turned inside out over this. When they see this thing laid out across the papers they'll do a mass Dutch act."

Her fingers trembled so hard they barely were able to hold the cigarette. I fished a packet of hotel matches out of my pocket, lit the butt for her and tossed them on the table. She choked once on the smoke, forced herself to a degree of composure. "You are so wrong, Tiger."

"Not me, sugar."

"You really wouldn't . . ."

"Try me and see."

She took a deep drag on the cigarette, snatched it away and snubbed it out in the ash tray until the butt came apart in fragments. Her eyes arched up, caught mine and she said, "I can't let you drag down the Caine name," in a cold, calculated tone that was the Rondine of old.

"How do you figure on stopping me? Vidor Churis?"

The pause before she spoke was a long one. There was a note of near-sympathy in her face and she said in a whisper, "You fool, you."

"I like your dogs, Rondine. They're the kind I know. I've been playing games with that type twenty years and left them lying stacked up behind me like cordwood. I'm surprised you aren't more subtle. There was a time when you worked every device a woman could and parlayed a smile and a figure into some first-rate kills. This new act of yours stinks. It's either too obvious or I'm getting jaded . . . I've had it pulled on me down in Mexico and twice in France. Each time the broad took the big fall because it takes more than an act to put a gun on me."

"Tiger . . ."

"Come here, Rondine. I'll let you take the act right to the end. Remember the kiss you gave me the last time? That was a real kiss, a real kiss of death. So come here, Rondine. I want to taste you again."

She stiffened in her seat, her eyes never leaving mine, both hands gripping the edge of her seat.

"I want to see if you taste the same knowing what you're doing to a fine family and with a young kid named Edith Caine lying dead in a hole somewhere. I want to know if having the smell of your own death in your nose can make you taste any different. Come here, Rondine."

She rose like an automaton at first, stood there momentarily with mind and body as taut as a bowstring.

"Come, my darling," I said. "I still have that same blaster on me. You might even have a chance to slip your hand inside my coat, grab the rod and spill my guts out again." I knew I was smiling. I could feel my lips tight across my teeth and the kill feeling chasing itself across my shoulders.

Something happened to her then. It started in her eyes and flirted down across her mouth. The tension went out of her shoulders bit by bit until she was the Rondine I had known so well, lovely, desirable, deadly . . . suddenly finding the situation to her liking and under her control. Each step across the room deliberate, the golden flesh of her thighs breaking through the opening of her gown as she walked toward me. Her pose was provocative, her breasts undulating beneath the sheer fabric totally unrestrained in their movement. The light was soft and kind to her and when it was behind her the glow outlined the sleek flow of her body.

I sat there and looked up at her, reading her mind. It wasn't hard.

She said, "Tell me how much you loved me, Tiger."

I had read it wrong. It had to be something else again.

"More than anyone could ever know."

"Do you still?"

"I told you there are some things that never change."

"As much as ever?"

"As much." I wasn't smiling any more. My stomach was tight and the words came out harsh and a little too loud.

"Once you would have done anything for me."

"That was a long time ago. Now there's only one thing I'm going to do for you. Kill you, Rondine."

"If . . . you must . . . can you do one thing for me?"

"Nothing."

She knelt on the couch beside me, then eased into a sitting position and her knee was a gentle pressure against my leg. The top of her gown had parted with the movement and the deep cleft between her breasts was an open invitation she made no attempt to hide.

"Please hear me," she said with almost innocent simplicity.

"Why?"

"Because you love me."

I reached out and pushed her knee away. "And how about me, kid? Tell me how much you still love me."

"Still?"

"You used to make beautiful love talk, baby. I used to lie in bed with you and listen to the sound of your voice and it could turn me inside out. All the while we were having each other whether it was in the mud or in a bed you'd tell me over and over how much you loved me, so let's hear you say it now. I want to see if you can still get that feeling in your voice."

"I think I loved you from the first moment I saw you, Tiger."

"Now you're being trite, kid. That used to be one of your favorite statements. Try something new."

Gently, she reached out and touched my face with her forefinger. "I love you, Tiger," she said.

And she reached me with it. She knew she did and I hated myself for feeling that slow wave of warmth that started in my brain because it was twenty years ago all over again.

"Can I ask you now?"

When I didn't answer she said, "Don't do anything to the Caine family."

"Killers don't change," I finally told her.

Her face remained impassive, but there was something new in her eyes. "I'm sure they don't."

I tried to stop what she did, but I couldn't. She leaned forward, eyes partly closed, her hand along the side of my face and then her mouth was on mine and the tip of her tongue searching and feeling. My fingers tightened on her arms, pinioning them and the past came closer and closer. I forced her shoulders back and the gown opened under the pressure and she was tight against me, a perfumed, hilly delight, fire-hot and moaning softly.

The incredible desire was there and I knew I was going to take her. I was going to do something I swore I'd never do again and couldn't help myself. But it was Rondine who made the move. Her breath jerked in her throat and she went rigid under my hands and tried to wrench herself away with a sudden sob. There was fright in her eyes and something else I couldn't fathom and, as quickly as it had started, it was over. I let her go and she twisted, grabbing for the front of her gown, and scrambled to her feet. She stood there breathing heavily, watching me, her mouth working until she half-blurted, "I'm . . . sorry. Truly . . ."

I grinned at her. The act was still going strong. A new act, a damn good one, but an act just the same. The only thing that surprised me was that she didn't make a try for my gun.

I eased out of the chair, got my hat and coat and turned to smile at her. "Soon, Rondine. I'll spoil it for you first and kill you. Sleep on it."

All the way out the door I knew her eyes were on my back and I was giving her one hell of a target, but somehow I knew she wasn't about to try one damn thing.

The rain was driving down now, whipping up the streets in front of the intermittent gusts that whistled around the buildings. All the cabs that came by were filled so I turned west and started walking. The last time I made the trip I had company and wound up with dead men at my feet. Maybe this time I'd have better luck.

By the time I reached Broadway I was soaked through my raincoat and still hadn't seen an empty cab. But there was an empty bar that was warm and dry so I went in for a drink. An old movie was running on the "Late Show" that got me caught up in it and it was an hour and a half before I left. I got a cab on the corner this time, told him the Chester Hotel and rode back still damp.

I knocked, but Toomey didn't answer so I supposed he

was asleep and stuck my key in the lock. I closed the door, flipped the light on and saw Toomey face down on the bed. But he wasn't asleep. There was a neat little hole at the base of his skull and a pool of red on the mattress that seeped up into the pillows. The body had barely lost any of its heat so the kill was only minutes old and I knew I had the answers.

Nicely timed, Rondine, I thought. A book of hotel matches carelessly left in your apartment, a phone call to a killer named Vidor Churis who gave me time to sack out, a passkey in the door, one nice shot with a silenced gun and out. The bad joke was on Toomey. The big joke was on the killer. He thought he had nailed me. He couldn't see Toomey's face while he napped and didn't think a positive make was necessary. It was my room and a guy asleep in my bed and it looked pat.

Chapter 12

The switchboard operator was a tired old guy who said a call had come in for me earlier, he gave the room number and was about to ring the room when the line went dead on the other end. Both he and the desk clerk said there had been traffic in and out of the lobby all night and neither had paid any special attention to people going either way.

I went back to the room, checked through it but found nothing. Later I'd get a report on the bullet, but it was still lodged in the body and I didn't want to probe for it.

There was one thing though. In Toomey's coat hanging on a hook in back of the door were two letters to me transshipped from the other hotel. One was a notice that my trunk had arrived by freight from Mexico. The other was from a German doctor specializing in plastic surgery who stated that although he never had her as a patient, she resembled a woman named Rondine Lund whom he had known when he was a medical officer in the Luftwaffe during the war. He understood that she was dead, but couldn't be certain.

Well, I could put him straight on that one.

My first call went through the relay to Martin Grady, the

second to Thomas Watford. He said to stay there until a team arrived but I wasn't about to. I gave him the picture as quickly as possible, said I'd check back with him on the slug that killed Toomey and hung up. I didn't have time to waste sweating out all the details of a police investigation no matter what agency handled it and if Hal Randolph was brought in he wasn't going to let me off the hook.

I got my gear together, went downstairs and paid the bill, leaving no forwarding address. Three blocks away I checked into another small commercial hotel under the name of Frank Wilson of Memphis, Tennessee. Just three blocks but in the complex of the city, twenty thousand people away.

As late as it was, I called Stephen Midros and got him out of bed.

His voice was a querulous, "Yes, please?"

"Tiger Mann, Midros. Hate to roust you out but something important has come up."

"Yes, yes, it is all right."

"I don't want to make any direct contacts, so you do this for me."

"Certainly."

"You know where to reach Gregory Hofta?"

"His home. He will be there. I spoke to him earlier tonight."

"Good. Have him get the address of Alexis Minner. He's a clerk at their Embassy . . ."

"Mr. Mann . . ." he stopped me. "This one is more than a clerk. He is dangerous."

"Hofta gave me his history. If his present assignment is just a cover then he'll be working with other people, too. He may be the lead I want."

"I was there when this man was in Hungary," Midros said carefully, keeping the emotion out of his voice that tried so hard to show itself. "He is a killer. Right now he enjoys diplomatic immunity and no matter what he does he can only be considered *persona non grata* and returned to Russia."

"He can do one other thing."

"What is that, Mr. Mann?"

"He can be buried."

Midros said nothing a moment, then a slight chuckle came over the receiver. "I wish you the best of luck, sir. Anything I can do to assist will be done. I will pass on your message at once."

"I'll call you back," I told him, said so long and hung up.

I needed sleep badly; too much had piled up and there was too much to come and I had to be right to finish it. I double-locked the door, checked the window and pulled the blinds shut, then flopped back on the bed.

How beautifully everything fit, I thought. They had to throw the package together in a hurry because I was something they had never planned on. Into the midst of their intricate planning that had taken years to set up, into their grand scheme to lock up the world through legalistic international maneuverings, comes one guy out of the past with one thing on his mind he never expected to find and that one guy could blow the basket for them.

Rondine knew what would happen. As soon as she left me that first day she had contacted her group and the order went out for an immediate hit.

Only I knew it would happen, too, and they shot up some pillows.

Ah, but she played it cute. She didn't know where to reach me so she contacted Wally Gibbons, and like a sucker took up my invitation to meet me at my hotel. Then she knew. Then she could pass it along and this time they came back in force for the second try and muffed it again because Toomey and I were ready for them.

She even knew the story would be quashed. The dirty ramifications of international politics aren't handled by local police and reporters are taboo. All you could do was play the game out as far as it would go until only one was left and that was the final answer, simple and complete.

Gretchen Lark put her finger on it when she inadvertently pointed up the way Rondine played Burton Selwick. He was the key, all right. He had the inside track and all the facts in his head. Rondine was a person to be trusted in his sights, a respected member of a fine old patriotic family, a countryman, a beautiful woman, one whom he had personally recommended for her position and one with whom he wouldn't be too guarded. She was on the inside, doing overtime work for him in addition to her regular duties and nobody knows more about the boss than his secretary. Or his work.

Rondine, it was a magnificent package!

You knew I'd visit you, kid. You knew I would want to be sure I knew how you did because I'm built that way. You knew I'd want to see how the plastic surgery worked and you were willing to take the chance because they had done such a good job you could afford it. You waited me out and had somebody standing by for the emergency. You had a gun and would have killed me yourself but I caught you on that one too and you had to pass the word down the line and it didn't take long. Two cars made the swing and tried for a hit on the street. That was a smart angle, calling in professional help. If they had made it nobody would have tied in the political bit. My reputation was enough to justify a kill like that and anybody could have done it, but it was still good thinking. Too bad it didn't work. Get your money back from the ones in the first car, sweetie, or are they still on the job? If they work it the usual way it's over for a while. You didn't tell them they were going after a big one and all contracts are canceled in their book. By now they'll realize what happened and you won't be getting them in again.

But it's the last one you're going to pay through the nose for, honey. You gave me plenty of time to get back to the hotel and fall asleep. You saw the book of matches and knew where I was. You didn't think I'd stop off for a few drinks and see a "Late Show" all the way through and your killer hit the wrong man. He's made too many mistakes to stay in business and now he's had it too.

And you know, stopping Burton Selwick's speech was a nice piece of cake. A delaying action. You got wind of what was going to happen and made sure you had time to work up a change of plans. What did you feed him for lunch . . . the same stuff we used on General Von Selter or the gook you dropped in the Greek's coffee that time in Athens? You didn't want to kill the old boy . . . he was too vital a source of information. Just putting him out of action was enough and his natural illness would cover up the real thing.

I grinned up at the ceiling and fell asleep, the .45 in my hand, a shell jacked into the chamber and the hammer on half-cock.

At ten A.M. I showered, shaved and got dressed. I called Stephen Midros and without discussion he simply said, "One-one-four-nine, Sixteenth. Upstairs over an Italian grocery store. There are four exits in the building, front, roof and two through the cellar, one on either side. Hofta advises extreme caution, the man is known to be an expert in all fields of murder."

"So am I, buddy."

"Will you need assistance?"

"Not at this point. I'll call for it if I do."

"We have a large organization, Mr. Mann, nothing official, but our people can be trusted and themselves have had experience in this sort of thing."

"Thanks. I appreciate it, but don't expose them to this. You might need what you have for the big play coming up."

"I understand."

I hung up, made sure I had the address down in my mind, slapped the gun in the holster and grabbed my coat and hat. Pay-off day was shaping up.

The apartment was the middle one of five that had just been renovated into a higher rent bracket, the occupants having the dubious advantage of living in the area of Greenwich Village. I toured the block, separating the funny ones from the real ones, stopping in a few stores to buy things I didn't need just to pick up the flavor of the locale.

Most of the permanent residents seemed to have international backgrounds, the older ones still speaking with thick accents and having mementos of life in another country on display behind counters and in their windows. A general sampling put them in the Slavic-German category with a few Italians sprinkled about. Twice I heard Russian spoken on the street in conversation, but nobody seemed anxious to exhibit that particular nationality with any artifacts.

Funny how patterns kept repeating themselves. Like Americans going across the ocean to Paris only to wind up in the American Bar or eating hot dogs that they wouldn't eat at home. There was always that unconscious search for your own kind, the innate desire to know you weren't alone. There was a sense of security, no matter how false, to hear a word spoken in a native tongue or taste back-yard spices on some familiar dish.

When I was ready I called Charlie Corbinet and told him to use the lever. Both Randolph and Watford wanted to talk to me but he would see that they were put off long enough for me to get this phase out of the way. What I wanted was a city fireman, in uniform, to accompany me on a simple inspection of the premises. All stops would have to come out because we were going to cross agencies and it had to be handled carefully. I said I would meet the one assigned on a corner two blocks away in an hour and got the "good-luck-and-go-ahead" signal from the Colonel on our old *Tike R.* code and hung up.

At ten after twelve a red city fire-chief sedan pulled to the curb and I got in. The driver was a young guy, the other a man in his fifties, with more the look of a cop than a fireman. There were burn scars on the backs of both his hands and another along the side of his face. He nodded, introduced himself as Captain Murray, the driver as Ron Kelly and wanted to know what the pitch was.

"Inspect all exits at One-one-four-nine, Sixteenth," I said.

"That's the Gorbatcher-Smith job. We went through there a week ago."

"Let's do it again."

He shrugged his shoulders. "No violations there. That's a good outfit and the super is on the ball. They complied with specs right down the line and the place is kept that way."

"Think of something."

"Can I ask any questions?"

"Sure."

"This came through some big channels. Police work?"

"Of a sort."

Murray grinned and nodded. "Okay, I get the picture. How do you want to handle it?"

"Regular routine," I said. "Nothing to draw any attention."

"No sweat. We pull spot checks all the time."

Kelly took us up the street and stopped in front of the buildings. A police cruiser passed, the cops waved casually and we threw them a wave back. Nobody on the street bothered giving us more than a first look. Cops and firemen were too common and unless there was some action nobody gave a damn what went on that wasn't their own business.

The superintendent was a middle-aged Italian who occupied the basement floor of the first building and he took so much pride in his job he was almost nappy about having an inspection run on him. He led the way through each building, smiling and talking, making us take note of the precision and cleanliness of the place and beamed every time Kelly made a check on the sheet on his clipboard that indicated an okay.

We wasted two hours on the farce, but I got to see what I wanted . . . the way in and out of the place from all angles, cellar to roof. There was a self-operated elevator that serviced the four flights of each building, an interior fireproof staircase and steel fire escapes that went down the back to the concrete courtyard.

Each fire escape was tested and as we passed the window of Alexis Minner's apartment I had a quick glimpse of the interior. He wasn't home, the super had told us that earlier, but on the kitchen table were two empty bottles of vodka, a half-full one and four used glasses.

Murray made an entry on the inspection form, went through the routine of the play and we went back outside. In the car he said, "Satisfied?"

"Yeah, thanks."

"You want anything else?"

"Not now. Which way you headed?"

"Back to the station, I have some work to clean up. Can I drop you off somewhere?"

I told him where to go. It wasn't far and I had some questions to ask. Maybe Gretchen Lark could answer them for me.

She came to the door in a knee-length paint-smeared smock, holding a brush between her teeth and a palette in her left hand while she opened the door. I took one look at her and laughed and she almost dropped the brush. "Well, this is a surprise, Tiger."

Only two buttons in the middle held the smock together and from the way it hung and the show of white at the closure I knew she didn't have anything under it. "You're going the Village route all the way. I like it."

Gretchen grimaced, glanced down at herself nervously and didn't seem to know what to do with her hands. She finally pushed her hair back with her forearm, gave me an impatient look and waved me in. "Look at me! I'm a mess. I wasn't expecting anybody."

"You look great."

"Oh sure." She glanced back at me over her shoulder. *"You men!"*

Gretchen dipped her brush in a peculiarly shaded apothecary jar half filled with solvent, picked up a few others and placed them beside it until they were soaked, swished them around and wiped them off, putting them on a table beside her easel.

I walked over and took another look at the study. Burton Selwick was a real British lion, proud, dignified, all his strength of character coming to life through his eyes and the set of his jaw.

"Like it?"

"He looks a shade strained. From here I'd say he was sick."

She stepped back, frowned at the portrait, turned the easel to catch a different light and, after several moments studying it, nodded slowly. "My fault, I've always had a flair for realism. Do you think I should soften it?"

"Hell, I'm no painter. If it's for his wife I'd make him pretty, that's all."

"It might be a good idea."

"How is he anyway?"

"Much better."

"What hit him down there?"

"Nothing more than I told you. He keeps having these ulcer attacks. Last year it was gallstones and he had them out, but that job of his doesn't invite peace and tranquility. He's a walking medicine cabinet. I think he eats more pills then he does food. Now, if you don't mind, I'd like to put something on. It's too early to be entertaining in the buff."

I let out a laugh. "Honey, it's never too early for that."

"*Men*," she said again and walked away.

While she dressed I went back to the portrait of Selwick. From the time I first met him a few days ago until now he had changed. There was little of the jocular type he seemed to be; it was more like he was hiding in the shadow of pain behind a mask of imperturbability. Chin up and all that sort of thing.

The chair that he was posed in was an ornate prop, but in the picture it appeared to be a throne. giving him a regal aspect. I sat in it myself and wondered if Gretchen painted him wearing nothing but a smock like she did when she was alone. I grinned at the thought because Selwick was just a little too dignified to sit through it. It would have shown on his face.

Beside the chair was an end table that didn't show in the picture and I flipped open the box on it. Selwick's medicine cabinet. There must've been a dozen bottles of assorted pills and capsules there, most from chain pharmacies in the city.

Gretchen came out in a sweater-and-skirt combination, her hair loose and flowing again and the paint smudges gone from her face. She smelled of a cross between turpentine and Chanel No. 5. She pointed to the box I had open on the table. "See what I mean? He sits there and eats them like candy."

"The doctors must know what they're doing," I said.

"Sometimes, although I don't always agree with their remedies."

"No?"

She finally got her belt adjusted and patted her hips down. "I used to be a nurse." She laughed, the tinkly one that sounded so nice. "Funny, but I wanted to try everything. I was good at it, but after a while the excitement seemed to pale. I guess I wasn't what you call dedicated."

"You should have tried getting married. You would have been good at that."

"Someday, Tiger, someday perhaps. There are still a lot of worlds to conquer and although I am only a woman I want to see what life is made up of before I settle down to diapers and dishes." She perched on an unpainted bar stool and swung her leg on either side. "Now, what do we do? It's Saturday afternoon and I'm hungry, if that's any kind of a hint at all."

"So let's eat," I said.

"Where?"

"Oh, there ought to be some local slop chute that serves up the rare and exotic."

"I'm thinking of that wonderful place you took me the last time, the *Hall of the Two Sisters*."

"No floor show at this hour but the chow is good."

"Can we go back?"

"Why not? Only don't ask for an interpretation of the menu."

"I wouldn't dare."

Dell hadn't arrived at the *Hall of the Two Sisters* when we got there but Joe Swan had and let us through with a big grin and a whistle-and-wink when he saw Gretchen. Swan handled most of the smuggling contacts, specialized in gems and blew the whistle on anybody he knew about handling narcotics. He had a special hate for *horse* because he lost a wife who was given an overdose by some wise punk at a party and wound up killing him. Down at headquarters he was treated with respect not given the ordinary informer or stoolie and although three rub-outs had been tried, Swan was still up at bat.

He got a waiter to get us our spot, suggested the specialty of the house and when we were halfway through came in to say he had something special to show me, the leer indicating it was of a sexy nature not intended for tender feminine eyes and Gretchen gave me the raised-brow look and sighed fatuously.

But it wasn't that. Dell was back in his office and after he closed the door he said, "I have information for you, Tiger. Your man with the stiff finger."

I waited.

"He has been seen."

"Where, Dell?"

"Not too far from here. In the section between Fourteenth and Fourth Street."

"Who got on to him?"

"Two people. One is a newsdealer who remembered the hand. He bought a copy of a foreign newspaper that is sold in the section. The other was a contact, Marty Lehman, a junkie. He's a peddler. The man you're looking for purchased three caps of H."

"Somebody steered him to Marty," I said.

"Not necessarily. Marty, unfortunately, is well known in that section. He took a chance with your man and charged him well above the going price for the goods. He passed it through a door and remembered the hand well. The man paid, Marty was clear and satisfied and so was the customer." Dell moved behind his desk and sat down. "Have you learned something?"

"It's coming together. The big thing is that he's an addict."

"That is important in a man."

"He'd almost have to be to be a killer."

Dell smiled and shook his head. "Tell me, Tiger, have you ever used this terrible thing?"

"I'm not about to, buddy."

"Yet you have killed."

"Just killers, Dell. They are animals who need killing badly. I don't have to get hyped up for that job."

"Please be careful. I like your business."

When I got back to the table Gretchen said, "How was she?"

"The great Oriental mystery is a secret no longer. They are all alike. The slant is only in their eyes."

"Dirty man."

"Just curious," I said. "Eat up. I have things to do."

"Can I go?"

"No."

"Why not?"

"Business. Broads aren't an asset when you're setting a deal. They're too damn distracting."

"Will I see you again?"

"Maybe."

"When?"

I pushed away from the table and called the waiter in for the check. "You sure you want to?"

Her eyes had a mist over them and a rueful smile tugged at her mouth. "Yes, Tiger, I'm sure. You make me feel foolish saying it, but there hasn't been too much in my life, not really. I guess that's why I do so many things that seem strange to those who know me. Since you . . . well, I feel funny inside."

"Don't kid. If anything happens it can hurt."

"What can happen?"

"It's a rough business."

"Please don't scare me."

I felt pleasant and relaxed and thoughts of the past and the present were very close in my mind. There was no future after Rondine, but there had never been any future anyway so it really didn't matter at all. Maybe with Gretchen Lark, but who could tell? You didn't parade any checkered flag past the grandstand until after you had won the race and it wasn't over yet.

"Can you tell me?" she asked.

"You wouldn't believe it."

"Try and see."

I leaned back in the chair and felt for the words. "Suppose I have to kill somebody."

"Is it necessary?"

"Essential."

"Then there is no choice, is there?"

"No choice at all, baby."

"Who is this person?"

"Not one . . . several. Maybe just two. There have been others. I've killed before."

She studied me intently, her eyes filled with quiet passion. "I know that, Tiger. It's something I can feel in you. Whatever it is you have to do, you'll do it. Just don't leave me."

"I won't."

"When do you have to do this?"

I moved my shoulders and frowned. "Tonight maybe."

"You'll be careful?"

"I'm always careful."

"You will be back?"

"Later."

"I'll wait for you," she said gently.

At five I let her out of the cab and had the driver take me back uptown to Ernie Bentley's new workshop. It was a cross between a laboratory and a miniature machine shop and he was working at a microscope when I got there.

When I was at Minner's apartment I got the name of the lock on his door and asked Ernie to fix me up with a master key for the make. He said he'd have to make six, one of which would fit and would take twenty minutes to complete.

While I waited I called Charlie Corbinet, got him as he was about to leave the office and asked him about the bullet that killed Toomey.

"Matches one gun that was used on you."

"The guy must be nuts to hang onto the piece. If he's picked up with it he's had it."

"Not with diplomatic immunity."

"*If* he has it. We may not be talking about the same one. I'm thinking he might be smart enough to dump that rod."

"Tiger . . ."

"What?"

"In '41 you were issued an Army Colt automatic. Do you still have it?"

"Okay, I get the point."

"Do you have anything for me?" Corbinet asked.

"Are you ready to work with probables?"

"Anything."

"They seem to be located in the Village. If we push them hard they'll have to move fast and won't have the time to be careful. The improvisation is coming from their end, not ours. They're the ones running scared."

"Then move fast, boy. This coming week is a critical point in our history. If that leak is still there we can lose everything."

"It won't be," I said. "If necessary I know one way of stopping it."

"We may have to do it that way."

"Did you see a report on Selwick?"

"I have it on the desk in front of me. They used a stomach pump and all known tests on him. Negative. His condition is a natural one."

"Clever," I said.

"What's that?"

"There are ways to do anything if you have the right means. I can name you two poisons that can kill without leaving a trace and will be diagnosed as natural death."

"Selwick didn't die," he reminded me. "He was in good health except for an organic disorder. Several top medical authorities attested to that."

"You ought to remember what we did to Krouse and Gettler that time in '45 to get them off the planning committee and put it directly in the hands of Hitler who we knew would louse up the situation."

Before he could answer, I laughed and hung up.

Ernie finished the keys, dropped them in my palm and said, "Martin Grady called. We've been working on something you might find useful. He suggested you consider it."

"Like what?"

He held out three black spheres half the size of golf balls. One had a line around its perimeter. "Remember the torpedoes you got as a kid on the Fourth of July? You could hit a sidewalk or a wall with them and they'd blow?"

"Yeah. Fun. The little pebbles inside could gouge an eye out."

"They work the same way, only these have the intensity of a hand grenade."

"Stable?"

Ernie shrugged eloquently. "They're new. They worked fine under lab conditions. Keep them in your pocket and don't jiggle them too much."

"Thanks a bunch."

"I'd suggest you keep them wrapped in a handkerchief or in different pockets. Someplace where they won't rattle around. And don't hang your coat near a radiator. Anything over a hundred degrees will set them off."

"What's their primary purpose?"

"Same as a grenade. If you have something to pack them with the charge becomes directional and can take a steel fire door down. The one with the white line around it has an incendiary capacity."

"Thermite?"

"We've progressed, Tiger. Something like it only better. Devlin used it in Yugoslavia to get through the safe he got the Morvitch papers out of."

I dropped one in each side pocket of my raincoat and put the fireball job inside my jacket. "You hear about Toomey?"

"Grady told me," he said. "I'm happy to stay inside and leave the field work up to you idiots."

"You'll never meet any broads in here," I told him.

"Hell, I got more than I can handle at home. If you use those things let me know how they work. Anything can be improved."

"Sure, buddy."

There was a column in the evening papers about the dead man being found in the Chester Hotel. He was identified as a small businessman from a Midwestern city with a passion for gambling, a known welsher and a person upon whom murder had been tried before. The story said he arrived late that evening and occupied a room just vacated and was probably killed by person or persons unknown with whom he had gambled, lost and refused to pay off. Whoever wrote the story made it look like an old story and a warning to the sheep who came East to be fleeced. The big boys take a dim view of the type.

I.A.T.S. were on their toes and had the local police department following their line whether they liked it or not. If the story held, Vidor Churis might take an easy breath. He'd have time for another try at me without any heat on him. A bad kill wouldn't concern him. He'd know I was still around and he could move with some latitude, knowing the cops were on the wrong trail. He couldn't make a fast move and would have to wait for me, and this wasn't going to happen again. Not if I could help it.

But I could stir things up a little.

I called Rondine.

I said, "It's Tiger, doll."

Her breathing was audible in my ear.

"First the others, then you," was all I said. I heard her sob before I put the phone on the hook.

Rain again. I walked in it and watched it wash the streets down with the angular fury of the small storm that seemed to hover above the city. I walked past the row of newly renovated buildings and spotted the apartment that belonged to Alexis Minner. And company.

Funny, how birds always looked for a common nesting place. Dell's tip put Vidor Churis in the same neighborhood, a hodge-podge of nationalities where an accent or conversation in a foreign tongue wouldn't be out of place at all. The area was peopled by those of queer habits and odd customs and by nature wouldn't be looking for spots on someone else's back. It was an end of New York where privacy meant being lost in a crowd and you could be drinking buddies with your neighbor at a bar five blocks away and never find out he lived next door to you until you walked home with him one night.

There would have to be some liaison between the Embassy and the operatives and what better place than the apartment of a supposedly minor clerk who was, in actuality, a director and executor of kill operations taking orders from the big boss, Stovetsky.

It wasn't Moscow. It was New York. It wasn't a dictatorship, it was a democracy and they could move without being harassed by secret police and tapped phones. They worked in an atmosphere of trust and respectability and stuck our noses in it, utilizing every advantage our country was sucker enough to give them.

Crime? Hell. Our diplomats walked on tippy toes for fear of making a single bad move. Oh, don't offend anybody . . . let them get away with murder, park their cars by hydrants, make our government a joke all the way down into Mau-Mau territory, needle the nithead countries until they tear our flag down in student uprisings and shoot up our nationals, snipe at our military . . . and then don't slap them down, don't even bitch about . . . instead, try to remove the intelligence officers who gave the command to shoot if shot at and protect our interests. Make it appear that we were to blame because this country was rich and smart and powerful and everyone else downtrodden because of it.

Brother, what would the militiamen who fought at Concord or the pioneers who cleared the land of hostile Indians say to that! John Paul Jones had a damn good answer to that one . . . so did the commander at the ridge of Bunker Hill.

We made it the hard way and now the clunkers wanted to take it away and the eggheads were willing to give it to them. But there were some of us who weren't going to let it go. There are ways of doing things and if there had to be a modern-day tea party we could do that too. If we had to stand in line abreast and challenge officialdom, red tape and radical thinking, it would be done.

They'd never expect it. They knew the usual pattern of things, the way the compromise would come or the total backdown when the propaganda pressure went on. But let them know there was more to us than what they thought and some revisions would be made. Fast. Nobody liked to die at all.

Who was it that had called it the *day of the guns?* It was back again. You can't win with scared diplomacy, but a bullet on the way to somebody's gut doesn't know any fear at all and moves too fast to be stopped. It has a power all its own of changing the shape of things instantly and instituting a propaganda factor that sticks in a person's mind all his life. They could stand up to words and would hold down a gun themselves, but what they did when the big hole in the end was pointed at them and they saw the hammer go back was a different story entirely and if ever there was a moment of truth it was then, and not in a bull ring.

I called Wally Gibbons from a drugstore and finally got him at his office. He was excited, but kept his voice down. "Where the hell are you, Tiger?"

"Why?"

"Buddy, you have everybody on your neck. You know they've bugged me three times in the last two hours trying to make a contact?"

"Who are 'they'?"

"Come on, I can read between the lines. They don't show badges but I know who they are. I've seen them work before. You're hot, feller."

"Tell them anything you want to."

"Like what? I'm only a Broadway columnist, remember? Only there are other types on this paper and when Ted Huston who handles the political end saw those guys up here he leaned on me for my bit in it. Something big is rattling our guys and theirs and they're in a huddle like never before. The Russians have been at a top-level meeting all day and the British and Americans have decided to scrap their differences and hit this thing together. Now on top of all this scrambling going on they take time out to look for my old friend, Tiger Mann."

"Nice of them," I said.

"Give me the pitch, will you? If I have to do a cover-up, the least I can have is a track on the business."

"I told you you'd get it all, Wally. We're almost there so don't put anything out until I call it in."

"Sure . . . thanks . . . you're a great help. Not even a human-interest line except for Burton Selwick."

"Now what?"

"Oh, staunch British devotion to duty. He's up out of a sick bed calling the signals at the joint meeting. Vincent Harley Case is doing all his leg work for him, but Selwick's on the mound. Next week is going to be a turning point in international politics."

"Great. Maybe they'll cut taxes."

"Look, Tiger . . . I'll be here all night. If you feel like talking, give me a call. I got a creepy feeling you're some kind of a time bomb ready to go off."

I laughed at him, said so long and hung up. Without knowing it Wally had tossed the dice for me and came up with a point. Now I had to make it the hard way.

And it was time.

The windows in Alexis Minner's apartment were dark and if they were in a tight huddle I'd have an opportunity to get inside. This time I didn't cruise past the building for a final look. I just turned in the doorway, used the stairs to get to his floor and went to the door. I rang twice, got no answer and took out the set of keys Ernie Bentley had made up. The second one fit, opened it and I walked inside.

As I did I felt the slightest wispy touch of something across my cheek and swore at myself for being so damn careless. Minner had put a check on his door someplace.

I found the thread with the pencil flash on the floor. It was about two inches long, black and as fine as a hair. He would have rigged it from the outside, a trick that could only be done as you closed the door from the hallway, and without it in place he'd know either someone was inside or the place had been broken into.

It wasted a full half-hour, but I managed to get the thread back where I imagined it would have been and hoped he wouldn't look too carefully if he got back unexpectedly. If there was any edge of surprise, I wanted it myself.

When I closed the blinds over the window I flicked on the light switch, saw that it turned on a single globe in the small alcove, then rigged the bulb with some tinfoil so that when it went on again it would burn out in a normal fashion after a second or so. That set, I opened the blinds and used the flash to get the furniture located and feel my way around.

The apartment was an expensive place and had been tastefully decorated. Apparently Alexis Minner wasn't concerned about bourgeois décor. There were cigarette burns on every piece of furniture, butts in flower pots, candy dishes and a few ground into the rug. Two vodka bottles and one of Scotch were on the table and some more dirty glasses along with the remains of a sausage.

At one side there were adjoining bedrooms with twin beds in each. Although they were made up, the cigarette burns on each side of the night table between them said all had been occupied and might well still be. Even though one guy rented the apartment, he could have visitors as he pleased and with just the single superintendent and neighbors who liked their privacy, it would be simple enough for them to come and go as they pleased without causing any comment.

Before going through the dresser drawers I looked for any thread checks like he had on the door and didn't find any. There wasn't much of anything else, either. The occupants might stay here a long while, but they were ready for a quick move out at any time. There weren't enough clothes to take up two suitcases.

The bathroom was the cleanest room in the place. Maybe they never used it. There was dust in the shower stall and tub. A glass on the sink held tiny pieces of soap and I could remember them doing that in Europe during the war years. Some things had a stubborn pattern that couldn't be wiped out, like trying to get too many shaves out of a blade.

Nobody had bothered to clean up the kitchen. The bottles and glasses were still there and a couple of flies had dropped into one and died there. The closets on the wall held a miscellaneous assortment of canned foods and spices, more like emergency stuff than a steady diet. The last one you could smell before you opened it because there were a half-dozen smoked sausages hung from the cup hooks on top.

I grimaced, started to close it and saw the corner of the box on the shelf. It was of heavy cardboard, about eight inches square and pieces of tissue packing were sticking out of the fold-in top. I flipped it open, separated the tissue and saw the bottles inside that reflected pale blue back into the light of the pencil flash.

Very gently I eased the cap off and smelled the contents, then tasted it to make sure. *Sodium pentothal*. Interesting. There were ways of using the stuff to get things out of a person the easy way. Two of the other bottles were clear glass and didn't take any tasting to determine the contents. One was prussic acid and the other strychnine.

This bunch was ready for anything and it wasn't subtlety.

I put everything back the way I had found it and closed the closet door. Legally, anyone could own the stuff so there wasn't any great necessity of hiding it. Especially if you had diplomatic immunity and never expected a search of the premises.

Which led to some curious speculation.

I began to poke around some more.

With what little clothes they had it was improbable that they'd use the washer-dryer combination that was set in the niche in the wall. I started on the washer and went through it first, but it was the dryer that paid off. I had no definite idea of what I hoped to find, but thought it would be guns.

It wasn't.

It was a packet of brand-new thousand-dollar bills wrapped in wax paper and stuffed in the area just forward of the heating unit. If anyone had ever turned the machine on, forty-one grand would have gone up in smoke. I slipped out three of them, repacked the rest and put them back where I found them.

Let me be right in what I was thinking and there were going to be a few people declared *persona non grata* tomorrow.

But that day might be a long way off.

I heard a key go into the lock on the front door and the murmur of voices, a satisfied grunt and some low-key laughter. I said, "Damn!" to myself, ripped the .45 out and got behind the kitchen door. There were at least three of them there and they'd be pros, so what had to be done had to be done fast.

Someone flipped the light on and it glowed for no more than a second. It went out in a bluish flare with a soft popping noise and in that brief interval I saw one thing that brought back a minute from a few days ago. The one in front was wearing a funny velour hat with a feather in the band and the last time I saw him he had been directing the bit when the others shot up the pillows in my bed and I was on a ledge outside, forty floors above the street.

There was one other thing, too. The second guy had his right hand in a bandage and there was a trace of crimson seeping through the gauze. I had them locked in tight now and there was no doubt about it. These three were part of a kill team and the one with the bad mitt could be the guy I nailed in the corridor of the hotel.

One thing I *was* sure of. None of them was Vidor Churis and none had what could be described as having a round mouth. Two more were someplace else and I wanted them too.

With a thick-tongued accent one said, "Burned out. I'll get the lamp, Alexis."

I came around the door the same instant the light switched on and the one in the velour hat screamed out, "Nyet!" and I knew the odds had changed. The guy had been around too much and had probably pulled the same stunt before and he was in a dive going for a gun as I lined up on him.

The other two needed only that one hoarse shout to move and they were down and furniture was in the way and all I could do was pitch off to one side and go for the floor. The first shots from Minner's gun blasted into the woodwork where I had been and smashed back into the kitchen.

Something flew through the air, hit the lamp and knocked it over in a shower of glass and a flash of yellow and the room was blacker than before because my eyes were not accommodated to the darkness.

The only advantage I had was that it had happened to them too and with three of them scattered around they couldn't risk random shots without risking their own necks. The blast of the gun still reverberated in everyone's ears and before it could fade and let the small noises back I skittered ten feet closer to the wall where the one was with the bandaged hand and I could hear him breathing only a little distance away from me.

I eased off my shoes, threw one across the room and it hit and bounced against a chair. Nobody fell for it. I couldn't wait. I couldn't give them time to let their eyes and ears get adjusted to the darkness. Any move I made had to be quick while they were on edge and not thinking. They couldn't be sure I was alone, but it wouldn't take long for them to realize how the situation stood.

The only thing that annoyed me was that I couldn't see their faces without exposing my position and I didn't want to take a chance of getting myself knocked off when the odds were in their favor. But one had a funny velour hat on with a feather in the band and if I saw that again I'd recognize it.

My hands felt the legs of the table and a heavy chair to the side. I tried to remember how the furniture was placed, recalled the details and began to edge around the chair. It couldn't have taken longer than a minute, but time seemed to drag on and on as I inched along.

The first thing I saw was a small luminous glow and knew it was the watch on the guy's left wrist. The job was going to take both hands, so I shoved the .45 in my waistband where I could get at it quickly and got ready. I took my time about how I was going to do it, located the approximate position of his head and neck, gathered myself and made the final jump of three feet. I landed on his back with my fingers tearing through the skin at his throat and felt his windpipe crack and burst as I forced his head back.

Even then, seconds before he died, he was able to drum his feet against the floor, just once, but it was enough. That reflex action of dying agony spelled it out for the others and I knew what was coming. I rolled fast, pulling the guy on top of me when the shots blazed out from across the room. Four of the slugs thudded sickeningly into the guy and made him jerk against my stomach. One came right through him and slammed into my hip like a fist but I knew it was spent and never penetrated.

Then the noise was over and only the smell of cordite and blood was left. I felt for the .45. My hands never found it. Sometime during the struggle it had come out of my belt and was on the floor.

I used the body as a shield and pushed forward behind the sofa, feeling to see if there was a gun someplace. Either the guy hadn't felt up to carrying one because of his hand or he didn't have one on him. So the odds stayed down.

One shot winked out of the corner and there was the sound of hands and feet scrambling along the floor to duck a return bullet. I had maybe ten seconds before they knew what I was doing, so I rolled on my back, doubled up my knees with my feet against the body of the dead man and gave the body a shove that sent it rolling into the furniture.

I was running after the first roll of the guns. I could hear the bullets slapping into dead meat and the guy I hit never knew he was dying until he was dead. I snapped his neck, then his back while Alexis Minner was still throwing bullets into a corpse across the room and had his gun in my hand and the target in my sights.

The slob ran out of ammo with a laugh thinking he had nailed me and said, "Gorge . . ."

I said, "Don't reload, pal. You're in the sights and I have you lined up."

For one horrible instant he stopped breathing and I knew how he was feeling. His guts were inside out and his brain going a mile a minute to fathom the situation. There was a lamp on the table beside me and I reached up and snapped it on.

Alexis Minner was face down on the floor, one hand in a pocket going after another clip for his gun and his head was turned toward me with eyes showing white all around the irises and nostrils flared to the fullest with the wildest kind of fear imaginable.

Before I could talk he said hoarsely, "I am a diplomat. I have immunity. This is my house."

"But I have the gun."

For some reason, he started to smile. His nerves were geared tight and the fear came out in a smile. "This will mean . . . trouble for you."

"Sure."

"There will be police."

Two dead men, one to either side of me. They weren't killed by my bullets. They died under my hands, one with his own bullets in him, but they were dead and we both were pros and now he was trying to snake out from under.

"I'll give the cops maybe five minutes, Alexis."

This time he pulled his hand out of his pocket deliberately, wanting me to see that it was empty.

"It will be too late," I said.

Now his eyes were half-closed, his tongue flicking in and out, trying to hide what he felt inside.

"Who's on the inside, buddy?"

"What is that?"

"Don't stall, you bastard. You haven't got that much time left. Who's on the inside?"

"I . . . do not know what you mean."

"Die silent then."

He tried the old dodge, the indignant bit. He half raised himself to look at me squarely. "I come here as a diplomat attached to the Embassy. You have . . . invaded my privacy." He glanced toward the pair of bodies. "You have done this . . . you. The police will see that you . . ."

"Know who I am?" I asked him. I walked over and stood there with his friend's Tokarev in my fist.

"I am a diplomat and . . ."

"Know who I am?" I repeated. "I killed some of your friends. You have me on your 'A' list and if you keep a copy of your BTO-5's around you know my category."

"Mr. Mann . . ."

Now he knew my name well enough. He was scared and could try to play it out. But all the while he was thinking and when old-time pros start thinking you start to watch out.

I said, "You paid out some of those new grand notes you have hidden in the machine in the kitchen to somebody else who hired a contract killer. Who, Alexis?"

His eyes made an appealing gesture and I knew he was playing it for time. Somebody would have heard the shots and the report was in by now. In half a minute a squad car would come screaming around the corner. But Alexis was well brainwashed. Well trained. He could be scared, but he wasn't going to talk, and that type you don't waste time on.

I grinned at him, let him see all the choppers in a fat smile, leveled the gun and when he tried to make the one last move toward his pants leg, shot him squarely between the horns. The whole back of his head came off and splashed up against the wall.

There was one thing I had to be sure of. I took the two Tokarev 7.65's, ran to the bathroom and fired a shot from each into the five gallons of water in the toilet reservoir. Each bullet spun out dead before it reached the bottom . . . I got them out and dropped them in my pocket, then went back to the living room.

I found my .45 where it had fallen and for the first time felt lucky. I could make this deal stick all the way with a little fast talk and ballistics would prove me out if there were any cooperation at all.

I wiped the guns first, then got them back in the hands of the ones who had owned them, making sure prints were all over them, then took two minutes to go around the room and wipe out any prints I had left when I touched the furniture. Not everything will hold a print and I don't make stupid mistakes in handling things that did without gloves, so I wasn't worried about the rest of the place.

Somewhere outside a siren was whining and I knew it

was time to go. Another joined it, so I ran to the kitchen, opened the window, closed it after I was on the fire escape and got down to the courtyard below. From there it was easy to hop the fence, go out through the areaway between the buildings and start walking toward the band of street lights and then north six blocks where I flagged a cab down and told him to drive me to Charlie Corbinet's house. After I settled back I checked my watch and the whole damn business couldn't have taken more than a few minutes. Three dead men in a few minutes.

Good score, Tiger. Your playing is up to par.

Chapter 13

If Ernie Bentley had more at home than he could take care of, he was showing it pretty well. He was still in the lab playing with miniature explosive charges when I walked in, and though the entry looked casual and easy, I knew I had been checked out on a closed-circuit TV downstairs and if I hadn't been right, I would have been dead.

I said, "Hi, lover."

Ernie never bothered to look up. "Now what."

"You have microphotos of the bullets from Toomey?"

"What's this, amateur night?"

"So?"

"Certainly. You want to see the slides?"

I tossed the two slugs down beside him. "Make a comparison test."

"Now?"

"Right now."

He snapped a light off, threw a couple of switches and picked up the slugs. While he was busy running the photos I walked to the window and looked down at New York in the shadows below.

It wasn't like being uptown. Here it was quiet and mean and dark, with all the latent streaks of hatred and animosity that go to build a city. Down there people were thinking and planning, and according to statistics, somebody would die violently within four blocks of this place tonight.

Hell, I could tell them where three of them were already if the police hadn't found them yet.

Ernie processed the slides as quickly as he could, set them in the machine and projected them on a screen. The left one killed Toomey. Its nose was blunted and there was a twist to the conical shape, but each land and leed had left an indelible groove on the metal.

The first one didn't measure up, but the second one did. It came from Alexis Minner's gun and now, even in death, he didn't have to worry about diplomatic immunity. He was on a meathook nobody could get off and there he had to hang. Those fat-faced Russian slobs wouldn't even dare try a push after what we had and what I had set up. Before the Washington agencies or I.A.T.S. could get on it New York's Finest would have it photographed, fingerprinted and processed and no matter how hard the District pushed for jurisdiction, the locals wouldn't let it out of their laps. It had better be good or it was no go no matter what.

This time it was pretty good.

So Minner killed Toomey . . . his other gun hands were on record, and in a fit of remorse, or a fight over the money they had to find, three guys had gone down. Maybe some bright boy would tie up the angles and figure me into it, but here, at least, I.A.T.S. kept quiet and Martin Grady's loot paid off excuses. Hell, maybe patriotism would even come into the picture.

But it wasn't the end yet. The noose wasn't tight enough.

Ernie said, "Use the goof balls yet?"

"Saving them for an emergency."

"Look, I found something out. They're good for about forty-eight hours. For some reason the instability becomes acute after that and you don't need heat or impact to set them off. The shells are too thin and there is an evaporation factor involved. Give yourself about twelve hours to be on the safe side and drop them down a toilet somewhere."

"What happens then?"

"They dissolve. No trouble."

"How long did you have them before you handed them over?"

"I'm getting old," Ernie said, "or maybe I just hate you

field men. Limit it down. I just cut six hours off their expiration date. If I were you I'd make sure they were either used or destroyed before . . ." he looked at his watch . . . "two A.M. Monday morning. Of course, if you want to be part of a grand experiment. . . ."

"Drop dead," I said.

He went back to his microscope and peered down the lenses. "I have a radio tuned to police frequencies," he mentioned.

"Good for you."

"They got to the house."

"How about that."

"Think you ought to write a report before you leave? You may not have another chance."

"Faith. Nothing like it."

Ernie shrugged his shoulders elaborately and looked up from his microscope. "Tiger . . . I'm an inside type. You field men scare hell out of me. I know what you do and help do it, but you wouldn't catch me dead with a gun in my hand or any of the tools I dream up. Sometimes I sit here and wonder what goes on outside there and when I think about it long enough I get the cold shakes because I know I'm a part of it. I'm in this for money and nobody has enough to pay me for what I do or what I think except Martin Grady. But when those times come when my conscience starts working on my mind I try to figure out just where I stand. I look at you field men with your goddamn bullet scars and that wild, cold look in your eyes and know you can kill without a thought and man, I get scared. Am I a man or a bug?"

I took a long time before I spoke. "You're a man, buddy."

"Thanks. Sometimes I wonder."

"Play your part. You're important. Some things we can do alone. Some things we can't. At least you go home at night to a wife and lie in bed safe and sound and it isn't a bad thing to know you have. Try sweating out one day alone in a mud hut with a native whore so you can get one tiny piece of information or eat chicken heads and snakes to get inside a ritual and nail down a name that belongs to a guy you have to disembowel because he swallowed a piece of paper with an address or phone number written on it. Think of how it is to spray a compound full of people who have archaic weapons wanting to fill your hide with poison darts and watch them fall when even they know they're out of range, but to stay alive you pump all those bodies full of .45 slugs or Schamuser bullets or occasionally lob a grenade through an open window and watch chunks of arms and legs sail out of the wreckage. Buddy, you're lucky. You don't know how lucky. Stay with your chemicals, but when you start thinking, feel what we have to think when the possibilities are that you can be eaten alive by ants or tossed into a sinkhole with a weight tied to your feet and know you're dead, real dead in a few seconds and there's no way out."

Ernie's smile was pathetic. He'd like to try it, but he didn't dare. He had a wife at home. "Why don't you get married?" he asked me.

"Who the hell would have me?"

"A woman."

"There are only girls and broads left."

"I hear one time you loved a woman."

"If you're really hungry I'll make you eat that goddamn microscope," I said.

His eyes went up and down me and at last he got the answer. I could see it go through his analytical mind and come up with the tape all neatly punched and classified. "I'll stay where I am," he said. Then he added, "Why don't you find a broad and get married?"

"Shut up, Ernie."

"No . . . no kidding. I heard about you and somebody a long time ago. What happened?"

"I said, shut up." My voice felt like a rasp in my throat.

"Psycho?" Ernie asked gently.

I turned around, looked at him and smiled. "I've killed friends too, Ernie, so lay off me."

"No, I won't. You got an itch for a broad. What happened?"

"Nothing happened yet."

"But it will? You're in love, sucker."

"She tried to kill me," I said.

"Kill her then. What do you have left?"

"I never had anything to start with. I died a long time ago. Now lay off me."

"I can't. We're in the same racket. I need you and you need me. You got a problem . . . oh hell, I know all about it, Tiger. You had one and you found her again. What now?"

I grinned, my mouth tight and my eyes pulled down into little slits. "Dead," I said. "She died."

"Happy landings," he told me and went back to his microscope.

I hopped a cab up to Charlie Corbinet's apartment, called him from the lobby to make sure he was alone, then went up. It was a small place, almost military in appearance. It functioned as a second office to him with filing cabinets, a large working desk and a rack full of handguns and rifles on the wall.

"Coffee, Tiger?"

"A quick one."

He poured out two, sat down casually and said, "I just had a call. There has been a triple killing downtown. One happened to be attached to the Russian delegation."

"How about that."

"Yes, Tiger, how about that? Care to offer an explanation?"

"No."

He picked up the coffee cup and looked into it, thought a moment then sipped it. "At this moment the police are a little baffled. The bullets from one gun killed a man named Toomey. They found a good deal of money in the place so the shooting could have been over that."

"It wasn't."

"I didn't think so. Now, what's the visit about?"

I pulled out the three thousand-dollar bills I had taken from Minner's cache and laid them down in front of the Colonel. "Run a check on these serial numbers. See if they are from the same batch as the other one I gave you."

He fingered the bills, frowned and reached for the phone. He had to go through two other numbers and a fifteen-minute wait before he had his party, then the conversation was brief. He read off the numbers, nodded, said something I didn't get, then put the phone back.

"You hit it, Tiger."

"Okay, so that dough was earmarked for the rough stuff. Alexis Minner arranged for that contract kill through somebody else and this is the money that was used in the pay-off. The Reds may start to sound off loud about this but when you slap it down in front of them they'll cut and run like dogs. My suggestion is to let the papers have it . . . spread it all over the front pages."

"You know better than that. This is still an age of diplomacy," he said.

"Balls. It's about time the public was wised up to what these slobs are pulling. They come over here acting like they own us, get privileged enough to commit murder without too much fear of reprisal and then bitch when they're caught at it. Now I want you to understand something, Colonel . . . I'm not tied to any stupid rules of diplomatic protocol and convention. I don't give one hoot in hell what the eggheads in Washington think. I've been there when they've loused up the situations so badly we had to slink off with our tails between our legs. Nobody's going to stop me from doing what I want to do. Either I.A.T.S. or some other agency can make this thing public, or I will. I have a guy standing by who will go down the line on it and if it has to come out that way a lot of the college boys in striped pants will be reaching for their hats."

"You're asking for it, you know."

"Screw it, Colonel. I'm the one who's a target. They don't put me up there without realizing the consequences. They got what they wanted . . . almost. There's a little more left to do and it won't take long. There's still time enough to round the story out and polish it off to suit propaganda needs if they want to play it that way. I'll give them one day to get ready, no more."

"It's incidents like this that can cause a war," he reminded me.

I finished the coffee and put the cup on the table. "You got it wrong. They can't afford a blowup. They aren't that tough. We may seem like we can be pushed easily, but they know that when the chips are down we can wipe them out and nothing will stop us. If we can't be pushed they'll back down until they can control things again, but right now we have the ball and it's about time we ran it a little."

"Very well. I'll submit the suggestion. If they don't agree, I'll remind them of the alternative. You know the possibilities, don't you?"

"Sure, so let them try spotting me like they did Vance in L.A. When our own kind play it rough with us we let out all the stops. Martin Grady will have them screaming through their ears again."

"I hope you know what you're doing."

"I've been around, Colonel."

"And where do you go from here?"

"To find Vidor Churis."

"The same way you found the others?" A hard smile worked at the corners of his mouth.

"Maybe."

I sat back and looked at him without really seeing him at all. There was a sharp turn in the picture somewhere and it had been pulling at my mind all night. It was one of those little things that is there without being seen you know can be the crux of the whole affair.

What?

Someplace I had picked up the key then laid it down again without realizing it.

Corbinet said, "Got it yet?" He knew what I was thinking.

I shook my head. "It'll come. Maybe it doesn't mean anything, maybe it does. If one thing doesn't show up something else will."

"Don't go playing hunches. You can die that way."

"You can die either way, Colonel." I got up and put on my hat. "Thanks for the coffee."

"My pleasure. I'll see what they want to do with this angle of attack." He flapped the three bills against his fingers. "They may want a statement from you."

"No doubt. It will make nice reading in the papers."

"In view of the situation Hal Randolph may want to handle it differently. It can be done if it is warranted. In either case you are still on the spot, Tiger. Our Russian friends won't take this lying down."

"I'm on their 'A' list now," I grinned, "but there's a difference this time."

"What's that?"

"They're on mine," I told him.

The ticket window of the *Grenoble Theater* was just opening as I arrived. A half-dozen people were in line, a couple with kids, and I waited until they had gone inside before I shoved my money through the slit. The woman there passed back the ticket and the change without ever looking up, then went back to her evening paper as I walked away.

I took the same seat I had before and sat there with the .45 in my lap under my raincoat and waited. There was no sign of Vidor Churis or his round-mouthed friend. I did the same thing for the second show with the same result, then filed out with the rest.

If Churis was going to make the show he had one more day to do it in otherwise I'd lose a possible contact for three weeks. The previews of coming attractions all were of different language films for that period of time. The only other chance was that Newark Control could come up with another lead and to check it out I called them.

Negative.

I tried Dell on his private line and got the same thing, but he said he would put the word out to expedite matters if possible, then suggested that I take in the special show that night. Something new from Paris, France. If the lady was broad-minded she would enjoy it too.

Saturday night. The loneliest night in the week.

So I called the lady to see if she was broad-minded enough and Gretchen said, "Tiger Mann, I have never, repeat . . . never, seen anyone who was so offhanded about asking for a date."

"It's not that late."

"Do you know it's after eleven?"

"I'm a night people."

"What have you been doing?"

"Causing trouble. Now I'm tired. I'd like to see you. Dell has a new act coming into the *Hall of the Two Sisters* we can catch if you shake it up. That is, if you can take it. His shows get pretty rough."

She laughed, a pretty sound, full of life. "You talked me into it, Tiger. Will you come to get me?"

"Grab a cab and meet me there. It'll be quicker."

"Okay, lover boy. But there are times when I'd like to belt you one."

It took me ten minutes to get to the *Hall* and Dell was there to meet me. I told him my broad-minded girl would be along shortly and to bring her to the booth. When he had relayed the word to his other doorman he led the way up the steps, down to the end and parted the curtains for me.

I told the Arab waiter to bring a pair of drinks and pointed to the table. "Join me for one, Dell."

"Certainly, Tiger. We do not often get a chance to drink together, no?"

"Any news?"

"As I said, it is difficult. The man you want is . . . elusive. I have dealt with these types before as have you. They don't frequent public places, preferring to stay in their holes until they are needed."

"You seem to have the guy pinned down pretty well," I said.

Dell gave me his usual generous shrug. "It is that I know you better, Tiger. The ones you want are generally of the same sort. They have nearly identical habits. Something in their mind makes them do it."

"They have to come out once in a while."

"Yes," he said, "it is so. There are necessities and peculiarities that make them reveal themselves eventually. I have posted my people and if the one with the stiff finger or the round mouth shows himself, you will know about it immediately." He raised his drink in a silent toast and finished it.

The waiter came in then, swept the curtains aside and

Gretchen Lark stood there, a fitted white trench coat hugging the beautiful curves of her body like a glove. We both stood up and Dell nodded approvingly.

"Ah," he said, "now you can be alone. The show will start shortly."

"Come on in, kitten."

She smiled, unbuckled the coat and tossed it over the back of the chair. The black sheath she had on had an open throat that cut down in a generous V, exposing the cleft of her breasts in a daring sweep you couldn't take your eyes off.

"You look sexy," I said.

"I'm supposed to."

I signaled the waiter for two more drinks and lit her cigarette for her. Across the flame her eyes became serious. "I've been worried about you."

"Why?"

"Because the last time . . ." she didn't finish.

"I'm still here."

"Did you . . . do what you had to do?"

"Somewhat."

Gretchen exhaled a thin stream of smoke, watching me intently. "Tiger . . . I hope it can always be like this for us. I . . . don't know what these things are you do . . . I think I prefer not to know. But please be careful."

"Relax."

She reached over and took my hand. Her fingers were long and cool and there was a bluish pigment stain on the side of her palm she couldn't get off.

"How is the picture coming?"

"One more sitting will finish it, but who knows when Mr. Selwick will be back? This will be a busy week-end for him."

"He ought to be glad to take a break with you."

She smiled and her teeth showed even and startlingly white. "He is. He's a dear, you know. Whenever he isn't feeling well he'll tell me he's ready for another sitting." She giggled then. "It's a wonder the painting doesn't show him with a pill in his mouth."

"Take that crazy smock off and he'll get a better expression."

"I don't think his wife would appreciate it. She's pretty starchy from what he tells me. Anyway, he just likes to sit there and think. Nobody bothers him, no phones ring and he makes a fine subject. Sometimes he just sleeps." She squeezed my hand. "When am I going to paint you?"

"Nude?" I laughed.

"Naturally."

"That'll be the day," I said.

From the orchestra came a weird chord of sound. The lights dimmed around the room and a tinted spot hit the floor. The dancers moved into it slowly, suggestively, preparing the audience for what was to come.

A Japanese team joined them, were followed by four Hawaiians who put more vibrancy in the hula than I had ever seen before. Then Dell's big act came in with a muted roll of drums.

There was no music, just the steady tempo of the drums. The pair that strutted in dressed in the ordinary stage attire of the Parisian *apache* dancers, peak cap, rough jacket and red pants on one, a black slitted satin skirt and loose scarlet blouse on the other, was the tallest couple I had ever seen. Both were well over six feet four, both wearing smiles of the oddest nature I had ever seen.

The beginning of the act was almost commonplace and Gretchen said, "I thought this was supposed to be something special."

"I don't know the gimmick," I told her, "but it will be. Watch."

Bit by bit the tempo increased and the pair went through the classical motions of the act. Then they began to improvise. As the woman struggled with the man in the mock dance-fight, things began happening to their clothes. It almost began to look as if it were real and had they not kept such close rapport with the music it would have been believable.

Again, it was those at the tables below who attested to what the act was designed for. I could see them, tense and drawn, unable to look away even to touch their drinks.

The two dancers came at each other, hands grabbing and clawing. The girl was nearly naked, fighting her partner off, and as he stripped away the last shred of cloth from her body she grabbed his shirt, tore it, took him to the floor and in the melee of the struggle, to the rising sound of the drums, he lost everything he had on.

And then the specialty of the act was plain for all to see.

They were both women.

They were both contortionists.

I picked up my drink and watched Gretchen. Her face was livid and a small pulse beat showed near her temple. When Dell came through the curtain, motioned to me with his finger to follow, she hardly noticed him.

At the corner of the balcony out of sight from any of the

others he leaned toward my ear and said, "One of my people has seen your man."

"Which one?"

He held out a rigid forefinger. "He was first seen in a delicatessen store, then followed to a theater."

"The *Grenoble?*"

Dell nodded soberly. "You have a good system of your own too, no?"

"Everything helps."

"Indeed. He inquired of the attendant who was closing the theater if the picture would play tomorrow."

Good boy, Churis. Nostalgia will kill you yet.

"He get an address?"

"Unfortunately, no. My . . . man . . . has a slight allergy for police and there was one standing on the corner. You see . . . he is wanted for something or other. He was forced to give up tailing him."

"That places him in two general areas, but both close enough to be related. He's not shopping in any one store apparently."

"It's still in the Village?"

"Looks that way."

"Tomorrow is your day, Tiger?"

"All the way."

I thanked him and went back to the booth. On the floor the dance had come to a torrid end that was unbelievable and the audience was sitting in shocked silence, but making no move to avoid the scene. They were enjoying every lascivious moment of it and when the lights darkened momentarily, to light up again and show the floor empty, you could hear the slow letting out of breaths long held in.

Gretchen had a look of guilt not quite concealed by the nervous smile she gave me. "That was terrible!" she said.

"I told you it would be rough."

"But did you see them?" She pointed to the tables on the floor. "The faces on those women . . ."

"You should have looked in the mirror yourself." I grinned.

"But . . . but they knew what to expect."

"It takes all kinds to make a world, kid. I've seen far worse in the capitals of some of the most cultured countries in Europe."

"And you get up and walk away from it!" She laughed behind her hand and said, "Did your friend offer us a room again?"

"It was better than that." Before I had to lie to her I said, "Ready to go?"

"Whenever you like."

"Let's go then. I'll drive you home."

"For a nightcap?"

"It's polite to wait till you're asked. No, no nightcap. Tonight I want sack time and a chance to think."

We told Dell good night and he called a cab for us. I gave Gretchen's address, flicked a match for her cigarette and watched how her mouth formed around the tube, tinting it with her lipstick.

"Pretty," I told her.

"Prettier than Edith Caine?" she teased.

"Different type."

"She's the jealous type. She doesn't like to show it, but women can tell."

"You mention I saw you?"

"Uh-huh. I call her every day anyway. I don't think she was pleased at all when I told her." She let out that silly laugh again. "Frankly, Tiger, I don't care. Do you mind?"

"I'm here, sugar."

She glanced at me sidewise. "Something always happens to your face when you speak about her."

"Does it?"

"Were you . . . ever in love with her?"

I leaned my head back and stared at the ceiling. "A long time ago. Twenty years."

"But . . ." I could feel the puzzled frown on her face and it wasn't something I wanted to talk about.

"Maybe someday I'll tell you about it."

The cab pulled to the curb and I told him to wait. I got out, helped Gretchen out and walked to the building with her. She turned, her lips moist and her eyes soft. "Thanks for the date, Tiger."

I kissed her easily, feeling her mouth tremble beneath mine, the restraint inside her. "I'll call you earlier the next time," I said.

She winked and went up the steps. When the inside door closed I started back to the cab and had one second to spot the car coming down the street. It was like a whistle going off in my head, a sudden premonition of what was going to happen and I threw myself to the side and hit the pavement behind a pair of ash cans as the first stacatto thunder from a tommy gun rolled out of the window.

The slugs tore into metal, spraying a cloud of dust in the air, ricocheting off the walls of the building behind me. One tugged at my coat and another careened off the sidewalk sending a shower of stone into my face. I couldn't move, couldn't go for my gun without losing the protection of the cans. The cabbie didn't wait for anything more. He jammed the cab in gear, pulled away from the curb with rubber burning behind him, slipped around the black sedan and raced for the intersection.

This time they wanted to make sure. The car screeched to a stop, the door opened and a guy cradling the tommy under his arm ran to where I was. He had his back to the others when I went for the .45, shielding me from anything they could throw. He didn't think I could have been alive and didn't have the gun up. My first shot hit the butt of the gun, slammed him halfway around with a hoarse yell of terror, the tommy sailing out of his hands.

I didn't have to hit him again. The others did it for me. I dropped behind the cans when they started pumping shots at me and some of them caught the guy in the back and pitched him head first against the curb with a sickening thud. Somebody yelled in the car, the door slammed shut and it took off down the street with a foot jammed hard on the accelerator. The police car that suddenly nosed around the corner to block off the exit almost caught it. The driver wrenched on the wheel to get around him and couldn't hold it. There was one awful moment when the sedan was on its two right wheels, then it went rolling across the intersection with glass and metal fragments spewing from the body and, with a ghastly explosion, burst into a billowing sheet of bright yellow flame that turned the night into day.

Both cops were at the pyre and the people pouring out of the buildings in odd pieces of clothing hurriedly thrown on were hurrying toward the wreck with morbid curiosity. Nobody paid any attention to me at all. Later the cabbie would make a report, but at least I had time to get out of there.

Thanks again, Rondine. You talk to Gretchen and know I see her on occasion. You plant your men where you know you'll have a definite contact sooner or later and wait it out. But you've slipped badly, baby. Time was when you'd do the job yourself. I sure must be a sword over your head. Each minute I'm getting closer and closer, and now you're running with your tongue hanging out. How will you feel now, doll? What will happen to your guts when you get the word that they didn't make the hit? What will be your next move?

Three blocks away, I flagged down a cab and went back to my hotel. I cleaned the .45, stowed it away, took a shower and laid down on the sack. Only then did I get a sudden, chilling thought. I had those damn pellets in my pockets all the time and in that fall I took behind the garbage cans I could have blown myself into little tiny pieces.

I picked up the phone, dialed Gretchen's number and, before it finished ringing the first time, she answered, her voice taut with fear. "Me, baby," I said.

"Oh, Tiger!" There was relief now and for a moment she couldn't talk. Then: "Right after I left you . . . I had just started upstairs . . ."

"I know. I was there."

"You . . . are all right, aren't you?"

"No trouble."

She seemed to be crying but not wanting me to know it. "They were after . . . you, weren't they?"

"It looks that way. Part of the business."

"Tiger . . ."

"Come off it, girl . . . it's the way I am and the way I'm going to stay. Quit worrying about me."

"I can't help it."

"So I'm okay. I just wanted to let you know. Now get some sleep."

I cut the connection so I wouldn't have to go into any explanations. The next number was Charlie Corbinet's. He answered with a sleepy hello, but came to fast when he knew it was me.

"They made another try, Colonel. You'd better check it out." I gave him the details and added, "My guess is they're all dead, but if you get make on them they'll be part of that contract bunch from Chicago. You'd better alert Randolph on this and have them keep it quiet. The usual story of a mob rub-out might do it. They killed one of their own men when he got in the line of fire so the slugs will match their guns."

"I'm afraid it will be more than that, Tiger. Randolph won't stand still for any more of this. He'll want to see you personally."

"Randolph can go jump, Charlie. He plays it my way. This thing is tied up with the international picture and if he doesn't want to blow the whole deal he'll go along. If you have to, go over his head. You'll get cooperation there if you need it."

"That's just what I might have to do."

"Good. Randolph swung a tail on Edith Caine. You hear anything about it yet?"

141

"Nothing there. She's been very quiet. All other leads petered out."

"When the stakes are high you have to play the cards close to your vest."

"Tiger . . ."

"What?"

"Monday the new proposition comes up in the U.N. There's no time left any more."

"There's enough," I said and hung up. I lay back in bed, switched the light off and stared into the darkness.

All I could see was Rondine's face.

And the rest of her.

We were back in the loft again and she was naked and beautiful and she loved me. I could feel the satin of her skin and the soft-hard curves of her body and smell the delicious warmth of her body and knew what the explosion of love was like.

Chapter 14

Rain tapping the window woke me up at seven. Outside it was another soggy, dull day, but it was Sunday and the streets were practically empty. It was like being in a ball park after the game was over, nothing left but the debris of cigarette and candy wrappers and a handful of lackadaisical keepers trying to clean up.

I shaved, went downstairs for breakfast, had the desk send up a typewriter then wrote out a report in triplicate, sealed it in an envelope and dropped it down the chute by the elevator. Martin Grady was going to have a lot of interesting reading. So was Wally Gibbons. So would the public. It was about time.

At noon I went down to the street to a pay phone and put in a call to Thomas Watford. There was a touch of anger in his voice and he told me that unless I turned myself into the office there would be trouble. Since the Minner affair they wanted me out of the way before there were any more complications.

I said, "How did the Soviets react?"

"It was they who hushed it up," he said laconically. "They

chose to announce that it was a personal disagreement between three former friends that led to the killing."

"And the city police?"

"They accepted it, of course, under our instructions. However, with the bullets from the gun and the money they found certain facts are evident and will be useful, but we are not going to allow anyone else to pursue this case."

"Meaning me?"

"Meaning you, Mr. Mann. I think it will be better if you are placed in custody in view of the situation last night. There is no need for unnecessary deaths."

"You wanted a target, buddy."

"Not any longer."

"Tough."

He waited a few seconds then said, "It might be well if I gave you a certain piece of information. Friday afternoon a congressional committee started proceedings against Martin Grady and those in his employ. He will be *subpoenaed* this week and his entire organization investigated."

I laughed at him. "They'll get their fingers burned, Watford. Martin Grady reaches into pretty high places. Sometimes he does it with money, other times with means that are slightly immoral but very necessary to get the edge he needs. Some of those congressmen can be leaving themselves wide open. I hope they have a private practice to retire to."

"The Congress of the United States is not to be intimidated."

"They're only men, buddy. If some are afraid to do things the right way, private individuals will do it for them. All Grady has to do is give them the true picture of a few instances and the lid will come down hard. But thanks for the warning anyway."

"You will be under indictment yourself, Mr. Mann."

"That won't be anything new either."

"It will keep you out of our hair."

"I'll make a deal with you."

"No deals."

"You have no choice," I told him. He didn't answer, but he was still listening. "Call off the dogs until tomorrow. If the air isn't cleared by then I'll be around. Well?"

He took his time, finally saying, "All right. Nothing can happen on a Sunday, I'm sure."

"I'm glad *you* are," I said.

I ducked out of the booth, got across the street to the diagonal corner and looked at my watch. It took the police car forty-five seconds to get there. Thomas Watford's methods of tracing a call could use some polishing up. Hell, I gave him enough time.

Wasting a rainy Sunday in the city wasn't easy. It took two double features in Times Square movie houses to bring me up to supper and then I had another hour before the *Grenoble Theater* opened. To kill off the minutes I walked there, running the pieces of the puzzle through my mind trying to get it to make sense.

War was like that. You stopped the other guy without having to know his schemes or intentions. You just stopped him and it ended right there. If you didn't, he took over and you'd find out what he wanted the hard way. So now we did it from back to front. Find a killer. Find Vidor Churis and you found who sent him. It wouldn't be hard to make him talk. I knew enough ways myself. It might take a little time, but that would just make him talk louder and faster. Find out how the Soviets arranged for the leak in our security. Kill Rondine and you stopped the leak. But you had to break up their organization to do it or they'd find another way.

At seven the ticket window opened and I bought the first pasteboard. One more time through the movie and I'd know all the dialog. I was even beginning to make sense out of it already.

I sat there in the semidarkness of the theater with my hand to my face trying to look bored. No more than twenty people came in before the lights dimmed and the picture started. None of them was him.

Had it not been for the slightly furtive manner of the guy I never would have spotted him, but the uneasy glance around he gave and the way he picked his seat was enough. He could have taken the one I had if I hadn't been there first. Instead, he took the back row on the opposite side, walked through the empty row to the side aisle and sat down. His hands were in his lap and I knew he wasn't taking any chances either.

There was one advantage going for me. If I had to take him in here he'd be engrossed in the picture. You could see the way he was settling down, nodding at the dialog, pleased with the action the way a kid would be at a cowboy show.

How's your hand, you pig? I thought.

My watch said almost eight. If I were going to move, it would have too be now. A fake trip to the men's room to see if he was covering himself with anyone else, take that one first, then get back to Churis. I wrapped my fingers around the butt of the .45 and thumbed the hammer back off half-cock.

Then the first move came from his side. Another man moved into the darkness of the corner, leaned over and spoke to Churis and I caught a glimpse of white as he passed something to him. He couldn't see it there, got up and went around the curtain to the lobby.

Damn!

I took the risk of being seen and lifted the heavy drapes behind my head. The two of them were standing there, Churis with his forefinger at a still, awkward angle as he held the note, the other guy facing him as though he was always saying "Oh!" His mouth was round, all right. There was the puckered scar tissue from a burn all around it and when he wasn't speaking he held it in that peculiar way that made him look as if he had a hole in his face.

When Churis finished the note he took a quick look around, struck a match and let the paper flare up until it reached his fingers, then dropped the pieces in a standing ash tray filled with sand, stirring up the charred bits into powder. He nodded for the other one to follow him and went out the front door.

I gave them ten seconds, no more. When I spotted them they were on the corner looking for a cab. I saw one coming, going the other way, crossed the street and flagged it down.

When I got in I pointed to the pair still on the corner and told the driver, "Go up a block and swing around. When those guys grab a taxi, follow it."

The driver looked at my face and gave me a grin. "Police business?"

"Damn right," I said.

"Think it'll be a chase?"

"No."

"Look, if those are the punks who have been pulling a stick-up on the cabbies I can have them locked in tight in five seconds."

"Never mind, I'll take care of it."

"Sure, officer. You want help you can use my radio. We're the only outfit that's got 'em," he said proudly.

"Just follow them."

He went ahead, made the turn and headed back as Churis and the other one were climbing in a cab. They headed downtown toward the Village with us a half-block behind, well screened by the traffic. The street they turned in was one of the ones due for demolition, a remnant of the original section, now a flat-faced mass of crumbling brownstone and wood of odd shapes and sizes.

Some of the top floors facing north had skylights built into them for the benefit of the artist bunch that seemed to find this place so fascinating and the air was filled with the smells of cooking kept down by the mantle of misty air that lay like a blanket over the city. Each streetlight was a yellow glow encased in haze, throwing no light at all. A yellow-haired guy with a sweater over his shoulders like a cape strutted by walking a collie, but, outside him, the street was deserted.

I got out on the corner, paid off the cab after spotting the building they went into and stood across the street waiting to see if any lights flashed on in the building. None did, so the chances were their apartment faced the back. There were three floors in the building, the cellar being closed with a padlock on the outside.

Two minutes went by.

I crossed over and went inside.

Kids were bawling on the first floor so that wouldn't be it. On the second floor the strong odor of garlic-charged spaghetti sauce seeped out under the door from the front apartment and the sounds of some kind of soirée from the back one.

That left one possible. The top rear apartment.

The lower stairs had creaked and groaned all the way up and I didn't want to announce myself to a funeral. I went back down, into the next building and ran up to the top floor. Somebody peered out the door on the second landing when they heard my feet, but went back inside after I passed him. When I reached the door that led to the roof I squeezed the handle, fought it until the latch gave and swung the door outward on rusty hinges.

At the rampart between the two buildings I swung my legs over, grabbed the tiles and let myself down as far as I could go and dropped the remaining two feet to the next level. I hit easily, but stood there anyway in case they heard the *thump*, the rod in my hand pointed at the kiosk door on the roof. They'd be dead if they came at me through there, not knowing where I stood.

Nothing happened so I started across the roof, trying to keep the gravel from crunching under my feet. I was almost at the door when I saw the pinpoint of light in the roof and made out a V-shaped skylight that had been painted black on the inside. I eased over, knelt down beside it and put my eye close to the one spot that a brush had missed.

They were there all right, talking rapidly in Russian, Vidor

Churis pacing the floor like a caged animal. He reached in his pocket, pulled out a flat automatic, checked it absently and put it back, only to glance at his watch. I looked at my own. It was almost eight-thirty.

A quiet Sunday night.

Right on the half-hour he picked up the phone and when he did I plastered my ear to the window to see if I could catch the clicks of the dial and read off the number he was calling. I couldn't get it all, but I got part of the conversation. It was in English, this time, garbled, but one word came out loud and clear.

Selwick.

He said something else I didn't get then I heard him hang up and went back to peering through the peephole. Once again the conversation switched languages and Churis was giving the other one instructions. He was reaching for his coat and the other was nodding until Churis was done talking, then he walked over to a chair, switched on the TV and Churis left.

I didn't bother about noise now. I ran to the door, grabbed the knob and the damn thing came off in my hand! I had to check myself to take it easy and fit it back on the square shaft that protruded through the door. When I did I had to stick the .45 back in the holster to use both hands to turn it. Long ago the door had warped and only opened a foot, but it could have been wide open without doing me any good. From the sill to the landing the stairs were piled high with boxes and the remains of broken baby carriages and there was no way of getting through the mess at all.

Downstairs an outside door slammed shut and I knew Vidor Churis was gone on an assignment. But the other one would know whom he called. I got back to the skylight, saw the guy still in front of the TV with the sound up loud, felt for the metal edge of the glass and hoped it wasn't locked.

This time I was lucky. It lifted. I set it in place, got a length of broom handle from the junk in the doorway and held it ready. I lifted the skylight, propped it and was through it before the guy in the chair heard me. He came up with a startled yell, stood there immobile as I hit the floor and fell, then made a dash for a table across the room and I knew he was going for a gun. He had it in his hand as I got the .45 out and when he spun around I shot him right through the middle and he folded over backward knocking the table and lamp sidewise in a heap.

Even then he tried to lift the gun, but couldn't do it.

He was dying with his intestines all churned to pieces and hanging out his back and he was still trying to kill me. I knelt down beside him and smelled the fetid odor of his breath mixing with the blood that was spilling onto the floor.

"Churis," I said. "Where did he go?"

All he did was hate me with his eyes, his mouth in that startled "O" shape, but white now and twisting with pain.

I put the .45 next to the other hole in his belly. "You won't die any quicker," I said, "But you'll hurt more."

He knew I would do it. He could read my eyes the way I could his and all the fear in his mind overflowed into one garbled, unfinished sentence. "Selwick . . . the girl . . ."

Then he died.

And I knew whom he had called.

Rondine. Edith Caine. If they couldn't play with Selwick any more they'd make sure he died before he figured out that he had been made a sucker.

I stood there in the middle of the room trying to sort out the possibles, my ears listening hard for the first sound of a siren. From downstairs came a burst of roaring laughter and everybody joining into a raucous party song. Here in the room the TV was going above normal. I let a couple of minutes pass and then I got it. The .45 made a big bang, but for once nobody heard it. Noise was the commonplace here and the other racket drowned it out.

The possibility then. On schedule, Churis called Rondine and was told Selwick could be induced to go to her place and Churis could take him there. How would they do it? Alexis had enough toxic goodies in his apartment to knock off a hundred people, but would have to be better than that.

No, Rondine knew the ropes. She'd be subtle about it. Some of the other things were lining up now. Like the sodium pentothal, truth serum. How easy it could be if Selwick did have to take an occasional needle for his illness. She could switch contents, put Selwick out and question him until she had the answers.

That was Rondine, all right.

Okay, cutie, here I come.

I went to the door, not the usual door, but a steel, fireproof affair double-locked with heavy Yales and a barrel bolt. Vidor Churis wasn't taking any chances on somebody busting in on him. He should have thought of doing more to the skylight than painting it black.

I eased out and let the door close behind me. The cops

would have a fine time breaking in to see what the stench was that was coming from behind it.

I called Burton Selwick's apartment from a drugstore and got the clipped voice of a servant on the other end. He said no, he was sorry, but Mr. Selwick had left a short time before. I identified myself as Dr. Lane attached to the American Embassy, saying that I had treated Mr. Selwick when he had his last attack and idly wondered if my British colleague had called earlier. He had wanted to check Mr. Selwick before he attended Monday's session. Both embassies were naturally concerned.

The servant said yes, Mr. Selwick left in response to a phone call from a woman without saying where he was going. Almost as a second thought I inquired if his employer had been taking the dosage by hypodermic as was prescribed. The man on the other end was quite certain since he had seen marks on his arms at various times.

When I put the phone back the picture was clear and bright. They had been getting Selwick under a needle and extracting the information from him. Now he'd be ready for another dosage and the next day's plans would be right out in the open.

Then exit Selwick in a convenient "accident."

I got a cab and reached Edith Caine's apartment at nine forty-five. The stake-outs had changed, but I spotted them and got inside and looked for the other. He hadn't changed. He was still watching the elevator cables from the floor below and I went past him on the stairway.

I leaned on the bell and waited, hearing her feet come across the floor. She opened the door, took a sudden sharp breath and bit her lower lip between her teeth. Her face was drawn with fear and something else, shadows underlining her eyes, her body tense. But even then she was beautiful, so damn beautiful that when I killed her I was going to be killing myself.

She had on a skirt and blouse, part of the suit combinations she had always liked so well, a wide leather belt at her waist. She always used to keep her rod there in a professional-type holster, but this time it was someplace else. *Too bad, honey*.

"It's here, Rondine. Time has run out," I said.

Rondine-Edith Caine held the door open so I could step inside. I did, but I pushed her ahead of me where I could see her. I'd never let her get behind me again. She looked at the gun in my hand, shook her head slowly and said nothing, simply walked straight into the living room and sat in the middle of the couch with her legs together and a sad expression on her face.

I checked each of the rooms quickly, never letting her out of my sight, then went back and sat across from her. "Tell me about it, Rondine."

"There's nothing to tell," she said simply.

"What happened to the real Edith Caine, honey? What did the dead Diana Caine do that you could hold it over the Caine family's heads? That's the interesting part of the story. What's going to happen when it comes out?"

There were real tears in her eyes now and she was going to play the part right down to the end. I would have liked it better had she reverted to her true character, the one with the gun who could shoot a guy who loved her.

"Please stop it, Tiger."

"Why? I like to see you suffer. It's paying off for all those twenty years I had to."

"Tiger . . . what are you going to do?"

"Kill you."

She bit into her lip again. "Just . . . like that."

"No, I'll wait for the other to come. You aren't the only one."

The act again. The expression like she didn't understand and the quick lowering of her head so I wouldn't see what she was thinking. When she straightened up she wiped her eyes and said, "May I go to the bathroom? I look . . . terrible, I know."

Ah, vanity. Even in the face of death they had to look pretty. But if she was looking for razor blades she'd have to get them out of my pocket where I dropped them before. "Sure, go ahead," I said.

She got up, went to the bathroom, closed the door and I heard the sound of water running in the basin. I sat there thinking of how I was going to do it when I knew what was happening and raced to the door. She opened it before I could put my shoulder to it and I said, "Damn you, Rondine," because she had won again. I had forgotten that she had an extension telephone in there beside the tub.

"Nice. You got a call through. So now they won't be here. Churis will take him someplace else."

"Tiger . . ." she said, a curious note in her voice.

"I could make you talk, Rondine, but there isn't any time. Your pain level is too high. You could hold out too long. I saw you do it when the *maquis* had you and I got you out. I could kill you here, but I might not make it out in time to get Selwick off the hook and that means our whole country would take a fall. So we'll go out of here together and when I shoot you I'll shoot Vidor Churis too, and tie it all up in a nice, neat package."

"Selwick?"

I gave her a shove toward the closet. "Don't play coy with me, baby. Your boys have him and I know where he'll be taken. We have the Embassy and all their other buildings covered including most residences now. So he goes in one place where he'll be worked on . . . Churis's apartment.

"You almost had it made, Rondine. You called Selwick to come here, had Churis ready to move in behind him and between the two of you it would have been done. But you managed to intercept Churis and I can see him going up to Selwick on the street downstairs with the story that you had to leave and would meet him someplace else and your killer friend, Vidor Churis, was instructed to lead him there. Like a sheep to the slaughter. Okay, kid, we'll meet him. I've already been at Vidor's apartment and left a dead man behind to watch the place. Get your damn coat on."

I called a cab and asked for one to stand by downstairs. Both the stake-outs had been walking and if it was timed right we could be in a cab and gone before they got to their car.

Once again I bypassed the guy on the floor below, took the elevator down the rest of the way and saw the cab pulling up outside. I pushed Rondine through the door, got us into the cab and told him to take off in a hurry and only gave him the address after we made the turn. Back down the block and too late, the stake-outs were trying to swing around in the street and were blocked by traffic.

There was no activity on Churis's block at all. Nobody had heard the shot and nobody investigated yet, otherwise a prowl car would still be on the scene and half the neighborhood trying for a look at the premises. I gave the cabbie ten bucks and told him to wait. He was glad to.

Keeping Rondine ahead of me, I nudged her up the stairs. Each time she tried to speak I shut her up curtly. She was terrified now. She saw death written all over my face and knew I was a part of it. She knew what I was going to do and she was tasting it already.

At the door I stopped. I had forgotten about the mammoth feature of the thing. Inside, the TV was going loud enough to make any sound I made impossible to hear, but if they were there already they'd keep it up. Churis would guess what had happened and would be ready for a break in the attempt.

But not the way I was going to do it.

I got out one of the pellets Ernie Bentley had given me, the one with the ring around it. I used wads of paper from the junk on the stairs, wedged the pellet between the knob and the door jamb, wetting it down with a half full can of black paint, squeezing the mess until it had the consistency of mud and the capability of directing the charge where I wanted it to go.

Part of it I left exposed, took a cigarette from Rondine's bag while she stood there with amazement and terror a rigid mask on her face. I tore off a stub, lit it, set it on the exposed part of the pellet and moved her flat against the wall with me.

It was over in a minute, but when the thing went off, the concussion slammed against my eardrums like a sledge. The door flew inward, splinters flying everywhere, gray, choking smoke filling the hall. I grabbed her arm, spun her into the room first, shoved her aside and stood there with the .45 aimed at emptiness.

The dead guy was still saying "Oh," on the floor and downstairs doors were opening and voices yelling to ask what the hell was going on up there. I shouted back that it was all right . . . the oven blew but nobody was hurt and there was no damage. In a little while they'd be coming up to see for themselves.

And I was at the end of the road right then. The fox had been foxed. I lifted the gun and pointed it right at her head. She never moved. Too much had happened too fast and she seemed to be in a state of shock. Her eyes were on the body a long time and when they reached me they seemed lifeless.

You're getting old, Rondine, I thought. Plastic surgery can help the body, but the mind stays the same, getting older each day until you can't take it any more.

I couldn't do it alone now. I'd have to call in the others. I'd get wrung for it but it would be worth it. I went to the phone, the gun still on Rondine. I dialed Colonel Corbinet's number and held on until he answered. His voice said, "Hello . . . hello?"

Very slowly I put the phone back without answering him. On a pad beside the phone was a sheet of doodle paper and on it was written an address, a familiar address.

Gretchen Lark's.

I grinned at the scratching Vidor Churis had made and

knew what they had planned. Cute. Real cute. She was watching me now and some of the shock had left her eyes. I walked over, pointed out the door and when she left, stayed right behind her with the gun in her back. To a couple of nosy kids on the floor below I said my friend was upstairs taking care of the mess and with the TV still on loud they nodded and went back to their party stinking of beer.

In the cab the driver said, "What was that racket back there?"

"Crazy Village party."

"Always like that around here," he said.

Yeah. On Sunday, too. What else can happen on a quiet Sunday?

She couldn't contain herself any longer. Her clenched fist went to her mouth and the tears came, coursing down her cheeks. Huge, gulping sobs wracked her body and with an impulsive move she slammed her hand against me and if I hadn't grabbed it in mid-air it would have been over there in a fat mushroom of flame.

I squeezed her wrist and said, "Don't be anxious to die ahead of time. I still have two more of those nice little charges and impact sets them off. They're right in my pocket, honey, and a small jar blows them."

Instinctively, she pulled away, the fear back in her eyes. I told the cabbie to let us out on the next corner, paid him off while we were still two blocks away and held Rondine's arm while we walked. I wanted her in top shape when we got there.

And there would be time. They wouldn't kill Gretchen Lark or Selwick until she was there to give the order. It would have to be planned somehow, a love-nest suicide pact, and it would look logical as hell and only we would know the difference. There would be a ring of truth to it . . . a lovely woman painter doing a portrait of a famous man for whom she worked, the two of them falling in love, realizing the futility of it all, him with a wife in England and an illness that could kill him at any time. So they take the big out together. Just a quick dosage of strychnine forced down their throats would do the trick. It was available and the thing suicides would use.

But first they'd wait for the master planner to show. Selwick would have to be forced to talk first. I explained it to her, letting Rondine see how much of it I had down pat, watched her go white as each sentence came out of me and saw her nearly get sick when I described how I had killed Alexis Minner

154

and the two others. She stumbled and almost fell and I laughed and kept on with the story.

I said, "If I had killed you at first I could have stopped it cold right then, but I wanted to louse up your organization, Rondine. So far I did pretty well. You've gone all week trying to dump me because the critical time in the U.N. comes this week and you couldn't have anybody standing in the way of all those grand Soviet sneak plans. Nobody. You could guard against the agency boys but not against me."

We were outside the building then. She looked at me and said one word, softly: "Fool."

I prodded her. "Inside. You know where she lives."

At the door I took the .45 out and whispered, "Knock."

With some hesitancy she tapped on the door. Inside there was a sudden movement, the sound of feet on the floor and Gretchen said in a voice that was tinged with fear, "Yes . . . who is it?"

Behind her Churis would be standing with a gun, making her speak. She had a right to be scared. I tapped Rondine with the nose of the gun and stepped out of the way.

Rondine said, "Edith . . . Edith Caine."

A chain rattled on the door and a lock clicked. The door opened and when Gretchen saw Edith her face changed, went from relief to fear again, then I shoved her into Gretchen so they both hit the floor in a jumble of arms and legs and there in a corner with a gun in his hand was Vidor Churis and the first shot he got off went across my side with a searing, white hot stab of pain.

He only got the first one. The .45 caught him right at the bridge of the nose and everything seemed to come apart from there on up. Skull, brains and blood sprayed the wall like a bright wet flower and he flung his hands out so violently with the death jerk the Tokarev flew halfway across the room.

I ran to the door, slammed it shut, jerked Rondine to her feet and threw her violently into a chair so she could look at the figure of Burton Selwick in the chair facing her, eyes closed in a peaceful sleep, one sleeve rolled up above the elbow and a tiny red dot in the vein showing where the needle had gone in. Behind me, still gasping from the fall, Gretchen was getting up, but I didn't take my eyes off Rondine.

"Want to question him, baby? Want to see what they laid out for tomorrow's session? Think it can do you any good now? Or aren't you curious any more? I'd think you'd want to know what he'd have to say just to satisfy yourself."

"Tiger . . ."

"Shut up, Rondine. It makes nice listening. You were the one putting the squeeze on the old boy. We'll just back-check to be sure, but chances are you had him to your place many a time and needled him into a dream sleep supposedly to relax him and made him talk under the drug. Nice, baby, but not nice enough. You were the one who laid out the play to have me dumped. You were the one who knew where I'd be and how I'd move. You were trapped from the first second I saw you there in the restaurant and had to move from any angle at all to get rid of me without exposing yourself. The only thing I can't understand is why you moved so badly. You used to be a great operator. You could nearly outthink anybody. You could work in ways a person wouldn't dream of. You could scheme and plan and come up with a dilly in seconds . . . none of this crude stuff like contract killers. You would have known I could outthink you and be ready for something like sending a squad to nail me in bed. Why so stupid, Rondine?"

There was no fear at all in her eyes now. Instead, there was just the quiet acquiescence, resignation and deep, deep pity.

"I'm not Rondine," she said.

And I knew she was telling the truth!

There by the easel with the stems of her paintbrushes sticking out of the neck was a peculiarly colored pale blue bottle half filled with solvent and it was exactly the same as those filled with sodium pentothal that I had found in Alex Minner's cabinet!

From behind me Gretchen Lark said, "You really aren't very smart, Tiger. Throw your gun on the chair."

I didn't have to turn around to be sure. I knew she had me lined up. I eased the hammer down on the .45 and did what she told me to. The move made the bullet crease on my side blaze into life again and I clamped my teeth together. The belt on my raincoat was too tight and I began to feel sick.

Gretchen Lark walked around the side of me, pointed the gun at a chair near the wall and said, "Sit down."

Sweat was running into my eyes and dripping from my nose. I nodded, undid the belt of the coat, took it off and threw it next to Edith Caine. Then I sat down. I knew what she was waiting for. She had to make this look right and she was going to set it up. It wouldn't be too hard. I had enough kills behind me to make me look like a madman. The story would be easy. Selwick had come for a portrait sitting when Churis came in to drop him. I had charged in and during the resulting gunfight everybody but Gretchen got knocked off. She could even inflict a minor wound on herself to make it look good and the story would be believed.

The thought was there in her mind because she picked up Vidor Churis's gun and weighed it in her hand. Smilingly, Gretchen said, "The house is empty at this moment. If you're hoping someone heard the shots you'll be wrong, Tiger."

I looked at Edith Caine sitting there so quietly. "I've been wrong about a lot of things."

"Yes, you have," Gretchen told me. "But you did spoil a wonderful situation."

"Great."

"Don't you know how I was able to move against you, Tiger?"

I did now, but I let her say it.

"Burton was a lonely man. He was sick and overworked as well. His only real pleasure and chance to relax was when he came here to sit for his portrait. There were many things he took for his illness, but being a nurse I was able to prescribe other things too. They relieved his pain, of course, but with the use of simple truth serums, sodium pentothal, I extracted every secret he had and he never realized it. That's how I knew about you. He told me of meeting you the first day he saw you. He was sick then and came here to relax. When he mentioned the name Rondine which you called Edith here we realized what might happen. You see, Rondine isn't exactly unknown to us either.

"Then, it was Edith who told Burton Selwick that she was to meet you at your hotel and later he told me under deep sleep and we tried to kill you there. You handled yourself well, Tiger.

"Unfortunately, your friend had to die for you. I visited Edith at her apartment and saw the matches you left behind. That was very clumsy of you . . . or was it deliberate?" She thought a moment and nodded. "Yes, that *is* it. You did it deliberately thinking what you did about her. Or was it unconsciously, Tiger?"

She was right the last time.

"It was I who arranged for those so-called 'contract killers.' They weren't very good at all and after all the money we spent! I knew you'd go to her apartment that one night and had those men ready. I thought I had them ready again when you took me home from the *Hall of the Two Sisters*."

Gretchen smiled again, and dramatically paced the room, the gun never leaving my stomach where it was aimed. In her pacing she stopped by the window, perched on the sill

157

and changed guns in her hands so she had Churis's pointed at me with her right.

"Funny," she said, "all those elaborate plans that never seemed to work out and at the last moment you walk in all by yourself with an idiotic idea and turn your back on me. How strange fate is."

"Where is Rondine, Gretchen?" I said.

"Dead. A long time ago. She was shot by one of our agents when she tried to get some papers back to England that would possibly grant her some protection for her past crimes."

No, she wasn't dead. She was very much alive, sitting ten feet away facing me and I loved her with all my heart and knew she loved me. I said, "Who was Rondine, Edith?" because I had to know.

Her eyes were directly on mine, loving, forgiving, sorry that it had to come out this way. "Rondine was my oldest sister Diana. She didn't die in an air raid. She defected to the Nazis and worked for them against her own people. She was considered dead by the family and her name is never mentioned. She was the one shame they ever had."

She smiled, her eyes wet. "They tell me I look exactly like her, Tiger. I know what it must have meant to you to see me so suddenly. But I couldn't tell you, do you understand?" Her voice was soft, compassionate.

I still couldn't believe it. *That was Rondine sitting there!*

"Tiger . . . I couldn't expose what Rondine did to my family. I couldn't hurt them that much. I just had to put up with it."

"And I lost a good friend because you didn't have the nerve to talk." I couldn't keep the coldness out of my tone.

She dropped her eyes momentarily. "I—I'm sorry."

There was an amused smile on Gretchen's face as she listened to us, the gun never wavering in her hand. She had the back of Edith's head and my stomach in perfect target and she could afford the amusement. *But I couldn't look at Edith Caine in that chair and believe what she was telling me!*

There was one thing I saw. Edith was looking at Gretchen's reflection in the glass of a framed picture on the wall and one hand was already in the pocket of my coat. When it came out she had one of the pellets in her fingers and was getting it set on her knuckle and I felt a chill go over me that took all the fire out of my side and made me want to turn inside out.

I tried to yell for her not to do it but by then it was already done. She flipped the pellet back over her head toward Gretchen Lark's feet and she never noticed it coming. The moment I let myself go to the floor, Edith did too and if Gretchen got off a shot it was drowned out in the wild blast from across the room. The violence of the explosion threw furniture all over and tumbled the chair over Edith into me and knocked the unconscious figure of Burton Selwick into a stack of paintings, completely oblivious to whatever happened.

I shoved the chair away, got up and reached for Edith. There were smudges on her face and a trickle of blood coming down her cheek, but no more. She touched my face once, ran to Selwick to make sure he was all right, then we both turned to look at the hole where the window had been.

Someplace down below Gretchen Lark would be lying in fragments.

She turned, looked at me, knowing I hadn't taken my eyes off her for a long while, frowned at what she saw there and tried to speak. I beat her to it. "It could have been a beautiful plant, kid. Gretchen wasn't going to knock you off because you two pulled it together. She sat there with a gun on us and could have killed us any time, the sooner the better. She was just letting you have your fun until you gave the signal. But you protected your own hide again, just like that last time. To come out clean with me you saw an angle and played it. You knew I had those damn things in my coat and took the big chance, just the way Rondine always did. If it went right you knew you could get me to fall for that phony story because I love you and would be sucker enough to let it lie."

I had the .45 back in my hand again and the hammer was back.

She saw it.

But she wasn't afraid.

She said, "Do you really love me, Tiger?"

"Yes, I really do, Rondine, and now you get it."

"I love you, Tiger. As I told you before, I loved you from the first time I saw you. Did Rondine love you that way too?"

"Yes, Rondine, that's the way you always did." I lifted the snout of the gun.

"You made love to her many times, didn't you?"

Her hands went to her jacket, took it off and threw it on the floor. Slowly, she undid her blouse, pulled it out of her skirt and let it follow. In that strange way women have, she reached behind her back and unfastened the snaps on her bra and took it away deliberately, her breasts full and lovely, bursting with pride at having been relieved of their restraint.

I felt the gun in my hand shake and held it steady.

"No good, Rondine, the act won't work. You tried the same one before."

My words didn't stop her. Her fingers felt for the zipper on the side of the skirt, found it and pulled it down. She moved her hips, swayed and the skirt fell in a heap at her feet and with her thumbs she pushed down the slip on top of it.

Damn, my hand was no good, no good at all! The palm was slippery with sweat and muscles jerked and pulled up my back. My eyes seemed to burn and something was churning inside my mind. I felt an involuntary message of habit from my brain trying to tell my fingers to move, to pull the trigger, to kill her, kill her, kill her before it was too late, but my finger wouldn't move.

The last act of the tableau was complete because she had the wisp of pink nylon in her hand and she was naked before me, beautiful, lovely, desirable, legs as graceful and firm as a statue, belly flat and moving with the swell of her breathing, breasts hard and flamingly pink-tipped now, chestnut hair still soft and gleaming, skin satin-sweet and waiting.

The gun began to get too heavy to hold and I let it down. She was going to win after all. Two dead and one unconscious at our feet and she could still do this.

She said, "If you had Rondine then you'll know now for sure, Tiger."

I couldn't stop her when she walked to the couch. As languidly as a cat she lay down on it, her body and her eyes inviting me, wanting me. No, it was more than that. She was demanding me.

I had to. I was beyond choice. I loved her too much and too long. This was a Rondine I loved and had to have and to hell with the consequences.

She reached her arms up to me and smiled, the love in her eyes bright and shining. "Now you will find out, Tiger, my love. Now you will know," she said to me. "You see . . . I'm still a virgin."

And she was.